Children and Juvenile Justice

Children and Juvenile Justice

SECOND EDITION

Ellen Marrus
George Butler Research Professor of Law
University of Houston Law Center

Irene Merker Rosenberg
Late Royce R. Till Professor of Law
University of Houston Law Center

Carolina Academic Press
Durham, North Carolina

ISBN: 978-1-59460-901-5
LCCN: 2012940589

Carolina Academic Press
700 Kent Street
Durham, North Carolina 27701
Telephone (919) 489-7486
Fax (919) 493-5668
www.cap-press.com

Printed in the United States of America

In loving memory of Yoel ben Moshe Halevi *Z"L*, Yale L. Rosenberg, A.A. White Professor of Law, University of Houston Law Center. Beloved husband, school mate, best friend, colleague, co-author, and so much more.

I.M.R.

...

In memory of my grandmother, Rebecca Rosenblatt, who always believed I could accomplish whatever I set out to do. To my granddaughter, Rifqa, for being a very special and thoughtful young lady who lives up to the meaning of her name. I want to thank my daughter, Malikah, for her encouragement and support while I was working on this book.

This edition is also in memory of Irene Merker Rosenberg, my friend and coauthor, who passed away prior to the publication of this edition. Without her support this book would never had been written.

E.M.

Summary of Contents

Contents

Cases

Preface

When we sat down to begin work on the first edition of this book (which was a long time ago), we knew what we wanted to accomplish—to create a casebook that would combine theory, practice, and ethics. We hope we have succeeded.

At that time we both underestimated how difficult this project would be—the numerous decisions that would have to be made, the tedious detail work, the extensive research and culling of materials. We decided at that time that we might well do some things differently—we are told that this is the purpose of second editions. At that time I did not realize how much harder it would be to write the second edition. Between our two books, Irene became ill and passed away before the second edition was completed. It has been a difficult task to continue this work without the discussions, laughter, and arguments that we had with the first edition. I have kept much of the same philosophy with the second edition as we did with the first.

One of our decisions was to edit Supreme Court cases lightly. They provide the basic constitutional framework for analyzing juvenile justice issues in the United States. We believe that students should discover and experience the full import and flavor of the Court's opinions in order to be able to grapple with the Court's shifting approaches in resolving questions regarding the juvenile justice system. We want students to view the subject matter in all its constitutional complexity rather than as simplistic "sand box" law or "kiddie" court law. This continues in the second edition. When *Roper v. Simmons* was decided, we had many discussions about where to place the case in the book. I wanted to put it with the other constitutional law cases. Professor Rosenberg wanted to put it separate because "death is different." She won out in the first edition. However, when we first started to discuss this edition, Professor Rosenberg said something she rarely would admit, someone else was right. In this edition *Roper* appears in the chapter that includes the Supreme Court decisions, along with the cases that have followed the reasoning of the Court in *Roper*. We did so because just as the Court has always stated "death is different" the Court has also continued to say "children are different."

We have also used the Institute of Judicial Administration—American Bar Association's (IJA-ABA) Standards rather freely. Although they were written quite awhile ago, in general, they still provide the best source for what we consider the best practices.

In our efforts to make this a national case book, we used cases and statutes from many states. We think they are sufficiently representative of the juvenile justice systems in the United States. However, we recognize that most students want to know how the system works in their particular jurisdictions. To that end, we suggest that professors who use this book complement it with statutes from their home states.

We hope that our practice experience gives students greater access to the somewhat schizophrenic, secretive, and impenetrable juvenile justice world. We have tried to be neutral in our choice of materials and notes, but because we were both defense attorneys in large urban areas and share common views about the juvenile courts, some of our biases may be reflected in the book. We do not apologize for this, but we do want to make explicit what may be implicit.

Many ethical problems arise in juvenile practice. Unfortunately they are rarely acknowledged, and when they are, they are disposed of under the rubric of the "best interests of the child." We have tried to explore these issues openly. Some students may find this disconcerting, but we think discussion of such problems will force students to examine their own views about children and the adversarial process.

Both of us have used some version of these materials when teaching juvenile law. We want to thank our students at the University of Houston Law Center who helped compile the materials and were willing to be experimental subjects with the various versions. We, however, are responsible for any typos or editorial mistakes. We also want to thank the University of Houston Law Foundation for its financial support.

As before, I invite your criticism, comments, suggestions, and any observations as to what worked and what did not. Please contact Ellen Marrus, emarrus@uh.edu, with your ideas.

We hope that you and your students enjoy using the book.

June 2012
E.M. and I.M.R.

Acknowledgments

The excerpts from the articles and books cited below are reprinted with the kind permission of the copyright holders.

A CALL FOR JUSTICE: AN ASSESSMENT OF ACCESS TO COUNSEL AND QUALITY OF REPRESENTATION IN DELINQUENCY PROCEEDINGS (1995) (reprinted with the permission of the American Bar Association).

Janet E. Ainsworth, *Re-Imagining Childhood and Reconstructing The Legal Order: The Case for Abolishing the Juvenile Court*, 69 N.C.L. REV. 1083 (1991) (reprinted with the permission of the North Carolina Law Review).

Neal I. Aizenstein, *Note, Fourth Amendment—Searches By Public School Officials Valid On "Reasonable Grounds,"* 76 J. CRIM. L. & CRIMINOLOGY 898 (1985) (reprinted with the permission of the Journal of Criminal Law & Criminology).

Mary Berkheiser, *The Fiction of Juvenile Right to Counsel: Waiver in the Juvenile Courts*, 54 FLA. L. REV. 577 (2002) (reprinted with the permission of the Florida Law Review).

Allan Borowski and Mimi Ajzenstadt, *A Solution Without a Problem: Judges' Perspectives on the Impact of the Introduction of Public Defenders on Israel's Juvenile Courts*, 45 BRIT. J. CRIMINOLOGY 183 (2005) (reprinted with the permission of the British Journal of Criminology).

Emily Buss, *The Missed Opportunity in Gault*, 70 U. CHI. L. REV. 39 (2003) (reprinted with the permission of the University of Chicago Law Review).

Katherine Hunt Federle, *The Abolition of the Juvenile Court: A Proposal for the Preservation of Children's Rights*, 16 J. CONTEMP. L. 23 (1990) (reprinted with the permission of the Journal of Contemporary Law).

Barry C. Feld, *Race, Politics, and Juvenile Justice: The Warren Court and the Conservative "Backlash,"* 87 MINN. L. REV. 1447 (2003) (reprinted with the permission of the Minnesota Law Review).

Barry C. Feld, *The Constitutional Tension Between* Apprendi *and* McKeiver: *Sentence Enhancements Based on Delinquency Convictions and the Quality of Justice in Juvenile Courts*, 38 WAKE FOREST L. REV. 1111 (2003) (reprinted with the permission of the Wake Forest Law Review).

Barry C. Feld, BAD KIDS: RACE AND THE TRANSFORMATION OF THE JUVENILE COURT(1999) (reprinted with the permission of Oxford University Press).

Barry C. Feld, *The Transformation of the Juvenile Court*, 75 MINN. L. REV. 691 (1991) (reprinted with the permission of the Minnesota Law Review).

Barry C. Feld, *The Right to Counsel in Juvenile Court: An Empirical Study of When Lawyers Appear and the Difference They Make*, 79 J. CRIM. L. & CRIMINOLOGY 1185 (1989) (reprinted with the permission of the Journal of Criminal Law & Criminology).

Patrick Griffin, *Trying and Sentencing Juveniles as Adults: An Analysis of State Transfer and Blended Sentencing Laws*, (2003) (reprinted with the permission of the National Center for Juvenile Justice).

Thomas Grisso, *What We Know About Youths' Capacities as Trial Defendants* in T. Grisso & R. Schwartz (eds.), YOUTH ON TRIAL: A DEVELOPMENTAL PERSPECTIVE ON JUVENILE JUSTICE(2003) (reprinted with the permission of the author).

Charles W. Hardin, Jr., Comment, *Searching Public Schools: T.L.O. and the Exclusionary Rule*, 47 Ohio STATE L.J. 1099 (1986) (reprinted with the permission of the Ohio State Law Journal).

IJA-ABA JUVENILE JUSTICE STANDARDS ANNOTATED, Robert E. Shepherd, Jr., ed. (1996) (reprinted with the permission of the American Bar Association).

Ellen Marrus,"*That Isn't Fair, Judge*": *The Costs of Using Prior Juvenile Delinquency Adjudications in Criminal Court Sentencing*, 40 HOUS. L. REV. 1323 (2004) (reprinted with the permission of the author).

Ellen Marrus, *Best Interests Equals Zealous Advocacy: A Not So Radical View of Holistic Representation For Children Accused of Crime*, 62 MD. L. REV. 288 (2003) (reprinted with the permission of the author).

Ellen Marrus, *Effective Assistance of Counsel in the Wonderland of "Kiddie Court"—Why The Queen of Hearts Trumps* Strickland, 39 CRIM. L. BULL. 393 (2003) (reprinted with the permission of the Criminal Law Bulletin and the author).

Ellen Marrus and Irene Merker Rosenberg, *After* Roper v. Simmons: *Keeping Kids Out of Adult Criminal Court*, 42 SAN DIEGO L. REV. 1151 (2005) (reprinted with the permission of the San Diego Law Review and the authors).

Willie McCarney, *Responding to Juvenile Delinquency Restorative Justice: An International Perspective*, 3 J. CENTER FOR FAMILIES, CHILD. & CTS. 3 (2001) (reprinted with the permission of the Journal of the Center for Families, Children and Courts).

Anthony Platt, THE CHILD SAVERS: THE INVENTION OF DELINQUENCY(1977) (reprinted with the permission of University of Chicago Press).

Irene Merker Rosenberg, *Leaving Bad Enough Alone: A Response To The Juvenile Court Abolitionists*, 1993 WIS. L. REV. 163 (1993*)* (reprinted with the permission of the Wisconsin Law Review).

Irene Merker Rosenberg, *Winship Redux: 1970–1990*, 69 TEX. L. REV. 109 (1990) (reprinted with the permission of the Texas Law Review).

Irene Merker Rosenberg, *The Constitutional Rights of Children Charged With Crime: Proposal for a Return to the Not So Distant Past*, 27 U.C.L.A. L. REV. 656 (1980) (reprinted with the permission of the University of California Los Angeles Law Review).

Irene Merker Rosenberg and Yale L. Rosenberg, *The Legacy of the Stubborn and Rebellious Son*, 74 MICH. L. REV. 1097 (1976) (reprinted with the permission of the Michigan Law Review).

Robert E. Shepherd, Jr., *The Juvenile Court at 100: Birthday Cake or Funeral Pyre?*, 13 CRIMINAL JUSTICE 47 (1999) (reprinted with the permission of Criminal Justice).

Masami Izumida Tyson, *Revising Shonenho: a Call to a Reform That Makes the Already Effective Japanese Juvenile System Even More Effective*, 33 VAND. J. TRANSNAT'L. L. 739 (2000) (reprinted with the permission of the Vanderbilt Journal of Transnational Law).

Lois A. Weithorn, *Mental Hospitalization of Troublesome Youth: An Analysis of Skyrocketing Admission Rates*, 40 STAN. L. REV. 773 (1988) (reprinted with the permission of the Stanford Law Review).

Thomas Welch, *Delinquency Proceedings—Fundamental Fairness for the Accused in a Quasi-Criminal Forum*, 50 MINN. L. REV. 653 (1966) (reprinted with the permission of the Minnesota Law Review).

Children and Juvenile Justice

Chapter 1

The Juvenile Court System in the United States

A. Historical Perspectives

1. President's Commission on Law Enforcement, Task Force Report: Juvenile Delinquency and Youth Crime
2–4 (1967)

Development of the Idea of the Juvenile Court

The juvenile court emerged from the confluence of several streams of thought and practice, some of them centuries old, others relatively recent responses to changing social conditions.

The best known source of the idea of the juvenile court is summed up in the Latin phrase, *parens patriae*. From feudal days the English chancery court has exercised protective jurisdiction over all the children of the realm on behalf of the *pater patriae*, the King. While the chancery court traditionally had broad authority over the welfare of children, its jurisdiction was exercised almost exclusively on behalf of minors whose property rights were jeopardized, on the theory that it lacked the means with which to provide for impoverished, neglected minors. When the English legal system was transplanted to the United States, the chancery court's activities were extended to include protection of minors in danger of personal as well as property injury, and it is as inheritor of the chancery court's protective powers that the juvenile court in this country has most commonly been justified against constitutional attack.

The chancery court, however, dealt only with neglected and dependent children, not with children accused of criminal law violations, and the historical basis of the present-day juvenile court's delinquency jurisdiction has been a matter of some dispute. One opinion is that the institution of the juvenile court owes more to the criminal law than to chancery; other writers give the common law of crimes at least part of the credit. The common law had long presumed a child under 7 years incapable of felonious intent and therefore unable to be held criminally responsible, and a child between 7 and 14 years similarly incapable unless shown able to understand the consequences of his actions. It has been suggested, however, that the older adolescent now included in the juvenile court's province cannot really be considered without legal responsibility and that, while it may be historically correct to ascribe the juvenile court's delinquency jurisdiction to the criminal law, "its logical justification seems to lie in the recognition of the failure of the older criminal courts to prevent crime and in the experimentation in judicial methods and procedure."

3

A somewhat different view of the court's origins is that "these courts have developed as part and reflection of the growth of contemporary administrative and quasi-judicial tribunals," and that the *parens patriae* theory is the *ex post facto* justification offered for practices that in fact originated with the modern juvenile court. Similarly the Children's Bureau of the Department of Health, Education, and Welfare, emphasizing the uniqueness of juvenile court procedures, has characterized them as special statutory creations rather than direct descendants of chancery.

Although the 19th century movement for reform in treatment of children was a natural enough development in the humanizing of the criminal law, it may well have been accelerated and intensified by the social conditions then prevailing. Both industrialization and immigration were bringing people into cities by the thousands, with resulting overcrowding, disruption of family life, increase in vice and crime, and all the other destructive factors characteristic of rapid urbanization. Truancy and delinquency rose rapidly, and civic-minded men and women worried about the exposure of children to tobacco, alcohol, pornography, and street life in general. With the growing concern over environmental influences came the desire to rescue children and restore them to a healthful, useful life. In addition, throughout the 19th century there was a rising concern about official treatment of children—the growth of what has been called the spirit of social justice. The ascending social sciences, with their optimistic claims to diagnose and treat the problems underlying deviance, seemed to provide the ideal tool for implementing the dual goals of treating wayward children humanely and offsetting their deleterious surroundings. Philanthropic men and women such as the members of the Chicago Women's Club, emancipated intellectual feminists like the Hull House group, and professional penologists and reformers joined forces to achieve recognition of the greater vulnerability and salvageability of children—first in establishing separate institutions for youth and substituting noninstitutional supervision wherever feasible [;] and then in adopting physically separate court proceedings and finally in altering the very philosophy underlying judicial handling of children.

Thus, whatever its historical basis, the scene was set for the juvenile court's arrival by a variety of reforms that immediately preceded it. The growing trend was early evidenced in the founding of such institutions as New York City's House of Refuge (1825), in which children were to be separated from adult offenders and given corrective treatment rather than punishment. State reform and industrial schools for juveniles followed, the first in Massachusetts in 1847, all of them aimed at teaching youths discipline and an honest trade and instill[ing] dedication to advancement through hard work. The development of probation as a substitute for confinement in criminal cases, which began in Massachusetts in 1880, reflected the growing belief in application of the social sciences through treatment and supervision, as a means of preventing further criminality.

Awareness of the brutality of incarcerating children with adult criminals led to efforts to separate them before and during trial as well. In 1861 the mayor of Chicago was authorized to appoint a commissioner to hear and decide minor charges against boys between 6 and 17 years old to place them on probation or in a reformatory, power which the judges received in 1867. In 1869 a Massachusetts statute provided for the presence in court of an agent of the State in cases where the child might be committed to the State reformatory; the agent was also charged with finding foster homes in suitable cases and paying subsequent visits to them. A law of 1870 required separate hearings of children's cases in Suffolk County (Boston) and authorized a representative of the Commonwealth to investigate cases, attend trials, and protect children's interests. The separate trial statute was extended throughout the Commonwealth in 1872, followed in 1877 by provision for separate sessions, dockets, and court records in juvenile cases. New York established separate trials, dockets, and records in 1892. Rhode Island in 1898 instituted segregation of children under 16 years awaiting trial, separate arraignments and trials, special dockets and records, and presence at juvenile proceedings of public and private agents to protect the interests of the child.

But the reformers were not yet satisfied. Judge Julian Mack, a well-known early juvenile court judge, commented years later on the juvenile court's development out of the general movement to reform the treatment of children, "What we did not have was the conception that a child that broke the law was to be dealt with by the State as a wise parent would deal with a wayward child."

The juvenile court, then, was born in an aura of reform and it spread with amazing speed. The conception of the delinquent as a "wayward child" first specifically came to life in April 1899, when the Illinois legislature passed the Juvenile Court Act, creating the first statewide court especially for children. It did not create a new court; it did include most of the features that have since come to distinguish the juvenile court. The original act and the amendments to it that shortly followed brought together under one jurisdiction cases of dependency, neglect, and delinquency—the last comprehending incorrigibles and children threatened by immoral associations as well as criminal lawbreakers. Hearings were to be informal and nonpublic, records confidential, children detained apart from adults, a probation staff appointed. In short, children were not to be treated as criminals nor dealt with by the processes used for criminals.

A new vocabulary symbolized the new order. Petition instead of complaint, summons instead of warrant, initial hearing instead of arraignment, finding of involvement instead of conviction, disposition instead of sentence. The physical surroundings were important too. They should seem less imposing than a courtroom, with the judge at a desk or table instead of behind a bench[,] fatherly and sympathetic while still authoritative and sobering. The goals were to investigate, diagnose, and prescribe treatment, not to adjudicate guilt or fix blame. The individual's background was more important than the facts of a given incident, specific conduct relevant more as symptomatic of a need for the court to bring its helping powers to bear than as prerequisite to exercise of jurisdiction. Lawyers were unnecessary—adversary tactics were out of place, for the mutual aim of all was not to contest or object but to determine the treatment plan best for the child. That plan was to be devised by the increasingly popular psychologists and psychiatrists; delinquency was thought of almost as a disease, to be diagnosed by specialists and the patient kindly but firmly dosed. Even the judicial role began to attract extralegal specialists, men and women aware of and interested in the social and scientific developments of the day, and government supported professional personnel and service expanded and replaced the amateur volunteers.

Within a dozen years 22 states had followed the example of Illinois, and by 1925 there were juvenile courts in every State but two. Today there is a juvenile court act in every American jurisdiction, including the District of Columbia, with approximately 2,700 courts hearing children's cases. The alacrity with which State after State followed the Illinois example, however, must be considered in the context of the developing reform movement sketched above; the Illinois act was in many respects the reflection of an idea already widespread and the consolidation of previous efforts to realize it.

Furthermore, the mere passage of a juvenile court statute does not automatically establish a tribunal of the sort the reformers contemplated. A U.S. Children's Bureau survey in 1920 found that only 16 percent of all so-called juvenile courts in fact had separate hearings for children and an officially authorized probation service and recorded social information on children brought to court. A similar survey conducted by the Children's Bureau and this Commission in 1966 revealed significant gaps still existing between ideal and actual court structures, practices, and personnel. Indeed, it has been observed that "there is nothing uniform" in the operations of children's courts....

In fact, more children's courts than not are staffed by judges and other personnel who spend much of their time on civil, criminal, and other nonjuvenile matters, and many children's courts are unlike other courts only by virtue of their separate and more private hearings. Even among those few more specialized courts for children there are great differences in method, depending both on statutes and on the views and values of those in charge.

2. Robert E. Shepherd, Jr., *The Juvenile Court at 100: Birthday Cake or Funeral Pyre?*

13 Criminal Justice 47 (1999) (citations omitted)

One hundred years ago, in 1899, the Illinois legislature enacted a juvenile court act creating the first completely separate juvenile court in the world. However, the policy debates raging around the country in this centennial year make it uncertain whether there will be a birthday cake and a celebration or a funeral pyre for the mortally wounded traditional juvenile court. Early in the 19th century, juveniles were tried in criminal courts like everyone else, with their youth being most relevant on the question of criminal responsibility [via the infancy defense]....

In spite of the law's effort to temper the harshness of trying and punishing children as adults through the benign device of the infancy defense, young children were still at times sentenced to prison and occasionally to death, and executed. Dean Victor Streib has pointed out that at least 10 children were executed in this country prior to 1900 for crimes committed before their fourteenth birthdays. Virginia penitentiary records from 1876 reflect that a prisoner died from being scalded in a tub of boiling coffee—he was 10 years old. These excesses shocked the conscience of the public. Thus, Americans in the 19th century sought some more pervasive reform than just the defense of infancy to address the growing recognition of the distinctive nature of children and youth.

Houses of Refuge, Origins of "Child Saving"

Jury nullification began to play a significant role in the acquittal of children charged with crime in the early part of the 1800s, to the dismay of prosecutors. Quakers in New York City sought by creating the Society for the Prevention of Pauperism to establish a balance between those concerned about jury nullification and those others repelled by the harshness of imprisoning juvenile defendants in adult institutions. That organization, which later evolved into the Society for the Reformation of Juvenile Delinquents, founded the first House of Refuge in New York in 1825, with the expressed purpose "to receive and take ... all such children as shall be taken up or committed as vagrants, or convicted of criminal offenses." The children worked a full eight-hour day at trades such as tailoring, brass-nail manufacturing, and silver plating, in addition to attending school for another four hours. Many of them had not committed any criminal act, and a number were probably 19th century "status offenders."

In an early legal attack on the involuntary incarceration of children in such an institution, a father sought a writ of habeas corpus from the Pennsylvania Supreme Court declaring the commitment illegal. The court denied the writ and concluded that "it would be an act of extreme cruelty to release" the girl from the facility and refused to inquire into the procedures for commitment, the duration of her incarceration, or the conditions within the school. (*Ex parte Crouse*, 4 Wharton 9, 11 (Pa. 1838).) This decision is often credited with originating the use of the doctrine of *parens patriae* to justify informality and paternalism in dealing with children in the courts.

Reformatories

As the House of Refuge movement evolved into the slightly more punitive reform school, or reformatory, approach later in the last century, an occasional legal attack on the incarceration of a child in such a youth prison was successful. The reformatory was created in the middle of the century to 1) segregate young offenders from adult criminals; 2) imprison the young "for their own good" in order to remove them from bad home environments; 3) minimize court proceedings because the incarceration was for benevolent purposes; 4) provide indeterminate sentences to last until the youth is reformed; 5) use punishment only when other alternatives have been unavailing; 6) utilize military drill, physical exercise, and supervision to avoid idleness; 7) use a "cottage" approach located in rural areas; 8) [emphasize] education—preferably vocational in focus, work, and religion to accomplish reform of the youth; and 9) teach sobriety, thrift, industry, and prudence.

However, in an 1870 case the Illinois Supreme Court held it to be unconstitutional to confine in the Chicago Reform School a youth who had not been convicted of criminal conduct or afforded legal due process. (*People ex rel. O'Connell v. Turner*, 55 Ill. 280, 283–84, 287 (1870).) Two years later that school closed[,] and juveniles convicted of crimes were sent to a normal juvenile prison. It was against this backdrop in the last quarter of the 19th century that the juvenile court movement began.

The Illinois Juvenile Court Act

The 1899 Illinois Juvenile Court Act was in part a response to a growing incidence of jury nullification, to concerns about the dominance of sectarian industrial schools in a Chicago filling with immigrants, and to the reform-based opposition to the placement of youths in facilities with adults. Although the act did not radically change procedures in the existing courts that now would be sitting as juvenile courts in adjudicating cases involving children, it did reintroduce the *parens patriae* philosophy to govern such cases. In addition to giving the courts jurisdiction over children charged with crimes, the act also gave jurisdiction over a variety of behaviors and conditions. The act was unique in that it did create a special court, or jurisdiction for an existing court, for neglected, dependent, or delinquent children under age 16; define a rehabilitative rather than punishment purpose for that court; establish a policy of confidentiality for records of the court to minimize stigma; require the separation of juveniles from adults when incarcerated or placed in the same institution, as well as barring the detention of children under age 12 in jails altogether; and provide for the informality of procedures within the court. The court's procedures in Illinois were, indeed, quite brief and superficial, frequently consisting of the judge gaining the trust of the child through informal conversation and then asking the youth directly about the offenses charged. The first Chicago judge, Richard S. Tuthill, did send 37 boys on to the grand jury for adult handling in the first year of the court for not being fit for the treatment orientation of the court. His successor, Judge Julian Mack, described the court's goals in the following fashion:

> The child who must be brought into court should, of course, be made to know that he is face to face with the power of the state, but he should at the same time, and more emphatically, be made to feel that he is the object of its care and solicitude. The ordinary trappings of the courtroom are out of place in such hearings. The judge on a bench, looking down upon the boy standing at the

bar, can never evoke a proper sympathetic spirit. Seated at a desk, with the child at his side, where he can on occasion put his arm around his shoulder and draw the lad to him, the judge, while losing none of his judicial dignity, will gain immensely in the effectiveness of his work (Hon. Julian Mack, The Juvenile Court, 23 Harv. L. Rev.104 (1909)).

. . . .

Professionalization of Court Staffs

In the early days of the juvenile court, many of the service functions were performed through volunteers or by the court's own probation staff, which was largely untrained. It became clear early on that there was a greater need for professional staff to serve the court and its varied clientele. As these professional services became more common, the role of volunteers subsided into the background. Although this professionalization aided the court in one respect, it displaced the extensive use of influential and highly supportive volunteers.

Introduction of Status Offenses

The effort to expand the juvenile court movement beyond the urban areas was somewhat slower than the initial burst of legislative action in the first two decades of the 20th century. However, the post-World War II period witnessed a further development with the separation out of the jurisdictional categories for "status offenders" from the definitions of delinquency. New York created a new jurisdictional category, that of Persons in Need of Supervision (PINS), for runaways, truants, and other youth who had committed acts that would not be criminal if committed by an adult. Other states followed the lead. With the enactment of the federal Juvenile Justice and Delinquency Prevention Act in 1974, the approach of the states to these new categories of offenders was changed dramatically, as young people "convicted" of non-criminal misbehavior were removed from juvenile correctional facilities. . . .

[T]here is a somewhat schizophrenic aspect to the juvenile court's appearance after almost two decades of seemingly conflicting Supreme Court decisions about the parameters of due process in the [juvenile] court. Dean Roscoe Pound of the Harvard Law School has been quoted as saying that the juvenile court has become like "the illegitimate issue of an illicit relationship between the legal profession and the social work profession, and now no one wants to claim the little bastard."

3. Sanford J. Fox, *Juvenile Justice Reform: An Historical Perspective*

22 Stan. L. Rev. 1187, 1187–95, 1204–07, 1221–25, 1227–39
(1970) (citations omitted)

The opening of the New York House of Refuge in 1825 has been denominated "the first great event in child welfare" in the period before the Civil War. The second reform, probably the better known of the two, was the institution of the juvenile court by the Illinois legislature in 1899. *Gault* appears to mark a third great humanitarian effort. In assessing the potential impact of *Gault*, it is useful to consider the social and judicial evolution of these earlier reforms. An analysis of both the House of Refuge development and enactment of the Illinois Juvenile Court Act suggests that juvenile justice reform is a complex and highly ambivalent affair in which the goal of child welfare has been but one of many motivational elements. . . .

I. The House of Refuge as a Manifestation of American Optimism

The colonization of America was itself a reform movement, undertaken with a firm belief in man's ability to bring about earthly progress.... Many of the most enthusiastic reformers were Quakers. The movement to establish the House of Refuge, and its management after it opened, was guided by Quaker reformers who had gained prominence through earlier works of charity and reform.... Eventually the reformers focused on the plight of children. The House of Refuge, by offering food, shelter, and education to the homeless and destitute youth of New York, and by removing juvenile offenders from the prison company of adult convicts, partook of the same dynamic humanitarian fervor that had characterized their earlier projects.

A. The Campaign to Save Predelinquents

....

The objects of [the] House [of Refuge] reform ... were seen as children who were not yet truly criminal; the undertaking was a matter of crime and delinquency prevention, aimed at saving predelinquent youth. This concept of predelinquency was one of the central concepts of juvenile justice for well over a century following its emergence in New York reform thought in the early nineteenth century. A major corollary was the view that deviant children were victims rather than offenders, even though they might already have been convicted in a court.

Many children had, in fact, been convicted as disorderly persons, an offense that included "all persons wandering abroad and begging, and all idle persons, not having visible means of livelihood." But the reformers fully understood that these children were guilty of little more than being poor and neglected. The House reform was designed to deal with those who were still novices in antisocial conduct. As Thomas Eddy, one of the leaders of the movement, noted, the House was intended "solely for the confinement of boys sixteen years of age, considered as vagrants, or guilty of petty thefts or other minor offenses." There was no right to indictment or jury trial. In 1816 Chancellor Kent upheld summary conviction of disorderly persons and their imprisonment for up to 60 days. An emphasis on minor offenses, belief in the innocence of the children despite their wrongs, and summary commitment procedures were all central features of the predelinquency campaign that characterized the House of Refuge reform. Subsequent developments in juvenile treatment, including the appearance of a juvenile court in Chicago in 1899, were similarly concentrated on petty offenses and salvageable offenders. Major offenders were, from the beginning, left in the adult criminal system. A similar segregation of the reformables from the nonreformables came to occupy a prominent place in the later juvenile court acts. This central concern for morally untarnished minor offenders has been a characteristic of American juvenile justice from the outset.

A final aspect of the New York undertaking to be noted is the extent to which the reformers were engaged in crime prediction. The conditions of misery, the minor law breaking, and the habits of ignorance and vice were seen as prodromal signs of future antisocial conduct, and these predictive factors were commonly spelled out in legislation. Like other elements of the House reform, the use of statutory terms to describe conditions leading to crime is a thread that runs through more than a century of juvenile justice.

The early focus thus was on children who were not guilty of what was considered real crime. They were the class of youth that predominated in the population of the House....

B. The Emergence of Parens Patriae

The theoretical justification for subjecting predelinquent children to a coercive court commitment was furnished by the *parens patriae* doctrine. The role of this doctrine in American juvenile justice has been misunderstood due to a failure to recognize that the distinction between neglected children and delinquent children, which is of great importance in the twentieth century, had virtually no meaning in the nineteenth-century predelinquency system. In 1875 Mary Carpenter, the noted English penal reformer, spoke for all the reformers of the [1800s] when she declared that, as to children under 14: "All may be classed together under this age, for there is no distinction between pauper, vagrant, and criminal children, which would require a different system of treatment." In 1898 Illinois reformers reaffirmed the unitary nature of predelinquency by reporting: "If the child is the material out of which men and women are made, the neglected child is the material out of which paupers and criminals are made." Thus, when the nineteenth-century reformers spoke of *parens patriae*, they were dealing with neglected and criminal children; they were articulating the duty of the government to intervene in the lives of *all* children who might become a community crime problem.

This idea of the guardianship of juvenile deviants in order to prevent their punishment was soon picked up by the courts, and applied with almost uniform consistency during a long period in which the prediction-oriented predelinquency system of justice prevailed. The view espoused in *Gault* that "there is no trace of the [*parens patriae*] doctrine in the history of criminal jurisprudence," misses the crucial point that juvenile justice in America had no separate *criminal* jurisprudence, a fact not to be obscured by the administration of juvenile justice in the criminal courts. In those courts *parens patriae* was a cornerstone justification for state intervention in the jurisprudence that did exist regarding deviant, crime-prone children.

II. The Regressive Face of Reform

Support for the House was replete with a solicitous regard for saving victimized children from downward careers that would inevitably invoke harsh official punishments. Paradoxically these same children were the objects of open hostility emanating from the very reformers who supported the House. The terms these reformers employed could have been used to describe a system of criminal corrections. Thomas Eddy, for example, opined that the boys could "by proper discipline be subdued and reclaimed." ... This insistence on atonement and punishment is a common attitude toward deviance and perhaps is only surprising when seen as a part of a reform program for the granting of shelter, nourishment, education, and removal from adult prisons.

A. Nullification

For many of the boys who had committed punishable offenses, the reform meant the change from freedom to incarceration, rather than a transfer from prison to House. One of the features that characterized the prereform era was the outright acquittal of what officials and reformers considered an inordinately large number of boys brought up on minor charges of one sort or another. The District Attorney, for example, reported in 1823 that "[m]any ... have been discharged, from an unwillingness to imprison, in hope of reformation, or under peculiar circumstances." In speaking of cases of petty theft in the pre-House period, he later stated: "It was hardly ever that a jury would convict. They would rather that the culprit acknowledged to be guilty should be discharged altogether, than be confined in the prisons of the state and county."

In addition, cases were brought to the attention of the judicial agencies that would earlier have gone unreported. The District Attorney noted that "[f]ormerly, too many citizens were reluctant in bringing to the police office, young persons who were detected in the commission of crimes. This operated as an encouragement to depraved parents to send very young children to depredate on the community—if detected they knew no punishment would follow." Law enforcement officers must have seen as one of the great reform needs a more efficient system of juvenile justice that would close the gaps through which children were escaping apprehension and conviction.

B. Corporal Punishments

Once at the House, the boys found that the Society's President had made no idle promise when he declared that the program should be no school picnic. Punishment for infraction of the rules was severe. [These punishments included flagellation, solitary confinement, a restricted diet, a prohibition against speaking without permission, and being put in irons.]

C. Coerced Heresy

A substantial portion of the House population also experienced religious repression. The reformers were all Protestants, many of them actively so. The rehabilitation program, therefore, included Bible reading and chapel services that the inmates were required to attend. For the sizeable number of Catholics in the House this involuntary Protestantism was pure heresy.... The practice of coerced heresy continued during the nineteenth century as a common element in the administration of juvenile justice.

III. Sources of Reform

All of this suggests that the House of Refuge was not simply a manifestation of humanitarian concern for children needing help. It was, in fact, the following: (1) a retrenchment in correctional practices, (2) a regression in poor-law policy, (3) a reaction to the phenomenon of immigration, (4) a reflection of the repressive side of Quaker education. Old values were reaffirmed in the search for new forms....

IV. Endorsement by the Courts and Coercive Predictions

The philosophy of the House of Refuge movement illustrates the well-known historical truth that the decade of the [1820s] was a period of reaction and conservatism. In spite of the punitive and conservative aspects of the reform, however, the American judiciary interpreted the establishment of institutions patterned on the New York House of Refuge wholly as a matter of humanitarian progress. With but two short-lived exceptions, when commitments to these institutions were challenged as infringements of liberty, judicial opinions denied that disadvantage, forfeiture, and punishment existed in such houses at all. The unqualified adoption by the courts of the philanthropic protestations of the reformers and their disregard of any punitive purpose were major factors contributing to the creation of the myth that the New York House of Refuge marked a noble triumph in child welfare rather than the complex and ambivalent development that it was.

....

From the beginnings of a separate juvenile system in the early [1820s] through the enactment of juvenile court acts at the turn of the twentieth century, these ... basic predictive factors appeared in the legislation dealing with juvenile deviants. Thus the same law violations, idleness, and parental unfitness defined "juvenile offender" in Massachusetts in 1826 and the jurisdictional reach of the Illinois Juvenile Court Act in 1899. The presumption remained that this was all a means to the end of crime prevention. Rather than a significant reform, the Illinois Juvenile Court Act of 1899 was essentially a continuation of both the major goals and the means of the predelinquency program initiated in New York more than 70 years earlier.

. . . .

VI. The Illinois Juvenile Court Act

. . . .

B. *The Reform Movement and the 1899 Juvenile Court Act*

It has been proposed thus far that the 1899 legislation served to continue the process of coercive predictions as a program of crime prevention; that it was designed to continue, as well, the emphasis on family life; and that it was not the aim of the reformers to change the procedures whereby the courts participated in child-saving. There were, in addition, other reform goals influencing the 1899 legislation that should be noted.

1. Improving Institutions.

In 1871 Superintendent Turner of the Chicago Reform School echoed the concern expressed by reformers fifty years earlier—children ought not to be incarcerated with adults, and when set off by themselves they should be under a system of strict classification. The last quarter of the nineteenth century in Illinois proved to be much less fruitful for reformers, however, than was the first quarter in New York. Legislation made the Pontiac institution a place for more mature and experienced criminals. Reformers lamented that Pontiac had become incapable of caring for predelinquents. The alternative institutions to which children were sentenced were as bad.

Predelinquent children were also kept in poorhouses. In 1870 the Board of State Commissioners of Public Charities had warned: "[T]he children in the almshouse have little or no hope of ever being lifted, by any agency whatever, out of the pauper class. They are, almost without exception, uninstructed and untrained." There is some reason to believe that it was the problem of almshouse children about which the Illinois reformers marshaled in 1898 to do battle with the legislature....

There is consistent evidence from the most relevant sources for believing that the reform crusade was massing for a change in institutional conditions. If this is correct—if these urban crusaders were seeking reform of the institutions when they went to Springfield—then the legislation that resulted was a colossal failure. Institutional conditions were barely changed. Nothing was done about the children in the poorhouse; a provision to remove them was deleted from the final bill. Local jails remained as they were. The only change was the provision that forbade placing children under twelve in a jail or police station. They were to be confined in a "suitable place," although no money was provided to lease, build, or otherwise find such a place. A provision to pay for such special detention was deleted by the legislature....

2. Private Enterprise.

During the whole period of reform activity in Illinois, local jails and state reformatories took charge only of the criminal children. The dependent, ignorant, idle, and other noncriminal predelinquents became clients of private child welfare organizations. Four of these received subsidies from county government, and ran their own institutions—industrial and training schools. Other private groups ... functioned largely as family placement agencies, holding children only long enough to find foster homes for them.

The state charities commissioners were opposed to the practice of having private parties care for these children and called for the state to assume this responsibility....

The 1899 legislation definitively settled the issue of private enterprise versus government monopoly.... Its provisions were a crushing defeat for the charities commissioners and others who had similarly viewed the problem of predelinquency as an exclusive concern of government. The industrial schools came away from the 1899 legislative session with more business than ever before. The Juvenile Court Act authorized commitment to them of law violators as well as the predelinquents they had been receiving before....

The institutional issue and the private enterprise question were related. The predelinquency business that the industrial and training schools received under the Juvenile Court Act could not have been given to them if government facilities had been expanded to serve the same needs. Taking children out of the poorhouses would have required some institutional alternatives that would inevitably have competed with the privately maintained schools. Many of those who pressed vigorously for the industrial school interests could not have been very enthusiastic in their support for improvement in public institutions.

3. Religious Segregation.

The third major issue on which the charities commissioners and others aligned with them—including this time the state supreme court—were administered a resounding defeat... was the matter of religious segregation of predelinquent youth. In 1863 the Society for the Protection of Destitute Roman Catholic Children in the City of New York received its official state charter. It required that "whenever the parent, guardian, or next of kin of any Catholic child about to be finally committed, shall request the magistrate to commit the child to the Catholic institution, the magistrate shall grant the request." In Illinois there was no such explicit approval of religious segregation of this sort, but it existed nonetheless. By 1887 the four industrial schools that had been chartered and were operating were evenly divided between Catholic and Protestant managements; each religious group had a school for girls and one for boys.

. . . .

In summary, the 1899 Illinois Act (1) restated the belief in the value of coercive predictions, (2) continued nineteenth-century summary trials for children about whom the predictions were to be made, (3) made no improvements in the long-condemned institutional care furnished these same children, (4) codified the view that institutions should, even without badly needed financial help from the legislature, replicate family life, and that foster homes should be found for predelinquents, and (5) reinforced the private sectarian interests, whose role long had been decried by leading child welfare reformers in the area of juvenile care.

C. The Rise of the Juvenile Court

The establishment of the court was hailed as a new era in our criminal history, and it was widely imitated in other states. Why this new myth developed—that society had indeed turned a corner in its dealings with children—is an intriguing historical question that can only be treated briefly here. At the outset, it seems clear that a large number of interests benefitted from the legislation.... Illinois law spoke of probation for the first time; a rule against keeping young children in jails had been accepted. The Act was a reaffirmation of state concern for predelinquents and for prevention. Perhaps exaggeration to the point of announcing a novel idea in American jurisprudence served to mask the magnitude of the defeat suffered by opponents of industrial schools, private interests, and sectarianism.

In reality the law's policies could hardly be described as a milestone of progress. No one could applaud "An act to promote private sectarian agencies and to defeat institutional reform." A more appealing title was needed. It was a phrase, buried in one section that said the tribunal was to carry on the prevailing system, that was used to characterize the accomplishment. The phrase was "[the court] may, for convenience, be called the 'Juvenile Court.'" Although the legislation was actually titled "An Act to regulate the treatment and control of dependent, neglected and delinquent children," it came to be known as the Juvenile Court Law....

One can guess at reasons for the friendly reception given the new law. The same climate of welfare enthusiasm that produced child labor legislation and compulsory-school laws would have been fertile ground for acceptance of a juvenile court law. An era of progressivism helped to generate receptivity for any strongly supported welfare proposal, especially one that cost no money. Furthermore, it is quite possible that in other states, as in Illinois, the issue of private sectarian power was ready for political resolution. A widespread sense of failure in the century-long effort to provide for "the best interests" of lower-class children and a realization that reform schools—family as well as congregate—had struck out dismally could have led to a discomforting awareness that the American social and economic system needed reform as much as did deviant parents and their offspring. Along with a growing sense of *mea culpa* seared into the conscience of the ruling classes by Upton Sinclair, Lincoln Steffens, and the cadre of muckraking revivalists, such factors would have created a profound need for the dawn of *some* new era. Enthusiasm was easier than recognition that the juvenile court law changed nothing of substance.

VII. The Third Round of Reform

It was almost seventy years before the Supreme Court of the United States rendered a critical appraisal of juvenile courts in America. It would be a great mistake to believe that the *Gault* decision represented an appraisal of the juvenile court as it was created at the turn of the century. Much of the nineteenth-century system that the juvenile court served to perpetuate had died out before the Supreme Court took on a major part of the responsibility for the nature of juvenile justice in the [1960s].

The juvenile court eventually became irrelevant as an institution to funnel law violating children to private schools or agencies; the Illinois state government acquired a virtual monopoly in the care and treatment of these children. Similarly, the responsibility of the juvenile court to provide family placements for predelinquent children was nullified by the process of industrialization and urbanization that, early in this century, rendered the practice of exporting children from city streets to rural homes an anachronism. In theory, at least, the loss of country placements might have been compensated for by the development of foster homes within the city. But this has not happened; "juvenile delinquent" today does not mean an unfortunate child not completely responsible for his misbehavior. A juvenile delinquent is viewed as a junior criminal hardly less threatening to peace and order than his more mature counterpart. Just as the opprobrium attached to reform schools long ago identified them as the dead end of juvenile justice, so the connotations of "juvenile delinquency" have made the delinquents highly unattractive as members of another's household. The demands delinquents appear to make on potential foster parents have effectively ruled out home placement as a dispositional choice for the juvenile court.

An additional factor contributing to the loss of foster homes has been the change in the racial composition of the children brought to the courts. In 1939 it was noted that [an increasingly higher percentage of Negro children appeared before the juvenile courts]....

For reasons likely akin to those that have caused racial segregation elsewhere in the community, foster home placements seldom cross racial lines....

At the same time, there has been a lack of significant change in juvenile reformatories and training schools. Most hold to the nineteenth-century expectation that family-style institutional organization can produce long-term changes in character. In 1950 Albert

Deutsch revealed that the problems of political appointments, financial starvation, over-crowding, and untrained custodians that had haunted the first juvenile reformatories had persisted. He only found some new words in use:

> The disciplinary or punishment barracks—sometimes these veritable cell blocks were more forbidding than adult prisons—were known officially as "adjustment cottages," or "lost privileges cottages." Guards were "supervisors." Employees who were often little more than caretakers and custodians were called "cottage parents." Whips, paddles, blackjacks and straps were "tools of control." Isolation cells were "meditation rooms." ... Catch-words of the trade—"individualization of treatment," "rehabilitating the maladjusted"—rolled easily off the tongues of many institutional officials who not only didn't put these principles into practice but didn't even understand their meaning.

The call for family relations within institutions was nothing more than wishful thinking. Without ready access to family life for the children coming before it, the juvenile court lost much of its *raison d'etre*.

The greatest functional loss the juvenile court has suffered in the twentieth century, however, is its role in the predelinquency system of crime prevention. The predelinquency concept rested on the belief that society could recognize, and the law could describe, the conditions of childhood that would give rise to adult criminals, and that techniques were available—institutions, foster homes, probation, psychiatry—that could arrest the conditions and prevent the crime. Loss of any of the elements of this belief would undermine the fundamental function of the juvenile court; the twentieth century has eroded all of them.

The metamorphosis of the relationship between poverty and crime exemplifies the erosion of nineteenth-century crime prevention techniques. In contrast to the zeal of earlier reformers for rehabilitating idle and ignorant children, today it is widely acknowledged that the roots of delinquency go deeper. Both the incipient political power of the poor and the conscience of the liberals make such antipauper action unfeasible. But denial of the predictive relationship between the conditions of poverty and the phenomenon of crime is more fundamental. It is based upon the recognition that poverty is not always a matter of the moral deficiencies of the poor, and that, absent the assumption that immorality is inherent in poverty, the leap to the immorality of crime fails. When American society finally rejected the older view cannot be specified. It must have occurred, or been greatly reinforced, during the Great Depression when impersonal economic forces reduced to poverty great numbers of Americans whose moral credentials were not open to question.

Related to the evolution of this attitude toward the poor was a new conception of the problem of child neglect, one that served to remove neglected children from the class of predelinquents. Parental immoralities that used to be seen as warnings of oncoming criminality in children have become acceptable, albeit not ideal, factors in a child's home life....

In addition, it had become clear that the new institutions for predelinquents were heavily punitive and functioned much like the adult prisons. It was only the myth of the New York House of Refuge—the belief that it was not designedly punitive and prison-like from the outset—that sustained the conception that substantive penal law, too, could be bent to humanitarian purposes. In reality, however, children charged with criminal offenses had to contend with the popular view—expressed in the law by the *mens rea* concept—that crime is the result of a choice to behave wickedly....

The role of juvenile crime as a predictor was weakened by the growing belief that society, as well as the child, was at fault; the more each act of criminal behavior symbolized the failures of the community, the less sense it made to be preoccupied with crime as an incipient failure of character. ...

Changing the focus of treatment from the individual to the community at large became increasingly attractive, moreover, as evidence increasingly indicated that the reformation of individual children was more fantasy than fact. The idea that crime could be prevented by individual treatment of those who showed its early symptoms lost its claim to credibility. With the illusions gone, it became clear that the juvenile courts were really deciding criminal responsibility. One court observed: "While the juvenile court law provides that adjudication of a minor to be a ward of the court shall not be deemed a conviction of crime, nevertheless, for all practical purposes this is a legal fiction, presenting a challenge to credulity and doing violence to reason." ...

In some states, notably New York and California, legislation finally placed procedural concerns ahead of the long-dead judicial system of coercive predictions, but the passage of over a century produced little change. The juvenile court system had taken on a life of its own, and, though it lost its social relevance, neither the motive to change nor the institutional means for effecting change appeared.

It was upon this scene that the Supreme Court arrived to announce a "revolution in the procedural aspects of juvenile courts." Or did it? Procedural revolution in the juvenile courts may well be the most recent myth of juvenile justice reform. There seem to be several reasons to doubt that any such revolution has taken place, or is likely to in the near future.

It is one thing for the Supreme Court or a legislature to command that procedural rights be guaranteed but quite another for them to be enforced in the juvenile courts. The *Gault* opinion did little to provide the juvenile courts with the motivation to comply by dubbing them "kangaroo courts" and by calling for their "domestication" as if they were some beasts run amuck. But even if the Court had consciously attempted to motivate the country's juvenile courts to apply a system of procedural formalities and rights and to recognize that the nineteenth century had come and gone, it would be naive to assume that these courts would enthusiastically adopt the mandated system.

Central among the reasons for the failure of the revolution is the role of counsel. The granting of procedural rights can hardly become a reality for children without lawyers to assert them on their behalf. As a practical matter, there are indications that defense lawyers do not defend. Platt has already noted that the role of defense counsel in the juvenile court appears to be less defending his client than accommodating himself to the system of personal relationships, the philosophy, and the organizational needs of the juvenile court. ...

Nonetheless, the lawyers are the heroes of the current round of reform; procedural revolution could nominate no one for this role but he who is trained and skilled in the tactics of the revolt. Like the heroes of earlier juvenile justice reform movements, they are deemed capable of nothing but heroic action on behalf of children in trouble. Little is known or heard of the severities and repressions of the House of Refuge; masked, too, is the essential vacuousness of the 1899 Juvenile Court Act and its capitulation to special interests. There is a real danger that contemporary society generally, and the bar in particular, will ignore the darker, less respectable, and less generous side of reform and reformer.

Can there be a procedural revolution? The *Gault* decision accepted the standard propaganda ... and gave its sponsorship to ... [the] myth that the original juvenile court was a matter trading constitutional rights for promises of rehabilitation and humane treatment. The Court also created its own myth — that children were being brought back to a Golden Age of constitutional rights that they lost at the turn of the century. If procedural formalities once were the order of the day, then it is quite likely that they can be made so again; there is no pioneering involved, only restoration. But if the historical interpretation made here is sound, then there is little reason to suppose that such a Golden Age ever existed and much reason to suspect that it did not.

There is also the disquieting thought that historical continuities in the judicial administration of juvenile justice may extend to the resource-starvation that has characterized both juvenile and adult justice. Giving children procedural rights is a somewhat distorted way of formulating the prospective reform. The rights must be bought and paid for by the community. Skillful and experienced lawyers must be obtained. Court staff size must be vastly expanded to relieve the pressure to compromise that results when too many cases must be processed by too few people. Courtrooms need to be constructed so that cases can go forward without encountering a bottleneck of physical facilities. Training programs, especially those that would permit lawyers to acquire an understanding of the social and psychological setting in which they work, need to be figured in the cost. But if the community has been unwilling to pay for nineteenth-century institutions and twentieth-century courts, can it be assumed that it will suddenly become generous when asked to pay for a procedural system designed largely to serve the same deprived population that has traditionally been the "beneficiary" of the juvenile justice system?

The Supreme Court's endorsement of the view that children are now being returned what they once gave up serves to compound the already enormously difficult task of reversing public attitudes toward the deviant poor. The Court interprets the 1899 events as creating a quid pro quo relationship between the delinquents and the state. For their constitutional rights, so tradition tells it, the children were promised treatment and humane kindness. Will all of this now be rescinded as the rights are reconveyed? Will child welfare responsibilities assumed in 1899 be terminated and the state relieved of its obligations to allocate resources? With no call on the public purse, the youthful clients of the juvenile court may find their procedural rights as chimerical as the so-called benefits that were proposed for the juvenile offenders of earlier days.

In spite of all this, there is one foundation on which faith in the achievement of procedural reform might rest. Unlike the earlier reforms, the present one can be viewed as being made by lawyers for lawyers. It is a deeper and broader involvement than was undertaken by the Chicago lawyers in 1899. The procedural reforms now being pursued require, in addition to resources and reorganization, the development and application of lawyer's law — the technical rules derived from constitutional theory and the needs of an orderly litigation process. Perhaps if the bar seriously devotes itself to satisfying what might be seen as its own professional needs, the public can be persuaded to allocate the necessary resources. Skillful and zealous advocacy in legislative halls might accomplish what has thus far eluded the bar's humanitarian predecessors. A commitment of the bar's abilities and prestige to the cause of procedural justice for juveniles may also provide opportunities to correct other glaring deficiencies in the methods by which juvenile justice is presently administered; the relevant underlying public attitudes are, after all, the same. The first step is the recognition that history has frowned on similar efforts, and that the path of reform is a matter of complex social and psychological problems that must be confronted before procedural change can be truly accomplished.

4. Anthony Platt, The Child Savers: The Invention of Delinquency

152–53, 155–61 (1977) (citations omitted)

Criticism of the juvenile court system over the last fifty years has come from persons expressing two diametrically opposed ideological perspectives. To the "legal moralists," the juvenile court is a politically ineffective and morally improper means of controlling juvenile crime. To the "constitutionalists," the juvenile court is arbitrary, unconstitutional, and violates the principles of fair trial. The former view concerns the protection of society, the latter addresses the safeguarding of individual rights.

With regard to juvenile delinquency, the legal moralists argue that it is socially undesirable to allow predatory and harmful behavior to go unpunished. They further point out that most ordinary citizens view delinquency with "intolerance, indignation and disgust" and that it is the proper function of the law to give ceremonial expression to this moral revulsion. Some writers claim that failure to punish delinquency and immoral behavior is likely to weaken the moral fabric of society; according to A. L. Goodhart, for example, "a community which is too ready to forgive the wrongdoer may end by condoning the crime."

The legal moralists stress the important psycho-social functions of "theatrical justice," which are predicated upon the expressive capacity of the criminal law to ritually uphold institutionalized values. The resentment shown by many lawyers toward the juvenile court system embodies many of the traditional features of legal moralism: there is vigorous criticism of the ineffectiveness of the juvenile court in the "war against crime," an implicit hostility directed toward professional rivals, and a stern disapproval of permissive ideologies. Although the legal moralists do not necessarily advocate harsh punishments, their theoretical perspective is often used by law-enforcement officials, political campaigners and community organizations who seek severer penalties or corporal punishment as an answer to the "crime problem." The following manifesto by John Wigmore captures the essence and spirit of the legal moralists' argument with regard to juvenile justice:

> [T]he social workers and the psychologists and the psychiatrists know nothing of crime or wrong. They refer to "reactions" and "maladjustments" and "complexes." ... The people need to have the moral law dinned into their consciences every day in the year. The juvenile court does not do that. And to segregate a large share of daily crime into the juvenile court is to take a long step toward undermining the whole criminal law.... [T]here is no deterrence of the multitude; merely a "treatment" of the "maladjustment." Its actions have no more effect on the multitude than the surgical operations of the hospitals—not so much, to be sure, because many a citizen has been deterred from submitting to the surgeon's knife because of rumors of what happened to his friend. And so we say to the devoted social workers and the cold scientists: "Do not think that you have the right to demand that all crimes be handed over to your charge until you have looked a little more deeply into the criminal law and have a better comprehension of the whole of its functions."

The legal moralists view the criminal law as the symbolic expression of the institutionalized values which the criminal violates, so that punishment has an educative function which unites all noncriminals and conformists in the "emotional solidarity of aggression." Punishment—for the legal moralists—is not intended to have instrumental value other than to promote a sense of moral solidarity in the citizenry. The juvenile court, according to this perspective, fails to make juvenile delinquency unattractive as a role model and has deprived the criminal law of its efficacy as an instrument of moral education because it does not formally express condemnation of anti-social behavior.

Advocates of the constitutionalist perspective, on the other hand, are skeptical of the juvenile court's humanitarian goals and are particularly concerned about the invasion of personal rights under the pretext of "welfare" and "rehabilitation." Edward Lindsey, one of the earliest spokesmen for this point of view, observed in 1914 that, despite the sonorous rhetoric of "socialized justice," there had been no effort to provide proper care and protection for children." There is often a very real deprivation of liberty," said Lindsey, "nor is that fact changed by refusing to call it punishment or because the good of the child is stated to be the object." This constitutional position was later echoed by Paul Tappan, who suggested that the *parens patriae* argument is an *ex post facto* fiction designed to reconcile reform legislation with traditional legal dogma. Juvenile courts, as Tappan observed, are in fact more akin in spirit and in method to contemporary administrative agencies than to early equity. Many critics consider that the tendency to conceive of the juvenile court as either a "clinic" or "welfare agency," to the exclusion of its other considerable functions, contributes neither to understanding the institution nor to its rational use in serving the public interest.

In support of their criticism of the administration of juvenile justice, the constitutionalists have drawn upon a variety of social science studies. The evidence from these studies suggests that the publicized goals of the juvenile court are rarely achieved. Informal procedures and confidentiality in juvenile court do not necessarily guard juveniles against "degradation ceremonies." The juvenile court, despite any intentions to sympathize with juvenile problems, is structurally organized to make judgments about positive and negative social behavior. Juvenile justice is administered by a politically constituted authority which addresses juvenile misconduct through the threat of coercion. Judicial sanctions can be imposed in the case of either contrary conduct or contrary attitudes, for the juvenile court is authorized to demand certain forms of moral propriety and attitudinal responses, even without the presence of a social victim who is visible and suffering.

Despite attempts to purge "juvenile delinquency" of pejorative implications, it has come to have as much dramatic significance for community disapproval as the label of "criminal" which it replaced. The informal system of communication between school, social agency, and parents operates to disseminate the stigma throughout the adolescent's social world, thus identifying him as "delinquent," "troublemaker," and "problem child." The benevolent philosophy of the juvenile court often disguises the fact that the offender is regarded as a "non-person" who is immature, unworldly, and incapable of making effective decisions with regard to his own welfare and future. Genuine attention is rarely paid to how the offender feels and experiences his predicament; according to Elliot Studt, the present structural arrangement of the juvenile court is likely to invite regression and diminish self-respect in its "clients." David Matza alludes to the "sense of injustice" which is experienced by many adolescents when they are treated with condescension, inconsistency, hypocrisy, favoritism, or whimsy. Other writers have confirmed that authoritarian professionalism and pious intimacy in a courtroom setting are not conducive to trusting and cooperative relationships. Finally, the constitutionalists argue that juvenile institutions are no better and in some cases worse than adult prisons. On purely utilitarian grounds, reformatories are a dismal failure in deterring future criminal behavior.

To summarize, the essence of the constitutionalist argument is that the juvenile court system violates constitutional guarantees of due process and stigmatizes adolescents as "delinquents," thereby performing functions similar to those of the criminal courts.

5. Barry C. Feld, *Bad Kids: Race and the Transformation of the Juvenile Court*

75–78 (1999) (citations omitted)

Industrialization, urbanization, and immigration threatened the culture and character of Anglo-Protestant America. The juvenile court represents a specific example of Progressive reformers' generic solutions to four interrelated problems of modernization: how to impose the "traditional values of the native elite" on the larger society, how to separate politics from administration, how to distribute authority among various levels of government, and how to integrate the work of charity and government. Characteristically, Progressives delegated discretion to professionals to solve individual problems within a bureaucratic setting. The occupational status of judges and the invocation of science and medicine in the guise of the rehabilitative ideal legitimated coercive intervention. However, the juvenile court's primary goal "was not a new technology of rehabilitation, but a comprehensive administrative apparatus that coordinated and formalized routine practices of the past." The juvenile court provided legal authority for administrative discretion and provided continuity with earlier strategies to regulate the children of immigrants and the poor.

The juvenile court culminated a century-long evolution in the control of young offenders and their differentiation from adults. Although the earlier houses of refuge and reformatories provided specialized institutions for youths, the juvenile court completed the process and created a separate agency more extensively to regulate children. Juvenile court ideology postulated that children were immature, irresponsible, and needed care and guidance. The courts' jurisdiction affirmed the dependent status of children. Its dispositional authority enabled it to exercise control over children and to supervise their families.

Juvenile courts' authority to oversee children and their families embodied a conceptual contradiction. On the one hand, family life became increasingly privatized, it erected barriers between the domestic and outside worlds, and parents assumed greater responsibility to raise their own children. On the other hand, Progressives expanded the role of the state, assumed greater authority to intrude into private arrangements, and intervened when families failed in their obligations to their children. Progressives resolved the conflict between private autonomy and public authority by predicating *parens patriae* intervention on the failures of families, particularly those of the lower classes and immigrants. Although Progressives affirmed family privacy, the state provided the necessary counterweight to lower-class socialization gone awry. These contradictions inevitably skew the balance between social welfare and social control …"[C]hildren's institutions have been premised on class-biased conceptions of family deficiency, and they have embodied a class-differentiated conception of their goals…. The juvenile justice programs and the welfare system have consistently emphasized the need to watch over lower-class families and prevent their excesses…. [T]he fear of lower-class children has converted the promise to 'save the child' into the goal of protecting the community from their disruptive potential."

Progressives' belief in their own benevolence and in the superiority of their vision of childhood and society blinded them to the possibility of cultural conflict in defining and controlling youthful deviance. Notwithstanding their child-saving motivations, juvenile court reformers created a powerful instrument of coercive social control. When juvenile court reformers espoused a commitment to uplift the downtrodden, they also preserved the power and privilege of the status quo. The juvenile court embodied both reformers' compassion for the child and their class and ethnic antagonisms. The ideology of *parens patriae* stipulated personal inadequacy or moral deficiency as preconditions for social welfare intervention. Either the child must commit an offense or violate the undefined norms of childhood or her parents must fail to meet middle-class child-rearing standards before Progressives would provide public support. Thus, a negative connotation inevitably attached to all public intervention.

Progressives ignored the social structural implications of their own theories of delinquency and instead addressed deviance in terms of personal shortcomings. "The focus on social reform implied that the 'blame' for poverty and dependency lay in the social conditions created and maintained by these powerful people, rather than in poor and dependent individuals themselves." Social structure and political economy create the material inequalities that place the poor and marginalized at greater risk of crime, delinquency, and justice system intervention. Moreover, Progressives institutionalized childhood as a dependent social and legal status, and children least of all bore responsibility for their adverse circumstances. According to positivist theory, youths' detrimental family situations and injurious environmental conditions *caused* them to become delinquents. Despite the social structural implications of positivism, Progressive reformers chose to mend damaged individuals rather than to alter the social conditions that injured them or caused their misbehavior. Rather than proposing structural reforms to alleviate the conditions that they knew caused crime, they opted to "stand on the sidelines and administer first aid to the children who were the battle's victims." Saving children appealed to Progressives' humanitarian impulses without engendering a more radical critique and the more fundamental social changes it entailed. By minimizing social structural explanations and maximizing children's and parents' inadequacies and responsibilities for their own plights, Progressives simultaneously undermined support for programs for children. Labeling children and their parents as deficient creates a self fulfilling prophecy and reduces public responsibility to alleviate those personal deficits. In their reformative zeal, Progressives did not consider the depersonalizing consequences of defining children as dependent and objects for them to mold. They naively assumed that they could combine social welfare and social control and failed to recognize the potential conflicts between protecting children and protecting society. They did not appreciate the inherent contradictions of providing social welfare services in a coercive institution. Rather, they delegated to the subjective discretion of each judge and court worker the authority to resolve the fundamental antagonisms between voluntarism and coercion and between welfare and control without any formal guidance.

Progressive reformers failed to perceive the operational contradictions between treating and punishing, between *parens patriae* and coercion, or the rapidity with which juvenile justice operatives could subordinate rehabilitative considerations to custodial concerns. Although the juvenile court hoped to rehabilitate errant youths, protecting the community from dangerous youths constituted its primary responsibility. They did not fully appreciate the organizational tensions inherent in a multipurpose court that coerced a "voluntary" therapeutic relationship and subordinated the rule of law to discretionary professional expertise. The juvenile court combined features of a social service agency, welfare system, and mental health clinic with the coercive power of a court of law. Nor did they recognize that juvenile court intervention, or indeed any measure of social control, may aggravate and intensify the behaviors it seeks to reduce. In short, Progressives embedded a number of cultural contradictions in the juvenile court without attempting to reconcile them. They subsumed the clash between individualized sentences and equality and the rule of law in "sound discretion" and "scientific expertise." They evaded the contradictions between the offender and the offense, between the social worker's desire to help and the judge's inclination to punish by conceptualizing the judge as a social worker.

Although Progressive ideology recognized that social structural and environmental conditions "caused" delinquency, they defined juvenile courts' delinquency jurisdiction on the basis of children's offenses rather than their real needs. Instead of pursuing a social welfare agenda and reducing the adverse conditions that caused delinquency, they combined social welfare and penal social control in the juvenile court. They espoused deterministic causal explanations of delinquent behavior but then individualized their sanctions. But if state coercion for criminal offenses constitutes "punishment," then punishing people for behavior that "society" caused supports charges of hypocrisy. On the other hand, if deterministic explanations reduce offenders' personal responsibility for their behavior, then "treatment" erodes the expressive functions that the criminal law serves by blaming and condemning people's choices.

Finally, juvenile jurisprudence embodies the inherent administrative conflicts between individualized discretion and the rule of law. Through most of juvenile courts' history, appellate courts uncritically rejected children's legal contentions that juvenile courts punished them without due process of law, echoed the expansive language of *Crouse*, and upheld the state's *parens patriae* authority to "rescue" and "rehabilitate" young people. Indeed, juvenile courts represent such a universal fixture of childhood that questioning the promise of the "noble experiment" challenges the legitimacy of the social construction of childhood itself. Until *Gault*, appellate courts assumed compatibility between juvenile courts' twin goals of promoting the best interests of the child and the welfare of the state and rejected requests for procedural safeguards.

The United States Supreme Court's decisions in the 1960s and 1970s extended some constitutional procedural safeguards to juveniles. The decisions imposed some legal formality and a modicum of equality on a system designed to ignore legal considerations in favor of individual considerations and personal circumstances.

Notes

(a) Which of these authors has the most pessimistic view of the juvenile court system? Which one is the most optimistic? What factors motivate their opinions?

(b) To what extent should history affect one's approach to the contemporary juvenile court system and its deficiencies? For example, if the original purposes of the juvenile courts were not benevolent, does that mean they should be eliminated or drastically overhauled? Can the historical impetus for juvenile courts be purged?

(c) As we read and analyze the material in the book, keep the historical material in mind.

B. Children in the Courts

1. Early Cases

Exparte CROUSE
4 Whart. 9 (1839)

HABEAS CORPUS

The provisions of the acts of 23rd of March 1826, and 10th of April, 1835, which authorise the committal of infants to the House of Refuge, under certain circumstances, and their detention there, without a previous trial by jury, are not unconstitutional.

The petition for the *habeas corpus* was in the name of her father.

[T]he girl had been committed to the custody of the managers by virtue of a warrant under the hand and seal of a justice of the peace of the county of Philadelphia, which recited that complaint and due proof had been made before him by Mary Crouse, the mother of the said Mary Ann Crouse, "that the said infant by reason of vicious conduct, has rendered her control beyond the power of the said complainant, and made it manifestly requisite that from regard to the moral and future welfare of the said infant she should be placed under the guardianship of the managers of the House of Refuge;" and the said alderman certified that in his opinion the said infant was "a proper subject for the said House of Refuge." Appended to the warrant of commitment were the names and places of residence of the witnesses examined, and the substance of the testimony given by them respectively, upon which the adjudication of the magistrate was founded.

The House of Refuge was established in pursuance of an act of assembly passed on the 23rd day of March, 1826. The 6th section of that act declared that the managers should, "at their discretion, receive into the said House of Refuge, such children who shall be taken up or committed as vagrants, or upon any criminal charge, or duly convicted of criminal offences, as may be in the judgment of any Court, or of any alderman or justice of the peace, or of the managers of the Alms-house and house of employment, be deemed proper objects." By a supplement to the act passed on the 10th day of April 1835, it was declared, that in lieu of the provisions of the act of 1826, it should be lawful for the managers of the House of Refuge "at their discretion, to receive into their care and guardianship, infants, males under the age of twenty-one years, and females under the age of eighteen years, committed to their custody in either of the following modes, viz. First: infants committed by an alderman or justice of the peace on the complaint and due proof made to him by the parent, guardian or next friend of such infant, that by reason of incorrigible or vicious conduct such infant has rendered his or her control beyond the power of such parent, guardian or next friend, and made it manifestly requisite that from regard for the morals and future welfare of such infant, he or she should be placed under the guardianship of the managers of the House of Refuge. Second: infants committed by the authority aforesaid, where complaint and due proof have been made that such infant is a proper subject for the guardianship of the managers of the House of Refuge, in consequence of vagrancy, or of incorrigible or vicious conduct, and that from the moral depravity or otherwise of the parent or next friend in whose custody such infant may be, such parent or next friend is incapable or unwilling to exercise the proper care and discipline over such incorrigible or vicious infant. Third: infants committed by the Courts of this commonwealth in the mode provided by the act to which this is a supplement."

PER CURIAM.

The House of Refuge is not a prison, but a school. Where reformation, and not punishment, is the end, it may indeed be used as a prison for juvenile convicts who would else be committed to a common goal; and in respect to these, the constitutionality of the act which incorporated it, stands clear of controversy. It is only in respect of the application of its discipline to subjects admitted on the order of a court, a magistrate, or the managers of the Alms-house, that a doubt is entertained. The object of the charity is reformation, by training its inmates to industry; by imbuing their minds with principles of morality and religion; by furnishing them with means to earn a living; and, above all, by separating them from the corrupting influence of improper associates. To this end, may not the natural parents, when unequal to the task of education, or unworthy of it, be superseded by the *parens patriæ*, or common guardian of the community? It is to be remembered that the public has a paramount interest in the virtue and knowledge of its members, and that, of strict right, the business of education belongs to it. That parents are ordinarily entrusted with it, is because it can seldom be put into better hands; but where they are incompetent or corrupt, what is there to prevent the public from withdrawing their faculties, held, as they obviously are, at its sufferance? The right of parental control is a natural, but not an unalienable one. It is not excepted by the declaration of rights out of the subjects of ordinary legislation; and it consequently remains subject to the ordinary legislative power, which, if wantonly or inconveniently used, would soon be constitutionally restricted, but the competency of which, as the government is constituted, cannot be doubted. As to abridgment of indefeasible rights by confinement of the person, it is no more than what is borne, to a greater or less extent, in every school; and we know of no natural right to exemption from restraints which conduce to an infant's welfare. Nor is there a doubt of the propriety of their application in the particular instance. The infant has been snatched from a course which must have ended in confirmed depravity; and, not only is the restraint of her person lawful, but it would be an act of extreme cruelty to release her from it.

Remanded.

People ex rel O'Connell v. Turner

55 Ill. 280 (1870)

The return is, that the boy had been detained by authority of the mittimus, which accompanied the petition, the original of which was filed with an endorsement thereon by the sheriff of its due execution, by the delivery of the "body of the prisoner to the superintendent of the reform school."

It is admitted, that the relator is the father of the boy, alleged to be restrained of his liberty, and that he is of the age stated.

The only question for determination, is the power of the legislature to pass the laws, under which this boy was arrested and confined.

...

The first section [of the charter of the reform school] establishes "a school for the safe keeping, education, employment and reformation of all children between the ages of six and sixteen years, who are destitute of proper parental care, and growing up in mendicancy, ignorance, idleness or vice."

Section four, of the act of 1867, provides, that "whenever any police magistrate, or justice of the peace, shall have brought before him any boy or girl, within the ages of six or sixteen years, who he has reason to believe is a vagrant, or is destitute of proper parental care, or is growing up in mendicancy, ignorance, idleness or vice," he shall cause such boy or girl to be arrested, and, together with the witnesses, taken before one of the judges of the superior or circuit court of Cook county. The judge is empowered to issue a summons, or order in writing, to the child's father, mother, guardian, or whosoever may have the care of the child, in the order named, and if there be none such, to any person, at his discretion, to appear, at a time and place mentioned, and show cause why the child should not be committed to the "reform school," and upon return of due service of the summons, an investigation shall be had. The section then directs, "if, upon such examination, such judge shall be of opinion that said boy or girl is a proper subject for commitment to the reform school, and that his or her moral welfare, and the good of society, require that he or she should be sent to said school for employment, instruction and reformation, he shall so decide, and direct the clerk of the court of which he is judge, to make out a warrant of commitment to said reform school; and such child shall thereupon be committed."

Section nine, of the act of 1863, directs, that all persons between six and sixteen years of age, convicted of crime punishable by fine or imprisonment, who, in the opinion of the court, would be proper subjects for commitment, shall be committed to said school.

Section ten authorizes the confinement of the children, and that they "shall be kept, disciplined, instructed, employed and governed," until they shall be reformed and discharged, or shall have arrived at the age of twenty-one years; and that the sole authority to discharge shall be in the board of guardians.

The warrant of commitment does not indicate that the arrest was made for a criminal offense. Hence, we conclude that it was issued under the general grant of power, to arrest and confine for misfortune.

The contingencies enumerated, upon the happening of either of which the power may be exercised, are vagrancy, destitution of proper parental care, mendicancy, ignorance, idleness or vice. Upon proof of any one, the child is deprived of home, and parents, and friends, and confined for more than half of an ordinary life. It is claimed, that the law is administered for the moral welfare and intellectual improvement of the minor, and the good of society. From the record before us, we know nothing of the management. We are only informed that a father desires the custody of his child; and that he is restrained of his liberty. Therefore, we can only look at the language of the law, and the power granted.

What is proper parental care? The best and kindest parents would differ, in the attempt to solve the question. No two scarcely agree; and when we consider the watchful supervision, which is so unremitting over the domestic affairs of others, the conclusion is forced upon us, that there is not a child in the land who could not be proved, by two or more witnesses, to be in this sad condition. Ignorance, idleness, vice, are relative terms. Ignorance is always preferable to error, but, at most, is only venial. It may be general or it may be limited. Though it is sometimes said, that "idleness is the parent of vice," yet the former may exist without the latter. It is strictly an abstinence from labor or employment. If the child perform all its duties to parents and to society, the State has no right to compel it to labor. Vice is a very comprehensive term. Acts, wholly innocent in the estimation of many good men, would, according to the code of ethics of others, show fearful depravity. What is the standard to be? What extent of enlightenment, what amount of industry, what degree of virtue, will save from the threatened imprisonment? In our solicitude to form youth for the duties of civil life, we should not forget the rights which inhere both in parents and children. The principle of the absorption of the child in, and its complete subjection to the despotism of, the State, is wholly inadmissible in the modern civilized world.

The parent has the right to the care, custody and assistance of his child. The duty to maintain and protect it, is a principle of natural law. He may even justify an assault and battery, in the defense of his children, and uphold them in their law suits. Thus the law recognizes the power of parental affection, and excuses acts which, in the absence of such a relation, would be punished. Another branch of parental duty, strongly inculcated by writers on natural law, is the education of children. To aid in the performance of these duties, and enforce obedience, parents have authority over them. The municipal law should not disturb this relation, except for the strongest reasons. The ease with which it may be disrupted under the laws in question; the slight evidence required, and the informal mode of procedure, make them conflict with the natural right of the parent. Before any abridgment of the right, gross misconduct or almost total unfitness on the part of the parent, should be clearly proved. This power is an emanation from God, and every attempt to infringe upon it, except from dire necessity, should be resisted in all well governed States. "In this country, the hope of the child, in respect to its education and future advancement, is mainly dependent upon the father; for this he struggles and toils through life; the desire of its accomplishment operating as one of the most powerful incentives to industry and thrift. The violent abruption of this relation would not only tend to wither these motives to action, but necessarily, in time, alienate the father's natural affections."

. . .

These laws provide for the "safe keeping" of the child; they direct his "commitment," and only a "ticket of leave," or the uncontrolled discretion of a board of guardians, will permit the imprisoned boy to breathe the pure air of heaven outside his prison walls, and to feel the instincts of manhood by contact with the busy world. The mittimus terms him "a proper subject for commitment;" directs the superintendent to "take his body," and the sheriff endorses upon it, "executed by delivering the body of the within named prisoner." The confinement may be from one to fifteen years, according to the age of the child. Executive clemency can not open the prison doors, for no offense has been committed. The writ of habeas corpus, a writ for the security of liberty, can afford no relief, for the sovereign power of the State, as parens patriæ, has determined the imprisonment beyond recall. Such a restraint upon natural liberty is tyranny and oppression. If, without crime, without the conviction of any offense, the children of the State are to be thus confined for the "good of society," then society had better be reduced to its original elements, and free government acknowledged a failure.

In cases of writs of habeas corpus to bring up infants, there are other rights beside the rights of the father. If improperly or illegally restrained, it is our duty, *ex debito justitiæ*, to liberate. The welfare and rights of the child are also to be considered. The disability of minors does not make slaves or criminals of them. They are entitled to legal rights, and are under legal liabilities. An implied contract for necessaries is binding on them. The only act which they are under a legal incapacity to perform, is the appointment of an attorney. All their other acts are merely voidable or confirmable. They are liable for torts, and punishable for crime. Lord Kenyon said, "If an infant commit an assault, or utter slander, God forbid that he should not be answerable for it, in a court of justice." Every child over ten years of age may be found guilty of crime. For robbery, burglary or arson, any minor may be sent to the penitentiary. Minors are bound to pay taxes for the support of the government, and constitute a part of the militia, and are compelled to endure the hardship and privation of a soldier's life, in defense of the constitution and the laws; and yet it is assumed, that to them, liberty is a mere chimera. It is something of which they may have dreamed, but have never enjoyed the fruition.

Can we hold children responsible for crime; liable for their torts; impose onerous burdens upon them, and yet deprive them of the enjoyment of liberty, without charge or conviction of crime? The bill of rights declares, that "all men are, by nature, free and independent, and have certain inherent and inalienable rights—among these are life, liberty, and the pursuit of happiness." This language is not restrictive; it is broad and comprehensive, and declares a grand truth, that "all men," all people, everywhere, have the inherent and inalienable right to liberty. Shall we say to the children of the State, you shall not enjoy this right—a right independent of all human laws and regulations? It is declared in the constitution; is higher than constitution and law, and should be held forever sacred.

Even criminals can not be convicted and imprisoned without due process of law—without a regular trial, according to the course of the common law. Why should minors be imprisoned for misfortune? Destitution of proper parental care, ignorance, idleness and vice, are misfortunes, not crimes. In all criminal prosecutions against minors, for grave and heinous offenses, they have the right to demand the nature and cause of the accusation, and a speedy public trial by an impartial jury. All this must precede the final commitment to prison. Why should children, only guilty of misfortune, be deprived of liberty without "due process of law?"

It can not be said, that in this case, there is no imprisonment. This boy is deprived of a father's care; bereft of home influences; has no freedom of action; is committed for an uncertain time; is branded as a prisoner; made subject to the will of others, and thus feels that he is a slave. Nothing could more contribute to paralyze the youthful energies, crush all noble aspirations, and unfit him for the duties of manhood. Other means of a milder character; other influences of a more kindly nature; other laws less in restraint of liberty, would better accomplish the reformation of the depraved, and infringe less upon inalienable rights.

It is a grave responsibility to pronounce upon the acts of the legislative department. It is, however, the solemn duty of the courts to adjudge the law, and guard, when assailed, the liberty of the citizen. The constitution is the highest law; it commands and protects all. Its declaration of rights is an express limitation of legislative power, and as the laws under which the detention is had, are in conflict with its provisions, we must so declare.

It is therefore ordered, that Daniel O'Connell be discharged from custody.

C. An Overview of the Juvenile Justice System

1. The Changing Nature of the Juvenile Court as Reflected in the "Purposes" Sections of Juvenile Justice Codes

Most juvenile law statutory schemes contain a "purposes clause"[1] or a provision articulating the underlying objectives of the legislation. This clause is designed to provide guide-

---

1. *But see* Arizona and the District of Columbia statutes, which appear to have no purposes provisions.

lines for officials when they interpret and enforce the statutes governing the juvenile court system. The traditional approach was that juveniles were not fully culpable for their deviant behavior. The theory was that whereas adults ought to be punished or receive their "just deserts" for committing offenses or crimes, juveniles should be treated and rehabilitated. The juvenile court created in 1899 in Cook County, Illinois was devised to ensure that juvenile matters were adjudicated in a manner consistent with treatment and rehabilitation motives. Many states were influenced by Illinois' creation of a separate juvenile court and adopted the goals of care and guidance in dealing with juveniles. However, recently, many states have espoused a "get tough" attitude in dealing with alleged delinquents. This more recent trend is to downplay the care and rehabilitation aspects, and instead stress goals of punishment, deterrence, isolation, and protection of the community.

The research concerning the purposes clauses of juvenile court statutes yielded interesting results in the philosophical similarities and differences among the states. We have placed the states' purposes clauses into three main categories that often overlap: Traditional, Community Protection and Accountability, and Balanced. We did so by looking at the following linguistic variables in the statutes: (1) Rehabilitation/Treatment of the Juvenile; (2) Care, Guidance, and Control of the Juvenile; (3) Protection of the Juvenile; (4) Holding the Juvenile Accountable/Responsible for His or Her Behavior; (5) Punishment/Discipline of the Juvenile; (6) Protection of the Community or Public Safety; (7) Best Interests of the Juvenile; and (8) Best Interests of Society.

We could just as easily have made only two categories: traditional and balanced. We chose the tripartite classification because we concluded that some of the balanced jurisdictions were more punitive than others. All the statutory purposes can be viewed on a spectrum ranging from care, protection and rehabilitation to punishment, accountability and public safety.

Traditional

The traditional model focuses on the juvenile's rehabilitation and treatment, although the statute may also mention the best interests of the state. However, jurisdictions that fit into this model do not use the word punishment. Rather, traditional models echo the concept that delinquents need treatment rather than criminal sanctions.

Almost one-third of the states emphasize these traditional objectives in dealing with juvenile delinquency. Delaware's purpose section states that the objective is to "provide for the delinquent such wise conditions of modern education and training as will restore the largest possible portion of such delinquents to useful citizenship." Del. Code Ann. tit. 31, § 302 (2004). Massachusetts clearly distinguishes juveniles from adults: "they shall be treated, not as criminals, but as children in need of aid, encouragement and guidance." Mass. Gen. Law ch. 119, § 53 (West 2007). *See also Commonwealth v. Connor C.*, 738 N.E. 2d 731 (Mass 2000), in which the court noted that the "primary public policy of the Commonwealth remains one of rehabilitation and redemption of children who violate laws." Most of these traditional states, like Iowa, reiterate that juveniles should receive "care, guidance and control." Iowa Code § 232.1 (2003). *See also* Ga. Code Ann. § 15-11-1 (2002) (Georgia); Mich. Comp. Laws § 712A.1 (2004) (Michigan); Mo. Rev. Stat. § 211.011 (2004) (Missouri); Nev. Rev. Stat. § 62A.360 (Nevada); N.D. Cent. Code, § 27-20-01 (2003) (North Dakota); Ohio Rev. Code Ann. 211.01 (2004) (Ohio); R.I. Gen. Laws § 14-1-2 (2004) (Rhode Island); S.C. Code Ann. § 20-7-470 (2003) (South Carolina); Tenn. Code Ann. § 37-1-101 (2003) (Tennessee); Vt. Stat. Ann. tit. 33, § 5501 (2003) (Vermont); Wis. Stat. § 48.01 (2003) (Wisconsin).

New Hampshire acknowledges the need for the minor to accept "personal responsibility" but does not mention punishment or sanctions; rather it provides for "counseling, supervision, treatment, and rehabilitation." N.H. Rev. Stat. Ann. § 169-B:1 (2003). South Dakota falls into the traditional model, but its overall categorization remains open for debate. South Dakota, on its face, is a clear traditional model; it does not mention societal interests or punishment. Relevant sections assert that, "provisions of this chapter ... shall be liberally construed in favor of the child ... and for the purposes of affording guidance, control and rehabilitation of any child in need of supervision or any delinquent child." S.D. Codified Laws § 26-7A-6 (2003). However, South Dakota's Supreme Court in *State v. Harris*, 494 N.W. 2d 619 (1993), asserted that "it cannot be imagined that the legislature, in rewriting the juvenile laws in 1991, intended that the interests of the child only would be considered." Similarly, Montana's statute is difficult to categorize. The stated purpose is "to prevent and reduce youth delinquency through a system that does not seek retribution but that provides: (a) immediate, consistent, enforceable, and avoidable consequences of youths' actions; (b) a program of supervision, care, rehabilitation, detention, competency development, and community protection for youth...." Mont. Code Ann., § 41-5-102(2)(a)(b) (2003).

Community Protection and Accountability

The community protection and accountability model emphasizes the juvenile's accountability for his actions and the need to protect the community. States following this model also include references to the traditional objectives of care and treatment but stress punishment and sanctions as integral parts of the juvenile justice system. The rhetoric of these states indicates a willingness to impose punitive measures on juvenile delinquents for compromising the safety and security of the community. This model represents a clear shift from the traditional notion that juveniles should not be punished in the same manner as adults in recognition of their lesser culpability, immaturity, and potential for change.

Alaska, for example, requires the court to, "protect the community, impose accountability for violations of law, and equip juvenile offenders with the skills needed to live responsibly and productively." Alaska Stat. § 47.12.010 (2004). The particular provisions that define Alaska as a community protection and accountability model are found in subsections (2)–(4) of the same section, which state, "(2) protect citizens from juvenile crime; (3) hold each juvenile offender directly accountable for the offender's conduct; (4) provide swift and consistent consequences for crimes committed by juveniles." *Id.* California is included in this category because the statute first mentions public safety and protection, and authorizes punishment. Cal. Welf. & Inst. Code § 202 (2004). However, notions of rehabilitation are included, so this categorization is disputable. The Colorado General Assembly clearly places the interests of public safety as paramount and authorizes sanctions to bring about these ends. Colo. Rev. Stat. § 19-2-102 (2003). Texas does include some language referring to rehabilitation, but grammatical inference places the statute in the community protection and accountability model because the child's therapeutic needs take a backseat to public safety. The pertinent section of Texas's purpose provision stresses public protection: "(1) provide for the protection of the public and public safety; (2) consistent with the protection of the public and public safety: (A) promote the concept of punishment for criminal acts; ... (c) provide treatment, training, and rehabilitation that emphasizes the accountability and responsibility...." Tex. Fam. Code § 51.01 (Vernon 2004); *see also* Wyo. Stat. § 14-6-201 (which similarly states that all goals are to be effectuated consistent with the protection of the public and public safety). Washington places the utmost emphasis on "protecting the citizenry from criminal behavior" and also authorizes "punishment commensurate with the age, crime, and criminal history of the juvenile offender...." Wash. Rev. Code § 13.40.010 (2)(a)(d) (2004).

Balanced

The majority of states have attempted to strike a balance between the traditional and community protection and accountability models. Balanced states look more or less equally to the juvenile's well-being through rehabilitation, and accountability for the minor's deviant behavior. Often these clauses may cause confusion, as the new goals of punishment and protection may contradict traditional objectives of therapy and rehabilitation.

Provision (7) of the Alabama juvenile code exemplifies this tension by "hold[ing] a child found to be delinquent accountable for his or her actions to the extent of the child's age, education, mental, and physical condition, background, and all other relevant factors and to provide a program of supervision, care, and rehabilitation, including restitution by the child to the victim for his or her delinquent acts." Ala. Code § 12-15-101 (2004). Connecticut's provisions allow for the child to remain at home and emphasize the need for the child's family to be involved with his or her treatment. *See* Conn. Gen. Stat. § 46b-121h (2005); *see also* 705 Ill. Comp. Stat. 405/5-101 (2004) (Illinois); Kan. Stat. Ann. § 38-1601 (2003) (Kansas). Hawaii states in the same sentence its goals to "foster the rehabilitation of juveniles[,]" while "render[ing] appropriate punishment to offenders...." Haw. Rev. Stat. § 571-1 (2003). Idaho, in a lengthy section of legislative intent, combines rehabilitation methods with communal safeguarding devices. Idaho Code Ann. § 20-501 (2004). Maine presents a conflicting model by espousing not only "[t]o secure for any juvenile ... treatment, care, guidance and discipline[,]" but also "[t]o provide consequences, which may include those of a punitive nature...." Me. Rev. Stat. Ann. tit. 15, § 3002 (D)(F) (2003). Arkansas also takes this approach in its statute: "to protect society more effectively by substituting for retributive punishment, whenever possible, methods of offender rehabilitation and rehabilitative restitution, recognizing that the application of sanctions which are consistent with the seriousness of the offense is appropriate in all cases...." Ark. Code Ann. § 9-27-302 (3) (1999). This statute could be read to focus on rehabilitation instead of retribution, but the application of sanctions brings a punitive taint to the statute. Mississippi strikes a balance by including the traditional phrase, "care, guidance and control," but also mandating that the child be accountable and responsible, stressing the best interest of the state. Miss. Code Ann. § 43-21-103 (2004). Many other states simultaneously include the objectives of ensuring public safety, demanding juvenile accountability, and rehabilitating the delinquent. New York provides that the court should consider the needs and best interests of the respondent as well as the need for protection of the community, but does not provide guidelines when these objectives clash, as they often do. N.Y. Fam. Ct. Act § 301.1 (McKinney 2004). *See also* Ind. Code Ann. § 31-10-2-1 (2004) (Indiana); Ky. Rev. Stat. Ann. § 600.010 (2003) (Kentucky); La. Child. Code Ann. art. 801 (2004) (Louisiana); Md. Code Ann. § 3-8A-02 (2003) (Maryland); Minn. Stat. § 260B.001 (2003) (Minnesota); Neb. Rev. Stat. § 43-246 (2003) (Nebraska); N.J. Stat. Ann. § 2A:4A-21 (2004) (New Jersey); N.M. Stat. Ann. § 32A-2-2 (Michie 2004) (New Mexico); N.C. Gen. Stat. § 7B-1500 (2004) (North Carolina); Okla. Stat. tit. 10, § 7301-1.2 (2004) (Oklahoma); Or. Rev. Stat. § 419C.001 (2003) (Oregon); 42 Pa. Cons. Stat. § 6301 (2004) (Pennsylvania);Utah Code Ann. § 78-3a-102 (2004) (Utah); Va. Code Ann. § 16.1-227 (2004) (Virginia); W.Va. Code § 49-1-1 (2003) (West Virginia).

Notes

(a) Barry C. Feld, *Race, Politics, and Juvenile Justice: The Warren Court and the Conservative "Backlash,"* 87 Minn. L. Rev. 1447, 1572–73 (2003):

The recent "get tough" amendments to juvenile sentencing statutes have had a substantial and disproportionate impact on minority youths in correctional confinement. Examining the proportional changes in the racial composition of institutional populations for the period 1985–95, which corresponds with the era of "get tough" changes in sentencing laws, reveals that the overall numbers of youths in custody on any given day increased almost 40%. Despite the overall increase of youths in correctional custody, the proportion of white juveniles confined in public facilities declined 7%, while the percentage of black juveniles confined increased 63%. Thus, the overall increases in the numbers of youths confined and proportional changes in the racial composition of the correctional inmates reflect the sharp growth of minority youths in institutions. As a result, the proportion of white juveniles in custody declined from 44% to 32% of all incarcerated delinquents, while the proportion of black youths increased from 37% to 43% and that of Hispanics increased from 13% to 21% of all confined youths.

(b) Do you agree with the shift that juvenile courts have taken? Is there an alternative? What language would you use if you were responsible for developing the purposes section of the juvenile code?

(c) Many states have not only added notions of punishment, accountability and protection of society to their statutes, but have also increased the number of children formally referred to juvenile court, reduced diversion, lowered the age for waiver, and permitted harsher sanctions for juveniles adjudicated delinquent. See Chapter 7, *infra*.

(d) Some commentators take the position that the "get tough" statutes and lack of equal constitutional protection obviate the need for a separate juvenile court system. *See, e.g.*, Janet E. Ainsworth, *Re-Imagining Childhood and Reconstructing the Legal Order: The Case for Abolishing the Juvenile Court*, 69 N.C.L. Rev. 1083 (1991). For further discussion of the "abolitionist" movement see Chapter 2, *infra*.

2. Tracking a Typical Delinquency Case through the Juvenile Court

A child's first contact with the juvenile justice system will occur because of a referral to the police or a juvenile probation officer accusing the minor of committing a crime. Police officers often have discretion not to pursue the case in juvenile court, and can release the child to the parents' or guardians' custody immediately. The police may issue a warning or maintain a record of the child and alleged offense. If the child is held for further action, he or she can be released to parents or guardians or, depending on the child and the offense, placed in a detention facility.

The intake probation officer interviews the child, his or her parents, and witnesses, and obtains school and offense reports. The probation officer can either refer the child and his or her parents to community-based agencies or to the juvenile court for formal proceedings. If the latter occurs, the prosecutor files a petition alleging that the juvenile is a delinquent because he or she committed an act that constitutes a crime if committed by an adult. Instead of filing a delinquency petition, the prosecutor may file a request for waiver of the child to criminal court and trial as an adult. Various types of waiver statutes are discussed in depth in Chapter 7, *infra*.

If a delinquency petition is filed, the child appears before the court and, if the child is in custody, the court will conduct a detention hearing to determine whether the child should remain in detention or be released to his or her parents or guardian. Furthermore, the court will determine if the child is indigent and, if so, the judge inquires into whether the child wishes to be represented by counsel.

At the adjudicatory hearing the prosecutor presents evidence regarding the child's culpability, and the child can present a defense or remain silent. The adjudicatory hearing is much like a criminal bench trial. (Jury trials are very rare in juvenile court). If the allegations are not proved beyond a reasonable doubt, the trial judge is required to dismiss the charges. If, however, the court concludes that the minor committed the charged offense, an adjudication is made to that effect. The trial court then orders a probation investigation, and determines whether the child should return home or remain in custody pending the dispositional hearing.

At the dispositional hearing the probation department will report its recommendation, and the child may also present evidence regarding his or her sentence. A wide range of dispositional alternatives is available: discharge; remain at home or in a foster home under probation supervision; placement in a group home, residential treatment facility, mental hospital, or facility for the retarded; or commitment to a state training school. If the state has a blended or extended sentencing scheme, the child may be committed to a long prison term in adult facilities. See Chapter 7, *infra*.

If the child is placed on probation and he or she violates probation, a hearing is held. If the violation is proved, the child is subject to the same dispositions available at the initial sentencing proceedings.

If the child is placed in a facility, there will be placement reviews or extension of placement requests, which can result in transfer to harsher or more secure facilities or longer commitments. In some jurisdictions, the minor, when he or she reaches a certain age, can be transferred to an adult prison.

a. Flow Chart

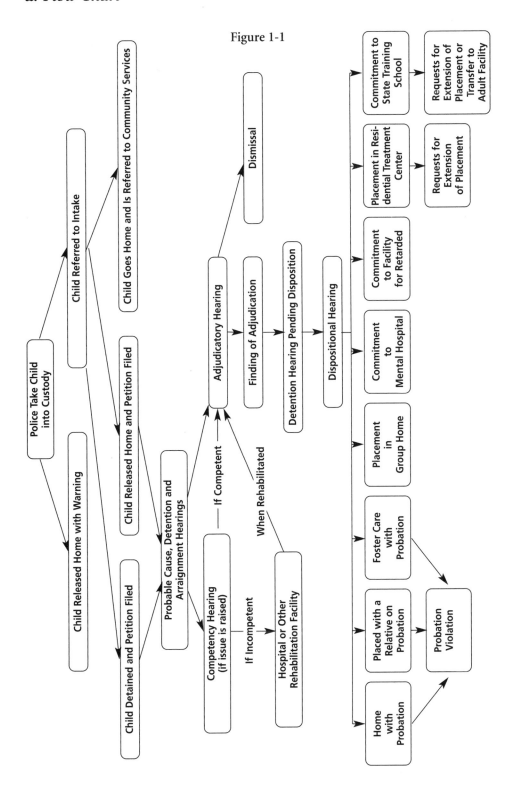

Figure 1-1

Chapter 2

The Supreme Court's Constitutional Domestication of the Juvenile Court

A. Introduction

Irene Merker Rosenberg, *The Constitutional Rights of Children Charged with Crime: Proposal for a Return to the Not So Distant Past*

27 UCLA L. Rev. 656, 658–60 (1980) (citations omitted)

Every state has a separate juvenile court system and separate treatment institutions that are purportedly concerned with rehabilitation and protection of the child charged with juvenile delinquency. The price of admission, concerning which the minor has no choice once she or he is charged with an offense, is often a relinquishment of specified constitutional rights afforded adults charged with crime, and, if adjudicated guilty, commitment to correctional facilities that [can] rival their adult prison counterparts for ineffectiveness and brutality....

While the Court often speaks benignly about juveniles, its holdings with respect to the constitutional rights of minors almost invariably embody standards which give them less protection than adults. Nowhere is the ambivalence toward children more clearly reflected than in the Court's decisions determining the constitutional guarantees of alleged juvenile delinquents—children charged with acts that, if committed by adults, would constitute crimes. Such cases pit adult compassion and understanding that immature youths are not fully responsible against adult anger at children who commit crimes. Nevertheless, one might question why, in view of age and competency differentials, the child is given less protection rather than more. The cases provide no explicit answers and often appear to rest primarily on the acceptance of myths and the use of labels such as *parens patriae*, rather than on analysis and proof.

An examination of the Court's delinquency decisions discloses that it initially employed a standard to determine both applicability and content of constitutional rights that could be used to maximize the protection afforded alleged juvenile delinquents. Turning away from that test, the Court retreated to a fundamental fairness standard that provided a substantially lower level of protection for children charged with crime.... [T]he Court [then] moved to an intermediate position, [but] the cases manifest an analytical confusion between the standard used for determining the applicability of constitutional rights to delinquents and the test utilized for ascertaining the content of those rights that are found to be applicable. Moreover, even when using the same standard for delinquency cases as it does for adult criminal trials, the Court's rulings nonetheless effectively dilute the constitutional safeguards afforded alleged delinquents and also have the potential effect of diminishing the content of implicated rights of adult criminal defendants. [The most recent Supreme Court rulings involving delinquents have reverted to fundamental fairness analyses and acceptance not only of the view that children are always in some sort of custody, but also of the principle that delinquency hearings and criminal trials are fundamentally different.]

The premises and assumptions, both stated and unstated, that appear to underlie the delinquency decisions do not lend support to the view that children charged with crime should be afforded less constitutional protection than their adult criminal counterparts at the adjudicatory hearing—the proceeding to determine guilt or innocence. Indeed, an analysis of each of the standards used by the Court indicates that even a test giving delinquents the same rights as adult defendants results in insufficient protection of minors.

B. The Supreme Court Cases

Kent v. United States
383 U.S. 541 (1966)

Mr. Justice FORTAS delivered the opinion of the Court.

This case is here on certiorari to the United States Court of Appeals for the District of Columbia Circuit. The facts and the contentions of counsel raise a number of disturbing questions concerning the administration by the police and the Juvenile Court authorities of the District of Columbia laws relating to juveniles.... Because we conclude that the Juvenile Court's order waiving jurisdiction of petitioner was entered without compliance with required procedures, we remand the case to the trial court.

Morris A. Kent, Jr., first came under the authority of the Juvenile Court of the District of Columbia in 1959. He was then aged 14. He was apprehended as a result of several housebreakings and an attempted purse snatching. He was placed on probation, in the custody of his mother who had been separated from her husband since Kent was two years old. Juvenile Court officials interviewed Kent from time to time during the probation period and accumulated a "Social Service" file.

On September 2, 1961, an intruder entered the apartment of a woman in the District of Columbia. He took her wallet. He raped her. The police found latent fingerprints in the apartment. They were developed and processed. They matched the fingerprints of Morris Kent, taken when he was 14 years old and under the jurisdiction of the Juvenile Court. At about 3 p.m. on September 5, 1961, Kent was taken into custody by the police. Kent was then 16 and therefore subject to the "exclusive jurisdiction" of the Juvenile Court. He was still on probation to that court as a result of the 1959 proceedings.

Upon being apprehended, Kent was taken to police headquarters where he was interrogated by police officers. It appears that he admitted his involvement in the offense which led to his apprehension and volunteered information as to similar offenses involving housebreaking, robbery, and rape. His interrogation proceeded from about 3 p.m. to 10 p.m. the same evening.

Some time after 10 p.m. petitioner was taken to the Receiving Home for Children. The next morning he was released to the police for further interrogation at police headquarters, which lasted until 5 p.m.

The record does not show when his mother became aware that the boy was in custody, but shortly after 2 p.m. on September 6, 1961, the day following petitioner's apprehension, she retained counsel.

Counsel, together with petitioner's mother, promptly conferred with the Social Service Director of the Juvenile Court. In a brief interview, they discussed the possibility that the Juvenile Court might waive jurisdiction and remit Kent to trial by the District Court. Counsel made known his intention to oppose waiver.

Petitioner was detained at the Receiving Home for almost a week. There was no arraignment during this time, no determination by a judicial officer of probable cause for petitioner's apprehension.

During this period of detention and interrogation, petitioner's counsel arranged for examination of petitioner by two psychiatrists and a psychologist. He thereafter filed with the Juvenile Court a motion for a hearing on the question of waiver of Juvenile Court jurisdiction, together with an affidavit of a psychiatrist certifying that petitioner "is a victim of severe psychopathology" and recommending hospitalization for psychiatric observation. Petitioner's counsel, in support of his motion to the effect that the Juvenile Court should retain jurisdiction of petitioner, offered to prove that if petitioner were given adequate treatment in a hospital under the aegis of the Juvenile Court, he would be a suitable subject for rehabilitation.

At the same time, petitioner's counsel moved that the Juvenile Court should give him access to the Social Service file relating to petitioner which had been accumulated by the staff of the Juvenile Court during petitioner's probation period, and which would be available to the Juvenile Court judge in considering the question whether it should retain or waive jurisdiction. Petitioner's counsel represented that access to this file was essential to his providing petitioner with effective assistance of counsel.

The Juvenile Court judge did not rule on these motions. He held no hearing. He did not confer with petitioner or petitioner's parents or petitioner's counsel. He entered an order reciting that after "full investigation, I do hereby waive" jurisdiction of petitioner and directing that he be "held for trial for (the alleged) offenses under the regular procedure of the U.S. District Court for the District of Columbia." He made no findings. He did not recite any reason for the waiver. He made no reference to the motions filed by petitioner's counsel. We must assume that he denied, *sub silentio*, the motions for a hearing, the recommendation for hospitalization for psychiatric observation, the request for access to the Social Service file, and the offer to prove that petitioner was a fit subject for rehabilitation under the Juvenile Court's jurisdiction.

Presumably, prior to entry of his order, the Juvenile Court judge received and considered recommendations of the Juvenile Court staff, the Social Service file relating to petitioner, and a report dated September 8, 1961 (three days following petitioner's apprehension), submitted to him by the Juvenile Probation Section. The Social Service file and the September 8 report were later sent to the District Court[,] and it appears that both of them referred to petitioner's mental condition. The September 8 report spoke of "a rapid deterioration of [petitioner's] personality structure and the possibility of mental illness." As stated, neither this report nor the Social Service file was made available to petitioner's counsel.

The provision of the Juvenile Court Act governing waiver expressly provides only for "full investigation." It states the circumstances in which jurisdiction may be waived and the child held for trial under adult procedures, but it does not state standards to govern the Juvenile Court's decision as to waiver. The provision reads as follows:

> "If a child sixteen years of age or older is charged with an offense which would amount to a felony in the case of an adult, or any child charged with an offense which if committed by an adult is punishable by death or life imprisonment, the judge may, after full investigation, waive jurisdiction and order such child held for trial under the regular procedure of the court which would have jurisdiction of such offense if committed by an adult; or such other court may exercise the powers conferred upon the juvenile court in this subchapter in conducting and disposing of such cases."

. . . .

Meanwhile, on September 25, 1961, shortly after the Juvenile Court order waiving its jurisdiction, petitioner was indicted by a grand jury of the United States District Court for the District of Columbia. The indictment contained eight counts alleging two instances of housebreaking, robbery, and rape, and one of housebreaking and robbery. On November 16, 1961, petitioner moved the District Court to dismiss the indictment on the grounds that the waiver was invalid. He also moved the District Court to constitute itself a Juvenile Court as authorized by the D. C. Code. After substantial delay occasioned by petitioner's appeal and habeas corpus proceedings, the District Court addressed itself to the motion to dismiss on February 8, 1963.

The District Court denied the motion to dismiss the indictment. The District Court ruled that it would not "go behind" the Juvenile Court judge's recital that his order was entered "after full investigation." It held that "The only matter before me is as to whether or not the statutory provisions were complied with and the Courts have held * * * with reference to full investigation, that that does not mean a quasi judicial or judicial hearing. No hearing is required."

On March 7, 1963, the District Court held a hearing on petitioner's motion to determine his competency to stand trial. The court determined that petitioner was competent.

At trial, petitioner's defense was wholly directed toward proving that he was not criminally responsible because "his unlawful act was the product of mental disease or mental defect." Extensive evidence, including expert testimony, was presented to support this defense. The jury found as to the counts alleging rape that petitioner was "not guilty by reason of insanity." Under District of Columbia law, this made it mandatory that petitioner be transferred to St. Elizabeth's Hospital, a mental institution, until his sanity is restored. On the six counts of housebreaking and robbery, the jury found that petitioner was guilty.[10]

Kent was sentenced to serve five to 15 years on each count as to which he was found guilty, or a total of 30 to 90 years in prison. The District Court ordered that the time to be spent at St. Elizabeth's on the mandatory commitment after the insanity acquittal be counted as part of the 30- to 90-year sentence. Petitioner appealed to the United States Court of Appeals for the District of Columbia Circuit. That court affirmed.

Before the Court of Appeals and in this Court, petitioner's counsel has urged a number of grounds for reversal. He argues that petitioner's detention and interrogation, de-

---

10. The basis for this distinction—that petitioner was "sane" for purposes of the housebreaking and robbery but "insane" for the purposes of the rape—apparently was the hypothesis, for which there is some support in the record, that the jury might find that the robberies had anteceded the rapes, and in that event, it might conclude that the housebreakings and robberies were not the products of his mental disease or defect, while the rapes were produced thereby.

scribed above, were unlawful. He contends that the police failed to follow the procedure prescribed by the Juvenile Court Act in that they failed to notify the parents of the child and the Juvenile Court itself; that petitioner was deprived of his liberty for about a week without a determination of probable cause which would have been required in the case of an adult; that he was interrogated by the police in the absence of counsel or a parent, without warning of his right to remain silent or advice as to his right to counsel, in asserted violation of the Juvenile Court Act and in violation of rights that he would have if he were an adult; and that petitioner was fingerprinted in violation of the asserted intent of the Juvenile Court Act and while unlawfully detained and that the fingerprints were unlawfully used in the District Court proceeding.

These contentions raise problems of substantial concern as to the construction of and compliance with the Juvenile Court Act. They also suggest basic issues as to the justifiability of affording a juvenile less protection than is accorded to adults suspected of criminal offenses, particularly where, as here, there is an absence of any indication that the denial of rights available to adults was offset, mitigated or explained by action of the Government, as *parens patriae*, evidencing the special solicitude for juveniles commanded by the Juvenile Court Act. However, because we remand the case on account of the procedural error with respect to waiver of jurisdiction, we do not pass upon these questions.

It is to petitioner's arguments as to the infirmity of the proceedings by which the Juvenile Court waived its otherwise exclusive jurisdiction that we address our attention. Petitioner attacks the waiver of jurisdiction on a number of statutory and constitutional grounds. He contends that the waiver is defective because no hearing was held; because no findings were made by the Juvenile Court; because the Juvenile Court stated no reasons for waiver; and because counsel was denied access to the Social Service file which presumably was considered by the Juvenile Court in determining to waive jurisdiction.

We agree that the order of the Juvenile Court waiving its jurisdiction and transferring petitioner for trial in the United States District Court for the District of Columbia was invalid. There is no question that the order is reviewable on motion to dismiss the indictment in the District Court, as specified by the Court of Appeals in this case. The issue is the standards to be applied upon such review.

We agree with the Court of Appeals that the statute contemplates that the Juvenile Court should have considerable latitude within which to determine whether it should retain jurisdiction over a child or—subject to the statutory delimitation—should waive jurisdiction. But this latitude is not complete. At the outset, it assumes procedural regularity sufficient in the particular circumstances to satisfy the basic requirements of due process and fairness, as well as compliance with the statutory requirement of a "full investigation." The statute gives the Juvenile Court a substantial degree of discretion as to the factual considerations to be evaluated, the weight to be given them and the conclusion to be reached. It does not confer upon the Juvenile Court a license for arbitrary procedure. The statute does not permit the Juvenile Court to determine in isolation and without the participation or any representation of the child the "critically important" question whether a child will be deprived of the special protections and provisions of the Juvenile Court Act. It does not authorize the Juvenile Court, in total disregard of a motion for hearing filed by counsel, and without any hearing or statement or reasons, to decide—as in this case— that the child will be taken from the Receiving Home for Children and transferred to jail along with adults, and that he will be exposed to the possibility of a death sentence instead of treatment for a maximum, in Kent's case, of five years, until he is 21.

We do not consider whether, on the merits, Kent should have been transferred; but there is no place in our system of law for reaching a result of such tremendous consequences without ceremony — without hearing, without effective assistance of counsel, without a statement of reasons. It is inconceivable that a court of justice dealing with adults, with respect to a similar issue, would proceed in this manner. It would be extraordinary if society's special concern for children, as reflected in the District of Columbia's Juvenile Court Act, permitted this procedure. We hold that it does not.

1.   The theory of the District's Juvenile Court Act, like that of other jurisdictions, is rooted in social welfare philosophy rather than in the *corpus juris*. Its proceedings are designated as civil rather than criminal. The Juvenile Court is theoretically engaged in determining the needs of the child and of society rather than adjudicating criminal conduct. The objectives are to provide measures of guidance and rehabilitation for the child and protection for society, not to fix criminal responsibility, guilt and punishment. The State is *parens patriae* rather than prosecuting attorney and judge. But the admonition to function in a "parental" relationship is not an invitation to procedural arbitrariness.

2.   Because the State is supposed to proceed in respect of the child as *parens patriae* and not as adversary, courts have relied on the premise that the proceedings are "civil" in nature and not criminal, and have asserted that the child cannot complain of the deprivation of important rights available in criminal cases. It has been asserted that he can claim only the fundamental due process right to fair treatment. For example, it has been held that he is not entitled to bail; to indictment by grand jury; to a speedy and public trial; to trial by jury; to immunity against self-incrimination; to confrontation of his accusers; and in some jurisdictions ... that he is not entitled to counsel.

While there can be no doubt of the original laudable purpose of juvenile courts, studies and critiques in recent years raise serious questions as to whether actual performance measures well enough against theoretical purpose to make tolerable the immunity of the process from the reach of constitutional guaranties applicable to adults. There is much evidence that some juvenile courts, including that of the District of Columbia, lack the personnel, facilities and techniques to perform adequately as representatives of the State in a *parens patriae* capacity, at least with respect to children charged with law violation. There is evidence, in fact, that there may be grounds for concern that the child receives the worst of both worlds: that he gets neither the protections accorded to adults nor the solicitous care and regenerative treatment postulated for children.

This concern, however, does not induce us in this case to accept the invitation to rule that constitutional guaranties which would be applicable to adults charged with the serious offenses for which Kent was tried must be applied in juvenile court proceedings concerned with allegations of law violation. The Juvenile Court Act and the decisions of the United States Court of Appeals for the District of Columbia Circuit provide an adequate basis for decision of this case, and we go no further.

3.   It is clear beyond dispute that the waiver of jurisdiction is a "critically important" action determining vitally important statutory rights of the juvenile. The Court of Appeals for the District of Columbia Circuit has so held. The statutory scheme makes this plain. The Juvenile Court is vested with "original and exclusive jurisdiction" of the child. This jurisdiction confers special rights and immunities. He is, as specified by the statute, shielded from publicity. He may be confined, but with rare exceptions he may not be jailed along with adults. He may be detained, but only until he is 21 years of age. The court is admonished by the statute to give preference to retaining the child in the custody of his parents "unless his welfare and the safety and protection of the public can not

be adequately safeguarded without * * * removal." The child is protected against consequences of adult conviction such as the loss of civil rights, the use of adjudication against him in subsequent proceedings, and disqualification for public employment.

The net, therefore, is that petitioner—then a boy of 16—was by statute entitled to certain procedures and benefits as a consequence of his statutory right to the "exclusive" jurisdiction of the Juvenile Court. In these circumstances, considering particularly that decision as to waiver of jurisdiction and transfer of the matter to the District Court was potentially as important to petitioner as the difference between five years' confinement and a death sentence, we conclude that, as a condition to a valid waiver order, petitioner was entitled to a hearing, including access by his counsel to the social records and probation or similar reports which presumably are considered by the court, and to a statement of reasons for the Juvenile Court's decision. We believe that this result is required by the statute read in the context of constitutional principles relating to due process and the assistance of counsel.

. . . .

We are of the opinion that the Court of Appeals misconceived the basic issue and the underlying values in this case. It did note ... that the determination of whether to transfer a child from the statutory structure of the Juvenile Court to the criminal processes of the District Court is "critically important." We hold that it is, indeed, a "critically important" proceeding. The Juvenile Court Act confers upon the child a right to avail himself of that court's "exclusive" jurisdiction. As the Court of Appeals has said, "It is implicit in [the Juvenile Court] scheme that non-criminal treatment is to be the rule—and the adult criminal treatment the exception which must be governed by the particular factors of individual cases."

Meaningful review requires that the reviewing court should review. It should not be remitted to assumptions. It must have before it a statement of the reasons motivating the waiver including, of course, a statement of the relevant facts. It may not "assume" that there are adequate reasons, nor may it merely assume that "full investigation" has been made. Accordingly, we hold that it is incumbent upon the Juvenile Court to accompany its waiver order with a statement of the reasons or considerations therefor. We do not read the statute as requiring that this statement must be formal or that it should necessarily include conventional findings of fact. But the statement should be sufficient to demonstrate that the statutory requirement of "full investigation" has been met; and that the question has received the careful consideration of the Juvenile Court; and it must set forth the basis for the order with sufficient specificity to permit meaningful review.

Correspondingly, we conclude that an opportunity for a hearing which may be informal, must be given the child prior to entry of a waiver order.... [T]he child is entitled to counsel in connection with a waiver proceeding, and ... counsel is entitled to see the child's social records. These rights are meaningless—an illusion, a mockery—unless counsel is given an opportunity to function.

The right to representation by counsel is not a formality. It is not a grudging gesture to a ritualistic requirement. It is of the essence of justice. Appointment of counsel without affording an opportunity for hearing on a "critically important" decision is tantamount to denial of counsel. There is no justification for the failure of the Juvenile Court to rule on the motion for hearing filed by petitioner's counsel, and it was error to fail to grant a hearing.

We do not mean by this to indicate that the hearing to be held must conform with all of the requirements of a criminal trial or even of the usual administrative hearing; but we do hold that the hearing must measure up to the essentials of due process and fair treatment.

With respect to access by the child's counsel to the social records of the child, we deem it obvious that since these are to be considered by the Juvenile Court in making its decision to waive, they must be made available to the child's counsel.... We cannot agree with the Court of Appeals in the present case that the statute is "ambiguous." The statute expressly provides that the record shall be withheld from "indiscriminate" public inspection, "except that such records or parts thereof *shall* be made available by rule of court or special order of court to such persons * * * as have a *legitimate interest* in the protection * * * of the child * * *." ... [W]e agree ... that counsel must be afforded to the child in waiver proceedings. Counsel, therefore, have a "legitimate interest" in the protection of the child, and must be afforded access to these records.

We do not agree with the Court of Appeals' statement, attempting to justify denial of access to these records, that counsel's role is limited to presenting "to the court anything on behalf of the child which might help the court in arriving at a decision; it is not to denigrate the staff's submissions and recommendations." On the contrary, if the staff's submissions include materials which are susceptible to challenge or impeachment, it is precisely the role of counsel to "denigrate" such matter. There is no irrebuttable presumption of accuracy attached to staff reports. If a decision on waiver is "critically important" it is equally of "critical importance" that the material submitted to the judge—which is protected by the statute only against "indiscriminate" inspection—be subjected, within reasonable limits having regard to the theory of the Juvenile Court Act, to examination, criticism and refutation. While the Juvenile Court judge may, of course, receive *ex parte* analyses and recommendations from his staff, he may not, for purposes of a decision on waiver, receive and rely upon secret information, whether emanating from his staff or otherwise. The Juvenile Court is governed in this respect by the established principles which control courts and quasi-judicial agencies of the Government.

For the reasons stated, we conclude that the Court of Appeals and the District Court erred in sustaining the validity of the waiver by the Juvenile Court. The Government urges that any error committed by the Juvenile Court was cured by the proceedings before the District Court. It is true that the District Court considered and denied a motion to dismiss on the grounds of the invalidity of the waiver order of the Juvenile Court, and that it considered and denied a motion that it should itself, as authorized by statute, proceed in this case to "exercise the powers conferred upon the juvenile court." [W]e agree ... that "the waiver question was primarily and initially one for the Juvenile Court to decide and its failure to do so in a valid manner cannot be said to be harmless error. It is the Juvenile Court, not the District Court, which has the facilities, personnel and expertise for a proper determination of the waiver issue."[32]

Ordinarily we would reverse the Court of Appeals and direct the District Court to remand the case to the Juvenile Court for a new determination of waiver. If on remand the decision were against waiver, the indictment in the District Court would be dismissed. However, petitioner has now passed the age of 21 and the Juvenile Court can no longer exercise jurisdiction over him. In view of the unavailability of a redetermination of the waiver

---

32. It also appears that the District Court requested and obtained the Social Service file and the probation staff's report of September 8, 1961, and that these were made available to petitioner's counsel. This did not cure the error of the Juvenile Court. Perhaps the point of it is that it again illustrates the maxim that while nondisclosure may contribute to the comfort of the staff, disclosure does not cause heaven to fall.

question by the Juvenile Court, it is urged by petitioner that the conviction should be vacated and the indictment dismissed. In the circumstances of this case, and in light of the remedy which the Court of Appeals fashioned, we do not consider it appropriate to grant this drastic relief.[33] Accordingly, we vacate the order of the Court of Appeals and the judgment of the District Court and remand the case to the District Court for a hearing *de novo* on waiver, consistent with this opinion. If that court finds that waiver was inappropriate, petitioner's conviction must be vacated. If, however, it finds that the waiver order was proper when originally made, the District Court may proceed, after consideration of such motions as counsel may make and such further proceedings, if any, as may be warranted, to enter an appropriate judgment.

Reversed and remanded.

Appendix to OPINION of the Court

Policy Memorandum No. 7, November 30, 1959

The authority of the Judge of the Juvenile Court of the District of Columbia to waive or transfer jurisdiction to the U.S. District Court for the District of Columbia is contained in the Juvenile Court Act. This section permits the Judge to waive jurisdiction "after full investigation" in the case of any child "sixteen years of age or older [who is] charged with an offense which would amount to a felony in the case of an adult, or any child charged with an offense which if committed by an adult is punishable by death or life imprisonment."

The statute sets forth no specific standards for the exercise of this important discretionary act, but leaves the formulation of such criteria to the Judge. A knowledge of the Judge's criteria is important to the child, his parents, his attorney, to the judges of the U.S. District Court for the District of Columbia, to the United States Attorney and his assistants, and to the Metropolitan Police Department, as well as to the staff of this court, especially the Juvenile Intake Section.

Therefore, the Judge has consulted with the Chief Judge and other judges of the U.S. District Court for the District of Columbia, with the United States Attorney, with representatives of the Bar, and with other groups concerned and has formulated the following criteria and principles concerning waiver of jurisdiction which are consistent with the basic aims and purpose of the Juvenile Court Act.

An offense falling within the statutory limitations (set forth above) will be waived if it has prosecutive merit and if it is heinous or of an aggravated character, or—even though less serious—if it represents a pattern of repeated offenses which indicate that the juvenile may be beyond rehabilitation under Juvenile Court procedures, or if the public needs the protection afforded by such action.

The determinative factors which will be considered by the Judge in deciding whether the Juvenile Court's jurisdiction over such offenses will be waived are the following:

1. The seriousness of the alleged offense to the community and whether the protection of the community requires waiver.

2. Whether the alleged offense was committed in an aggressive, violent, premeditated or willful manner.

---

33. Petitioner is in St. Elizabeth's Hospital for psychiatric treatment as a result of the jury verdict on the rape charges.

3. Whether the alleged offense was against persons or against property, greater weight being given to offenses against persons especially if personal injury resulted.

4. The prosecutive merit of the complaint, *i.e.*, whether there is evidence upon which a Grand Jury may be expected to return an indictment (to be determined by consultation with the United States Attorney).

5. The desirability of trial and disposition of the entire offense in one court when the juvenile's associates in the alleged offense are adults who will be charged with a crime in the U.S. District Court for the District of Columbia.

6. The sophistication and maturity of the juvenile as determined by consideration of his home, environmental situation, emotional attitude and pattern of living.

7. The record and previous history of the juvenile, including previous contacts with the Youth Aid Division, other law enforcement agencies, juvenile courts and other jurisdictions, prior periods of probation to this Court, or prior commitments to juvenile institutions.

8. The prospects for adequate protection of the public and the likelihood of reasonable rehabilitation of the juvenile (if he is found to have committed the alleged offense) by the use of procedures, services and facilities currently available to the Juvenile Court.

It will be the responsibility of any officer of the Court's staff assigned to make the investigation of any complaint in which waiver of jurisdiction is being considered to develop fully all available information which may bear upon the criteria and factors set forth above. Although not all such factors will be involved in an individual case, the Judge will consider the relevant factors in a specific case before reaching a conclusion to waive juvenile jurisdiction and transfer the case to the U.S. District Court for the District of Columbia for trial under the adult procedures of that Court.

Mr. Justice STEWART, with whom Mr. Justice BLACK, Mr. Justice HARLAN and Mr. Justice WHITE join, dissenting.

This case involves the construction of a statute applicable only to the District of Columbia. Our general practice is to leave undisturbed decisions of the Court of Appeals for the District of Columbia Circuit concerning the import of legislation governing the affairs of the District. It appears, however, that two cases decided by the Court of Appeals subsequent to its decision in the present case may have considerably modified the court's construction of the statute. Therefore, I would vacate this judgment and remand the case to the Court of Appeals for reconsideration in the light of its subsequent decisions.

Notes

(a) Although *Kent* is not a delinquency case, it was the first Supreme Court decision indicating that Due Process was applicable to children in juvenile court. Much earlier, however, the Supreme Court had decided two cases dealing with confessions made by children while within the jurisdiction of the juvenile court. As in *Kent*, the children were waived to criminal court to be tried as adults, and the confessions were used against them at trial. On appeal the Supreme Court reversed their convictions on the ground that the confessions were involuntary under the Due Process clause of the Fourteenth Amendment. So although these earlier cases did not deal with the applicability of constitutional guarantees in juvenile court, they did apply constitutional rights to children. See *Haley v. Ohio*, 332 U.S. 596 (1948); *Gallegos v. Colorado*, 370 U.S. 49 (1962).

(b) The *Kent* Court made clear that *parens patriae* concepts alone would not preclude application of Due Process for children facing waiver to adult court, and that the myths surrounding the beneficence of the juvenile court system would not be uncritically accepted. Because these same issues were pivotal in *In re Gault*, the *Kent* analysis provided an important constitutional backdrop for *Gault*, the landmark case delineating the constitutional rights of delinquents.

(c) On what authority does the Court reverse Kent's conviction? More specifically, is *Kent* decided on constitutional or statutory grounds? See Justice Stewart's dissenting opinion. Does it make any difference? Why?

(d) Justice Fortas noted the general lack of compliance with the requirements of the D.C. Juvenile Court Act, yet he took special pains not to rule on these legal issues, such as Kent's apprehension, interrogation, fingerprinting, and detention without probable cause. Why then did Justice Fortas mention them?

(e) Does Justice Fortas conclude on the merits that Kent should not have been waived over to criminal court? Should Kent have been transferred? Why?

(f) Are the criteria for waiver listed in the appendix to the opinion of the Court mandatory, that is, must all states pattern their waiver codes so as to include them? Can these criteria really assist a juvenile court judge in deciding whether to transfer a juvenile to adult criminal court? Does the requirement that the juvenile court judge give reasons for the transfer to criminal court assist in effective appellate court review? Which of these criteria do you think are most relevant to the juvenile court waiver decision?

(g) If the juvenile court had retained jurisdiction over Kent and adjudicated him a delinquent would that adjudication have resulted in inadequate protection for the public? The juvenile court's jurisdiction over minors continued only until the child's twenty-first birthday. In adult criminal court, however, Kent was sentenced to 30–90 years imprisonment. *See Kent v. United States*, 401 F.2d 408, 412 (D.C. Cir. 1968) (concluding on remand that Kent should not have been waived and that protection of the public could be assured by civil commitment of Kent to a psychiatric hospital that would have extended the juvenile court's jurisdiction beyond Kent's majority). *See also* Catherine J. Ross, *Disposition in a Discretionary Regime: Punishment and Rehabilitation in the Juvenile Justice System*, 36 B.C. L. Rev. 1037 (1995) (arguing that in *Kent* and *Gault* the lower courts imposed what "the Justices viewed as unreasonable penalties on minors, one by retaining juvenile jurisdiction, the other by waiving it[,]" *id.* at 1052).

(h) The specific issues concerning waiver will be discussed further in Chapter 7, *infra*.

In re Gault is a seminal decision that provides an analytical framework for evaluating whether constitutional rights should be applied in the juvenile courts, and, if so, what the content of those rights should be. Although the holding in *Gault* may be narrow, depending on how you read it, the opinion is an illuminating exposition of the philosophy and history of the juvenile court system and its failures. Special care should be given in reading the footnotes because they reveal much of the rationale and scope of the Court's rulings.

In re Gault

387 U.S. 1 (1967)

Mr. Justice FORTAS delivered the opinion of the Court.

This is an appeal from a judgment of the Supreme Court of Arizona affirming the dismissal of a petition for a writ of habeas corpus. The petition sought the release of Gerald Francis Gault, appellants' 15-year-old son, who had been committed as a juvenile delinquent to the State Industrial School by the Juvenile Court of Gila County, Arizona. The Supreme Court of Arizona affirmed dismissal of the writ against various arguments which included an attack upon the constitutionality of the Arizona Juvenile Code because of its alleged denial of procedural due process rights to juveniles charged with being "delinquents." The court agreed that the constitutional guarantee of due process of law is applicable in such proceedings. It held that Arizona's Juvenile Code is to be read as "impliedly" implementing the "due process concept." It then proceeded to identify and describe "the particular elements which constitute due process in a juvenile hearing." It concluded that the proceedings ending in commitment of Gerald Gault did not offend those requirements. We do not agree, and we reverse. We begin with a statement of the facts.

I

On Monday, June 8, 1964, at about 10 a.m., Gerald Francis Gault and a friend, Ronald Lewis, were taken into custody by the Sheriff of Gila County. Gerald was then still subject to a six months' probation order which had been entered on February 25, 1964, as a result of his having been in the company of another boy who had stolen a wallet from a lady's purse. The police action on June 8 was taken as the result of a verbal complaint by a neighbor of the boys, Mrs. Cook, about a telephone call made to her in which the caller or callers made lewd or indecent remarks. It will suffice for purposes of this opinion to say that the remarks or questions put to her were of the irritatingly offensive, adolescent, sex variety.

At the time Gerald was picked up, his mother and father were both at work. No notice that Gerald was being taken into custody was left at the home. No other steps were taken to advise them that their son had, in effect, been arrested. Gerald was taken to the Children's Detention Home. When his mother arrived home at about 6 o'clock, Gerald was not there. Gerald's older brother was sent to look for him at the trailer home of the Lewis family. He apparently learned then that Gerald was in custody. He so informed his mother. The two of them went to the Detention Home. The deputy probation officer, Flagg, who was also superintendent of the Detention Home, told Mrs. Gault "why Jerry was there" and said that a hearing would be held in Juvenile Court at 3 o'clock the following day, June 9.

Officer Flagg filed a petition with the court on the hearing day, June 9, 1964. It was not served on the Gaults. Indeed, none of them saw this petition until the habeas corpus hearing on August 17, 1964. The petition was entirely formal. It made no reference to any factual basis for the judicial action which it initiated. It recited only that "said minor is under the age of eighteen years, and is in need of the protection of this Honorable Court; [and that] said minor is a delinquent minor." It prayed for a hearing and an order regarding "the care and custody of said minor." Officer Flagg executed a formal affidavit in support of the petition.

On June 9, Gerald, his mother, his older brother, and Probation Officers Flagg and Henderson appeared before the Juvenile Judge in chambers. Gerald's father was … at work out of the city. Mrs. Cook, the complainant, was not there. No one was sworn at this hearing. No transcript or recording was made. No memorandum or record of the substance of the proceedings was prepared. Our information about the proceedings and the subsequent hearing on June 15, derives entirely from the testimony of the Juvenile Court Judge, Mr. and Mrs. Gault and Officer Flagg at the habeas corpus proceeding conducted two months later. From this, it appears that at the June 9 hearing Gerald was questioned by the judge about the telephone call. There was conflict as to what he said. His mother recalled that Gerald said he only dialed Mrs. Cook's number and handed the telephone to his friend, Ronald. Officer Flagg recalled that Gerald had admitted making the lewd remarks. Judge McGhee testified that Gerald "admitted making one of these [lewd] statements." At the conclusion of the hearing, the judge said he would "think about it." Gerald was taken back to the Detention Home. He was not sent to his own home with his parents. On June 11 or 12, after having been detained since June 8, Gerald was released and driven home. There is no explanation in the record as to why he was kept in the Detention Home or why he was released. At 5 p.m. on the day of Gerald's release, Mrs. Gault received a note signed by Officer Flagg. It was on plain paper, not letterhead. Its entire text was as follows:

"Mrs. Gault:

Judge McGHEE has set Monday June 15, 1964 at 11:00 A.M. as the date and time for further Hearings on Gerald's delinquency/s/Flagg"

At the appointed time on Monday, June 15, Gerald, his father and mother, Ronald Lewis and his father, and Officers Flagg and Henderson were present before Judge McGhee. Witnesses at the habeas corpus proceeding differed in their recollections of Gerald's testimony at the June 15 hearing. Mr. and Mrs. Gault recalled that Gerald again testified that he had only dialed the number and that the other boy had made the remarks. Officer Flagg agreed that at this hearing Gerald did not admit making the lewd remarks.[3] But Judge McGhee recalled that "there was some admission again of some of the lewd statements. He—he didn't admit any of the more serious lewd statements."[4] Again, the complainant, Mrs. Cook, was not present. Mrs. Gault asked that Mrs. Cook be present "so she could see which boy that done the talking, the dirty talking over the phone." The Juvenile Judge said "she didn't have to be present at that hearing." The judge did not speak to Mrs. Cook or communicate with her at any time. Probation Officer Flagg had talked to her once—over the telephone on June 9.

At this June 15 hearing a "referral report" made by the probation officers was filed with the court, although not disclosed to Gerald or his parents. This listed the charge as "Lewd Phone Calls." At the conclusion of the hearing, the judge committed Gerald as a juvenile delinquent to the State Industrial School "for the period of his minority [that is, until 21], unless sooner discharged by due process of law." An order to that effect was entered. It recites that "after a full hearing and due deliberation the Court finds that said minor is a delinquent child, and that said minor is of the age of 15 years."

No appeal is permitted by Arizona law in juvenile cases. On August 3, 1964, a petition for a writ of habeas corpus was filed with the Supreme Court of Arizona and referred by it to the Superior Court for hearing.

At the habeas corpus hearing on August 17, Judge McGhee was vigorously cross-examined as to the basis for his actions. He testified that he had taken into account the fact that Gerald was on probation. He was asked "under what section of * * * the code you found the boy delinquent?"

---

3. Officer Flagg also testified that Gerald had not, when questioned at the Detention Home, admitted having made any of the lewd statements, but that each boy had sought to put the blame on the other. There was conflicting testimony as to whether Ronald had accused Gerald of making the lewd statements during the June 15 hearing.

4. Judge McGhee also testified that Gerald had not denied "certain statements" made to him at the hearing by Officer Henderson.

His answer is set forth in the margin.[5] In substance, he concluded that Gerald came within ARS § 8-201, subsec. 6(a), which specifies that a "delinquent child" includes one "who has violated a law of the state or an ordinance or regulation of a political subdivision thereof." The law which Gerald was found to have violated is ARS § 13-377. This section of the Arizona Criminal Code provides that a person who "in the presence or hearing of any woman or child * * * uses vulgar, abusive or obscene language, is guilty of a misdemeanor * * *." The penalty specified in the Criminal Code, which would apply to an adult, is $5 to $50, or imprisonment for not more than two months. The judge also testified that he acted under ARS § 8-201, subsec. 6(d) which includes in the definition of a "delinquent child" one who, as the judge phrased it, is "habitually involved in immoral matters."[6]

Asked about the basis for his conclusion that Gerald was "habitually involved in immoral matters," the judge testified, somewhat vaguely, that two years earlier, on July 2, 1962, a "referral" was made concerning Gerald, "where the boy had stolen a baseball glove from another boy and lied to the Police Department about it." The judge said there was "no hearing," and "no accusation" relating to this incident, "because of lack of material foundation." But it seems to have remained in his mind as a relevant factor. The judge also testified that Gerald had admitted making other nuisance phone calls in the past which, as the judge recalled the boy's testimony, were "silly calls, or funny calls, or something like that."

The Superior Court dismissed the writ, and appellants sought review in the Arizona Supreme Court. That court stated that it considered appellants' assignments of error as urging (1) that the Juvenile Code is unconstitutional because it does not require that parents and children be apprised of the specific charges, does not require proper notice of a hearing, and does not provide for an appeal; and (2) that the proceedings and order relating to Gerald constituted a denial of due process of law because of the absence of adequate notice of the charge and the hearing; failure to notify appellants of certain constitutional rights including the rights to counsel and to confrontation, and the privilege against self-incrimination; the use of unsworn hearsay testimony; and the failure to make a record of the proceedings. Appellants further asserted that it was error for the Juvenile Court to remove Gerald from the custody of his parents without a showing and finding of their unsuitability, and alleged a miscellany of other errors under state law.

The Supreme Court handed down an elaborate and wide-ranging opinion affirming dismissal of the writ and stating the court's conclusions as to the issues raised by appel-

---

5. "Q. All right. Now, Judge, would you tell me under what section of the law or tell me under what section of—of the code you found the boy delinquent?

"A. Well, there is a—I think it amounts to disturbing the peace. I can't give you the section, but I can tell you the law, that when one person uses lewd language in the presence of another person, that it can amount to—and I consider that when a person makes it over the phone, that it is considered in the presence, I might be wrong, that is one section. The other section upon which I consider the boy delinquent is Section 8-201, Subsection (d), habitually involved in immoral matters."

6. [T]he section of the Arizona Juvenile Code which defines a delinquent child, reads:
"'Delinquent child' includes:
    (a) A child who has violated a law of the state or an ordinance or regulation of a political subdivision thereof.
    (b) A child who, by reason of being incorrigible, wayward or habitually disobedient, is uncontrolled by his parent, guardian or custodian.
    (c) A child who is habitually truant from school or home.
    (d) A child who habitually so deports himself as to injure or endanger the morals or health of himself or others."

lants and other aspects of the juvenile process. In their jurisdictional statement and brief in this Court, appellants do not urge upon us all of the points passed upon by the Supreme Court of Arizona. They urge that we hold the Juvenile Code of Arizona invalid on its face or as applied in this case because, contrary to the Due Process Clause of the Fourteenth Amendment, the juvenile is taken from the custody of his parents and committed to a state institution pursuant to proceedings in which the Juvenile Court has virtually unlimited discretion, and in which the following basic rights are denied:

1. Notice of the charges;

2. Right to counsel;

3. Right to confrontation and cross-examination;

4. Privilege against self-incrimination;

5. Right to a transcript of the proceedings; and

6. Right to appellate review.

We shall not consider other issues which were passed upon by the Supreme Court of Arizona. We emphasize that we indicate no opinion as to whether the decision of that court with respect to such other issues does or does not conflict with requirements of the Federal Constitution.[7]

II

The Supreme Court of Arizona held that due process of law is requisite to the constitutional validity of proceedings in which a court reaches the conclusion that a juvenile has been at fault, has engaged in conduct prohibited by law, or has otherwise misbehaved with the consequence that he is committed to an institution in which his freedom is curtailed. This conclusion is in accord with the decisions of a number of courts under both federal and state constitutions.

This Court has not heretofore decided the precise question. In *Kent v. United States*, we considered the requirements for a valid waiver of the "exclusive" jurisdiction of the Juvenile Court of the District of Columbia so that a juvenile could be tried in the adult criminal court of the District. Although our decision turned upon the language of the

---

7. For example, the laws of Arizona allow arrest for a misdemeanor only if a warrant is obtained or if it is committed in the presence of the officer. The Supreme Court of Arizona held that this is inapplicable in the case of juveniles.

The court also held that the judge may consider hearsay if it is "of a kind on which reasonable men are accustomed to rely in serious affairs."

"The informality of juvenile court hearings frequently leads to the admission of hearsay and unsworn testimony. It is said that 'close adherence to the strict rules of evidence might prevent the court from obtaining important facts as to the child's character and condition which could only be to the child's detriment.' The assumption is that the judge will give normally inadmissible evidence only its proper weight. It is also declared in support of these evidentiary practices that the juvenile court is not a criminal court, that the importance of the hearsay rule has been overestimated, and that allowing an attorney to make 'technical objections' would disrupt the desired informality of the proceedings. But to the extent that the rules of evidence are not merely technical or historical, but like the hearsay rule have a sound basis in human experience, they should not be rejected in any judicial inquiry. Juvenile court judges in Los Angeles, Tucson, and Wisconsin Rapids, Wisconsin report that they are satisfied with the operation of their courts despite application of unrelaxed rules of evidence."

It ruled that the correct burden of proof is that "the juvenile judge must be persuaded by clear and convincing evidence that the infant has committed the alleged delinquent act." Compare the "preponderance of the evidence" test, N.Y.Family Court Act § 744 (where maximum commitment is three years, §§ 753, 758).

statute, we emphasized the necessity that "the basic requirements of due process and fairness" [b]e satisfied in such proceedings. *Haley v. State of Ohio* involved the admissibility, in a state criminal court of general jurisdiction, of a confession by a 15-year-old boy. The Court held that the Fourteenth Amendment applied to prohibit the use of the coerced confession. Mr. Justice Douglas said, "Neither man nor child can be allowed to stand condemned by methods which flout constitutional requirements of due process of law." To the same effect is *Gallegos v. State of Colorado*. Accordingly, while these cases relate only to restricted aspects of the subject, they unmistakably indicate that, whatever may be their precise impact, neither the Fourteenth Amendment nor the Bill of Rights is for adults alone.

We do not in this opinion consider the impact of these constitutional provisions upon the totality of the relationship of the juvenile and the state. We do not even consider the entire process relating to juvenile "delinquents." For example, we are not here concerned with the procedures or constitutional rights applicable to the pre-judicial stages of the juvenile process, nor do we direct our attention to the post-adjudicative or dispositional process. We consider only the problems presented to us by this case. These relate to the proceedings by which a determination is made as to whether a juvenile is a "delinquent" as a result of alleged misconduct on his part, with the consequence that he may be committed to a state institution. As to these proceedings, there appears to be little current dissent from the proposition that the Due Process Clause has a role to play. The problem is to ascertain the precise impact of the due process requirement upon such proceedings.

From the inception of the juvenile court system, wide differences have been tolerated—indeed insisted upon—between the procedural rights accorded to adults and those of juveniles. In practically all jurisdictions, there are rights granted to adults which are withheld from juveniles. In addition to the specific problems involved in the present case, for example, it has been held that the juvenile is not entitled to bail, to indictment by grand jury, to a public trial or to trial by jury. It is frequent practice that rules governing the arrest and interrogation of adults by the police are not observed in the case of juveniles.

The history and theory underlying this development are well-known, but a recapitulation is necessary for purposes of this opinion. The Juvenile Court movement began in this country at the end of the last century. From the juvenile court statute adopted in Illinois in 1899, the system has spread to every State in the Union, the District of Columbia, and Puerto Rico.[14] The constitutionality of juvenile court laws has been sustained in over 40 jurisdictions against a variety of attacks.

The early reformers were appalled by adult procedures and penalties, and by the fact that children could be given long prison sentences and mixed in jails with hardened criminals. They were profoundly convinced that society's duty to the child could not be con-

---

14. *See* National Council of Juvenile Court Judges, Directory and Manual (1964), p. 1. The number of Juvenile Judges as of 1964 is listed as 2,987, of whom 213 are full-time Juvenile Court Judges. The Nat'l Crime Comm'n Report indicates that half of these judges have no undergraduate degree, a fifth have no college education at all, a fifth are not members of the bar, and three-quarters devote less than one-quarter of their time to juvenile matters. [A] detailed statistical study of Juvenile Court Judges ... indicates additionally that about a quarter of these judges have no law school training at all. About one-third of all judges have no probation and social work staff available to them; between eighty and ninety percent have no available psychologist or psychiatrist. Ibid. It has been observed that while "good will, compassion, and similar virtues are * * * admirably prevalent throughout the system * * * expertise, the keystone of the whole venture, is lacking." In 1965, over 697,000 delinquency cases (excluding traffic) were disposed of in these courts, involving some 601,000 children, or 2% of all children between 10 and 17.

fined by the concept of justice alone. They believed that society's role was not to ascertain whether the child was "guilty" or "innocent," but "What is he, how has he become what he is, and what had best be done in his interest and in the interest of the state to save him from a downward career." The child—essentially good, as they saw it—was to be made "to feel that he is the object of [the state's] care and solicitude," not that he was under arrest or on trial. The rules of criminal procedure were therefore altogether inapplicable. The apparent rigidities, technicalities, and harshness which they observed in both substantive and procedural criminal law were therefore to be discarded. The idea of crime and punishment was to be abandoned. The child was to be "treated" and "rehabilitated" and the procedures, from apprehension through institutionalization, were to be "clinical" rather than punitive.

These results were to be achieved, without coming to conceptual and constitutional grief, by insisting that the proceedings were not adversary, but that the state was proceeding as parens patriae. The Latin phrase proved to be a great help to those who sought to rationalize the exclusion of juveniles from the constitutional scheme; but its meaning is murky and its historic credentials are of dubious relevance. The phrase was taken from chancery practice, where, however, it was used to describe the power of the state to act in loco parentis for the purpose of protecting the property interests and the person of the child. But there is no trace of the doctrine in the history of criminal jurisprudence. At common law, children under seven were considered incapable of possessing criminal intent. Beyond that age, they were subjected to arrest, trial, and in theory to punishment like adult offenders. In these old days, the state was not deemed to have authority to accord them fewer procedural rights than adults.

The right of the state, as parens patriae, to deny to the child procedural rights available to his elders was elaborated by the assertion that a child, unlike an adult, has a right "not to liberty but to custody." He can be made to attorn to his parents, to go to school, etc. If his parents default in effectively performing their custodial functions—that is, if the child is "delinquent"—the state may intervene. In doing so, it does not deprive the child of any rights, because he has none. It merely provides the "custody" to which the child is entitled. On this basis, proceedings involving juveniles were described as "civil" not "criminal" and therefore not subject to the requirements which restrict the state when it seeks to deprive a person of his liberty.[22]

Accordingly, the highest motives and most enlightened impulses led to a peculiar system for juveniles, unknown to our law in any comparable context. The constitutional and theoretical basis for this peculiar system is—to say the least—debatable. And in practice, as we remarked in the *Kent* case, the results have not been entirely satisfactory. Juvenile Court history has again demonstrated that unbridled discretion, however benevolently motivated, is frequently a poor substitute for principle and procedure. In 1937, Dean Pound wrote: "The powers of the Star Chamber were a trifle in comparison with those of our juvenile courts * * *."[24] The absence of substantive standards has not necessarily meant that children receive careful, compassionate, individualized treatment. The

---

22. Even rules required by due process in civil proceedings, however, have not generally been deemed compulsory as to proceedings affecting juveniles. For example, constitutional requirements as to notice of issues, which would commonly apply in civil cases, are commonly disregarded in juvenile proceedings, as this case illustrates.

24. The 1965 Report of the United States Commission on Civil Rights, "Law Enforcement—A Report on Equal Protection in the South," pp. 80–83, documents numerous instances in which "local authorities used the broad discretion afforded them by the absence of safeguards (in the juvenile process)" to punish, intimidate, and obstruct youthful participants in civil rights demonstrations.

absence of procedural rules based upon constitutional principle has not always produced fair, efficient, and effective procedures. Departures from established principles of due process have frequently resulted not in enlightened procedure, but in arbitrariness. The Chairman of the Pennsylvania Council of Juvenile Court Judges has recently observed: "Unfortunately, loose procedures, high-handed methods and crowded court calendars, either singly or in combination, all too often, have resulted in depriving some juveniles of fundamental rights that have resulted in a denial of due process."

Failure to observe the fundamental requirements of due process has resulted in instances, which might have been avoided, of unfairness to individuals and inadequate or inaccurate findings of fact and unfortunate prescriptions of remedy. Due process of law is the primary and indispensable foundation of individual freedom. It is the basic and essential term in the social compact which defines the rights of the individual and delimits the powers which the state may exercise.[26] As Mr. Justice Frankfurter has said: "The history of American freedom is, in no small measure, the history of procedure." But, in addition, the procedural rules which have been fashioned from the generality of due process are our best instruments for the distillation and evaluation of essential facts from the conflicting welter of data that life and our adversary methods present. It is these instruments of due process which enhance the possibility that truth will emerge from the confrontation of opposing versions and conflicting data. "Procedure is to law what 'scientific method' is to science."

It is claimed that juveniles obtain benefits from the special procedures applicable to them which more than offset the disadvantages of denial of the substance of normal due process. As we shall discuss, the observance of due process standards, intelligently and not ruthlessly administered, will not compel the States to abandon or displace any of the substantive benefits of the juvenile process. But it is important, we think, that the claimed benefits of the juvenile process should be candidly appraised. Neither sentiment nor folklore should cause us to shut our eyes, for example, to such startling findings as that reported in an exceptionally reliable study of repeaters or recidivism conducted by the Standford Research Institute for the President's Commission on Crime in the District of Columbia. This Commission's Report states:

> "In fiscal 1966 approximately 66 percent of the 16- and 17-year-old juveniles referred to the court by the Youth Aid Division had been before the court previously. In 1965, 56 percent of those in the Receiving Home were repeaters. The

---

26. The impact of denying fundamental procedural due process to juveniles involved in "delinquency" charges is dramatized by the following considerations: (1) In 1965, persons under 18 accounted for about one-fifth of all arrests for serious crimes and over half of all arrests for serious property offenses, and in the same year some 601,000 children under 18, or 2% of all children between 10 and 17, came before juvenile courts. About one out of nine youths will be referred to juvenile court in connection with a delinquent act (excluding traffic offenses) before he is 18. Furthermore, most juvenile crime apparently goes undetected or not formally punished. Wheeler & Cottrell observe that "[A]lmost all youngsters have committed at least one of the petty forms of theft and vandalism in the course of their adolescence." "[S]elf-report studies reveal that perhaps 90 percent of all young people have committed at least one act for which they could have been brought to juvenile court." It seems that the rate of juvenile delinquency is also steadily rising. (2) In New York, where most juveniles are represented by counsel and substantial procedural rights are afforded, out of a fiscal year 1965–1966 a total of 10,755 juvenile proceedings involving boys, 2,242 were dismissed for failure of proof at the fact-finding hearing; for girls, the figures were 306 out of a total of 1,051. (3) In about one-half of the States, a juvenile may be transferred to an adult penal institution after a juvenile court has found him "delinquent." (4) In some jurisdictions a juvenile may be subjected to criminal prosecution for the same offense for which he has served under a juvenile court commitment. (5) In most of the States the juvenile may end in criminal court through waiver.

SRI study revealed that 61 percent of the sample Juvenile Court referrals in 1965 had been previously referred at least once and that 42 percent had been referred at least twice before."

Certainly, these figures and the high crime rates among juveniles to which we have referred, could not lead us to conclude that the absence of constitutional protections … is effective to reduce crime or rehabilitate offenders. We do not mean by this to … suggest that there are not aspects of the juvenile system relating to offenders which are valuable. But the features of the juvenile system which … are of unique benefit will not be impaired by constitutional domestication. For example, the commendable principles relating to the processing and treatment of juveniles separately from adults are in no way involved or affected by the procedural issues under discussion[30] Further, we are told that one of the important benefits of the special juvenile court procedures is that they avoid classifying the juvenile as a "criminal." The juvenile offender is now classed as a "delinquent." There is, of course, no reason why this should not continue. It is disconcerting, however, that this term has come to involve only slightly less stigma than the term "criminal" applied to adults[31] … [I]n practically all jurisdictions, statutes provide that an adjudication of the child as a delinquent shall not operate as a civil disability or disqualify him for civil service appointment. There is no reason why the application of due process requirements should interfere with such provisions.

Beyond this, it is frequently said that juveniles are protected by the process from disclosure of their deviational behavior. As the Supreme Court of Arizona phrased it in the present case, the summary procedures of Juvenile Courts are sometimes defended by a statement that it is the law's policy "to hide youthful errors from the full gaze of the public and bury them in the graveyard of the forgotten past." This claim of secrecy, however, is more rhetoric than reality. Disclosure of court records is discretionary with the judge in most jurisdictions. Statutory restrictions almost invariably apply only to the court records, and even as to those the evidence is that many courts routinely furnish information to the FBI and the military, and on request to government agencies and even to private employers. Of more importance are police records. In most States the police keep a complete file of juvenile "police contacts" and have complete discretion as to disclosure of juvenile records. Police departments receive requests for information from the FBI and other law-enforcement agencies, the Armed Forces, and social service agencies, and most of them generally comply. [I]n some jurisdictions information concerning juvenile police contacts is furnished private employers as well as government agencies.

In any event, there is no reason why, consistently with due process, a State cannot continue if it deems it appropriate, to provide and to improve provision for the confidentiality

---

30. Here again, however, there is substantial question as to whether fact and pretension, with respect to the separate handling and treatment of children, coincide.

While we are concerned only with procedure before the juvenile court in this case, … to the extent that the special procedures for juveniles are thought to be justified by the special consideration and treatment afforded them, there is reason to doubt that juveniles always receive the benefits of such a quid pro quo. …

The high rate of juvenile recidivism casts some doubt upon the adequacy of treatment afforded juveniles. In fact, some courts have recently indicated that appropriate treatment is essential to the validity of juvenile custody, and therefore that a juvenile may challenge the validity of his custody on the ground that he is not in fact receiving any special treatment.

31. "Theword 'delinquent' has today developed such invidious connotations that the terminology is in the process of being altered; the new descriptive phrase is 'persons in need of supervision,' usually shortened to 'pins.'" The N.Y. Family Court Act § 712 distinguishes between "delinquents" and "persons in need of supervision."

of records of police contacts and court action relating to juveniles. It is interesting to note, however, that the Arizona Supreme Court used the confidentiality argument as a justification for the type of notice which is here attacked as inadequate for due process purposes. The parents were given merely general notice that their child was charged with "delinquency." No facts were specified. The Arizona court held, however, as we shall discuss, that in addition to this general "notice," the child and his parents must be advised "of the facts involved in the case" no later than the initial hearing by the judge. Obviously, this does not "bury" the word about the child's transgressions. It merely defers the time of disclosure to a point when it is of limited use to the child or his parents in preparing his defense or explanation.

Further, it is urged that the juvenile benefits from informal proceedings in the court. The early conception of the Juvenile Court proceeding was one in which a fatherly judge touched the heart and conscience of the erring youth by talking over his problems, by paternal advice and admonition, and in which, in extreme situations, benevolent and wise institutions of the State provided guidance and help "to save him from downward career." Then, as now, goodwill and compassion were admirably prevalent. But recent studies have, with surprising unanimity, entered sharp dissent as to the validity of this gentle conception. They suggest that the appearance as well as the actuality of fairness, impartiality and orderliness—in short, the essentials of due process—may be a more impressive and more therapeutic attitude so far as the juvenile is concerned. For example, in a recent study, the sociologists Wheeler and Cottrell ... conclude as follows: "Unless appropriate due process of law is followed, even the juvenile who has violated the law may not feel that he is being fairly treated and may therefore resist the rehabilitative efforts of court personnel."[37] ... While due process requirements will, in some instances, introduce a degree of order and regularity to Juvenile Court proceedings to determine delinquency, and in contested cases will introduce some elements of the adversary system, nothing will require that the conception of the kindly juvenile judge be replaced by its opposite, nor do we here rule upon the question whether ordinary due process requirements must be observed with respect to hearings to determine the disposition of the delinquent child.

Ultimately, however, we confront the reality of that portion of the Juvenile Court process with which we deal in this case. A boy is charged with misconduct. The boy is committed to an institution where he may be restrained of liberty for years. It is of no constitutional consequence—and of limited practical meaning—that the institution to which he is committed is called an Industrial School ... [H]owever euphemistic the title, a "receiving home" or an "industrial school" for juveniles is an institution of confinement in which the child is incarcerated for a greater or lesser time. His world becomes "a building with whitewashed walls, regimented routine and institutional hours * * *." Instead of mother and father and sisters and brothers and friends and classmates, his world is peopled by guards, custodians, state employees, and "delinquents" confined with him for anything from waywardness to rape and homicide.

In view of this, it would be extraordinary if our Constitution did not require the procedural regularity and the exercise of care implied in the phrase "due process." Under our

---

37. The conclusion of the Nat'l Crime Comm'n Report is similar: "[T]here is increasing evidence that the informal procedures, contrary to the original expectation, may themselves constitute a further obstacle to effective treatment of the delinquent to the extent that they engender in the child a sense of injustice provoked by seemingly all-powerful and challengeless exercise of authority by judges and probation officers."

Constitution, the condition of being a boy does not justify a kangaroo court. The traditional ideas of Juvenile Court procedure, indeed, contemplated that time would be available and care would be used to establish precisely what the juvenile did and why he did it—was it a prank of adolescence or a brutal act threatening serious consequences to himself or society unless corrected? Under traditional notions, one would assume that in a case like that of Gerald Gault, where the juvenile appears to have a home, a working mother and father, and an older brother, the Juvenile Judge would have made a careful inquiry and judgment as to the possibility that the boy could be disciplined and dealt with at home, despite his previous transgressions.[41] Indeed, so far as appears in the record before us, except for some conversation with Gerald about his school work and his "wanting to go to * * * the Grand Canyon with his father," the points to which the judge directed his attention were little different from those that would be involved in determining any charge of violation of a penal statute.[42] The essential difference between Gerald's case and a normal criminal case is that safeguards available to adults were discarded in Gerald's case. The summary procedure as well as the long commitment was possible because Gerald was 15 years of age instead of over 18.

If Gerald had been over 18, he would not have been subject to Juvenile Court proceedings. For the particular offense immediately involved, the maximum punishment would have been a fine of $5 to $50, or imprisonment in jail for not more than two months. Instead, he was committed to custody for a maximum of six years. If he had been over 18 and had committed an offense to which such a sentence might apply, he would have been entitled to substantial rights under the Constitution of the United States as well as under Arizona's laws and constitution. The United States Constitution would guarantee him rights and protections with respect to arrest, search, and seizure, and pretrial interrogation. It would assure him of specific notice of the charges and adequate time to decide his course of action and to prepare his defense. He would be entitled to clear advice that he could be represented by counsel, and, at least if a felony were involved, the State would be required to provide counsel if his parents were unable to afford it. If the court acted on the basis of his confession, careful procedures would be required to assure its voluntariness. If the case went to trial, confrontation and opportunity for cross-examination would be guaranteed. So wide a gulf between the State's treatment of the adult and of the child requires a bridge sturdier than mere verbiage, and reasons more persuasive than cliché can provide. As Wheeler and Cottrell have put it, "The rhetoric of the juvenile court movement has developed without any necessarily close correspondence to the realities of court and institutional routines."

In *Kent*, we stated that the Juvenile Court Judge's exercise of the power of the state as parens patriae was not unlimited. We said that "the admonition to function in a 'parental' relationship is not an invitation to procedural arbitrariness." With respect to the waiver by the Juvenile Court to the adult court of jurisdiction over an offense committed by a youth, we said that "there is no place in our system of law for reaching a result of such tremendous consequences without ceremony—without hearing, without effective assis-

---

41. The Juvenile Judge's testimony at the habeas corpus proceeding is devoid of any meaningful discussion of this. He appears to have centered his attention upon whether Gerald made the phone call and used lewd words. He was impressed by the fact that Gerald was on six months' probation because he was with another boy who allegedly stole a purse—a different sort of offense, sharing the feature that Gerald was "along." And he even referred to a report which he said was not investigated because "there was no accusation because of lack of a material foundation."

42. While appellee's brief suggests that the probation officer made some investigation of Gerald's home life, etc., there is not even a claim that the judge went beyond the point stated in the text.

tance of counsel, without a statement of reasons." We announced with respect to such waiver proceedings that while "We do not mean * * * to indicate that the hearing to be held must conform with all of the requirements of a criminal trial or even of the usual administrative hearing; but we do hold that the hearing must measure up to the essentials of due process and fair treatment." We reiterate this view, here in connection with a juvenile court adjudication of "delinquency," as a requirement which is part of the Due Process Clause of the Fourteenth Amendment of our Constitution.[48]

We now turn to the specific issues which are presented to us in the present case.

III
NOTICE OF CHARGES

Appellants allege that the Arizona Juvenile Code is unconstitutional or alternatively that the proceedings before the Juvenile Court were constitutionally defective because of failure to provide adequate notice of the hearings. No notice was given to Gerald's parents when he was taken into custody on Monday, June 8. On that night, when Mrs. Gault went to the Detention Home, she was orally informed that there would be a hearing the next afternoon and was told the reason why Gerald was in custody. The only written notice Gerald's parents received at any time was a note on plain paper from Officer Flagg delivered on Thursday or Friday, June 11 or 12, to the effect that the judge had set Monday, June 15, "for further Hearings on Gerald's delinquency."

A "petition" was filed with the court on June 9 by Officer Flagg, reciting only that he was informed and believed that "said minor is a delinquent minor and that it is necessary that some order be made by the Honorable Court for said minor's welfare." The applicable Arizona statute provides for a petition to be filed in Juvenile Court, alleging in general terms that the child is "neglected, dependent or delinquent." The statute explicitly states that such a general allegation is sufficient, "without alleging the facts." There is no requirement that the petition be served and it was not served upon, given to, or shown to Gerald or his parents.[50]

The Supreme Court of Arizona rejected appellants' claim that due process was denied because of inadequate notice. It stated that "Mrs. Gault knew the exact nature of the charge against Gerald from the day he was taken to the detention home." The court also pointed out that the Gaults appeared at the two hearings "without objection." The court held that because "the policy of the juvenile law is to hide youthful errors from the full gaze of the public and bury them in the graveyard of the forgotten past," advance notice of the specific charges or basis for taking the juvenile into custody and for the hearing is not necessary. It held that the appropriate rule is that "the infant and his parents or guardian will

---

48. The Nat'l Crime Comm'n Report recommends that "Juvenile courts should make fullest feasible use of preliminary conferences to dispose of cases short of adjudication." Since this "consent decree" procedure would involve neither adjudication of delinquency nor institutionalization, nothing we say in this opinion should be construed as expressing any views with respect to such procedure. The problems of pre-adjudication treatment of juveniles, and of post-adjudication disposition, are unique to the juvenile process; hence what we hold in this opinion with regard to the procedural requirements at the adjudicatory stage has no necessary applicability to other steps of the juvenile process.

50. Arizona's Juvenile Code does not provide for notice of any sort to be given at the commencement of the proceedings to the child or his parents. Its only notice provision is ... if a person other than the parent or guardian is cited to appear, the parent or guardian shall be notified "by personal service" of the time and place of hearing. The procedure for initiating a proceeding ... seems to require that after a preliminary inquiry by the court, a determination may be made "that formal jurisdiction should be acquired." Thereupon the court may authorize a petition to be filed. It does not appear that this procedure was followed in the present case.

receive a petition only reciting a conclusion of delinquency.[51] But no later than the initial hearing by the judge, they must be advised of the facts involved in the case. If the charges are denied, they must be given a reasonable period of time to prepare."

We cannot agree with the court's conclusion that adequate notice was given in this case. Notice, to comply with due process requirements, must be given sufficiently in advance of scheduled court proceedings so that reasonable opportunity to prepare will be afforded, and it must "set forth the alleged misconduct with particularity." [N]o purpose of shielding the child from the public stigma of knowledge of his having been taken into custody and scheduled for hearing is served by the procedure approved by the court below. The "initial hearing" in the present case was a hearing on the merits. Notice at that time is not timely; and even if there were a conceivable purpose served by the deferral proposed by the court below, it would have to yield to the requirements that the child and his parents or guardian be notified, in writing, of the specific charge or factual allegations to be considered at the hearing, and that such written notice be given at the earliest practicable time, and in any event sufficiently in advance of the hearing to permit preparation. Due process of law requires notice of the sort we have described—that is, notice which would be deemed constitutionally adequate in a civil or criminal proceeding. It does not allow a hearing to be held in which a youth's freedom and his parents' right to his custody are at stake without giving them timely notice, in advance of the hearing, of the specific issues that they must meet. Nor, in the circumstances of this case, can it reasonably be said that the requirement of notice was waived.[54]

IV

RIGHT TO COUNSEL

Appellants charge that the Juvenile Court proceedings were fatally defective because the court did not advise Gerald or his parents of their right to counsel, and proceeded with the hearing, the adjudication of delinquency and the order of commitment in the absence of counsel for the child and his parents or an express waiver of the right thereto. The Supreme Court of Arizona pointed out that "[t]here is disagreement [among the various jurisdictions] as to whether the court must advise the infant that he has a right to counsel." It noted its own decision in *Arizona State Dept. of Public Welfare v. Barlow* to the effect "that the parents of an infant in a juvenile proceeding cannot be denied representation by counsel of their choosing." It referred to a provision of the Juvenile Code which it characterized as requiring "that the probation officer shall look after the interests of neglected, delinquent and dependent children," including representing their interests in court.[56] The

---

51. No such petition w[as] served or supplied in the present case.

54. Mrs. Gault's "knowledge" of the charge against Gerald, and/or the asserted failure to object, does not excuse the lack of adequate notice. Indeed, one of the purposes of notice is to clarify the issues to be considered, and as our discussion of the facts, supra, shows, even the Juvenile Court Judge was uncertain as to the precise issues determined at the two "hearings." Since the Gaults had no counsel and were not told of their right to counsel, we cannot consider their failure to object to the lack of constitutionally adequate notice as a waiver of their rights. Because of our conclusion that notice given only at the first hearing is inadequate, we need not reach the question whether the Gaults ever received adequately specific notice even at the June 9 hearing, in light of the fact they were never apprised of the charge of being habitually involved in immoral matters.

56. The section cited by the court, ARS § 8-204, subsec. C, reads as follows:

"The probation officer shall have the authority of a peace officer. He shall:

    1. Look after the interests of neglected, delinquent and dependent children of the county.

    2. Make investigations and file petitions.

    3. Be present in court when cases are heard concerning children and represent their interests.

    4. Furnish the court information and assistance as it may require.

court argued that "The parent and the probation officer may be relied upon to protect the infant's interests." Accordingly it rejected the proposition that "due process requires that an infant have a right to counsel." It said that juvenile courts have the discretion, but not the duty, to allow such representation; it referred specifically to the situation in which the Juvenile Court discerns conflict between the child and his parents as an instance in which this discretion might be exercised. We do not agree. Probation officers, in the Arizona scheme, are also arresting officers. They initiate proceedings and file petitions which they verify, as here, alleging the delinquency of the child; and they testify, as here, against the child. And here the probation officer was also superintendent of the Detention Home. The probation officer cannot act as counsel for the child. His role in the adjudicatory hearing, by statute and in fact, is as arresting officer and witness against the child. Nor can the judge represent the child. There is no material difference in this respect between adult and juvenile proceedings of the sort here involved. In adult proceedings, this contention has been foreclosed by decisions of this Court. A proceeding where the issue is whether the child will be found to be "delinquent" and subjected to the loss of his liberty for years is comparable in seriousness to a felony prosecution. The juvenile needs the assistance of counsel to cope with problems of law,[58] to make skilled inquiry into the facts, to insist upon regularity of the proceedings, and to ascertain whether he has a defense and to prepare and submit it. The child "requires the guiding hand of counsel at every step in the proceedings against him." We indicated our agreement with the United States Court of Appeals for the District of Columbia Circuit that the assistance of counsel is essential for purposes of waiver proceedings, so we hold now that it is equally essential for the determination of delinquency, carrying with it the awesome prospect of incarceration in a state institution until the juvenile reaches the age of 21.[60]

During the last decade, court decisions, experts, and legislatures have demonstrated increasing recognition of this view. In at least one-third of the States, statutes now provide for the right of representation by retained counsel in juvenile delinquency proceedings, notice of the right, or assignment of counsel, or a combination of these. In other States, court rules have similar provisions.[64]

The President's Crime Commission has recently recommended that in order to assure "procedural justice for the child," it is necessary that "Counsel * * * be appointed as a matter of course wherever coercive action is a possibility, without requiring any affirmative choice by child or parent."[65] As stated by the authoritative "Standards for Juvenile and Family Courts":

---

5. Assist in the collection of sums ordered paid for the support of children.

6. Perform other acts ordered by the court."

58. In the present proceeding, for example, although the Juvenile Judge believed that Gerald's telephone conversation was within the condemnation of ARS § 13-377, he suggested some uncertainty because the statute prohibits the use of vulgar language "in the presence or hearing of" a woman or child.

60. This means that the commitment, in virtually all cases, is for a minimum of three years since jurisdiction of juvenile courts is usually limited to age 18 and under.

64. Recognition of the right to counsel involves no necessary interference with the special purposes of juvenile court procedures; indeed, it seems that counsel can play an important role in the process of rehabilitation.

65. The Commission's statement of its position is very forceful:

"[N]o single action holds more potential for achieving procedural justice for the child in the juvenile court than provision of counsel. The presence of an independent legal representative of the child, or of his parent, is the keystone of the whole structure of guarantees that a minimum system of procedural justice requires. The rights to confront one's accusers, to cross-examine witnesses, to present evidence and testimony of one's own, to be unaffected

"As a component part of a fair hearing required by due process guaranteed under the 14th amendment, notice of the right to counsel should be required at all hearings and counsel provided upon request when the family is financially unable to employ counsel."

This statement was "reviewed" by the National Council of Juvenile Court Judges at its 1965 Convention and they "found no fault" with it. The New York Family Court Act contains the following statement:

"This act declares that minors have a right to the assistance of counsel of their own choosing or of law guardians[67] in neglect proceedings under article three and in proceedings to determine juvenile delinquency and whether a person is in need of supervision under article seven. This declaration is based on a finding that counsel is often indispensable to a practical realization of due process of law and may be helpful in making reasoned determinations of fact and proper orders of disposition."

The Act provides that "[a]t the commencement of any hearing" under the delinquency article of the statute, the juvenile and his parent shall be advised of the juvenile's "right to be represented by counsel chosen by him or his parent * * * by a law guardian assigned by the court * * *." The California Act (1961) also requires appointment of counsel.

We conclude that the Due Process Clause of the Fourteenth Amendment requires that in respect of proceedings to determine delinquency which may result in commitment to

---

by prejudicial and unreliable evidence, to participate meaningfully in the dispositional decision, [or] to take an appeal, have substantial meaning for the overwhelming majority of persons brought before the juvenile court only if they are provided with competent lawyers who can invoke those rights effectively. The most informal and well-intentioned of judicial proceedings are technical; few adults without legal training can influence or even understand them; certainly children cannot.... But with lawyers come records of proceedings; records make possible appeals which, even if they do not occur, impart by their possibility a healthy atmosphere of accountability.

Fears have been expressed that lawyers would make juvenile court proceedings adversary. No doubt this is partly true, but it is partly desirable. Informality is often abused. The juvenile courts deal with cases in which ... rules of evidence, confrontation of witnesses, and other adversary procedures are called for. They deal with many cases involving conduct that can lead to incarceration or close supervision for long periods, and therefore juveniles often need the same safeguards that are granted to adults. And in all cases children need advocates to speak for them and guard their interests, particularly when disposition decisions are made....

Fears also have been expressed that the formality lawyers would bring into juvenile court would defeat the therapeutic aims of the court. But informality has no necessary connection with therapy.... [I]n many instances lawyers, for all their commitment to formality, [possibly] could do more to further therapy for their clients than can the small, overworked social staffs of the courts. * * *

[I]t is essential that counsel be appointed by the juvenile court for those who are unable to provide their own. Experience under the prevailing systems in which children are free to seek counsel of their choice reveals how empty of meaning the right is for those typically the subjects of juvenile court proceedings. Moreover, providing counsel only when the child is sophisticated enough to be aware of his need and to ask for one or when he fails to waive his announced right [is] not enough, as experience in numerous jurisdictions reveals.

The Commission recommends:

COUNSEL SHOULD BE APPOINTED AS A MATTER OF COURSE WHEREVER COERCIVE ACTION IS A POSSIBILITY, WITHOUT REQUIRING ANY AFFIRMATIVE CHOICE BY CHILD OR PARENT."

67. These are lawyers designated, as provided by the statute, to represent minors.

an institution in which the juvenile's freedom is curtailed, the child and his parents must be notified of the child's right to be represented by counsel retained by them, or if they are unable to afford counsel, that counsel will be appointed to represent the child.

At the habeas corpus proceeding, Mrs. Gault testified that she knew that she could have appeared with counsel at the juvenile hearing. This knowledge is not a waiver of the right to counsel which she and her juvenile son had, as we have defined it. They had a right expressly to be advised that they might retain counsel and to be confronted with the need for specific consideration of whether they did or did not choose to waive the right. If they were unable to afford to employ counsel, they were entitled in view of the seriousness of the charge and the potential commitment, to appointed counsel, unless they chose waiver. Mrs. Gault's knowledge that she could employ counsel was not an "intentional relinquishment or abandonment" of a fully known right.

V

CONFRONTATION, SELF-INCRIMINATION,
CROSS-EXAMINATION

Appellants urge that the writ of habeas corpus should have been granted because of the denial of the rights of confrontation and cross-examination in the Juvenile Court hearings, and because the privilege against self-incrimination was not observed. The Juvenile Court Judge testified at the habeas corpus hearing that he had proceeded on the basis of Gerald's admissions at the two hearings. Appellants attack this on the ground that the admissions were obtained in disregard of the privilege against self-incrimination. If the confession is disregarded, appellants argue that the delinquency conclusion, since it was fundamentally based on a finding that Gerald had made lewd remarks during the phone call to Mrs. Cook, is fatally defective for failure to accord the rights of confrontation and cross-examination which the Due Process Clause of the Fourteenth Amendment of the Federal Constitution guarantees in state proceedings generally.

Our first question, then, is whether Gerald's admission was improperly obtained and relied on as the basis of decision, in conflict with the Federal Constitution. For this purpose, it is necessary briefly to recall the relevant facts.

Mrs. Cook, the complainant, ... was not called as a witness. Gerald's mother asked ... why Mrs. Cook was not present and the judge replied that "she didn't have to be present." So far as appears, Mrs. Cook was spoken to only once, by Officer Flagg, ... by telephone. The judge did not speak with her on any occasion. Gerald had been questioned by the probation officer after having been taken into custody. The exact circumstances of this questioning do not appear but any admissions Gerald may have made at this time do not appear in the record.[74] Gerald was also questioned by the Juvenile Court Judge at each of the two hearings. The judge testified in the habeas corpus proceeding that Gerald admitted making "some of the lewd statements * * * [but not] any of the more serious lewd statements." There was conflict and uncertainty among the witnesses at the habeas corpus proceeding—the Juvenile Court Judge, Mr. and Mrs. Gault, and the probation officer—as to what Gerald did or did not admit.

We shall assume that Gerald made admissions of the sort described by the Juvenile Court Judge, as quoted above. Neither Gerald nor his parents were advised that he did not have to testify or make a statement, or that an incriminating statement might result in his commitment as a "delinquent."

---

74. For this reason, we cannot consider the status of Gerald's alleged admissions to the probation officers.

The Arizona Supreme Court rejected appellants' contention that Gerald had a right to be advised that he need not incriminate himself. It said: "We think the necessary flexibility for individualized treatment will be enhanced by a rule which does not require the judge to advise the infant of a privilege against self-incrimination."

In reviewing this conclusion of Arizona's Supreme Court, we emphasize again that we are here concerned only with a proceeding to determine whether a minor is a "delinquent" and which may result in commitment to a state institution. Specifically, the question is whether, in such a proceeding, an admission by the juvenile may be used against him in the absence of clear and unequivocal evidence that the admission was made with knowledge that he was not obliged to speak and would not be penalized for remaining silent. In light of *Miranda v. State of Arizona*, we must also consider whether, if the privilege against self-incrimination is available, it can effectively be waived unless counsel is present or the right to counsel has been waived.

[T]he eliciting and use of confessions or admissions require careful scrutiny. Dean Wigmore states:

> "The ground of distrust of confessions made in certain situations is, in a rough and indefinite way, judicial experience. [E]nough [untrue confessions] have been verified to fortify the conclusion, based on ordinary observation of human conduct, that under certain stresses a person, especially one of defective mentality or peculiar temperament, may falsely acknowledge guilt. This possibility arises wherever the innocent person is placed in such a situation that the untrue acknowledgment of guilt is at the time the more promising of two alternatives between which he is obliged to choose; that is, he chooses any risk that may be in falsely acknowledging guilt, in preference to some worse alternative associated with silence.

> The principle, then, upon which a confession may be excluded is that it is, under certain conditions, testimonially untrustworthy * * *."

> This Court has emphasized that admissions and confessions of juveniles require special caution....

The privilege against self-incrimination is, of course, related to the question of the safeguards necessary to assure that admissions or confessions are reasonably trustworthy, that they are not the mere fruits of fear or coercion, but are reliable expressions of the truth. The roots of the privilege are, however, far deeper. They tap the basic stream of religious and political principle because the privilege reflects the limits of the individual's attornment to the state and—in a philosophical sense—insists upon the equality of the individual and the state. In other words, the privilege has a broader and deeper thrust than the rule which prevents the use of confessions which are the product of coercion because coercion is thought to carry with it the danger of unreliability. One of its purposes is to prevent the state, whether by force or by psychological domination, from overcoming the mind and will of the person under investigation and depriving him of the freedom to decide whether to assist the state in securing his conviction.

It would indeed be surprising if the privilege against self-incrimination were available to hardened criminals but not to children.

With respect to juveniles, both common observation and expert opinion emphasize that the "distrust of confessions made in certain situations" to which Dean Wigmore referred ... is imperative in the case of children from an early age through adolescence. In New York, for example, the recently enacted Family Court Act provides that the juvenile and his parents must be advised at the start of the hearing of his right to remain silent. The New York statute also provides that the police must attempt to communicate with the juvenile's parents before questioning him, and that absent "special circumstances" a confession may not be obtained from a child prior to notifying his parents or relatives and releasing the child either to them or to the Family Court. [T]he New York Court of Appeals [has] held that the privilege against self-incrimination applies in juvenile delinquency cases and requires the exclusion of involuntary confessions....

The authoritative "Standards for Juvenile and Family Courts" concludes that, "Whether or not transfer to the criminal court is a possibility, certain procedures should always be followed. Before being interviewed [by the police], the child and his parents should be informed of his right to have legal counsel present and to refuse to answer questions or be fingerprinted[83] if he should so decide."

Against the application to juveniles of the right to silence, it is argued that juvenile proceedings are "civil" and not "criminal," and therefore the privilege should not apply. It is true that the statement of the privilege in the Fifth Amendment, which is applicable to the States by reason of the Fourteenth Amendment, is that no person "shall be compelled in any criminal case to be a witness against himself." However, it is also clear that the availability of the privilege does not turn upon the type of proceeding in which its protection is invoked, but upon the nature of the statement or admission and the exposure which it invites. The privilege may, for example, be claimed in a civil or administrative proceeding, if the statement is or may be inculpatory.

It would be entirely unrealistic to carve out of the Fifth Amendment all statements by juveniles on the ground that these cannot lead to "criminal" involvement. In the first place, juvenile proceedings to determine "delinquency," which may lead to commitment to a state institution, must be regarded as "criminal" for purposes of the privilege against self-incrimination. To hold otherwise would be to disregard substance because of the feeble enticement of the "civil" label-of-convenience which has been attached to juvenile proceedings. Indeed, in over half of the States, there is not even assurance that the juvenile will be kept in separate institutions, apart from adult "criminals." In those States juveniles may be placed in or transferred to adult penal institutions after having been found "delinquent" by a juvenile court. For this purpose, at least, commitment is a deprivation of liberty. It is incarceration against one's will, whether it is called "criminal" or "civil." And our Constitution guarantees that no person shall be "compelled" to be a witness against himself when he is threatened with deprivation of his liberty—a command which this Court has broadly applied and generously implemented in accordance with the teaching of the history of the privilege and its great office in mankind's battle for freedom.

In addition, apart from the equivalence for this purpose of exposure to commitment as a juvenile delinquent and exposure to imprisonment as an adult offender, ... there is little or no assurance in Arizona, as in most if not all of the States, that a juvenile apprehended and interrogated by the police or even by the Juvenile Court itself will remain outside of the reach of adult courts as a consequence of the offense for which he has been taken into custody. In Arizona, as in other States, provision is made for Juvenile Courts to relinquish or waive jurisdiction to the ordinary criminal courts. In the present case, when Gerald Gault was interrogated concerning violation of a section of the Arizona Criminal

---

83. The issues relating to fingerprinting of juveniles are not presented here, and we express no opinion concerning them.

Code, it could not be certain that the Juvenile Court Judge would decide to "suspend" criminal prosecution in court for adults by proceeding to an adjudication in Juvenile Court.

It is also urged, as the Supreme Court of Arizona here asserted, that the juvenile and presumably his parents should not be advised of the juvenile's right to silence because confession is good for the child as the commencement of the assumed therapy of the juvenile court process, and he should be encouraged to assume an attitude of trust and confidence toward the officials of the juvenile process. This proposition has been subjected to widespread challenge on the basis of current reappraisals of the rhetoric and realities of the handling of juvenile offenders.

In fact, evidence is accumulating that confessions by juveniles do not aid in "individualized treatment," as the court below put it, and that compelling the child to answer questions, without warning or advice as to his right to remain silent, does not serve this or any other good purpose. In light of the observations of Wheeler and Cottrell, and others, ... where children are induced to confess by "paternal" urgings on the part of officials and the confession is then followed by disciplinary action, ... the child may well feel that he has been led or tricked into confession and that despite his confession, he is being punished.

Further, authoritative opinion has cast formidable doubt upon the reliability and trustworthiness of "confessions" by children.... The recent decision of the New York Court of Appeals, *In Matters of W. and S.* deals with a dramatic and, it is to be hoped, extreme example. Two 12-year-old Negro boys were taken into custody for the brutal assault and rape of two aged domestics, one of whom died as the result of the attack. One of the boys was schizophrenic and had been locked in the security ward of a mental institution at the time of the attacks. By a process that may best be described as bizarre, his confession was obtained by the police. A psychiatrist testified that the boy would admit 'whatever he thought was expected so that he could get out of the immediate situation.' The other 12-year-old also "confessed." Both confessions were in specific detail, albeit they contained various inconsistencies. The Court of Appeals ... concluded that the confessions were products of the will of the police instead of the boys. The confessions were therefore held involuntary....

A similar and equally instructive case has recently been decided by the Supreme Court of New Jersey. *In Interests of Carlo and Stasilowicz.* The body of a 10-year-old girl was found. She had been strangled. Neighborhood boys who knew the girl were questioned. The two appellants, aged 13 and 15, confessed to the police, with vivid detail and some inconsistencies. At the Juvenile Court hearing, both denied any complicity in the killing. They testified that their confessions were the product of fear and fatigue due to extensive police grilling. The Juvenile Court Judge found that the confessions were voluntary and admissible. On appeal ... the Supreme Court of New Jersey reversed. It rejected the State's argument that the constitutional safeguard of voluntariness governing the use of confessions does not apply in proceedings before the Juvenile Court. It pointed out that under New Jersey court rules, juveniles under the age of 16 accused of committing a homicide are tried in a proceeding which "has all of the appurtenances of a criminal trial," including participation by the county prosecutor, and requirements that the juvenile be provided with counsel, that a stenographic record be made, etc. It also pointed out that under New Jersey law, the confinement of the boys after reaching age 21 could be extended until they had served the maximum sentence which could have been imposed on an adult for such a homicide, here found to be second-degree murder carrying up to 30 years' imprisonment. The court concluded that the confessions were involuntary, stressing that the boys, contrary to statute, were placed in the police station and there interrogated;

that the parents of both boys were not allowed to see them while they were being inter-rogated;[94] that inconsistencies appeared among the various statements of the boys and with the objective evidence of the crime; and that there were protracted periods of questioning. The court noted the State's contention that both boys were advised of their constitutional rights before they made their statements, but it held that this should not be given "significant weight in our determination of voluntariness." Accordingly, the judgment of the Juvenile Court was reversed.

. . . .

We conclude that the constitutional privilege against self-incrimination is applicable in the case of juveniles as it is with respect to adults. We appreciate that special problems may arise with respect to waiver of the privilege by or on behalf of children, and that there may well be some differences in technique — but not in principle — depending upon the age of the child and the presence and competence of parents. The participation of counsel will, of course, assist the police, Juvenile Courts and appellate tribunals in administering the privilege. If counsel was not present for some permissible reason when an admission was obtained, the greatest care must be taken to assure that the admission was voluntary, in the sense not only that it was not coerced or suggested, but also that it was not the product of ignorance of rights or of adolescent fantasy, fright or despair.[96]

The "confession" of Gerald Gault was first obtained by Officer Flagg, out of the presence of Gerald's parents, without counsel and without advising him of his right to silence, as far as appears. The judgment of the Juvenile Court was stated by the judge to be based on Gerald's admissions in court. Neither "admission" was reduced to writing, and ... the process by which the "admissions" were obtained [was] lacking the certainty and order which are required of proceedings of such formidable consequences. Apart from the "admission," there was nothing upon which a judgment or finding might be based. There was no sworn testimony. Mrs. Cook, the complainant, was not present. The Arizona Supreme Court held that "sworn testimony must be required of all witnesses including police officers, probation officers and others who are part of or officially related to the juvenile court structure." We hold that this is not enough. No reason is suggested or appears for a different rule in respect of sworn testimony in juvenile courts than in adult tribunals. Absent a valid confession adequate to support the determination of the Juvenile Court, confrontation and sworn testimony by witnesses available for cross-examination were essential for a finding of "delinquency" and an order committing Gerald to a state institution for a maximum of six years.

The recommendations in the ..."Standards for Juvenile and Family Courts" are in general accord with our conclusions. They state that testimony should be under oath and that only competent, material and relevant evidence under rules applicable to civil cases should be admitted in evidence. The New York Family Court Act contains a similar provision.

As we said in *Kent*, with respect to waiver proceedings, "there is no place in our system of law of reaching a result of such tremendous consequences without ceremony * * *." We now hold that, absent a valid confession, a determination of delinquency and an order of commitment to a state institution cannot be sustained in the absence of sworn testimony subjected to the opportunity for cross-examination in accordance with our law and constitutional requirements.

---

94. The court held that this alone might be enough to show that the confessions were involuntary "even though, as the police testified, the boys did not wish to see their parents."

96. The N.Y.Family Court Act § 744(b) provides that "an uncorroborated confession made out of court by a respondent is not sufficient" to constitute the required "preponderance of the evidence."

VI
APPELLATE REVIEW AND TRANSCRIPT OF PROCEEDINGS

Appellants urge that the Arizona statute is unconstitutional under the Due Process Clause because, as construed by its Supreme Court, "there is no right of appeal from a juvenile court order * * *." The court held that there is no right to a transcript because there is no right to appeal and because the proceedings are confidential and any record must be destroyed after a prescribed period of time. Whether a transcript or other recording is made, it held, is a matter for the discretion of the juvenile court.

This Court has not held that a State is required by the Federal Constitution "to provide appellate courts or a right to appellate review at all." In view of the fact that we must reverse the Supreme Court of Arizona's affirmance of the dismissal of the writ of habeas corpus for other reasons, we need not rule on this question in the present case or upon the failure to provide a transcript or recording of the hearings — or, indeed, the failure of the Juvenile Judge to state the grounds for his conclusion. [As we said in] *Kent*, "* * * it is incumbent upon the Juvenile Court to accompany its waiver order with a statement of the reasons or considerations therefor." As the present case illustrates, the consequences of failure to provide an appeal, to record the proceedings, or to make findings or state the grounds for the juvenile court's conclusion may be to throw a burden upon the machinery for habeas corpus, to saddle the reviewing process with the burden of attempting to reconstruct a record, and to impose upon the Juvenile Judge the unseemly duty of testifying under cross-examination as to the events that transpired in the hearings before him.

For the reasons stated, the judgment of the Supreme Court of Arizona is reversed and the cause remanded for further proceedings not inconsistent with this opinion. It is so ordered.

Judgment reversed and cause remanded with directions.

Mr. Justice BLACK, concurring.

The juvenile court laws of Arizona and other States, as the Court points out, are the result of plans promoted by humane and forward-looking people to provide a system of courts, procedures, and sanctions deemed to be less harmful and more lenient to children than to adults. For this reason such state laws generally provide less formal and less public methods for the trial of children. In line with this policy, both courts and legislators have shrunk back from labeling these laws as "criminal" and have preferred to call them "civil." This, in part, was to prevent the full application to juvenile court cases of the Bill of Rights safeguards, including notice as provided in the Sixth Amendment,[1] the right to counsel guaranteed by the Sixth,[2] the right against self-incrimination guaranteed by the Fifth,[3] and the right to confrontation guaranteed by the Sixth.[4] The Court here holds, however, that these four Bill of Rights safeguards apply to protect a juvenile accused in a juvenile court on a charge under which he can be imprisoned for a term of years. This holding strikes a well-nigh fatal blow to much that is unique about the juvenile courts in

---

1. "In all criminal prosecutions, the accused shall enjoy the right * * * to be informed of the nature and cause of the accusation * * *." Also requiring notice is the Fifth Amendment's provision that "No person shall be held to answer for a capital, or otherwise infamous crime, unless on a presentment or indictment of a Grand Jury * * *."

2. "In all criminal prosecutions, the accused shall * * * have the Assistance of Counsel in his defence."

3. "No person * * * shall be compelled in any criminal case to be a witness against himself * * *."

4. "In all criminal prosecutions, the accused shall enjoy the right * * * to be confronted with the witnesses against him * * *."

the Nation. For this reason, there is much to be said for the position of my Brother STEW-ART that we should not pass on all these issues until they are more squarely presented. But since the majority of the Court chooses to decide all of these questions, I must either do the same or leave my views unexpressed on the important issues determined. In these circumstances, I feel impelled to express my views.

The juvenile court planners envisaged a system that would practically immunize juveniles from "punishment" for "crimes" in an effort to save them from youthful indiscretions and stigmas due to criminal charges or convictions. I agree with the Court, however, that this exalted ideal has failed of achievement since the beginning of the system. Indeed, the state laws from the first one on contained provisions, written in emphatic terms, for ar-resting and charging juveniles with violations of state criminal laws, as well as for taking juveniles by force of law away from their parents and turning them over to different in-dividuals or groups or for confinement within some state school or institution for a num-ber of years. The latter occurred in this case. Young Gault was arrested and detained on a charge of violating an Arizona penal law by using vile and offensive language to a lady on the telephone. If an adult, he could only have been fined or imprisoned for two months for his conduct. As a juvenile, however, he was put through a more or less secret, infor-mal hearing by the court, after which he was ordered, or more realistically, "sentenced," to confinement in Arizona's Industrial School until he reaches 21 years of age. Thus, in a juvenile system designed to lighten or avoid punishment for criminality, he was ordered by the State to six years' confinement in what is in all but name a penitentiary or jail.

Where a person, infant or adult, can be seized by the State, charged, and convicted for violating a state criminal law, and then ordered by the State to be confined for six years, I think the Constitution requires that he be tried in accordance with the guaran-tees of all the provisions of the Bill of Rights made applicable to the States by the Four-teenth Amendment. Undoubtedly this would be true of an adult defendant, and it would be a plain denial of equal protection of the laws — an invidious discrimination — to hold that others subject to heavier punishments could, because they are children, be denied these same constitutional safeguards. I consequently agree with the Court that the Arizona law as applied here denied to the parents and their son the right of notice, right to counsel, right against self-incrimination, and right to confront the witnesses against young Gault. Appellants are entitled to these rights, not because "fairness, impartiality and orderli-ness — in short, the essentials of due process" — require them and not because they are "the procedural rules which have been fashioned from the generality of due process," but because they are specifically and unequivocally granted by provisions of the Fifth and Sixth Amendments which the Fourteenth Amendment makes applicable to the States.

A few words should be added because of the opinion of my Brother HARLAN who rests his concurrence and dissent on the Due Process Clause alone. He reads that clause alone as allowing this Court "to determine what forms of procedural protection are necessary to guarantee the fundamental fairness of juvenile proceedings" in a fashion consistent with the "traditions and conscience of our people." He believes that the Due Process Clause gives this Court the power, upon weighing a "compelling public interest," to impose on the States only those specific constitutional rights which the Court deems "imperative" and "necessary" to comport with the Court's notions of "fundamental fairness."

. . . .

I do not believe that the Constitution vests any such power in judges, either in the Due Process Clause or anywhere else. Consequently, I do not vote to invalidate this Arizona law on the ground that it is "unfair" but solely on the ground that it violates the Fifth and

Sixth Amendments made obligatory on the States by the Fourteenth Amendment. It is enough for me that the Arizona law as here applied collides head-on with the Fifth and Sixth Amendments in the four respects mentioned. The only relevance to me of the Due Process Clause is that it would, of course, violate due process or the "law of the land" to enforce a law that collides with the Bill of Rights.

Mr. Justice WHITE, concurring.

I join the Court's opinion except for Part V. I also agree that the privilege against compelled self-incrimination applies at the adjudicatory stage of juvenile court proceedings. I do not, however, find an adequate basis in the record for determination whether that privilege was violated in this case. The Fifth Amendment protects a person from being "compelled" in any criminal proceeding to be a witness against himself. Compulsion is essential to a violation. It may be that when a judge, armed with the authority he has or which people think he has, asks questions of a party or a witness in an adjudicatory hearing, that person, especially if a minor, would feel compelled to answer, absent a warning to the contrary or similar information from some other source. The difficulty is that the record made at the habeas corpus hearing, which is the only information we have concerning the proceedings in the juvenile court, does not directly inform us whether Gerald Gault or his parents were told of Gerald's right to remain silent; nor does it reveal whether the parties were aware of the privilege from some other source, just as they were already aware that they had the right to have the help of counsel and to have witnesses on their behalf. The petition for habeas corpus did not raise the Fifth Amendment issue nor did any of the witnesses focus on it.

I have previously recorded my views with respect to what I have deemed unsound applications of the Fifth Amendment. These views, of course, have not prevailed. But I do hope that the Court will proceed with some care in extending the privilege, with all its vigor, to proceedings in juvenile court, particularly the nonadjudicatory stages of those proceedings.

For somewhat similar reasons, I would not reach the questions of confrontation and cross-examination which are also dealt with in Part V of the opinion.

Mr. Justice HARLAN, concurring in part and dissenting in part.

I

. . . .

The proper issue here is ... not whether the State may constitutionally treat juvenile offenders through a system of specialized courts, but whether the proceedings in Arizona's juvenile courts include procedural guarantees which satisfy the requirements of the Fourteenth Amendment. Among the first premises of our constitutional system is the obligation to conduct any proceeding in which an individual may be deprived of liberty or property in a fashion consistent with the "traditions and conscience of our people." The importance of these procedural guarantees is doubly intensified here. First, many of the problems with which Arizona is concerned are among those traditionally confined to the processes of criminal justice; their disposition necessarily affects in the most direct and substantial manner the liberty of individual citizens. Quite obviously, systems of specialized penal justice might permit erosion, or even evasion, of the limitations placed by the Constitution upon state criminal proceedings. Second, we must recognize that the character and consequences of many juvenile court proceedings have in fact closely resembled those of ordinary criminal trials. Nothing before us suggests that juvenile courts were intended as a device to escape constitutional constraints, but I entirely agree with the Court that we are nonetheless obliged to examine with circumspection the procedural guarantees the State has provided.

The central issue here, and the principal one upon which I am divided from the Court, is the method by which the procedural requirements of due process should be measured. It must at the outset be emphasized that the protections necessary here cannot be determined by resort to any classification of juvenile proceedings either as criminal or as civil, whether made by the State or by this Court. Both formulae are simply too imprecise to permit reasoned analysis of these difficult constitutional issues. The Court should instead measure the requirements of due process by reference both to the problems which confront the State and to the actual character of the procedural system which the State has created. The Court has for such purposes chiefly examined three connected sources: first, the 'settled usages and modes of proceeding;' second, the 'fundamental principles of liberty and justice which lie at the base of all our civil and political institutions;' and third, the character and requirements of the circumstances presented in each situation.

The Court has repeatedly emphasized that determination of the constitutionally required procedural safeguards in any situation requires recognition both of the 'interests affected' and of the 'circumstances involved.' In particular, a 'compelling public interest' must, under our cases, be taken fully into account in assessing the validity under the due process clauses of state or federal legislation and its application. Such interests would never warrant arbitrariness or the diminution of any specifically assured constitutional right, but they are an essential element of the context through which the legislation and proceedings under it must be read and evaluated.

No more evidence of the importance of the public interests at stake here is required than that furnished by the opinion of the Court; it indicates that "some 601,000 children under 18, or 2% of all children between 10 and 17, came before juvenile courts" in 1965, and that "about one-fifth of all arrests for serious crimes" in 1965 were of juveniles. The Court adds that the rate of juvenile crime is steadily rising. All this, as the Court suggests, indicates the importance of these due process issues, but it mirrors no less vividly that state authorities are confronted by formidable and immediate problems involving the most fundamental social values. The state legislatures have determined that the most hopeful solution for these problems is to be found in specialized courts, organized under their own rules and imposing distinctive consequences. The terms and limitations of these systems are not identical, nor are the procedural arrangements which they include, but the States are uniform in their insistence that the ordinary processes of criminal justice are inappropriate, and that relatively informal proceedings, dedicated to premises and purposes only imperfectly reflected in the criminal law, are instead necessary.

....

These ... considerations, which I believe to be fair distillations of relevant judicial history, suggest three criteria by which the procedural requirements of due process should be measured here: first, no more restrictions should be imposed than are imperative to assure the proceedings' fundamental fairness; second, the restrictions which are imposed should be those which preserve, so far as possible, the essential elements of the State's purpose; and finally, restrictions should be chosen which will later permit the orderly selection of any additional protections which may ultimately prove necessary. In this way, the Court may guarantee the fundamental fairness of the proceeding, and yet permit the State to continue development of an effective response to the problems of juvenile crime.

II

Measured by these criteria, only three procedural requirements should, in my opinion, now be deemed required of state juvenile courts by the Due Process Clause of the Fourteenth Amendment: first, timely notice must be provided to parents and children of the nature and terms of any juvenile court proceeding in which a determination affecting their rights or interests may be made; second, unequivocal and timely notice must be given that counsel may appear in any such proceeding in behalf of the child and its parents, and that in cases in which the child may be confined in an institution, counsel may, in circumstances of indigency, be appointed for them; and third, the court must maintain a written record, or its equivalent, adequate to permit effective review on appeal or in collateral proceedings. These requirements would guarantee to juveniles the tools with which their rights could be fully vindicated, and yet permit the States to pursue without unnecessary hindrance the purposes which they believe imperative in this field. Further, their imposition now would later permit more intelligent assessment of the necessity under the Fourteenth Amendment of additional requirements, by creating suitable records from which the character and deficiencies of juvenile proceedings could be accurately judged. I turn to consider each of these three requirements.

The Court has consistently made plain that adequate and timely notice is the fulcrum of due process, whatever the purposes of the proceeding. Notice is ordinarily the prerequisite to effective assertion of any constitutional or other rights; without it, vindication of those rights must be essentially fortuitous. So fundamental a protection can neither be spared here nor left to the "favor or grace" of state authorities.

Provision of counsel and of a record, like adequate notice, would permit the juvenile to assert very much more effectively his rights and defenses, both in the juvenile proceedings and upon direct or collateral review. The Court has frequently emphasized their importance in proceedings in which an individual may be deprived of his liberty; this reasoning must include with special force those who are commonly inexperienced and immature. The facts of this case illustrate poignantly the difficulties of review without either an adequate record or the participation of counsel in the proceeding's initial stages. At the same time, these requirements should not cause any substantial modification in the character of juvenile court proceedings: counsel, although now present in only a small percentage of juvenile cases, have apparently already appeared without incident in virtually all juvenile courts;[3] and the maintenance of a record should not appreciably alter the conduct of these proceedings.

The question remains whether certain additional requirements, among them the privilege against self-incrimination, confrontation, and cross-examination, must now, as the Court holds, also be imposed. I share in part the views expressed in my Brother WHITE'S concurring opinion, but believe that there are other, and more deep-seated, reasons to defer, at least for the present, the imposition of such requirements.

Initially, I must vouchsafe that I cannot determine with certainty the reasoning by which the Court concludes that these further requirements are now imperative. The Court begins from the premise, to which it gives force at several points, that juvenile courts need not satisfy "all of the requirements of a criminal trial." It therefore scarcely suffices to explain the selection of these particular procedural requirements for the Court to declare that juvenile court proceedings are essentially criminal, and thereupon to recall that

---

3. The statistical evidence here is incomplete, but Skoler & Tenney ... indicate that some 91% of the juvenile court judges whom they polled favored representation by counsel in their courts.

these are requisites for a criminal trial. Nor does the Court's voucher of "authoritative opinion," which consists of four extraordinary juvenile cases, contribute materially to the solution of these issues. The Court has, even under its own premises, asked the wrong questions: the problem here is to determine what forms of procedural protection are necessary to guarantee the fundamental fairness of juvenile proceedings, and not which of the procedures now employed in criminal trials should be transplanted intact to proceedings in these specialized courts.

In my view, the Court should approach this question in terms of the criteria, described above, which emerge from the history of due process adjudication. Measured by them, there are compelling reasons at least to defer imposition of these additional requirements. First, quite unlike notice, counsel, and a record, these requirements might radically alter the character of juvenile court proceedings. The evidence from which the Court reasons that they would not is inconclusive, and other available evidence suggests that they very likely would. At the least, it is plain that these additional requirements would contribute materially to the creation in these proceedings of the atmosphere of an ordinary criminal trial, and would, even if they do no more, thereby largely frustrate a central purpose of these specialized courts. Further, these are restrictions intended to conform to the demands of an intensely adversary system of criminal justice; the broad purposes which they represent might be served in juvenile courts with equal effectiveness by procedural devices more consistent with the premises of proceedings in those courts. As the Court apparently acknowledges, the hazards of self-accusation, for example, might be avoided in juvenile proceedings without the imposition of all the requirements and limitations which surround the privilege against self-incrimination. The guarantee of adequate notice, counsel, and a record would create conditions in which suitable alternative procedures could be devised; but, unfortunately, the Court's haste to impose restrictions taken intact from criminal procedure may well seriously hamper the development of such alternatives. Surely this illustrates that prudence and the principles of the Fourteenth Amendment alike require that the Court should now impose no more procedural restrictions than are imperative to assure fundamental fairness, and that the States should instead be permitted additional opportunities to develop without unnecessary hindrance their systems of juvenile courts.

I find confirmation for these views in two ancillary considerations. First, it is clear that an uncertain, but very substantial number of the cases brought to juvenile courts involve children who are not in any sense guilty of criminal misconduct. Many of these children have simply the misfortune to be in some manner distressed; others have engaged in conduct, such as truancy, which is plainly not criminal.[6] Efforts are now being made to develop effective, and entirely noncriminal, methods of treatment for these children. In such cases, the state authorities are in the most literal sense acting in loco parentis; they are, by any standard, concerned with the child's protection, and not with his punishment. I do not question that the methods employed in such cases must be consistent with the constitutional obligation to act in accordance with due process, but certainly the Fourteenth Amendment does not demand that they be constricted by the procedural guarantees devised for ordinary criminal prosecutions. [T]he various classifications of juvenile court proceedings are, as the vagaries of the available statistics illustrate, often ar-

---

6. Estimates of the number of children in this situation brought before juvenile courts range from 26% to some 48%; variation seems chiefly a product both of the inadequacy of records and of the difficulty of categorizing precisely the conduct with which juveniles are charged. By any standard, the number of juveniles involved is "considerable."

bitrary or ambiguous; it would therefore be imprudent, at the least, to build upon these classifications rigid systems of procedural requirements which would be applicable, or not, in accordance with the descriptive label given to the particular proceeding. It is better ... to begin by now requiring the essential elements of fundamental fairness in juvenile courts, whatever the label given by the State to the proceedings; in this way the Court could avoid imposing unnecessarily rigid restrictions, and yet escape dependence upon classifications which may often prove to be illusory. Further, the provision of notice, counsel, and a record would permit orderly efforts to determine later whether more satisfactory classifications can be devised, and if they can, whether additional procedural requirements are necessary for them under the Fourteenth Amendment.

Second, ... juvenile crime and juvenile courts are both now under earnest study throughout the country. [T]his Court, by imposing these rigid procedural requirements, may inadvertently have served to discourage these efforts to find more satisfactory solutions for the problems of juvenile crime, and may thus now hamper enlightened development of the systems of juvenile courts. [T]he Fourteenth Amendment does not compel the law to remain passive in the midst of change; to demand otherwise denies "every quality of the law but its age."

III

Finally, I turn to assess the validity of this juvenile court proceeding under the criteria discussed in this opinion. Measured by them, the judgment below must, in my opinion, fall. Gerald Gault and his parents were not provided adequate notice of the terms and purposes of the proceedings in which he was adjudged delinquent; they were not advised of their rights to be represented by counsel; and no record in any form was maintained of the proceedings. It follows, for the reasons given in this opinion, that Gerald Gault was deprived of his liberty without due process of law, and I therefore concur in the judgment of the Court.

Mr. Justice STEWART, dissenting.

The Court today uses an obscure Arizona case as a vehicle to impose upon thousands of juvenile courts throughout the Nation restrictions that the Constitution made applicable to adversary criminal trials. I believe the Court's decision is wholly unsound as a matter of constitutional law, and sadly unwise as a matter of judicial policy.

Juvenile proceedings are not criminal trials. They are not civil trials. They are simply not adversary proceedings. Whether treating with a delinquent child, a neglected child, a defective child, or a dependent child, a juvenile proceeding's whole purpose and mission is the very opposite of the mission and purpose of a prosecution in a criminal court. The object of the one is correction of a condition. The object of the other is conviction and punishment for a criminal act.

In the last 70 years many dedicated men and women have devoted their professional lives to the enlightened task of bringing us out of the dark world of Charles Dickens in meeting our responsibilities to the child in our society. The result has been the creation in this century of a system of juvenile and family courts in each of the 50 States. There can be no denying that in many areas the performance of these agencies has fallen disappointingly short of the hopes and dreams of the courageous pioneers who first conceived them. For a variety of reasons, the reality has sometimes not even approached the ideal, and much remains to be accomplished in the administration of public juvenile and family agencies—in personnel, in planning, in financing, perhaps in the formulation of wholly new approaches.

I possess neither the specialized experience nor the expert knowledge to predict with any certainty where may lie the brightest hope for progress in dealing with the serious problems of juvenile delinquency. But I am certain that the answer does not lie in the Court's opinion in this case, which serves to convert a juvenile proceeding into a criminal prosecution.

The inflexible restrictions that the Constitution so wisely made applicable to adversary criminal trials have no inevitable place in the proceedings of those public social agencies known as juvenile or family courts. And to impose the Court's long catalog of requirements upon juvenile proceedings in every area of the country is to invite a long step backwards into the nineteenth century. In that era there were no juvenile proceedings, and a child was tried in a conventional criminal court will all the trappings of a conventional criminal trial. So it was that a 12-year-old boy named James Guild was tried in New Jersey for killing Catharine Beakes. A jury found him guilty of murder, and he was sentenced to death by hanging. The sentence was executed. It was all very constitutional.[2]

A State in all its dealings must, of course, accord every person due process of law. And due process may require that some of the same restrictions which the Constitution has placed upon criminal trials must be imposed upon juvenile proceedings. For example, I suppose that all would agree that a brutally coerced confession could not constitutionally be considered in a juvenile court hearing. But it surely does not follow that the testimonial privilege against self-incrimination is applicable in all juvenile proceedings. Similarly, due process clearly requires timely notice of the purpose and scope of any proceedings affecting the relationship of parent and child. But it certainly does not follow that notice of a juvenile hearing must be framed with all the technical niceties of a criminal indictment.

In any event, there is no reason to deal with issues such as these in the present case. The Supreme Court of Arizona found that the parents of Gerald Gault "knew of their right to counsel, to subpoena and cross examine witnesses, of the right to confront the witnesses against Gerald and the possible consequences of a finding of delinquency." It further found that "Mrs. Gault knew the exact nature of the charge against Gerald from the day he was taken to the detention home." And, as Mr. Justice WHITE correctly points out, no issue of compulsory self-incrimination is presented by this case.

I would dismiss the appeal.

Notes

(a) What precisely is the holding in *Gault*? What are the constitutional bases of the *Gault* holding? Does it make a difference which constitutional source is utilized? Consider Irene Merker Rosenberg, *The Constitutional Rights of Children Charged With*

---

2. "Thus, also, in very modern times, a boy of ten years old was convicted on his own confession of murdering his bedfellow, there appearing in his whole behavior plain tokens of a mischievous discretion; and as sparing this boy merely on account of his tender years might be of dangerous consequence to the public, by propagating a notion that children might commit such atrocious crimes with impunity, it was unanimously agreed by all the judges that he was a proper subject of capital punishment."

Crime: Proposal for a Return to the Not So Distant Past, 27 UCLA L. Rev. 656, 665–68 (1980).

(b) Under the majority opinion what is the scope of each right applicable in juvenile court proceedings, and to whom does this right belong?

(c) How do Justice Harlan's dissenting and concurring opinion and Justice Black's concurring opinion differ from Justice Fortas' majority opinion? Which is broader or narrower?

(d) Which opinion provides the greatest potential for constitutional protection of children in juvenile court?

(e) What is Justice Stewart so concerned about? Is it a realistic fear?

(f) What is Justice White's assumption in his concurring opinion regarding the scope of the privilege against self-incrimination in juvenile court?

(g) Is *Gault* just a procedural case? *See* Barry C. Feld, *Race, Politics, and Juvenile Justice: The Warren Court and the Conservative "Backlash,"* 87 Minn. L. Rev. 1447, 1484 (2003). "Gault's 'Due Process Revolution' demonstrated the link between procedure and substance, because once the Court required some procedural safeguards at trial, state laws and practices began to transform the juvenile court from the social welfare agency that the Progressives intended it to be into a formal legal institution. This 'constitutional domestication' was the first step in the procedural and substantive convergence between the juvenile and the adult criminal justice systems."

(h) For a different perspective on the *Gault* decision see Emily Buss, *The Missed Opportunity in Gault*, 70 U. Chi. L. Rev. 39, 39, 41–43 (2003), arguing that *Gault*:

> foreclosed any thoughtful consideration of the changes required to make the juvenile justice system fair to children. The direct product of *Gault* is a set of rights ill-tailored to serve either the aims of the juvenile justice system or the interests of the children who hold those rights. More broadly, *Gault's* error helped establish a pattern of analysis which has stunted the development of children's constitutional rights overall. . . .
>
> That the state's treatment of Gerald Gault was fundamentally unfair was clearly right. Less clear, however, were the changes required to make the juvenile justice system fair for children. By simply limiting its consideration to those procedural protections afforded adults, the Court avoided giving this second question [of providing juveniles with rehabilitative treatment rather than punishment] any serious attention. Focused exclusively on adult-derived rights, the Court produced a juvenile justice system whose procedures are poorly designed to meet its goals and out of step with childhood.
>
> In finding Gerald Gault's treatment unconstitutional, the Court neither challenged the substantive goals of the juvenile justice system nor argued for its abolition. To the contrary, the Court acknowledged the system's value and its distinct "substantive benefits." But it dismissed concerns that importing adult procedural protections into the system would undermine these goals. This was, the Court explained, both because these criminal procedural rights, "intelligently and not ruthlessly administered," were compatible with the goals of the juvenile justice system and because these goals were not being achieved without these rights. It is this second argument that seems to have had more force for the Court: Because a world with no procedural rights had failed to produce a fair system for children, affording children adult rights would surely be an improvement.

....

A fundamentally fair juvenile justice proceeding might well look very different from a fundamentally fair criminal justice proceeding, and the effect of the Due Process Clause should be to guarantee both. The fault of the juvenile justice system's design, then, was not in its rejection of the admittedly ill-fitting adult set of procedures, but in its failure to replace those procedural requirements with others more true to the juvenile justice vision. The fault of the Court, in turn, was to assume that the only solution to this procedural deficit was to reimpose the very sort of protections the reformers had rejected. In this way, *Gault* established the false dichotomy between the juvenile justice system's lofty aims on the one hand and the Constitution's concern for fairness on the other, which the Court claimed to balance against each other in subsequent cases.

In re Winship

397 U.S. 358 (1970)

Mr. Justice BRENNAN delivered the opinion of the Court.

Constitutional questions decided by this Court concerning the juvenile process have centered on the adjudicatory stage at "which a determination is made as to whether a juvenile is a 'delinquent' as a result of alleged misconduct on his part, with the consequence that he may be committed to a state institution." *Gault* decided that, although the Fourteenth Amendment does not require that the hearing at this stage conform with all the requirements of a criminal trial or even of the usual administrative proceeding, the Due Process Clause does require application during the adjudicatory hearing of "the essentials of due process and fair treatment." This case presents the single, narrow question whether proof beyond a reasonable doubt is among the "essentials of due process and fair treatment" required during the adjudicatory stage when a juvenile is charged with an act which would constitute a crime if committed by an adult.[1]

Section 712 of the New York Family Court Act defines a juvenile delinquent as "a person over seven and less than sixteen years of age who does any act which, if done by an adult, would constitute a crime." During a 1967 adjudicatory hearing, conducted pursuant to § 742 of the Act, a judge in New York Family Court found that appellant, then a 12-year-old boy, had entered a locker and stolen $112 from a woman's pocketbook. The petition which charged appellant with delinquency alleged that his act, "if done by an adult, would constitute the crime or crimes of Larceny." The judge acknowledged that the proof might not establish guilt beyond a reasonable doubt, but rejected appellant's contention that such proof was required by the Fourteenth Amendment. The judge relied instead on § 744(b) of the New York Family Court Act which provides that "[a]ny deter-

---

1. Thus, we do not see how it can be said in dissent that this opinion "rests entirely on the assumption that all juvenile proceedings are 'criminal prosecutions,' hence subject to constitutional limitations." As in *Gault*, "we are not here concerned with * * * the pre-judicial stages of the juvenile process, nor do we direct our attention to the post-adjudicative or dispositional process." In New York, the adjudicatory stage of a delinquency proceeding is clearly distinct from both the preliminary phase of the juvenile process and from its dispositional stage. Similarly, we intimate no view concerning the constitutionality of the New York procedures governing children "in need of supervision[,]" nor do we consider whether there are other "essentials of due process and fair treatment" required during the adjudicatory hearing of a delinquency proceeding. Finally, we have no occasion to consider appellant's argument that § 744(b) is a violation of the Equal Protection Clause, as well as a denial of due process.

mination at the conclusion of [an adjudicatory] hearing that a [juvenile] did an act or acts must be based on a preponderance of the evidence."[2] During a subsequent dispositional hearing, appellant was ordered placed in a training school for an initial period of 18 months, subject to annual extensions of his commitment until his 18th birthday—six years in appellant's case. The Appellate Division of the New York Supreme Court, First Judicial Department, affirmed without opinion. The New York Court of Appeals then affirmed by a four-to-three vote, expressly sustaining the constitutionality of § 744(b). [The Court cited to several decisions in different jurisdictions that were in accord with the New York Court of Appeals ruling.] … We reverse.

I

The requirement that guilt of a criminal charge be established by proof beyond a reasonable doubt dates at least from our early years as a Nation. The "demand for a higher degree of persuasion in criminal cases was recurrently expressed from ancient times, [though] its crystallization into the formula 'beyond a reasonable doubt' seems to have occurred as late as 1798. It is now accepted in common law jurisdictions as the measure of persuasion by which the prosecution must convince the trier of all the essential elements of guilt." Although virtually unanimous adherence to the reasonable-doubt standard in common-law jurisdictions may not conclusively establish it as a requirement of due process, such adherence does "reflect a profound judgment about the way in which law should be enforced and justice administered."

Expressions in many opinions of this Court indicate that it has long been assumed that proof of a criminal charge beyond a reasonable doubt is constitutionally required. Mr. Justice Frankfurter stated that "[i]t [is] the duty of the Government to establish * * * guilt beyond a reasonable doubt. This notion—basic in our law and rightly one of the boasts of a free society—is a requirement and a safeguard of due process of law in the historic, procedural content of 'due process.'" In a similar vein, the Court said in *Brinegar*, that "[g]uilt in a criminal case must be proved beyond a reasonable doubt and by evidence confined to that which long experience in the common-law tradition, to some extent embodied in the Constitution, has crystallized into rules of evidence consistent with that standard. These rules are historically grounded rights of our system, developed to safeguard men from dubious and unjust convictions, with resulting forfeitures of life, liberty and property." *Davis v. United States* stated that the requirement is implicit in "constitutions * * * [which] recognize the fundamental principles that are deemed essential for the protection of life and liberty." In *Davis* a murder conviction was reversed because the trial judge instructed the jury that it was their duty to convict when the evidence was equally balanced regarding the sanity of the accused. This Court said: "On the contrary, he is entitled to an acquittal of the specific crime charged, if upon all the evidence, there is reasonable doubt whether he was capable in law of committing [the] crime. * * * No man should be deprived of his life under the forms of law unless the jurors who try him are able, upon their consciences, to say that the evidence before them * * * is sufficient to show beyond a reasonable doubt the existence of every fact necessary to constitute the crime charged."

The reasonable-doubt standard plays a vital role in the American scheme of criminal procedure. It is a prime instrument for reducing the risk of convictions resting on factual

---

2. The ruling appears in the following portion of the hearing transcript:
"Counsel: Your Honor is making a finding by the preponderance of the evidence.
"Court: Well, it convinces me.
"Counsel: It's not beyond a reasonable doubt, Your Honor.
"Court: That is true * * * Our statute says a preponderance and a preponderance it is."

error. The standard provides concrete substance for the presumption of innocence—that bedrock "axiomatic and elementary" principle whose "enforcement lies at the foundation of the administration of our criminal law." As the dissenters in the New York Court of Appeals observed, and we agree, "a person accused of a crime * * * would be at a severe disadvantage, a disadvantage amounting to a lack of fundamental fairness, if he could be adjudged guilty and imprisoned for years on the strength of the same evidence as would suffice in a civil case."

The requirement of proof beyond a reasonable doubt has this vital role in our criminal procedure for cogent reasons. The accused during a criminal prosecution has at stake interest of immense importance, both because of the possibility that he may lose his liberty upon conviction and because of the certainty that he would be stigmatized by the conviction. Accordingly, a society that values the good name and freedom of every individual should not condemn a man for commission of a crime when there is reasonable doubt about his guilt. As we said in *Speiser v. Randall*, "There is always in litigation a margin of error, representing error in factfinding, which both parties must take into account. Where one party has at stake an interest of transcending value—as a criminal defendant his liberty—this margin of error is reduced as to him by the process of placing on the other party the burden of * * * persuading the factfinder at the conclusion of the trial of his guilt beyond a reasonable doubt. Due process commands that no man shall lose his liberty unless the Government has borne the burden of * * * convincing the factfinder of his guilt." To this end, the reasonable-doubt standard is indispensable, for it "impresses on the trier of fact the necessity of reaching a subjective state of certitude of the facts in issue."

Moreover, use of the reasonable-doubt standard is indispensable to command the respect and confidence of the community in applications of the criminal law. It is critical that the moral force of the criminal law not be diluted by a standard of proof that leaves people in doubt whether innocent men are being condemned. It is also important in our free society that every individual going about his ordinary affairs have confidence that his government cannot adjudge him guilty of a criminal offense without convincing a proper factfinder of his guilt with utmost certainty.

Lest there remain any doubt about the constitutional stature of the reasonable-doubt standard, we explicitly hold that the Due Process Clause protects the accused against conviction except upon proof beyond a reasonable doubt of every fact necessary to constitute the crime with which he is charged.

II

We turn to the question whether juveniles, like adults, are constitutionally entitled to proof beyond a reasonable doubt when they are charged with violation of a criminal law. The same considerations that demand extreme caution in factfinding to protect the innocent adult apply as well to the innocent child. We do not find convincing the contrary arguments of the New York Court of Appeals[;] *Gault* rendered untenable much of the reasoning relied upon by that court to sustain the constitutionality of § 744(b). The Court of Appeals indicated that a delinquency adjudication "is not a 'conviction'; that it affects no right or privilege, including the right to hold public office or to obtain a license; and a cloak of protective confidentiality is thrown around all the proceedings." The court said further: "The delinquency status is not made a crime; and the proceedings are not criminal. There is, hence, no deprivation of due process in the statutory provision [challenged by appellant] * * *. In effect the Court of Appeals distinguished the proceedings in question here from a criminal prosecution by use of what *Gault* called the "'civil' label-of-convenience which has been attached to juvenile proceedings." But *Gault* expressly rejected that distinction as a reason for holding the Due Process Clause inapplicable to a juvenile proceeding. The Court of Appeals also attempted to justify the preponderance standard on the related ground that juvenile proceedings are designed "not to punish, but to save the child." Again, however, *Gault* expressly rejected this justification. We made clear in that decision that civil labels and good intentions do not themselves obviate the need for criminal due process safeguards in juvenile courts, for "[a] proceeding where the issue is whether the child will be found to be 'delinquent' and subjected to the loss of his liberty for years is comparable in seriousness to a felony prosecution."

Nor do we perceive any merit in the argument that to afford juveniles the protection of proof beyond a reasonable doubt would risk destruction of beneficial aspects of the juvenile process.[4] Use of the reasonable-doubt standard during the adjudicatory hearing will not disturb New York's policies that a finding that a child has violated a criminal law does not constitute a criminal conviction, that such a finding does not deprive the child of his civil rights, and that juvenile proceedings are confidential. Nor will there be any effect on the informality, flexibility, or speed of the hearing at which the factfinding takes place. And the opportunity during the post-adjudicatory or dispositional hearing for a wide-ranging review of the child's social history and for his individualized treatment will remain unimpaired. Similarly, there will be no effect on the procedures distinctive to juvenile proceedings that are employed prior to the adjudicatory hearing.

The Court of Appeals observed that "a child's best interest is not necessarily, or even probably, promoted if he wins in the particular inquiry which may bring him to the juvenile court." It is true, of course, that the juvenile may be engaging in a general course of conduct inimical to his welfare that calls for judicial intervention. But that intervention cannot take the form of subjecting the child to the stigma of a finding that he violated a criminal law and to the possibility of institutional confinement on proof insufficient to convict him were he an adult.

We conclude, as we concluded regarding the essential due process safeguards applied in *Gault*, that the observance of the standard of proof beyond a reasonable doubt "will not compel the States to abandon or displace any of the substantive benefits of the juvenile process."

Finally, we reject the Court of Appeals' suggestion that there is, in any event, only a "tenuous difference" between the reasonable-doubt and preponderance standards. The suggestion is singularly unpersuasive. In this very case, the trial judge's ability to distinguish between the two standards enabled him to make a finding of guilt that he conceded he might not have made under the standard of proof beyond a reasonable doubt. Indeed, the trial judge's action evidences the accuracy of the observation of commentators that "the preponderance test is susceptible to the misinterpretation that it calls on the trier of fact merely to perform an abstract weighing of the evidence in order to determine which side has produced the greater quantum, without regard to its effect in convincing his mind of the truth of the proposition asserted."[6]

---

4. Appellee, New York City, apparently concedes as much in its Brief, page 8, where it states:
   "A determination that the New York law unconstitutionally denies due process because it does not provide for use of the reasonable doubt standard probably would not have a serious impact if all that resulted would be a change in the quantum of proof."

6. Compare this Court's rejection of the preponderance standard in deportation proceedings, where we ruled that the Government must support its allegations with "clear, unequivocal, and convincing evidence." Although we ruled in *Woodby* that deportation is not tantamount to a criminal conviction, we found that since it could lead to "drastic deprivations," it is impermissible for a per-

III

In sum, the constitutional safeguard of proof beyond a reasonable doubt is as much required during the adjudicatory stage of a delinquency proceeding as are those constitutional safeguards applied in *Gault*—notice of charges, right to counsel, the rights of confrontation and examination, and the privilege against self-incrimination. We therefore hold, in agreement with Chief Judge Fuld in dissent in the Court of Appeals, "that where a 12-year-old child is charged with an act of stealing which renders him liable to confinement for as long as six years, then, as a matter of due process * * * the case against him must be proved beyond a reasonable doubt."

Reversed.

Mr. Justice HARLAN, concurring.

No one, I daresay, would contend that state juvenile court trials are subject to no federal constitutional limitations. Differences have existed, however, among the members of this Court as to what constitutional protections do apply.

The present case draws in question the validity of a New York statute that permits a determination of juvenile delinquency, founded on a charge of criminal conduct, to be made on a standard of proof that is less rigorous than that which would obtain had the accused been tried for the same conduct in an ordinary criminal case. While I am in full agreement that this statutory provision offends the requirement of fundamental fairness embodied in the Due Process Clause of the Fourteenth Amendment, I am constrained to add something to what my Brother BRENNAN has written for the Court, lest the true nature of the constitutional problem presented become obscured or the impact on state juvenile court systems of what the Court holds today be exaggerated.

I

Professor Wigmore, in discussing the various attempts by courts to define how convinced one must be to be convinced beyond a reasonable doubt, wryly observed: "The truth is that no one has yet invented or discovered a mode of measurement for the intensity of human belief. Hence there can be yet no successful method of communicating intelligibly * * * a sound method of self analysis for one's belief."

Notwithstanding Professor Wigmore's skepticism, we have before us a case where the choice of the standard of proof has made a difference: the juvenile court judge below forthrightly acknowledged that he believed by a preponderance of the evidence, but was not convinced beyond a reasonable doubt, that appellant stole $112 from the complainant's pocketbook. Moreover, even though the labels used for alternative standards of proof are vague and not a very sure guide to decisionmaking, the choice of the standard for a particular variety of adjudication does, I think, reflect a very fundamental assessment of the comparative social costs of erroneous factual determinations.

To explain why I think this so, I begin by stating two propositions, neither of which I believe can be fairly disputed. First, in a judicial proceeding in which there is a dispute about the facts of some earlier event, the factfinder cannot acquire unassailably accurate knowledge of what happened. Instead, all the fact-finder can acquire is a belief of what probably happened. The intensity of this belief—the degree to which a factfinder is convinced that a given act actually occurred—can, of course, vary. In this regard, a standard of proof represents an attempt to instruct the fact-finder concerning the degree of

---

son to be "banished from this country upon no higher degree of proof than applies in a negligence case."

confidence our society thinks he should have in the correctness of factual conclusions for a particular type of adjudication. Although the phrases 'preponderance of the evidence' and 'proof beyond a reasonable doubt' are quantitatively imprecise, they do communicate to the finder of fact different notions concerning the degree of confidence he is expected to have in the correctness of his factual conclusions.

A second proposition, which is really nothing more than a corollary of the first, is that the trier of fact will sometimes, despite his best efforts, be wrong in his factual conclusions. In a lawsuit between two parties, a factual error can make a difference in one of two ways. First, it can result in a judgment in favor of the plaintiff when the true facts warrant a judgment for the defendant. The analogue in a criminal case would be the conviction of an innocent man. On the other hand, an erroneous factual determination can result in a judgment for the defendant when the true facts justify a judgment in plaintiff's favor. The criminal analogue would be the acquittal of a guilty man.

The standard of proof influences the relative frequency of these two types of erroneous outcomes. If, for example, the standard of proof for a criminal trial were a preponderance of the evidence rather than proof beyond a reasonable doubt, there would be a smaller risk of factual errors that result in freeing guilty persons, but a far greater risk of factual errors that result in convicting the innocent. Because the standard of proof affects the comparative frequency of these two types of erroneous outcomes, the choice of the standard to be applied in a particular kind of litigation should, in a rational world, reflect an assessment of the comparative social disutility of each.

When one makes such an assessment, the reason for different standards of proof in civil as opposed to criminal litigation becomes apparent. In a civil suit between two private parties for money damages, for example, we view it as no more serious in general for there to be an erroneous verdict in the defendant's favor than for there to be an erroneous verdict in the plaintiff's favor. A preponderance of the evidence standard therefore seems peculiarly appropriate for, as explained most sensibly,[3] it simply requires the trier of fact "to believe that the existence of a fact is more probable than its nonexistence before [he] may find in favor of the party who has the burden to persuade the [judge] of the fact's existence."

In a criminal case, on the other hand, we do not view the social disutility of convicting an innocent man as equivalent to the disutility of acquitting someone who is guilty. As Mr. Justice Brennan wrote for the Court in *Speiser v. Randall*:

> "There is always in litigation a margin of error, representing error in factfinding, which both parties must take into account. Where one party has at stake an interest of transcending value—as a criminal defendant his liberty—this margin of error is reduced as to him by the process of placing on the other party the burden * * * of persuading the fact-finder at the conclusion of the trial of his guilt beyond a reasonable doubt."

In this context, I view the requirement of proof beyond a reasonable doubt in a criminal case as bottomed on a fundamental value determination of our society that it is far worse to convict an innocent man than to let a guilty man go free. It is only because of the nearly complete and long-standing acceptance of the reasonable-doubt standard by the States in criminal trials that the Court has not before today had to hold explicitly that

---

3. The preponderance test has been criticized, justifiably in my view, when it is read as asking the trier of fact to weigh in some objective sense the quantity of evidence submitted by each side rather than asking him to decide what he believes most probably happened.

due process, as an expression of fundamental procedural fairness,[5] requires a more stringent standard for criminal trials than for ordinary civil litigation.

II

When one assesses the consequences of an erroneous factual determination in a juvenile delinquency proceeding in which a youth is accused of a crime, I think it must be concluded that, while the consequences are not identical to those in a criminal case, the differences will not support a distinction in the standard of proof. First, and of paramount importance, a factual error here, as in a criminal case, exposes the accused to a complete loss of his personal liberty through a state-imposed confinement away from his home, family, and friends. And, second, a delinquency determination, to some extent at least, stigmatizes a youth in that it is by definition bottomed on a finding that the accused committed a crime.[6] Although there are no doubt costs to society (and possibly even to the youth himself) in letting a guilty youth go free, I think here, as in a criminal case, it is far worse to declare an innocent youth a delinquent. I therefore agree that a juvenile court judge should be no less convinced of the factual conclusion that the accused committed the criminal act with which he is charged than would be required in a criminal trial.

III

I wish to emphasize, as I did in my separate opinion in *Gault*, that there is no automatic congruence between the procedural requirements imposed by due process in a criminal case, and those imposed by due process in juvenile cases.[7] It is of great importance, in my view, that procedural strictures not be constitutionally imposed that jeop-

---

5. In dissent my Brother BLACK again argues that, apart from the specific prohibitions of the first eight amendments, any procedure spelled out by a legislature — no matter how unfair — passes constitutional muster under the Due Process Clause. He bottoms his conclusion on history that he claims demonstrates (1) that due process means "law of the land"; (2) that any legislative enactment, ipso facto, is part of the law of the land; and (3) that the Fourteenth Amendment incorporates the prohibitions of the Bill of Rights and applies them to the States. I cannot refrain from expressing my continued bafflement at my Brother BLACK'S insistence that due process, whether under the Fourteenth Amendment or the Fifth Amendment, does not embody a concept of fundamental fairness as part of our scheme of constitutionally ordered liberty. His thesis flies in the face of a course of judicial history reflected in an unbroken line of opinions that have interpreted due process to impose restraints on the procedures government may adopt in its dealing with its citizens, see, e.g., the cases cited in my dissenting opinions in *Poe v. Ullman* and *Duncan v. Louisiana*, as well as the uncontroverted scholarly research respecting the intendment of the Due Process Clause of the Fourteenth Amendment. Indeed, with all respect, the very case cited in Brother BLACK'S dissent as establishing that "due process of law" means "law of the land" rejected the argument that any statute, by the mere process of enactment, met the requirements of the Due Process Clause.

6. The New York statute was amended to distinguish between a "juvenile delinquent," *i.e.*, a youth "who does any act which, if done by an adult, would constitute a crime," N.Y. Family Court Act § 712 (1963), and a "[p]erson in need of supervision" (PINS) who is a person "who is an habitual truant or who is incorrigible, ungovernable or habitually disobedient and beyond the lawful control of parent or other lawful authority." The PINS category was established in order to avoid the stigma of finding someone to be a "juvenile delinquent" unless he committed a criminal act. The Legislative Committee report stated: "'Juvenile delinquent' is now a term of disapproval. The judges of the Children's Court and the Domestic Relations Court of course are aware of this and also aware that government officials and private employers often learn of an adjudication of delinquency." Moreover, the powers of the police and courts differ in these two categories of cases. Thus, in a PINS type case, the consequences of an erroneous factual determination are by no means identical to those involved here.

7. In *Gault*, for example, I agreed with the majority that due process required (1) adequate notice of the "nature and terms" of the proceedings; (2) notice of the right to retain counsel, and an obligation on the State to provide counsel for indigents "in cases in which the child may be confined"; and (3) a written record "adequate to permit effective review." Unlike the majority, however, I thought

ardize "the essential elements of the State's purpose" in creating juvenile courts. In this regard, I think it worth emphasizing that the requirement of proof beyond a reasonable doubt that a juvenile committed a criminal act before he is found to be a delinquent does not (1) interfere with the worthy goal of rehabilitating the juvenile, (2) make any significant difference in the extent to which a youth is stigmatized as a "criminal" because he has been found to be a delinquent, or (3) burden the juvenile courts with a procedural requirement that will make juvenile adjudications significantly more time consuming, or rigid. Today's decision simply requires a juvenile court judge to be more confident in his belief that the youth did the act with which he has been charged.

With these observations, I join the Court's opinion, subject only to the constitutional reservations expressed in my opinion in *Gault*.

Mr. Chief Justice BURGER, with whom Mr. Justice STEWART joins, dissenting.

The Court's opinion today rests entirely on the assumption that all juvenile proceedings are "criminal prosecutions," hence subject to constitutional limitations. This derives from earlier holdings, which, like today's holding, were steps eroding the differences between juvenile courts and traditional criminal courts. The original concept of the juvenile court system was to provide a benevolent and less formal means than criminal courts could provide for dealing with the special and often sensitive problems of youthful offenders. Since I see no constitutional requirement of due process sufficient to overcome the legislative judgment of the States in this area, I dissent from further straitjacketing of an already overly restricted system. What the juvenile court system needs is not more but less of the trappings of legal procedure and judicial formalism; the juvenile court system requires breathing room and flexibility in order to survive, if it can survive the repeated assaults from this Court.

Much of the judicial attitude manifested by the Court's opinion today and earlier holdings in this field is really a protest against inadequate juvenile court staffs and facilities; we "burn down the stable to get rid of the mice." The lack of support and the distressing growth of juvenile crime have combined to make for a literal breakdown in many if not most juvenile courts. Constitutional problems were not seen while those courts functioned in an atmosphere where juvenile judges were not crushed with an avalanche of cases.

My hope is that today's decision will not spell the end of a generously conceived program of compassionate treatment intended to mitigate the rigors and trauma of exposing youthful offenders to a traditional criminal court; each step we take turns the clock back to the pre-juvenile-court era. I cannot regard it as a manifestation of progress to transform juvenile courts into criminal courts, which is what we are well on the way to accomplishing. We can only hope the legislative response will not reflect our own by having these courts abolished.

Mr. Justice BLACK, dissenting.

The majority states that "many opinions of this Court indicate that it has long been assumed that proof of a criminal charge beyond a reasonable doubt is constitutionally required." I have joined in some of those opinions, as well as the dissenting opinion of Mr. Justice Frankfurter in *Leland v. Oregon*. The Court has never clearly held, however, that proof beyond a reasonable doubt is either expressly or impliedly commanded by any provision of the Constitution. The Bill of Rights, which in my view is made fully applicable to the States by the Fourteenth Amendment, does by express language provide for, among

---

it unnecessary at the time of *Gault* to impose the additional requirements of the privilege against self-incrimination, confrontation, and cross-examination.

other things, a right to counsel in criminal trials, a right to indictment, and the right of a defendant to be informed of the nature of the charges against him. And in two places the Constitution provides for trial by jury, but nowhere in that document is there any statement that conviction of crime requires proof of guilt beyond a reasonable doubt. The Constitution thus goes into some detail to spell out what kind of trial a defendant charged with crime should have, and I believe the Court has no power to add to or subtract from the procedures set forth by the Founders. I realize that it is far easier to substitute individual judges' ideas of "fairness" for the fairness prescribed by the Constitution, but I shall not at any time surrender my belief that that document itself should be our guide, not our own concept of what is fair, decent, and right. That this old "shock-the-conscience" test is what the Court is relying on, rather than the words of the Constitution, is clearly enough revealed by the reference of the majority to "fair treatment" and to the statement by the dissenting judges in the New York Court of Appeals that failure to require proof beyond a reasonable doubt amounts to a "lack of fundamental fairness." As I have said time and time again, I prefer to put my faith in the words of the written Constitution itself rather than to rely on the shifting, day-to-day standards of fairness of individual judges.

....

II

I admit a strong, persuasive argument can be made for a standard of proof beyond a reasonable doubt in criminal cases—and the majority has made that argument well—but it is not for me as a judge to say for that reason that Congress or the States are without constitutional power to establish another standard that the Constitution does not otherwise forbid. It is quite true that proof beyond a reasonable doubt has long been required in federal criminal trials. It is also true that this requirement is almost universally found in the governing laws of the States. And as long as a particular jurisdiction requires proof beyond a reasonable doubt, then the Due Process Clause commands that every trial in that jurisdiction must adhere to that standard. But when, as here, a State through its duly constituted legislative branch decides to apply a different standard, then that standard, unless it is otherwise unconstitutional, must be applied to insure that persons are treated according to the "law of the land." The State of New York has made such a decision, and in my view nothing in the Due Process Clause invalidates it.

Notes

(a) Irene Merker Rosenberg, *Winship Redux: 1970 to 1990*, 69 Tex. L. Rev. 109, 109–13 (1990).

> I was the trial attorney who represented Samuel Winship—the Winship of *In re Winship* reasonable-doubt fame—in the New York City Bronx County family court in 1967. I am the anonymous lawyer in footnote 2 of the Supreme Court's opinion who nudged the unnamed trial judge into conceding that the prosecution had not established Samuel's guilt of delinquency based on an act of larceny beyond a reasonable doubt, a concession on which both the majority and the concurring opinions relied. I am not claiming footnote 2 as my fifteen minutes of Warholian fame. It does, however, serve very nicely as a nostalgic introduction to some thoughts about the *Winship* case on the occasion of its twentieth anniversary.

> I started working as a trial attorney for the Family Court Division of the New York City Legal Aid Society in February 1967. The Society, a charitable nonprofit

organization, had a contract with the state to provide legal representation for juveniles from indigent families. The governing statute referred to such lawyers as law guardians—a not too oblique legislative attempt to inhibit zealous adversarial representation of children. Training for new attorneys in 1967 was minimal (one observed for two days and then got thrown in), and the work load in the Bronx office was staggering—each attorney handled about 250 cases at a time. The courthouse was old and filthy; the noise level, a dull roar. Children, their parents, witnesses, and police officers waited for hours and then were shuffled in and out of the two courtrooms.

The youthful respondents accused of committing acts that would be crimes if committed by adults, almost all of whom were blacks and Puerto Ricans, were presumed to be guilty, and the judges were impatient to get down to brass tacks—the disposition, the sentence. The adjudicatory hearing, which determined guilt or innocence, was a mere formality. "Legal" objections, viewed as obstreperous interferences with the so-called rehabilitative process, were treated with the utmost contempt. Some judges genuinely tried to help the children appearing before them, but only a few judges believed that the rules of law applied in the juvenile courts.

The Family Court Act required the state to prove the alleged delinquent's culpability by a preponderance of the evidence, the same standard we use for redistributing money in a civil action. I can recall only a few cases in which a judge found that the state had not met its burden. Yet in many proceedings a reasonable doubt existed, and I would venture that more than a few innocent children were convicted, or in the euphemistic vocabulary of the juvenile courts, adjudicated delinquent. The preponderance standard contributed in large part to the arbitrariness of the family court. Findings of fact—that is, convictions—were for the most part unreviewable; the judges knew it and they let you know that they knew it.

The institutions to which the delinquents were sent were truly awful. The myth of beneficence was just that. Inevitably, one was struck by the realization that the state was treating children very much like criminals without affording them most of the procedural protections guaranteed to adults. That state of affairs led me finally to argue at Samuel's trial, an otherwise run-of-the-mill larceny case, that the preponderance standard violated both equal protection and due process. Because the state requires proof of guilt beyond a reasonable doubt for adult larcenists, setting a lower standard for juveniles accused of committing the same offense denies them equal protection; furthermore, finding someone guilty of a criminal act and subjecting him or her to incarceration and stigmatization without overwhelming evidence of culpability offends due process notions of fundamental fairness. The juvenile court judge was an honest man and agreed that the evidence against Samuel might not show guilt beyond a reasonable doubt (there was a shaky alibi witness), but he concluded that the statute required only a preponderance of the evidence and that it was up to the appellate courts to determine constitutionality.

I asked the Legal Aid Society to appeal Samuel's case, and the powers that be agreed. Three years later, the Supreme Court of the United States made Samuel Winship's name a landmark in criminal law jurisprudence.

I must confess that I did not perceive the true essence or scope of the constitutional value at stake in *Winship*. I saw it primarily from the point of view of a litigator in the trenches—a "kiddie case" that would provide a precedent for asserting that other procedural guarantees applied to juveniles. For that reason, the Court's refusal to decide the case on the narrower equal protection claim was puzzling and a little disheartening, but I took comfort from Justice Brennan's analysis equating criminal trials and delinquency adjudicatory hearings in the standard-of-proof context. I paid little attention to the Court's ruling as it applied to adult defendants.

(b) Is Justice Brennan's analysis in *Winship* compatible with Justice Fortas' opinion in *Gault*?

(c) Although *Winship* is clearer than the *Gault* decision, it is not without its own ambiguities. Chief among them is the Court's first ruling that the reasonable doubt standard applies in criminal trials, even though that issue was not raised by the parties. Why did Justice Brennan do that? Does it undermine a broad reading of the *Gault* decision?

(d) What is the exact holding in *Winship* regarding the juvenile courts? Could the Court have decided the case by relying on another constitutional provision? Why did the Court not do that? Does it make a difference?

(e) What is the nature of the debate between Justices Harlan and Black? Why did Justice Black, who concurred in the *Gault* decision, dissent in *Winship*? Is there a way he could have concurred in the judgment without violating his principles regarding constitutional interpretation? If there was, why did he not do so? In *Griffin v. Illinois*, 351 U.S. 12 (1956), a plurality of the Court held that states must provide indigents appealing their convictions a transcript sufficient to facilitate appellate review even though there is no explicit constitutional right to appellate review. The plurality opinion rested on two constitutional sources—Due Process and Equal Protection. Justice Black was the author of that opinion. Is it consistent with his view in *Winship*, a view he had articulated many times in other cases, including ones predating *Griffin*?

(f) In the Chief Justice's dissenting opinion he criticizes the majority decision. Is his assumption about the majority ruling accurate?

(g) Does Justice Harlan's concurring opinion add anything to the majority opinion? Is his concurring opinion in *Winship* consistent with the reasoning in his concurring and dissenting opinion in *Gault*?

(h) Does or should *Winship* apply to involuntary civil commitments to state mental hospitals, deportation proceedings or denaturalization hearings? *See Addington v. Texas*, 441 U.S. 418 (1979); *Woodby v. INS*, 385 U.S. 276 (1966); *Schmeiderman v. United States*, 320 U.S. 118 (1976). In all these cases the Court held that *Winship* did not apply, and the appropriate standard of proof in such cases was clear and convincing evidence.

Ivan V. v. New York

407 U.S. 203 (1972)

PER CURIAM.

The Court held in *In re Winship*, decided March 31, 1970, that proof beyond a reasonable doubt is among the essentials of due process and fair treatment that must be afforded at the adjudicatory stage when a juvenile is charged with an act that would constitute a crime if committed by an adult. In this case, on January 6, 1970, before *Winship* was decided, petitioner was adjudged a delinquent in the Family Court of Bronx County, New York, on a finding, based on the preponderance-of-evidence standard, that, at knifepoint, he forcibly took a bicycle from another boy, an act that, if done by an adult, would constitute the crime of robbery in the first degree. On direct appeal, the Appellate Division, First Department, reversed on the ground that *Winship* should be retroactively applied to all cases still in the appellate process. The New York Court of Appeals reversed the Appellate Division, holding that *Winship* was not to be applied retroactively. We disagree with the holding of the Court of Appeals that *Winship* is not to be applied retroactively.

"Where the major purpose of new constitutional doctrine is to overcome an aspect of the criminal trial that substantially impairs its truth-finding function and so raises serious questions about the accuracy of guilty verdicts in past trials, the new rule has been given complete retroactive effect. Neither good faith reliance by state or federal authorities on prior constitutional law or accepted practice, nor severe impact on the administration of justice has sufficed to require prospective application in these circumstances."

Winship expressly held that the reasonable doubt standard "is a prime instrument for reducing the risk of convictions resting on factual error. The standard provides concrete substance for the presumption of innocence—that bedrock 'axiomatic and elementary' principle whose 'enforcement lies at the foundation of the administration of our criminal law' * * *'Due process commands that no man shall lose his liberty unless the Government has borne the burden of * * * convincing the factfinder of his guilt.' To this end, the reasonable doubt standard is indispensable, for it 'impresses on the trier of fact the necessity of reaching a subjective state of certitude of the facts in issue.'"

Plainly, then, the major purpose of the constitutional standard of proof beyond a reasonable doubt announced in *Winship* was to overcome an aspect of a criminal trial that substantially impairs the truth-finding function, and *Winship* is thus to be given complete retroactive effect.

The CHIEF JUSTICE took no part in the consideration or decision of this case.

Notes

(a) What is the holding in *Ivan V.*? Would the ruling have any practical effect on children who had been adjudicated delinquent prior to the decision and who are no longer pending in the appellate process? Presumably children who had been adjudicated delinquent and were still in placement regarding a charge that had not been proven beyond a reasonable doubt would be released or retried. Beyond that, would children who had been adjudicated delinquent based on a preponderance of the evidence and who had completed their sentences derive any benefit from the ruling in *Winship*? In that connection, see Ellen Marrus, *"That Isn't Fair, Judge": The Costs of Using Prior Juvenile Delinquency Adjudications in Criminal Court Sentencing*, 40 Hous. L. Rev. 1323, 1329 (2004):

> The U.S. Supreme Court recently refused to grant certiorari in two cases raising a related sentencing issue that is dividing the lower courts. The question is seemingly straightforward and narrow: whether government can use juvenile delinquency adjudications obtained [in a jurisdiction] without a right to a jury trial as a predicate for increasing an adult offender's sentence in criminal court beyond the statutorily mandated maximum for that crime.... The answer, however, is not simple. The Justices undoubtedly will be closely divided on the matter, and the resolution will have important repercussions both in criminal sentencing law and the juvenile court system. To decide that such adjudications can be considered prior convictions in criminal court will destroy the image of the juvenile courts as benevolent institutions designed to help children in trouble, shielding

their wrongdoing from public scrutiny and giving them a second chance. However, if the Court were to hold that such adjudications cannot be used in criminal court, either to enhance punishment beyond the statutory maximum or as an element of the crime per *Apprendi v. New Jersey*, 530 U.S. 466 (2000), it would disguise the character of the defendant. This would make sentencing [in criminal court] less accurate and may be unfair to other defendants who do not have a juvenile court history.

(b) The Court's analytical approach to the retroactivity problem was governed by *Linkletter v. Walker*, 381 U.S. 618 (1965) and *Stovall v. Denno*, 388 U.S. 293 (1967), in which the Court created a framework for determining this issue. The three prong test governing whether a right was to be applied retroactively or prospectively required the Court to balance the following factors: (1) the purpose of the new ruling, (2) the extent to which law enforcement relied on the old rule, and (3) the effect on the administration of justice. That framework has been abandoned by the Court and replaced by *Teague v. Lane*, 489 U.S. 288 (1989), in which the Court held that new rulings are always to be applied retroactively to cases pending on direct appeal at the time the new ruling is issued. However, new rulings are not to be applied to cases on collateral review with two exceptions: when the new ruling places certain types of conduct beyond the power of the criminal law, or, if it "mandates new watershed rules of procedure that effect the accuracy in fact-finding." Would the result in *Ivan V.* have been any different under the *Teague* ruling?

McKeiver v. Pennsylvania
403 U.S. 528 (1971)

Mr. Justice BLACKMUN announced the judgments of the Court and an opinion in which THE CHIEF JUSTICE, Mr. Justice STEWART, and Mr. Justice WHITE join.

These cases present the narrow but precise issue whether the Due Process Clause of the Fourteenth Amendment assures the right to trial by jury in the adjudicative phase of a state juvenile court delinquency proceeding.

I

The issue arises understandably, for the Court in a series of cases already has emphasized due process factors protective of the juvenile.

....

From these six cases *Haley, Gallegos, Kent, Gault, DeBacker,* and *Winship*—it is apparent that:

1. Some of the constitutional requirements attendant upon the state criminal trial have equal application to that part of the state juvenile proceeding that is adjudicative in nature. Among these are the rights to appropriate notice, to counsel, to confrontation and to cross-examination, and the privilege against self-incrimination. Included, also, is the standard of proof beyond a reasonable doubt.

2. The Court, however, has not yet said that all rights constitutionally assured to an adult accused of crime also are to be enforced or made available to the juvenile in his delinquency proceeding. Indeed, the Court specifically has refrained from going that far:

   "We do not mean by this to indicate that the hearing to be held must conform with all of the requirements of a criminal trial or even of the usual administrative hearing; but we do hold that the hearing must measure up to the essentials of due process and fair treatment."

3. The Court, although recognizing the high hopes and aspirations of Judge Julian Mack, the leaders of the Jane Addams School and the other supporters of the juvenile court concept, has also noted the disappointments of the system's performance and experience and the resulting widespread disaffection. There have been, at one and the same time, both an appreciation for the juvenile court judge who is devoted, sympathetic, and conscientious, and a disturbed concern about the judge who is untrained and less than fully imbued with an understanding approach to the complex problems of childhood and adolescence. There has been praise for the system and its purposes, and there has been alarm over its defects.

4. The Court has insisted that these successive decisions do not spell the doom of the juvenile court system or even deprive it of its "informality, flexibility, or speed." On the other hand, a concern precisely to the opposite effect was expressed by two dissenters in *Winship.*

II

With this substantial background already developed, we turn to the facts of the present cases:

No. 322. Joseph McKeiver, then age 16, in May 1968 was charged with robbery, larceny, and receiving stolen goods (felonies under Pennsylvania law), as acts of juvenile delinquency. At the time of the adjudication hearing he was represented by counsel.[2] His request for a jury trial was denied and his case was heard by [a juvenile court] Judge. McKeiver was adjudged a delinquent upon findings that he had violated a law of the Commonwealth. On appeal, the Superior Court affirmed without opinion.

Edward Terry, then age 15, in January 1969 was charged with assault and battery on a police officer and conspiracy (misdemeanors under Pennsylvania law) as acts of juvenile delinquency. His counsel's request for a jury trial was denied and his case was heard by [a juvenile court] Judge. Terry was adjudged a delinquent on the charges. This followed an adjudication and commitment in the preceding week for an assault on a teacher. He was committed, as he had been on the earlier charge, to the Youth Development Center at Cornwells Heights. On appeal, the Superior Court affirmed without opinion.

The Supreme Court of Pennsylvania granted leave to appeal in both cases and consolidated them. The single question considered, as phrased by the court, was "whether there is a constitutional right to a jury trial in juvenile court." The answer, one justice dissenting, was in the negative....

McKeiver's offense was his participating with 20 or 30 youths who pursued three young teenagers and took 25 cents from them; ... McKeiver never before had been arrested and had a record of gainful employment; ... the testimony of two of the victims was described by the court as somewhat inconsistent and as "weak"; and ... Terry's offense consisted of hitting a police officer with his fists and with a stick when the officer broke up a boys' fight Terry and others were watching.

---

2. At McKeiver's hearing his counsel advised the court that he had never seen McKeiver before and "was just in the middle of interviewing" him. The court allowed him five minutes for the interview. Counsel's office, Community Legal Services, however, had been appointed to represent McKeiver five months earlier.

No. 128. Barbara Burrus and approximately 45 other black children, ranging in age from 11 to 15 years,[3] were the subjects of juvenile court summonses issued in Hyde County, North Carolina, in January 1969.

The charges arose out of a series of demonstrations in the county in late 1968 by black adults and children protesting school assignments and a school consolidation plan. Petitions were filed by North Carolina state highway patrolmen. Except for one relating to James Lambert Howard, the petitions charged the respective juveniles with wilfully impeding traffic. The charge against Howard was that he wilfully made riotous noise and was disorderly in the O. A. Peay School in Swan Quarter; interrupted and disturbed the school during its regular sessions; and defaced school furniture. The acts so charged are misdemeanors under North Carolina law.

The several cases were consolidated into groups for hearing before … [the] juvenile court. The same lawyer appeared for all the juveniles. Over counsel's objection, made in all except two of the cases, the general public was excluded. A request for a jury trial in each case was denied.

The evidence as to the juveniles other than Howard consisted solely of testimony of highway patrolmen. No juvenile took the stand or offered any witness. The testimony was to the effect that on various occasions the juveniles and adults were observed walking along Highway 64 singing, shouting, clapping, and playing basketball. As a result, there was interference with traffic. The marchers were asked to leave the paved portion of the highway and they were warned that they were committing a statutory offense. They either refused or left the roadway and immediately returned. The juveniles and participating adults were taken into custody. Juvenile petitions were then filed with respect to those under the age of 16.

The evidence as to Howard was that on the morning of December 5, he was in the office of the principal of the O. A. Peay School with 15 other persons while school was in session and was moving furniture around; that the office was in disarray; that as a result the school closed before noon; and that neither he nor any of the others was a student at the school or authorized to enter the principal's office.

In each case the court found that the juvenile had committed "an act for which an adult may be punished by law." A custody order was entered declaring the juvenile a delinquent "in need of more suitable guardianship" and committing him to the custody of the County Department of Public Welfare for placement in a suitable institution "until such time as the Board of Juvenile Correction or the Superintendent of said institution may determine, not inconsistent with the laws of this State." The court, however, suspended these commitments and placed each juvenile on probation for either one or two years conditioned upon his violating none of the State's laws, upon his reporting monthly to the County Department of Welfare, upon his being home by 11 p.m. each evening, and upon his attending a school approved by the Welfare Director. None of the juveniles has been confined on these charges.

On appeal, the cases were consolidated into two groups. The North Carolina Court of Appeals affirmed. In its turn the Supreme Court of North Carolina deleted that portion of the order in each case relating to commitment, but otherwise affirmed. Two justices dissented without opinion. We granted certiorari.

….

---

3. In North Carolina juvenile court procedures are provided only for persons under the age of 16.

IV

The right to an impartial jury "[i]n all criminal prosecutions" under federal law is guaranteed by the Sixth Amendment. Through the Fourteenth Amendment that requirement has now been imposed upon the States "in all criminal cases which—were they to be tried in a federal court—would come within the Sixth Amendment's guarantee." This is because the Court has said it believes "that trial by jury in criminal cases is fundamental to the American scheme of justice."

This, of course, does not automatically provide the answer to the present jury trial issue, if for no other reason than that the juvenile court proceeding has not yet been held to be a "criminal prosecution," within the meaning and reach of the Sixth Amendment, and also has not yet been regarded as devoid of criminal aspects merely because it usually has been given the civil label.

Little, indeed, is to be gained by any attempt simplistically to call the juvenile court proceeding either "civil" or "criminal." The Court carefully has avoided this wooden approach. Before *Gault* was decided in 1967, the Fifth Amendment's guarantee against self-incrimination had been imposed upon the state criminal trial. So, too, had the Sixth Amendment's rights of confrontation and cross-examination. Yet the Court did not automatically and peremptorily apply those rights to the juvenile proceeding. A reading of *Gault* reveals the opposite. And the same separate approach to the standard-of-proof issue is evident from the carefully separated application of the standard, first to the criminal trial, and then to the juvenile proceeding, displayed in *Winship*.

Thus, accepting "the proposition that the Due Process Clause has a role to play," our task here with respect to trial by jury, as it was in *Gault* with respect to other claimed rights, "is to ascertain the precise impact of the due process requirement."

V

The Pennsylvania juveniles' basic argument is that they were tried in proceedings "substantially similar to a criminal trial." They say that a delinquency proceeding in their State is initiated by a petition charging a penal code violation in the conclusory language of an indictment; that a juvenile detained prior to trial is held in a building substantially similar to an adult prison; that in Philadelphia juveniles over 16 are, in fact, held in the cells of a prison; that counsel and the prosecution engage in plea bargaining; that motions to suppress are routinely heard and decided; that the usual rules of evidence are applied; that the customary common-law defenses are available; that the press is generally admitted in the Philadelphia juvenile courtrooms; that members of the public enter the room; that arrest and prior record may be reported by the press (from police sources, however, rather than from the juvenile court records); that, once adjudged delinquent, a juvenile may be confined until his majority in what amounts to a prison (see *In re Bethea* describing the state correctional institution at Camp Hill as a "maximum security prison for adjudged delinquents and youthful criminal offenders"); and that the stigma attached upon delinquency adjudication approximates that resulting from conviction in an adult criminal proceeding.

The North Carolina juveniles particularly urge that the requirement of a jury trial would not operate to deny the supposed benefits of the juvenile court system; that the system's primary benefits are its discretionary intake procedure permitting disposition short of adjudication, and its flexible sentencing permitting emphasis on rehabilitation; that realization of these benefits does not depend upon dispensing with the jury; that adjudication of factual issues on the one hand and disposition of the case on the other are very different matters with very different purposes; that the purpose of the former is indistinguishable from that of the criminal trial; that the jury trial provides an independent protective factor; that experience has shown that jury trials in juvenile courts are manageable; that no reason exists why protection traditionally accorded in criminal proceedings should be denied young people subject to involuntary incarceration for lengthy periods; and that the juvenile courts deserve healthy public scrutiny.

VI

All the litigants here agree that the applicable due process standard in juvenile proceedings, as developed by *Gault* and *Winship*, is fundamental fairness. As that standard was applied in those two cases, we have an emphasis on factfinding procedures. The requirements of notice, counsel, confrontation, cross-examination, and standard of proof naturally flowed from this emphasis. But one cannot say that in our legal system the jury is a necessary component of accurate factfinding. There is much to be said for it, to be sure, but we have been content to pursue other ways for determining facts. Juries are not required, and have not been, for example, in equity cases, in workmen's compensation, in probate, or in deportation cases. Neither have they been generally used in military trials. In *Duncan* the Court stated, "We would not assert, however, that every criminal trial—or any particular trial—held before a judge alone is unfair or that a defendant may never be as fairly treated by a judge as he would be by a jury." In *DeStefano*, for this reason and others, the Court refrained from retrospective application of *Duncan*, an action it surely would have not taken had it felt that the integrity of the result was seriously at issue. And in *Williams v. Florida*, the Court saw no particular magic in a 12-man jury for a criminal case, thus revealing that even jury concepts themselves are not inflexible.

We must recognize, as the Court has recognized before, that the fond and idealistic hopes of the juvenile court proponents and early reformers of three generations ago have not been realized. The devastating commentary upon the system's failures as a whole, contained in the President's Commission on Law Enforcement and Administration of Justice, Task Force Report, reveals the depth of disappointment in what has been accomplished. Too often the juvenile court judge falls far short of that stalwart, protective, and communicating figure the system envisaged.[4] The community's unwillingness to provide people and facilities and to be concerned, the insufficiency of time devoted, the scarcity of professional help, the inadequacy of dispositional alternatives, and our general lack of knowledge all contribute to dissatisfaction with the experiment.[5]

---

4. "A recent study of juvenile court judges * * * revealed that half had not received undergraduate degrees; a fifth had received no college education at all; a fifth were not members of the bar."

5. "What emerges, then, is this: In theory the juvenile court was to be helpful and rehabilitative rather than punitive. In fact the distinction often disappears, not only because of the absence of facilities and personnel but also because of the limits of knowledge and technique. In theory the court's action was to affix no stigmatizing label. In fact a delinquent is generally viewed by employers, schools, the armed services—by society generally—as a criminal. In theory the court was to treat children guilty of criminal acts in noncriminal ways. In fact it labels truants and runaways as junior criminals. In theory the court's operations could justifiably be informal, its findings and decisions made without observing ordinary procedural safeguards, because it would act only in the best interest of the child. In fact it frequently does nothing more nor less than deprive a child of liberty without due process of law—knowing not what else to do and needing, whether admittedly or not, to act in the community's interest even more imperatively than the child's. In theory it was to exercise its protective powers to bring an errant child back into the fold. In fact there is increasing reason to believe that its intervention reinforces the juvenile's unlawful impulses. In theory it was to concentrate on each case the best of current social science learning. In fact it has often become a vested interest in its turn, loathe to cooperate with innovative programs or avail itself of forward-looking methods."

The Task Force Report, however, also said, "To say that juvenile courts have failed to achieve their goals is to say no more than what is true of criminal courts in the United States. But failure is most striking when hopes are highest."

Despite all these disappointments, all these failures, and all these shortcomings, we conclude that trial by jury in the juvenile court's adjudicative stage is not a constitutional requirement. We so conclude for a number of reasons:

1. The Court has refrained, in the cases heretofore decided, from taking the easy way with a flat holding that all rights constitutionally assured for the adult accused are to be imposed upon the state juvenile proceeding....

2. There is a possibility, at least, that the jury trial, if required as a matter of constitutional precept, will remake the juvenile proceeding into a fully adversary process and will put an effective end to what has been the idealistic prospect of an intimate, informal protective proceeding.

3. The Task Force Report, although concededly pre-*Gault*, is notable for its not making any recommendation that the jury trial be imposed upon the juvenile court system. This is so despite its vivid description of the system's deficiencies and disappointments. Had the Commission deemed this vital to the integrity of the juvenile process, or to the handling of juveniles, surely a recommendation or suggestion to this effect would have appeared. The intimations, instead, are quite the other way. Further, it expressly recommends against abandonment of the system and against the return of the juvenile to the criminal courts.[6]

4. The Court specifically has recognized by dictum that a jury is not a necessary part even of every criminal process that is fair and equitable.

5. The imposition of the jury trial on the juvenile court system would not strengthen greatly, if at all, the fact-finding function, and would, contrarily, provide an attrition of the juvenile court's assumed ability to function in a unique manner. It would not remedy the defects of the system. Meager as has been the hoped-for advance in the juvenile field, the alternative would be regressive, would lose what has been gained, and would tend once again to place the juvenile squarely in the routine of the criminal process.

---

6. "Nevertheless, study of the juvenile courts does not necessarily lead to the conclusion that the time has come to jettison the experiment and remand the disposition of children charged with crime to the criminal courts of the country. As trying as are the problems of the juvenile courts, the problems of the criminal courts, particularly those of the lower courts, which would fall heir to much of the juvenile court jurisdiction, are even graver; and the ideal of separate treatment of children is still worth pursuing. What is required is rather a revised philosophy of the juvenile court based on the recognition that in the past our reach exceeded our grasp. The spirit that animated the juvenile court movement was fed in part by a humanitarian compassion for offenders who were children. That willingness to understand and treat people who threaten public safety and security should be nurtured, not turned aside as hopeless sentimentality, both because it is civilized and because social protection itself demands constant search for alternatives to the crude and limited expedient of condemnation and punishment. But neither should it be allowed to outrun reality. The juvenile court is a court of law, charged like other agencies of criminal justice with protecting the community against threatening conduct. Rehabilitating offenders through individualized handling is one way of providing protection, and appropriately the primary way in dealing with children. But the guiding consideration for a court of law that deals with threatening conduct is nonetheless protection of the community. The juvenile court, like other courts, is therefore obliged to employ all the means at hand, not excluding incapacitation, for achieving that protection. What should distinguish the juvenile from the criminal courts is greater emphasis on rehabilitation, not exclusive preoccupation with it."

6. The juvenile concept held high promise. We are reluctant to say that, despite disappointments of grave dimensions, it still does not hold promise, and we are particularly reluctant to say, as do the Pennsylvania appellants here, that the system cannot accomplish its rehabilitative goals. So much depends on the availability of resources, on the interest and commitment of the public, on willingness to learn, and on understanding as to cause and effect and cure. In this field, as in so many others, one perhaps learns best by doing. We are reluctant to disallow the States to experiment further and to seek in new and different ways the elusive answers to the problems of the young, and we feel that we would be impeding that experimentation by imposing the jury trial. The States, indeed, must go forward. If, in its wisdom, any State feels the jury trial is desirable in all cases, or in certain kinds, there appears to be no impediment to its installing a system embracing that feature. That, however, is the State's privilege and not its obligation.

7. Of course there have been abuses. The Task Force Report has noted them. We refrain from saying at this point that those abuses are of constitutional dimension. They relate to the lack of resources and of dedication rather than to inherent unfairness.

8. There is, of course, nothing to prevent a juvenile court judge, in a particular case where he feels the need, or when the need is demonstrated, from using an advisory jury.

9. "The fact that a practice is followed by a large number of states is not conclusive in a decision as to whether that practice accords with due process, but it is plainly worth considering in determining whether the practice 'offends some principle of justice so rooted in the traditions and conscience of our people as to be ranked as fundamental.'" It therefore is of more than passing interest that at least 28 States and the District of Columbia by statute deny the juvenile a right to a jury trial in cases such as these. The same result is achieved in other States by judicial decision. In 10 States statutes provide for a jury trial under certain circumstances.

10. Since *Gault* and since *Duncan* the great majority of States, in addition to Pennsylvania and North Carolina, that have faced the issue have concluded that the considerations that led to the result in those two cases do not compel trial by jury in the juvenile court.

11. Stopping short of proposing the jury trial for juvenile proceedings are the Uniform Juvenile Court Act, § 24(a), approved in July 1968 by the National Conference of Commissioners on Uniform State Laws; the Standard Juvenile Court Act, Art. V, § 19, proposed by the National Council on Crime and Delinquency; and the Legislative Guide for Drafting Family and Juvenile Court Acts, § 29(a).

12. If the jury trial were to be injected into the juvenile court system as a matter of right, it would bring with it into that system the traditional delay, the formality, and the clamor of the adversary system and, possibly, the public trial. It is of interest that these very factors were stressed by the District Committee of the Senate when, through Senator Tydings, it recommended, and Congress then approved, as a provision in the District of Columbia Crime Bill, the abolition of the jury trial in the juvenile court.

13. Finally, the arguments advanced by the juveniles here are, of course, the identical arguments that underlie the demand for the jury trial for criminal proceedings. The arguments necessarily equate the juvenile proceeding — or at least the adjudicative phase of it — with the criminal trial. Whether they should be so

equated is our issue. Concern about the inapplicability of exclusionary and other rules of evidence, about the juvenile court judge's possible awareness of the juvenile's prior record and of the contents of the social file; about repeated appearances of the same familiar witnesses in the persons of juvenile and probation officers and social workers—all to the effect that this will create the likelihood of pre-judgment—chooses to ignore it seems to us, every aspect of fairness, of concern, of sympathy, and of paternal attention that the juvenile court system contemplates.

If the formalities of the criminal adjudicative process are to be superimposed upon the juvenile court system, there is little need for its separate existence. Perhaps that ultimate disillusionment will come one day, but for the moment we are disinclined to give impetus to it.

Affirmed.

Mr. Justice WHITE, concurring.

Although the function of the jury is to find facts, that body is not necessarily or even probably better at the job than the conscientious judge. Nevertheless, the consequences of criminal guilt are so severe that the Constitution mandates a jury to prevent abuses of official power by insuring, where demanded, community participation in imposing serious deprivations of liberty and to provide a hedge against corrupt, biased, or political justice. We have not, however, considered the juvenile case a criminal proceeding within the meaning of the Sixth Amendment and hence automatically subject to all of the restrictions normally applicable in criminal cases. The question here is one of due process of law and I join the plurality opinion concluding that the States are not required by that clause to afford jury trials in juvenile courts where juveniles are charged with improper acts.

The criminal law proceeds on the theory that defendants have a will and are responsible for their actions. A finding of guilt establishes that they have chosen to engage in conduct so reprehensible and injurious to others that they must be punished to deter them and others from crime. Guilty defendants are considered blameworthy; they are branded and treated as such, however much the State also pursues rehabilitative ends in the criminal justice system.

For the most part, the juvenile justice system rests on more deterministic assumptions. Reprehensible acts by juveniles are not deemed the consequence of mature and malevolent choice but of environmental pressures (or lack of them) or of other forces beyond their control. Hence the state legislative judgment not to stigmatize the juvenile delinquent by branding him a criminal; his conduct is not deemed so blameworthy that punishment is required to deter him or others. Coercive measures, where employed, are considered neither retribution nor punishment. Supervision or confinement is aimed at rehabilitation, not at convincing the juvenile of his error simply by imposing pains and penalties. Nor is the purpose to make the juvenile delinquent an object lesson for others, whatever his own merits or demerits may be. A typical disposition in the juvenile court where delinquency is established may authorize confinement until age 21, but it will last no longer and within that period will last only so long as his behavior demonstrates that he remains an unacceptable risk if returned to his family. Nor is the authorization for custody until 21 any measure of the seriousness of the particular act that the juvenile has performed.

Against this background and in light of the distinctive purpose of requiring juries in criminal cases, I am satisfied with the Court's holding. To the extent that the jury is a buffer to the corrupt or overzealous prosecutor in the criminal law system, the distinctive intake policies and procedures of the juvenile court system to a great extent obviate this important function of the jury. As for the necessity to guard against judicial bias, a system eschewing blameworthiness and punishment for evil choice is itself an operative force against prejudice and short-tempered justice. Nor where juveniles are involved is there the same opportunity for corruption to the juvenile's detriment or the same temptation to use the courts for political ends.

Not only are those risks that mandate juries in criminal cases of lesser magnitude in juvenile court adjudications, but the consequences of adjudication are less severe than those flowing from verdicts of criminal guilt. This is plainly so in theory, and in practice there remains a substantial gulf between criminal guilt and delinquency, whatever the failings of the juvenile court in practice may be. Moreover, to the extent that current unhappiness with juvenile court performance rests on dissatisfaction with the vague and overbroad grounds for delinquency adjudications, with faulty judicial choice as to disposition after adjudication, or with the record of rehabilitative custody, whether institutional or probationary, these shortcomings are in no way mitigated by providing a jury at the adjudicative stage.

For me there remain differences of substance between criminal and juvenile courts. They are quite enough for me to hold that a jury is not required in the latter. Of course, there are strong arguments that juries are desirable when dealing with the young, and States are free to use juries if they choose. They are also free if they extend criminal court safeguards to juvenile court adjudications, frankly to embrace condemnation, punishment, and deterrence as permissible and desirable attributes of the juvenile justice system. But the Due Process Clause neither compels nor invites them to do so.

Mr. Justice BRENNAN, concurring in the judgment in No. 322 and dissenting in No. 128.

I agree with the plurality opinion's conclusion that the proceedings below in these cases were not "criminal prosecutions" within the meaning of the Sixth Amendment. For me, therefore, the question in these cases is whether jury trial is among the "essentials of due process and fair treatment." This does not, however, mean that the interests protected by the Sixth Amendment's guarantee of jury trial in all "criminal prosecutions" are of no importance in the context of these cases. The Sixth Amendment, where applicable, commands … a particular procedure, that is, trial by jury. The Due Process Clause commands not a particular procedure, but only a result: …"fundamental fairness * * * [in] factfinding." In the context of these and similar juvenile delinquency proceedings, what this means is that the States are not bound to provide jury trials on demand so long as some other aspect of the process adequately protects the interests that Sixth Amendment jury trials are intended to serve.[1]

In my view, therefore, the due process question cannot be decided upon the basis of general characteristics of juvenile proceedings, but only in terms of the adequacy of a particular state procedure to "protect the [juvenile] from oppression by the Government," and to protect him against "the compliant, biased, or eccentric judge."

Examined in this light, I find no defect in the Pennsylvania cases before us. The availability of trial by jury allows an accused to protect himself against possible oppression by what is in essence an appeal to the community conscience, as embodied in the jury that

---

1. "A criminal process which was fair and equitable but used no juries is easy to imagine. It would make use of alternative guarantees and protections which would serve the purposes that the jury serves in the English and American systems." This conclusion is, of course, inescapable in light of our decisions that petty criminal offenses may be tried without a jury notwithstanding the defendant's request.

hears his case. To some extent, however, a similar protection may be obtained when an accused may in essence appeal to the community at large, by focusing public attention upon the facts of his trial, exposing improper judicial behavior to public view, and obtaining, if necessary, executive redress through the medium of public indignation. Of course, the Constitution, in the context of adult criminal trials, has rejected the notion that public trial is an adequate substitution for trial by jury in serious cases. But in the context of juvenile delinquency proceedings, I cannot say that it is beyond the competence of a State to conclude that juveniles who fear that delinquency proceedings will mask judicial oppression may obtain adequate protection by focusing community attention upon the trial of their cases. For, however much the juvenile system may have failed in practice, its very existence as an ostensibly beneficent and noncriminal process for the care and guidance of young persons demonstrates the existence of the community's sympathy and concern for the young. Juveniles able to bring the community's attention to bear upon their trials may therefore draw upon a reservoir of public concern unavailable to the adult criminal defendant. In the Pennsylvania cases before us, there appears to be no statutory ban upon admission of the public to juvenile trials. Appellants themselves, without contradiction, assert that "the press is generally admitted" to juvenile delinquency proceedings in Philadelphia. Most important, the record in these cases is bare of any indication that any person whom appellants sought to have admitted to the courtroom was excluded. In these circumstances, I agree that the judgment in No. 322 must be affirmed.

The North Carolina cases, however, present a different situation. North Carolina law either permits or requires exclusion of the general public from juvenile trials. In the cases before us, the trial judge "ordered the general public excluded from the hearing room and stated that only officers of the court, the juveniles, their parents or guardians, their attorney and witnesses would be present for the hearing," notwithstanding petitioners' repeated demand for a public hearing. The cases themselves, which arise out of a series of demonstrations by black adults and juveniles who believed that the Hyde County, North Carolina, school system unlawfully discriminated against black schoolchildren, present a paradigm of the circumstances in which there may be a substantial "temptation to use the courts for political ends." And finally, neither the opinions supporting the judgment nor the respondent in No. 128 has pointed to any feature of North Carolina's juvenile proceedings that could substitute for public or jury trial in protecting the petitioners against misuse of the judicial process. Accordingly, I would reverse the judgment in No. 128.

Mr. Justice HARLAN, concurring in the judgments.

If I felt myself constrained to follow *Duncan*, which extended the Sixth Amendment right of jury trial to the States, I would have great difficulty, upon the premise seemingly accepted in my Brother BLACKMUN's opinion, in holding that the jury trial right does not extend to state juvenile proceedings. That premise is that juvenile delinquency proceedings have in practice actually become in many, if not all, respects criminal trials. But see my concurring and dissenting opinion in *Gault*. If that premise be correct, then I do not see why, given *Duncan*, juveniles as well as adults would not be constitutionally entitled to jury trials, so long as juvenile delinquency systems are not restructured to fit their original purpose. When that time comes I would have no difficulty in agreeing with [m]y Brother BLACKMUN, and indeed with my Brother WHITE, the author of *Duncan*, that juvenile delinquency proceedings are beyond the pale of *Duncan*.

I concur in the judgments in these cases, however, on the ground that criminal jury trials are not constitutionally required of the States, either as a matter of Sixth Amendment law or due process.

Mr. Justice DOUGLAS, with whom Mr. Justice BLACK and Mr. Justice MARSHALL concur, dissenting.

These cases from Pennsylvania and North Carolina present the issue of the right to a jury trial for offenders charged in juvenile court and facing a possible incarceration until they reach their majority. I believe the guarantees of the Bill of Rights, made applicable to the States by the Fourteenth Amendment, require a jury trial.

. . . .

Conviction of each of the [charged] crimes would subject a person, whether juvenile or adult, to imprisonment in a state institution. In the case of these students the possible term was six to 10 years; it would be computed for the period until an individual reached the age of 21. Each asked for a jury trial which was denied. The trial judge stated that the hearings were juvenile hearings, not criminal trials. But the issue in each case was whether they had violated a state criminal law. The trial judge found in each case that the juvenile had committed "an act for which an adult may be punished by law" and held in each case that the acts of the juvenile violated one of the criminal statutes cited above. The trial judge thereupon ordered each juvenile to be committed to the state institution for the care of delinquents and then placed each on probation for terms from 12 to 24 months.

We held in *Gault*, that "neither the Fourteenth Amendment nor the Bill of Rights is for adults alone." As we noted in that case, the Juvenile Court movement was designed to avoid procedures to ascertain whether the child was "guilty" or "innocent" but to bring to bear on these problems a "clinical" approach. It is, of course, not our task to determine as a matter of policy whether a "clinical" or "punitive" approach to these problems should be taken by the States. But where a State uses its juvenile court proceedings to prosecute a juvenile for a criminal act and to order "confinement" until the child reaches 21 years of age or where the child at the threshold of the proceedings faces that prospect, then he is entitled to the same procedural protection as an adult. . . .

Just as courts have sometimes confused delinquency with crime, so have law enforcement officials treated juveniles not as delinquents but as criminals. As noted in the President's Crime Commission Report:

> "In 1965, over 100,000 juveniles were confined in adult institutions. Presumably most of them were there because no separate juvenile detention facilities existed. Nonetheless, it is clearly undesirable that juveniles be confined with adults."

Even when juveniles are not incarcerated with adults the situation may be no better. One Pennsylvania correctional institution for juveniles is a brick building with barred windows, locked steel doors, a cyclone fence topped with barbed wire, and guard towers. A former juvenile judge described it as "a maximum security prison for adjudged delinquents."

In the present cases imprisonment or confinement up to 10 years was possible for one child and each faced at least a possible five-year incarceration. No adult could be denied a jury trial in those circumstances. The Fourteenth Amendment, which makes trial by jury provided in the Sixth Amendment applicable to the States, speaks of denial of rights to "any person," not denial of rights to "any adult person"; and we have held indeed that where a juvenile is charged with an act that would constitute a crime if committed by an adult, he is entitled to be tried under a standard of proof beyond a reasonable doubt.

In *DeBacker v. Brainard*, Mr. Justice Black and I dissented from a refusal to grant a juvenile, who was charged with forgery, a jury trial merely because the case was tried before *Duncan* was decided. Mr. Justice Black, after noting that a juvenile being charged with a criminal act was entitled to certain constitutional safeguards, viz., notice of the issues, benefit of counsel, protection against compulsory self-incrimination, and confrontation of the witnesses against him, added:

> "I can see no basis whatsoever in the language of the Constitution for allowing persons like appellant the benefit of those rights and yet denying them a jury trial, a right which is surely one of the fundamental aspects of criminal justice in the English-speaking world."

I added that by reason of the Sixth and Fourteenth Amendments the juvenile is entitled to a jury trial "as a matter of right where the delinquency charged is an offense that, if the person were an adult, would be a crime triable by jury. Such is this case, for behind the facade of delinquency is the crime of forgery."

Practical aspects of these problems are urged against allowing a jury trial in these cases.* They have been answered by Judge DeCiantis of the Family Court of Providence, Rhode Island, in a case entitled In the *Matter of McCloud*.... A juvenile was charged with the rape of a 17-year-old female and [the] Judge granted a motion for a jury trial.... He concluded that "the real traumatic" experience of incarceration without due process is "the feeling of being deprived of basic rights."...

[Judge DeCiantis went] on to say that "[t]rial by jury will provide the child with a safeguard against being prejudged" by a judge who may well be prejudiced by reports already submitted to him by the police or caseworkers in the case....

These cases should be remanded for trial by jury....

Notes

(a) How does Justice Blackmun view the *Gault* and *Winship* opinions in terms of their constitutional analyses?

(b) What type of constitutional analysis does Justice Blackmun use in *McKeiver*? How does Justice Blackmun's analysis differ from the *Gault* and *Winship* opinions?

---

* The Public Defender Service for the District of Columbia and the Neighborhood Legal Services Program of Washington, D.C., have filed a brief amicus in which the results of a survey of jury trials in delinquency cases in the 10 States requiring jury trials plus the District of Columbia are set forth. The cities selected were mostly large metropolitan areas. Thirty juvenile courts processing about 75,000 juvenile cases a year were canvassed: "[W]e discovered that during the past five and a half years, in 22 out of 26 courts surveyed, cumulative requests for jury trials totaled 15 or less. In the remaining five courts in our sample, statistics were unavailable. During the same period, in 26 out of 29 courts the cumulative number of jury trials actually held numbered 15 or less, with statistics unavailable for two courts in our sample. For example, in Tulsa, Oklahoma, counsel is present in 100% of delinquency cases, but only one jury trial has been requested and held during the past five and one-half years. In the Juvenile Court of Fort Worth, Texas, counsel is also present in 100% of the cases, and only two jury trials have been requested since 1967. The Juvenile Court in Detroit, Michigan, reports that counsel is appointed in 70–80% of its delinquency cases, but thus far in 1970, it has had only four requests for a jury. Between 1965 and 1969 requests for juries were reported as 'very few.'

In only four juvenile courts in our sample has there clearly been a total during the past five and one-half years of more than 15 jury trial requests and/or more than 15 such trials held." The four courts showing more than 15 requests for jury trials were Denver, Houston, Milwaukee, and Washington, D.C.

(c) How does Justice Blackmun articulate the test that he uses in reaching his conclusion?

(d) Given that the Court in *Duncan v. Louisiana*, 391 U.S. 145 (1968), concluded that jury trials in criminal cases are fundamental in our Anglo-American system of justice, how can Justice Blackmun deny that right to juvenile delinquents?

(e) Why did Justice Brennan concur in affirming one judgment (from Pennsylvania), and dissent with respect to the other judgment (from North Carolina)?

(f) Why did Justice Harlan concur in the judgment rather than concur in Justice Blackmun's plurality opinion, which could have then been a majority opinion?

(g) What is the basis of Justice Douglas' dissenting opinion? Justice Douglas referred to an opinion by Judge DeCiantis, granting a Rhode Island juvenile charged with rape of a 17-year-old female the right to a jury. In his opinion, Judge DeCiantis discussed several issues relating to jury trials in juvenile court. He argued that juveniles charged with crimes would be more traumatized by being deprived of basic rights; that jury trials would aid in rehabilitation; that there is no evidence that allowing jury trials would cause a backlog; that juvenile proceedings are not secret and that permitting a jury would not interfere with the goal of confidentiality; and that trial by jury is a safeguard against the child being prejudged because of the judge's access to probation reports.

(h) Are trial judges really worse than jurors in terms of accuracy in fact-finding? Most defendants in criminal cases plead guilty. Consider also that in criminal court defendants who request jury trials and are convicted usually face longer sentences than if they had pled guilty. That is also true in juvenile court. Why then is *McKeiver* viewed with such alarm? Harry Kalven and Hans Zeisel, in THE AMERICAN JURY (1966), conducted an empirical study of jury behavior. They concluded that judges and juries disagree in about 25% of criminal cases. In the majority of those cases the jury showed more leniency than the judge. *Id.* at 56–57. These results have recently been replicated. *See* Theodore Eisenberg et al., *Judge-Jury Agreement in Criminal Cases: A Partial Replication of Kalven & Zeisel's The American Jury*, 2 J. EMPIRICAL LEGAL STUD. 171 (2004). Kalven and Zeisel concluded that the reasons for the disparity related to evidentiary factors, facts that only the judge knew, disparity of counsel, jury sentiments about the particular defendant, and jury sentiment about the particular law. Kalven & Zeisel, *supra* at 106. It is thus clear that the jury is responding to factors unrelated to the technical guilt of the defendant, and exercises its authority to acquit defendants based on equitable factors. *Id.* at 285. The *McKeiver* ruling thus deprives juveniles of jury lenity, the equity dispensing function of the American jury system, and assures a greater conviction rate for juveniles accused of crime than adults facing the same charge.

See Irene Merker Rosenberg, *Leaving Bad Enough Alone: A Response to the Juvenile Court Abolitionists*, 1993 Wis. L. Rev. 163 (1993). *See also* Janet E. Ainsworth, *Re-Imagining Childhood and Reconstructing the Legal Order: The Case for Abolishing the Juvenile Court*, 69 N.C. L. Rev. 1083 (1991).

(i) Are there ways for lawyers to diminish the difficulties inherent in bench trials in juvenile court? *See* Martin Guggenheim & Randy Hertz, *Reflections on Judges, Juries, and Justice: Ensuring the Fairness of Juvenile Delinquency Trials*, 33 Wake Forest L. Rev. 553 (1998).

(j) *DeBacker v. Brainard* presented, by state habeas corpus, a challenge to a Nebraska statute providing that juvenile court hearings "shall be conducted by the judge without a jury in an informal manner." However, because that appellant's hearing had antedated *Duncan v. Louisiana* and because *Duncan* and *Bloom* had been given only prospective application by *DeStefano v. Woods*, DeBacker's case was deemed an inappropriate one for resolution of the jury trial issue. His appeal was therefore dismissed. Justice Black and Justice Douglas, in separate dissents, took the position that a juvenile is entitled to a jury trial at the adjudicative stage. Justice Black described this as "a right which is surely one of the fundamental aspects of criminal justice in the English-speaking world," and Justice Douglas described it as a right required by the Sixth and Fourteenth Amendments "where the delinquency charged is an offense that, if the person were an adult, would be a crime triable by jury."

Breed v. Jones
421 U.S. 519 (1975)

Mr. Chief Justice BURGER delivered the opinion of the Court.

We granted certiorari to decide whether the prosecution of respondent as an adult, after Juvenile Court proceedings which resulted in a finding that respondent had violated a criminal statute and a subsequent finding that he was unfit for treatment as a juvenile, violated the Fifth and Fourteenth Amendments to the United States Constitution.

On February 9, 1971, a petition was filed in the Superior Court of California, County of Los Angeles, Juvenile Court, alleging that respondent, then 17 years of age, was a person described by Cal.Welf. & Inst'ns Code[1] in that, on or about February 8, while armed with a deadly weapon, he had committed acts which, if committed by an adult, would constitute the crime of robbery in violation of [the California] Penal Code. The following day, a detention hearing was held, at the conclusion of which respondent was ordered detained pending a hearing on the petition.[2]

The jurisdictional or adjudicatory hearing was conducted on March 1.[3] After taking testimony from two prosecution witnesses and respondent, the Juvenile Court found that

---

1. As of the date of filing of the petition in this case, Cal. Welf. & Inst'ns Code § 602 (1966) provided:

> "Any person under the age of 21 years who violates any law of this State or of the United States or any ordinance of any city or county of this State defining crime or who, after having been found by the juvenile court to be a person described by Section 601, fails to obey any lawful order of the juvenile court, is within the jurisdiction of the juvenile court, which may adjudge such person to be a ward of the court." An amendment in 1971, not relevant here, lowered the jurisdictional age from 21 to 18.

2. The probation officer was required to present a prima facie case that respondent had committed the offense alleged in the petition. Respondent was represented by court-appointed counsel at the detention hearing and thereafter.

3. At the time of the hearing, Cal. Welf. & Inst'ns Code § 701 (1966) provided:

> "At the hearing, the court shall first consider only the question whether the minor is a person described by Sections 600, 601, or 602, and for this purpose, any matter or information relevant and material to the circumstances or acts which are alleged to bring him within the jurisdiction of the juvenile court is admissible and may be received in evidence; however, *a preponderance of evidence*, legally admissible in the trial of criminal cases, must be adduced to support a finding that the minor is a person described by Section 602, and *a preponderance of evidence*, legally admissible in the trial of civil cases must be adduced to support a finding that the minor is a person described by Sections 600 or 601. When it appears that the minor has made an extrajudicial admission or confession and denies the same at the hearing, the court may continue the hearing for not to exceed seven days to enable the probation officer to subpoena witnesses to attend the hearing to prove the allegations of the petition. If the minor is not represented by counsel at the hearing, it shall be deemed that objections that could have been made to the evidence were made." (Emphasis added.)

the allegations in the petition were true and that respondent was a person described by § 602, and it sustained the petition. The proceedings were continued for a dispositional hearing,[4] pending which the court ordered that respondent remain detained.

At a hearing conducted on March 15, the Juvenile Court indicated its intention to find respondent "not * * * amenable to the care, treatment and training program available through the facilities of the juvenile court" under § 707.[5] Respondent's counsel orally moved "to continue the matter on the ground of surprise," contending that respondent "was not informed that it was going to be a fitness hearing." The court continued the matter for one week, at which time, having considered the report of the probation officer assigned to the case and having heard her testimony, it declared re-

---

A 1971 amendment substituted "proof beyond a reasonable doubt supported by evidence" for the language in italics. Respondent does not claim that the standard of proof at the hearing failed to satisfy due process. Hereafter, the § 701 hearing will be referred to as the adjudicatory hearing.

4. At the time, Cal. Welf. & Inst'ns Code § 702 (Supp.1968) provided:

"After hearing such evidence, the court shall make a finding, noted in the minutes of the court, whether or not the minor is a person described by Sections 600, 601, or 602. If it finds that the minor is not such a person, it shall order that the petition be dismissed and the minor be discharged from any detention or restriction theretofore ordered. If the court finds that the minor is such a person, it shall make and enter its findings and order accordingly and shall then proceed to hear evidence on the question of the proper disposition to be made of the minor. Prior to doing so, it may continue the hearing, if necessary, to receive the social study of the probation officer or to receive other evidence on its own motion or the motion of a parent or guardian for not to exceed 10 judicial days if the minor is detained during such continuance, and if the minor is not detained, it may continue the hearing to a date not later than 30 days after the date of filing of the petition. The court may, for good cause shown continue the hearing for an additional 15 days, if the minor is not detained. The court may make such order for detention of the minor or his release from detention, during the period of the continuance, as is appropriate."

5. At the time, Cal. Welf. & Inst'ns Code § 707 (Supp. 1967) provided:

"At any time during a hearing upon a petition alleging that a minor is, by reason of violation of any criminal statute or ordinance, a person described in Section 602, when substantial evidence has been adduced to support a finding that the minor was 16 years of age or older at the time of the alleged commission of such offense and that the minor would not be amenable to the care, treatment and training program available through the facilities of the juvenile court, or if, at any time after such hearing, a minor who was 16 years of age or older at the time of the commission of an offense and who was committed therefor by the court to the Youth Authority, is returned to the court by the Youth Authority pursuant to Section 780 or 1737.1, the court may make a finding noted in the minutes of the court that the minor is not a fit and proper subject to be dealt with under this chapter, and the court shall direct the district attorney or other appropriate prosecuting officer to prosecute the person under the applicable criminal statute or ordinance and thereafter dismiss the petition or, if a prosecution has been commenced in another court but has been suspended while juvenile court proceedings are held, shall dismiss the petition and issue its order directing that the other court proceedings resume. In determining whether the minor is a fit and proper subject to be dealt with under this chapter, the offense, in itself, shall not be sufficient to support a finding that such minor is not a fit and proper subject to be dealt with under the provisions of the Juvenile Court Law. A denial by the person on whose behalf the petition is brought of any or all of the facts or conclusions set forth therein or of any inference to be drawn therefrom is not, of itself, sufficient to support a finding that such person is not a fit and proper subject to be dealt with under the provisions of the Juvenile Court Law. The court shall cause the probation officer to investigate and submit a report on the behavioral patterns of the person being considered for unfitness."

spondent "unfit for treatment as a juvenile,"[6] and ordered that he be prosecuted as an adult.[7]

Thereafter, respondent filed a petition for a writ of habeas corpus in Juvenile Court, raising the same double jeopardy claim now presented. Upon the denial of that petition, respondent sought habeas corpus relief in the California Court of Appeal, Second Appellate District. Although it initially stayed the criminal prosecution pending against respondent, that court denied the petition. The Supreme Court of California denied respondent's petition for a hearing.

After a preliminary hearing respondent was ordered held for trial in Superior Court, where an information was subsequently filed accusing him of having committed robbery, while armed with a deadly weapon, on or about February 8, 1971. Respondent entered a plea of not guilty, and he also pleaded that he had "already been placed once in jeopardy and convicted of the offense charged, by the judgment of the ... Juvenile Court, rendered * * * on the 1st day of March, 1971." By stipulation, the case was submitted to the court on the transcript of the preliminary hearing. The court found respondent guilty of robbery in the first degree and ordered that he be committed to the California Youth Authority.[8] No appeal was taken from the judgment of conviction.

On December 10, 1971, respondent, through his mother as guardian ad litem, filed the instant petition for a writ of habeas corpus in the United States District Court for the Central District of California. In his petition he alleged that his transfer to adult court pursuant to § 707 and subsequent trial there "placed him in double jeopardy." The District Court denied the petition, rejecting respondent's contention that jeopardy attached at his adjudicatory hearing. It concluded that the "distinctions between the preliminary procedures and hearings provided by California law for juveniles and a criminal trial are many and apparent and the effort of [respondent] to relate them is unconvincing," and that "even assuming jeopardy attached during the preliminary juvenile proceedings * * * it is clear that no new jeopardy arose by the juvenile proceeding sending the case to the criminal court."

The Court of Appeals reversed, concluding that applying double jeopardy protection to juvenile proceedings would not "impede the juvenile courts in carrying out their basic goal of rehabilitating the erring youth," and that the contrary result might "do irreparable harm to or destroy their confidence in our judicial system." The court therefore held that the Double Jeopardy Clause "is fully applicable to juvenile court proceedings."

---

6. The Juvenile Court noted: "This record I have read is one of the most threatening records I have read about any Minor who has come before me. We have, as a matter of simple fact, no less than three armed robberies, each with a loaded weapon. The degree of delinquency which that represents, the degree of sophistication which that represents and the degree of impossibility of assistance as a juvenile which that represents, I think is overwhelming * * *"

7. In doing so, the Juvenile Court implicitly rejected respondent's double jeopardy argument, made at both the original § 702 hearing and in a memorandum submitted by counsel prior to the resumption of that hearing after the continuance.

8. The authority for the order of commitment derived from Cal. Welf. & Inst'ns Code § 1731.5 (Supp. 1971). At the time of the order, Cal. Welf. & Inst'ns Code § 1771 (1966) provided: "Every person convicted of a felony and committed to the authority shall be discharged when such person reaches his 25th birthday, unless an order for further detention has been made by the committing court pursuant to Article 6 (commencing with Section 1800) or unless a petition is filed under Article 5 of this chapter. In the event such a petition under Article 5 is filed, the authority shall retain control until the final disposition of the proceeding under Article 5."

Turning to the question whether there had been a constitutional violation in this case, the Court of Appeals pointed to the power of the Juvenile Court to "impose severe restrictions upon the juvenile's liberty," in support of its conclusion that jeopardy attached in respondent's adjudicatory hearing.[9] It rejected petitioner's contention that no new jeopardy attached when respondent was referred to Superior Court and subsequently tried and convicted, finding "continuing jeopardy" principles advanced by petitioner inapplicable. Finally, the Court of Appeals observed that acceptance of petitioner's position would "allow the prosecution to review in advance the accused's defense and, as here, hear him testify about the crime charged," a procedure it found offensive to "our concepts of basic, even-handed fairness." The court therefore held that once jeopardy attached at the adjudicatory hearing, a minor could not be retried as an adult or a juvenile "absent some exception to the double jeopardy prohibition," and that there "was none here."

We granted certiorari because of a conflict between Courts of Appeals and the highest courts of a number of States on the issue presented in this case and similar issues and because of the importance of final resolution of the issue to the administration of the juvenile-court system.

I

The parties agree that, following his transfer from Juvenile Court, and as a defendant to a felony information, respondent was entitled to the full protection of the Double Jeopardy Clause of the Fifth Amendment, as applied to the States through the Fourteenth Amendment. In addition, they agree that respondent was put in jeopardy by the proceedings on that information, which resulted in an adjudication that he was guilty of robbery in the first degree and in a sentence of commitment. Finally, there is no dispute that the petition filed in Juvenile Court and the information filed in Superior Court related to the "same offence" within the meaning of the constitutional prohibition. The point of disagreement between the parties, and the question for our decision, is whether, by reason of the proceedings in Juvenile Court, respondent was "twice put in jeopardy."

II

Jeopardy denotes risk. In the constitutional sense, jeopardy describes the risk that is traditionally associated with a criminal prosecution. Although the constitutional language, "jeopardy of life or limb," suggests proceedings in which only the most serious penalties can be imposed, the Clause has long been construed to mean something far broader than its literal language.[10] At the same time, however, we have held that the risk to which the Clause refers is not present in proceedings that are not "essentially criminal."

Although the juvenile-court system had its genesis in the desire to provide a distinctive procedure and setting to deal with the problems of youth, including those manifested by antisocial conduct, our decisions in recent years have recognized that there is a gap between the originally benign conception of the system and its realities. With the exception of *McKeiver v. Pennsylvania*, the Court's response to that perception has been to make applicable in juvenile proceedings constitutional guarantees associated with traditional criminal prosecutions. In so doing the Court has evinced awareness of the threat which such a process

---

9. In reaching this conclusion, the Court of Appeals ... noted that "California concedes that jeopardy attaches when the juvenile is adjudicated a ward of the court."

10. Distinctions which in other contexts have proved determinative of the constitutional rights of those charged with offenses against public order have not similarly confined the protection of the Double Jeopardy Clause.

represents to the efforts of the juvenile court system, functioning in a unique manner, to ameliorate the harshness of criminal justice when applied to youthful offenders. That the system has fallen short of the high expectations of its sponsors in no way detracts from the broad social benefits sought or from those benefits that can survive constitutional scrutiny.

We believe it is simply too late in the day to conclude, as did the District Court in this case, that a juvenile is not put in jeopardy at a proceeding whose object is to determine whether he has committed acts that violate a criminal law and whose potential consequences include both the stigma inherent in such a determination and the deprivation of liberty for many years.[11] For it is clear under our cases that determining the relevance of constitutional policies, like determining the applicability of constitutional rights, in juvenile proceedings, requires that courts eschew "the 'civil' label-of-convenience which has been attached to juvenile proceedings," and that "the juvenile process * * * be candidly appraised."

As we have observed, the risk to which the term jeopardy refers is that traditionally associated with "actions intended to authorize criminal punishment to vindicate public justice." Because of its purpose and potential consequences, and the nature and resources of the State, such a proceeding imposes heavy pressures and burdens—psychological, physical, and financial—on a person charged. The purpose of the Double Jeopardy Clause is to require that he be subject to the experience only once "for the same offence."

In *In re Gault*, this Court concluded that, for purposes of the right to counsel, a "proceeding where the issue is whether the child will be found to be 'delinquent' and subjected to the loss of his liberty for years is comparable in seriousness to a felony prosecution." The Court stated that the term "delinquent" had "come to involve only slightly less stigma than the term 'criminal' applied to adults," and that, for purposes of the privilege against self-incrimination, "commitment is a deprivation of liberty. It is incarceration against one's will, whether it is called 'criminal' or 'civil.'"

Thus, in terms of potential consequences, there is little to distinguish an adjudicatory hearing such as was held in this case from a traditional criminal prosecution. For that reason, it engenders elements of "anxiety and insecurity" in a juvenile, and imposes a "heavy personal strain." And we can expect that, since our decisions implementing fundamental fairness in the juvenile court system, hearings have been prolonged, and some of the burdens incident to a juvenile's defense increased, as the system has assimilated the process thereby imposed.

We deal here, not with "the formalities of the criminal adjudicative process," but with an analysis of an aspect of the juvenile-court system in terms of the kind of risk to which jeopardy refers. Under our decisions we can find no persuasive distinction in that regard between the proceeding conducted in this case pursuant to §701 and a criminal prosecution, each of which is designed "to vindicate [the] very vital interest in enforcement of criminal laws." We therefore conclude that respondent was put in jeopardy at the adjudicatory hearing. Jeopardy attached when respondent was "put to trial before the trier of the facts," that is, when the Juvenile Court, as the trier of the facts, began to hear evidence.

III

Petitioner argues that, even assuming jeopardy attached at respondent's adjudicatory hearing, the procedures by which he was transferred from Juvenile Court and tried on a felony information in Superior Court did not violate the Double Jeopardy Clause. The ar-

---

11. At the time of respondent's dispositional hearing, permissible dispositions included commitment to the California Youth Authority until he reached the age of 21 years. Petitioner has conceded that the "adjudicatory hearing is, in every sense, a court trial."

gument is supported by two distinct, but in this case overlapping, lines of analysis. First, petitioner reasons that the procedure violated none of the policies of the Double Jeopardy Clause or that, alternatively, it should be upheld by analogy to those cases which permit retrial of an accused who has obtained reversal of a conviction on appeal. Second, pointing to this Court's concern for "the juvenile court's assumed ability to function in a unique manner," petitioner urges that, should we conclude traditional principles "would otherwise bar a transfer to adult court after a delinquency adjudication," we should avoid that result here because it "would diminish the flexibility and informality of juvenile court proceedings without conferring any additional due process benefits upon juveniles charged with delinquent acts."

A

We cannot agree with petitioner that the trial of respondent in Superior Court on an information charging the same offense as that for which he had been tried in Juvenile Court violated none of the policies of the Double Jeopardy Clause. For, even accepting petitioner's premise that respondent "never faced the risk of more than one punishment," we have pointed out that "the Double Jeopardy Clause * * * is written in terms of potential or risk of trial and conviction, not punishment." And we have recently noted:

> "The policy of avoiding multiple trials has been regarded as so important that exceptions to the principle have been only grudgingly allowed. Initially, a new trial was thought to be unavailable after appeal, whether requested by the prosecution or the defendant. * * * It was not until 1896 that it was made clear that a defendant could seek a new trial after conviction, even though the Government enjoyed no similar right. * * * Following the same policy, the Court has granted the Government the right to retry a defendant after a mistrial only where "there is a manifest necessity for the act, or the ends of public justice would otherwise be defeated."

Respondent was subjected to the burden of two trials for the same offense; he [w]as twice put to the task of marshaling his resources against those of the State, twice subjected to the "heavy personal strain" which such an experience represents. We turn, therefore, to inquire whether either traditional principles or "the juvenile court's assumed ability to function in a unique manner," *McKeiver v. Pennsylvania*, supports an exception to the "constitutional policy of finality" to which respondent would otherwise be entitled.

B

In denying respondent's petitions for writs of habeas corpus, the California Court of Appeal first, and the United States District Court later, concluded that no new jeopardy arose as a result of his transfer from Juvenile Court and trial in Superior Court. In the view of those courts, the jeopardy that attaches at an adjudicatory hearing continues until there is a final disposition of the case under the adult charge.

The phrase "continuing jeopardy" describes both a concept and a conclusion. As originally articulated by Mr. Justice Holmes in his dissent in *Kepner v. United States*, the concept has proved an interesting model for comparison with the system of constitutional protection which the Court has in fact derived from the rather ambiguous language and history of the Double Jeopardy Clause. Holmes' view has "never been adopted by a majority of this Court."

The conclusion, "continuing jeopardy," as distinguished from the concept, has occasionally been used to explain why an accused who has secured the reversal of a conviction on appeal may be retried for the same offense. Probably a more satisfactory explanation lies in analysis of the respective interests involved. Similarly, the fact that the proceedings against respondent had not "run their full course," within the contemplation of the California Welfare and Institutions Code at the time of transfer, does not satisfactorily explain why respondent should be deprived of the constitutional protection against a second trial. If there is to be an exception to that protection in the context of the juvenile court system, it must be justified by interests of society, reflected in that unique institution, or of juveniles themselves, of sufficient substance to render tolerable the costs and burdens, noted earlier, which the exception will entail in individual cases.

C

The possibility of transfer from juvenile court to a court of general criminal jurisdiction is a matter of great significance to the juvenile. See *Kent v. United States*. At the same time, there appears to be widely shared agreement that not all juveniles can benefit from the special features and programs of the juvenile-court system and that a procedure for transfer to an adult court should be available. This general agreement is reflected in the fact that an overwhelming majority of jurisdictions permits transfer in certain circumstances. As might be expected, the statutory provisions differ in numerous details. Whatever their differences, however, such transfer provisions represent an attempt to impart to the juvenile-court system the flexibility needed to deal with youthful offenders who cannot benefit from the specialized guidance and treatment contemplated by the system.

We do not agree with petitioner that giving respondent the constitutional protection against multiple trials in this context will diminish flexibility and informality to the extent that those qualities relate uniquely to the goals of the juvenile-court system.[15] We agree that such a holding will require, in most cases, that the transfer decision be made prior to an adjudicatory hearing. To the extent that evidence concerning the alleged offense is considered relevant,[16] it may be that, in those cases where transfer is considered and rejected, some added burden will be imposed on the juvenile courts by reason of duplicative proceedings. Finally, the nature of the evidence considered at a transfer hearing may in some States require that, if transfer is rejected, a different judge preside at the adjudicatory hearing.

We recognize that juvenile courts, perhaps even more than most courts, suffer from the problems created by spiraling caseloads unaccompanied by enlarged resources and manpower. And courts should be reluctant to impose on the juvenile-court system any additional requirements which could so strain its resources as to endanger its unique functions. However, the burdens that petitioner envisions appear to us neither qualita-

---

15. That the flexibility and informality of juvenile proceedings are diminished by the application of due process standards is not open to doubt. Due process standards inevitably produce such an effect, but that tells us no more than that the Constitution imposes burdens on the functioning of government and especially of law enforcement institutions.

16. Under Cal.Welf. & Inst'ns Code § 707 (1972), the governing criterion with respect to transfer, assuming the juvenile is 16 years of age [and] is charged with a violation of a criminal statute or ordinance, is amenability "to the care, treatment and training program available through the facilities of the juvenile court." The section further provides that neither "the offense, in itself" nor a denial by the juvenile of the facts or conclusions set forth in the petition shall be "sufficient to support a finding that (he) is not a fit and proper subject to be dealt with under the provisions of the Juvenile Court law." The California Supreme Court has held that the only factor a juvenile court must consider is the juvenile's "behavior pattern as described in the probation officer's report," but that it may also consider, inter alia, the nature and circumstances of the alleged offense. In contrast to California, which does not require any evidentiary showing with respect to the commission of the offense, a number of jurisdictions require a finding of probable cause to believe the juvenile committed the offense before transfer is permitted. In addition, two jurisdictions appear presently to require a finding of delinquency before the transfer of a juvenile to adult court.

tively nor quantitatively sufficient to justify a departure in this context from the fundamental prohibition against double jeopardy.

A requirement that transfer hearings be held prior to adjudicatory hearings affects not at all the nature of the latter proceedings. More significantly, such a requirement need not affect the quality of decisionmaking at transfer hearings themselves. In *Kent v. United States*, the Court held that hearings under the statute there involved "must measure up to the essentials of due process and fair treatment." However, the Court has never attempted to prescribe criteria for, or the nature and quantum of evidence that must support, a decision to transfer a juvenile for trial in adult court. We require only that, whatever the relevant criteria, and whatever the evidence demanded, a State determine whether it wants to treat a juvenile within the juvenile-court system before entering upon a proceeding that may result in an adjudication that he has violated a criminal law and in a substantial deprivation of liberty, rather than subject him to the expense, delay, strain, and embarrassment of two such proceedings.[18]

Moreover, we are not persuaded that the burdens petitioner envisions would pose a significant problem for the administration of the juvenile-court system. The large number of jurisdictions that presently require that the transfer decision be made prior to an adjudicatory hearing, and the absence of any indication that the juvenile courts in those jurisdictions have not been able to perform their task within that framework, suggest the contrary. The likelihood that in many cases the lack of need or basis for a transfer hearing can be recognized promptly reduces the number of cases in which a commitment of resources is necessary. In addition, we have no reason to believe that the resources available to those who recommend transfer or participate in the process leading to transfer decisions are inadequate to enable them to gather the information relevant to informed decision prior to an adjudicatory hearing.[20]

To the extent that transfer hearings held prior to adjudication result in some duplication of evidence if transfer is rejected, the burden on juvenile courts will tend to be offset somewhat by the cases in which, because of transfer, no further proceedings in juvenile court are required. Moreover, when transfer has previously been rejected, juveniles may well be more likely to admit the commission of the offense charged, thereby obviating the need for adjudicatory hearings, than if transfer remains a possibility. Finally, we note that those States which presently require a different judge to preside at an adjudicatory hearing if transfer is rejected also permit waiver of that requirement.[21] Where the requirement is not waived, it is difficult to see a substantial strain on judicial resources.

Quite apart from our conclusions with respect to the burdens on the juvenile-court system envisioned by petitioner, we are persuaded that transfer hearings prior to adjudication

---

18. We note that nothing decided today forecloses States from requiring, as a prerequisite to the transfer of a juvenile, substantial evidence that he committed the offense charged, so long as the showing required is not made in an adjudicatory proceeding. The instant case is not one in which the judicial determination was simply a finding of, *e.g.*, probable cause. Rather, it was an adjudication that respondent had violated a criminal statute.

20. We intimate no views concerning the constitutional validity of transfer following the attachment of jeopardy at an adjudicatory hearing where the information which forms the predicate for the transfer decision could not, by the exercise of due diligence, reasonably have been obtained previously.

21. "The reason for this waiver provision is clear. A juvenile will ordinarily not want to dismiss a judge who has refused to transfer him to a criminal court. There is a risk of having another judge assigned to the case who is not as sympathetic. Moreover, in many cases, a rapport has been established between the judge and the juvenile, and the goal of rehabilitation is well on its way to being met."

will aid the objectives of that system. What concerns us here is the dilemma that the possibility of transfer after an adjudicatory hearing presents for a juvenile, a dilemma to which the Court of Appeals alluded. Because of that possibility, a juvenile, thought to be the beneficiary of special consideration, may in fact suffer substantial disadvantages. If he appears uncooperative, he runs the risk of an adverse adjudication, as well as of an unfavorable dispositional recommendation.[22] If, on the other hand, he is cooperative, he runs the risk of prejudicing his chances in adult court if transfer is ordered. We regard a procedure that results in such a dilemma as at odds with the goal that, to the extent fundamental fairness permits, adjudicatory hearings be informal and nonadversary. Knowledge of the risk of transfer after an adjudicatory hearing can only undermine the potential for informality and cooperation which was intended to be the hallmark of the juvenile-court system. Rather than concerning themselves with the matter at hand, establishing innocence or seeking a disposition best suited to individual correctional needs, the juvenile and his attorney are pressed into a posture of adversary wariness that is conducive to neither.[23]

IV

We hold that the prosecution of respondent in Superior Court, after an adjudicatory proceeding in Juvenile Court, violated the Double Jeopardy Clause of the Fifth Amendment, as applied to the States through the Fourteenth Amendment. The mandate of the Court of Appeals, which was stayed by that court pending our decision, directs the District Court "to issue a writ of habeas corpus directing the state court, within 60 days, to vacate the adult conviction of Jones and either set him free or remand him to the juvenile court for disposition." Since respondent is no longer subject to the jurisdiction of the California Juvenile Court, we vacate the judgment and remand the case to the Court of Appeals for such further proceedings consistent with this opinion as may be appropriate in the circumstances.

So ordered.

Judgment vacated and case remanded.

Notes

(a) Is the *Breed* opinion more like *Gault* and *Winship* or *McKeiver*? Why?

(b) Could the Court have reached the conclusion it did in *Breed* by using the analytical approach of the *McKeiver* Court? Explain.

(c) Chief Justice Burger insists that he is not departing from *McKeiver*, yet he distinguishes it away. How? Is his reason persuasive?

(d) How does the *Breed* Court view the prior delinquency cases in terms of constitutional analysis?

---

22. Although denying respondent's petition for a writ of habeas corpus, the judge of the Juvenile Court noted: 'If he doesn't open up with a probation officer there is of course the danger that the probation officer will find that he is so uncooperative that he cannot make a recommendation for the kind of treatment you think he really should have and, yet, as the attorney worrying about what might happen a[t] the disposition hearing, you have to advise him to continue to more or less stand upon his constitutional right not to incriminate himself * * *."

23. With respect to the possibility of "making the juvenile proceedings confidential and not being able to be used against the minor," the judge of the Juvenile Court observed: "I must say that doesn't impress me because if the minor admitted something in the Juvenile Court and named his companions nobody is going to eradicate from the minds of the district attorney or other people the information they obtained."

(e) Given *McKeiver*, how do you explain the *Breed* Court's unanimous decision invalidating the California statute? What do you think is motivating the Justices?

(f) What test did the Court use to determine the applicability of the double jeopardy clause to juvenile court hearings? Did the Court use the same test to determine the content of the double jeopardy clause in juvenile court hearings? How do they differ?

(g) Based on *Breed*, what is the result in the following hypo?

A is charged with delinquency based on an underlying act of robbery. During his adjudicatory hearing the judge declares a mistrial because she is going out of town for two weeks and will not be able to conclude the case. A objects, but is overruled. At the second adjudicatory hearing A is found to be a delinquent. Is A's adjudication constitutional?

(h) In answering these questions consider the following:

Irene Merker Rosenberg, *The Constitutional Rights of Children Charged With Crime: Proposal For a Return to the Not So Distant Past*, 27 UCLA L. Rev. 656, 681–84 (1980):

> One may wonder why the [*Breed*] Court unanimously adopted what appears to be a functional equivalence standard and utilized a double jeopardy analysis, rather than employing a fundamental fairness-due process approach....
>
> At the same time, following the approach established in *McKeiver*, the Court in *Breed* carefully examined whether the particular constitutional right would strengthen the juvenile court system. This analysis was not, however, undertaken in the context of determining the *applicability of* the right, but rather for the purpose of ascertaining its *content*. *Breed* is the first case since *Gault* in which the Court was called upon to decide not only whether a particular right applied to delinquency proceedings, but also whether there was a violation of that right. In *McKeiver* and *Winship*, the issues of applicability and content were collapsed, because the particular state laws would concededly have violated the implicated constitutional rights, and the only issue in each case was whether the particular safeguard applied to juveniles. In *Winship*, once it was decided that the reasonable doubt standard applied to delinquency cases, it was clear that the state statute authorizing a preponderance standard was unconstitutional on its face. In *McKeiver*, the content issue was never reached because the Court found against the juveniles on the question of applicability. *Breed* is not that simple. The state argued not only that jeopardy did not attach at the juvenile adjudicatory hearing, but also that even if it did there was nonetheless no violation of the double jeopardy clause for three reasons: the challenged state procedure violated none of the policies underlying the double jeopardy provision; there was "continuing jeopardy"; and even if the procedure would violate double jeopardy as traditionally interpreted, a different result should obtain in juvenile court because its unique benefits would be impaired by a contrary ruling.
>
> The first two arguments, based on the contention that the state procedure in question would not violate the traditional standard governing double jeopardy, were quickly disposed of by the Court. The Chief Justice then focused on the third argument, which was aimed at establishing a lesser content for the double jeopardy clause in juvenile proceedings. Were this argument accepted, the clause would apply to delinquency adjudicatory hearings, but would not prohibit all of the practices it would forbid in adult criminal trials-only those whose proscription would not impair the special benefits of the juvenile justice system.

Utilizing reasoning similar to that which would have supported a fundamental fairness rationale for invalidation of the California procedure, Chief Justice Burger concluded that the double jeopardy prohibition in this context would strengthen the juvenile court. He reasoned that requiring the state to opt for either waiver to the adult court or a delinquency prosecution in the juvenile court would enable the youth to cooperate fully with the probation officer without fear that any resulting evidence could be used in criminal court. Thus, the fundamental fairness concept may have been one factor used in deciding whether the unique benefits of the juvenile court would be served by traditional interpretation of the content of a particular right.

Because the California procedure placed the child in an untenable dilemma—the youth's cooperation in an effort to avoid waiver might prejudice subsequent defense efforts in criminal court, but refusal to cooperate might result in a harsher disposition in juvenile court, including a recommendation for waiver—the *Breed* Court rejected the state's unique-benefits argument in the particular case. Yet in so reasoning, the *Breed* Court appears to have accepted the logic of this content-limiting argument. By doing so, the Court creates what can be called a conditional functional equivalence test to determine the content of constitutional rights in delinquency proceedings. Delinquency adjudicatory hearings are viewed as the functional equivalent of adult criminal trials, and any right granted to adult defendants will receive the same interpretation in juvenile proceedings if it satisfies the additional condition the Court imposes: such an interpretation must strengthen, or at least not impair, the unique functioning of the juvenile court. Thus, *Breed* appears to make functional equivalence the test for determining the applicability of a constitutional right, whereas conditional functional equivalence is used to ascertain the content of a right that has been found applicable.

Swisher v. Brady
438 U.S. 204 (1978)

Mr. Chief Justice BURGER delivered the opinion of the Court.

This is an appeal from a three-judge District Court for the District of Maryland. Nine minors, appellees here, brought an action under 42 U.S.C. § 1983, seeking a declaratory judgment and injunctive relief to prevent the State from filing exceptions with the Juvenile Court to proposed findings and recommendations made by masters of that court. The minors' claim was based on an alleged violation of the Double Jeopardy Clause of the Fifth Amendment, as applied to the States through the Fourteenth Amendment....

I

In order to understand the present Maryland scheme for the use of masters in juvenile court proceedings, it is necessary to trace briefly the history both of antecedent schemes and of this and related litigation.

Prior to July 1975, the use of masters in Maryland juvenile proceedings was governed by Rule 908(e), Maryland Rules of Procedure. It provided that a master "shall hear such cases as may be assigned to him by the court." The Rule further directed that, at the conclusion of the hearing, the master transmit the case file and his "findings and recommendations" to the Juvenile Court. If no party filed exceptions to these findings and recommendations, they were to be "promptly * * * confirmed, modified or remanded by the judge." If, however, a party filed exceptions—and in delinquency hearings, only the

State had the authority to do so—then, after notice, the Juvenile Court judge would "hear the entire matter or such specific matters as set forth in the exceptions *de novo*."[1]

In the city of Baltimore, after the State filed a petition alleging that a minor had committed a delinquent act,[2] the clerk of the Juvenile Court generally would assign the case to one of seven masters.[4] In the ensuing unrecorded hearing, the State would call its witnesses and present its evidence in accordance with the rules of evidence applicable in criminal cases. The minor could offer evidence in defense. At the conclusion of the presentation of evidence, the master usually would announce his findings and contemplated recommendations. In a minority of those cases where the recommendations favored the minor's position, the State would file exceptions, whereupon the Juvenile Court judge would try the case *de novo*.[5]

In 1972, a Baltimore City Master concluded, after a hearing, that the State had failed to show beyond a reasonable doubt that a minor, William Anderson, had assaulted and robbed a woman. His recommendation to the Juvenile Court judge reflected that conclusion. The State filed exceptions. Anderson responded with a motion to dismiss the notice of exceptions, contending that Rule 908(e), with its provision for a *de novo* hearing, violated the Double Jeopardy Clause. The Juvenile Court judge ruled that juvenile proceedings as such were not outside the scope of the Double Jeopardy Clause. He then held that the proceeding before him on the State's exceptions would violate Anderson's right not to be twice put in jeopardy and, on that basis, granted the motion to dismiss. The judge granted the same relief to similarly situated minors, including several who later initiated the present litigation.

The State appealed and the Court of Special Appeals reversed. That court assumed, for purposes of its decision, that jeopardy attached at the commencement of the initial hearing before the master. It held, however: "[T]here is *no adjudication* by reason of the master's findings and recommendations. The proceedings before the master and his findings and recommendations are simply the first phase of the hearing which continues with the consideration by the juvenile judge. Whether the juvenile judge, in the absence of exceptions, accepts the master's findings or recommendations, modifies them or remands them, or whether, when exceptions are filed, he hears the matter himself *de novo*, there is merely a continuance of the hearing and the initial jeopardy. In other words, *the hearing*, and the jeopardy thereto attaching, terminate only upon a valid adjudication *by the juvenile judge*, not upon the findings and recommendations of the master."

On this basis, the court concluded that the *de novo* hearing was not a second exposure to jeopardy. On appeal by the minors, the Court of Appeals affirmed, although on a rationale different from that of the intermediate appellate court. It held that "a hearing before a master is not such a hearing as places a juvenile in jeopardy." Central to this holding was the court's conclusion that masters in Maryland serve only as ministerial assistants to judges; although authorized to hear evidence, report findings, and make recommendations to the judge, masters are entrusted with none of the judicial power of the State, including the *sine qua non* of judicial office—the power to enter a binding judgment.

---

1. Rule 908(e) was the sole authority for the use of masters in juvenile causes. The practice was not treated in Maryland statutes.

2. Maryland, like 39 other States, defines a delinquent act as one that, if committed by an adult, would violate a criminal statute.

4. In 1974, of 5,345 delinquency hearings conducted in the Juvenile Court, 5,098 were held before masters. The remaining 247 were assigned in the first instance to the judge.

5. In 1974, the Juvenile Court judge conducted 80 *de novo*, or "exceptions," hearings in delinquency matters. All hearings before the judge were recorded.

In November 1974, five months after the Court of Appeals' decision, nine juveniles sought federal habeas corpus relief, contending that by taking exceptions to masters' recommendations favorable to them the State was violating their rights under the Double Jeopardy Clause. These same nine minors also initiated a class action under 42 U.S.C. § 1983 in which they sought a declaratory judgment and injunctive relief against the future operation of Rule 908(e). The sole constitutional basis for their complaint was, again, the Double Jeopardy Clause. A three-judge court was convened to hear this matter, and it is the judgment of that court we now review.

Before either the three-judge District Court or the single judge reviewing the habeas corpus petitions could act, the Maryland Legislature enacted legislation which, for the first time, provided a statutory basis for the use of masters in juvenile court proceedings. In doing so, it modified slightly the scheme previously operative under Rule 908(e). The new legislation required that hearings before a master be recorded and that, at their conclusion, the master submit to the Juvenile Court judge written findings of fact, conclusions of law, and recommendations. Either party was authorized to file exceptions and could elect a hearing on the record or a *de novo* hearing before the judge. The legislature specified that the master's "proposals and recommendations * * * for juvenile causes do not constitute orders or final action of the court." Accordingly, the judge could, even in the absence of exceptions, reject a master's recommendations and conduct a *de novo* hearing or, if the parties agreed, a hearing on the record.

In June 1975, within two months of the enactment of § 3-813 and before its July 1, 1975 effective date, the single-judge United States District Court held that the Rule 908.e provision for a *de novo* hearing on the State's exceptions violated the Double Jeopardy Clause. In that court's view, a juvenile was placed in jeopardy as soon as the State offered evidence in the hearing before a master. The court also concluded that to subject a juvenile to a *de novo* hearing before the Juvenile Court judge was to place him in jeopardy a second time. Accordingly, it granted habeas corpus relief to the six petitioners already subjected by the State to a *de novo* hearing. The petitions of the remaining three, who had not yet been brought before the Juvenile Court judge, were dismissed without prejudice as being premature.

In response to both the enactment of § 3-813 and the decision in [the federal district court], the Maryland Court of Appeals, in the exercise of its rulemaking power, promulgated a new rule, and the one currently in force, Rule 911, to govern the use of masters in juvenile proceedings. Rule 911 differs from the statute in significant aspects. First, in order to emphasize the nonfinal nature of a master's conclusions, it stresses that all of his "FINDINGS, CONCLUSIONS, RECOMMENDATIONS OR * * * ORDERS" ARE ONLY *PROPOSED*. Second, the State no longer has power to secure a *de novo* hearing before the Juvenile Court judge after unfavorable proposals by the master. The State still may file exceptions, but the judge can act on them only on the basis of the record made before the master and "such additional [relevant] evidence * * * to which the parties raise no objection."[8] The judge retains his power to accept, reject, or modify the master's proposals, to remand to the master for further hearings, and to supplement the record for his own review with additional evidence to which the parties do not object.[9]

---

8. The juvenile, after filing exceptions, can still elect either a *de novo* hearing or a hearing on the record.

9. "Rule 911, in its entirety, provides:

  a. *Authority*

    1. Detention or Shelter Care.

A master is authorized to order detention or shelter care in accordance with Rule 912 (Detention or Shelter Care) subject to an immediate review by a judge if requested by any party.

Thus, Rule 911 is a direct product of the desire of the State to continue using masters to meet the heavy burden of juvenile court caseloads while at the same time assuring that their use not violate the constitutional guarantee against double jeopardy. To this end, the Rule permits the presentation and recording of evidence in the absence of the only officer authorized by the state constitution to serve as the factfinder and judge.

After the effective date of Rule 911, July 1, 1975, the plaintiffs in the § 1983 action amended their complaint to bring Rule 911 within its scope. They continued to challenge the state procedure, however, only on the basis of the Double Jeopardy Clause. Other juveniles intervened as the ongoing work of the juvenile court brought them within the definition of the proposed class. Their complaints in intervention likewise rested only on the Double Jeopardy Clause.

The three-judge District Court certified the proposed class under Fed. Rule Civ. Proc. 23(b)(2) to consist of all juveniles involved in proceedings where the State had filed exceptions to a master's proposed findings of nondelinquency. That court then held that a juvenile subjected to a hearing before a master is placed in jeopardy, even though the master has no power to enter a final order. It also held that the Juvenile Court judge's review of the record constitutes a "second proceeding at which [the juvenile] must once again marshal whatever resources he can against the State's and at which the State is given a second opportunity to obtain a conviction." Accordingly, the three-judge District Court enjoined the defendant state officials from taking exceptions to either a master's proposed finding of nondelinquency or his proposed disposition.

---

2. Other Matters.

A master is authorized to hear any cases and matters assigned to him by the court, except a hearing on a waiver petition. The findings, conclusions and recommendations of a master do not constitute orders or final action of the court.

b. *Report to the Court.*

Within ten days following the conclusion of a disposition hearing by a master, he shall transmit to the judge the entire file in the case, together with a written report of his proposed findings of fact, conclusions of law, recommendations and proposed orders with respect to adjudication and disposition. A copy of his report and proposed order shall be served upon each party as provided by Rule 306 (Service of Pleadings and Other Papers).

c. *Review by Court if Exceptions Filed.*

Any party may file exceptions to the master's proposed findings, conclusions, recommendations or proposed orders. Exceptions shall be in writing, filed with the clerk within five days after the master's report is served upon the party, and shall specify those items to which the party excepts, and whether the hearing is to be *de novo* or on the record. A copy shall be served upon all other parties pursuant to Rule 306 (Service of Pleadings and Other Papers).

Upon the filing of exceptions, a prompt hearing shall be scheduled on the exceptions. An excepting party other than the State may elect a hearing *de novo* or a hearing on the record. If the State is the excepting party, the hearing shall be on the record, supplemented by such additional evidence as the judge considers relevant and to which the parties raise no objection. In either case the hearing shall be limited to those matters to which exceptions have been taken.

d. *Review by Court in Absence of Exceptions.*

In the absence of timely and proper exceptions, the master's proposed findings of fact, conclusions of law and recommendations may be adopted by the court and the proposed or other appropriate orders may be entered based on them. The court may remand the case to the master for further hearings, or may, on its own motion, schedule and conduct a further hearing supplemented by such additional evidence as the court considers relevant and to which the parties raise no objection. Action by the court under this section shall be taken within two days after the expiration of the time for filing exceptions."

We noted probable jurisdiction solely to determine whether the Double Jeopardy Clause prohibits state officials, acting in accordance with Rule 911, from taking exceptions to a master's proposed findings.[11]

II

The general principles governing this case are well established.

"A State may not put a defendant in jeopardy twice for the same offense. The constitutional protection against double jeopardy unequivocally prohibits a second trial following an acquittal. The public interest in the finality of criminal judgments is so strong that an acquitted defendant may not be retried even though 'the acquittal was based upon an egregiously erroneous foundation.' * * * If the innocence of the accused has been confirmed by a final judgment, the Constitution conclusively presumes that a second trial would be unfair.

Because jeopardy attaches before the judgment becomes final, the constitutional protection also embraces the defendant's 'valued right to have his trial completed by a particular tribunal.' * * * Consequently, as a general rule, the prosecutor is entitled to one, and only one, opportunity to require an accused to stand trial."

In the application of these general principles, the narrow question here[12] is whether the State in filing exceptions to a master's proposals, pursuant to Rule 911, thereby "re-

---

11. The State did not contend, either in the District Court or here, that appellees' suit for injunctive relief should be dismissed under the abstention doctrine of *Younger v. Harris*. In these circumstances, we are not inclined to examine the application of the doctrine *sua sponte*. See *Ohio Bureau of Employment Services v. Hodory* ("If the State voluntarily chooses to submit to a federal forum, principles of comity do not demand that the federal court force the case back into the State's own system").

There is also a mootness question in this case. At the time of final argument before the District Court, Fields, the last in a series of intervening plaintiffs, was the only named plaintiff with a live controversy against the State. By that time, the State had either withdrawn its exceptions against the other named plaintiffs or completed the adjudicatory process by securing a ruling, one way or the other, from the Juvenile Court judge. After final argument, but before the District Court announced its decision, the State withdrew its exceptions to the master's proposals respecting Fields. Nevertheless, the District Court, at the outset of its decision, granted Fields' motion to intervene and certified the class.

We conclude that under the principles announced in *Sosna v. Iowa*, the State's action, with respect to the original named plaintiffs and the intervenors, did not deprive the District Court of the power to certify the class action when it did and that, accordingly, a live controversy presently exists between the unnamed class members and the State. In *Sosna*, we observed: "There may be cases in which the controversy involving the named plaintiffs is such that it becomes moot as to them before the district court can reasonably be expected to rule on a certification motion. In such instances, whether the certification can be said to 'relate back' to the filing of the complaint may depend upon the circumstances of the particular case and especially the reality of the claim that otherwise the issue would evade review."

Here the rapidity of judicial review of exceptions to masters' proposals creates mootness questions with respect to named plaintiffs, and even perhaps with respect to a series of intervening plaintiffs appearing thereafter, "before the district court can reasonably be expected to rule on a certification motion."

In cases such as this one where mootness problems are likely to arise, district courts should heed strictly the requirement of Fed. Rule Civ. Proc. 23(c)(1) that "*[a]s soon as practicable* after the commencement of an action brought as a class action, the court shall determine by order whether it is to be so maintained." (Emphasis added.)

12. The State contends that jeopardy does not attach at the hearing before the master. Our decision in *Breed v. Jones*, however, suggests the contrary conclusion. "We believe it is simply too late in the day to conclude * * * that a juvenile is not put in jeopardy at a proceeding whose object is to de-

quire[s] an accused to stand trial" a second time. We hold that it does not. Maryland has created a system with Rule 911 in which an accused juvenile is subjected to a single proceeding which begins with a master's hearing and culminates with an adjudication by a judge.

Importantly, a Rule 911 proceeding does not impinge on the purposes of the Double Jeopardy Clause. A central purpose "of the prohibition against successive trials" is to bar "the prosecution [from] another opportunity to supply evidence which it failed to muster in the first proceeding." A Rule 911 proceeding does not provide the prosecution that forbidden "second crack." The State presents its evidence once before the master. The record is then closed, and additional evidence can be received by the Juvenile Court judge only with the consent of the minor.

The Double Jeopardy Clause also precludes the prosecutor from "enhanc[ing] the risk that an innocent defendant may be convicted," by taking the question of guilt to a series of persons or groups empowered to make binding determinations. Appellees contend that in its operation Rule 911 gives the State the chance to persuade two such factfinders: first the master, then the Juvenile Court judge. In support of this contention they point to evidence that juveniles and their parents sometimes consider the master "the judge" and his recommendations "the verdict." Within the limits of jury trial rights, and other constitutional constraints, it is for the State, not the parties, to designate and empower the factfinder and adjudicator. And here Maryland has conferred those roles only on the Juvenile Court judge. Thus, regardless of which party is initially favored by the master's proposals, and regardless of the presence or absence of exceptions, the judge is empowered to accept, modify, or reject those proposals.[14]

Finally, there is nothing in the record to indicate that the procedure authorized under Rule 911 unfairly subjects the defendant to the embarrassment, expense, and ordeal of a second trial proscribed in *Green v. United States*. Indeed, there is nothing to indicate that the juvenile is even brought before the judge while he conducts the "hearing on the record," or that the juvenile's attorney appears at the "hearing" and presents oral argument or written briefs. But even if there were such participation or appearance, the burdens are more akin to those resulting from a judge's permissible request for post-trial briefing or argument following a bench trial than to the "expense" of a full-blown second trial contemplated by the Court in *Green*.

In their effort to characterize a Rule 911 proceeding as two trials for double jeopardy purposes, appellees rely on two decisions of this Court, *Breed v. Jones*, and *United States v. Jenkins*.

In *Breed*, we held that a juvenile was placed twice in jeopardy when, after an adjudicatory hearing in Juvenile Court on a charge of delinquent conduct, he was transferred to adult criminal court, tried, and convicted for the same conduct. All parties conceded that jeopardy attached at the second proceeding in criminal court. The State contended,

---

termine whether he has committed acts that violate a criminal law and whose potential consequences include both the stigma inherent in such a determination and the deprivation of liberty for many years." The California juvenile proceeding reviewed in *Breed* involved the use of a referee, or master, and was not materially different—for purposes of analysis of attachment of jeopardy—from a Rule 911 proceeding.

It is not essential to decision in this case, however, to fix the precise time when jeopardy attaches.

14. It is not usual in a criminal proceeding for the evidence to be presented and recorded in the absence of the one authorized to determine guilt. But if there are any objections to such a system, they do not arise from the guarantees of the Double Jeopardy Clause.

however, that jeopardy did not attach in the Juvenile Court proceeding, although that proceeding could have culminated in a deprivation of the juvenile's liberty. We rejected this contention and also the contention that somehow jeopardy "continued" from the first to the second trial. *Breed* is therefore inapplicable to the Maryland scheme, where juveniles are subjected to only one proceeding, or "trial."

Appellees also stress this language from *Jenkins*:

> "[I]t is enough for purposes of the Double Jeopardy Clause * * * that further proceedings of some sort, devoted to the resolution of factual issues, going to the elements of the offense charged, would have been required upon reversal and remand. *Even if the District Court were to receive no additional evidence, it would still be necessary for it to make supplemental findings.* * * * [To do so] would violate the Double Jeopardy Clause."

Although we doubt that the Court's decision in a case can be correctly identified by reference to three isolated sentences, any language in *Jenkins* must now be read in light of our subsequent decision in *United States v. Scott*. In *Scott* we held that it is not all proceedings requiring the making of supplemental findings that are barred by the Double Jeopardy Clause, but only those that follow a previous trial ending in an acquittal; in a conviction either not reversed on appeal or reversed because of insufficient evidence, see *Burks v. United States, supra*, or in a mistrial ruling not prompted by "manifest necessity." A Juvenile Court judge's decision terminating a Rule 911 proceeding follows none of those occurrences. Furthermore, *Jenkins* involved appellate review of the final judgment of a trial court fully empowered to enter that judgment. Nothing comparable occurs in a Rule 911 proceeding.

To the extent the Juvenile Court judge makes supplemental findings in a manner permitted by Rule 911 — either *sua sponte*, in response to the State's exceptions, or in response to the juvenile's exceptions, and either on the record or on a record supplemented by evidence to which the parties raise no objection — he does so without violating the constraints of the Double Jeopardy Clause.

Accordingly, we reverse and remand for further proceedings consistent with this opinion.

It is so ordered.

Mr. Justice MARSHALL, with whom Mr. Justice BRENNAN and Mr. Justice POWELL join, dissenting.

Appellees are a class of juveniles who, following adjudicatory hearings on charges of criminal conduct, were found nondelinquent by a "master." Because the State has labeled the master's findings as "proposed," the Court today allows the State in effect to appeal those findings to a "judge," who is empowered to reverse the master's findings and convict the juvenile. The Court's holding is at odds with the constitutional prohibition against double jeopardy, made applicable to the States by the Due Process Clause of the Fourteenth Amendment, and specifically held to apply to juvenile proceedings in *Breed v. Jones*.

The majority does not purport to retreat from our holding in *Breed*. Yet the Court reaches a result that it would not countenance were this a criminal prosecution against an adult, for the juvenile defendants here are placed twice in jeopardy just as surely as if an adult defendant, after acquittal in a trial court, were convicted on appeal. In addition to violating the Double Jeopardy Clause, Maryland's scheme raises serious due process questions because the judge making the final adjudication of guilt has not heard the evidence and may reverse the master's findings of nondelinquency based on the judge's review of a cold record. For these reasons, I dissent.

I

While the first inquiry in any double jeopardy case must be whether jeopardy has attached, I agree with the Court that jeopardy does attach at the master's hearing. In *Breed v. Jones*, we held that jeopardy attaches "at a proceeding whose object is to determine whether [a juvenile] has committed acts that violate a criminal law." The master's hearing clearly has this as an object. Under Maryland law, the master is empowered to conduct a full "adjudicatory hearing," in order "to determine whether the allegations in the petition * * * are true."[1] And it is at this hearing that the State introduces the evidence on which it seeks to have the determination of guilt or innocence rest.

My disagreement with the Court lies in its misapplication of well-settled double jeopardy rules applicable once jeopardy has attached. As the Court itself recognizes, the Double Jeopardy Clause "unequivocally prohibits a second trial following an acquittal". Just as unequivocally, it prevents the prosecution from seeking review or reversal of a judgment of acquittal on appeal. And even where the first trial does not end in a final judgment, the "defendant's valued right to have his trial completed by a particular tribunal," absent a "'manifest necessity'" for terminating the first proceedings, is protected by this Clause.

These rules are designed to serve the underlying purposes of the Double Jeopardy Clause, the most fundamental of which is to protect an accused from the governmental harassment and oppression that can so easily arise from the massed power of the State in confrontation with an individual. As the Court recognizes, the Double Jeopardy Clause serves to preclude the State from having "'another opportunity to supply evidence which it failed to muster in the first proceeding'"; to avoid the risk that a defendant, though in fact innocent, may be convicted by a successive decisionmaker; and to prevent the State from unfairly subjecting a defendant "to the embarrassment, expense, and ordeal of a second trial." It is against these touchstones of law that the Maryland scheme must be evaluated.

A

After rejecting the State's chief argument—that jeopardy does not attach in hearings before a master—the Court reaches its result primarily by ignoring the undisputed fact that state law commits to the master a factfinding function. Admittedly, the Maryland proceedings are somewhat difficult to classify into the customary pigeonholes of double jeopardy analysis, but that is precisely because the State has engaged in a novel redefini-

---

1. Thus, unlike a preliminary hearing (to which the State analogizes a master's hearing), where the inquiry is one of probable cause, the adjudicatory hearing conducted by the master is the beginning of the unitary process designated by the State of Maryland to determine the truth of the charges. The Maryland Court of Special Appeals has rejected the State's argument that masters' hearings are not adjudicatory: "We think it within the clear contemplation of the Maryland law that the 'adjudicatory hearing' is that phase of the total proceeding whereto witnesses are summonsed [*sic*]; whereat they are sworn, confronted with the alleged delinquent, examined and cross-examined; whereat their demeanor is observed, their credibility assessed and their testimony * * * transcribed by a court reporter; whereat the alleged delinquent is represented by counsel and where he enjoys the right to remain silent * * * whereat the State's Attorney marshals and presents the [State's] evidence * * *; and whereat the presiding judge or master makes and announces his finding. * * *

"Conversely, we think it * * * equally clear * * * that the 'adjudicatory hearing' is not that phase of the proceeding, frequently conducted *ex parte* and * * * *in camera*, whereat the supervising judge ratifies, modifies or rejects the finding and recommendations of the master."

Although the *Brown* opinion was rendered prior to Maryland's revision of its rules relating to the use of masters, the record before us indicates that the character of the hearing has not materially changed since that decision.

tion of trial and appellate functions in a quasi-criminal proceeding, intentionally designed to avoid the constraints of the Double Jeopardy Clause.[2] While a State is, of course, free to designate a "master," a "judge," or some other officer to conduct juvenile adjudicatory hearings, our Constitution is not so fragile an instrument that its substantive prohibitions may be evaded by formal designations that fail to correspond with the actual functions performed.

Viewing the master and judge in terms of their relative functions, I think the appropriate analogy is between a trial judge and an appellate court with unusually broad powers of review. In the cases before us, the masters had made unequivocal findings, on the facts, that the State had not proved its case, and the State sought to have the judge overturn these findings.[3] By ignoring these functional considerations, the Court permits the State to circumvent the protections of the Double Jeopardy Clause by a mere change in the formal definitions of finality. The Court thus makes the linchpin of its holding a formalism that belies our insistence that "courts eschew * * * 'label[s]-of-convenience' * * * attached to juvenile proceedings and that 'the juvenile process * * * be candidly appraised.'"

(1)

The Court describes the Maryland system as one permitting "the presentation and recording of evidence in the absence of the only officer authorized by the state constitution * * * and by statute * * * to serve as the factfinder and judge." It is inaccurate, however, to say that only the judge is "authorized" under Maryland law to act as a factfinder.[4] The master does not simply act as a referee at the hearing, deciding evidentiary questions and creating a record placed before the judge. Rather, Rule 911 directs that, at the end of the disposition hearing (which follows the adjudicatory hearing), the master "transmit to the judge the entire file in the case, together with a written report of his proposed findings of fact, conclusions of law, recommendations and proposed orders with respect to adjudication and disposition."[5]

---

2. In response to an earlier decision holding that a second hearing before the judge, when the State excepted to the master's findings of nondelinquency, violated the Double Jeopardy Clause, the State of Maryland modified its procedures to preclude a new hearing before the juvenile judge on the State's exceptions, unless both "parties" consent. Following passage of these amended rules, the State moved to dismiss the instant proceeding as moot; the motion was denied.

3. For example, in one instance, the State's case rested on the identification testimony of the victim of a bicycle theft. At the close of the evidence the master announced that, because he was not persuaded beyond a reasonable doubt of the accuracy of the witness' identification, especially since it was uncorroborated, he found the defendant not guilty. On the State's exception, the juvenile judge convicted the defendant.

4. It is not disputed here that, under the Maryland State Constitution, the State may validly delegate to masters authority to make proposed findings of fact under Rule 911.

5. We therefore need not rely on appellees' statistical proof, convincing as it may be, to conclude that in Maryland masters are supposed to find facts. Appellees' evidence, however, supports this interpretation of Maryland law.

In Baltimore City in 1975 and 1976, there were seven masters and one Juvenile Court Judge. The District Court found that, except when the State filed an exception, all of the masters' recommended findings of nondelinquency had been approved by the judge.

Moreover, the first judge presented with appellees' double jeopardy claim—the state trial judge serving as the only Juvenile Court Judge in Baltimore from 1967–1975—agreed with the juveniles that permitting the State to take exceptions violated the Double Jeopardy Clause. His conclusion rested in part on his perception that "it is impossible for the Judge * * *, who also carries a full docket of cases himself, to exercise any independent, meaningful judgment in the overwhelming majority of the many thousands of [masters'] orders put before him each year * * *. With this being the case it is difficult to see how realistically a Master can be called only an adviser * * *. [T]he Master conducts, for all intents and purposes, full blown and complete proceedings through the adjudicatory and dispositional

That Maryland contemplates an actual factfinding function for the master is emphasized by the fact that neither the Rule nor the statute requires the "judge" to read the entire record, listen to the tape recording of the adjudicatory hearing, or otherwise expose himself to the full factual record as it was presented to the master. Indeed, the Rule expressly recognizes that the judge may enter his order "based on" the master's findings. Rule 911(d). The master himself thus serves as a factfinder of first instance; while his findings are only "proposed," they may be accepted by the judge without an independent review of the entire record.

(2)

In *Kepner v. United States*, we held that the Double Jeopardy Clause prohibited an appellate court in the Philippines from reversing a verdict of acquittal rendered by the trial court in a bench trial and entering a verdict of guilty.[6] The Government had argued that, under controlling Spanish law, "[t]he original trial is a unitary and continuous thing, and is not complete until the appellate court has pronounced judgment." This Court, however, held that American constitutional law governed and that the Double Jeopardy Clause prohibited the Government from appealing a judgment of acquittal entered by the first trier of facts. In so holding, the Court rejected Mr. Justice Holmes' "continuing jeopardy" argument, an argument that we have consistently refused to adopt, and to which the State's position here bears an uncomfortable resemblance.

There are, of course, differences between *Kepner* and the instant case. In *Kepner* the court of first instance apparently had authority to enter an adjudication that would be final absent an appeal by either party, whereas here the masters do not have power to enter a final order of acquittal. But as we have repeatedly emphasized, an "acquittal" is not necessarily determined by the form of the order. As the *Kepner* Court noted in support of its holding that a bench acquittal could not be appealed, a jury verdict of acquittal, even when not followed by a formal judgment of the trial court, bars further proceedings under the Double Jeopardy Clause. Here, while the master does not formally make a final adjudication, in all other respects his proposed finding of nondelinquency is fully equivalent to an acquittal: after a plenary adjudicatory hearing, he makes "a resolution, correct or not, of some or all of the factual elements of the offense charged." And the State's exception to the master's finding of nondelinquency engenders the same anxiety and burden as would a State's appeal from an adult court's verdict of acquittal.

The Court's rationale allows States to avoid the *Kepner* holding by the simple expedient of changing the definitions of finality without changing the functions performed by judges at different levels of decision. The decision today might well be read to hold that the Double Jeopardy Clause is no bar to structuring a juvenile justice system or, for that

---

phases and * * * as a practical matter he imposes sanctions and can effectively deprive youngsters of their freedom."

The Juvenile Court Judge's decision was ultimately reversed on appeal.

A report of the State Commission on Juvenile Justice in January 1977, after spending 18 months studying the Maryland juvenile courts, reached the same conclusion: "[W]ithout bearing legal responsibility for his decisions, the Master's recommended decisions become, in effect, final orders of the Court."

6. In *Kepner*, the Court was technically construing an Act of Congress extending certain procedural protections to criminal trials conducted in the Philippines, which was a United States possession. However, the Court made clear that it construed the statutory language to incorporate the constitutional principles of double jeopardy, and its decision is thus properly regarded by the Court today as a constitutional one.

matter, an adult criminal justice system so as to have several layers of adjudication, none of which is final until the State has exhausted its last appeal.[8] This proliferation of levels at which a defendant—juvenile or adult—must defend himself against an adjudication of guilt is precisely the kind of evil that the Double Jeopardy Clause was designed to forbid. Yet under the Court's rationale, this is seemingly permissible so long as the State takes care to define the lower levels of decisionmaking as only "proposed" or "tentative" in nature, thereby commingling traditional trial and appellate functions.

B

Even if the master's findings are not regarded as an acquittal, the Double Jeopardy Clause does more than simply protect acquittals from review on direct appeal. It also protects the defendant's right to go to judgment before a "particular tribunal" once jeopardy has attached, absent a "'manifest necessity'" justifying termination of the first proceeding. This rule is designed in part to ensure that the government not be able to bolster its case by additional evidence or arguments, once it believes that its evidence has not persuaded the first tribunal. But the Maryland system is structured so as to give the State precisely this type of proscribed opportunity, where it disagrees with the favorable rulings of the first trier of fact.

As recognized by the Court, jeopardy attaches at the master's hearing. This hearing is a formal, adjudicatory proceeding at which the State's witnesses testify and are cross-examined; the juvenile may present evidence in his own defense; and the juvenile is entitled to counsel and to remain silent. Presentation of evidence at that proceeding is keyed to the reactions and attitudes of the presiding master, who acts, for purposes of the adjudicatory hearing, as the "particular tribunal." A juvenile who has had such a hearing may justifiably expect that, when the master who has heard all this evidence announces a finding in his favor, it will be final. But a juvenile tried before a master in Maryland is never, as a matter of law, entitled to have his trial "completed" before the master, since his recommendations must be confirmed by the judge and may be ignored by him.

Thus, endemic to the Maryland system is a kind of interrupted proceeding which ensures that the defendant cannot get the benefit of the first trier of fact's reaction to the evidence. The system thereby poses a substantial risk that innocent defendants may be found guilty, since it allows the State a second opportunity to persuade a decisionmaker of the juvenile's guilt, after the first trier of fact has concluded that the State has not proved its case. Unless justified by a "manifest necessity"—not present here—the Double Jeopardy Clause condemns such a system. The "underlying idea" of the Double Jeopardy Clause "is that the State with all its resources and power should not be allowed to make repeated attempts to convict an individual for an alleged offense, thereby subjecting him to embarrassment, expense and ordeal and compelling him to live in a continuing state of anxiety and insecurity, as well as enhancing the possibility that even though innocent he may be found guilty."

For these reasons, I conclude that the Maryland Rule, insofar as it permits a judge to review and set aside a master's findings favorable to the defendant on the facts of the case, violates the Double Jeopardy Clause.

---

8. Thus, for example, a State might provide that in all bench trials, a judgment of acquittal does not become "final" for a certain amount of time in which an appellate court may review it. While this is an unlikely eventuality, it points up the fallacy in the Court's reasoning. Fortunately, the damage done by the Court's holding today is limited in its application by the Sixth Amendment right to a jury trial. Not only would it offend the Double Jeopardy Clause for a jury's verdict of acquittal to be set aside (whether or not a judgment were entered on the verdict), but it would also dilute the constitutional right to a jury trial in criminal cases. The jury trial right has been held inapplicable to juvenile proceedings, however.

II

As the majority accurately states, the only issue raised in the complaints or focused upon in the parties' briefs was that of double jeopardy. It is argued by *amicus*, however, that the Maryland system, even if it were found to avoid double jeopardy problems, violates the Due Process Clause by permitting ultimate factfinding by a judge who did not actually conduct the trial. The Court does not reach this issue, apparently believing that it is not properly presented here.[10] It is thus important to emphasize that the Maryland system and ones like it have not been held constitutional today; the Court's only holding is that such systems are not unconstitutional under the Double Jeopardy Clause. It is entirely open to this Court, and lower courts, to find in another case that a system like that in Maryland violates the Due Process Clause.

In *In re Winship*, we held that a juvenile accused of a crime may be convicted only upon proof beyond a reasonable doubt, even if he is prosecuted in a juvenile court. The rationale of *Winship* suggests that the Due Process Clause requires the most reliable procedures to be used in making the reasonable-doubt determination in juvenile proceedings. As we have repeatedly emphasized: "To experienced lawyers it is commonplace that the outcome of a lawsuit — and hence the vindication of legal rights — depends more often on how the factfinder appraises the facts than on a disputed construction of a statute * * * Thus the procedures by which the facts of the case are determined assume an importance fully as great as the validity of the substantive rule of law to be applied."

Over 30 years ago, we recognized the importance to a reliable factfinding process of hearing live witnesses. The issue there was whether, on a federal habeas corpus petition, a District Judge could utilize a United States Commissioner to hold the evidentiary hearing and make recommended findings of fact and conclusions of law. Although our holding that the prisoner had a right to testify and present his evidence before a judge was a statutory one, our reasoning went to the fundamental nature of the kind of factfinding on which many judicial determinations must rest:

> "One of the essential elements of the determination of the crucial facts is the weighing and appraising of the testimony. * * * We cannot say that an appraisal of the truth of the prisoner's oral testimony by a master or commissioner is, in the light of the purpose and object of the proceeding, the equivalent of the judge's own exercise of the function of the trier of the facts."

Four Terms ago, we adhered to this view, holding that the successor habeas corpus statute also required the district judge personally to conduct evidentiary hearings in habeas corpus cases. We not only disapproved the practice of referring evidentiary hearings to masters, but also held that the judge's listening to an electronic recording of the testimony was no substitute for his personally hearing and observing the witnesses to evaluate their credibility.

---

10. Although the Court does not reach this issue, I believe it would be within its power to do so. Affirming the judgment below on this ground would not have the effect of expanding the relief granted: an injunction against the State's taking of exceptions. While the due process claim was not raised in appellees' complaints, it was argued in substance to the District Court in opposition to appellants' motion to dismiss the complaint. Moreover, appellees' brief here makes the following argument: "It is only logical to assume that if a case is tried before enough judicial officers, one of them will eventually conclude that the defendant is guilty beyond a reasonable doubt * * *. [S]uch a process would emasculate this Court's decision in *In re Winship*." While this is not identical to the due process argument urged by *amicus*, it illustrates the intimate relationship between the double jeopardy and due process problems inherent in the Maryland scheme.

These decisions arose in the context of habeas corpus proceedings, where the prisoner has the burden of demonstrating that he is being held in violation of the Constitution. In a criminal proceeding, where the issue posed is the threshold one of whether a defendant has been proved guilty of a crime beyond a reasonable doubt, the same considerations surely have at least as much force. Indeed, the need for achieving the most reliable determinations of evidentiary facts, and particularly of credibility, exists *a fortiori* where the factual determinations must be made beyond a reasonable doubt.

As the Maryland courts have held, and as is self-evident from the structure of Rule 911, the master's function at the hearing is, in large part, to assess the credibility of the witnesses. That function simply cannot be replicated by the "judge," acting in his essentially appellate capacity reviewing the record; as *amicus* cogently notes, "[t]rials-by-transcript can never be more than trials by substantial evidence." It would thus appear that the Maryland system of splitting the hearing of evidence from the final adjudication violates the Due Process Clause.

It is no answer to this problem that the juvenile defendant may elect to submit additional material to the judge when the State takes an exception to the master's finding. In the first place, the State apparently must agree to the supplementation of the record, and can thus stymie a defendant's efforts to persuade the judge that he is not guilty. But more importantly, when a juvenile seeks to reopen the proceeding before the judge—in order to avoid having a case decided against him on the basis of a cold record in violation of the Due Process Clause—he is being subjected to a second trial of the sort clearly prohibited by the Double Jeopardy Clause. The constitutionality of forcing a juvenile to such a choice between fundamental rights is questionable at best.

III

That the current Maryland scheme cannot pass constitutional muster does not necessarily mean that the idea of using masters, or some other class of specially trained or selected personnel for juvenile court adjudications, is either unconstitutional or unwise. Using masters to adjudicate the more common charges may save scarce judicial resources for the more difficult cases. It may also aid the ultimate goals of a juvenile justice system by ensuring that the decisionmakers have some familiarity with the special problems of juvenile dispositions. But the State must find a way of implementing this concept without jeopardizing the constitutional rights of juveniles. Whether it does so by endowing masters with the power to make final adjudications or by some other means, matters not. What does matter is that, absent compelling circumstances not present here, the system of juvenile justice in this country must not be permitted to fall below the minimum constitutional standards set for adult criminal proceedings.

Accordingly, I dissent.

Notes

(a) Is *Swisher* compatible with *Breed*? In what ways?

(b) What happened to the *Breed* Court's test relating to the unique benefits of the juvenile court system? Using that test what should be the result in *Swisher*?

(c) The *Swisher* majority upheld the Maryland court rule using only Double Jeopardy analysis. Is the Due Process claim stronger or weaker?

(d) In what way (or ways) is *Swisher* different from the Court's prior delinquency cases in terms of constitutional analysis?

Fare v. Michael C.

442 U.S. 707 (1979)

Mr. Justice BLACKMUN delivered the opinion of the Court.

In *Miranda v. Arizona,* this Court established certain procedural safeguards designed to protect the rights of an accused, under the Fifth and Fourteenth Amendments, to be free from compelled self-incrimination during custodial interrogation. The Court specified, among other things, that if the accused indicates in any manner that he wishes to remain silent or to consult an attorney, interrogation must cease, and any statement obtained from him during interrogation thereafter may not be admitted against him at his trial.

In this case, the State of California, in the person of its acting chief probation officer, attacks the conclusion of the Supreme Court of California that a juvenile's request, made while undergoing custodial interrogation, to see his *probation officer* is *per se* an invocation of the juvenile's Fifth Amendment rights as pronounced in *Miranda.*

I

Respondent Michael C. was implicated in the murder of Robert Yeager. The murder occurred during a robbery of the victim's home on January 19, 1976. A small truck registered in the name of respondent's mother was identified as having been near the Yeager home at the time of the killing, and a young man answering respondent's description was seen by witnesses near the truck and near the home shortly before Yeager was murdered.

On the basis of this information, Van Nuys, Cal., police took respondent into custody at approximately 6:30 p.m. on February 4. Respondent then was 16 years old and on probation to the Juvenile Court. He had been on probation since the age of 12. Approximately one year earlier he had served a term in a youth corrections camp under the supervision of the Juvenile Court. He had a record of several previous offenses, including burglary of guns and purse snatching, stretching back over several years.

Upon respondent's arrival at the Van Nuys station house two police officers began to interrogate him. The officers and respondent were the only persons in the room during the interrogation. The conversation was tape-recorded. One of the officers initiated the interview by informing respondent that he had been brought in for questioning in relation to a murder. The officer fully advised respondent of his *Miranda* rights. The following exchange then occurred, as set out in the opinion of the California Supreme Court,

Q. ... Do you understand all of these rights as I have explained them to you?

A. Yeah.

Q. Okay, do you wish to give up your right to remain silent and talk to us about this murder?

A. What murder? I don't know about no murder.

Q. I'll explain to you which one it is if you want to talk to us about it.

A. Yeah, I might talk to you.

Q. Do you want to give up your right to have an attorney present here while we talk about it?

A. *Can I have my probation officer here?*

Q. Well I can't get a hold of your probation officer right now. You have the right to an attorney.

A. How I know you guys won't pull no police officer in and tell me he's an attorney?

Q. Huh?

A. [How I know you guys won't pull no police officer in and tell me he's an attorney?]

Q. Your probation officer is Mr. Christiansen.

A. Yeah.

Q. Well I'm not going to call Mr. Christiansen tonight. There's a good chance we can talk to him later, but I'm not going to call him right now. If you want to talk to us without an attorney present, you can. If you don't want to, you don't have to. But if you want to say something, you can, and if you don't want to say something you don't have to. That's your right. You understand that right?

A. Yeah.

Q. Okay, will you talk to us without an attorney present?

A. Yeah[,] I want to talk to you.

Respondent thereupon proceeded to answer questions put to him by the officers. He made statements and drew sketches that incriminated him in the Yeager murder.

Largely on the basis of respondent's incriminating statements, probation authorities filed a petition in Juvenile Court alleging that respondent had murdered Robert Yeager, and that respondent therefore should be adjudged a ward of the Juvenile Court. Respondent thereupon moved to suppress the statements and sketches he gave the police during the interrogation. He alleged that the statements had been obtained in violation of *Miranda* in that his request to see his probation officer at the outset of the questioning constituted an invocation of his Fifth Amendment right to remain silent, just as if he had requested the assistance of an attorney. Accordingly, respondent argued that since the interrogation did not cease until he had a chance to confer with his probation officer, the statements and sketches could not be admitted against him in the Juvenile Court proceedings. In so arguing, respondent relied by analogy on the decision in *People v. Burton*, where the Supreme Court of California had held that a minor's request, made during custodial interrogation, to see his parents constituted an invocation of the minor's Fifth Amendment rights.

In support of his suppression motion, respondent called his probation officer, Charles P. Christiansen, as a witness. Christiansen testified that he had instructed respondent that if at any time he had "a concern with his family," or ever had "a police contact," he should get in touch with his probation officer immediately. The witness stated that, on a previous occasion, when respondent had had a police contact and had failed to communicate with Christiansen, the probation officer had reprimanded him. This testimony, respondent argued, indicated that when he asked for his probation officer, he was in fact asserting his right to remain silent in the face of further questioning.

In a ruling from the bench, the court denied the motion to suppress. It held that the question whether respondent had waived his right to remain silent was one of fact to be determined on a case-by-case basis, and that the facts of this case showed a "clear waiver" by respondent of that right. The court observed that the transcript of the interrogation revealed that respondent specifically had told the officers that he would talk with them, and that this waiver had come at the outset of the interrogation and not after prolonged questioning. The court noted that respondent was a "16 and a half year old minor who has been through the court system before, has been to [probation] camp, has a probation officer, [and is not] a young, naive minor with no experience with the courts." Accordingly, it found that on the facts of the case respondent had waived his Fifth Amendment rights, notwithstanding the request to see his probation officer.[2]

On appeal, the Supreme Court of California took the case by transfer from the California Court of Appeal and, by a divided vote, reversed. The court held that respondent's "request to see his probation officer at the commencement of interrogation negated any possible willingness on his part to discuss his case with the police [and] thereby invoked his Fifth Amendment privilege." The court based this conclusion on its view that, because of the juvenile court system's emphasis on the relationship between a probation officer and the probationer, the officer was "a trusted guardian figure who exercises the authority of the state as *parens patriae* and whose duty it is to implement the protective and rehabilitative powers of the juvenile court." As a consequence, the court found that a minor's request for his probation officer was the same as a request to see his parents during interrogation, and thus under the rule of *Burton* constituted an invocation of the minor's Fifth Amendment rights.

The fact that the probation officer also served as a peace officer, and, whenever a proceeding against a juvenile was contemplated, was charged with a duty to file a petition alleging that the minor had committed an offense, did not alter, in the court's view, the fact that the officer in the eyes of the juvenile was a trusted guardian figure to whom the minor normally would turn for help when in trouble with the police. Relying on *Burton*, the court ruled that it would unduly restrict *Miranda* to limit its reach in a case involving a minor to a request by the minor for an attorney, since it would be "'fatuous to assume that a minor in custody will be in a position to call an attorney for assistance and it is unrealistic to attribute no significance to his call for help from the only person to whom he normally looks—a parent or guardian.'" The court dismissed the concern expressed by the State that a request for a probation officer could not be distinguished from a request for one's football coach, music teacher, or clergyman on the ground that the probation officer, unlike those other figures in the juvenile's life, was charged by statute to represent the interests of the juvenile.

The court accordingly held that the probation officer would act to protect the minor's Fifth Amendment rights in precisely the way an attorney would act if called for by the accused. In so holding, the court found the request for a probation officer to be a *per se* invocation of Fifth Amendment rights in the same way the request for an attorney was found in *Miranda* to be, regardless of what the interrogation otherwise might reveal. In rejecting a totality-of-the-circumstances inquiry, the court stated:

> "Here, however, we face conduct which, regardless of considerations of capacity, coercion or voluntariness, per se invokes the privilege against self-incrimination.

---

2. The California Court of Appeal ... noted that since the Juvenile Court's findings of fact resolved against respondent his contention that the confession had been coerced from him by threats and promises, it would have to "conclude that there was a knowing and intelligent waiver of the minor's *Miranda* rights unless it can be said that the request to speak to a probation officer was in and of itself sufficient to invoke" respondent's Fifth Amendment privilege. It refused to extend the rule of *People v. Burton* to include a request for a probation officer, finding it difficult to distinguish such a request from a request to see "one's football coach, music teacher or clergyman." Even if the *Burton* rule were applicable, the court held, there was sufficient evidence of an affirmative waiver of his rights by respondent to distinguish *Burton,* where the California Supreme Court had noted that there was "nothing in the way of affirmative proof that defendant did not intend to assert his privilege."

Thus our question turns not on whether the [respondent] had the ability, capacity or willingness to give a knowledgeable waiver, and hence whether he acted voluntarily, but whether, when he called for his probation officer, he exercised his Fifth Amendment privilege. We hold that in doing so he no less invoked the protection against self-incrimination than if he asked for the presence of an attorney."

The court went on to conclude that since the State had not met its "burden of proving that a minor who requests to see his probation officer does not intend to assert his Fifth Amendment privilege," the trial court should not have admitted the confessions obtained after respondent had requested his probation officer.[3]

The State of California petitioned this Court for a writ of certiorari. Mr. Justice REHNQUIST, as Circuit Justice, stayed the execution of the mandate of the Supreme Court of California. Because the California judgment extending the *per se* aspects of *Miranda* presents an important question about the reach of that case, we thereafter issued the writ.

II

We note at the outset that it is clear that the judgment of the California Supreme Court rests firmly on that court's interpretation of federal law. This Court, however, has not heretofore extended the *per se* aspects of the *Miranda* safeguards beyond the scope of the holding in the *Miranda* case itself.[4] We therefore must examine the California court's decision to determine whether that court's conclusion so to extend *Miranda* is in harmony

---

3. Two justices concurred in the court's opinion and judgment. They expressed concern that a probation officer's public responsibilities would make it difficult for him to offer legal advice to a minor implicated in a crime, and that a minor advised to cooperate with the police, perhaps even to confess, justifiably could complain later "that he had been subjected to a variation of the Mutt-and-Jeff technique criticized in *Miranda*: initial interrogating by overbearing officers, then comforting by a presumably friendly and gentle peace officer in the guise of a probation officer."

Two justices dissented. They would have affirmed respondent's conviction on the basis of the finding of the Juvenile Court that, in light of all the circumstances surrounding the interrogation of respondent, there was sufficient affirmative proof that respondent had waived his privilege.

The dissenters pointed out that the opinion of the court was confusing in holding, on the one hand, that the request for a probation officer was *per se* an invocation of the minor's Fifth Amendment rights, and, on the other, that reversal was required because the State had not carried its burden of proving that respondent, by requesting his probation officer, did not intend thereby to assert his Fifth Amendment privilege.

There may well be ambiguity in this regard. On the basis of that ambiguity, respondent argues that the California court did not establish a *per se* rule, but held only that on the facts here respondent's request to see his probation officer constituted an invocation of his Fifth Amendment rights. The decision in *People v. Randall*, upon which the California court relied in both *Burton* and the present case, however, indicates that the court did indeed establish a *per se* rule in this case. In *Randall*, the court stated that even though a suspect might have invoked his Fifth Amendment rights by asking for counsel or by stating he wished to remain silent, it might be possible that subsequent voluntary statements of the accused, not prompted by custodial interrogation, would be admissible if the State could show that they were the product of the voluntary decision of the accused to waive the rights he had asserted.

Randall thus indicates that the *per se* language employed by the California Supreme Court in this case is compatible with the finding that the State could have negated the *per se* effect of the request for a probation officer by showing that, notwithstanding his *per se* invocation of his rights, respondent later voluntarily decided to waive those rights and volunteer statements. In light of *Randall*, and in light of the strong *per se* language used by the California Supreme Court in its opinion in this case, we think that any ambiguity in that opinion must be resolved in favor of a conclusion that the court did in fact establish a *per se* rule.

4. Indeed, this Court has not yet held that *Miranda* applies with full force to exclude evidence obtained in violation of its proscriptions from consideration in juvenile proceedings, which for certain purposes have been distinguished from formal criminal prosecutions. We do not decide that issue

with *Miranda's* underlying principles. For it is clear that "a State may not impose * * * greater restrictions as a matter of *federal constitutional law* when this Court specifically refrains from imposing them."

The rule the Court established in *Miranda* is clear. In order to be able to use statements obtained during custodial interrogation of the accused, the State must warn the accused prior to such questioning of his right to remain silent and of his right to have counsel, retained or appointed, present during interrogation. "Once [such] warnings have been given, the subsequent procedure is clear.

If the individual indicates in any manner, at any time prior to or during questioning, that he wishes to remain silent, the interrogation must cease. At this point he has shown that he intends to exercise his Fifth Amendment privilege; any statement taken after the person invokes his privilege cannot be other than the product of compulsion, subtle or otherwise. * * * If the individual states that he wants an attorney, the interrogation must cease until an attorney is present. At that time, the individual must have an opportunity to confer with the attorney and to have him present during any subsequent questioning. If the individual cannot obtain an attorney and he indicates that he wants one before speaking to police, they must respect his decision to remain silent."

Any statements obtained during custodial interrogation conducted in violation of these rules may not be admitted against the accused, at least during the State's case in chief.

Whatever the defects, if any, of this relatively rigid requirement that interrogation must cease upon the accused's request for an attorney, *Miranda's* holding has the virtue of informing police and prosecutors with specificity as to what they may do in conducting custodial interrogation, and of informing courts under what circumstances statements obtained during such interrogation are not admissible. This gain in specificity, which benefits the accused and the State alike, has been thought to outweigh the burdens that the decision in *Miranda* imposes on law enforcement agencies and the courts by requiring the suppression of trustworthy and highly probative evidence even though the confession might be voluntary under traditional Fifth Amendment analysis.[*]

The California court in this case, however, significantly has extended this rule by providing that a request by a juvenile for his probation officer has the same effect as a request for an attorney. Based on the court's belief that the probation officer occupies a position as a trusted guardian figure in the minor's life that would make it normal for the minor to turn to the officer when apprehended by the police, and based as well on the state-law requirement that the officer represent the interest of the juvenile, the California decision found that consultation with a probation officer fulfilled the role for the juvenile that consultation with an attorney does in general, acting as a "'protective [device] * * * to dispel the compulsion inherent in custodial surroundings.'"

The rule in *Miranda*, however, was based on this Court's perception that the lawyer occupies a critical position in our legal system because of his unique ability to protect the Fifth Amendment rights of a client undergoing custodial interrogation. Because of this special ability of the lawyer to help the client preserve his Fifth Amendment rights once the client becomes enmeshed in the adversary process, the Court found that "the right to have counsel present at the interrogation is indispensable to the protection of the Fifth

---

today. In view of our disposition of this case, we assume without deciding that the *Miranda* principles were fully applicable to the present proceedings.

* [Prior to *Miranda*, determinations of volunariness of confessions in state court proceedings were made under the *Due Process* clause of the *Fourteenth Amendment*.— Eds.]

Amendment privilege under the system" established by the Court. Moreover, the lawyer's presence helps guard against overreaching by the police and ensures that any statements actually obtained are accurately transcribed for presentation into evidence.

The *per se* aspect of *Miranda* was thus based on the unique role the lawyer plays in the adversary system of criminal justice in this country. Whether it is a minor or an adult who stands accused, the lawyer is the one person to whom society as a whole looks as the protector of the legal rights of that person in his dealings with the police and the courts. For this reason, the Court fashioned in *Miranda* the rigid rule that an accused's request for an attorney is *per se* an invocation of his Fifth Amendment rights, requiring that all interrogation cease.

A probation officer is not in the same posture with regard to either the accused or the system of justice as a whole. Often he is not trained in the law, and so is not in a position to advise the accused as to his legal rights. Neither is he a trained advocate, skilled in the representation of the interests of his client before both police and courts. He does not assume the power to act on behalf of his client by virtue of his status as adviser, nor are the communications of the accused to the probation officer shielded by the lawyer-client privilege.

Moreover, the probation officer is the employee of the State which seeks to prosecute the alleged offender. He is a peace officer, and as such is allied, to a greater or lesser extent, with his fellow peace officers. He owes an obligation to the State, notwithstanding the obligation he may also owe the juvenile under his supervision. In most cases, the probation officer is duty bound to report wrongdoing by the juvenile when it comes to his attention, even if by communication from the juvenile himself. Indeed, when this case arose, the probation officer had the responsibility for filing the petition alleging wrongdoing by the juvenile and seeking to have him taken into the custody of the Juvenile Court. It was respondent's probation officer who filed the petition against him, and it is the acting chief of probation for the State of California, a probation officer, who is petitioner in this Court today.[5]

In these circumstances, it cannot be said that the probation officer is able to offer the type of independent advice that an accused would expect from a lawyer retained or as-

---

5. When this case arose, a California statute provided that a proceeding in juvenile court to declare a minor a ward of the court was to be commenced by the filing of a petition by a probation officer. This provision since has been amended to provide that most such petitions are to be filed by the prosecuting attorney. Respondent argues that, whatever the status of the probation officer as a peace officer at the time this case arose, the amendment indicates that in the future a probation officer is not to be viewed as a legal adversary of the accused juvenile. Consequently, respondent believes that any holding of this Court with regard to respondent's 1976 request for a probation officer will be mere dictum with regard to a juvenile's similar request today.

We disagree. The fact that a California probation officer in 1976 was responsible for initiating a complaint is only one factor in our analysis. The fact remains that a probation officer does not fulfill the role in our system of criminal justice that an attorney does, regardless of whether he acts merely as a counselor or has significant law enforcement duties. And in California, as in many States, the other duties of a probation officer are incompatible with the view that he may act as a counselor to a juvenile accused of crime. The very California statute that imposes upon the probation officer the duty to represent the interests of the juvenile also provides: "It shall be the duty of the probation officer to prepare for every hearing [of criminal charges against a juvenile] a social study of the minor, containing such matters as may be relevant to a proper disposition of the case."

Similarly, a probation officer is required, upon the order of the juvenile court or the Youth Authority, to investigate the circumstances surrounding the charge against the minor and to file written reports and recommendations. And a probation officer in California continues to have the powers and authority of a peace officer in connection with any violation of a criminal statute that is discovered by the probation officer in the course of his probation activities. The duties of a peace officer, like the investigative and reporting duties of probation officers, are incompatible with the role of legal adviser to a juvenile accused of crime.

signed to assist him during questioning. Indeed, the probation officer's duty to his employer in many, if not most, cases would conflict sharply with the interests of the juvenile. For where an attorney might well advise his client to remain silent in the face of interrogation by the police, and in doing so would be "exercising [his] good professional judgment * * * to protect to the extent of his ability the rights of his client," *Miranda,* a probation officer would be bound to advise his charge to cooperate with the police. The justices who concurred in the opinion of the California Supreme Court in this case aptly noted: "Where a conflict between the minor and the law arises, the probation officer can be neither neutral nor in the minor's corner." It thus is doubtful that a general rule can be established that a juvenile, in every case, looks to his probation officer as a "trusted guardian figure" rather than as an officer of the court system that imposes punishment.

By the same token, a lawyer is able to protect his client's rights by learning the extent, if any, of the client's involvement in the crime under investigation, and advising his client accordingly. To facilitate this, the law rightly protects the communications between client and attorney from discovery. We doubt, however, that similar protection will be afforded the communications between the probation officer and the minor. Indeed, we doubt that a probation officer, consistent with his responsibilities to the public and his profession, could withhold from the police or the courts facts made known to him by the juvenile implicating the juvenile in the crime under investigation.

We thus believe it clear that the probation officer is not in a position to offer the type of legal assistance necessary to protect the Fifth Amendment rights of an accused undergoing custodial interrogation that a lawyer can offer. The Court in *Miranda* recognized that "the attorney plays a vital role in the administration of criminal justice under our Constitution." It is this pivotal role of legal counsel that justifies the *per se* rule established in *Miranda,* and that distinguishes the request for counsel from the request for a probation officer, a clergyman, or a close friend. A probation officer simply is not necessary, in the way an attorney is, for the protection of the legal rights of the accused, juvenile or adult. He is significantly handicapped by the position he occupies in the juvenile system from serving as an effective protector of the rights of a juvenile suspected of a crime.

The California Supreme Court, however, found that the close relationship between juveniles and their probation officers compelled the conclusion that a probation officer, for purposes of *Miranda,* was sufficiently like a lawyer to justify extension of the *per se* rule. The fact that a relationship of trust and cooperation between a probation officer and a juvenile might exist, however, does not indicate that the probation officer is capable of rendering effective legal advice sufficient to protect the juvenile's rights during interrogation by the police, or of providing the other services rendered by a lawyer. To find otherwise would be "an extension of the *Miranda* requirements [that] would cut this Court's holding in that case completely loose from its own explicitly stated rationale." Such an extension would impose the burdens associated with the rule of *Miranda* on the juvenile justice system and the police without serving the interests that rule was designed simultaneously to protect. If it were otherwise, a juvenile's request for almost anyone he considered trustworthy enough to give him reliable advice would trigger the rigid rule of *Miranda.*

Similarly, the fact that the State has created a statutory duty on the part of the probation officer to protect the interests of the juvenile does not render the probation officer any more capable of rendering legal assistance to the juvenile or of protecting his legal rights, especially in light of the fact that the State has also legislated a duty on the part of the officer to report wrongdoing by the juvenile and serve the ends of the juvenile court system. The State cannot transmute the relationship between probation officer and juvenile offender into the type of relationship between attorney and client that was essential to the holding of *Miranda* simply by legislating an amorphous "duty to advise and care for the juvenile defendant." Though such a statutory duty might serve to distinguish to some degree the probation officer from the coach and the clergyman, it does not justify the extension of *Miranda* to requests to see probation officers. If it did, the State could expand the class of persons covered by the *Miranda per se* rule simply by creating a duty to care for the juvenile on the part of other persons, regardless of whether the logic of *Miranda* would justify that extension.

Nor do we believe that a request by a juvenile to speak with his probation officer constitutes a *per se* request to remain silent. As indicated, since a probation officer does not fulfill the important role in protecting the rights of the accused juvenile that an attorney plays, we decline to find that the request for the probation officer is tantamount to the request for an attorney. And there is nothing inherent in the request for a probation officer that requires us to find that a juvenile's request to see one necessarily constitutes an expression of the juvenile's right to remain silent. As discussed below, courts may take into account such a request in evaluating whether a juvenile in fact had waived his Fifth Amendment rights before confessing. But in other circumstances such a request might well be consistent with a desire to speak with the police. In the absence of further evidence that the minor intended in the circumstances to invoke his Fifth Amendment rights by such a request, we decline to attach such overwhelming significance to this request.

We hold, therefore, that it was error to find that the request by respondent to speak with his probation officer *per se* constituted an invocation of respondent's Fifth Amendment right to be free from compelled self-incrimination. It therefore was also error to hold that because the police did not then cease interrogating respondent the statements he made during interrogation should have been suppressed.

III

Miranda further recognized that after the required warnings are given the accused, "[i]f the interrogation continues without the presence of an attorney and a statement is taken, a heavy burden rests on the government to demonstrate that the defendant knowingly and intelligently waived his privilege against self-incrimination and his right to retained or appointed counsel." We noted in *North Carolina v. Butler*, that the question whether the accused waived his rights "is not one of form, but rather whether the defendant in fact knowingly and voluntarily waived the rights delineated in the *Miranda* case." Thus, the determination whether statements obtained during custodial interrogation are admissible against the accused is to be made upon an inquiry into the totality of the circumstances surrounding the interrogation, to ascertain whether the accused in fact knowingly and voluntarily decided to forgo his rights to remain silent and to have the assistance of counsel.

This totality-of-the-circumstances approach is adequate to determine whether there has been a waiver even where interrogation of juveniles is involved. We discern no persuasive reasons why any other approach is required where the question is whether a juvenile has waived his rights, as opposed to whether an adult has done so. The totality approach permits—indeed, it mandates—inquiry into all the circumstances surrounding the interrogation. This includes evaluation of the juvenile's age, experience, education, background, and intelligence, and into whether he has the capacity to understand the warnings given him, the nature of his Fifth Amendment rights, and the consequences of waiving those rights.

Courts repeatedly must deal with these issues of waiver with regard to a broad variety of constitutional rights. There is no reason to assume that such courts—especially juvenile courts, with their special expertise in this area—will be unable to apply the totality-of-the-circumstances analysis so as to take into account those special concerns that are present when young persons, often with limited experience and education and with immature judgment, are involved. Where the age and experience of a juvenile indicate that his request for his probation officer or his parents is, in fact, an invocation of his right to remain silent, the totality approach will allow the court the necessary flexibility to take this into account in making a waiver determination. At the same time, that approach refrains from imposing rigid restraints on police and courts in dealing with an experienced older juvenile with an extensive prior record who knowingly and intelligently waives his Fifth Amendment rights and voluntarily consents to interrogation.

In this case, we conclude that the California Supreme Court should have determined the issue of waiver on the basis of all the circumstances surrounding the interrogation of respondent. The Juvenile Court found that under this approach, respondent in fact had waived his Fifth Amendment rights and consented to interrogation by the police after his request to see his probation officer was denied. Given its view of the case, of course, the California Supreme Court did not consider this issue, though it did hold that the State had failed to prove that, notwithstanding respondent's request to see his probation officer, respondent had not intended to invoke his Fifth Amendment rights.

We feel that the conclusion of the Juvenile Court was correct. The transcript of the interrogation reveals that the police officers conducting the interrogation took care to ensure that respondent understood his rights. They fully explained to respondent that he was being questioned in connection with a murder. They then informed him of all the rights delineated in *Miranda*, and ascertained that respondent understood those rights. There is no indication in the record that respondent failed to understand what the officers told him. Moreover, after his request to see his probation officer had been denied, and after the police officer once more had explained his rights to him, respondent clearly expressed his willingness to waive his rights and continue the interrogation. Further, no special factors indicate that respondent was unable to understand the nature of his actions. He was a 16-year-old juvenile with considerable experience with the police. He had a record of several arrests. He had served time in a youth camp, and he had been on probation for several years. He was under the full-time supervision of probation authorities. There is no indication that he was of insufficient intelligence to understand the rights he was waiving, or what the consequences of that waiver would be. He was not worn down by improper interrogation tactics or lengthy questioning or by trickery or deceit.

On these facts, we think it clear that respondent voluntarily and knowingly waived his Fifth Amendment rights. Respondent argues, however, that any statements he made during interrogation were coerced. Specifically, respondent alleges that the police made threats and promises during the interrogation to pressure him into cooperating in the hope of obtaining leniency for his cooperative attitude. He notes also that he repeatedly told the officers during his interrogation that he wished to stop answering their questions, but that the officers ignored his pleas. He argues further that the record reveals that he was afraid that the police would coerce him, and that this fear caused him to cooperate. He points out that at one point the transcript revealed that he wept during the interrogation.

Review of the entire transcript reveals that respondent's claims of coercion are without merit. As noted, the police took care to inform respondent of his rights and to ensure that he understood them. The officers did not intimidate or threaten respondent in any way. Their questioning was restrained and free from the abuses that so concerned the Court in *Miranda*. The police did indeed indicate that a cooperative attitude would be to respondent's benefit, but their remarks in this regard were far from threatening or coercive. And respondent's allegation that he repeatedly asked that the interrogation cease goes too far: at some points he did state that he did not know the answer to a question put to him or that he could not, or would not, answer the question, but these statements were not assertions of his right to remain silent.

IV

We hold, in short, that the California Supreme Court erred in finding that a juvenile's request for his probation officer was a *per se* invocation of that juvenile's Fifth Amendment rights under *Miranda*. We conclude, rather, that whether the statements obtained during subsequent interrogation of a juvenile who has asked to see his probation officer, but who has not asked to consult an attorney or expressly asserted his right to remain silent, are admissible on the basis of waiver remains a question to be resolved on the totality of the circumstances surrounding the interrogation. On the basis of the record in this case, we hold that the Juvenile Court's findings that respondent voluntarily and knowingly waived his rights and consented to continued interrogation, and that the statements obtained from him were voluntary, were proper, and that the admission of those statements in the proceeding against respondent in Juvenile Court was correct.

The judgment of the Supreme Court of California is reversed, and the case is remanded for further proceedings not inconsistent with this opinion.

It is so ordered.

Mr. Justice MARSHALL, with whom Mr. Justice BRENNAN and Mr. Justice STEVENS join, dissenting.

. . . .

As this Court has consistently recognized, the coerciveness of the custodial setting is of heightened concern where, as here, a juvenile is under investigation. In *Haley v. Ohio* the plurality reasoned that because a 15-year-old minor was particularly susceptible to overbearing interrogation tactics, the voluntariness of his confession could not "be judged by the more exacting standards of maturity." The Court reiterated this point in *Gallegos v. Colorado*, observing that a 14-year-old suspect could not "be compared with an adult in full possession of his senses and knowledgeable of the consequences of his admissions." The juvenile defendant, in the Court's view, required "the aid of more mature judgment as to the steps he should take in the predicament in which he found himself. A lawyer or an adult relative or friend could have given the petitioner the protection which his own immaturity could not."

And, in *In re Gault*, the Court admonished that "the greatest care must be taken to assure that [a minor's] admission was voluntary."

It is therefore critical in the present context that we construe *Miranda's* prophylactic requirements broadly to accomplish their intended purpose—"dispel [ling] the compulsion inherent in custodial surroundings." To effectuate this purpose, the Court must ensure that the "protective device" of legal counsel be readily available, and that any intimation of a desire to preclude questioning be scrupulously honored. Thus, I believe *Miranda* requires that interrogation cease whenever a juvenile requests an adult who is obligated to represent his interests. Such a request, in my judgment, constitutes both an attempt to obtain advice and a general invocation of the right to silence. For, as the California Supreme Court recognized, "'[i]t is fatuous to assume that a minor in custody will be in a position to call an attorney for assistance,'" or that he will trust the police to obtain a lawyer for him.[1] A juvenile in these circumstances will likely turn to his parents, or another adult responsible for his welfare, as the only means of securing legal counsel. Moreover, a request for such adult assistance is surely inconsistent with a present desire to speak freely. Requiring a strict verbal formula to invoke the protections of *Miranda* would "protect the knowledgeable accused from stationhouse coercion while abandoning the young person who knows no more than to ask for the * * * person he trusts."

On my reading of *Miranda*, a California juvenile's request for his probation officer should be treated as a *per se* assertion of Fifth Amendment rights. The California Supreme Court determined that probation officers have a statutory duty to represent minors' interests and, indeed, are "trusted guardian figure[s]" to whom a juvenile would likely turn for assistance. In addition, the court found, probation officers are particularly well suited to assist a juvenile "on such matters as to whether or not he should obtain an attorney" and "how to conduct himself with police." Hence, a juvenile's request for a probation officer may frequently be an attempt to secure protection from the coercive aspects of custodial questioning.[2]

This Court concludes, however, that because a probation officer has law enforcement duties, juveniles generally would not call upon him to represent their interests, and if they did, would not be well served. But that conclusion ignores the California Supreme Court's express determination that the officer's responsibility to initiate juvenile proceedings did not negate his function as personal adviser to his wards. I decline to second-guess that court's assessment of state law. Further, although the majority here speculates that probation officers have a duty to advise cooperation with the police—a proposition suggested only in the concurring opinion of two justices below—respondent's probation officer instructed all his charges "not to go and admit openly to an offense, [but rather] to get some type of advice from * * * parents or a lawyer." Absent an explicit statutory provision or judicial holding, the officer's assessment of the obligations imposed by state law is entitled to deference by this Court.

Thus, given the role of probation officers under California law, a juvenile's request to see his officer may reflect a desire for precisely the kind of assistance *Miranda* guarantees an accused before he waives his Fifth Amendment rights. At the very least, such a request signals a desire to remain silent until contact with the officer is made. Because the Court's contrary determination withdraws the safeguards of *Miranda* from those most in need of protection, I respectfully dissent.

Mr. Justice POWELL, dissenting.

Although I agree with the Court that the Supreme Court of California misconstrued *Miranda v. Arizona*, I would not reverse the California court's judgment. This Court repeatedly has recognized that "the greatest care" must be taken to assure that an alleged con-

---

1. The facts of the instant case are illustrative. When the police offered to obtain an attorney for respondent, he replied: "How I know you guys won't pull no police officer in and tell me he's an attorney?" Significantly, the police made no attempt to allay that concern.

2. The Court intimates that construing a request for a probation officer as an invocation of the Fifth Amendment privilege would undermine the specificity of *Miranda's* prophylactic rules. Yet the Court concedes that the statutory duty to "advise and care for the juvenile defendant," distinguishes probation officers from other adults, such as coaches and clergymen. Since law enforcement officials should be on notice of such legal relationships, they would presumably have no difficulty determining whether a suspect has asserted his Fifth Amendment rights.

Although I agree with my Brother POWELL that, on the facts here, respondent was not "subjected to a fair interrogation free from inherently coercive circumstances," I do not believe a case-by-case approach provides police sufficient guidance, or affords juveniles adequate protection.

fession of a juvenile was voluntary. Respondent was a young person, 16 years old at the time of his arrest and the subsequent prolonged interrogation at the stationhouse. Although respondent had had prior brushes with the law, and was under supervision by a probation officer, the taped transcript of his interrogation—as well as his testimony at the suppression hearing—demonstrates that he was immature, emotional,[2] and uneducated, and therefore was likely to be vulnerable to the skillful, two-on-one, repetitive style of interrogation to which he was subjected.

When given *Miranda* warnings and asked whether he desired an attorney, respondent requested permission to "have my probation officer here," a request that was refused. That officer testified later that he had communicated frequently with respondent, that respondent had serious and "extensive" family problems, and that the officer had instructed respondent to call him immediately "at any time he has a police contact, even if they stop him and talk to him on the street." The reasons given by the probation officer for having so instructed his charge were substantially the same reasons that prompt this Court to examine with special care the circumstances under which a minor's alleged confession was obtained. After stating that respondent had been "going through problems," the officer observed that "many times the kids don't understand what is going on, and what they are supposed to do relative to police * * *." This view of the limited understanding of the average 16-year-old was borne out by respondent's question when, during interrogation, he was advised of his right to an attorney: "How I know you guys won't pull no police officer in and tell me he's an attorney?" It was during this part of the interrogation that the police had denied respondent's request to "have my probation officer here."

The police then proceeded, despite respondent's repeated denial of any connection to the murder under investigation, persistently to press interrogation until they extracted a confession. In *In re Gault,* in addressing police interrogation of detained juveniles, the Court stated:

> "If counsel was not present for some permissible reason when an admission was obtained [from a child], the greatest care must be taken to assure that the admission was voluntary, in the sense not only that it was not coerced or suggested, but also that it was not the product of ignorance of rights or of adolescent fantasy, fright or despair."

It is clear that the interrogating police did not exercise "the greatest care" to assure that respondent's "admission was voluntary."[4] In the absence of counsel, and having refused to call the probation officer, they nevertheless engaged in protracted interrogation.

Although I view the case as close, I am not satisfied that this particular 16-year-old boy, in this particular situation, was subjected to a fair interrogation free from inherently coercive circumstances. For these reasons, I would affirm the judgment of the Supreme Court of California.

---

2. The Juvenile Court Judge observed that he had "heard the tapes" of the interrogation, and was "aware of the fact that Michael [respondent] was crying at the time he talked to the police officers."

4. Minors who become embroiled with the law range from the very young up to those on the brink of majority. Some of the older minors become fully "street-wise," hardened criminals, deserving no greater consideration than that properly accorded all persons suspected of crime. Other minors are more of a child than an adult. As the Court indicated in *In re Gault,* the facts relevant to the care to be exercised in a particular case vary widely. They include the minor's age, actual maturity, family environment, education, emotional and mental stability, and, of course, any prior record he might have.

Notes

(a) What is the holding in *Michael C.*?

(b) Is the ruling in *Michael C.* more likely to affect adults or juveniles? Why?

(c) In holding that the totality of the circumstances test used in determining waiver of *Miranda* rights by adults also applied to waivers by children, what opportunity did the *Michael C.* majority bypass?

(d) Does the Court's totality of the circumstances approach make sense for juveniles? Why?

(e) In *Haley v. Ohio*, 332 U.S. 596 (1948), the United States Supreme Court invalidated a confession taken from a fifteen-year-old that was used as evidence against him at his trial for murder after he was waived to adult court. Haley was questioned by relays of police officers for five hours between midnight and 5:00. He was subsequently held incommunicado for five days. Using a due process totality of the circumstances test the Court found that the confession was not voluntary. Haley's age was the focus of the Court's analysis:

> What transpired would make us pause for careful inquiry if a mature man were involved. And when, as here, a mere child—an easy victim of the law—is before us, special care in scrutinizing the record must be used. Age 15 is a tender and difficult age for a boy of any race. He cannot be judged by the more exacting standards of maturity. That which would leave a man cold and unimpressed can overawe and overwhelm a lad in his early teens. This is the period of great instability which the crisis of adolescence produces. *Id.* at 599.

(f) Similarly, in *Gallegos v. Colorado*, 370 U.S. 49 (1962), the confession of a fourteen-year-old used at his criminal trial for murder was held involuntary under the due process totality of the circumstances test. Again the Court stressed the age of the defendant and the lack of adult advice during the interrogation process:

> [A]dvice as to [the juvenile's] detention and rights [should come] from someone concerned with securing [the juvenile] those rights.... A lawyer or an adult relative or friend could [give a juvenile] the protection which his own immaturity could not. Adult advice [could put a juvenile] on a less unequal footing with his interrogators. Without some adult protection against this inequality, a [juvenile] would not be able to know, let alone assert, such constitutional rights....
>
> There is no guide to the decision of cases such as this, except the totality of circumstances.... The youth of the petitioner, the long detention, the failure to send for his parents, the failure immediately to bring him before the judge of the Juvenile Court, the failure to see to it that he had the advice of a lawyer or a friend—all these combine to make us conclude that the formal confession on which this conviction may have rested was obtained in violation of due process. *Id.* at 54–55.

(g) In *Gault*, Justice Fortas discussed several state cases dealing with children's confessions that ultimately proved to be involuntary as well as untrue. The Court concluded "that the constitutional privilege against self-incrimination is applicable in the case of juveniles as it is with respect to adults." 387 U.S. at 55.

However, the ultimate holding applying the privilege to delinquents was limited to in-court admissions. This was what presumably enabled the Court in *Michael C.* to conclude that it had "not yet held that *Miranda* applies with full force to exclude evidence obtained in violation of its proscriptions from consideration in juvenile proceedings...." Indeed, given the holding in *Gault* regarding the privilege against self-incrimination, is it so clear that *Miranda* applies at all to juvenile proceedings?

(h) Notwithstanding the lack of a specific holding that *Miranda* fully applies to minors as well as adults, all states require, at the least, that *Miranda* warnings be given to children during custodial interrogation regarding a crime. Several states, however, go further and require either parental presence or the presence of an interested adult or that an attorney be consulted prior to waiver. Some of these jurisdictions limit the special protection to juveniles of a certain age. Still others mandate electronic recording of the interrogation or that the minor be brought before a magistrate. Is there a downside to requiring the presence of a parent or interested adult during custodial interrogation? See Ellen Marrus, *Can I Talk Now?: Why* Miranda *Does Not Offer Adolescents Adequate Protections*, 79 TEMP. L. REV. 515 (2006).

(i) In *Yarborough v. Alvarado*, 541 U.S. 652 (2004), the Court, 5–4, held that the state court's determination that it was not necessary to take the seventeen-year-old suspect's age into account when considering whether he was held in custody for *Miranda* purposes, was not an unreasonable application of clearly established federal law, which is required for issuance of a writ of habeas corpus under the federal habeas corpus statute. *Id.* at 664, 669. The Court made clear, however, that its ruling did not depend on the deferential standard of the federal habeas corpus statute. The Court noted that "[t]here is an important conceptual difference between the *Miranda* custody test and the line of cases from other contexts considering age and experience. The *Miranda* custody inquiry is an objective test[,]" and does not permit an inquiry into subjective matters such as age and experience. *Id.* at 667. The Court conceded, however, that in determining the voluntariness of a suspect's confession, courts should consider the suspect's age and experience. *Id.* at 668.

Justice O'Connor concurred, stating that "[t]here may be cases in which a suspect's age will be relevant to the *Miranda* 'custody' inquiry. In this case, however, Alvarado was almost 18 years old at the time of his interview. It is difficult to expect police to recognize that a suspect is a juvenile when he is so close to the age of majority. Even when police do know a suspect's age, it may be difficult for them to ascertain what bearing it has on the likelihood that the suspect would feel free to leave. That is especially true here; 17-year-olds vary widely in their reactions to police questioning, and many can be expected to behave as adults." *Id.* at 669.

Justice Breyer, dissenting, argued that "[in] this case, Alvarado's youth is an objective circumstance that was known to the police. It is not a special quality, but rather a widely shared characteristic that generates commonsense conclusions about behavior and perception. To focus on the circumstance of age in a case like this does not complicate the 'in custody' inquiry. And to say that courts should ignore widely shared, objective characteristics, like age, on the ground that only a (large) *minority* of the population possesses them would produce absurd results, the present instance being a case in point." *Id.* at 674–75.

(j) Consider the following excerpts from two non-delinquency cases that were decided in 1979, the same year of the *Michael C.* ruling.

In *Addington v. Texas*, 441 U.S. 418 (1979), the Court held unanimously that in involuntary commitments of mentally ill persons the proper constitutional standard of proof was clear and convincing. The majority distinguished criminal and delinquency prosecutions from involuntary commitments, stating that:

> The Court [in *Winship*] saw no controlling difference in loss of liberty and stigma between a conviction for an adult and a delinquency adjudication for a juvenile.

Winship recognized that the basic issue — whether the individual in fact committed a criminal act — was the same in both proceedings. There being no meaningful distinctions between the two proceedings, we required the state to prove the juvenile's act and intent beyond a reasonable doubt.

... Unlike the delinquency proceeding in *Winship,* a civil commitment proceeding can in no sense be equated to a criminal prosecution. *Id.* at 427–28.

In *Bellotti v. Baird*, 443 U.S. 622 (1979) (plurality opinion), the Court concluded that a state law requiring a pregnant minor to obtain either parental permission or court approval to receive an abortion unconstitutionally burdened the minor's privacy rights. The decision rested on fundamental fairness grounds and cited *McKeiver* with approval. The Court noted:

The Court's concern for the vulnerability of children is demonstrated in its decisions dealing with minors' claims to constitutional protections against deprivations of liberty or property interests by the State. With respect to many of these claims, we have concluded that the child's right is virtually coextensive with that of an adult....

These rulings [including *Gault, Winship,* and *Breed*] have not been made on the uncritical assumption that the constitutional rights of children are indistinguishable from those of adults. Indeed, our acceptance of juvenile courts distinct from the adult criminal justice system assumes that juvenile offenders constitutionally may be treated differently from adults.... [T]he State is entitled to adjust its legal system to account for children's vulnerability and their needs for "concern, * * * sympathy, and * * * paternal attention." *Id.* at 634–35.

How do these cases rest alongside the *Gault* line of cases?

Schall v. Martin
467 U.S. 253 (1984)

Justice REHNQUIST delivered the opinion of the Court.

Section 320.5(3)(b) of the New York Family Court Act authorizes pretrial detention of an accused juvenile delinquent based on a finding that there is a "serious risk" that the child "may before the return date commit an act which if committed by an adult would constitute a crime."[1] Appellees brought suit on behalf of a class of all juveniles detained pursuant to that provision. The District Court struck down § 320.5(3)(b) as permitting detention without due process of law and ordered the immediate release of all class members. The Court of Appeals for the Second Circuit affirmed, holding the provision "unconstitutional

---

1. New York Jud.Law § 320.5 (McKinney 1983) (Family Court Act (hereinafter FCA)) provides, in relevant part:

"1. At the initial appearance, the court in its discretion may release the respondent or direct his detention. * * *

3. The court shall not direct detention unless it finds and states the facts and reasons for so finding that unless the respondent is detained;

(a) there is a substantial probability that he will not appear in court on the return date; or

(b) there is a serious risk that he may before the return date commit an act which if committed by an adult would constitute a crime." Appellees have only challenged pretrial detention under § 320.5(3)(b). Thus, the propriety of detention to ensure that a juvenile appears in court on the return date, pursuant to § 320.5(3)(a), is not before the Court.

as to all juveniles" because the statute is administered in such a way that "the detention period serves as punishment imposed without proof of guilt established according to the requisite constitutional standard." We noted probable jurisdiction, and now reverse. We conclude that preventive detention under the FCA serves a legitimate state objective, and that the procedural protections afforded pretrial detainees by the New York statute satisfy the requirements of the Due Process Clause of the Fourteenth Amendment to the United States Constitution.

I

Appellee Gregory Martin was arrested on December 13, 1977, and charged with first-degree robbery, second-degree assault, and criminal possession of a weapon based on an incident in which he, with two others, allegedly hit a youth on the head with a loaded gun and stole his jacket and sneakers. Martin had possession of the gun when he was arrested. He was 14 years old at the time and, therefore, came within the jurisdiction of New York's Family Court.[4] The incident occurred at 11:30 at night, and Martin lied to the police about where and with whom he lived. He was consequently detained overnight.[5]

A petition of delinquency was filed,[6] and Martin made his "initial appearance" in Family Court on December 14th, accompanied by his grandmother.[7] The Family Court Judge, citing the possession of the loaded weapon, the false address given to the police, and the lateness of the hour as evidencing a lack of supervision, ordered Martin detained under §320.5(3)(b). A probable cause hearing was held five days later, on December 19th, and

---

4. In New York, a child over the age of 7 but less than 16 is not considered criminally responsible for his conduct. If he commits an act that would constitute a crime if committed by an adult, he comes under the exclusive jurisdiction of the Family Court. That court is charged not with finding guilt and affixing punishment, but rather with determining and pursuing the needs and best interests of the child insofar as those are consistent with the need for the protection of the community. Juvenile proceedings are, thus, civil rather than criminal, although because of the restrictions that may be placed on a juvenile adjudged delinquent, some of the same protections afforded accused adult criminals are also applicable in this context.

5. When a juvenile is arrested, the arresting officer must immediately notify the parent or other person legally responsible for the child's care. Ordinarily, the child will be released into the custody of his parent or guardian after being issued an "appearance ticket" requiring him to meet with the probation service on a specified day. If, however, he is charged with a serious crime, one of several designated felonies, or if his parent or guardian cannot be reached, the juvenile may be taken directly before the Family Court. The Family Court judge will make a preliminary determination as to the jurisdiction of the court, appoint a law guardian for the child, and advise the child of his or her rights, including the right to counsel and the right to remain silent.

Only if, as in Martin's case, the Family Court is not in session and special circumstances exist, such as an inability to notify the parents, will the child be taken directly by the arresting officer to a juvenile detention facility. If the juvenile is so detained, he must be brought before the Family Court within 72 hours or the next day the court is in session, whichever is sooner. The propriety of such detention, prior to a juvenile's initial appearance in Family Court, is not at issue in this case. Appellees challenged only judicially ordered detention.

6. A delinquency petition, prepared by the "presentment agency," originates delinquency proceedings. The petition must contain, *inter alia*, a precise statement of each crime charged and factual allegations which "clearly apprise" the juvenile of the conduct which is the subject of the accusation. The petition is not deemed sufficient unless the allegations of the factual part of the petition, together with those of any supporting depositions which may accompany it, provide reasonable cause to believe that the juvenile committed the crime or crimes charged. Also, nonhearsay allegations in the petition and supporting deposition must establish, if true, every element of each crime charged and the juvenile's commission thereof. The sufficiency of a petition may be tested by filing a motion to dismiss.

7. The first proceeding in Family Court following the filing of the petition is known as the initial appearance even if the juvenile has already been brought before the court immediately following his arrest.

probable cause was found to exist for all the crimes charged. At the factfinding hearing held December 27–29, Martin was found guilty on the robbery and criminal possession charges. He was adjudicated a delinquent and placed on two years' probation.[8] He had been detained pursuant to § 320.5(3)(b), between the initial appearance and the completion of the factfinding hearing, for a total of 15 days.

Appellees Luis Rosario and Kenneth Morgan, both age 14, were also ordered detained pending their factfinding hearings. Rosario was charged with attempted first-degree robbery and second-degree assault for an incident in which he, with four others, allegedly tried to rob two men, putting a gun to the head of one of them and beating both about the head with sticks. At the time of his initial appearance, on March 15, 1978, Rosario had another delinquency petition pending for knifing a student, and two prior petitions had been adjusted.[9] Probable cause was found on March 21. On April 11, Rosario was released to his father, and the case was terminated without adjustment on September 25, 1978.

Kenneth Morgan was charged with attempted robbery and attempted grand larceny for an incident in which he and another boy allegedly tried to steal money from a 14-year-old girl and her brother by threatening to blow their heads off and grabbing them to search their pockets. Morgan, like Rosario, was on release status on another petition (for robbery and criminal possession of stolen property) at the time of his initial appearance on March 27, 1978. He had been arrested four previous times, and his mother refused to come to court because he had been in trouble so often she did not want him home. A probable-cause hearing was set for March 30, but was continued until April 4, when it was combined with a factfinding hearing. Morgan was found guilty of harassment and petit lar-

---

8. The "factfinding" is the juvenile's analogue of a trial. As in the earlier proceedings, the juvenile has a right to counsel at this hearing. Evidence may be suppressed on the same grounds as in criminal cases, and proof of guilt, based on the record evidence, must be beyond a reasonable doubt. If guilt is established, the court enters an appropriate order and schedules a dispositional hearing.

The dispositional hearing is the final and most important proceeding in the Family Court. If the juvenile has committed a designated felony, the court must order a probation investigation and a diagnostic assessment. Any other material and relevant evidence may be offered by the probation agency or the juvenile. Both sides may call and cross-examine witnesses and recommend specific dispositional alternatives. The court must find, based on a preponderance of the evidence, that the juvenile is delinquent and requires supervision, treatment, or confinement. Otherwise, the petition is dismissed.

If the juvenile is found to be delinquent, then the court enters an order of disposition. Possible alternatives include a conditional discharge; probation for up to two years; nonsecure placement with, perhaps, a relative or the Division for Youth; transfer to the Commissioner of Mental Health; or secure placement. Unless the juvenile committed one of the designated felonies, the court must order the least restrictive available alternative consistent with the needs and best interests of the juvenile and the need for protection of the community.

9. Every accused juvenile is interviewed by a member of the staff of the Probation Department. This process is known as "probation intake." In the course of the interview, which lasts an average of 45 minutes, the probation officer will gather what information he can about the nature of the case, the attitudes of the parties involved, and the child's past history and current family circumstances. His sources of information are the child, his parent or guardian, the arresting officer, and any records of past contacts between the child and the Family Court. On the basis of this interview, the probation officer may attempt to "adjust," or informally resolve, the case. Adjustment is a purely voluntary process in which the complaining witness agrees not to press the case further, while the juvenile is given a warning or agrees to counseling sessions or, perhaps, referral to a community agency. In cases involving designated felonies or other serious crimes, adjustment is not permitted without written approval of the Family Court. If a case is not informally adjusted, it is referred to the "presentment agency."

ceny and was ordered placed with the Department of Social Services for 18 months. He was detained a total of eight days between his initial appearance and the factfinding hearing.

On December 21, 1977, while still in preventive detention pending his factfinding hearing, Gregory Martin instituted a habeas corpus class action on behalf of "those persons who are, or during the pendency of this action will be, preventively detained pursuant to" § 320.5(3)(b) of the FCA. Rosario and Morgan were subsequently added as additional named plaintiffs. These three class representatives sought a declaratory judgment that § 320.5(3)(b) violates the Due Process and Equal Protection Clauses of the Fourteenth Amendment.

In an unpublished opinion, the District Court certified the class.[10] The court also held that appellees were not required to exhaust their state remedies before resorting to federal habeas because the highest state court had already rejected an identical challenge to the juvenile preventive detention statute. Exhaustion of state remedies, therefore, would be "an exercise in futility."

At trial, appellees offered in evidence the case histories of 34 members of the class, including the three named petitioners. Both parties presented some general statistics on the relation between pretrial detention and ultimate disposition. In addition, there was testimony concerning juvenile proceedings from a number of witnesses, including a legal aid attorney specializing in juvenile cases, a probation supervisor, a child psychologist, and a Family Court Judge. On the basis of this evidence, the District Court rejected the equal protection challenge as "insubstantial,"[11] but agreed with appellees that pretrial detention under the FCA violates due process.[12] The court ordered that "all class members in custody pursuant to Family Court Act Section [320.5(3)(b)] shall be released forthwith."

The Court of Appeals affirmed. After reviewing the trial record, the court opined that "the vast majority of juveniles detained under [§ 320.5(3)(b)] either have their petitions dismissed before an adjudication of delinquency or are released after adjudication." The court concluded from that fact that § 320.5(3)(b) "is utilized principally, not for preventive purposes, but to impose punishment for unadjudicated criminal acts." The early release of so many of those detained contradicts any asserted need for pretrial confinement

---

10. We have never decided whether Federal Rule of Civil Procedure 23, providing for class actions, is applicable to petitions for habeas corpus relief. Although appellants contested the class certification in the District Court, they did not raise the issue on appeal; nor do they urge it here. Again, therefore, we have no occasion to reach the question.

11. The equal protection claim, which was neither raised on appeal nor decided by the Second Circuit, is not before us.

12. The District Court gave three reasons for this conclusion. First, under the FCA, a juvenile may be held in pretrial detention for up to five days without any judicial determination of probable cause. Relying on *Gerstein v. Pugh*, the District Court concluded that pretrial detention without a prior adjudication of probable cause is, itself, a per se violation of due process.

Second, after a review of the pertinent scholarly literature, the court noted that "no diagnostic tools have as yet been devised which enable even the most highly trained criminologists to predict reliably which juveniles will engage in violent crime." *A fortiori*, the court concluded, a Family Court judge cannot make a reliable prediction based on the limited information available to him at the initial appearance. Moreover, the court felt that the trial record was "replete" with examples of arbitrary and capricious detentions.

Finally, the court concluded that preventive detention is merely a euphemism for punishment imposed without an adjudication of guilt. The alleged purpose of the detention—to protect society from the juvenile's criminal conduct—is indistinguishable from the purpose of post-trial detention. And given "the inability of trial judges to predict which juveniles will commit crimes," there is no rational connection between the decision to detain and the alleged purpose, even if that purpose were legitimate.

to protect the community. The court therefore concluded that § 320.5(3)(b) must be declared unconstitutional as to all juveniles. Individual litigation would be a practical impossibility because the periods of detention are so short that the litigation is mooted before the merits are determined.[13]

II

There is no doubt that the Due Process Clause is applicable in juvenile proceedings. "The problem," we have stressed, "is to ascertain the precise impact of the due process requirement upon such proceedings." We have held that certain basic constitutional protections enjoyed by adults accused of crimes also apply to juveniles[: (notice of charges, right to counsel, privilege against self-incrimination, right to confrontation and cross-examination); (proof beyond a reasonable doubt); (double jeopardy)]. But the Constitution does not mandate elimination of all differences in the treatment of juveniles. See, e.g., *McKeiver v. Pennsylvania* (no right to jury trial). The State has "a parens patriae interest in preserving and promoting the welfare of the child," which makes a juvenile proceeding fundamentally different from an adult criminal trial. We have tried, therefore, to strike a balance—to respect the "informality" and "flexibility" that characterize juvenile proceedings, and yet to ensure that such proceedings comport with the "fundamental fairness" demanded by the Due Process Clause.

The statutory provision at issue in these cases, § 320.5(3)(b), permits a brief pretrial detention based on a finding of a "serious risk" that an arrested juvenile may commit a crime before his return date. The question before us is whether preventive detention of juveniles pursuant to § 320.5(3)(b) is compatible with the "fundamental fairness" required by due process. Two separate inquiries are necessary to answer this question. First, does preventive detention under the New York statute serve a legitimate state objective? And, second, are the procedural safeguards contained in the FCA adequate to authorize the pretrial detention of at least some juveniles charged with crimes?

A

Preventive detention under the FCA is purportedly designed to protect the child and society from the potential consequences of his criminal acts. When making any detention decision, the Family Court judge is specifically directed to consider the needs and best interests of the juvenile as well as the need for the protection of the community. In *Bell v. Wolfish*, we left open the question whether any governmental objective other than ensuring a detainee's presence at trial may constitutionally justify pretrial detention. As an initial matter, therefore, we must decide whether, in the context of the juvenile system, the combined interest in protecting both the community and the juvenile himself from the consequences of future criminal conduct is sufficient to justify such detention.

The "legitimate and compelling state interest" in protecting the community from crime cannot be doubted. We have stressed before that crime prevention is "a weighty social objective," and this interest persists undiluted in the juvenile context. The harm suffered by the victim of a crime is not dependent upon the age of the perpetrator.[14] And the harm

---

13. Judge Newman concurred separately. He was not convinced that the record supported the majority's statistical conclusions. But he thought that the statute was procedurally infirm because it granted unbridled discretion to Family Court judges to make an inherently uncertain prediction of future criminal behavior.

14. In 1982, juveniles under 16 accounted for 7.5 percent of all arrests for violent crimes, 19.9 percent of all arrests for serious property crime, and 17.3 percent of all arrests for violent and serious property crimes combined. U.S. Dept. of Justice, Federal Bureau of Investigation, Crime in the United States 176–177 (1982) ("violent crimes" include murder, nonnegligent manslaughter, forcible

to society generally may even be greater in this context given the high rate of recidivism among juveniles.

The juvenile's countervailing interest in freedom from institutional restraints, even for the brief time involved here, is undoubtedly substantial as well. But that interest must be qualified by the recognition that juveniles, unlike adults, are always in some form of custody. Children, by definition, are not assumed to have the capacity to take care of themselves. They are assumed to be subject to the control of their parents, and if parental control falters, the State must play its part as parens patriae. In this respect, the juvenile's liberty interest may, in appropriate circumstances, be subordinated to the State's "parens patriae interest in preserving and promoting the welfare of the child."

The New York Court of Appeals, in upholding the statute at issue here, stressed at some length "the desirability of protecting the juvenile from his own folly."[15] Society has a legitimate interest in protecting a juvenile from the consequences of his criminal activity—both from potential physical injury which may be suffered when a victim fights back or a policeman attempts to make an arrest and from the downward spiral of criminal activity into which peer pressure may lead the child. *See Eddings v. Oklahoma* (minority "is a time and condition of life when a person may be most susceptible to influence and to psychological damage"); *Belloti v. Baird* (juveniles "often lack the experience, perspective, and judgment to recognize and avoid choices that could be detrimental to them").

The substantiality and legitimacy of the state interests underlying this statute are confirmed by the widespread use and judicial acceptance of preventive detention for juveniles. Every State, as well as the United States in the District of Columbia, permits preventive detention of juveniles accused of crime. A number of model juvenile justice acts also contain provisions permitting preventive detention. And the courts of eight States, including the New York Court of Appeals, have upheld their statutes with specific reference to protecting the juvenile and the community from harmful pretrial conduct, including pretrial crime.

"The fact that a practice is followed by a large number of states is not conclusive in a decision as to whether that practice accords with due process, but it is plainly worth considering in determining whether the practice 'offends some principle of justice so rooted in the traditions and conscience of our people as to be ranked as fundamental.' In light of the uniform legislative judgment that pretrial detention of juveniles properly promotes the interests both of society and the juvenile, we conclude that the practice serves a legitimate

---

rape, robbery, and aggravated assault; "serious property crimes" include burglary, larceny—theft, motor vehicle theft, and arson).

15. Our society recognizes that juveniles in general are in the earlier stages of their emotional growth, that their intellectual development is incomplete, that they have had only limited practical experience, and that their value systems have not yet been clearly identified or firmly adopted. * * *

"For the same reasons that our society does not hold juveniles to an adult standard of responsibility for their conduct, our society may also conclude that there is a greater likelihood that a juvenile charged with delinquency, if released, will commit another criminal act than that an adult charged with crime will do so. To the extent that self-restraint may be expected to constrain adults, it may not be expected to operate with equal force as to juveniles. Because of the possibility of juvenile delinquency treatment and the absence of second-offender sentencing, there will not be the deterrent for the juvenile which confronts the adult. Perhaps more significant is the fact that in consequence of lack of experience and comprehension the juvenile does not view the commission of what are criminal acts in the same perspective as an adult. * * * There is the element of gamesmanship and the excitement of 'getting away' with something and the powerful inducement of peer pressures. All of these commonly acknowledged factors make the commission of criminal conduct on the part of juveniles in general more likely than in the case of adults."

regulatory purpose compatible with the "fundamental fairness" demanded by the Due Process Clause in juvenile proceedings.[18]

Of course, the mere invocation of a legitimate purpose will not justify particular restrictions and conditions of confinement amounting to punishment. It is axiomatic that "[d]ue process requires that a pretrial detainee not be punished." Even given, therefore, that pretrial detention may serve legitimate regulatory purposes, it is still necessary to determine whether the terms and conditions of confinement under § 320.5(3)(b) are in fact compatible with those purposes. "A court must decide whether the disability is imposed for the purpose of punishment or whether it is but an incident of some other legitimate governmental purpose." Absent a showing of an express intent to punish on the part of the State, that determination generally will turn on "whether an alternative purpose to which [the restriction] may rationally be connected is assignable for it, and whether it appears excessive in relation to the alternative purpose assigned [to it]."

There is no indication in the statute itself that preventive detention is used or intended as a punishment. First of all, the detention is strictly limited in time. If a juvenile is detained at his initial appearance and has denied the charges against him, he is entitled to a probable-cause hearing to be held not more than three days after the conclusion of the initial appearance or four days after the filing of the petition, whichever is sooner.[19] If the Family Court judge finds probable cause, he must also determine whether continued detention is necessary pursuant to § 320.5(3)(b).

Detained juveniles are also entitled to an expedited factfinding hearing. If the juvenile is charged with one of a limited number of designated felonies, the factfinding hearing must be scheduled to commence not more than 14 days after the conclusion of the initial appearance. If the juvenile is charged with a lesser offense, then the factfinding hearing must be held not more than three days after the initial appearance.[20] In the latter case, since the times for the probable-cause hearing and the factfinding hearing coincide, the two hearings are merged.

Thus, the maximum possible detention under § 320.5(3)(b) of a youth accused of a serious crime, assuming a 3-day extension of the factfinding hearing for good cause shown, is 17 days. The maximum detention for less serious crimes, again assuming a 3-day extension for good cause shown, is six days. These time frames seem suited to the limited purpose of providing the youth with a controlled environment and separating him from improper influences pending the speedy disposition of his case.

The conditions of confinement also appear to reflect the regulatory purposes relied upon by the State. When a juvenile is remanded after his initial appearance, he cannot, absent exceptional circumstances, be sent to a prison or lockup where he would be exposed to adult criminals. Instead, the child is screened by an "assessment unit" of the Department of Juvenile Justice. The assessment unit places the child in either nonsecure or secure detention. Nonsecure detention involves an open facility in the community, a sort

---

18. Appellees argue that some limit must be placed on the categories of crimes that detained juveniles must be accused of having committed or being likely to commit. But the discretion to delimit the categories of crimes justifying detention, like the discretion to define criminal offenses and prescribe punishments, resides wholly with the state legislatures.

19. For good cause shown, the court may adjourn the hearing, but for no more than three additional court days.

20. In either case, the court may adjourn the hearing for not more than three days for good cause shown. The court must state on the record the reason for any adjournment.

of "halfway house," without locks, bars, or security officers where the child receives schooling and counseling and has access to recreational facilities.

Secure detention is more restrictive, but it is still consistent with the regulatory and parens patriae objectives relied upon by the State. Children are assigned to separate dorms based on age, size, and behavior. They wear street clothes provided by the institution and partake in educational and recreational programs and counseling sessions run by trained social workers. Misbehavior is punished by confinement to one's room. We cannot conclude from this record that the controlled environment briefly imposed by the State on juveniles in secure pretrial detention "is imposed for the purpose of punishment" rather than as "an incident of some other legitimate governmental purpose."

The Court of Appeals, of course, did conclude that the underlying purpose of § 320.5(3)(b) is punitive rather than regulatory. But the court did not dispute that preventive detention might serve legitimate regulatory purposes or that the terms and conditions of pretrial confinement in New York are compatible with those purposes. Rather, the court invalidated a significant aspect of New York's juvenile justice system based solely on some case histories and a statistical study which appeared to show that "the vast majority of juveniles detained under [§ 320.5(3)(b)] either have their petitions dismissed before an adjudication of delinquency or are released after adjudication." The court assumed that dismissal of a petition or failure to confine a juvenile at the dispositional hearing belied the need to detain him prior to fact-finding and that, therefore, the pretrial detention constituted punishment. Since punishment imposed without a prior adjudication of guilt is per se illegitimate, the Court of Appeals concluded that no juveniles could be held pursuant to § 320.5(3)(b).

There are some obvious flaws in the statistics and case histories relied upon by the lower court.[21] But even assuming it to be the case that "by far the greater number of juveniles incarcerated under [§ 320.5(3)(b)] will never be confined as a consequence of a disposition imposed after an adjudication of delinquency," we find that to be an insufficient ground for upsetting the widely shared legislative judgment that preventive detention serves an important and legitimate function in the juvenile justice system. We are unpersuaded by the Court of Appeals' rather cavalier equation of detentions that do not lead to continued confinement after an adjudication of guilt and "wrongful" or "punitive" pretrial detentions.

Pretrial detention need not be considered punitive merely because a juvenile is subsequently discharged subject to conditions or put on probation. In fact, such actions reinforce the original finding that close supervision of the juvenile is required. Lenient but supervised disposition is in keeping with the Act's purpose to promote the welfare and development of the child.[22] As the New York Court of Appeals noted:

---

21. For example, as the Court of Appeals itself admits, the statistical study on which it relied mingles indiscriminately detentions under § 320.5(3)(b) with detentions under § 320.5(3)(a). The latter provision applies only to juveniles who are likely not to appear on the return date if not detained, and appellees concede that such juveniles may be lawfully detained. Furthermore, the 34 case histories on which the court relied were handpicked by appellees' counsel from over a 3-year period. The Court of Appeals stated that appellants did not contest the representativeness of these case histories. Appellants argue, however, that there was no occasion to contest their representativeness because the case histories were not even offered by appellees as a representative sample, and were not evaluated by appellees' expert statistician or the District Court in that light. We need not resolve this controversy.

22. Judge Quinones testified that detention at disposition is considered a "harsh solution." At the dispositional hearing, the Family Court judge usually has "a much more complete picture of the youngster" and tries to tailor the least restrictive dispositional order compatible with that picture.

"It should surprise no one that caution and concern for both the juvenile and society may indicate the more conservative decision to detain at the very outset, whereas
the later development of very much more relevant information may prove that
while a finding of delinquency was warranted, placement may not be indicated."

Even when a case is terminated prior to fact finding, it does not follow that the decision
to detain the juvenile pursuant to § 320.5(3)(b) amounted to a due process violation. A
delinquency petition may be dismissed for any number of reasons collateral to its merits, such as the failure of a witness to testify. The Family Court judge cannot be expected
to anticipate such developments at the initial hearing. He makes his decision based on the
information available to him at that time, and the propriety of the decision must be
judged in that light. Consequently, the final disposition of a case is "largely irrelevant" to
the legality of a pretrial detention.

It may be, of course, that in some circumstances detention of a juvenile would not
pass constitutional muster. But the validity of those detentions must be determined on a
case-by-case basis. Section 320.5(3)(b) is not invalid "on its face" by reason of the ambiguous
statistics and case histories relied upon by the court below.[23] We find no justification for
the conclusion that, contrary to the express language of the statute and the judgment of
the highest state court, § 320.5(3)(b) is a punitive rather than a regulatory measure. Preventive detention under the FCA serves the legitimate state objective, held in common with
every State in the country, of protecting both the juvenile and society from the hazards
of pretrial crime.

B

Given the legitimacy of the State's interest in preventive detention, and the nonpuni-
tive nature of that detention, the remaining question is whether the procedures afforded
juveniles detained prior to fact-finding provide sufficient protection against erroneous
and unnecessary deprivations of liberty.[24] In *Gerstein v. Pugh*, we held that a judicial determination of probable cause is a prerequisite to any extended restraint on the liberty of
an adult accused of crime. We did not, however, mandate a specific time-table. Nor did
we require the "full panoply of adversary safeguards — counsel, confrontation, cross-examination, and compulsory process for witnesses." Instead, we recognized "the desirability of flexibility and experimentation by the States." *Gerstein* arose under the Fourth
Amendment, but the same concern with "flexibility" and "informality," while yet ensuring adequate predetention procedures, is present in this context.

In many respects, the FCA provides far more predetention protection for juveniles
than we found to be constitutionally required for a probable-cause determination for
adults in *Gerstein*. The initial appearance is informal, but the accused juvenile is given

---

23. Several amici argue that similar statistics obtain throughout the country. But even if New
York's experience were duplicated on a national scale, that fact would not lead us, as amici urge, to
conclude that every State and the United States are illicitly punishing juveniles prior to their trial. On
the contrary, if such statistics obtain nationwide, our conclusion is strengthened that the existence of
the statistics in these cases is not a sufficient ground for striking down New York's statute. As already
noted: "The fact that a practice is followed by a large number of states is not conclusive in a decision
as to whether that practice accords with due process, but it is plainly worth considering in determining whether the practice 'offends some principle of justice so rooted in the traditions and conscience
of our people as to be ranked as fundamental.'"

24. Appellees urge the alleged lack of procedural safeguards as an alternative ground for upholding the judgment of the Court of Appeals. The court itself intimated that it would reach the same result on that ground, and Judge Newman, in his concurrence, relied expressly on perceived procedural
flaws in the statute. Accordingly, we deem it necessary to consider the question.

full notice of the charges against him and a complete stenographic record is kept of the hearing. The juvenile appears accompanied by his parent or guardian.[25] He is first informed of his rights, including the right to remain silent and the right to be represented by counsel chosen by him or by a law guardian assigned by the court. The initial appearance may be adjourned for no longer than 72 hours or until the next court day, whichever is sooner, to enable an appointed law guardian or other counsel to appear before the court. When his counsel is present, the juvenile is informed of the charges against him and furnished with a copy of the delinquency petition. A representative from the presentment agency appears in support of the petition.

The nonhearsay allegations in the delinquency petition and supporting depositions must establish probable cause to believe the juvenile committed the offense. Although the Family Court judge is not required to make a finding of probable cause at the initial appearance, the youth may challenge the sufficiency of the petition on that ground. Thus, the juvenile may oppose any recommended detention by arguing that there is not probable cause to believe he committed the offense or offenses with which he is charged. If the petition is not dismissed, the juvenile is given an opportunity to admit or deny the charges.[26]

With the consent of the victim or complainant and the juvenile, the court may also refer a case to the probation service for adjustment. If the case is subsequently adjusted, the petition is then dismissed.

At the conclusion of the initial appearance, the presentment agency makes a recommendation regarding detention. A probation officer reports on the juvenile's record, including other prior and current Family Court and probation contacts, as well as relevant information concerning home life, school attendance, and any special medical or developmental problems. He concludes by offering his agency's recommendation on detention. Opposing counsel, the juvenile's parents, and the juvenile himself may all speak on his behalf and challenge any information or recommendation. If the judge does decide to detain the juvenile under § 320.5(3)(b), he must state on the record the facts and reasons for the detention.[27]

As noted, a detained juvenile is entitled to a formal, adversarial probable-cause hearing within three days of his initial appearance, with one 3-day extension possible for good cause shown.[28] The burden at this hearing is on the presentment agency to call witnesses and offer evidence in support of the charges. Testimony is under oath and subject to

---

25. If the juvenile's parent or guardian fails to appear after reasonable and substantial efforts have been made to notify such person, the court must appoint a law guardian for the child.

26. If the child chooses to remain silent, he is assumed to deny the charges. With the consent of the court and of the presentment agency, the child may admit to a lesser charge. If he wishes to admit to the charges or to a lesser charge, the court must, before accepting the admission, advise the child of his right to a factfinding hearing and of the possible specific dispositional orders that may result from the admission. The court must also satisfy itself that the child actually did commit the acts to which he admits.

27. Given that under *Gerstein* a probable-cause hearing may be informal and nonadversarial, a Family Court judge could make a finding of probable cause at the initial appearance. That he is not required to do so does not, under the circumstances, amount to a deprivation of due process. Appellees fail to point to a single example where probable cause was not found after a decision was made to detain the child.

28. The Court in *Gerstein* indicated approval of pretrial detention procedures that supplied a probable-cause hearing within five days of the initial detention. The brief delay in the probable-cause hearing may actually work to the advantage of the juvenile since it gives his counsel, usually appointed at the initial appearance pursuant to FCA § 320.2(2), time to prepare.

cross-examination. The accused juvenile may call witnesses and offer evidence in his own behalf. If the court finds probable cause, the court must again decide whether continued detention is necessary under § 320.5(3)(b). Again, the facts and reasons for the detention must be stated on the record.

In sum, notice, a hearing, and a statement of facts and reasons are given prior to any detention under § 320.5(3)(b). A formal probable-cause hearing is then held within a short while thereafter, if the factfinding hearing is not itself scheduled within three days. These flexible procedures have been found constitutionally adequate under the Fourth Amendment, see *Gerstein v. Pugh*, and under the Due Process Clause, see *Kent v. United States*. Appellees have failed to note any additional procedures that would significantly improve the accuracy of the determination without unduly impinging on the achievement of legitimate state purposes.[29]

Appellees argue, however, that the risk of erroneous and unnecessary detentions is too high despite these procedures because the standard for detention is fatally vague. Detention under § 320.5(3)(b) is based on a finding that there is a "serious risk" that the juvenile, if released, would commit a crime prior to his next court appearance. We have already seen that detention of juveniles on that ground serves legitimate regulatory purposes. But appellees claim, and the District Court agreed, that it is virtually impossible to predict future criminal conduct with any degree of accuracy. Moreover, they say, the statutory standard fails to channel the discretion of the Family Court judge by specifying the factors on which he should rely in making that prediction. The procedural protections noted above are thus, in their view, unavailing because the ultimate decision is intrinsically arbitrary and uncontrolled.

Our cases indicate, however, that from a legal point of view there is nothing inherently unattainable about a prediction of future criminal conduct. Such a judgment forms an important element in many decisions,[30] and we have specifically rejected the contention, based on the same sort of sociological data relied upon by appellees and the District Court, "that it is impossible to predict future behavior and that the question is so vague as to be meaningless."

We have also recognized that a prediction of future criminal conduct is "an experienced prediction based on a host of variables" which cannot be readily codified. Judge Quinones of the Family Court testified at trial that he and his colleagues make a determination under § 320.5(3)(b) based on numerous factors including the nature and seriousness of the charges; whether the charges are likely to be proved at trial; the juvenile's prior record; the adequacy and effectiveness of his home supervision; his school situation,

---

29. Judge Newman, in his concurrence below, offered a list of statutory improvements. These suggested changes included: limitations on the crimes for which the juvenile has been arrested or which he is likely to commit if released; a determination of the likelihood that the juvenile committed the crime; an assessment of the juvenile's background; and a more specific standard of proof. The first and second of these suggestions have already been considered. We need only add to the discussion in n. 18 that there is no indication that delimiting the category of crimes justifying detention would improve the accuracy of the § 320.5(3)(b) determination in any respect. The third and fourth suggestions are discussed in text, *infra*.

30. *See Jurek;* (death sentence imposed by jury); *Greenholtz* (grant of parole); *Morrissey* (parole revocation). A prediction of future criminal conduct may also form the basis for an increased sentence under the "dangerous special offender" statute. Under § 3575(f), a "dangerous" offender is defined as an individual for whom "a period of confinement longer than that provided for such [underlying] felony is required for the protection of the public from further criminal conduct by the defendant." The statute has been challenged numerous times on the grounds that the standard is unconstitutionally vague. Every Court of Appeals considering the question has rejected that claim.

if known; the time of day of the alleged crime as evidence of its seriousness and a possible lack of parental control; and any special circumstances that might be brought to his attention by the probation officer, the child's attorney, or any parents, relatives, or other responsible persons accompanying the child. The decision is based on as much information as can reasonably be obtained at the initial appearance.

Given the right to a hearing, to counsel, and to a statement of reasons, there is no reason that the specific factors upon which the Family Court judge might rely must be specified in the statute. As the New York Court of Appeals concluded, "to a very real extent Family Court must exercise a substitute parental control for which there can be no particularized criteria." There is also no reason, we should add, for a federal court to assume that a state court judge will not strive to apply state law as conscientiously as possible.

It is worth adding that the Court of Appeals for the Second Circuit was mistaken in its conclusion that "[i]ndividual litigation * * * is a practical impossibility because the periods of detention are so short that the litigation is mooted before the merits are determined." In fact, one of the juveniles in the very case histories upon which the court relied was released from pretrial detention on a writ of habeas corpus issued by the State Supreme Court. New York courts also have adopted a liberal view of the doctrine of "capable of repetition, yet evading review" precisely in order to ensure that pretrial detention orders are not unreviewable. In *People ex rel. Wayburn v. Schupf*, the court declined to dismiss an appeal from the grant of a writ of habeas corpus despite the technical mootness of the case.

"Because the situation is likely to recur * * * and the substantial issue may otherwise never be reached (in view of the predictably recurring happenstance that, however expeditiously an appeal might be prosecuted, fact-finding and dispositional hearings normally will have been held and a disposition made before the appeal could reach us), * * * we decline to dismiss [the appeal] on the ground of mootness."

The required statement of facts and reasons justifying the detention and the stenographic record of the initial appearance will provide a basis for the review of individual cases. Pretrial detention orders in New York may be reviewed by writ of habeas corpus brought in State Supreme Court. And the judgment of that court is appealable as of right and may be taken directly to the Court of Appeals if a constitutional question is presented. Permissive appeal from a Family Court order may also be had to the Appellate Division. Or a motion for reconsideration may be directed to the Family Court judge. These postdetention procedures provide a sufficient mechanism for correcting on a case-by-case basis any erroneous detentions ordered under § 320.5(3). Such procedures may well flesh out the standards specified in the statute.

III

The dissent would apparently have us strike down New York's preventive detention statute on two grounds: first, because the preventive detention of juveniles constitutes poor public policy, with the balance of harms outweighing any positive benefits either to society or to the juveniles themselves and, second, because the statute could have been better drafted to improve the quality of the decisionmaking process. But it is worth recalling that we are neither a legislature charged with formulating public policy nor an American Bar Association committee charged with drafting a model statute. The question before us today is solely whether the preventive detention system chosen by the State of New York and applied by the New York Family Court comports with constitutional standards. Given the regulatory purpose for the detention and the procedural protections that precede its imposition, we conclude that § 320.5(3)(b) of the New York FCA is not invalid under the Due Process Clause of the Fourteenth Amendment.

The judgment of the Court of Appeals is

Reversed.

Justice MARSHALL, with whom Justice BRENNAN and Justice STEVENS join, dissenting.

The New York Family Court Act governs the treatment of persons between 7 and 16 years of age who are alleged to have committed acts that, if committed by adults, would constitute crimes. The Act contains two provisions that authorize the detention of juveniles arrested for offenses covered by the Act[2] for up to 17 days pending adjudication of their guilt.[3] Section 320.5(3)(a) empowers a judge of the New York Family Court to order detention of a juvenile if he finds "there is a substantial probability that [the juvenile] will not appear in court on the return date." Section 320.5(3)(b), the provision at issue in these cases, authorizes detention if the judge finds "there is a serious risk [the juvenile] may before the return date commit an act which if committed by an adult would constitute a crime."

There are few limitations on § 320.5(3)(b). Detention need not be predicated on a finding that there is probable cause to believe the child committed the offense for which he was arrested. The provision applies to all juveniles, regardless of their prior records or the severity of the offenses of which they are accused. The provision is not limited to the prevention of dangerous crimes; a prediction that a juvenile if released may commit a minor misdemeanor is sufficient to justify his detention. Aside from the reference to "serious risk," the requisite likelihood that the juvenile will misbehave before his trial is not specified by the statute.

The Court today holds that preventive detention of a juvenile pursuant to § 320.5(3)(b) does not violate the Due Process Clause. Two rulings are essential to the Court's decision: that the provision promotes legitimate government objectives important enough to justify the abridgment of the detained juveniles' liberty interests, and that the provision incorporates procedural safeguards sufficient to prevent unnecessary or arbitrary impairment of constitutionally protected rights. Because I disagree with both of those rulings, I dissent.

I

The District Court made detailed findings, which the Court of Appeals left undisturbed, regarding the manner in which § 320.5(3)(b) is applied in practice. Unless clearly erroneous, those findings are binding upon us, and must guide our analysis of the constitutional questions presented by these cases.

The first step in the process that leads to detention under § 320.5(3)(b) is known as "probation intake." A juvenile may arrive at intake by one of three routes: he may be brought there directly by an arresting officer; he may be detained for a brief period after his arrest and then taken to intake; he may be released upon arrest and directed to appear at a designated time. The heart of the intake procedure is a 10- to 40-minute interview of the

---

2. Ironically, juveniles arrested for very serious offenses are not subject to preventive detention under this or any other provision.

3. Strictly speaking, "guilt" is never adjudicated under the Act; nor is the juvenile ever given a trial. Rather, whether the juvenile committed the offense is ascertained in a "factfinding hearing." In most respects, however, such a hearing is the functional equivalent of an ordinary criminal trial. For example, the juvenile is entitled to counsel and the State bears the burden of demonstrating beyond a reasonable doubt that the juvenile committed the offense of which he is accused. For convenience, the ensuing discussion will use the terminology associated with adult criminal proceedings when describing the treatment of juveniles in New York.

juvenile, the arresting officer, and sometimes the juvenile's parent or guardian. The objectives of the probation officer conducting the interview are to determine the nature of the offense the child may have committed and to obtain some background information on him.

On the basis of the information derived from the interview and from an examination of the juvenile's record, the probation officer decides whether the case should be disposed of informally ("adjusted") or whether it should be referred to the Family Court. If the latter, the officer makes an additional recommendation regarding whether the juvenile should be detained. "There do not appear to be any governing criteria which must be followed by the probation officer in choosing between proposing detention and parole. * * *"

The actual decision whether to detain a juvenile under § 320.5(3)(b) is made by a Family Court judge at what is called an "initial appearance"—a brief hearing resembling an arraignment.[5] The information on which the judge makes his determination is very limited. He has before him a "petition for delinquency" prepared by a state agency, charging the juvenile with an offense, accompanied with one or more affidavits attesting to the juvenile's involvement. Ordinarily the judge has in addition the written report and recommendation of the probation officer. However, the probation officer who prepared the report rarely attends the hearing. Nor is the complainant likely to appear. Consequently, "[o]ften there is no one present with personal knowledge of what happened."

In the typical case, the judge appoints counsel for the juvenile at the time his case is called. Thus, the lawyer has no opportunity to make an independent inquiry into the juvenile's background or character, and has only a few minutes to prepare arguments on the child's behalf. The judge ordinarily does not interview the juvenile, makes no inquiry into the truth of allegations in the petition, and does not determine whether there is probable cause to believe the juvenile committed the offense.[6] The typical hearing lasts between 5 and 15 minutes, and the judge renders his decision immediately afterward.

Neither the statute nor any other body of rules guides the efforts of the judge to determine whether a given juvenile is likely to commit a crime before his trial. In making

---

5. If the juvenile is detained upon arrest, this hearing must be held on the next court day or within 72 hours, whichever comes first.

6. The majority admits that "the Family Court judge is not required to make a finding of probable cause at the initial appearance," but contends that the juvenile has the option to challenge the sufficiency of the petition for delinquency on the ground that it fails to establish probable cause. None of the courts that have considered the constitutionality of New York's preventive-detention system has suggested that a juvenile has a statutory right to a probable-cause determination before he is detained. The provisions cited by the majority for its novel reading of the statute provide only shaky support for its contention. FCA § 315.1, which empowers the juvenile to move to dismiss a petition lacking allegations sufficient to satisfy § 311.2, provides that "[a] motion to dismiss under this section must be made within the time provided for in section 332.2." Section 332.2, in turn, provides that pretrial motions shall be made within 30 days after the initial appearance and before the factfinding hearing. If the juvenile has been detained, the judge is instructed to "hear and determine pre-trial motions on an expedited basis," but is not required to rule upon such motions peremptorily. In sum, the statutory scheme seems to contemplate that a motion to dismiss a petition for lack of probable cause, accompanied with "supporting affidavits, exhibits and memoranda of law," would be filed sometime after the juvenile is detained under § 320.5(3)(b). And there is no reason to expect that the ruling on such a motion would be rendered before the juvenile would in any event be entitled to a probable-cause hearing under § 325.1(2). That counsel for a juvenile ordinarily is not even appointed until a few minutes prior to the initial appearance confirms this interpretation. The lesson of this foray into the tangled provisions of the New York Family Court Act is that the majority ought to adhere to our usual policy of relying whenever possible for interpretation of a state statute upon courts better acquainted with its terms and applications.

detention decisions, "each judge must rely on his own subjective judgment, based on the limited information available to him at court intake and whatever personal standards he himself has developed in exercising his discretionary authority under the statute." Family Court judges are not provided information regarding the behavior of juveniles over whose cases they have presided, so a judge has no way of refining the standards he employs in making detention decisions.

After examining a study of a sample of 34 cases in which juveniles were detained under § 320.5(3)(b)[7] along with various statistical studies of pretrial detention of juveniles in New York,[8] the District Court made findings regarding the circumstances in which the provision habitually is invoked. Three of those findings are especially germane to appellees' challenge to the statute. First, a substantial number of "first offenders" are detained pursuant to § 320.5(3)(b). For example, at least 5 of the 34 juveniles in the sample had no prior contact with the Family Court before being detained and at least 16 had no prior adjudications of delinquency.[9] Second, many juveniles are released—for periods ranging from five days to several weeks—after their arrests and are then detained under § 320.5(3)(b), despite the absence of any evidence of misconduct during the time between their arrests and "initial appearances." Sixteen of the thirty-four cases in the sample fit this pattern. Third, "the overwhelming majority" of the juveniles detained under § 320.5(3)(b) are released either before or immediately after their trials, either unconditionally or on parole. At least 23 of the juveniles in the sample fell into this category.

Finally, the District Court made a few significant findings concerning the conditions associated with "secure detention" pursuant to § 320.5(3)(b).[10] In a "secure facility," "[t]he juveniles are subjected to strip-searches, wear institutional clothing and follow institutional regimen. At Spofford [Juvenile Detention Center], which is a secure facility, some

---

7. The majority refuses to consider the circumstances of these 34 cases, dismissing them as unrepresentative, and focuses instead on the lurid facts associated with the cases of the three named appellees. I cannot agree that the sample is entitled to so little weight. There was uncontested testimony at trial to the effect that the 34 cases were typical. At no point in this litigation have appellants offered an alternative selection of instances in which § 320.5(3)(b) has been invoked. And most importantly, despite the fact that the District Court relied heavily on the sample when assessing the manner in which the statute is applied, appellants did not dispute before the Court of Appeals the representativeness of the 34 cases. When the defendants in a plaintiff class action challenge on appeal neither the certification of the class, nor the plaintiffs' depiction of the character of the class, we ought to analyze the case as it comes to us and not try to construct a new version of the facts on the basis of an independent and selective review of the record.

8. As the Court of Appeals acknowledged, there are defects in all of the available statistical studies. Most importantly, none of the studies distinguishes persons detained under § 320.5(3)(a) from persons detained under § 320.5(3)(b). However, these flaws did not disable the courts below from making meaningful—albeit rough—generalizations regarding the incidence of detention under the latter provision. Especially when conjoined with the sample of 34 cases submitted by appellees, the studies are sufficient to support the three findings enumerated in the text. Even the majority, though it chastises appellees for failing to assemble better data, does not suggest that those findings are clearly erroneous.

9. The figures in the text are taken from the District Court's summary of the 34 cases in the sample. Review of the transcripts of the hearings in those cases reveals the actual number to be 9 and 23, respectively.

10. The state director of detention services testified that, in 1978, approximately six times as many juveniles were admitted to "secure facilities" as to "non-secure facilities." These figures are not broken down as to persons detained under § 320.5(3)(a) and persons detained under § 320.5(3)(b). There seems no dispute, however, that most of the juveniles held under the latter provision are subjected to "secure detention."

juveniles who have had dispositional determinations and were awaiting placement (long term care) commingle with those in pretrial detention (short term care)."

It is against the backdrop of these findings that the contentions of the parties must be examined.

II

A

As the majority concedes, the fact that § 320.5(3)(b) applies only to juveniles does not insulate the provision from review under the Due Process Clause. * * * Examination of the provision must of course be informed by a recognition that juveniles have different needs and capacities than adults, but the provision still "must measure up to the essentials of due process and fair treatment."

To comport with "fundamental fairness," § 320.5(3)(b) must satisfy two requirements. First, it must advance goals commensurate with the burdens it imposes on constitutionally protected interests. Second, it must not punish the juveniles to whom it applies.

The majority only grudgingly and incompletely acknowledges the applicability of the first of these tests, but its grip on the cases before us is undeniable. It is manifest that § 320.5(3)(b) impinges upon fundamental rights. If the "liberty" protected by the Due Process Clause means anything, it means freedom from physical restraint. Only a very important government interest can justify deprivation of liberty in this basic sense.[11]

The majority seeks to evade the force of this principle by discounting the impact on a child of incarceration pursuant to § 320.5(3)(b). The curtailment of liberty consequent upon detention of a juvenile, the majority contends, is mitigated by the fact that "juveniles, unlike adults, are always in some form of custody." In any event, the majority argues, the conditions of confinement associated with "secure detention" under § 320.5(3)(b) are not unduly burdensome. These contentions enable the majority to suggest that § 320.5(3)(b) need only advance a "legitimate state objective" to satisfy the strictures of the Due Process Clause.[12]

The majority's arguments do not survive scrutiny. Its characterization of preventive detention as merely a transfer of custody from a parent or guardian to the State is difficult to take seriously. Surely there is a qualitative difference between imprisonment and the condition of being subject to the supervision and control of an adult who has one's best interests at heart. And the majority's depiction of the nature of confinement under § 320.5(3)(b) is insupportable on this record. As noted above, the District Court found that secure detention entails incarceration in a facility closely resembling a jail and that

---

11. This principle underlies prior decisions of the Court involving various constitutional provisions as they relate to pretrial detention. In *Gerstein* we relied in part on the severity of "[t]he consequences of prolonged detention" in construing the Fourth Amendment to forbid pretrial incarceration of a suspect for an extended period of time without "a judicial determination of probable cause." In *Stack v. Boyle*, we stressed the importance of a person's right to freedom until proved guilty in construing the Eighth Amendment to proscribe the setting of bail "at a figure higher than an amount reasonably calculated to" assure the presence of the accused at trial.

12. The phrase "legitimate governmental objective" appears at several points in the opinion of the Court in *Bell v. Wolfish*, and the majority may be relying implicitly on that decision for the standard it applies in these cases. If so, the reliance is misplaced. *Wolfish* was exclusively concerned with the constitutionality of conditions of pretrial incarceration under circumstances in which the legitimacy of the incarceration itself was undisputed; the Court avoided any discussion of the showing a State must make in order to justify pretrial detention in the first instance. The standard employed by the Court in *Wolfish* thus has no bearing on the problem before us.

pretrial detainees are sometimes mixed with juveniles who have been found to be delinquent. Evidence adduced at trial reinforces these findings. For example, Judge Quinones, a Family Court Judge with eight years of experience, described the conditions of detention as follows:

> "Then again, Juvenile Center, as much as we might try, is not the most pleasant place in the world. If you put them in detention, you are liable to be exposing these youngsters to all sorts of things. They are liable to be exposed to assault, they are liable to be exposed to sexual assaults. You are taking the risk of putting them together with a youngster that might be much worse than they, possibly might be, and it might have a bad effect in that respect."

Many other observers of the circumstances of juvenile detention in New York have come to similar conclusions.[13]

In short, fairly viewed, pretrial detention of a juvenile pursuant to § 320.5(3)(b) gives rise to injuries comparable to those associated with imprisonment of an adult. In both situations, the detainee suffers stigmatization and severe limitation of his freedom of movement. Indeed, the impressionability of juveniles may make the experience of incarceration more injurious to them than to adults; all too quickly juveniles subjected to preventive detention come to see society at large as hostile and oppressive and to regard themselves as irremediably "delinquent." Such serious injuries to presumptively innocent persons — encompassing the curtailment of their constitutional rights to liberty — can be justified only by a weighty public interest that is substantially advanced by the statute.[15]

The applicability of the second of the two tests is admitted even by the majority. In *Bell v. Wolfish*, the Court held that an adult may not be punished prior to determination that he is guilty of a crime. The majority concedes, as it must, that this principle applies to juveniles. Thus, if the only purpose substantially advanced by § 320.5(3)(b) is punishment, the provision must be struck down.

For related reasons, § 320.5(3)(b) cannot satisfy either of the requirements discussed above that together define "fundamental fairness" in the context of pretrial detention.

B

Appellants and the majority contend that § 320.5(3)(b) advances a pair of intertwined government objectives: "protecting the community from crime," and "protecting a juvenile from the consequences of his criminal activity." More specifically, the majority ar-

---

13. All of the 34 juveniles in the sample were detained in Spofford Juvenile Center, the detention facility for New York City. Numerous studies of that facility have attested to its unsavory characteristics. Conditions in Spofford have been successfully challenged on constitutional grounds (by a group of inmates of a different type), but nevertheless remain grim. Not surprisingly, a former New York City Deputy Mayor for Criminal Justice has averred that "Spofford is, in many ways, indistinguishable from a prison."

15. This standard might be refined in one of two ways. First, it might be argued that, because § 320.5(3)(b) impinges upon "[l]iberty from bodily restraint," which has long been "recognized as the core of the liberty protected by the Due Process Clause," the provision can pass constitutional muster only if it promotes a "compelling" government interest. Alternatively, it might be argued that the comparatively brief period of incarceration permissible under the provision warrants a slight lowering of the constitutional bar. Applying the principle that the strength of the state interest needed to legitimate a statute depends upon the degree to which the statute encroaches upon fundamental rights[;] it might be held that an important — but not quite "compelling" — objective is necessary to sustain § 320.5(3)(b). In the present context, there is no need to choose between these doctrinal options, because § 320.5(3)(b) would fail either test.

gues that detaining a juvenile for a period of up to 17 days prior to his trial has two desirable effects: it protects society at large from the crimes he might have committed during that period if released; and it protects the juvenile himself "both from potential physical injury which may be suffered when a victim fights back or a policeman attempts to make an arrest and from the downward spiral of criminal activity into which peer pressure may lead the child."

Appellees and some amici argue that public purposes of this sort can never justify incarceration of a person who has not been adjudicated guilty of a crime, at least in the absence of a determination that there exists probable cause to believe he committed a criminal offense. We need not reach that categorical argument in these cases because, even if the purposes identified by the majority are conceded to be compelling, they are not sufficiently promoted by detention pursuant to § 320.5(3)(b) to justify the concomitant impairment of the juveniles' liberty interests.[18] To state the case more precisely, two circumstances in combination render § 320.5(3)(b) invalid in toto: in the large majority of cases in which the provision is invoked, its asserted objectives are either not advanced at all or are only minimally promoted; and, as the provision is written and administered by the state courts, the cases in which its asserted ends are significantly advanced cannot practically be distinguished from the cases in which they are not.

1

Both of the courts below concluded that only occasionally and accidentally does pretrial detention of a juvenile under § 320.5(3)(b) prevent the commission of a crime. Three subsidiary findings undergird that conclusion. First, Family Court judges are incapable of determining which of the juveniles who appear before them would commit offenses before their trials if left at large and which would not. In part, this incapacity derives from the limitations of current knowledge concerning the dynamics of human behavior. On the basis of evidence adduced at trial, supplemented by a thorough review of the secondary literature, the District Court found that "no diagnostic tools have as yet been devised which enable even the most highly trained criminologists to predict reliably which juveniles will engage in violent crime." The evidence supportive of this finding is overwhelming. An independent impediment to identification of the defendants who would misbehave if released is the paucity of data available at an initial appearance. The judge must make his decision whether to detain a juvenile on the basis of a set of allegations regarding the child's alleged offense, a cursory review of his background and criminal record, and the recommendation of a probation officer who, in the typical case, has seen the child only once. In view of this scarcity of relevant information, the District Court credited the testimony of appellees' expert witness, who "stated that he would be surprised if recommendations based on intake interviews were better than chance and assessed the judge's subjective prognosis about the probability of future crime as only 4% better than chance—virtually wholly unpredictable."[20]

---

18. An additional reason for not reaching appellees' categorical objection to the purposes relied upon by the State is that the Court of Appeals did not pass upon the validity of those objectives. We are generally chary of deciding important constitutional questions not reached by a lower court.

20. The majority brushes aside the District Court's findings on this issue with the remark that "a prediction of future criminal conduct * * * forms an important element in many decisions, and we have specifically rejected the contention * * * 'that it is impossible to predict future behavior and that the question is so vague as to be meaningless.'" Whatever the merits of the decisions upon which the majority relies, they do not control the problem before us. In each of the cases in which the Court has countenanced reliance upon a prediction of future conduct in a decisionmaking process impinging upon life or liberty, the affected person had already been convicted of a crime. The constitutional

Second, § 320.5(3)(b) is not limited to classes of juveniles whose past conduct suggests that they are substantially more likely than average juveniles to misbehave in the immediate future. The provision authorizes the detention of persons arrested for trivial offenses[21] and persons without any prior contacts with juvenile court. Even a finding that there is probable cause to believe a juvenile committed the offense with which he was charged is not a prerequisite to his detention.[22]

Third, the courts below concluded that circumstances surrounding most of the cases in which § 320.5(3)(b) has been invoked strongly suggest that the detainee would not have committed a crime during the period before his trial if he had been released. In a significant proportion of the cases, the juvenile had been released after his arrest and had not committed any reported crimes while at large; it is not apparent why a juvenile would be more likely to misbehave between his initial appearance and his trial than between his arrest and initial appearance. Even more telling is the fact that "the vast majority" of persons detained under § 320.5(3)(b) are released either before or immediately after their trials. The inference is powerful that most detainees, when examined more carefully than at their initial appearances, are deemed insufficiently dangerous to warrant further incarceration.[23]

The rarity with which invocation of § 320.5(3)(b) results in detention of a juvenile who otherwise would have committed a crime fatally undercuts the two public purposes assigned to the statute by the State and the majority. The argument that § 320.5(3)(b) serves "the State's 'parens patriae interest in preserving and promoting the welfare of the child,'" now appears particularly hollow. Most juveniles detained pursuant to the provision are not benefitted thereby, because they would not have committed crimes if left to their own devices (and thus would not have been exposed to the risk of physical injury or the perils of the cycle of recidivism). On the contrary, these juveniles suffer several serious harms: deprivation of liberty and stigmatization as "delinquent" or "dangerous," as well as impairment of their ability to prepare their legal defenses. The benefits even to

---

limitations upon the kinds of factors that may be relied on in making such decisions are significantly looser than those upon decisionmaking processes that abridge the liberty of presumptively innocent persons. Cf. *United States v. Tucker* ("[A] trial judge in the federal judicial system generally has wide discretion in determining what sentence to impose. * * * [B]efore making that determination, a judge may appropriately conduct an inquiry broad in scope, largely unlimited either as to the kind of information he may consider, or the source from which it may come").

21. For example, Tyrone Parson, aged 15, one of the members of the sample, was arrested for enticing others to play three-card monte. After being detained for five days under § 320.5(3)(b), the petition against him was dismissed on the ground that "the offense alleged did not come within the provisions of the penal law."

In contrast to the breadth of the coverage of the Family Court Act, the District of Columbia adult preventive-detention statute that was upheld in *United States v. Edwards*, authorizes detention only of persons charged with one of a prescribed set of "dangerous crime[s]" or "crime[s] of violence."

Prediction whether a given person will commit a crime in the future is especially difficult when he has committed only minor crimes in the past. Cf. *Baldasar v. Illinois*("No court can predict with confidence whether a misdemeanor defendant is likely to become a recidivist").

22. By contrast, under the District of Columbia statute, the judge is obliged before ordering detention to find, inter alia, a "substantial probability" that the defendant committed the serious crime for which he was arrested.

23. Both courts below made this inference. Indeed, the New York Court of Appeals, in upholding the statute, did not disagree with this explanation of the incidence of its application.

Release (before or after trial) of some of the juveniles detained under § 320.5(3)(b) may well be due to a different factor: the evidence against them may be insufficient to support a finding of guilt. It is conceivable that some of those persons are so crime-prone that they would have committed an offense if not detained. But even the majority does not suggest that persons who could not be convicted of any crimes may nevertheless be imprisoned for the protection of themselves and the public.

those few juveniles who would have committed crimes if released are not unalloyed; the gains to them are partially offset by the aforementioned injuries. In view of this configuration of benefits and harms, it is not surprising that Judge Quinones repudiated the suggestion that detention under § 320.5(3)(b) serves the interests of the detainees.

The argument that § 320.(3)(b) protects the welfare of the community fares little better. Certainly the public reaps no benefit from incarceration of the majority of the detainees who would not have committed any crimes had they been released. Prevention of the minor offenses that would have been committed by a small proportion of the persons detained confers only a slight benefit on the community. Only in occasional cases does incarceration of a juvenile pending his trial serve to prevent a crime of violence and thereby significantly promote the public interest. Such an infrequent and haphazard gain is insufficient to justify curtailment of the liberty interests of all the presumptively innocent juveniles who would have obeyed the law pending their trials had they been given the chance.[26]

2

The majority seeks to deflect appellees' attack on the constitutionality of § 320.5(3)(b) by contending that they have framed their argument too broadly. It is possible, the majority acknowledges, that "in some circumstances detention of a juvenile [pursuant to § 320.5(3)(b)] would not pass constitutional muster. But the validity of those detentions must be determined on a case-by-case basis." The majority thus implies that, even if the Due Process Clause is violated by most detentions under § 320.5(3)(b) because those detainees would not have committed crimes if released, the statute nevertheless is not invalid "on its face" because detention of those persons who would have committed a serious crime comports with the Constitution. Separation of the properly detained juveniles from the improperly detained juveniles must be achieved through "case-by-case" adjudication.

There are some obvious practical impediments to adoption of the majority's proposal. Because a juvenile may not be incarcerated under § 320.5(3)(b) for more than 17 days, it would be impracticable for a particular detainee to secure his freedom by challenging the constitutional basis of his detention; by the time the suit could be considered, it would have been rendered moot by the juvenile's release or long-term detention pursuant to a delinquency adjudication.[27] Nor could an individual detainee avoid the problem of moot-

---

26. Some amici contend that a preventive-detention statute that, unlike § 320.5(3)(b), covered only specific categories of juveniles and embodied stringent procedural safeguards would result in incarceration only of juveniles very likely to commit crimes of violence in the near future. It could be argued that, even though such a statute would unavoidably result in detention of some juveniles who would not have committed any offenses if released (because of the impossibility of reliably predicting the behavior of individual persons), the gains consequent upon the detention of the large proportion who would have committed crimes would be sufficient to justify the injuries to the other detainees. To decide the cases before us, we need not consider either the feasibility of such a scheme or its constitutionality.

27. The District Court, whose knowledge of New York procedural law surely exceeds ours, concluded that "[t]he short span of pretrial detention makes effective review impossible." The majority dismisses this finding, along with a comparable finding by the Court of Appeals as "mistaken." But neither of the circumstances relied upon by the majority supports its confident judgment on this point. That the New York courts suspended their usual rules of mootness in order to consider an attack on the constitutionality of the statute as a whole, in no way suggests that they would be willing to do so if an individual detainee challenged the constitutionality of § 320.5(3)(b) as applied to him. The majority cites one case in which a detainee did obtain his release by securing a writ of habeas corpus. However, that case involved a juvenile who was not given a probable-cause hearing within six days of his detention—a patent violation of the state statute. That a writ of habeas corpus could be obtained on short notice to remedy a glaring statutory violation provides no support for the ma-

ness by filing a suit for damages or for injunctive relief. This Court's declaration that § 320.5(3)(b) is not unconstitutional on its face would almost certainly preclude a finding that detention of a juvenile pursuant to the statute violated any clearly established constitutional rights; in the absence of such a finding all state officials would be immune from liability in damages. And, under current doctrine pertaining to the standing of an individual victim of allegedly unconstitutional conduct to obtain an injunction against repetition of that behavior, it is far from clear that an individual detainee would be able to obtain an equitable remedy.

But even if these practical difficulties could be surmounted, the majority's proposal would be inadequate. Precisely because of the unreliability of any determination whether a particular juvenile is likely to commit a crime between his arrest and trial, no individual detainee would be able to demonstrate that he would have abided by the law had he been released. In other words, no configuration of circumstances would enable a juvenile to establish that he fell into the category of persons unconstitutionally detained rather than the category constitutionally detained.[28] Thus, to protect the rights of the majority of juveniles whose incarceration advances no legitimate state interest, § 320.5(3)(b) must be held unconstitutional "on its face."

C

The findings reviewed in the preceding section lend credence to the conclusion reached by the courts below: § 320.5(3)(b) "is utilized principally, not for preventive purposes, but to impose punishment for unadjudicated criminal acts."

The majority contends that, of the many factors we have considered in trying to determine whether a particular sanction constitutes "punishment," the most useful are "whether an alternative purpose to which [the sanction] may rationally be connected is assignable for it, and whether it appears excessive in relation to the alternative purpose assigned." Assuming, *arguendo*, that this test is appropriate, it requires affirmance in these cases. The alternative purpose assigned by the State to § 320.5(3)(b) is the prevention of crime by the detained juveniles. But, as has been shown, that objective is advanced at best sporadically by the provision. Moreover, § 320.5(3)(b) frequently is invoked under circumstances in which it is extremely unlikely that the juvenile in question would commit a crime while awaiting trial. The most striking of these cases involve juveniles who have been at large without mishap for a substantial period of time prior to their initial appearances, and detainees who are adjudged delinquent and are nevertheless released into the community. In short, § 320.5(3)(b) as administered by the New York courts surely "appears excessive in relation to" the putatively legitimate objectives assigned to it.

The inference that § 320.5(3)(b) is punitive in nature is supported by additional materials in the record. For example, Judge Quinones and even appellants' counsel acknowledged that one of the reasons juveniles detained pursuant to § 320.5(3)(b) usually are released after the determination of their guilt is that the judge decides that their pre-

---

jority's suggestion that individual detainees could effectively petition for release by challenging the constitutionality of their detentions.

28. This problem is exacerbated by the fact that Family Court judges, when making findings justifying a detention pursuant to § 320.5(3)(b), do not specify whether there is a risk that the juvenile would commit a serious crime or whether there is a risk that he would commit a petty offense. A finding of the latter sort should not be sufficient under the Due Process Clause to justify a juvenile's detention. But a particular detainee has no way of ascertaining the grounds for his incarceration.

trial detention constitutes sufficient punishment. Another Family Court Judge admitted using "preventive detention" to punish one of the juveniles in the sample.[29]

In summary, application of the litmus test the Court recently has used to identify punitive sanctions supports the finding of the lower courts that preventive detention under § 320.5(3)(b) constitutes punishment. Because punishment of juveniles before adjudication of their guilt violates the Due Process Clause, the provision cannot stand.

III

If the record did not establish the impossibility, on the basis of the evidence available to a Family Court judge at a § 320.5(3)(b) hearing, of reliably predicting whether a given juvenile would commit a crime before his trial, and if the purposes relied upon by the State were promoted sufficiently to justify the deprivations of liberty effected by the provision, I would nevertheless still strike down § 320.5(3)(b) because of the absence of procedural safeguards in the provision. As Judge Newman, concurring in the Court of Appeals observed, "New York's statute is unconstitutional because it permits liberty to be denied, prior to adjudication of guilt, in the exercise of unfettered discretion as to an issue of considerable uncertainty—likelihood of future criminal behavior."

Appellees point out that § 320.5(3)(b) lacks two crucial procedural constraints. First, a New York Family Court judge is given no guidance regarding what kinds of evidence he should consider or what weight he should accord different sorts of material in deciding whether to detain a juvenile.[30] For example, there is no requirement in the statute that the judge take into account the juvenile's background or current living situation. Nor is a judge obliged to attach significance to the nature of a juvenile's criminal record or the severity of the crime for which he was arrested.[31] Second, § 320.5(3)(b) does not specify how likely it must be that a juvenile will commit a crime before his trial to warrant his detention. The provision indicates only that there must be a "serious risk" that he will commit an offense and does not prescribe the standard of proof that should govern the judge's determination of that issue.[32]

Not surprisingly, in view of the lack of directions provided by the statute, different judges have adopted different ways of estimating the chances whether a juvenile will misbehave in the near future. "Each judge follows his own individual approach to [the detention] determination." This discretion exercised by Family Court judges in making detention decisions gives rise to two related constitutional problems. First, it creates an excessive risk that juveniles will be detained "erroneously"—i.e., under circumstances in which no public interest would be served by their incarceration. Second, it fosters arbi-

---

29. [In] the initial appearance of Ramon Ramos, …: "This business now of being able to get guns, is now completely out of proportion. We are living in a jungle. We are living in a jungle, and it is time that these youths that are brought before the Court, know that they are in a Court, and that if these allegations are true, that they are going to pay the penalty.

"As for the reasons I just state[d] on the record, * * * I am remand[ing] the respondent to the Commissioner of Juvenile Justice, secure detention."

30. The absence of any limitations on the sorts of reasons that may support a determination that a child is likely to commit a crime if released means that the statutory requirement that the judge state "reasons" on the record, does not meaningfully constrain the decisionmaking process.

31. "Whether the juvenile was a first offender with no prior conduct, whether the court was advised that the juvenile was an obedient son or was needed at home, whether probation intake recommended parole, the case histories in this record disclose that it was not unusual for the court to discount these considerations and order remand based on a 5 to 15 minute evaluation."

32. Cf. *Addington v. Texas* ("clear and convincing" proof constitutionally required to justify civil commitment to mental hospital).

trariness and inequality in a decisionmaking process that impinges upon fundamental rights.

A

One of the purposes of imposing procedural constraints on decisions affecting life, liberty, or property is to reduce the incidence of error. In *Mathews v. Eldridge*, the Court identified a complex of considerations that has proved helpful in determining what protections are constitutionally required in particular contexts to achieve that end:

> "[I]dentification of the specific dictates of due process generally requires consideration of three distinct factors: First, the private interest that will be affected by the official action; second, the risk of an erroneous deprivation of such interest through the procedures used, and the probable value, if any, of additional or substitute procedural safeguards; and finally, the Government's interest, including the function involved and the fiscal and administrative burdens that the additional or substitute procedural requirement would entail."

As Judge Newman recognized, a review of these three factors in the context of New York's preventive-detention scheme compels the conclusion that the Due Process Clause is violated by § 320.5(3)(b) in its present form. First, the private interest affected by a decision to detain a juvenile is personal liberty. Unnecessary abridgment of such a fundamental right should be avoided if at all possible.

Second, there can be no dispute that there is a serious risk under the present statute that a juvenile will be detained erroneously — *i.e.*, despite the fact that he would not commit a crime if released. The findings of fact reviewed in the preceding sections make it apparent that the vast majority of detentions pursuant to § 320.5(3)(b) advance no state interest; only rarely does the statute operate to prevent crime. This high incidence of demonstrated error should induce a reviewing court to exercise utmost care in ensuring that no procedures could be devised that would improve the accuracy of the decisionmaking process. Opportunities for improvement in the extant regime are apparent even to a casual observer. Most obviously, some measure of guidance to Family Court judges regarding the evidence they should consider and the standard of proof they should use in making their determinations would surely contribute to the quality of their detention determinations.[33]

The majority purports to see no value in such additional safeguards, contending that … estimating the likelihood that a given juvenile will commit a crime in the near future involves subtle assessment of a host of variables, the precise weight of which cannot be determined in advance. A review of the hearings that resulted in the detention of the juveniles included in the sample of 34 cases reveals the majority's depiction of the decisionmaking process to be hopelessly idealized. For example, the operative portion of the initial appearance of Tyrone Parson, the three-card monte player, consisted of the following:

---

33. Judge Newman, concurring below, pointed to three other protections lacking in § 320.5(3)(b): "the statute places no limits on the crimes for which the person subject to detention has been arrested * * *, the judge ordering detention is not required to make any evaluation of the degree of likelihood that the person committed the crime of which he is accused[,] * * * [and] the statute places no limits on the type of crimes that the judge believes the detained juvenile might commit if released." In my view, the absence of these constraints is most relevant to the question whether the ends served by the statute can justify its broad reach. However, as Judge Newman observed, they could also be considered procedural flaws. Certainly, a narrowing of the categories of persons covered by § 320.5(3)(b), along the lines sketched by Judge Newman, would reduce the incidence of error in the application of the provision.

"COURT OFFICER: Will you identify yourself.

* * *

"TYRONE PARSON: Tyrone Parson, Age 15.

"THE COURT: Miss Brown, how many times has Tyrone been known to the Court?

* * *

"MISS BROWN: Seven times.

"THE COURT: Remand the respondent."[35]

This kind of parody of reasoned decisionmaking would be less likely to occur if judges were given more specific and mandatory instructions regarding the information they should consider and the manner in which they should assess it.

Third and finally, the imposition of such constraints on the deliberations of the Family Court judges would have no adverse effect on the State's interest in detaining dangerous juveniles and would give rise to insubstantial administrative burdens. For example, a simple directive to Family Court judges to state on the record the significance they give to the seriousness of the offense of which a juvenile is accused and to the nature of the juvenile's background would contribute materially to the quality of the decisionmaking process without significantly increasing the duration of initial appearances.

In summary, the three factors enumerated in *Mathews* in combination incline overwhelmingly in favor of imposition of more stringent constraints on detention determinations under § 320.5(3)(b). Especially in view of the impracticability of correcting erroneous decisions through judicial review, the absence of meaningful procedural safeguards in the provision renders it invalid.

B

A principle underlying many of our prior decisions in various doctrinal settings is that government officials may not be accorded unfettered discretion in making decisions that impinge upon fundamental rights. Two concerns underlie this principle: excessive discretion fosters inequality in the distribution of entitlements and harms, inequality which is especially troublesome when those benefits and burdens are great; and discretion can mask the use by officials of illegitimate criteria in allocating important goods and rights.

So, in striking down on vagueness grounds a vagrancy ordinance, we emphasized the "unfettered discretion it places in the hands of the * * * police." Such flexibility was deemed constitutionally offensive because it "permits and encourages an arbitrary and discriminatory enforcement of the law." Partly for similar reasons, we have consistently held violative of the First Amendment ordinances which make the ability to engage in constitutionally protected speech "contingent upon the uncontrolled will of an official — as by requiring a permit or license which may be granted or withheld in the discretion of such official." ...

The concerns that powered these decisions are strongly implicated by New York's preventive-detention scheme. The effect of the lack of procedural safeguards constraining detention decisions under § 320.5(3)(b) is that the liberty of a juvenile arrested even for a petty crime is dependent upon the "caprice" of a Family Court judge. The absence of meaningful guidelines creates opportunities for judges to use illegitimate criteria when deciding whether juveniles should be incarcerated pending their trials — for example, to

---

35. Parson's case is not unique. The hearings accorded Juan Santiago and Daniel Nelson, for example, though somewhat longer in duration, were nearly as cavalier and undiscriminating.

detain children for the express purpose of punishing them. Even the judges who strive conscientiously to apply the law have little choice but to assess juveniles' dangerousness on the basis of whatever standards they deem appropriate.[37] The resultant variation in detention decisions gives rise to a level of inequality in the deprivation of a fundamental right too great to be countenanced under the Constitution.

IV

The majority acknowledges—indeed, founds much of its argument upon—the principle that a State has both the power and the responsibility to protect the interests of the children within its jurisdiction. Yet the majority today upholds a statute whose net impact on the juveniles who come within its purview is overwhelmingly detrimental. Most persons detained under the provision reap no benefit and suffer serious injuries thereby. The welfare of only a minority of the detainees is even arguably enhanced. The inequity of this regime, combined with the arbitrariness with which it is administered, is bound to disillusion its victims regarding the virtues of our system of criminal justice. I can see—and the majority has pointed to—no public purpose advanced by the statute sufficient to justify the harm it works.

I respectfully dissent.

Notes

(a) What type of constitutional analysis does the Court use in *Schall*?

(b) How does the majority describe the prior delinquency cases? Is the description accurate? Is it complete?

(c) How does Justice Rehnquist reach the conclusion that preventive detention serves a legitimate state interest?

(d) How was Justice Rehnquist able to overcome the vagueness challenge to the "serious risk" criterion?

(e) Is *Schall* solely a "kiddie" case? See *United States v. Salerno*, 481 U.S. 739 (1987) (relying on *Schall* to uphold the constitutionality of the 1984 Bail Reform Act permitting preventive detention). Given the *Schall* Court's view that criminal cases and juvenile proceedings are "fundamentally different," why is *Schall* an appropriate support for *Salerno*? Is there a danger in using "kiddie" cases in this way?

(f) In grappling with these questions consider the following excerpt from *The Supreme Court 1983 Term*, 98 Harv. L. Rev. 130, 134–37 (1984):

> The *Schall* decision marks a turning point in the Court's juvenile procedure jurisprudence. With one persuasively justified exception, the Court had previously extended various constitutional protections associated with criminal prosecutions to juvenile proceedings as each of the issues arose. By declining to apply to juveniles an important constitutional guarantee afforded adult offenders—the assurance that "the Fourth Amendment requires a judicial determination of probable cause as a prerequisite to extended restraint of liberty following arrest"—the Court has signaled a reluctance to impose any further procedural constraints on the juvenile justice system. In reaching its conclusion, the *Schall* majority in-

---

37. "It is clear that the judge decides on pretrial detention for a variety of reasons—as a means of protecting the community, as the policy of the judge to remand, as an express punitive device, or because of the serious nature of the charge[,] among others."

voked reasoning and assumptions that, though dubious, might well be applied in future juvenile justice cases. Indeed, the Court's willingness to ignore the district court's findings and defer to state officials has implications for criminal procedure not only for juveniles, but for adults as well.

The *Schall* opinion resurrects the phrase *parens patriae* and elevates it to talismanic significance. The Court's use of this doctrine to justify infringement of juveniles' liberty interests by the juvenile courts is surprising, given the general disapproval of the *parens patriae* rationale reflected in the Court's landmark juvenile justice decisions. In *In re Gault*, the Court took a jaundiced view of the injustices perpetrated against juveniles under the guise of this doctrine, and later cases have further discredited it. The *Schall* Court's implicit assumption that, in light of the state's benevolent motives, there is little difference from the child's point of view whether she is in parental or institutional custody is indeed "difficult to take seriously" and contradicts the Court's prior decisions.

The revival of the *parens patriae* rationale allowed the Court to treat the liberty interests of juveniles as less substantial than those of adults. The *Schall* majority set forth a "legitimate state objective" test as the detention statute's first constitutional hurdle. Although the phrase appears in a previous opinion by Justice Rehnquist, *Bell v. Wolfish*, that case dealt with the constitutionality of "double-bunking" and other conditions of pretrial detention for adult offenders the legitimacy of whose incarceration was undisputed. *Schall*, however, involved a situation in which the legitimacy of the detention itself was at issue. Thus, the use of the "legitimate state objective" test relegates the fundamental liberty interests of presumptively innocent juveniles to the same reduced level of constitutional scrutiny as lesser interests of adults who have already been legally deprived of their liberty.

Moreover, the "legitimate state objective" standard is surprisingly easy to satisfy and has the potential to affect future children's rights cases significantly. In this particular case, however, the statute apparently failed to promote the government interests regardless of whether those interests were deemed compelling or merely legitimate. The real problem with the Court's analysis lies in the Court's blithe acceptance of the appellants' assertions that the detention provision had actually fulfilled its alleged objectives. In reaching its conclusion that the statute was justified by a legislative purpose of protecting both society and the juvenile from the youth's misconduct, the Court paid no heed to its usual practice of accepting a lower court's findings of fact unless "clearly erroneous," and ignored legislative history, the testimony of a judge who administered the provision, scientific authority, and common sense.

New Jersey v. T.L.O.
469 U.S. 325 (1985)

Justice WHITE delivered the opinion of the Court.

We granted certiorari in this case to examine the appropriateness of the exclusionary rule as a remedy for searches carried out in violation of the Fourth Amendment by public school authorities. Our consideration of the proper application of the Fourth Amendment to the public schools, however, has led us to conclude that the search that gave rise to the case now before us did not violate the Fourth Amendment. Accordingly, we here address only the questions of the proper standard for assessing the legality of searches conducted by public school officials and the application of that standard to the facts of this case.

I

On March 7, 1980, a teacher at Piscataway High School in Middlesex County, N.J., discovered two girls smoking in a lavatory. One of the two girls was the respondent T.L.O., who at that time was a 14-year-old high school freshman. Because smoking in the lavatory was a violation of a school rule, the teacher took the two girls to the Principal's office, where they met with Assistant Vice Principal Theodore Choplick. In response to questioning by Mr. Choplick, T.L.O.'s companion admitted that she had violated the rule. T.L.O., however, denied that she had been smoking in the lavatory and claimed that she did not smoke at all.

Mr. Choplick asked T.L.O. to come into his private office and demanded to see her purse. Opening the purse, he found a pack of cigarettes, which he removed from the purse and held before T.L.O. as he accused her of having lied to him. As he reached into the purse for the cigarettes, Mr. Choplick also noticed a package of cigarette rolling papers. In his experience, possession of rolling papers by high school students was closely associated with the use of marihuana. Suspecting that a closer examination of the purse might yield further evidence of drug use, Mr. Choplick proceeded to search the purse thoroughly. The search revealed a small amount of marihuana, a pipe, a number of empty plastic bags, a substantial quantity of money in one-dollar bills, an index card that appeared to be a list of students who owed T.L.O. money, and two letters that implicated T.L.O. in marihuana dealing.

Mr. Choplick notified T.L.O.'s mother and the police, and turned the evidence of drug dealing over to the police. At the request of the police, T.L.O.'s mother took her daughter to police headquarters, where T.L.O. confessed that she had been selling marihuana at the high school. On the basis of the confession and the evidence seized by Mr. Choplick, the State brought delinquency charges against T.L.O. in the Juvenile and Domestic Relations Court of Middlesex County.[1] Contending that Mr. Choplick's search of her purse violated the Fourth Amendment, T.L.O. moved to suppress the evidence found in her purse as well as her confession, which, she argued, was tainted by the allegedly unlawful search. The Juvenile Court denied the motion to suppress. Although the court concluded that the Fourth Amendment did apply to searches carried out by school officials, it held that

"a school official may properly conduct a search of a student's person if the official has a reasonable suspicion that a crime has been or is in the process of being committed, *or* reasonable cause to believe that the search is necessary to maintain school discipline or enforce school policies."

Applying this standard, the court concluded that the search conducted by Mr. Choplick was a reasonable one. The initial decision to open the purse was justified by Mr. Choplick's well-founded suspicion that T.L.O. had violated the rule forbidding smoking in the lavatory. Once the purse was open, evidence of marihuana violations was in plain view, and Mr. Choplick was entitled to conduct a thorough search to determine the nature and extent of T.L.O.'s drug-related activities. Having denied the motion to suppress, the court

---

1. T.L.O. also received a 3-day suspension from school for smoking cigarettes in a nonsmoking area and a 7-day suspension for possession of marihuana. On T.L.O.'s motion, the Superior Court of New Jersey, Chancery Division, set aside the 7-day suspension on the ground that it was based on evidence seized in violation of the Fourth Amendment.

on March 23, 1981, found T.L.O. to be a delinquent and on January 8, 1982, sentenced her to a year's probation.

On appeal from the final judgment of the Juvenile Court, a divided Appellate Division affirmed the trial court's finding that there had been no Fourth Amendment violation, but vacated the adjudication of delinquency and remanded for a determination whether T.L.O. had knowingly and voluntarily waived her Fifth Amendment rights before confessing. T.L.O. appealed the Fourth Amendment ruling, and the Supreme Court of New Jersey reversed the judgment of the Appellate Division and ordered the suppression of the evidence found in T.L.O.'s purse.

The New Jersey Supreme Court agreed with the lower courts that the Fourth Amendment applies to searches conducted by school officials. The court also rejected the State of New Jersey's argument that the exclusionary rule should not be employed to prevent the use in juvenile proceedings of evidence unlawfully seized by school officials. Declining to consider whether applying the rule to the fruits of searches by school officials would have any deterrent value, the court held simply that the precedents of this Court establish that "if an official search violates constitutional rights, the evidence is not admissible in criminal proceedings."

With respect to the question of the legality of the search before it, the court agreed with the Juvenile Court that a warrantless search by a school official does not violate the Fourth Amendment so long as the official "has reasonable grounds to believe that a student possesses evidence of illegal activity or activity that would interfere with school discipline and order." However, the court, with two justices dissenting, sharply disagreed with the Juvenile Court's conclusion that the search of the purse was reasonable. According to the majority, the contents of T.L.O.'s purse had no bearing on the accusation against T.L.O., for possession of cigarettes (as opposed to smoking them in the lavatory) did not violate school rules, and a mere desire for evidence that would impeach T.L.O.'s claim that she did not smoke cigarettes could not justify the search. Moreover, even if a reasonable suspicion that T.L.O. had cigarettes in her purse would justify a search, Mr. Choplick had no such suspicion, as no one had furnished him with any specific information that there were cigarettes in the purse. Finally, leaving aside the question whether Mr. Choplick was justified in opening the purse, the court held that the evidence of drug use that he saw inside did not justify the extensive "rummaging" through T.L.O.'s papers and effects that followed.

We granted the State of New Jersey's petition for certiorari. Although the State had argued in the Supreme Court of New Jersey that the search of T.L.O.'s purse did not violate the Fourth Amendment, the petition for certiorari raised only the question whether the exclusionary rule should operate to bar consideration in juvenile delinquency proceedings of evidence unlawfully seized by a school official without the involvement of law enforcement officers. When this case was first argued last Term, the State conceded for the purpose of argument that the standard devised by the New Jersey Supreme Court for determining the legality of school searches was appropriate and that the court had correctly applied that standard; the State contended only that the remedial purposes of the exclusionary rule were not well served by applying it to searches conducted by public authorities not primarily engaged in law enforcement.

Although we originally granted certiorari to decide the issue of the appropriate remedy in juvenile court proceedings for unlawful school searches, our doubts regarding the wisdom of deciding that question in isolation from the broader question of what limits, if any, the Fourth Amendment places on the activities of school authorities prompted us to order reargument on that question.[2] Having heard argument on the legality of the search of T.L.O.'s purse, we are satisfied ... the search did not violate the Fourth Amendment.[3]

II

In determining whether the search at issue in this case violated the Fourth Amendment, we are faced initially with the question whether that Amendment's prohibition on unreasonable searches and seizures applies to searches conducted by public school officials. We hold that it does.

It is now beyond dispute that "the Federal Constitution, by virtue of the Fourteenth Amendment, prohibits unreasonable searches and seizures by state officers." Equally indisputable is the proposition that the Fourteenth Amendment protects the rights of students against encroachment by public school officials:

> "The Fourteenth Amendment, as now applied to the States, protects the citizen against the State itself and all of its creatures—Boards of Education not excepted. These have, of course, important, delicate, and highly discretionary functions, but none that they may not perform within the limits of the Bill of Rights. That they are educating the young for citizenship is reason for scrupulous protection of Constitutional freedoms of the individual, if we are not to strangle the free mind at its source and teach youth to discount important principles of our government as mere platitudes."

These two propositions—that the Fourth Amendment applies to the States through the Fourteenth Amendment, and that the actions of public school officials are subject to the

---

2. State and federal courts considering these questions have struggled to accommodate the interests protected by the Fourth Amendment and the interest of the States in providing a safe environment conducive to education in the public schools. Some courts have resolved the tension between these interests by giving full force to one or the other side of the balance. Thus, in a number of cases courts have held that school officials conducting in-school searches of students are private parties acting *in loco parentis* and are therefore not subject to the constraints of the Fourth Amendment. At least one court has held, on the other hand, that the Fourth Amendment applies in full to in-school searches by school officials and that a search conducted without probable cause is unreasonable; others have held or suggested that the probable-cause standard is applicable at least where the police are involved in a search, or where the search is highly intrusive.

The majority of courts that have addressed the issue of the Fourth Amendment in the schools have, like the Supreme Court of New Jersey in this case, reached a middle position: the Fourth Amendment applies to searches conducted by school authorities, but the special needs of the school environment require assessment of the legality of such searches against a standard less exacting than that of probable cause. These courts have, by and large, upheld warrantless searches by school authorities provided that they are supported by a reasonable suspicion that the search will uncover evidence of an infraction of school disciplinary rules or a violation of the law.

Although few have considered the matter, courts have also split over whether the exclusionary rule is an appropriate remedy for Fourth Amendment violations committed by school authorities. The Georgia courts have held that although the Fourth Amendment applies to the schools, the exclusionary rule does not. Other jurisdictions have applied the rule to exclude the fruits of unlawful school searches from criminal trials and delinquency proceedings.

3. In holding that the search of T.L.O.'s purse did not violate the Fourth Amendment, we do not implicitly determine that the exclusionary rule applies to the fruits of unlawful searches conducted by school authorities. The question whether evidence should be excluded from a criminal proceeding involves two discrete inquiries: whether the evidence was seized in violation of the Fourth Amendment, and whether the exclusionary rule is the appropriate remedy for the violation. Neither question is logically antecedent to the other, for a negative answer to either question is sufficient to dispose of the case. Thus, our determination that the search at issue in this case did not violate the Fourth Amendment implies no particular resolution of the question of the applicability of the exclusionary rule.

limits placed on state action by the Fourteenth Amendment—might appear sufficient to answer the suggestion that the Fourth Amendment does not proscribe unreasonable searches by school officials. On reargument, however, the State of New Jersey has argued that the history of the Fourth Amendment indicates that the Amendment was intended to regulate only searches and seizures carried out by law enforcement officers; accordingly, although public school officials are concededly state agents for purposes of the Fourteenth Amendment, the Fourth Amendment creates no rights enforceable against them.[4]

It may well be true that the evil toward which the Fourth Amendment was primarily directed was the resurrection of the pre-Revolutionary practice of using general warrants or "writs of assistance" to authorize searches for contraband by officers of the Crown. But this Court has never limited the Amendment's prohibition on unreasonable searches and seizures to operations conducted by the police. Rather, the Court has long spoken of the Fourth Amendment's strictures as restraints imposed upon "governmental action"— that is, "upon the activities of sovereign authority." Accordingly, we have held the Fourth Amendment applicable to the activities of civil as well as criminal authorities: building inspectors, Occupational Safety and Health Act inspectors, and even firemen entering privately-owned premises to battle a fire, are all subject to the restraints imposed by the Fourth Amendment. As we [have] observed "[t]he basic purpose of this Amendment, as recognized in countless decisions of this Court, is to safeguard the privacy and security of individuals against arbitrary invasions by governmental officials." Because the individual's interest in privacy and personal security "suffers whether the government's motivation is to investigate violations of criminal laws or breaches of other statutory or regulatory standards," it would be "anomalous to say that the individual and his private property are fully protected by the Fourth Amendment only when the individual is suspected of criminal behavior."

Notwithstanding the general applicability of the Fourth Amendment to the activities of civil authorities, a few courts have concluded that school officials are exempt from the dictates of the Fourth Amendment by virtue of the special nature of their authority over schoolchildren. Teachers and school administrators, it is said, act *in loco parentis* in their dealings with students: their authority is that of the parent, not the State, and is therefore not subject to the limits of the Fourth Amendment.

Such reasoning is in tension with contemporary reality and the teachings of this Court. We have held school officials subject to the commands of the First Amendment, and the Due Process Clause of the Fourteenth Amendment. If school authorities are state actors for purposes of the constitutional guarantees of freedom of expression and due process, it is difficult to understand why they should be deemed to be exercising parental rather than public authority when conducting searches of their students. More generally, the Court has recognized that "the concept of parental delegation" as a source of school authority is not entirely "consonant with compulsory education laws." Today's public school officials do not merely exercise authority voluntarily conferred on them by individual parents; rather, they act in furtherance of publicly mandated educational and disciplinary policies.... In carrying out searches and other disciplinary functions pursuant to such policies, school officials act as representatives of the State, not merely as surrogates for the parents, and they cannot claim the parents' immunity from the strictures of the Fourth Amendment.

---

4. Cf. *Ingraham v. Wright*, (holding that the Eighth Amendment's prohibition of cruel and unusual punishment applies only to punishments imposed after criminal convictions and hence does not apply to corporal punishment of schoolchildren by public school officials).

III

To hold that the Fourth Amendment applies to searches conducted by school authorities is only to begin the inquiry into the standards governing such searches. Although the underlying command of the Fourth Amendment is always that searches and seizures be reasonable, what is reasonable depends on the context within which a search takes place. The determination of the standard of reasonableness governing any specific class of searches requires "balancing the need to search against the invasion which the search entails." On one side of the balance are arrayed the individual's legitimate expectations of privacy and personal security; on the other, the government's need for effective methods to deal with breaches of public order.

We have recognized that even a limited search of the person is a substantial invasion of privacy. We have also recognized that searches of closed items of personal luggage are intrusions on protected privacy interests, for "the Fourth Amendment provides protection to the owner of every container that conceals its contents from plain view." A search of a child's person or of a closed purse or other bag carried on her person,[5] no less than a similar search carried out on an adult, is undoubtedly a severe violation of subjective expectations of privacy.

Of course, the Fourth Amendment does not protect subjective expectations of privacy that are unreasonable or otherwise "illegitimate." To receive the protection of the Fourth Amendment, an expectation of privacy must be one that society is "prepared to recognize as legitimate." The State of New Jersey has argued that because of the pervasive supervision to which children in the schools are necessarily subject, a child has virtually no legitimate expectation of privacy in articles of personal property "unnecessarily" carried into a school. This argument has two factual premises: (1) the fundamental incompatibility of expectations of privacy with the maintenance of a sound educational environment; and (2) the minimal interest of the child in bringing any items of personal property into the school. Both premises are severely flawed.

Although this Court may take notice of the difficulty of maintaining discipline in the public schools today, the situation is not so dire that students in the schools may claim no legitimate expectations of privacy. We have recently recognized that the need to maintain order in a prison is such that prisoners retain no legitimate expectations of privacy in their cells, but it goes almost without saying that "[t]he prisoner and the schoolchild stand in wholly different circumstances, separated by the harsh facts of criminal conviction and incarceration." We are not yet ready to hold that the schools and the prisons need be equated for purposes of the Fourth Amendment.

Nor does the State's suggestion that children have no legitimate need to bring personal property into the schools seem well anchored in reality. Students at a minimum must bring to school not only the supplies needed for their studies, but also keys, money, and the necessaries of personal hygiene and grooming. In addition, students may carry on

---

5. We do not address the question, not presented by this case, whether a schoolchild has a legitimate expectation of privacy in lockers, desks, or other school property provided for the storage of school supplies. Nor do we express any opinion on the standards (if any) governing searches of such areas by school officials or by other public authorities acting at the request of school officials. Compare *Zamora v. Pomeroy* ("Inasmuch as the school had assumed joint control of the locker it cannot be successfully maintained that the school did not have a right to inspect it"), and *People v. Overton* (school administrators have power to consent to search of a student's locker), with *State v. Engerud* ("We are satisfied that in the context of this case the student had an expectation of privacy in the contents of his locker * * *. For the four years of high school, the school locker is a home away from home. In it the student stores the kind of personal 'effects' protected by the Fourth Amendment").

their persons or in purses or wallets such nondisruptive yet highly personal items as photographs, letters, and diaries. Finally, students may have perfectly legitimate reasons to carry with them articles of property needed in connection with extracurricular or recreational activities. In short, schoolchildren may find it necessary to carry with them a variety of legitimate, noncontraband items, and there is no reason to conclude that they have necessarily waived all rights to privacy in such items merely by bringing them onto school grounds.

Against the child's interest in privacy must be set the substantial interest of teachers and administrators in maintaining discipline in the classroom and on school grounds. Maintaining order in the classroom has never been easy, but in recent years, school disorder has often taken particularly ugly forms: drug use and violent crime in the schools have become major social problems. Even in schools that have been spared the most severe disciplinary problems, the preservation of order and a proper educational environment requires close supervision of schoolchildren, as well as the enforcement of rules against conduct that would be perfectly permissible if undertaken by an adult. "Events calling for discipline are frequent occurrences and sometimes require immediate, effective action." Accordingly, we have recognized that maintaining security and order in the schools requires a certain degree of flexibility in school disciplinary procedures, and we have respected the value of preserving the informality of the student-teacher relationship.

How, then, should we strike the balance between the schoolchild's legitimate expectations of privacy and the school's equally legitimate need to maintain an environment in which learning can take place? It is evident that the school setting requires some easing of the restrictions to which searches by public authorities are ordinarily subject. The warrant requirement, in particular, is unsuited to the school environment: requiring a teacher to obtain a warrant before searching a child suspected of an infraction of school rules (or of the criminal law) would unduly interfere with the maintenance of the swift and informal disciplinary procedures needed in the schools. Just as we have in other cases dispensed with the warrant requirement when "the burden of obtaining a warrant is likely to frustrate the governmental purpose behind the search," we hold today that school officials need not obtain a warrant before searching a student who is under their authority.

The school setting also requires some modification of the level of suspicion of illicit activity needed to justify a search. Ordinarily, a search—even one that may permissibly be carried out without a warrant—must be based upon "probable cause" to believe that a violation of the law has occurred. However, "probable cause" is not an irreducible requirement of a valid search. The fundamental command of the Fourth Amendment is that searches and seizures be reasonable, and although "both the concept of probable cause and the requirement of a warrant bear on the reasonableness of a search, * * * in certain limited circumstances neither is required." Thus, we have in a number of cases recognized the legality of searches and seizures based on suspicions that, although "reasonable," do not rise to the level of probable cause. Where a careful balancing of governmental and private interests suggests that the public interest is best served by a Fourth Amendment standard of reasonableness that stops short of probable cause, we have not hesitated to adopt such a standard.

We join the majority of courts that have examined this issue in concluding that the accommodation of the privacy interests of schoolchildren with the substantial need of teachers and administrators for freedom to maintain order in the schools does not require strict adherence to the requirement that searches be based on probable cause to believe that the subject of the search has violated or is violating the law. Rather, the legality of a search of a student should depend simply on the reasonableness, under all the circumstances, of the search. Determining the reasonableness of any search involves a twofold inquiry: first, one must consider "whether the * * * action was justified at its inception"; second, one must determine whether the search as actually conducted "was reasonably related in scope to the circumstances which justified the interference in the first place." Under ordinary circumstances, a search of a student by a teacher or other school official[7] will be "justified at its inception" when there are reasonable grounds for suspecting that the search will turn up evidence that the student has violated or is violating either the law or the rules of the school.[8] Such a search will be permissible in its scope when the measures adopted are reasonably related to the objectives of the search and not excessively intrusive in light of the age and sex of the student and the nature of the infraction.[9]

This standard will, we trust, neither unduly burden the efforts of school authorities to maintain order in their schools nor authorize unrestrained intrusions upon the privacy of schoolchildren. By focusing attention on the question of reasonableness, the standard will spare teachers and school administrators the necessity of schooling themselves in the niceties of probable cause and permit them to regulate their conduct according to the dictates of reason and common sense. At the same time, the reasonableness standard should ensure that the interests of students will be invaded no more than is necessary to achieve the legitimate end of preserving order in the schools.

IV

There remains the question of the legality of the search in this case. We recognize that the "reasonable grounds" standard applied by the New Jersey Supreme Court in its consideration of this question is not substantially different from the standard that we have adopted today. Nonetheless, we believe that the New Jersey court's application of that

---

7. We here consider only searches carried out by school authorities acting alone and on their own authority. This case does not present the question of the appropriate standard for assessing the legality of searches conducted by school officials in conjunction with or at the behest of law enforcement agencies, and we express no opinion on that question.

8. We do not decide whether individualized suspicion is an essential element of the reasonableness standard we adopt for searches by school authorities. In other contexts, however, we have held that although "some quantum of individualized suspicion is usually a prerequisite to a constitutional search or seizure[,] * * * the Fourth Amendment imposes no irreducible requirement of such suspicion." Exceptions to the requirement of individualized suspicion are generally appropriate only where the privacy interests implicated by a search are minimal and where "other safeguards" are available "to assure that the individual's reasonable expectation of privacy is not 'subject to the discretion of the official in the field.'" Because the search of T.L.O.'s purse was based upon an individualized suspicion that she had violated school rules, we need not consider the circumstances that might justify school authorities in conducting searches unsupported by individualized suspicion.

9. Our reference to the nature of the infraction is not intended as an endorsement of Justice STEVENS' suggestion that some rules regarding student conduct are by nature too "trivial" to justify a search based upon reasonable suspicion. We are unwilling to adopt a standard under which the legality of a search is dependent upon a judge's evaluation of the relative importance of various school rules. The maintenance of discipline in the schools requires not only that students be restrained from assaulting one another, abusing drugs and alcohol, and committing other crimes, but also that students conform themselves to the standards of conduct prescribed by school authorities. We have "repeatedly emphasized the need for affirming the comprehensive authority of the States and of school officials, consistent with fundamental constitutional safeguards, to prescribe and control conduct in the schools." The promulgation of a rule forbidding specified conduct presumably reflects a judgment on the part of school officials that such conduct is destructive of school order or of a proper educational environment. Absent any suggestion that the rule violates some substantive constitutional guarantee, the courts should, as a general matter, defer to that judgment and refrain from attempting to distinguish between rules that are important to the preservation of order in the schools and rules that are not.

standard to strike down the search of T.L.O.'s purse reflects a somewhat crabbed notion of reasonableness. Our review of the facts surrounding the search leads us to conclude that the search was in no sense unreasonable for Fourth Amendment purposes.[10]

The incident that gave rise to this case actually involved two separate searches, with the first—the search for cigarettes—providing the suspicion that gave rise to the second—the search for marihuana. Although it is the fruits of the second search that are at issue here, the validity of the search for marihuana must depend on the reasonableness of the initial search for cigarettes, as there would have been no reason to suspect that T.L.O. possessed marihuana had the first search not taken place. Accordingly, it is to the search for cigarettes that we first turn our attention.

The New Jersey Supreme Court pointed to two grounds for its holding that the search for cigarettes was unreasonable. First, the court observed that possession of cigarettes was not in itself illegal or a violation of school rules. Because the contents of T.L.O.'s purse would therefore have "no direct bearing on the infraction" of which she was accused (smoking in a lavatory where smoking was prohibited), there was no reason to search her purse.[11] Second, even assuming that a search of T.L.O.'s purse might under some circumstances be reasonable in light of the accusation made against T.L.O., the New Jersey court concluded that Mr. Choplick in this particular case had no reasonable grounds to suspect that T.L.O. had cigarettes in her purse. At best, according to the court, Mr. Choplick had "a good hunch."

Both these conclusions are implausible. T.L.O. had been accused of smoking, and had denied the accusation in the strongest possible terms when she stated that she did not smoke at all. Surely it cannot be said that under these circumstances, T.L.O.'s possession of cigarettes would be irrelevant to the charges against her or to her response to those charges. T.L.O.'s possession of cigarettes, once it was discovered, would both corroborate the report that she had been smoking and undermine the credibility of her defense to the charge of smoking. To be sure, the discovery of the cigarettes would not prove that T.L.O. had been smoking in the lavatory; nor would it, strictly speaking, necessarily be inconsistent with her claim that she did not smoke at all. But it is universally recognized that evidence, to be relevant to an inquiry, need not conclusively prove the ultimate fact in issue, but only have "any tendency to make the existence of any fact that is of consequence to the determination of the action more probable or less probable than it would be without the evidence." The relevance of T.L.O.'s possession of cigarettes to the question whether she had been smoking and to the credibility of her denial that she smoked supplied the necessary "nexus" between the item searched for and the infraction under investigation.

---

10. Of course, New Jersey may insist on a more demanding standard under its own Constitution or statutes. In that case, its courts would not purport to be applying the Fourth Amendment when they invalidate a search.

11. Justice STEVENS interprets these statements as a holding that enforcement of the school's smoking regulations was not sufficiently related to the goal of maintaining discipline or order in the school to justify a search under the standard adopted by the New Jersey court. We do not agree that this is an accurate characterization of the New Jersey Supreme Court's opinion. The New Jersey court did not hold that the school's smoking rules were unrelated to the goal of maintaining discipline or order, nor did it suggest that a search that would produce evidence bearing directly on an accusation that a student had violated the smoking rules would be impermissible under the court's reasonable-suspicion standard; rather, the court concluded that any evidence a search of T.L.O.'s purse was likely to produce would not have a sufficiently direct bearing on the infraction to justify a search—a conclusion with which we cannot agree. JUSTICE STEVENS' suggestion that the New Jersey Supreme Court's decision rested on the perceived triviality of the smoking infraction appears to be a reflection of his own views rather than those of the New Jersey court.

Thus, if Mr. Choplick in fact had a reasonable suspicion that T.L.O. had cigarettes in her purse, the search was justified despite the fact that the cigarettes, if found, would constitute "mere evidence" of a violation.

Of course, the New Jersey Supreme Court also held that Mr. Choplick had no reasonable suspicion that the purse would contain cigarettes. This conclusion is puzzling. A teacher had reported that T.L.O. was smoking in the lavatory. Certainly this report gave Mr. Choplick reason to suspect that T.L.O. was carrying cigarettes with her; and if she did have cigarettes, her purse was the obvious place in which to find them. Mr. Choplick's suspicion that there were cigarettes in the purse was not an "inchoate and unparticularized suspicion or 'hunch,'" rather, it was the sort of "common-sense conclusio[n] about human behavior" upon which "practical people"—including government officials—are entitled to rely. Of course, even if the teacher's report were true, T.L.O. *might* not have had a pack of cigarettes with her; she might have borrowed a cigarette from someone else or have been sharing a cigarette with another student. But the requirement of reasonable suspicion is not a requirement of absolute certainty: "sufficient probability, not certainty, is the touchstone of reasonableness under the Fourth Amendment. * * *" Because the hypothesis that T.L.O. was carrying cigarettes in her purse was itself not unreasonable, it is irrelevant that other hypotheses were also consistent with the teacher's accusation. Accordingly, it cannot be said that Mr. Choplick acted unreasonably when he examined T.L.O.'s purse to see if it contained cigarettes.[12]

Our conclusion that Mr. Choplick's decision to open T.L.O.'s purse was reasonable brings us to the question of the further search for marihuana once the pack of cigarettes was located. The suspicion upon which the search for marihuana was founded was provided when Mr. Choplick observed a package of rolling papers in the purse as he removed the pack of cigarettes. Although T.L.O. does not dispute the reasonableness of Mr. Choplick's belief that the rolling papers indicated the presence of marihuana, she does contend that the scope of the search Mr. Choplick conducted exceeded permissible bounds when he seized and read certain letters that implicated T.L.O. in drug dealing. This argument, too, is unpersuasive. The discovery of the rolling papers concededly gave rise to a reasonable suspicion that T.L.O. was carrying marihuana as well as cigarettes in her purse. This suspicion justified further exploration of T.L.O.'s purse, which turned up more evidence of drug-related activities: a pipe, a number of plastic bags of the type commonly used to store marihuana, a small quantity of marihuana, and a fairly substantial amount of money. Under these circumstances, it was not unreasonable to extend the search to a separate zippered compartment of the purse; and when a search of that compartment revealed an index card containing a list of "people who owe me money" as well as two letters, the inference that T.L.O. was involved in marihuana trafficking was substantial enough to jus-

---

12. T.L.O. contends that even if it was reasonable for Mr. Choplick to open her purse to look for cigarettes, it was not reasonable for him to reach in and take the cigarettes out of her purse once he found them. Had he not removed the cigarettes from the purse, she asserts, he would not have observed the rolling papers that suggested the presence of marihuana, and the search for marihuana could not have taken place. T.L.O.'s argument is based on the fact that the cigarettes were not "contraband," as no school rule forbade her to have them. Thus, according to T.L.O., the cigarettes were not subject to seizure or confiscation by school authorities, and Mr. Choplick was not entitled to take them out of T.L.O.'s purse regardless of whether he was entitled to peer into the purse to see if they were there. Such hairsplitting argumentation has no place in an inquiry addressed to the issue of reasonableness. If Mr. Choplick could permissibly search T.L.O.'s purse for cigarettes, it hardly seems reasonable to suggest that his natural reaction to finding them—picking them up—could be a constitutional violation. We find that neither in opening the purse nor in reaching into it to remove the cigarettes did Mr. Choplick violate the Fourth Amendment.

tify Mr. Choplick in examining the letters to determine whether they contained any further evidence. In short, we cannot conclude that the search for marihuana was unreasonable in any respect.

Because the search resulting in the discovery of the evidence of marihuana dealing by T.L.O. was reasonable, the New Jersey Supreme Court's decision to exclude that evidence from T.L.O.'s juvenile delinquency proceedings on Fourth Amendment grounds was erroneous. Accordingly, the judgment of the Supreme Court of New Jersey is

Reversed.

Justice POWELL, with whom Justice O'CONNOR joins, concurring.

I agree with the Court's decision, and generally with its opinion. I would place greater emphasis, however, on the special characteristics of elementary and secondary schools that make it unnecessary to afford students the same constitutional protections granted adults and juveniles in a nonschool setting.

In any realistic sense, students within the school environment have a lesser expectation of privacy than members of the population generally. They spend the school hours in close association with each other, both in the classroom and during recreation periods. The students in a particular class often know each other and their teachers quite well. Of necessity, teachers have a degree of familiarity with, and authority over, their students that is unparalleled except perhaps in the relationship between parent and child. It is simply unrealistic to think that students have the same subjective expectation of privacy as the population generally. But for purposes of deciding this case, I can assume that children in school — no less than adults — have privacy interests that society is prepared to recognize as legitimate.

However one may characterize their privacy expectations, students properly are afforded some constitutional protections. In an often quoted statement, the Court said that students do not "shed their constitutional rights * * * at the schoolhouse gate." The Court also has "emphasized the need for affirming the comprehensive authority of the states and of school officials * * * to prescribe and control conduct in the schools." The Court has balanced the interests of the student against the school officials' need to maintain discipline by recognizing qualitative differences between the constitutional remedies to which students and adults are entitled.

In *Goss v. Lopez,* the Court recognized a constitutional right to due process, and yet was careful to limit the exercise of this right by a student who challenged a disciplinary suspension. The only process found to be "due" was notice and a hearing described as "rudimentary"; it amounted to no more than "the disciplinarian * * * informally discuss[ing] the alleged misconduct with the student minutes after it has occurred." In *Ingraham v. Wright,* we declined to extend the Eighth Amendment to prohibit the use of corporal punishment of schoolchildren as authorized by Florida law. We emphasized in that opinion that familiar constraints in the school, and also in the community, provide substantial protection against the violation of constitutional rights by school authorities. "[A]t the end of the school day, the child is invariably free to return home. Even while at school, the child brings with him the support of family and friends and is rarely apart from teachers and other pupils who may witness and protest any instances of mistreatment." The *Ingraham* Court further pointed out that the "openness of the public school and its supervision by the community afford significant safeguards" against the violation of constitutional rights.

The special relationship between teacher and student also distinguishes the setting within which schoolchildren operate. Law enforcement officers function as adversaries of criminal suspects. These officers have the responsibility to investigate criminal activity, to locate and arrest those who violate our laws, and to facilitate the charging and bringing of such persons to trial. Rarely does this type of adversarial relationship exist between school authorities and pupils.[1] Instead, there is a commonality of interests between teachers and their pupils. The attitude of the typical teacher is one of personal responsibility for the student's welfare as well as for his education.

The primary duty of school officials and teachers, as the Court states, is the education and training of young people. A State has a compelling interest in assuring that the schools meet this responsibility. Without first establishing discipline and maintaining order, teachers cannot begin to educate their students. And apart from education, the school has the obligation to protect pupils from mistreatment by other children, and also to protect teachers themselves from violence by the few students whose conduct in recent years has prompted national concern. For me, it would be unreasonable and at odds with history to argue that the full panoply of constitutional rules applies with the same force and effect in the schoolhouse as it does in the enforcement of criminal laws.[2]

In sum, although I join the Court's opinion and its holding,[3] my emphasis is somewhat different.

Justice BLACKMUN, concurring in the judgment.

I join the judgment of the Court and agree with much that is said in its opinion. I write separately, however, because I believe the Court omits a crucial step in its analysis of whether a school search must be based upon probable-cause. The Court correctly states that we have recognized limited exceptions to the probable-cause requirement "[w]here a careful balancing of governmental and private interests suggests that the public interest is best served" by a lesser standard. I believe that we have used such a balancing test, rather than strictly applying the Fourth Amendment's Warrant and Probable-Cause Clause, only when we were confronted with "a special law enforcement need for greater flexibility." I pointed out in *United States v. Place*:

> "While the Fourth Amendment speaks in terms of freedom from unreasonable [searches], the Amendment does not leave the reasonableness of most [searches] to the judgment of courts or government officers; the Framers of the Amendment balanced the interests involved and decided that a [search] is reasonable only if supported by a judicial warrant based on probable cause."

Only in those exceptional circumstances in which special needs, beyond the normal need for law enforcement, make the warrant and probable-cause requirement impracticable, is a court entitled to substitute its balancing of interests for that of the Framers.

Thus, for example, in determining that police can conduct a limited "stop and frisk" upon less than probable cause, this Court relied upon the fact that "as a practical matter" the stop and frisk could not be subjected to a warrant and probable-cause require-

---

1. Unlike police officers, school authorities have no law enforcement responsibility or indeed any obligation to be familiar with the criminal laws. Of course, as illustrated by this case, school authorities have a layman's familiarity with the types of crimes that occur frequently in our schools: the distribution and use of drugs, theft, and even violence against teachers as well as fellow students.

2. As noted above, decisions of this Court have never held to the contrary. The law recognizes a host of distinctions between the rights and duties of children and those of adults.

3. The Court's holding is that "when there are reasonable grounds for suspecting that [a] search will turn up evidence that the student has violated or is violating either the law or the rules of the school," a search of the student's person or belongings is justified. This is in accord with the Court's summary of the views of a majority of the state and federal courts that have addressed this issue.

ment, because a law enforcement officer must be able to take immediate steps to assure himself that the person he has stopped to question is not armed with a weapon that could be used against him. Similarly, this Court's holding that a roving Border Patrol may stop a car and briefly question its occupants upon less than probable cause was based in part upon "the absence of practical alternatives for policing the border."

The Court's implication that the balancing test is the rule rather than the exception is troubling for me because it is unnecessary in this case. The elementary and secondary school setting presents a special need for flexibility justifying a departure from the balance struck by the Framers. As Justice POWELL notes, "[w]ithout first establishing discipline and maintaining order, teachers cannot begin to educate their students." Maintaining order in the classroom can be a difficult task. A single teacher often must watch over a large number of students, and, as any parent knows, children at certain ages are inclined to test the outer boundaries of acceptable conduct and to imitate the misbehavior of a peer if that misbehavior is not dealt with quickly. Every adult remembers from his own schooldays the havoc a water pistol or peashooter can wreak until it is taken away. Thus, the Court has recognized that "[e]vents calling for discipline are frequent occurrences and sometimes require immediate, effective action." Indeed, because drug use and possession of weapons have become increasingly common among young people, an immediate response frequently is required not just to maintain an environment conducive to learning, but to protect the very safety of students and school personnel.

Such immediate action obviously would not be possible if a teacher were required to secure a warrant before searching a student. Nor would it be possible if a teacher could not conduct a necessary search until the teacher thought there was probable cause for the search. A teacher has neither the training nor the day-to-day experience in the complexities of probable cause that a law enforcement officer possesses, and is ill-equipped to make a quick judgment about the existence of probable cause. The time required for a teacher to ask the questions or make the observations that are necessary to turn reasonable grounds into probable cause is time during which the teacher, and other students, are diverted from the essential task of education. A teacher's focus is, and should be, on teaching and helping students, rather than on developing evidence against a particular troublemaker.

Education "is perhaps the most important function" of government, and government has a heightened obligation to safeguard students whom it compels to attend school. The special need for an immediate response to behavior that threatens either the safety of schoolchildren and teachers or the educational process itself justifies the Court in excepting school searches from the warrant and probable-cause requirement, and in applying a standard determined by balancing the relevant interests. I agree with the standard the Court has announced, and with its application of the standard to the facts of this case. I therefore concur in its judgment.

Justice BRENNAN, with whom Justice MARSHALL joins, concurring in part and dissenting in part.

I fully agree with Part II of the Court's opinion. Teachers, like all other government officials, must conform their conduct to the Fourth Amendment's protections of personal privacy and personal security. As Justice STEVENS points out, this principle is of particular importance when applied to schoolteachers, for children learn as much by example as by exposition. It would be incongruous and futile to charge teachers with the task of embuing their students with an understanding of our system of constitutional democracy, while at the same time immunizing those same teachers from the need to respect constitutional protections.

I do not, however, otherwise join the Court's opinion. Today's decision sanctions school officials to conduct full-scale searches on a "reasonableness" standard whose only definite content is that it is *not* the same test as the "probable cause" standard found in the text of the Fourth Amendment. In adopting this unclear, unprecedented, and unnecessary departure from generally applicable Fourth Amendment standards, the Court carves out a broad exception to standards that this Court has developed over years of considering Fourth Amendment problems. Its decision is supported neither by precedent nor even by a fair application of the "balancing test" it proclaims in this very opinion.

I

Three basic principles underly this Court's Fourth Amendment jurisprudence. First, warrantless searches are *per se* unreasonable, subject only to a few specifically delineated and well-recognized exceptions. Second, full-scale searches—whether conducted in accordance with the warrant requirement or pursuant to one of its exceptions—are "reasonable" in Fourth Amendment terms only on a showing of probable cause to believe that a crime has been committed and that evidence of the crime will be found in the place to be searched. Third, categories of intrusions that are substantially less intrusive than full-scale searches or seizures may be justifiable in accordance with a balancing test even absent a warrant or probable cause, provided that the balancing test used gives sufficient weight to the privacy interests that will be infringed.

Assistant Vice Principal Choplick's thorough excavation of T.L.O.'s purse was undoubtedly a serious intrusion on her privacy. Unlike the searches in *Terry v. Ohio,* the search at issue here encompassed a detailed and minute examination of respondent's pocketbook, in which the contents of private papers and letters were thoroughly scrutinized.[1] Wisely, neither petitioner nor the Court today attempts to justify the search of T.L.O.'s pocketbook as a minimally intrusive search in the *Terry* line. To be faithful to the Court's settled doctrine, the inquiry therefore must focus on the warrant and probable-cause requirements.

A

I agree that schoolteachers or principals, when not acting as agents of law enforcement authorities, generally may conduct a search of their students' belongings without first obtaining a warrant. To agree with the Court on this point is to say that school searches may justifiably be held to that extent to constitute an exception to the Fourth Amendment's warrant requirement. Such an exception, however, is not to be justified, as the Court apparently holds, by assessing net social value through application of an unguided "balancing test" in which "the individual's legitimate expectations of privacy and personal security" are weighed against "the government's need for effective methods to deal with breaches of public order." The Warrant Clause is something more than an exhortation to this Court to maximize social welfare as *we* see fit. It requires that the authorities must obtain a warrant before conducting a full-scale search. The undifferentiated governmental interest in law enforcement is insufficient to justify an exception to the warrant requirement. Rather, some *special* governmental interest beyond the need merely to apprehend lawbreakers is necessary to justify a categorical exception to the warrant requirement. For the most part, special governmental needs suffi-

---

1. A purse typically contains items of a highly personal nature. Especially for shy or sensitive adolescents, it could prove extremely embarrassing for a teacher or principal to rummage through its contents, which could include notes from friends, fragments of love poems, caricatures of school authorities, and items of personal hygiene.

cient to override the warrant requirement flow from "exigency" — that is, from the press of time that makes obtaining a warrant either impossible or hopelessly infeasible. Only after finding an extraordinary governmental interest of this kind do we — or ought we — engage in a balancing test to determine if a warrant should nonetheless be required.[2]

To require a showing of some extraordinary governmental interest before dispensing with the warrant requirement is not to undervalue society's need to apprehend violators of the criminal law. To be sure, forcing law enforcement personnel to obtain a warrant before engaging in a search will predictably deter the police from conducting some searches that they would otherwise like to conduct. But this is not an unintended *result* of the Fourth Amendment's protection of privacy; rather, it is the very *purpose* for which the Amendment was thought necessary. Only where the governmental interests at stake exceed those implicated in any ordinary law enforcement context — that is, only where there is some extraordinary governmental interest involved — is it legitimate to engage in a balancing test to determine whether a warrant is indeed necessary.

In this case, such extraordinary governmental interests do exist and are sufficient to justify an exception to the warrant requirement. Students are necessarily confined for most of the schoolday in close proximity to each other and to the school staff. I agree with the Court that we can take judicial notice of the serious problems of drugs and violence that plague our schools. As Justice BLACKMUN notes, teachers must not merely "maintain an environment conducive to learning" among children who "are inclined to test the outer boundaries of acceptable conduct," but must also "protect the very safety of students and school personnel." A teacher or principal could neither carry out essential teaching functions nor adequately protect students' safety if required to wait for a warrant before conducting a necessary search.

B

I emphatically disagree with the Court's decision to cast aside the constitutional probable-cause standard when assessing the constitutional validity of a schoolhouse search. The Court's decision jettisons the probable-cause standard — the only standard that finds support in the text of the Fourth Amendment — on the basis of its Rohrschach-like "balancing test." Use of such a "balancing test" to determine the standard for evaluating the validity of a full-scale search represents a sizable innovation in Fourth Amendment analysis. This innovation finds support neither in precedent nor policy and portends a dangerous weakening of the purpose of the Fourth Amendment to protect the privacy and security of our citizens. Moreover, even if this Court's historic understanding of the Fourth Amendment were mistaken and a balancing test of some kind were appropriate, any such test that gave adequate weight to the privacy and security interests protected by the Fourth Amendment would not reach the preordained result the Court's conclusory analysis reaches today. Therefore, because I believe that the balancing test used by the Court today is flawed both in its inception and in its execution, I respectfully dissent.

1

An unbroken line of cases in this Court have held that probable cause is a prerequisite for a full-scale search.... Under our past decisions probable cause — which exists where "the facts and circumstances within [the officials'] knowledge and of which they

---

2. Administrative search cases involving inspection schemes have recognized that "if inspection is to be effective and serve as a credible deterrent, unannounced, even frequent, inspections are essential. In this context, the prerequisite of a warrant could easily frustrate inspection * * *."

had reasonably trustworthy information [are] sufficient in themselves to warrant a man of reasonable caution in the belief" that a criminal offense had occurred and the evidence would be found in the suspected place — is the constitutional minimum for justifying a full-scale search, regardless of whether it is conducted pursuant to a warrant or within one of the exceptions to the warrant requirement.

Our holdings that probable cause is a prerequisite to a full-scale search are based on the relationship between the two Clauses of the Fourth Amendment. The first Clause ("The right of the people to be secure in their persons, houses, papers and effects, against unreasonable searches and seizures, shall not be violated * * *") states the purpose of the Amendment and its coverage. The second Clause (" * * * and no Warrants shall issue but upon probable cause * * *") gives content to the word "unreasonable" in the first clause. "For all but * * * narrowly defined intrusions, the requisite 'balancing' has been performed in centuries of precedent and is embodied in the principle that seizures are 'reasonable' only if supported by probable cause."

I therefore fully agree with the Court that "the underlying command of the Fourth Amendment is always that searches and seizures be reasonable." But this "underlying command" is not directly interpreted in each category of cases by some amorphous "balancing test." Rather, the provisions of the Warrant Clause — a warrant and probable cause — provide the yardstick against which official searches and seizures are to be measured. The Fourth Amendment neither requires nor authorizes the conceptual free-for-all that ensues when an unguided balancing test is used to assess specific categories of searches. If the search in question is more than a minimally intrusive *Terry* stop, the constitutional probable-cause standard determines its validity.

To be sure, the Court recognizes that probable cause "ordinarily" is required to justify a full-scale search and that the existence of probable cause "bears on" the validity of the search. Yet the Court fails to cite any case in which a full-scale intrusion upon privacy interests has been justified on less than probable cause. The line of cases begun by *Terry v. Ohio* provides no support, for they applied a balancing test only in the context of minimally intrusive searches that served crucial law enforcement interests. The search in *Terry* itself, for instance, was a "limited search of the outer clothing." The type of border stop at issue in *United States v. Brignoni-Ponce,* usually "consume[d] no more than a minute"; the Court explicitly noted that "any further detention * * * must be based on consent or probable cause." *See also United States v. Hensley* (momentary stop); *United States v. Place* (brief detention of luggage for canine "sniff"); *Pennsylvania v. Mimms* (*per curiam*) (brief frisk after stop for traffic violation); *United States v. Martinez-Fuerte* (characterizing intrusion as "minimal"); *Adams v. Williams* (stop and frisk). In short, all of these cases involved " 'seizures' so substantially less intrusive than arrests that the general rule requiring probable cause to make Fourth Amendment 'seizures' reasonable could be replaced by a balancing test."

Nor do the "administrative search" cases provide any comfort for the Court. In *Camara v. Municipal Court*, the Court held that the probable-cause standard governed even administrative searches. Although the *Camara* Court recognized that probable-cause standards themselves may have to be somewhat modified to take into account the special nature of administrative searches, the Court did so only after noting that "because [housing code] inspections are neither personal in nature nor aimed at the discovery of evidence of crime, they involve a relatively limited invasion of the urban citizen's privacy." Subsequent administrative search cases have similarly recognized that such searches intrude upon areas whose owners harbor a significantly decreased expectation of privacy, thus circumscribing the injury to Fourth Amendment interests caused by the search.

Considerations of the deepest significance for the freedom of our citizens counsel strict adherence to the principle that no search may be conducted where the official is not in possession of probable cause—that is, where the official does not know of "facts and circumstances [that] warrant a prudent man in believing that the offense has been committed." The Fourth Amendment was designed not merely to protect against official intrusions whose social utility was less as measured by some "balancing test" than its intrusion on individual privacy; it was designed in addition to grant the individual a zone of privacy whose protections could be breached only where the "reasonable" requirements of the probable-cause standard were met. Moved by whatever momentary evil has aroused their fears, officials—perhaps even supported by a majority of citizens—may be tempted to conduct searches that sacrifice the liberty of each citizen to assuage the perceived evil. But the Fourth Amendment rests on the principle that a true balance between the individual and society depends on the recognition of "the right to be let alone—the most comprehensive of rights and the right most valued by civilized men." That right protects the privacy and security of the individual unless the authorities can cross a specific threshold of need, designated by the term "probable cause." I cannot agree with the Court's assertions today that a "balancing test" can replace the constitutional threshold with one that is more convenient for those enforcing the laws but less protective of the citizens' liberty; the Fourth Amendment's protections should not be defaced by "a balancing process that overwhelms the individual's protection against unwarranted official intrusion by a governmental interest said to justify the search and seizure."

2

I thus do not accept the majority's premise that "[t]o hold that the Fourth Amendment applies to searches conducted by school authorities is only to begin the inquiry into the standards governing such searches." For me, the finding that the Fourth Amendment applies, coupled with the observation that what is at issue is a full-scale search, is the end of the inquiry. But even if I believed that a "balancing test" appropriately replaces the judgment of the Framers of the Fourth Amendment, I would nonetheless object to the cursory and shortsighted "test" that the Court employs to justify its predictable weakening of Fourth Amendment protections. In particular, the test employed by the Court vastly overstates the social costs that a probable-cause standard entails and, though it plausibly articulates the serious privacy interests at stake, inexplicably fails to accord them adequate weight in striking the balance.

The Court begins to articulate its "balancing test" by observing that "the government's need for effective methods to deal with breaches of public order" is to be weighed on one side of the balance. Of course, this is not correct. It is not the government's need for effective enforcement methods that should weigh in the balance, for ordinary Fourth Amendment standards—including probable cause—may well permit methods for maintaining the public order that are perfectly effective. If that were the case, the governmental interest in having effective standards would carry no weight at all as a justification for *departing* from the probable-cause standard. Rather, it is the costs of applying probable cause as opposed to applying some lesser standard that should be weighed on the government's side.[5]

---

5. I speak of the "government's side" only because it is the terminology used by the Court. In my view, this terminology itself is seriously misleading. The government is charged with protecting the privacy and security of the citizen, just as it is charged with apprehending those who violate the criminal law. Consequently, the government has *no* legitimate interest in conducting a search that unduly intrudes on the privacy and security of the citizen. The balance is not between the rights of the government and the rights of the citizen, but between opposing conceptions of the constitutionally legitimate means of carrying out the government's varied responsibilities.

In order to tote up the costs of applying the probable-cause standard, it is thus necessary first to take into account the nature and content of that standard, and the likelihood that it would hamper achievement of the goal — vital not just to "teachers and administrators" — of maintaining an effective educational setting in the public schools. The seminal statement concerning the nature of the probable-cause standard is found in *Carroll v. United States*. *Carroll* held that law enforcement authorities have probable cause to search where "the facts and circumstances within their knowledge and of which they had reasonably trustworthy information [are] sufficient in themselves to warrant a man of reasonable caution in the belief" that a criminal offense had occurred. In *Brinegar v. United States*, the Court amplified this requirement, holding that probable cause depends upon "the factual and practical considerations of everyday life on which reasonable and prudent men, not legal technicians, act."

Two Terms ago, in *Illinois v. Gates,* this Court expounded at some length its view of the probable-cause standard. Among the adjectives used to describe the standard were "practical," "fluid," "flexible," "easily applied," and "nontechnical." The probable-cause standard was to be seen as a "commonsense" test whose application depended on an evaluation of the "totality of the circumstances."

Ignoring what *Gates* took such great pains to emphasize, the Court today holds that a new "reasonableness" standard is appropriate because it "will spare teachers and school administrators the necessity of schooling themselves in the niceties of probable cause and permit them to regulate their conduct according to the dictates of reason and commonsense." I had never thought that our pre-*Gates* understanding of probable cause defied either reason or common sense. But after *Gates*, I would have thought that there could be no doubt that this "nontechnical," "practical," and "easily applied" concept was eminently serviceable in a context like a school, where teachers require the flexibility to respond quickly and decisively to emergencies.

A consideration of the likely operation of the probable-cause standard reinforces this conclusion. Discussing the issue of school searches, Professor LaFave has noted that the cases that have reached the appellate courts "strongly suggest that in most instances the evidence of wrongdoing prompting teachers or principals to conduct searches is sufficiently detailed and specific to meet the traditional probable cause test."[6] The problems that have caused this Court difficulty in interpreting the probable-cause standard have largely involved informants. However, three factors make it likely that problems involving informants will not make it difficult for teachers and school administrators to make probable-cause decisions. This Court's decision in *Gates* applying a "totality of the circumstances" test to determine whether an informant's tip can constitute probable cause renders the test easy for teachers to apply. The fact that students and teachers interact daily in the school building makes it more likely that teachers will get to know students who supply information; the problem of informants who remain anonymous even to the teachers — and who are therefore unavailable for verification or further questioning — is unlikely to arise. Finally, teachers can observe the behavior of students under suspicion to corroborate any doubtful tips they do receive.

As compared with the relative ease with which teachers can apply the probable-cause standard, the amorphous "reasonableness under all the circumstances" standard freshly coined by the Court today will likely spawn increased litigation and greater uncertainty among teachers and administrators. Of course, as this Court should know, an essential

---

6. It should be noted that Professor LaFave reached this conclusion in 1978, *before* this Court's decision in *Gates* made clear the "flexibility" of the probable-cause concept.

purpose of developing and articulating legal norms is to enable individuals to conform their conduct to those norms. A school system conscientiously attempting to obey the Fourth Amendment's dictates under a probable-cause standard could, for example, consult decisions and other legal materials and prepare a booklet expounding the rough outlines of the concept. Such a booklet could be distributed to teachers to provide them with guidance as to when a search may be lawfully conducted. I cannot but believe that the same school system faced with interpreting what is permitted under the Court's new "reasonableness" standard would be hopelessly adrift as to when a search may be permissible. The sad result of this uncertainty may well be that some teachers will be reluctant to conduct searches that are fully permissible and even necessary under the constitutional probable-cause standard, while others may intrude arbitrarily and unjustifiably on the privacy of students.[7]

One further point should be taken into account when considering the desirability of replacing the constitutional probable-cause standard. The question facing the Court is not whether the probable-cause standard should be replaced by a test of "reasonableness under all the circumstances." Rather, it is whether traditional Fourth Amendment standards should recede before the Court's new standard. Thus, although the Court today paints with a broad brush and holds its undefined "reasonableness" standard applicable to *all* school searches, I would approach the question with considerably more reserve. I would not think it necessary to develop a single standard to govern all school searches, any more than traditional Fourth Amendment law applies even the probable-cause standard to *all* searches and seizures. For instance, just as police officers may conduct a brief stop and frisk on something less than probable cause, so too should teachers be permitted the same flexibility. A teacher or administrator who had reasonable suspicion that a student was carrying a gun would no doubt have authority under ordinary Fourth Amendment doctrine to conduct a limited search of the student to determine whether the threat was genuine. The "costs" of applying the traditional probable-cause standard must therefore be discounted by the fact that, where additional flexibility is necessary and where the intrusion is minor, traditional Fourth Amendment jurisprudence itself displaces probable cause when it determines the validity of a search.

A legitimate balancing test whose function was something more substantial than reaching a predetermined conclusion acceptable to this Court's impressions of what authority teachers need would therefore reach rather a different result than that reached by the Court today. On one side of the balance would be the costs of applying traditional Fourth Amendment standards—the "practical" and "flexible" probable-cause standard where a full-scale intrusion is sought, a lesser standard in situations where the intrusion is much less severe and the need for greater authority compelling. Whatever costs were toted up on this side would have to be discounted by the costs of applying an unprecedented and ill-defined

---

7. A comparison of the language of the standard ("reasonableness under all the circumstances") with the traditional language of probable cause ("facts sufficient to warrant a person of reasonable caution in believing that a crime had been committed and the evidence would be found in the designated place") suggests that the Court's new standard may turn out to be probable cause under a new guise. If so, the additional uncertainty caused by this Court's innovation is surely unjustifiable; it would be naive to expect that the addition of this extra dose of uncertainty would do anything other than "burden the efforts of school authorities to maintain order in their schools." If, on the other hand, the new standard permits searches of students in instances when probable cause is absent—instances, according to this Court's consistent formulations, when a person of reasonable caution would not think it likely that a violation existed or that evidence of that violation would be found—the new standard is genuinely objectionable and impossible to square with the premise that our citizens have the right to be free from arbitrary intrusions on their privacy.

"reasonableness under all the circumstances" test that will leave teachers and administrators uncertain as to their authority and will encourage excessive fact-based litigation.

On the other side of the balance would be the serious privacy interests of the student, interests that the Court admirably articulates in its opinion, but which the Court's new ambiguous standard places in serious jeopardy. I have no doubt that a fair assessment of the two sides of the balance would necessarily reach the same conclusion that, as I have argued above, the Fourth Amendment's language compels—that school searches like that conducted in this case are valid only if supported by probable cause.

II

Applying the constitutional probable-cause standard to the facts of this case, I would find that Mr. Choplick's search violated T.L.O.'s Fourth Amendment rights. After escorting T.L.O. into his private office, Mr. Choplick demanded to see her purse. He then opened the purse to find evidence of whether she had been smoking in the bathroom. When he opened the purse, he discovered the pack of cigarettes. At this point, his search for evidence of the smoking violation was complete.

Mr. Choplick then noticed, below the cigarettes, a pack of cigarette rolling papers. Believing that such papers were "associated" with the use of marihuana, he proceeded to conduct a detailed examination of the contents of her purse, in which he found some marihuana, a pipe, some money, an index card, and some private letters indicating that T.L.O. had sold marihuana to other students. The State sought to introduce this latter material in evidence at a criminal proceeding, and the issue before the Court is whether it should have been suppressed.

On my view of the case, we need not decide whether the initial search conducted by Mr. Choplick—the search for evidence of the smoking violation that was completed when Mr. Choplick found the pack of cigarettes—was valid. For Mr. Choplick at that point did not have probable cause to continue to rummage through T.L.O.'s purse. Mr. Choplick's suspicion of marihuana possession at this time was based *solely* on the presence of the package of cigarette papers. The mere presence without more of such a staple item of commerce is insufficient to warrant a person of reasonable caution in inferring both that T.L.O. had violated the law by possessing marihuana and that evidence of that violation would be found in her purse. Just as a police officer could not obtain a warrant to search a home based solely on his claim that he had seen a package of cigarette papers in that home, Mr. Choplick was not entitled to search possibly the most private possessions of T.L.O. based on the mere presence of a package of cigarette papers. Therefore, the fruits of this illegal search must be excluded and the judgment of the New Jersey Supreme Court affirmed.

III

In the past several Terms, this Court has produced a succession of Fourth Amendment opinions in which "balancing tests" have been applied to resolve various questions concerning the proper scope of official searches. The Court has begun to apply a "balancing test" to determine whether a particular category of searches intrudes upon expectations of privacy that merit Fourth Amendment protection. It applies a "balancing test" to determine whether a warrant is necessary to conduct a search. In today's opinion, it employs a "balancing test" to determine what standard should govern the constitutionality of a given category of searches. Should a search turn out to be unreasonable after application of all of these "balancing tests," the Court then applies an additional "balancing test" to decide whether the evidence resulting from the search must be excluded.

All of these "balancing tests" amount to brief nods by the Court in the direction of a neutral utilitarian calculus while the Court in fact engages in an unanalyzed exercise of judicial will. Perhaps this doctrinally destructive nihilism is merely a convenient umbrella under which a majority that cannot agree on a genuine rationale can conceal its differences. And it may be that the real force underlying today's decision is the belief that the Court purports to reject—the belief that the unique role served by the schools justifies an exception to the Fourth Amendment on their behalf. If so, the methodology of today's decision may turn out to have as little influence in future cases as will its result, and the Court's departure from traditional Fourth Amendment doctrine will be confined to the schools.

On my view, the presence of the word "unreasonable" in the text of the Fourth Amendment does not grant a shifting majority of this Court the authority to answer *all* Fourth Amendment questions by consulting its momentary vision of the social good. Full-scale searches unaccompanied by probable cause violate the Fourth Amendment. I do not pretend that our traditional Fourth Amendment doctrine automatically answers all of the difficult legal questions that occasionally arise. I do contend, however, that this Court has an obligation to provide some coherent framework to resolve such questions on the basis of more than a conclusory recitation of the results of a "balancing test." The Fourth Amendment itself supplies that framework and, because the Court today fails to heed its message, I must respectfully dissent.

Justice STEVENS, with whom Justice MARSHALL joins, and with whom Justice BRENNAN joins as to Part I, concurring in part and dissenting in part.

Assistant Vice Principal Choplick searched T.L.O.'s purse for evidence that she was smoking in the girls' restroom. Because T.L.O.'s suspected misconduct was not illegal and did not pose a serious threat to school discipline, the New Jersey Supreme Court held that Choplick's search of her purse was an unreasonable invasion of her privacy and that the evidence which he seized could not be used against her in criminal proceedings. The New Jersey court's holding was a careful response to the case it was required to decide.

The State of New Jersey sought review in this Court, first arguing that the exclusionary rule is wholly inapplicable to searches conducted by school officials, and then contending that the Fourth Amendment itself provides no protection at all to the student's privacy. The Court has accepted neither of these frontal assaults on the Fourth Amendment. It has, however, seized upon this "no smoking" case to announce "the proper standard" that should govern searches by school officials who are confronted with disciplinary problems far more severe than smoking in the restroom. Although I join Part II of the Court's opinion, I continue to believe that the Court has unnecessarily and inappropriately reached out to decide a constitutional question. More importantly, I fear that the concerns that motivated the Court's activism have produced a holding that will permit school administrators to search students suspected of violating only the most trivial school regulations and guidelines for behavior.

I

The question the Court decides today—whether Mr. Choplick's search of T.L.O.'s purse violated the Fourth Amendment—was not raised by the State's petition for writ of certiorari. That petition only raised one question: "Whether the Fourth Amendment's exclusionary rule applies to searches made by public school officials and teachers in school." The State quite properly declined to submit the former question because "[it] did not wish to present what might appear to be solely a factual dispute to this Court." Since this Court has twice had the threshold question argued, I believe that it should expressly consider the merits of the New Jersey Supreme Court's ruling that the exclusionary rule applies.

The New Jersey Supreme Court's holding on this question is plainly correct. As the state court noted, this case does not involve the use of evidence in a school disciplinary proceeding; the juvenile proceedings brought against T.L.O. involved a charge that would have been a criminal offense if committed by an adult. Accordingly, the exclusionary rule issue decided by that court and later presented to this Court concerned only the use in a criminal proceeding of evidence obtained in a search conducted by a public school administrator.

Having confined the issue to the law enforcement context, the New Jersey court then reasoned that this Court's cases have made it quite clear that the exclusionary rule is equally applicable "whether the public official who illegally obtained the evidence was a municipal inspector, or a school administrator or law enforcement official." It correctly concluded "that if an official search violates constitutional rights, the evidence is not admissible in criminal proceedings."

When a defendant in a criminal proceeding alleges that she was the victim of an illegal search by a school administrator, the application of the exclusionary rule is a simple corollary of the principle that "all evidence obtained by searches and seizures in violation of the Constitution is, by that same authority, inadmissible in a state court." The practical basis for this principle is, in part, its deterrent effect, and as a general matter it is tolerably clear to me, as it has been to the Court, that the existence of an exclusionary remedy does deter the authorities from violating the Fourth Amendment by sharply reducing their incentive to do so. In the case of evidence obtained in school searches, the "overall educative effect" of the exclusionary rule adds important symbolic force to this utilitarian judgment.

Justice Brandeis was both a great student and a great teacher. It was he who wrote:

> "Our Government is the potent, the omnipresent teacher. For good or for ill, it teaches the whole people by its example. Crime is contagious. If the Government becomes a lawbreaker, it breeds contempt for law; it invites every man to become a law unto himself; it invites anarchy."

Those of us who revere the flag and the ideals for which it stands believe in the power of symbols. We cannot ignore that rules of law also have a symbolic power that may vastly exceed their utility.

Schools are places where we inculcate the values essential to the meaningful exercise of rights and responsibilities by a self-governing citizenry. If the Nation's students can be convicted through the use of arbitrary methods destructive of personal liberty, they cannot help but feel that they have been dealt with unfairly.[9] The application of the exclusionary rule in criminal proceedings arising from illegal school searches makes an important statement to young people that "our society attaches serious consequences to a violation of constitutional rights," and that this is a principle of "liberty and justice for all."

---

9. Justice BRENNAN has written of an analogous case:

"We do not know what class petitioner was attending when the police and dogs burst in, but the lesson the school authorities taught her that day will undoubtedly make a greater impression than the one her teacher had hoped to convey. I would grant certiorari to teach petitioner another lesson: that the Fourth Amendment protects '[t]he right of the people to be secure in their persons, houses, papers, and effects, against unreasonable searches and seizures' * * *. Schools cannot expect their students to learn the lessons of good citizenship when the school authorities themselves disregard the fundamental principles underpinning our constitutional freedoms."

Thus, the simple and correct answer to the question presented by the State's petition for certiorari would have required affirmance of a state court's judgment suppressing evidence. That result would have been dramatically out of character for a Court that not only grants prosecutors relief from suppression orders with distressing regularity, but also is prone to rely on grounds not advanced by the parties in order to protect evidence from exclusion. In characteristic disregard of the doctrine of judicial restraint, the Court avoided that result in this case by ordering reargument and directing the parties to address a constitutional question that the parties, with good reason, had not asked the Court to decide. Because judicial activism undermines the Court's power to perform its central mission in a legitimate way, I dissented from the reargument order. I have not modified the views expressed in that dissent, but since the majority has brought the question before us, I shall explain why I believe the Court has misapplied the standard of reasonableness embodied in the Fourth Amendment.

II

The search of a young woman's purse by a school administrator is a serious invasion of her legitimate expectations of privacy. A purse "is a common repository for one's personal effects and therefore is inevitably associated with the expectation of privacy." Although such expectations must sometimes yield to the legitimate requirements of government, in assessing the constitutionality of a warrantless search, our decision must be guided by the language of the Fourth Amendment: "The right of the people to be secure in their persons, houses, papers and effects, against *unreasonable* searches and seizures, shall not be violated * * *." In order to evaluate the reasonableness of such searches, "it is necessary 'first to focus upon the governmental interest which allegedly justifies official intrusion upon the constitutionally protected interests of the private citizen,' for there is 'no ready test for determining reasonableness other than by balancing the need to search [or seize] against the invasion which the search [or seizure] entails.'"

The "limited search for weapons" in *Terry* was justified by the "immediate interest of the police officer in taking steps to assure himself that the person with whom he is dealing is not armed with a weapon that could unexpectedly and fatally be used against him." When viewed from the institutional perspective, "the substantial need of teachers and administrators for freedom to maintain order in the schools," is no less acute. Violent, unlawful, or seriously disruptive conduct is fundamentally inconsistent with the principal function of teaching institutions which is to educate young people and prepare them for citizenship. When such conduct occurs amidst a sizable group of impressionable young people, it creates an explosive atmosphere that requires a prompt and effective response.

Thus, warrantless searches of students by school administrators are reasonable when undertaken for those purposes. But the majority's statement of the standard for evaluating the reasonableness of such searches is not suitably adapted to that end. The majority holds that "a search of a student by a teacher or other school official will be 'justified at its inception' when there are reasonable grounds for suspecting that the search will turn up evidence *that the student has violated or is violating* either the law or *the rules of the school*." This standard will permit teachers and school administrators to search students when they suspect that the search will reveal evidence of even the most trivial school regulation or precatory guideline for student behavior. The Court's standard for deciding whether a search is justified "at its inception" treats all violations of the rules of the school as though they were fungible. For the Court, a search for curlers and sunglasses in order to enforce the school dress code[16] is apparently just as important as a search for evidence of heroin addiction or violent gang activity.

The majority, however, does not contend that school administrators have a compelling need to search students in order to achieve optimum enforcement of minor school regulations. To the contrary, when minor violations are involved, there is every indication that the informal school disciplinary process, with only minimum requirements of due process, can function effectively without the power to search for enough evidence to prove a criminal case. In arguing that teachers and school administrators need the power to search students based on a lessened standard, the United States as *amicus curiae* relies heavily on empirical evidence of a contemporary crisis of violence and unlawful behavior that is seriously undermining the process of education in American schools. A standard better attuned to this concern would permit teachers and school administrators to search a student when they have reason to believe that the search will uncover *evidence that the student is violating the law or engaging in conduct that is seriously disruptive of school order, or the educational process.*

This standard is properly directed at "[t]he sole justification for the [warrantless] search." In addition, a standard that varies the extent of the permissible intrusion with the gravity of the suspected offense is also more consistent with common-law experience and this Court's precedent. Criminal law has traditionally recognized a distinction between essentially regulatory offenses and serious violations of the peace, and graduated the response of the criminal justice system depending on the character of the violation.[21] The application of a similar distinction in evaluating the reasonableness of warrantless searches and seizures "is not a novel idea."

In *Welsh,* police officers arrived at the scene of a traffic accident and obtained information indicating that the driver of the automobile involved was guilty of a first offense of driving while intoxicated—a civil violation with a maximum fine of $200. The driver had left the scene of the accident, and the officers followed the suspect to his home where they arrested him without a warrant. Absent exigent circumstances, the warrantless invasion of the home was a clear violation of *Payton v. New York.* In holding that the war-

---

16. Parent-Student Handbook of Piscataway [N.J.] H.S. (1979). A brief survey of school rule books reveals that, under the majority's approach, teachers and school administrators may also search students to enforce school rules regulating:

    (i) secret societies;

    (ii) students driving to school;

    (iii) parking and use of parking lots during school hours;

    (iv) smoking on campus;

    (v) the direction of traffic in the hallways;

    (vi) student presence in the hallways during class hours without a pass;

    (vii) profanity;

    (viii) school attendance of interscholastic athletes on the day of a game, meet or match;

    (ix) cafeteria use and cleanup;

    (x) eating lunch off-campus; and

    (xi) unauthorized absence.

21. Throughout the criminal law this dichotomy has been expressed by classifying crimes as misdemeanors or felonies, *malum prohibitum* or *malum in se,* crimes that do not involve moral turpitude or those that do, and major or petty offenses.

Some codes of student behavior also provide a system of graduated response by distinguishing between violent, unlawful, or seriously disruptive conduct, and conduct that will only warrant serious sanctions when the student engages in repetitive offenses. Indeed, at Piscataway High School a violation of smoking regulations that is "[a] student's first offense will result in assignment of up to three (3) days of after school classes concerning hazards of smoking."

rantless arrest for the "noncriminal, traffic offense" in *Welsh* was unconstitutional, the Court noted that "application of the exigent-circumstances exception in the context of a home entry should rarely be sanctioned when there is probable cause to believe that only a minor offense * * * has been committed."

The logic of distinguishing between minor and serious offenses in evaluating the reasonableness of school searches is almost too clear for argument. In order to justify the serious intrusion on the persons and privacy of young people that New Jersey asks this Court to approve, the State must identify "some real immediate and serious consequences." While school administrators have entirely legitimate reasons for adopting school regulations and guidelines for student behavior, the authorization of searches to enforce them "displays a shocking lack of all sense of proportion."[24]

The majority offers weak deference to these principles of balance and decency by announcing that school searches will only be reasonable in scope "when the measures adopted are reasonably related to the objectives of the search and not excessively intrusive in light of the age and sex of the student *and the nature of the infraction.*" The majority offers no explanation why a two-part standard is necessary to evaluate the reasonableness of the ordinary school search. Significantly, in the balance of its opinion the Court pretermits any discussion of the nature of T.L.O.'s infraction of the "no smoking" rule.

The "rider" to the Court's standard for evaluating the reasonableness of the initial intrusion apparently is the Court's perception that its standard is overly generous and does not, by itself, achieve a fair balance between the administrator's right to search and the student's reasonable expectations of privacy. The Court's standard for evaluating the "scope" of reasonable school searches is obviously designed to prohibit physically intrusive searches of students by persons of the opposite sex for relatively minor offenses. The Court's effort to establish a standard that is, at once, clear enough to allow searches to be upheld in nearly every case, and flexible enough to prohibit obviously unreasonable intrusions of young adults' privacy only creates uncertainty in the extent of its resolve to prohibit the latter. Moreover, the majority's application of its standard in this case — to permit a male administrator to rummage through the purse of a female high school student in order to obtain evidence that she was smoking in a bathroom — raises grave doubts in my mind whether its effort will be effective.[25] Unlike the Court, I believe the nature of the suspected infraction is a matter of first importance in deciding whether *any* invasion of privacy is permissible.

III

The Court embraces the standard applied by the New Jersey Supreme Court as equivalent to its own, and then deprecates the state court's application of the standard as reflecting "a somewhat crabbed notion of reasonableness." There is no mystery, how-

---

24. While a policeman who sees a person smoking in an elevator in violation of a city ordinance may conduct a full-blown search for evidence of the smoking violation in the unlikely event of a custodial arrest, it is more doubtful whether a search of this kind would be reasonable if the officer only planned to issue a citation to the offender and depart. In any case, the majority offers no rationale supporting its conclusion that a student detained by school officials for questioning, on reasonable suspicion that she has violated a school rule, is entitled to no more protection under the Fourth Amendment than a criminal suspect under custodial arrest.

25. One thing is clear under any standard — the shocking strip searches that are described in some cases have no place in the schoolhouse. ("It does not require a constitutional scholar to conclude that a nude search of a 13-year-old child is an invasion of constitutional rights of some magnitude"). To the extent that deeply intrusive searches are ever reasonable outside the custodial context, it surely must only be to prevent imminent, and serious harm.

ever, in the state court's finding that the search in this case was unconstitutional; the decision below was not based on a manipulation of reasonable suspicion, but on the trivial character of the activity that promoted the official search. The New Jersey Supreme Court wrote:

> "We are satisfied that when a school official has reasonable grounds to believe that a student possesses evidence of *illegal activity or activity that would interfere with school discipline and order,* the school official has the right to conduct a reasonable search for such evidence."

> "In determining whether the school official has reasonable grounds, courts should consider 'the child's age, history, and school record, *the prevalence and seriousness of the problem in the school to which the search was* directed, the exigency to make the search without delay, and the probative value and reliability of the information used as a justification for the search.'"

The emphasized language in the state court's opinion focuses on the character of the rule infraction that is to be the object of the search.

In the view of the state court, there is a quite obvious and material difference between a search for evidence relating to violent or disruptive activity, and a search for evidence of a smoking rule violation. This distinction does not imply that a no-smoking rule is a matter of minor importance. Rather, like a rule that prohibits a student from being tardy, its occasional violation in a context that poses no threat of disrupting school order and discipline offers no reason to believe that an immediate search is necessary to avoid unlawful conduct, violence, or a serious impairment of the educational process.

A correct understanding of the New Jersey court's standard explains why that court concluded in T.L.O.'s case that "the assistant principal did not have reasonable grounds to believe that the student was concealing in her purse evidence of criminal activity or evidence of activity that *would seriously interfere with school discipline or order.*" The importance of the nature of the rule infraction to the New Jersey Supreme Court's holding is evident from its brief explanation of the principal basis for its decision:

> "A student has an expectation of privacy in the contents of her purse. Mere possession of cigarettes did not violate school rule or policy, since the school allowed smoking in designated areas. The contents of the handbag had no direct bearing on the infraction.

> "The assistant principal's desire, legal in itself, to gather evidence to impeach the student's credibility at a hearing on the disciplinary infraction does not validate the search."[28]

Like the New Jersey Supreme Court, I would view this case differently if the Assistant Vice Principal had reason to believe T.L.O.'s purse contained evidence of criminal activity, or of an activity that would seriously disrupt school discipline. There was, however, absolutely no basis for any such assumption—not even a "hunch."

---

28. The court added:
>   "Moreover, there were not reasonable grounds to believe that the purse contained cigarettes, if they were the object of the search. No one had furnished information to that effect to the school official. He had, at best, a good hunch. No doubt good hunches would unearth much more evidence of crime on the persons of students and citizens as a whole. But more is required to sustain a search."

   It is this portion of the New Jersey Supreme Court's reasoning—a portion that was not necessary to its holding—to which this Court makes its principal response.

In this case, Mr. Choplick overreacted to what appeared to be nothing more than a minor infraction—a rule prohibiting smoking in the bathroom of the freshmen's and sophomores' building. It is, of course, true that he actually found evidence of serious wrongdoing by T.L.O., but no one claims that the prior search may be justified by his unexpected discovery. As far as the smoking infraction is concerned, the search for cigarettes merely tended to corroborate a teacher's eyewitness account of T.L.O.'s violation of a minor regulation designed to channel student smoking behavior into designated locations. Because this conduct was neither unlawful nor significantly disruptive of school order or the educational process, the invasion of privacy associated with the forcible opening of T.L.O.'s purse was entirely unjustified at its inception.

A review of the sampling of school search cases relied on by the Court demonstrates how different this case is from those in which there was indeed a valid justification for intruding on a student's privacy. In most of them the student was suspected of a criminal violation; in the remainder either violence or substantial disruption of school order or the integrity of the academic process was at stake. Few involved matters as trivial as the no-smoking rule violated by T.L.O. The rule the Court adopts today is so open-ended that it may make the Fourth Amendment virtually meaningless in the school context. Although I agree that school administrators must have broad latitude to maintain order and discipline in our classrooms, that authority is not unlimited.

IV

The schoolroom is the first opportunity most citizens have to experience the power of government. Through it passes every citizen and public official, from schoolteachers to policemen and prison guards. The values they learn there, they take with them in life. One of our most cherished ideals is the one contained in the Fourth Amendment: that the government may not intrude on the personal privacy of its citizens without a warrant or compelling circumstance. The Court's decision today is a curious moral for the Nation's youth. Although the search of T.L.O.'s purse does not trouble today's majority, I submit that we are not dealing with "matters relatively trivial to the welfare of the Nation. There are village tyrants as well as village Hampdens, but none who acts under color of law is beyond reach of the Constitution."

I respectfully dissent.

Notes

(a) Given the *Schall* Court's conclusion that children are always in some form of custody and that juvenile court judges act in *loco parentis*, how could Justice White conclude in *T.L.O.* that the Fourth Amendment constrains public school officials?

(b) Why did the *T.L.O.* Court fail to cite to any of the prior delinquency cases? Are they not relevant?

(c) Is the *T.L.O.* Court's holding that reasonableness standards govern the constitutionality of searches of school children by school officials compatible with the prior delinquency cases? Note that the dissenting opinions refer to T.L.O.'s trial as a *criminal* proceeding. Was it?

(d) Why did Justice Powell find it necessary to write a concurring opinion?

(e) Is the *T.L.O.* Court's conclusion regarding the standard for school searches supported by its Fourth Amendment precedent?

(f) What Fourth Amendment issues in the public school context were left unresolved by the Court?

(g) In answering these questions consider the following material:

Neal I. Aizenstein, Note, *Fourth Amendment — Searches by Public School Officials Valid on "Reasonable Grounds,"* 76 J. Crim. L. & Criminology 898, 908, 931–32 (1985):

> The T.L.O. decision is flawed in several respects. First, although the Court initially stressed the importance of students' rights to privacy in holding that the fourth amendment's prohibition on unreasonable searches and seizures applies to searches conducted by school officials, the Court then minimized the fourth amendment protection afforded to students by using a balancing test to carve out an unprecedented exception to the probable cause standard for full-scale searches conducted in public schools. Second, even if the balancing test employed by the Court was warranted by traditional fourth amendment analysis, the "reasonable grounds" standard adopted by the Court will promote unjustified searches in public schools since the privacy rights of students were not given adequate weight in the Court's balancing of the relevant interests.
>
> . . . .
>
> Despite the Court's adoption of a relaxed fourth amendment standard in T.L.O., students may not necessarily be subjected to unnecessary intrusions of privacy. Although the fourth amendment is the primary means used to assess the validity of searches conducted by school officials, there are other constitutional and statutory grounds for challenging the validity of a search. First, states that have constitutional provisions corresponding to the fourth amendment of the Federal Constitution may insist on a more demanding standard than "reasonable grounds." The "reasonable grounds" standard only represents the minimum amount of protection against unreasonable searches and seizures that must be provided to students in public schools. Second, state legislation may be enacted that requires the exclusion of evidence obtained through school searches conducted without probable cause. For example, one state is presently considering legislation which provides that no contraband seized pursuant to a search without probable cause shall be admissible in any adjudication brought under the juvenile court. Thus, although the "reasonable grounds" standard adopted in *T.L.O.* will minimize the fourth amendment protection available to students, alternative means may exist to provide students with adequate protection against unreasonable intrusions of privacy.

(h) Charles W. Hardin, Jr., Comment, *Searching Public Schools: T.L.O. and the Exclusionary Rule,* 47 Ohio St. L. J. 1099, 1104–05 (1986).

> [T]he majority's standard fails to adequately advise school officials as to when they may lawfully undertake a search. The majority states that its approach will "spare teachers and school administrators the necessity of schooling themselves in the niceties of probable cause." But the majority overlooks the fact that its standard requires school officials to educate themselves in the niceties of reasonableness. This will be particularly difficult in light of the majority's failure to clearly define reasonableness. The probable cause standard, by contrast, is a fairly well-defined legal concept as evidenced by the many decisions delineating its contours. Justice Brennan argues that a school system could consult these "decisions and other legal materials and prepare a booklet expounding the rough outlines of

the concept. Such a booklet could be distributed to teachers to provide them with guidance as to when a search may be lawfully conducted." The majority simply ignores this logical suggestion and expounds a standard which, at best, provides little guidance to school officials.

Third, the majority mistakenly views the probable cause standard as unworkable in the schoolhouse search situation. This view runs counter to that expressed by the Court in *Illinois v. Gates*, in which, Justice Brennan notes, the probable cause standard was described as "'practical,' 'fluid,' 'flexible,' 'easily applied,' and 'nontechnical.'" Moreover, teachers and school administrators are a generally well-educated group, which, with a minimal amount of instruction, would appear quite capable of comprehending and administering this "nontechnical" standard.

(i) Given the level of drugs, weapons, assaults, murders, and disruptive behavior in public schools nationally, does *T.L.O.* and the special needs doctrine not provide valuable tools for assuring safe school environments? Are better alternatives available?

(j) Random Urine Testing in the Public Schools

After *T.L.O.* the Court decided two other Fourth Amendment cases involving public school students. Neither case explicitly involved the constitutional rights of children charged with crime. That is, although the justices upheld random searches of public school students, the Court did not determine whether the fruits of such searches were admissible in juvenile or criminal court, and indeed did not decide if the results of such tests could be made available to police authorities. The latter factor, however, did seem important to the majority in each case. The cases are nonetheless relevant because they reflect the Court's continuing willingness to contract the Fourth Amendment protections of students, which may spill over into the area of rights of alleged delinquents in juvenile court, and because the "special needs" analysis used in these cases comports more with fundamental fairness views rather than with the functional equivalence approach of *Breed*.

In *Vernonia School District v. Acton*, 515 U.S. 646 (1995), the Court upheld a public school district's policy authorizing random urinalysis drug testing of grade school and high school students who voluntarily participated in interscholastic athletic programs. Because of the school environment the Court concluded that the case involved "special needs," which eliminated the necessity of a warrant, probable cause, or even individualized suspicion. Instead, the Court used a balancing test that included assessing the individual privacy right, the nature of the intrusion on that right, and the competing governmental interests. The majority found that student athletes' privacy expectations were even more diminished than those of ordinary students, and that the governmental intrusion was negligible, whereas the governmental concern was "important-indeed, perhaps compelling."

In *Board of Education of Independent School District No. 92 of Pottawatemie County v. Earls*, 536 U.S. 822 (2002), the Court went beyond *Acton* and upheld random drug testing of all students who participated in *any* extracurricular school activities, including the National Honor Society, Future Farmers of America, band, choir, and Future Homemakers of America. Even the concurring Justice was concerned about the scope of the school policy in question and the nature of the intrusion. Indeed, Justice Breyer noted that "not everyone would agree with this Court's characterization of … urine sampling as 'negligible.'" Furthermore, he was persuaded by the facts that the test results were not shared with police of-ficials, that the only consequence of positive drug results was suspension from the extracurricular activity, and that students had a choice whether to participate in the activity, thus giving "conscientious objectors" a way out. Extracurricular activities, however, are a vital part of students' education and an important fac-tor in college admissions. Moreover, unlike athletics, students are much less likely to be injured when engaging in extracurricular activities such as the chess club.

The next question to come before the Court will probably concern the con-stitutionality of random drug testing of *all* students. Justice Breyer's concurring opinion, which is necessary to form a majority in *Earls*, suggests that he would not be receptive to across-the-board drug testing of all students.

(k) Some Unanswered Questions

1. Does the Exclusionary Rule of the Fourth Amendment Apply to Delinquency Hearings?

Still undecided is whether the exclusionary rule of the Fourth Amendment ap-plies to either police or school searches resulting in delinquency charges. The Court recently decided *Florida v. J.L.*, 529 U.S. 266 (2000), a case involving a minor charged with delinquency based on possession of a firearm. The Court held in a narrow opin-ion that an anonymous tip alone was insufficient to justify a stop and frisk under *Terry v. Ohio*. The result of the ruling is that the firearm should have been suppressed at the child's adjudicatory hearing because State law prohibited the use of illegally seized evidence in delinquency hearings. Thus, the Court did not have to reach the issue of whether the exclusionary rule is required in delinquency cases as a matter of federal law. In a sense, that issue is, at this point in time at least, not pressing, because all states seem to have explicitly or implicitly determined that the exclusionary rule applies, at least to non-school searches of minors by police officers. On the other hand, courts specifically addressing the issue of whether a search by school officials implicates the exclusionary rule have generally rejected that argument.

Whether the exclusionary rule would apply even in criminal court if the search were conducted by a school official is not clear. In some states juveniles are consid-ered adults at the age of 16 or 17 when they are still in high school. The Court uses a balancing test in determining whether the exclusionary rule is to be applied in crim-inal court. So far the Court has excluded magistrates, judicial clerks, and legislators as officials who can trigger the exclusionary rule. Based on these decisions it is un-likely that the Court would require application of the exclusionary rule for searches by school officials, even in criminal court cases. School searches by police officers are another matter. If, however, the special needs exception also applies to school searches by police officers, the exclusionary rule would be almost irrelevant, because almost all action can be viewed as reasonable per *T.L.O.* For a discussion of these is-sues see Irene Merker Rosenberg, *A Door Left Open: Applicability of the Fourth Amend-ment Exclusionary Rule to Juvenile Delinquency Proceedings*, 24 AM. J. CRIM. L. 29–61 (1996).

2. Does Equal Protection Require That Delinquents Be Afforded the Same Proce-dural Protection as Adults Charged with Crime?

The United States Supreme Court has never resolved a juvenile delinquency case on equal protection grounds, even when explicitly invited to do so. *See, e.g., In re Win-ship*, 397 U.S. at 358 n.1. Instead, the Court has always looked to due process—fun-damental fairness, or, occasionally, to explicit guarantees in the Bill of Rights. Compare

McKeiver v. Pennsylvania, finding no due process violation for denying juveniles the right to a jury trial with *Breed v. Jones*, holding that the double jeopardy clause applies to delinquency adjudicatory hearings. Justice Black, concurring in *In re Gault*, and true to his total incorporation theory, concluded that the Arizona law in question violated the Fifth and Sixth Amendments rather than due process in the fundamental fairness sense of the term. He also stated that "[w]here a person, infant or adult, can be seized by the State, charged, and convicted for violating a state criminal law, and then ordered by the State to be confined for six years, I think the Constitution requires that he be tried in accordance with the guarantees of all the provisions made applicable to the States by the Fourteenth Amendment. Undoubtedly this would be true of an adult defendant, and it would be a plain denial of equal protection of the laws — an invidious discrimination — to hold that others subject to heavier punishments could, because they are children, be denied these same constitutional safeguards."* In *McKeiver*, Justice Black joined Justice Douglas' dissenting opinion which alluded to the former's equal protection argument in *Gault*, and noted that the Fourteenth Amendment "speaks of denial of rights to any person, not to any adult person."

Why does the Court shy away from equal protection analysis in delinquency cases?

Roper v. Simmons
543 U.S. 551 (2005)

Justice KENNEDY delivered the opinion of the Court.

I

At the age of 17, when he was still a junior in high school, Christopher Simmons, the respondent here, committed murder. About nine months later, after he had turned 18, he was tried and sentenced to death. There is little doubt that Simmons was the instigator of the crime. Before its commission Simmons said he wanted to murder someone. In chilling, callous terms he talked about his plan, discussing it for the most part with two friends, Charles Benjamin and John Tessmer, then aged 15 and 16 respectively. Simmons proposed to commit burglary and murder by breaking and entering, tying up a victim, and throwing the victim off a bridge. Simmons assured his friends they could "get away with it" because they were minors.

The three met at about 2 a.m. on the night of the murder, but Tessmer left before the other two set out.... Simmons and Benjamin entered the home of the victim, Shirley Crook, after reaching through an open window and unlocking the back door. Simmons turned on a hallway light. Awakened, Mrs. Crook called out, "Who's there?" In response Simmons entered Mrs. Crook's bedroom, where he recognized her from a previous car accident involving them both. Simmons later admitted this confirmed his resolve to murder her.

Using duct tape to cover her eyes and mouth and bind her hands, the two perpetrators put Mrs. Crook in her minivan and drove to a state park. They reinforced the bindings, covered her head with a towel, and walked her to a railroad trestle spanning the Meramec River. There they tied her hands and feet together with electrical wire, wrapped her whole face in duct tape and threw her from the bridge, drowning her in the waters below.

---

* [Conceivably, Justice Black may be intimating that equal protection would be available only in cases in which the juvenile's punishment was equal to or greater than that given to an adult convicted of the same offense. In *Gault*, an adult convicted of the same offense as Gerald would have been subject to a fine and two months imprisonment, whereas Gerald received a six year sentence.— Eds.]

By the afternoon of September 9, Steven Crook had returned home from an overnight trip, found his bedroom in disarray, and reported his wife missing. On the same afternoon fishermen recovered the victim's body from the river. Simmons, meanwhile, was bragging about the killing, telling friends he had killed a woman "because the bitch seen my face."

The next day, after receiving information of Simmons' involvement, police arrested him at his high school and took him to the police station in Fenton, Missouri. They read him his Miranda rights. Simmons waived his right to an attorney and agreed to answer questions. After less than two hours of interrogation, Simmons confessed to the murder and agreed to perform a videotaped reenactment at the crime scene.

The State charged Simmons with burglary, kidnaping, stealing, and murder in the first degree. As Simmons was 17 at the time of the crime, he was outside the criminal jurisdiction of Missouri's juvenile court system. He was tried as an adult. At trial the State introduced Simmons' confession and the videotaped reenactment of the crime, along with testimony that Simmons discussed the crime in advance and bragged about it later. The defense called no witnesses in the guilt phase. The jury having returned a verdict of murder, the trial proceeded to the penalty phase.

The State sought the death penalty. As aggravating factors, the State submitted that the murder was committed for the purpose of receiving money; was committed for the purpose of avoiding, interfering with, or preventing lawful arrest of the defendant; and involved depravity of mind and was outrageously and wantonly vile, horrible, and inhuman. The State called Shirley Crook's husband, daughter, and two sisters, who presented moving evidence of the devastation her death had brought to their lives.

In mitigation Simmons' attorneys first called an officer of the Missouri juvenile justice system, who testified that Simmons had no prior convictions and that no previous charges had been filed against him. Simmons' mother, father, two younger half brothers, a neighbor, and a friend took the stand to tell the jurors of the close relationships they had formed with Simmons and to plead for mercy on his behalf. Simmons' mother, in particular, testified to the responsibility Simmons demonstrated in taking care of his two younger half brothers and of his grandmother and to his capacity to show love for them.

During closing arguments, both the prosecutor and defense counsel addressed Simmons' age, which the trial judge had instructed the jurors they could consider as a mitigating factor. Defense counsel reminded the jurors that juveniles of Simmons' age cannot drink, serve on juries, or even see certain movies, because "the legislatures have wisely decided that individuals of a certain age aren't responsible enough." Defense counsel argued that Simmons' age should make "a huge difference to [the jurors] in deciding just exactly what sort of punishment to make." In rebuttal, the prosecutor gave the following response: "Age, he says. Think about age. Seventeen years old. Isn't that scary? Doesn't that scare you? Mitigating? Quite the contrary I submit. Quite the contrary."

The jury recommended the death penalty after finding the State had proved each of the three aggravating factors submitted to it. Accepting the jury's recommendation, the trial judge imposed the death penalty.

Simmons obtained new counsel, who moved in the trial court to set aside the conviction and sentence. One argument was that Simmons had received ineffective assistance at trial. To support this contention, the new counsel called as witnesses Simmons' trial attorney, Simmons' friends and neighbors, and clinical psychologists who had evaluated him.

Part of the submission was that Simmons was "very immature," "very impulsive," and "very susceptible to being manipulated or influenced." The experts testified about Simmons' background including a difficult home environment and dramatic changes in behavior, accompanied by poor school performance in adolescence. Simmons was absent from home for long periods, spending time using alcohol and drugs with other teenagers or young adults. The contention by Simmons' postconviction counsel was that these matters should have been established in the sentencing proceeding.

The trial court found no constitutional violation by reason of ineffective assistance of counsel and denied the motion for postconviction relief. In a consolidated appeal from Simmons' conviction and sentence, and from the denial of postconviction relief, the Missouri Supreme Court affirmed. The federal courts denied Simmons' petition for a writ of habeas corpus.

After these proceedings in Simmons' case had run their course, this Court held that the Eighth and Fourteenth Amendments prohibit the execution of a mentally retarded person. *Atkins v. Virginia*. Simmons filed a new petition for state postconviction relief, arguing that the reasoning of *Atkins* established that the Constitution prohibits the execution of a juvenile who was under 18 when the crime was committed.

The Missouri Supreme Court agreed ... and set aside Simmons' death sentence and resentenced him to "life imprisonment without eligibility for probation, parole, or release except by act of the Governor."

We granted certiorari, and now affirm.

II

The Eighth Amendment provides: "Excessive bail shall not be required, nor excessive fines imposed, nor cruel and unusual punishments inflicted." The provision is applicable to the States through the Fourteenth Amendment. As the Court explained in *Atkins*, the Eighth Amendment guarantees individuals the right not to be subjected to excessive sanctions. The right flows from the basic "'precept of justice that punishment for crime should be graduated and proportioned to [the] offense.'" By protecting even those convicted of heinous crimes, the Eighth Amendment reaffirms the duty of the government to respect the dignity of all persons.

The prohibition against "cruel and unusual punishments," like other expansive language in the Constitution, must be interpreted according to its text, by considering history, tradition, and precedent, and with due regard for its purpose and function in the constitutional design. To implement this framework we have established the propriety and affirmed the necessity of referring to "the evolving standards of decency that mark the progress of a maturing society" to determine which punishments are so disproportionate as to be cruel and unusual.

In *Thompson v. Oklahoma*, a plurality of the Court determined that our standards of decency do not permit the execution of any offender under the age of 16 at the time of the crime. The plurality opinion explained that no death penalty State that had given express consideration to a minimum age for the death penalty had set the age lower than 16. The plurality also observed that "[t]he conclusion that it would offend civilized standards of decency to execute a person who was less than 16 years old at the time of his or her offense is consistent with the views that have been expressed by respected professional organizations, by other nations that share our Anglo-American heritage, and by the leading members of the Western European community." The opinion further noted that juries imposed the death penalty on offenders under 16 with exceeding rarity; the last execution of an offender for a crime committed under the age of 16 had been carried out in 1948, 40 years prior.

Bringing its independent judgment to bear on the permissibility of the death penalty for a 15-year-old offender, the *Thompson* plurality stressed that "[t]he reasons why juveniles are not trusted with the privileges and responsibilities of an adult also explain why their irresponsible conduct is not as morally reprehensible as that of an adult." According to the plurality, the lesser culpability of offenders under 16 made the death penalty inappropriate as a form of retribution, while the low likelihood that offenders under 16 engaged in "the kind of cost-benefit analysis that attaches any weight to the possibility of execution" made the death penalty ineffective as a means of deterrence.

The next year, in *Stanford v. Kentucky*, the Court, over a dissenting opinion joined by four Justices, referred to contemporary standards of decency in this country and concluded the Eighth and Fourteenth Amendments did not proscribe the execution of juvenile offenders over 15 but under 18. The Court noted that 22 of the 37 death penalty States permitted the death penalty for 16-year-old offenders, and, among these 37 States, 25 permitted it for 17-year-old offenders. These numbers, in the Court's view, indicated there was no national consensus "sufficient to label a particular punishment cruel and unusual." A plurality of the Court also "emphatically reject [ed]" the suggestion that the Court should bring its own judgment to bear on the acceptability of the juvenile death penalty.

The same day the Court decided *Stanford*, it held that the Eighth Amendment did not mandate a categorical exemption from the death penalty for the mentally retarded. In reaching this conclusion it stressed that only two States had enacted laws banning the imposition of the death penalty on a mentally retarded person convicted of a capital offense. According to the Court, "the two state statutes prohibiting execution of the mentally retarded, even when added to the 14 States that have rejected capital punishment completely, [did] not provide sufficient evidence at present of a national consensus."

Three Terms ago the subject was reconsidered in *Atkins*. We held that standards of decency have evolved since *Penry* and now demonstrate that the execution of the mentally retarded is cruel and unusual punishment. The Court noted objective indicia of society's standards, as expressed in legislative enactments and state practice with respect to executions of the mentally retarded. When *Atkins* was decided only a minority of States permitted the practice, and even in those States it was rare. On the basis of these indicia the Court determined that executing mentally retarded offenders "has become truly unusual, and it is fair to say that a national consensus has developed against it."

The inquiry into our society's evolving standards of decency did not end there. The *Atkins* Court neither repeated nor relied upon the statement in *Stanford* that the Court's independent judgment has no bearing on the acceptability of a particular punishment under the Eighth Amendment. Instead we returned to the rule, established in decisions predating *Stanford*, that "'the Constitution contemplates that in the end our own judgment will be brought to bear on the question of the acceptability of the death penalty under the Eighth Amendment.'" Mental retardation, the Court said, diminishes personal culpability even if the offender can distinguish right from wrong. The impairments of mentally retarded offenders make it less defensible to impose the death penalty as retribution for past crimes and less likely that the death penalty will have a real deterrent effect. Based on these considerations and on the finding of national consensus against executing the mentally retarded, the Court ruled that the death penalty constitutes an excessive sanction for the entire category of mentally retarded offenders, and that the Eighth Amendment "'places a substantive restriction on the State's power to take the life' of a mentally retarded offender."

Just as the *Atkins* Court reconsidered the issue decided in *Penry*, we now reconsider the issue decided in *Stanford*. The beginning point is a review of objective indicia of consensus, as expressed in particular by the enactments of legislatures that have addressed the question. This data gives us essential instruction. We then must determine, in the exercise of our own independent judgment, whether the death penalty is a disproportionate punishment for juveniles.

III

A

The evidence of national consensus against the death penalty for juveniles is similar, and in some respects parallel, to the evidence *Atkins* held sufficient to demonstrate a national consensus against the death penalty for the mentally retarded. When *Atkins* was decided, 30 States prohibited the death penalty for the mentally retarded. This number comprised 12 that had abandoned the death penalty altogether, and 18 that maintained it but excluded the mentally retarded from its reach. By a similar calculation in this case, 30 States prohibit the juvenile death penalty, comprising 12 that have rejected the death penalty altogether and 18 that maintain it but, by express provision or judicial interpretation, exclude juveniles from its reach. *Atkins* emphasized that even in the 20 States without formal prohibition, the practice of executing the mentally retarded was infrequent. Since *Penry*, only five States had executed offenders known to have an IQ under 70. In the present case, too, even in the 20 States without a formal prohibition on executing juveniles, the practice is infrequent. Since *Stanford*, six States have executed prisoners for crimes committed as juveniles. In the past 10 years, only three have done so: Oklahoma, Texas, and Virginia. In December 2003 the Governor of Kentucky decided to spare the life of Kevin Stanford, and commuted his sentence to one of life imprisonment without parole, with the declaration that "'[w]e ought not be executing people who, legally, were children.'" By this act the Governor ensured Kentucky would not add itself to the list of States that have executed juveniles within the last 10 years even by the execution of the very defendant whose death sentence the Court had upheld in *Stanford*.

There is, to be sure, at least one difference between the evidence of consensus in *Atkins* and in this case. Impressive in *Atkins* was the rate of abolition of the death penalty for the mentally retarded. Sixteen States that permitted the execution of the mentally retarded at the time of *Penry* had prohibited the practice by the time we heard *Atkins*. By contrast, the rate of change in reducing the incidence of the juvenile death penalty, or in taking specific steps to abolish it, has been slower. Five States that allowed the juvenile death penalty at the time of *Stanford* have abandoned it in the intervening 15 years-four through legislative enactments and one through judicial decision.

Though less dramatic than the change from *Penry* to *Atkins* ("telling," to borrow the word *Atkins* used to describe this difference), we still consider the change from *Stanford* to this case to be significant. As noted in *Atkins*, with respect to the States that had abandoned the death penalty for the mentally retarded since *Penry*, "[i]t is not so much the number of these States that is significant, but the consistency of the direction of change." In particular we found it significant that, in the wake of *Penry*, no State that had already prohibited the execution of the mentally retarded had passed legislation to reinstate the penalty. The number of States that have abandoned capital punishment for juvenile offenders since *Stanford* is smaller than the number of States that abandoned capital punishment for the mentally retarded after *Penry*; yet we think the same consistency of direction of change has been demonstrated. Since *Stanford*, no State that previously prohibited capital punishment for juveniles has reinstated it. This fact, coupled with the trend toward abolition of the juvenile death penalty, carries special force in light of the general popularity of anticrime legislation, and in light of the particular trend in recent years toward cracking down on juvenile crime in other respects. Any difference between this case and *Atkins* with respect to the pace of abolition is thus counterbalanced by the consistent direction of the change.

The slower pace of abolition of the juvenile death penalty over the past 15 years, moreover, may have a simple explanation. When we heard *Penry*, only two death penalty States had already prohibited the execution of the mentally retarded. When we heard *Stanford*, by contrast, 12 death penalty States had already prohibited the execution of any juvenile under 18, and 15 had prohibited the execution of any juvenile under 17. If anything, this shows that the impropriety of executing juveniles between 16 and 18 years of age gained wide recognition earlier than the impropriety of executing the mentally retarded. In the words of the Missouri Supreme Court: "It would be the ultimate in irony if the very fact that the inappropriateness of the death penalty for juveniles was broadly recognized sooner than it was recognized for the mentally retarded were to become a reason to continue the execution of juveniles now that the execution of the mentally retarded has been barred."

Petitioner cannot show national consensus in favor of capital punishment for juveniles but still resists the conclusion that any consensus exists against it. Petitioner supports this position with, in particular, the observation that when the Senate ratified the International Covenant on Civil and Political Rights (ICCPR), it did so subject to the President's proposed reservation regarding Article 6(5) of that treaty, which prohibits capital punishment for juveniles. This reservation at best provides only faint support for petitioner's argument. First, the reservation was passed in 1992; since then, five States have abandoned capital punishment for juveniles. Second, Congress considered the issue when enacting the Federal Death Penalty Act in 1994, and determined that the death penalty should not extend to juveniles. The reservation to Article 6(5) of the ICCPR provides minimal evidence that there is not now a national consensus against juvenile executions.

As in *Atkins*, the objective indicia of consensus in this case—the rejection of the juvenile death penalty in the majority of States; the infrequency of its use even where it remains on the books; and the consistency in the trend toward abolition of the practice—provide sufficient evidence that today our society views juveniles, in the words *Atkins* used respecting the mentally retarded, as "categorically less culpable than the average criminal."

B

A majority of States have rejected the imposition of the death penalty on juvenile offenders under 18, and we now hold this is required by the Eighth Amendment.

Because the death penalty is the most severe punishment, the Eighth Amendment applies to it with special force. Capital punishment must be limited to those offenders who commit "a narrow category of the most serious crimes" and whose extreme culpability makes them "the most deserving of execution." This principle is implemented throughout the capital sentencing process. States must give narrow and precise definition to the aggravating factors that can result in a capital sentence. In any capital case a defendant has wide latitude to raise as a mitigating factor "any aspect of [his or her] character or record and any of the circumstances of the offense that the defendant proffers as a basis for a sentence less than death." There are a number of crimes that beyond question are severe in absolute terms, yet the death penalty may not be imposed for their commission. The death penalty may not be imposed on certain classes of offenders, such as juveniles under 16, the insane, and the mentally retarded, no matter how heinous the crime. These rules vindicate the underlying principle that the death penalty is reserved for a narrow category of crimes and offenders.

Three general differences between juveniles under 18 and adults demonstrate that juvenile offenders cannot with reliability be classified among the worst offenders. First, as any parent knows and as the scientific and sociological studies respondent and his amici cite tend to confirm, "[a] lack of maturity and an underdeveloped sense of responsibility are found in youth more often than in adults and are more understandable among the young. These qualities often result in impetuous and ill-considered actions and decisions." It has been noted that "adolescents are overrepresented statistically in virtually every category of reckless behavior." In recognition of the comparative immaturity and irresponsibility of juveniles, almost every State prohibits those under 18 years of age from voting, serving on juries, or marrying without parental consent.

The second area of difference is that juveniles are more vulnerable or susceptible to negative influences and outside pressures, including peer pressure. This is explained in part by the prevailing circumstance that juveniles have less control, or less experience with control, over their own environment.

The third broad difference is that the character of a juvenile is not as well formed as that of an adult. The personality traits of juveniles are more transitory, less fixed.

These differences render suspect any conclusion that a juvenile falls among the worst offenders. The susceptibility of juveniles to immature and irresponsible behavior means "their irresponsible conduct is not as morally reprehensible as that of an adult." Their own vulnerability and comparative lack of control over their immediate surroundings mean juveniles have a greater claim than adults to be forgiven for failing to escape negative influences in their whole environment. The reality that juveniles still struggle to define their identity means it is less supportable to conclude that even a heinous crime committed by a juvenile is evidence of irretrievably depraved character. From a moral standpoint it would be misguided to equate the failings of a minor with those of an adult, for a greater possibility exists that a minor's character deficiencies will be reformed. Indeed, "[t]he relevance of youth as a mitigating factor derives from the fact that the signature qualities of youth are transient; as individuals mature, the impetuousness and recklessness that may dominate in younger years can subside."

In *Thompson*, a plurality of the Court recognized the import of these characteristics with respect to juveniles under 16, and relied on them to hold that the Eighth Amendment prohibited the imposition of the death penalty on juveniles below that age. We conclude the same reasoning applies to all juvenile offenders under 18.

Once the diminished culpability of juveniles is recognized, it is evident that the penological justifications for the death penalty apply to them with lesser force than to adults. We have held there are two distinct social purposes served by the death penalty: "'retribution and deterrence of capital crimes by prospective offenders.'" As for retribution, we remarked in *Atkins* that "[i]f the culpability of the average murderer is insufficient to justify the most extreme sanction available to the State, the lesser culpability of the mentally retarded offender surely does not merit that form of retribution." The same conclusions follow from the lesser culpability of the juvenile offender. Whether viewed as an attempt to express the community's moral outrage or as an attempt to right the balance for the wrong to the victim, the case for retribution is not as strong with a minor as with an adult. Retribution is not proportional if the law's most severe penalty is imposed on one whose culpability or blameworthiness is diminished, to a substantial degree, by reason of youth and immaturity.

As for deterrence, it is unclear whether the death penalty has a significant or even measurable deterrent effect on juveniles, as counsel for the petitioner acknowledged at oral argument. In general we leave to legislatures the assessment of the efficacy of various criminal penalty schemes. Here, however, the absence of evidence of deterrent effect is of special concern because the same characteristics that render juveniles less culpable than adults suggest as well that juveniles will be less susceptible to deterrence. In particular, as the plurality observed in *Thompson*, "[t]he likelihood that the teenage offender has made the kind of cost-benefit analysis that attaches any weight to the possibility of execution is so remote as to be virtually nonexistent." To the extent the juvenile death penalty might have residual deterrent effect, it is worth noting that the punishment of life imprisonment without the possibility of parole is itself a severe sanction, in particular for a young person.

In concluding that neither retribution nor deterrence provides adequate justification for imposing the death penalty on juvenile offenders, we cannot deny or overlook the brutal crimes too many juvenile offenders have committed. Certainly it can be argued, although we by no means concede the point, that a rare case might arise in which a juvenile offender has sufficient psychological maturity, and at the same time demonstrates sufficient depravity, to merit a sentence of death. Indeed, this possibility is the linchpin of one contention pressed by petitioner and his amici. They assert that even assuming the truth of the observations we have made about juveniles' diminished culpability in general, jurors nonetheless should be allowed to consider mitigating arguments related to youth on a case-by-case basis, and in some cases to impose the death penalty if justified. A central feature of death penalty sentencing is a particular assessment of the circumstances of the crime and the characteristics of the offender. The system is designed to consider both aggravating and mitigating circumstances, including youth, in every case. Given this Court's own insistence on individualized consideration, petitioner maintains that it is both arbitrary and unnecessary to adopt a categorical rule barring imposition of the death penalty on any offender under 18 years of age.

We disagree. The differences between juvenile and adult offenders are too marked and well understood to risk allowing a youthful person to receive the death penalty despite insufficient culpability. An unacceptable likelihood exists that the brutality or cold-blooded nature of any particular crime would overpower mitigating arguments based on youth as a matter of course, even where the juvenile offender's objective immaturity, vulnerability, and lack of true depravity should require a sentence less severe than death. In some cases a defendant's youth may even be counted against him. In this very case, as we noted above, the prosecutor argued Simmons' youth was aggravating rather than mitigating. While this sort of overreaching could be corrected by a particular rule to ensure that the mitigating force of youth is not overlooked, that would not address our larger concerns.

It is difficult even for expert psychologists to differentiate between the juvenile offender whose crime reflects unfortunate yet transient immaturity, and the rare juvenile offender whose crime reflects irreparable corruption. As we understand it, this difficulty underlies the rule forbidding psychiatrists from diagnosing any patient under 18 as having antisocial personality disorder, a disorder also referred to as psychopathy or sociopathy, and which is characterized by callousness, cynicism, and contempt for the feelings, rights, and suffering of others. If trained psychiatrists with the advantage of clinical testing and observation refrain, despite diagnostic expertise, from assessing any juvenile under 18 as having antisocial personality disorder, we conclude that States should refrain from asking jurors to issue a far graver condemnation—that a juvenile offender merits the death penalty. When a juvenile offender commits a heinous crime, the State can exact forfeiture of some of the most basic liberties, but the State cannot extinguish his life and his potential to attain a mature understanding of his own humanity.

Drawing the line at 18 years of age is subject, of course, to the objections always raised against categorical rules. The qualities that distinguish juveniles from adults do not disappear when an individual turns 18. By the same token, some under 18 have already attained a level of maturity some adults will never reach. For the reasons we have discussed, however, a line must be drawn. The plurality opinion in *Thompson* drew the line at 16. In the intervening years the *Thompson* plurality's conclusion that offenders under 16 may not be executed has not been challenged. The logic of *Thompson* extends to those who are under 18. The age of 18 is the point where society draws the line for many purposes between childhood and adulthood. It is, we conclude, the age at which the line for death eligibility ought to rest.

These considerations mean *Stanford* should be deemed no longer controlling on this issue. To the extent *Stanford* was based on review of the objective indicia of consensus that obtained in 1989, it suffices to note that those indicia have changed. It should be observed, furthermore, that the *Stanford* Court should have considered those States that had abandoned the death penalty altogether as part of the consensus against the juvenile death penalty; a State's decision to bar the death penalty altogether of necessity demonstrates a judgment that the death penalty is inappropriate for all offenders, including juveniles. Last, to the extent *Stanford* was based on a rejection of the idea that this Court is required to bring its independent judgment to bear on the proportionality of the death penalty for a particular class of crimes or offenders, it suffices to note that this rejection was inconsistent with prior Eighth Amendment decisions. It is also inconsistent with the premises of our recent decision in *Atkins*.

In holding that the death penalty cannot be imposed upon juvenile offenders, we take into account the circumstance that some States have relied on *Stanford* in seeking the death penalty against juvenile offenders. This consideration, however, does not outweigh our conclusion that *Stanford* should no longer control in those few pending cases or in those yet to arise.

IV

Our determination that the death penalty is disproportionate punishment for offenders under 18 finds confirmation in the stark reality that the United States is the only country in the world that continues to give official sanction to the juvenile death penalty. This reality does not become controlling, for the task of interpreting the Eighth Amendment remains our responsibility. Yet at least from the time of the Court's decision in *Trop*, the Court has referred to the laws of other countries and to international authorities as instructive for its interpretation of the Eighth Amendment's prohibition of "cruel and unusual punishments."

As respondent and a number of amici emphasize, Article 37 of the United Nations Convention on the Rights of the Child, which every country in the world has ratified save for the United States and Somalia, contains an express prohibition on capital punishment for crimes committed by juveniles under 18. No ratifying country has entered a reservation to the provision prohibiting the execution of juvenile offenders. Parallel prohibitions are contained in other significant international covenants.

Respondent and his amici have submitted, and petitioner does not contest, that only seven countries other than the United States have executed juvenile offenders since 1990:

Iran, Pakistan, Saudi Arabia, Yemen, Nigeria, the Democratic Republic of Congo, and China. Since then each of these countries has either abolished capital punishment for juveniles or made public disavowal of the practice. In sum, it is fair to say that the United States now stands alone in a world that has turned its face against the juvenile death penalty.

Though the international covenants prohibiting the juvenile death penalty are of more recent date, it is instructive to note that the United Kingdom abolished the juvenile death penalty before these covenants came into being. The United Kingdom's experience bears particular relevance here in light of the historic ties between our countries and in light of the Eighth Amendment's own origins. The Amendment was modeled on a parallel provision in the English Declaration of Rights of 1689, which provided: "[E]xcessive Bail ought not to be required nor excessive Fines imposed; nor cruel and unusual Punishments inflicted." As of now, the United Kingdom has abolished the death penalty in its entirety; but, decades before it took this step, it recognized the disproportionate nature of the juvenile death penalty; and it abolished that penalty as a separate matter.

It is proper that we acknowledge the overwhelming weight of international opinion against the juvenile death penalty, resting in large part on the understanding that the instability and emotional imbalance of young people may often be a factor in the crime. The opinion of the world community, while not controlling our outcome, does provide respected and significant confirmation for our own conclusions.

Over time, from one generation to the next, the Constitution has come to earn the high respect and even, as Madison dared to hope, the veneration of the American people. The document sets forth, and rests upon, innovative principles original to the American experience, such as federalism; a proven balance in political mechanisms through separation of powers; specific guarantees for the accused in criminal cases; and broad provisions to secure individual freedom and preserve human dignity. These doctrines and guarantees are central to the American experience and remain essential to our present-day self-definition and national identity. Not the least of the reasons we honor the Constitution, then, is because we know it to be our own. It does not lessen our fidelity to the Constitution or our pride in its origins to acknowledge that the express affirmation of certain fundamental rights by other nations and peoples simply underscores the centrality of those same rights within our own heritage of freedom.

* * *

The Eighth and Fourteenth Amendments forbid imposition of the death penalty on offenders who were under the age of 18 when their crimes were committed. The judgment of the Missouri Supreme Court setting aside the sentence of death imposed upon Christopher Simmons is affirmed.

It is so ordered.

Justice STEVENS, with whom Justice GINSBURG joins, concurring.

Perhaps even more important than our specific holding today is our reaffirmation of the basic principle that informs the Court's interpretation of the Eighth Amendment. If the meaning of that Amendment had been frozen when it was originally drafted, it would impose no impediment to the execution of 7-year-old children today. The evolving standards of decency that have driven our construction of this critically important part of the Bill of Rights foreclose any such reading of the Amendment. In the best tradition of the common law, the pace of that evolution is a matter for continuing debate; but that our understanding of the Constitution does change from time to time has been settled since John Marshall breathed life into its text. If great lawyers of his day—Alexander Hamilton, for example—were sitting with us today, I would expect them to join Justice KENNEDY's opinion for the Court. In all events, I do so without hesitation.

Justice O'CONNOR, dissenting.

The Court's decision today establishes a categorical rule forbidding the execution of any offender for any crime committed before his 18th birthday, no matter how deliberate, wanton, or cruel the offense. Neither the objective evidence of contemporary societal values, nor the Court's moral proportionality analysis, nor the two in tandem suffice to justify this ruling.

* * *

C

Seventeen-year-old murderers must be categorically exempted from capital punishment, the Court says, because they "cannot with reliability be classified among the worst offenders." That conclusion is premised on three perceived differences between "adults," who have already reached their 18th birthdays, and "juveniles," who have not. First, juveniles lack maturity and responsibility and are more reckless than adults. Second, juveniles are more vulnerable to outside influences because they have less control over their surroundings. And third, a juvenile's character is not as fully formed as that of an adult. Based on these characteristics, the Court determines that 17-year-old capital murderers are not as blameworthy as adults guilty of similar crimes; that 17-year-olds are less likely than adults to be deterred by the prospect of a death sentence; and that it is difficult to conclude that a 17-year-old who commits even the most heinous of crimes is "irretrievably depraved." The Court suggests that "a rare case might arise in which a juvenile offender has sufficient psychological maturity, and at the same time demonstrates sufficient depravity, to merit a sentence of death." However, the Court argues that a categorical age-based prohibition is justified as a prophylactic rule because "[t]he differences between juvenile and adult offenders are too marked and well understood to risk allowing a youthful person to receive the death penalty despite insufficient culpability."

It is beyond cavil that juveniles as a class are generally less mature, less responsible, and less fully formed than adults, and that these differences bear on juveniles' comparative moral culpability. But even accepting this premise, the Court's proportionality argument fails to support its categorical rule.

First, the Court adduces no evidence whatsoever in support of its sweeping conclusion, that it is only in "rare" cases, if ever, that 17-year-old murderers are sufficiently mature and act with sufficient depravity to warrant the death penalty. The fact that juveniles are generally less culpable for their misconduct than adults does not necessarily mean that a 17-year-old murderer cannot be sufficiently culpable to merit the death penalty. At most, the Court's argument suggests that the average 17-year-old murderer is not as culpable as the average adult murderer. But an especially depraved juvenile offender may nevertheless be just as culpable as many adult offenders considered bad enough to deserve the death penalty. Similarly, the fact that the availability of the death penalty may be less likely to deter a juvenile from committing a capital crime does not imply that this threat cannot effectively deter some 17-year-olds from such an act. Surely there is an age below which no offender, no matter what his crime, can be deemed to have the cognitive or emotional maturity necessary to warrant the death penalty. But at least at the margins between adolescence and adulthood—and especially for 17-year-olds such as respondent—the relevant differences between "adults" and "juveniles" appear to be a matter of degree, rather than of kind. It follows that a legislature may reasonably conclude that at least some 17-year-olds can act with sufficient moral culpability, and can be sufficiently deterred by the threat of execution, that capital punishment may be warranted in an appropriate case.

* * *

The Court's proportionality argument suffers from a second and closely related defect: It fails to establish that the differences in maturity between 17-year-olds and young "adults" are both universal enough and significant enough to justify a bright-line prophylactic rule against capital punishment of the former. The Court's analysis is premised on differences in the aggregate between juveniles and adults, which frequently do not hold true when comparing individuals. Although it may be that many 17-year-old murderers lack sufficient maturity to deserve the death penalty, some juvenile murderers may be quite mature. Chronological age is not an unfailing measure of psychological development, and common experience suggests that many 17-year-olds are more mature than the average young "adult." In short, the class of offenders exempted from capital punishment by today's decision is too broad and too diverse to warrant a categorical prohibition. Indeed, the age-based line drawn by the Court is indefensibly arbitrary—it quite likely will protect a number of offenders who are mature enough to deserve the death penalty and may well leave vulnerable many who are not.

For purposes of proportionality analysis, 17-year-olds as a class are qualitatively and materially different from the mentally retarded. "Mentally retarded" offenders, as we understood that category in *Atkins*, are defined by precisely the characteristics which render death an excessive punishment. A mentally retarded person is, "by definition," one whose cognitive and behavioral capacities have been proven to fall below a certain minimum. Accordingly, for purposes of our decision in *Atkins*, the mentally retarded are not merely less blameworthy for their misconduct or less likely to be deterred by the death penalty than others. Rather, a mentally retarded offender is one whose demonstrated impairments make it so highly unlikely that he is culpable enough to deserve the death penalty or that he could have been deterred by the threat of death, that execution is not a defensible punishment. There is no such inherent or accurate fit between an offender's chronological age and the personal limitations which the Court believes make capital punishment excessive for 17-year-old murderers. Moreover, it defies common sense to suggest that 17-year-olds as a class are somehow equivalent to mentally retarded persons with regard to culpability or susceptibility to deterrence. Seventeen-year-olds may, on average, be less mature than adults, but that lesser maturity simply cannot be equated with the major, lifelong impairments suffered by the mentally retarded.

The proportionality issues raised by the Court clearly implicate Eighth Amendment concerns. But these concerns may properly be addressed not by means of an arbitrary, categorical age-based rule, but rather through individualized sentencing in which juries are required to give appropriate mitigating weight to the defendant's immaturity, his susceptibility to outside pressures, his cognizance of the consequences of his actions, and so forth. In that way the constitutional response can be tailored to the specific problem it is meant to remedy. The Eighth Amendment guards against the execution of those who are "insufficiently culpable," in significant part, by requiring sentencing that "reflect[s] a reasoned moral response to the defendant's background, character, and crime." Accordingly, the sentencer in a capital case must be permitted to give full effect to all constitutionally relevant mitigating evidence. A defendant's youth or immaturity is, of course, a paradigmatic example of such evidence.

Although the prosecutor's apparent attempt to use respondent's youth as an aggravating circumstance in this case is troubling, that conduct was never challenged with specificity in the lower courts and is not directly at issue here. As the Court itself suggests, such "overreaching" would best be addressed, if at all, through a more narrowly tailored remedy. The Court argues that sentencing juries cannot accurately evaluate a youthful offender's maturity or give appropriate weight to the mitigating characteristics related to youth. But, again, the Court presents no real evidence—and the record appears to contain none-supporting this claim. Perhaps more importantly, the Court fails to explain why this duty should be so different from, or so much more difficult than, that of assessing and giving proper effect to any other qualitative capital sentencing factor. I would not be so quick to conclude that the constitutional safeguards, the sentencing juries, and the trial judges upon which we place so much reliance in all capital cases are inadequate in this narrow context.

D

I turn, finally, to the Court's discussion of foreign and international law. Without question, there has been a global trend in recent years towards abolishing capital punishment for under-18 offenders. Very few, if any, countries other than the United States now permit this practice in law or in fact. While acknowledging that the actions and views of other countries do not dictate the outcome of our Eighth Amendment inquiry, the Court asserts that "the overwhelming weight of international opinion against the juvenile death penalty ... does provide respected and significant confirmation for [its] own conclusions." Because I do not believe that a genuine national consensus against the juvenile death penalty has yet developed, and because I do not believe the Court's moral proportionality argument justifies a categorical, age-based constitutional rule, I can assign no such confirmatory role to the international consensus described by the Court. In short, the evidence of an international consensus does not alter my determination that the Eighth Amendment does not, at this time, forbid capital punishment of 17-year-old murderers in all cases.

Nevertheless, I disagree with Justice SCALIA's contention that foreign and international law have no place in our Eighth Amendment jurisprudence. Over the course of nearly half a century, the Court has consistently referred to foreign and international law as relevant to its assessment of evolving standards of decency. This inquiry reflects the special character of the Eighth Amendment, which, as the Court has long held, draws its meaning directly from the maturing values of civilized society. Obviously, American law is distinctive in many respects, not least where the specific provisions of our Constitution and the history of its exposition so dictate. But this Nation's evolving understanding of human dignity certainly is neither wholly isolated from, nor inherently at odds with, the values prevailing in other countries. On the contrary, we should not be surprised to find congruence between domestic and international values, especially where the international community has reached clear agreement—expressed in international law or in the domestic laws of individual countries—that a particular form of punishment is inconsistent with fundamental human rights. At least, the existence of an international consensus of this nature can serve to confirm the reasonableness of a consonant and genuine American consensus. The instant case presents no such domestic consensus, however, and the recent emergence of an otherwise global consensus does not alter that basic fact.

* * *

Reasonable minds can differ as to the minimum age at which commission of a serious crime should expose the defendant to the death penalty, if at all. Many jurisdictions have abolished capital punishment altogether, while many others have determined that even the most heinous crime, if committed before the age of 18, should not be punishable by death. Indeed, were my office that of a legislator, rather than a judge, then I, too, would be inclined to support legislation setting a minimum age of 18 in this context. But a significant number of States, including Missouri, have decided to make the death penalty potentially available for 17-year-old capital murderers such as respondent. Without a clearer showing that a genuine national consensus forbids the execution of such offenders, this Court should not substitute its own "inevitably subjective judgment" on how best to resolve this difficult moral question for the judgments of the Nation's democratically elected legislatures. I respectfully dissent.

Justice SCALIA, with whom THE CHIEF JUSTICE and Justice THOMAS join, dissenting.

In urging approval of a constitution that gave life-tenured judges the power to nullify laws enacted by the people's representatives, Alexander Hamilton assured the citizens of New York that there was little risk in this, since "[t]he judiciary ... ha[s] neither FORCE nor WILL but merely judgment." But Hamilton had in mind a traditional judiciary, "bound down by strict rules and precedents which serve to define and point out their duty in every particular case that comes before them." Bound down, indeed. What a mockery today's opinion makes of Hamilton's expectation, announcing the Court's conclusion that the meaning of our Constitution has changed over the past 15 years—not, mind you, that this Court's decision 15 years ago was wrong, but that the Constitution has changed. The Court reaches this implausible result by purporting to advert, not to the original meaning of the Eighth Amendment, but to "the evolving standards of decency," of our national society. It then finds, on the flimsiest of grounds, that a national consensus which could not be perceived in our people's laws barely 15 years ago now solidly exists. Worse still, the Court says in so many words that what our people's laws say about the issue does not, in the last analysis, matter: "[I]n the end our own judgment will be brought to bear on the question of the acceptability of the death penalty under the Eighth Amendment." The Court thus proclaims itself sole arbiter of our Nation's moral standards—and in the course of discharging that awesome responsibility purports to take guidance from the views of foreign courts and legislatures. Because I do not believe that the meaning of our Eighth Amendment, any more than the meaning of other provisions of our Constitution, should be determined by the subjective views of five Members of this Court and like-minded foreigners, I dissent.

I

* * *

Today's opinion provides a perfect example of why judges are ill equipped to make the type of legislative judgments the Court insists on making here. To support its opinion that States should be prohibited from imposing the death penalty on anyone who committed murder before age 18, the Court looks to scientific and sociological studies, picking and choosing those that support its position. It never explains why those particular studies are methodologically sound; none was ever entered into evidence or tested in an adversarial proceeding.

We need not look far to find studies contradicting the Court's conclusions. As petitioner points out, the American Psychological Association (APA), which claims in this case that scientific evidence shows persons under 18 lack the ability to take moral responsibility for their decisions, has previously taken precisely the opposite position before this very Court. In its brief in Hodgson, the APA found a "rich body of research" showing that juveniles are mature enough to decide whether to obtain an abortion without parental involvement. The APA brief, citing psychology treatises and studies too numerous to list here, asserted: "[B]y middle adolescence (age 14–15) young people develop abilities similar to adults in reasoning about moral dilemmas, understanding social rules and laws, [and] reasoning about interpersonal relationships and interpersonal problems." Given the nuances of scientific methodology and conflicting views, courts—which can only consider the limited evidence on the record before them—are ill equipped to determine which view of science is the right one. Legislatures "are better qualified to weigh and 'evaluate the results of statistical studies in terms of their own local conditions and with a flexibility of approach that is not available to the courts.' "

Even putting aside questions of methodology, the studies cited by the Court offer scant support for a categorical prohibition of the death penalty for murderers under 18. At most, these studies conclude that, on average, or in most cases, persons under 18 are unable to take moral responsibility for their actions. Not one of the cited studies opines that all individuals under 18 are unable to appreciate the nature of their crimes.

Moreover, the cited studies describe only adolescents who engage in risky or antisocial behavior, as many young people do. Murder, however, is more than just risky or antisocial behavior. It is entirely consistent to believe that young people often act impetuously and lack judgment, but, at the same time, to believe that those who commit premeditated murder are—at least sometimes—just as culpable as adults. Christopher Simmons, who was only seven months shy of his 18th birthday when he murdered Shirley Crook, described to his friends beforehand—"[i]n chilling, callous terms," as the Court puts it, ante, at 1187—the murder he planned to commit. He then broke into the home of an innocent woman, bound her with duct tape and electrical wire, and threw her off a bridge alive and conscious. In their amici brief, the States of Alabama, Delaware, Oklahoma, Texas, Utah, and Virginia offer additional examples of murders committed by individuals under 18 that involve truly monstrous acts. In Alabama, two 17-year-olds, one 16-year-old, and one 19-year-old picked up a female hitchhiker, threw bottles at her, and kicked and stomped her for approximately 30 minutes until she died. They then sexually assaulted her lifeless body and, when they were finished, threw her body off a cliff. They later returned to the crime scene to mutilate her corpse. Other examples in the brief are equally shocking. Though these cases are assuredly the exception rather than the rule, the studies the Court cites in no way justify a constitutional imperative that prevents legislatures and juries from treating exceptional cases in an exceptional way—by determining that some murders are not just the acts of happy-go-lucky teenagers, but heinous crimes deserving of death.

Moreover, the age statutes the Court lists "set the appropriate ages for the operation of a system that makes its determinations in gross, and that does not conduct individualized maturity tests." The criminal justice system, by contrast, provides for individualized consideration of each defendant. In capital cases, this Court requires the sentencer to make an individualized determination, which includes weighing aggravating factors and mitigating factors, such as youth. In other contexts where individualized consideration is provided, we have recognized that at least some minors will be mature enough to make difficult decisions that involve moral considerations. For instance, we have struck down abortion statutes that do not allow minors deemed mature by courts to bypass parental notification provisions. It is hard to see why this context should be any different. Whether to obtain an abortion is surely a much more complex decision for a young person than whether to kill an innocent person in cold blood.

The Court concludes, however, that juries cannot be trusted with the delicate task of weighing a defendant's youth along with the other mitigating and aggravating factors of his crime. This startling conclusion undermines the very foundations of our capital sentencing system, which entrusts juries with "mak[ing] the difficult and uniquely human judgments that defy codification and that 'buil[d] discretion, equity, and flexibility into a legal system.'" The Court says that juries will be unable to appreciate the significance of a defendant's youth when faced with details of a brutal crime. This assertion is based on no evidence; to the contrary, the Court itself acknowledges that the execution of under-18 offenders is "infrequent" even in the States "without a formal prohibition on executing juveniles," suggesting that juries take seriously their responsibility to weigh youth as a mitigating factor.

The Court's contention that the goals of retribution and deterrence are not served by executing murderers under 18 is also transparently false. The argument that "[r]etribution is not proportional if the law's most severe penalty is imposed on one whose culpability or blameworthiness is diminished," is simply an extension of the earlier, false generalization that youth always defeats culpability. The Court claims that "juveniles will be less susceptible to deterrence," because "'[t]he likelihood that the teenage offender has made the kind of cost-benefit analysis that attaches any weight to the possibility of execution is so remote as to be virtually nonexistent.'" The Court unsurprisingly finds no support for this astounding proposition, save its own case law. The facts of this very case show the proposition to be false. Before committing the crime, Simmons encouraged his friends to join him by assuring them that they could "get away with it" because they were minors. This fact may have influenced the jury's decision to impose capital punishment despite Simmons' age. Because the Court refuses to entertain the possibility that its own unsubstantiated generalization about juveniles could be wrong, it ignores this evidence entirely.

III

Though the views of our own citizens are essentially irrelevant to the Court's decision today, the views of other countries and the so-called international community take center stage.

… That the Senate and the President—those actors our Constitution empowers to enter into treaties, have declined to join and ratify treaties prohibiting execution of under-18 offenders can only suggest that our country has either not reached a national consensus on the question, or has reached a consensus contrary to what the Court announces. That the reservation to the ICCPR was made in 1992 does not suggest otherwise, since the reservation still remains in place today. It is also worth noting that, in addition to barring the execution of under-18 offenders, the United Nations Convention on the Rights of the Child prohibits punishing them with life in prison without the possibility of release. If we are truly going to get in line with the international community, then the Court's reassurance that the death penalty is really not needed, since "the punishment of life imprisonment without the possibility of parole is itself a severe sanction," gives little comfort.

It is interesting that whereas the Court is not content to accept what the States of our Federal Union say, but insists on inquiring into what they do (specifically, whether they in fact apply the juvenile death penalty that their laws allow), the Court is quite willing to believe that every foreign nation—of whatever tyrannical political makeup and with however subservient or incompetent a court system—in fact adheres to a rule of no death penalty for offenders under 18. Nor does the Court inquire into how many of the countries that have the death penalty, but have forsworn (on paper at least) imposing that penalty on offenders under 18, have what no State of this country can constitutionally have: a mandatory death penalty for certain crimes, with no possibility of mitigation by the sentencing authority, for youth or any other reason. I suspect it is most of them. To forbid the death penalty for juveniles under such a system may be a good idea, but it says nothing about our system, in which the sentencing authority, typically a jury, always can, and almost always does, withhold the death penalty from an under-18 offender except, after considering all the circumstances, in the rare cases where it is warranted. The foreign authorities, in other words, do not even speak to the issue before us here.

More fundamentally, however, the basic premise of the Court's argument—that American law should conform to the laws of the rest of the world—ought to be rejected out of hand. In fact the Court itself does not believe it. In many significant respects the laws of most other countries differ from our law—including not only such explicit provisions of our Constitution as the right to jury trial and grand jury indictment, but even many interpretations of the Constitution prescribed by this Court itself.

... I do not believe that approval by "other nations and peoples" should buttress our commitment to American principles any more than (what should logically follow) disapproval by "other nations and peoples" should weaken that commitment. Foreign sources are cited today, not to underscore our "fidelity" to the Constitution, our "pride in its origins," and "our own [American] heritage." To the contrary, they are cited to set aside the centuries-old American practice—a practice still engaged in by a large majority of the relevant States—of letting a jury of 12 citizens decide whether, in the particular case, youth should be the basis for withholding the death penalty. What these foreign sources "affirm," rather than repudiate, is the Justices' own notion of how the world ought to be, and their diktat that it shall be so henceforth in America. The Court's parting attempt to downplay the significance of its extensive discussion of foreign law is unconvincing. "Acknowledgment" of foreign approval has no place in the legal opinion of this Court unless it is part of the basis for the Court's judgment—which is surely what it parades as today.

IV

To add insult to injury, the Court affirms the Missouri Supreme Court without even admonishing that court for its flagrant disregard of our precedent in *Stanford*. Until today, we have always held that "it is this Court's prerogative alone to overrule one of its precedents." That has been true even where "'changes in judicial doctrine' ha[ve] significantly undermined" our prior holding, and even where our prior holding "appears to rest on reasons rejected in some other line of decisions." Today, however, the Court silently approves a state-court decision that blatantly rejected controlling precedent.

Notes

(a) Although capital cases are often viewed as *sui generis*, and therefore not of strong precedential value in other contexts, could it be argued that the developmental and psychological distinctions between adults and adolescents, differences that the *Roper* Court believed was constitutionally relevant regarding execution, should also be considered in other scenarios? In other words, should there be special constitutional protection for children in juvenile court? For example, should *Roper* be relevant in determining the extent of punishment for juveniles who commit serious criminal acts, what Professor Barry Feld calls a "youth discount," or whether there should be a categorical bar against waiver of children to criminal court, or whether the standard for determining ineffective assistance of counsel for delinquent minors tried in juvenile court should be different from that of adults in criminal court, or whether the test for admissibility of confessions should be more stringent than for adults or whether juvenile records should be admissible in adult criminal sentencing proceedings? In later cases the Court is applying the rationale used in *Roper* to other juvenile matters.

(b) The United Nations Convention on the Rights of the Child (CRC) discussed in the *Roper* case, is the primary international law document dealing with juvenile justice systems. It was ratified in 1989 by all member nations except the United States and Somalia. There are two Articles that specifically speak to the rights of children charged with crimes, Articles 37 and 40. The pertinent provision of Article 37 is as follows:

States Parties shall ensure that:

(a) No child shall be subjected to torture or other cruel, inhuman or degrading treatment or punishment. Neither capital punishment nor life imprisonment without possibility of release shall be imposed for offences committed by persons below eighteen years of age;

Allegedly the United States did not ratify the CRC because of the prohibition of capital punishment for juveniles. After *Roper v. Simmons*, invalidating the death penalty for individuals who committed capital offenses when they were under the age of eighteen, that reason is no longer operative. However, there are other provisions that may be viewed as impinging on the sovereignty of the United States and are likely to prevent the United States from ratifying it in the near future.

Safford Unified School District v. April Redding
129 S. Ct. 2633 (2009)

Justice SOUTER delivered the opinion of the Court.

The issue here is whether a 13-year-old student's Fourth Amendment right was violated when she was subjected to a search of her bra and underpants by school officials acting on reasonable suspicion that she had brought forbidden prescription and over-the-counter drugs to school. Because there were no reasons to suspect the drugs presented a danger or were concealed in her underwear, we hold that the search did violate the Constitution, but because there is reason to question the clarity with which the right was established, the official who ordered the unconstitutional search is entitled to qualified immunity from liability.

I

The events immediately prior to the search in question began in 13-year-old Savana Redding's math class at Safford Middle School one October day in 2003. The assistant principal of the school, Kerry Wilson, came into the room and asked Savana to go to his office. There, he showed her a day planner, unzipped and open flat on his desk, in which there were several knives, lighters, a permanent marker, and a cigarette. Wilson asked Savana whether the planner was hers; she said it was, but that a few days before she had lent it to her friend, Marissa Glines. Savana stated that none of the items in the planner belonged to her.

Wilson then showed Savana four white prescription-strength ibuprofen 400-mg pills, and one over-the-counter blue naproxen 200-mg pill, all used for pain and inflammation but banned under school rules without advance permission. He asked Savana if she knew anything about the pills. Savana answered that she did not. Wilson then told Savana that he had received a report that she was giving these pills to fellow students; Savana denied it and agreed to let Wilson search her belongings. Helen Romero, an administrative assistant, came into the office, and together with Wilson they searched Savana's backpack, finding nothing.

At that point, Wilson instructed Romero to take Savana to the school nurse's office to search her clothes for pills. Romero and the nurse, Peggy Schwallier, asked Savana to remove her jacket, socks, and shoes, leaving her in stretch pants and a T-shirt (both without pockets), which she was then asked to remove. Finally, Savana was told to pull her bra out and to the side and shake it, and to pull out the elastic on her underpants, thus exposing her breasts and pelvic area to some degree. No pills were found.

Savana's mother filed suit against Safford Unified School District # 1, Wilson, Romero, and Schwallier for conducting a strip search in violation of Savana's Fourth Amendment rights.

We granted certiorari, and now affirm in part, reverse in part, and remand.

II

The Fourth Amendment "right of the people to be secure in their persons ... against unreasonable searches and seizures" generally requires a law enforcement officer to have probable cause for conducting a search. "Probable cause exists where 'the facts and circumstances within [an officer's] knowledge and of which [he] had reasonably trustworthy information [are] sufficient in themselves to warrant a man of reasonable caution in the belief that' an offense has been or is being committed," and that evidence bearing on that offense will be found in the place to be searched.

In *T.L.O.*, we recognized that the school setting "requires some modification of the level of suspicion of illicit activity needed to justify a search," and held that for searches by school officials "a careful balancing of governmental and private interests suggests that the public interest is best served by a Fourth Amendment standard of reasonableness that stops short of probable cause." We have thus applied a standard of reasonable suspicion to determine the legality of a school administrator's search of a student, and have held that a school search "will be permissible in its scope when the measures adopted are reasonably related to the objectives of the search and not excessively intrusive in light of the age and sex of the student and the nature of the infraction."

A number of our cases on probable cause have an implicit bearing on the reliable knowledge element of reasonable suspicion, as we have attempted to flesh out the knowledge component by looking to the degree to which known facts imply prohibited conduct. At the end of the day, however, we have realized that these factors cannot rigidly control, and we have come back to saying that the standards are "fluid concepts that take their substantive content from the particular contexts" in which they are being assessed.

Perhaps the best that can be said generally about the required knowledge component of probable cause for a law enforcement officer's evidence search is that it raise a "fair probability," or a "substantial chance," of discovering evidence of criminal activity. The lesser standard for school searches could as readily be described as a moderate chance of finding evidence of wrongdoing.

III

A

In this case, the school's policies strictly prohibit the nonmedical use, possession, or sale of any drug on school grounds, including "'[a]ny prescription or over-the-counter drug, except those for which permission to use in school has been granted pursuant to Board policy.'" A week before Savana was searched, another student, Jordan Romero (no relation of the school's administrative assistant), told the principal and Assistant Principal Wilson that "certain students were bringing drugs and weapons on campus," and that he had been sick after taking some pills that "he got from a classmate." On the morning of October 8, the same boy handed Wilson a white pill that he said Marissa Glines had given him. He told Wilson that students were planning to take the pills at lunch.

Wilson learned from Peggy Schwallier, the school nurse, that the pill was Ibuprofen 400 mg, available only by prescription. Wilson then called Marissa out of class. Outside the classroom, Marissa's teacher handed Wilson the day planner, found within Marissa's reach, containing various contraband items. Wilson escorted Marissa back to his office.

In the presence of Helen Romero, Wilson requested Marissa to turn out her pockets and open her wallet. Marissa produced a blue pill, several white ones, and a razor blade. Wilson asked where the blue pill came from, and Marissa answered, "'I guess it slipped in when she gave me the IBU 400s.'" When Wilson asked whom she meant, Marissa replied, "'Savana Redding.'" Wilson then enquired about the day planner and its contents; Marissa denied knowing anything about them. Wilson did not ask Marissa any followup questions to determine whether there was any likelihood that Savana presently had pills: neither asking when Marissa received the pills from Savana nor where Savana might be hiding them.

Schwallier did not immediately recognize the blue pill, but information provided through a poison control hotline indicated that the pill was a 200-mg dose of an anti-inflammatory drug, generically called naproxen, available over the counter. At Wilson's direction, Marissa was then subjected to a search of her bra and underpants by Romero and Schwallier, as Savana was later on. The search revealed no additional pills.

It was at this juncture that Wilson called Savana into his office and showed her the day planner. Their conversation established that Savana and Marissa were on friendly terms: while she denied knowledge of the contraband, Savana admitted that the day planner was hers and that she had lent it to Marissa. Wilson had other reports of their friendship from staff members, who had identified Savana and Marissa as part of an unusually rowdy group at the school's opening dance in August, during which alcohol and cigarettes were found in the girls' bathroom. Wilson had reason to connect the girls with this contraband, for Wilson knew that Jordan Romero had told the principal that before the dance, he had been at a party at Savana's house where alcohol was served. Marissa's statement that the pills came from Savana was thus sufficiently plausible to warrant suspicion that Savana was involved in pill distribution.

This suspicion of Wilson's was enough to justify a search of Savana's backpack and outer clothing. If a student is reasonably suspected of giving out contraband pills, she is reasonably suspected of carrying them on her person and in the carryall that has become an item of student uniform in most places today. If Wilson's reasonable suspicion of pill distribution were not understood to support searches of outer clothes and backpack, it would not justify any search worth making. And the look into Savana's bag, in her presence and in the relative privacy of Wilson's office, was not excessively intrusive, any more than Romero's subsequent search of her outer clothing.

B

Here it is that the parties part company, with Savana's claim that extending the search at Wilson's behest to the point of making her pull out her underwear was constitutionally unreasonable. The exact label for this final step in the intrusion is not important, though strip search is a fair way to speak of it. Romero and Schwallier directed Savana to remove her clothes down to her underwear, and then "pull out" her bra and the elastic band on her underpants. Although Romero and Schwallier stated that they did not see anything when Savana followed their instructions, we would not define strip search and its Fourth Amendment consequences in a way that would guarantee litigation about who was looking and how much was seen. The very fact of Savana's pulling her underwear away from her body in the presence of the two officials who were able to see her necessarily exposed her breasts and pelvic area to some degree, and both subjective and reasonable societal expectations of personal privacy support the treatment of such a search as categorically distinct, requiring distinct elements of justification on the part of school authorities for going beyond a search of outer clothing and belongings.

Savana's subjective expectation of privacy against such a search is inherent in her account of it as embarrassing, frightening, and humiliating. The reasonableness of her expectation (required by the Fourth Amendment standard) is indicated by the consistent experiences of other young people similarly searched, whose adolescent vulnerability intensifies the patent intrusiveness of the exposure. The common reaction of these adolescents simply registers the obviously different meaning of a search exposing the body from the experience of nakedness or near undress in other school circumstances. Changing for gym is getting ready for play; exposing for a search is responding to an accusation reserved for suspected wrongdoers and fairly understood as so degrading that a number of communities have decided that strip searches in schools are never reasonable and have banned them no matter what the facts may be, see, e.g., New York City Dept. of Education, Reg. No. A-432, p. 2 (2005), online at http://docs.nycenet.edu/docushare/dsweb/Get/Document-21/A-432.pdf ("Under no circumstances shall a strip-search of a student be conducted").

The indignity of the search does not, of course, outlaw it, but it does implicate the rule of reasonableness as stated in *T.L.O.*, that "the search as actually conducted [be] reasonably related in scope to the circumstances which justified the interference in the first place." The scope will be permissible, that is, when it is "not excessively intrusive in light of the age and sex of the student and the nature of the infraction."

Here, the content of the suspicion failed to match the degree of intrusion. Wilson knew beforehand that the pills were prescription-strength ibuprofen and over-the-counter naproxen, common pain relievers equivalent to two Advil, or one Aleve. He must have been aware of the nature and limited threat of the specific drugs he was searching for, and while just about anything can be taken in quantities that will do real harm, Wilson had no reason to suspect that large amounts of the drugs were being passed around, or that individual students were receiving great numbers of pills.

Nor could Wilson have suspected that Savana was hiding common painkillers in her underwear. Petitioners suggest, as a truth universally acknowledged, that "students ... hid[e] contraband in or under their clothing," and cite a smattering of cases of students with contraband in their underwear. But when the categorically extreme intrusiveness of a search down to the body of an adolescent requires some justification in suspected facts, general background possibilities fall short; a reasonable search that extensive calls for suspicion that it will pay off. But nondangerous school contraband does not raise the specter of stashes in intimate places, and there is no evidence in the record of any general practice among Safford Middle School students of hiding that sort of thing in underwear; neither Jordan nor Marissa suggested to Wilson that Savana was doing that, and the preceding search of Marissa that Wilson ordered yielded nothing. Wilson never even determined when Marissa had received the pills from Savana; if it had been a few days before, that would weigh heavily against any reasonable conclusion that Savana presently had the pills on her person, much less in her underwear.

In sum, what was missing from the suspected facts that pointed to Savana was any indication of danger to the students from the power of the drugs or their quantity, and any reason to suppose that Savana was carrying pills in her underwear. We think that the combination of these deficiencies was fatal to finding the search reasonable.

In so holding, we mean to cast no ill reflection on the assistant principal, for the record raises no doubt that his motive throughout was to eliminate drugs from his school and protect students from what Jordan Romero had gone through. Parents are known to over-react to protect their children from danger, and a school official with responsibility for safety may tend to do the same. The difference is that the Fourth Amendment places limits on the official, even with the high degree of deference that courts must pay to the educator's professional judgment.

We do mean, though, to make it clear that the *T.L.O.* concern to limit a school search to reasonable scope requires the support of reasonable suspicion of danger or of resort to underwear for hiding evidence of wrongdoing before a search can reasonably make the quantum leap from outer clothes and backpacks to exposure of intimate parts. The meaning of such a search, and the degradation its subject may reasonably feel, place a search that intrusive in a category of its own demanding its own specific suspicions.

IV

A school official searching a student is "entitled to qualified immunity where clearly established law does not show that the search violated the Fourth Amendment." To be established clearly, however, there is no need that "the very action in question [have] previously been held unlawful." The unconstitutionality of outrageous conduct obviously will be unconstitutional, this being the reason, as Judge Posner has said, that "[t]he easiest cases don't even arise." But even as to action less than an outrage, "officials can still be on notice that their conduct violates established law … in novel factual circumstances."

T.L.O. directed school officials to limit the intrusiveness of a search, "in light of the age and sex of the student and the nature of the infraction," and as we have just said at some length, the intrusiveness of the strip search here cannot be seen as justifiably related to the circumstances. But we realize that the lower courts have reached divergent conclusions regarding how the *T.L.O.* standard applies to such searches.

A number of judges have read *T.L.O.* as the en banc minority of the Ninth Circuit did here. The Sixth Circuit upheld a strip search of a high school student for a drug, without any suspicion that drugs were hidden next to her body. And other courts considering qualified immunity for strip searches have read *T.L.O.* as "a series of abstractions, on the one hand, and a declaration of seeming deference to the judgments of school officials, on the other," which made it impossible "to establish clearly the contours of a Fourth Amendment right … [in] the wide variety of possible school settings different from those involved in *T.L.O.*" itself. Ibid.

We think these differences of opinion from our own are substantial enough to require immunity for the school officials in this case. We would not suggest that entitlement to qualified immunity is the guaranteed product of disuniform views of the law in the other federal, or state, courts, and the fact that a single judge, or even a group of judges, disagrees about the contours of a right does not automatically render the law unclear if we have been clear. That said, however, the cases viewing school strip searches differently from the way we see them are numerous enough, with well-reasoned majority and dissenting opinions, to counsel doubt that we were sufficiently clear in the prior statement of law. We conclude that qualified immunity is warranted.

V

The strip search of Savana Redding was unreasonable and a violation of the Fourth Amendment, but petitioners Wilson, Romero, and Schwallier are nevertheless protected from liability through qualified immunity. Our conclusions here do not resolve, however, the question of the liability of petitioner Safford Unified School District # 1 under *Monell v. New York City Dept. of Social Servs.*, a claim the Ninth Circuit did not address. The judgment of the Ninth Circuit is therefore affirmed in part and reversed in part, and this case is remanded for consideration of the *Monell* claim.

It is so ordered.

Justice STEVENS, with whom Justice GINSBURG joins, concurring in part and dissenting in part.

In *New Jersey v. T.L.O.*, the Court established a two-step inquiry for determining the reasonableness of a school official's decision to search a student. First, the Court explained, the search must be "'justified at its inception'" by the presence of "reasonable grounds for suspecting that the search will turn up evidence that the student has violated or is violating either the law or the rules of the school." Second, the search must be "permissible in its scope," which is achieved "when the measures adopted are reasonably related to the objectives of the search and not excessively intrusive in light of the age and sex of the student and the nature of the infraction."

Nothing the Court decides today alters this basic framework. It simply applies *T.L.O.* to declare unconstitutional a strip search of a 13-year-old honors student that was based on a groundless suspicion that she might be hiding medicine in her underwear. This is, in essence, a case in which clearly established law meets clearly outrageous conduct. I have long believed that "'[i]t does not require a constitutional scholar to conclude that a nude search of a 13-year-old child is an invasion of constitutional rights of some magnitude.'" The strip search of Savana Redding in this case was both more intrusive and less justified than the search of the student's purse in *T.L.O.* Therefore, while I join Parts I–III of the Court's opinion, I disagree with its decision to extend qualified immunity to the school official who authorized this unconstitutional search.

The Court of Appeals properly rejected the school official's qualified immunity defense, and I would affirm that court's judgment in its entirety.

Justice GINSBURG, concurring in part and dissenting in part.

I agree with the Court that Assistant Principal Wilson's subjection of 13-year-old Savana Redding to a humiliating stripdown search violated the Fourth Amendment. But I also agree with JUSTICE STEVENS, that our opinion in *New Jersey v. T.L.O.*, "clearly established" the law governing this case.

Fellow student Marissa Glines, caught with pills in her pocket, accused Redding of supplying them. Asked where the blue pill among several white pills in Glines's pocket came from, Glines answered: "I guess it slipped in when she gave me the IBU 400s." Asked next "who is she ?", Glines responded: "Savana Redding." As the Court observes, no followup questions were asked. Wilson did not test Glines's accusation for veracity by asking Glines when did Redding give her the pills, where, for what purpose. Any reasonable search for the pills would have ended when inspection of Redding's backpack and jacket pockets yielded nothing. Wilson had no cause to suspect, based on prior experience at the school or clues in this case, that Redding had hidden pills—containing the equivalent of two Advils or one Aleve—in her underwear or body. To make matters worse, Wilson did not release Redding, to return to class or to go home, after the search. Instead, he made her sit on a chair outside his office for over two hours. At no point did he attempt to call her parent. Abuse of authority of that order should not be shielded by official immunity.

In contrast to *T.L.O.*, where a teacher discovered a student smoking in the lavatory, and where the search was confined to the student's purse, the search of Redding involved her body and rested on the bare accusation of another student whose reliability the Assistant Principal had no reason to trust. The Court's opinion in *T.L.O.* plainly stated the controlling Fourth Amendment law: A search ordered by a school official, even if "justified at its inception," crosses the constitutional boundary if it becomes "excessively intrusive in light of the age and sex of the student and the nature of the infraction."

Here, "the nature of the [supposed] infraction," the slim basis for suspecting Savana Redding, and her "age and sex," establish beyond doubt that Assistant Principal Wilson's order cannot be reconciled with this Court's opinion in *T.L.O.* Wilson's treatment of Redding was abusive and it was not reasonable for him to believe that the law permitted it. I join Justice STEVENS in dissenting from the Court's acceptance of Wilson's qualified immunity plea, and would affirm the Court of Appeals' judgment in all respects.

Justice THOMAS, concurring in the judgment in part and dissenting in part.

I agree with the Court that the judgment against the school officials with respect to qualified immunity should be reversed. Unlike the majority, however, I would hold that the search of Savana Redding did not violate the Fourth Amendment. The majority imposes a vague and amorphous standard on school administrators. It also grants judges sweeping authority to second-guess the measures that these officials take to maintain discipline in their schools and ensure the health and safety of the students in their charge. This deep intrusion into the administration of public schools exemplifies why the Court should return to the common-law doctrine of in loco parentis under which "the judiciary was reluctant to interfere in the routine business of school administration, allowing schools and teachers to set and enforce rules and to maintain order." But even under the prevailing Fourth Amendment test established by *New Jersey v. T.L.O.*, all petitioners, including the school district, are entitled to judgment as a matter of law in their favor.

I

"Although the underlying command of the Fourth Amendment is always that searches and seizures be reasonable, what is reasonable depends on the context within which a search takes place.". Thus, although public school students retain Fourth Amendment rights under this Court's precedent, those rights "are different ... than elsewhere; the 'reasonableness' inquiry cannot disregard the schools' custodial and tutelary responsibility for children," For nearly 25 years this Court has understood that "[m]aintaining order in the classroom has never been easy, but in more recent years, school disorder has often taken particularly ugly forms: drug use and violent crime in the schools have become major social problems." In schools, "[e]vents calling for discipline are frequent occurrences and sometimes require immediate, effective action."

For this reason, school officials retain broad authority to protect students and preserve "order and a proper educational environment" under the Fourth Amendment. This authority requires that school officials be able to engage in the "close supervision of schoolchildren, as well as ... enforc[e] rules against conduct that would be perfectly permissible if undertaken by an adult." Ibid. Seeking to reconcile the Fourth Amendment with this unique public school setting, the Court in *T.L.O.* held that a school search is "reasonable" if it is "'justified at its inception'" and "'reasonably related in scope to the circumstances which justified the interference in the first place.'" The search under review easily meets this standard.

A

A "search of a student by a teacher or other school official will be 'justified at its inception' when there are reasonable grounds for suspecting that the search will turn up evidence that the student has violated or is violating either the law or the rules of the school." As the majority rightly concedes, this search was justified at its inception because there were reasonable grounds to suspect that Redding possessed medication that violated school rules. A finding of reasonable suspicion "does not deal with hard certainties, but with probabilities."

Furthermore, in evaluating whether there is a reasonable "particularized and objective" basis for conducting a search based on suspected wrongdoing, government officials must consider the "totality of the circumstances." School officials have a specialized understanding of the school environment, the habits of the students, and the concerns of the community, which enables them to "'formulat[e] certain common-sense conclusions about human behavior.'" And like police officers, school officials are "entitled to make an assessment of the situation in light of [this] specialized training and familiarity with the customs of the [school]."

Here, petitioners had reasonable grounds to suspect that Redding was in possession of prescription and nonprescription drugs in violation of the school's prohibition of the "non-medical use, possession, or sale of a drug" on school property or at school events. As an initial matter, school officials were aware that a few years earlier, a student had become "seriously ill" and "spent several days in intensive care" after ingesting prescription medication obtained from a classmate. Fourth Amendment searches do not occur in a vacuum; rather, context must inform the judicial inquiry. In this instance, the suspicion of drug possession arose at a middle school that had "a history of problems with students using and distributing prohibited and illegal substances on campus."

The school's substance-abuse problems had not abated by the 2003–2004 school year, which is when the challenged search of Redding took place. School officials had found alcohol and cigarettes in the girls' bathroom during the first school dance of the year and noticed that a group of students including Redding and Marissa Glines smelled of alcohol. Several weeks later, another student, Jordan Romero, reported that Redding had hosted a party before the dance where she served whiskey, vodka, and tequila. Romero had provided this report to school officials as a result of a meeting his mother scheduled with the officials after Romero "bec[a]me violent" and "sick to his stomach" one night and admitted that "he had taken some pills that he had got[ten] from a classmate." At that meeting, Romero admitted that "certain students were bringing drugs and weapons on campus." One week later, Romero handed the assistant principal a white pill that he said he had received from Glines. He reported "that a group of students [were] planning on taking the pills at lunch."

School officials justifiably took quick action in light of the lunchtime deadline. The assistant principal took the pill to the school nurse who identified it as prescription-strength 400-mg Ibuprofen. A subsequent search of Glines and her belongings produced a razor blade, a Naproxen 200-mg pill, and several Ibuprofen 400-mg pills. When asked, Glines claimed that she had received the pills from Redding. A search of Redding's planner, which Glines had borrowed, then uncovered "several knives, several lighters, a cigarette, and a permanent marker." Thus, as the majority acknowledges, the totality of relevant circumstances justified a search of Redding for pills.

B

The remaining question is whether the search was reasonable in scope. Under *T.L.O.*, "a search will be permissible in its scope when the measures adopted are reasonably related to the objectives of the search and not excessively intrusive in light of the age and sex of the student and the nature of the infraction." The majority concludes that the school officials' search of Redding's underwear was not "'reasonably related in scope to the circumstances which justified the interference in the first place,'" notwithstanding the officials' reasonable suspicion that Redding "was involved in pill distribution." According to the majority, to be reasonable, this school search required a showing of "danger to the students from the power of the drugs or their quantity" or a "reason to suppose that [Redding] was carrying pills in her underwear." Each of these additional requirements is an unjustifiable departure from bedrock Fourth Amendment law in the school setting, where this Court has heretofore read the Fourth Amendment to grant considerable leeway to school officials. Because the school officials searched in a location where the pills could have been hidden, the search was reasonable in scope under *T.L.O.*

1

The majority finds that "subjective and reasonable societal expectations of personal privacy support ... treat[ing]" this type of search, which it labels a "strip search," as "categorically distinct, requiring distinct elements of justification on the part of school authorities for going beyond a search of clothing and belongings." Thus, in the majority's view, although the school officials had reasonable suspicion to believe that Redding had the pills on her person, they needed some greater level of particularized suspicion to conduct this "strip search." There is no support for this contortion of the Fourth Amendment.

The Court has generally held that the reasonableness of a search's scope depends only on whether it is limited to the area that is capable of concealing the object of the search.

In keeping with this longstanding rule, the "nature of the infraction" referenced in *T.L.O.* delineates the proper scope of a search of students in a way that is identical to that permitted for searches outside the school—i.e., the search must be limited to the areas where the object of that infraction could be concealed. A search of a student therefore is permissible in scope under *T.L.O.* so long as it is objectively reasonable to believe that the area searched could conceal the contraband. The dissenting opinion below correctly captured this Fourth Amendment standard, noting that "if a student brought a baseball bat on campus in violation of school policy, a search of that student's shirt pocket would be patently unjustified."

The analysis of whether the scope of the search here was permissible under that standard is straightforward. Indeed, the majority does not dispute that "general background possibilities" establish that students conceal "contraband in their underwear." It acknowledges that school officials had reasonable suspicion to look in Redding's backpack and outer clothing because if "Wilson's reasonable suspicion of pill distribution were not understood to support searches of outer clothes and backpack, it would not justify any search worth making." The majority nevertheless concludes that proceeding any further with the search was unreasonable. But there is no support for this conclusion. The reasonable suspicion that Redding possessed the pills for distribution purposes did not dissipate simply because the search of her backpack turned up nothing. It was eminently reasonable to conclude that the backpack was empty because Redding was secreting the pills in a place she thought no one would look.

Redding would not have been the first person to conceal pills in her undergarments. Nor will she be the last after today's decision, which announces the safest place to secrete contraband in school.

2

The majority compounds its error by reading the "nature of the infraction" aspect of the *T.L.O.* test as a license to limit searches based on a judge's assessment of a particular school policy. According to the majority, the scope of the search was impermissible because the school official "must have been aware of the nature and limited threat of the specific drugs he was searching for" and because he "had no reason to suspect that large amounts of the drugs were being passed around, or that individual students were receiving great numbers of pills." Thus, in order to locate a rationale for finding a Fourth Amendment violation in this case, the majority retreats from its observation that the school's firm no-drug policy "makes sense, and there is no basis to claim that the search was unreasonable owing to some defect or shortcoming of the rule it was aimed at enforcing."

Even accepting the majority's assurances that it is not attacking the rule's reasonableness, it certainly is attacking the rule's importance. This approach directly conflicts with *T.L.O.* in which the Court was "unwilling to adopt a standard under which the legality of a search is dependent upon a judge's evaluation of the relative importance of school rules." Indeed, the Court in *T.L.O.* expressly rejected the proposition that the majority seemingly endorses — that "some rules regarding student conduct are by nature too 'trivial' to justify a search based upon reasonable suspicion."

The majority's decision in this regard also departs from another basic principle of the Fourth Amendment: that law enforcement officials can enforce with the same vigor all rules and regulations irrespective of the perceived importance of any of those rules. "In a long line of cases, we have said that when an officer has probable cause to believe a person committed even a minor crime in his presence, the balancing of private and public interests is not in doubt. The arrest is constitutionally reasonable." The Fourth Amendment rule for searches is the same: Police officers are entitled to search regardless of the perceived triviality of the underlying law. As we have explained, requiring police to make "sensitive, case-by-case determinations of government need," for a particular prohibition before conducting a search would "place police in an almost impossible spot."

The majority has placed school officials in this "impossible spot" by questioning whether possession of Ibuprofen and Naproxen causes a severe enough threat to warrant investigation. Had the suspected infraction involved a street drug, the majority implies that it would have approved the scope of the search. In effect, then, the majority has replaced a school rule that draws no distinction among drugs with a new one that does. As a result, a full search of a student's person for prohibited drugs will be permitted only if the Court agrees that the drug in question was sufficiently dangerous. Such a test is unworkable and unsound. School officials cannot be expected to halt searches based on the possibility that a court might later find that the particular infraction at issue is not severe enough to warrant an intrusive investigation.

A rule promulgated by a school board represents the judgment of school officials that the rule is needed to maintain "school order" and "a proper educational environment." Teachers, administrators, and the local school board are called upon both to "protect the ... safety of students and school personnel" and "maintain an environment conducive to learning." They are tasked with "watch[ing] over a large number of students" who "are inclined to test the outer boundaries of acceptable conduct and to imitate the misbehavior of a peer if that misbehavior is not dealt with quickly." In such an environment, something as simple as a "water pistol or peashooter can wreak [havoc] until it is taken away." The danger posed by unchecked distribution and consumption of prescription pills by students certainly needs no elaboration.

Judges are not qualified to second-guess the best manner for maintaining quiet and order in the school environment. Such institutional judgments, like those concerning the selection of the best methods for "restrain[ing students] from assaulting one another, abusing drugs and alcohol, and committing other crimes," "involve a host of policy choices that must be made by locally elected representatives, rather than by federal judges interpreting the basic charter of Government for the entire country." It is a mistake for judges to assume the responsibility for deciding which school rules are important enough to allow for invasive searches and which rules are not.

3

Even if this Court were authorized to second-guess the importance of school rules, the Court's assessment of the importance of this district's policy is flawed. It is a crime to possess or use prescription-strength Ibuprofen without a prescription. By prohibiting unauthorized prescription drugs on school grounds—and conducting a search to ensure students abide by that prohibition—the school rule here was consistent with a routine provision of the state criminal code. It hardly seems unreasonable for school officials to enforce a rule that, in effect, proscribes conduct that amounts to a crime.

Moreover, school districts have valid reasons for punishing the unauthorized possession of prescription drugs on school property as severely as the possession of street drugs; "[t]eenage abuse of over-the-counter and prescription drugs poses an increasingly alarming national crisis." As one study noted, "more young people ages 12–17 abuse prescription drugs than any illicit drug except marijuana—more than cocaine, heroin, and methamphetamine combined." And according to a 2005 survey of teens, "nearly one in five (19 percent or 4.5 million) admit abusing prescription drugs in their lifetime."

School administrators can reasonably conclude that this high rate of drug abuse is being fueled, at least in part, by the increasing presence of prescription drugs on school campuses. In a 2008 survey, "44 percent of teens sa[id] drugs are used, kept or sold on the grounds of their schools." The risks posed by the abuse of these drugs are every bit as serious as the dangers of using a typical street drug.

Teenagers are nevertheless apt to "believe the myth that these drugs provide a medically safe high." At least some of these injuries and deaths are likely due to the fact that "[m]ost controlled prescription drug abusers are poly-substance abusers," a habit that is especially likely to result in deadly drug combinations. Furthermore, even if a child is not immediately harmed by the abuse of prescription drugs, research suggests that prescription drugs have become "gateway drugs to other substances of abuse."

Admittedly, the Ibuprofen and Naproxen at issue in this case are not the prescription painkillers at the forefront of the prescription-drug-abuse problem. But they are not without their own dangers. As nonsteroidal anti-inflammatory drugs (NSAIDs), they pose a risk of death from overdose.

If a student with a previously unknown intolerance to Ibuprofen or Naproxen were to take either drug and become ill, the public outrage would likely be directed toward the school for failing to take steps to prevent the unmonitored use of the drug. In light of the risks involved, a school's decision to establish and enforce a school prohibition on the possession of any unauthorized drug is thus a reasonable judgment.

* * *

In determining whether the search's scope was reasonable under the Fourth Amendment, it is therefore irrelevant whether officials suspected Redding of possessing prescription-strength Ibuprofen, nonprescription-strength Naproxen, or some harder street drug. Safford prohibited its possession on school property. Reasonable suspicion that Redding was in possession of drugs in violation of these policies, therefore, justified a search extending to any area where small pills could be concealed. The search did not violate the Fourth Amendment.

II

By declaring the search unreasonable in this case, the majority has "'surrender[ed] control of the American public school system to public school students'" by invalidating school policies that treat all drugs equally and by second-guessing swift disciplinary decisions made by school officials. The Court's interference in these matters of great concern to teachers, parents, and students illustrates why the most constitutionally sound approach to the question of applying the Fourth Amendment in local public schools would in fact be the complete restoration of the common-law doctrine of in loco parentis.

"[I]n the early years of public schooling," courts applied the doctrine of in loco parentis to transfer to teachers the authority of a parent to "'command obedience, to control stubbornness, to quicken diligence, and to reform bad habits.'" So empowered, schoolteachers and administrators had almost complete discretion to establish and enforce the rules they believed were necessary to maintain control over their classrooms. The perils of judicial policymaking inherent in applying Fourth Amendment protections to public schools counsel in favor of a return to the understanding that existed in this Nation's first public schools, which gave teachers discretion to craft the rules needed to carry out the disciplinary responsibilities delegated to them by parents.

If the common-law view that parents delegate to teachers their authority to discipline and maintain order were to be applied in this case, the search of Redding would stand. There can be no doubt that a parent would have had the authority to conduct the search at issue in this case. Parents have "immunity from the strictures of the Fourth Amendment" when it comes to searches of a child or that child's belongings.

As acknowledged by this Court, this principle is based on the "societal understanding of superior and inferior" with respect to the "parent and child" relationship. In light of this relationship, the Court has indicated that a parent can authorize a third-party search of a child by consenting to such a search, even if the child denies his consent. Certainly, a search by the parent himself is no different, regardless of whether or not a child would prefer to be left alone.

Restoring the common-law doctrine of in loco parentis would not, however, leave public schools entirely free to impose any rule they choose. "If parents do not like the rules imposed by those schools, they can seek redress in school boards or legislatures; they can send their children to private schools or home school them; or they can simply move." Indeed, parents and local government officials have proved themselves quite capable of challenging overly harsh school rules or the enforcement of sensible rules in insensible ways.

For example, one community questioned a school policy that resulted in "an 11-year-old [being] arrested, handcuffed, and taken to jail for bringing a plastic butter knife to school." In another, "[a]t least one school board member was outraged" when 14 elementary-school students were suspended for "imitating drug activity" after they combined Kool-Aid and sugar in plastic bags. Individuals within yet another school district protested a "'zero-tolerance' policy toward weapons" that had become "so rigid that it force[d] schools to expel any student who belongs to a military organization, a drum-and-bugle corps or any other legitimate extracurricular group and is simply transporting what amounts to harmless props."

These local efforts to change controversial school policies through democratic processes have proven successful in many cases.

In the end, the task of implementing and amending public school policies is beyond this Court's function. Parents, teachers, school administrators, local politicians, and state officials are all better suited than judges to determine the appropriate limits on searches conducted by school officials. Preservation of order, discipline, and safety in public schools is simply not the domain of the Constitution. And, common sense is not a judicial monopoly or a Constitutional imperative.

III

"[T]he nationwide drug epidemic makes the war against drugs a pressing concern in every school." And yet the Court has limited the authority of school officials to conduct searches for the drugs that the officials believe pose a serious safety risk to their students. By doing so, the majority has confirmed that a return to the doctrine of in loco parentis is required to keep the judiciary from essentially seizing control of public schools. Only then will teachers again be able to "'govern the[ir] pupils, quicken the slothful, spur the indolent, restrain the impetuous, and control the stubborn'" by making "'rules, giv[ing] commands, and punish[ing] disobedience'" without interference from judges. By deciding that it is better equipped to decide what behavior should be permitted in schools, the Court has undercut student safety and undermined the authority of school administrators and local officials. Even more troubling, it has done so in a case in which the underlying response by school administrators was reasonable and justified. I cannot join this regrettable decision. I, therefore, respectfully dissent from the Court's determination that this search violated the Fourth Amendment.

Notes

(a) In earlier cases the Court used *T.L.O.* to allow extensive searches and drug testing of children in schools (*see Vernonia School District v. Acton*, 515 U.S. 646 (1995) and *Board of Education of Independent School District No. 92 of Pottawatemie County v. Earls*, 536 U.S. 822 (2002)), but in *Redding* the Court states that the school went too far in conducting a strip search of a student. Does this case contradict the earlier decisions?

(b) Would the Court have reached a different conclusion if the school had found any illegal substances or dangerous prescription drugs during the search?

Terrance Jamar Graham v. Florida
130 S.Ct. 2011 (2010)

Justice KENNEDY delivered the opinion of the Court.

The issue before the Court is whether the Constitution permits a juvenile offender to be sentenced to life in prison without parole for a nonhomicide crime. The sentence was imposed by the State of Florida. Petitioner challenges the sentence under the Eighth Amendment's Cruel and Unusual Punishments Clause, made applicable to the States by the Due Process Clause of the Fourteenth Amendment.

I

Petitioner is Terrance Jamar Graham. He was born on January 6, 1987. Graham's parents were addicted to crack cocaine, and their drug use persisted in his early years. Graham was diagnosed with attention deficit hyperactivity disorder in elementary school. He began drinking alcohol and using tobacco at age 9 and smoked marijuana at age 13.

In July 2003, when Graham was age 16, he and three other school-age youths attempted to rob a barbeque restaurant in Jacksonville, Florida. One youth, who worked at the restaurant, left the back door unlocked just before closing time. Graham and another youth, wearing masks, entered through the unlocked door. Graham's masked accomplice twice struck the restaurant manager in the back of the head with a metal bar. When the manager started yelling at the assailant and Graham, the two youths ran out and escaped in a car driven by the third accomplice. The restaurant manager required stitches for his head injury. No money was taken.

Graham was arrested for the robbery attempt. Under Florida law, it is within a prosecutor's discretion whether to charge 16- and 17-year-olds as adults or juveniles for most felony crimes. Graham's prosecutor elected to charge Graham as an adult. The charges against Graham were armed burglary with assault or battery, a first-degree felony carrying a maximum penalty of life imprisonment without the possibility of parole, and attempted armed-robbery, a second-degree felony carrying a maximum penalty of 15 years' imprisonment.

On December 18, 2003, Graham pleaded guilty to both charges under a plea agreement. Graham wrote a letter to the trial court. After reciting "this is my first and last time getting in trouble," he continued "I've decided to turn my life around." Graham said "I made a promise to God and myself that if I get a second chance, I'm going to do whatever it takes to get to the [National Football League]."

The trial court accepted the plea agreement. The court withheld adjudication of guilt as to both charges and sentenced Graham to concurrent 3-year terms of probation. Graham was required to spend the first 12 months of his probation in the county jail, but he received credit for the time he had served awaiting trial, and was released on June 25, 2004.

Less than 6 months later, on the night of December 2, 2004, Graham again was arrested. The State's case was as follows: Earlier that evening, Graham participated in a home invasion robbery. His two accomplices were Meigo Bailey and Kirkland Lawrence, both 20-year-old men. According to the State, at 7 p.m. that night, Graham, Bailey, and Lawrence knocked on the door of the home where Carlos Rodriguez lived. Graham, followed by Bailey and Lawrence, forcibly entered the home and held a pistol to Rodriguez's chest. For the next 30 minutes, the three held Rodriguez and another man, a friend of Rodriguez, at gunpoint while they ransacked the home searching for money. Before leaving, Graham and his accomplices barricaded Rodriguez and his friend inside a closet.

The State further alleged that Graham, Bailey, and Lawrence, later the same evening, attempted a second robbery, during which Bailey was shot. Graham, who had borrowed his father's car, drove Bailey and Lawrence to the hospital and left them there. As Graham drove away, a police sergeant signaled him to stop. Graham continued at a high speed but crashed into a telephone pole. He tried to flee on foot but was apprehended. Three handguns were found in his car.

When detectives interviewed Graham, he denied involvement in the crimes. He said he encountered Bailey and Lawrence only after Bailey had been shot. One of the detectives told Graham that the victims of the home invasion had identified him. He asked Graham, "Aside from the two robberies tonight how many more were you involved in?" Graham responded, "Two to three before tonight." The night that Graham allegedly committed the robbery, he was 34 days short of his 18th birthday.

On December 13, 2004, Graham's probation officer filed with the trial court an affidavit asserting that Graham had violated the conditions of his probation by possessing a firearm, committing crimes, and associating with persons engaged in criminal activity. The trial court held hearings on Graham's violations about a year later, in December 2005 and January 2006. The judge who presided was not the same judge who had accepted Graham's guilty plea to the earlier offenses.

Graham maintained that he had no involvement in the home invasion robbery; but, even after the court underscored that the admission could expose him to a life sentence on the earlier charges, he admitted violating probation conditions by fleeing. The State presented evidence related to the home invasion, including testimony from the victims. The trial court noted that Graham, in admitting his attempt to avoid arrest, had acknowledged violating his probation. The court further found that Graham had violated his probation by committing a home invasion robbery, by possessing a firearm, and by associating with persons engaged in criminal activity.

The trial court held a sentencing hearing. Under Florida law the minimum sentence Graham could receive absent a downward departure by the judge was 5 years' imprisonment. The maximum was life imprisonment. Graham's attorney requested the minimum nondeparture sentence of 5 years. A presentence report prepared by the Florida Department of Corrections recommended that Graham receive an even lower sentence — at most 4 years' imprisonment. The State recommended that Graham receive 30 years on the armed burglary count and 15 years on the attempted armed robbery count.

After hearing Graham's testimony, the trial court explained the sentence it was about to pronounce:

> "Mr. Graham, as I look back on your case, yours is really candidly a sad situation. You had, as far as I can tell, you have quite a family structure. You had a lot of people who wanted to try and help you get your life turned around including the court system, and you had a judge who took the step to try and give you direction through his probation order to give you a chance to get back onto track. And at the time you seemed through your letters that that is exactly what you wanted to do. And I don't know why it is that you threw your life away. I don't know why.

> "But you did, and that is what is so sad about this today is that you have actually been given a chance to get through this, the original charge, which were very serious charges to begin with.... The attempted robbery with a weapon was a very serious charge.

>   ....

> "[I]n a very short period of time you were back before the Court on a violation of this probation, and then here you are two years later standing before me, literally the — facing a life sentence as to — up to life as to count 1 and up to 15 years as to count 2.

> "And I don't understand why you would be given such a great opportunity to do something with your life and why you would throw it away. The only thing that I can rationalize is that you decided that this is how you were going to lead your life and that there is nothing that we can do for you. And as the state pointed out, that this is an escalating pattern of criminal conduct on your part and that we can't help you any further. We can't do anything to deter you. This is the way you are going to lead your life, and I don't know why you are going to. You've made that decision. I have no idea. But, evidently, that is what you decided to do.

> "So then it becomes a focus, if I can't do anything to help you, if I can't do anything to get you back on the right path, then I have to start focusing on the

community and trying to protect the community from your actions. And, unfortunately, that is where we are today is I don't see where I can do anything to help you any further. You've evidently decided this is the direction you're going to take in life, and it's unfortunate that you made that choice.

"I have reviewed the statute. I don't see where any further juvenile sanctions would be appropriate. I don't see where any youthful offender sanctions would be appropriate. Given your escalating pattern of criminal conduct, it is apparent to the Court that you have decided that this is the way you are going to live your life and that the only thing I can do now is to try and protect the community from your actions."

The trial court found Graham guilty of the earlier armed burglary and attempted armed robbery charges. It sentenced him to the maximum sentence authorized by law on each charge: life imprisonment for the armed burglary and 15 years for the attempted armed robbery. Because Florida has abolished its parole system, a life sentence gives a defendant no possibility of release unless he is granted executive clemency.

Graham filed a motion in the trial court challenging his sentence under the Eighth Amendment. The motion was deemed denied after the trial court failed to rule on it within 60 days. The First District Court of Appeal of Florida affirmed, concluding that Graham's sentence was not grossly disproportionate to his crimes. The court took note of the seriousness of Graham's offenses and their violent nature, as well as the fact that they "were not committed by a pre-teen, but a seventeen-year-old who was ultimately sentenced at the age of nineteen." The court concluded further that Graham was incapable of rehabilitation. Although Graham "was given an unheard of probationary sentence for a life felony, ... wrote a letter expressing his remorse and promising to refrain from the commission of further crime, and ... had a strong family structure to support him," the court noted, he "rejected his second chance and chose to continue committing crimes at an escalating pace." The Florida Supreme Court denied review.

II

The Eighth Amendment states: "Excessive bail shall not be required, nor excessive fines imposed, nor cruel and unusual punishments inflicted." To determine whether a punishment is cruel and unusual, courts must look beyond historical conceptions to "'the evolving standards of decency that mark the progress of a maturing society.'" "This is because '[t]he standard of extreme cruelty is not merely descriptive, but necessarily embodies a moral judgment. The standard itself remains the same, but its applicability must change as the basic mores of society change.'"

The Cruel and Unusual Punishments Clause prohibits the imposition of inherently barbaric punishments under all circumstances. For the most part, however, the Court's precedents consider punishments challenged not as inherently barbaric but as disproportionate to the crime. The concept of proportionality is central to the Eighth Amendment. Embodied in the Constitution's ban on cruel and unusual punishments is the "precept of justice that punishment for crime should be graduated and proportioned to [the] offense."

The Court's cases addressing the proportionality of sentences fall within two general classifications. The first involves challenges to the length of term-of-years sentences given all the circumstances in a particular case. The second comprises cases in which the Court implements the proportionality standard by certain categorical restrictions on the death penalty.

In the first classification the Court considers all of the circumstances of the case to determine whether the sentence is unconstitutionally excessive. Under this approach, the

Court has held unconstitutional a life without parole sentence for the defendant's seventh nonviolent felony, the crime of passing a worthless check. In other cases, however, it has been difficult for the challenger to establish a lack of proportionality. In *Harmelin v. Michigan*, the offender was sentenced under state law to life without parole for possessing a large quantity of cocaine. A closely divided Court upheld the sentence. The controlling opinion concluded that the Eighth Amendment contains a "narrow proportionality principle," that "does not require strict proportionality between crime and sentence" but rather "forbids only extreme sentences that are 'grossly disproportionate' to the crime." Again closely divided, the Court rejected a challenge to a sentence of 25 years to life for the theft of a few golf clubs under California's so-called three-strikes recidivist sentencing scheme. The Court has also upheld a sentence of life with the possibility of parole for a defendant's third nonviolent felony, the crime of obtaining money by false pretenses, and a sentence of 40 years for possession of marijuana with intent to distribute and distribution of marijuana.

The controlling opinion in *Harmelin* explained its approach for determining whether a sentence for a term of years is grossly disproportionate for a particular defendant's crime. A court must begin by comparing the gravity of the offense and the severity of the sentence. "[I]n the rare case in which [this] threshold comparison ... leads to an inference of gross disproportionality" the court should then compare the defendant's sentence with the sentences received by other offenders in the same jurisdiction and with the sentences imposed for the same crime in other jurisdictions. If this comparative analysis "validate[s] an initial judgment that [the] sentence is grossly disproportionate," the sentence is cruel and unusual.

The second classification of cases has used categorical rules to define Eighth Amendment standards. The previous cases in this classification involved the death penalty. The classification in turn consists of two subsets, one considering the nature of the offense, the other considering the characteristics of the offender. With respect to the nature of the offense, the Court has concluded that capital punishment is impermissible for nonhomicide crimes against individuals. In cases turning on the characteristics of the offender, the Court has adopted categorical rules prohibiting the death penalty for defendants who committed their crimes before the age of 18, *Roper v. Simmons*, or whose intellectual functioning is in a low range, *Atkins v. Virginia*.

In the cases adopting categorical rules the Court has taken the following approach. The Court first considers "objective indicia of society's standards, as expressed in legislative enactments and state practice" to determine whether there is a national consensus against the sentencing practice at issue. Next, guided by "the standards elaborated by controlling precedents and by the Court's own understanding and interpretation of the Eighth Amendment's text, history, meaning, and purpose," the Court must determine in the exercise of its own independent judgment whether the punishment in question violates the Constitution.

The present case involves an issue the Court has not considered previously: a categorical challenge to a term-of-years sentence. The approach in cases such as Harmelin and Ewing is suited for considering a gross proportionality challenge to a particular defendant's sentence, but here a sentencing practice itself is in question. This case implicates a particular type of sentence as it applies to an entire class of offenders who have committed a range of crimes. As a result, a threshold comparison between the severity of the penalty and the gravity of the crime does not advance the analysis. Here, in addressing the question presented, the appropriate analysis is the one used in cases that involved the categorical approach, specifically *Atkins*, *Roper*, and *Kennedy*.

III

A

The analysis begins with objective indicia of national consensus. "[T]he 'clearest and most reliable objective evidence of contemporary values is the legislation enacted by the country's legislatures.'" Six jurisdictions do not allow life without parole sentences for any juvenile offenders. Seven jurisdictions permit life without parole for juvenile offenders, but only for homicide crimes. Thirty-seven States as well as the District of Columbia permit sentences of life without parole for a juvenile nonhomicide offender in some circumstances. Federal law also allows for the possibility of life without parole for offenders as young as 13. Relying on this metric, the State and its amici argue that there is no national consensus against the sentencing practice at issue.

This argument is incomplete and unavailing. "There are measures of consensus other than legislation." Actual sentencing practices are an important part of the Court's inquiry into consensus. Here, an examination of actual sentencing practices in jurisdictions where the sentence in question is permitted by statute discloses a consensus against its use. Although these statutory schemes contain no explicit prohibition on sentences of life without parole for juvenile nonhomicide offenders, those sentences are most infrequent. According to a recent study, nationwide there are only 109 juvenile offenders serving sentences of life without parole for nonhomicide offenses.

The State contends that this study's tally is inaccurate because it does not count juvenile offenders who were convicted of both a homicide and a nonhomicide offense, even when the offender received a life without parole sentence for the nonhomicide. This distinction is unpersuasive. Juvenile offenders who committed both homicide and nonhomicide crimes present a different situation for a sentencing judge than juvenile offenders who committed no homicide. It is difficult to say that a defendant who receives a life sentence on a nonhomicide offense but who was at the same time convicted of homicide is not in some sense being punished in part for the homicide when the judge makes the sentencing determination. The instant case concerns only those juvenile offenders sentenced to life without parole solely for a nonhomicide offense.

Florida further criticizes this study because the authors were unable to obtain complete information on some States and because the study was not peer reviewed. The State does not, however, provide any data of its own. Although in the first instance it is for the litigants to provide data to aid the Court, we have been able to supplement the study's findings* ...

It becomes all the more clear how rare these sentences are, even within the jurisdictions that do sometimes impose them, when one considers that a juvenile sentenced to life without parole is likely to live in prison for decades. Thus, these statistics likely reflect nearly all juvenile nonhomicide offenders who have received a life without parole sentence stretching back many years. It is not certain that this opinion has iden-

---

* [The study the court looked at was not able to obtain a definitive tally for Nevada, Utah, or Virginia. It did show that Nevada has five juvenile nonhomicide offenders serving life without parole sentences, Utah has none, and Virginia has eight. After the study was complete an Oklahoma defendant was sentenced to life without parole for a rape and stabbing at the age of 16. The numbers from the study, in addition to the ones above, show that there are 123 juvenile non-homicide offenders serving life without parole sentences. 77 of that total are serving sentences imposed by Florida, with the remaining 46 imprisoned in California, Delaware, Iowa, Louisiana, Mississippi, Nebraska, Nevada, Oklahoma, South Carolina, and Virginia. Thus, only 11 jurisdictions nationwide in fact impose life without parole sentences on juvenile nonhomicide offenders.—Eds.]

tified every juvenile nonhomicide offender nationwide serving a life without parole sentence, for the statistics are not precise. The available data, nonetheless, are sufficient to demonstrate how rarely these sentences are imposed even if there are isolated cases that have not been included in the presentations of the parties or the analysis of the Court.

It must be acknowledged that in terms of absolute numbers juvenile life without parole sentences for nonhomicides are more common than the sentencing practices at issue in some of this Court's other Eighth Amendment cases. This contrast can be instructive, however, if attention is first given to the base number of certain types of offenses. For example, in the year 2007 (the most recent year for which statistics are available), a total of 13,480 persons, adult and juvenile, were arrested for homicide crimes. That same year, 57,600 juveniles were arrested for aggravated assault; 3,580 for forcible rape; 34,500 for robbery; 81,900 for burglary; 195,700 for drug offenses; and 7,200 for arson. See Dept. of Justice, Office of Juvenile Justice and Delinquency Prevention, Statistical Briefing Book, online at http://ojjdp.ncjrs.org/ojstatbb/ (as visited May 14, 2010, and available in Clerk of Court's case file). Although it is not certain how many of these numerous juvenile offenders were eligible for life without parole sentences, the comparison suggests that in proportion to the opportunities for its imposition, life without parole sentences for juveniles convicted of nonhomicide crimes is as rare as other sentencing practices found to be cruel and unusual.

The evidence of consensus is not undermined by the fact that many jurisdictions do not prohibit life without parole for juvenile nonhomicide offenders. The Court confronted a similar situation in Thompson, where a plurality concluded that the death penalty for offenders younger than 16 was unconstitutional. A number of States then allowed the juvenile death penalty if one considered the statutory scheme. As is the case here, those States authorized the transfer of some juvenile offenders to adult court; and at that point there was no statutory differentiation between adults and juveniles with respect to authorized penalties. The plurality concluded that the transfer laws show "that the States consider 15-year-olds to be old enough to be tried in criminal court for serious crimes (or too old to be dealt with effectively in juvenile court), but tells us nothing about the judgment these States have made regarding the appropriate punishment for such youthful offenders."

The same reasoning obtains here. Many States have chosen to move away from juvenile court systems and to allow juveniles to be transferred to, or charged directly in, adult court under certain circumstances. Once in adult court, a juvenile offender may receive the same sentence as would be given to an adult offender, including a life without parole sentence. But the fact that transfer and direct charging laws make life without parole possible for some juvenile nonhomicide offenders does not justify a judgment that many States intended to subject such offenders to life without parole sentences.

For example, under Florida law a child of any age can be prosecuted as an adult for certain crimes and can be sentenced to life without parole. The State acknowledged at oral argument that even a 5-year-old, theoretically, could receive such a sentence under the letter of the law. All would concede this to be unrealistic, but the example underscores that the statutory eligibility of a juvenile offender for life without parole does not indicate that the penalty has been endorsed through deliberate, express, and full legislative consideration. Similarly, the many States that allow life without parole for juvenile nonhomicide offenders but do not impose the punishment should not be treated as if they have expressed the view that the sentence is appropriate. The sentencing practice now under consideration is exceedingly rare. And "it is fair to say that a national consensus has developed against it."

B

Community consensus, while "entitled to great weight," is not itself determinative of whether a punishment is cruel and unusual. In accordance with the constitutional design, "the task of interpreting the Eighth Amendment remains our responsibility." The judicial exercise of independent judgment requires consideration of the culpability of the offenders at issue in light of their crimes and characteristics, along with the severity of the punishment in question. In this inquiry the Court also considers whether the challenged sentencing practice serves legitimate penological goals.

Roper established that because juveniles have lessened culpability they are less deserving of the most severe punishments. As compared to adults, juveniles have a "'lack of maturity and an underdeveloped sense of responsibility'"; they "are more vulnerable or susceptible to negative influences and outside pressures, including peer pressure"; and their characters are "not as well formed." These salient characteristics mean that "[i]t is difficult even for expert psychologists to differentiate between the juvenile offender whose crime reflects unfortunate yet transient immaturity, and the rare juvenile offender whose crime reflects irreparable corruption." Accordingly, "juvenile offenders cannot with reliability be classified among the worst offenders." A juvenile is not absolved of responsibility for his actions, but his transgression "is not as morally reprehensible as that of an adult."

No recent data provide reason to reconsider the Court's observations in *Roper* about the nature of juveniles. As petitioner's amici point out, developments in psychology and brain science continue to show fundamental differences between juvenile and adult minds. For example, parts of the brain involved in behavior control continue to mature through late adolescence. Juveniles are more capable of change than are adults, and their actions are less likely to be evidence of "irretrievably depraved character" than are the actions of adults. It remains true that "[f]rom a moral standpoint it would be misguided to equate the failings of a minor with those of an adult, for a greater possibility exists that a minor's character deficiencies will be reformed." These matters relate to the status of the offenders in question; and it is relevant to consider next the nature of the offenses to which this harsh penalty might apply.

The Court has recognized that defendants who do not kill, intend to kill, or foresee that life will be taken are categorically less deserving of the most serious forms of punishment than are murderers. There is a line "between homicide and other serious violent offenses against the individual." Serious nonhomicide crimes "may be devastating in their harm … but 'in terms of moral depravity and of the injury to the person and to the public,' … they cannot be compared to murder in their 'severity and irrevocability.'" This is because "[l]ife is over for the victim of the murderer," but for the victim of even a very serious nonhomicide crime, "life … is not over and normally is not beyond repair." Although an offense like robbery or rape is "a serious crime deserving serious punishment," those crimes differ from homicide crimes in a moral sense.

It follows that, when compared to an adult murderer, a juvenile offender who did not kill or intend to kill has a twice diminished moral culpability. The age of the offender and the nature of the crime each bear on the analysis.

As for the punishment, life without parole is "the second most severe penalty permitted by law." It is true that a death sentence is "unique in its severity and irrevocability," yet life without parole sentences share some characteristics with death sentences that are shared by no other sentences. The State does not execute the offender sentenced to life without parole, but the sentence alters the offender's life by a forfeiture that is irrevocable. It deprives the convict of the most basic liberties without giving hope of restoration, except perhaps by executive clemency—the remote possibility of which does not mitigate the harshness of the sentence. As one court observed in overturning a life without parole sentence for a juvenile defendant, this sentence "means denial of hope; it means that good behavior and character improvement are immaterial; it means that whatever the future might hold in store for the mind and spirit of [the convict], he will remain in prison for the rest of his days."

The Court has recognized the severity of sentences that deny convicts the possibility of parole. In *Rummel*, the Court rejected an Eighth Amendment challenge to a life sentence for a defendant's third nonviolent felony but stressed that the sentence gave the defendant the possibility of parole. Noting that "parole is an established variation on imprisonment of convicted criminals," it was evident that an analysis of the petitioner's sentence "could hardly ignore the possibility that he will not actually be imprisoned for the rest of his life." And in *Solem*, the only previous case striking down a sentence for a term of years as grossly disproportionate, the defendant's sentence was deemed "far more severe than the life sentence we considered in *Rummel*," because it did not give the defendant the possibility of parole.

Life without parole is an especially harsh punishment for a juvenile. Under this sentence a juvenile offender will on average serve more years and a greater percentage of his life in prison than an adult offender. A 16-year-old and a 75-year-old each sentenced to life without parole receive the same punishment in name only. This reality cannot be ignored.

The penological justifications for the sentencing practice are also relevant to the analysis. Criminal punishment can have different goals, and choosing among them is within a legislature's discretion. It does not follow, however, that the purposes and effects of penal sanctions are irrelevant to the determination of Eighth Amendment restrictions. A sentence lacking any legitimate penological justification is by its nature disproportionate to the offense. With respect to life without parole for juvenile nonhomicide offenders, none of the goals of penal sanctions that have been recognized as legitimate-retribution, deterrence, incapacitation, and rehabilitation.

Retribution is a legitimate reason to punish, but it cannot support the sentence at issue here. Society is entitled to impose severe sanctions on a juvenile nonhomicide offender to express its condemnation of the crime and to seek restoration of the moral imbalance caused by the offense. But "[t]he heart of the retribution rationale is that a criminal sentence must be directly related to the personal culpability of the criminal offender." The case becomes even weaker with respect to a juvenile who did not commit homicide. *Roper* found that "[r]etribution is not proportional if the law's most severe penalty is imposed" on the juvenile murderer. The considerations underlying that holding support as well the conclusion that retribution does not justify imposing the second most severe penalty on the less culpable juvenile nonhomicide offender.

Deterrence does not suffice to justify the sentence either. *Roper* noted that "the same characteristics that render juveniles less culpable than adults suggest ... that juveniles will be less susceptible to deterrence." Because juveniles' "lack of maturity and underdeveloped sense of responsibility ... often result in impetuous and ill-considered actions and decisions," they are less likely to take a possible punishment into consideration when making decisions. This is particularly so when that punishment is rarely imposed. That the sentence deters in a few cases is perhaps plausible, but "[t]his argument does not overcome other objections." Even if the punishment has some connection to a valid penological goal, it must be shown that the punishment is not grossly disproportionate in light of the justification offered. Here, in light of juvenile nonhomicide offenders' diminished moral responsibility, any limited deterrent effect provided by life without parole is not enough to justify the sentence.

Incapacitation, a third legitimate reason for imprisonment, does not justify the life without parole sentence in question here. Recidivism is a serious risk to public safety, and so incapacitation is an important goal. But while incapacitation may be a legitimate penological goal sufficient to justify life without parole in other contexts, it is inadequate to justify that punishment for juveniles who did not commit homicide. To justify life without parole on the assumption that the juvenile offender forever will be a danger to society requires the sentencer to make a judgment that the juvenile is incorrigible. The characteristics of juveniles make that judgment questionable. "It is difficult even for expert psychologists to differentiate between the juvenile offender whose crime reflects unfortunate yet transient immaturity, and the rare juvenile offender whose crime reflects irreparable corruption." As one court concluded in a challenge to a life without parole sentence for a 14-year-old, "incorrigibility is inconsistent with youth."

Here one cannot dispute that this defendant posed an immediate risk, for he had committed, we can assume, serious crimes early in his term of supervised release and despite his own assurances of reform. Graham deserved to be separated from society for some time in order to prevent what the trial court described as an "escalating pattern of criminal conduct," but it does not follow that he would be a risk to society for the rest of his life. Even if the State's judgment that Graham was incorrigible were later corroborated by prison misbehavior or failure to mature, the sentence was still disproportionate because that judgment was made at the outset. A life without parole sentence improperly denies the juvenile offender a chance to demonstrate growth and maturity. Incapacitation cannot override all other considerations, lest the Eighth Amendment's rule against disproportionate sentences be a nullity. Finally there is rehabilitation, a penological goal that forms the basis of parole systems. The concept of rehabilitation is imprecise; and its utility and proper implementation are the subject of a substantial, dynamic field of inquiry and dialogue. It is for legislatures to determine what rehabilitative techniques are appropriate and effective.

A sentence of life imprisonment without parole, however, cannot be justified by the goal of rehabilitation. The penalty forswears altogether the rehabilitative ideal. By denying the defendant the right to reenter the community, the State makes an irrevocable judgment about that person's value and place in society. This judgment is not appropriate in light of a juvenile nonhomicide offender's capacity for change and limited moral culpability. A State's rejection of rehabilitation, moreover, goes beyond a mere expressive judgment. As one amicus notes, defendants serving life without parole sentences are often denied access to vocational training and other rehabilitative services that are available to other inmates.

In sum, penological theory is not adequate to justify life without parole for juvenile nonhomicide offenders. This determination; the limited culpability of juvenile nonhomicide offenders; and the severity of life without parole sentences all lead to the conclusion that the sentencing practice under consideration is cruel and unusual. This Court now holds that for a juvenile offender who did not commit homicide the Eighth Amendment forbids the sentence of life without parole. This clear line is necessary to prevent the possibility that life without parole sentences will be imposed on juvenile nonhomicide offenders who are not sufficiently culpable to merit that punishment. Because "[t]he age of 18 is the point where society draws the line for many purposes between childhood and adulthood," those who were below that age when the offense was committed may not be sentenced to life without parole for a nonhomicide crime.

A State is not required to guarantee eventual freedom to a juvenile offender convicted of a nonhomicide crime. What the State must do, however, is give defendants like Graham some meaningful opportunity to obtain release based on demonstrated maturity and rehabilitation. It is for the State, in the first instance, to explore the means and mechanisms for compliance. It bears emphasis, however, that while the Eighth Amendment forbids a State from imposing a life without parole sentence on a juvenile nonhomicide offender, it does not require the State to release that offender during his natural life. Those who commit truly horrifying crimes as juveniles may turn out to be irredeemable, and thus deserving of incarceration for the duration of their lives. The Eighth Amendment does not foreclose the possibility that persons convicted of nonhomicide crimes committed before adulthood will remain behind bars for life. It does forbid States from making the judgment at the outset that those offenders never will be fit to reenter society.

C

Categorical rules tend to be imperfect, but one is necessary here. Two alternative approaches are not adequate to address the relevant constitutional concerns. First, the State argues that the laws of Florida and other States governing criminal procedure take sufficient account of the age of a juvenile offender. Here, Florida notes that under its law prosecutors are required to charge 16- and 17-year-old offenders as adults only for certain serious felonies; that prosecutors have discretion to charge those offenders as adults for other felonies; and that prosecutors may not charge nonrecidivist 16- and 17-year-old offenders as adults for misdemeanors. The State also stresses that "in only the narrowest of circumstances" does Florida law impose no age limit whatsoever for prosecuting juveniles in adult court.

Florida is correct to say that state laws requiring consideration of a defendant's age in charging decisions are salutary. An offender's age is relevant to the Eighth Amendment, and criminal procedure laws that fail to take defendants' youthfulness into account at all would be flawed. Florida, like other States, has made substantial efforts to enact comprehensive rules governing the treatment of youthful offenders by its criminal justice system.

The provisions the State notes are, nonetheless, by themselves insufficient to address the constitutional concerns at issue. Nothing in Florida's laws prevents its courts from sentencing a juvenile nonhomicide offender to life without parole based on a subjective judgment that the defendant's crimes demonstrate an "irretrievably depraved character." This is inconsistent with the Eighth Amendment. Specific cases are illustrative. In Graham's case the sentencing judge decided to impose life without parole—a sentence greater than that requested by the prosecutor—for Graham's armed burglary conviction. The judge did so because he concluded that Graham was incorrigible: "[Y]ou decided that this is how you were going to lead your life and that there is nothing that we can do for you.... We can't do anything to deter you."

Another example comes from *Sullivan v. Florida*, No. 08-7621. *Sullivan* was argued the same day as this case, but the Court has now dismissed the writ of certiorari in *Sullivan* as improvidently granted. The facts, however, demonstrate the flaws of Florida's system. The petitioner, Joe Sullivan, was prosecuted as an adult for a sexual assault committed when he was 13 years old. Noting Sullivan's past encounters with the law, the sentencing judge concluded that, although Sullivan had been "given opportunity after opportunity to upright himself and take advantage of the second and third chances he's been given," he had demonstrated himself to be unwilling to follow the law and needed to be kept away from society for the duration of his life. The judge sentenced Sullivan to life without parole. As these examples make clear, existing state laws, allowing the imposition of these sentences based only on a discretionary, subjective judgment by a judge or jury that the offender is irredeemably depraved, are insufficient to prevent the possibility that the offender will receive a life without parole sentence for which he or she lacks the moral culpability.

Another possible approach would be to hold that the Eighth Amendment requires courts to take the offender's age into consideration as part of a case-specific gross disproportionality inquiry, weighing it against the seriousness of the crime. This approach would allow courts to account for factual differences between cases and to impose life without parole sentences for particularly heinous crimes. Few, perhaps no, judicial responsibilities are more difficult than sentencing. The task is usually undertaken by trial judges who seek with diligence and professionalism to take account of the human existence of the offender and the just demands of a wronged society.

The case-by-case approach to sentencing must, however, be confined by some boundaries. The dilemma of juvenile sentencing demonstrates this. For even if we were to assume that some juvenile nonhomicide offenders might have "sufficient psychological maturity, and at the same time demonstrat[e] sufficient depravity," to merit a life without parole sentence, it does not follow that courts taking a case-by-case proportionality approach could with sufficient accuracy distinguish the few incorrigible juvenile offenders from the many that have the capacity for change. *Roper* rejected the argument that the Eighth Amendment required only that juries be told they must consider the defendant's age as a mitigating factor in sentencing. The Court concluded that an "unacceptable likelihood exists that the brutality or cold-blooded nature of any particular crime would overpower mitigating arguments based on youth as a matter of course, even where the juvenile offender's objective immaturity, vulnerability, and lack of true depravity should require a sentence less severe than death." Here, as with the death penalty, "[t]he differences between juvenile and adult offenders are too marked and well understood to risk allowing a youthful person to receive" a sentence of life without parole for a nonhomicide crime "despite insufficient culpability."

Another problem with a case-by-case approach is that it does not take account of special difficulties encountered by counsel in juvenile representation. As some amici note, the features that distinguish juveniles from adults also put them at a significant disadvantage in criminal proceedings. Juveniles mistrust adults and have limited understandings of the criminal justice system and the roles of the institutional actors within it. They are less likely than adults to work effectively with their lawyers to aid in their defense. Difficulty in weighing long-term consequences; a corresponding impulsiveness; and reluctance to trust defense counsel seen as part of the adult world a rebellious youth rejects, all can lead to poor decisions by one charged with a juvenile offense. These factors are likely to impair the quality of a juvenile defendant's representation. A categorical rule avoids the risk that, as a result of these difficulties, a court or jury will erroneously conclude that a particular juvenile is sufficiently culpable to deserve life without parole for a nonhomicide.

Finally, a categorical rule gives all juvenile nonhomicide offenders a chance to demonstrate maturity and reform. The juvenile should not be deprived of the opportunity to achieve maturity of judgment and self-recognition of human worth and potential. In *Roper*, that deprivation resulted from an execution that brought life to its end. Here, though by a different dynamic, the same concerns apply. Life in prison without the possibility of parole gives no chance for fulfillment outside prison walls, no chance for reconciliation with society, no hope. Maturity can lead to that considered reflection which is the foundation for remorse, renewal, and rehabilitation. A young person who knows that he or she has no chance to leave prison before life's end has little incentive to become a responsible individual. In some prisons, moreover, the system itself becomes complicit in the lack of development. As noted above, it is the policy in some prisons to withhold counseling, education, and rehabilitation programs for those who are ineligible for parole consideration. A categorical rule against life without parole for juvenile nonhomicide offenders avoids the perverse consequence in which the lack of maturity that led to an offender's crime is reinforced by the prison term.

Terrance Graham's sentence guarantees he will die in prison without any meaningful opportunity to obtain release, no matter what he might do to demonstrate that the bad acts he committed as a teenager are not representative of his true character, even if he spends the next half century attempting to atone for his crimes and learn from his mistakes. The State has denied him any chance to later demonstrate that he is fit to rejoin society based solely on a nonhomicide crime that he committed while he was a child in the eyes of the law. This the Eighth Amendment does not permit.

D

There is support for our conclusion in the fact that, in continuing to impose life without parole sentences on juveniles who did not commit homicide, the United States adheres to a sentencing practice rejected the world over. This observation does not control our decision. The judgments of other nations and the international community are not dispositive as to the meaning of the Eighth Amendment. But "'[t]he climate of international opinion concerning the acceptability of a particular punishment'" is also "'not irrelevant.'" The Court has looked beyond our Nation's borders for support for its independent conclusion that a particular punishment is cruel and unusual.

Today we continue that longstanding practice in noting the global consensus against the sentencing practice in question. A recent study concluded that only 11 nations authorize life without parole for juvenile offenders under any circumstances; and only 2 of them, the United States and Israel, ever impose the punishment in practice. An updated version of the study concluded that Israel's "laws allow for parole review of juvenile offenders serving life terms," but expressed reservations about how that parole review is implemented. But even if Israel is counted as allowing life without parole for juvenile offenders, that nation does not appear to impose that sentence for nonhomicide crimes; all of the seven Israeli prisoners whom commentators have identified as serving life sentences for juvenile crimes were convicted of homicide or attempted homicide.

Thus, as petitioner contends and respondent does not contest, the United States is the only Nation that imposes life without parole sentences on juvenile nonhomicide offenders. We also note, as petitioner and his amici emphasize, that Article 37(a) of the United Nations Convention on the Rights of the Child, Nov. 20, 1989, 1577 U.N.T.S. 3 (entered into force Sept. 2, 1990), ratified by every nation except the United States and Somalia, prohibits the imposition of "life imprisonment without possibility of release ... for offences committed by persons below eighteen years of age." As we concluded in *Roper* with respect to the juvenile death penalty, "the United States now stands alone in a world that has turned its face against" life without parole for juvenile nonhomicide offenders.

The State's amici stress that no international legal agreement that is binding on the United States prohibits life without parole for juvenile offenders and thus urge us to ignore the international consensus. These arguments miss the mark. The question before us is not whether international law prohibits the United States from imposing the sentence at issue in this case. The question is whether that punishment is cruel and unusual. In that inquiry, "the overwhelming weight of international opinion against" life without parole for nonhomicide offenses committed by juveniles "provide[s] respected and significant confirmation for our own conclusions."

The debate between petitioner's and respondent's amici over whether there is a binding jus cogens norm against this sentencing practice is likewise of no import. The Court has treated the laws and practices of other nations and international agreements as relevant to the Eighth Amendment not because those norms are binding or controlling but because the judgment of the world's nations that a particular sentencing practice is inconsistent with basic principles of decency demonstrates that the Court's rationale has respected reasoning to support it.

* * *

The Constitution prohibits the imposition of a life without parole sentence on a juvenile offender who did not commit homicide. A State need not guarantee the offender eventual release, but if it imposes a sentence of life it must provide him or her with some realistic opportunity to obtain release before the end of that term. The judgment of the First District Court of Appeal of Florida is reversed, and the case is remanded for further proceedings not inconsistent with this opinion.

It is so ordered.

Justice STEVENS, with whom Justice GINSBURG and Justice SOTOMAYOR join, concurring.

In his dissenting opinion, Justice THOMAS argues that today's holding is not entirely consistent with the controlling opinions in *Lockyer v. Andrade, Ewing v. California, Harmelin v. Michigan,* and *Rummel v. Estelle.* Given that "evolving standards of decency" have played a central role in our Eighth Amendment jurisprudence for at least a century, this argument suggests the dissenting opinions in those cases more accurately describe the law today than does Justice THOMAS' rigid interpretation of the Amendment. Society changes. Knowledge accumulates. We learn, sometimes, from our mistakes. Punishments that did not seem cruel and unusual at one time may, in the light of reason and experience, be found cruel and unusual at a later time; unless we are to abandon the moral commitment embodied in the Eighth Amendment, proportionality review must never become effectively obsolete.

While Justice THOMAS would apparently not rule out a death sentence for a $50 theft by a 7-year-old, the Court wisely rejects his static approach to the law. Standards of decency have evolved since 1980. They will never stop doing so.

Chief Justice ROBERTS, concurring in the judgment.

I agree with the Court that Terrance Graham's sentence of life without parole violates the Eighth Amendment's prohibition on "cruel and unusual punishments." Unlike the majority, however, I see no need to invent a new constitutional rule of dubious provenance in reaching that conclusion. Instead, my analysis is based on an application of this Court's precedents, in particular (1) our cases requiring "narrow proportionality" review of noncapital sentences and (2) our conclusion in *Roper v. Simmons,* that juvenile offenders are generally less culpable than adults who commit the same crimes.

These cases expressly allow courts addressing allegations that a noncapital sentence violates the Eighth Amendment to consider the particular defendant and particular crime at issue. The standards for relief under these precedents are rigorous, and should be. But here Graham's juvenile status—together with the nature of his criminal conduct and the extraordinarily severe punishment imposed—lead me to conclude that his sentence of life without parole is unconstitutional.

I

Our Court has struggled with whether and how to apply the Cruel and Unusual Punishments Clause to sentences for noncapital crimes. Some of my colleagues have raised serious and thoughtful questions about whether, as an original matter, the Constitution was understood to require any degree of proportionality between noncapital offenses and their corresponding punishments. Neither party here asks us to reexamine our precedents requiring such proportionality, however, and so I approach this case by trying to apply our past decisions to the facts at hand.

A

Graham's case arises at the intersection of two lines of Eighth Amendment precedent. The first consists of decisions holding that the Cruel and Unusual Punishments Clause embraces a "narrow proportionality principle" that we apply, on a case-by-case basis, when asked to review noncapital sentences. This "narrow proportionality principle" does not grant judges blanket authority to second-guess decisions made by legislatures or sentencing courts. On the contrary, a reviewing court will only "rarely" need "to engage in extended analysis to determine that a sentence is not constitutionally disproportionate".

We have "not established a clear or consistent path for courts to follow" in applying the highly deferential "narrow proportionality" analysis. We have, however, emphasized the primacy of the legislature in setting sentences, the variety of legitimate penological schemes, the state-by-state diversity protected by our federal system, and the requirement that review be guided by objective, rather than subjective, factors. Most importantly, however, we have explained that the Eighth Amendment "'does not require strict proportionality between crime and sentence'"; rather, "'it forbids only extreme sentences that are "grossly disproportionate" to the crime.'"

Our cases indicate that courts conducting "narrow proportionality" review should begin with a threshold inquiry that compares "the gravity of the offense and the harshness of the penalty." This analysis can consider a particular offender's mental state and motive in committing the crime, the actual harm caused to his victim or to society by his conduct, and any prior criminal history.

Only in "the rare case in which a threshold comparison of the crime committed and the sentence imposed leads to an inference of gross disproportionality," should courts proceed to an "intrajurisdictional" comparison of the sentence at issue with those imposed on other criminals in the same jurisdiction, and an "interjurisdictional" comparison with sentences imposed for the same crime in other jurisdictions. If these subsequent comparisons confirm the inference of gross disproportionality, courts should invalidate the sentence as a violation of the Eighth Amendment.

B

The second line of precedent relevant to assessing Graham's sentence consists of our cases acknowledging that juvenile offenders are generally—though not necessarily in every case-less morally culpable than adults who commit the same crimes. This insight animated our decision in *Thompson v. Oklahoma*, in which we invalidated a capital sentence imposed on a juvenile who had committed his crime under the age of 16. More recently, in *Roper*, we extended the prohibition on executions to those who committed their crimes before the age of 18.

Both *Thompson* and *Roper* arose in the unique context of the death penalty, a punishment that our Court has recognized "must be limited to those offenders who commit 'a narrow category of the most serious crimes' and whose extreme culpability makes them 'the most deserving of execution.'" *Roper*'s prohibition on the juvenile death penalty followed from our conclusion that "[t]hree general differences between juveniles under 18 and adults demonstrate that juvenile offenders cannot with reliability be classified among the worst offenders." These differences are a lack of maturity and an underdeveloped sense of responsibility, a heightened susceptibility to negative influences and outside pressures, and the fact that the character of a juvenile is "more transitory" and "less fixed" than that of an adult. Together, these factors establish the "diminished culpability of juveniles," "render suspect any conclusion" that juveniles are among "the worst offenders" for whom the death penalty is reserved.

Today, the Court views *Roper* as providing the basis for a new categorical rule that juveniles may never receive a sentence of life without parole for nonhomicide crimes. I disagree. In *Roper*, the Court tailored its analysis of juvenile characteristics to the specific question whether juvenile offenders could constitutionally be subject to capital punishment. Our answer that they could not be sentenced to death was based on the explicit conclusion that they "cannot with reliability be classified among the worst offenders."

This conclusion does not establish that juveniles can never be eligible for life without parole. A life sentence is of course far less severe than a death sentence, and we have never required that it be imposed only on the very worst offenders, as we have with capital punishment. Treating juvenile life sentences as analogous to capital punishment is at odds with our longstanding view that "the death penalty is different from other punishments in kind rather than degree." It is also at odds with *Roper* itself, which drew the line at capital punishment by blessing juvenile sentences that are "less severe than death" despite involving "forfeiture of some of the most basic liberties." Indeed, *Roper* explicitly relied on the possible imposition of life without parole on some juvenile offenders.

But the fact that *Roper* does not support a categorical rule barring life sentences for all juveniles does not mean that a criminal defendant's age is irrelevant to those sentences. On the contrary, our cases establish that the "narrow proportionality" review applicable to noncapital cases itself takes the personal "culpability of the offender" into account in examining whether a given punishment is proportionate to the crime. There is no reason why an offender's juvenile status should be excluded from the analysis. Indeed, given *Roper*'s conclusion that juveniles are typically less blameworthy than adults, an offender's juvenile status can play a central role in the inquiry.

Justice THOMAS disagrees with even our limited reliance on *Roper* on the ground that the present case does not involve capital punishment. That distinction is important— indeed, it underlies our rejection of the categorical rule declared by the Court. But *Roper*'s conclusion that juveniles are typically less culpable than adults has pertinence beyond capital cases, and rightly informs the case-specific inquiry I believe to be appropriate here.

In short, our existing precedent already provides a sufficient framework for assessing the concerns outlined by the majority. Not every juvenile receiving a life sentence will prevail under this approach. Not every juvenile should. But all will receive the protection that the Eighth Amendment requires.

II

Applying the "narrow proportionality" framework to the particular facts of this case, I conclude that Graham's sentence of life without parole violates the Eighth Amendment.

A

I begin with the threshold inquiry comparing the gravity of Graham's conduct to the harshness of his penalty. There is no question that the crime for which Graham received his life sentence—armed burglary of a nondomicil with an assault or battery—is "a serious crime deserving serious punishment." So too is the home invasion robbery that was the basis of Graham's probation violation. But these crimes are certainly less serious than other crimes, such as murder or rape.

As for Graham's degree of personal culpability, he committed the relevant offenses when he was a juvenile—a stage at which, *Roper* emphasized, one's "culpability or blameworthiness is diminished, to a substantial degree, by reason of youth and immaturity." Graham's age places him in a significantly different category from the defendants in *Rummel*, *Harmelin*, and *Ewing*, all of whom committed their crimes as adults. Graham's youth made him relatively more likely to engage in reckless and dangerous criminal activity than an adult; it also likely enhanced his susceptibility to peer pressure. There is no reason to believe that Graham should be denied the general presumption of diminished culpability that *Roper* indicates should apply to juvenile offenders. If anything, Graham's in-court statements—including his request for a second chance so that he could "do whatever it takes to get to the NFL"—underscore his immaturity.

The fact that Graham committed the crimes that he did proves that he was dangerous and deserved to be punished. But it does not establish that he was particularly dangerous—at least relative to the murderers and rapists for whom the sentence of life without parole is typically reserved. On the contrary, his lack of prior criminal convictions, his youth and immaturity, and the difficult circumstances of his upbringing noted by the majority, all suggest that he was markedly less culpable than a typical adult who commits the same offenses.

Despite these considerations, the trial court sentenced Graham to life in prison without the possibility of parole. This is the second-harshest sentence available under our precedents for any crime, and the most severe sanction available for a nonhomicide offense. Indeed, as the majority notes, Graham's sentence far exceeded the punishment proposed by the Florida Department of Corrections (which suggested a sentence of four years), and the state prosecutors (who asked that he be sentenced to 30 years in prison for the armed burglary). No one in Graham's case other than the sentencing judge appears to have believed that Graham deserved to go to prison for life.

Based on the foregoing circumstances, I conclude that there is a strong inference that Graham's sentence of life imprisonment without parole was grossly disproportionate in violation of the Eighth Amendment. I therefore proceed to the next steps of the proportionality analysis.

B

Both intrajurisdictional and interjurisdictional comparisons of Graham's sentence confirm the threshold inference of disproportionality.

Graham's sentence was far more severe than that imposed for similar violations of Florida law, even without taking juvenile status into account. For example, individuals who commit burglary or robbery offenses in Florida receive average sentences of less than 5 years and less than 10 years, respectively. Florida's juvenile criminals receive similarly low sentences— typically less than five years for burglary and less than seven years for robbery. Graham's life without parole sentence was far more severe than the average sentence imposed on those convicted of murder or manslaughter, who typically receive under 25 years in prison. As the Court explained in *Solem*, "[i]f more serious crimes are subject to the same penalty, or to less serious penalties, that is some indication that the punishment at issue may be excessive."

Finally, the inference that Graham's sentence is disproportionate is further validated by comparison to the sentences imposed in other domestic jurisdictions. As the majority opinion explains, Florida is an outlier in its willingness to impose sentences of life without parole on juveniles convicted of nonhomicide crimes.

III

So much for Graham. But what about Milagro Cunningham, a 17-year-old who beat and raped an 8-year-old girl before leaving her to die under 197 pounds of rock in a recycling bin in a remote landfill? Or Nathan Walker and Jakaris Taylor, the Florida juveniles who together with their friends gang-raped a woman and forced her to perform oral sex on her 12-year-old son? The fact that Graham cannot be sentenced to life without parole for his conduct says nothing whatever about these offenders, or others like them who commit nonhomicide crimes far more reprehensible than the conduct at issue here. The Court uses Graham's case as a vehicle to proclaim a new constitutional rule-applicable well beyond the particular facts of Graham's case—that a sentence of life without parole imposed on any juvenile for any nonhomicide offense is unconstitutional. This categorical conclusion is as unnecessary as it is unwise.

A holding this broad is unnecessary because the particular conduct and circumstances at issue in the case before us are not serious enough to justify Graham's sentence. In reaching this conclusion, there is no need for the Court to decide whether that same sentence would be constitutional if imposed for other more heinous nonhomicide crimes.

A more restrained approach is especially appropriate in light of the Court's apparent recognition that it is perfectly legitimate for a juvenile to receive a sentence of life without parole for committing murder. This means that there is nothing inherently unconstitutional about imposing sentences of life without parole on juvenile offenders; rather, the constitutionality of such sentences depends on the particular crimes for which they are imposed. But if the constitutionality of the sentence turns on the particular crime being punished, then the Court should limit its holding to the particular offenses that Graham committed here, and should decline to consider other hypothetical crimes not presented by this case.

In any event, the Court's categorical conclusion is also unwise. Most importantly, it ignores the fact that some nonhomicide crimes—like the ones committed by Milagro Cunningham, Nathan Walker, and Jakaris Taylor—are especially heinous or grotesque, and thus may be deserving of more severe punishment.

Those under 18 years old may as a general matter have "diminished" culpability relative to adults who commit the same crimes, but that does not mean that their culpability is always insufficient to justify a life sentence. It does not take a moral sense that is fully developed in every respect to know that beating and raping an 8-year-old girl and leaving her to die under 197 pounds of rocks is horribly wrong. The single fact of being 17 years old would not afford Cunningham protection against life without parole if the young girl had died—as Cunningham surely expected she would—so why should it do so when she miraculously survived his barbaric brutality?

The Court defends its categorical approach on the grounds that a "clear line is necessary to prevent the possibility that life without parole sentences will be imposed on juvenile nonhomicide offenders who are not sufficiently culpable to merit that punishment." It argues that a case-by-case approach to proportionality review is constitutionally insufficient because courts might not be able "with sufficient accuracy [to] distinguish the few incorrigible juvenile offenders from the many that have the capacity for change."

The Court is of course correct that judges will never have perfect foresight—or perfect wisdom—in making sentencing decisions. But this is true when they sentence adults no less than when they sentence juveniles. It is also true when they sentence juveniles who commit murder no less than when they sentence juveniles who commit other crimes.

Our system depends upon sentencing judges applying their reasoned judgment to each case that comes before them. As we explained in *Solem*, the whole enterprise of proportionality review is premised on the "justified" assumption that "courts are competent to judge the gravity of an offense, at least on a relative scale." Indeed, "courts traditionally have made these judgments" by applying "generally accepted criteria" to analyze "the harm caused or threatened to the victim or society, and the culpability of the offender."

* * *

Terrance Graham committed serious offenses, for which he deserves serious punishment. But he was only 16 years old, and under our Court's precedents, his youth is one factor, among others, that should be considered in deciding whether his punishment was unconstitutionally excessive. In my view, Graham's age — together with the nature of his criminal activity and the unusual severity of his sentence — tips the constitutional balance. I thus concur in the Court's judgment that Graham's sentence of life without parole violated the Eighth Amendment.

I would not, however, reach the same conclusion in every case involving a juvenile offender. Some crimes are so heinous, and some juvenile offenders so highly culpable, that a sentence of life without parole may be entirely justified under the Constitution. As we have said, "successful challenges" to noncapital sentences under the Eighth Amendment have been — and, in my view, should continue to be — "exceedingly rare." But Graham's sentence presents the exceptional case that our precedents have recognized will come along. We should grant Graham the relief to which he is entitled under the Eighth Amendment. The Court errs, however, in using this case as a vehicle for unsettling our established jurisprudence and fashioning a categorical rule applicable to far different cases.

Justice THOMAS, with whom Justice SCALIA joins, and with whom Justice ALITO joins as to Parts I and III, dissenting.

The Court holds today that it is "grossly disproportionate" and hence unconstitutional for any judge or jury to impose a sentence of life without parole on an offender less than 18 years old, unless he has committed a homicide. Although the text of the Constitution is silent regarding the permissibility of this sentencing practice, and although it would not have offended the standards that prevailed at the founding, the Court insists that the standards of American society have evolved such that the Constitution now requires its prohibition.

The news of this evolution will, I think, come as a surprise to the American people. Congress, the District of Columbia, and 37 States allow judges and juries to consider this sentencing practice in juvenile nonhomicide cases, and those judges and juries have decided to use it in the very worst cases they have encountered.

The Court does not conclude that life without parole itself is a cruel and unusual punishment. It instead rejects the judgments of those legislatures, judges, and juries regarding what the Court describes as the "moral" question of whether this sentence can ever be "proportionat[e]" when applied to the category of offenders at issue here.

I am unwilling to assume that we, as members of this Court, are any more capable of making such moral judgments than our fellow citizens. Nothing in our training as judges qualifies us for that task, and nothing in Article III gives us that authority.

I respectfully dissent.

* * *

II
A

* * *

More recently, however, the Court has held that the Clause authorizes it to proscribe not only methods of punishment that qualify as "cruel and unusual," but also any punishment that the Court deems "grossly disproportionate" to the crime committed. This latter interpretation is entirely the Court's creation. As has been described elsewhere at length, there is virtually no indication that the Cruel and Unusual Punishments Clause originally was understood to require proportionality in sentencing. Here, it suffices to recall just two points. First, the Clause does not expressly refer to proportionality or invoke any synonym for that term, even though the Framers were familiar with the concept, as evidenced by several founding-era state constitutions that required (albeit without defining) proportional punishments. In addition, the penal statute adopted by the First Congress demonstrates that proportionality in sentencing was not considered a constitutional command.

The Court has nonetheless invoked proportionality to declare that capital punishment—though not unconstitutional per se—is categorically too harsh a penalty to apply to certain types of crimes and certain classes of offenders. In adopting these categorical proportionality rules, the Court intrudes upon areas that the Constitution reserves to other (state and federal) organs of government. The Eighth Amendment prohibits the government from inflicting a cruel and unusual method of punishment upon a defendant. Other constitutional provisions ensure the defendant's right to fair process before any punishment is imposed. But, as members of today's majority note, "[s]ociety changes," and the Eighth Amendment leaves the unavoidably moral question of who "deserves" a particular nonprohibited method of punishment to the judgment of the legislatures that authorize the penalty, the prosecutors who seek it, and the judges and juries that impose it under circumstances they deem appropriate.

The Court has nonetheless adopted categorical rules that shield entire classes of offenses and offenders from the death penalty on the theory that "evolving standards of decency" require this result. The Court has offered assurances that these standards can be reliably measured by "'objective indicia'" of "national consensus," such as state and federal legislation, jury behavior, and (surprisingly, given that we are talking about "national" consensus) international opinion. Yet even assuming that is true, the Framers did not provide for the constitutionality of a particular type of punishment to turn on a "snapshot of American public opinion" taken at the moment a case is decided. By holding otherwise, the Court pretermits in all but one direction the evolution of the standards it describes, thus "calling a constitutional halt to what may well be a pendulum swing in social attitudes," and "stunt[ing] legislative consideration" of new questions of penal policy as they emerge.

But the Court is not content to rely on snapshots of community consensus in any event. Instead, it reserves the right to reject the evidence of consensus it finds whenever its own "independent judgment" points in a different direction. The Court thus openly claims the power not only to approve or disapprove of democratic choices in penal policy based on evidence of how society's standards have evolved, but also on the basis of the Court's "independent" perception of how those standards should evolve, which depends on what the Court concedes is "'"necessarily ... a moral judgment"'" regarding the propriety of a given punishment in today's society.

The categorical proportionality review the Court employs in capital cases thus lacks a principled foundation. The Court's decision today is significant because it does not merely apply this standard — it remarkably expands its reach. For the first time in its history, the Court declares an entire class of offenders immune from a noncapital sentence using the categorical approach it previously reserved for death penalty cases alone.

B

Until today, the Court has based its categorical proportionality rulings on the notion that the Constitution gives special protection to capital defendants because the death penalty is a uniquely severe punishment that must be reserved for only those who are "most deserving of execution." Of course, the Eighth Amendment itself makes no distinction between capital and noncapital sentencing, but the "'bright line'" the Court drew between the two penalties has for many years served as the principal justification for the Court's willingness to reject democratic choices regarding the death penalty.

Today's decision eviscerates that distinction. "Death is different" no longer. The Court now claims not only the power categorically to reserve the "most severe punishment" for those the Court thinks are "'the most deserving of execution,'" but also to declare that "less culpable" persons are categorically exempt from the "second most severe penalty." No reliable limiting principle remains to prevent the Court from immunizing any class of offenders from the law's third, fourth, fifth, or fiftieth most severe penalties as well.

The Court's departure from the "death is different" distinction is especially mystifying when one considers how long it has resisted crossing that divide. Indeed, for a time the Court declined to apply proportionality principles to noncapital sentences at all, emphasizing that "a sentence of death differs in kind from any sentence of imprisonment, no matter how long." Based on that rationale, the Court found that the excessiveness of one prison term as compared to another was "properly within the province of legislatures, not courts," precisely because it involved an "invariably … subjective determination, there being no clear way to make 'any constitutional distinction between one term of years and a shorter or longer term of years.'"

Even when the Court broke from that understanding in its 5-to-4 decision in *Solem* (striking down as "grossly disproportionate" a life-without-parole sentence imposed on a defendant for passing a worthless check), the Court did so only as applied to the facts of that case; it announced no categorical rule. Moreover, the Court soon cabined *Solem*'s rationale. The controlling opinion in the Court's very next noncapital proportionality case emphasized that principles of federalism require substantial deference to legislative choices regarding the proper length of prison sentences. That opinion thus concluded that "successful challenges to the proportionality of [prison] sentences [would be] exceedingly rare."

They have been rare indeed. In the 28 years since *Solem*, the Court has considered just three such challenges and has rejected them all, largely on the theory that criticisms of the "wisdom, cost-efficiency, and effectiveness" of term-of-years prison sentences are "appropriately directed at the legislature[s]," not the courts. The Court correctly notes that those decisions were "closely divided," but so was *Solem* itself, and it is now fair to describe *Solem* as an outlier.

Remarkably, the Court today does more than return to *Solem*'s case-by-case proportionality standard for noncapital sentences; it hurtles past it to impose a categorical proportionality rule banning life-without-parole sentences not just in this case, but in every case involving a juvenile nonhomicide offender, no matter what the circumstances. Neither the Eighth Amendment nor the Court's precedents justify this decision.

III

The Court asserts that categorical proportionality review is necessary here merely because Graham asks for a categorical rule, and because the Court thinks clear lines are a good idea. I find those factors wholly insufficient to justify the Court's break from past practice. First, the Court fails to acknowledge that a petitioner seeking to exempt an entire category of offenders from a sentencing practice carries a much heavier burden than one seeking case-specific relief under *Solem*. Unlike the petitioner in *Solem*, Graham must establish not only that his own life-without-parole sentence is "grossly disproportionate," but also that such a sentence is always grossly disproportionate whenever it is applied to a juvenile nonhomicide offender, no matter how heinous his crime. Second, even applying the Court's categorical "evolving standards" test, neither objective evidence of national consensus nor the notions of culpability on which the Court's "independent judgment" relies can justify the categorical rule it declares here.

A

According to the Court, proper Eighth Amendment analysis "begins with objective indicia of national consensus," and "[t]he clearest and most reliable objective evidence of contemporary values is the legislation enacted by the country's legislatures". As such, the analysis should end quickly, because a national "consensus" in favor of the Court's result simply does not exist. The laws of all 50 States, the Federal Government, and the District of Columbia provide that juveniles over a certain age may be tried in adult court if charged with certain crimes. Forty-five States, the Federal Government, and the District of Columbia expose juvenile offenders charged in adult court to the very same range of punishments faced by adults charged with the same crimes. Eight of those States do not make life-without-parole sentences available for any nonhomicide offender, regardless of age. All remaining jurisdictions—the Federal Government, the other 37 States, and the District-authorize life-without-parole sentences for certain nonhomicide offenses, and authorize the imposition of such sentences on persons under 18. Only five States prohibit juvenile offenders from receiving a life-without-parole sentence that could be imposed on an adult convicted of the same crime.

No plausible claim of a consensus against this sentencing practice can be made in light of this overwhelming legislative evidence. The sole fact that federal law authorizes this practice singlehandedly refutes the claim that our Nation finds it morally repugnant. The additional reality that 37 out of 50 States (a supermajority of 74%) permit the practice makes the claim utterly implausible. Not only is there no consensus against this penalty, there is a clear legislative consensus in favor of its availability.

Undaunted, however, the Court brushes this evidence aside as "incomplete and unavailing," declaring that "'[t]here are measures of consensus other than legislation.'" And although the Court has never decided how many state laws are necessary to show consensus, the Court has never banished into constitutional exile a sentencing practice that the laws of a majority, let alone a supermajority, of States expressly permit.

Moreover, the consistency and direction of recent legislation—a factor the Court previously has relied upon when crafting categorical proportionality rules, underscores the consensus against the rule the Court announces here. In my view, the Court cannot point to a national consensus in favor of its rule without assuming a consensus in favor of the two penological points it later discusses: (1) Juveniles are always less culpable than similarly-situated adults, and (2) juveniles who commit nonhomicide crimes should always receive an opportunity to demonstrate rehabilitation through parole. But legislative trends make that assumption untenable.

First, States over the past 20 years have consistently increased the severity of punishments for juvenile offenders. This, in my view, reveals the States' widespread agreement that juveniles can sometimes act with the same culpability as adults and that the law should permit judges and juries to consider adult sentences-including life without parole — in those rare and unfortunate cases.

Second, legislatures have moved away from parole over the same period. Congress abolished parole for federal offenders in 1984 amid criticism that it was subject to "gamesmanship and cynicism". In light of these developments, the argument that there is nationwide consensus that parole must be available to offenders less than 18 years old in every nonhomicide case simply fails.

B

The Court nonetheless dismisses existing legislation, pointing out that life-without-parole sentences are rarely imposed on juvenile nonhomicide offenders — 123 times in recent memory by the Court's calculation, spread out across 11 States. Based on this rarity of use, the Court proclaims a consensus against the practice, implying that laws allowing it either reflect the consensus of a prior, less civilized time or are the work of legislatures tone-deaf to moral values of their constituents that this Court claims to have easily discerned from afar.

This logic strains credulity. It has been rejected before. ("[T]he relative infrequency of jury verdicts imposing the death sentence does not indicate rejection of capital punishment per se. Rather, [it] … may well reflect the humane feeling that this most irrevocable of sanctions should be reserved for a small number of extreme cases"). It should also be rejected here. That a punishment is rarely imposed demonstrates nothing more than a general consensus that it should be just that — rarely imposed. It is not proof that the punishment is one the Nation abhors.

The Court nonetheless insists that the 26 States that authorize this penalty, but are not presently incarcerating a juvenile nonhomicide offender on a life-without-parole sentence, cannot be counted as approving its use. The mere fact that the laws of a jurisdiction permit this penalty, the Court explains, "does not indicate that the penalty has been endorsed through deliberate, express, and full legislative consideration."

But this misapplies the Court's own evolving standards test, "[i]t is not the burden of [a State] to establish a national consensus approving what their citizens have voted to do; rather, it is the 'heavy burden' of petitioners to establish a national consensus against it." In light of this fact, the Court is wrong to equate a jurisdiction's disuse of a legislatively authorized penalty with its moral opposition to it. The fact that the laws of a jurisdiction permit this sentencing practice demonstrates, at a minimum, that the citizens of that jurisdiction find tolerable the possibility that a jury of their peers could impose a life-without-parole sentence on a juvenile whose nonhomicide crime is sufficiently depraved.

The recent case of 16-year-old Keighton Budder illustrates this point. Just weeks before the release of this opinion, an Oklahoma jury sentenced Budder to life without parole after hearing evidence that he viciously attacked a 17-year-old girl who gave him a ride home from a party. Budder allegedly put the girl's head "'into a headlock and sliced her throat,'" raped her, stabbed her about 20 times, beat her, and pounded her face into the rocks alongside a dirt road. Miraculously, the victim survived.

Budder's crime was rare in its brutality. The sentence the jury imposed was also rare. According to the study relied upon by this Court, Oklahoma had no such offender in its prison system before. Without his conviction, therefore, the Court would have counted

Oklahoma's citizens as morally opposed to life-without-parole sentences for juveniles nonhomicide offenders.

Yet Oklahoma's experience proves the inescapable flaw in that reasoning: Oklahoma citizens have enacted laws that allow Oklahoma juries to consider life-without-parole sentences in juvenile nonhomicide cases. Oklahoma juries invoke those laws rarely—in the unusual cases that they find exceptionally depraved. I cannot agree with the Court that Oklahoma citizens should be constitutionally disabled from using this sentencing practice merely because they have not done so more frequently. If anything, the rarity of this penalty's use underscores just how judicious sentencing judges and juries across the country have been in invoking it.

This fact is entirely consistent with the Court's intuition that juveniles generally are less culpable and more capable of growth than adults. Graham's own case provides another example. Graham was statutorily eligible for a life-without-parole sentence after his first crime. But the record indicates that the trial court did not give such a sentence serious consideration at Graham's initial plea hearing. It was only after Graham subsequently violated his parole by invading a home at gunpoint that the maximum sentence was imposed.

In sum, the Court's calculation that 123 juvenile nonhomicide life-without-parole sentences have been imposed nationwide in recent memory, even if accepted, hardly amounts to strong evidence that the sentencing practice offends our common sense of decency.

Finally, I cannot help but note that the statistics the Court finds inadequate to justify the penalty in this case are stronger than those supporting at least one other penalty this Court has upheld. Not long ago, this Court, joined by the author of today's opinion, upheld the application of the death penalty against a 16-year-old, despite the fact that no such punishment had been carried out on a person of that age in this country in nearly 30 years. Whatever the statistical frequency with which life-without-parole sentences have been imposed on juvenile nonhomicide offenders in the last 30 years, it is surely greater than zero.

In the end, however, objective factors such as legislation and the frequency of a penalty's use are merely ornaments in the Court's analysis, window dressing that accompanies its judicial fiat. By the Court's own decree, "[c]ommunity consensus ... is not itself determinative." Only the independent moral judgment of this Court is sufficient to decide the question.

C

Lacking any plausible claim to consensus, the Court shifts to the heart of its argument: its "independent judgment" that this sentencing practice does not "serv[e] legitimate penological goals." The Court begins that analysis with the obligatory preamble that "'[t]he Eighth Amendment does not mandate adoption of any one penological theory,'" then promptly mandates the adoption of the theories the Court deems best.

First, the Court acknowledges that, at a minimum, the imposition of life-without-parole sentences on juvenile nonhomicide offenders serves two "legitimate" penological goals: incapacitation and deterrence. By definition, such sentences serve the goal of incapacitation by ensuring that juvenile offenders who commit armed burglaries, or those who commit the types of grievous sex crimes described by THE CHIEF JUSTICE, no longer threaten their communities. That should settle the matter, since the Court acknowledges that incapacitation is an "important" penological goal. Yet, the Court finds this goal "inadequate" to justify the life-without-parole sentences here. A similar fate befalls deterrence. The Court acknowledges that such sentences will deter future juvenile offenders, at least to some degree, but rejects that penological goal, not as illegitimate, but as insufficient.

The Court looks more favorably on rehabilitation, but laments that life-without-parole sentences do little to promote this goal because they result in the offender's permanent incarceration. Of course, the Court recognizes that rehabilitation's "utility and proper implementation" are subject to debate. But that does not stop it from declaring that a legislature may not "forswea[r] ... the rehabilitative ideal." In other words, the Eighth Amendment does not mandate "any one penological theory (internal quotation marks omitted), just one the Court approves.

Ultimately, however, the Court's "independent judgment" and the proportionality rule itself center on retribution—the notion that a criminal sentence should be proportioned to "'the personal culpability of the criminal offender.'" The Court finds that retributive purposes are not served here for two reasons.

1

First, quoting *Roper*, the Court concludes that juveniles are less culpable than adults because, as compared to adults, they "have a '"lack of maturity and an underdeveloped sense of responsibility,"'" and "their characters are 'not as well formed.'" As a general matter, this statement is entirely consistent with the evidence recounted above that judges and juries impose the sentence at issue quite infrequently, despite legislative authorization to do so in many more cases. Our society tends to treat the average juvenile as less culpable than the average adult. But the question here does not involve the average juvenile. The question, instead, is whether the Constitution prohibits judges and juries from ever concluding that an offender under the age of 18 has demonstrated sufficient depravity and incorrigibility to warrant his permanent incarceration.

In holding that the Constitution imposes such a ban, the Court cites "developments in psychology and brain science" indicating that juvenile minds "continue to mature through late adolescence," and that juveniles are "more likely [than adults] to engage in risky behaviors". But even if such generalizations from social science were relevant to constitutional rulemaking, the Court misstates the data on which it relies.

The Court equates the propensity of a fairly substantial number of youths to engage in "risky" or antisocial behaviors with the propensity of a much smaller group to commit violent crimes. But research relied upon by the amici cited in the Court's opinion differentiates between adolescents for whom antisocial behavior is a fleeting symptom and those for whom it is a lifelong pattern. That research further suggests that the pattern of behavior in the latter group often sets in before 18. ("The well-documented resistance of antisocial personality disorder to treatments of all kinds seems to suggest that the life-course-persistent style is fixed sometime before age 18"). And, notably, it suggests that violence itself is evidence that an adolescent offender's antisocial behavior is not transient.

In sum, even if it were relevant, none of this psychological or sociological data is sufficient to support the Court's "'moral'" conclusion that youth defeats culpability in every case.

The Court responds that a categorical rule is nonetheless necessary to prevent the "'unacceptable likelihood'" that a judge or jury, unduly swayed by "'the brutality or cold-blooded nature'" of a juvenile's nonhomicide crime, will sentence him to a life-without-parole sentence for which he possesses "'insufficient culpability.'" I find that justification entirely insufficient. The integrity of our criminal justice system depends on the ability of citizens to stand between the defendant and an outraged public and dispassionately determine his guilt and the proper amount of punishment based on the evidence presented. That process necessarily admits of human error. But so does the process of judging in which we engage. As between the two, I find far more "unacceptable" that this Court, swayed by studies reflecting the general tendencies of youth, decree that the people of this country are not fit to decide for themselves when the rare case requires different treatment.

2

That is especially so because, in the end, the Court does not even believe its pronouncements about the juvenile mind. If it did, the categorical rule it announces today would be most peculiar because it leaves intact state and federal laws that permit life-without-parole sentences for juveniles who commit homicides. The Court thus acknowledges that there is nothing inherent in the psyche of a person less than 18 that prevents him from acquiring the moral agency necessary to warrant a life-without-parole sentence. Instead, the Court rejects overwhelming legislative consensus only on the question of which acts are sufficient to demonstrate that moral agency.

The Court is quite willing to accept that a 17-year-old who pulls the trigger on a firearm can demonstrate sufficient depravity and irredeemability to be denied reentry into society, but insists that a 17-year-old who rapes an 8-year-old and leaves her for dead does not. Thus, the Court's conclusion that life-without-parole sentences are "grossly disproportionate" for juvenile nonhomicide offenders in fact has very little to do with its view of juveniles, and much more to do with its perception that "defendants who do not kill, intend to kill, or foresee that life will be taken are categorically less deserving of the most serious forms of punishment than are murderers."

That the Court is willing to impose such an exacting constraint on democratic sentencing choices based on such an untestable philosophical conclusion is remarkable. The question of what acts are "deserving" of what punishments is bound so tightly with questions of morality and social conditions as to make it, almost by definition, a question for legislative resolution. It is true that the Court previously has relied on the notion of proportionality in holding certain classes of offenses categorically exempt from capital punishment. But never before today has the Court relied on its own view of just deserts to impose a categorical limit on the imposition of a lesser punishment. Its willingness to cross that well-established boundary raises the question whether any democratic choice regarding appropriate punishment is safe from the Court's ever-expanding constitutional veto.

IV

Although the concurrence avoids the problems associated with expanding categorical proportionality review to noncapital cases, it employs noncapital proportionality analysis in a way that raises the same fundamental concern. Although I do not believe *Solem* merits *stare decisis* treatment, Graham's claim cannot prevail even under that test (as it has been limited by the Court's subsequent precedents). *Solem* instructs a court first to compare the "gravity" of an offender's conduct to the "harshness of the penalty" to determine whether an "inference" of gross disproportionality exists. Only in "the rare case" in which such an inference is present should the court proceed to the "objective" part of the inquiry—an intra- and inter-jurisdictional comparison of the defendant's sentence with others similarly situated.

Under the Court's precedents, I fail to see how an "inference" of gross disproportionality arises here. The concurrence notes several arguably mitigating facts—Graham's "lack of prior criminal convictions, his youth and immaturity, and the difficult circumstances of his upbringing." But the Court previously has upheld a life-without-parole sentence imposed on a first-time offender who committed a nonviolent drug crime. Graham's conviction for an actual violent felony is surely more severe than that offense. As for Graham's age, it is true that *Roper* held juveniles categorically ineligible for capital punishment, but as the concurrence explains, *Roper* was based on the "explicit conclusion that [juveniles] 'cannot with reliability be classified among the worst offenders'"; it did "not establish that juveniles can never be eligible for life without parole." In my view, *Roper*'s principles are thus not generally applicable outside the capital sentencing context.

By holding otherwise, the concurrence relies on the same type of subjective judgment as the Court, only it restrains itself to a case-by-case rather than a categorical ruling. The concurrence is quite ready to hand Graham "the general presumption of diminished culpability" for juveniles, ante, at 2040, apparently because it believes that Graham's armed burglary and home invasion crimes were "certainly less serious" than murder or rape, ibid. It recoils only from the prospect that the Court would extend the same presumption to a juvenile who commits a sex crime. I simply cannot accept that these subjective judgments of proportionality are ones the Eighth Amendment authorizes us to make.

The "objective" elements of the *Solem* test provide no additional support for the concurrence's conclusion. The concurrence compares Graham's sentence to "similar" sentences in Florida and concludes that Graham's sentence was "far more severe." But strangely, the concurrence uses average sentences for burglary or robbery offenses as examples of "similar" offenses, even though it seems that a run-of-the-mill burglary or robbery is not at all similar to Graham's criminal history, which includes a charge for armed burglary with assault, and a probation violation for invading a home at gunpoint.

And even if Graham's sentence is higher than ones he might have received for an armed burglary with assault in other jurisdictions, this hardly seems relevant if one takes seriously the principle that "'[a]bsent a constitutionally imposed uniformity inimical to traditional notions of federalism, some State will always bear the distinction of treating particular offenders more severely than any other State.'" Applying *Solem*, the Court has upheld a 25-years-to-life sentence for theft under California's recidivist statute, despite the fact that the State and its amici could cite only "a single instance of a similar sentence imposed outside the context of California's three strikes law, out of a prison population [then] approaching two million individuals." It has also upheld a life-without-parole sentence for a first-time drug offender in Michigan charged with possessing 672 grams of cocaine despite the fact that only one other State would have authorized such a stiff penalty for a first-time drug offense, and even that State required a far greater quantity of cocaine (10 kilograms) to trigger the penalty. Graham's sentence is certainly less rare than the sentences upheld in these cases, so his claim fails even under *Solem*.

* * *

Both the Court and the concurrence claim their decisions to be narrow ones, but both invite a host of line-drawing problems to which courts must seek answers beyond the strictures of the Constitution. The Court holds that "[a] State is not required to guarantee eventual freedom to a juvenile offender convicted of a nonhomicide crime," but must provide the offender with "some meaningful opportunity to obtain release based on demonstrated maturity and rehabilitation." But what, exactly, does such a "meaningful" opportunity entail? When must it occur? And what Eighth Amendment principles will govern review by the parole boards the Court now demands that States empanel? The Court provides no answers to these questions, which will no doubt embroil the courts for years.

V

The ultimate question in this case is not whether a life-without-parole sentence 'fits' the crime at issue here or the crimes of juvenile nonhomicide offenders more generally, but to whom the Constitution assigns that decision. The Florida Legislature has concluded that such sentences should be available for persons under 18 who commit certain crimes, and the trial judge in this case decided to impose that legislatively authorized sentence here. Because a life-without-parole prison sentence is not a "cruel and unusual" method of punishment under any standard, the Eighth Amendment gives this Court no authority to reject those judgments.

It would be unjustifiable for the Court to declare otherwise even if it could claim that a bare majority of state laws supported its independent moral view. The fact that the Court categorically prohibits life-without-parole sentences for juvenile nonhomicide offenders in the face of an overwhelming legislative majority in favor of leaving that sentencing option available under certain cases simply illustrates how far beyond any cognizable constitutional principle the Court has reached to ensure that its own sense of morality and retributive justice pre-empts that of the people and their representatives.

Justice ALITO, dissenting.

I join Parts I and III of Justice THOMAS's dissenting opinion. I write separately to make two points.

First, the Court holds only that "for a juvenile offender who did not commit homicide the Eighth Amendment forbids the sentence of life without parole." Nothing in the Court's opinion affects the imposition of a sentence to a term of years without the possibility of parole. Indeed, petitioner conceded at oral argument that a sentence of as much as 40 years without the possibility of parole "probably" would be constitutional.

Second, the question whether petitioner's sentence violates the narrow, as-applied proportionality principle that applies to noncapital sentences is not properly before us in this case. Although petitioner asserted an as-applied proportionality challenge to his sentence before the Florida courts, he did not include an as-applied claim in his petition for certiorari or in his merits briefs before this Court.

Notes

(a) If children are different and the juvenile justice system was designed to recognize these differences should dispositions for juveniles be different than those sanctions imposed on adults in similar cases? Are such severe penalties as life without possibility of parole ever appropriate for children? If so, under what circumstances?

(b) Although the Court found LWOP to be an inappropriate sentence for a juvenile in nonhomicide cases, would the Court find it appropriate in all homicide cases? Are lengthy sentences where a juvenile must serve a minimum amount of time any different to the juvenile? Are harsh sentences appropriate for juveniles if the system is meant to be rehabilitative and give children another chance? Should the type of sanction used with a juvenile depend on the offense and where the matter is heard, i.e. juvenile court or criminal court?

J.D.B. v. North Carolina

131 S. Ct. 2394 (2011)

Justice SOTOMAYOR delivered the opinion of the Court. Justices KENNEDY, GINS-BURG, BREYER and KAGAN joined.

This case presents the question whether the age of a child subjected to police questioning is relevant to the custody analysis of Miranda v. Arizona. It is beyond dispute that children will often feel bound to submit to police questioning when an adult in the same circumstances would feel free to leave. Seeing no reason for police officers or courts to blind themselves to that commonsense reality, we hold that a child's age properly informs the Miranda custody analysis.

I

A

Petitioner J.D.B. was a 13-year-old, seventh-grade student attending class at Smith Middle School in Chapel Hill, North Carolina when he was removed from his classroom by a uniformed police officer, escorted to a closed-door conference room, and questioned by police for at least half an hour.

This was the second time that police questioned J.D.B. in the span of a week. Five days earlier, two home break-ins occurred, and various items were stolen. Police stopped and questioned J.D.B. after he was seen behind a residence in the neighborhood where the crimes occurred. That same day, police also spoke to J.D. B.'s grandmother—his legal guardian—as well as his aunt.

Police later learned that a digital camera matching the description of one of the stolen items had been found at J.D. B.'s middle school and seen in J.D. B.'s possession. Investigator DiCostanzo, the juvenile investigator with the local police force who had been assigned to the case, went to the school to question J.D.B. Upon arrival, DiCostanzo informed the uniformed police officer on detail to the school (a so-called school resource officer), the assistant principal, and an administrative intern that he was there to question J.D.B. about the break-ins. Although DiCostanzo asked the school administrators to verify J.D. B.'s date of birth, address, and parent contact in-formation from school records, neither the police officers nor the school administrators contacted J.D. B.'s grandmother.

The uniformed officer interrupted J.D. B.'s afternoon social studies class, removed J.D.B. from the classroom, and escorted him to a school conference room. There, J.D.B. was met by DiCostanzo, the assistant principal, and the administrative intern. The door to the conference room was closed. With the two police officers and the two administrators present, J.D.B. was questioned for the next 30 to 45 minutes. Prior to the commencement of questioning, J.D.B. was given neither Miranda warnings nor the opportunity to speak to his grandmother. Nor was he informed that he was free to leave the room.

Questioning began with small talk—discussion of sports and J.D. B.'s family life. DiCostanzo asked, and J.D.B. agreed, to discuss the events of the prior weekend. Denying any wrongdoing, J.D.B. explained that he had been in the neighborhood where the crimes occurred because he was seeking work mowing lawns. DiCostanzo pressed J.D.B. for additional detail about his efforts to obtain work; asked J.D.B. to explain a prior incident, when one of the victims returned home to find J.D.B. behind her house; and confronted J.D.B. with the stolen camera. The assistant principal urged J.D.B. to "do the right thing," warning J.D.B. that "the truth always comes out in the end."

Eventually, J.D.B. asked whether he would "still be in trouble" if he returned the "stuff." In response, DiCostanzo explained that return of the stolen items would be helpful, but "this thing is going to court" regardless. ("[W]hat's done is done[;] now you need to help yourself by making it right"). DiCostanzo then warned that he may need to seek a secure custody order if he believed that J.D.B. would continue to break into other homes. When J.D.B. asked what a secure custody order was, DiCostanzo explained that "it's where you get sent to juvenile detention before court."

After learning of the prospect of juvenile detention, J.D.B. confessed that he and a friend were responsible for the break-ins. DiCostanzo only then informed J.D.B. that he could refuse to answer the investigator's questions and that he was free to leave. Asked whether he understood, J.D.B. nodded and provided further detail, including information about the location of the stolen items. Eventually J.D.B. wrote a statement, at DiCostanzo's request. When the bell rang indicating the end of the schoolday, J.D.B. was allowed to leave to catch the bus home.

B

Two juvenile petitions were filed against J.D. B., each alleging one count of breaking and entering and one count of larceny. J.D. B.'s public defender moved to suppress his statements and the evidence derived therefrom, arguing that suppression was necessary because J.D.B. had been "interrogated by police in a custodial setting without being afforded Miranda warning[s]," and because his statements were involuntary under the totality of the circumstances test. After a suppression hearing at which DiCostanzo and J.D.B. testified, the trial court denied the motion, deciding that J.D.B. was not in custody at the time of the schoolhouse interrogation and that his statements were voluntary. As a result, J.D.B. entered a transcript of admission to all four counts, renewing his objection to the denial of his motion to suppress, and the court adjudicated J.D.B. delinquent.

A divided panel of the North Carolina Court of Appeals affirmed. The North Carolina Supreme Court held, over two dissents, that J.D.B. was not in custody when he confessed, "declin[ing] to extend the test for custody to include consideration of the age ... of an individual subjected to questioning by police."

We granted certiorari to determine whether the Miranda custody analysis includes consideration of a juvenile suspect's age.

II
A

Any police interview of an individual suspected of a crime has "coercive aspects to it." Only those interrogations that occur while a suspect is in police custody, however, "heighte[n] the risk" that statements obtained are not the product of the suspect's free choice.

By its very nature, custodial police interrogation entails "inherently compelling pressures." Even for an adult, the physical and psychological isolation of custodial interrogation can "undermine the individual's will to resist and ... compel him to speak where he would not otherwise do so freely." Indeed, the pressure of custodial interrogation is so immense that it "can induce a frighteningly high percentage of people to confess to crimes they never committed." That risk is all the more troubling—and recent studies suggest, all the more acute—when the subject of custodial interrogation is a juvenile.

Recognizing that the inherently coercive nature of custodial interrogation "blurs the line between voluntary and involuntary statements," this Court in *Miranda* adopted a set of prophylactic measures designed to safeguard the constitutional guarantee against self-incrimination. Prior to questioning, a suspect "must be warned that he has a right to remain silent, that any statement he does make may be used as evidence against him, and that he has a right to the presence of an attorney, either retained or appointed." And, if a suspect makes a statement during custodial interrogation, the burden is on the Government to show, as a "prerequisit[e]" to the statement's admissibility as evidence in the Government's case in chief, that the defendant "voluntarily, knowingly and intelligently" waived his rights.

Because these measures protect the individual against the coercive nature of custodial interrogation, they are required "'only where there has been such a restriction on a person's freedom as to render him "in custody."'" As we have repeatedly emphasized, whether a suspect is "in custody" is an objective inquiry.

"Two discrete inquiries are essential to the determination: first, what were the circumstances surrounding the interrogation; and second, given those circumstances, would a reasonable person have felt he or she was at liberty to terminate the interrogation and leave. Once the scene is set and the players' lines and actions are reconstructed, the court must apply an objective test to resolve the ultimate inquiry: was there a formal arrest or restraint on freedom of movement of the degree associated with formal arrest."

Rather than demarcate a limited set of relevant circumstances, we have required police officers and courts to "examine all of the circumstances surrounding the interrogation," including any circumstance that "would have affected how a reasonable person" in the suspect's position "would perceive his or her freedom to leave." On the other hand, the "subjective views harbored by either the interrogating officers or the person being questioned" are irrelevant. The test, in other words, involves no consideration of the "actual mindset" of the particular suspect subjected to police questioning.

The benefit of the objective custody analysis is that it is "designed to give clear guidance to the police." Police must make in-the-moment judgments as to when to administer Miranda warnings. By limiting analysis to the objective circumstances of the interrogation, and asking how a reasonable person in the suspect's position would understand his freedom to terminate questioning and leave, the objective test avoids burdening police with the task of anticipating the idiosyncrasies of every individual suspect and divining how those particular traits affect each person's subjective state of mind.

B

The State and its amici contend that a child's age has no place in the custody analysis, no matter how young the child subjected to police questioning. We cannot agree. In some circumstances, a child's age "would have affected how a reasonable person" in the suspect's position "would perceive his or her freedom to leave." That is, a reasonable child subjected to police questioning will sometimes feel pressured to submit when a reasonable adult would feel free to go. We think it clear that courts can account for that reality without doing any damage to the objective nature of the custody analysis.

A child's age is far "more than a chronological fact." It is a fact that "generates commonsense conclusions about behavior and perception." Such conclusions apply broadly to children as a class. And, they are self-evident to anyone who was a child once himself, including any police officer or judge.

Time and again, this Court has drawn these commonsense conclusions for itself. We have observed that children "generally are less mature and responsible than adults," that they "often lack the experience, perspective, and judgment to recognize and avoid choices that could be detrimental to them," that they "are more vulnerable or susceptible to ... outside pressures" than adults and so on. Addressing the specific context of police interrogation, we have observed that events that "would leave a man cold and unimpressed can overawe and overwhelm a lad in his early teens." Describing no one child in particular, these observations restate what "any parent knows"—indeed, what any person knows—about children generally.

Our various statements to this effect are far from unique. The law has historically reflected the same assumption that children characteristically lack the capacity to exercise mature judgment and possess only an incomplete ability to understand the world around them. Like this Court's own generalizations, the legal disqualifications placed on children as a class—e.g., limitations on their ability to alienate property, enter a binding contract enforceable against them, and marry without parental consent—exhibit the settled understanding that the differentiating characteristics of youth are universal.

Indeed, even where a "reasonable person" standard otherwise applies, the common law has reflected the reality that children are not adults. In negligence suits, for instance, where liability turns on what an objectively reasonable person would do in the circumstances, "[a]ll American jurisdictions accept the idea that a person's childhood is a relevant circumstance" to be considered.

As this discussion establishes, "[o]ur history is replete with laws and judicial recognition" that children cannot be viewed simply as miniature adults. We see no justification for taking a different course here. So long as the child's age was known to the officer at the time of the interview, or would have been objectively apparent to any reasonable officer, including age as part of the custody analysis requires officers neither to consider circumstances "unknowable" to them ... The same "wide basis of community experience" that makes it possible, as an objective matter, "to determine what is to be expected" of children in other contexts, likewise makes it possible to know what to expect of children subjected to police questioning.

In other words, a child's age differs from other personal characteristics that, even when known to police, have no objectively discernible relationship to a reasonable person's understanding of his freedom of action. *Alvarado*, holds, for instance, that a suspect's prior interrogation history with law enforcement has no role to play in the custody analysis because such experience could just as easily lead a reasonable person to feel free to walk away as to feel compelled to stay in place. Because the effect in any given case would be "contingent [on the] psycholog[y]" of the individual suspect, the Court explained, such experience cannot be considered without compromising the objective nature of the custody analysis. A child's age, however, is different. Precisely because childhood yields objective conclusions like those we have drawn ourselves—among others, that children are "most susceptible to influence," and "outside pressures,"—considering age in the custody analysis in no way involves a determination of how youth "subjectively affect[s] the mindset" of any particular child.

In fact, in many cases involving juvenile suspects, the custody analysis would be nonsensical absent some consideration of the suspect's age. This case is a prime example. Were the court precluded from taking J.D.B.'s youth into account, it would be forced to evaluate the circumstances present here through the eyes of a reasonable person of average years. In other words, how would a reasonable adult understand his situation, after being removed from a seventh-grade social studies class by a uniformed school resource officer; being encouraged by his assistant principal to "do the right thing"; and being warned by a police investigator of the prospect of juvenile detention and separation from his guardian and primary caretaker? To describe such an inquiry is to demonstrate its absurdity. Neither officers nor courts can reasonably evaluate the effect of objective circumstances that, by their nature, are specific to children without accounting for the age of the child subjected to those circumstances.

Indeed, although the dissent suggests that concerns "regarding the application of the *Miranda* custody rule to minors can be accommodated by considering the unique circumstances present when minors are questioned in school," the effect of the schoolhouse setting cannot be disentangled from the identity of the person questioned. A student — whose presence at school is compulsory and whose disobedience at school is cause for disciplinary action — is in a far different position than, say, a parent volunteer on school grounds to chaperone an event, or an adult from the community on school grounds to attend a basketball game. Without asking whether the person "questioned in school" is a "minor," the coercive effect of the schoolhouse setting is unknowable.

Our prior decision in *Alvarado* in no way undermines these conclusions. In that case, we held that a state-court decision that failed to mention a 17-year-old's age as part of the *Miranda* custody analysis was not objectively unreasonable under the deferential standard of review set forth by the Antiterrorism and Effective Death Penalty Act of 1996 (AEDPA). Like the North Carolina Supreme Court here, we observed that accounting for a juvenile's age in the *Miranda* custody analysis "could be viewed as creating a subjective inquiry." We said nothing, however, of whether such a view would be correct under the law. ("[W]hether the [state court] was right or wrong is not the pertinent question under AEDPA"). To the contrary, Justice O'Connor's concurring opinion explained that a suspect's age may indeed "be relevant to the 'custody' inquiry."

Reviewing the question *de novo* today, we hold that so long as the child's age was known to the officer at the time of police questioning, or would have been objectively apparent to a reasonable officer, its inclusion in the custody analysis is consistent with the objective nature of that test. This is not to say that a child's age will be a determinative, or even a significant, factor in every case. It is, however, a reality that courts cannot simply ignore.

III

The State and its amici offer numerous reasons that courts must blind themselves to a juvenile defendant's age. None is persuasive.

To start, the State contends that a child's age must be excluded from the custody inquiry because age is a personal characteristic specific to the suspect himself rather than an "external" circumstance of the interrogation. Despite the supposed significance of this distinction, however, at oral argument counsel for the State suggested without hesitation that at least some undeniably personal characteristics — for instance, whether the individual being questioned is blind — are circumstances relevant to the custody analysis. Thus, the State's quarrel cannot be that age is a personal characteristic, without more.

The State further argues that age is irrelevant to the custody analysis because it "go[es] to how a suspect may internalize and perceive the circumstances of an interrogation." But the same can be said of every objective circumstance that the State agrees is relevant to the custody analysis: Each circumstance goes to how a reasonable person would "internalize and perceive" every other. Indeed, this is the very reason that we ask whether the objective circumstances "add up to custody," instead of evaluating the circumstances one by one.

In the same vein, the State and its amici protest that the "effect of ... age on [the] perception of custody is internal." But the whole point of the custody analysis is to determine whether, given the circumstances, "a reasonable person [would] have felt he or she was ... at liberty to terminate the interrogation and leave." Because the *Miranda* custody inquiry turns on the mindset of a reasonable person in the suspect's position, it cannot be the case that a circumstance is subjective simply because it has an "internal" or "psychological" impact on perception. Were that so, there would be no objective circumstances to consider at all.

Relying on our statements that the objective custody test is "designed to give clear guidance to the police," the State next argues that a child's age must be excluded from the analysis in order to preserve clarity. Similarly, the dissent insists that the clarity of the custody analysis will be destroyed unless a "one-size-fits-all reasonable-person test" applies. In reality, however, ignoring a juvenile defendant's age will often make the inquiry more artificial, and thus only add confusion. And in any event, a child's age, when known or apparent, is hardly an obscure factor to assess. Though the State and the dissent worry about gradations among children of different ages, that concern cannot justify ignoring a child's age altogether. Just as police officers are competent to account for other objective circumstances that are a matter of degree such as the length of questioning or the number of officers present, so too are they competent to evaluate the effect of relative age. Indeed, they are competent to do so even though an interrogation room lacks the "reflective atmosphere of a [jury] deliberation room." The same is true of judges, including those whose childhoods have long since passed. In short, officers and judges need no imaginative powers, knowledge of developmental psychology, training in cognitive science, or expertise in social and cultural anthropology to account for a child's age. They simply need the common sense to know that a 7-year-old is not a 13-year-old and neither is an adult.

There is, however, an even more fundamental flaw with the State's plea for clarity and the dissent's singular focus on simplifying the analysis: Not once have we excluded from the custody analysis a circumstance that we determined was relevant and objective, simply to make the fault line between custodial and noncustodial "brighter." Indeed, were the guiding concern clarity and nothing else, the custody test would presumably ask only whether the suspect had been placed under formal arrest. But we have rejected that "more easily administered line," recognizing that it would simply "enable the police to circumvent the constraints on custodial interrogations established by *Miranda*."

Finally, the State and the dissent suggest that excluding age from the custody analysis comes at no cost to juveniles' constitutional rights because the due process voluntariness test independently accounts for a child's youth. To be sure, that test permits consideration of a child's age, and it erects its own barrier to admission of a defendant's inculpatory statements at trial. ("[C]ourts should be instructed to take particular care to ensure that [young children's] incriminating statements were not obtained involuntarily"). But *Miranda*'s procedural safeguards exist precisely because the voluntariness test is an inadequate barrier when custodial interrogation is at stake. To hold, as the State requests, that a child's age is never relevant to whether a suspect has been taken into custody—and thus to ignore the very real differences between children and adults—would be to deny children the full scope of the procedural safeguards that Miranda guarantees to adults.

* * *

The question remains whether J.D.B. was in custody when police interrogated him. We remand for the state courts to address that question, this time taking account of all of the relevant circumstances of the interrogation, including J.D. B.'s age at the time. The judgment of the North Carolina Supreme Court is reversed, and the case is remanded for proceedings not inconsistent with this opinion.

It is so ordered.

Justice ALITO, with whom THE CHIEF JUSTICE, Justice SCALIA, and Justice THOMAS join, dissenting.

The Court's decision in this case may seem on first consideration to be modest and sensible, but in truth it is neither. It is fundamentally inconsistent with one of the main justifications for the *Miranda* rule: the perceived need for a clear rule that can be easily applied in all cases. And today's holding is not needed to protect the constitutional rights of minors who are questioned by the police.

Miranda's prophylactic regime places a high value on clarity and certainty. Dissatisfied with the highly fact-specific constitutional rule against the admission of involuntary confessions, the *Miranda* Court set down rigid standards that often require courts to ignore personal characteristics that may be highly relevant to a particular suspect's actual susceptibility to police pressure. This rigidity, however, has brought with it one of *Miranda*'s principal strengths—"the ease and clarity of its application" by law enforcement officials and courts. A key contributor to this clarity, at least up until now, has been *Miranda*'s objective reasonable-person test for determining custody.

Miranda's custody requirement is based on the proposition that the risk of unconstitutional coercion is heightened when a suspect is placed under formal arrest or is subjected to some functionally equivalent limitation on freedom of movement. When this custodial threshold is reached, *Miranda* warnings must precede police questioning. But in the interest of simplicity, the custody analysis considers only whether, under the circumstances, a hypothetical reasonable person would consider himself to be confined.

Many suspects, of course, will differ from this hypothetical reasonable person. Some, including those who have been hardened by past interrogations, may have no need for Miranda warnings at all. And for other suspects—those who are unusually sensitive to the pressures of police questioning—*Miranda* warnings may come too late to be of any use. That is a necessary consequence of *Miranda*'s rigid standards, but it does not mean that the constitutional rights of these especially sensitive suspects are left unprotected. A vulnerable defendant can still turn to the constitutional rule against actual coercion and contend that that his confession was extracted against his will.

Today's decision shifts the *Miranda* custody determination from a one-size-fits-all reasonable-person test into an inquiry that must account for at least one individualized characteristic—age—that is thought to correlate with susceptibility to coercive pressures. Age, however, is in no way the only personal characteristic that may correlate with pliability, and in future cases the Court will be forced to choose between two unpalatable alternatives. It may choose to limit today's decision by arbitrarily distinguishing a suspect's age from other personal characteristics—such as intelligence, education, occupation, or prior experience with law enforcement—that may also correlate with susceptibility to coercive pressures. Or, if the Court is unwilling to draw these arbitrary lines, it will be forced to effect a fundamental transformation of the *Miranda* custody test—from a clear, easily applied prophylactic rule into a highly fact-intensive standard resembling the voluntariness test that the *Miranda* Court found to be unsatisfactory.

For at least three reasons, there is no need to go down this road. First, many minors subjected to police interrogation are near the age of majority, and for these suspects the one-size-fits-all *Miranda* custody rule may not be a bad fit. Second, many of the difficulties in applying the *Miranda* custody rule to minors arise because of the unique circumstances present when the police conduct interrogations at school. The *Miranda* custody rule has always taken into account the setting in which questioning occurs, and accounting for the school setting in such cases will address many of these problems. Third, in cases like the one now before us, where the suspect is especially young, courts applying the constitutional voluntariness standard can take special care to ensure that incriminating statements were not obtained through coercion.

Safeguarding the constitutional rights of minors does not require the extreme makeover of *Miranda* that today's decision may portend.

I

In the days before *Miranda*, this Court's sole metric for evaluating the admissibility of confessions was a voluntariness standard rooted in both the Fifth Amendment's Self-Incrimination Clause and the Due Process Clause of the Fourteenth Amendment. The question in these voluntariness cases was whether the particular "defendant's will" had been "overborne." Courts took into account both "the details of the interrogation" and "the characteristics of the accused," and then "weigh[ed] ... the circumstances of pressure against the power of resistance of the person confessing."

All manner of individualized, personal characteristics were relevant in this voluntariness inquiry. Among the most frequently mentioned factors were the defendant's education, physical condition, intelligence, and mental health. The suspect's age also received prominent attention in several cases. The weight assigned to any one consideration varied from case to case. But all of these factors, along with anything else that might have affected the "individual's ... capacity for effective choice," were relevant in determining whether the confession was coerced or compelled.

The all-encompassing nature of the voluntariness inquiry had its benefits. It allowed courts to accommodate a "complex of values," and to make a careful, highly individualized determination as to whether the police had wrung "a confession out of [the] accused against his will." But with this flexibility came a decrease in both certainty and predictability, and the voluntariness standard proved difficult "for law enforcement officers to conform to, and for courts to apply in a consistent manner."

In *Miranda*, the Court supplemented the voluntariness inquiry with a "set of prophylactic measures" designed to ward off the "'inherently compelling pressures' of custodial interrogation." *Miranda* greatly simplified matters by requiring police to give suspects standard warnings before commencing any custodial interrogation. But with this rigidity comes increased clarity. *Miranda* provides "a workable rule to guide police officers," and an administrable standard for the courts. As has often been recognized, this gain in clarity and administrability is one of *Miranda's* "principal advantages."

No less than other facets of *Miranda*, the threshold requirement that the suspect be in "custody" is "designed to give clear guidance to the police." Custody under *Miranda* attaches where there is a "formal arrest" or a "restraint on freedom of movement" akin to formal arrest. This standard is "objective" and turns on how a hypothetical "reasonable person in the position of the individual being questioned would gauge the breadth of his or her freedom of action."

Until today, the Court's cases applying this test have focused solely on the "objective circumstances of the interrogation," not the personal characteristics of the interrogated. Relevant factors have included such things as where the questioning occurred, how long it lasted, what was said, any physical restraints placed on the suspect's movement, and whether the suspect was allowed to leave when the questioning was through. The totality of these circumstances—the external circumstances, that is, of the interrogation itself—is what has mattered in this Court's cases. Personal characteristics of suspects have consistently been rejected or ignored as irrelevant under a one-size-fits-all reasonable-person standard.

For example, in *Berkemer v. McCarty*, police officers conducting a traffic stop questioned a man who had been drinking and smoking marijuana before he was pulled over. Although the suspect's inebriation was readily apparent to the officers at the scene, the Court's analysis did not advert to this or any other individualized consideration. Instead, the Court focused only on the external circumstances of the interrogation itself. The opinion concluded that a typical "traffic stop" is akin to a "Terry stop" and does not qualify as the equivalent of "formal arrest."

California v. Beheler, is another useful example. There, the circumstances of the interrogation were "remarkably similar" to the facts of the Court's earlier decision in *Oregon v. Mathiason*, the suspect was "not placed under arrest," he "voluntarily [came] to the police station," and he was "allowed to leave unhindered by police after a brief interview." A California court in *Beheler* had nonetheless distinguished *Mathiason* because the police knew that Beheler "had been drinking earlier in the day" and was "emotionally distraught." In a summary reversal, this Court explained that the fact "[t]hat the police knew more" personal information about Beheler than they did about Mathiason was "irrelevant." Neither one of them was in custody under the objective reasonable-person standard.

The glaring absence of reliance on personal characteristics in these and other custody cases should come as no surprise. To account for such individualized considerations would be to contradict *Miranda's* central premise. The *Miranda* Court's decision to adopt its inflexible prophylactic requirements was expressly based on the notion that "[a]ssessments of the knowledge the defendant possessed, based on information as to his age, education, intelligence, or prior contact with authorities, can never be more than speculation."

II

In light of this established practice, there is no denying that, by incorporating age into its analysis, the Court is embarking on a new expansion of the established custody standard. And since *Miranda* is this Court's rule, "not a constitutional command," it is up to the Court "to justify its expansion." This the Court fails to do.

In its present form, *Miranda's* prophylactic regime already imposes "high cost[s]" by requiring suppression of confessions that are often "highly probative" and "voluntary" by any traditional standard. Nonetheless, a "core virtue" of *Miranda* has been the clarity and precision of its guidance to "police and courts" ... The Court has, however, repeatedly cautioned against upsetting the careful "balance" that *Miranda* struck, and it has "refused to sanction attempts to expand [the] *Miranda* holding" in ways that would reduce its "clarity." Given this practice, there should be a "strong presumption" against the Court's new departure from the established custody test. In my judgment, that presumption cannot be overcome here.

A

The Court's rationale for importing age into the custody standard is that minors tend to lack adults' "capacity to exercise mature judgment" and that failing to account for that "reality" will leave some minors unprotected under *Miranda* in situations where they perceive themselves to be confined. I do not dispute that many suspects who are under 18 will be more susceptible to police pressure than the average adult. As the Court notes, our pre-*Miranda* cases were particularly attuned to this "reality" in applying the constitutional requirement of voluntariness in fact. It is no less a "reality," however, that many persons over the age of 18 are also more susceptible to police pressure than the hypothetical reasonable person. Yet the Miranda custody standard has never accounted for the personal characteristics of these or any other individual defendants.

Indeed, it has always been the case under *Miranda* that the unusually meek or compliant are subject to the same fixed rules, including the same custody requirement, as those who are unusually resistant to police pressure. *Miranda's* rigid standards are both overinclusive and underinclusive. They are overinclusive to the extent that they provide a windfall to the most hardened and savvy of suspects, who often have no need for *Miranda's* protections. And *Miranda's* requirements are underinclusive to the extent that they fail to account for "frailties," "idiosyncrasies," and other individualized considerations that might cause a person to bend more easily during a confrontation with the police. Members of this Court have seen this rigidity as a major weakness in *Miranda's* "code of rules for confessions." But if it is, then the weakness is an inescapable consequence of the *Miranda* Court's decision to supplement the more holistic voluntariness requirement with a one-size-fits-all prophylactic rule.

That is undoubtedly why this Court's *Miranda* cases have never before mentioned "the suspect's age" or any other individualized consideration in applying the custody standard. And unless the Miranda custody rule is now to be radically transformed into one that takes into account the wide range of individual characteristics that are relevant in determining whether a confession is voluntary, the Court must shoulder the burden of explaining why age is different from these other personal characteristics.

Why, for example, is age different from intelligence? Suppose that an officer, upon going to a school to question a student, is told by the principal that the student has an I.Q. of 75 and is in a special-education class. Are those facts more or less important than the student's age in determining whether he or she "felt ... at liberty to terminate the interrogation and leave"? An I.Q. score, like age, is more than just a number. And an individual's intelligence can also yield "conclusions" similar to those "we have drawn ourselves" in cases far afield of *Miranda*.

How about the suspect's cultural background? Suppose the police learn that a suspect they wish to question is a recent immigrant from a country in which dire consequences often befall any person who dares to attempt to cut short any meeting with the police. Is this really less relevant than the fact that a suspect is a month or so away from his 18th birthday?

The defendant's education is another personal characteristic that may generate "conclusions about behavior and perception." Under today's decision, why should police officers and courts "blind themselves," to the fact that a suspect has "only a fifth-grade education"? Alternatively, what if the police know or should know that the suspect is "a college-educated man with law school training"? How are these individual considerations meaningfully different from age in their "relationship to a reasonable person's understanding of his freedom of action"? The Court proclaims that "[a] child's age ... is different," but the basis for this *ipse dixit* is dubious.

I have little doubt that today's decision will soon be cited by defendants—and perhaps by prosecutors as well—for the proposition that all manner of other individual characteristics should be treated like age and taken into account in the *Miranda* custody calculus. Indeed, there are already lower court decisions that take this approach.

In time, the Court will have to confront these issues, and it will be faced with a difficult choice. It may choose to distinguish today's decision and adhere to the arbitrary proclamation that "age ... is different." Or it may choose to extend today's holding and, in doing so, further undermine the very rationale for the *Miranda* regime.

B

If the Court chooses the latter course, then a core virtue of *Miranda* — the "ease and clarity of its application" — will be lost. However, even today's more limited departure from *Miranda's* one-size-fits-all reasonable-person test will produce the very consequences that prompted the *Miranda* Court to abandon exclusive reliance on the voluntariness test in the first place: The Court's test will be hard for the police to follow, and it will be hard for judges to apply.

The Court holds that age must be taken into account when it "was known to the officer at the time of the interview," or when it "would have been objectively apparent" to a reasonable officer. The first half of this test overturns the rule that the "initial determination of custody" does not depend on the "subjective views harbored by ... interrogating officers." The second half will generate time-consuming satellite litigation over a reasonable officer's perceptions. When, as here, the interrogation takes place in school, the inquiry may be relatively simple. But not all police questioning of minors takes place in schools. In many cases, courts will presumably have to make findings as to whether a particular suspect had a sufficiently youthful look to alert a reasonable officer to the possibility that the suspect was under 18, or whether a reasonable officer would have recognized that a suspect's I.D. was a fake. The inquiry will be both "time-consuming and disruptive" for the police and the courts. It will also be made all the more complicated by the fact that a suspect's dress and manner will often be different when the issue is litigated in court than it was at the time of the interrogation.

Even after courts clear this initial hurdle, further problems will likely emerge as judges attempt to put themselves in the shoes of the average 16-year-old, or 15-year-old, or 13-year-old, as the case may be. Consider, for example, a 60-year-old judge attempting to make a custody determination through the eyes of a hypothetical, average 15-year-old. Forty-five years of personal experience and societal change separate this judge from the days when he or she was 15 years old. And this judge may or may not have been an average 15-year-old. The Court's answer to these difficulties is to state that "no imaginative powers, knowledge of developmental psychology, [or] training in cognitive science" will be necessary. Judges "simply need the common sense," the Court assures, "to know that a 7-year-old is not a 13-year-old and neither is an adult." It is obvious, however, that application of the Court's new rule demands much more than this.

Take a fairly typical case in which today's holding may make a difference. A 16-year-old moves to suppress incriminating statements made prior to the administration of *Miranda* warnings. The circumstances are such that, if the defendant were at least 18, the court would not find that he or she was in custody, but the defendant argues that a reasonable 16-year-old would view the situation differently. The judge will not have the luxury of merely saying: "It is common sense that a 16-year-old is not an 18-year-old. Motion granted." Rather, the judge will be required to determine whether the differences between a typical 16-year-old and a typical 18-year-old with respect to susceptibility to the pressures of interrogation are sufficient to change the outcome of the custody determination. Today's opinion contains not a word of actual guidance as to how judges are supposed to go about making that determination.

C

Petitioner and the Court attempt to show that this task is not unmanageable by pointing out that age is taken into account in other legal contexts. In particular, the Court relies on the fact that the age of a defendant is a relevant factor under the reasonable-person standard applicable in negligence suits. But negligence is generally a question for the jury, the members of which can draw on their varied experiences with persons of different ages. It also involves a *post hoc* determination, in the reflective atmosphere of a deliberation room, about whether the defendant conformed to a standard of care. The Miranda custody determination, by contrast, must be made in the first instance by police officers in the course of an investigation that may require quick decision making.

Equally inapposite are the Eighth Amendment cases the Court cites in support of its new rule. Those decisions involve the "judicial exercise of independent judgment" about the constitutionality of certain punishments. Like the negligence standard, they do not require on-the-spot judgments by the police.

Nor do state laws affording extra protection for juveniles during custodial interrogation provide any support for petitioner's arguments. States are free to enact additional restrictions on the police over and above those demanded by the Constitution or *Miranda*. In addition, these state statutes generally create clear, workable rules to guide police conduct. Today's decision, by contrast, injects a new, complicating factor into what had been a clear, easily applied prophylactic rule.

III

The Court's decision greatly diminishes the clarity and administrability that have long been recognized as "principal advantages" of *Miranda*'s prophylactic requirements. But what is worse, the Court takes this step unnecessarily, as there are other, less disruptive tools available to ensure that minors are not coerced into confessing.

As an initial matter, the difficulties that the Court's standard introduces will likely yield little added protection for most juvenile defendants. Most juveniles who are subjected to police interrogation are teenagers nearing the age of majority. These defendants' reactions to police pressure are unlikely to be much different from the reaction of a typical 18-year-old in similar circumstances. A one-size-fits-all *Miranda* custody rule thus provides a roughly reasonable fit for these defendants.

In addition, many of the concerns that petitioner raises regarding the application of the *Miranda* custody rule to minors can be accommodated by considering the unique circumstances present when minors are questioned in school. The *Miranda* custody rule has always taken into account the setting in which questioning occurs, restrictions on a suspect's freedom of movement, and the presence of police officers or other authority figures.

Finally, in cases like the one now before us, where the suspect is much younger than the typical juvenile defendant, courts should be instructed to take particular care to ensure that incriminating statements were not obtained involuntarily. The voluntariness inquiry is flexible and accommodating by nature, and the Court's precedents already make clear that "special care" must be exercised in applying the voluntariness test where the confession of a "mere child" is at issue. If *Miranda*'s rigid, one-size-fits-all standards fail to account for the unique needs of juveniles, the response should be to rigorously apply the constitutional rule against coercion to ensure that the rights of minors are protected. There is no need to run *Miranda* off the rails.

* * *

The Court rests its decision to inject personal characteristics into the *Miranda* custody inquiry on the principle that judges applying *Miranda* cannot "blind themselves to ... commonsense reality." *Miranda* frequently requires judges to blind themselves to the reality that many un-Mirandized custodial confessions are "by no means involuntary" or coerced. It also requires police to provide a rote recitation of *Miranda* warnings that many suspects already know and could likely recite from memory. Under today's new, "reality"-based approach to the doctrine, perhaps these and other principles of our *Miranda* jurisprudence will, like the custody standard, now be ripe for modification. Then, bit by bit, *Miranda* will lose the clarity and ease of application that has long been viewed as one of its chief justifications.

Notes

(a) If age is to be a factor in determining if a suspect is in custody during interrogation for purposes of *Miranda*, should not age be a factor in determining the appropriateness of the *Miranda* warnings and should interrogations for juveniles be handled differently than with adults?

(b) How does *J.D.B.* differ from *Roper* and *Graham*?

C. Abolition of the Juvenile Court System

1. Katherine Hunt Federle, *The Abolition of the Juvenile Court: A Proposal for the Preservation of Children's Rights*
16 J. Contemp. L. 23, 49–50 (1990)

The true stumbling block to a juvenile jurisprudence is the concept of power and capacity. Once overcome, the development and implementation of a jurisprudence sensitive to children's rights requires little restructuring of our present legal system. Rights are recognized and enforced by the courts which act as restraints on unfettered state power. No longer may we justify discriminatory treatment of children based on childhood. The abolition of the juvenile court is essential to the preservation of children's legal rights.

The abolition of the juvenile court will insure the adoption of a rights-based jurisprudence for children. The separate juvenile system, which has meaning only as long as a viable justification for treating children differently exists, no longer bears a relationship to the present reality of childhood. The elimination of the juvenile system will guarantee that those charged with violating the law will receive the full panoply of protections both constitutional and statutory. The criminal court will have jurisdiction over all those accused of criminal offenses. No longer will the courts resort to legal gymnastics in attempting to exonerate legal doctrine discriminating against children. The accused, whether an adult or a child, will receive the same guarantees and protections consistent with the Anglo-American legal system of individual rights.

Those who participate in such a court will reinforce the child's rights model. The attorney, who previously saw her role as guardian, will advance the interests of her client regardless of the client's age. The judge will no longer be a parental figure but will be a neutral and impartial arbiter of justice. Charging decisions by the prosecuting attorney will no longer reflect a highly interventionist parens patriae model but one consistent with concerns for community safety. Police behavior will conform to constitutional requisites in the revised system because of its adversarial nature. Finally, sentencing will be proportional to the seriousness of the crime rather than to the attitude of the child.

The abolition of the juvenile court proffers a more coherent legal model for the treatment of law violators. Criminalizing the juvenile court creates legal inconsistencies in the way children are treated. Automatic waiver provisions inherently contradict the concept of child incompetence and eliminate the very justification for a separate juvenile court. These provisions permit children to be tried as adults simply because they have been accused of an enumerated crime. Waiver, however, is no longer needed in the revised system because criminal courts traditionally are responsive to community concerns about crime and safety.

Status offense jurisdiction has no place in the revised legal system. Parents, schools, and other nonjudicial agencies will be required to deal with behavior with which the courts have had little success. Parents and teachers must learn to seek out nonlegal alternatives for the problems of truancy and incorrigibility. This will spur the creation of community-based alternatives to misbehavior. Removing the court from intervention in the daily lives of children is economical and will result in savings to the community.

The abolition of the juvenile court need not preclude an emphasis on rehabilitation and treatment of the young offender. Many criminal codes provide for alternatives to incarceration, and rehabilitation and treatment are not inconsistent with the exercise of the criminal court's jurisdiction. An alternative sentencing model for child offenders provides such an option and is not without precedent. In the federal system, for example, special sentencing provisions existed for adult offenders under the age of twenty-two. While alternative sentencing options and facilities for child offenders are consistent with the child's rights model, they may also have an ameliorative effect on sentencing schemes for adults. Thus, children's participation in the criminal system may force a revision of the proportionality doctrine.

2. Janet E. Ainsworth, *Re-Imagining Childhood and Reconstructing the Legal Order: The Case for Abolishing the Juvenile Court*
69 N.C.L. Rev. 1083, 1118–26, 1130–33 (1991)

Having an autonomous juvenile justice system with its own distinctive procedures made sense in a world that viewed the categories of "child" and "adult" as inherently antithetical in their essential attributes. Once the imagined nature of childhood changed and the child-adult dichotomy blurred, however, the ideological justification for a separate juvenile jurisprudence evaporated. With its philosophical underpinnings no longer consonant with the current social construction of childhood, the juvenile court now lacks a rationale for its continued existence other than sheer institutional inertia. All things being equal, inertia might not be an insupportable basis for maintaining the juvenile court. After all, dismantling the system would entail at least some political and economic costs. Indeed, overcoming the vested interests of such an entrenched institution could take a heroic political effort of will. Yet all things are not equal. Perpetuating an anachronistic juvenile court exacts its own costs, both ideological and practical. These costs compel me to conclude that the juvenile court ought to be abolished.

....

To the extent that today's juvenile court preserves its legacy of greater procedural informality than the adult criminal court, the procedural contrast between the two systems is the most salient feature of the juvenile justice system. This contrast may be more of a liability to the juvenile court than traditionally has been assumed, however. When juvenile court practice diverges from that observed in other courts, juvenile court seems less like a court at all. As Martha Minow observed, "due process notions are familiar to every child in this culture." Raised on a steady television diet of fictional courtroom drama and local news coverage of notorious criminal trials, American young people have an image of what a court proceeding should look like. The perfunctory bench trial typical of the juvenile court is not what they imagine a trial to be.

The gulf between the archetypical trial and its actualized caricature has significance for juveniles beyond the obvious conceptual dissonance it engenders. Like any other litigants, juvenile defendants invest the legal system with legitimacy only insofar as they see it to be a just system. That perception of justice is affected not merely by the litigants' degree of satisfaction with the outcome of the case, or its distributive justice, but also by their belief in its prescriptive fairness, or its procedural justice.

Extensive sociological research has explored the somewhat counter-intuitive notion that how one is treated in court may be at least as important as the ultimate verdict in shaping one's opinion about whether a system is just. According to these studies, the key factors contributing to a sense of procedural justice are consistency in the process, control of the process by the litigant, respectful treatment of the litigant, and ethicality of the fact-finder. Consistency in the process means both that the system always follows prescribed rules and that everyone is treated equally within the system. Process control is the litigant's ability to determine which issues will be contested and upon what basis the contest will proceed. Respectful treatment of the litigant connotes more than just courteous interchange; it also includes investing the litigant with the full complement of rights possessed by other actors in the system. Ethicality of the fact-finder entails a sense that the judge is honest, non-biased, forthright and non-arbitrary in adjudication.

Even in its current "constitutionally domesticated" version, juvenile court procedural practice cuts against these core notions of procedural justice. Treating juveniles differently from adults—by denying them jury trials, for example—violates the consistency norm of equal treatment for all and reminds the young that they do not have all of the rights assigned to full-fledged members of the society. Similarly, the paternalistic tendencies that juvenile court engenders in its functionaries undermines the norm of litigant process control. From judges to probation officers to defense counsel, juvenile court professionals all too frequently assume that juvenile accuseds are incapable of exercising sound judgment in making the decisions that affect their cases. Confidence in the ethicality of the fact-finder is undercut by the dual roles of the juvenile court judge as finder of fact and sentencing authority. Particularly for the repeat offender, the judge's knowledge of the accused's background and previous criminal record creates the unseemly appearance that guilt has been pre-judged. In the sentencing role, expressions by the judge of paternalistic concern for the juvenile accused coupled with stern judicial sanctioning likewise is inconsistent with the normative model of adjudicatorial behavior. All of these divergences from procedural justice norms strongly suggest that, in the eyes of juvenile respondents, the legitimacy of juvenile court is suspect.

As a consequence of this loss of legitimacy of the juvenile court, the process of legal socialization for a large segment of our youth has broken down. Legal socialization, or the inculcation of a society's approved norms and values regarding the law, has been described as a primary mechanism of social control. The legal system, along with the schools, has been considered the most important institution involved in legal socialization. In a legal culture as deeply permeated by due process concepts as ours, strict observance of procedural rights in and of itself contributes to an inculcation of the values of the social and political order. If juveniles perceive their exposure to the legal system as unjust, however, the legal socialization process fails. Ironically, conserving the current legal order may be possible only at the expense of abolishing the present dual system of adult and juvenile criminal jurisdiction.

3. Barry C. Feld, *The Transformation of the Juvenile Court*

75 Minn. L. Rev. 691, 717–25 (1991)

A strong, nationwide movement, both in theory and in practice, is repudiating therapeutic, individualized dispositions in favor of punitive sentences. When the Court decided *McKeiver* in 1971, no states used determinate or mandatory minimum sentences or administrative guidelines. In the middle to late 1970s, several states adopted "designated felony" and serious offender laws and sentencing guidelines. Since 1980, at least eleven more states have adopted determinate or mandatory minimum sentence laws or administrative guidelines, so that now about one-third of the states explicitly use punitive sentencing strategies. These formal changes and actual practices eliminate most of the differences between juvenile and adult sentencing. Imposing mandatory or determinate sentences on the basis of offense and prior record contradicts any therapeutic purposes and precludes consideration of a youth's "real needs." Revised juvenile purpose clauses and court decisions eliminate even rhetorical support for rehabilitation. As a result, "the purposes of the juvenile process have become more punitive, its procedures formalistic, adversarial and public, and the consequences of conviction much more harsh." All these changes repudiate the original assumptions that juvenile courts operate in a child's "best interests," that youths should be treated differently than adults, and that rehabilitation is an indeterminate process that cannot be limited by fixed-time punishment.

. . . .

The recent changes in juvenile court jurisdiction, sentencing, and procedures reflect ambivalence about the role of juvenile courts and the control of children. As juvenile courts converge procedurally and substantively with criminal courts, is there any reason to maintain a separate court whose only distinctions are procedures under which no adult would agree to be tried?

The juvenile court is at a philosophical crossroads that cannot be resolved by simplistic formulations, such as treatment versus punishment. In reality, there are no practical or operational differences between the two. Acknowledging that juvenile courts punish, imposes an obligation to provide all criminal procedural safeguards because, in the words of *Gault*, "the condition of being a boy does not justify a kangaroo court." While procedural parity with adults may sound the death-knell of the juvenile court, to fail to do so perpetuates injustice. To treat similarly situated juveniles differently, to punish them in the name of treatment, and to deny them basic safeguards fosters a sense of injustice that thwarts any efforts to rehabilitate.

Abolishing juvenile courts is desirable both for youths and society. After more than two decades of constitutional and legislative reform, juvenile courts continue to deflect, co-opt, ignore, or absorb ameliorative tinkering with minimal institutional change. Despite its transformation from a welfare agency to a criminal court, the juvenile court remains essentially unreformed. The quality of justice youths receive would be intolerable if it were adults facing incarceration. Public and political concerns about drugs and youth crime foster a "get tough" mentality to repress rather than rehabilitate young offenders. With fiscal constraints, budget deficits, and competition from other interest groups, there is little likelihood that treatment services for delinquents will expand. Coupling the emergence of punitive policies with our societal unwillingness to provide for the welfare of children in general, much less to those who commit crimes, there is simply no reason to believe that the juvenile court can be rehabilitated.

Without a juvenile court, an adult criminal court that administers justice for young offenders could provide children with all the procedural guarantees already available to adult defendants and additional enhanced protections because of the children's vulnerability and immaturity. The only virtue of the contemporary juvenile court is that juveniles convicted of serious crimes receive shorter sentences than do adults. Youthfulness, however, long has been recognized as a mitigating, even if not an excusing, condition at sentencing. The common law's infancy defense presumed that children below age fourteen lacked criminal capacity, emphasized their lack of fault, and made youthful irresponsibility explicit. Youths older than fourteen are mature enough to be responsible for their behavior, but immature enough as to not deserve punishment commensurate with adults. If shorter sentences for diminished responsibility is the rationale for punitive juvenile courts, then providing an explicit "youth discount" to reduce adult sentences can ensure an intermediate level of just punishment. Reduced adult sentences do not require young people to be incarcerated with adults; existing juvenile prisons allow the segregation of offenders by age.

Full procedural parity in criminal courts coupled with mechanisms to expunge records, restore civil rights, and the like can more adequately protect young people than does the current juvenile court. Abolishing juvenile courts, however, should not gloss over the many deficiencies of criminal courts such as excessive case loads, insufficient sentencing options, ineffective representation, and over-reliance on plea bargains. These are characteristics of juvenile courts as well.

Ideological changes in strategies of social control and the conception of children produced the juvenile court. One of these ideas, strategies of social control, no longer distinguishes juvenile from criminal courts. Despite their inability to prevent or reduce youth crime, juvenile courts survive and even prosper. Despite statutory and judicial reforms, official discretion arguably has increased rather than decreased. Why, even without empirical support, does the ideology of therapeutic justice persist so tenaciously?

The answer is that the social control is directed at children. Despite humanitarian claims of being a child-centered nation, our cultural conception of children supports institutional arrangements that deny the personhood of young people. In legal doctrine, children are not entitled to liberty, but to custody. We care less about other people's children than we do our own, especially when those children are of other colors or cultures.

Children, especially by adolescence, are more competent than the law acknowledges. We can recognize young people's competence as a basis for greater autonomy without equating it with full criminal responsibility. Many social institutions—families, schools, the economy, and the law—systematically disable adolescents, deny them opportunities to be responsible and autonomous, and then use the resulting immaturity to justify imposing further disabilities. Rejecting the juvenile court's premise that young people are inherently irresponsible can begin a process of reexamining childhood that extends to every institution that touches their lives.

4. Irene Merker Rosenberg, *Leaving Bad Enough Alone: A Response to the Juvenile Court Abolitionists*

1993 WIS. L. REV. 163, 165–76, 184–85 (1993)

I oppose the abolitionists despite hard-earned experience that tugs me in their direction. In the late 1960s and early 1970s, I was an attorney for the Family Court Branch of the Legal Aid Society in New York City, representing indigent children in delinquency, supervision, and neglect cases. This stint left me with highly negative views of the juvenile court. The judges were by and large uncaring and ignorant of both the rudiments of due process and the basic principles of child development and psychology; the probation department had an overwhelming caseload; and the state facilities in which the minors were detained and to which they were committed were walking Eighth Amendment violations. In addition, I have been writing and teaching about juvenile justice and children's rights for almost twenty years, and I am aware of the various ways in which the states do not fulfill their promises to provide care, treatment, and rehabilitation, and to assure adequate procedural protection. And yet, as much as I agree with Barry Feld that the juvenile courts impose punishment in the name of treatment and give reduced constitutional and procedural protection to children, I do not share his belief in the abolitionist solution, even though it is prompted by a despair that I do share. The proposed alternative of trial in the adult criminal courts, where I have also practiced, is even worse than what we now have [in juvenile court].

Before deciding whether to abandon the juvenile courts, two basic questions must be addressed: (1) is the disparity in procedural and constitutional protection between the adult and juvenile courts significant enough to justify opting out of the juvenile justice system; and (2) if children are tried in the criminal courts, will their immaturity and vulnerability be taken into account adequately in assessing culpability and determining sentences? In my view, the answers to these questions are no and no.

First, the abolitionists claim that there is a significant disparity between the constitutional and procedural rights afforded adults charged with crime and children charged with delinquency. In my opinion, these differences are not as substantial as they appear to be, or at least not substantial enough to be a basis for giving up on the juvenile justice system. The conceded inequality in safeguards should not blind us to the incremental changes over the years that have benefitted children. The *Gault* line of cases does give alleged delinquents significant constitutional protection. Indeed, in cases such as *In re Winship* and *Breed v. Jones*, applying the reasonable doubt standard and the double jeopardy requirement to delinquency adjudicatory proceedings, the Supreme Court treated delinquency and adult criminal trials as functionally equivalent for purposes of the implicated constitutional guarantees.

Moreover, even where the Court has given juveniles less, as in *New Jersey v. T.L.O.*, the disparity is often more apparent than real. In *T.L.O.*, the majority concluded that school officials could conduct warrantless searches of students without adhering to the probable cause requirement; school searches need only be reasonable under all the circumstances. By virtue of this decision, public school students seem to be accorded less Fourth Amendment protection than adults. School searches, however, come within the category of so-called administrative inspections, and searches of adults in such contexts are also upheld without adherence to either the warrant or probable cause requirements. Furthermore, even with respect to traditional criminal searches, the *Illinois v. Gates* standard, which determines probable cause based on a totality of the circumstances, is not that different from the reasonableness test articulated in *T.L.O.*

To be sure, in *Schall v. Martin*, which upheld a vague preventive detention law for alleged delinquents, the Court made much of the differences between children and adults, and used these distinctions as a basis for giving children less constitutional protection. The *Schall* holding clearly allowed the state substantial leeway in detaining minors accused of crime and reinvigorated a constricted due process methodology for ascertaining the rights of alleged delinquents. Yet, in the end *Schall* was simply a prelude to the Court's decision in *United States v. Salerno*, rejecting substantive due process and Eighth Amendment challenges to the federal preventive detention statute governing adults. Thus, notwithstanding *Schall*'s emphatic pronouncement that children are entitled to custody rather than liberty, *Salerno*, which relies on *Schall*, put adults in roughly the same position as far as preventive detention is concerned.

The major setback for juveniles was denial of the right to a jury trial in *McKeiver v. Pennsylvania*. As Professor Ainsworth has noted, in the insular world of the juvenile courts, a jury is necessary to protect children from oppression by the government and to assure more accurate and impartial fact-finding. I do not, however, view the loss of even this right as catastrophic. After all, there are relatively few jury trials in the adult criminal court. Instead, the right to trial by jury is primarily a chip to be used in the poker game of plea bargaining — a game of far greater seriousness in the adult courts, where the sentencing stakes, at least for serious offenses, are much higher. Nonetheless, denial of the jury trial to juveniles as a matter of federal constitutional law is significant. One way of dealing with the problem is state law reform. In fact, a number of states already grant juveniles such a right as a matter of state law, and the "New Federalism" is an opportunity for advocates to push for jury trials in juvenile courts.

More broadly, I think we have not sufficiently appreciated that in a substantial number of jurisdictions state law gives children many of the same rights as adult defendants, and sometimes more. Texas, for example, has a very generous Family Code providing, *inter alia*, jury trials with unanimous verdicts, a Fourth Amendment exclusionary rule, and enhanced *Miranda* protections. This is not to say that juvenile and adult rights are coterminous in Texas — the police, for instance can arrest a juvenile without a warrant in cases where state law would require one for adults. And, to add insult to injury, that diminished level of protection travels with the minor to criminal court if he or she is transferred for trial as an adult. On the other hand, a child has greater rights than an adult regarding confessions, and that enhanced protection also applies in criminal court if the juvenile is waived over. It is questionable whether such increased protection would be preserved if the juvenile courts were abolished and children were instead tried as adults in the criminal courts.

In determining whether to abandon the juvenile courts because of the disparity in protection, it is also necessary to make a realistic assessment of the constitutional safeguards available in the criminal courts. The Burger and Rehnquist Courts have, after all, taken their toll. Much of *Miranda* has been eviscerated, and the Fourth Amendment and the exclusionary rule are being severely constricted. If children are tried in the criminal courts, they will receive only this diluted constitutional protection, and since minors are less likely to invoke their rights and more likely to waive them, effectively they will still receive less protection than adults. While it is true that the latest Supreme Court decisions give juvenile little more than the right to fundamental fairness, that also is just about all the Justices are now affording to adult defendants. Even the revered Sixth Amendment right to counsel, deemed essential for safeguarding all other guarantees in the Bill of Rights, is very much under attack.

In addition, this low level of constitutional protection granted to adults is available only theoretically. Nationwide, approximately 90% of defendants plead guilty. A series of Supreme Court decisions establishes that if a defendant does plead guilty, almost all antecedent constitutional violations are waived. So even if children were tried in the criminal courts where they would be entitled to the same guarantees as adults, it is just as likely, if not more so, that they would join the vast majority of their older counterparts who waive such protection to secure the purported benefit of a reduced sentence. In any event, do we really want the child's fate to be determined on an ad hoc basis by individual prosecutors and defense attorneys pursuant to plea bargaining, rather than by a juvenile court judge who has at least some obligation to act in the youth's best interest?

It seems to me that underlying the views of the abolitionists, at least unconsciously, is a somewhat idealized or romanticized vision of adult courts in which the criminal guarantees of the Bill of Rights are meaningfully enforced. Yes, there is a right to trial by jury that is missing in the juvenile court unless supplied by state law. Yes, there is a right to counsel that, as Professor Feld has pointed out, is too often denied in practice in juvenile court. And I surely would not denigrate either of these important safeguards. At the same time, however, the reality of adult criminal proceedings is crowded courtrooms in which justice is dispensed through waivers and pleas negotiated by defense attorneys who are often less than zealous and well-prepared advocates, and in which racism is at least as much a fact of life as in juvenile court. For the most part, the typical criminal court in urban areas is a harsh, tough, mean institution cranking out pleas, with a few pauses for individualized attention. It is no place for an adult defendant to be, much less a child. Given such an environment in the criminal courts, will children really perceive the criminal justice process as fairer than the juvenile courts, as Professor Ainsworth has suggested?

Initially, perhaps there would be a burst of concern for the kiddie defendants. But once the glow wore off, and that would not take long, it would be back to business as usual: treadmill processing for adults both over and under the age of eighteen. Let us face it: As bad as the juvenile courts are, the adult criminal courts are worse. Adding a new class of defendants to an already overburdened system can only exacerbate the situation, all to the detriment of children.

That brings me to the second question. Professor Feld and other abolitionists believe that if children are tried in criminal court, rationales will be developed to give them special protection in ascertaining guilt and punishment. While I agree that is what children should get, I am not so sure that is what they will get. This looks a lot like having your cake and eating it too, a difficult request to be making in these hard-nosed, law-and-order times. On the one hand, the abolitionists are asking that children be treated as adults in order to secure equal constitutional guarantees, and on the other, they are asking that children be treated as children in order to protect their unique disabilities. While it is true that taking competency differentials of juveniles into account is simply a means of attaining parity with adults, skeptical legislators may consider these demands internally inconsistent. Thus, although Professor Ainsworth argues that, according to social science research, "the adult-child distinction is a false dichotomy that can no longer support disparate justice systems," she also asserts that after abolition youth will continue to be viewed as a mitigating factor in adult court sentencing. But assuming such a "false dichotomy," puzzled legislators and judges might be pardoned for asking why youth should then be a basis for more lenient punishment.

If states are unwilling to give minors enhanced constitutional and procedural protection when they are within the supposedly benevolent confines of the juvenile court, why would they do so in the criminal court? Bringing children within the criminal jurisdiction is an assertion by the state that minors do not deserve specialized treatment. While it is true that the state will no longer have the bogus rehabilitation argument as a basis for diminishing constitutional protection, the state may argue that because it has elected to treat children and adults the same, there is no reason to give youngsters enhanced safeguards.

Moreover, it is unclear whether the common law infancy defense, which Barry Feld believes will be available for children in criminal court, is constitutionally mandated as a matter of federal law. As the plurality noted in *Powell v. Texas*, "this court has never articulated a general constitutional doctrine of mens rea." In his concurring opinion, Justice Black agreed that "the legislatures have always been allowed wide freedom to determine the extent to which moral culpability should be a prerequisite to conviction of a crime."

. . . .

Abandoning the juvenile court is an admission that its humane purposes were misguided or unattainable. I do not believe that. We should stay and fight — fight for a reordering of societal resources, one that will protect and nourish children. For example, Mark Soler of the Youth Law Center in San Francisco, has argued that the juvenile court must be re-imagined so as to focus on the child's dispositional needs, making the court serve a coordinating function that assures the provision of a wide range of services that benefit the child. Other commentators stress the need for enhanced constitutional and procedural protection in the adjudicative stage of the proceedings. These differing goals are not inconsistent. We can and should seek both procedural and dispositional reform in the juvenile courts.

Despite all their failings, of which there are many, the juvenile courts do afford benefits that are unlikely to be replicated in the criminal courts, such as the institutionalized intake diversionary system, anonymity, diminished stigma, shorter sentences, and recognition of rehabilitation as a viable goal. We should build on these strengths rather than abandon ship.

Notes

(a) What is the most persuasive argument in favor of abolition of the juvenile court?

(b) What is the best argument against abolition of the juvenile court?

(c) Is it likely that the abolitionists' position will win out? Why?

(d) If *McKeiver*, holding that the right to a jury trial does not apply to delinquency hearings, were reversed, or if all states provided jury trials in juvenile adjudicatory proceedings, do you think that abolitionists would change their position? Why?

(e) Do the recent Supreme Court cases; *Roper*, *Graham*, and *J.D.B.*; diminish or strengthen the position of the abolitionists to eliminate the juvenile courts?

Chapter 3

Right to Counsel in the Juvenile Court: Theory and Practice

A. The Various Stages of a Delinquency Proceeding at Which the Right to Counsel Could Theoretically Apply

1. Ellen Marrus, *Best Interests Equals Zealous Advocacy: A Not So Radical View of Holistic Representation for Children Accused of Crime*

62 Md. L. Rev. 288, 303–12 (2003)

[As with the other constitutional rights granted to delinquents by the *Gault* Court, the right to counsel applies] only to the adjudicatory hearing, at which guilt or innocence of a penal offense is determined. Most jurisdictions, however, have as a matter of state law, extended the right to counsel to dispositional hearings where the "sentence" is imposed....

[There are, however, several other stages of delinquency proceedings where the right to counsel could theoretically apply — intake, detention, revocation of probation, placement review, placement extension, and appeal. *See* discussion in Chapter 1, *supra*. Representation at these other stages is less frequent than at adjudicatory and dispositional hearings. With respect to each of these stages we will examine the way counsel's representation, if it were afforded, could affect the child].

Intake probation officers often determine whether to refer alleged delinquents to court or to divert them to community based agencies. Whether a child is referred to court depends on a variety of factors including: [the child's] admission of guilt, evidence of guilt, seriousness of the offense, [his or her] prior record, school attendance, and home environment. It is in effect a dispositional hearing at the front end of the proceeding, and if one values representation at the latter stage, it would be just as valuable at intake. Alternatively, the intake process could be viewed as a preliminary hearing, which for criminal defendants is a "critical stage" of the proceedings requiring the appointment of counsel for indigents. Furthermore, any information gathered at the intake level [in juvenile court] is often used by probation officers for detention and dispositional recommendations and may be relayed to prosecutors [and judges]. These conditions make the presence of counsel a necessity rather than a luxury. Nonetheless, the right to counsel at intake is a rarity.

Detention hearings decide whether the child is to be released or remanded to a juvenile facility, and are thus akin to bail hearings at which defendants in criminal court have the right to legal representation. Detention affects the ability of the attorney to gather information and can be harmful to the child's development, even assuming the remand facility is safe. Additionally, a child who is detained is more likely to be adjudicated a delinquent than one who is returned home and is more likely to be placed in a locked facility at disposition. [T]he right to counsel at detention hearings is becoming more widespread, but as of [now], is not universal.

Adjudicatory hearings settle whether a child committed the alleged criminal acts, and [are], except for the lack of a jury in most jurisdictions, [much like] adult criminal trials. The court considers whether there is proof beyond a reasonable doubt that the person charged committed a violation of the penal law. Of course, *Gault* makes representation at this stage constitutionally mandatory. [T]his right to counsel, however, is generally subject to waiver, and as a result many children appear without counsel at these critical hearings. Furthermore, the lack of a jury, the inbred nature of the juvenile court bureaucracy, and the secrecy surrounding juvenile court hearings tend to make trials in juvenile court overly informal and mask the momentous consequences.

The dispositional hearing is analogous to an adult criminal sentencing proceeding where counsel is constitutionally required. As noted above, the *Gault* Court did not mandate counsel at this stage in juvenile court, yet, in most jurisdictions, assigned counsel will represent the child at both the adjudicatory and dispositional hearings. [C]ounsel's role in juvenile dispositional hearings is both more important and more complicated than in adult sentencing hearings. Even though there are mandatory commitments for some offenses in juvenile court, there are generally more sentencing options than in criminal court. Additionally, the programs used by juvenile probation vary in degree of treatment and structure. Whether the child goes to a prison-like training school, a residential treatment center, is placed in foster care, or remains at home on probation is of great importance to the child's future development. Indeed, one might argue that it is at this stage that defense counsel's active participation can be most effective [in] protecting his or her client. Unfortunately, it is here that many attorneys defer to the "expert" recommendations of an overworked probation department.

Similarly, probation revocation hearings are essentially the same as adult revocation proceedings. The court considers whether the probationer violated the terms of his or her probation and the appropriate sanction. The violations can be the commission of criminal law offenses or of specific terms of probation, such as failure to report to the probation officer or failure to keep away from persons convicted of crime. Furthermore, for children, the violation can even be something as simple as failing to attend school or staying out late at night. For adults, there [is] no federal constitutional right ... to counsel at a probation revocation hearing [either under the Sixth Amendment or the Due Process Clause of the Fourteenth Amendment]. However, the Court in *Gagnon v. Scarpelli* held that in certain circumstances due process would require ... an attorney if there are substantial reasons which "make revocation inappropriate;" the defendant makes a "colorable claim" that he did not violate probation; and the probationer appears to be incapable of speaking for himself. That last factor alone, in the context of juvenile revocation proceedings, could mandate a per se right to counsel for juvenile probationers. Most jurisdictions, however, grant counsel at a juvenile probation revocation proceeding only under certain circumstances.

Placement reviews and extension of placement requests are also critically important for the child. These actions can result in transfers to harsher and more secure facilities or commitments to longer periods of incarceration and supervision. These proceedings are akin to parole decisions, loss of good time determinations, transfers, and disciplinary actions, and as such, require no right to counsel as they are viewed as correctional decisions. [M]any of the factors going into these ultimate decisions can be based on disputed facts, yet an attorney is viewed as an intruder rather than as someone who can act as an advocate for the child-client. [Moreover], very few states assign counsel at such proceedings for adults or children.

Adult defendants are entitled to counsel on their first appeal as a matter of Fourteenth Amendment due process and equal protection, even though the Supreme Court has never held that appellate review is of constitutional proportions in criminal cases. The *Gault* Court declined to determine whether due process requires a transcript and appellate review of juvenile proceedings. Nonetheless, all jurisdictions provide appellate review in both criminal and juvenile cases as a matter of state law. However, many states do not grant juveniles a right to appointed counsel for appeals. Yet, how can a minor navigate the complex and arcane rules of appellate review? Without legal expertise, errors below cannot be rectified; therefore, juvenile trial court decisions are effectively insulated from corrective appellate review. At all stages of juvenile delinquency proceedings (intake, detention, adjudication, disposition, revocation, placement review, placement extension, and appeal), the role of counsel for children is critical, but is often lacking. [Yet, a]s the *Gault* Court note[d], "The child 'requires the guiding hand of counsel at every step in the proceedings against him.'"

2. IJA-ABA Juvenile Justice Standards Annotated: Standards Relating to Counsel for Private Parties

74–75, 80 (Robert E. Shepherd, Jr., ed. 1996)

Part II. Provision and Organization of Legal Services

2.3 Types of proceedings.

(a) Delinquency and in need of supervision proceedings.

(i) Counsel should be provided for any juvenile subject to delinquency or in need of supervision proceedings.

(ii) Legal representation should also be provided the juvenile in all proceedings arising from or related to a delinquency or in need of supervision action, including mental competency, transfer, post-disposition, probation revocation, and classification, institutional transfer, disciplinary or other administrative proceedings related to the treatment process which may substantially affect the juvenile's custody, status or course of treatment. The nature of the forum and the formal classification of the proceedings is irrelevant for this purpose.

. . . .

2.4 Stages of proceedings.

(a) Initial provision of counsel.

(i) When a juvenile is taken into custody, placed in detention or made subject to an intake process, the authorities taking such action have the responsibility promptly to notify the juvenile's lawyer, if there is one, or advise the juvenile with respect to the availability of legal counsel.

(ii) In administrative or judicial postdispositional proceedings which may affect the juvenile's custody, status or course of treatment, counsel should be available at the earliest stage of the decisional process, whether the respondent is present or not. Notification of counsel and, where necessary, provision of counsel in such proceedings is the responsibility of the judicial or administrative agency.

....

Part IV. Initial Stages of Representation

4.1 Prompt action to protect the client.

Many important rights of clients involved in juvenile court proceedings can be protected only by prompt advice and action. Lawyers should immediately inform clients of their rights and pursue any investigatory or procedural steps necessary to protection of the client's interests.

B. The Reality of the Right to Counsel in Juvenile Court

1. Anthony M. Platt, *The Child Savers: The Invention of Delinquency*

164–72 (1977)

There is strong ideological and organizational pressure from legislatures, judges, and legal commentators to repress adversary tactics in juvenile court. The Florida legislature, for example, has responded to *Gault* with a provision for legal representation through the state division of youth services. This provision reinforces the traditional policy of benign paternalism by assuming that state officials will act in the best interests of young persons charged with crimes. Most juvenile court judges deny the importance of adversary trials and "see the lawyer's chief value as lying in the areas of interpretation of the court's approach and securing cooperation in the court's disposition rather than more traditional roles of fact elicitation and preservation of legal rights."

Recent studies of the work of lawyers in Chicago's juvenile court provide some insight into the impact of the *Gault* decision. Less than 3 percent of the city's 13,605 listed attorneys filed appearances in the year following the passage of Illinois' juvenile court act in 1965. Lawyers in the upper echelons of their profession came into contact with juvenile court by accident only. Juvenile cases are given even lower priority than traffic or misdemeanor cases. Prior to governmental funding of legal programs to the poor through the Office of Economic Opportunity, some lawyers from influential firms donated time and money on a voluntary basis. Now, however, most of these lawyers come into contact with juvenile court only as a favor to a friend or an influential client. With the expansion of public defender and legal aid programs, members of large and medium-size firms have less and less to do with the problems of poor people.

Private lawyers in juvenile court are typically small-fee practitioners who have solo practices and do predominantly trial work. Like most small-fee work, juvenile cases are rarely profitable, and the effort they require often seems out of proportion to the seriousness of the case, the fee, and the good that can be accomplished. Furthermore, lawyers are only sporadically given priority on the hearing of cases and are not accorded special respect by court functionaries. Under these circumstances, it is understandable why the small-fee lawyer feels uncomfortable in a system which does not acknowledge the informal practices characteristic of his work in other courts. Lawyers who are forced to sit about the court building soon become insensitive to its depressing surroundings and the rows of poor people waiting for officialdom to intervene in their lives. The hypocrisy of private hearings becomes apparent as juveniles are led in handcuffs through the public corridors. The consensus among lawyers is that juvenile court is a dreary and discouraging place.

Small-fee lawyers do not generally regard juvenile court as a punitive organization. They are well aware that the court lacks the formal procedures available in other courts, but find this limitation unobjectionable in practice. The views of lawyers about the rights of children differ quite fundamentally from those expressed by the Supreme Court and academics. Lawyers apply different standards to juvenile clients because they are children, not necessarily because lawyers have been constrained by the court's welfare orientation. A lawyer typically has conscientious reservations about helping a juvenile to "beat a case" and, if a case is won on a technicality, he feels obliged to personally warn his client against the dangers of future misconduct.

Lawyers see it as part of their duty as adults and public officials to sit down and talk with juveniles on their own level, to impress them with the importance of telling the truth, to deter them from committing similar acts in the future, and to reinforce to the child what the judge has said. The client is in turn expected to show penitence and gratitude—human qualities which are similarly appreciated by juvenile court judges. Any attempt at defense tactics is complicated by the unpredictability of juvenile clients who have poor memories, don't remember, don't have the social and intellectual maturity of an adult, are likely to blurt out and convict themselves, and easily spill the beans. A lawyer is hesitant to put on the witness stand a client who is likely to "crack on cross-examination" or "clam up" and convict himself through silence.

A juvenile client poses further special problems of defense because his whole family is involved in the legal proceeding. Although a lawyer appears on behalf of a juvenile, he is usually hired by and therefore responsible to the juvenile's parents. A client is consulted for factual and biographical information, and instructed how to dress and behave in court, but others decide what should be done to him. Lawyers from influential firms who represent children from a background similar to their own find that juvenile court is a reasonable place to do business because all parties to the case share parental pessimism about "troublesome" youth.

The *Gault* decision encouraged legal aid and public defender offices to send lawyers into juvenile court. In Chicago, the juvenile court public defender maintains two seemingly conflicting definitions of his job. As an officer of the court, whose prevailing ethic is child saving, he sees himself as a social worker with a law degree. As a social worker, he must acknowledge that juveniles are naturally dependent and require supervision by mature adults. At the same time, however, he is a defense attorney who takes pride in the craft of advocacy.

The public defender resolves this dilemma by doing what is best for a kid. If he considers his client a good kid, he will do everything to have the charge dismissed or will plead guilty in return for a warning or light sentence, such as probation. Bad kids are given up on. The public defender assumes, along with all juvenile court functionaries that little can be done to "help" these clients. He pleads them guilty and cooperates to process them into reformatories. They have long records, they are charged with serious offenses, and they are likely to antagonize judges with their poor school record. The public defender does not waste his time or credit on bad kids because a serious effort on their behalf would only jeopardize his chances with more worthy defendants.

Although the public defender enjoys the contest of a trial, advocacy is nevertheless a limited commodity in Chicago's juvenile court. Appeals are rare and impractical, jury trials are not allowed, police testimony is rarely challenged, and witnesses are often unreliable when faced with cross-examination. Also, the public defender is more than a personal social worker or lawyer for individual clients. He is an "officer of the court" and an employee of a system in which he must operate from day to day.

2. Janet E. Ainsworth, *Re-Imagining Childhood and Reconstructing the Legal Order: The Case for Abolishing the Juvenile Court*

69 N.C.L. Rev. 1083, 1126–30 (1991)

. . . .

In the literature on the contemporary juvenile court, a harsh indictment of the legal counsel available to juveniles is a repeated refrain. Notwithstanding that more than twenty years ago the Supreme Court constitutionally guaranteed legal counsel to juveniles charged with crimes, the most recent empirical studies reveal that a shockingly high proportion of juveniles still are tried without lawyers. As it turns out, those juveniles may be the lucky ones; over and over again, studies have shown that juveniles with lawyers fare worse in juvenile court than those proceeding without counsel, being more likely to be incarcerated and jailed for longer periods than if represented pro se.

These statistics reveal only the correlation between legal representation and more severe dispositions, and not why this disadvantage exists. One possibility is that lawyers hurt their clients through sheer incompetence and inadequacy in their advocacy. Another is that lawyers in juvenile court may deliberately solicit harsher penalties, believing that such dispositions are in their clients' best interests in the long run. Still another explanation is that juvenile court judges may display conscious or unconscious antagonism toward the idea of attorneys in juvenile court, and take out their hostility on the represented clients. Or it may be that the juvenile court judge has prejudged the case and predetermined the likely sentence before the proceedings began, and to save the system time and money, encourages waiver of counsel in those cases where the probable sanction is comparatively light. What is clear, however, is that all of these factors find factual support in current studies of the juvenile court.

As is demonstrated in two in-depth examinations of juvenile court procedures, trials in juvenile court are frequently "only marginally contested," marked by "lackadaisical defense efforts." Defense counsel generally make few objections, and seldom move to exclude evidence on constitutional grounds. Defense witnesses rarely are called, and the cross-examination of prosecution witnesses is "frequently perfunctory and reveals no design or rationale on the part of the defense attorney." Closing arguments are sketchy when they are made at all. Watching these trials, one gets the overall impression that defense counsel prepare minimally or not at all. The New York State Bar Association study estimated that in forty-five percent of all juvenile trials, counsel was "seriously inadequate"; in only five percent could the performance of defense counsel be considered "effective representation."

One explanation for the abysmal performance of defense counsel is that lawyers in juvenile court are all too frequently both inexperienced and overworked. Particularly in jurisdictions where juveniles have no right to jury trials, public defender offices often assign their greenest attorneys to juvenile court to season them. Supervision from senior attorneys is not always what might be desired, and caseloads in these high volume courts are crushing. Moreover, in a forum without jury trials, there is a tendency for lawyers to cut corners in these cases of comparatively low public visibility, a tendency often tacitly encouraged by judges anxious to process cases as expeditiously as possible. Under these circumstances, it is no wonder that juvenile bench trials are seldom models of zealous defense advocacy.

In addition, defense lawyers who routinely practice in juvenile court face tremendous institutional pressures to cooperate in maintaining a smoothly functioning court system. The defense lawyer who is seen as obstreperous in her advocacy will be reminded subtly, or overtly if necessary, that excessive zeal in representing her juvenile clients is inappropriate and counter-productive. If she ignores these signals to temper her advocacy, the appointed defense lawyer is vulnerable to direct attacks, such as having her fees slashed or being excluded from the panel of lawyers from which the court makes indigent appointments. Seldom are such crude measures necessary, however. For most defense lawyers, withstanding the psychological debilitation attendant upon being the sustained focus of judicial and prosecutorial disapproval is hopeless.

Perhaps the most pervasive and insidious reason for less than zealous defense advocacy is the ambiguity felt by many juvenile court lawyers concerning their proper role. The legacy of decades of paternalistic parens patriae ideology is still evident in the attitudes of many defense lawyers, who cannot help thinking of themselves as charged, at least in part, with a responsibility to act in their clients' long term best interests rather than scrupulously to safeguard their legal rights. Despite the clear ethical mandate to represent juveniles on the same terms and with the same zeal as they would adults, many defenders nevertheless find themselves deeply torn between their professional obligation to press their clients' legitimate legal claims and their paternalistic inclination to help the court address their clients' often desperate social needs. Even lawyers who have not internalized this role conflict may face external pressure from judges and probation officers to conform to a guardian-like role.

In all of these ways, the institution of the autonomous and distinct juvenile court inherently discourages effective assistance of counsel for juvenile defendants. As long as a separate juvenile court system exists, separate advocacy models appear to be the inevitable result. Although rooting out paternalistic attitudes toward children cannot be accomplished by fiat, abolishing the juvenile court would go a long way toward ensuring that juveniles charged with crimes get the same caliber of legal counsel, operating under the same standards of zealous advocacy, as adult defendants receive.

3. A Call For Justice: An Assessment of Access to Counsel and Quality of Representation in Delinquency Proceedings

4–5, 6–7 (1995)

This report [by the American Bar Association Juvenile Justice Center, in conjunction with the Youth Law Center and Juvenile Law Center], is a national assessment of the current state of representation of youth in juvenile court and an evaluation of training, support, and other needs of practitioners. The assessment sought information about excellent work being done in the field as well as problems in representation of youth. It examines all stages of representation, from the time of arrest to the time of discharge from the juvenile justice system, and covers all regions of the country, including urban, suburban, and rural areas.

THE ASSESSMENT

The assessment consisted of a national survey of hundreds of juvenile defenders, site visits to a variety of jurisdictions, interviews with people working in the field, client interviews, an extensive literature search, and meetings and consultation with the project's national Advisory Board. The assessment focused on public defenders and court-appointed counsel. We also examined the small but important role played by law school clinical programs and non-profit children's law centers. We compared our observations with the Juvenile Justice Standards developed by the Institute for Judicial Administration and the American Bar Association.

ASSESSMENT RESULTS

We observed many attorneys who vigorously and enthusiastically represented their young clients. Those lawyers challenged the prosecution to prove its case through pertinent evidentiary objections, motions, arguments, and contested hearings. In court, they were articulate and prepared. Their arguments were supported with relevant facts and law. When their clients were faced with lengthy incarceration, they often provided the court with compelling alternatives. The children they represented appeared to understand the proceedings. There was ongoing communication between children and their attorneys, both in and out of court. The attorneys made good use of family members, other significant adults, experts, and potential service providers to demonstrate to the court the appropriateness of non-institutional placements.

But this type of vigorous representation was not widespread, or even very common. Often what we were told in interviews and what was reported in mail survey responses did not square with what we personally observed in courtrooms and detention centers. The assessment raised serious concerns that the interests of many young people in juvenile court are significantly compromised, and that many children are literally left defenseless.

[The assessment was concerned with the high rate of waiver of counsel by children, heavy caseloads, late appointment of counsel, lack of pre-trial preparation and motion practice, lack of support staff, lack of training, failure to aggressively pursue sound defenses at trial, and lack of appeals. States followed this investigation with individual state reports that found the same problems the national group did. So far twelve states have participated in the assessment process—Georgia, Kentucky, Louisiana, Maine, Maryland, Montana, North Carolina, Ohio, Pennsylvania, Texas, Virginia, and Washington. These individual reports are on line at www.abanet.org/crimjust/juvjus/assessments.html].

4. Indigency

a. Ellen Marrus, *Best Interests Equals Zealous Advocacy: A Not So Radical View of Holistic Representation for Children Accused of Crime*

62 Md. L. Rev. 288, 312–26 (2003)

Like adults, the child's right to appointed counsel is dependent on indigency, which is a flexible criterion. Often this means ... the *Gault* right to counsel is problematic. Theoretically, there are two possible approaches that courts could take. One is a per se presumption that the child, who is the accused, has no source of financial resources to pay counsel absent a trust fund or movie star status. The parents' resources would simply not be relevant, either before or after the proceedings. Currently, no state takes that position, although it is one that would serve the best interests of the child. Under such an approach, the minor is assured of appointed counsel without reference to parental finances, which removes a source of tension between parent and child in this context. Moreover, most children in juvenile court come from poor families. Thus, hearings to ferret out the small minority who are able to retain counsel are inefficient and has serious implications for the question of waiver of counsel.

The second approach, which is used by all states, determines indigency based on the parents' resources. Jurisdictions, however, use two different methods of ascertaining the parents' ability to pay for counsel. In the first method, the determination of indigency is made at the beginning of the case. If the parents are not deemed indigent, the courts will not appoint an attorney, leaving it to the parents' discretion to retain counsel. In other jurisdictions, courts appoint counsel to represent the child *ab initio*, and indigency is ascertained after the fact. If the parents are found able to afford counsel, the court will recoup the attorney's fees from them after the delinquency proceedings are concluded. Although it may superficially appear that the answer to the question of indigency is thus largely procedural, in fact, there are enormous substantive ramifications from the way in which indigency is evaluated.

When a court determines indigency based on the parents' income before trial, it makes the ability of the juvenile to obtain representation dependent on a third party's resources over which the child has no control. This means that if a judge determines that the parents' income is sufficient to hire an attorney, the court will not appoint one. If the parents do not obtain legal representation for their child, he or she will be unrepresented, unless the court orders the parents to retain counsel under pain of contempt or appoints counsel for the child and orders the parents to reimburse the attorney. In contrast, when the court appoints counsel at the beginning of the case and determines indigency at the end of the proceedings, the child is assured of representation throughout the case.

The substantive issue of what constitutes indigency is also problematic. Many courts will find that parents are not indigent, even when the family has few resources and can barely make ends meet. Thus, the working poor may be left without adequate representation, subjected to contempt proceedings, or faced with reimbursal orders.

Although parents may barely surpass the guidelines for indigency, they may choose not to hire an attorney for various reasons. Parents with limited circumstances, may, for example, decide that hiring a lawyer is not as important as paying rent, buying food, buying a new car needed for work, providing a talented child with music lessons or a sick sibling with special medical treatment. Parents, poor or well-to-do, may have other reasons for not retaining counsel. They may have been experiencing difficulties with their offspring or they may think the child needs to be taught a lesson and that a lawyer would interfere with that [objective]. Also, they may take the position that there is no reason to hire a lawyer because the child is guilty of committing the delinquent act, and they may not be aware of the possible legal defenses and the need for representation at disposition. Alternatively, parents may not hire a lawyer even when the child says he is innocent, on the theory that the juvenile court system is benign and the judge will believe their child's version of the facts. Finally, parents may choose not to hire an attorney because they want the child removed from their home, thus placing the interests of the parents and child in direct conflict.

Even though it is preferable for courts to appoint counsel at the beginning of the proceedings and determine the parents' ability to reimburse the state afterwards, there are serious consequences even to that approach. Forcing parents to pay for retained counsel when they are unable or unwilling to pay an attorney may exacerbate existing family tensions and result in further acting-out by the child. Moreover, as we will see, imposing such a financial obligation on the parents may also affect the issue of waiving counsel.

b. IJA-ABA Juvenile Justice Standards Annotated: Standards Relating to Pretrial Court Proceedings

254 (Robert E. Shepherd, Jr., ed. 1996)

Part V: Respondent's Right To Counsel

5.3 Juvenile's eligibility for court-appointed counsel; parent-juvenile conflicts.

In any delinquency proceeding, if counsel has not been retained for the juvenile, and if it does not appear that counsel will be retained, the court should appoint counsel. No reimbursement should be sought from the parent or the juvenile for the cost of court-appointed counsel for the juvenile, regardless of the parent's or juvenile's financial resources.

5. Waiver of the Right to Counsel

a. Barry C. Feld, *The Right to Counsel in Juvenile Court: An Empirical Study of When Lawyers Appear and the Difference They Make*

79 J. Crim. L. & Criminology 1185, 1200–01 (1989)

Evaluations of rates of representation in Minnesota also indicate that a majority of youths are unrepresented. Professor Folded reported enormous county-by-county variations within Minnesota in rates of representation, ranging from a high of over 90% to a low of less than 10%. A substantial minority of youths removed from their homes or confined in state juvenile correctional institutions lacked representation at the time of their adjudication and disposition. Significant numbers of unrepresented juveniles continue to be incarcerated in other jurisdictions as well.

There are a variety of possible explanations for why so many youths are still unrepresented: parental reluctance to retain an attorney; inadequate or non-existent public-defender legal services in nonurban areas; a judicial encouragement of and readiness to find a waiver of the right to counsel in order to ease administrative burdens on the courts; cursory and misleading judicial advisories of rights that inadequately convey the importance of the right to counsel and suggest that the waiver litany is simply a meaningless technicality; a continuing judicial hostility to an advocacy role in traditional treatment-oriented courts; or a judicial predetermination of dispositions with nonappointment of counsel where probation or nonincarceration is the anticipated outcome. Whatever the reasons and despite *Gault*'s promise of counsel, many juveniles facing potentially coercive state action never see a lawyer, waive their right to counsel without consulting an attorney or appreciating the legal consequences of relinquishing counsel, and face the prosecutorial power of the state alone and unaided.

b. Thomas Grisso, *What We Know About Youths' Capacities as Trial Defendants*

YOUTH ON TRIAL: A DEVELOPMENTAL PERSPECTIVE ON JUVENILE JUSTICE
148–49, 154–55 (Thomas Grisso & Robert G. Schwartz, eds. 2000)

Understanding the legal process and one's choices in it requires knowing not only that one has certain rights, but also knowing what a right is. Defendants' decisions about waiving the right to avoid self-incrimination (for example, in the context of a guilty plea) or waiving the right to a jury trial will be ill-informed if they do not conceptualize a right as a legal entitlement, providing protection that authorities in the justice system cannot arbitrarily set aside.

According to theoretical views of children's development of conceptualizations of laws and rules, most preadolescent children are expected to have a *preconventional* view of laws as mandates that are made and controlled by persons in authority. Cognitive and social development early in adolescence makes possible the capacity, although not automatically or uniformly realized, for development of a *conventional* concept of law. This perspective conceptualizes laws as consensual agreements among members of society for the collective benefit. A third, more abstract conceptualization of law as derived from universal principles also is possible (*postconventional*).

Read found that about one third of delinquent fifteen- to sixteen-year-olds saw rights as conditional rather than automatic. In two studies with a broad age range of delinquent adolescents, less than one quarter (compared with about one half of adult ex-offenders) defined a right in a way that indicated that it was an entitlement ("You can do it no matter what"). They tended more often to construe a right as something one is "allowed to do." Thus, when asked "what should happen" if a judge at a hearing discovers that a youth "wouldn't talk to the police," one-half to two-thirds of adolescents (but only 30 percent of adults) did not recognize that the court should not penalize a defendant for having asserted a right to avoid self-incrimination....

These comparisons of delinquent adolescents with adults suggest that a larger proportion of delinquent youths bring to the defendant role an incomplete comprehension of the concept and meaning of a right as it applies to adversarial legal proceedings.

....

Beliefs about Legal Counsel

Studies ... indicated that even most young adolescents understand that defense counsel plays an advocacy role. But does this necessarily mean that they believe that this advocacy is available in their own cases? [One study] ... found that a majority of high school students believed that attorneys and police officers are dishonest. A majority of juvenile defendants in several studies voiced disappointment in their lawyers' advocacy after delinquency hearings, and many have said that they trusted their probation officers more than their attorneys. Such attitudes are not conducive to collaborative interactions between lawyers and adolescent clients.

Other studies have documented adolescents' more specific misbeliefs or distortions of the attorney-client role that might interfere with their collaboration. [One study] ... found that, compared with nineteen-year-olds, a greater number of younger adolescents (and a substantial proportion of sixteen-year-olds as well) incorrectly believed that the attorney was authorized to tell judges or police officers what was discussed in confidential attorney-defendant conversations. When I asked detained juveniles ... why defendants must be truthful with their lawyers, about one third of them (but only about 10 percent of adult ex-offenders) believed that this was necessary so that the lawyer could decide whether or not to advocate the defendant's interests, whether to report the defendant's guilt to the court, or whether to "let him go or send him up." Adolescents often seem to believe that defense attorneys defend the innocent but become more like police officers for the guilty.

c. Ellen Marrus, *Best Interests Equals Zealous Advocacy: A Not So Radical View of Holistic Representation for Children Accused of Crime*
62 Md. L. Rev. 288, 316–20 (2003)

Per *Gault*, every jurisdiction provides the right to counsel for juveniles accused of crime, at least at the adjudicatory hearing. That right, however, is not to the automatic assignment of counsel, but rather is the right to choose whether to have counsel. This, of course, raises the issue of waiver, an issue that is particularly critical when dealing with youthful offenders.

Although states are currently inconsistent in their handling of waivers of counsel by juveniles, there are two main approaches for determining when waiver of counsel by juveniles is appropriate. The first category does not allow a juvenile to waive the right to counsel under any circumstances. In effect, these states find the adult's right to self-representation and the requirement that the waiver of counsel and guilty pleas be an intentional relinquishment of a known right inapplicable to alleged delinquents. In other words, a child may neither waive counsel, nor represent herself, even if it is only to plead guilty. Jurisdictions in the second category allow children to waive their right to counsel at any stage, so long as it is knowing, intelligent, and voluntary.

In the first category, the courts or the legislatures have presumably determined that counsel's participation in the proceedings is necessary to assure due process for the child and at the same time is helpful to the court. In addition, they may view it as unlikely that any child can make a knowing and intelligent waiver of counsel. Even if some minors do have the capacity to waive, some courts may believe they are few in number, and a per se rule is more efficient than trying to look at all the circumstances to determine if a child is making a knowing and voluntary waiver.

In the jurisdictions that permit children to dispense with counsel, courts set different criteria for the acceptability of a waiver. In some instances, courts may permit children to waive the right to counsel on their own, presumably after the court explains the nature of the proceedings and the possible consequences, or they may only be able to waive counsel if they first consult with an attorney or their parents. There are several difficulties with this approach, even when parents and attorneys must be consulted first. Studies indicate that children may not be able to make knowing or intelligent waivers on their own, at least with respect to the limited right to counsel to protect their Fifth Amendment interests. For example, Dr. Thomas Grisso has shown that fifteen-year-olds cannot fully comprehend their rights under *Miranda*, no matter how simply explained, and therefore cannot make knowing and intelligent waivers. While sixteen- and seventeen-year-olds may have a slightly easier task in understanding the impact of waiving these legal rights, they still do not have the same grasp of the concepts as an adult. Further, although it may be easier for a child to understand why it would be more important to have a lawyer in court proceedings rather than during custodial interrogations, it is doubtful that most children can make that distinction.

Furthermore, it is much easier for an adult in a position of authority, such as a judge or parent, to pressure a child into waiving counsel than it would be to apply this pressure to an adult. For example, judges may inform minors that the court wants to help them and return them home quickly, or that if they want a lawyer, the case would have to be adjourned. Particularly if the child is also under the strain of detention, he or she may feel that involvement by an attorney would only exacerbate the problem further. Judges, especially those who must be elected, may have incentives for getting children to waive counsel, such as saving state or county funds, expediting hearings, and imposing harsh punishment to maintain a law and order reputation. Indeed, there are studies indicating that judges impose harsher punishment on children who do not waive their right to counsel.

If a parent does not want to be responsible for the costs involved in retaining an attorney or otherwise does not want counsel representing the child, the parent may encourage the child to waive legal representation. Even an attorney consultation before the child can waive his or her right to counsel may not be sufficient to protect the minor. Since the lawyer is not yet retained or appointed, and has no relationship with the youth, he or she may not spend sufficient time with the child to explain the consequences and to elicit sufficient facts about the case in order to properly advise the child of the benefits an attorney can provide. Moreover, the attorney may have an incentive to get alleged delinquents to waive counsel so that he or she may maintain a good relationship with the judge.

[In general], I believe children should be able to make the ultimate decisions in legal proceedings. Therefore, if an attorney represents to the court that he has explained the consequences and ramifications of waiver, and in his opinion, the child understands what he or she is giving up, and the judge inquires of the juvenile to assure that he or she understands the right to counsel and the consequences of waiver, the court should accept the child's waiver. However, based on my experience in the juvenile court system, I ultimately opt for a per se rule prohibiting waiver of counsel by minors. I simply do not believe that the standards-based approach to waiver in this context is one that is sufficiently protective of children, nor do I believe that appellate review will properly ferret out the cases in which the court accepted improper waivers. Mandatory counsel also prevents overbearing judges and parents from influencing a child to waive counsel and prevents judges from imposing punishment based on the child's choice of waiver. Therefore, I believe the per se rule is desirable for the child and the courts.

Nevertheless, this position is fraught with its own dangers. The children are more likely to distrust the attorneys and simply see them as another government official foisted on them. In such cases, it will be difficult for counsel to elicit the necessary information and provide a proper defense. Moreover, the attorney may still cater to overbearing judges by pleading his or her client guilty. On balance, I still conclude that the court must assign counsel to represent children appearing in juvenile court regardless of the child's wishes. After that point, however, as I will explain later, the accused child should determine how the defense is to be conducted.

d. Mary Berkheiser, *The Fiction of Juvenile Right to Counsel: Waiver in the Juvenile Courts*

54 Fla. L. Rev. 577, 640–45 (2002)

Society too has an interest in assuring that the trial process is fair and in keeping with the commands of due process. Juvenile waiver of the right to counsel impairs the fairness of delinquency proceedings because lawyers are themselves the means of securing a fair trial and maintaining due process throughout the proceedings. Moreover, courts which freely permit juveniles to waive their right to counsel undermine their own "institutional interest in the rendition of just verdicts." Due process guarantees every juvenile facing a delinquency adjudication a fundamental, absolute right to a fair trial, just as it does adult criminal defendants. "Where, for one reason or another, the proceedings fall short of the standard the Constitution imposes, and a defendant does not receive a fair trial, he is deprived of due process of law." Thus, it is "not only the defendant who 'suffers the consequences' when a fair trial is denied, but the justice system itself. Put another way, the state has a compelling interest, related to its own political legitimacy, in ensuring both fair procedures and reliable outcomes in criminal trials * * *." The same reasoning applies to juveniles facing delinquency adjudication and possible confinement to a juvenile institution.

Juvenile courts that sacrifice the right to counsel for judicial expediency unduly jeopardize both the accused juvenile's rights and their own and the public's interest in a fair trial. The state has no legitimate interest in the perpetuation of procedures which place juveniles' substantial liberty interests at risk of deprivation when those same procedures violate the most basic right of all Americans accused of criminal acts to a fair trial. To the contrary, the state has a paramount interest in ensuring a fair system of juvenile justice, just as the juvenile defendant has a paramount interest in minimizing the risk of an unwarranted loss of his liberty.

Mandatory appointment of counsel also may overcome the sometimes prejudicial effects of selective appointment of counsel. Although a 1970 study showed that providing counsel to juveniles resulted in fewer dismissals and commitments to juvenile institutions, later research reported the opposite result in connection with dispositions. Represented juveniles often received more severe treatment than those who were not represented. Juvenile court judges' resistance to and even resentment of, defense lawyers may explain the latter result. However, if all children receive representation by counsel, judges will no longer be able to penalize those who appear before them with counsel, for to do so would mean penalizing everyone. As bad as some juvenile courts are, they are unlikely to divorce themselves completely from the rehabilitative aims of the juvenile court. If some judges remain recalcitrant voters and appointing bodies will have to exercise their will and refuse to retain them.

. . . .

In sum, the automatic appointment of nonwaivable counsel furthers the interests of everyone: the juvenile facing delinquency charges, the juvenile court, the juvenile justice system, and the public at large.

The analysis here would be incomplete, however, if it did not address the concerns of some that a per se rule of nonwaivability would contradict important principles of developmental psychology, juvenile justice, and due process. One commentator has cited the Supreme Court's adoption of due process as the constitutional basis for juvenile rights to buttress her arguments in favor of adolescent autonomy, stating "the Court reminds us of the law's intrinsic respect for the dignity of persons, whether children, adolescents, or adults. Though not explicitly addressed by the Court, implicit in its rulings affording constitutional rights to adolescents is the corollary ability to exercise or waive those rights * * *." Moreover, studies have shown that youthful offenders are more likely to respond positively to court intervention when they are active participants in the process than when the process is simply imposed upon them. Social scientists have further observed that "[w]hen young people are helped to take responsibility for their actions in programs designed to foster positive development in the way they think, how they define themselves in their families and with peers, their view of right and wrong, and their recovery from abuse, they are unlikely to be dangerous once they become adults."

These principles form the basis for opposition to a prohibition against juvenile waiver of right to counsel.

. . . .

[M]andating representation by counsel, [however,] does not deny juveniles the opportunity to exercise their individual autonomy. As clients, juveniles maintain the ability to actively participate in the judicial process and to accept personal responsibility for their decisions concerning, *inter alia*, whether to accept a plea and waive the right to a trial and whether to testify at trial. The only decision that is taken out of their hands by the proposed prohibition is whether to waive the right to counsel. Given the studies of juvenile courts' implementation of *Gault* and the results of the case law research conducted for this Article, continued reliance on juvenile court judges to conduct waiver proceedings that give due attention to the particular needs of juveniles is not sound public policy. Instead, prohibiting waiver and assuring that every child facing delinquency charges in juvenile court has the assistance of counsel will provide the due process that is lacking in many juvenile courts today. Taking this one bold step also should help restore confidence in a juvenile justice system that many believe has lost its way.

e. IJA-ABA Juvenile Justice Standards Annotated: Standards Relating to Pretrial Court Proceedings

254–55 (Robert E. Shepherd, Jr., ed. 1996)

Part V: Respondent's Right to Counsel

5.2 Notification of the juvenile's right to counsel.

As soon as a juvenile's right to counsel attaches under standard 5.1 B, the authorities should advise the juvenile that representation by counsel is mandatory, that there is a right to employ private counsel, and that if private counsel is not retained, counsel will be provided without cost.

Part VI: Waiver Of The Juvenile's Rights: The Role Of Parents And Guardians Ad Litem In The Delinquency Proceedings

Waiver of the Juvenile's Rights

6.1 Waiver of the juvenile's rights: in general.

A. Any right accorded to the respondent in a delinquency case by these standards or by federal, state, or local law may be waived in the manner described below. A juvenile's right to counsel may not be waived.

6. The Role of Parents and the Right to Counsel

a. Ellen Marrus, *Best Interests Equals Zealous Advocacy: A Not So Radical View of Holistic Representation for Children Accused of Crime*

62 Md. L. Rev. 288, 320–21, 325 (2003)

An attorney representing adults in criminal court usually has to deal only with her client. In juvenile court there is an added wrinkle—the parents. In *Gault*, Justice Fortas recognized the parental interest in delinquency cases and required that both the child and parent be advised of the right to counsel. However, he also made clear that counsel was to be appointed to "represent the child." Many parents find it difficult to believe that the child is the client, and therefore, the one who makes the ultimate decisions. They feel entitled to sit in on attorney-client interviews and to determine the direction of the representation. In doing so, parents often clash with the attorney on what should be done. Additionally, parents will often try to subvert their children's decision-making power by telling them they must do what they (the parents) want. Furthermore, some parents will provide information to the probation department which is then used against the child, and indeed, parental complaints are the basis for many petitions for violation of probation.

In the criminal courts, relatives and friends are under no illusion as to the consequences of the criminal proceeding. Therefore, they tend to look to the attorney as the expert who can shield the defendant from criminal sanctions. On the other hand, parents do not always understand what can happen to their children in juvenile court, because they may view it as a therapeutic institution. In such cases, the parents see the attorney as an intruder who may stand in the way of what [they view] is beneficial to the child.

. . . .

In sum, parents of children alleged to be delinquents can be an impediment to zealous advocacy by insisting on sitting in on attorney-client interviews, demanding that their children plead guilty, testifying against their children, or trying to hide neglectful behavior including their own complicity in the crime [with which the child is charged]. Not all parents present such problems and it is helpful when parents are on the child's side. The attorney, however, must be aware at all times that the child, not the parent, is the client. If there is a clash between parent and child, the child must come first.

b. IJA-ABA Juvenile Justice Standards Annotated: Standards Relating to Pretrial Court Proceedings

138 (Robert E. Shepherd, Jr., ed. 1996)

Part VIII: Standards For The Defense Attorney

8.1 Conflicts of Interest.

The potential for conflict of interest between an accused juvenile and his or her parents should be clearly recognized and acknowledged. In every case, doubt as to a conflict should be resolved by the appointment of separate counsel for the child and by advising parents of their right to counsel and, if they are unable to afford counsel, of their right to have the court appoint such counsel. All parties should be informed by the initial attorney that he or she is counsel for the juvenile, and that in the event of disagreement between a parent or guardian and the juvenile, the attorney is required to serve exclusively the interests of the accused juvenile.

c. Consider This Hypothetical

An attorney is representing a child who is accused of larceny. The child comes from a poor family in which expensive sneakers are a luxury, and he readily admits to his attorney that he stole a fellow student's Nike shoes. In addition, the boy has problems in school with bouts of absenteeism. After the interview, he advises his attorney that he does not want to plead guilty and asks the attorney to meet with his parents to explain his decision to have a trial notwithstanding his guilt. When the parents are told that their son committed the crime, but does not want to plead guilty, the parents react with anger and want to force him to plead. The consequences of their child's being adjudicated a delinquent are explained to them, including, because of his school problems, possible placement in a state facility. The parents are also told a good likelihood exists that the sneakers are inadmissible because they were obtained as a result of an unlawful search and seizure. Without this evidence, the child can not be convicted. The parents insist their child plead guilty. What is the attorney's appropriate course of action?

C. Models of Representation

1. Emily Buss, *The Missed Opportunity in Gault*

70 U. CHI. L. REV. 39, 51 (2003)

The achievement of the special aims of the juvenile justice system all depends on a juvenile's effective participation. The special developmental status of children suggests that effective participation requires a set of procedures very different from those afforded adults. But just as with adults, these procedures will need to be protected as rights to withstand the compromising pressures of resource limitations and power disparities.

To secure children's meaningful participation, their proceedings must be comfortable, comprehensible, and swift. Children should be allowed to speak directly with witnesses rather than left to watch their lawyer's formal, and likely inscrutable, examinations. Lawyers might still serve an important role as legal advisors, while relinquishing the role of spokesperson to their child clients. Because judges have no special expertise in communicating with children or assessing their needs, they might be replaced by other more qualified decisionmakers. Social service professionals would have the benefit of subject matter expertise, whereas non-professional adults known to the child might be in the best position to secure the comfortable participation of that child. Whoever the decisionmaker, the child should be afforded a meaningful opportunity to speak with her directly at considerable length on more than one occasion. To ensure that the accused appreciates the connection between self and offense, and offense and response, proceedings should last no longer than a few weeks from the time of the accusation to the time of final disposition.

2. Leslie Abramson, The Defense Is Ready: Life in the Trenches of Criminal Law

105 (1997)

With adults, it's ethically appropriate to do whatever your client wants, so long as it's legal.... But when it's a kid who's being wrongheaded, you have to recognize that the child doesn't necessarily have the maturity to make wise choices. You overrule him when necessary. And you try to do something that will make his life better, even if he doesn't see the logic.

3. Thomas Welch, *Delinquency Proceedings—Fundamental Fairness for the Accused in a Quasi-Criminal Forum*

50 MINN. L. REV. 653, 695 (1966)

The attorney who participates in juvenile proceedings must leave his criminal court strategy behind. He must contribute his own efforts toward implementing the philosophy of the juvenile court. If the procedures used are questionable within the context of juvenile court, he should seek to revise them on appeal and elsewhere. However, he must critically appraise his own approach to the juvenile forum to avoid dogmatisms borrowed wholesale from criminal law. Maximum resistance is not always in his client's best interests. His client is one who is presumed by all of society to be incapable of deciding his ultimate best interests. His role must include that of confidant and spokesman, yet he must temper his resistance to the court by recognizing that the child may be headed for greater difficulty in the future. Counsel may invite future trouble if his actions indicate to the child that the court is a state institution which will only impose on the individual. Further, he must maintain and defend his client's rightful standing in the proceedings, and yet leave room for the state's legitimate interests once it has justified its right to act.

4. Ellen Marrus, *Best Interests Equals Zealous Advocacy: A Not So Radical View of Holistic Representation For Children Accused of Crime*

62 MD. L. REV. 288, 334, 341–42, 345–47 (2003)

The model of holistic lawyering that I propose permits, and indeed requires the lawyer to act as a lawyer. While zealous advocacy informs the entire model, the attorney also is associated with other professionals in a team. The combined skills of each team member contribute to the kind of advocacy that truly ensures the best interests of the child. This model requires money, access to professionals in other disciplines, a keen appreciation of the dangers of the juvenile court system, attitudinal changes regarding the attorney child-client relationship, the necessity for adversarial representation, and expertise in child development and criminal, juvenile, and civil court law and practice. Even attorneys with limited means can employ aspects of this model....

Simply stated, my proposal of ideal holistic lawyering for minors charged with juvenile delinquency encompasses a team approach. The team should include attorneys who specialize in juvenile law, social workers, educators, therapists, psychologists, psychiatrists, investigators, and criminal and civil law attorneys who work together to provide high quality representation for the child-client.

. . . .

Children, when properly informed of all matters by the team, can make good decisions regarding their representation. Unless there are compelling circumstances, the child, if he or she wishes, should be present for team meetings and have access to reports. The issues must be explained in a way that is child-friendly, and the client should be urged to provide feedback and direction to team members. Children in juvenile court often do not understand what is happening to them, what the possible consequences are, or how selecting different choices can affect their lives. At the very least, children in juvenile court have to be kept informed. Many children will ultimately ask the lawyer to make the decision, particularly when the juvenile is very young. That is fine, because the child is deciding to let the lawyer decide. What is important is that the child knows he or she has a say in the outcome. Of course, the older the child, the greater the likelihood that the child, after being informed, will elect to make the ultimate decision. Realistically, however, based on my experience, almost all children, even older adolescents, will elect to follow their attorney's recommendation. That too is fine, because the child is still the decisionmaker.

. . . .

Is there a downside to my model of holistic lawyering, particularly if it results in a factually guilty child's acquittal? While it may be distasteful for some to facilitate such a result, I view it as no worse than doing the same for an adult defendant. Indeed, an argument could be made that "getting children off" in juvenile court is even more important than in adult criminal court. Many children commit criminal acts, even serious ones, and then outgrow their impulsive behavior even without juvenile court intervention. In fact, it is more likely that the child will develop normally without the labeling and incarceration that the juvenile court imposes. Studies show that children adjudicated delinquents are more likely to become recidivists as adults.

But are we teaching the child that crime is okay as long as you have good lawyers? Furthermore, are trials not simply a waste of time and resources since most children are, in fact, guilty, and there is usually enough evidence to support an adjudication of delinquency? Starting backwards with the "efficiency" and "everyone charged is guilty" arguments, the difficulty is that most adults charged with a crime are also guilty. Yet few argue that they should not have a right to test the government's proof, even though the lawyer in defense of a "guilty" person may have to cross-examine witnesses who are telling the truth so as to make it appear that they are lying or mistaken. Moreover, there is an even stronger argument that children, even if guilty, should have a trial. A trial brings home to children the realization that they committed criminal acts and are deserving of punishment. A guilty plea may obviate that lesson and children may feel that they are being punished for their confession of guilt rather than their criminal acts. Furthermore, a plea of not guilty necessarily slows down the treadmill dispensing of justice that is prevalent both in adult and juvenile court. The judge is forced to listen and see the child not just as another burglar, but as an individual with unique characteristics. I am not suggesting that there should be a trial in every case. For various strategic and tactical reasons it may be better for the child to plead guilty, such as in cases where the facts are so horrendous it would be better that the judge not hear the gruesome and overwhelming evidence.

With respect to the argument that getting guilty children off can result in future crime because it engenders an attitude of being able to get away with anything as long as you have a good lawyer, it is well to remember that such a belief is grounded in reality. By insisting on proof beyond a reasonable doubt, the child is learning another, perhaps more important lesson; he or she is valued by the system, and that the system, although imperfect, assures that individuals count and that it is better to free a guilty person than to convict an innocent one. It has also been shown that when people understand how the system works and the rules to be followed, they are more likely to become law-abiding citizens. Alternatively, children may see the acquittal as getting a second chance, particularly when they are told why they "got off." Children are likely to recognize that the circumstances leading to the acquittal may not occur again in the future and will take this opportunity as a way of staying out of trouble.

5. Ten Core Principles for Providing Quality Delinquency Representation Through Public Defense Delivery Systems

National Juvenile Defender Center

PREAMBLE

A. Goals of These Principles

The Ten Core Principles for Providing Quality Delinquency Representation through Public Defense Delivery Systems provide criteria by which a public defense delivery system may fully implement the holding of *In re Gault*. These Principles offer guidance to public defense leaders and policymakers regarding the role of public defenders, contract attorneys, or assigned counsel in delivering zealous, comprehensive and quality legal representation on behalf of children facing both delinquency and criminal proceedings. In applying these Principles, advocates should always be guided by defense counsel's primary responsibility to zealously defend clients against the charges leveled against them and to protect their due process rights.

Delinquency cases are complex and their consequences have significant implications for children and their families. Therefore, every child client must have access to qualified, well-resourced defense counsel. These resources should include the time and skill to adequately communicate with a client so that lawyer and client can build a trust-based attorney-client relationship and so that the lawyer is prepared to competently represent the client's interests. These Principles elucidate the parameters of this critical relationship already well established in legal ethics rules and opinions.

In 1995, the American Bar Association's Juvenile Justice Center published A Call for Justice: An Assessment of Access to Counsel and Quality of Representation in Delinquency Proceedings, a national study that revealed major failings in juvenile defense across the nation. Since that time, numerous state-based assessments have documented in detail the manner in which these failings result in lifelong, harmful consequences for our nation's children. These Principles provide public defense leaders and policymakers a guide to rectifying systemic deficits and to providing children charged with criminal behavior the high quality counsel to which they are entitled.

B. The Representation of Children and Adolescents is a Specialty.

Public defense delivery systems must recognize that children and adolescents are different from adults. Advances in brain research cited favorably by the Supreme Court *in Roper v. Simmons* confirm that children and young adults do not possess the same cognitive, emotional, decision-making or behavioral capacities as adults. Public defense delivery systems must provide training regarding the stages of child and adolescent development.

Public defense delivery systems must emphasize that juvenile defense counsel has an obligation to maximize each client's participation in his or her own case in order to ensure that the client understands the court process and to facilitate informed decision making by the client. Defense attorneys owe their juvenile clients the same duty of loyalty that adult criminal clients enjoy. This coextensive duty of loyalty requires the juvenile defense attorney to advocate for the child client's expressed interests with the legal knowledge, skill, thoroughness and preparation reasonably necessary for the representation.

C. Public Defense Delivery Systems Must Pay Particular Attention to the Most Vulnerable and Over-Represented Groups of Children in the Delinquency System.

Because research has demonstrated that involvement in the juvenile court system increases the likelihood that a child will subsequently be convicted and incarcerated as an adult, public defense delivery systems should pay special attention to providing high quality representation for the most vulnerable and over-represented groups of children in the delinquency system.

Nationally, children of color are severely over-represented at every stage of the juvenile justice process. Defenders must zealously advocate for the elimination of the disproportionate representation of minority youth in juvenile courts and detention facilities.

Children with mental health and developmental disabilities are also overrepresented in the juvenile justice system. Defenders must address these needs and secure appropriate assistance for these clients as an essential component of quality legal representation.

Drug- and alcohol-dependent juveniles and those dually diagnosed with addiction and mental health disorders are more likely to become involved with the juvenile justice system. Defenders must advocate for appropriate treatment services for these clients.

Research shows that the population of girls in the delinquency system is increasing, and that girls' issues are distinct from boys'. Gender-based interventions and the programmatic needs of girls in the juvenile delinquency system, who have frequently suffered from abuse and neglect, must be assessed and appropriate gender-based services developed and funded.

The special issues presented by lesbian, gay, bisexual and transgender youth require increased awareness and training to ensure that advocacy on their behalf addresses their needs.

TEN PRINCIPLES

1. The Public Defense Delivery System Upholds Juveniles' Constitutional Rights Throughout the Delinquency Process and Recognizes The Need For Competent and Diligent Representation.

   A. Competent and diligent representation is the bedrock of a juvenile defense attorney's responsibilities.

   B. The public defense delivery system ensures that children do not waive appointment of counsel and that defense counsel are assigned at the earliest possible stage of the delinquency proceedings.

   C. The public defense delivery system recognizes that the delinquency process is adversarial and provides children with continuous legal representation throughout the proceedings including, but no limited to, detention, pre-trial motions or hearings, adjudication, disposition, post-disposition, probation, appeal, expungement and sealing of records.

   D. The public defense delivery system includes the active participation of the private bar or conflict office whenever a conflict of interest arises for the primary defender service provider or when the caseload justifies the need for outside counsel.

2. The Public Defense Delivery System Recognizes that Legal Representation of Children is a Specialized Area of the Law.

A.   The public defense delivery system recognizes that representing children in delinquency proceedings is a complex specialty in the law that is different from, but equally as important as, the representation of adults in criminal proceedings. The public defense delivery system further acknowledges the specialized nature of representing juveniles prosecuted as adults following transfer/waiver proceedings.

B.   The public defense delivery system leadership promotes respect for juvenile defense team members and values the provision of quality, zealous and comprehensive delinquency representation services.

C.   The public defense delivery system encourages experienced attorneys to provide delinquency representation and strongly discourages use of delinquency representation as a training assignment for new attorneys or future adult court advocates.

3. The Public Defense Delivery System Supports Quality Juvenile Delinquency Representation Through Personnel and Resource Parity.

A.   The public defense delivery system encourages juvenile specialization without limiting access to promotions, financial advancement, or personnel benefits for attorneys and support staff.

B.   The public defense delivery system provides a professional work environment and adequate operational resources such as office space, furnishings, technology, confidential client interview areas and current legal research tools. The system includes juvenile representation resources in budgetary planning to ensure parity in the allocation of equipment and resources.

4. The Public Defense Delivery System Uses Expert and Ancillary Services to Provide Quality Juvenile Defense Services.

A.   The public defense delivery system supports requests for expert services throughout the delinquency process whenever individual juvenile case representation requires these services for quality representation. These services include, but are not limited to, evaluation by and testimony of mental health professionals, education specialists, forensic evidence examiners, DNA experts, ballistics analysts and accident reconstruction experts.

B.   The public defense delivery system ensures the provision of all litigation support services necessary for the delivery of quality services, including, but not limited to, interpreters, court reporters, social workers, investigators, paralegals and other support staff.

5. The Public Defense Delivery System Supervises Attorneys and Staff and Monitors Work and Caseloads.

A.   The leadership of the public defense delivery system monitors defense counsel's workload to promote quality representation. The workload of public defense attorneys, including appointed and other work, should never be so large that it interferes with competent and diligent representation or limits client contact. Factors that impact the number of cases an attorney can appropriately handle include case complexity and available support services.

B.   The leadership of the public defense delivery system adjusts attorney case assignments and resources to guarantee the continued delivery of quality juvenile defense services.

6. The Public Defense Delivery System Supervises and Systematically Reviews Juvenile Staff According to National, State and/or Local Performance Guidelines or Standards.

A. The public defense delivery system provides supervision and management direction for attorneys and team members who provide defense services to children.

B. The leadership of the public defense delivery system clearly defines the organization's vision and adopts guidelines consistent with national, state and/or local performance standards.

C. The public defense delivery system provides systematic reviews for all attorneys and staff representing juveniles, whether they are contract defenders, assigned counsel or employees of defender offices.

7. The Public Defense Delivery System Provides and Requires Comprehensive, Ongoing Training and Education for All Attorneys and Support Staff Involved in the Representation of Children.

A. The public defense delivery system recognizes juvenile delinquency defense as a specialty that requires continuous training in unique areas of the law. The public defense delivery system provides and mandates training on topics including detention advocacy, litigation and trial skills, dispositional planning, post-dispositional practice, educational rights, appellate advocacy and procedure and administrative hearing representation.

B. Juvenile team members have a comprehensive understanding of the jurisdiction's juvenile law procedure, and the collateral consequences of adjudication and conviction.

C. Team members receive training to recognize issues that arise in juvenile cases and that may require assistance from specialists in other disciplines. Such disciplines include, but are not limited to:

    1) Administrative appeals 2) Child welfare and entitlements 3) Special Education 4) Dependency court/abuse and neglect court process 5) Immigration 6) Mental health, physical health and treatment 7) Drug addiction and substance abuse

D. Training for team members emphasizes understanding of the needs of juveniles in general and of specific populations of juveniles in particular, including in the following areas:

    1) Child and adolescent development 2) Racial, ethnic and cultural understanding 3) Communicating and building attorney-client relationships with children and adolescents 4) Ethical issues and considerations of juvenile representation 5) Competency and capacity 6) Role of parents/guardians 7) Sexual orientation and gender identity awareness 8) Transfer to adult court and waiver hearings 9) Zero tolerance, school suspension and expulsion policies

E. Team members are trained to understand and use special programs and resources that are available in the juvenile system and in the community, such as:

    1) Treatment and problem solving courts 2) Diversionary programs 3) Community-based treatment resources and programs 4) Gender-specific programming

8. The Public Defense Delivery System Has an Obligation to Present Independent Treatment and Disposition Alternatives to the Court.

A. The public defense delivery system ensures that attorneys consult with clients and, independent from court or probation staff, actively seek out and advocate for treatment and placement alternatives that serve the unique needs and dispositional requests of each child, consistent with the client's expressed interests.

B. The leadership and staff of the public defense delivery system works in partnership with other juvenile justice agencies and community leaders to minimize custodial detention and the incarceration of children and to support the creation of continuum of community-based, culturally sensitive and gender-specific treatment alternatives.

C. The public defense delivery system provides independent post-disposition monitoring of each child's treatment, placement or program to ensure that rehabilitative needs are met. If clients' expressed needs are not effectively addressed, attorneys are responsible for intervention and advocacy before the appropriate authority.

9. The Public Defense Delivery System Advocates for the Educational Needs of Clients.

A. The public defense delivery system recognizes that access to education and to an appropriate educational curriculum is of paramount importance to juveniles facing delinquency adjudication and disposition.

B. The public defense delivery system advocates, either through direct representation or through collaborations with community-based partners, for the appropriate provision of the individualized educational needs of clients.

10. The Public Defense Delivery System Promotes Fairness and Equity For Children

A. The public defense delivery system demonstrates strong support of the right to counsel and due process in delinquency courts to promote a juvenile justice system that is fair, non-discriminatory and rehabilitative.

B. The public defense delivery system recognizes that disproportionate representation of minority youth in the juvenile justice system is contrary to notions of fairness and equality. The public defense delivery system works to draw attention to, and zealously advocates for the elimination of, disproportionate minority contact.

D. Why Effective Assistance of Counsel Standards Applicable to Adult Defendants Are Insufficient to Protect Delinquents in Juvenile Court

1. Ellen Marrus, *Effective Assistance of Counsel in the Wonderland of "Kiddie Court" — Why the Queen of Hearts Trumps* Strickland

39 Crim. L. Bull. 393, 393–95, 417–24 (2003)

Do children accused of delinquency in juvenile court have a right to effective assistance of counsel, and, if they do, is that right coterminous with that of adult defendants in criminal court? Since *In re Gault* grants the right to counsel to delinquents at adjudicatory hearings in juvenile court, it would seem obvious that the concomitant right to effective assistance of counsel granted in *Strickland v. Washington* to adult defendants, should also be applicable to children, at least to the same degree. Courts entertaining effective assistance of counsel claims in juvenile court matters seem to take that position, notwithstanding the Supreme Court's more recent views that adult criminal trials and delinquency adjudicatory hearings are different, and that delinquents are not automatically entitled to the same rights as adult defendants.

Assuming, however, that *Strickland* applies with full force to delinquents, the question is whether that case will protect children in the same way it purports to do for adults. [T]he *Strickland* Court's analysis places a heavy burden on the defendant, and many argue that the fluid *Strickland* standards do little to ensure effective assistance of counsel to adults charged with crime. Applying *Strickland* to children who will, by and large, be unable to meet the two prong test of *Strickland*, both because of their competency differentials, and their inability to communicate effectively with attorneys, dilutes the right to effective assistance of counsel for children. Furthermore, the peculiarities of juvenile court practice and the best interest standard make it less likely that counsel will, in fact perform as a zealous advocate, thus making *Strickland*'s emphasis on prevailing professional norms a danger for minors in juvenile court.

. . . .

Given the differences between children and adults and criminal court and juvenile court, how should *Strickland* apply in delinquency proceedings so as to assure that minors accused of crime receive effective assistance of counsel? One of the difficulties with applying *Strickland* to juvenile cases is its emphasis on reasonableness under prevailing professional norms. In juvenile court the general level of counsel's competence, at least as measured by the criterion of zealous advocacy, is lower than in criminal court where concededly advocacy is also often *de minimis*. Furthermore, the expectations of counsel in juvenile court and criminal court differ from the viewpoint of judges, the attorneys themselves, and probably the accused.

The best interest of the child is the dominant platitude in juvenile court. This amorphous standard, at least as generally applied, insists that adversarial representation of the child is inappropriate, and that the lawyer should act instead as, at best, a guardian ad litem, representing the child's best interests, an often elusive goal. If a child is guilty of an offense, the theory is that the lawyer should not try to win the case, because that will prevent the court from "helping" the juvenile and may foster future criminality. Indeed, in extreme cases, some judges take the position that if a youth has been referred to juvenile court, whether he is guilty of the particular offense is irrelevant. The minor needs help and he or she should plead guilty so as to allow the court to give the child the treatment he or she so obviously requires, even though there is a paucity of successful treatment options. If the probation department proposes that the adjudicated delinquent be committed to a state youth prison, that should be accepted by the defense attorney, without any attempt to contradict the recommendation or to find an alternative placement.

This best interest standard not only prevails among judges, prosecutors, and probation officials, but unfortunately also permeates the juvenile court defense bar, including both assigned private counsel and public defender offices. Indeed, very often the attorney does not believe that juvenile court sanctions are of major consequence, and therefore the disposition is of little import. Thus, what is considered effective representation in juvenile court would clearly fall below the *Strickland* standard of competence in adult criminal court, even though the child faces serious restrictions of his or her liberty. Furthermore, *Strickland* emphasizes prevailing professional norms. If that is taken literally, it would institutionalize all the defects of juvenile court representation.

Not only is the approach to representation different in juvenile court, it is also less adequate than in criminal court. While it is true that most cases in criminal court are disposed of by plea bargaining, it is understood that it is the job of defendant's counsel to cut the best deal he or she can. In juvenile court there is, in effect, no real plea bargaining, there are just pleas, a significantly higher number than in criminal court, which itself has a very high percentage of pleas. The probation department in juvenile court has no vested interest in obtaining an adjudication by plea. That problem is up to the prosecution, who generally has little institutional interest in the child's disposition, and usually has little influence on the sentence. Thus, defense attorneys often plead their clients guilty without investigating the case or exploring the strength of the prosecutor's evidence or getting a commitment as to disposition.

Juvenile court is often viewed as a training ground for "green" attorneys who, after having practiced on the child-clients, will move up to misdemeanor and felony cases. Prosecutors in juvenile court are not always part of the regular district attorney offices, and, they too, often do not know how to do trials. This contributes to the informal atmosphere of the hearing and reinforces the view that this is not an adversarial proceeding.

Even if a case goes to trial, many attorneys do not view them as a quasi-criminal proceeding that could result in deprivation of their client's freedom. They do very little pretrial motion work, and often neglect to subpoena necessary records. The trials are called hearings, and are far and few between. When there is a trial, the attorneys do not always know the criminal law or the rules of evidence, and do not press hostile witnesses. Preparation of defense witnesses for testifying is minimal. Furthermore, it is not uncommon for lawyers to put their clients on the stand and tell them to tell the court what happened, or to let the judge speak directly to their clients. Moreover, they make no objection when the judge takes over questioning of witnesses, which gives the appearance that the judge is partial to the prosecution's side, which, unfortunately, is often a reality. An example of such judicial behavior involved a fifteen-year old boy who was in court for an adjudicatory hearing. After the prosecution rested its case, and before the defense was presented, the judge turned to the boy and demanded that he tell him why he robbed the store. Since children will often automatically respond to authority figures, the juvenile answered the judge and incriminated himself, and the attorney did not object. The child, apparently thinking this was a good defense, said he needed the money to buy new sneakers.

Adding to the problem is that, in all but a few jurisdictions, there is no right to a jury trial, and the atmosphere in juvenile court is dangerously informal. Lawyers tend to be more zealous in front of a jury than a judge, if for no other reason that they do not want to be embarrassed before the public. The judge, who has usually seen the child's probation file to determine detention, who has presided over other hearings involving the same child, is impatient, and tells counsel to move along, move along. Judges often refuse to hear oral argument and summarily dismiss "technical" objections, using the old saw, "I'll take it for what it's worth." Trials rarely last more than a few hours.

Also adding to the mix is the fact that most juvenile hearings are closed, so the public and news media cannot monitor what goes on in these secret inquisitorial courts, leaving the judges and court personnel to believe that they are not constrained by the normal restrictions on arbitrary behavior. The confidentiality screen which is touted as necessary to protect the child, instead often serves as a shield to questionable, and, indeed, clearly unconstitutional judicial behavior.

Strickland gives deference to attorneys' tactics and strategies. But of what value is it when lawyers in the juvenile court system, by and large, do not engage in tactical or strategic planning?

. . . .

Concededly, representing children in juvenile court is extremely difficult. The difference between adults and children that may require additional protections for the child-client, also makes the defense attorney's job more challenging. An attorney practicing in juvenile court needs to know criminal law, juvenile law, civil law (since juvenile courts are deemed civil courts), education law, child development, and a good grasp of the private dispositional alternatives for children. As difficult as it may be, however, that is what is necessary to assure effective assistance of counsel in juvenile court.

One way to overcome the inherent problems of representation in juvenile court, is to require the attorney practicing there to perform certain acts. This checklist approach would constitute minimal standards for representing children in juvenile court—interviewing the client and witnesses, adequately investigating the facts and law, subpoenaing police records, refusing to plead unless it is in the child's interest to do so, listening to the child, exploring alternate placements, and taking probation's recommendation with a grain of salt.

A checklist also helps to ensure that institutionally the juvenile defense bar provides competent representation. It is a guide to lawyers about their legal duties to their clients in juvenile court. This is critical, because as it now stands, as noted above, many lawyers who practice in juvenile court do not engage in zealous advocacy. Furthermore, the checklist allows defense lawyers to represent their clients with zeal without fear of repercussions from judges. The checklist approach in juvenile court is supported by the *Gault* decision itself. Justice Fortas noted,

> The juvenile needs the assistance of counsel to cope with problems of law, to make skilled inquiry into the facts, to insist upon regularity of the proceedings, and to ascertain whether he has a defense and to prepare and submit it. The child "requires the guiding hand of counsel at every step in the proceedings against him."

Indeed, even in *Strickland*, the Court while debating the "basic duties" of an attorney, and disavowing a checklist approach, noted that the basic duties did not "exhaustively define the obligations of counsel."

Such a categorical approach would help with the first prong of *Strickland*. What about the prejudice prong?

In many states counsel is not appointed to prosecute appeals from juvenile court, and the child is, therefore, deprived of review. The lawyers' incompetence gets buried in the trial court. Children in the youth facilities are not as savvy as their adult counterparts in prison, who have access to writ writers and some semblance of a law library. Even in states in which the trial lawyer may proceed with an appeal, he or she may try to induce the client not to seek review. Even if the child insists on an appeal, which is unusual, the trial lawyer is not likely to raise his or her own errors. Even if independent counsel is assigned to pursue an appeal or to seek a writ, child clients are much less able to help their attorneys establish an ineffective assistance of counsel claim. Their memories are short lived, and they often have no idea of what strategy planning, if any, that the lawyer engaged in. Since most cases are resolved by plea, with a bare record, there will be no way to establish that the attorney did not act as a zealous advocate, nor that had he done so, there was a substantial probability that the outcome would have been different. The huge caseloads in juvenile court and the best interest standard, often result in attorneys doing little investigation, neglecting to conduct extensive interviews with witnesses or clients, file necessary motions, or to subpoena records, and whose files tend to consist of a single page with the hearing dates. Even if the attorney was subpoenaed for a hearing on effective assistance of counsel, he or she would probably not be able to reconstruct the particular case. Thus, requiring children to prove prejudice is simply a way of barring ineffective assistance claims for minors.

If there is a *Gideon* violation, no counsel at all, the defendant need not prove that lack of counsel prejudiced his or her case. Even if the evidence against the defendant is overwhelming, prejudice is presumed because the deprivation is "easy to identify" and prevent, and for which the prosecution is "directly responsible." Furthermore, the Court alleges that prejudice in these situations "is so likely that case-by-case inquiry into prejudice is not worth the cost." One might also argue that in such circumstances, it would be impossible to prove prejudice because of the cold and bare record which hides almost everything or more likely nothing.

If the defendant is represented by counsel, but there is a conflict of interest, the Court says that there is no requirement to prove prejudice. Prejudice is presumed if there is an actual "conflict of interest and the defendant proves that counsel actively represented conflicting interests," and that "an actual conflict of interest adversely affected his lawyer's performance."

Claims of ineffective assistance of counsel, however, do require proof of prejudice [unless a complete breakdown of the adversarial process has occurred]. Why? If a lawyer has committed egregious errors, it is as if the defendant had no counsel. Just as with a *Gideon* violation, prejudice is irrelevant in this context. The constitutional violation occurs with the lack of proper representation, not with whether the outcome of the case would be different.

Just as children cannot help to establish the first prong of *Strickland*, egregious errors, they cannot help to establish prejudice. The very factors that highlight the differences between adults and children also operate to hinder the child-client in assisting with the establishment of prejudice. As Justice Marshall noted in dissent in *Strickland*, "evidence of injury to the defendant may be missing from the record precisely because of the incompetence of defense counsel."

In my view, a child should not have the burden of proving prejudice. The prejudice should be presumed from the violation. At the very least the burden of disproving prejudice should be on the prosecution, as with harmless error analysis. Applying *Strickland* to children in the same way as it is applied to adults, is simply another way of institutionalizing the inadequate representation of minors in juvenile court. If the Court is serious about alleged delinquents being entitled to competent counsel, then it must conform *Strickland* to the needs of children in juvenile court. Conceptually, this would not be difficult because the right to counsel in juvenile court was granted as a matter of Due Process rather than the Sixth Amendment. Due Process focuses on fundamental fairness which can only be accomplished if representation in juvenile court is substantially improved.

Note

After the Court's decision in *Burger v. Kemp*, 483 U.S. 776 (1987), holding that counsel's failure to investigate and present mitigating evidence at sentencing was reasonable, the Court seemed to move toward easing the *Strickland* standards in similar circumstances. In *Williams v. Taylor*, 529 U.S. 362 (2000), the Court held that the attorney's failure to introduce extensive mitigating evidence at the sentencing stage of a capital case "fell short of professional standards" and that a reasonable probability existed that such an error would have affected the outcome. Similarly, in *Wiggins v. Smith*, 539 U.S. 510 (2003), the Court found that counsel's failure to conduct a thorough investigation regarding mitigating circumstances was unreasonable and prejudicial. In both cases, the Court rejected claims of strategy.

Why the apparent shift? One possibility is that the cases involved the death penalty. The Court had earlier held that all mitigating factors could be introduced at sentencing in a capital case so as to assure "a reasoned moral response." *Lockett v. Ohio*, 438 U.S. 586 (1978). Yet the *Burger* discussion, also involving the death penalty, made it clear that defense attorneys could circumvent the *Lockett* ruling by making "strategic" decisions not to present mitigating evidence, thus making the outcomes in capital cases less reliable in terms of assessing culpability.

Another possibility is the flood of academic commentary attacking the Court's application of *Strickland* in various contexts. In effect, said the commentators, establishing ineffective assistance of counsel was nearly impossible absent some evidence of defendant's innocence or strong indications of lesser culpability.

This movement would appear to be of little value to juvenile delinquents when punishment is viewed as treatment, and the sentences generally are not as lengthy as in criminal court. Conversely, one could argue the increased use of determinate sentencing in juvenile court, see Chapter 7, *infra*, which can yield forty year sentences, should be protected by the "modified" *Strickland* approach. Furthermore, in *Wiggins,* the Court cited the ABA Standards relating to the death penalty, and therefore it might realistically be expected to apply the ABA Standards for the representation of juveniles.

Chapter 4

Juvenile Delinquency Proceedings: State Statutes and Cases

A. Infancy Defense — Introduction

The infancy defense prohibits criminal punishment for children of certain ages. It is based on the theory that children lack the general mens rea to be morally blameworthy. At common law a tripartite classification defined a child's criminal capacity. For children below the age of 7 there was an irrebuttable presumption of infancy; from 7–14 the presumption of infancy was rebuttable, allowing the state to show that the particular juvenile was morally culpable; minors over 14 were presumed responsible for their acts.

The juvenile courts in the United States are viewed as civil in nature. Although children alleged to be delinquent are accused of committing criminal acts, thus implicating the state's police power, because the offenders are minors, the state's *parens patriae* interests are also triggered. It is argued, therefore, that the civil label and purportedly nonadversarial nature of the proceedings render the infancy defense inappropriate in the juvenile court system because its invocation could frustrate the very purpose of these courts, that is, treatment of the juvenile.

Recently, legislators have abandoned or subordinated the treatment model of the juvenile courts. Because of growing public opinion that juvenile delinquency is out of control and that juvenile courts are failing to impose punishment for wrongdoing, states are now demanding accountability from juveniles, and many allow stringent, punitive sanctions for deviant behavior. Furthermore, in the late 1960s and early 1970s, the Supreme Court applied some constitutional safeguards to juvenile court delinquency actions. The effect of this "constitutional domestication" of the juvenile courts and the call for accountability by youths, make the juvenile court landscape look similar to criminal courts. These significant changes have caused many to reconsider whether the infancy defense does in fact have a place in juvenile court proceedings. However, in more recent years the competency of juveniles to stand trial has been raised more often. This is sometimes done through an infancy defense, but is also being challenged through competency statutes. For a more complete summary of juvenile competency statues and the restoration provisions *see* Richard E. Redding Lynda E. Frost, *Adjudicative Competence in the Modern Juvenile Court*, 9 VA. J. SOC. POL'Y. & L. 353 (2001).

1. Cases

In re Tyvonne

558 A.2d 661 (Conn. 1989)

GLASS, Associate Justice.

In this case we decide whether the common law defense of infancy applies to juvenile delinquency proceedings.

[The minor, 8 years old, was charged with shooting another child. At the delinquency proceeding, after the state completed its case, the respondent made an oral motion for judgment of acquittal, claiming that the state had introduced no evidence to rebut the common law presumption that children between the ages of seven and fourteen are incapable of harboring mens rea. The trial court reserved decision on the motion for acquittal, and granted the respondent's motion for an examination to determine his competency.]

When the hearing resumed..., the report evaluating the respondent's competency was filed and proof of his competency was waived.[1] The trial court then denied the respondent's motion for judgment of acquittal. At the completion of the hearing, the trial court made an adjudication that the respondent was a delinquent based on a finding that he had committed assault in the second degree.... The trial court also ordered a preliminary investigation and a psychological evaluation of the respondent's mother and grandmother. At the disposition hearing on October 26, 1987, the trial court committed the respondent to the department of children and youth services (DCYS) for a period not to exceed four years.[2]

On appeal, the respondent assigns as error the trial court's denial of his motion for judgment of acquittal. He asserts that Connecticut's juvenile justice legislation does not expressly or implicitly eliminate the common law infancy defense from delinquency proceedings. He further argues that because the original goals of rehabilitation and remediation in the juvenile justice system have not been attained, there is no justification for excluding the infancy defense from juvenile delinquency proceedings. Consequently, he claims, the trial court erred in not requiring the state to rebut the presumption that he was incapable of committing the offense underlying the delinquency adjudication. We are not persuaded.

I

The respondent argues that, even though the legislature may abolish common law rules statutes in derogation of the common law must be strictly construed. He asserts that because the juvenile justice legislation is silent with respect to the common law infancy defense, the common law presumptions must apply to delinquency proceedings. The state argues, however, that Connecticut's juvenile justice legislation implicitly abolishes the defense and, further, that application of the defense in delinquency proceedings would frustrate the legislation's remedial objectives.

---

1. The competency evaluation ... was conducted by the diagnostic clinic of the department of mental health. [T]he ... unanimous opinion of the clinical team [was] that the respondent was able to understand the delinquency proceedings.

2. The respondent's attorney filed a petition with the trial court seeking an adjudication that the respondent was an "uncared for" child, ... defined as one "who is homeless or whose home cannot provide the specialized care which his physical, emotional or mental condition requires." The trial court found that the respondent was an uncared for child. In addition to the four year commitment based on the delinquency adjudication, the trial court ordered a commitment of eighteen months based on the adjudication that the respondent was an uncared for child.

"Down through the centuries the law has attempted to save offending children from the rigidity of the criminal law applicable to adults, but the history of the law has disclosed that such attempts were only sporadic and in many instances accomplished very little. As early as the fifth century B.C., the Twelve Tables made the theft of crops at night a capital crime, but a youthful offender could escape with a fine double the value and a flogging. The Romans promulgated the defense of *infantia* which provided absolute immunity for those children who were incapable of speech. Puberty was established as the upper limit of eligibility for mitigated treatment. Between infancy and puberty, criminal responsibility depended on a combination of three factors—the proximity of age to either infancy or puberty, the nature of the offense, and the mental capacity of the offender.

"By the seventeenth century, the Roman classification of criminal responsibility became the basis of the English common-law approach, so that children under seven were incapable of committing a crime while those between seven and fourteen were presumed incapable. Such presumption, however, was rebuttable by strong and clear evidence. Those [fourteen and over] were subject to the same criminal laws as were adults." In a case decided after the enactment of Connecticut's juvenile justice legislation, we observed in dictum that the common law principles had applied to criminal prosecutions of children in Connecticut.

The common law defense of infancy, like the defense of insanity, differs from the criminal law's requirement of "mens rea" or criminal intent. The law recognized that while a child may have actually intended to perform a criminal act, children in general could not reasonably be presumed capable of differentiating right from wrong. The presumptions of incapacity were created to avoid punishing those who, because of age, could not appreciate the moral dimensions of their behavior, and for whom the threat of punishment would not act as a deterrent. Although a number of states have codified the common law rule by statute[,] there is no statutory infancy defense in Connecticut.

The concept of juvenile delinquency did not exist at common law. In most states, including Connecticut, legislation was enacted that rendered children under a certain age liable as "delinquents" for committing acts that, if committed by an adult, would be criminal.... Even though the Superior Court is Connecticut's trial court of general jurisdiction, and juvenile matters are heard in the Superior Court, juvenile proceedings are conducted separately from all other business of the Superior Court. Delinquency is defined as follows: "[A] child may be found 'delinquent' (1) who has violated any federal or state law or municipal or local ordinance * * * or (2) who has violated any order of the superior court. * * *" An important feature of the legislation since its inception is presently expressed in General Statutes § 46b-145, which provides: "No child shall be prosecuted for an offense before the Superior Court, nor shall the adjudication of such court that a child is delinquent in any case be deemed a conviction of crime except as provided in sections 46b-126 and 46b-127."[3]

Shortly after the creation of the juvenile justice system, we addressed the issue whether a delinquency proceeding is tantamount to a criminal prosecution. [W]e stated that "the Act [creating the juvenile justice system] is not of a criminal nature. * * *" "The Act is but an exercise by the State of its * * * power over the welfare of its children," and a juvenile subjected to delinquency proceedings "[is] tried for no offense," but "[comes] under the operation of the law in order that he might not be tried for any offense." Since [then] we have on several occasions recognized that ... juvenile proceedings are fundamentally different from criminal proceedings.

---

3. The exceptions refer to juvenile cases subject to transfer to the regular criminal docket.

The rehabilitative nature of our juvenile justice system is most saliently evidenced by the statutory provisions pertaining to the disposition of delinquent juveniles. Under General Statutes § 46b-134, the trial court may not render a disposition of the case of any delinquent child until the trial court receives from the probation officer assigned to the case a comprehensive background report on the child's characteristics, history and home life. The disposition of a child found delinquent for a serious juvenile offense may be made only after the court receives a complete evaluation of the child's physical and psychological health. General Statutes § 46b-140(a) provides in part that upon an adjudication of delinquency, the trial court may place the juvenile "in the care of any institution or agency which is permitted by law to care for children, order the child to remain in his own home or in the custody of a relative or any other fit person subject to the supervision of the probation officer or withhold or suspend execution of any judgment." The court may also order the juvenile to perform public service or to make restitution when appropriate, provided that the child and his parent or guardian consent to such an order.

Significantly, commitment of the child to DCYS may be made only if the court finds that "its probation services or other services available to the court are not adequate for such child. * * *" Prior to any such commitment, however, the court must "consult with [DCYS] to determine the placement which will be in the best interest of such child." When the trial court determines that a commitment must be made, it may commit the child to DCYS for an indeterminate period not to exceed two years, or in the case of a child found delinquent for committing a serious juvenile offense, for an indeterminate period not to exceed four years. DCYS may petition for an extension of the commitment of a child originally committed for two years. An extension may not exceed an additional two years, and may only be ordered when, after a hearing, it is found to be in the best interests of the child.

Several other provisions of the General Statutes and the Practice Book delineate fundamental distinctions between delinquency and criminal proceedings. For example, Practice Book § 1034(1) provides that a juvenile delinquency hearing "shall not be conducted as a criminal trial; the proceedings shall be at all times as informal as the requirements of due process and fairness permit." Further, unlike the records of convicted criminals, the records of juvenile delinquency proceedings generally are confidential....

It is clear from our analysis that the purpose of the comprehensive statutory treatment of "juvenile delinquents" is clinical and rehabilitative, rather than retributive or punitive. As we recently observed, "[t]he objective of juvenile court proceedings is to 'determin[e] the needs of the child and of society rather than to adjudicat[e] criminal conduct. The objectives are to provide measures of guidance and rehabilitation * * * not to fix criminal responsibility, guilt and punishment.' Thus the child found delinquent is not perceived as a criminal guilty of one or more offenses, but rather as a child in need of guidance and rehabilitative services." In effect, the statutes regulating juvenile misconduct represent a system-wide displacement of the common law.

With the enactment of juvenile justice legislation nationwide, several courts have addressed the issue whether the infancy defense applies to delinquency proceedings. Most have held that, in the absence of legislation codifying or adopting the defense, incapacity is not a defense in delinquency proceedings. These courts observe that because a delinquency adjudication is not a criminal conviction, it is unnecessary to determine whether the juvenile understood the moral implications of his or her behavior. In addition, some decisions recognize that the defense would frustrate the remedial purposes of juvenile justice legislation.

Because Connecticut's juvenile justice system is designed to provide delinquent minors with guidance and rehabilitation, we agree with the courts that hold that the common law infancy defense, created to protect children from being punished as criminals, has no place in delinquency proceedings. We also agree that the legislature could decide that the infancy defense would unnecessarily interfere with the state's legitimate efforts to provide structured forms of guidance for children who have committed acts of delinquency. It could conclude that the defense inevitably would exclude those children most in need of guidance from a system designed to instill socially responsible behavior. To construe the legislature's silence as indicating an intent to preserve the infancy defense in delinquency proceedings is unwarranted in light of the legislation's obvious and singular remedial objectives. We are not persuaded that recognition of the defense would advance the interests of either the child or society.[4]

II

Relying on a number of decisions in other states, however, the respondent argues that the rehabilitative objectives of juvenile justice have become defunct, and cannot justify excluding the infancy defense from delinquency proceedings. Most of the decisions holding the infancy defense applicable to juvenile proceedings have been based on specific legislation adopting the defense, and therefore are irrelevant to the present case.

Some courts, however, have held that even absent pertinent legislation, the common law infancy defense applies to delinquency proceedings. These courts advance the notion that the United States Supreme Court decisions in *Kent*, *Gault*, and *Winship* reflect the evolving reality that the true objectives of juvenile justice legislation are not rehabilitation and treatment, but accountability and punishment.

Kent, *Gault* and *Winship* establish that the state may not suspend fundamental protections of due process in juvenile proceedings. A particular procedure must be followed if it is required as a matter of "fundamental fairness." The precise principle emerging from *Kent* and *Gault* is that states may not rely on superficial exhortations of "rehabilitation" to justify procedural arbitrariness in delinquency proceedings. As the court observed in *Gault*, "[j]uvenile [c]ourt history has again demonstrated that unbridled discretion, however benevolently motivated, is frequently a poor substitute for principle and procedure."

The respondent does not argue that the United States Supreme Court's juvenile decisions require the common law incapacity defense in delinquency proceedings as a matter of fundamental constitutional fairness. Nor does he suggest that the exclusion of the incapacity defense introduces procedural arbitrariness. Instead, the respondent gleans from those cases the proposition that since the juvenile justice system punishes rather than rehabilitates, there is no good reason not to recognize incapacity as a defense. We are not persuaded, however, that *Kent* and *Gault* warrant the proposition that the respondent discerns.

We acknowledge that the United States Supreme Court has opined that the rehabilitative goals of the various state juvenile courts have often not been attained. The Court has made it quite clear that states may not deny juveniles fundamental due process rights simply by labeling delinquency proceedings "civil," or by asserting that the purpose of delinquency proceedings is rehabilitative. Thus, the parens patriae doctrine does not support inroads on basic constitutional guarantees simply because a state claims that its ju-

---

4. Nothing in this opinion should be construed to deter the legislature from considering the desirability of a floor for such juvenile proceedings in recognition of the fact that the clinical and rehabilitative needs of a four or eight year old are different from those of a fourteen or fifteen year old.

venile justice system is "rehabilitative" rather than "punitive." The United States Supreme Court, however, has expressly refused to hold that the rehabilitative goals of the various systems of juvenile justice may under no circumstances justify appropriate differential treatment of a child adjudicated a delinquent. Further, the Court has never suggested that such differential treatment, based on the juvenile justice systems' fundamentally non-punitive objectives, is intrinsically illegitimate....

We do not discern in *Kent* and its progeny an abandonment of the rehabilitative focus of juvenile justice. The respondent has not presented us with any grounds for concluding that the rehabilitative objectives of Connecticut's juvenile justice system are contradicted in practice. We therefore decline to adopt the somewhat cynical view expressed by some writers that the ideals of the juvenile justice system are now bankrupt, and have necessarily succumbed to the corrosive effects of institutionalization.

Further, we are not persuaded by the respondent's argument that the statutory treatment of juveniles who commit "serious juvenile offenses" requires a conclusion that there is no genuine difference between juvenile and criminal proceedings. The four year maximum commitment term for serious juvenile offenders certainly contemplates the possibility of a serious restriction on the juvenile's liberty. But as we have already observed, any commitment order must be predicated on a determination that other options not involving commitment are inadequate to address the child's needs. In addition, placement of the child in a program or facility must be based on the child's best interests. We cannot infer from these provisions a legislative intent to inflict retribution on the serious juvenile offender.

Finally, we reject the respondent's argument that the common law presumption should apply in this case because the offense charged was a serious juvenile offense. We acknowledge that the commission of a serious juvenile offense is a prerequisite to the transfer of a juvenile case to the Superior Court criminal docket. Another prerequisite to such a transfer, however, is that the child must have committed the offense after attaining the age of fourteen. In the present case, the respondent was eight years of age at the time of the predicate offense.

There is no error.

Notes

(a) *Accord, State v. D.H.*, 340 So.2d 1163 (Fla. 1976); *Gammons v. Berlat*, 696 P.2d 700 (Ariz. 1985); *In the Interest of G.T.*, 597 A.2d 638, 642 (Pa. Super. Ct. 1990).

(b) Footnote 2 of the court's opinion in *In re Tyvonne* notes that Tyvonne was also adjudicated "an uncared" for child and committed for eighteen months. Why were both adjudications necessary? Are they inconsistent? Could the neglect adjudication be viewed as a defense to the delinquency charges?

State v. Q.D. and M.S.
685 P.2d 557 (Wash. 1984)

DIMMICK, Justice.

Two juveniles appeal from separate adjudications which found that they had committed offenses which if committed by an adult would be crimes. The Court of Appeals, in these consolidated appeals, certified to this court the questions whether the statutory presumption of infant incapacity, RCW 9A.04.050,[5] applies to juvenile adjudications, and if it does, what standard of proof is required to rebut the presumption. Each defendant argues that the trial court's determinations of capacity were erroneous under any standard....

We hold that (1) RCW 9A.04.050 applies to juvenile adjudications, (2) the standard of proof necessary to rebut the presumption of incapacity is clear and convincing proof....

I
APPLICABILITY OF RCW 9A.04.050 TO JUVENILE COURTS

Counsel for both the State and the defendants urge us to hold that the infant incapacity defense in RCW 9A.04.050 applies to juvenile proceedings. We so hold.

At common law, children below the age of 7 were conclusively presumed to be incapable of committing crime, and children over the age of 14 were presumed capable and treated as adults. Children between these ages were rebuttably presumed incapable of committing crime. Washington codified these presumptions amending the age of conclusive incapacity to 7, and presumed capacity to 12 years of age. As recently as 1975, the Legislature again included the infancy defense in the criminal code. The purpose of the presumption is to protect from the criminal justice system those individuals of tender years who are less capable than adults of appreciating the wrongfulness of their behavior.

The infancy defense fell into disuse during the early part of the century with the advent of reforms intended to substitute treatment and rehabilitation for punishment of juvenile offenders. This parens patriae system, believed not to be a criminal one, had no need of the infancy defense.

The juvenile justice system in recent years has evolved from *parens patriae* scheme to one more akin to adult criminal proceedings. The United States Supreme Court has been critical of the *parens patriae* scheme as failing to provide safeguards due an adult criminal defendant, while subjecting the juvenile defendant to similar stigma, and possible loss of liberty. This court has acknowledged Washington's departure from a strictly *parens patriae* scheme to a more criminal one, involving both rehabilitation and punishment. Being a criminal defense, RCW 9A.04.050 should be available to juvenile proceedings that are criminal in nature.

The principles of construction of criminal statutes, made necessary by our recognition of the criminal nature of juvenile court proceedings, also compel us to conclude that RCW 9A.04.050 applies to proceedings in juvenile courts.

A finding that RCW 9A.04.050 does not apply to juvenile courts would render that statute meaningless or superfluous contrary to rules of construction. Juvenile courts have exclusive jurisdiction over all individuals under the chronological age of 18 who have committed acts designated criminal if committed by an adult. Declination of jurisdiction and transfer to adult court is limited to instances where it is in the best interest of the juvenile or the public. Thus, all juveniles who can avail themselves of the infancy defense will come under the jurisdiction of the juvenile court, and most will remain there. Implied statutory repeals are found not to exist where the two statutes can be reconciled and given effect. Goals of the Juvenile Justice Act of 1977 include accountability for crim-

---

5. RCW 9A.04.050 provides in part: "Children under the age of eight years are incapable of committing crime. Children of eight and under twelve years of age are presumed to be incapable of committing crime, but this presumption may be removed by proof that they have sufficient capacity to understand the act or neglect, and to know that it was wrong."

inal behavior and punishment commensurate with age and crime. A goal of the criminal code is to safeguard conduct that is not culpable. The infancy defense which excludes from criminal condemnation persons not capable of culpable, criminal acts, is consistent with the overlapping goals of the Juvenile Justice Act of 1977 and the Washington Criminal Code.

II
STANDARD OF PROOF UNDER RCW 9A.04.050

The State has the burden of rebutting the statutory presumption of incapacity of juveniles age 8 and less than 12 years. Capacity must be found to exist separate from the specific mental element of the crime charged. While capacity is similar to the mental element of a specific crime or offense, it is not an element of the offense, but is rather a general determination that the individual understood the act and its wrongfulness. Both defendants liken the incapacity presumption to a jurisdictional presumption. Were capacity an element of the crime, proof beyond a reasonable doubt would be required. But capacity, not being an element of the crime, does not require as stringent a standard of proof.

Few jurisdictions have ruled on the appropriate standard of proof necessary to rebut the presumption of incapacity, and fewer still have discussed their reasoning for preferring one standard over another. It appears that other states have split between requiring proof beyond a reasonable doubt, and clear and convincing proof....

[W]e [have] held that the burden of proof [in involuntary commitment proceedings] should be by clear, cogent and convincing evidence. In so holding, we recognized that the preponderance of the evidence standard was inadequate, but the proof beyond a reasonable doubt standard imposed a burden which, as a practical matter, was unreasonably difficult, thus undercutting the State's legitimate interests.

The Legislature, by requiring the State to rebut the presumption of incapacity, has assumed a greater burden than the minimal proof imposed by the preponderance of the evidence standard. On the other hand, to require the State to prove capacity beyond a reasonable doubt when the State must also prove the specific mental element of the charged offense by the same standard, is unnecessarily duplicative. Frequently, the same facts required to prove mens rea will be probative of capacity, yet the overlap is not complete. Capacity to be culpable must exist in order to maintain the specific mental element of the charged offense. Once the generalized determination of capacity is found, the State must prove beyond a reasonable doubt that the juvenile defendant possessed the specific mental element. The clear and convincing standard reflects the State's assumption of a greater burden than does the preponderance of the evidence standard. At the same time, the liberty interest of the juvenile is fully protected by the requirement of proof beyond a reasonable doubt of the specific mental element. We therefore require the State to rebut the presumption of incapacity by clear and convincing evidence.

III
EVIDENCE OF CAPACITY

....

The issue of capacity was first raised on M.S.'s motion to dismiss at the end of the trial. The judge stated in response to arguments of counsel that he was persuaded by the confidence in defendant's maturity held by the mother of the victim and her own parents in permitting her to assume the responsibility for babysitting. Contrary to defendant's arguments that the trial judge created a prima facie proof of capacity based solely on babysitting, there was other evidence to support his finding of capacity. The defendant waited until she and the victim were alone evidencing a desire for secrecy. The defendant later admonished the victim not to tell what happened, further supporting the finding that the defendant knew the act was wrong. Lastly, the defendant was less than 3 months from the age at which capacity is presumed to exist. There was clear and convincing circumstantial evidence that M.S. understood the act of indecent liberties and knew it to be wrong.

Finally, in response to the parties' requests for guidelines concerning the forum of the capacity hearing, we find the separate hearing in Q.D.'s case, and the single hearing of capacity and the substantive charge in M.S.'s case to be appropriate under the different circumstances in each. In Q.D.'s case, prior criminal history was the basis for attempting to prove capacity, and thus a separate hearing avoided prejudice. In M.S.'s case, the facts of the offense were offered to show capacity, and a separate hearing would be unduly repetitive. Rather than delineating a rigid rule, the circumstances should dictate whether a separate hearing is appropriate.... In the event that it is necessary to show capacity by proof of both criminal history and the particular facts of the offense charged, caution should be employed to prevent the introduction of evidence of prior history from prejudicing the determination on the merits.

Accord, In re Manuel, 865 P.2d 718 (Cal. 1994); *In re William A.*, 548 A.2d 130 (Md. 1988); *In the Interest of C.P.*, 514 A.2d 850 (N.J. 1986).

2. Irene Merker Rosenberg, *Leaving Bad Enough Alone: A Response to the Juvenile Court Abolitionists*

1993 Wis. L. Rev. 163, 175–80 (1993)

[I]t is unclear whether the common law infancy defense ... is constitutionally mandated as a matter of federal law. As the plurality noted in *Powell v. Texas*, "this Court has never articulated a general constitutional doctrine of mens rea." In his concurring opinion, Justice Black agreed that "the legislatures have always been allowed wide freedom to determine the extent to which moral culpability should be a prerequisite to conviction of a crime."

The infancy defense is viewed as an aspect of mens rea in its general sense—that is, an ability to appreciate the wrongfulness of one's conduct, one's moral blameworthiness—and thus not a material element of the crime to which *In re Winship* applies. In *Patterson v. New York*, the Supreme Court upheld a state statue requiring the defendant to prove extreme emotional disturbance in order to be convicted of manslaughter rather than murder, in part because the state has the power to punish any intentional killing as murder, that is, the state is not required to recognize or prove mitigating factors that show reduced culpability.... [I]f *Patterson* teaches that states need not recognize defenses based on diminished moral culpability, such as extreme emotional disturbance, then presumably refusal to allow the infancy defense would likewise withstand constitutional attack.

The strongest argument supporting the infancy defense as constitutionally mandated stems from the Court's ruling in *Medina v. California*, in which the Justices upheld a state law placing the burden of proving incompetency to stand trial on the defendant. The Court reaffirmed *Patterson*, emphasizing that decision's deference to the states in matters of criminal procedure. Using a two-pronged test, the majority rejected the due process claim, finding that the rule was neither fundamentally unfair nor offensive to any "principle of justice so rooted in the traditions and conscience of our people as to be ranked as fundamental." With respect to the latter test, the Court asserted that "historical practice is probative of whether a procedural rule can be characterized as fundamental." Given the deep historical roots of the infancy defense at common law and in the United States, this acknowledgment supports constitutionalization of the infancy defense. At the same time, however, in its discussion of the fundamental fairness prong, the *Medina* Court distinguished incompetency from insanity by noting, "we have not said that the Constitution requires the States to recognize the insanity defense," a statement also applicable to infancy.

Even assuming, however, that the infancy defense were either constitutionally mandated or afforded as a matter of state law, it might be insufficiently protective of children.... The irrebuttable presumption for those under seven would be invoked in very few cases because there are few crimes committed by children so young, and when they are, the state generally chooses not to prosecute them.... At the other end of the spectrum, children over fourteen are presumed to be criminally responsible, and many of the juveniles accused of serious crimes fall within that age bracket, making the infancy defense irrelevant in such cases. Thus, the defense generally would be applicable only to children between seven and fourteen ... and a large number of juveniles accused of crime do fall within that age bracket. Many of those within this intermediate category are approaching fourteen, however, and unfortunately the rebuttable presumption decreases in strength as the child gets older. Therefore, the closer a child is to fourteen, the less evidence the state needs to prove capacity. Moreover, the prosecutor can establish capacity simply by showing consciousness of wrongdoing, not an onerous burden, especially since many jurisdictions allow that burden to be met by inferences from the very circumstances of the crime. Finally, since it is based on chronological rather than mental age, and is concerned with cognitive rather than volitional capacity, the infancy defense would not, in my view, give children parity in the criminal courts.

Infancy, of course, would be constitutionally relevant insofar as it relates to mens rea in the specific sense, that is, the mental state required by definition of the crime. If the offense with which a child is charged has such a mens rea element, then *Winship* requires that it be proved beyond a reasonable doubt. Evidence relating to that mens rea requirement would be admissible, and, presumably, that would include evidence that the child was too immature to form the requisite intent. For example, in a larceny case, testimony that the minor defendant was too young to form the intent to deprive the owner of his or her property permanently would be relevant. As with the general mens rea infancy defense, however, it is unlikely to affect children over the age of ten, most of whom have a good sense of mine and thine.

Notes

(a) Given the recent developments in the juvenile justice system, particularly those involving harsher punishment of delinquents, see Chapter 7, *infra*, should the infancy defense apply in delinquency cases?

(b) If the infancy defense were applicable in juvenile court, would that lend support to those advocating its abolition?

B. Age Limitations

The absence of the infancy defense in juvenile court is even more troublesome when considered in the context of the age limits, both upper and lower, that states set for defining a delinquent child. While each state, of course, has the authority to determine its own age limits for delinquency, surprising agreement exists among them. The upper limits range from 15 to 17. By far the overwhelming upper age limit is 17. The more surprising aspect is the lower age limit. Most jurisdictions have no lower age limit. Of those that do, ten seems to be the most common. The rest have either seven or six. As a matter of practice, however, very few children under the age of seven are brought to juvenile court on delinquency charges. But every now and then a five or six year old makes the newspapers for homicide or assaulting a teacher. It is in those cases that the defendant's inability to invoke the infancy defense makes it difficult for the juvenile court to make an accurate assessment of moral culpability and mens rea. Also relevant to this issue is whether juvenile court jurisdiction is based on age at the time of the offense, or at the time the petition is filed or when the child is actually tried.

State Juvenile Court Delinquency Jurisdiction

Upper Limit: means Juvenile Court no longer has jurisdiction on child's Nth birthday

Lower Limit: means Juvenile Court begins to have jurisdiction on child's Nth birthday

	Upper Limit	Lower Limit	State Statute
Alabama	18		Ala. Code § 12-15-114
Alaska	18		Alaska Stat. § 47.12.020
Arizona	18		Ariz. Rev. Stat. § 8-202 & 8-201
Arkansas	18	10	Ark. Code Ann. § 9-27-303
California	18		Cal. Welf. & Inst. Code § 602
Colorado	18	10	Colo. Rev. Stat. 19-2-104
Connecticut	16		Conn. Gen. Stat. § 46b-120
Delaware	18		Del. Code Ann. tit. 10, § 901
D.C.	18		D.C. Code § 16-2301
Florida	18		Fla. Stat. § 39.013
Georgia	17		Ga. Code Ann. § 15-11-28
Hawaii	18	*	Haw. Rev. Stat. § 571-11
Idaho	18		Idaho Code Ann. § 20-502 & 2-505
Illinois	17		705 Ill. Comp. Stat. 405/5-120
Indiana	18		Burns Ind. Code Ann. 31-37-1-1 & 31-30-1-4
Iowa	18		Iowa Code § 232.8, 232.2
Kansas	18	10	Kan. Stat. Ann. § 38-2302, 38-2304
Kentucky	18		Ky. Rev. Stat. Ann. § 610.010, 600.020
Louisiana	17	10	La. Child. Code Ann. Art. 804
Maine	18		Me. Rev. Stat. Ann. tit. 15, § 3101, 3003
Maryland	18		Md. Code Ann. & Jud. Proc. § 3-8A-03, 3-8A-01
Massachusetts	17	7	Mass. Gen. Laws Ann. ch. 119, § 52
Michigan	17		Mich. Comp. Laws Serv. § 712A.2
Minnesota	18		Minn. Stat. § 260B.101
Mississippi	18	10	Miss. Code Ann. § 43-21-151, 43-21-105
Missouri	17		Mo. Rev. Stat. § 211.031
Montana	18		Mont. Code Ann., § 41-5-203, 41-5-103
Nebraska	18		Neb. Rev. Stat. § 43-245 & 43-247
Nevada	18		Nev. Rev. Stat. § 62A.030, 62A.070, 62B.330
New Hampshire	17		N.H. Rev. Stat. Ann. § 169-B:2, 169-B:3

New Jersey	18		N.J. Stat. Ann. § 2A:4A-22 & 2A:4A-23
New Mexico	18		N.M. Stat. Ann. § 32A-1-8, 32A-1-4
New York	16	7	N.Y. Fam. Ct. Act § 301.2, 302.1
North Carolina	16	6	N.C. Gen. Stat. § 7B-1501
North Dakota	18		N.D. Cent. Code § 27-20-03,02
Ohio	18		Ohio Rev. Code Ann. § 2151.23, 2152.02
Oklahoma	18		Okla. Stat. Tit. 10, § 7301-1.3
Oregon	18		Or. Rev. Stat. § 419C.005
Pennsylvania	18	10	42 Pa. Cons. Stat. § 6302
Rhode Island	18		R.I. Gen. Laws § 14-1-5, 14-1-3
South Carolina	17		S.C. Code Ann. § 63-19-20
South Dakota	18	10	S.D. Codified Laws § 26-8C-2, 26-7A-1
Tennessee	18		Tenn. Code Ann. § 37-1-102, 37-1-103
Texas	17	10	Tex. Fam. Code Ann. § 51.02, 51.04
Utah	18		Utah Code Ann. § 78A-6-103
Vermont	16	10	Vt. Stat. Ann. tit. 33, § 5102, 5103
Virginia	18		Va. Code Ann. § 16.1-228, 16.1-241
Washington	18		Wash. Rev. Code § 13.40.020,13.40.030
West Virginia	18		W. Va. Code § 49-1-2, 49-5-2
Wisconsin	17		Wis. Stat. § 48.02, 48.13
Wyoming	18		Wyo. Stat. Ann. § 14-1-101 & 14-6-201, 14-6-203

* Although Hawaii has no lower age limit for juvenile jurisdiction, its juvenile code provides that children under the age of 12 cannot be proceeded against without the written recommendation of a licensed psychologist or psychiatrist.

Notes

(a) Why do you think that most states have no lower age limits for juvenile delinquency? Is it simply a matter of inartful drafting or the result of a particular policy decision by the state? If so, what is driving this decision?

(b) In determining whether juvenile court jurisdiction should end at the age of 18, consider the following excerpt relating to brain development:

Cordia Wallas, *What Makes Teens Tick*, Time, May 10, 2004, at 57, 65.

In light of what has been learned, [from various MRI and other scientific studies], it seems almost arbitrary that our society has decided that a young American is ready to drive a car at sixteen, to vote and serve in the Army at eighteen and to drink alcohol at twenty-one. [Dr. J.] Giedd, [Chief of brain imaging in the Child Psychiatry Branch at the National Institute of Mental Health,] says the best estimate for when the brain is truly mature is 25, the age at which you can rent a car. "Avis must have some pretty sophisticated neuroscientists," he jokes. Now that we have scientific evidence that the adolescent brain is not quite up to scratch, some legal scholars and child advocates argue that minors should never be tried as adults and should be spared the death penalty. Last year, in an official statement that summarized current research on the adolescent brain, the American Bar Association urged all State Legislatures to ban the death penalty for juveniles. "For social and biological reasons," it read, "teens have increased difficulty making mature decisions and understanding the consequences of their actions."

(c) In *Roper v. Simmons*, 543 U.S. 551, 568–78 (2005), excerpted and discussed in Chapter 2, *infra*, the Court relied on scientific evidence regarding brain maturation in adolescents and determined that the death penalty for minors under eighteen violated the cruel and unusual punishment clause of the Eighth Amendment.

Does *Roper* have any relevance to the various age limits in delinquency statutes?

C. Special Problems Relating to Juvenile Court Age Limits

Commonwealth v. A Juvenile
534 N.E.2d 809 (Mass. App. Ct. 1989)

The primary question before us is whether John Jarvis could properly be adjudicated a delinquent child without the Commonwealth's proving to the jury that Jarvis was between the ages of seven and seventeen. The record does not include a transcript, and the case is before us on a stipulation and findings of the trial judge.

The findings set forth the following facts. No affirmative evidence was introduced at trial to show that Jarvis was a juvenile. His counsel, at the close of the Commonwealth's case, moved for a required finding of not guilty on the ground that there was insufficient evidence to find his client delinquent. He never proffered as a basis for the motion that the Commonwealth had omitted to prove that his client was a juvenile, and the motion was denied after a hearing. The judge [instructed] the jury:

> "In order to find [John Jarvis] delinquent, the Commonwealth must prove the following beyond a reasonable doubt:
>
> First: That he is between the age of seven and seventeen;
>
> Second: That he committed [an offence against the Commonwealth].
>
> In order to find that he [committed an offence against the Commonwealth], the Commonwealth must prove all the elements of that offense beyond a reasonable doubt...."

Jarvis does not argue that he was not between the ages of seven and seventeen or that Worcester Juvenile Court did not, in fact, have jurisdiction. Rather, he claims, his age is a "jurisdictional fact" that must be proved to the jury in the Juvenile Court, a court of limited jurisdiction.

We reject that contention. As Jarvis acknowledges, the age of a juvenile is not an element of the offense of delinquency. It is the juvenile's conduct and not his age which constitutes the offense. Age is a condition which entitles him to treatment deemed by the Legislature less onerous than that accorded to an adult under the criminal law.

Age is also a matter usually within the juvenile's knowledge. In this case the exact date of birth appears on the complaint. Where, as here, the delinquent made no claim either in the trial court or in this court that he was not in fact between the ages alleged in the complaint, he may not challenge the adjudication of delinquency on the ground that the Commonwealth has not proved age.

This conclusion accords with the "clear legislative intent to give a broad application to the specialized juvenile offender procedure." To require specific proof of age might needlessly make it difficult for the Commonwealth to invoke the protection of the act for the benefit of minors and might delay, if not defeat, its protective purpose. [The s]tate may have difficulty obtaining proof such as the testimony of a parent, a birth certificate, or an admission by the alleged delinquent. We thus hold that when no claim is made that the alleged delinquent is not a juvenile, evidence of age need not be produced by the Commonwealth, and no specific finding by the judge or the jury as to age is necessary.

Choco v. United States
383 A.2d 333 (D.C. 1978)

Appellant is charged by indictment with burglary I, burglary II, and four counts of willful failure to appear in court proceedings in violation of conditions of release. By pretrial motion, appellant moved that she be treated as a juvenile and that her case be transferred from the Criminal Division of the Superior Court to the Family Division. The judge of the Criminal Division determined, after an evidentiary hearing, that appellant was not a juvenile. Appellant asserts that the government did not bear its burden of proving that she was not a juvenile. The government argues that the trial court's finding was supported by the evidence but that we have no jurisdiction to entertain this appeal because it is from a non-final order. We hold that the order is presently appealable and reverse.

. . . .

A defendant's asserted right to disposition in juvenile proceedings ... is forever lost if not resolved in her favor before jeopardy has attached. The ruling in this case meets all the tests of finality....

At the evidentiary hearing, appellant introduced evidence which, if believed, would have established her birth date as May 4, 1960. The government, on the other hand, introduced the testimony of two expert witnesses. The first of these, a forensic dentist, testified that appellant was, in May 1977, between the ages of seventeen and twenty years, "toward the lower end." The other expert witness for the government, a pediatric radiologist, testified that appellant's age, in June 1977, was "in excess of eighteen years." From this testimony the hearing judge concluded that the appellant was more then sixteen years of age when the burglary was committed and that she should, therefore, be treated as an adult.

Appellant asserts that the finding was not supported by the evidence and that the hearing judge erred in not finding appellant's age "beyond a reasonable doubt." The government argues that the finding was supported by the record and that, while it must prove age by a preponderance of the evidence, it need do no more.

We need not reach the issue of which standard is applicable to the resolution of this jurisdictional fact. In order for appellant to be subject to criminal prosecution, absent transfer from the family division, she must have been sixteen years of age on April 17, 1975, the date of the alleged burglary. *A fortiori*, appellant must have been eighteen years of age on April 17, 1977. Evidence that appellant was between seventeen and twenty, or in excess of eighteen in May or June 1977, tended to prove only that appellant attained eighteen years of age sometime before May or June 1977, not that she attained that age by April 17, 1977. The finding that appellant had attained the age of sixteen on April 17, 1975, therefore, is without support in the record.

The government having failed to bear its burden of proof on this jurisdictional fact, the court must, on remand, transfer this case to the Family Division. Such transfer, we note, does not preclude re-transfer of appellant's case for criminal prosecution under the provisions of the D.C. Code. The government's failure of proof that appellant was sixteen years of age on April 17, 1975, does not foreclose proof that she was at least fifteen years of age on that date, or that she is at least eighteen years of age at present, and, therefore, eligible for transfer for criminal prosecution upon the further findings required by [the] D.C. Code.

Commonwealth of Pennsylvania v. Iafrate
561 A.2d 1244 (Pa. Super. Ct. 1989)[1]

This is an appeal of a judgment of sentence following a trial by jury where the Appellant was found guilty of one count of simple assault, not guilty on another count of simple assault, and not guilty of the summary offense of obstructing and loitering.

This conviction stemmed from an incident which occurred at 8:15 p.m. on September 29, 1985, involving Appellant and a police officer. The police officer attempted to issue a loitering citation to Appellant who was kneeling on the curb next to a car parked on a heavily traveled portion of the public thoroughfare. Appellant was arrested that evening. The next day, September 30, was Appellant's eighteenth birthday. Prior to trial, Appellant filed a motion to quash and transfer the case to juvenile court. This motion was denied and Appellant was tried as an adult.

In this appeal, Appellant ... claims the trial court erred in denying his motion to transfer his case to Juvenile Court....

Prior to trial, Appellant filed a motion to transfer his case to Juvenile Court. * * * As defined by statute, a child is an individual who is under eighteen (18) years of age. Thus if Appellant were a child at the time the crime was committed, then a transfer to Juvenile Court would have been required.

According to common and accepted usage, an individual is seventeen years of age until his or her eighteenth birthday, the anniversary of the date of birth. Therefore, it is generally and commonly understood that prior to that birthday a person is "under eighteen years of age."

However, the common law of this state does not follow this prevailing usage, and instead, for reasons founded on arcane principles of early common law, a person is deemed to attain a given age on the day before his or her birthday.

Thus, because we are constrained by precedent from our court and from the Pennsylvania Supreme Court, we must affirm the trial court's holding that Appellant was not a "child" on the day before his eighteenth birthday, and was not entitled to trial under the Juvenile Act.

However, we would ask the Supreme Court of Pennsylvania and General Assembly of Pennsylvania to take note of this archaic rule. Because we, as an intermediate appellate court, can not decide to change established precedent, we ask that these bodies reconsider whether they intended that Pennsylvania statutes which specify certain ages for the purposes of determining attainment of majority, should be construed according to this common law method of age computation which unnecessarily complicates matters and contravenes accepted usage.

---

1. This case was reversed, 594 A.2d 293, 295–96 (Pa. 1991) ("For purposes of the [Juvenile] Act [only], an individual becomes a year older on the day of his birthday and not the day before." *Id.* at 295.).

We are aware of several states which have changed the common law rule, either legislatively or judicially. We would urge the same course here, noting the words of Justice Holmes:

> It is revolting to have no better reason for a rule of law than that so it was laid down in the time of Henry the IV. It is still more revolting if the grounds upon which it was laid down have vanished long since, and the rule simply persists from blind imitation of the past.

In the Matter of M.E.
982 S.W.2d 528 (Tex. App. 1998)

M.E. argues that the juvenile court lacked jurisdiction over her because she was married when she committed the offenses for which she was adjudicated delinquent. We disagree and affirm.

. . . .

In her sole point of error, M.E. argues that married persons under the age of eighteen should be tried in criminal court, rather then juvenile court. She bases this argument on the fact that such persons are considered to be emancipated in other contexts. She also points out that in certain circumstances the juvenile court may waive its jurisdiction and transfer a juvenile for trial in criminal court. We recognize that married juveniles are treated as adults under many aspects of the civil law. [The Texas Family Code provides that] "[e]xcept as expressly provided by statute or by the constitution, a person, regardless of age, who has been married in accordance with the law of this state has the capacity and power of an adult, including the capacity to contract." Nevertheless, the thesis that married juveniles are not subject to juvenile court jurisdiction is contradicted by the language of the Juvenile Justice Code, rejected by case law, and contrary to reason.

The Juvenile Justice Code confers upon juvenile courts exclusive original jurisdiction over "proceedings in all cases involving the delinquent conduct * * * engaged in by a person who was a child within the meaning of this title at the time he engaged in the conduct." "Child," in turn, is defined as a person who is: (A) ten years of age or older and under 17 years of age; or (B) seventeen years of age or older and under 18 years of age who is alleged or found to have engaged in delinquent conduct or conduct indicating a need for supervision as a result of acts committed before becoming 17 years of age. The statute thus defines "child" only with reference to age, and not with reference to marital status.

We are charged with applying the literal text of statutes. Based on the literal text of section 51.02 (2), we conclude that a person who falls within the statute's age limits is a "child" and is subject to juvenile court jurisdiction regardless of his or her marital status.

Two ... statutes in the Juvenile Justice Code reinforce our conclusion that married juveniles are subject to juvenile court jurisdiction. Section 51.03 (e) excludes married persons from the definition of "child" for purposes of certain conduct indicating a need for supervision. This statute thus recognizes that married persons are ordinarily included within the definition of "child." Additionally, § 51.02 (10) defines "party" to include the child who is the subject of the proceedings or "the child's parent, *spouse*, guardian, or guardian ad litem." This statute recognizes that persons subject to juvenile court jurisdiction may be married. We also note that M.E.'s argument has been rejected by courts construing the predecessors to the current Juvenile Justice Code.

Finally, M.E. asserts that it is wrong to subject married juveniles to the "vagaries" of the juvenile justice system. This argument should be made to the legislature rather than this court. It bears pointing out, however, that one of the purposes of juvenile adjudications is to avoid branding a child a criminal and to allow her to retain rights that would be lost to an adult offender. Although a juvenile offender is afforded the important constitutional protections provided to adult offenders in criminal court, she does not encounter the same legal disabilities upon her release as an adult offender would. It is difficult to perceive how this system is unfair; indeed, the adjudication rather than conviction is considered preferable.

Because it is undisputed that M.E. was under 17 when she committed these offenses she was a "child" subject to juvenile court jurisdiction.

Note

Usually young persons charged with criminal acts want to be tried in juvenile court rather than criminal court. Why is M.E. so anxious to be tried in criminal court?

Commonwealth of Pennsylvania v. Anderson
630 A.2d 47 (Pa. Super. Ct. 1993)

The relevant facts and procedural history of this case may be summarized as follows. In 1985, while at age sixteen (16), appellee allegedly participated in a fight with another teenager in a playground and struck the teenager in the head with a baseball bat. Subsequently, appellee was arrested and charged with possession of an instrument of crime, ... possession of a weapon, recklessly endangering another person, simple assault, and aggravated assault. Appellee failed to appear for his scheduled hearing in the Family Court Division. Due to appellee's failure to appear, a bench warrant was issued.

In 1988, while at age nineteen (19), appellee allegedly committed the offense of retail theft. According to the record, appellee once again failed to appear for his scheduled hearing. As a result, the Philadelphia Municipal Court issued another bench warrant for appellee's arrest.

In 1991, appellee, at age twenty-two (22), was arrested on other charges. The Commonwealth recharged appellee as an adult with the crimes he allegedly committed at the age of sixteen (16). Also at this time, the Family Court Division lifted appellee's first bench warrant and transferred the case to the Trial Division on the ground that the appellee was no longer a "child" as defined in the Juvenile Act.

The court in the Trial Division heard and granted appellee's oral motion to dismiss charges on the ground that the court in the Trial Division of the Court of Common Pleas lacked jurisdiction over juvenile offenders. The Trial Division then remanded the case to the Juvenile Division and quashed all bills of information. However, the Trial Division court later vacated its order granting appellee's motion to reconsider the Commonwealth's petition.... Nonetheless, following reconsideration, the Trial Division court affirmed its decision to dismiss for lack of subject matter jurisdiction and denied relief to the Commonwealth. The Commonwealth filed this timely appeal.

In its appeal, the Commonwealth argues that appellee, who committed crimes at age sixteen (16), then remained on fugitive status until recaptured at age twenty-two (22), is no longer a child as defined by the Juvenile Act. Therefore, the Trial Division court erred in dismissing the charges against appellee on the ground that the court has no jurisdiction because the appellee is no longer a child within the definition of the Juvenile Act. The Commonwealth further asserts that appellee can be tried as an adult in the Trial Division because appellee, by virtue of his sustained fugitive status, forfeited his opportunity to benefit from being tried as a child in the Family Court Division.

Appellee, on the other hand, contends that he should still be considered a child under the Juvenile Act because he is being charged with crimes allegedly committed at age sixteen (16). Appellee concludes that he should be tried in the Family Court Division.

The Juvenile Court Act defines a child as follows: "'Child.' An individual who: (1) is under the age of 18 years; (2) is under the age of 21 years who committed an act of delinquency before reaching the age of 18 years; or (3) was adjudicated dependent before reaching the age of 18 years and who, while engaged in a course of instruction or treatment, requests the court to retain jurisdiction until the course has been completed, but in no event shall a child remain in a course of instruction or treatment past the age of 21 years."

In the instant case, although appellee allegedly committed certain crimes before reaching the age of eighteen (18), he is now over the age of twenty-one (21). Appellee's current age places him outside the Juvenile Act's definition of a child. Therefore, the Juvenile Act does not apply to him. The inapplication of the Act to the appellee, however, does not mean that he inhabits a jurisdictional limbo between the Family Court Division and the Trial Division. Because of his current age, appellee is not a child. Thus, he should be tried as an adult in the Trial Division.

Appellee would have been tried as a child if it were not for his deliberate avoidance of the justice system. The instance case is analogous to *Commonwealth v. Sims*. In *Sims*, appellant refused to reveal his age to the Trial Division trial court. On appeal, appellant claimed that the trial court lacked jurisdiction because it never properly ascertained that appellant was a child at the time of trial. This Court held that "the Juvenile Act provided appellant the opportunity to request that his case be transferred to Juvenile Court and appellant failed to avail himself of this opportunity" by not divulging his correct age. Even if the appellant had been a minor at the time of trial, which was not determined, he waived his right to be transferred to Family Court Division by refusing to reveal his age.

Similarly, appellee, by virtue of his flight, denied himself the opportunity to be tried in the Family Court Division. Specifically, appellee did not appear at his scheduled hearing in Family Court in 1985. Appellee's action thus forfeited any benefits that he might have derived from the Juvenile Court System. See *Commonwealth v. Jones* (holding that appellant's voluntary escape acts as *per se* forfeiture of his right to appeal).

As an alternative argument, appellee points out that the Commonwealth had appellee in its control at age nineteen (19) when he was arrested for retail theft. Appellee contends that the Commonwealth should have seized the opportunity to recharge appellee with his previous crimes at that time because, at age nineteen (19) he would still be considered a child under the Juvenile Act. Appellee concludes that the Commonwealth should be barred from recharging appellee as an adult with those crimes allegedly committed at age sixteen (16) due to the Commonwealth's failure to recharge appellee at age nineteen (19), when it had the opportunity to due so.

Yet, the appellee failed to proffer record evidence that the Commonwealth was even aware of appellee's prior juvenile charges. Appellee also neglects to present any evidence that he informed the Commonwealth that he was available to be tried on the juvenile charges, that he requested that the Commonwealth try him as a juvenile, or that he otherwise availed himself of the benefits of the Juvenile Act when they were his as of right. Thus, appellee's alternative argument is groundless.

Note

The result in *Anderson* depends in large part on the wording of the statute. What if juvenile court jurisdiction depends on age at the time of the criminal act without regard to age at the time of trial. Consider the following scenario: A man thirty-five years of age is charged with killing a person when he was twelve years of age (the evidence did not become available until the present time). Currently, and at the time of the murder, the statute in that jurisdiction defines a delinquent child as a person under the age of 18 who commits an act which if committed by an adult would constitute a crime. The age limitation depends solely on the age at the time of the act. Under the statute waiver is not permitted unless the child is 15 or over. Furthermore, all dispositions end when the child is 21. How should this case be handled? Given the statute, what result? From time to time such cases do arise.

D. Taking a Juvenile into Custody

1. Summons

State v. S.C.W.

718 So. 2d 320 (Fla. Dist. Ct. App. 1998)

The State has filed two petitions for certiorari or mandamus in four juvenile proceedings. The State wants this court to compel the trial court to issue an order to take each child into state custody because each child failed to appear for a juvenile delinquency proceeding after a summons was mailed to his or her last known address. We deny the petitions. If a child has been released from state custody before a petition for delinquency is filed and without receiving a notice to appear pursuant to Florida Rule of Juvenile Procedure 8.045, we conclude that proper notice for purposes of § 985.207(1)(c), Florida Statutes (1997), is not accomplished by first class mail. Even if a juvenile does not appear for arraignment when properly noticed, we conclude that a trial court has discretion to decline to issue an order to take the child into custody under the language of § 985.207.

. . . .

The parties involved in these cases have analyzed the legal question as one of jurisdiction over the person of the juvenile. The State argues that the trial court had jurisdiction over the person of the juveniles in these cases because § 985.219(7), Florida Statutes (1997), provides that the court's jurisdiction "shall attach to the child" when a summons is served on the child and a guardian or "when the child is taken into custody with or without service of summons and before or after the filing of a petition, whichever first occurs. * * *" "Taken into custody" has a statutory definition. [It] ... means the status of a child immediately when temporary physical control over the child is attained by a person authorized by law, pending the child's release, detention, placement, or other disposition as authorized by law.

The State argues that the juveniles were taken into custody by the deputy sheriffs or by officials at the juvenile assessment centers, and that the court had jurisdiction over their persons from that moment forward — even if no petition alleging delinquency was ever filed.

This argument is too simplistic because the issue is whether a pickup order must be signed by the judge in these cases, not whether the court has some level of jurisdiction over the juvenile. The concepts of "custody" and "taken into custody" are used many times in chapter 985 and in the Florida Rules of Juvenile Procedure. For example, a child "taken into custody" may be released to an assessment center, that in turn may "release" the child from custody. Indeed, the title of the section concerning the type of pickup orders at issue in this case is "Taking a Child Into Custody." Thus, a child may be "taken into custody" for failure to appear at a hearing, even though he or she was already "taken into custody" by a law enforcement officer. Finally, "taken into custody" is also a term used to determine the period for speedy trial in juvenile cases. Thus, it appears that the analysis used to determine whether a pickup order may issue must involve a more precise analysis.

Section 985.207(1)(c) states that a child "may" be taken into custody "for failing to appear at a court hearing after being properly served." Upon the face of this statute, the dispositive issues in this case are: (1) whether a juvenile is "properly served" when the summons and petition are mailed, first class, to the juvenile's last known address, and (2) whether a trial judge must sign a pickup order for a child eligible for pickup under this statue whenever the State requests such an order.

We agree with the trial court that proper notice for purposes of § 985.207(1)(c) requires more than a simple letter to a last known address. Even if a child has been "taken into custody," Florida Rule of Juvenile Procedure 8.040(a) requires that a summons be issued and served upon a child "who is not detained." If it is likely that such service will be difficult or impossible, the State always has the option of giving the child actual notice while he or she is detained by employing the notice to appear procedures in rule 8.045. Those procedures, which were not used in these cases, expressly provide for an order to take into custody if the child does not appear.

2. Probable Cause

Lanes v. Texas

767 S.W.2d 789 (Tex. Crim. App. 1989)

Opinion on Appellant's Petition for Discretionary Review

WHITE, Judge.

Appellant, a juvenile certified for trial as an adult under § 54.02 [of the] Family Code, was convicted of burglary of a habitation. Punishment was assessed at twenty years imprisonment.

The Ninth Court of Appeals affirmed the conviction holding, *inter alia*, that a fingerprint order, issued pursuant to § 51.15 [of the] Family Code, provided sufficient probable cause to arrest and fingerprint a juvenile.[6] Appellant petitioned this Court for discretionary review arguing that, independent of the § 51.15 probable cause requirement to fingerprint a child, Article I, Section 9 of the Texas Constitution and the Fourth and Fourteenth Amendments of the United States Constitution require probable cause to arrest a child in order to obtain his fingerprints. Because this raises a question of first im-

---

6. The validity of the arrest is determined solely upon appellant's rights as a juvenile. The fact that appellant was later certified and tried as an adult has no retroactive impact on his initial arrest which was made prior to certification.

pression, i.e, whether the probable cause requirement of Art. I, §9 and the Fourth Amendment applies in full force to a juvenile arrest, we granted appellant's petition. After having carefully considered the issues, we now hold that [they do].

The facts of the case can be simply stated. Pursuant to a constant order from the juvenile court authorizing the taking of appellant's fingerprints, a police officer arrested appellant at his high school, transported him to the police station and took his fingerprints. The trial court as well as the Court of Appeals found that this order provided sufficient authority for an arrest. We disagree.

The issue presented is whether the probable cause requisite of Art. I, §9 of the Texas Constitution and the Fourth Amendment of the U.S. Constitution, applicable to the states through the Fourteenth, applies to the arrest of a child. This precise issue has not been decided by our Court or the U.S. Supreme Court. It has, however, long been settled that the Fourth Amendment is, to some undetermined extent, applicable to juvenile proceedings. This rule was best expressed in the seminal opinion on juvenile rights — *In re Gault*.

....

One of the fundamental goals of the juvenile system is rehabilitation. Essential to a rehabilitative environment is the proper attitudinal setting. Children have the strongest sense of justice — a product of youth, energy, and innocence. Such an inherent sense of justice, however, is fragile and can easily be turned to cynicism, helplessness, disillusionment and disrespect. Not only would such an attitude be contra — rehabilitative, but it could breed dissension and reactionary criminal behavior.

A child arrested without valid reason by a seemingly all-powerful and challengeless exercise of police power would instantly intuit the injustice and react accordingly. Even a juvenile who has violated the law but is unfairly arrested will feel deceived and thus resist any rehabilitative efforts. Inherent in youth is a malleable nature, and example can be the most formidable teacher. We must institutionalize justice in order to engender it among our youth. Affording a child the essentials of basic human dignity and announcing a respect for their autonomy through the extension of constitutional privacy protections can only further these efforts.

Other important goals of the Texas juvenile scheme include protection of the community and the child. We as a society have decided that evidence less than that which would convince a reasonable man that an offense is being or has been committed does not constitute a sufficient showing of guilt to validate the deprivation of personal freedom attendant to an arrest. Thus, implicit in the probable cause requirement is the presumption of innocence. The community need not be protected from a child who has presumptively not committed an offense. Nor does a child need to be protected from himself when he is not in trouble. Thus, requiring probable cause can only help to prevent such erroneous and unnecessary arrests.

The Texas juvenile system also seeks to avoid the taint of criminality in order to prevent recidivism and promote rehabilitation. The best method of avoiding attachment of a criminal taint is keeping the child completely out of the system. Studies are legion which conclude that once a child is arrested and becomes involved in the juvenile system the chances are almost non-existent that he can later withdraw himself or be cleansed of the criminal taint. Even a single arrest can brand a child as a delinquent to outsiders. He could be stigmatized as criminal by teachers, parents, employers, and law enforcement officers and could be labeled as "cool" among his peers. Both reputations would be injurious. Discrimination by parents, teachers, employers, and police would severely limit the child's educational or employment goals or subject him to unwarranted arrests or police purview. Peer pressure could result in the child striving to live up to his "cool" reputation by committing other crimes. Requiring probable cause to arrest a child can only serve to reduce the risk that innocent youths will be so erroneously stigmatized.

An almost unavoidable consequence of arrest is detention. Pre-trial detention can be extremely destructive to a child's life and act as the determinative factor toward recidivism. The impressionability of juveniles can make even the most minimal experience of incarceration extremely injurious, and such injury is compounded where confinement is unfounded. All too quickly juveniles subjected to detention come to view society at large as "oppressive" and "hostile" and to "regard themselves as irremediably 'delinquent.'" ... Such negative self-labeling is clearly counter-rehabilitative and can easily lead to self-fulfilling prophecy. It seems appropriate to require some probable cause evidence of wrongdoing before subjecting a child to the possibility of such detriment.

Further, the disruption that detention causes in a child's everyday life runs counter to any rehabilitative efforts. If the child is attending school, a week's absence while in detention would undoubtedly cause him to fall behind in his work thus enhancing disillusionment and contributing to the possibility that he will drop out. Further, if employed, the child's absence from work could cause loss of employment which further entangles him in a downward spiral. Lack of education and a poor employment record—two major causes of recidivism—can only serve to perpetuate delinquency. An arresting officer makes the first and, thus, most important decision of whether the child will be arrested and introduced into a system plagued with such negative possibilities. Such a momentous and determinative decision should at least be based on facts sufficient to sustain a reasonable belief that an offense was being or had been committed.

A further purpose of the juvenile system is preservation of the family environment either at home or, when detention is a necessity, to perpetuate a family-type atmosphere in the detention facility. Obviously, the optimal method of family preservation is keeping the family intact. [R]equiring some evidence of wrongdoing before disrupting the family and removing the child can only further this goal.

The old adage that a child, by virtue of his age, has no right to freedom but only a right to custody since he is presumably under constant parental control, does not withstand scrutiny or application in the instant context. Assuredly, a child is or should be under constant parental authority, but this comprises an entirely different form of custody than that of State detention. No one seriously argues anymore that State custody in any way approximates the family environment. Quite to the contrary, one judge summarized the realities of pre-trial detention thus:

> "Over half a million juveniles annually detained in 'junior jails,' another several
> hundred thousand in adult jails, penned like cattle, demoralized by lack of activities and trained staff. Often brutalized. Over half the facilities in which juveniles
> are held have no psychiatric or social work staff. A fourth have no school program. The median age of detainees is fourteen; the novice may be sodomized
> within a matter of hours. Many have not been charged with a crime at all." ...

The foregoing discussion renders the conclusion that the purposes of the Texas juvenile system and the probable cause requirement of Art. I, §9 are in harmony. The limitations imposed by these two protective entities do not conflict or undermine one another, but rather accommodate and enhance the goals sought by both. Probable cause protects the sanctity of personal freedom through the prevention of unnecessary arrests. The juvenile system was designed to protect and rehabilitate children. We in no way see how imposing a probable cause requirement will deter juvenile court from pursuing its ameliorative goals.

The final consideration to be factored in is the realistic fact that, even at the expense of procedural protections, the exalted ideals of the juvenile system have failed in achievement. Reading [the U.S. Supreme Court] cases elicits a growing sense of frustration in that the Court over a span of forty years constantly criticized yet patiently abided and awaited the success of a [failing] system. . . .

In *McKeiver*, one of the more recent cases, the Court, after an extensive discussion of the failings of the juvenile system and whether it should be abandoned, noted, "[p]erhaps that ultimate disillusionment will come one day, but for the moment we are disinclined to give impetus to it." The juvenile justice system will soon be 100 years old. At this point in time this Court is prepared to realistically face and, to some extent, rebuff the system's failings.

Research and program analysis evaluations have shown that the efficacy of the juvenile system's rehabilitative institutions is challengeable. Patience and the passage of time have failed to vindicate the system. Quite to the contrary, there is ample historical as well as current data to demonstrate that juvenile justice has been a consistently retrogressive social enterprise. Although there are examples of quality probation and other treatment services, the truth is that these are few and far between. The majority of our youths are falling through rehabilitative cracks. Juveniles are often either exposed to experimental therapeutic techniques that are demeaning or violate fairness, or they are banished to institutions that fail to offer any treatment or accord with even minimal constitutional requisites. The system is clearly far more punitive than rehabilitative. One scholar estimates that juveniles receive 100 times more punishment than treatment.

Further, reality fails to reflect the protective and professional intentions expected of all participants in the system. In this area in particular the gap between rhetoric and reality is phenomenal. The success of the system is completely dependent upon the availability of resources and on the interest, expertise, commitment and concern of the system's participants. Too often juvenile court personnel fall "far short" of being the "stalwart," sympathetic, paternalistic, and "communicating" professionals envisaged by the system. The "community's unwillingness" to provide funding for staff and facilities, the "insufficiency of time devoted" the "scarcity"of truly professional resources, the "inadequacy of dispositional alternatives," and the "general lack" of diagnostic expertise all contribute to the system's failing. Once again, time has served to exacerbate rather than absolve these problems. Our juveniles are being thrust into a precarious system where all personnel are presumed to consider the child's best interests, yet none has the time, training, resources or sometimes even the inclination to do so. Thus, as one juvenile court judge has aptly summarized, "loose procedure, high-handed methods, and crowded court calendars" have resulted in "arbitrariness" and assembly line dispositions.

Nor does the palatable terminology of the juvenile system alter this reality. The adoption of a soft vocabulary in an attempt to dispel labeling and promote professionalism has been ineffective. Words such as "detention," "juvenile delinquent," and "commitment" have proven no less severe or to carry no less of a criminal taint. Further, utilization of medical terminology has not rendered treatment which is medically founded. Reality reflects that the juvenile court's unique terminology consists of nothing more than euphemisms unable to alter the punitive consequences inherent in any kind of judicial intervention.

Although the denial of certain procedural protections could be countenanced by the founder's goals, when these goals fail in achievement, then the time has come for change. It is now poignantly evident that good intentions alone cannot replace constitutional safeguards. Reincarnated is Grandfather *Gault's* announcement that the "condition of being a boy does not justify a kangaroo court." In the face of the unpredictable and arbitrary dispositional and rehabilitative atmosphere of the system, procedure must become the unifying stalwart of fairness, uniformity and predictability.

This is not to say that the rehabilitative intent of the juvenile processes should be completely overridden; nor do we mean to denigrate the admirable aspirations and ideals of the founders. Even in the face of the system's failures, we are not convinced that current practice does not contain the philosophical progeny from which a truly rehabilitative, treatment-oriented system can be created. We do, however, intend to eschew the protective "label-of-convenience" and extinguish the heretofore blinding aspects of tradition, sentiment, naive faith, and habit in order to set the stage for candid judicial confrontation of the realities of the system.

The failure of the juvenile system is not merely a legalistic problem or a singular problem of the individual involved. It is a problem shared by all. Society as a whole shares not only the blame for the system's failures but also will undoubtedly carry the economic and emotional burden of its repeat offenders. We are now attempting to evolve a new methodology to truly provide a child with the best of both the juvenile and criminal worlds—the treatment model of the juvenile system and the procedural protections of the adult. Thus, while we dispel the antiquated and unrealistic resistance to procedural safeguards, we continue to embrace a rehabilitative and treatment oriented spirit.

Based on the foregoing analysis, we now extend the probable cause requirement of Art. I, § 9 and the Fourth Amendment to juvenile proceedings. Our holding today represents an accommodation between the aspirations of the juvenile court and the grim realities of the system. Although we are adopting another requisite of the criminal system, we find that requiring probable cause for arrest will not compel abandonment or displacement of the juvenile system's commendable rehabilitative intentions. Such a requisite places minimal fetters on police discretion in making decisions that concern fundamental rights of personal privacy and freedom and have the potential for particularly detrimental effects on a child's life. This holding is also in the line with Texas statutory guidelines for a juvenile arrest....

Further, in light of the most recent caselaw in this area, there is great need for application of this probable cause protection. Most recently, in *Vasquez v. State,* this Court held that the Article 14.04, V.A.C.C.P. warrant requirement is not applicable to juveniles. We determined that to require a warrant would unnecessarily restrict the flexibility of protective police action. This holding was predicated upon the expectation that the officer would himself have probable cause to arrest. Thus, juveniles can freely be arrested without a warrant. Since there is no unbiased judicial probable cause determination prior to arrest, at the very least, law enforcement officers can be expected to personally have probable cause for a juvenile arrest and also be held responsible for a reasonable articulation of such at a later hearing. The hope is that through this requirement dubious or unjust arrests will be generally deterred and prevented from the outset.

Also relatively recently, the U.S. Supreme Court held in *Schall* that juveniles can properly be subject to pre-trial detention without a judicial determination of probable cause for up to six days. The *Schall* Court further announced that juveniles can properly be denied any opportunity to pre-trial release. Thus, once a juvenile is arrested he can be subjected to continual incarceration for a disruptively lengthy period of time without an unbiased judicial determination that such incarceration is at all warranted. This is especially true in Texas, where there is no statutory requirement of a judicial probable cause determination for pretrial detention. Although caselaw mandates a finding of probable cause for valid extended detention, it is not clear that such a determination is routinely made. As discussed *ante*, detention can be extremely detrimental and contra to the goals of the juvenile court, especially when it is unjustified; thus, a minimal probable cause restriction at the time of arrest can only serve to help prevent such detriment.

Finally, imposition of a probable cause requirement will not severely limit or disrupt proper law enforcement since it is not an ultra-restrictive requirement. Rather, it was purposely designed as a realistic, practical, and workable determination to be based upon the "totality of the circumstances" presented. Because the probable cause standard is a commonsense test, its application is sufficiently flexible to ensure reasonable law enforcement as well as juvenile protection. The probable cause requirement rests on the principal that a true balance between an individual—whether youth or adult—and the government depends on the recognition and respect of "the right to be let alone—the most comprehensive of rights and the right most valued by civilized men." Today we are proudly able to afford such a right to juveniles.

Application of this law to the instant facts requires reversal....

The statute expressly states that, in order to fingerprint a child, not only must one of the exceptions to the general prohibition be met, but also it must be "otherwise authorized by law." § 51.15(f). As was recognized in the Draftsman['s] comment to the Family Code, this additional proviso explicitly emphasizes the fact that seizure of a juvenile in order to take fingerprints must comport with constitutional requisites.

It is agreed that the officers had authority to fingerprint appellant pursuant to the 51.15 consent order; however, this order in no way conferred authority to arrest. At a suppression hearing, the State carries the burden of either producing a warrant and supporting affidavit or establishing evidentiary facts sufficient to show probable cause. In the instant case the State did not come forward with a warrant, but only introduced the fingerprint consent form. The State and the Court of Appeals seem to argue that this form takes the place of an arrest warrant, thus shifting the burden of proof back to appellant. This argument does not withstand scrutiny. The bare-bones fingerprint consent order neither facially confers authority to arrest nor evinces any factual probable cause basis. Further, there is nothing on the face of the order which exhibits any judicial intent to authorize an arrest. Having none of the protective characteristics or purposes of a warrant, this order simply cannot take the place of such.

Without a warrant, the State carried the burden of establishing the validity of the arrest. This burden the State wholly failed to carry. At the suppression hearing, the judge who issued the order did not testify and no facts were elicited concerning probable cause. Thus we find that appellant's fingerprints were taken during an illegal juvenile arrest which was not founded on probable cause. Because the only direct evidence linking appellant to the scene of the crime was his fingerprints, we cannot say beyond a reasonable doubt that their introduction made no contribution to the verdict. Consequently, we reverse the holding of the Court of Appeals and remand this cause to the trial court.

Notes

(a) How persuasive is the *Lane* court's distinction of *Vasquez*? *Vasquez* appears in Chapter 7, *infra*.

(b) Is the court's reasoning consistent with the Supreme Court's opinion in *Schall v. Martin* in Chapter 2, *supra*?

3. Resisting Arrest

In the Matter of Hartsfield
531 S.W.2d 149 (Tex. Civ. App. 1975)

Appellant [argues] that a juvenile cannot violate a law of this State by resisting arrest because § 52.01(b) provides that the taking of a child into custody is not an arrest. No cases have been cited nor have we found any construing the effect of this section of the Family Code. However, there are cases decided under the Family Code which state that a juvenile was arrested.

A purpose of Title 3, which includes § 52.01, is to remove from children committing unlawful acts the taint of criminality. The objective of § 52.01(b) is to avoid the stigmatizing effect of an arrest upon a child. However, the Legislature did not intend by the enactment of § 52.01(b), to permit a child to forcefully resist arrest.

A person is arrested when he has been actually placed under restraint or "Taken into Custody * * *." We hold that the term, "arrest", as used in Tex. Penal Code Ann. § 38.03, includes the taking into custody of a juvenile.

4. Confessions

In the Matter of J.B.J.
86 S.W.3d 810 (Tex. App. 2002)

Under Texas law, a person taking a child into custody must promptly notify the child's parent, guardian, or custodian of that fact and of the reason for taking the child into custody. JBJ contends the officers took him into custody upon leaving the school, which the State concedes, and failed to promptly notify a parent, a point that the State challenges. JBJ claims that the violation of the statute renders his confession inadmissible, and that the trial court should have granted his motion to suppress.

The juvenile has the burden to raise non-compliance with the Family Code's requirements. Once the juvenile raises the issue, the State has the burden to demonstrate compliance.

Application of Law to the Facts

JBJ claims the officers violated § 52.02(b)(1). No violation of his constitutional rights or of any other statutory provision is claimed on appeal. JBJ argues only that a parent was not "promptly notified" when he was taken into custody, and for that reason his confession should have been suppressed. We are required to decide whether an approximate hour and a half time frame meets the prompt notification requirement of the Texas Family Code.

The Family Code does not provide us with a definition of "promptly" in this context. We look first to the meaning of "promptly" as the word is commonly used. The adjective "prompt" generally means "ready and quick to act as occasion demands; immediately or instantly at hand." *Black's Law Dictionary* defines the adverb "promptly" as doing something "without delay" and "with reasonable speed." These definitions suggest the meaning of the word "promptly" in § 52.02(b) includes consideration of what is reasonable speed under the circumstances.

We note that the words "prompt" or "promptly" are employed in other sections of the Juvenile Justice Code. For example, on referral of a child's case to the office designated by the juvenile court, the office shall promptly give notice of the referral and a statement of the reason for the referral to the child's parents. In § 53.01, the Code provides that "[w]hen custody of a child is given to the office or official designated by the juvenile board, the intake officer, probation officer, or other person authorized by the court shall promptly give notice of the whereabouts of the child and a statement of the reason the child was taken into custody to the child's parent, guardian, or custodian unless the notice given under § 52.02(b) provided fair notice of the child's present whereabouts." In § 53.012(a), the prosecutor is required to promptly review the circumstances and allegations of a referral.

In contrast to these uses of the word "promptly," the Juvenile Justice Code also contains a section that provides that a detention hearing, subject to certain exceptions, shall be held "promptly, but not later than the second working day after the child is taken into custody[.]" The fact that the parental notification provision gives no specific time deadline suggests that a determination of whether notification was "promptly" given requires consideration of the circumstances of the specific case. We believe courts must determine what constitutes prompt parental notification ... by determining whether, considering the circumstances of the particular case, the notification was with reasonable speed.

In *Vann,* the court cited the following four factors that have been considered by other courts in determining whether parental notification was prompt under the circumstances of a particular case: (1) the length of time the juvenile was in custody before the police notified a parent, guardian, or custodian; (2) whether notification occurred after the police obtained a statement; (3) the ease with which the police were ultimately able to contact the appropriate adult; and (4) what the police did during the period of delay. We note some of the factors considered by other courts seem targeted at assessing whether the parental notification attempts were made in good faith or were reasonable under the circumstances. In determining whether parental notification was given with reasonable speed under the circumstances, we believe the factors noted in *Vann* are relevant considerations.

The Court of Criminal Appeals has emphasized the necessity of strict compliance with the Texas Family Code provisions regarding juveniles. Specifically, the parental notification requirement of § 52.02(b) has been the subject of court decisions in criminal cases, where courts generally have strictly applied the requirement. And we note that violation of the parental notification requirement, along with its effect on the admissibility of confessions of juveniles, has also been the subject recently of various courts of appeals['] decisions. The parental notification statute requires strict compliance. However, we do not believe that the necessity for strict compliance precludes our consideration of the totality of the circumstances or of the reasonableness of the efforts to notify the parents. We conclude these considerations are within the meaning of the word "promptly" as used in § 52.02(b).

Here, the parental notification responsibility was delegated by Detective Page to the C.I.S.D. police officer. We recognize that delegation of the parental notification responsibility to another officer may be necessary, and in fact may result in faster parental notification; but once the notification requirement is delegated to another officer, that officer must comply with the requirements of § 52.02(b).

We conclude, considering the reasonable speed exercised under the circumstances of this case, the parental notification here was prompt. We view the evidence in a light most favorable to the trial court's ruling when, as here, there are no findings of fact. Before being taken into custody by Detective Page, J.B.J. "confessed to what she asked." The juvenile then gave the school officer his residence number. JBJ told the officer his mother was not at home. The officer repeatedly tried to call the mother. When the mother still had not arrived home, the officer then called the father at work. Contact was made at that point with a parent—approximately one hour and a half after JBJ was taken into custody. No evidence suggests the attempts to notify the child's parents were less than good faith efforts. No claim is made here of a violation of constitutional rights or of a violation of some other statutory provision. It is undisputed that the confession was taken in compliance with the requirements of §51.095, which governs the admissibility of a statement of a child. Considering the totality of the circumstances in this case and applying the law to the facts, we conclude no violation of §52.02(b) occurred.

Appellant's issue is overruled. The order adjudicating JBJ as having engaged in delinquent conduct is affirmed.

. . . .

DON BURGESS, Justice, concurring.

I concur in the result, but respectfully disagree with the majority's analysis....

The majority utilizes the totality of the circumstances construct in determining whether a violation of the notification statute occurred. No other Texas court has utilized this construct in this manner. If voluntariness of the confession were the issue, then the totality of the circumstances would be considered in making that determination. This appeal does not challenge the voluntariness of the confession; therefore the totality of the circumstances construct is applied inappropriately.

Even with a determination that the notification was not prompt, the judgment must still be affirmed. The Court of Criminal Appeals has concluded that before a juvenile's confession can be excluded, there must be a causal connection between the Family Code violation and the making of the statement. There is no evidence of such a causal connection. Therefore, the trial judge was correct in denying the motion to suppress.

Note

J.B.J. suggests that there are four bases for arguing that a juvenile's confession should be excluded: *Miranda*, the due process clause of the Fourteenth Amendment, the state constitution, or a state statute.

In the Interest of R.L.J.
336 So. 2d 132 (Fla. Dist. Ct. App. 1976)

SMITH, Judge.

Wakulla County deputy sheriff Bailey asked appellant R. L. J., then 14 years old, to go to the sheriff's office for questioning. Bailey there gave the boy warnings required for custodial interrogation by *Miranda v. Arizona*, elicited his confession to breaking and entering a dwelling with intent to commit a misdemeanor, and delivered him to an intake officer of the Division of Youth Services. R. L. J. was adjudicated a delinquent[3] and he now appeals, urging that evidence of his confession should have been suppressed. His lawyer asserts that deputy Bailey made "an unconstitutional arrest" and that neither *Miranda*

---

3. The conviction was unsupported by an explicit trial court finding that appellant's confession was voluntary. Our disposition of the case makes unnecessary the usual remand for a finding on that issue.

warnings nor other intervening circumstances "sufficiently attenuated the taint" of the illegal arrest to "break, for Fourth (and Fourteenth) Amendment purposes, the causal connection between the illegality and the confession." A parallel question arises under Section 12 of Florida's Declaration of Rights, which protects "[t]he right of the people to be secure in their persons * * * against unreasonable * * * seizures. * * *"

Deputy Bailey had a well-founded suspicion, not amounting to probable cause for arrest, that appellant participated in recent burglaries. Bailey decided to question the youth and went to his home, where appellant's father told Bailey that appellant was with his brother-in-law, also a suspect. Bailey explained his wish to question appellant at the sheriff's office and, according to Bailey's testimony, appellant's father replied that he had no objection. Bailey drove to the brother-in-law's house and found appellant in the yard with his brother-in-law. When he asked appellant "if I might talk with him for a little while down at the sheriff's office," appellant inquired, "Why?" Bailey replied that "I would rather wait and go to the sheriff's office and I would explain it to him there." Appellant then "agreed to ride down to the sheriff's office with me in order for me to talk with him." Bailey did not advise the youth he was not obligated to go along for questioning. Appellant explained:

"Well, I figured that him a law officer, you had to, you [k]now, had to go with him."

At the sheriff's office Bailey read *Miranda* warnings to appellant from a card and after 30 to 40 minutes of questioning, obtained the confession which was received in evidence.

I.

Bailey made no arrest "in the technical and restricted sense" when he asked appellant to accompany him to headquarters for questioning. But the absence of a formal arrest does not end the inquiry. The Fourth Amendment monitors arrests whether announced or unannounced, and it applies a rule of reason to both greater and lesser intrusions on protected privacy. Thus, regardless of whether deputy Bailey thought he had "arrested" appellant, and in spite of his disclaimer, any personal seizure unjustified by Fourth Amendment standards must be shown ... not to have influenced the confession on which the State seeks to rely.

The threshold issue, then, is whether there was a personal seizure as defined in *Terry*:

"Obviously, not all personal intercourse between policemen and citizens involves 'seizures' of persons. Only when the officer, by means of physical force or show of authority, has in some way restrained the liberty of a citizen may we conclude that a 'seizure' has occurred."

The record shows that appellant moved progressively into a state of custody from the moment deputy Bailey asserted authority to request appellant's presence at headquarters without explanation. By increments appellant was thereafter "deprived of his freedom of action" in a "significant way." He was 14 and a felony suspect. At first he tentatively challenged the requested interview by asking its purpose. When Bailey parried that inquiry, and so tacitly asserted his will and authority to proceed without explanation, the acquiescing youth was taken by patrol car for questioning at headquarters "in a police-dominated atmosphere."

Considering appellant's youth, the deputy's methods and the purposeful formality of the headquarters visitation, we find that appellant's liberty was restrained to a degree cognizable under the Fourth Amendment. The deputy's Miranda warnings were themselves an acknowledgment—though assuredly not a conclusive one—that the imminent interrogation was custodial and therefore attended by guaranties of the Fifth Amendment, which "is in 'intimate relation' with the Fourth." Appellant was in custody.

II.

Miranda warnings were given and there was no evidence that appellant's confession was coerced by physical deprivation, persistent interrogation or other constraints which the Fifth and Fourteenth Amendments have long been held to condemn. But this was no momentary on-scene intrusion of the sort which the Fourth Amendment accommodates for field investigation. Appellant's detention was more concentrated, lengthier and more purposeful than that, and his privacy interests were therefore more substantial than those of one who, though free to go, is stopped on the street for routine questioning.

It is argued for appellant that a person under 18 cannot voluntarily submit to detention for interrogation in Florida because custodial interrogation without arrest is unauthorized by § 39.03(1), F.S., specifying occasions when a child "may be taken into custody." The cited statute provides that "(a) child may be taken into custody * * *(b) [f]or a delinquent act, pursuant to the laws of arrest * * *," and in other circumstances not here pertinent.

We cannot agree that Florida's statutory enumeration of occasions for taking juveniles into custody forbids custodial questioning of juveniles in all events. Chapter 39 does not purport to govern all relationships between police and juveniles. Its principal concern, as its title indicates, is orderly and sensitive "judicial treatment" of juveniles. That phrase implies a concern for adjudicatory standards and for appropriate ancillary processes. Section 39.01(30) defines "taken into custody," the linchpin phrase of appellant's argument, as

> "the status of a temporary physical control of a child by a person authorized by this chapter, pending his release, detention, or placement."

The statute refers to a child's "release" as his release "to a parent, a responsible adult relative, or an adult approved by the court"; to a child's "detention" as his delivery after parental notice "to the appropriate intake officer or * * *detention home or shelter"; and to his "placement" as judicial release to an adult not a relative. We think the statute was not intended to forbid a brief and otherwise lawful investigative custody which is simply ended, without ceremony, when its legitimate purpose has been served. In these events formal "release, detention, or placement" is rarely "pending" or necessarily desirable. To read chapter 39 as prohibiting all custodial interrogation of nonarrested juveniles would encourage marginally valid arrests for investigative purposes, deprive law enforcement authorities of a means to exonerate innocent suspects, and unduly deter apprehension of many felons. We decline to give chapter 39 an effect so obviously unintended by the legislature.

. . . .

III.

No Florida statute having intervened to prevent appellant's headquarters interrogation, we must base our decision on whether appellant voluntarily submitted to the detention process.

We must first acknowledge that society often has strong interests in encouraging voluntary relinquishment of Fourth Amendment protections at police request. "It is an act of responsible citizenship for individuals to give whatever information they may have to aid in law enforcement" and, as Mr. Justice Frankfurter said, close interrogation of criminal suspects "is often indispensable to crime detection" and a matter of "compelling necessity." So, while one in custody may not be induced without warning to give incriminating answers, the Fourth Amendment permits police to propound questions to closely held suspects not only because the voluntary answers of the guilty may incriminate but also because voluntary answers by the innocent may exculpate: "The questions which these suspected witnesses are asked may serve to clear them. They may serve, directly or indirectly, to lead the police to other suspects than the persons questioned."

Because of these considerations, the Fourth Amendment does not prevent voluntary submission to a search and does not require that a person be informed explicitly, in the manner prerequisite to waiver of Fifth Amendment rights, that he need not consent to a search. In the same way, we think, the Fourth Amendment permits voluntary but uncautioned submissions to "seizures" of the order we consider here. An officer's spontaneous warning that the suspect need not go to headquarters for interrogation may conclusively demonstrate that the subsequent submission was voluntary, but such a warning is not indispensable. The Supreme Court held in *Watson* that "the absence of proof that Watson knew he could withhold his consent, though it may be a factor in the overall judgment, is not to be given controlling significance."

Reviewing all aspects of deputy Bailey's diversion, detention and custodial interrogation of R.L.J., we must conclude that the boy's submission to it was the product of an overborne will and not the result of a "free and unconstrained choice." It is not of controlling significance here that R.L.J. "figured that him a law officer, you had to * * *go with him," and that Bailey said nothing to the contrary. Yet that is a factor in the judgment, made weighty here because appellant was a suspect 14 years old and, for all that appears, of no unusual maturity. The decisive fact is that R.L.J. asked deputy Bailey the reason for the requested headquarters interrogation, and the deputy declined to say until they were at headquarters. He thereby overbore the youth's will, and postponed to a more advantageous moment R.L.J.'s decision on whether to acquiesce in the investigation. We hold that the State cannot constitutionally invite such a suspect to relinquish Fourth Amendment privacies, withhold the information or explanation the suspect thinks necessary to his decision and then characterize as voluntary the resulting submission to authority.

IV.

There is no indication here that R.L.J.'s confession was not "induced by the continuing effects of unconstitutional custody." By *Brown* criteria, the "temporal proximity" of seizure and confession was immediate, the purpose of the seizure was fulfilled as Bailey intended, and no ameliorating circumstances isolated the detention from the confession, as did Wong Sun's arraignment and release from custody. As in *Brown*, the unlawful detention here both in design and in execution, was investigatory. The confession was a direct and purposeful consequence of the detention. As in the case of James Wah Troy in *Wong Sun* and that of Brown himself, "there was no intervening event of significance whatsoever." The confession was the effect of unconstitutional custody.

5. IJA-ABA Juvenile Justice Standards: Standards Relating to Police Handling of Juvenile Problems

Robert E. Shepherd, Jr., ed.

....

Part III: The Authority of the Police to Handle Juvenile Delinquency and Criminal Problems

....

3.2 Police investigation into criminal matters should be similar whether the suspect is an adult or a juvenile. Juveniles, therefore, should receive at least the same safeguards available to adults in the criminal justice system. This should apply to:

A.   preliminary investigations (*e.g.*, stop and frisk);

    B.   the arrest process;

    C.   search and seizure;

    D.   questioning;

    E.   pretrial identification; and

    F.   prehearing detention and release.

For some investigative procedures, greater constitutional safeguards are needed because of the vulnerability of juveniles. Juveniles should not be permitted to waive constitutional rights on their own. In certain investigative areas not governed by constitutional guidelines, guidance to police officers should be provided either legislatively or administratively by court rules or through police agency policies.

Standards Relating to Interim Status: The Release, Control and Detention of Accused Juvenile Offenders Between Arrest and Disposition

. . . .

Part II: Definitions

. . . .

2.2 Arrest.

The taking of an accused juvenile into custody in conformity with the law governing the arrest of persons believed to have committed a crime.

2.3 Custody.

Any interval during which an accused juvenile is held by the arresting police authorities.

. . . .

Part VII: Standards for the Juvenile Court

7.1 Authority to issue summons in lieu of arrest warrant.

Judges should be authorized to issue a summons (which may be served by certified mail or in person) rather than an arrest warrant in every case in which a complaint, information, indictment, or petition is filed or returned against an accused juvenile not already in custody.

7.2 Policy favoring summons over warrant.

In the absence of reasonable grounds indicating that, if an accused juvenile is not promptly taken into custody, he or she will flee to avoid prosecution, the court should prefer the issuance of a summons over the issuance of an arrest warrant.

7.3 Application for summons or warrant.

Whenever an application for a summons or warrant is presented, the court should require all available information relevant to an interim status decision, the reasons why a summons or warrant should be issued, and information concerning the juvenile's schooling or employment that might be affected by service of a summons or warrant at particular times of the day.

7.4 Arrest Warrant to specify initial interim status.

    A. Every warrant issued by a court for the arrest of a juvenile should specify an interim status for the juvenile. The court may order the arresting officer to release the juvenile with a citation, or to place the juvenile in any other interim status permissible under these standards.

B. The warrant should indicate on its face the interim status designated. if any form of detention is ordered, the warrant should indicate the place to which the accused juvenile should be taken, if other than directly to court. In each such case, the court should simultaneously file a written statement indicating the reasons why no measure short of detention would suffice.

7.5 Service of summons or warrant.

In the absence of compelling circumstances that prompt the issuing court to specify to the contrary, a summons or warrant should not be served on an accused juvenile while in school or at a place of employment.

Notes

(a) Reconcile the confession cases in this section with *Fare v. Michael C.* in Chapter 2, *supra*.

(b) After *Fare v. Michael C.*, many states gave juveniles accused of delinquency enhanced Fifth Amendment protection. Does the Court's opinion in *Roper*, see Chapter 7, *infra*, and its view of adolescents' immaturity and impulsiveness require, or at least favor, greater protections in the juvenile confession area?

(c) Should the extent of constitutional or statutory protection of juveniles who are subjected to custodial interrogations depend on whether the minor is tried in juvenile court or criminal court? What are the difficulties in making such a distinction?

(d) As a matter of policy, should children's confessions ever be used in court? Why?

E. The Intake Process

1. Statutes

a. *Cal. Welf. & Inst. Code* § 653.5

Application to commence proceedings; affidavits

(a) Whenever any person applies to the probation officer to commence proceedings in the juvenile court, the application shall be in the form of an affidavit alleging that there was or is within the county, or residing therein, a minor within the provisions of Section 602 [defining delinquency], or that a minor committed an offense described in Section 602 within the county, and setting forth facts in support thereof. The probation officer shall immediately make any investigation he or she deems necessary to determine whether proceedings in the juvenile court shall be commenced. If the probation officer determines that it is appropriate to offer services to the family to prevent or eliminate the need for removal of the minor from his or her home, the probation officer shall make a referral to those services.

(b) Except as provided in subdivision (c), if the probation officer determines that proceedings pursuant to Section 650 should be commenced to declare a person to be a ward of the juvenile court on the basis that he or she is a person described in Section 602, the probation officer shall cause the affidavit to be taken to the prosecuting attorney.

. . . .

The prosecuting attorney shall within his or her discretionary power institute proceedings in accordance with his or her role as public prosecutor pursuant to subdivision (b) of Section 650 and Section 26500 of the Government Code. However, if it appears to the prosecuting attorney that the affidavit was not properly referred, that the offense for which the minor was referred should be charged as a misdemeanor, or that the minor may benefit from a program of informal supervision, he or she shall refer the matter to the probation officer for whatever action the probation officer may deem appropriate.

b. *Cal. Rules of Court, Rule 1405*

Factors to consider

(a) [Settlement at intake (§ 653.5)] In determining whether a matter not described in rule 1404(d) should be settled at intake, the social worker or probation officer shall consider:

(1) Whether there is sufficient evidence of a condition or conduct to bring the child within the jurisdiction of the court;

(2) If the alleged condition or conduct is not considered serious, whether the child has previously presented significant problems in the home, school, or community;

(3) Whether the matter appears to have arisen from a temporary problem within the family which has been or can be resolved;

(4) Whether any agency or other resource in the community is available to offer services to the child and the child's family to prevent or eliminate the need for removal of the child from the child's home;

(5) The attitudes of the child, the parent or guardian, and any affected persons;

(6) The age, maturity, and capabilities of the child;

(7) The dependency or delinquency history, if any, of the child;

(8) The recommendation, if any, of the referring party or agency; and

(9) Any other circumstances that indicate that settling the matter at intake would be consistent with the welfare of the child and the protection of the public.

(b) [Informal supervision] In determining whether to undertake a program of informal supervision of a child not described by rule 1404(d), the social worker or probation officer shall consider:

(1) If the condition or conduct is not considered serious, whether the child has had a problem in the home, school, or community which indicates that some supervision would be desirable;

(2) Whether the child and the parent or guardian seem able to resolve the matter with the assistance of the social worker or probation officer and without formal court action;

(3) Whether further observation or evaluation by the social worker or probation officer is needed before a decision can be reached;

(4) The attitudes of the child and the parent or guardian;

(5) The age, maturity, and capabilities of the child;

(6) The dependency or delinquency history, if any, of the child;

(7) The recommendation, if any, of the referring party or agency;

(8) The attitudes of affected persons; and

(9) Any other circumstances that indicate that a program of informal supervision would be consistent with the welfare of the child and the protection of the public.

(c) [**Filing of petition**] In determining whether to file a petition under section 300 or 601 or to request the prosecuting attorney to file a petition under section 602, the social worker or probation officer shall consider:

(1) Whether any of the statutory criteria listed in rules 1482 and 1483 relating to the fitness of the child are present;

(2) Whether the alleged conduct would be a felony;

(3) Whether the alleged conduct involved physical harm or the threat of physical harm to person or property;

(4) If the alleged condition or conduct is not serious, whether the child has had serious problems in the home, school, or community which indicate that formal court action is desirable;

(5) If the alleged condition or conduct is not serious, whether the child is already a ward or dependent of the court;

(6) Whether the alleged condition or conduct involves a threat to the physical or emotional health of the child;

(7) Whether a chronic serious family problem exists after other efforts to resolve the problem have been made;

(8) Whether the alleged condition or conduct is in dispute and, if proven, whether court-ordered disposition appears desirable;

(9) The attitudes of the child and the parent or guardian;

(10) The age, maturity, and capabilities of the child;

(11) Whether the child is on probation or parole;

(12) The recommendation, if any, of the referring party or agency;

(13) The attitudes of affected persons;

(14) Whether any other referrals or petitions are pending; and

(15) Any other circumstances that indicate that the filing of a petition is necessary to promote the welfare of the child or to protect the public.

c. *Cal. Rules of Court, Rule 1404*

Intake; guidelines

(a) [**Role of juvenile court**] The presiding judge of the juvenile court shall initiate meetings and cooperate with the probation department, welfare department, prosecuting attorney, law enforcement, and other persons and agencies performing an intake function to establish and maintain a fair and efficient intake program designed to promote swift and objective evaluation of the circumstances of any referral and to pursue an appropriate course of action.

(b) [**Purpose of intake program**] The intake program shall be designed to:

(1) Provide for settlement at intake of:

(A) Matters over which the juvenile court has no jurisdiction;

(B) Matters in which there is insufficient evidence to support a petition; and

(C) Matters which are suitable for referral to a nonjudicial agency or program available in the community;

(2) Provide for a program of informal supervision of the child under sections 301 and 654; and

(3) Provide for the commencement of proceedings in the juvenile court only when necessary for the welfare of the child or protection of the public.

(c) [**Investigation at intake (§ 653.5)**] The probation officer may or the social worker shall conduct an investigation and determine whether:

(1) The matter should be settled at intake by:

(A) Taking no action;

(B) Counseling the child and any others involved in the matter; or

(C) Referring the child, the child's family, and any others involved to other agencies and programs in the community for the purpose of receiving services to prevent or eliminate the need for removal;

(2) A program of informal supervision should be undertaken for not more than six months under section 301 or 654; or

(3) A petition should be filed under section 300 or 601, or the prosecuting attorney should be requested to file a petition under section 602.

(d) [**Mandatory referrals to the prosecuting attorney (§ 653.5)**] Notwithstanding subdivision (c), the probation officer may refer to the prosecuting attorney, within 48 hours, all affidavits requesting that a petition be filed under section 602 if it appears to the probation officer that:

(1) The child, regardless of age:

(A) Is alleged to have committed an offense listed in section 707(b);

(B) Has been referred for the sale or possession for sale of a controlled substance under Chapter 2 of Division 10 of the Health and Safety Code;

(C) Has been referred for a violation of section 11350 or 11377 of the Health and Safety Code at a school, or for a violation of section 245.5, 626.9, or 626.10 of the Penal Code;

(D) Has been referred for a violation of section 186.22 of the Penal Code;

(E) Has previously been placed on informal supervision under section 654; or

(F) Has been referred for an alleged offense in which restitution to the victim exceeds $1,000;

(2) The child was 16 years of age or older on the date of the alleged offense and the referral is for a felony offense;

(3) The child was under 16 years of age on the date of the alleged offense and the referral is not the first referral for a felony offense; or....

Except for the offenses listed in paragraph (1)(C), the provisions of this subdivision shall not apply to narcotics and drug offenses listed in section 1000 of the Penal Code.

(e) [**Informal supervision (§§ 301, 654)**]

(1) If the child is placed on a program of informal supervision for not more than six months under section 301, the social worker may file a petition at any time during the six-month period. If the objectives of a service plan under section 301 have not been achieved

within six months, the social worker may extend the period up to an additional six months, with the consent of the parent or guardian.

(2) If a child is placed on a program of informal supervision for not more than six months under section 654, the probation officer may file a petition under section 601, or request that one be filed by the prosecuting attorney under section 602, at any time during the six-month period, or within 90 days thereafter. If a child on informal supervision under section 654 has not participated in the specific programs within 60 days, the probation officer shall immediately file a petition under section 601, or request that one be filed by the prosecuting attorney under section 602, unless the probation officer determines that the interests of the child and the community can be protected adequately by continuing under section 654.

d. *Tex. Family Code* § 53.01

Preliminary Investigation and Determinations; Notice to Parents

(a) On referral of a person believed to be a child or on referral of the person's case to the office or official designated by the juvenile board, the intake officer, probation officer, or other person authorized by the board shall conduct a preliminary investigation to determine whether:

(1) the person referred to juvenile court is a child within the meaning of this title; and

(2) there is probable cause to believe the person:

(A) engaged in delinquent conduct or conduct indicating a need for supervision; or

(B) is a nonoffender who has been taken into custody and is being held solely for deportation out of the United States.

(b) If it is determined that the person is not a child or there is no probable cause, the person shall immediately be released.

(c) When custody of a child is given to the office or official designated by the juvenile board, the intake officer, probation officer, or other person authorized by the board shall promptly give notice of the whereabouts of the child and a statement of the reason the child was taken into custody to the child's parent, guardian, or custodian unless the notice given under Section 52.02(b) provided fair notice of the child's present whereabouts.

(d) Unless the juvenile board approves a written procedure proposed by the office of the prosecuting attorney and chief juvenile probation officer which provides otherwise, if it is determined that the person is a child and, regardless of a finding of probable cause, or a lack thereof, there is an allegation that the child engaged in delinquent conduct of the grade of felony, or conduct constituting a misdemeanor offense involving violence to a person or the use or possession of a firearm, illegal knife, or club, as those terms are defined by Section 46.01, Penal Code, or prohibited weapon, as described by Section 46.05, Penal Code, the case shall be promptly forwarded to the office of the prosecuting attorney, accompanied by:

(1) all documents that accompanied the current referral; and

(2) a summary of all prior referrals of the child to the juvenile court, juvenile probation department, or a detention facility.

e. *Tex. Family Code* § 53.012

Review by Prosecutor

(a) The prosecuting attorney shall promptly review the circumstances and allegations of a referral made under Section 53.01 for legal sufficiency and the desirability of prosecution and may file a petition without regard to whether probable cause was found under Section 53.01.

(b) If the prosecuting attorney does not file a petition requesting the adjudication of the child referred to the prosecuting attorney, the prosecuting attorney shall:

(1) terminate all proceedings, if the reason is for lack of probable cause; or

(2) return the referral to the juvenile probation department for further proceedings.

(c) The juvenile probation department shall promptly refer a child who has been returned to the department under Subsection (b)(2) and who fails or refuses to participate in a program of the department to the prosecuting attorney for review of the child's case and determination of whether to file a petition.

f. *Fla. Statute* § 985.21

Intake and case management

....

[(4)](b) The juvenile probation officer, upon determining that the report, affidavit, or complaint complies with the standards of a probable cause affidavit and that the interest of the child and the public will be best served, may recommend that a delinquency petition not be filed. If such a recommendation is made, the juvenile probation officer shall advise in writing the person or agency making the report, affidavit, or complaint, the victim, if any, and the law enforcement agency having investigative jurisdiction of the offense of the recommendation and the reasons therefor; and that the person or agency may submit, within 10 days after the receipt of such notice, the report, affidavit, or complaint to the state attorney for special review. The state attorney, upon receiving a request for special review, shall consider the facts presented by the report, affidavit, or complaint, and by the juvenile probation officer who made the recommendation that no petition be filed, before making a final decision as to whether a petition or information should or should not be filed.

(c) Subject to the interagency agreement authorized under this paragraph, the juvenile probation officer for each case in which a child is alleged to have committed a violation of law or delinquent act and is not detained shall submit a written report to the state attorney, including the original report, complaint, or affidavit, or a copy thereof, including a copy of the child's prior juvenile record, within 20 days after the date the child is taken into custody. In cases in which the child is in detention, the intake office report must be submitted within 24 hours after the child is placed into detention. The intake office report may include a recommendation that a petition or information be filed or that no petition or information be filed, and may set forth reasons for the recommendation. The State Attorney and the Department of Juvenile Justice may, on a district-by-district basis, enter into interagency agreements denoting the cases that will require a recommendation and those for which a recommendation is unnecessary.

(d) The state attorney may in all cases take action independent of the action or lack of action of the juvenile probation officer, and shall determine the action which is in the best interest of the public and the child. If the child meets the criteria requiring prosecution as an adult pursuant to § 985.226, the state attorney shall request the court to transfer and certify the child for prosecution as an adult or shall provide written reasons to the court for not making such request. In all other cases, the state attorney may:

1. File a petition for dependency;

2. File a petition pursuant to chapter 984;

3. File a petition for delinquency;

4. File a petition for delinquency with a motion to transfer and certify the child for prosecution as an adult;

5. File an information pursuant to § 985.227;

6. Refer the case to a grand jury;

7. Refer the child to a diversionary, pretrial intervention, arbitration, or mediation program, or to some other treatment or care program if such program commitment is voluntarily accepted by the child or the child's parents or legal guardians; or

8. Decline to file.

(e) In cases in which a delinquency report, affidavit, or complaint is filed by a law enforcement agency and the state attorney determines not to file a petition, the state attorney shall advise the clerk of the circuit court in writing that no petition will be filed thereon.

. . . .

(5) Prior to requesting that a delinquency petition be filed or prior to filing a dependency petition, the juvenile probation officer may request the parent or legal guardian of the child to attend a course of instruction in parenting skills, training in conflict resolution, and the practice of nonviolence; to accept counseling; or to receive other assistance from any agency in the community which notifies the clerk of the court of the availability of its services. Where appropriate, the juvenile probation officer shall request both parents or guardians to receive such parental assistance. The juvenile probation officer may, in determining whether to request that a delinquency petition be filed, take into consideration the willingness of the parent or legal guardian to comply with such request. The parent or guardian must provide the juvenile probation officer with identifying information, including the parent's or guardian's name, address, date of birth, social security number, and driver's license number or identification card number in order to comply with § 985.2311.

2. Informal Adjustment Contract

Informal Adjustment Contract   Petition # _____

INFORMAL ADJUSTMENT AGREEMENT TERMS

A preliminary investigation has been made and it has been determined that you are eligible to enter an Informal Agreement.

Informal Adjustment is a six-month program of supervision by the Harris County Juvenile Probation Department. A Probation Officer and/or Counselor will work with you during this period of time. The agreement is subject to any or all conditions to be determined by the Probation Officer and/or Counselor. These conditions are listed on the back of this form.

YOU DO NOT HAVE TO CONSENT TO THE INFORMAL ADJUSTMENT PERIOD. IF YOU DO NOT CHOOSE TO DO SO, YOUR CASE WILL BE HEARD IN THE FAMILY DISTRICT COURT.

If you agree to the Informal Adjustment period, you understand that:

1. There is no obligation to consent to the Informal Adjustment Agreement. This is a voluntary program.

2. Any statements made by you concerning the case cannot be used against you.

3. You may request that this Agreement be terminated at any time during the six-month period and ask for a Court Hearing.

4. The Probation Officer will cancel the Agreement if you fail to fulfill the terms of the Agreement. The case will be returned for a Court Hearing.

5. This Agreement includes the conditions listed on the back of this form.

THIS CASE WILL BE DISMISSED IF INFORMAL ADJUSTMENT IS SUCCESSFULLY COMPLETED WITHIN A PERIOD OF TIME NOT EXCEEDING SIX (6) MONTHS.

Harris County Juvenile Prob.	Juvenile
Date	Parent/Guardian/Custodian
Probation Officer/Coun.	

CONDITIONS*

1. I will enroll/re-enroll in school within ten (10) days and notify my Probation Officer/Counselor.

2. I will enroll in a Vocational Training and Employment Program within ten (10) days and notify my Probation Officer/Counselor.

3. I will enroll in a Drug Abuse Program within ten (10) days and notify my Probation Officer/Counselor.

4. If employed full-time, I will complete an application for a federal Certificate of Age and return said form to the Probation Officer/Counselor within ten (10) days.

5. I will enroll in a counseling program within ten (10) days and notify my Probation Officer/Counselor.

6. I will notify my Probation Officer/Counselor immediately if I am suspended or expelled from school.

7. I will complete the required number of Informal Adjustment Progress Reports and deliver said reports to my Probation Officer/Counselor.

8. I will participate in the following program(s):

   _____ a. Red Cross Community Service Program for _____ hours.

   _____ b. Inhalant Abuse Program, sponsored by AAMA.

   _____ c. Juvenile Alcoholic Awareness Program.

   _____ d. Alief Outreach Counseling Program.

   _____ e. Workshops/ Programs:

   _____

   _____

   _____

9. I will complete restitution requirements of $_____ to _____ by _____ and according to the following terms: _____

10. I will not violate any laws of the State of Texas or any of its Political Subdivisions.

3. Cases

In the Matter of Elizabeth J.
413 N.Y.S. 2d 867 (N.Y. Fam. Ct. 1979)

This motion to dismiss the [delinquency] petition or in the alternative that the court accept an admission to a charge or charges contained in the petition and place the child on probation is denied. The application was made before me at an Intake Part on supporting papers and marked submitted.

The Respondent, now 16 years, 2 months old, made admissions to burglary in November 1978 before a Kings County Family Court Judge. The disposition on those petitions and on another alleging assault in the 2nd degree, was 2 years on probation, upon special conditions.

This petition alleging attempted petit larceny, possession of burglary's tools, and possession of a weapon was filed on September 22, 1978, and was pending when the other two admissions were made in November. That court was aware of the instant petition, and of the Probation Court Liaison Officer's … [view of] the disposition when it made its decision in November.

Law Guardian argues that since Respondent is on probation, doing well (i. e., has not had any police contact since the September petition) and since Family Court does not punish or vindicate private wrongs, but supervises, treats, or confines, if necessary, there is no necessity for further probation or further disposition. It is argued that the instant petition be dismissed, or, in the alternative, an admission accepted, with a probation disposition, to run concurrently with the probation already ordered. The Corporation Counsel is opposed.

The respondent-movant relies on two cases wherein the court granted motions to dismiss without the consent of the petitioner or complainant, who were represented by the corporation counsel. These cases were grounded on the proposition that there must be a need for court intervention to supervise, treat, or confine a child. Since these cases were decided, §711 of the F.C.A., one of the sections upon which movant proceeds has been amended. Laws of 1976, chapter 878, was enacted, and F.C.A. §711 now provides: "In any juvenile delinquency proceeding under this article, the court shall consider the needs and best interests of the respondent as well as the need for the protection of the community."

This additional factor requiring consideration can only be weighed after there has been a finding of fact and after a second hearing on disposition. At a dispositional hearing the court should have before it a current investigation and report from the Probation Department as to respondent's present needs for treatment, supervision or confinement, with due consideration for protection of the community. This petition may not be dismissed at this juncture on these papers. This decision is not meant to imply that a disposition agreeable to both parties may not be effected without a trial in an all purpose part.

In re M.D.
527 N.E.2d 286 (Ohio 1988)

HOLMES, Justice.

This case presents an issue involving the prosecution of juveniles under the age of thirteen as delinquents for conduct, characterized as "playing doctor," allegedly constituting felony sex crimes. [Four children were involved, a boy and girl age five and two girls, nine and twelve. The twelve year old was prosecuted for acts between the five year olds.] We hold that to bring such charges in juvenile court, under the instant circumstances, is contrary to [law], violates the intake policy of the Juvenile Court, and public policy in general, and thus constitutes a denial of due process of law. We must, therefore, reverse the judgment of the court of appeals and vacate the adjudication of delinquency in this case.

As a threshold matter, we must consider the doctrine of waiver, relied on by the court of appeals in affirming the trial court. In *State v. Awan* (1986), this court held in the syllabus:

> "Failure to raise at the trial court level the issue of the constitutionality of a statute or its application, which issue is apparent at the time of trial, constitutes a waiver of such issue and a deviation from this state's orderly procedure, and therefore *need not* be heard for the first time on appeal."

We find the court of appeals erred in relying on this doctrine in the instant case. Appellant, in her motion to dismiss the complaint against her in the trial court, argued that her prosecution for complicity to rape was repugnant to [statutes], and local intake policy as to juvenile sex offenses, all of which, she argued, "implicates not only rights under the Constitution but also the psychological and social well-being of young children." We grant that the constitutional challenge was here made in general terms. However, the due process considerations of appellant's arguments are apparent, and sufficient to avoid the waiver issue.

Furthermore, ... the waiver doctrine announced in *Awan* is discretionary. In the criminal context, Crim. R. 52(B) provides that "[p]lain errors or defects affecting substantial rights may be noticed although they were not brought to the attention of the court." Thus, even where waiver is clear, this court reserves the right to consider constitutional challenges to the application of statutes in specific cases of plain error or where the rights and interests involved may warrant it.

In considering appellant's constitutional challenge herein, we are somewhat hampered, as was the court of appeals, by appellant's failure to provide a transcript of the proceedings below. We must, therefore, presume the validity of the proceedings in juvenile court. We are not, however, required to affirm on this basis alone, as appellant challenges only the discretion initially exercised by the prosecutor in bringing the instant charges. Such a challenge may be decided on the documents and exhibits found in the record certified to this court, in addition to the findings of the juvenile court below. Our review leads to the inescapable conclusion that the conduct of appellant and the other children involved herein did not constitute a sexual assault or complicity thereto, as proscribed by [statute], but rather could more accurately be characterized as childhood curiosity and exploration.

The events giving rise to the instant charges did not meet each element of the offense of complicity to rape. R.C. 2923.03 provides, in pertinent part:

> "(A) No person, acting with the kind of culpability required for the commission of an offense, shall do any of the following:
>
> " * * *
>
> "(4) Cause an innocent or irresponsible person to commit the offense.
>
> " * * *
>
> "(C) *No person shall be convicted of complicity under this section unless an offense is actually committed,* but a person may be convicted of complicity in an attempt to commit an offense in violation of § 2923.02 of the Revised Code."

It is axiomatic, as reflected in subsection (c) of this statute, that an offense must actually be committed before a person may be convicted as an accomplice. Here, the underlying offense of rape did not occur. We emphasize, first, that all sections of the Revised Code defining offenses must be liberally construed in favor of the accused.

The offense of rape is generally defined in R.C. 2907.02 as follows:

"(A)(1) No person shall engage in sexual conduct with another who is not the spouse of the offender or who is the spouse of the offender but is living separate and apart from the offender, when either of the following apply:

" * * *

"(b) The other person is less than thirteen years of age, whether or not the offender knows the age of such person."

The key term in this section is "sexual conduct," which is specifically defined in R.C. 2907.01(A):

"(A) 'Sexual conduct' means vaginal intercourse between a male and female, and anal intercourse, fellatio, and cunnilingus between persons regardless of sex. Penetration, however slight, is sufficient to complete vaginal or anal intercourse."

Fellatio is the only proscribed act which resembles what occurred herein. Although fellatio is not defined in the Revised Code, our construction of that term according to common usage is guided by its dictionary definition, *i.e.,* "the practice of obtaining sexual satisfaction by oral stimulation of the penis." In addition, other jurisdictions that have considered the term have defined fellatio to encompass elements of either stimulation or sexual satisfaction, or both. Finally, we note that mere penetration of the oral cavity is not sufficient to complete the offense, unlike vaginal or anal intercourse. Here, the record demonstrates neither an element of sexual satisfaction nor of oral stimulation. We seriously doubt whether either element is physiologically or emotionally possible in a child of the tender age of five, and the record presented to us does not suggest otherwise. Furthermore, it is a well-established presumption that an infant under the age of fourteen is incapable of committing the crime of rape, rebuttable only upon proof that such child has reached the age of puberty. Fellatio did not occur here, thus no rape was committed to which appellant could be an accessory.

Adjudicating a child as "delinquent" under circumstances where, as here, the child has neither committed a crime nor violated a lawful order of the juvenile court is obviously contrary to R.C. Chapter 2151. Even assuming, however, given the paucity of the record before us, that the conduct here technically involved a "rape" as that term is statutorily defined, we hold that prosecution of M.D. under these circumstances violates the underlying public policy of this state as expressed in R.C. Chapter 2151 and the Rules of Juvenile Procedure. R.C. 2151.01 provides, in pertinent part:

"The sections in Chapter 2151, of the Revised Code, with the exception of those sections providing for the criminal prosecution of adults, shall be liberally interpreted and construed so as to effectuate the following purposes:

"(A) To provide for the care, protection, and mental and physical development of children subject to Chapter 2151 of the Revised Code;

"(B) To protect the public interest in removing the consequences of criminal behavior and the taint of criminality from children committing delinquent acts and to substitute therefor a program of supervision, care, and rehabilitation;
* * *."

The best interests of the child and the welfare and protection of the community are paramount considerations in every juvenile proceeding in this state. This is further emphasized in the Rules of Juvenile Procedure.[5] These goals are effectuated at every step in the juvenile court system, but are most effectively met at the initial intake of the juvenile by the juvenile court. The overriding rule upon intake of a child is that formal court action should be a last resort to resolving juvenile problems. Juv. R. 9 provides:

> "(A) Court action to be avoided.

> "In all appropriate cases formal court action should be avoided and other community resources utilized to ameliorate situations brought to the attention of the court.

> "(B) Screening; referral.

> "Information that a child is within the court's jurisdiction may be informally screened prior to the filing of a complaint to determine whether the filing of a complaint is in the best interest of the child and the public."

That rule is reflected in the intake policy of the Cuyahoga County Juvenile Court as it relates to allegations of statutory rape between children who are under thirteen years of age:

> "Rape—Complaint shall be taken and set before a JUDGE unless subject is under age 13 years, in which case the matter may be diverted."

A memorandum from the legal department of the . . . Juvenile Court attached to the record in this case further emphasizes this policy:

> "In situations where there is an allegation of sexual conduct involving no force and both the alleged offender and the victim are under 13 years of age, charges are not to be taken under the above statute. As an alternative, the intake mediator may consider unruly charges on one or both children."

The prosecution of M.D. under the facts as found by the trial court below constitutes a significant variance from this specific, local intake policy, and fails to conform to the general policies of R.C. Chapter 2151. Nothing in the record or in the arguments of the prosecutor persuades us that the "best interest of the child and the public" were served by the filing of the instant complaint. Quite to the contrary, legal counsel for the family of the alleged five-year-old "rapist" petitioned the juvenile court judge prior to trial to dismiss this action, as "the trauma which the impending trial is causing and could cause the family is far more serious than the alleged acts, which * * *[the family] truly believe[s] [were] just kids playing doctor."

Nor was the "care, protection, and mental and physical development of children" provided for herein. The report . . . of a mental health counselor who was assigned to M.D.'s case after her being adjudicated delinquent below indicates a normal pre-teen who enjoys being with her friends, listening to music, roller skating and swimming. The battery of tests and evaluations performed on her "gave no compelling evidence to suggest or support * * * [her] involvement in the crime for which she has been found guilty. Her profile deviates markedly when compared with the profiles of other sex offenders. * * *

---

5. Juv. R. 1(B) provides, in part:
    "These rules shall be liberally interpreted and construed so as to effectuate the following purposes:
    "* * *

    "(3) to provide for the care, protection, and mental and physical development of children subject to the jurisdiction of the juvenile court, and to protect the welfare of the community; and
    "(4) to protect the public interest by treating children as persons in need of supervision, care and rehabilitation."

Negative community relationships as identified by * * * [her] and her parents and supported by the testing are of particular concern. * * * [She] (and her family) ha[ve] had to endure incredible and persistent harassment as a result of this incident." Appellant has been saddled with the "taint of criminality" by this adjudication for a felony sex offense under circumstances where "sex" played but a minute role.

It was inappropriate that this case was filed in juvenile court. The case having been filed, it reasonably devolved on the juvenile judge to dismiss it pursuant to the mandates of R.C. Chapter 2151. The failure to dismiss resulted in a denial of M.D.'s constitutional rights to due process under the law, which should have been vindicated by the court of appeals. We proceed to rectify that court's failure to do so, and accordingly reverse the judgment of the court of appeals, and hereby vacate appellant's adjudication as a delinquent child.

In re Armondo A.

3 Cal. App. 4th 1185 (Cal. Ct. App. 1992)

DABNEY, Associate Justice.

A juvenile court petition was filed May 21, 1990, alleging that minor, Armondo A., violated Vehicle Code § 10851, felony automobile theft. Before the petition had been filed, the probation officer had determined, pursuant to Welfare and Institutions Code § 654, that informal supervision would not be appropriate for minor's circumstances. Upon minor's request, the court referred the matter to the probation department for reconsideration of informal supervision. On August 15 and 22, the court held hearings for consideration of informal supervision and denied the minor's request.

On August 23, 1990, the minor admitted the allegation in the petition as a misdemeanor. The court declared minor to be a ward of the court and determined the maximum period of confinement would be one year. Minor was placed on formal probation in the custody of his parents.

On appeal, minor contends the juvenile court failed to properly exercise its discretion in determining his eligibility for informal supervision. He also asserts he was denied due process in the hearing on this matter.

Facts

The underlying facts of the petition are not relevant to the issues in this case; however, we set them out briefly as background.

Minor was found in possession of a vehicle which had been stolen. The rear window of the car was broken, and the ignition lock was punched. Minor told police he had found the car in an alley and knew it was stolen. He said he started the car with fingernail clippers and had been driving the car for three or four days.

Discussion

I. *Informal Supervision: Court's Determination*

Minor contends the trial court erred in failing to make an independent determination of his suitability for informal supervision. The transcript of the hearing on this issue reveals that the court limited its decision to a review of the probation officer's discretionary decision and did not exercise its independent discretion. The court stated, "I will certainly give the discretionary decision by the probation office a fair review, but I don't think I have to hear testimony." The court indicated it understood that it could overrule the probation officer, dismiss the petition and direct that minor be given informal supervision; however, it limited its decision to "whether or not the investigation was fair and that the probation officer exercised her discretion properly."

"If a petition has been filed by the prosecuting attorney to declare a minor a ward of the court under § 602, the court may, without adjudging the minor a ward of the court and with the consent of the minor and the minor's parents or guardian, continue any hearing on a petition for six months and order the minor to participate in a program of supervision as set forth in § 654." Section 654 allows the probation officer to delineate a program of informal supervision in lieu of filing a petition or requesting the prosecuting attorney to file a petition to declare the minor a ward. The probation officer is guided in this decision by the factors listed in California Rules of Court, Rule 1405(b).

Section 654 further provides: "The program of supervision of the minor undertaken pursuant to this section may call for the minor to obtain care and treatment for the misuse of or addiction to controlled substances from a county mental health service or other appropriate community agency. The program of supervision shall require the parents * * * of the minor to participate with the minor in counseling or education programs, including, but not limited to, parent education and parenting programs operated by community colleges, school districts, or other appropriate agencies designated by the court if the program of supervision is pursuant to the procedure prescribed in § 654.2." It further provides for other services which may be designated as part of the minor's informal probation.

Because the district attorney had filed a petition in this case, the court's decision whether to grant informal supervision was subject to § 654.2. That section was enacted in 1989, and no case law exists which assists us in our determination of whether the court's decision pursuant to this section is merely a review of the probation officer's earlier decision or an independent exercise of its own discretion.

Section 654.2 does not mention a review of the probation officer's discretion. Instead, it suggests the court must exercise its own discretion in its decision whether informal supervision is appropriate. If the language of a statute is clear, its plain meaning should be followed.

In interpreting statutes, the courts must construe them to give effect to the Legislature's intent. The Legislature intended to address juvenile delinquency at its inception and at the earliest signs of delinquency with a less structured program. To meet this objective it gave the courts more authority to deal with minors before they become habitual criminals. Section 654.2 created a new power in the juvenile courts by allowing them to order informal supervision after a petition had been filed. This power is in addition to the probation officer's already existing prepetition discretion.

It appears that § 654.2 creates a new power in the court to grant informal probation supervision in a postpetition setting independently of the probation officer's pre-petition discretion. Therefore, the juvenile court's refusal to exercise its independent discretion in determining whether informal supervision was appropriate was error. The court's failure to exercise its discretion requires that the case be reversed and remanded to the juvenile court where minor may withdraw his admission to the § 602 petition. The juvenile court shall conduct a new hearing on minor's suitability for informal probation supervision. At this hearing, the court shall exercise its independent discretion in determining the matter.

II. *Evidence Admissible at Section 654.2 Hearing*

To assist the juvenile court in the conduct of the hearing on remand, we address minor's second issue. Minor argues he was denied due process when the court refused to consider the evidence he proffered to show that he was a suitable candidate for informal probation.[2] At the hearing on informal probation, the court limited the evidence to the probation officer's testimony concerning her investigation and basis for her decision. The court stated, "If you are suggesting testimony, that I have to endure testimony from witnesses, I don't think that's the law." The court later added, "But to say that the court also must endure all of the testimony, that's not true. The decision is whether or not the investigation was fair and that the probation officer exercised her discretion properly. And that's solely the function of the information from the probation officer. It has nothing to do with what the family has to contribute to the court."

Our inquiry concerns what evidence the juvenile court must consider when making an independent determination pursuant to § 654.2 of whether informal probation is appropriate. The general language of § 654.2 does not assist our inquiry.[3] Logically, if the court is to make an independent determination of a minor's suitability for informal supervision, it should weigh all relevant evidence.

Furthermore, § 202, subdivision (d) provides that "Juvenile courts and other public agencies charged with enforcing, interpreting, and administering the juvenile court law shall consider the safety and protection of the public and the best interests of the minor in all deliberations pursuant to this chapter." Section 680 mandates, "The judge of the juvenile court shall control all proceedings during the hearings with a view to the expeditious and effective ascertainment of the jurisdictional facts and the ascertainment of *all information relative to the present condition and future welfare of the person upon whose behalf the petition is brought.*"

Due process also requires that the juvenile court consider all relevant evidence in exercising its discretion. Juvenile court proceedings must conform to constitutional guaranties of due process of law.

The Attorney General argues that probation is a privilege and not a right; therefore, due process is not relevant to our inquiry. The Attorney General also contends that the minor should have presented all his evidence to the probation office, which administers the informal supervision program and which would then report all evidence to the juvenile court. The Attorney General relies on *People v. Ramirez*, which held that due process entitles the patient-inmate an opportunity to respond to the grounds for his exclusion from the California Rehabilitation Center (CRC) by being given the opportunity to "respond orally before a responsible official." That court held that confrontation, cross-examination, and other formal hearing rights were not necessary to preserve due process.

In *Ramirez,* the director of CRC, who administers the CRC, made an initial determination which the court then reviewed. Here, the probation office administers informal probation. The minor may provide any information relevant to the informal probation determination to the probation officer. The probation officer then must report all relevant information to the juvenile court. If the juvenile court feels that more information is necessary, it may always request a supplemental report from the probation officer. The court shall examine all of this evidence, keeping in mind the factors listed in California Rules of Court, and make an independent determination of minor's eligibility for informal proba-

---

2. Minor's further contentions that he was denied due process when the court limited cross-examination intended to show whether the probation officer performed an adequate investigation and when the probation officer failed to conduct a sufficient investigation are rendered moot by our decision.

3. If the Legislature is dismayed at our interpretation of this statute, we invite them to clarify § 654.2.

tion. As in *Ramirez*, due process does not require a formal hearing with confrontation and cross-examination. The court shall consider all relevant evidence as presented by the probation officer. Minor shall have the opportunity to present all evidence relevant to this determination to the probation officer for inclusion in its report to the court.

The case is reversed and remanded to the juvenile court with directions to allow minor to withdraw his admission to the allegation in the petition and to exercise its independent discretion pursuant to §654.2.

In the Matter of Frank H.
337 N.Y.S.2d 118 (N.Y. Fam. Ct. 1972)

The petition alleges that the respondent "while acting in concert with one other, also apprehended, was in a 1971 Pontiac Le Mans — no registration — the property of Robbins Reef Buick Corporation 44 Hannah Street, Staten Island, New York. The respondent had no permission to use the above vehicle * * *."

The respondent, on his first appearance before the court, was assigned counsel pursuant to article 18-B of the County Law. When the assigned attorney appeared in this proceeding, he made a motion to vacate the petition and send the case back to intake for consideration de novo on the ground that the respondent had been denied his constitutional right to counsel at the intake stage of the Family Court proceeding. The court directed that the respondent's attorney file a memorandum of law in his behalf. The fact-finding hearing has not commenced pending decision on the motion by the court.

The sole question for determination is whether the initial intake conference is a critical stage in the proceedings within the meaning of the constitutional guarantee of the right to counsel thereby depriving the respondent of this right. This initial intake conference occurs before a petition is ordered drawn and prior to the holding of a Family Court hearing.

The intake procedure of the Family Court insofar as it applies to juvenile delinquency cases is provided for in §734 of the Family Court Act and section 2506.3 of the Uniform Family Court Rules. Section 2506.3 provides in part:

> "The probation service is authorized to confer with any person seeking to originate a juvenile delinquency or person in need of supervision proceeding under Article 7 of the Family Court Act, with the potential respondent and other interested persons concerning the advisability of filing a petition under said Article and to attempt to adjust suitable cases before a petition is filed * * *."

The intake officer can adjust a case at intake where the accused youth denies his guilt of any offense. Intake process in juvenile courts is a specialized proceeding in the constellation of court services and procedures. There are more social than legal issues involved. Adjustment is not mandatory and the Rules specifically provide that the probation service may not prevent any person or complainant from having access to the court if he insists that a petition be filed. It permits informal adjustments to be made at intake but includes provisions designed to protect the rights of the parties in this process. No person can be compelled to appear at any conference, produce any papers or visit any place.

Under §734(c) of the Family Court Act, "Efforts at adjustment pursuant to rules of court * * * may not extend for a period of more than two months without leave of a judge of the court, who may extend the period for an additional sixty days."

Intake is not a legal term and with the exception of juvenile and family courts, is foreign to the court file. Its use in juvenile and family courts has no doubt been adopted from the field of social welfare. In the welfare field, the client has complete freedom of choice. He comes to the agency and he may or may not decide to accept the service if offered. At the same time, the agency also has freedom of choice. It may or may not accept the client for service, particularly in the private welfare field.

The same is not true with court intake. The "client" defined as the person complained about or alleged to be in a situation necessitating action, has no freedom of choice. Here the request for action is initiated by someone other than the client. Whatever freedom of choice exists as to whether action will be taken rests in the court, not in the client. Unlike the private welfare agency, the court's authority to deny the right to file a petition is controlled by the nature of the case. Certainly giving the court this power can be justified and is fairly well established, at least by custom in delinquency cases.

Delinquency cases involve offenses which if committed by an adult would be a crime. Here the State is usually a party to the action. The decisions made at intake level, affect individual and community rights—the right of the child and family to personal freedom and privacy and at the same time the right of the child and family to receive the services of the State for care, protection and treatment.

The New York Family Court Act provides for due process of law in § 711, stating: "The purpose of this article is to provide a due process of law (a) for considering a claim that a person is a juvenile delinquent or a person in need of supervision and (b) for devising an appropriate order of disposition for any person adjudged a juvenile delinquent or in need of supervision." The landmark case in the area of due process for juveniles is *In re Gault*. In this case, the New York Family Court Act was quoted with approval on several occasions. In determining whether the *Gault* decision and the New York Family Court Act should be expanded to provide a right of counsel at intake proceedings it is first necessary to examine the relevant provisions of the Family Court Act and the specific holdings of *Gault*.

Section 241 of the Family Court Act provides: "that minors who are the subject of family court proceedings should be represented by counsel of their own choosing or by law guardians. This declaration is based on a finding that counsel is often indispensable to a practical realization of due process of law and may be helpful in making reasoned determinations of fact and proper orders of disposition."

This act preceded *Gault* by some five years and obviously the right to counsel in juvenile proceedings already existed in New York at the time of that case. *Gault* is limited to adjudicatory hearings resulting in incarceration. The question then becomes whether right to counsel also exists at intake proceedings. No specific answers to whether the intake stage of a juvenile delinquency proceeding is a critical stage of the proceedings wherein the right to counsel attaches [are] supplied by § 241 or the entire Family Court Act. Nor does *Gault* provide any answers to this specific question.

The answer does, however, lie in § 735 of the Family Court Act indicating strong legislative intent that no counsel is necessary at the intake stage of proceedings. This section provides that: "No statement made during a preliminary conference may be admitted into evidence at a fact-finding hearing or, if the proceeding is transferred to a criminal court, at any time prior to a conviction."

[S]ection [2506.3(d)] makes inadmissible at a fact-finding hearing any statement made during a preliminary conference carried on under probation service connected with the Family Court and does not refer to questioning by police and statements made to police which are not within the proscription of this section.

This preserves the spirit of cooperation which it is to be hoped prevails, at a preliminary conference such as intake and guards against self-incrimination, a prohibition in

Gault. Furthermore, § 734(b) provides that: "The probation service may not prevent any person who wishes to file a petition under this article from having access to the court for that purpose." This is further protection to the respondent because this is still the pre-fact-finding hearing level where the presiding judge, rather than the intake officer, will make the determination as to whether or not a petition will issue.

Counsel for respondent elaborates at length in his memorandum of law on holdings in adult criminal cases which find preliminary conferences to be a critical stage of the proceedings requiring Constitutional safeguards. However, these all refer to police custodial interrogations. Intake officers do not make arrests or charge anyone with acts which if committed by adults would be crimes. This is all done before the respondent arrives at the intake door.

In other words, § 735 accomplishes in effect what *Miranda* accomplishes: If the juvenile is to be encouraged to make admissions, despite the privilege against self-incrimination, he should be protected against the use of such admissions at ensuing proceedings. Furthermore, there can be no unnecessary detention of the juvenile in the Family Court. If the probation service for any reason should not release the child before the filing of a petition, he must be brought before a judge of the Family Court and "the judge shall hold a hearing for the purpose of making a preliminary determination of whether the court appears to have jurisdiction over the child. At the commencement of the hearing, the judge shall advise the child of his right to remain silent, his right to be represented by counsel of his own choosing, and of his right to have a law guardian assigned * * *. He [the Judge] must also allow the child a reasonable time to send for his parents or other person legally responsible for his care, and for counsel, and adjourn the hearing for that purpose."

Thus both *Gault* and the New York Family Court Act provide for counsel at adjudication at the very least. The question is how far *Gault* can be expanded. In fact, *Gault* stated "we are not here concerned with the procedures or constitutional rights applicable to the pre-judicial stages of the juvenile process * * *."

The threat of self-incrimination is mitigated by the exclusion provision of § 735. Counsel for the respondent argues that the mere presence of counsel for the respondent at the intake level will prevent the issuance of a petition. This is not necessarily true and is a legal non sequitur. The fact that a petition may issue and a record created for the juvenile depends on what develops at the subsequent fact-finding hearing. The petition may be dismissed for lack of credible or legal evidence. The standard of proof is now "beyond a reasonable doubt" rather than mere preponderance. Is the intake level to be designated a critical stage for the juvenile because it determines whether an official record of delinquency adjudication will become part of the child's dossier? Intake referral for petition per se would not create an institutional commitment. It may well be that the desired openness of the intake interview can be maintained with counsel present as well as absent at least where under § 735 of the Family Court Act admissions made by the juvenile may not be used at the hearing.

To require counsel at intake would be an intolerable burden on an already overburdened court. The lack of manpower is both frightful and appalling. This is a valid argument entitled to great weight and has great relevancy. If there was no § 735 of the Family Court Act with its exclusionary rule, the argument would have no merit over the greater right to be represented at a critical stage of the proceeding, for it would then become truly a critical stage of the proceedings where counsel would be required.

In addition, … under § 735 of the Family Court Act there is an absolute prohibition of the use of any statements or confession made at the intake interview, even though voluntarily made and without coercion or undue influence or even where a waiver of that right was knowingly and intelligently made. Contrast this with admission statements and confessions, voluntarily made, after *Miranda* warnings or waiver of such rights, intelligently and knowingly made, in adult criminal proceedings where such statements or confessions, voluntarily made can be used against the respondent or defendant.

What greater right then does the juvenile need at intake proceedings than the tremendous protection afforded him under the exclusionary rule of § 735 of the Family Court Act or the equally great right of having the court or judge determine whether or not any petition will issue against him if a petitioner does not wish an adjustment at intake level and insists upon a petition being drawn.

If intake proceedings are to be classified as critical stages of proceedings despite all the legal protections for the juveniles above enumerated as already in existing law, rules and procedures, then there would be no need for intake proceedings for accused juveniles in furtherance of Family Court policy of rehabilitation and not punishment for crime and petitions should be drawn automatically in all cases and set down for fact-finding hearings.

There is, accordingly, no basis … [to] exten[d] … *Gault* to provide counsel at the intake level. There are no abuses in the pre-hearing stage as to impose the procedural requirement of counsel for the respondent at the intake interview. There is no present violation of due process clause of the 14th Amendment by not providing such counsel at the informal intake conference.

Motion to vacate the petition and send the case back to intake for consideration de novo on the ground that the respondent had been denied his constitutional right to counsel at the intake stage of the present Family Court proceeding is denied.

Notes

(a) The New York statute involved in *Frank H.* prohibits the use of a juvenile's intake statement during the fact finding hearing. Can it be used at any other stage of the proceedings?

(b) Is it realistic to believe that a judge who has had access to probation files will ignore an admission of guilt made at intake? Compare IJA-ABA Juvenile Justice Standards, § 2.12, regarding intake procedures.

4. IJA-ABA Juvenile Justice Standards

Robert E. Shepherd, Jr., ed.

a. Standards Relating to the Juvenile Probation Function: Intake and Predisposition Investigative Services

. . . .

Part II: Juvenile Court Intake

General Standards

2.1. Availability and utilization of intake services.

Intake services should be available to and utilized by all juvenile courts.

. . . .

2.4 Nonjudicial disposition of a complaint.

. . . .

E. A nonjudicial disposition should be utilized only under the following conditions

1. A nonjudicial disposition should take the form of an agreement of a contractual nature under which the intake officer promises not to file a petition in exchange for certain commitments by the juvenile and his or her parents or legal guardian or both with respect to their future conduct and activities.

2. The juvenile and his or her parents or legal guardian should voluntarily and intelligently enter into the agreement.

. . . .

2.8 Disposition in best interests of juvenile and community.

A. If the intake officer determines that the complaint is legally sufficient, the officer should determine what disposition of the complaint is most appropriate and desirable from the standpoint of the best interests of the juvenile and the community. This involves a determination as to whether a judicial disposition of the complaint would cause undue harm to the juvenile or exacerbate the problems that led to his or her delinquent acts, whether the juvenile presents a substantial danger to others, and whether the referral of the juvenile to the court has already served as a desired deterrent.

B. The officer should determine what disposition is in the best interests of the juvenile and the community in light of the following:

1. The seriousness of the offense that the alleged delinquent conduct constitutes should be considered in making an intake dispositional decision. A petition should ordinarily be filed against a juvenile who has allegedly engaged in delinquent conduct constituting a serious offense, which should be determined on the basis of the nature and extent of harm to others produced by the conduct.

2. The nature and number of the juvenile's prior contacts with the juvenile court should be considered in making an intake dispositional decision.

3. The circumstances surrounding the alleged delinquent conduct, including whether the juvenile was alone or in the company of other juveniles who also participated in the alleged delinquent conduct, should be considered in making an intake dispositional decision. If a petition is filed against one of the juveniles, a petition should ordinarily be filed against the other juveniles for substantially similar conduct.

4. The age and maturity of the juvenile may be relevant to an intake dispositional decision.

5. The juvenile's school attendance and behavior, the juvenile's family situation and relationships, and the juvenile's home environment may be relevant to an intake dispositional decision.

6. The attitude of the juvenile to the alleged delinquent conduct and to law enforcement and juvenile court authorities may be relevant to an intake dispositional decision, but a nonjudicial disposition of the complaint or the unconditional dismissal of the complaint should not be precluded for the sole reason that the juvenile denies the allegations of the complaint.

7. A nonjudicial disposition of the complaint or the unconditional dismissal of the complaint should not be precluded for the sole reason that the complainant opposes dismissal.

8. The availability of services to meet the juvenile's needs both within and outside the juvenile justice system should be considered in making an intake dispositional decision.

9. The factors that are not relevant to an intake dispositional decision include but are not necessarily limited to the juvenile's race, ethnic background, religion, sex, and economic status.

. . . .

Section IV: Intake Procedures

. . . .

2.9 Necessity for and desirability of written guidelines and rules.

Juvenile probation agencies and other agencies responsible for intake services should develop and publish written guidelines and rules with respect to intake procedures.

2.10 Initiation of intake proceedings and receipt of complaint by intake officer.

A. An intake officer should initiate proceedings upon receipt of a complaint.

B. Any complaint that serves as the basis for the filing of a petition should be sworn to and signed by a person who has personal knowledge of the facts or is informed of them and believes they are true.

2.11 Intake investigation.

A. Prior to making a dispositional decision, the intake officer should be authorized to conduct a preliminary investigation in order to obtain information essential to the making of the decision.

B. In the course of the investigation the intake officer may:

1. interview or otherwise seek information from the complainant, a victim of, witness to, or coparticipant in the delinquent conduct allegedly engaged in by the juvenile;

2. check existing court records, the records of law enforcement agencies, and other public records of a nonprivate nature;

3. conduct interviews with the juvenile and his or her parents or legal guardian in accordance with the requirements set forth in Standard 2.14.

C. If the officer wishes to make any additional inquiries, he or she should do so only with the consent of the juvenile and his or her parents or legal guardian.

D. It is the responsibility of the complainant to furnish the intake officer with the information sufficient to establish the jurisdiction of the court over the juvenile and to support the charges against the juvenile. If the officer believes the information to be deficient in this respect, he or she may notify the complainant of the need for additional information.

2.12 Juvenile's privilege against self-incrimination at intake.

A. A juvenile should have a privilege against self-incrimination in connection with questioning by intake personnel during the intake process.

B. Any statement made by a juvenile to an intake officer or other information derived directly or indirectly from such a statement is inadmissible in evidence in any judicial proceeding prior to a formal finding of delinquency unless the statement was made after consultation with and in the presence of counsel.

2.13 Juvenile's right to assistance of counsel at intake.

A juvenile should have an unwaivable right to the assistance of counsel at intake:

A. in connection with any questioning in accordance with Standard 2.14 or other questioning by intake personnel; and

B. in conjunction with any discussions or negotiations regarding a nonjudicial disposition, including discussions and negotiations in the course of a dispositional conference in accordance with Standard 2.14.

2.14 Intake interviews and dispositional conferences.

A. If the intake officer deems it advisable, the officer may request and arrange an interview with the juvenile and his or her parents or legal guardian.

B. Participation in an intake interview by the juvenile and his or her parents or legal guardian should be voluntary. They should have the right to refuse to participate in an interview, and the officer should have no authority to compel their attendance.

C. At the time the request to attend the interview is made, the intake officer should inform the juvenile and his or her parents or legal guardian either in writing or orally that attendance is voluntary and that the juvenile has the right to be represented by counsel.

D. At the commencement of the interview, the intake officer should:

1. explain to the juvenile and his or her parents or legal guardian that a complaint has been made and explain the allegations of the complaint;

2. explain the function of the intake process, the dispositional powers of the intake officer, and intake procedures;

3. explain that participation in the intake interview is voluntary and that they may refuse to participate; and

4. notify them of the right of the juvenile to remain silent and the right to counsel as heretofore defined in Standard 2.13.

E. Subsequent to the intake interview, the intake officer may schedule one or more dispositional conferences with the juvenile and his or her parents or legal guardian in order to effect a nonjudicial disposition.

F. Participation in a dispositional conference by a juvenile and his or her parents or legal guardian should be voluntary. They should have the right to refuse to participate, and the intake officer should have no authority to compel their attendance.

G. The intake officer may conduct dispositional conferences in accordance with the procedures for intake interviews set forth in subsections D and E.

2.15 Length of intake process.

A decision at the intake level as to the disposition of a complaint should be made as expeditiously as possible. The period within which the decision is made should not exceed thirty (30) days from the date the complaint is filed in cases in which the juvenile who is the subject of a complaint has not been placed in detention or shelter care facilities.

Section V: Scope of Intake Officer's Dispositional Powers

. . . .

2.16 Role of intake officer and prosecutor in filing of petition: right of complainant to file a petition.

A. If the intake officer determines that a petition should be filed, the officer should submit a written report to the appropriate prosecuting official requesting that a petition should be filed. The officer should also submit a written statement of his or her decision and of the reasons for the decision to the juvenile and his or her parents or legal guardian. All petitions should be countersigned and filed by the appropriate prosecuting official. The prosecutor may refuse the request of the intake officer to file a petition. Any determination by the prosecutor that a petition should not be filed should be final.

B. If the intake officer determines that a petition should not be filed, the officer should notify the complainant of his or her decision and of the reasons for the decision and should advise the complainant that he or she may submit the complaint to the appropriate prosecuting official for review. Upon receiving a request for review, the prosecutor should consider the facts presented by the complainant, consult with the intake officer who made the initial decision, and then make the final determination as to whether a petition should be filed.

C. In the absence of a complainant's request for a review of the intake officer's determination that a petition should not be filed, the intake officer should notify the appropriate prosecuting official of the officer's decision not to request the filing of a petition in those cases in which the conduct charged would constitute a crime if committed by an adult. The prosecutor should have the right in all such cases, after consultation with the intake officer, to file a petition.

. . . .

Part VI. Intake, Early Disposition and Detention

6.1 Intake and early disposition, generally.

Whenever the nature and circumstances of the case permit, counsel should explore the possibility of an early diversion from the formal juvenile court process through subjudicial agencies and other community resources. Participation in pre- or non-judicial stages of the juvenile court process may well be critical to such diversion, as well as to protection of the client's rights.

6.2 Intake hearings.

A. In jurisdictions where intake hearings are held prior to reference of a juvenile court matter for judicial proceedings, the lawyer should be familiar with and explain to the client and, if the client is a minor, to the client's parents, the nature of the hearing, the procedures to be followed, the several dispositions available, and their probable consequences. The lawyer should further advise the client of his or her rights at the intake hearing, including privilege against self-incrimination where appropriate, and of the use that may later be made of the client's statements.

B. The lawyer should be prepared to make to the intake hearing officer arguments concerning the jurisdictional sufficiency of the allegations made and to present facts and circumstances relating to the occurrence of and the client's responsibility for the acts or conditions charged or to the necessity for official treatment of the matter.

6.3 Early disposition

A. When the client admits the acts or conditions alleged in the juvenile court proceedings and after investigation the lawyer is satisfied that the admission is factually supported and that the court would have jurisdiction to act, the lawyer should, with the client's consent, consider developing or cooperating in the development of a plan for informal or voluntary adjustment of the case.

B. A lawyer should not participate in an admission of responsibility by the client for purposes of securing informal or early disposition when the client denies responsibility for the acts or conditions alleged.

Notes

(a) Given that there are very few jury trials in juvenile court, and that judges are the factfinders, what procedures should be established at intake to prevent bias?

(b) The decision in *Frank H.* is the norm. Given the consequences if a child is referred to juvenile court, should intake be viewed as a critical stage of the proceeding requiring the appointment of counsel? Moreover, even if a child is not referred to juvenile court, does he or she face consequences from merely signing an adjustment contract?

F. Pre-Trial Detention Hearings

1. Statutes

a. *N.Y. Family Court Act § 320.5*

The initial appearance; release or detention

1. At the initial appearance, the court in its discretion may release the respondent or direct his detention.

2. Rules of court shall define permissible terms and conditions of release. The court may in its discretion release the respondent upon such terms and conditions as it deems appropriate. The respondent shall be given a written copy of any such terms and conditions. The court may modify or enlarge such terms and conditions at any time prior to the expiration of the respondent's release.

3. The court shall not direct detention unless it finds and states the facts and reasons for so finding that unless the respondent is detained:

    (a) there is a substantial probability that he will not appear in court on the return date; or

    (b) there is a serious risk that he may before the return date commit an act which if committed by an adult would constitute a crime.

4. At the initial appearance the presentment agency may introduce the respondent's previous delinquency findings entered by a family court. If the respondent has been fingerprinted for the current charge pursuant to § 306.1, the presentment agency may also introduce the fingerprint records maintained by the division of criminal justice services. The clerk of court and the probation service shall cooperate with the presentment agency in making available the appropriate records. At the conclusion of the initial appearance such fingerprint records shall be returned to the presentment agency and shall not be made a part of the court record.

5. Upon a finding of facts and reasons which support a detention order pursuant to subdivision three of this section, the court shall also determine and state in any order directing detention:

    (a) whether the continuation of the respondent in the respondent's home would be contrary to the best interests of the respondent based upon, and limited to, the facts and circumstances available to the court at the time of the initial appearance; and

    (b) where appropriate and consistent with the need for protection of the community, whether reasonable efforts were made prior to the date of the court appearance that resulted in the detention order issued in accordance with this section to prevent or eliminate the need for removal of the respondent from his or her home or, if the respondent had been removed from his or her home prior to the initial appearance, where appropriate and consistent with the need for protection of the community, whether reasonable efforts were made to make it possible for the respondent to safely return home.

b. *Tex. Family Code § 53.02*

Release from Detention

(a) If a child is brought before the court or delivered to a detention facility as authorized by §§ 51.12(a)(3) and (4), the intake or other authorized officer of the court shall immediately make an investigation and shall release the child unless it appears that his detention is warranted under Subsection (b). The release may be conditioned upon requirements reasonably necessary to insure the child's appearance at later proceedings, but the conditions of the release must be in writing and filed with the office or official designated by the court and a copy furnished to the child.

(b) A child taken into custody may be detained prior to hearing on the petition only if:

    (1) the child is likely to abscond or be removed from the jurisdiction of the court;

    (2) suitable supervision, care, or protection for the child is not being provided by a parent, guardian, custodian, or other person;

    (3) the child has no parent, guardian, custodian, or other person able to return the child to the court when required;

    (4) the child may be dangerous to himself or herself or the child may threaten the safety of the public if released;

    (5) the child has previously been found to be a delinquent child or has previously been convicted of a penal offense punishable by a term in jail or prison and is likely to commit an offense if released; or

    (6) the child's detention is required under Subsection (f).

(c) If the child is not released, a request for detention hearing shall be made and promptly presented to the court, and an informal detention hearing as provided in § 54.01 of this code shall be held promptly, but not later than the time required by § 54.01 of this code.

c. *Tex. Family Code § 54.01*

Detention Hearing

(a) Except as provided by Subsection (p), if the child is not released under § 53.02, a detention hearing without a jury shall be held promptly, but not later than the second working day after the child is taken into custody; provided, however, that when a child is detained on a Friday or Saturday, then such detention hearing shall be held on the first working day after the child is taken into custody.

(b) Reasonable notice of the detention hearing, either oral or written, shall be given, stating the time, place, and purpose of the hearing. Notice shall be given to the child and, if they can be found, to his parents, guardian, or custodian. Prior to the commencement of the hearing, the court shall inform the parties of the child's right to counsel and to appointed counsel if they are indigent and of the child's right to remain silent with respect to any allegations of delinquent conduct, conduct indicating a need for supervision, or conduct that violates an order of probation imposed by a juvenile court.

(c) At the detention hearing, the court may consider written reports from probation officers, professional court employees, or professional consultants in addition to the testimony of witnesses. Prior to the detention hearing, the court shall provide the attorney for the child with access to all written matter to be considered by the court in making the detention decision. The court may order counsel not to reveal items to the child or his parent, guardian, or guardian ad litem if such disclosure would materially harm the treatment and rehabilitation of the child or would substantially decrease the likelihood of receiving information from the same or similar sources in the future.

(d) A detention hearing may be held without the presence of the child's parents if the court has been unable to locate them. If no parent or guardian is present, the court shall appoint counsel or a guardian ad litem for the child.

(e) At the conclusion of the hearing, the court shall order the child released from detention unless it finds that:

(1) he is likely to abscond or be removed from the jurisdiction of the court;

(2) suitable supervision, care, or protection for him is not being provided by a parent, guardian, custodian, or other person;

(3) he has no parent, guardian, custodian, or other person able to return him to the court when required;

(4) he may be dangerous to himself or may threaten the safety of the public if released; or

(5) he has previously been found to be a delinquent child or has previously been convicted of a penal offense punishable by a term in jail or prison and is likely to commit an offense if released.

(f) Unless otherwise agreed in the memorandum of understanding under §37.011, Education Code, a release may be conditioned on requirements reasonably necessary to insure the child's appearance at later proceedings, but the conditions of the release must be in writing and a copy furnished to the child. In a county with a population greater than 125,000, if a child being released under this section is expelled under §37.007, Education Code, the release shall be conditioned on the child's attending a juvenile justice alternative education program pending a deferred prosecution or formal court disposition of the child's case.

(g) No statement made by the child at the detention hearing shall be admissible against the child at any other hearing.

(h) A detention order extends to the conclusion of the disposition hearing, if there is one, but in no event for more than 10 working days. Further detention orders may be made following subsequent detention hearings. The initial detention hearing may not be waived but subsequent detention hearings may be waived in accordance with the requirements of § 51.09. Each subsequent detention order shall extend for no more than 10 working days, except that in a county that does not have a certified juvenile detention facility, as described by § 51.12(a)(3), each subsequent detention order shall extend for no more than 15 working days.

(i) A child in custody may be detained for as long as 10 days without the hearing described in Subsection (a) of this section if:

(1) a written request for shelter in detention facilities pending arrangement of transportation to his place of residence in another state or country or another county of this state is voluntarily executed by the child not later than the next working day after he was taken into custody;

(2) the request for shelter contains:

(A) a statement by the child that he voluntarily agrees to submit himself to custody and detention for a period of not longer than 10 days without a detention hearing;

(B) an allegation by the person detaining the child that the child has left his place of residence in another state or country or another county of this state, that he is in need of shelter, and that an effort is being made to arrange transportation to his place of residence; and

(C) a statement by the person detaining the child that he has advised the child of his right to demand a detention hearing under Subsection (a) of this section; and

(3) the request is signed by the juvenile court judge to evidence his knowledge of the fact that the child is being held in detention.

(j) The request for shelter may be revoked by the child at any time, and on such revocation, if further detention is necessary, a detention hearing shall be held not later than the next working day in accordance with Subsections (a) through (g) of this section.

(k) Notwithstanding anything in this title to the contrary, the child may sign a request for shelter without the concurrence of an adult specified in § 51.09 of this code.

(l) The juvenile board may appoint a referee to conduct the detention hearing. The referee shall be an attorney licensed to practice law in this state. Before commencing the detention hearing, the referee shall inform the parties who have appeared that they are entitled to have the hearing before the juvenile court judge or a substitute judge authorized by § 51.04(f). If a party objects to the referee conducting the detention hearing, an authorized judge shall conduct the hearing within 24 hours. At the conclusion of the hearing, the referee shall transmit written findings and recommendations to the juvenile court judge or substitute judge. The juvenile court judge or substitute judge shall adopt, modify, or reject the referee's recommendations not later than the next working day after the day that the judge receives the recommendations. Failure to act within that time results in release of the child by operation of law. A recommendation that the child be released operates to secure the child's immediate release, subject to the power of the juvenile court judge or substitute judge to reject or modify that recommendation. The effect of an order detaining a child shall be computed from the time of the hearing before the referee.

(m) The detention hearing required in this section may be held in the county of the designated place of detention where the child is being held even though the designated place of detention is outside the county of residence of the child or the county in which the alleged delinquent conduct, conduct indicating a need for supervision, or probation violation occurred.

(n) An attorney appointed by the court under § 51.10(c) because a determination was made under this section to detain a child who was not represented by an attorney may request on behalf of the child and is entitled to a de novo detention hearing under this section. The attorney must make the request not later than the 10th working day after the date the attorney is appointed. The hearing must take place not later than the second working day after the date the attorney filed a formal request with the court for a hearing.

(o) The court or referee shall find whether there is probable cause to believe that a child taken into custody without an arrest warrant or a directive to apprehend has engaged in delinquent conduct, conduct indicating a need for supervision, or conduct that violates an order of probation imposed by a juvenile court. The court or referee must make the finding within 48 hours, including weekends and holidays, of the time the child was taken into custody. The court or referee may make the finding on any reasonably reliable information without regard to admissibility of that information under the Texas Rules of Evidence. A finding of probable cause is required to detain a child after the 48th hour after the time the child was taken into custody. If a court or referee finds probable cause, additional findings of probable cause are not required in the same cause to authorize further detention.

(p) If a child is detained in a county jail or other facility as provided by § 51.12(l) and the child is not released under § 53.02(f), a detention hearing without a jury shall be held promptly, but not later than the 24th hour, excluding weekends and holidays, after the time the child is taken into custody.

(q) If a child has not been released under § 53.02 or this section and a petition has not been filed under § 53.04 or § 54.05 concerning the child, the court shall order the child released from detention not later than:

(1) the 30th working day after the date the initial detention hearing is held, if the child is alleged to have engaged in conduct constituting a capital felony, an aggravated controlled substance felony, or a felony of the first degree; or

(2) the 15th working day after the date the initial detention hearing is held, if the child is alleged to have engaged in conduct constituting an offense other than an offense listed in Subdivision (1) or conduct that violates an order of probation imposed by a juvenile court.

(q-1) The juvenile board may impose an earlier deadline than the specified deadlines for filing petitions under Subsection (q) and may specify the consequences of not filing a petition by the deadline the juvenile board has established. The juvenile board may authorize but not require the juvenile court to release a respondent from detention for failure of the prosecutor to file a petition by the juvenile board's deadline.

(r) On the conditional release of a child from detention by judicial order under Subsection (f), the court, referee, or detention magistrate may order that the child's parent, guardian, or custodian present in court at the detention hearing engage in acts or omissions specified by the court, referee, or detention magistrate that will assist the child in complying with the conditions of release. The order must be in writing and a copy furnished to the parent, guardian, or custodian. An order entered under this subsection may be enforced as provided by Chapter 61.

2. Detention Forms and Assessments

Arizona

Option 390A   **JUVENILE DETENTION SCREENING**   File Number _____

JV Number _____

Juvenile Name _____   DOB _____

Warrant status at screening _____   Age _____

Legal status at time of screening _____

Are there any 13-501 charges? _____

Location (S/D) _____ Date Screened _____ Time Screened

Referring Agency _____ Zip code _____

Detained (Y/N) Reason for Screening _____ (valid codes)

Complaint Number _____ Advisory date _____ time _____

Last complaint nbr _____

Screening PO _____ PO/SUPV Notified (Y/N) High Profile

Notes

Preliminary Questions on 13-501 A and B (must detain per Rule 38 (5))

A. **MOST SERIOUS PRESENTING CHARGE OR PETITIONED OFFENSE**
    (choose only one item indicating the most serious charge)
    12 — Class I Felony   4 — Class V Felony
    10 — Class II Felony   3 — Class VI Felony
    8 — Class III Felony   2 — All Misdemeanors
    6 — Class IV Felony   0 — Status Offenses   A. _____

B. **ADDITIONAL PRESENTING CHARGES OR PETITIONED OFFENSES**
    (select only one, highest point value)
    3 — Two or more additional felonies
    2 — One additional felony
    1 — One or more additional misdemeanors   B. _____

C. **PRIOR HISTORY** *(covers all adjudicated offenses) (select only one, highest point value)*
    5 — Two or more prior felonies Class I–III
    4 — Two or more prior felonies Class IV–VI
    3 — One or more technical VOP
    2 — One prior felony
    1 — Two or more prior misdemeanors   C. _____

D. **LEGAL STATUS** *(select only one, highest point value)*
    12 — FOJ FELONY OFFENSE (if scores in this category, Juvenile MUST be detained)
    5 — On Parole, Adult Probation or remanded on any offense
    5 — Felony (petitioned/charged) while awaiting a (n) Adv., Adj., Dispo. or Transfer Hearing
    4 — Misdemeanor (petitioned/charged) while awaiting a(n) Adv., Adj., Dispo. or Transfer Hearing
    3 — On JIPS or Electronic Monitoring
    2 — On Standard Probation or probation in any county or Home Detention
    1 — In Residential Placement, DAP or Southwest Key ATD   D. _____

E. **WARRANTS** *(if scores in this category, Juvenile MUST be detained)*
    12 — DOJC 901 Warrant
    12 — Temporary Custody Warrant or FTA/Mandatory Warrant (mandatory detention) E. _____

F. **MITIGATING FACTORS** *(can decrease total by 1 or 2 points) (max. –2)*
    1 — Availability of parents to supervise
    1 — Attitude of juvenile
    1 — Police input   F. _____

G. AGGRAVATING FACTORS *(can increase total by 2 to 5 points) (max. +5)*

    5 — Driver in vehicle theft

    3 — Specific threat/Injury to person

    3 — Offense committed in aggressive, offensive or hostile manner

    3 — Possession or use of weapon

    2 — Gang related presenting offense   G. _____

H. RISK — OVERRIDE

Juvenile may be detained regardless of points IF CIRCUMSTANCES EXIST THAT POSE A SERIOUS THREAT TO LIFE: for instance, an immediate suicide risk, severe chemical dependency, a serious threat to child's life from others, a serious threat to family members by the juvenile, or return to dangerous environment.   H. _____

I. TOTAL *(Sum of A through G)*   I. _____

SCORING: 12 AND UP DETAIN 11 AND BELOW RELEASE

RISK ASSESSMENT INSTRUMENTS—Oregon

MULTNOMAH COUNTY DEPARTMENT OF JUVENILE JUSTICE SERVICES

RISK ASSESSMENT INSTRUMENT (RAI) III

This paper form is to be used only when electronic **RAI** is unavailable.
It *must* be entered into the electronic **RAI** as soon as it is available.

Date/time youth brought to DELH/Admissions:	Date/Time of Intake Screening:
YOUTH'S NAME:	Case # Ref.# DOB:

SPECIAL DETENTION CASES	(CIRCLE "DETAIN" FOR ALL APPLICABLE CATEGORIES)	
Escape from secure custody		Detain
Arrest warrant (Detain with limited exception, see definitions) Type of Warrant: Fail to appear ☐ Judicial Officer opposes release ☐ (Check all that apply) Unable to locate ☐ Judicial Officer opposes release ☐ Other (specify:_____) ☐ Judicial Officer opposes release ☐ If Judicial Officer doesn't oppose, do not treat as a special detention cases. Screen according to policy.		Detain
In custody youth summoned for hearing		Detain
Court ordered (Check all that apply) Community Detention Violation ☐ Day Reporting Violation ☐ Electronic Monitoring Violation ☐ Law Violation ☐ Probation Violation ☐ Other (specify:_____) ☐		Detain

MOST SERIOUS INSTANT OFFENSE	(CIRCLE HIGHEST APPLICABLE SCORE)
Intentional homicide (aggravated murder, murder)	17
Attempted Murder or Class A Felonies involving violence or use or threatened use of a weapon (including Rape 1, Sodomy 1, and Unlawful Sexual Penetration 1 involving forcible compulsion)	12
Class B Felonies involving violence or use or threatened use of a weapon	8
Rape 1, Sodomy 1, Sexual Penetration 1 **not** involving forcible compulsion	7
Class C Felony involving violence or use or threatened use of a weapon	6
All other Class A and B Felonies	5
All other Class C Felonies	3
Misdemeanor involving violence, or possession, use or threatened use of a weapon	3
All other Misdemeanors	1
Probation/Parole Violation	1
Other, e.g., status offense (MIP, runaway, curfew, etc.)	0
SCORE RANGE 0 - 17 SCORE	

ADDITIONAL CURRENT OFFENSES	(IF APPLICABLE, CIRCLE HIGHEST SCORE)
Two or more unrelated additional current Felonies	3
One unrelated additional current Felony	2
SCORE RANGE 0 - 3 SCORE	

LEGAL STATUS	(CIRCLE ALL THAT APPLY)

RISK ASSESSMENT INSTRUMENTS — Oregon (Page 2)

Currently under Juvenile Justice/OYA or other state or County supervision: **(Check all that apply)**	**EITHER:** Parole ☐ Probation ☐	2
	OR: (If this section applies, score <u>either</u> 2 or 1, <u>not</u> both.) Deferred Disposition ☐ Informal Disposition ☐ Formal Accountability Agreement ☐ DJJS Diversion ☐ Other (Specify:____) ☐	1
Above referenced status is for felony violent/assaultive law violation or domestic violence or unlawful possession of a firearm.		1
Pending trial (or disposition) on a law violation/probation violation (petition filed). Score only most serious pending offense using the " Most Serious Instant Offense" values. No score for misdemeanor petitions over 6 months old, unless there is an outstanding warrant.		17 12 8 7 6 5 3 1 0
Youth is on a conditional release. (Check all that apply, but score only 1 point.) Community Detention ☐ Electronic Monitoring ☐ House Arrest ☐ Other (specify:_____) ☐		1
	SCORE RANGE 0 - 21 **SCORE TOTAL**	

ALL WARRANTS (EXCLUDING TRAFFIC AND DEPENDENCY) HISTORY:

Score two (2) points for each warrant (excluding traffic and dependency warrants) during the past 18 months (maximum 20 points).	20 18 16 14 12 10 8 6 4 2
SCORE RANGE 0 - 20 **SCORE**	

PRIOR SUSTAINED OFFENSE   **(IF APPLICABLE CIRCLE HIGHEST SCORE)**

Two or more prior felony adjudications (true findings)	3
One prior felony adjudication, or three or more prior misdemeanor adjudications (true findings)	2
Two prior misdemeanor adjudications (true findings)	1
SCORE RANGE 0 - 3 **SCORE**	

MITIGATING FACTORS   **(CIRCLE ALL THAT APPLY)**

Regular school attendance or employed	-1
Responsible adult to assure supervision and return to Court	-1

RISK ASSESSMENT INSTRUMENTS — Oregon (Page 3)

No Law Violation referrals within past year *(applies only to youth with a prior history of law violations)*	-1
First Law Violation referral at age 16 or older	-1
First Law Violation referral (instant offense)	-1
Not on probation, first UTL warrant and unaware of warrant.	-2
No FTA warrant history *(youth <u>must</u> have had a delinquency Court appearance history)*	-2
SCORE RANGE -9 TO 0 SCORE TOTAL	

AGGRAVATING FACTORS (CIRCLE ALL THAT APPLY)	
No verifiable local community ties	3
Possession of a firearm during instant offense without use or threatened use	2
Reported history of runaways from home within past six (6) months (2 or more) **OR** 1 run away from home and 1 run from placement	1
Reported history of runaways from out-of-home placement within past six (6) months (2 or more)	2
Multiple victims in instant offense	1
Documented threats to victim/witness (instant offense)	1
SCORE RANGE 0 - 10 SCORE TOTAL	

TOTAL RISK	
SCORE	

DECISION SCALE/DECISION	**OVERRIDE**	
Special Detention Cases ☐	Detain	☐
12 - Over Detain ☐	Conditional Release	☐
7 - 11 Conditional Release ☐ 0 - 6 Unconditional Release ☐	Unconditional Release ☐ Approved by:_____ Reason:_____
SUMMONS	_____ _____
	Y N	_____ _____
Preliminary Hearing Summons ☐ ☐ (Summons to prelim if score over 6 or youth is being released on a warrant, on a charge involving a weapon, on a UUMV charge, domestic violence, or is being placed in a shelter care placement that requires a prelim.)	_____ _____ _____
Shelter Placement Y N ☐ ☐	
	Y N
Does youth meet statutory criteria for detention ☐ ☐ (If no, youth **MUST** be released.)	

RISK ASSESSMENT INSTRUMENTS — Oregon (Page 4)

REASON FOR ADMISSION OF YOUTH HELD PENDING A PRELIMINARY HEARING

Probable cause that <u>one or more</u> of the following exists:

☐ Committed any felony crime
☐ Committed a crime involving infliction of
physical injury to another person
☐ Possession of a firearm (ORS. 166.250)
☐ Escape from a juvenile detention facility
☐ Out-of-State runaway

☐ Probation/parole violator
☐ Fugitive from another jurisdiction

☐ APB from state training school
☐ Violation of conditional release
☐ FTA after summons, citation or subpoena

AND

☐ No means less restrictive of the youth's liberty
gives reasonable assurance that the youth will
attend hearing; **OR**

☐ The youth's behavior endangers the physical welfare
of the youth or another person, or endangers the
community.

THIRTY-SIX (36)-HOUR HOLD (OVERRIDE/SUPERVISORY APPROVAL REQUIRED)

Youth can be held 36 hours from the time first taken into police custody <u>to develop a release plan</u> if: they are brought in on a law violation; a parent of guardian cannot be found or will not take responsibility for the youth, shelter is not available; and <u>the youth cannot be released safely</u> on recognizance or conditionally. What is the date and time
of the police custody?_____Release must be no later than: (date/time)
REASON:_____
_____

Fill out the table below only when the electronic RAI is unavailable <u>and</u> only if youth is detained. The following table is the method used by the electronic RAI to automatically compute the CMS score.

COMPUTATION OF THE CMS SCORE	
Client's Risk Assessment Instrument (RAI) Score	
Add CMS points for each of the current (police) allegations (not just most serious allegation)	
Add CMS points for each "Person" or "Property" allegation that has been filed in a petition	
Add CMS points for each allegation that has been found true	
Add 2 points for each warrant issued (excluding traffic/dependency warrants) within the last 18 months	
Capacity Management System (CMS) Score TOTAL	

This paper RAI does not include notification and narrative information found on the face sheet. Include this information when transferring to the electronic RAI.

ATTENTION: Fill out CMS Early Release Plan form on all youth detained with RAI score of less than 12.

Multnomah County Department of Juvenile And Adult Community Justice
RISK ASSESSMENT INSTRUMENT (RAI) III
FACTOR DEFINITIONS

The Detention Risk Assessment Instrument (RAI) will be applied to all juveniles brought to detention admissions, even if it is apparent that the youth should be released. Below are the only exceptions at this point in time:

- Contracted Housing beds
- Parole, Close Custody or Community Safety beds
- Material Witness holds
- Measure 11 allegations (RAI is completed but youth is held regardless of score)
- Status offenders who are not on Probation or not out of state runaways
- AITP/Program Placements

The Intake worker will attempt to obtain objective, verifiable information in completing the RAI and will also include all available information from other counties and jurisdictions. When confirming information is not available, staff will otherwise rely on the youth's or parent's self-report. The following work day, JCCs will be responsible for filling out a work sheet to add or adjust any additional available information.

If a youth is detained based on their special detention status or upon accruing a risk score of twelve (12) or more, the youth will appear before a judicial officer on the following work day, unless they have been Court ordered to be held in detention.

<u>SPECIAL DETENTION CASES</u>

- Escape from secure custody. This applies to a youth who is on escape status from a youth correction facility or other "secure" detention setting.

- **Juvenile Corrections APB/Parole violator community safety hold.** APB (All Points Bulletin) issued by Oregon Department of Corrections/Oregon Youth Authority. Intake worker will contact the parole officer or youth correction facility to confirm the APB and to further confirm whether the youth should be held. The parole violator community safety hold is reserved only for those Department of Corrections/Oregon Youth Authority parole violators who have been ordered into designated "community safety beds" following a preliminary parole revocation hearing or as directed by specific Multnomah County Juvenile and Adult Community Justice staff responsible for these youth.

- **Arrest warrant.** All youth brought to detention following their arrest based on a warrant will be screened utilizing the RAI. If a Multnomah County Judicial Officer does not oppose release prior to the preliminary hearing, (indicated by **not** checking the related box on the warrant), the youth is eligible for release based on their RAI score. If released, the youth will <u>always</u> be put on the maximum supervision level of Community Detention and summonsed to appear at a preliminary hearing the next judicial day regardless of their RAI score.

  If the judicial officer opposes release prior to the preliminary hearing (indicated by **checking** the related box on the warrant), the youth will be held in detention pending the preliminary hearing.

- **Two prior misdemeanor adjudications (true findings).** A misdemeanor adjudication or "true finding" includes only those charges where jurisdiction has been established by the Court subsequent to a trial or admission by the youth.

<u>*MITIGATING FACTORS*</u>

- **Regular school attendance or employed.** Allows for occasional truancy (two to three un-excused absences in most recent school month). Employed assumes at least 15 hours per week if not attending school.

- **Responsible adult to assure in supervision and return to Court.** Responsible adult would include a friend, neighbor, or relative who does not relate to the youth as a peer but rather as an individual who is concerned about the youth's best interests and clearly agrees to appropriately supervise the youth and <u>assure</u> their return to Court.

- **No Law Violation referrals within past year (applies only to youth with a prior history of law violations).** Law violation referrals exclude any status offense such as curfew or MIP but does include law violation referrals from any and all jurisdictions.

- **First Law Violation referral at age 16 or older.** Law violation referrals exclude any status offense such as curfew or MIP but does include law violation referrals from any and all jurisdictions.

- **First Law Violation referral (instant offense).** Law violation referrals exclude any status offense such as curfew or MIP but does include law violation referrals from any and all jurisdictions.

- **Not on Probation, in custody on first warrant which is an UTL and unaware of warrant.** This is for the rare situation where the youth and family really did not know about the UTL warrant and the youth is not on probation.

- **No FTA history (youth <u>must</u> have had a delinquency Court appearance history)** Youth has demonstrated the ability to make it to delinquency hearings and has no FTA history.

AGGRAVATING FACTORS

- No verifiable local community ties. **The youth is unable to provide information that can be verified by the Intake worker regarding residence (independent living, with friends or relatives), school enrollment or employment. If the youth reports a residence address but no telephone number, the Intake worker will request police assistance to contact individuals at the reported address in order to verify said residence and community ties. The Intake worker will also make every effort to eliminate any language barriers through the use of appropriate interpreters.**

- **Possession of a firearm during instant offense, but without use or threatened** use. Example: A youth found to be in possession of a gun when arrested for UUMV, PCS, Criminal Mischief or any such other law violation that did not require the use or threatened use of a gun.

- **Reported history of runaways from home within past six (6) months (2 or more) OR 1 run away from home and 1 run away from placement.** Runaways must have been reported to law enforcement or confirmed by parent/guardian/JCC to Intake worker.

- **Reported history of runaways from out-of-home placement within the past six (6) months (2 or more).** Runaways must have been reported to law enforcement or confirmed by parent/guardian/JCC to Intake worker.

- **Multiple victims in instant offense.** Determination of whether there are multiple victims is established by the police crime report or "incident" report which will clearly list each victim for the instant offense.

- **Victim/witness threats (instant offense).** Threats must be documented and made directly to victims or witnesses as opposed to angry statements made to an Intake worker or others regarding allegations that the youth claims to be false or inaccurate.

ADDENDUM
MEASURE 11/SUCCESSOR STATUTE CRIMES

Aggravated Murder	Kidnap II**
Murder	Rape I
Attempt Aggravated Murder	Rape II
Conspiracy to Commit	Robbery I
Aggravated Murder	Robbery II — (see ** below)
Attempt Murder	Sodomy I
Conspiracy to Commit Murder	Sodomy II
Manslaughter I	Unlawful Sexual Penetration I
Manslaughter II	Unlawful Sexual Penetration II
Assault I	Sexual Abuse I
Assault II (see ** below)	Compelling Prostitution — (see ** below)
Kidnap I	Arson I — (see ** below)

** SB 1049 … "Revises BM11 … creates possibility of guideline sentence for assault 2, kidnap 2 and robbery 2 under certain circumstances of the crime and if the accused meets certain criminal history criterion. Also adds crimes of arson 1 if threat to serious physical injury, using child in sexually explicit display and compelling prostitution."

PEORIA COUNTY [Illinois]
JUVENILE DETENTION CENTER SCREENING INSTRUMENT

DATE: _____ TIME: _____

REFERRAL FROM: _____ WITH: _____
(PRINT POLICE OFFICER'S NAME)   (PRINT LAW ENFORCEMENT AGENCY'S NAME)

MINOR: _____ SCREENER: _____
(PRINT JUVENILE'S NAME)   (PRINT YOUR NAME)

REFER TO POINT VALUES PAGE (SCORE EACH ITEM) SCORE

A. **Most Serious Alleged Current Offense**   0–12 _____
(Choose only one item indicating the most serious charge)
Charge: _____

B. **Additional Current/Pending Offenses**
Two or more additional current felonies   4
One additional felony   3
One or more additional current misdemeanors   1
None   0 _____

C. **Prior Arrest**
Two or more prior major (offenses in 12 category) felonies   5
Three or more arrests in last 30 days   4
One prior major felony; two or more other felonies   3
One other felony   2
Two or more prior misdemeanors; one prior misdemeanor weapons offense   1
None   0

D. **SUBTOTAL I (Sum of A, B, and C)**   _____

E. **Risk of Failure to Appear**
Active delinquent warrant/request for apprehension/delinquent offense
while on court-ordered home detention   10
Absconded from court-ordered residential placement or violated home detention   8
Habitual absconder or history of absconding to avoid court appearance   6
Prior delinquent warrant issued   3
None of above   0

F. **SUBTOTAL II (Enter the larger of D or E)**   _____

G. **Legal Status**
On parole   4
On probation or supervision or previously on probation, parole, or supervision   3
Pending court; pending prior delinquency referrals to S.A. for petition request   2
None of above   0 _____

H. **TOTAL (Sum of F and G)**   _____

AUTO HOLD—ALL CHARGES IN THE 12 OR 10 CATEGORY; WARRANTS OR REQUEST FOR APPREHENSION, AS WELL AS ANY VIOLENT OFFENSE WHERE A LAW ENFORCEMENT OFFICER, TEACHER, OR SCHOOL ADMINISTRATOR, OR THE JUVENILE'S PARENT IS THE VICTIM (includes staff members of Court-ordered placement facilities)

SCORING: 10 AND UP Detain.
              7 to 9 May Release (non-secure options can be utilized if feasible and appropriate).
              0 to 6 Release to parent or guardian or to a responsible adult relative.

PEORIA COUNTY [Illinois]
JUVENILE DETENTION CENTER SCREENING INSTRUMENT (continued)

Screen Date:	Screen Time: A.M./P.M.		Screener:	
Youth Officer:			District:	
Minor Respondent:			DOB:	Age:

Sex: ❏ Male ❏ Female   Race: ❏ White ❏ Black ❏ Hispanic ❏ Asian ❏ Other YD:

Factor	Family Folder Number:	Score	
1.	**MOST SERIOUS INSTANT OFFENSE:** *(Choose only one item indicating the most serious charge)*		
	Automatic Transfer Cases	15	
	Violent Felonies-(Murder, Armed Robbery with Handgun, Home Invasion, ACSA, UUW-Gun, Agg Batt-Bodily Harm, Agg Vehicular Invasion, Agg Discharge of a Firearm, Agg Battery with a firearm)	15	
	Other Forcible Felonies- (Robbery, Kidnapping, Intimidation, CSA, Hate Crime, Agg Batt, Vehicle Invasion)	10	
	Other Offenses		
	Felony Sale of Cannabis (Class 1 or 2 felony amount, Arson, DCS	10	
	PCS w/int deliver, Residential Burglary, UUW (not a gun), Possession Explosives	7	
	Felony Possession of Narcotics/Drugs for Sale or Other Felonies,	5	
	Misdemeanor Possession of Narcotics/Drugs or Other Weapons Possession	3	
	Other Misdemeanors	2	
	Not Picked up on New Offense *(WARRANT)*	0	
2.	**PRIOR COURT REFERRALS** *(Choose only one item)*		
	Prior IDOC commitment	7	
	Prior court referral within the last 24 hour period	5	
	Prior court referral within the last seven days	4	
	Six or more total court referrals within the last 12 months (#_____)	3	
	One to five court referrals within the last 12 months (#_____)	2	
	No court referrals within the last 12 months	0	
3.	**PAST FINDINGS OF DELINQUENCY - CLOSED PROCEEDINGS** *(Choose only one item)*		
	Past Finding of Delinquency on a violent felony	5	
	Past Finding of Delinquency on a felony	4	
	Past Finding of Delinquency on a misdemeanor *(# of findings x 1 up to a total of 3 points)*	1/2/3	
	No Past Finding of Delinquency	0	
4.	**CURRENT CASE STATUS** *(Choose only one item)*		
	IPS		
		6	
	Probation (#_____) Supervision (#_____) Multiple Disposition Dates	5	
	Probation (#_____) Supervision (#_____) Single Disposition Date	3	
	Not an active case	0	
5.	**PETITIONS PENDING ADJUDICATION** *(Choose only one item)*		
	3 Petitions Pending (#_____)	3	
	2 Petitions Pending	2	
	1 Petition Pending	1	
	No Petitions Pending	0	
6.	**UNDER PRE-ADJUDICATORY ORDER OF HOME CONFINEMENT**	4	
7.	**WARRANT CASES** *(Choose only one item)*		
	Category 1: Mandatory Detention	15	
	Category 2: Non-Mandatory Detention	8	
		TOTAL SCORE	

DECISION SCALE   Score 0-9   **AUTHORIZE RELEASE** with notice of prioritized date for § 5 - 12 Conference)
Score 10-14   **COMPLETE NON-SECURE DETENTION OPTIONS FORM**
Score 15 +   **AUTHORIZE DETENTION** (for minors 13 years of age and older)
(Complete non-secure custody options for minors under 13 years of age before placement into secure detention)

ADMINISTRATIVE OVERRIDE *(Supervisory approval is required)*
❏ Yes   ❏ No   REASON;
FINAL DECISION   ❏ Detain   ❏ Release   ❏ Release With Conditions
MR lives at:
Apt: City: State: Zip:
MR lives with: Relation: Phone:

Source: Cook County Juvenile Probation Department Detention Screening Instrument

COLORADO "SB94"
JUVENILE DETENTION SCREENING AND ASSESSMENT GUIDE

3. Cases

Moss v. Weaver

525 F.2d 1258 (5th Cir. 1976)

GODBOLD, Circuit Judge:

Ronald Moss filed this class action seeking declaratory and injunctive relief against the judges of the Juvenile and Family Division of the Circuit Court of Dade County, Florida, and against the state attorney for that county. The suit challenges the juvenile court judges' practice of imposing pretrial detention upon accused juvenile delinquents without determining whether there is probable cause to believe that the accused has committed an offense. The District Court found the practice unconstitutional and ordered that no accused delinquent could be held in custody without a showing of probable cause made in an adversary proceeding. We affirm, except that we hold that the Constitution does not require a hearing as full as that prescribed by the District Court.

Under Florida law a juvenile taken into custody on a charge of violating the criminal law is brought within 48 hours to a "pre-detention hearing," where the court decides whether to release or detain him pending a formal "adjudicatory hearing." The applicable statute specifies three factors for the judge to consider: whether detention is necessary to protect the person or property of the child or of others; whether a parent or guardian is available and able to provide adequate care and supervision for the child; and whether the parent or guardian convincingly assures the court of the child's future presence at the adjudicatory hearing. The parties agree that in practice the seriousness of the alleged offense is also frequently taken into consideration. If a decision is made to detain the child, money bail is not available.

The District Court concluded that this scheme embodied fatal constitutional infirmities. The court quoted from *Cooley v. Stone* to the effect that the Fourth Amendment's prohibition on penal custody without a prompt judicial determination of probable cause applies to adults and juveniles alike. As an alternative rationale the court found that "the classical principles of procedural due process of law" dictate a similar result, saying: "(D)ue process of law requires at a minimum that a showing of probable cause be made by competent, sworn testimony, and that witnesses be subject to cross-examination."

Some months after the District Court's order was entered, the Supreme Court handed down a ruling affirming in part and reversing in part our decision in *Pugh v. Rainwater*, on which the District Court had relied. In *Gerstein v. Pugh*, the Court had before it a class action brought on behalf of persons in Florida arrested and detained under a prosecutor's information. The Court held that Florida's failure to accord the plaintiffs a probable cause determination by a magistrate, and not just by a prosecutor, violated the Fourth Amendment. The Court was explicit in maintaining that the Fourth Amendment rather than the procedural due process guarantees of the Fourteenth controlled the case. The [*Gerstein*] Court noted:

> "The historical basis of the probable cause requirement is quite different from the relatively recent application of variable procedural due process in debtor-creditor disputes and termination of government-created benefits. The Fourth Amendment was tailored explicitly for the criminal justice system, and its balance between individual and public interests always has been thought to define the 'process that is due' for seizures of person or property in criminal cases, including the detention of suspects pending trial. * * * Moreover, the Fourth

Amendment probable cause determination is in fact only the first stage of an elaborate system, unique in jurisprudence, designed to safeguard the rights of those accused of criminal conduct."

Upon examining the judgment below in light of *Gerstein v. Pugh*, our proper course is clear. First, we affirm the District Court's opinion insofar as it discerned a Fourth Amendment violation in Florida's current juvenile justice system. A finding of probable cause—*i.e.*, of "facts and circumstances sufficient to warrant a prudent man in believing that the [suspect] had committed or was committing an offense,"—is central to the Amendment's protections against official abuse of power. Pretrial detention is an onerous experience, especially for juveniles, and the Constitution is affronted when this burden is imposed without adequate assurance that the accused has in fact committed the alleged crime. This case presents none of the circumstances *Gerstein* described as temporarily suspending the Amendment's command.

Attempting to distinguish away the Supreme Court's disapproval of analogous procedures for adults in the Dade County criminal justice system, the defendants invite us to test juvenile rights by a more flexible standard of "fundamental fairness," citing *McKeiver*. Assuming for argument's sake that fundamental fairness is the correct standard, Dade County's current procedures for pretrial detention of juveniles fail to pass muster. Florida may properly direct its juvenile court judges to make a decision about the child's welfare when they consider whether he should be released pending his adjudicatory hearing. But if they do not find release desirable on that basis, the Fourth Amendment's principles dictate that they must not detain him unless they also find probable cause to believe him guilty. These strong principles embedded in the Bill of Rights are not to be put aside merely because the pre-detention hearing is not formally viewed as part of a criminal case. Functionally it is similar. And the Supreme Court [in *Gault*] has recently told us that: "determining the relevance of constitutional policies, like determining the applicability of juvenile rights, in juvenile proceedings, requires that courts eschew 'the 'civil' label-of-convenience which has been attached to juvenile proceedings,' * * * and that 'the juvenile process * * * be candidly appraised.'"

The second point emerging from our reading of *Gerstein* is that the District Court erred in ordering that the finding of probable cause must be made on "competent, sworn testimony," with witnesses subject to cross-examination. Such requirements cannot be founded on the Fourteenth Amendment, for, as already noted, the Supreme Court has declined to employ due process analysis on this issue. Nor does the Fourth Amendment itself require adversary safeguards in the probable cause inquiry. As *Gerstein* pointed out, the standard of proof in a probable cause inquiry is low. There is no exacting insistence on certainty, as there is under a reasonable doubt or even a preponderance standard. Accordingly, there is less need for the assurances of reliability that the adversary system provides. The Court also observed in *Gerstein* that the question of probable cause has for many years been resolved "in a nonadversary proceeding on hearsay and written testimony," usually in the context of a magistrate's decision whether or not to issue an arrest warrant. And, finally, the Court suggested that pretrial delay might be exacerbated by a holding that the Fourth Amendment requires adversary hearings in every case of pretrial detention.

We know of no unique features of the juvenile courts by which *Gerstein*'s reasoning could be distinguished. On the contrary, it is normally assumed that the distinctive advantages of juvenile tribunals derive from their informal nature. We are apprehensive that these advantages, to the extent that they now exist, might be lessened if juvenile proceedings were freighted with the requirements of trial-type procedures. We share the doubts of the four

Justices in *McKeiver* who warned against subjecting the juvenile court system to "the traditional delay, the formality, and the clamor of the adversary system."

In the past the state public defender has been appointed to represent indigent juveniles, and the District Court specifically assumed in its decree that this practice would continue. Accordingly, we are not required to decide whether juveniles have a constitutional right to counsel at the pre-detention hearing. We note, however, that in *Gerstein* the Supreme Court decided that in Florida's adult criminal justice system "the probable cause determination is not a 'critical stage' in the prosecution that would require appointed counsel." And, as we have concluded above, in a juvenile pre-detention hearing there is no guaranteed right to hear and cross-examine witnesses. Contrast *In re Gault*, (a juvenile court proceeding where delinquency is determined and commitment to an institution may result is a critical stage); *Kent v. U.S.*, (a juvenile court proceeding on the issue of whether it should waive jurisdiction is a critical stage).

Doe v. State
487 P.2d 47 (Alaska 1971)

CONNOR, Justice.

On January 8, 1970, a petition was filed in the superior court asking that John Doe be declared a delinquent child. The petition, signed by a probation-parole officer, charged John Doe, then a child of sixteen, with having sold, on December 23, 1969, one-half a tablet of [LSD] to one Fred Lee Williams for three dollars. This act was alleged in the petition to be in violation of [law]. A summons was issued on January 8, 1970, directing John Doe to appear before the juvenile judge the following day at 2:30 p.m., to "assist the Court in rendering a final determination in the above-entitled action."

John Doe appeared with his parents at the 2:30 p. m. hearing on January 9, 1970. Mr. Irwin Ravin was appointed as counsel for John Doe at that time. The child denied the petition, and the superior court prepared to commence immediately with the adjudication of the merits of the petition. John Doe's counsel indicated that he was not ready and asked for a continuance so that he could prepare the defense. January 9, 1970, was a Friday. The court continued the hearing until the following Monday morning. With the hearing on the merits now set for Monday, the court inquired of the district attorney whether he wished to be heard on the subject of John Doe's detention over the weekend. The district attorney stated:

> "This defendant has threatened one of our witnesses and our witnesses have been [the] subject of threats generally and there are threats out in the community and threats against life and I—I would ask for that reason that he be detained."

John Doe's attorney denied knowledge of any threats and objected to the district attorney's hearsay statement. He further stated that John Doe had never previously been before the children's court; that there had been no showing under the rules that the child should be detained; that detention would hamper the preparation of the defense; and that the state had had knowledge of John Doe's alleged conduct since December 23, 1969, but had not asked until January 9, 1970, that the boy be placed in custody. The court ordered that "this defendant be committed to the detention home over this weekend so that he'll be present at 9:00 or shortly thereafter for the hearing in this case." A commitment order was issued.[2]

---

2. The order itself stated that the grounds for detention were that the boy would harm himself or harm others.

....

1. Right to Release Pending the Adjudication Hearing.

Appellant John Doe asks this court to hold that children have a constitutional right to bail under the Alaska Constitution, or in the alternative, that the Alaska Rules of Children's Procedure contravene the bail provision of the Alaska Constitution to the extent that they allow detention of children for reasons other than availability for trial.

Children's Rule 7(b) provides:

> "No juvenile shall be detained nor may any detention be continued prior to a first hearing of the case unless the court finds at a detention inquiry, which must be held not more than 48 hours after the juvenile has been taken into custody, not excluding weekends and holidays, that:
>
>> (1) Detention is necessary to protect the juvenile from others; or
>>
>> (2) The juvenile will not be available for subsequent court proceedings; or
>>
>> (3) The juvenile will cause harm to himself or to others if he is not detained."

While the United States Supreme Court has not held that children must be afforded due process rights in the preadjudication stages of the juvenile process, we believe that due process safeguards are necessary not only at the adjudicative hearing, but at any stage which may result in deprivation of the child's liberty.

Under the Alaska Constitution, all persons accused of a criminal offense are entitled to be released on bail except for capital offenses where the proof is evident or the presumption great. [As] we stated [in *Reeves*]:

> "The purpose of bail in the administration of criminal justice is to insure the defendant's appearance at trial."

We held in that case that while an adult criminal defendant has a constitutional right to be released on bail (except in certain capital cases), he does not have an absolute right to be released on his own recognizance, without bail, if he is financially unable to post the bond. We cited with approval ... however, the following language: "the right to release is heavily favored and * * * the requirement of security for bond may, in a proper case, be dispensed with. * * * For there may be other deterrents to jumping bail [that] in a given case may offer a deterrent at least equal to that of the threat of forfeiture."

Therefore, in adult criminal prosecutions, the central consideration with respect to pretrial release is whether the defendant will appear for trial. This is true for setting the amount of bail and for ruling on applications to be released on one's own recognizance. Society's interest in pretrial freedom for persons accused of crimes is strong. Under both the United States and Alaska Constitutions, excessive bail may not be imposed. Excessive bail has been held to be that which goes beyond the amount reasonably necessary to assure the defendant's presence at trial. The presumption of innocence, central to our system of criminal justice, also dictates in favor of pretrial release[:]

> "Unless this right to bail before trial is preserved, the presumption of innocence, secured only after centuries of struggle, would lose its meaning."

Certain problems peculiar to children are encountered in children's proceedings, however, which make a blanket application of the right to pre-adjudication release upon adequate assurance of future court appearance unworkable and undesirable from the child's viewpoint. In some cases, a parent whose child has become involved in delinquency proceedings may be unwilling to take the child back into the home pending an adjudication hearing. In other cases, a child may not wish to return to his home, or facts adduced at a detention inquiry may show that he should not return home, because the child fears he will be in danger of abuse at the hands of his parents. But the existence of these problems does not mean that the right to remain free pending an adjudication proceeding should be denied to children. Other courts have found that the children's rules can be construed and applied so that children are provided with an adequate substitute for bail.

In [another] case, we held that the fundamental constitutional right of public trial by jury must be afforded children in delinquency adjudication proceedings, in spite of the possible interference with the benevolent motives of the children's court system which have, in the past, justified denial of those rights. We believe, however, because of the peculiarities of children's proceedings, that the present adult bail system would be practically unsuitable as a device for securing the child's future appearance before the court, and would not necessarily result in the child's release. Because contracts entered into by minors have been held to be voidable, a bail bondsman surely would be unwilling to deal directly with a child in providing a bail bond. Unless the child's parents are willing and financially able to secure the bond, the child's right to bail will not result in release. Where the child's parents are not able to assure the bail bondsman of their financial security, the often criticized injustices of the adult bail system as applied to indigents would be visited upon the child.

Thus we are faced with conflicting interests. A child who is charged under the children's rules with an act which would be a crime, if committed by an adult, should have no less right to pre-adjudication freedom than an adult criminal defendant has pending trial. On the other hand, a child is in need of some care and supervision. If his parents are not willing to care for the child or if harm will come to the child in his present home situation, the children's court should not allow the child to return or remain at home; yet the child cannot be released entirely on his own responsibility. While these are serious conflicts, we believe they can be reconciled.

We hold that a child has the right to remain free pending an adjudication that the child is delinquent, dependent, or in need of supervision, where the facts supporting the petition involve an act which, if committed by an adult, would be a crime, and where the court has been given reasonable assurance that the child will appear at future court proceedings. If the facts produced at the inquiry show that the child cannot return or remain at home, every effort must be made to place the child in a situation where his freedom will not be curtailed. Only if there is clearly no alternative available may the child be committed to a detention facility and deprived of his freedom.

In the case at bar, the superior court apparently based its detention order on the statement made by the district attorney that John Doe had threatened prosecution witnesses. [D]ue process standards must be observed at a detention inquiry since it may result in the deprivation of the child's liberty. Due process requires at the very least that detention orders be based on competent, sworn testimony, that the child have the right to be represented by counsel at the detention inquiry, and that the detention order state with particularity the facts supporting it.[12]

We hold, therefore, that the superior court's detention order in this case was invalid on several grounds: first, because it was based on an unsworn, hearsay statement; sec-

---

12. Children's Rule 13 states in part: "All testimony in the juvenile court shall be given under oath or affirmation subject to the following exceptions: (1) In its discretion the court may permit the introduction of a verified statement * * *concerning the existence of a juvenile matter, the jurisdiction of the court to entertain the matter, or the temporary detention or release therefrom of a juvenile."

ond, because it was based upon the court's belief, unsupported by any evidence, that the child would engage in unlawful activity if not detained; and third, because the order did not contain any statement of the facts on which the order was based.

The state argues that because review of the detention order was not sought immediately upon its issuance, appellant cannot raise the issue now on appeal. Although the cases cited by the state in its brief in support of this argument do not mention the mootness doctrine as such, we believe that this is the rationale of these decisions which hold that an order denying bail or setting excessive bail must be appealed from immediately. Once the trial is completed, the pretrial detention necessarily ends, and a decision on the question of pretrial bail can have no effect on an appealing defendant.

Ordinarily we will refrain from deciding questions where the facts have rendered the legal issues moot. But where the matter is one of grave public concern and is recurrent but is capable of evading review, we have undertaken review even though the question may be technically moot. There is little question that preadjudication detention of children is a matter of public concern, and that it is likely to recur. Further, a decision not to seek immediate review of a detention order in a children's proceeding may not be a purely tactical one, but may involve serious considerations of the child's welfare. Therefore, we find this to be an appropriate case in which to apply the exception to the mootness doctrine.

Notes

(a) Review *Schall v. Martin* in Chapter 2, *supra*.

(b) Does *Schall* have any impact on *Moss*? Why? See Justice Mosk's dissenting opinion in the following case.

Alfredo A.
865 P.2d 56 (Cal. 1994) Opinion on Rehearing

LUCAS, Chief Justice.

....

California's postarrest juvenile detention statutes are plainly designed to protect the arrested minor's Fourth Amendment rights. The arresting officer must, within 24 hours of the arrest, prepare a written summary of the probable cause for taking the minor into temporary custody. In contrast to adult criminal proceedings, the statutory presumptions *require* "immediate release" of the minor to the custody of his or her parents or legal guardian unless specific factors warranting extended detention are found to exist. Even when such factors supportive of further detention are found to exist, the juvenile arrestee must nonetheless be released within 48 hours unless a wardship petition is filed within that initial 48-hour period. And, if a wardship petition is filed, a formal, adversarial detention hearing, which incorporates a probable cause determination, and at which counsel is provided for both the minor and his parents or guardian, must be conducted "as soon as possible but in any event [no later than] the expiration of the next judicial day after a petition to declare the minor a ward * * * has been filed" (*i.e.,* no later than 72 hours after arrest, excluding "nonjudicial days"). At that detention hearing, the juvenile court will consider "[t]he circumstances and gravity of the alleged offense" in determining whether extended pretrial detention is warranted under all the facts and circumstances.

In light of the foregoing, we therefore conclude that the United States Supreme Court's adoption of the strict 48-hour rule in *McLaughlin*, was neither foreseen nor intended by that court to be rigidly operable in juvenile postarrest detention proceedings. Given the fundamental differences between juvenile and adult detention proceedings recognized in a long line of that Court's decisions, we will not infer otherwise, absent an express and definitive ruling from the high Court to the contrary.

As has been shown, our Legislature, in its wisdom, has enacted a comprehensive statutory scheme governing postarrest juvenile detention that is designed to implement specific policies and procedures deemed to be in the juvenile detainees' best interests, while balancing their fundamental constitutional rights against the well-recognized need for "informality" and "flexibility" in juvenile criminal justice systems. Our juvenile courts, of course, are duty bound to comply with both constitutional and statutory requirements. Having examined the integrated components of California's juvenile detention statutes, we conclude that the Constitution, as interpreted by the United States Supreme Court's pertinent decisions reviewed herein, requires no more than that *juvenile* arrestees be afforded a judicial determination of "probable cause" for any postarrest detention extending beyond the 72-hour period immediately following a warrantless arrest.

In light of these conclusions, it follows that the formal detention hearing provided for in section 632, subdivision (a), may also serve to fulfill the constitutional requirement when the court at such a hearing, *where it is held within 72 hours of the juvenile's arrest*, makes a determination that sufficient probable cause exists for the extended postarrest detention of the juvenile. Consistent with our analysis and conclusions herein, if the 72-hour period immediately following arrest includes one or more "nonjudicial days," such that the juvenile court is unable or unwilling to provide a full statutory detention hearing within that period, then the Constitution independently requires that the juvenile be afforded a separate, timely judicial determination of probable cause for any extended period of detention beyond the 72 hours following arrest.

....

The judgment of the Court of Appeal is affirmed.

ARABIAN, Justice, concurring and dissenting.

I concur in the lead opinion insofar as it requires prompt probable cause determinations for juveniles within 72 hours of warrantless arrest. I respectfully dissent, however, from the due process analysis by which the lead opinion reaches this conclusion. Petitioner does not dispute his postarrest detention on that basis; nor does he raise such a challenge to any provision of the juvenile court law governing wardship detentions in general. Rather, he asserts that, like any adult in comparable circumstances, a detained minor is entitled to a probable cause determination of suspected criminal activity within 48 hours of a warrantless arrest as mandated by the decision in ... *McLaughlin*. As framed by petitioner, the only issue before us is whether the rule of *McLaughlin* applies to juveniles. Accordingly, we are constrained to refract his contentions solely through a Fourth Amendment prism, for that is the limited nature of the constitutional claim. The specificity of the question demands an equally precise answer, not the due process circuity submitted in the lead opinion.

While I agree with Justice Mosk that we should pursue a Fourth Amendment tack in resolving this case, I conclude that for juvenile detainees a probable cause determination within 72 hours satisfies the constitutional mandate of "promptness." I am unpersuaded *McLaughlin* is dispositive or controlling here. Factually, that case involved only adults. In assessing the protections afforded minors, the United States Supreme Court has consciously "refrained * * * from taking the easy way with a flat holding that all rights constitutionally assured for the adult accused are to be imposed on the state juvenile proceeding." Thus, I do not construe the holding in *McLaughlin* to extend perforce to juveniles simply because it does not expressly restrict its scope to adults. In my view, the issue warrants an independent examination, bearing in mind both the general nature of the Fourth Amendment guaranty with its rubric of reasonableness and the particularized concerns of the juvenile justice system.

Since any official detention can adversely affect a minor as critically and undeniably as it does an adult, juveniles do have a protectable liberty interest with respect to such restraint, even though they are generally subject to greater restriction of their freedom by virtue of their minority. Moreover, while juveniles do not ipso facto possess the same constitutional rights as adults, it is now a settled proposition that the "promptness" requirement of *Gerstein* embraces all warrantless detentions regardless of the detainee's age. The question remains, however, to quantify the mandate of *Gerstein* for juveniles as the United States Supreme Court has done for adults in *McLaughlin*. Although we lack a direct answer, decisions of the high court provide some useful contours to the analytical framework.

In general, the juvenile context is highly relevant in determining whether and to what extent a particular constitutional principle applies to minors. Depending upon the interest at stake, this circumstance may dictate that juveniles have rights coextensive with adults, may debar them entirely, or may necessitate some modification of rights.

. . . .

[T]he Supreme Court has continually emphasized in its analyses the need to maintain a measure of flexibility to accommodate the special attention with which our society still endeavors to treat youthful offenders. I believe this concern to maximize individualized response is particularly relevant to the question of probable cause determinations because the detention of juveniles implicates additional considerations related to their minority. It also segues with the explicit premise of the Fourth Amendment, which proscribes only "unreasonable" seizures.

These collateral matters do not necessarily preclude probable cause determinations within a shorter period; indeed, as both Justice Mosk and Justice George argue in their dissents, every effort should be made to minimize the period of detention at this juncture in the adjudicatory process. Nevertheless, they provide a rational basis on which to premise some latitude beyond the 48-hour limit delineated in *McLaughlin*. Moreover, even with respect to adult detentions, the Supreme Court has reiterated that "probable cause determinations must be prompt—not immediate" to maintain a necessary measure of "'flexibility' and 'experimentation'" within each state's criminal justice system. These latter considerations are all the more significant in the juvenile justice system, which seeks to provide intervention and rehabilitation, not simply punishment.

I therefore conclude that under the Fourth Amendment the circumstances of a juvenile differ sufficiently from those of an adult that the "promptness" requirement of *Gerstein* is satisfied if a juvenile detainee is provided a probable cause determination within 72 hours following a warrantless arrest with no extension of time for nonjudicial days.

MOSK, Justice, dissenting.

. . . .

In *Gerstein* the United States Supreme Court held that the Fourth Amendment mandates, as a prerequisite to extended restraint of liberty, a prompt judicial determination

that there is probable cause to believe that a person has in fact committed a criminal offense following a warrantless arrest based on suspicion thereof.

In *McLaughlin*, the court defined "promptness" under *Gerstein* as generally within 48
hours of the warrantless arrest.

Thus, under the Fourth Amendment as construed by *Gerstein* and *McLaughlin*, a law-
abiding person wrongfully arrested without a warrant is guaranteed his freedom within
about 48 hours.

Today, a majority of this court refuses to honor that guarantee when the person in
question happens to be a juvenile.

I cannot join in such a breach of our constitutional obligation.

. . . .

Whatever differentiation may be justified in some areas for adults and juveniles under
the Fourth Amendment is not justified here. In *McLaughlin,* the court predicated *Gerstein's* promptness requirement on the proposition that "[a] State has no legitimate interest
in detaining for extended periods individuals who have been arrested without probable
cause." This applies to *all* individuals — whether or not they have attained the age of majority. When probable cause is lacking, detention is unsupported as a matter of law. That
proposition does not depend on how old the detainee is. The presence of youth does not
make up for the absence of probable cause.

I recognize that the state, as *parens patriae,* may have a legitimate interest in detaining a juvenile for criminal activity prior to trial. That interest, however, is not served by
holding *Gerstein's* promptness requirement inapplicable. Without question, an adult arrested without probable cause must be released as soon as reasonably possible. The reason: grounds for detention are lacking. So too, a juvenile arrested without probable cause
must be released as soon as reasonably possible. The reason is the same. Absent probable cause, the state's exercise of its power to preserve and promote the welfare of the child
is without support. For juveniles as for adults, *Gerstein's* promptness requirement operates to conserve and allocate resources by limiting the class of detainees to those who are
properly subject to detention. Of course, the state, as *parens patriae,* may have a legitimate interest in detaining a juvenile for reasons *unrelated to criminal activity.* But no such
interest is implicated here.

I also recognize that, in detaining a juvenile for criminal activity prior to trial, the
state may use means and/or facilities different from those it uses for adults. That fact,
however, is not determinative. It simply cannot be said that the restraint of liberty imposed on a juvenile is somehow less significant, in and of itself, than that imposed on
an adult. Indeed, "[p]retrial detention is an onerous experience, *especially for juveniles*
* * *."

Moreover, it appears that since *Gerstein* was decided, all reported decisions that have
considered the question ... have held or stated, expressly or impliedly, that *Gerstein* is
applicable to *all* "persons" or "individuals," juveniles as well as adults.

Therefore, I conclude that *Gerstein's* promptness requirement is indeed applicable to
juveniles.

. . . .

McLaughlin declares, both expressly and impliedly, from beginning to end, that its definition of "promptness" extends to "probable cause determinations" generally. It does
not purport to limit its scope to adults or even to qualify its meaning for juveniles.

I do not see in *McLaughlin* itself any basis to restrict its definition of "promptness" against juveniles....

Neither do I discover any support outside *McLaughlin* to condition its definition of "promptness" against juveniles. As stated, juveniles as well as adults are entitled to the protections of the Fourth Amendment. As also stated, the basic criterion of the constitutional provision is "reasonableness." The definition articulated by the *McLaughlin* court serves to give content to this test. No reason appears to deny its benefit to juveniles. Unquestionably, "it is not enough to say that probable cause determinations must be 'prompt'" when the state acts as enforcer of the criminal law for the sake of the community generally. The same is true when the state acts as *parens patriae* for the benefit of the child. The word "prompt" is no less "vague" in the latter situation than in the former. As noted, under the Fourth Amendment as construed by *Gerstein* and *McLaughlin,* a law-abiding person wrongfully arrested without a warrant is guaranteed his freedom within about 48 hours. It would be unreasonable to hold that when the person in question happens to be a juvenile, the guaranty is illusory.

Therefore, I conclude that *McLaughlin's* definition of "promptness" does in fact operate in the juvenile setting.

In conducting my analysis, I have not overlooked *Schall v. Martin,*which was decided nine years after *Gerstein* and seven years before *McLaughlin.*

....

Schall is based on the Fourteenth Amendment's due process clause. *Gerstein* and *McLaughlin,* by contrast, rest on the Fourth Amendment. Indeed, the *Schall* Court effectively declared that its reach did not extend to the Fourth Amendment question presented here when it expressly noted that it was solely concerned with "*judicially ordered* detention." Moreover, the *Schall* Court referred only to formal, adversarial probable cause hearings, and not the informal, nonadversarial judicial probable cause determinations discussed in *Gerstein* and *McLaughlin.* Lastly, and perhaps most important, the *Schall* Court dealt with a situation in which the juvenile was already detained pursuant to court order—unlike the situation here, where he was not.

To be sure, at one point in its opinion the *Schall* Court stated: "In *Gerstein* * * *, we held that a judicial determination of probable cause is a prerequisite to any extended restraint on the liberty of an *adult* accused of crime." And at another point: "In many respects, the [New York statutory scheme] provides far more predetention protection for juveniles than we found to be constitutionally required for a probable-cause determination for *adults* in *Gerstein.*"

The *Schall* Court's dicta, isolated and irrelevant as they are, cannot reasonably be read as an after-the-fact attempt to limit *Gerstein* to adults, but must be viewed merely as a reflection of the general factual context out of which *Gerstein* arose. Indeed, it appears that no reported decision—with the singular exception of the opinion of the Court of Appeal below—has construed these words to impose such a limitation. This is certainly true of *McLaughlin.* In that case, the Court could easily have used this language, which was cited by the parties and amici curiae therein, to limit *Gerstein* to adults. Conspicuously, it did not do so.

It can perhaps be argued that there is tension between *Schall* and *McLaughlin.* The former implies that a formal, adversarial probable cause hearing within at most nine days of the warrantless arrest of a juvenile who is already in court-ordered preventive detention suffices for the Fourteenth Amendment's due process clause. By contrast, the latter holds that a judicial probable cause determination, albeit informal and nonadversarial, is required by the Fourth Amendment generally within 48 hours of a warrantless arrest.

Any such tension, however, must necessarily be resolved in favor of the later-decided *McLaughlin* and against the earlier-decided *Schall*. By its terms, the *Schall* implication depends on *Gerstein*'s "undefined" promptness requirement and *Gerstein*'s consequent approval of a delay of five days between a warrantless arrest and a formal, adversarial probable cause hearing. The *McLaughlin* holding, however, expressly defines "promptness" as generally within 48 hours and thereby withdraws approval of a 5-day delay. Therefore, the *Schall* implication simply does not survive the *McLaughlin* holding.

Note

Which opinion is most persuasive? Which opinion is most consistent with the goal or goals of the juvenile justice system?

4. Detention Facilities

Martarella v. Kelley
349 F. Supp. 575 (S.D.N.Y. 1972)

LASKER, District Judge.

. . . .

[W]e come to the legal questions raised on the merits of the case.

The Constitutionality of Common Custody of PINS and JDs:[16] In arguing that the New York regulations violate the equal protection clause because they prohibit neglected children from being housed with JDs but do not give the same "protection" to PINS, plaintiffs rely on the rationale of *Baxstrom v. Herold.*

In *Baxstrom,* the Court held that it was arbitrary and capricious to deny to a mentally ill prisoner whose sentence was about to expire, but who was held for further custody in a hospital under the jurisdiction of the Department of Correction, the procedural protection granted all other persons civilly committed to mental hospitals. "Equal protection," the Court stated "does not require that all persons be dealt with identically, but it does require that a distinction made have some relevance to the purpose for which the classification is made."

The question before us is whether the distinction between PINS and neglected children which allows the former, but not the latter, to be held in common custody with JDs has some relevance to the purpose for which the classification is made. We believe that it does.

It is true, of course, that a PINS and a neglected child—as distinct from a JD—have in common that neither is charged with acts of a criminal nature; but this fact alone does not require the state to treat PINS and neglected children identically if a rational basis

---

16. The Family Court Act itself as originally enacted in 1962 did not authorize placement of PINS in a maximum security institution. In 1964, 1965 and 1966 temporary amendments to the Act authorized institutionalization of PINS in the same facilities as JDs—primarily because there was no place else to send them. It was only in 1968 that the Act was permanently amended to permit such common custody. The Commonwealth of Massachusetts has recently eliminated all secure custodial institutions and substituted community-oriented programs and other alternative treatment methods that do not involve confinement.

exists for some other mode of action. The rationality demanded by the Equal Protection clause is not to be found in legal designations or labels, but must derive from the facts.

From the evidence before us we conclude that the distinction made in the custody and treatment of PINS and neglected children bears a reasonable relation to the purpose for which the classification is made.

. . . .

Judge Kelley articulated the distinction [between PINS and neglected children] clearly: a PINS is himself charged with misbehavior; in the case of a neglected child, the parent is the "defendant". Neglected children are victims, PINS are (non-criminal) offenders, or at least socially maladjusted. The neglected child is sinned against rather than sinning. On the other hand, a PINS' personal behavior is the cause of his subjection to legal authority.

While realism compels acknowledgment that the lines are often blurred, and that the PINS' maladjustment is frequently caused by misguidance or mistreatment by parents or other authority (as may be equally true of JDs) the acknowledgment does not vitiate the rationality of the distinction. For these reasons we find no violation of the equal protection clause.

. . . .

The Constitutionality of Physical Conditions at the Center: Plaintiffs contend that the physical conditions at the centers are so hazardous and unhealthy that holding them in custody there constitutes cruel and unusual punishment.

There is no doubt that the Eighth Amendment's prohibition of cruel and unusual punishment is not restricted to instances of particular punishment inflicted on a given individual but also applies to mere confinement to an institution which is "characterized by conditions and practices so bad as to be shocking to the conscience of reasonably civilized people." Plaintiffs argue that conditions at the centers fall within the parameters of those decisions and violate the Eighth Amendment.

Since the trial of the case Zerega [girls' facility] has been closed, and the claim as to it is, therefore, moot. We find the remaining contentions to have merit as to Manida [girls' secure facility surrounded by high wall] but not as to Spofford [boys' secure facility surrounded by high wall].

As we have indicated in the factual discussion, Manida was constructed in 1904, and is in a general state of decay; its plaster falling, paint peeling, and cracks in walls and ceilings. Showers have often been in such disrepair that they were unuseable. The Stone Commission Report criticized its gymnasium as "merely a medium-sized dilapidated room with two large poles in the center which restrict any mobile activity." It stated that a HEW expert consultant in 1963, submitted a report to the Director of the Centers in which he concluded that Manida was unsuitable for the detention of children, and that the condition had not been improved. Indeed the defendants have stipulated that Manida is an inappropriate facility for child detention. . . .

The word "unsuitable" is a euphemism for conditions that in their totality violate the Eighth Amendment rights of the young girls who are held in custody at Manida although not even charged with crime.

The situation is different at Spofford. With all its drawbacks, including its architectural resemblance to a small prison of modern construction, Spofford is a relatively contemporary building (built in 1958) whose physical conditions, although they should be improved, are acceptable and, at the least, correctable. None of the deficiencies at Spofford can reasonably be classified as hazardous. The Stone Report stated that Spofford "does not appear to be in such condition as to represent a physical danger to its occupants and thereby require immediate replacement" and it includes positive advantages, such as school rooms, game rooms, room for religious services, gymnasium, swimming pool and an outdoor playing yard.

While we do not adhere to the view that the Eighth Amendment comes into play only if the facility in question is a chamber of horrors, we do not find that the physical conditions alone at Spofford are such that confinement there constitutes cruel and unusual punishment.

Does the Program at the Centers Provide Treatment which Constitutionally Justifies Holding PINS in Secure Detention? We come to the final and most difficult legal issue in this case, which has poignantly presented questions of the rights of children in urban American society: The right to treatment.

. . . .

Although the concept of the right to "effective treatment" was first articulated not much more than a decade ago, it has come into nearly full flower in the intervening period, and has been applied to the mentally ill, sexual psychopaths, defective delinquents, persons committed following acquittal by reason of insanity, drug addicts and children, whether delinquent or merely in need of supervision.

Even before the development of the doctrine of the right to treatment for all persons held in noncriminal custody, the courts asserted an analogous right for children derived from due process concepts and statutes.

There can be no doubt that the right to treatment, generally, for those held in non-criminal custody (whether based on due process, equal protection or the Eighth Amendment, or a combination of them) has by now been recognized by the Supreme Court, the lower federal courts and the courts of New York.

. . . .

Judge Bazelon's seminal opinion in *Rouse v. Cameron* dealt more directly with the issue of the right to treatment, and is generally regarded as the leading case. Rouse was involuntarily hospitalized in a mental hospital after having been acquitted of a misdemeanor by reason of insanity. He petitioned for a writ of habeas corpus, claiming the right to be discharged in the absence of receiving treatment. The court sustained his argument on statutory grounds but with considerable emphasis on the constitutional questions raised, observing that:

> "absent treatment, the hospital is transform[ed] * * * into a penitentiary where one could be held indefinitely for no convicted offense, * * *."

The opinion emphasized issues of due process, but suggested the equal protection clause and the Eighth Amendment, citing *Robinson v. California* [holding unconstitutional a statute that made the status of being a drug addict a crime] as other constitutional foundations for the right to treatment.

. . . .

New York judges (including defendants here) have been equally alert to sustain the right to treatment [as have] a significant number of decisions of courts outside New York....

In sum, the law has developed to a point which justifies the assertion that:

> "A new concept of substantive due process is evolving in the therapeutic realm.
> This concept is founded upon a recognition of the concurrency between the

state's exercise of sanctioning powers and its assumption of the duties of social responsibility. Its implication is that effective treatment must be the *quid pro quo* for society's right to exercise its *parens patriae* controls. Whether specifically recognized by statutory enactment or implicitly derived from the constitutional requirements of due process, the right to treatment exists."

We move on, then, to determining the criteria by which the court should measure the centers' programs to determine whether they furnish "regenerative" or "effective" treatment. The decisions and literature on this difficult point are considerably less numerous and voluminous than on the subject of the right itself. Nevertheless, the courts and commentators have made at least exploratory efforts towards the formulation of such standards.

We start with the observations of Judge Bazelon in *Rouse* that: (1) The institution need not demonstrate that its treatment program will cure or improve, but only that there is "a bona fide effort to do so," (2) The effort must be to provide treatment adequate in light of present knowledge, (3) The fact that science has not reached finality of judgment as the most effective therapy cannot relieve the court of its duty to render an informed decision and (4) Continued failure to provide suitable adequate treatment cannot be justified by lack of staff or facilities, since, as the Supreme Court stated in *Watson v. City of Memphis*, "The rights here asserted are, like all such rights, *present* rights; * * * and, unless there is an overwhelmingly compelling reason, they are to be promptly fulfilled."

. . . .

[W]e find that the treatment of children who stay at the centers for a truly temporary period may be minimally acceptable. However, in the light of the solemn meaning which the phrase "bona fide" has acquired through the ages we find that there has not been a bona fide effort to treat the child who is a long termer at the centers, nor is the treatment of such a child adequate in the light of present knowledge. Even those defense witnesses who approved the secure detention of PINS, described as the justification for such detention, treatment programs and facilities vastly superior to those which prevail at the centers. Without attempting to delineate in detail the differences between those institutions and the centers, we emphasize the substantial differences in ratio of professional personnel to children and in the training of counselors, case-workers and other supporting personnel. The conclusion is inescapable that the shortage of key staff members at the centers, their lack of training, the poor communication among them, the shortage of information available about the child to those who treat him, and the other deficiencies noted in the discussion of facts above, results in a failure to provide adequate treatment for the long term detainee.

The distinction in measuring the adequacy of treatment for true temporary detainees, on one hand, and long termers on the other, is justified by the facts and the law. It is a reasonable inference that factually a treatment program for a temporary detainee need not provide in depth what is necessary for adequate treatment of the long termer, or, put another way, the child who is truly temporarily detained does not suffer deprivation of constitutional proportions, while the long termers do. We recognize the dangers of all generalizations, this one included, as well as the difficulty of estimating the magic moment at which the deprivation becomes unacceptable—an estimate which can best be made by the parties themselves, with expert assistance if necessary. But the difficulty of the issue does not eliminate the necessity for all concerned, including the court, to find a handle to the problem.

. . . .

We recognize the danger that in deciding these issues the court may be "tempted to act as super-legislature and super-executive," but that risk lies in the realm of remedy rather than analysis. In any event, we agree with the *Rouse* court that the difficulties of decision ["c]annot relieve the court of its duty to render an informed decision."]

It is the job of courts to decide issues. This is particularly true when we are dealing with the rights of children growing up in the difficult conditions of modern urban life.

Martarella v. Kelley
359 F. Supp. 478 (S.D.N.Y. 1973)

LASKER, District Judge.

This civil rights action is brought by children defined under § 732 of New York's Family Court Act as Persons In Need of Supervision.[1] They alleged that the conditions in which they are and have been held in the Juvenile Detention Centers of New York City, violate the Eighth Amendment of the Constitution. After a nonjury trial we held, by opinion filed October 16, 1972, that the physical conditions at Manida center were constitutionally inadequate, that they were adequate at Spofford, and that the issue as to Zerega, which had by then been closed, was moot. We also ruled that the rights of those who were held in long-term detention—a category whose definition was deferred—were violated because no adequate plan of treatment was provided for them.

[I]t is Ordered, Adjudged and Decreed:

1. That defendants are enjoined from failing to implement, in accordance with their respective responsibilities under law, the standards set forth in Appendix A annexed hereto and incorporated in this Order.

2. That the use of Manida Juvenile Center as a detention facility shall be discontinued no later than August 15, 1973.

3. Jurisdiction of this action is retained to assure the execution of this Order and to permit such modifications, if any, as may be necessary from time to time in the light of the rights and duties of the parties.

APPENDIX A

1. "Long-term detention" is defined as custody of a child in a secure detention facility for 30 or more days of continuous or substantially continuous detention from the date of admission.

2. This appendix establishes minimal standards for the treatment of children held in long-term detention, as well as conditions which must occur or exist prior to the child's 30th day of detention to assure the effectiveness of the treatment plan.

3. "A secure detention facility" is defined as a facility (whether now or hereafter in existence) characterized by physically restrictive construction and procedures which are intended to prevent a child from departing from the facility at will.

---

1. The defendants properly point out that, if standards of treatment are to be set for PINS (plaintiffs here), they should be the same for the delinquent children with whom PINS are housed at the Center, even though the delinquent children are not included in the plaintiff class; that is, that the improvement for PINS should not be at the expense of JDs by diverting personnel to one group exclusively. We agree with this view, and have considered the impact of our Order on the institution as a whole.

4. Any caseworker employed in a secure detention facility shall possess a Bachelor's Degree and shall have taken courses in social work or the behavioral sciences, which, together with his demonstrated aptitude and work experience, shall, in the good faith opinion of the appropriate administrator of the facility, qualify him to act as a caseworker for children who have behavioral problems or are emotionally disturbed. Every caseworker shall participate in in-service training.

5. Any recreational worker employed in a secure detention facility shall have undergone training in physical education or shall possess such demonstrated aptitude and work experience as shall, in the good faith opinion of the appropriate administrator of the facility, qualify him to supervise the recreation of children who have behavioral problems or are emotionally disturbed. Every recreation worker shall participate in in-service training.

6. Any children's counselor employed by a secure detention facility shall possess a high school diploma and have completed two years (60 credits) of college education. He shall have performed two years of community or institutional work with children and shall possess a demonstrated aptitude which, in the good faith opinion of the appropriate administrator of the facility, qualifies him to act as a counselor for children who have behavioral problems or are emotionally disturbed. Every children's counselor shall participate in in-service training.

7. In-service training shall consist of (a) appropriate orientation to agency rules, procedures and policies and, special needs including therapeutic approaches, of children who have behavioral problems or are emotionally disturbed and who are confined in secure detention and (b) a continuing program of seminars or work shops, conducted by persons with appropriate experience, for the purpose of developing special skills and methods of dealing with such children.

8. "Treatment" is defined as a therapeutic living situation for a child, including his grouping with other children; the adequacy and competency of staff members dealing with him or his case; diagnosis of his emotional and psychological needs and on the basis of such diagnosis and all other information about the child that is available, and the provision of appropriate mental health, case work, educational, recreational and medical services for him.

9. A child confined to a secure detention facility shall be afforded treatment appropriate to his individual need as determined by a suitably constituted team of staff members who have responsibility for his case.

10. On the day the child is remanded by the Family Court to a secure detention facility, the Family Court Judge and the Probation Department shall cause to accompany him a copy of the social information compiled by the Probation Department from any source including prior probation records, interviews with the child, family, guardian or any public or private agency having previous knowledge of the child, as for example, schools, mental hygiene or child guidance clinics, Department of Social Services or hospitals.

11. All reasonably available information of the type described in Paragraph 10 above, which has not been collected by the Probation Department and forwarded to the secure detention facility on the day of the child's admission, shall be obtained and forwarded as soon as practicable after the child's admission.

12. As soon as practicable after the child's admission to a secure detention facility, he shall be assigned to and confer with a caseworker who has reviewed the material received from the Probation Department referred to above. That caseworker shall remain the child's caseworker during his confinement to the extent that his doing so will not inter-

fere with the establishment of the working team referred to in Paragraph 13 below and its ability to carry out its function.

13. As soon as practicable after the admission of the child to a secure detention facility and no later than 10 days thereafter, he shall be observed and evaluated for the purpose of assignment to a permanent living unit. Such evaluation and determination shall take into consideration all relevant factors including his maturity, emotional development, emotional and psychiatric history, findings of fact, or, if they are known, the charges against him, and evidence of drug use and shall not be made on the basis of age, size and aggressiveness only. The evaluation and assignment process shall be conducted by a team including, to the extent appropriate, a caseworker, counselor, teacher, psychiatrist or psychologist and physician. The assignment and interim treatment plan developed, and the reasons therefor, shall be in writing, signed by the person responsible for leading the team, and a copy of the plan shall be given to the child's Probation Officer, and, if authorized by the child, to his attorney or law guardian. Unless the counselor on the permanent living unit was a member of the evaluation team, the person responsible for leading the team shall give the counselor an interpretation of the child's need and such information as is necessary to ensure appropriate handling of the child.

14. Each child shall be afforded no less than two hours a day on school days, and three hours a day on nonschool days, of planned and structured recreational activity.

15. Each child shall be afforded reasonable access to a psychiatrist in accordance with his needs in appropriate instances including consultation and crisis intervention.

16. A child who attempts suicide shall be afforded immediate treatment in a psychiatric hospital unless a psychiatrist examines him immediately after his attempt and states in writing that such hospitalization is not necessary.

17. Each child shall be afforded an individualized treatment program including the components listed below in Paragraphs 18 through 26.

18. Each such child shall be assigned to a living unit, therapeutic for him as determined by the evaluation team, and containing no more than the number of children which can be appropriately cared for on the basis of their individual needs.

19. There shall be no less than two counselors for each 20 children.

20. There shall be no less than one recreation worker for each 15 children during recreational activities.

21. There shall be no less than one caseworker for every 15 children. When a child is returned to the detention facility after a period of release, he shall be reassigned to his last caseworker whenever practicable.

22. The child's caseworker shall confer at reasonable intervals with the child's counselor.

23. No later than the 20th day of a child's confinement, there shall be a full case conference between the child's counselor, caseworker, probation officer, and any examining or treating psychiatrist or psychologist and one of the child's teachers, at which an individualized long treatment plan shall be formulated and recorded. Each child held in long-term detention shall have the right to implementation of such long range treatment plan to the fullest possible extent.

24. A full case conference as to the child shall be held thereafter at suitable intervals to review his treatment plan and progress and to provide such revisions in the plan, if any, as are determined necessary. Each such conference shall be reported in writing and any revisions determined shall be implemented as indicated.

25. A complete file for each child shall be maintained and shall contain a copy of all reports referred to in the paragraphs above, and shall be available to personnel having direct responsibility for the child. All information contained in such file shall be considered privileged and confidential. A summary of the pertinent findings in such file shall be sent to the child's Probation Officer. On consent of the child, his attorney or law guardian shall be permitted access to the file.

26. There being no dispute as to the value of the appointment of an independent ombudsman to hear and act on grievances of children held in long-term detention, the administrator of the secure detention facilities shall within 30 days of the filing of this Order submit to the Court a plan for the appointment of such an official. The plan shall include a description of the qualifications and duties of the ombudsman and procedures for his appointment.

Note

For a discussion of the right to treatment, see materials in Chapter 5, *infra*.

A.J. v. Kierst

56 F.3d 849 (8th Cir. 1995)

Pursuant to 42 U.S.C. §§ 1983 and 1988, A.J., a 16-year-old minor, filed this class action in the United States District Court for the Western District of Missouri on behalf of himself and others similarly situated to challenge the constitutionality of certain policies, practices, and conditions at the Jackson County Juvenile Justice Center ("JCJJC"). The district court ultimately certified a class to consist of all persons who had been detained at the JCJJC since November 15, 1989. A.J. and the class sought injunctive relief, and A.J. individually claimed monetary damages for injuries he incurred as a result of the center's allegedly unconstitutional practices. The court granted summary judgment to defendants on overcrowding and the use of floor mattresses,[3] two of a number of issues alleged by plaintiffs to be unconstitutional, and held in favor of defendants on all remaining issues after a court trial. The court granted summary judgment to defendants on A.J.'s claim that he received improper medical care and denied summary judgment on A.J.'s claim that he was unlawfully placed in isolation. A.J.'s isolation claim was ultimately tried to a jury, which awarded $42 in damages. The court awarded attorney's fees in the sum of $24,428 to one of plaintiffs' counsel on A.J.'s jury claim after declining to award fees to plaintiffs' other counsel.

On appeal plaintiffs argue that the district court (1) erred as a matter of law in granting summary judgment against plaintiffs on the issues of overcrowding and the use of floor mattresses; (2) abused its discretion in conditioning communications between plaintiffs' counsel and class members on the requirements that plaintiffs exhaust alternative resources and demonstrate a compelling need; and (3) erred in its rulings on various issues at trial which, combined, denied plaintiffs their right to a fair trial. In addition, plaintiffs argue the court erred in limiting attorneys' fees to one attorney and in holding that plaintiffs did not "prevail" under 42 U.S.C. § 1988 on their claims for injunctive relief.

---

3. In addition, the court granted summary judgment on plaintiffs' claims with respect to health and safety concerns and the physical condition of the center. Upon motion by plaintiffs, the court set aside its summary judgment on plaintiffs' health and safety claims and allowed those claims to be tried.

We affirm the district court's order granting summary judgment in defendants' favor. We agree with plaintiffs that the district court erred in conditioning communications between plaintiffs' counsel and class members on the requirements that plaintiffs exhaust other resources and demonstrate a compelling need, but hold that the court's order restricting access resulted in no prejudice to plaintiffs on the two issues appealed by them: overcrowding and the use of floor mattresses. We further find that the court's rulings at trial did not, either individually or collectively, deprive plaintiffs of their right to a fair trial. Finally, we find that the district court erred in limiting attorneys' fees to only one attorney for A.J.'s successful jury claim, but that the court did not err in denying fees for plaintiffs' injunctive claims.

I.

A. *Summary Judgment Claim*

We first address plaintiffs' argument that the district court erred in granting summary judgment to defendants on the issues of overcrowding and the use of floor mattresses....

The question before us is whether the record, when viewed in the light most favorable to the nonmoving party, shows that there is no genuine issue as to any material fact and that the moving party is entitled to judgment as a matter of law....

In memoranda of law filed with the district court the parties agreed that the Due Process Clause of the Fourteenth Amendment, and not the Cruel and Unusual Punishments Clause of the Eighth Amendment, is the appropriate measuring stick for evaluating conditions in a juvenile facility. The due process standard was applied by the district court which ... noted that "'[t]he 'evolving standards of decency' against which courts evaluate the constitutionality of * * *conditions certainly provide greater protection for juveniles than for adults.'" We note, as did the district court, that the Supreme Court has not yet articulated the appropriate federal standard by which to judge conditions in state juvenile facilities [and has expressly reserved] the question whether the Eighth Amendment applies to juvenile institutions. We agree with the court that, by virtue of plaintiffs' status as pretrial detainees, the more protective Fourteenth Amendment, and not the Eighth Amendment, applies. "[J]uveniles * * * who have not been convicted of crimes, have a due process interest in freedom from unnecessary bodily restraint which entitles them to closer scrutiny of their conditions of confinement than that accorded convicted criminals."

In applying the due process standard to juveniles, we cannot ignore the reality that assessments of juvenile conditions of confinement are necessarily different from those relevant to assessments of adult conditions of confinement. Juveniles subject to pretrial detention have "not as yet had a 'judicial determination of probable cause which the Fourth Amendment requires as a prerequisite to extended restraint of liberty following arrest[;]'" [they] are, in some instances, before the court on charges in unverified petitions, *e.g.*, delinquency petitions filed on information and belief; and are in a system whose purpose is rehabilitative, not penal, in nature. In addition, juveniles are frequently detained for reasons entirely separate from those associated with adjudication of charges. Some are detained as a result of neglect or abusive home environments and are held in protective custody, *e.g.*, are "status offenders"; some are runaways; some are simply undisciplined. For these reasons, we conclude that, as a general matter, the due process standard applied to juvenile pretrial detainees should be more liberally construed than that applied to adult detainees.

Plaintiffs do not dispute that overcrowding alone is insufficient to create a due process violation. In evaluating overcrowded conditions courts have looked to a number of factors, including the size of detainees' living space, the length of time detainees spend in their cell each day, the length of time of their confinement, and their opportunity for exercise.

Rooms at the JCJJC are approximately 69 feet in size. Prior to July 1990 the center lodged as many as three youths in a room due to an unprecedented increase in the number of juveniles. To accommodate the additional youths, floor mattresses were used in rooms in addition to already existing single beds. In July 1990 the facility terminated its practice of lodging more than one juvenile in a room. Beds affixed to the walls were removed, leaving only one bed per room. A dormitory is currently used to accommodate youths for sleeping purposes when there is a "special need," in which case floor mattresses are used. The juveniles' rooms are used primarily for sleeping. There is evidence that detainees are required to remain locked in their rooms for "nap time" immediately after school from 2:30 p.m. until 4:30 p.m. to allow for staff shift changes. Except when sleeping at night and during "nap time" in the afternoon, detainees are not restricted to their rooms. They are permitted to move about in common areas and have access to a game room, or dayroom, which is of "ample" size (53 square feet per juvenile). The dayroom is lined with windows that allow natural light into the room. It is equipped with tables, chairs, books, and televisions. The juveniles, additionally, have access to an indoor gymnasium equipped with a basketball court and weight equipment, which is "used frequently during the day," although activities appear to be disorganized and unplanned. According to JCJJC statistics, the average length of stay per juvenile in 1989, the year A.J. was detained, was thirteen days. The average length of stay per juvenile was ten days in 1990 and 1991.[4] These facts, in our view, do not constitute deprivations of such magnitude as to violate plaintiffs' due process rights.[5]

The district court similarly did not err in concluding that no violation existed with respect to the center's use of floor mattresses. It is uncontroverted that juveniles were subjected to sleeping on floor mattresses in their rooms when the population at the center peaked in the late 80s. They were required to do so, however, only for the relatively short period of time they were detained. Floor mattresses, as noted, are now used in the dormitory for sleeping purposes when there is a special need (apparently to accommodate additional youths when the center is at full capacity). Based on the totality of circumstances presented here, we do not believe that the center's past and present use of floor mattresses amounts to a deprivation of such severity as to deprive plaintiffs of their due process rights.[7]

B. *Access Claim*

Plaintiffs' counsel sought repeatedly to interview the juveniles detained at the JCJJC to prove the existence of past or present unconstitutional conditions of confinement. The

---

4. Plaintiffs dispute the court's factual findings with respect to juveniles' average length of detention, noting that "there was substantial evidence before the court that children were confined in the JCJJC for much longer than the 'brief period of time'" relied upon by the court. Specifically, they refer to the findings of one of their expert witnesses, Ira Schwartz, who reported that "[m]any youths are being held in … the JCJJC awaiting placement and * * *three of these youth had been at the JCJJC for five months." However true this may be, we do not see how this fact renders unreliable the district court's representations of the average number of days a juvenile is detained.

5. We note in this regard that the Supreme Court found it acceptable to house two adult pretrial detainees in 75 square feet of space containing a double bunk bed where they were confined to this area for six to seven hours a day (primarily for sleeping purposes) and were detained for generally less than sixty days.

7. We note that had we concluded that the conditions were violative of plaintiffs' constitutional rights, we would be faced with the separate task of reviewing the record for evidence regarding the likelihood that the conditions would reoccur. Because we hold that the complained of conditions do not rise to the level of a constitutional violation, however, we need not pursue that inquiry.

first such attempt occurred at a May 1990 hearing when counsel requested an order grant-ing access to the juveniles then detained at the center. The court denied plaintiffs' request on the grounds that each of the juveniles detained at the facility was represented by coun-sel, either personally retained or court-appointed, and that each was free to raise issues pertaining to constitutional deprivations on his or her own. In a July 3, 1990, order the court reaffirmed its position, explicitly requiring that plaintiffs' counsel exhaust alterna-tive resources and demonstrate a compelling need before the court would consider dis-turbing "the long-established protection of confidentiality for juveniles" under Missouri law. Plaintiffs again moved the court for access in July 1991, arguing that the juveniles had a right of access to class counsel separate and apart from their right to counsel on delin-quency charges and that they could not prepare their case for trial without access to the juveniles. At a status conference on September 6, 1991, in response to counsel's final re-quest to interview the juveniles, the court denied access stating that the necessary infor-mation concerning the policies and practices at the JCJJC could be obtained by reviewing the files and interviewing the employees of the center. By order dated October 3, 1991, the district court formally denied plaintiffs' motion for access.

Plaintiffs argue that neither the court's initial order of July 3, 1990, conditioning com-munication with class members on a showing of compelling need (a standard they as-sert finds no support in caselaw) nor its final order of October 3, 1991, reveals any factual basis for the court's "sweeping ban on communications." [T]he district court erred, they argue, in denying communications between plaintiffs' counsel and class members absent a clear record and specific findings that reflect the need for a ban. The court's order deny-ing communications, plaintiffs argue, additionally restricted class members' rights to due process. As a result of the ban, plaintiffs assert that counsel was unable to inform the ju-veniles of the existence of the lawsuit or to obtain critical factual information about the conditions of their confinement, thus preventing A.J. and class counsel, as class repre-sentatives, from adequately fulfilling their duties under Fed.R.Civ.P. 23.

In response, defendants argue the district court's denial of access to class members was not an absolute ban on communications. The court rather required plaintiffs' coun-sel to make some showing that the information they sought from the juveniles was not available from other sources and that they had a compelling need for contact with mem-bers of the class that overcame the juveniles' rights to confidentiality. Defendants rely on Missouri statutory provisions regarding the rights of juveniles in court proceedings which, they maintain, establish a clear statutory requirement of confidentiality. Section 211.271.3 of the Missouri Statutes provides that "reports and records of the juvenile court * * * shall not be used for any purpose whatsoever in any proceeding, civil or criminal * * *." Sec-tion 211.321.1 further provides that

> "[records of juvenile court proceedings] as well as all information obtained and social records prepared in the discharge of official duty for the court shall not be open to inspection or their contents disclosed, *except by order of the court to per-sons having a legitimate interest therein* * * *."

There are only four situations, defendants maintain, in which juvenile courts in Missouri have found such a "legitimate interest": (1) where the information is sought for the pur-poses of identification; (2) where the juvenile is charged with a serious crime for which he can be charged as an adult; (3) where a party seeks to impeach a juvenile witness; and (4) where the juvenile is not a party to the action. Because plaintiffs' request did not fall within any of the recognized exceptions, defendants argue they cannot overcome the statutes' qualified prohibition against disclosing records of juvenile court proceedings. Defendants further argue that plaintiffs' counsel had the burden of showing a compelling need for access to individual detainees, which counsel failed to do. Plaintiffs were provided with a plethora of records describing the conditions at the JCJJC, visually inspected the center, and had access to employees who worked there. These resources, they contend, were more than adequate to allow plaintiffs to prepare and present their case.

It cannot reasonably be disputed that the court's conditions on communications between counsel and class members "created at least potential difficulties for [plaintiffs] as they sought to vindicate the legal rights of [the juveniles]." Plaintiffs argued before the district court, and we agree, that the juveniles' perceptions of the institution, its staff, and its programs are relevant components of a comprehensive evaluation of institutional policy, for "proving a case of overcrowding is not [accomplished] simply [by] adding up the number of juveniles detained at any given time and dividing it by the number of beds * * *." The question before us is whether the district court's "limiting order * * * is consistent with the general policies embodied in Rule 23, which governs class actions in federal court."

A trial judge has broad authority to supervise a class action and to issue orders regulating the conduct of parties and counsel. That discretion, however, is not unlimited and "indeed is bounded by the relevant provisions of the Federal Rules [of Civil Procedure]." An order limiting communications between parties and potential class members must be based "on a clear record and specific findings that reflect a weighing of the need for a limitation and the potential interference with the rights of the parties.... [S]uch a weighing—identifying the potential abuses being addressed—should result in a carefully drawn order that limits speech as little as possible, consistent with the rights of the parties under the circumstances."

Contrary to this well-established law the district court made no discernible effort to weigh the state's interest in protecting the confidentiality of juveniles against the potential interference with the class members' rights. Apart from announcing that Missouri law mandates the imposition of strict measures of confidentiality to protect juveniles, the court made no findings of fact with respect to whether plaintiffs' counsel were engaged in or likely to engage in abusive tactics.[9] Additionally, the court rendered no findings with respect to whether access would be disruptive of administrative procedures at the JCJJC or would otherwise compromise the safety of the juveniles and staff.

We are unaware of any cases, and defendants cite none, which hold that counsel for plaintiffs in class action proceedings have the burden of first exhausting alternative means of collecting information and demonstrating a compelling need before they will be permitted access to class members absent evidence of present or potential abuse. Requiring plaintiffs to first exhaust alternative resources puts plaintiffs in the awkward, if not untenable, position of having to first muster enough evidence to prove precisely that which influenced their decision to seek access in the first instance. Although we are mindful of the district court's power under Rule 23 to restrict certain communications, the court may not exercise that power "'without a specific record showing by the moving party of the particular abuses by which it is threatened.'"[10]

---

9. The court did not identify, and we are unable to find, any of the following abuses that courts and scholars have recognized as potentially hazardous in class action suits: (1) solicitation of direct representation of class members who are not formal parties; (2) solicitation of funds and agreements to pay fees; (3) solicitation by defendants of requests to opt out; and (4) communications with class members that misrepresent the status or effect of the pending action.

10. The district court's concern that plaintiffs' motive for communicating with the juveniles was "to generate litigation" and to launch a fishing expedition "to go after money damages" is entirely unsupported by the record. There is no proof that plaintiffs' counsel wished to "'drum up' participation in the proceeding," or recruit plaintiffs for damage claims. Plaintiffs' counsel assured the district court at the September 6, 1991, status hearing that they had specifically disavowed any interest in

Defendants' argument that Missouri law weighs heavily against granting access is equally unconvincing. The relied upon statutes are not dispositive of the issue of whether communications between class counsel and juvenile class members is necessarily prohibited. The statutes specifically refer to "reports" and "records" of juvenile court proceedings, which, as is true in most states, are judiciously guarded. No mention is made, however, of the need to restrict communications between juveniles and counsel in class action or other proceedings, and we decline to stretch the statutes' reach that far. The district court understandably was concerned that direct communications with the juveniles, and testimony generated as a result thereof, might lead to breaches of confidentiality. The court, however, could have issued a carefully drawn order requiring adherence to procedures that would have ensured the confidentiality of the juveniles (*e.g.,* a protective order limiting access to the juveniles' records to designated individuals), while at the same time permitting plaintiffs' counsel sufficient latitude to gather facts and advocate on behalf of the class.

We are additionally unpersuaded that the court properly restricted communications on the ground that the juveniles were already represented by independent counsel in delinquency and other matters before the Juvenile Court. Once the class was formed and certified, class counsel, and not counsel appointed or retained to represent the juveniles on altogether separate matters, had the obligation to represent class members, for judgment on the class's claims would have barred further action by the juveniles individually.

Accordingly, we find that the district court abused its discretion in conditioning communications between plaintiffs' counsel and class members on the requirements that plaintiffs exhaust alternative resources and demonstrate a compelling need.

Having concluded that the district court erred in imposing unwarranted conditions on communications between counsel and class members, there remains the question of whether the court's grant of summary judgment on the two issues appealed by plaintiffs, overcrowding and the use of floor mattresses, should be set aside on the ground that the court's order restricting access materially hindered plaintiffs' efforts to marshall enough evidence to sustain their burden on summary judgment. Because we find that the court's order restricting access did not prejudice plaintiffs with respect to these two issues, we do not believe that the court's grant of summary judgment should be set aside. Had plaintiffs appealed the district court's denial of relief on the other practices, policies, and conditions challenged by plaintiffs, we might have reached a contrary result. The record on the issues of overcrowding and the use of floor mattresses, however, is sufficiently clear to allow us to affirm the court's decision that neither produced deprivations of such magnitude as to constitute violations of plaintiffs' due process rights.

....

Notes

(a) Harsh Medicine—Last of three articles: Mistreating Tiffany

A Spotty Record of Health Care For Children in City Detention

Paul von Zielbauer

N.Y. Times 3/1/05

---

pursuing damage claims and that, even if given the opportunity to represent the juveniles in such claims, they would not do so.

It was early February 2000, and Judge Paula J. Hepner said she could hardly believe what a doctor in the city's juvenile justice system had done to the girl standing before her in Brooklyn Family Court.

The girl, Tiffany S., was 14, with a history of suicide threats and a set of serious psychological problems well documented by doctors at a psychiatric hospital for children. They had treated her bipolar disorder with powerful medicines and, knowing that she was facing detention, had recommended that she keep receiving them when the Department of Juvenile Justice took her into custody.

But soon after Tiffany entered the system, Dr. Ralph L. Williams—an employee of Prison Health Services and the only full-time doctor for 19 juvenile centers across the city—stopped her medications. Instead, he placed her on Ritalin, a drug meant to treat attention deficit hyperactivity disorder.

It took only days for Tiffany to deteriorate. Soon, she said in an interview, she was hallucinating, fighting with other girls and spending hours staring at a wall. As an additional measure, she said, a Prison Health employee asked her to sign a pledge not to kill herself.

Judge Hepner ordered Tiffany back to the hospital, records show, and moved to hold Dr. Williams in criminal contempt. In doing so, Judge Hepner joined at least five other judges who would order more vigorous treatment by Prison Health, a company that cares for hundreds of thousands of inmates in New York State and across the country.

[In] May [2000], for instance, Judge Philip C. Segal of Brooklyn Family Court held the juvenile justice commissioner—whose agency represented Prison Health in court—in contempt after the company staff neglected to give a 13-year-old boy his H.I.V. medication. Later that month, Harold J. Lynch, a judge in the Bronx, ordered a 13-year-old girl in the agency's custody returned to the Bronx Children's Psychiatric Center. The girl, court records show, had tried to kill herself after a Prison Health doctor discarded her psychiatric medications and gave her Ritalin instead.

"This is not just a single case," Judge Lynch told city lawyers. "It's many cases."

But those cases are only one distressing facet of what would be a four-year effort by Prison Health to provide care to young people in the city's network of juvenile detention centers and group homes—a job that made the company about $15 million in revenue before it was replaced in 2003. Independent investigations have criticized the quality of that care. Questions have also been raised by some city officials about whether the company was forthright with various other city agencies about its work at Juvenile Justice.

Of the roughly 500 youngsters, ages 7 through 16, who were in custody on any given day, some had committed serious crimes. Others had been turned over by parents who could not or would not care for them. Still others were there simply because there was nowhere else to go. One thing is clear about most of them: they were sick and in need of help.

Prison Health, a profit-making corporation with a troubling record in many states, appears to have poorly served many of those youngsters, according to a review of its work, based on court records and audits, as well as interviews with children, judges, Legal Aid Society lawyers and current and former Juvenile Justice employees. The results, those documents and interviews make clear, were often confusion and mistreatment throughout the company's time in the juvenile justice system, from January 1999 to April 2003.

For the 5,000 youngsters who passed through each year, the one full-time doctor Prison Health employed oversaw a staff composed mostly of part-time physician assistants, social workers and nurses. Sometimes, current and former counselors who worked at Juvenile Justice said, the medical staff mistakenly gave children medication that had not been prescribed to them. One counselor said that to avoid further errors, Polaroid photos were stapled to medical files to help nurses match names with faces.

The only independent audit of the company's medical care, commissioned by the Juvenile Justice Department in 2003, six months after Prison Health had already left, found that patient records had been in disarray, and that no doctor had appeared to consult them anyway. Many children with serious illnesses received no follow-up care, the audit said, and most teenagers were not tested for sexually transmitted diseases. The audit was never made public.

"The work was poor and put young people at risk," the city comptroller, William C. Thompson Jr., said in an interview. "I'd almost say deplorable."

Juvenile Justice officials have said they were "generally satisfied" with the company. The agency declined interview requests for this article for five months, until aides to Mayor Michael R. Bloomberg ordered the department's spokesman to answer questions about Prison Health's tenure. Even then, in two interviews, department officials would not discuss the company's record.

Richard D. Wright, the president and chief executive of Prison Health, defended its work and the services it offered youngsters in custody. "There were a lot of professional people dedicated to that contract," he said in an interview. "We thought that they were sufficient to deal with the workload."

Prison Health's performance at Juvenile Justice is the least known aspect of its long and lucrative work in New York. The care the company provided in upstate county jails in recent years has been assailed by state investigators. And its work at the jail complex on Rikers Island has been consistently, if not always diligently monitored by New York City, which awarded the company a new $300 million contract in January.

But the care Prison Health provided children in the juvenile system, the city comptroller now says, should have been examined by the city when the company was seeking the Rikers contract in 2000.

Prison Health took over care at Juvenile Justice in 1999 when it bought EMSA Correctional Care, a smaller competitor that had been doing the job for three years. When it was vying for the Rikers contract, though, Prison Health listed EMSA in disclosure statements as an affiliate and indicated that EMSA was still working at Juvenile Justice.

The city comptroller now says that Prison Health was in charge of providing juvenile care from the time it bought EMSA, and that EMSA existed only on paper. The comptroller says that the company misled the city, and that as a result, the city missed an opportunity to get a hard look at Prison Health's work in its own backyard before it hired the company for its adult jails.

Prison Health says that its filings properly listed EMSA as a separate concern in 2000. The city agencies in charge of awarding the Rikers contract, the Health and Hospitals Corporation and the Mayor's Office of Contract Services, say they found no problem with Prison Health's disclosures.

Over the years, as Prison Health has expanded nationally, followed by accusations of flawed care by regulators, many of its critics have wondered how it kept winning new contracts, sometimes in a county or state next to one it had left under a cloud. In New York City, anger among judges and lawyers in the juvenile justice system did not prevent the company from landing a huge jail contract across town.

Of course, caring for youngsters inside the city's three jail-like detention centers and 16 less restrictive group homes can be as dangerous and frustrating as caring for adult inmates. Few young people entering the system have received consistent health care and, as a result, lack any medical record to guide doctors. Often, there are not even family members to question.

For many of them, as a result, detention offers the only opportunity to get a physical or dental examination, or even talk to an adult willing to listen. Proper medical and mental health care, say experts and the department's own employees, is vital in helping them become productive adults.

That care has improved under the two companies hired to replace Prison Health, say city officials and lawyers working in the Family Court system. It could hardly have gotten worse, said Jennifer Baum, a Legal Aid lawyer who represented many youngsters during Prison Health's tenure.

"I saw troubled and needy children being mistreated by shabby medical care," she said.

By the time Prison Health Services acquired it, EMSA had been treating the city's incarcerated children since 1996. EMSA had more experience with children than Prison Health, but it had problems, too.

In Westchester County, EMSA had paid $750,000 to settle a lawsuit by the parents of a 17-year-old girl who hanged herself at the jail there in 1996, after a psychiatrist stopped her antidepressant medication. The doctor, Harvey N. Lothringer, had pleaded guilty to second-degree manslaughter three decades before, admitting that he dismembered the body of a young woman who had died during an illegal abortion he performed, and then flushed her remains down a toilet. He spent four years in prison, but in 1973, the State Board of Regents declared the doctor "rehabilitated" and restored his medical license. He began working for EMSA in 1996.

At Juvenile Justice, counselors and Legal Aid lawyers said they had found EMSA's medical staff too small to properly treat all the children who needed help. But a little less than a year after Prison Health arrived, taking responsibility for the care, that private grumbling turned public.

Prompted by complaints from Ms. Baum, a half-dozen Family Court judges filed at least 12 court orders or contempt motions in 2000 to force Juvenile Justice to fix mistakes in care. In one instance, Dr. Joseph K. Youngerman of the Bronx Children's Psychiatric Center pleaded with Judge Lynch to help the suicidal 13-year-old girl who had been taken off her medication; if he could not, the doctor wrote, the center would take her back — "to spare her (and us all) any repeat" of her breakdown.

For nearly two years, though, those concerns remained buried in court files. Then, in 2002, the city comptroller, during a routine review, uncovered several problems.

He urged Prison Health to re-examine its staffing, which provided only one full-time psychiatrist and one part-time physician for all medical services. The company, the comptroller's office found, did not provide the group counseling required in its contract. There was no system, the comptroller said, to ensure that children taking psychiatric drugs received them on days they were sent to court; unmedicated, they sometimes broke down in front of a judge.

Indeed, several employees said that they sometimes were told that drugs for some of the children were unavailable or simply unnecessary, leaving them to handle the untreated patients.

"If they get disruptive," said one longtime counselor at a group home, "the staff has to put them in a restraining position, and then you end up with a child-abuse charge."

For reasons that its spokesman declined to disclose, the Department of Juvenile Justice commissioned its own review in 2003. It was a rare move, and it came only after Prison Health had left.

This would be the only outside medical audit. Done by IPRO, a well-known nonprofit health-care auditing firm, it found serious deficiencies, showing that things had been even worse than the comptroller's office had thought.

Medical charts had been badly disorganized, the audit said, and "there was little evidence of an oversight physician" reviewing them. Young people who developed medical problems were "almost never" seen by a doctor, but typically examined instead by a nurse, the audit said.

About one in six youngsters with chronic health problems like epilepsy, sickle cell anemia and kidney disease never received follow-up treatment while in custody. Tests critical to running an institution full of troubled young people were so haphazardly administered that fewer than one-third of the eligible girls received a Pap test, and only about 1 in 5 eligible youngsters were tested for gonorrhea, chlamydia and syphilis.

But Prison Health was by now largely beyond accountability. It had left the previous April, when the Department of Juvenile Justice replaced it with two other companies: Health Star Plus, which now provides medical care, and Forensic Health Services, which handles mental health services. Department officials, who had given Prison Health mostly satisfactory evaluations during its four years, would not discuss the problems raised by the audit.

"At this point, we have new providers," said Scott Trent, a department spokesman. "It's a new contract. It's entirely irrelevant."

(b) Recently the Casey Foundation has funded research to develop alternative detention programs for children accused of delinquency in order to decrease the number of children detained in locked detention facilities. Given the impact of detention on children, even when limited, what policies should communities be developing? Should communities also be considering the recent developmental research, the ABA Standards (that follow), and safety concerns of the community?

5. IJA-ABA Juvenile Justice Standards Relating to Interim Status: The Release, Control and Detention of Accused Juvenile Offenders between Arrest and Disposition

Robert E. Shepherd, Jr., ed.

. . . .

Part VI: Standards For The Juvenile Facility Intake Official

6.6 Guidelines for status decision.

A. Mandatory release. The intake official should release the accused juvenile unless the juvenile:

    1. is charged with a crime of violence which in the case of an adult would be punishable by a sentence of one year or more, and which if proven is likely to result in commitment to a secure institution, and one or more of the following additional factors is present:

        a. the crime charged is a class one juvenile offense;

        b. the juvenile is an escapee from an institution or other placement facility to which he or she was sentenced under a previous adjudication of criminal conduct;

        c. the juvenile has a demonstrable recent record of willful failure to appear at juvenile proceedings, on the basis of which the official finds that no measure short of detention can be imposed to reasonably ensure appearance; or

    2. has been verified to be a fugitive from another jurisdiction, an official of which has formally requested that the juvenile be placed in detention.

    B. Mandatory detention. A juvenile who is excluded from mandatory release under subsection A should not, pro tanto, be automatically detained. No category of alleged conduct or background in and of itself should justify a failure to exercise discretion to release.

    C. Discretionary situations.

    1. Release vs. detention. In every situation in which the release of an arrested juvenile is not mandatory, the intake official should first consider and determine whether the juvenile qualifies for an available diversion program, or whether any form of control short of detention is available to reasonably reduce the risk of flight or misconduct. If no such measure will suffice, the official should explicitly state in writing the reasons for rejecting each of these forms of release.

    2. Unconditional vs. conditional or supervised release. In order to minimize the imposition of release conditions on persons who would appear in court without them, and present no substantial risk in the interim, each jurisdiction should develop guidelines for the use of various forms of release based upon the resources and programs available, and analysis of the effectiveness of each form of release.

    3. Secure vs. nonsecure detention. Whenever an intake official determines that detention is the appropriate interim status, secure detention may be selected only if clear and convincing evidence indicates the probability of serious physical injury to others, or serious probability of flight to avoid appearance in court. Absent such evidence, the accused should be placed in an appropriate form of nonsecure detention, with a foster home to be preferred over other alternatives.

Part VII: Standards For The Juvenile Court

. . . .

7.6 Release Hearing.

    A. Timing. An accused juvenile taken into custody should, unless sooner released, be accorded a hearing in court within [twenty-four hours] of the filing of the petition for a release hearing. . . .

    B. Notice. Actual notice of the detention review hearing should be given to the accused juvenile, the parents, and their attorneys, immediately upon an intake official's decision that the juvenile will not be released prior to the hearing.

C. Rights. An attorney for the accused juvenile should be present at the hearing in addition to the juvenile's parents, if they attend. There should be a strong presumption against the validity of a waiver of any constitutional or statutory right of the juvenile, and no waiver should be valid unless made in writing by the juvenile and his or her counsel.

D. Information. At the review hearing, information relevant to the interim status of an accused juvenile, other than information bearing on the nature and circumstances of the offense charged and the weight of the evidence against the accused juvenile, need not conform to the rules pertaining to the admissibility of evidence in a court of law.

E. Disclosure. The juvenile and the attorney should have full access to all information and records upon which a judge relies in refusing to release the juvenile from detention, or in imposing conditions of supervision.

F. Probable cause. At the time of the initial detention hearing, the burden should be on the state to demonstrate that there is probable cause to believe that the juvenile committed the offense charged.

G. Notice of right to appeal. Whenever a court orders detention, or denies release upon review of an order of detention, it should simultaneously inform the juvenile, orally and in writing, of his or her rights to an automatic seven-day review under Standard 7.9 and to immediate appellate review under Standard 7.12.

7.7 Guidelines for Status decisions.

A. Release alternatives. The court may release the juvenile on his or her own recognizance, on conditions, under supervision, including release on a temporary, nonovernight basis to the attorney if so requested for the purpose of preparing the case, or into a diversion program.

B. Mandatory release. Release by the court should be mandatory when the state fails to establish probable cause to believe the juvenile committed the offense charged or in any situation in which the arresting officer or intake official was required to release the juvenile but failed to do so, unless the court is in possession of additional information which justifies detention under these standards.

C. Discretionary situations. In all other cases, the court should review all factors that officials earlier in the process were required by these standards to have considered. The court should review with particularity the adequacy of the reasons for detention recorded by the police and the intake official.

D. Written reasons. A written statement of the finding of facts and reasons why no measure short of detention would suffice should be made part of the order and filed immediately after the hearing by any judge who declines to release an accused juvenile from detention. An order continuing the juvenile in detention should be construed as authorizing nonsecure detention only, unless it contains an express direction to the contrary, supported by reasons. If the court orders release under a form of control to which the juvenile objects, the court should upon request by the attorney for the juvenile, record the facts and reasons why unconditional release was denied.

7.8 Judicial participation.

A. Every juvenile court judge should visit each secure facility under the jurisdiction of that court at least once every [sixty days].

B. Whenever feasible, a judge other than the one who presided at the detention hearing should preside at the trial.

7.9 Continuing detention review.

A. The court should hold a detention review hearing at or before the end of each seven-day period in which a juvenile remains in interim detention. At the first detention review hearing after the expiration of the time prescribed for execution of the dispositional order, the judge must execute such order forthwith, or fully explain on the record the reasons for the delay, or release the juvenile.

B. A list of all juveniles held in any form of interim detention, together with the length of such detention and the reasons for detention, should be prepared by the intake official and presented weekly to the presiding judge. Such reports, with names deleted, should simultaneously be made public to describe the number, duration, and reasons for interim detention of juveniles.

. . . .

7.12 Appellate review of detention decision.

The attorney for the juvenile may at any time, upon notice to the prosecutor, appeal and be entitled to an immediate hearing within [twenty-four hours] on notice or motion from a court order imposing detention or denying release from detention. A copy of the order and written statement of reasons should accompany such appeal, and decisions on appeal should be filed at the conclusion of the hearing.

Part VIII: Standards For The Defense Attorney

. . . .

8.2 Duties.

It should be the duty of counsel for an accused juvenile to explore promptly the least restrictive form of release, the alternatives to detention, and the opportunities for detention review, at every stage of the proceedings where such an inquiry would be relevant.

8.3 Visit detention facility.

Whenever an accused juvenile is held in some form of detention, the attorney should periodically visit the juvenile, at no less than seven day intervals, and review personally his or her well-being, the conditions of the facility, and opportunities to relax the conditions of detention or to secure release. A report on each such visit should be retained in the attorney's permanent file of the case.

. . . .

Part IX: Standards For The Prosecutor

9.1 Duties.

The prosecutor should review the charges, evidence, and the background of the juvenile prior to the initial court hearing in every case in which an accused juvenile is held in detention. On the basis of such review, the prosecutor should move at the initial hearing to dismiss the charges if prosecution is not warranted, to reduce charges to the extent excessive, and to eliminate detention or unduly restrictive control to the extent necessary to bring the juvenile's interim status into compliance with these standards.

. . . .

9.3 Visit detention facilities.

Each prosecutor should, in the same manner required of judges under Standard 7.8 and defense counsel under Standard 8.3, visit at least once every [sixty days] each secure detention facility in which accused juveniles prosecuted by his or her office are lodged.

G. Adjudicatory Hearings

1. The Criminal — Civil Dichotomy

a. *Tex. Family Code § 51.17*

Procedure and Evidence

(a) Except for the burden of proof to be borne by the state in adjudicating a child to be delinquent or in need of supervision under Section 54.03(f) or otherwise when in conflict with a provision of this title, the Texas Rules of Civil Procedure govern proceedings under this title.

(b) Discovery in a proceeding under this title is governed by the Code of Criminal Procedure and by case decisions in criminal cases.

(c) Except as otherwise provided by this title, the Texas Rules of Evidence applicable to criminal cases and Chapter 38, Code of Criminal Procedure, apply in a judicial proceeding under this title.

(d) When on the motion for appointment of an interpreter by a party or on the motion of the juvenile court, in any proceeding under this title, the court determines that the child, the child's parent or guardian, or a witness does not understand and speak English, an interpreter must be sworn to interpret for the person as provided by Article 38.30, Code of Criminal Procedure.

(e) In any proceeding under this title, if a party notifies the court that the child, the child's parent or guardian, or a witness is deaf, the court shall appoint a qualified interpreter to interpret the proceedings in any language, including sign language, that the deaf person can understand, as provided by Article 38.31, Code of Criminal Procedure.

(f) Any requirement under this title that a document contain a person's signature, including the signature of a judge or a clerk of the court, is satisfied if the document contains the signature of the person as captured on an electronic device or as a digital signature. Article 2.26, Code of Criminal Procedure, applies in a proceeding held under this title.

b. *N.Y. Family Court Act § 165*

Procedure

(a) Where the method of procedure in any proceeding in which the family court has jurisdiction is not prescribed by this act, the procedure shall be in accord with rules adopted by the administrative board of the judicial conference or, if none has been adopted, with the provisions of the civil practice act to the extent they are suitable to the proceeding involved. Upon the effective date of the CPLR, where the method of procedure in any proceeding in which the family court has jurisdiction is not prescribed, the provisions of the civil practice law and rules shall apply to the extent that they are appropriate to the proceedings involved.

(b) In any proceeding commenced pursuant to the provisions of the social services law in which the family court has exercised jurisdiction, the provisions of articles one, two and eleven of the family court act shall apply to the extent that they do not conflict with the specific provisions of the social services law.

c. *N.Y. Fam. Court Act § 303.2*

Double jeopardy

The provisions of article forty of the criminal procedure law concerning double jeopardy shall apply to juvenile delinquency proceedings.

d. *In the Matter of S.L.L.*

906 S.W.2d 190 (Tex. App. 1995) (per curiam)

....

Juvenile delinquency proceedings are both civil and criminal in nature. In light of the very real possibility of loss of liberty faced by the juvenile respondent, juvenile proceedings have been characterized as "quasi-criminal," with procedural requirements similar to those in adult prosecutions. Consequently, many of the rights afforded by the Code of Criminal Procedure to adult criminal defendants are provided to the juvenile in the Family Code. However, the Family Code does not mirror precisely the Code of Criminal Procedure, creating "gaps and ambiguities between the civil and criminal law."

These gaps may be quite substantial. For instance, while an adult defendant is afforded the right to bail, the juvenile respondent is not. Similarly, the legislature specifically granted the right to withdraw a plea entered pursuant to a plea agreement to adult defendants in 1977. However, no concomitant right exists in the Family Code for the juvenile respondent. In effect, juveniles are now in the same position that adults occupied before the 1977 amendment.

e. *In the Matter of J.R.*

907 S.W.2d 107 (Tex. App. 1995) (per curiam)

....

Although juvenile delinquency proceedings are considered civil proceedings, they are quasi-criminal in nature. One court has characterized juvenile proceedings as essentially criminal trials, involving criminal issues on appeal. Aspects of juvenile proceedings governed by the rules of criminal proceedings include the State's burden of proof, the right to trial by jury, the privilege against self-incrimination, the right to trial and confrontation of witnesses, and confessions. The juvenile is guaranteed the constitutional rights an adult would have in a criminal proceeding because the juvenile delinquency proceedings seek to deprive the juvenile of his liberty.

2. The Differences and Similarities between Rights and Rules Applicable in Criminal Trials and Those in Delinquency Adjudicatory Hearings

a. *N.Y. Family Court Act § 342.1*

The fact-finding hearing; order of procedure

The order of the fact-finding hearing shall be as follows:

1. The court shall permit the parties to deliver opening addresses. If both parties deliver opening addresses, the presentment agency's address shall be delivered first.

2. The presentment agency must offer evidence in support of the petition.

3. The respondent may offer evidence in his defense.

4. The presentment agency may offer evidence in rebuttal of the respondent's evidence, and the respondent may then offer evidence in rebuttal of the presentment agency's evidence. The court may in its discretion permit the parties to offer further rebuttal or sur-rebuttal evidence in this pattern. In the interest of justice, the court may permit either party to offer evidence upon rebuttal which is not technically of a rebuttal nature but more properly a part of the offering party's original case.

5. At the conclusion of the evidence, the respondent shall have the right to deliver a summation.

6. The presentment agency shall then have the right to deliver a summation.

7. The court must then consider the case and enter a finding.

b. *N.Y. Family Court Act § 342.2*

Evidence in fact-finding hearings; required quantum

1. Only evidence that is competent, material and relevant may be admitted at a fact-finding hearing.

2. Any determination at the conclusion of a fact-finding hearing that a respondent committed an act or acts which if committed by an adult would be a crime must be based on proof beyond a reasonable doubt.

c. *Tex. Family Code § 54.03*

Adjudication Hearing

(a) A child may be found to have engaged in delinquent conduct or conduct indicating a need for supervision only after an adjudication hearing conducted in accordance with the provisions of this section.

(b) At the beginning of the adjudication hearing, the juvenile court judge shall explain to the child and his parent, guardian, or guardian ad litem:

(1) the allegations made against the child;

(2) the nature and possible consequences of the proceedings, including the law relating to the admissibility of the record of a juvenile court adjudication in a criminal proceeding;

(3) the child's privilege against self-incrimination;

(4) the child's right to trial and to confrontation of witnesses;

(5) the child's right to representation by an attorney if he is not already represented; and

(6) the child's right to trial by jury.

(c) Trial shall be by jury unless jury is waived in accordance with Section 51.09. If the hearing is on a petition that has been approved by the grand jury under Section 53.045, the jury must consist of 12 persons and be selected in accordance with the requirements in criminal cases. Jury verdicts under this title must be unanimous.

(d) Except as provided by § 54.031, only material, relevant, and competent evidence in accordance with the Texas Rules of Evidence applicable to criminal cases and Chapter 38, Code of Criminal Procedure, may be considered in the adjudication hearing. Except in a detention or discretionary transfer hearing, a social history report or social service file shall not be viewed by the court before the adjudication decision and shall not be viewed by the jury at any time.

(e) A child alleged to have engaged in delinquent conduct or conduct indicating a need for supervision need not be a witness against nor otherwise incriminate himself. An extrajudicial statement which was obtained without fulfilling the requirements of this title or of the constitution of this state or the United States, may not be used in an adjudication hearing. A statement made by the child out of court is insufficient to support a finding of delinquent conduct or conduct indicating a need for supervision unless it is corroborated in whole or in part by other evidence. An adjudication of delinquent conduct or conduct indicating a need for supervision cannot be had upon the testimony of an accomplice unless corroborated by other evidence tending to connect the child with the alleged delinquent conduct or conduct indicating a need for supervision; and the corroboration is not sufficient if it merely shows the commission of the alleged conduct. Evidence illegally seized or obtained is inadmissible in an adjudication hearing.

(f) At the conclusion of the adjudication hearing, the court or jury shall find whether or not the child has engaged in delinquent conduct or conduct indicating a need for supervision. The finding must be based on competent evidence admitted at the hearing. The child shall be presumed to be innocent of the charges against the child and no finding that a child has engaged in delinquent conduct or conduct indicating a need for supervision may be returned unless the state has proved such beyond a reasonable doubt. In all jury cases the jury will be instructed that the burden is on the state to prove that a child has engaged in delinquent conduct or is in need of supervision beyond a reasonable doubt. A child may be adjudicated as having engaged in conduct constituting a lesser included offense as provided by Articles 37.08 and 37.09, Code of Criminal Procedure.

(g) If the court or jury finds that the child did not engage in delinquent conduct or conduct indicating a need for supervision, the court shall dismiss the case with prejudice.

(h) If the finding is that the child did engage in delinquent conduct or conduct indicating a need for supervision, the court or jury shall state which of the allegations in the petition were found to be established by the evidence. The court shall also set a date and time for the disposition hearing.

(i) In order to preserve for appellate or collateral review the failure of the court to provide the child the explanation required by Subsection (b), the attorney for the child must comply with Rule 33.1, Texas Rules of Appellate Procedure, before testimony begins or, if the adjudication is uncontested, before the child pleads to the petition or agrees to a stipulation of evidence.

3. Cases

In re Corcoran

587 N.E.2d 957 (Ohio Ct. App. 1990)

On June 23, 1988, appellant, Michael Corcoran, and his friend, Tim Bravchok, both thirteen years old, entered The Pampered Pet, a pet store located in the Bainbridge Commons in Bainbridge Township, Ohio. They proceeded to a thirty-five gallon aquarium containing six to eight gerbils, whereupon, Bravchok asked the appellant whether he should drop some super glue on one of the gerbils. The appellant responded by saying it did not matter to him. Bravchok then dripped some glue on the back of one of the gerbils.

An employee of The Pampered Pet, Julia Ann Fretter, saw the boys standing by the gerbil cage but did not witness the gluing incident. After the boys had left the store, Fretter discovered the glue on the gerbil and telephoned the police, whereupon the boys were located and questioned by the police.

On July 22, 1988, a complaint was filed in the Geauga County Common Pleas Court, Juvenile Division. The complaint alleged that the appellant was a delinquent child [for violating] the criminal mischief statute. A hearing was scheduled for September 19, 1988 but was continued upon motion of the state because one of the key witnesses was in the hospital. The hearing was rescheduled for November 14, 1988.

On November 14, 1988, the hearing was continued to December 28, 1988. The juvenile court stated that this second continuance was "for good cause shown."

The appellant filed a motion to dismiss on November 23, 1988, which was subsequently denied by the juvenile court. On December 12, 1988, the appellant filed a motion to dismiss pursuant to Juv.R. 9. The juvenile court denied this motion on December 13, 1988.

On December 28, 1988, a hearing was held on the matter and the appellant was adjudged to be a delinquent child.

. . . .

In his first assignment of error, the appellant contends that the trial court erred in not avoiding formal court proceedings, in denying his motion to dismiss, and in conducting the hearing in the manner of a criminal trial.

Juv. R. 9(A) states:

> "In all appropriate cases formal court action should be avoided and other community resources utilized to ameliorate situations brought to the attention of the court."

In the instant cause, the appellant filed a motion to dismiss based on Juv.R. 9 prior to the hearing. The appellant requested an outright dismissal and did not suggest that other community resources be utilized to ameliorate the situation. It is clear from the language of Juv.R. 9 that formal court action is permissible in appropriate cases, and that it is within the discretion of the juvenile court to proceed in such a manner.

According to R.C. 2151.01 among the purposes of the law involving juveniles is to provide for the care, protection, and mental and physical development of children, as well as to assure a fair hearing in which their constitutional and other legal rights are recognized and enforced. With this in mind, providing the appellant with the necessary care, protection, and mental development would not have been achieved by simply dismissing the case because he claimed no wrongdoing.

Juv. R. 27 and R.C. 2151.35 state that a juvenile hearing may be held in an informal manner. The appellant argues that it was error for the juvenile court to fail to conduct the hearing in an informal manner, yet once again that decision is within the discretion of the juvenile court. Further, a review of the partial transcript that appellant has provided fails to indicate that the appellant was prejudiced by the manner in which the hearing was conducted or that his constitutional rights were not protected.

The appellant's first assignment of error is without merit.

In his second assignment of error, the appellant argues that the juvenile court erred in concluding that he was an accomplice or a participant based on his failure to stop Tim Bravchok from putting glue on the gerbil. In essence, the appellant asserts that the juvenile court's finding that he was an accomplice was against the manifest weight of the evidence.

The Ohio Supreme Court has held, with respect to the standard of review:

"Judgments supported by some competent, credible evidence going to all the essential elements of the case will not be reversed by a reviewing court as being against the manifest weight of the evidence."

In addition, App. R. 9(B) provides, in part:

"* * * If the appellant intends to urge on appeal that a finding or conclusion is unsupported by the evidence or is contrary to the weight of the evidence, he shall include in the record a transcript of all evidence relevant to such findings or conclusion. * * *"

In the present case, the original proceedings were transcribed by the use of a video recording system. The appellant provided this court a copy of these videotapes but provided only a partial written transcript of the videotapes [those favorable to his cause]. For purposes of filing, the videotaped copy of the proceedings was sufficient; however, [to challenge the weight of the evidence,] App. R. 9(A) [provides]:

"[C]ounsel shall type or print those portions of such transcript necessary for the court to determine the questions presented, certify their accuracy, and append such copy of the portions of the transcripts to their briefs. * * *"

. . . .

The appellant's failure to include in the record transcribed portions of all the testimony relevant to his claim ... prevents this court from addressing the issue. Instead, a presumption of regularity of the proceedings below arises.

[T]he ... second assignment of error is overruled.

In his third assignment of error, the appellant claims the juvenile court erred in not providing him a speedy trial as required by the Ohio Constitution and R.C. 2945.71(B)(1). The appellant specifically asserts that he should have been brought to trial within forty-five days pursuant to R.C. 2945.71(B)(1). The Ohio Supreme Court determined that the statutory speedy trial provisions of R.C. 2945.71(c) do not apply to delinquency proceedings. The court stated:

"* * * We find it unnecessary to decide whether a minor has a constitutional right to a speedy disposition of juvenile charges pending against him. * * *Juv. R. 29(A) provides:

"'The date for the adjudicatory hearing shall be set when the complaint is filed, or as soon thereafter as is practicable. If the child who is the subject of the complaint is in detention or shelter care, the hearing shall be held not later than ten days after the filing of the complaint; upon a showing of good cause the adjudicatory hearing may be continued and detention or shelter care extended.'"

Subsequently, the Court of Appeals for Coshocton County held that "* * * the statutory speedy trial provisions for adults in Ohio do not apply to juveniles * * *."

Concerning the appellant's constitutional argument, the United States Supreme Court has held that four factors are relevant in determining whether the Sixth Amendment right to a speedy trial has been violated. These factors include: (1) the length of the delay, (2) the reason for the delay, (3) whether and when the defendant asserted the right to a speedy trial, and (4) whether the defendant was prejudiced by the delay.

Although the Ohio Supreme Court has not applied these factors to juvenile cases, there is no indication in the case *sub judice* that the appellant was prejudiced in any way due to the delay.

....

Judgment affirmed.

In re Good

692 N.E.2d 1072 (Ohio Ct. App. 1997)

On January 30, 1996, the Butler County Court of Common Pleas, Juvenile Division, held that defendant-appellant, Milton Good, Jr., was a delinquent child. Appellant was found to have violated R.C. 2911.01 (aggravated robbery) and R.C. 2929.71 (possession of a firearm while committing a felony). The court committed appellant to the Department of Youth Services for a minimum term of twelve months for the aggravated robbery charge and for a three-year term for the firearm possession charge, to be served prior to and consecutively to the aggravated robbery commitment. Appellant's maximum term is not to extend beyond his twenty-first birthday. Appellant appeals the court's delinquency finding. We affirm.

....

Assignment of Error No. 1:

> "The trial court erred by denying him due process and equal protection of the law as guaranteed to him by the Sixth and Fourteenth Amendments of the United States Constitution."

The complaint on file ("original complaint") does not contain a firearm specification. Appellant argues that since the original complaint does not contain a firearm specification, it was improper for the court to find that appellant violated R.C. 2929.71. There is a handwritten firearm specification in the court file following the original complaint, but it is not attached to the original complaint and has not been file-stamped by the court. Appellee contends that normally "the court" files an initial complaint (in this case the original complaint and the handwritten firearm specification) and then later files a typed formal complaint based upon the initial complaint. Appellee surmises that there was a typed formal complaint ("typed complaint") that contained the firearm specification, but it is now missing. Appellee supposes that the reason for the loss of the formal complaint was a clerical error.

In a criminal case, a court has no authority to impose the three-year sentence for offenses involving a firearm as provided in R.C. 2929.71 if the indictment does not include a firearm specification. However, this is a juvenile case, not a criminal case. A complaint in juvenile court alleging delinquency does not need to be read as strictly as a criminal indictment. Juvenile court is neither criminal nor penal in nature, but is an administrative police regulation of a corrective nature. The purpose of the proceeding is to determine whether a child is delinquent. A child is delinquent if the child "violates any law of this state, the United States, or any ordinance or regulation of a political subdivision of the state which would be a crime if committed by an adult."

Being found a juvenile delinquent is different from being found guilty of a crime in Ohio. A juvenile delinquency proceeding has different rules than a criminal trial. For example, a juvenile court hears and determines all cases without a jury, a juvenile court can conduct its hearings in an informal manner, and the general public may be excluded from a juvenile court hearing.

In the present case, the court did not commit error by finding that appellant violated R.C. 2929.71. Although the typed complaint is missing, the court record contains the original complaint, which states that appellant had committed "aggravated armed robbery." The record also indicates that appellant was informed of the charges against him by the court, including the firearm specification, at a hearing held on January 19, 1996, eleven days prior to the proceeding on January 30, 1996 at which he was adjudicated delinquent. Appellant therefore knew the charges against him prior to being adjudicated delinquent.

Further, even if the strict requirements of R.C. 2941.141 are applied, and the original complaint did not have the firearm specification, appellant's counsel did not object. Failure to object to a defect in the complaint in a juvenile proceeding constitutes a waiver. We find that the strict requirements of *State v. Loines*, which held that sentencing a defendant without a firearm specification is plain error, do not apply in this case because it is a juvenile case. For the foregoing reasons, the trial court's determination that appellant violated R.C. 2929.71 will be upheld.

Appellant also alleges that his due process rights were violated. Due process requires that before being found delinquent, a juvenile must be given a written notice of the alleged misconduct. *In re Gault.* We cannot say conclusively that a typed complaint that included a firearm specification was ever prepared in this case. However, the existing record would lead a reasonable person to believe that appellant had prior notice of his alleged misconduct.

The original complaint (written on the day of appellant's arrest) states that appellant is accused of "aggravated armed robbery." At the January 19, 1996 hearing, the court stated the nature of the charges against appellant and their numerical designations. At the delinquency hearing on January 30, 1996, the court again informed appellant of the possible consequences "just so it is clear for [appellant] and his mother." There is no evidence that indicates that appellant did not receive sufficient notice of the charges against him or of the penalties. Based upon the record that exists, appellant was not denied due process. Appellant's first assignment of error is accordingly overruled.

In re J.S.

438 A.2d 1125 (Vt. 1981)

A juvenile, J.S., appeals from an order of the juvenile court allowing the public to attend proceedings to adjudge him a delinquent child for his alleged participation in the murder of one girl and the sexual assault of another.

In an attempt to comply with the confidentiality provisions of our juvenile shield law, one trial judge issued an order of closure which barred the public from the proceedings. The Burlington Free Press was granted permission to intervene for the sole purpose of being heard on its petition for access to any and all of the proceedings involving J.S. A second trial judge granted the petition, holding that 33 V.S.A. § 651(c) [shield law] violated the First Amendment. He ordered that J.S.'s juvenile proceedings be held in open court and that the public and the news media be permitted to attend.

J.S. sought relief from this order by two means. He was granted this interlocutory appeal from the order opening the proceedings, and at the same time he filed a petition for extraordinary relief, seeking to vacate the order and to exclude the public.

A majority of this Court in a previous order disqualified the office of the State's Attorney of Chittenden County, which had not opposed public access, from representing the State. The office of the Attorney General now appears for the State, and also on its own behalf to defend the constitutionality of our juvenile statutes.

The principal question before us is whether the limited holding of *Richmond Newspapers, Inc. v. Virginia*, that the First Amendment contains a right of access to criminal trials extends to a juvenile proceeding to determine delinquency and treatment. We must also consider additional arguments put forward by the Free Press in support of public proceedings.

Only a brief recital of the facts is necessary to enable us to grapple with the legal issues raised in this appeal. Two 12-year-old Essex Junction girls were brutally assaulted by two persons in or near an area park. One was killed. The other, left for dead, managed to survive. J.S. and a 16-year-old are the alleged assailants. J.S., who is 15, has been charged as a juvenile delinquent and will have his proceedings heard in juvenile court. The 16-year-old is awaiting trial as an adult in superior court on charges of first-degree murder and sexual assault.

Our juvenile shield law requires that juvenile court proceedings be confidential. The relevant portions of that law provide:

> (c) Except in hearings to declare a person in contempt of court, the general public shall be excluded from hearings under this chapter and only the parties, their counsel, witnesses and other persons accompanying a party for his assistance and such other persons as the court finds to have a proper interest in the case or in the work of the court, may be admitted by the court. If the court finds that it is to the best interest and welfare of the child, his presence may be temporarily excluded, except while a charge of his delinquency is being heard at the hearing on the petition.
>
> (d) There shall be no publicity given by any person to any proceedings under the authority of this chapter except with the consent of the child and his parent or guardian.

On appeal, J.S. contends that 33 V.S.A. § 651(c) mandates that the juvenile proceedings be closed to the public and the news media, and that closed proceedings are perfectly consistent with the United States and Vermont Constitutions. The State, in effect, concurs. Both J.S. and the State ask us to reverse the court below and close the proceedings.

The Free Press makes three arguments in support of public proceedings: (1) The court below was correct in holding that 33 V.S.A. § 651(c) was unconstitutional. (2) Even if the statute is constitutional, the proceedings should be public because the court below erroneously found itself without discretion under § 651(c) to admit reporters, and in the proper exercise of that discretion, they should be admitted. (3) Even if we disagree with the first two arguments, the publicity involving J.S. has been and will be so pervasive that the reasons for confidentiality no longer exist, so a special exception from the general requirement of confidentiality should be made in this case to allow public access. We disagree with all three arguments and therefore reverse.

I.

The Free Press claims that *Richmond Newspapers* dictates that the general public and the news media have a First Amendment right to attend juvenile delinquency proceedings and to publicly report what they see and hear in the juvenile court during those proceedings.

The question facing the Supreme Court in the *Richmond Newspapers* case, however, was whether the public and press possess a constitutional right of access to criminal trials. The Supreme Court concluded that such a right existed. The plurality held that the combination of the unbroken tradition of open criminal trials at common law and the fact that openness of criminal trials serves important First Amendment goals requires public access, absent overriding interests. That limited holding, however, does not extend to the case at hand.

Far from a tradition of openness, juvenile proceedings are almost invariably closed. All 50 states, in fact, have some sort of juvenile shield law to limit public access. Further, juvenile proceedings are not criminal prosecutions, a fact which makes at least some of the First Amendment purposes served by open criminal trials inapplicable. Finally, inherent in the very nature of juvenile proceedings are compelling interests in confidentiality which the Supreme Court itself has endorsed in cases cited below, and which we hold override any remaining First Amendment goals which access might serve.

A.

The holding in *Richmond Newspapers* applies only to criminal trials. Our juvenile law expressly provides that juvenile proceedings are not criminal. The very purpose of the juvenile delinquency law is to provide an alternative to criminal prosecutions of children. Thus, the Legislature has stated:

(a) The purposes of this chapter are:

* * *

(2) to remove from children committing delinquent acts the taint of criminality and the consequences of criminal behavior * * *.

* * *

(b) The provisions of this chapter shall be construed as superseding the provisions of the criminal law of this state to the extent the same are inconsistent herewith.

. . . .

An order of the juvenile court in proceedings under this chapter shall not be deemed a conviction of crime * * *.

. . . .

We [have] underscored the fundamental characteristic of a juvenile proceeding:

"It is a protective proceeding entirely concerned with the welfare of the child, and is not punitive. The procedures supersede the provisions of the criminal law and laws affecting minors in conflict with the authorizations of the juvenile court statutes. The inquiry relates to proper custody for the child, not his guilt or innocence as a criminal offender."

The only issue in a juvenile proceeding is "the care, needs and protection of the minor and his rehabilitation and restoration to useful citizenship."

B.

The court below compared the similarities and differences of juvenile proceedings and criminal trials, cited the United States Supreme Court decisions in *Breed v. Jones*, *In re Winship*, and *In re Gault*, and concluded that a juvenile proceeding was a criminal prosecution for the purposes of the First Amendment. The differences and similarities it discussed were irrelevant in light of the fundamental distinction between the punitive purpose of a criminal prosecution and the rehabilitative purpose of a juvenile proceeding. The cases cited by the court below do not support the proposition for which they were cited. Each merely extended certain procedural protections to the juvenile. Nothing in any one of them suggests that the Legislature may not further protect the juvenile by closing the proceedings. If anything, the great concern for the welfare of the child that they demonstrate suggests that the child's interests should prevail when in conflict with public access. To the extent that they are relevant at all, the precedents cited by the court below indicate that confidentiality is appropriate.

Thus it appears to us that a juvenile proceeding is so unlike a criminal prosecution that the limited right of access described in *Richmond Newspapers* does not govern. Certainly, neither the United States nor Vermont Constitutions expressly mandate a right of access. Nor do our opinions or those of the United States Supreme Court hint that such a right exists. The court below was in error when it held otherwise.

C.

Even if there were some constitutional right of access which presumptively reached juvenile proceedings, public access would not automatically follow. Rather, the First Amendment interests would first have to be weighed against the countervailing interests in confidentiality.

The punitive purpose of criminal proceedings raises First Amendment issues which are not present here. There, public access serves as a check against unjust conviction, excessive punishment and the undeserved taint of criminality. The juvenile proceeding, by contrast, involves no criminal conviction, no punishment, and, when confidential, no taint of criminality. Thus fewer First Amendment interests are at stake here than was the case in *Richmond Newspapers*.

The other side of the balance, however, is more heavily weighted here than in *Richmond Newspapers*. The compelling interests in confidential juvenile proceedings have been recognized and implicitly endorsed by the United States Supreme Court.

Justice Rehnquist has reiterated the Supreme Court's concern for maintaining the confidentiality of juvenile proceedings:

> "It is a hallmark of our juvenile justice system in the United States that virtually from its inception at the end of the last century its proceedings have been conducted outside of the public's full gaze and the youths brought before our juvenile courts have been shielded from publicity. This insistence on confidentiality is born of a tender concern for the welfare of the child, to hide his youthful errors and 'bury them in the graveyard of the forgotten past.' The prohibition of publication of a juvenile's name is designed to protect the young person from the stigma of his misconduct and is rooted in the principle that a court concerned with juvenile affairs serves as a rehabilitative and protective agency of the State."

Even *Davis v. Alaska*, cited by the Free Press for the proposition that the State's interest in keeping juvenile matters confidential must yield to an overwhelming First Amendment right, supports the opposite conclusion. The Court there assumed the propriety of confidentiality in juvenile proceedings when it said, "We do not and need not challenge the State's interest as a matter of its own policy in the administration of criminal justice to seek to preserve the anonymity of a juvenile offender." If a right of access existed, there certainly could be no anonymity.

The holding in the *Davis* case only went so far as to protect the defendant's Sixth Amendment right to cross-examination in the context of the factual situation confronting that court. The Court concluded that the State's witness, a juvenile called to identify the defendant, must submit to cross-examination about his juvenile delinquency record, because the defendant's right outweighed the state interest.

Any right of the Free Press to report what takes place in juvenile court is hardly equivalent to the defendant's right to cross-examine the witness who fingered him as the prime suspect in a breaking and entering case, especially where a possible motive of the juvenile for turning State's witness was to take the heat off himself as a suspect in the same crime.

There are, however, many reasons why the State's compelling interests in the confidential juvenile proceedings override the countervailing interests of the public and the news media in access to those proceedings and the news media's interest in publicly disseminating what its reporters learn while attending.

Publication of the youth's name could impair the rehabilitative goals of the juvenile justice system. Confidential proceedings protect the delinquent from the stigma of conduct which may be outgrown and avoids the possibility that the adult is penalized for what he used to be, or worse yet, the possibility that the stigma becomes self-perpetuating, thereby making change and growth impossible. Publication of a delinquent's name may handicap his prospects for adjustment into society, for acceptance by the public, or it may cause him to lose employment opportunities. Public proceedings could so embarrass the youth's family members that they withhold their support in rehabilitative efforts.

The argument of the Free Press that its pervasive newspaper publicity has already compromised these goals and so it ought to be allowed to attend and publicize the proceedings concerning J.S., ignores still another purpose served by confidentiality. Publicity sometimes serves as a reward for the hardcore juvenile delinquent, thereby encouraging him to commit further antisocial acts to attract attention. Further, the legislative goals of expunging the juvenile's delinquency record are vitiated if the same information could at any subsequent time be obtained freely from newspaper morgues.

Neither the Vermont nor the United States Constitution, as interpreted by the United States Supreme Court or our Court, provides a right of public access which overrides the compelling interests served by our juvenile confidentiality shield statutes. The trial court erred in holding otherwise and must be reversed.

II.

The Free Press insists, however, that its reporters are among those persons contemplated by the Legislature as having "a proper interest in the case or in the work of the court," and that the second judge erred when he intimated in his order that the statute gave him no discretion to grant news reporters access to juvenile proceedings.

This argument collides with 33 V.S.A. § 651(d), which specifically prohibits any of those persons admitted under § 651(c) from publicly disseminating information gained from a juvenile hearing "except with the consent of the child and his parent or guardian." No provision is made in either § 651(c) or § 651(d) to give the judge discretion to permit public dissemination of these proceedings.

The Free Press, however, would have us hold that § 651(c) gives the judge discretion to admit their reporters and that § 651(d) forbids them from publishing what they learn once admitted. So construed, they say, § 651(d) is unenforceable as an unconstitutional prior restraint of the press in violation of the First Amendment.

This statutory interpretation runs afoul of common sense and the canons of construction which we observe to keep ourselves within the bounds of judicial authority. Our function is not to pass upon the validity of a legislative concern or the wisdom of the means the Legislature chooses to address that concern, but merely to make sure that no constitutional bounds are exceeded.

When faced with a choice, we assume that the Legislature intended a constitutional result and construe statutes accordingly. Further, we avoid a construction which leads to absurd or irrational results. Reading § 651(c) and § 651(d) together, to give effect to each, leads to the inescapable result that a desire to publicly disseminate the facts of a juvenile proceeding is not "a proper interest in the case or in the work of the court."

These two sections of the juvenile shield law are clear and unambiguous. The Legislature did not intend that either the news media or the general public should attend juvenile hearings or report what transpired there. We do not base this conclusion on a single sentence or word or phrase in a sentence, but we have looked at the provisions of the whole juvenile law, and to its objects and its policy.

III.

The Free Press and other members of the news media apparently obtained the name of J.S. and his involvement in the murder and sexual assault of the two young girls in Essex Junction after examining the affidavits of probable cause in the two cases pending against the 16-year-old adult in superior court. Information about the juvenile will inevitably be disclosed at the adult's trial. Because this legally obtained information has been flagrantly publicized by the news media, and because more is to come, the Free Press next argues there is no longer any reason for the confidentiality imposed by 33 V.S.A. §651(c) and §651(d) and the Court should drop the barriers for this case as a special exception.

This argument also has several flaws. First, as we have already noted, publicity sometimes serves as a reward for incorrigible delinquents, encouraging the very behavior sought to be deterred. Secondly, this approach calls for a case by case analysis to determine if, when, and to what extent access to juvenile proceedings should be limited. Third, such a case by case analysis lets the news media determine which juvenile proceedings will be open to the public simply by turning up the volume of publicity concerning any case that strikes their fancy. Fourth, decisions to open proceedings will then be based, not on the child's needs, but on chance circumstances. Finally, it is not just the name of delinquents which are protected by the juvenile shield law. Other matters which surface in a juvenile proceeding are just as worthy of anonymity as the juvenile's name. They include the very fact of the adjudication of delinquency and the taint of criminality emanating therefrom; the specific program of treatment, training and rehabilitation ordered and the locale in which it takes place; the name of the individual or organization to whom custody of the juvenile may be entrusted; the fact and conditions of probation; disposition reports and recommendations made by the commissioner of social and rehabilitation services or the commissioner of corrections to the juvenile court; the disposition order of the juvenile court; law enforcement reports and files concerning the minor, as well as fingerprints and photographs, and the files and records of the juvenile court itself, including dismissal of the petition. These are all part and parcel of the record of a young person's life which the Legislature shielded from public access.

IV.

To summarize, the Free Press has failed to establish that any right of access to J.S.'s juvenile proceeding is contained in the United States or Vermont Constitutions. The juvenile shield law does not give the court below discretion to make the proceedings public. The fact that J.S.'s name is already a household word in Essex Junction, and that the nature of the offense and his alleged participation with a named adult defendant in certain crimes will be disclosed in the trial of the adult, is no reason to dismantle our juvenile court system. Confidential proceedings continue to serve overriding interests.

Any limitations in the juvenile justice system will not be cured by a public trial of J.S. If the Free Press feels that the underlying purposes of our juvenile laws are outmoded and no longer valid, it should not look to this Court, but to the Legislature to change the law. Only the Legislature has the power to relax the limitations imposed by 33 V.S.A. §651(c) and §651(d) upon the general public and the news media if it believes that would be more desirable than the present law. As of the commencement of these juvenile proceedings against J.S., however, the legislative intent is clear. Juveniles, as a class, are shielded from public exposure of any proceedings conducted in juvenile court to determine delinquency.

The order of the District Court of Vermont, Unit No. 2, Chittenden Circuit, granting the public and the press the right to attend any and all proceedings in juvenile court concerning J.S. is reversed.

Notes

(a) *Review* Justice Brennan's concurring and dissenting opinion in *McKeiver*, Chapter 2, *supra*, and compare it to the above opinion.

(b) Are the reasons courts give for diminished constitutional protection in adjudicatory hearings based on enhancing the benefit of the juvenile court system, or are other factors informing such decisions?

(c) How do you think minors react to the knowledge that their adjudicatory hearings are not the same as adult criminal trials in terms of constitutional protections?

(d) Is there a principled way to resolve the civil-criminal dichotomy in juvenile courts?

(e) Notwithstanding the civil label, an adjudication of guilt in juvenile court has abiding consequences. Consider the following excerpts.

4. Ellen Marrus,"That Isn't Fair, Judge": *The Costs of Using Prior Juvenile Delinquency Adjudications in Criminal Court Sentencing*

40 Hous. L. Rev. 1323, 1343–47 (2004)

There are several issues concerning the use of juvenile adjudications in criminal court. The first question is whether juvenile adjudications may be used in criminal court for any purpose. That is, can the judge be informed of a prior adjudication as part of the sentencing report prepared by probation? The adjudications in such cases are not used to enhance the defendant's sentence beyond the statutory maximum, but they can be used by the judge to determine the actual sentence within the boundaries set by the legislature. In other words, if a crime is punishable by one to ten years, the judge can use the prior adjudication to give the maximum. That is in fact the overwhelming majority rule in the United States at both the state and federal levels. The reasoning is that judges need to have all the information so as to have an accurate history about the defendant. In some state courts we do not know how influential that factor is because the judge usually does not articulate why a greater sentence that is within the statutory limits is being set for a particular defendant. Thus, the impact of the prior adjudication may be obscured in the actual sentence imposed by the judge. Moreover, the plea bargain, which is the usual method of determining the sentence, may not reflect whether prior adjudications were considered. However, in federal courts and some states, the judge has to articulate the factors taken into consideration, and points are given for each such factor, even when the sentence is within the statutory limits for the offense.

A minority of states make it impossible to use juvenile adjudications in criminal sentencing. In these states, the juvenile records are either expunged or sealed and thus cannot be used for any purpose in criminal court, not even as part of the defendant's history.

The next category is whether juvenile adjudications can be used as sentencing enhancers in criminal court, allowing punishment beyond the statutory maximum for the particular offense. Although there is a deeper split than that regarding the use of prior juvenile adjudications as merely part of the sentencing history, the majority rule in the states is that juvenile adjudications can be used as sentence enhancers. However, in some of these states, the use of prior adjudications depends on a variety of factors, such as the age of the youth in juvenile court, the type of offense, and the length of time that has elapsed. A few states are silent on the matter. With respect to federal courts, of those that have addressed the issue, only the Ninth Circuit prohibits the use of juvenile adjudications as enhancers beyond the statutory maximum. There are several reasons given for allowing juvenile adjudications to be used as enhancers in criminal court. One, the juvenile courts are governed by due process safeguards, such as the right to counsel and proof beyond a reasonable doubt, that ensure the accuracy of factfinding. The lack of a jury trial is dismissed on the ground that judges are accurate factfinders. Thus, a finding of guilt by the judge is sufficient to assure due process. Two, repeat offenders are simply more culpable and have not learned to obey the law. This fact does not differ if it is based on a prior juvenile adjudication or an adult conviction. Indeed, some take the position that juvenile crime is a valid indicator of a "bad" kid who will grow up to become a "bad" adult criminal. Three, confidentiality of juvenile records is still maintained because sentencing reports are released not to the public, but only to those authorized to review such information.

The minority argues that juvenile adjudications are different from criminal convictions and that allowing the criminal court to, in effect, turn an adjudication into a conviction is unfair. The lack of a jury trial in juvenile court is viewed with much greater suspicion regarding the accuracy of factfinding. Moreover, it is not always apparent whether counsel has been offered and properly waived in juvenile court as required by *Gault*. In addition, juvenile proceedings are considered civil in nature and, therefore, may follow different rules of evidence than in criminal proceedings. There is not always a clear record or transcript of the proceedings, making it difficult to determine whether due process was followed. Masters or referees are permitted to hear juvenile matters in many states, and although they do not make a finding of guilt, they do give a recommendation to the judge. Thus, the state, in effect, is able to seek a finding of guilt twice.

Although most states allow the use of juvenile adjudications in criminal sentencing, there are serious consequences flowing from such action. Some of these consequences are subtle. Courts often do not carefully examine the factors that must be considered in reaching an appropriate decision regarding this matter.

5. Barry C. Feld, *The Constitutional Tension between* Apprendi *and* McKeiver: *Sentence Enhancements Based on Delinquency Convictions and the Quality of Justice in Juvenile Courts*

38 WAKE FOREST L. REV. 1111, 1184–90 (2003)

Despite the tradition of confidentiality and restricted access to juvenile records, the use of prior delinquency convictions to enhance adult sentences has a long lineage. Even prior to the adoption of state and federal sentencing guidelines, courts regularly approved the use of delinquency records to enhance the sentences of adult offenders. However, some states limit the impact of delinquency convictions on criminal sentences because of concerns about the quality of procedural justice in juvenile courts. In addition, the factual ambiguity of delinquency adjudications sometimes makes it difficult for criminal courts to determine for what offense the juvenile court actually convicted a youth when it uses those convictions for sentence enhancements or other collateral purposes.

A number of states' sentencing guidelines and the United States Sentencing Guidelines include some juvenile prior convictions in an adult defendant's criminal history score. Under California's "three-strikes" sentencing law, some juvenile felony convictions constitute "strikes" for purposes of sentence enhancements. Sentencing judges often assert the importance of access to defendants' prior records of juvenile convictions to distinguish errant offenders from recidivists. In *United States v. Davis*, the court observed that "These pubescent transgressions, when considered along with adult offenses, help the sentencing judge to determine whether the defendant has simply taken one wrong turn from the straight and narrow or is a criminal recidivist." In *United States v. McDonald*, the Court noted the policy conflict between confidentiality and punishing repeat offenders:

> Setting aside a conviction may allow a youth who has slipped to regain his footing by relieving him of the social and economic disabilities associated with a criminal record. But if a juvenile offender turns into a recidivist, the case for conferring the benefit dissipates. Society's stronger interest is in punishing appropriately an unrepentant criminal.

Although states often use delinquency adjudications for sentence enhancements, it is wrong to equate delinquency convictions with adult criminal convictions and to count them as one-for-one equivalents. Even though juvenile offenders may cause the same physical harm or property loss as older actors, their choices to engage in that conduct are not as culpable or blameworthy as that of older offenders and should not be weighted the same as adult prior convictions. Youths' ability to exercise self-control and the qualities of their judgment and decision-making are not developmentally comparable to those of adults. Youths and adults "differ in their breadth of experience, short-term versus long-term temporal perspective, attitude toward risk, impulsivity, and the importance they attach to peer influences." These differences affect their maturity of judgment, their self-control, and their culpability. State laws treat juveniles differently from adults in a host of areas — e.g., serving on a jury, voting, marrying, driving, and drinking — because of their lack of experience, propensity to engage in risky behavior, and immature judgment. I have argued that youths deserve less severe punishment than do adults when they commit the same crimes — a "youth discount" — because of their diminished responsibility. Some states' sentencing laws formally recognize youthfulness as a mitigating factor. The same principle of lesser consequences for the reduced culpability of youths applies to the weight given to their prior convictions as well as to their current sentences.

States' expanded uses of juveniles' prior records to enhance the sentences of young adult offenders raise troubling issues in light of the quality of procedural justice by which juvenile courts originally obtained those convictions. As noted above, juvenile courts in many states adjudicate as many as half of all youths delinquent without the assistance of counsel, including many convicted of felonies, and the vast majority of states deny juveniles access to a jury trial. As a result, a substantial number of delinquency adjudications occur that would not result in criminal convictions or pleas if defendants received all procedural safeguards.

6. IJA-ABA Juvenile Justice Standards Relating to Adjudication

PART I: Requisites for Adjudication Proceedings to Begin

1.1 Written petition.

A. Each jurisdiction should provide by law that the filing of a written petition giving the respondent adequate notice of the charges is a requisite for adjudication proceedings to begin.

B. If appropriate challenge is made to the legal sufficiency of the petition, the judge of the juvenile court should rule on that challenge before calling upon the respondent to plead.

1.2 Attorneys for respondent and the government.

The juvenile court should not begin adjudication proceedings unless the respondent is represented by an attorney who is present in court and the government is represented by an attorney who is present in court.

1.3 Presence of respondent.

A. The presence of the respondent should be required for adjudication proceedings to begin.

B. The respondent should be afforded the right to be present throughout adjudication proceedings, although the juvenile court should be permitted to proceed without a respondent who is voluntarily absent after adjudication proceedings have begun.

1.4 Presence of parents of respondent and others.

A. Subject to subsection D of this standard, parents and other persons required by law to be notified of adjudication proceedings should be entitled to be present throughout the proceedings.

. . . .

1.5 Opportunity to prepare for adjudication proceedings.

A. The juvenile court should determine whether the attorneys for the respondent and the government have had a reasonable opportunity to prepare for adjudication proceedings.

B. Attorneys for the respondent and the government have an obligation to exercise due diligence in preparation for adjudication proceedings and an obligation to make any motion for continuance at such time as to cause the least possible disruption of the work of the juvenile court.

PART IV: Contested Adjudication Procedures

4.1 Trial by jury.

A. Each jurisdiction should provide by law that the respondent may demand trial by jury in adjudication proceedings when the respondent has denied the allegations of the petition.

B. Each jurisdiction should provide by law that the jury may consist of as few as [six] persons and that the verdict of the jury must be unanimous.

4.2 Rules of evidence.

The rules of evidence employed in the trial of criminal cases should be used in delinquency adjudication proceedings when the respondent has denied the allegations of the petition.

4.3 Burden of proof.

Each jurisdiction should provide by law that the government is required to adduce proof beyond a reasonable doubt that the respondent engaged in the conduct alleged when the respondent has denied the allegations of the petition.

4.4 Social information.

A. Except in preadjudication hearings in which social history information concerning the respondent is relevant and admissible, such as a detention hearing or a hearing to consider transfer to criminal court for prosecution as an adult, the judge of the juvenile court should not view a social history report or receive social history information concerning a respondent who has not been adjudicated delinquent.

B. Each jurisdiction should provide by law that when a jury is the trier of fact, it should not view a social history report or receive social history information concerning the respondent.

PART VI: Public Access to Adjudication Proceedings.

6.1 Right to a public trial.

Each jurisdiction should provide by law that a respondent in juvenile court adjudication proceeding has a right to a public trial.

6.2 Implementing the right to a public trial.

A. Each jurisdiction should provide by law that the respondent, after consulting with counsel, may waive the right to a public trial.

B. Each jurisdiction should provide by law that the judge of the juvenile court has discretion to permit members of the public who have a legitimate interest in the proceedings or in the work of the court, including representatives of the news media, to view adjudication proceedings when the respondent has waived the right to a public trial.

C. The judge of the juvenile court should honor any request by the respondent, respondent's attorney, or family that specified members of the public be permitted to observe the respondent's adjudication proceeding when the respondent has waived the right to a public trial.

D. The judge of the juvenile court should use judicial power to prevent distractions from and disruptions of adjudication proceedings and should use that power to order removed from the courtroom any member of the public causing a distraction or disruption.

6.3 Prohibiting disclosure of respondent's identity

A. Each jurisdiction should provide by law that members of the public permitted by the judge of the juvenile court to observe adjudication proceedings may not disclose to others the identity of the respondent when the respondent has waived the right to a public trial.

B. Each jurisdiction should provide by law that the judge of the juvenile court should announce to members of the public present to view an adjudication proceeding when the respondent has waived the right to a public trial that they may not disclose to others the identity of the respondent.

H. Dispositional Hearings

1. Statutes

a. *Tex. Family Code* § 54.04 (a), (b), (c), (d) (1) (2)

Disposition Hearing

(a) The disposition hearing shall be separate, distinct, and subsequent to the adjudication hearing. There is no right to a jury at the disposition hearing unless the child is in jeopardy of a determinate sentence under Subsection (d)(3) or (m), in which case, the child is entitled to a jury of 12 persons to determine the sentence.

(b) At the disposition hearing, the juvenile court may consider written reports from probation officers, professional court employees, or professional consultants in addition to the testimony of witnesses. Prior to the disposition hearing, the court shall provide the attorney for the child with access to all written matter to be considered in disposition. The court may order counsel not to reveal items to the child or the child's parent, guardian, or guardian ad litem if such disclosure would materially harm the treatment and rehabilitation of the child or would substantially decrease the likelihood of receiving information from the same or similar sources in the future.

(c) No disposition may be made under this section unless the child is in need of rehabilitation or the protection of the public or the child requires that disposition be made. If the court or jury does not so find, the court shall dismiss the child and enter a final judgment without any disposition. No disposition placing the child on probation outside the child's home may be made under this section unless the court or jury finds that the child, in the child's home, cannot be provided the quality of care and level of support and supervision that the child needs to meet the conditions of the probation.

(d) If the court or jury makes the finding specified in Subsection (c) allowing the court to make a disposition in the case:

(1) the court or jury may, in addition to any order required or authorized under Section 54.041 or 54.042, place the child on probation on such reasonable and lawful terms as the court may determine:

(A) in the child's own home or in the custody of a relative or other fit person; or

(B) subject to the finding under Subsection (c) on the placement of the child outside the child's home, in:

(i) a suitable foster home; or

(ii) a suitable public or private institution or agency, except the Texas Youth Commission;

(2) if the court or jury found at the conclusion of the adjudication hearing that the child engaged in delinquent conduct that violates a penal law of this state or the United States of the grade of felony or, if the requirements of Subsection (s) or (t) are met, of the grade of misdemeanor, and if the petition was not approved by the grand jury under Section

53.045, the court may commit the child to the Texas Youth Commission without a determinate sentence.

b. *Cal. Welf. & Inst. Code § 727*

Order for care, supervision, custody, maintenance and support of
ward of court; placement; counseling; parental participation

(a) When a minor is adjudged a ward of the court on the ground that he or she is a person described by Section 601 or 602 the court may make any and all reasonable orders for the care, supervision, custody, conduct, maintenance, and support of the minor, including medical treatment, subject to further order of the court. To facilitate coordination and cooperation among government agencies, the court may, after giving notice and an opportunity to be heard, join in the juvenile court proceedings any agency that the court determines has failed to meet a legal obligation to provide services to the minor. However, no governmental agency shall be joined as a party in a juvenile court proceeding in which a minor has been ordered committed to the Department of the Youth Authority. In any proceeding in which an agency is joined, the court shall not impose duties upon the agency beyond those mandated by law. Nothing in this section shall prohibit agencies which have received notice of the hearing on joinder from meeting prior to the hearing to coordinate services for the minor.

The court has no authority to order services unless it has been determined through the administrative process of an agency that has been joined as a party, that the minor is eligible for those services. With respect to mental health assessment, treatment, and case management services pursuant to Chapter 26.5 of the Government Code, the court's determination shall be limited to whether the agency has complied with that chapter.

In the discretion of the court, a ward may be ordered to be on probation without supervision of the probation officer. The court, in so ordering, may impose on the ward any and all reasonable conditions of behavior as may be appropriate under this disposition. In all other cases, the court shall order the care, custody, and control of the minor to be under the supervision of the probation officer who may place the minor in any of the following:

(1) The approved home of a relative, or the approved home of a nonrelative, extended family member as defined in Section 362.7. When a decision has been made to place the minor in the home of a relative, the court may authorize the relative to give legal consent for the minor's medical, surgical, and dental care and education as if the relative caretaker were the custodial parent of the minor.

(2) A suitable licensed community care facility.

(3) With a foster family agency to be placed in a suitable licensed foster family home or certified family home which has been certified by the agency as meeting licensing standards.

(b) When a minor has been adjudged a ward of the court on the ground that he or she is a person described in Section 601 or 602 and the court finds that notice has been given in accordance with Section 661, and when the court orders that a parent or guardian shall retain custody of that minor either subject to or without the supervision of the probation officer, the parent or guardian may be required to participate with that minor in a counseling or education program including, but not limited to, parent education and parenting programs operated by community colleges, school districts, or other appropriate agencies designated by the court.

(c) The juvenile court may direct any and all reasonable orders to the parents and guardians of the minor who is the subject of any proceedings under this chapter as the court deems necessary and proper to carry out subdivisions (a) and (b), including orders to appear before a county financial evaluation officer and orders directing the parents or guardians to ensure the minor's regular school attendance and to make reasonable efforts to obtain appropriate educational services necessary to meet the needs of the minor.

When counseling or other treatment services are ordered for the minor, the parent, guardian, or foster parent shall be ordered to participate in those services, unless participation by the parent, guardian, or foster parent is deemed by the court to be inappropriate or potentially detrimental to the child.

c. *Cal. Welf. & Inst. Code* § 730

Minor violating criminal law; ward of court;
commitment to juvenile home; requiring ward to work

(a) When a minor is adjudged a ward of the court on the ground that he or she is a person described by Section 602, the court may order any of the types of treatment referred to in Section 727, and as an additional alternative, may commit the minor to a juvenile home, ranch, camp, or forestry camp. If there is no county juvenile home, ranch, camp, or forestry camp within the county, the court may commit the minor to the county juvenile hall.

(b) When a ward described in subdivision (a) is placed under the supervision of the probation officer or committed to the care, custody, and control of the probation officer, the court may make any and all reasonable orders for the conduct of the ward including the requirement that the ward go to work and earn money for the support of his or her dependents or to effect reparation and in either case that the ward keep an account of his or her earnings and report the same to the probation officer and apply these earnings as directed by the court. The court may impose and require any and all reasonable conditions that it may determine fitting and proper to the end that justice may be done and the reformation and rehabilitation of the ward enhanced.

(c) When a ward described in subdivision (a) is placed under the supervision of the probation officer or committed to the care, custody, and control of the probation officer, and is required as a condition of probation to participate in community service or graffiti cleanup, the court may impose a condition that if the minor unreasonably fails to attend or unreasonably leaves prior to completing the assigned daily hours of community service or graffiti cleanup, a law enforcement officer may take the minor into custody for the purpose of returning the minor to the site of the community service or graffiti cleanup.

d. *Cal. Welf. & Inst. Code* § 731

Minors violating laws defining crime and adjudged ward of court;
orders court may issue; maximum confinement period.

(a) If a minor is adjudged a ward of the court on the ground that he or she is a person described by Section 602, the court may order any of the types of treatment referred to in Sections 727 and 730 and, in addition, may order the ward to make restitution, to pay a fine up to the amount of two hundred fifty dollars ($250) for deposit in the county treasury if the court finds that the minor has the financial ability to pay the fine, or to participate in uncompensated work programs or the court may commit the ward to a sheltered-care facility or may order that the ward and his or her family or guardian participate in a program of professional counseling as arranged and directed by the probation officer as a condition of continued custody of that minor or may commit the minor to the Department of the Youth Authority.

(b) A minor committed to the Department of the Youth Authority may not be held in physical confinement for a period of time in excess of the maximum period of imprisonment which could be imposed upon an adult convicted of the offense or offenses which brought or continued the minor under the jurisdiction of the juvenile court. A minor committed to the Department of the Youth Authority also may not be held in physical confinement for a period of time in excess of the maximum term of physical confinement set by the court based upon the facts and circumstances of the matter or matters which brought or continued the minor under the jurisdiction of the juvenile court, which may not exceed the maximum period of adult confinement as determined pursuant to this section. This section does not limit the power of the Youth Authority Board to retain the minor on parole status for the period permitted by Section 1769.

2. Cases

State ex rel. D.D.H.

269 S.E.2d 401 (W. Va. 1980)

In this case we shall endeavor, with some apprehension, to clarify the proper procedures at the dispositional stage of a juvenile proceeding. The facts of these three consolidated cases provide an excellent opportunity to explore the nature of the juvenile disposition. Indeed this particular child's journey into the juvenile justice system constitutes a veritable primer on how a juvenile should not be handled by the courts under either our prior rulings or the applicable sections of the W.Va. Code.

On 25 April 1979, a delinquency petition was filed against petitioner, then a twelve-year-old female, charging her with four crimes that would be felonious had they been committed by an adult....

Having determined that the delinquency conviction must be reversed, we turn to the dispositional stage of the proceeding so that upon remand a proper record can be made. Petitioner, who was thirteen years old at the time of the disposition and had never been adjudicated delinquent, was committed to the most restrictive alternative available, the Industrial Home for Girls in Salem, West Virginia. At the dispositional hearing, which was held 5 July 1979, the court relied primarily on the testimony of a social worker for the Department of Welfare, Joseph Corbin, who recommended that the petitioner be placed in the West Virginia Industrial School. He testified that he contacted two other less restrictive alternatives, namely, the Burlington United Methodist Home for Children and Youth, and Davis-Stuart, Inc., both of which refused to accept petitioner. Upon cross-examination, it became clear that counsel for petitioner had suggested the Odyssey House, a group home in Morgantown, to Mr. Corbin, but that he had not pursued that possibility because he was unfamiliar with the facility. Testimony was also received from a police officer, Raymond Burcker, who said that he had seen the petitioner out late at night standing outside a bar on at least two occasions. Petitioner's mother appeared as a witness, and she testified that she had been very sick during the past year and that she had sought the aid of the Welfare Department to place petitioner in a foster home. Apparently the Welfare Department did not respond.

The court relied upon the recommendation of Dr. Bradley Soulee that petitioner "has a lot more potential to develop were she in a more highly structured environment than she has been in the past." While concluding that she had an extremely chaotic family life and a number of behavioral problems such as truancy, car theft, and drug abuse, Dr. Soulee also found petitioner to be "alert, articulate, behaviorally appropriate, and * * *cooperative * * *throughout the interview." The recommendation for a structured environment was seconded by Dr. Roberts, a clinical psychologist who tested petitioner.

The Court also considered the report on petitioner completed by the social service worker, Joseph Corbin. He reported that: petitioner's home should have been condemned as unfit for human habitation; petitioner's mother had been hospitalized for several weeks during the winter of 1979 with cervical cancer; petitioner's stepfather deserted the family as soon as the medical problem appeared; petitioner's stepfather had a drinking and drug problem which prompted him physically to abuse the petitioner; petitioner's father deserted her mother three weeks after petitioner was born; petitioner's mother had been a welfare client since D.D.H. was born; and, although petitioner had missed over 100 days of school her only major behavioral problem was stealing on one occasion.

I

At the outset it is important to recognize that the juvenile law in West Virginia has been in substantial turmoil since this Court's decision in *State ex rel. Harris v. Calendine*, which, among other things, prompted an entire revision of the statutory juvenile law. Historically, protecting society from juvenile delinquency and helping juvenile offenders modify their behavior have been seen as complementary goals of the juvenile law; however, it is now generally recognized that caring for the juvenile and controlling the juvenile are often quite contradictory processes. Much of our juvenile law at the moment is predicated upon a healthy skepticism about the capacity of the State and its agents to help children when they are incarcerated in one of the juvenile detention facilities. Thus, the control of juveniles and the treatment of juveniles (if that expression can be used without conjuring Kafkaesque images) are frequently irreconcilable goals. Furthermore, children can be dangerous, destructive, abusive, and otherwise thoroughly anti-social, which prompts an entirely understandable expectation in society of protection, even if we have matured beyond expecting retribution.

The dispositional stage of a juvenile proceeding is designed to do something which is almost impossible, namely, to reconcile: (1) society's interest in being protected from dangerous and disruptive children; (2) society's interest in nurturing its children in such a way that they will be productive and successful adults; (3) society's interest in providing a deterrent to other children who, but for the specter of the juvenile law, would themselves become disruptive and unamenable to adult control; (4) the citizens' demand that children be responsible for invasion of personal rights; and, (5) the setting of an example of care, love, and forgiveness by the engines of the state in the hope that such qualities will be emulated by the subject children. While retribution is considered an unhealthy instinct and, conceivably, an immoral instinct in an enlightened society, nonetheless, State imposed retribution has historically been the quid pro quo of the State's monopoly of force and its proscription of individual retribution. Retribution is merely another way of saying that children are to be treated as responsible moral agents.

II

It is possible to make the dispositional stage of a juvenile proceeding so burdensome in requiring exhaustive examination of all "less restrictive alternatives," no matter how speculative, that we, in effect, direct lower courts to abandon all hope of confining a child. That is not the clear purport, however, of W.Va. Code, 49-5-13(b) (1978) which says:

> In disposition the court shall not be limited to the relief sought in the petition and shall give precedence to the least restrictive of the following alternatives consistent with the best interests and welfare of the public and the child * * *.

W.Va. Code 49-5-13(b)(5) (1978) says:

> Upon a finding that no less restrictive alternative would accomplish the requisite rehabilitation of the child, and upon an adjudication of delinquency, commit the child to an industrial home or correctional institution for children. Commitments shall not exceed the maximum term for which an adult could have been sentenced for the same offense, with discretion as to discharge to rest with the director of the institution, who may release the child and return him to the court for further disposition; * * *.

. . . .

Chapter 49 of the W.Va. Code covering child welfare is clearly committed to the rehabilitative model. As we noted in *State ex rel. Harris v. Calendine,* the Legislature could choose to punish children guilty of criminal conduct in the same manner as it punishes adults, but as a matter of public policy the Legislature provided instead for a comprehensive system of child welfare. The aim of this system is to protect and rehabilitate children, not to punish them.

The rehabilitative model requires a great deal of information about the child at the dispositional hearing. Much of that information must necessarily focus on the critical issue of whether it is possible for the State or other social service agencies to help the child. Although helping the child is the first concern of the juvenile law, it is not the only concern, since at the operational rather than theoretical level, the rehabilitative approach has dramatic limitations, preeminent among which is that it interferes both with the deterrence of other children and the protection of society. While Code 49-5-13(b) explicitly recognizes this problem, we have not yet refined an approach which intelligently uses procedure to arrive at sufficient information to permit a balancing of the child's liberty interest with society's need for protection and deterrence.

III

There is no alternative in our efforts to reconcile the competing goals of the juvenile justice system but to enter reluctantly into a brief discussion of the age-old philosophical controversy about free will and determinism. Neither this Court nor anyone else in the world will ever definitively answer the question of whether mankind is determined or is possessed of free will. The philosophy of the law has generally accepted that at times people are determined while at other times they have free will. Pragmatically our legal tradition has answered the question by rules which recognize that men are guided entirely neither by external forces nor by free will; every person is influenced by both but is never totally controlled by either.

As perplexing as the philosophical argument over free will versus determinism may be, no single concept is as critical to the dispositional stage of a juvenile proceeding. The facts of the case before us clearly show a child whose sorrows are largely the result of external forces. That she is difficult, ungovernable, and unmanageable is not disputed in the elaborate record before us, yet she was to the social forces around her the "wingless fly in the hands of small boys." On the other hand, hypothetically, we can envisage a child from a perfect middle class background, selling drugs to other children for no apparent reason other than the allure of enormous profits. To speculate that deep inside that child's psyche there is some hidden, predetermining factor is not adequate for the "deterrent" or "responsibility" purposes of the juvenile law. Furthermore, it is a negation of our entire tradition to say that every social transgression is the result of "illness." Many a very sane and well adjusted person has found the allure of illegal profits compelling. Children can, and often do, engage in delinquent conduct for no better reason than that they prefer having money to not having money.

Her home as reported by Joseph Corbin, the social worker, also paints a grim picture: * * *The complex ... should have been condemned several years ago as unfit for human habitation. Charles Town has shut off all city services and water to the apartments due to non-payment of bills. As far as sanitary conditions, one goes outdoors in the weeds, which have all but taken over the area. Not only is Mrs. _____ and her three children living in the apartment, she is also allowing her brother, _____, and his female companion to reside there also.

Some things we have enough knowledge to treat and other things we do not have enough knowledge to treat. Broken homes, uncaring parents, learning disabilities, Dickensian poverty, parental abuse, and an unhealthy environment are all things which the State, "solicitous of the welfare of its children but also mindful of other demands upon the State budget for humanitarian purposes," can begin to cure. Where, however, no factor or factors can be isolated which we can treat, or which our over-all view of the State's role in providing social justice deems not worthy of a treatment approach, we must, for want of any other reasonable alternative, accept the free will model, the goals of which are deterrence and juvenile responsibility.

IV

At the dispositional stage of the juvenile proceeding there are a number of actors whose roles have been established by statute. The first major actor is obviously the judge who is entitled to request the juvenile probation officer or State department worker to make an investigation of the environment of the child and the alternative dispositions possible. The second actor is the probation officer or State department worker who must fulfill this obligation, and the third actor is the counsel for the petitioner who is entitled to review any report made by the probation officer or welfare worker seventy-two hours before the dispositional hearing. In addition there is the child and his parents, guardian, or adult relatives, and the representatives of any social service agencies, including the schools, which have been involved in the case. Since the threshold question at any dispositional hearing is whether the child is delinquent because of his own free will or for environmental reasons which society can attack directly, all of the actors in the dispositional drama should concentrate their attention initially on that one subject. Obviously this is a question which the trial judge has always answered in his own mind. However, the thrust of the formal procedural model which has been evolving is that this question be developed on the record and reasons for determining a particular disposition be articulated for appellate review. We shall now focus on the role of each major actor.

THE ROLE OF COURT APPOINTED COUNSEL:

The dispositional stage of any juvenile proceeding may be the most important stage in the entire process;[12] therefore, it is the obligation of any court appointed or retained counsel to continue active and vigorous representation of the child through that stage. We have already held that counsel has a duty to investigate all resources available to find the

---

12. "Since the majority of juvenile delinquency hearings involve pleas of guilty, * * *the disposition decision may be the most critical stage of all and the one most urgently requiring an advocate for the child."

least restrictive alternative, and here we confirm that holding. Court appointed counsel must make an independent investigation of the child's background. Counsel should present to the court any facts which could lead the court to conclude that the child's environment is a major contributing factor to his misbehavior. In this regard counsel should investigate the child's performance in school, his family background, the level of concern and leadership on the part of his parents, the physical conditions under which the child is living, and any health problems. Counsel must also inform himself in detail about the facilities both inside and outside the State of West Virginia which are able to help children.

Armed with adequate information, counsel can then present the court with all reasonable alternative dispositions to incarceration and should have taken the initial steps to secure the tentative acceptance of the child into those facilities. It is not sufficient to suggest upon the record as an abstract proposition that there are alternatives; it is the affirmative obligation of counsel to advise the court of the exact terms, conditions, and costs of such alternatives, whether the Department of Welfare or any other source can pay for such alternative, and under what conditions any alternative facilities would be willing to accept the child.

The faithful discharge of these duties requires substantial industry; however, appointed counsel is entitled to be compensated for his time up to the statutory limit set for the criminal charges fund. Furthermore, energetic advocacy implies that the court must accommodate an adversarial proceeding at the disposition stage. In the case at bar, the court reacted to the legitimate efforts of the appointed attorney to arrange an alternative disposition by finding him in contempt and removing him from his appointment. Such practices are obviously condemned since it is envisaged that the child shall have an advocate who will make a record.

The court undermined the efforts of counsel from the outset of the trial: counsel was given approximately thirty minutes to prepare before the first detention hearing, after which petitioner was placed in the Jefferson County Jail; after counsel obtained release of petitioner she was again placed in the Jefferson County Jail for failing to attend school and counsel received no notice of the second detention hearing; after counsel obtained release of petitioner she was arrested and taken before the court who placed her in the Morgan County Jail again without notice or presence of the child's counsel and with no record save the summary order; after petitioner was adjudicated delinquent, counsel represented the willingness of the Odyssey House in Morgantown to take petitioner for a trial period but the court refused all less restrictive alternatives; and, after placement in the Industrial Home for Girls counsel continued actively to pursue probation for petitioner to which the court reacted by withdrawing the appointment of counsel and requiring his appearance at a contempt hearing. This conduct is so unjustifiable that the State chose not even to address the validity of the contempt citation in its brief. We grant the writ of prohibition in connection with the contempt charges.

THE ROLE OF THE PROBATION OFFICER OR WELFARE WORKER:

The probation officer or welfare worker when requested by the judge is also responsible for discovering whether there are forces which are at work upon the child which either the Department of Welfare or other social service agencies can correct. In the case before us it is obvious that the petitioner had no adult supervision whatsoever and that she was left to fend for herself in the back streets. Obviously, before incarcerating a first offender like the petitioner it would have been incumbent upon the Department of Welfare to find a suitable environment for her. The record amply demonstrates from the history of the petitioner after this Court released her from the industrial school, that the petitioner is a somewhat unmanageable and ungovernable child who, at the time, would not remain in a juvenile refuge. Nonetheless, absent at least one predisposition incidence of flight from a reasonable alternative, it was quite improper for the court to place her in the first instance in the industrial school. Upon remand the court must focus on her level of cooperation at the time she is again considered for disposition at the remand.

The record before us also demonstrates that the Department of Welfare did not intervene with this child upon her initial arrest, although any inquiry into her background would have disclosed at the detention hearing that she was in need of help. The appropriate time for the Department of Welfare or the juvenile probation officer to intervene is at the first sign of trouble.

THE ROLE OF THE COURT:

It is the obligation of the court to hear all witnesses who might shed light upon the proper disposition of a child and before incarcerating a child, to find facts upon the record which would lead a reasonable appellate court to conclude in the words of the statute, either that "no less restrictive alternative would accomplish the requisite rehabilitation of the child * * *" or "the welfare of the public" requires incarceration. Where the court directs incarceration, he should affirmatively find upon the record either that the child's behavioral problem is not the result of social conditions beyond the child's control, but rather of an intentional failure on the part of the child to conform his actions to the law, or that the child will be dangerous if any other disposition is used, or that the child will not cooperate with any rehabilitative program absent physical restraint. Where the court concludes that simple punishment will be a more effective rehabilitative device than anything else, the conclusion is certainly legitimate and within the discretion of the trial court; nonetheless, the trial court must elaborate on the record his reasons for that conclusion.

If the proceeding is merely the last in a long series involving the same child, the court should set forth any "less restrictive alternatives" which have already been tried and the actions of the child after those alternatives were implemented. Even when the child's behavior results from environmental factors, the court may find the child to pose an imminent danger to society because he will flee from all but secure facilities and, therefore, conclude that incarceration is the only reasonable alternative.

The court has a duty to insure that the child's social history is reviewed intelligently so that an individualized treatment plan may be designed when appropriate. This information also insures that the disposition decision is not made simply by reference to the very misbehavior which is the ground for the juvenile proceeding. The effectiveness of treatment is disputed to say the least, and this is particularly true whenever commitment to an institution is involved. Therefore, the judge making the dispositional determination should not place a child who is not dangerous and who can be accommodated elsewhere in an institution under the guise of "treating" the child.

While in the hearing before this Court it appeared that progress has been made in providing basic education and counseling in the State's industrial schools, the fact that these schools have improved does not make them the proper place for "rehabilitation" unless it appears that the child is either dangerous or must be restrained in a secure facility in order to prevent his flight.

THE ROLE OF THE CHILD:

When we are dealing with children between the ages of twelve and eighteen it must be recognized that no placement plan short of a secure, prison-like facility is capable of having a beneficial effect without the cooperation of the child. Therefore, it is impossible to avoid the conclusion that there is an affirmative obligation on the part of the child to co-operate. Certainly one instance of a child failing to follow some Rhadamanthine ruling of a circuit court does not justify instant removal to an industrial school, but a consistent course of noncooperation, particularly when combined with a predilection to commit dangerous or destructive acts does justify the court in resorting to commitment. This rule must be tempered, however, by the conclusion that where the agents of the State are gross incompetents and where the treatment and rehabilitative programs prescribed for the child are unreasonable, this Court will not permit incarceration where the true fault lies with the State and not with the child.

When however, there is a consistent pattern of noncooperation which makes alternative rehabilitative programs impossible, the court should set forth the facts upon the record so that this Court will understand why the trial court concludes that there are no alternatives to placement in an institution.

V

In reaching the conclusion that rehabilitation alone does not exhaust the goals of a juvenile disposition, and that responsibility and deterrence are also important elements in our juvenile philosophy, we have not simply embraced a conservative theory that juvenile delinquents need to be punished. Liberals and conservatives alike may find solace in this opinion because we acknowledge what has been an unspoken conclusion: our treatment looks a lot like punishment. At first glance an agreement among commentators at both philosophical poles may appear strange; however, both share the conclusion that treatment is often disguised punishment. Liberals are pleased that juvenile courts must exercise restraint in resorting to questionable "treatments" at the dispositional stage and conservatives are pleased that it has been admitted that punishment can be a viable goal of any given juvenile disposition.

While the conservatives talk about punishment as "retribution" and the cornerstone of "responsibility," the liberal child advocates speak in terms of the "right to punishment." Once the rehabilitative model is accepted, the next fight is always to show that "treatment" is often a caricature [of] something worthy of a story of Kafka or a Soviet mental hospital. Therefore, while the conservatives throw up their hands because they believe punishment works better than treatment, the juvenile advocates return increasingly to punishment on the grounds that punishment is much less punishing than "treatment." Therefore, while our opinion in this case is hardly definitive, it is designed to give guidance concerning the factors to be developed in the record. In the final analysis, since we are dealing with a love of things irreconcilable, the successful implementation of the juvenile law must rest in the sound discretion of the trial court. A record which discloses conclusively that the trial court has considered all relevant factual material and dispositional theories will permit us to make an intelligent review, keeping in mind that discretionary, dispositional decisions of the trial courts should only be reversed where they are not supported by the evidence or are wrong as a matter of law.

Accordingly, … the judgment … adjudging petitioner delinquent is reversed and the case is remanded.…

McGRAW, Justice, concurring:

While the press of business at term's end has lessened the opportunity of everyone on the court to reflect upon Justice Neely's majority opinion, I offer these comments.

While trudging through the turgid prose, I had little cause to stumble over the answers to the questions which this case presented. I am moved to comment upon the extensive dicta which could be interpreted by the unwary to foreshadow a drift by this Court toward a "punishment model" of treatment for juvenile offenders. While the majority opinion's discussion may be revealing, it should not be viewed as constituting an endorsement by this Court of all the attendant legal concepts it purportedly encompasses. I believe that characterization in terms of liberal and conservative political philosophies is inappropriate to the issues at hand. These issues do not lend themselves to simplistic partisan political analysis. Reasonable people of good will, of whatever political persuasion, desire decent, rehabilitative treatment for troubled children. Judicial opinions should not be seen as attempting to dance the razor's edge between political extremes.

Elious Tyler, Jr., A Delinquent Child v. Texas
512 S.W.2d 46 (Tex. Civ. App. 1974)

The appellant, Elious Tyler, a juvenile, was charged with theft of personal property of a value less than $50. In accordance with the requirements of the Texas Family Code, two distinct hearings were had. In the first—the adjudication hearing—the juvenile affirmed the charges in writing and was adjudged to have engaged in delinquent conduct. No complaint is made of this proceeding.

At a subsequent disposition hearing, appellant was committed to the care, custody, and control of the Texas Youth Council. It is this hearing of which appellant complains in this review. His sole point of error is that § 54.04(b) denies his constitutional right to be confronted by and to cross-examine witnesses against him. The section challenged provides:

> "(b) At the disposition hearing, the juvenile court may consider written reports from probation officers, professional court employees, or professional consultants in addition to the testimony of witnesses. Prior to the disposition hearing, the court shall provide the attorney for the child with access to all written matter to be considered by the court in disposition. The court may order counsel not to reveal items to the child or his parent, guardian, or guardian ad litem if such disclosure would materially harm the treatment and rehabilitation of the child or would substantially decrease the likelihood of receiving information from the same or similar sources in the future."

In this disposition hearing, the court permitted the probation officer to testify regarding the contents of the "Analysis of the Factors" which contained opinions of a psychologist. The psychologist did not appear....

[O]ur legislature has determined that children should be treated with some difference than adults in criminal matters. The motives behind these differences are noble, intended to shield children from the consequences of criminal trials, convictions, and punishment. The procedure emanates from compassion, and society's hope that gentleness, understanding, and rehabilitation to the young offender will prevent the same person, on reaching adulthood, from criminal conduct. Indeed, we reject the contention that § 54.04(b) deprives a child of a basic constitutional right. If we are to apply all our rules and procedures of criminal law to children, we might as well abolish Title 3 and treat them in the same fashion as adults. We believe this action would be regressive. We are confident that the approach of Title 3 is another step by mankind in its effort to find a better and a more just way of life.

. . . .

Here there is no complaint that appellant was not accorded due process in the adjudication hearing. In the disposition hearing, there is good reason to give the judge the latitude afforded by § 54.04(b) to consider all factors in deciding what disposition to make. Any possible danger to the child is removed by the requirement that the court provide the attorney for the child with all written matter to be considered by the court in disposition. We conclude that § 54.04 of Title 3 of the Family Code is not unconstitutional as denying due process; we overrule appellant's point of error and affirm the judgment of the trial court.

In the Matter of L.G.
728 S.W.2d 939 (Tex. 1987)

Appellant, a sixteen-year-old girl, was found by a jury to have engaged in delinquent conduct by knowingly or intentionally possessing a controlled substance, cocaine. The trial court's order committed appellant to the Texas Youth Commission. We will affirm that part of the court's order adjudicating that appellant engaged in delinquent conduct; however, in all other respects the judgment of the trial court is vacated.

THE CONTROVERSY

Appellant and two other minors were videotaped during school hours on private property near Lockhart High School. The videotape showed appellant and the two other girls engaging in conduct consistent with the ingestion of cocaine. None of the powdery substance apparently consumed by the girls, was recovered by the authorities, so no chemical analysis of any sort was made. Appellant was nevertheless adjudicated delinquent for possessing cocaine based on the testimony by one of the girls that appellant had stated she had some cocaine, and that appellant and the other girls decided to "sniff" or "snort" the cocaine.

The original order of adjudication and disposition filed on August 27, 1985, failed to state any reasons for the trial court's disposition committing appellant to the Texas Youth Commission. Consequently, appellant filed a motion for statement of reasons for disposition. In response, the trial court on December 17, 1985, entered what is entitled "Order of Adjudication and Disposition Nunc Pro Tunc," which specified as reasons for its disposition the following:

1. The conduct made the basis of this juvenile petition involved the use of cocaine, a penalty group I controlled substance.

2. The use of said controlled substance took place during the school hours within a close proximity to the Lockhart High School campus.

3. The use of said controlled substance took place in public view in the presence of other students.

4. The child's acquisition of said controlled substance occurred in a classroom during school hours.

5. The child involved other students in the use of said controlled substance.

After reviewing the order, we found the reasons given for the specific disposition amounted to little more than a recitation of the details of the delinquent conduct engaged in by appellant. We noted in particular the absence of any explanation why appellant was committed to the Texas Youth Commission, especially in light of an extremely favorable juvenile probation report. Hence, we sustained appellant's seventh point of error addressing the adequacy of the reasons stated in the order of disposition, and we remanded the cause to the trial court with instructions for the trial judge to render a proper disposition order specifically stating the reasons for the disposition chosen and to file that corrected order with this Court.

The amended order of adjudication and disposition filed by the trial court is identical to the December 17, 1985 order, with the exception of the following two sentences which we will quote in full:

> The court further finds that the best interest of the child and the best interest of society will be served by committing her to the care, custody, and control of the Texas Youth Commission *because there exists in the community of Lockhart, Texas, where this conduct occurred, a great public awareness and concern about the problem of drug abuse in both the schools and the community at large.* Because of the findings stated above, the court believes that the best interests of society in insuring that conduct of the nature involved in this case is not to be tolerated, particularly in the school system, far outweigh any interests to be served by placing the child on probation.

. . . .

DISPOSITION

. . . .

In appellant's eighth and ninth points of error, she challenges the sufficiency of the evidence to support the trial court's disposition order committing appellant to the Texas Youth Commission. [A] trial court may commit a child to the Texas Youth Commission following a hearing in which the child has been adjudicated delinquent. In challenging a court's order of disposition on appeal, the child must show that the trial court "abused its discretion" in making the disposition it did.

One of the many reasons underlying the Tex. Fam. Code § 54.04(f) requirement that the trial court specifically state its reasons for the disposition ordered is that it furnishes a basis for the appellate court to determine whether the reasons recited are supported by the evidence and whether they are sufficient to justify the order of disposition.

After reviewing cases in other contexts upholding the trial court's disposition order committing a delinquent child to the Texas Youth Commission, we find a definite fact pattern is present. These cases denote a proper commitment when the delinquent child involved has engaged in some type of violent activity which makes them potentially dangerous to the public, or has been given a negative recommendation for probation. . . .

The juvenile probation report on appellant which represents the *only* evidence in the record regarding disposition indicates appellant should have been placed on probation. The probability of appellant successfully completing probation was rated as good. This prediction was based on several factors, including the existence of a supportive family, the lack of any prior juvenile referrals, and the existence of a stable academic school record. In addition, . . . the probation report denotes an absence of any antisocial behavioral characteristics necessitating a structured environment such as the Texas Youth Commission. In fact, the record shows the contrary since it reflects appellant served as President of the Future Homemakers of America during her sophomore and junior high school years and engaged in activities such as tennis, volleyball, and baseball. The present record, therefore, indicates that appellant has in the past engaged in activities consistent with normal, healthy teenage socialization. Absent is *any evidence* of a need for the strict environment of the Texas Youth Commission.

[The] Texas Family Code provides that Title 3, covering delinquent children, shall be construed to effectuate the purposes of providing care, protection, and the wholesome moral, mental, and physical development of children *along with* the protection of the welfare of the community. Subsection (4) provides that these purposes are to be achieved *whenever possible* in a family environment and that the child is to be separated from his parents *only* when it is necessary for his welfare or it is in the interest of public safety. There is no evidence in the record to support the trial court's conclusion that commitment to the Texas Youth Commission is warranted under the circumstances, nor is there any evidence that the delinquent conduct *alone* requires that the public be protected. Furthermore, we find no language in the Family Code indicating a public interest in "deterring" criminal activity which is preeminent over any interest in the rehabilitation of the child in his home environment. Based on the language noted above, we find just the opposite.

While we may not substitute our decision for the trial court's decision, we also may not affirm its decision when there is no evidence in the record to support the conclusions made. Under the evaluation made of the child in the probation report, the trial court may have been justified in disagreeing with those conclusions. However, when the *only* evidence in the record is to the effect that local services were available and that appellant could have been rehabilitated locally, there then became no basis for the reasons given in the order, *i.e.,* there was no evidence to support the reasons given. Appellant's eighth point of error alleging there existed no evidence to support the trial court's dispositional order is therefore sustained.

In the Interest of S.J., A Child
304 N.W.2d 685 (N.D. 1981)

S. J. appeals from an order issued by the Juvenile Court of Stutsman County on March 31, 1981, denying her motion for a stay of disposition. S. J. has submitted to this court a motion to stay the order of disposition entered by the juvenile court. We deny the motion for a stay of the juvenile court's order of disposition.

On January 19, 1981, a petition was filed in the Juvenile Court of Stutsman County which alleged that S. J. was a delinquent child because S. J. and another juvenile had committed the offense of robbery. At a hearing held on February 3, 1981, the juvenile court determined that S. J. was a delinquent child. On March 31, 1981, a dispositional hearing was held and the juvenile court ordered that S. J. be placed in the care, custody, and control of the Superintendent of the State Industrial School until she attained the age of eighteen, which will occur on August 20, 1981.

. . . .

We have previously stated that our scope of review under the North Dakota Century Code is equivalent to the former procedure of trial de novo. Thus, we are not bound by the "clearly erroneous" rule found in Rule 52(a) of the North Dakota Rules of Civil Procedure, in matters arising under Chapter 27–20, N.D.C.C. Despite the fact that we are not bound by the clearly erroneous rule, we ascribe appreciable weight to the juvenile court's findings of fact. . . .

In arriving at an order of disposition of a delinquent child, the best interests of the child and the State of North Dakota must be considered. S. J. asserts that a stay of the order of disposition would be proper because the delinquent child who accompanied her in the robbery received a stay despite the fact that such child was sixteen years of age. S. J. argues that the denial of the motion for a stay results in a form of retribution or punishment contrary to one of the purposes of the Uniform Juvenile Court Act, which purpose is to remove from children committing delinquent acts the taint of criminality and the consequences of criminal behavior and to substitute a program of treatment, training, and rehabilitation.

In support of her contention, S. J. relies upon the affidavit of Doctor Awad A. Ismir, who determined that S. J. presented little danger to society if she were released and that she could return to the family home as long as she was placed in the custody of the State Youth Authority. The juvenile court considered and rejected this proposal as an ineffective method of disposition because S. J.'s past history indicated that she had difficulty adjusting to restrictions imposed at her family home. S. J. had lived by herself and with relatives and, in each case, her living arrangements were unsuccessful. In addition, S. J. had not attended school for some time. These facts lead us to conclude that the district court's order of disposition was proper because the structured environment of the State Industrial School accounts for S. J.'s best interests in view of her past behavior. By placing her in the care, custody, and control of the Superintendent of the State Industrial School, the juvenile court has provided the means by which S. J. may receive the necessary treatment, rehabilitation, and correction.

For reasons stated in this opinion, the motion for a stay of the order of disposition is denied.

Note

Are there only two alternative dispositions for juveniles in North Dakota?

In the Matter of J.M.
546 N.W.2d 383 (S.D. 1996)

J.M., a minor child, appeals the trial court's order terminating the jurisdiction of the juvenile court and returning custody of him to his mother. We affirm.

FACTS

J.M. was born on November 2, 1979. He has an older brother and two younger sisters who reside with his mother and stepfather. In May 1990 at the age of ten, J.M. was adjudicated a delinquent child after cashing a forged check. Upon satisfactory completion of the terms and conditions of probation in July 1991, J.M. was discharged from probation and the juvenile court's jurisdiction was formally terminated.

In October 1991 when J.M. was eleven years old, he was again adjudicated a delinquent child, having committed the offense of intentional damage to property in the second degree. Custody of J.M. was temporarily transferred from his mother and stepfather to his grandmother and stepgrandfather (grandparents) pending the completion of a predispositional case study. On November 6, 1991, the juvenile court placed J.M. on probation for an indefinite period of time. One of the terms of his probation was that "during the entire period of said probation [J.M.] shall demean himself as a law-abiding citizen and shall not commit any Federal, State or local crime." The court also placed guardianship and custody of J.M. in his grandparents, while granting liberal visitation to J.M.'s mother and stepfather. The court concluded its order by stating: "It is the goal, in this Juvenile proceeding, to reunite this family as a functional family unit on or about June 1, 1992[.]"

On June 10, 1992, following a review hearing, the trial court ordered continued probation and continued guardianship and custody of J.M. with the grandparents. The court reiterated its goal of reuniting J.M. with his mother and stepfather.

Following another review hearing in October 1992 the court continued J.M.'s probation but returned custody of J.M. to his mother and stepfather. In May 1993 the court again continued J.M.'s probation but transferred guardianship and custody of J.M. back to the grandparents. J.M.'s mother received visitation rights. In September 1993 and June 1994 the court continued J.M.'s probation and custody with the grandparents, while increasing visitation with his mother.

On December 5, 1994, the trial court entered an order discharging J.M. from probation and terminating the jurisdiction of the juvenile court. The court's order indicated that J.M. had satisfactorily complied with the terms and conditions of probation....

Did the trial court abuse its discretion by discharging J.M. from probation, returning him to the custody of his mother, and terminating its jurisdiction?

In reviewing a court's order of disposition in a delinquency proceeding, we consider whether or not the trial court abused its discretion or otherwise committed an error of law requiring reversal. We conclude a trial court's determination that the juvenile has satisfied the terms of the dispositional plan is likewise subject to an abuse of discretion standard of review.

As part of his probation, J.M. was required to "demean himself as a law-abiding citizen" and refrain from committing "any Federal, State or local crime." He was also required to fully comply "with the rules and regulations imposed for his conduct by his custodians." As noted above, upon successful completion of probation, the juvenile court must terminate its jurisdiction.

The evidence is overwhelming that J.M. complied with the terms of his probation. Since being adjudicated delinquent in 1991, J.M. has not committed any violations of the law. He has excelled in school and participated in extracurricular sports. He does not present any serious discipline problems at home or at school.

J.M. does not dispute these facts, or even appear to deny that he has complied with the terms of his probation. Instead, J.M. argues that the court should have continued its jurisdiction and permitted him to remain in the custody of his grandparents. At the June 25, 1995 hearing, J.M. testified about his desire to remain with his grandparents, where he is happy and doing well in school. He expressed concern that, if he is returned to his mother's home, he will revert to his previous delinquent behavior. J.M. did not testify that his mother or stepfather are abusive or neglectful, but emphasized his preference for living with his grandparents. Likewise, a home study requested by the court recommended J.M. be permitted to remain with his grandparents. The home study did not identify J.M's mother or stepfather as unfit, but noted J.M.'s warmer relationship with his grandparents and his fears that his education and reputation would suffer if he lived with his parents.

However, the terms of [the statute] are emphatic. Upon successful completion of probation, a delinquent child shall be released from probation and the jurisdiction of the court shall be terminated. The law does not permit the trial court to continue its jurisdiction over a fully rehabilitated child so as to avoid returning the child to capable parents. It would seem that J.M. and the grandparents are having difficulty distinguishing between the review of a custody determination and the termination of juvenile delinquency proceedings.

[The statute] provides an avenue for removing children from the home of abusive or neglectful parents. Unable to make a showing of parental unfitness under this chapter, J.M. cannot insist on the unlawful extension of a delinquency proceeding to achieve a permanent change in custody. We conclude the trial court did not abuse its discretion or commit an error of law by releasing J.M. from probation, returning him to the custody of his parents, and terminating the court's jurisdiction.

Note

After this decision, what are J.M.'s alternatives?

In the Interest of B.B., A Minor Child
516 N.W.2d 874 (Iowa 1994)

In this case we review the dispositional orders of the juvenile court placing a minor adjudged delinquent in the Iowa State Training School for Boys. The minor, B.B., appeals the orders arguing: (1) the initial dispositional order was not supported by sufficient evidence and was therefore an abuse of discretion; (2) the initial dispositional order went beyond the issues presented by the parties and constituted unfair surprise; and (3) the funding caps placed on group foster care pursuant to [the] Iowa Code violate his constitutional rights of due process and equal protection. We affirm.

I. Background Facts and Proceedings.

B.B. first came before the juvenile court in 1990 for committing fifth-degree theft. Later that year he committed two simple assaults. Disposition on the theft and the first of the simple assault offenses included informal adjustment agreements requiring B.B. to do community service work. After the second simple assault B.B. was adjudged delinquent. The court ordered him to remain in the custody of his mother under formal probation to the Department of Juvenile Court Services (JCS).

In the first six months of 1992, B.B. was referred to the juvenile court three times, once for the offense of third-degree theft and twice for the offense of simple assault. B.B. was adjudicated on the theft charge. The juvenile court ordered B.B. to remain in his mother's home under the supervision of JCS and comply with a probation contract. The contract required that B.B. participate in family therapy until he was successfully discharged.

In October 1992, the Waterloo police department referred B.B. to JCS for the offense of possession of a counterfeit controlled substance with the intent to deliver. The juvenile court adjudged B.B. delinquent and placed him under the supervision of JCS. The probation contract was continued.

At the dispositional hearing in February 1993, evidence was introduced that B.B. had violated the terms of his probation contract several times and the family had never followed through with the requirement for family counseling. JCS recommended that B.B. be placed in group foster care. The parties stipulated, however, that such a placement would violate the regional plan for group foster care.

The juvenile court concluded that the least restrictive placement available under the circumstances was at the Iowa State Training School for Boys in Eldora, Iowa. Accordingly, the court transferred guardianship of B.B. to the Director of the Department of Human Services (Department) for placement at the State Training School.

B.B. appealed to the district court from this order. First, he argued that the cap placed on group foster care denied him due process and equal protection. Secondly, he claimed the juvenile court abused its discretion in ordering B.B. to be placed in the State Training School. The district court rejected these arguments. B.B. appealed to this court.

At the review hearing in August 1993, the juvenile court decided to continue guardianship of B.B. with the Department but return the care, custody, and control of B.B. to his mother. The court approved a behavioral contract executed by the parties. It also ordered that if B.B. violated the contract, the court should be informed and mittimus would be issued without hearing.

B.B. later violated several conditions of the behavioral contract. After a hearing the juvenile court recommitted B.B. to the State Training School. The court stated B.B. should be placed in highly structured group foster care when an opening became available.

B.B. appealed the order recommitting him to the State Training School. Upon B.B.'s motion we consolidated his two appeals.

II. *Scope of Review.*

Our scope of review of juvenile court proceedings is de novo. We review both questions of law and fact.

....

IV. *Due Process.*

B.B. contends that Iowa Code § 232.143, which establishes a cap on the number of children in group foster care, violates his substantive due process rights. He asserts that the State's interest in the public fisc should not outweigh his interest in being placed in the least restrictive setting, here, group foster care.

Under the Due Process Clause of the Fifth and Fourteenth Amendments to the United States Constitution, the state is forbidden from infringing on certain fundamental liberty interests, regardless of the process provided, unless the infringement is narrowly tailored to serve a compelling state interest. Substantive due process analysis requires that we first identify the asserted right and whether it is "fundamental." We then decide whether the action infringing that right is narrowly tailored to serve a compelling state interest.

The right asserted by B.B. here is the right to the least restrictive placement.[1] B.B. argues that his liberty is less restricted in group foster care than it would be at the State Training School. We accept this premise, although we note that the juvenile court's order designated a "*highly structured*" group foster care setting. The question then becomes whether B.B. has an absolute right to the least restrictive placement. In other words, is B.B. entitled to a placement that is less restrictive than the placement ordered even though the less restrictive placement is not authorized by the legislature or is otherwise unavailable? We think neither state law nor the constitution gives him this right.

A. *State law.* Iowa law requires the juvenile court to enter "the least restrictive dispositional order appropriate in view of the seriousness of the delinquent act, the child's culpability * * *, the age of the child and the child's prior record." In the same statute, the legislature provides that the court cannot order group foster care placement if the placement is not in accordance with the regional plan established pursuant to § 232.143. We do not consider one portion of a statute in isolation, but rather construe it in context with other portions of the statute. Thus, we must read the entire statute to determine the meaning of the requirement that the court enter "the least restrictive dispositional order appropriate."

---

1. B.B. does not claim that the cap on group foster care dispositions deprives him of an adequate placement. More specifically, he does not allege that placement at the State Training School was an inappropriate alternative placement at the time he was recommitted to that facility. Therefore, this case does not present the issue of whether B.B. has been denied a right to minimally adequate care and treatment while in the state's custody.

Certainly the legislature did not intend to give a juvenile the right to be placed in the least restrictive setting despite the unavailability of a less restrictive placement when in the same statute purportedly giving such a right the legislature limits the number of group foster care placements. We conclude that in deciding which disposition is the least restrictive, the juvenile court is confined to consideration of those facilities which have a bed available and in which the juvenile can be legally placed. Since B.B. could not legally be placed in group foster care, he had no right under state law to such a placement, although it might be less restrictive than assignment to the State Training School.

B. *Constitutional right.* We must now consider whether the liberty interest protected by the Due Process Clause entitles B.B. to the least restrictive placement. Both the United States Supreme Court and the Eighth Circuit Court of Appeals have considered similar claims. We find these cases instructive.

In the *Flores* case, the Supreme Court considered whether juvenile aliens detained by the government had a right to placement with a private custodian rather than in a child-care institution. The Court held that if institutional custody is constitutional, it does not become unconstitutional just because there may be a more desirable form of child care for the juvenile. The Court stated:

> "The best interests of the child" is likewise not an absolute and exclusive consti-
> tutional criterion for the government's exercise of the custodial responsibilities
> that it undertakes, which must be reconciled with many other responsibilities.
> Thus, child-care institutions operated by the state in the exercise of its parens
> patriae authority * * *are not constitutionally required to be funded at such a
> level as to provide the *best* schooling or the *best* health care available; nor does
> the Constitution require them to substitute, wherever possible, private non-
> adoptive custody for institutional care. * * *Minimum standards must be met,
> and the child's fundamental rights must not be impaired; but the decision to go
> beyond those requirements—to give one or another of the child's additional in-
> terests priority over other concerns that compete for public funds and adminis-
> trative attention—is a policy judgment rather than a constitutional imperative.

. . . .

Here, B.B. does not claim that institutional custody of him is unconstitutional. There-fore, we start with the basic premise that placement of B.B. in some form of child care institution does not violate his constitutional rights. We must then consider B.B.'s claim that he is entitled to a particular form of institutional custody—the least restrictive place-ment. This claim is very similar to the claims of the juvenile aliens in *Flores* who asserted a right to a specific form of custody by the government and the claim of the adult plain-tiff in *Hanson* who asserted a right to placement in the least restrictive environment. For the reasons discussed in *Flores* and *Hanson*, we hold that a juvenile has no constitutional right to the least restrictive form of institutional placement. *See Gary W. v. State of Louisiana*(no constitutional right to the least restrictive confinement conceivable; state must provide care in the best "available" environment).

Even if such a right did exist, it is not a "fundamental" right. Therefore, substantive due process demands, at the most, that there be a reasonable fit between the govern-mental purpose and the means chosen to advance that purpose. Here the state's goals are to reduce spending on group foster care and to encourage the development of alternatives to group foster care placements. Limitations on the number of placements in group fos-ter care "reasonably fit" these goals. Indeed, it is difficult to imagine a more direct man-ner in which to control spending and reallocate limited resources.

In summary, we hold that B.B. has no right under state law or the Due Process Clause to be placed in the least restrictive form of institutional custody regardless of the availability of a less restrictive placement. Therefore, the juvenile court did not err in placing B.B. in the State Training School pending the availability of space in a group foster care facility.

V. *Equal Protection.*

The United States and Iowa Constitutions guarantee the equal protection of the laws to all persons. B.B. claims that § 232.143 violates his right of equal protection because it serves to treat him differently than similarly situated juveniles who require group foster care merely because he falls within the class of juveniles referred at a time when the caps have been reached. B.B. argues the statute unreasonably allocates group foster care among children needing such care on a first-come-first-served basis rather than based on need.

The first step we take in applying an equal protection analysis is to determine the appropriate standard of review. A rational basis test applies unless the challenged statute involves a suspect classification or a fundamental right. Suspect classifications are generally based on race, alienage, or national origin. Fundamental rights include the right to vote, the right to interstate travel, and other rights, such as those guaranteed by the First Amendment, which are considered essential to individual liberty.

We have already decided in our consideration of B.B.'s substantive due process claim that no fundamental right is asserted in this case. We also conclude that no suspect classification is implicated. The statute challenged here is state social legislation which is entitled to broad deference. Therefore, the rational basis test is applicable.

Under the rational basis test, a statute is constitutional unless the classification bears no rational relationship to a legitimate governmental interest. The Equal Protection Clause does not require that social legislation produce a rational result in each case. If there is a rational basis for the program as a whole, the fact that it produces seemingly arbitrary consequences in some individual cases will not render it unconstitutional.

We believe the statute is not unreasonable in allocating the limited group foster care available on a first-come-first-served basis. B.B. argues that group foster care should be assigned on the basis of need. Allocating this type of placement based on need would be impracticable, expensive, and adversely affect the stability of group foster care placements.

The amount of time and resources that would be required to compare the relative needs of all juveniles for whom group foster care is the least restrictive form of placement would be substantial. Additionally, a recomparison of these juveniles would theoretically be necessary every time the juvenile court recommends group foster care for another juvenile. Allocating group foster care based on relative need would also result in the disruption of placements. A juvenile placed in group foster care could conceivably be taken out of a group foster care facility later because a newly adjudicated juvenile's need for group foster care is identified as greater. The very real practical difficulties in allocating group foster care on the basis of relative need demonstrate the reasonableness of the system of priority chosen by the legislature.

Therefore, we conclude the statutory method for placing children in group foster care is rational. Consequently, B.B. was not deprived of equal protection of the laws merely because he was temporarily denied the least restrictive institutional setting for addressing his needs.

In the Matter of the Interests of A.L.J., A Minor
836 P.2d 307 (Wyo. 1992)

Appellant A.L.J., a minor, appeals from the trial court's finding that he committed a delinquent act by recklessly endangering others and from the court's order of disposition pertaining to his probation conditions.

We affirm in part and vacate in part.

....

Appellant claims that the probation condition requiring him to submit to random chemical testing for the presence of alcohol violates his right to be free from unreasonable searches and seizures as guaranteed by the Fourth Amendment to the United States Constitution and the Wyoming Constitution. Appellant bases his contention on *Pena v. State*, which involved an adult parolee. In *Pena*, we found that, while parolees have lesser Fourth Amendment protections than law abiding citizens have, a parole officer, before he makes a search, must still have a "reasonable suspicion" that the parolee committed a parole violation. On the basis of the holding in *Pena*, Appellant argues that, since urinalysis is a search, his probation condition should have included a requirement that the probation officer must reasonably suspect that a probation violation exists before he orders a test.

Appellant's argument necessarily assumes that: (a) urinalysis is a search; (b) Fourth Amendment protections apply to juveniles; and (c) adult and juvenile probationers are entitled to the same Fourth Amendment protections. We agree with Appellant's first assumption and adopt the Supreme Court's finding in *Skinner v. Railway Labor Executives' Association*, that the testing of urine is a search. For this case, we can assume, without deciding, that Fourth Amendment protections apply to juveniles in adjudicatory proceedings.[1] However, the Fourth Amendment protections which apply to adult *probationers* do not necessarily apply to juvenile probationers.[2] The dispositional phase of juvenile proceedings requires broad judicial discretion to accommodate the unique rehabilitative needs of juveniles. We hold that it is within the court's discretion to allow a probation officer to search a juvenile without reasonably suspecting that a probation violation exists.

Other courts have recognized that minors' constitutional rights available in the adjudicatory stage are not necessarily applicable in the dispositional stage. The Supreme Court has found that in adjudicatory hearings minors are entitled to those rights which comport with due process and fair treatment under the Fourteenth Amendment to the United States Constitution. However, the Supreme Court in *In re Gault*, recognizing the uniqueness of the disposition stage, specifically limited its finding to the adjudicatory stage.

This difference between the adjudicative and dispositional phases reflects the broad discretion judges need for making an appropriate disposition. Wyoming requires that, when entering an order of disposition, the court must do what is best suited for the public safety, the preservation of families, and the physical, mental, and moral welfare of the child. To fulfill this mandate and to address the rehabilitative needs of juveniles, the court must have flexibility when it is formulating the probation conditions.

---

1. [See discussion of this issue in Chapter 2, *supra*.—Eds.]

2. [In *Griffin v. Washington*, 483 U.S. 868 (1987), the Court held full Fourth Amendment protections did not apply to adult probationers.—Eds.]

(f) As a part of any order of disposition and the terms and conditions thereof, the court may:

. . . .

(vi) Impose any demands, requirements, limitations, restrictions or restraints on the child, and do all things with regard to the child that his parents might reasonably and lawfully do under similar circumstances;

(vii) As a condition of permitting the child to live in the home, order the child * * *into counseling, treatment or another program designed to rectify problems which contributed to the adjudication.

Both of these provisions are broad enough to encompass chemical testing. In this case, alcohol was being consumed at the party. Appellant's background showed that he had previously been involved in an alcohol-related incident. The testing-for-alcohol condition was designed to avoid any future problems involving alcohol. We believe that, under these circumstances, the chemical-testing condition was appropriate.

Appellant next contests probation condition (n) which states, "Said minor's parents shall cooperate in all respects with said minor's probation officer and allow residential checks at the discretion of said officer." As he did in his argument concerning the chemical-testing condition, Appellant argues that the probation officer must reasonably suspect that a probation violation exists before he searches the minor's residence. Our constitutional analysis regarding chemical testing is applicable to the probation condition requiring residential checks. Appellant's Fourth Amendment rights were not violated by the court allowing the probation officer to make residential checks without reasonably suspecting the existence of a probation violation. The condition was clearly within the court's discretion. Residential checks are an appropriate probation condition because they allow the probation officer to verify that the minor is not consuming alcohol or otherwise violating his probation conditions.

Appellant's probation condition (1) states:

> Said minor's driving privileges are hereby revoked. Said minor shall not drive a motor vehicle until January 20, 1991. Thereafter, if said minor is arrested or ticketed for a traffic violation or violates any condition contained herein, then said minor's driving privilege shall be automatically deemed revoked by virtue of this Court order.

Appellant contends that this condition is beyond the court's statutory authority. Pursuant to [the statute], the court may "[r]estrict or restrain the child's driving privileges for a period of time the court deems appropriate, and if necessary to enforce the restrictions the court may take possession of the child's driver's license." Appellant objects to the court using the word "revoke" as opposed to using the words "restrict or restrain." In the context of condition (1), we see no discernible difference between "revoking" and "restraining or restricting" the child's driving privileges. By revoking the child's driving *privileges,* the court is not revoking the child's driver's license.

Appellant's probation condition (p) requires him to reimburse the public defender for the cost of his defense. Appellant claims that the trial court must inquire into his ability to reimburse the public defender before it can order reimbursement. We agree.

The State argues that the trial judge had sufficient knowledge to conclude that Appellant had the capacity to reimburse the public defender. The basis for this claim is that, at the dispositional hearing, Appellant's father testified to Appellant's steady work history. This evidence was not sufficient to qualify as an inquiry into Appellant's ability to pay.

[The statute] allows the court to order the child to pay for the cost of his defense; however, the statute does not specifically require the court to inquire into the child's ability to pay:

"The application of restitution and cost repayment statutes without a judicial finding of ability to pay are statutes designed as debt collecting devices masquerading as penal laws and contravene the constitutional prohibition against imprisonment for debt."

We hold that the court must inquire and find that the juvenile has the ability to pay before the court can order reimbursement of attorney fees, and we vacate that probation condition requiring Appellant to reimburse the public defender.

Equal Protection

Appellant argues that his three-year probation term violates the Equal Protection Clauses of the Wyoming and United States Constitutions. He relies upon *Hicklin v. State,* for the proposition that a probation term cannot exceed the maximum imprisonment term. Since the maximum sentence for reckless endangerment is one year, Appellant claims that his three-year probation term denies him equal protection under the law.

The right to equal protection under the law mandates that all persons similarly situated shall be treated alike, both in the privileges conferred and in the liabilities imposed. When claiming an equal protection violation, the claimant must initially show that the classification in question treats similarly situated persons unequally. Adults placed on probation after they have been criminally prosecuted are not similarly situated to juveniles placed on probation after they have been adjudicated delinquents; therefore, Appellant's argument must fail.

By enacting a juvenile code separate from the criminal code, Wyoming's legislature has recognized that juveniles and adults are not similarly situated. Juvenile proceedings are designed to rehabilitate and protect the juvenile, not to punish him. These goals of rehabilitation and protection are reflected throughout the juvenile code. Proceedings in juvenile court are equitable as opposed to being criminal. Juveniles are not convicted; they are merely adjudicated delinquents. By treating juveniles more gently than it treats adults, the legislature is compensating for juveniles' inherent lack of experience and maturity.

Since juvenile probations and adult probations are not similarly situated, Appellant suffered no denial of his right to equal protection under the law.

Affirmed in part and vacated in part.

URBIGKIT, Chief Justice, concurring in part and dissenting in part.

For a different reason than given by Justice Cardine, I cannot join in concurrence with the entire majority opinion. Directly stated, I do not find persons to be constitutionally second-class, or no-class, citizens under either the federal or state constitution when younger than some age limit, which is from time to time readjusted by the legislature to establish the juvenile court jurisdictional age limit by changing the age of majority.

I find no constitutional basis for the conversion of the misdemeanor offense for an adult into a confinement sentence of five days in jail and three years probation for a juvenile. An adult convicted of reckless endangerment cannot be confined or placed on probation for a term to exceed one year. The same criminal offense is utilized under this court's decision for the appellant, the only difference being age, to be subjected to a criminal felony conviction penalty extended to three years. That divergence, even if found to be justified in state statute, is, in my opinion, unconstitutional under the Wyoming Constitution in violating both due process and equal protection.

This is not a youth-out-of-control juvenile court protective action. It is criminal conduct, prosecuted under the juvenile statute for an adult crime where, even if the youth had been prosecuted as an adult, the maximum confinement sentence, including periods of probation, could not have exceeded one year. Here, where this appellant was prosecuted as a minor under the juvenile code, we add judicial opportunity to confine and punish for a total time of three years.

This case involves punishment of appellant for the commission of a crime....

We are presented with an explicitly directed criminal proceeding relating to punishment assessed by society for the commission of a criminal offense. The criminal nature of the proceeding and the required recognition of constitutional interests surely is not in question in 1992. These proceedings can no longer be characterized as civil, where punitive disturbance of liberty interests of the individual as retribution for criminal conduct is presented....

The due process nature of the Wyoming juvenile code proceeding is statutorily recognized by the right to counsel, to be provided a jury trial and to exercise the privilege against self-incrimination. At their first appearance before the court the child and his parents, guardian or custodian shall be advised by the court of their right to be represented by counsel at every stage of the proceedings including appeal, and to employ counsel of their own choice....

Specific issues inculcated into the majority decision which remain undiscussed in the opinion include: (1) a basic discrimination based on age in punishment against a minor in severity of sentence (when he is prosecuted as a minor instead of charged under the adult crime status and dependent on the happenstance of being younger or older than the age of majority); (2) conversion of a criminal misdemeanor into a felony punishment status by utilization of the juvenile code in substitution of the adult criminal court system; and (3) continuation of the juvenile court inflicted punishment into adulthood from the initial juvenile court sentence.

The first examination is to determine whether this proceeding is criminal in nature and consequently requires application of associative constitutional protection under both the Wyoming and United States Constitutions. The United States Supreme Court has taken a forceful, but not necessarily consistent, pathway. The clearest recognition of the essential criminal nature of this kind of juvenile court proceeding was provided in *Breed*. Earlier recognition of the reality can be followed from *Kent v. United States,* to *Application of Gault,* and then continued in philosophic adaptation in *In re Winship,* to *Bellotti v. Baird.*

. . . .

The exception to the constitutionally required protective designation is found in *McKeiver v. Pennsylvania,* which considered the right to a jury trial for due process in juvenile court proceedings. That case has no Wyoming relevance since the Wyoming statute guarantees that right which honors the state constitutional criteria....

Reasoned consideration of the juvenile court system requires recognition of the fundamental nature of the liberty interest to then be related to a conclusion that it does not first arise with attained adulthood. In 1987, Chief Justice Rehnquist acknowledged "the individual's strong interest in liberty." We do not minimize the importance and fundamental nature of this right.

Thoughtfully examined principles would lead to the conclusion that the fundamental interest of liberty is no less real for a juvenile faced with incarceration or probation than is the case for an adult.

Notes

(a) Is a dispositional hearing in juvenile court significantly different from a sentencing proceeding in criminal court? Should it be? If so, how?

(b) Would a sentencing grid be feasible in juvenile court? Why?

(c) What standard of review should appellate courts use to assure compliance with the purposes of the juvenile court? Is the abuse of discretion standard on appeal sufficient to provide guidelines and to make clear that dispositional orders are not immune from reversal?

3. IJA-ABA Juvenile Justice Standards: Standards Relating to Dispositional Procedures

Robert E. Shepherd, Jr., ed.

Part I: Dispositional Authority

1.1 Authority vested in judge.

Authority to determine and impose the appropriate disposition should be vested in the juvenile court judge.

Part II: Dispositional Information

2.1 General principles.

A. Information that is relevant and material to disposition may be obtained by persons acting on behalf of the juvenile court only after an adjudication, with the exceptions noted hereafter.

B. The sources for dispositional information and the techniques for gathering such information are subject to legal standards, as provided in Standards 2.2 and 2.3.

C. The information required for the imposition of an appropriate disposition should be directly related to the stated objectives for the selection and imposition of available dispositional alternatives and the nature and quantum of discretion vested in the judge.

D. It should not be assumed that more information is also better information, or that the accumulation of dispositional information, particularly of the subjective and evaluative type, is necessarily an aid to decision making.

E. Dispositional information should be subject to rules governing admissibility and burdens of persuasion as provided in Standard 2.5.

F. Information relating to disposition should be broadly shared among the parties to the proceeding and any individual or agency officially designated as appropriate for the custody or care of the juvenile, as provided in Standard 2.4.

G. Any such information should not be considered a public record.

2.2 Obtaining information.

A. No investigation for dispositional purposes should be undertaken by representatives of the state, nor any additional information of record gathered, until it has been determined that the juvenile has engaged in the conduct alleged in the charging instrument, unless the juvenile and the juvenile's attorney consent in writing to an earlier undertaking.

B. Information in the form of oral or written statements relevant to disposition may be obtained from the juvenile, subject to the following limitations:

1. The statement should be voluntary as determined by the totality of circumstances surrounding the questioning, and the juvenile should have full knowledge of the possible adverse dispositional consequences that may ensue.

2. In determining voluntariness, special consideration should be given to the susceptibility of the juvenile to any coercion, exhortations, or inducements which may have been used.

3. The juvenile should be afforded the right to consult with and be advised by counsel prior to any questioning by a representative of the state when such questioning is designed to elicit dispositional information.

4. It should clearly appear of record that the juvenile was advised that the information solicited may be used in a dispositional proceeding and that it may result in adverse dispositional consequences.

2.3 Information base.

A. The information essential to a disposition should consist of the juvenile's age; the nature and circumstances of the offense or offenses upon which the underlying adjudication is based, such information not being limited to that which was or may be introduced at the adjudication; and any prior record of adjudicated delinquency and disposition thereof.

B. Information concerning the social situation or the personal characteristics of the juvenile, including the results of psychological testing, psychiatric evaluations, and intelligence testing, may be considered as relevant to a disposition.

C. The social history may include information concerning the family and home situation; school records, in accordance with the *Juvenile Records and Information Systems* volume; any prior contacts with social agencies; and other similar items. The social history report should be in writing and should indicate clearly the sources of the information, the number of contacts made with such sources, and the total time expended on investigation and preparation.

D. When the state seeks to obtain and utilize information concerning the personal characteristics of the juvenile, such information should first be sought without resort to any form of confinement or institutionalization.

1. In the unusual case, where some form of confinement or institutionalization is represented by the state as being a necessary condition for obtaining this information, and the juvenile or his or her attorney objects, the court should conduct a hearing on the issue and determine whether the proposed confinement is necessary.

2. At such hearing the juvenile prosecutor should set forth the reasons for considering the information relevant to the dispositional decision. The juvenile prosecutor should also indicate what nonconfining alternatives were explored and demonstrate their inefficacy or unavailability. An order for examination and confinement under this standard should be limited to a maximum of thirty days, and should specify the nature and objectives of the examinations to be undertaken, as well as the place where such examinations are to be conducted.

2.4 Sharing information.

A. No dispositional decision should be made on the basis of a fact or opinion that is not disclosed to the attorney for the juvenile. Should there be a compelling reason for nondisclosure to the juvenile, as for example when the names of prospective adoptive parents appear, the court may advise the attorney for the juvenile not to disclose.

B. The information that may be developed in accordance with Part II should be shared sufficiently prior to any predisposition conference which may be held, and sufficiently prior to the disposition hearing to allow for independent investigation, verification, and the development of rebuttal information.

C. The right of access to dispositional information creates a professional obligation that counsel for the juvenile avail himself or herself of the opportunity.

D. The juvenile prosecutor has a right to disclosure of dispositional information coextensive with that of the attorney for the juvenile.

2.5 Rules of evidence.

A. Dispositional information should be relevant and material.

B. When a more severe dispositional alternative is selected in preference to a less severe one, the selection of such alternative should be supported by a preponderance of the evidence.

PART VI: Formal Disposition Hearing

6.3 Conduct of the hearing.

As soon as practicable after the adjudication and any predisposition conference that may be held, a full disposition hearing should be conducted at which the judge should:

A. be advised as to any stipulations or disagreements concerning dispositional facts;

B. allow the juvenile prosecutor and the attorney for the juvenile to present evidence, in the form of written presentations or by witnesses, concerning the appropriate disposition;

C. afford the juvenile and the juvenile's parents or legal guardian an opportunity to address the court;

D. hear argument by the attorney for the juvenile and the juvenile prosecutor concerning the appropriate disposition;

E. allow both attorneys to question any documents and cross-examine any witnesses;

F. allow both attorneys to examine any person who prepares any report concerning the juvenile, unless the attorney expressly waives that right.

PART VII: Imposition and Correction of Disposition

7.1 Findings and formal requisites.

A. The judge should determine the appropriate disposition as expeditiously as possible after the dispositional hearing, and when the disposition is imposed;

1. Make specific findings on all controverted issues of fact and on the weight attached to all significant dispositional facts in arriving at the disposition decision;

2. State for the record, in the presence of the juvenile, the reasons for selecting the particular disposition and the objective or objectives desired to be achieved thereby;

3. When the disposition involves any deprivation of liberty or any form of coercion, indicate for the record those alternative dispositions, including particular places and programs, that were explored and the reason for their rejection;

4. State with particularity the precise terms of the disposition that is imposed, including credit for any time previously spent in custody; and,

5. Advise the juvenile and the juvenile's attorney of the right to appeal and of the procedure to be followed if the appellant is unable to pay the cost of an appeal.

B. The court may correct an illegal disposition at any time and may correct a disposition imposed in an illegal manner within [120 days] of the imposition of the disposition.

Standards Relating to Dispositions

PART I: General Purposes and Limitations

1.1 Purpose.

The purpose of the juvenile correctional system is to reduce juvenile crime by maintaining the integrity of the substantive law proscribing certain behavior and by developing individual responsibility for lawful behavior. This purpose should be pursued through means that are fair and just, that recognize the unique characteristics and needs of juveniles, and that give juveniles access to opportunities for personal and social growth.

1.2 Coercive dispositions: definition and requirements.

A disposition is coercive when it limits the freedom of action of the adjudicated juvenile in any way that is distinguishable from that of a nonadjudicated juvenile and when the failure or refusal to comply with the disposition may result in further enforcement action. The imposition of any coercive disposition by the state imposes the obligation to act with fairness and to avoid arbitrariness. This obligation includes the following requirements:

A. Adjudicated violation of substantive law.

No coercive disposition may be imposed unless there has been an adjudicated violation of the substantive law.

B. Specification of disposition by statute.

No coercive disposition may be imposed unless pursuant to a statute that prescribes the particular disposition with reasonable specificity

C. Procedural regularity and fairness.

The imposition and implementation of all coercive dispositions should conform to standards governing procedural regularity and fairness.

D. Information concerning obligations.

Juveniles should be given adequate information concerning the obligations imposed on them by all coercive dispositions and the consequences of failure to meet such obligations. Such information should be given in the language primarily spoken by the juvenile.

E. Legislatively determined maximum dispositions.

The maximum severity and duration of all coercive dispositions should be determined by the legislature, which should limit them according to the seriousness of the offense for which the juvenile has been adjudicated.

F. Judicially determined dispositions.

The nature and duration of all coercive dispositions should be determined by the court at the time of sentencing, within the limitations established by the legislature.

G. Availability of resources.

No coercive disposition should be imposed unless the resources necessary to carry out the disposition are shown to exist. If services required as part of a disposition are not available, an alternative disposition no more severe should be employed.

H. Physical safety.

No coercive disposition should subject the juvenile to unreasonable risk of physical harm.

I. Prohibition of collateral disabilities.

No collateral disabilities extending beyond the term of the disposition should be imposed by the court, by operation of law, or by any person or agency exercising authority over the juvenile.

PART II: Dispositional Criteria

2.1 Least restrictive alternative.

In choosing among statutorily permissible dispositions, the court should employ the least restrictive category and duration of disposition that is appropriate to the seriousness of the offense, as modified by the degree of culpability indicated by the circumstances of the particular case, and by the age and prior record of the juvenile. The imposition of a particular disposition should be accompanied by a statement of the facts relied on in support of the disposition and the reasons for selecting the disposition and rejecting less restrictive alternatives.

2.2 Needs and desires of the juvenile.

Once the category and duration of the disposition have been determined, the choice of a particular program within the category should include consideration of the needs and desires of the juvenile.

PART III: Dispositions

3.1 Nominal: reprimand and release.

The court may reprimand the juvenile for the unlawful conduct, warn against future offenses, and release him or her unconditionally.

3.2 Conditional.

The court may sentence the juvenile to comply with one or more conditions, which are specified below, none of which involves removal from the juvenile's home. Such conditions should not interfere with the juvenile's schooling, regular employment, or other activities necessary for normal growth and development.

A. Suspended sentence.

The court may suspend imposition or execution of a more severe, statutorily permissible sentence with the provision that the juvenile meet certain conditions agreed to by him or her and specified in the sentencing order. Such conditions should not exceed, in severity or duration, the maximum sanction permissible for the offense.

B. Financial.

1. Restitution.

a. Restitution should be directly related to the juvenile's offense, the actual harm caused, and the juvenile's ability to pay.

b. The means to carry out a restitution order should be available.

c. Either full or partial restitution may be ordered.

d. Repayment may be required in a lump sum or in installments.

e. Consultation with victims may be encouraged but not required. Payments may be made directly to victims, or indirectly, through the court.

f. The juvenile's duty of repayment should be limited in duration; in no event should the time necessary for repayment exceed the maximum term permissible for the offense.

2. Fine.

a. Imposition of a fine is most appropriate in cases where the juvenile has derived monetary gain from the offense.

b. The amount of the fine should be directly related to the seriousness of the juvenile's offense and the juvenile's ability to pay.

c. Payment of a fine may be required in a lump sum or installments.

d. Imposition of a restitution order is preferable to imposition of a fine.

e. The juvenile's duty of payment should be limited in duration; in no event should the time necessary for payment exceed the maximum term permissible for the offense.

3. Community service.

a. In sentencing a juvenile to perform community service, the judge should specify the nature of the work and the number of hours required.

b. The amount of work required should be related to the seriousness of the juvenile's offense.

c. The juvenile's duty to perform community service should be limited in duration; in no event should the duty to work exceed the maximum term permissible for the offense.

C. Supervisory.

1. Community supervision.

The court may sentence the juvenile to a program of community supervision, requiring him or her to report at specified intervals to a probation officer or other designated individual and to comply with any other reasonable conditions that are designed to facilitate supervision and are specified in the sentencing order.

2. Day custody.

The court may sentence the juvenile to a program of day custody, requiring him or her to be present at a specified place for all or part of every day or of certain days. The court also may require the juvenile to comply with any other reasonable conditions that are designed to facilitate supervision and are specified in the sentencing order.

D. Remedial.

1. Remedial programs.

The court may sentence the juvenile to a community program of academic or vocational education or counseling, requiring him or her to attend sessions designed to afford access to opportunities for normal growth and development. The duration of such programs should not exceed the maximum term permissible for the offense.

2. Prohibition of coercive imposition of certain programs.

This standard does not permit the coercive imposition of any program that may have harmful effects. Any such program should comply with the requirements of Standard 4.3 concerning informed consent.

3.3 Custodial.

A. Custodial disposition defined.

A Custodial disposition is one in which a juvenile is removed coercively from his or her home.

B. Presumption against custodial dispositions.

There should be a presumption against coercively removing a juvenile from his or her home, and this category of sanction should be reserved for the most serious or repetitive offenses. It should not be used as a substitute for a judicial finding of neglect, which should conform to the standards in the Abuse and Neglect volume.

C. Exclusiveness of custodial dispositions.

A custodial disposition is an exclusive sanction and should not be used simultaneously with other sanctions. However, this does not prevent the imposition of a custodial disposition for a specified period of time to be followed by a conditional disposition for a specified period of time, provided that the total duration of the disposition does not exceed the maximum term of a custodial disposition permissible for the offense.

D. Continuous and intermittent confinement.

Custodial confinement may be imposed on a continuous or an intermittent basis, not to exceed the maximum term permissible for the offense. Intermittent confinement includes:

1. night custody

2. weekend custody.

E. Levels of Custody.

Levels of custody include nonsecure residences and secure facilities.

1. Nonsecure residences.

No court should sentence a juvenile to reside in a nonsecure residence unless the juvenile is at least ten years old and unless the court finds that any less severe disposition would be grossly inadequate to the needs of the juvenile and that such needs can be met by placing the juvenile in a particular nonsecure residence.

2. Secure facilities.

a. A juvenile may be sentenced to a period of confinement in a secure facility; such a disposition, however, should be a last resort, reserved only for the most serious or repetitive offenses.

b. No court should sentence a juvenile to confinement in a secure facility unless the juvenile is at least twelve years old and unless the court finds that such confinement is necessary to prevent the juvenile from causing injury to the person or substantial property interests of another.

c. Secure facilities should be coeducational, located near population centers as close as possible to the juvenile's home, and limited in population.

PART IV: Provision of Services

4.1 Right to Services.

All publicly funded services to which nonadjudicated juveniles have access should be made available to adjudicated delinquents. In addition, juveniles adjudicated delinquent should have access to all services necessary for their normal growth and development.

A. Obligations of correctional agencies.

Correctional agencies have an affirmative obligation to ensure that juveniles under their supervision obtain all services to which they are entitled.

B. Purchase of services.

Services may be provided directly by correctional agencies or obtained, by purchase or otherwise, from other public or private agencies. Whichever method is employed, agencies providing services should set standards governing the provision of services and establish monitoring procedures to ensure compliance with such standards.

C. Prohibition against increased dispositions.

Neither the severity nor the duration of a disposition should be increased in order to ensure access to services.

D. Obligation of correctional agency and sentencing court.

If access to all required services is not being provided to a juvenile under the supervision of a correctional agency, the agency has the obligation to so inform the sentencing court. In addition, the juvenile, his or her parents, or any other interested party may inform the court of the failure to provide services. The court also may act on its own initiative. If the court determines that access to all required services in fact is not being provided, it should employ the following:

1. Reduction of disposition or discharge.

Unless the court can ensure that the required services are provided forthwith, it should reduce the nature of the juvenile's disposition to a less severe disposition that will ensure the juvenile access to the required services, or discharge the juvenile.

2. Affirmative orders.

In addition, the sentencing court, or any other court with the requisite jurisdiction, may order the correctional agency or other public agencies to make the required services available in the future.

4.2 Right to refuse services; exceptions.

Juveniles who have been adjudicated delinquent have the right to refuse all services, subject to the following exceptions:

A. Participation legally required of all juveniles.

Juveniles who have been adjudicated delinquent may be required to participate in all types of programs in which participation is legally required of juveniles who have not been adjudicated delinquent.

B. Prevention of clear harm to physical health.

Juveniles may be required to participate in certain programs in order to prevent clear harm to their physical health.

C. Remedial dispositions.

Juveniles subject to a conditional disposition may be required to participate in any program specified in the sentencing order, pursuant to Standard 3.2 D.

4.3 Requirement of informed consent to participate in certain programs.

Informed, written consent should be obtained before a juvenile may be required to participate in any program designed to alter or modify his or her behavior if that program may have harmful effects.

A. Juveniles below the age of sixteen.

If the juvenile is under the age of sixteen, his or her consent and the consent of his or her parent or guardian should be obtained.

B. Juveniles above the age of sixteen.

If the juvenile is sixteen or older, only the juvenile's consent need be obtained.

C. Withdrawal of consent.

Any such consent may be withdrawn at any time.

PART V: Modification and Enforcement of Dispositional Orders

Dispositional orders may be modified as follows.

5.1 Reduction because disposition inequitable.

A juvenile, his or her parents, the correctional agency with responsibility for the juvenile, or the sentencing court on its own motion may petition the sentencing court (or an appellate court) at any time during the course of the disposition to reduce the nature or the duration of the disposition on the basis that it exceeds the statutory maximum; was imposed in an illegal manner; is unduly severe with reference to the seriousness of the offense, the culpability of the juvenile, or the dispositions given by the same or other courts to juveniles convicted of similar offenses; or if it appears at the time of the application that by doing so it can prevent an unduly harsh or inequitable result.

5.2 Reduction because services not provided.

The sentencing court should reduce a disposition or discharge the juvenile when it appears that access to required services is not being provided, pursuant to Standard 4.1 D.

5.3 Reduction for good behavior.

The correctional agency with responsibility for a juvenile may reduce the duration of the juvenile's disposition by an amount not to exceed [5] percent of the original disposition if the juvenile has refrained from major infractions of the dispositional order or of the reasonable regulations governing any facility to which the juvenile is assigned.

5.4 Enforcement when juvenile fails to comply.

The correctional agency with responsibility for a juvenile may petition the sentencing court if it appears that the juvenile has willfully failed to comply with any part of the dispositional order. In the case of a remedial sanction, compliance is defined in terms of attendance at the specified program, and not in terms of performance.

If, after a hearing, it is determined that the juvenile in fact has not complied with the order and that there is no excuse for the noncompliance, the court may do one of the following:

A. Warning and order to comply.

The court may warn the juvenile of the consequences of failure to comply and order him or her to make up any missed time, in the case of supervisory, remedial, or custodial sanctions or community work; or missed payment, in the case of restitution or fines.

B. Modification of conditions and/or imposition of additional conditions.

If it appears that a warning will be insufficient to induce compliance, the court may modify existing conditions or impose additional conditions calculated to induce compliance, provided that the conditions do not exceed the maximum sanction permissible for the offense. The duration of the disposition should remain the same, with the addition of any missed time or payments ordered to be made up.

C. Imposition of more severe disposition.

If it appears that there are no permissible conditions reasonably calculated to induce compliance, the court may sentence the juvenile to the next most severe category of sanctions for the remaining duration of the disposition. The duration of the disposition should remain the same, except that the court may add some or all of the missed time to the remainder of the disposition.

D. Commission of a new offense.

Where conduct is alleged that constitutes a willful failure to comply with the dispositional order and also constitutes a separate offense, prosecution for the new offense is preferable to modification of the original order. The preference for separate prosecution in no way precludes the imposition of concurrent dispositions.

Notes

(a) Do these standards correct the deficiencies in juvenile court dispositional hearings? How?

(b) How would you address the tensions inherent in juvenile court dispositional hearings?

I. International and Comparative Law

1. Convention on the Rights of the Child

As noted in Chapter 2, *supra*, the Convention on the Rights of the Child is the major international law document relating to children charged with crime. Article 37 states in pertinent part:

(b) No child shall be deprived of his or her liberty unlawfully or arbitrarily. The arrest, detention or imprisonment of a child shall be in conformity with the law and shall be used only as a measure of last resort and for the shortest appropriate period of time;

(c) Every child deprived of liberty shall be treated with humanity and respect for the inherent dignity of the human person and in a manner which takes into account the needs of persons of his or her age. In particular, every child deprived of liberty shall be separated from adults unless it is considered in the child's best interest not to do so and shall have the right to maintain contact with his or her family through correspondence and visits, save in exceptional circumstances;

(d) Every child deprived of his or her liberty shall have the right to prompt access to legal and other appropriate assistance, as well as the right to challenge the legality of the deprivation of his or her liberty before a court or other competent, independent and impartial authority and to a prompt decision on any such action.

Article 40

1. States Parties recognize the right of every child alleged as, accused of, or recognized as having infringed the penal law to be treated in a manner consistent with the promotion of the child's sense of dignity and worth, which reinforces the child's respect for the human rights and fundamental freedoms of others and which takes into account the child's age and the desirability of promoting the child's reintegration and the child's assuming a constructive role in society.

2. To this end and having regard to the relevant provisions of international instruments, States Parties shall, in particular, ensure that:

    (a) No child shall be alleged as, be accused of, or recognized as having infringed the penal law by reason of acts or omissions that were not prohibited by national or international law at the time they were committed.

    (b) Every child alleged as or accused of having infringed the penal law has at least the following guarantees:

        (i) To be presumed innocent until proven guilty according to law;

        (ii) To be informed promptly and directly of the charges against him or her, and if appropriate, through his or her parents or legal guardians and to have legal or other appropriate assistance in the preparation and presentation of his or her defence;

        (iii) To have the matter determined without delay by a competent, independent and impartial authority or judicial body in a fair hearing according to the law, in the presence of legal or other appropriate assistance and, unless it is considered not to be in the best interest of the child, in particular, taking into account his or her age or situation, his or her parents or legal guardians;

        (iv) Not to be compelled to give testimony or to confess guilt; to examine or have examined adverse witnesses and to obtain the participation and examination of witnesses on his or her behalf under conditions of equality;

        (v) If considered to have infringed the penal law, to have his decision and any measures imposed in consequence thereof reviewed by a higher competent, independent and impartial authority or judicial body according to law;

        (vi) To have the free assistance of an interpreter if the child cannot understand or speak the language used;

        (vii) To have his or her privacy fully respected at all stages of the proceedings.

3. States Parties shall seek to promote the establishment of laws, procedures, authorities and institutions specifically applicable to children alleged as, accused of, or recognized as having infringed the penal law, and, in particular:

    (a) The establishment of a minimum age below which children shall be presumed not to have the capacity to infringe the penal law;

    (b) Whenever appropriate and desirable, measures for dealing with such children without resorting to judicial proceedings, providing that human rights and legal safeguards are fully respected.

4. A variety of dispositions, such as care, guidance and supervision orders; counseling; probation; foster care; education and vocational training programmes and other alternatives to institutional care shall be available to ensure that children are dealt with in a manner appropriate to their well-being and proportionate both to their circumstances and the offence.

Notes

(a) How do these provisions compare to the various juvenile justice systems in the United States? Do states need to change their laws to comply with Articles 37 and 40?

(b) For further discussions of the CRC see: Cynthia Price Cohen & Susan Kilbourn, *Jurisprudence of the Committee on the Rights of the Child: A Guide for Research and Analysis*, 19 Mich. J. Int'l. L. 633 (1998); Roger J.R. Levesque, *Future Visions of Juvenile Justice: Lessons from International and Comparative Law*, 29 Creighton L. Rev. 1563 (1996); Martha Minnow, *Whatever Happened to Children's Rights?*, 8 Minn. L. Rev. 267 (1995); Roger R. Levesque, *The International Litigation of Children's Human Rights: Too Radical for American Adolescents?* 9 Conn. J. Int'l. L. 237 (1994).

2. Comparative Systems

There are a number of different juvenile justice systems in the world ranging from punitive models using criminal sanctions to those emphasizing social welfare programs.

a. Masami Izumida Tyson, *Revising Shonenho: A Call to a Reform That Makes the Already Effective Japanese Juvenile System Even More Effective*

33 Vand. J. Transnat'l L. 739, 743–50 (2000)

II. *Shonenho*: The Japanese Juvenile Law

The protective nature of *Shonenho* is based on an assumption that delinquency, as discussed in *Shonenho*, has two components. The first component is that which harms others, and the second is that which harms the juvenile himself. When the juvenile commits delinquent acts, he often harms others. Because these acts label the juvenile as "delinquent," and he subsequently may be shunned by society, there is harm to the juvenile himself. By putting the juvenile offender through rehabilitation programs and by taking the juvenile out of circumstances in which he committed the delinquent acts, *Shonenho* seeks to protect the juvenile from the harm and stigma he put on himself. *Shonenho's* goal is to erase the offense completely, not only from the juvenile's own past, but also from the mind of the rest of society.

A. The Purpose of *Shonenho*: Protecting the Juvenile Offender

. . . .

Shonenho ... contains no reference to retribution or punishment of juvenile offenders. The focus is on reforming the juvenile. The principle of making protection the main focus is known as *hogoshugi*. *Hogo* is translated as "protection" or "care" and "patronage" or "to keep from harm." ... Juvenile crimes are often referred to as *shonen no hogo jiken*, loosely translated as "a crime that calls for a juvenile's protection." The hearing, conducted in Family Court, and the "penalty" phase of a juvenile crime, are sometimes collectively referred to as *hogo-tetsuzuki*, or "the process of protection [of the juvenile]." The punishment component is found in the fact that the juvenile is forced to undergo reform, even if he does not feel it is necessary. It is clear that *Shonenho* has been designed so that punishment is not the primary focus.

. . . .

The fact that punishment is not one of the main purposes of the juvenile system distinguishes it from the adult criminal system.... [For this reason and because of the] presumption that juvenile crimes are in some way related to problems within the juvenile's home or family [juvenile crimes were moved to Family Courts].

. . . .

[*Shonenho* also] forbids the publication of any information that may lead to the identification of the juvenile offender. It prevents the juvenile from being identified after he has been rehabilitated.... There are two main reasons for this guarantee. First, it allows the Family Court to understand what kind of "help" the juvenile needs in order for him to change or to be removed from the circumstances that caused him to commit a crime. The Family Court must extensively and carefully investigate the juvenile's private information such as his upbringing and details about his family. It would be a violation of the juvenile's privacy to release such information to the public. Second, once the juvenile is rehabilitated, and when he attempts to return to society-at-large, it would be against the spirit of *Shonenho* to have him suffer then because of a mistake of his youth.

B. The Juvenile Criminal Process

. . . .

1. The Investigation and Trial

After a juvenile is arrested, he is sent to the prosecutor within forty-eight hours. Thus, the police are entitled to a maximum of forty-eight hours in which to conduct all their questioning before the juvenile is transferred to the prosecutor for further questioning. After the juvenile is transferred, the prosecutor has twenty-four hours in which to question the juvenile. If it is absolutely necessary to conduct additional questioning and investigating, the prosecutor may request an extension for ten days. If still more time is absolutely necessary, he may request a second ten-day extension.... *Shonenho's* purpose here is to prevent the juvenile from experiencing excessive pressure from the prosecutor, as well as to keep to a minimum a situation in which the juvenile is in solitary confinement....

The juvenile trial system, or the hearing, is arranged so that the juvenile offender is given ample opportunity to express his opinions freely, but those who accused him are not. All juvenile cases are held in front of a single judge. A court-appointed investigator presents the information to the judge. The judge hears the evidence and other pertinent information and then makes a decision based on what he has heard. The only people allowed at the hearing are the juvenile, the judge, the court-appointed investigator, the guardian, and in some cases, the chaperon as well. The prosecutor is not allowed to attend the hearing. These rules create a system in which all participants are on the "same side," working toward the same goals — to ensure a "gentle and amicable" atmosphere and to protect the juvenile.

. . . .

The Family Court can reach one of five possible decisions: (1) no trial necessary [similar to when the charges are dropped in adult criminal court]; (2) no decision necessary (*fushobun*) [equivalent to an acquittal and allows for observation by a court social worker after the acquittal]; (3) requirement of counseling at the Children's Counseling Services; (4) further investigation by the public prosecutor [if it is determined that the defendant is over the age of twenty and therefore not a juvenile or if he is over the age of sixteen and committed a crime punishable by death, he then enters the adult system]; and 5) decision to protect (*hogo-shobun*)—that is, the juvenile is sent to either reform school or a juvenile correctional institution [this is similar to a guilty verdict, but the concept is still to protect the juvenile rather than punish him].

b. Willie McCarney, Ph.D., Lay Magistrate, Belfast, Northern Ireland, *Responding to Juvenile Delinquency Restorative Justice An International Perspective*

3 J. Center for Families, Child. & Cts. 3, 6–7 (2001)

FAMILY GROUP (OR COMMUNITY) CONFERENCING

The family-group-conferencing approach to criminal justice originated in New Zealand in 1989 as a result of several factors.

One was a movement that resulted from the anger felt by New Zealand's Maori and Pacific Island communities toward the previous youth justice system. That system regarded young people as individuals in their own right, not as members who had obligations to their wider family and whose wider family had obligations to them. This anger helped spur an attempt to include ancient Maori traditions of resolving disputes within the criminal justice process. The second major factor was the international recognition of victims' interests and the way in which they had been overlooked in the past. Third, international recognition that institutions as then constituted were part of the problem and not the solution led to calls for reform.

The result was enactment of a radical new set of practices for dealing with young offenders under the Children, Young Persons and Their Families Act of 1989. The vision of New Zealand's legislation was to harness community strengths and community wisdom and to connect victims and offenders as individual people in a way that the criminal justice system had previously failed to do.

Quite apart from the issues pressing for change in the way young offenders were dealt with, there was a concern on the "care" side that professionals were failing to keep children safe through professional case management and that the community needed to be involved to bring its collective wisdom and strengths to the problems of child abuse and neglect. At the time, a number of pilot programs involved families in the development of care plans to help resolve neglect and abuse cases and to promote child protection. Today New Zealand's welfare system uses conferencing as the central diversionary device on the dependency side.

Conferencing encourages the participation of a wide collection of people who are "concerned" in some way about the offense. They include those who are concerned for the well-being of either the victim or the offender, those who have concerns about the offense and its consequences, and those who may be able to contribute toward a solution to the problem presented by the offense. This collection of people—who might also include those who are indirectly affected by the offense—have been described as making up a "community of interest," and the whole approach is sometimes referred to as a "communitarian" model. However, the community in question is not a geographical entity as such, nor does it comprise "representatives" (whether elected, appointed, or self-appointed).

. . . .

The New Zealand conferencing approach has a number of distinctive features . . .

1. It is integrated and fully incorporated into the youth justice system as a whole (which deals with those over the age of 14 but not older than 17).

2. There is an effective "gate-keeping" procedure whereby both traditional means of obtaining a suspect's appearance at court—arrest and summons—are carefully restricted. The aim of this procedure is to ensure that young persons are diverted from court wherever possible. Thus, no arrest can be effected unless it is needed to prevent further offending, absconding of the young person, or interference with witnesses or evidence.

3. Furthermore, no summons can be issued without first referring the matter to a youth justice coordinator, who will then convene a family group conference (FGC), which recommends for or against prosecution, with a presumption in favor of diversion. All members of the FGC (including the young person) must agree to the proposed diversionary program, and its implementation is essentially consensual.

4. Where the young person has been arrested, the court must refer all matters (charges) that are not denied to an FGC, which recommends a disposition to the court. This usually consists of a plan of action incorporating a "restorative outcome" (e.g., apology, financial reparation, work for the victim or for the community, a curfew, or some undertaking relating to future behavior). The plan normally nominates persons to supervise its implementation, and the court is asked to adjourn proceedings for a suitable duration to allow for this to happen. Occasionally, an FGC recommends a sanction for imposition by the court.

5. Apart from murder and manslaughter, which for public-policy reasons are excluded from the youth court, every offense (including indictable-only offenses and all the other very serious charges) must be dealt with by means of a family group conference. In the case of indictable-only charges, the young person's case may be adjudicated in adult court. The young person who wishes to admit the charge may be given the right to remain in the youth court and be dealt with there rather than be transferred to the adult court. In practice, the emphasis is on keeping such cases in the youth court unless all the options and strengths of the family- and community-based youth court have been exhausted and no other options remain.

6. All FGCs are facilitated and convened by a youth justice coordinator, who is an employee of the department of social welfare. Those in attendance will be the young person, members of the (extended) family, the victim (if willing to participate), a youth advocate (if requested by the young person), a police officer (usually from the specialist youth aid division), a social worker (in certain cases only), and anyone else the family wishes. The last category could include a representative from a relevant community organization (for example, an addiction treatment agency or a community-work sponsor).

7. The youth court nearly always accepts FGC plans. Outstanding successes have been achieved in instances of very serious offending without the need for any formal court sanctions. If the plan is carried out as agreed, the proceedings are usually withdrawn. If the plan is not implemented satisfactorily, the court can impose its own sanctions. In both serious and nonserious cases where family or community intervention has been ineffective and it has fallen to the court to sentence the youth, the court has a wide range of sanctions available. Such instances, however, are quite rare. If there is a referral to the district court, the available sanctions include imprisonment for up to five years. The court thus acts both as a "quality-control" mechanism that is capable of coming into play in

the event of patently unsatisfactory recommendations, and as a "default" procedure in cases where plans break down.

c.   Allan Borowski & Mimi Ajzenstadt, *A Solution without a Problem: Judges' Perspectives on the Impact of the Introduction of Public Defenders on Israel's Juvenile Courts*

45 Brit. J. Criminology 183, 190–95 (2005)

....

The first Juvenile Court was established in Tel Aviv in 1950, within two years of Israel's becoming an independent state. Today, young Israelis (12–17-year-olds) accused of engaging in criminal behavior are processed either by a specialized Juvenile Court or, in the case of more serious offences, by a court of higher jurisdiction, namely the District Court, constituted as a Juvenile Court.

....

[T]he Youth Law of 1971 allowed for the appointment of defence counsel. Further, despite the strong influence of the British legal tradition on Israel's legal system stemming from Britain's League of Nations' Mandate over Palestine, held between 1921 and 1948, this law also, rather curiously, allowed juveniles without legal representation to be assisted by the judge in cross-examining witnesses. In practice, however, legal representation was comparatively rare.

In this respect, Israel, until the introduction of the new regulation [appointment of public defenders in the juvenile courts], had much in common with the juvenile courts of such Western countries as the United States, Canada, England and Australia—as these courts formerly operated. For Israel's Juvenile Courts and, until the 1970s and 1980s, those in many other Western countries, were substantially driven in legislation, policy and practice by the 'welfare' or parens patriae model of juvenile justice.

Indeed, the extent to which this model imbued Israel's juvenile justice system is reflected in the following observations of David Reifen, Israel's first Juvenile Court judge:

> * * * [T]he juvenile court is properly regarded as a child welfare agency [whose] function is the rehabilitation and social care of juvenile offenders.* * * The technical problem, therefore, is to make the maximum use * * * of [the court] for the purpose of promoting or initiating change in delinquent attitudes and behavior patterns. The situation in which an offender is compelled to give an account of himself and his actions to a court * * * has a powerful influence. * * * The tension created by the court is of great value for it can be used therapeutically.* * *

Although it is 30 years since Reifen's book was published, Israel's juvenile justice system has remained substantially immune from the sorts of philosophical shifts that have taken place elsewhere.

This faith is ... reflected in the central role played by social work-trained juvenile probation officers in the juvenile justice system.

[D]uring the period covered by this study, the Israeli Government provided sufficient resources to the PDO [Public Defender Office] ... to ensure that all youngsters appearing in the Juvenile Court and who had not engaged a private attorney (most cases) could do so with a lawyer present. Israel's public defenders are either employees of the PDO or are private legal practitioners engaged by the PDO. The employees carry their own caseload and also supervise the private practitioners who are engaged by the PDO. A budgetary appropriation designed to try to ensure near universal legal representation stands in contrast to most other countries where budgetary constraints invariably lead to the rationing of access to publicly funded legal representation. In consequence, many youngsters, unlike in Israel, appear in court without a defence attorney.

. . . .

The data for this study were gathered between late 2000 and early 2002. Thus, this study, like the analysis of any social process, captures only one segment—in this case, the early stages—of the changes flowing from the introduction of public defenders in Israel's Juvenile Court. Forty in-depth interviews of between one and two hours' duration were conducted. They were conducted at six urban sites across Israel. Of the 40 interviewees, six were Juvenile Court judges (there are only eight in the whole country), 14 were public defenders employed by the Public Defenders' Office, 12 were juvenile probation officers, and eight were prosecutors. In the case of each of these four groups, interviewing ceased at the point at which additional interviewing had ceased to yield new findings (redundancy). Further, this study utilized purposive sampling. We selected those judges who, through allowing the researchers to document diverse variations and identify important common themes, were best placed to help to address the research question.

. . . .

Findings

The analysis of the data generated by the judges' interviews yielded six major themes. These revolved around: (1) the need for public defenders, (2) the problems associated with public defender representation, (3) the ideal and (4) the actual roles played by public defenders, (5) the judges' attitudes towards the public defenders, and (6) whether the introduction of public defenders signified a shift in the court's underlying philosophy.

A Solution Without a Problem

One of the first themes that emerged from the data analysis was that the judges viewed public defenders as unessential accoutrements in their courts. The judges were quite emphatic that public defenders were unnecessary. Judge 3, for example, felt that "the public defender was not a missing element in the court prior to their introduction [and is] not really a necessary element today."

The judges viewed public defenders as unnecessary because they represented a solution to a problem that did not, in fact, exist. The judges attached no credence to the notion that public defenders offered greater protection of the young person's rights because these rights, in their view, had never been threatened. Again, Judge 3's comments are illustrative: "I don't know of any violation of boy's rights before the public defender was introduced." And the reason that they had never been threatened is that the judges saw themselves as the guardians of these rights, as required by the 1971 Youth Law. Indeed, their role in this regard had diminished since the arrival on the scene of public defenders. As Judge 5 put it, "I always saw myself as protecting the child's rights. Now there is someone else to do it. * * * The juvenile's rights were always protected."

. . . .

The Solution as the Cause of Further Problems

. . . .

The public defenders were perceived as a problem by the judges in so far as the former's role demanded that they interpose themselves between the judge and the youngster. Thus, according to Judge 3, "the child is led by the lawyer" and so "the public defender is a barrier between me and the boy" (Judge 5). As a result, the judge's direct interaction with the youngster—a key element of the therapeutic benefit of the court hearing—has substantially diminished, allowing the accused to disengage both from the judge and the proceedings. Not only has this eroded the role of the judge, but it also "* * * damages the treatment and rehabilitation of the child" (Judge 4).

The Ideal Role of the Public Defender: Defender of the Court

The judges were quite clear about what they believe to be the appropriate role of public defenders: an important theme that emerged from the data analysis was that public defenders should be agents of the court in advancing the best interests of the child. An important means of achieving this end was to facilitate the smooth functioning of the court as a therapeutic medium through (1) the public defender's cooperation with all of the other court actors, and (2) his/her encouragement of the young defendant to cooperate with the legal proceedings.

Judge 5, for instance, maintained that the public defender needs to be the partner of the judge, for example, in "emphasizing the seriousness of what happened. He should say that this is a very serious offence but that maybe the boy should be given a chance." In Judge 2's view, the public defender's role is "* * * not just * * * to have the court find the boy not guilty. He also has to make sure that the boy becomes a law-abiding and useful person to society." The public defender is, therefore, "* * * society's representative" (Judge 5). A good lawyer, in Judge 1's estimation, "is one who succeeds in explaining to the family that he is there [to serve] the juvenile's best interest."

Judge 6 put it most succinctly:

> "* * * a lawyer who sees his duty when representing a minor as equal to (the same as) his duty when representing an adult is not doing justice to the minor."

The Actual Role of the Public Defender: In the Service of Disservice

. . . .

And, in doing what lawyers do, the public defenders, more often than not, do their young clients a great disservice—yet another major theme that emerged from the data analysis. How so? One dimension of this disservice is the delay experienced by the youngster in accessing necessary treatment due to the protracted nature of case processing. Indeed, not only does the extended time involved in bringing a case to a conclusion delay treatment, but it may also render it useless when eventually provided.

> For the boys this time is critical. Sometimes the boys need treatment and nothing happens. By the time the trial is over it [treatment] will be a waste of time. (Judge 3)

Another dimension of this disservice arises from the young client's being exposed to "unhelpful" aspects of the court's procedures. Thus, in Judge 5's view, the public defenders:

> * * * do not understand that they should not argue with the prosecutor regarding an indictment in the court in front of the boy or his parents. They should argue with the prosecutor somewhere else. They are causing damage to the boy and his family.

And a third dimension of this disservice is that the legal advantages secured by the public defender (e.g. dismissal of some charges, reduction in their seriousness, etc.) in the final analysis "may not necessarily serve the best interests of the child" (Judge 1). As Judge 5 observed:

* * * when the lawyer seeks to reduce the charge, this encourages the boy and confuses him regarding behavioral norms. The public defender does not understand that he is harming the boy (Judge 5).

Notes

(a) How do these systems compare to the various juvenile justice systems in the United States? Which models are in the "best interests" of the child and which emphasize public safety?

(b) Regarding the Israeli study above, compare the National Juvenile Defender Center Assessment, and the Marrus article on zealous advocacy in Chapter 3, *supra*.

(c) For descriptions and analyses of additional types of juvenile justice systems, see JUVENILE LAW VIOLATORS, HUMAN RIGHTS, AND THE DEVELOPMENT OF NEW JUVENILE JUSTICE SYSTEMS (Eric L. Jensen & Jorgen Jepsen, eds.) (2006).

Chapter 5

Constitutional Restraints on Practices in Juvenile Correctional Facilities

One of the key purposes of the juvenile codes was, and is, to rehabilitate youngsters who came within the court's jurisdiction. While many states now have amended their statutes to reflect that punishment of wrongdoers is also an objective, such shifts have not resulted in entirely eliminating rehabilitation as a goal. Indeed, one of the reasons given for disparate constitutional protection of children is that they would ultimately benefit from the treatment and rehabilitative options available only to the juvenile courts. No one, however, made sure that the minors committed to state facilities were actually being properly treated.

Starting in the 1960s several lawsuits were filed, and the trials exposed extreme cruelty and lack of treatment in the particular juvenile facilities. The cases, particularly those filed in federal court, made clear that some constitutional restraints govern the state's correctional and rehabilitative facilities. While some changes were made in response to judicial decrees, many of the underlying practices still prevailed, although perhaps in a less visible way. The states did, however, turn to other forms of treatment which supporters touted as having none of the drawbacks of the facilities in the earlier era. But these new treatment options have their own problems, many of which mirror the earlier practices that had been banned.

A. Cases from the 1970s

Inmates of the Boys' Training School v. Affleck
346 F. Supp. 1354 (D.R.I. 1972)

PETTINE, Chief Judge.

The indignities suffered by juveniles who did not respond well to their confinement to the Boys Training School and the attempts of Training School officials to cope with the disciplinary and running-away problems presented by such juveniles led to the institution of this Civil Rights action. Confinement of these juveniles in the maximum security Adult Correctional Institution, in the resuscitated relic of a former women's prison, in dim and cold steel cellblocks, and in a wing of the adult medium security prison is argued to violate plaintiffs' constitutional rights to due process, and equal protection, and to constitute cruel and unusual punishment.

Five named plaintiffs, for themselves and on behalf of a class, seek a preliminary injunction stopping confinement of juveniles in the Adult Correctional Institution Maxi-

461

mum Security building; in the solitary confinement cells of the Medium-Minimum Security building of the A.C.I.; and in Annex B, the old women's reformatory. They also seek to stop transfers of juveniles to the Youth Correctional Center (Annex C) of the Medium-Minimum Security Building and isolation of any juvenile in a room for more than two hours without a psychiatrist's certificate, and in any event, for more than 24 hours within a seven-day period. They also seek to define certain minimum requirements for conditions of confinement. While they do not seek to close Annex C immediately, they seek the return to the Training School of those juveniles transferred there without a judicial hearing.

Further prayers for relief raise, at the outside, important questions of the philosophy of treatment of juvenile offenders and, at base, vital questions of what rights juveniles retain in their confinement at state correctional centers. Arguing that these juveniles have a right to rehabilitative treatment, plaintiffs seek institution of vocational training, a drug rehabilitation program, and a psychiatric counseling program at the Boys' Training School. They also seek a full day of schooling for juveniles under the age of sixteen, three hours of outdoors athletics, and the right of the juveniles to obtain food daily from the canteen unless a meal is served after six p. m. daily.

Jurisdiction exists under 28 U.S.C. § 1343. This has been certified as a class action.

. . . .

This action raises questions of substantial constitutional import and will not be dismissed. As the Supreme Court recently held summary placement of an inmate in solitary confinement states a cause of action under 42 U.S.C.A. § 1983. This law suit goes to the conditions of confinement of juveniles and, as such, is well within the jurisdiction of the federal courts.

The intercession of a federal court into a state correctional system is a matter of much gravity and is not done here lightly. The Court, having entered a consent decree recently in a case concerning conditions at the Rhode Island Adult Correctional Institutions, was hopeful that the issues in this case could be similarly resolved, and accordingly, has encouraged the parties to negotiate their differences. Such efforts were unavailing; rather, as the record in this action demonstrates, this Court has had great difficulty in securing compliance from defendants with even customary discovery orders. In the circumstances of this case, the Court finds no equitable reason to withhold from ruling.

. . . .

Findings of Fact

The class of inmates at the Boys Training School may be divided into five sub-classes, depending on the reason for commitment: 1) those voluntarily committed by their parents; 2)those awaiting trial; 3) those convicted of delinquency; 4) those adjudicated wayward; and 5) those found to be dependent or neglected.

Most of the boys at the Training School are housed in cottages on the School grounds. For reasons concerned mostly with discipline and escape problems, some boys have been transferred from the cottages to functionally distinct and geographically separate institutions, known as Annex B, Annex C, Annex C cellblock, and the Maximum Security building of the Adult Correctional Institution (ACI). Some juveniles in Annex C and its cellblock were transferred there directly pursuant to court proceedings. As stipulated by the parties, juveniles otherwise are transferred to Annex B, Annex C and its cellblock, and Maximum Security without judicial hearing. It has been the past practice of defendants to effectuate these transfers without administrative hearing or prior notice. There are no specific rules or regulations which indicate what offenses will result in transfer of a juvenile to Maximum Security.

A registered nurse and a licensed practical nurse, located in the main building at the BTS, are on duty from 6:30 a. m. to 3 p. m. on weekdays, and on call for emergencies until 10 p. m. There is no psychiatrist or clinical psychologist on the BTS staff. A routine physical examination is given on entrance of a boy to the Training School. There is evidence, and I so find, of at least two probable suicide attempts by boys who received no medical or psychiatric care proximately following the attempts. The response of BTS supervisors to these suicide attempts was solitary confinement. There is other evidence indicating that the boys have not received adequate medical care; however, there is also contradicting evidence.

The decisions to transfer juveniles to the Maximum Security Building of the ACI is made by the Superintendent of the BTS, subject to the approval of the Assistant Director for Correctional Services. Administrative transfers to Annex C are made on the decision of the Superintendent of the BTS alone. Boys detained at the BTS pending a court hearing have been administratively transferred both to the ACI and to Annex C. Boys confined to the BTS for truancy have been administratively transferred to Annex C.

Annex B

Annex B is a wing of the old women's reformatory built in 1863 and contains dingy cement rooms, approximately six feet by eight feet. Each room is furnished only with a bed, a sink, and a toilet. The toilet is flushed from outside the room by BTS personnel. The only opening in these cells is a barred window on the far wall, which opens onto a catwalk from which the inmate is observed.

Two of these cells are stripped isolation cells, containing nothing but a toilet, and a mattress on the floor. The cells have, at times, not had artificial lighting. In one of the cells, the window is boarded over, rendering it completely dark at times. These cells are known as "bug-out" rooms and are used for solitary confinement of boys.

The boys confined to Annex B are never allowed to go outside and exercise. Indeed they are almost never allowed out of their cells. They are allowed out of their cells only to take daily showers and to get meal trays. Meals are eaten in the rooms. Some boys, who have been in Annex B for a specified period of time, are allowed out of their cells to watch television for a short time. There are a few magazines and books available. A teacher provides one and a half hours daily of education to some boys. This education consists chiefly of working math problems.

No nurse or doctor is on duty at Annex B. Medical care for an inmate must first be requested by a staff member. Even when medical care was so requested in Annex B, it was usually not forthcoming.

Boys are confined to Annex B for periods ranging from a few days to two and a half months. No visitors, and this includes parents, are allowed.

The solitary confinement cells in Annex B are used to punish infractions by boys committed after they are confined to Annex B. Boys have been kept in these "bug-out" rooms a maximum of three to seven days. One inmate testified, and I accept his testimony as true, that he was confined to the solitary confinement cell for a week, wearing only his underwear. The room was dark and was cold. He was not given toilet paper, soap, sheets, blanket, or change of clothes. He was not allowed to leave the room. His testimony is corroborated by similar testimony from other boys who have been confined there. Boys do not receive a physical or psychiatric examination either prior to, during, or after confinement in the "bug-out" room.

There is no psychiatrist or clinical psychologist on the Training School staff or engaged in regular counseling at the school. Psychiatric help has been requested for inmates by staff members and not received. There is an obvious need for psychiatric aid as the following incident demonstrates.

A staff member testified, and I accept his testimony as true, that while on duty at Annex B he observed a boy attempting to hang himself. He managed to get the boy down. Requesting instructions and assistance from his superiors, the staff member was told to put the boy in the "bug-out" room. He did. Once in the room the boy started banging his head into the wall. The staff member removed the hysterical boy from the room. Assistance arrived in the form of two employees of the BTS, one a truck driver. They stayed and talked to the boy for a short period of time then instructed the staff member to put the boy back in the "bug-out" room. Disobeying these instructions, the staff member talked with the boy in his office for several hours until the boy was calmer. No trained psychiatric help was given.

During the past year, Annex B, including the two isolation rooms has enjoyed full occupancy. This Court ordered Annex B closed in January, 1972, by temporary restraining order. Defendants have agreed to continue the restraining order and have not since used Annex B.

Annex B was considered to be less severe confinement than Annex C by Training School officials.

Annex C

Annex C, which is a closed-off wing of the Medium-Minimum Security building of the Adult Correctional Institution, is a series of rooms on either side of a long corridor. One or two boys occupy a room, secured by a locked door. The windows are barred and many are broken, rendering the rooms cold. Some windows and the bars on the windows have been broken by boys in escape attempts. Annex C is far from escape proof.

Annex C contains 16 rooms, 15 are used for the boys and one room is used for staff. There is also a shower room and a recreation room. Access is had to an outdoors fenced-in yard. The basic furnishings of each room are a desk, a chair, beds, and a small table. There is a small window in the door of the cell. Clothing, bedding, and toilet articles are issued.

Meals are taken in the adult cafeteria where the boys have some contact with adult inmates, although this contact is generally limited by BTS personnel. Breakfast is at 7 a. m.; lunch, at 11 a. m.; and dinner at 3 p. m. After 3 p. m. candy is available at the canteen for some of the boys. For those without the canteen privileges there is nothing to eat for the 16 hour period between 3 p. m. and 7 a. m.

In spite of the presence of the exercise yard, it appears that the boys are rarely allowed outside for exercise. It is alleged that boys have not used the yard since Summer of 1971. There is no nurse and no doctor on duty in Annex C, nor do they make regular visits there. There is a locked medicine chest available, but the boys complain that their medicine is not given to them.

There is a "level" program at Annex C, that is, depending on his progress, a boy may be advanced to a different level with more privileges. One variant with the different levels is the amount of time a boy is allowed out of his cell. When not in their cells, the primary recreational activities in which the boys engage are watching television, roaming the hall, playing cards or doing calisthenics.

Boys under sixteen years of age are required to receive some educational training. A teacher comes for two hours a day. He teaches two groups, each of which receives an hour of education. Education primarily consists of doing mathematics problems. There are no math textbooks but there is a history book on which tests but not lessons are given. It is unclear whether boys over 17 years of age are allowed to participate in this education. There are inmates who have surpassed the level of education taught at Annex C so find it useless. Students have been, at times, excluded from this schooling by BTS officials.

There is no vocational training. A counselor comes regularly, but, as testified, the plaintiffs may individually see him for only ten minutes weekly or less. The visitors allowed other than the counselor are professionals such as attorneys. There are no activities such as arts or crafts, nor are there individualized programs. There is a ping-pong table some of the inmates are allowed to use. While defendants have submitted a schedule indicating there are "Human Relations" sessions, the overwhelming weight of the evidence to date is that there have not been any such sessions.

I accept as true the statement in plaintiffs' affidavits that boys are locked in their rooms for 24 hour periods for such offenses as inability to perform an exercise during calisthenics, "kidding around" with roommates, and making noise to get the guards to let them out to go to the bathroom. I also accept as true that guards sometimes ignore the boys' requests to go to the toilet or to open the window.

Transfers to Annex C are frequently grounded on escape attempts, and are accomplished without notice or hearing. There is evidence that the Assistant Director for Youth Services and the Superintendent of the BTS consider Annex C to be in need of change.

Annex C Cellblock

Located on the floor above Annex C is a series of small, dimly lit, steel-barred cells used for solitary confinement. Each cell is approximately eight feet by four feet, containing a metal slab bed and mattress, sink, and toilet. Boys confined there are released only to take showers, about twice a week. They get no exercise. The inmate's attorney, but not his family, is allowed to visit him there. Because windows on the wall opposite the cellblock are broken, the cells are cold. There is a small hole in the bars, through which meals, sometimes cold, are passed.

At times reading materials and toilet articles are given to the boys, at times they are withheld. Confinement to the cellblock is frequently for 15 day maximum periods. Clean sheets or underwear is not provided during the stay.

The offenses for which a boy is confined to the cellblock include running away, fighting, assault on guards, and homosexual behaviour.

There is no nurse or doctor on duty or who makes regular visits. A staff member testified, and I find as true, that on one occasion on coming on duty in the cellblock he discovered that a boy had slit his wrists, which were still bleeding and covered with bloody towels. Notifying other staff of this and requesting medical care for the boy, he was told they already knew of it. No doctor came to attend the boy during the next eight hours, nor was any other care forthcoming.

Maximum Security

Juveniles have been transferred from the Boys Training School to cells amidst the adult population of sections of the Maximum Security Building at the ACI. The juveniles are subject to the same rules, punishments, and opportunities as the adult inmates. While rehabilitative programs are generally available, the juveniles have not participated in them.

They have continual contact with adult inmates and learn from these inmates the tricks of the trade of crime. They have been the subject of homosexual overtures and threats from adult inmates.

The ACI contains adult male convicts who are convicted of felonies or misdemeanors and adults accused of committing felonies and misdemeanors.

. . . .

Conclusions of Law

This suit is concerned with the rights of boys confined to the Boys Training School. Not all of these boys have been convicted of violation of the criminal laws. Some are there because they are "wayward" children. Among such "wayward" boys, are boys who are found to be truants from schools, disobedient boys, and boys who have run away from home "without good or sufficient cause."[1] Parents may voluntarily commit their sons to the Training School. Boys may be sent there because of "idleness." Other boys may end up at the Training School because they have been found to be "dependent" or "neglected" by their parents. It is possible for a boy to be committed to the BTS not for something he does, but for what he is, that is, "neglected." Furthermore, boys who have been accused of "delinquency" but who have not been tried before the Family Court of Rhode Island may be committed to the Training School. All of these boys, without distinction as to how they came to the Training School, have been subject to the Superintendent's discretion to transfer them to Annex B, and Annex C and its cellblock, and the Maximum Security Building of the ACI.

The purpose of removing a juvenile from his family enunciated by the Rhode Island legislature is "to secure for him custody, care and discipline as nearly as possible equivalent to that which should have been given by his parents." He is to be removed from his parents only when "his welfare or the safety and protection of the public cannot be safeguarded without such removal."

The purpose of confinement of juveniles under Rhode Island law is "instruction and reformation," not punishment. An adjudication upon a juvenile does not have the effect of a conviction[,] nor is such a child deemed a criminal.

Juvenile adjudicative proceedings must be conducted in compliance with the standards of Due Process of law, because, as was held by the United States Supreme Court:

> "Ultimately, however, we confront the reality of that portion of the Juvenile Court process with which we deal in this case. A boy is charged with misconduct. The boy is committed to an institution where he may be restrained of liberty for years. It is of no constitutional consequence — and of limited practical meaning — that the institution to which he is committed is called an Industrial School. The fact of the matter is that, however, euphemistic the title, a 'receiving home' or an 'industrial school' for juveniles is an institution of confinement in which the child is incarcerated for a greater or lesser time. His world becomes 'a building with whitewashed walls, regimented routine and institutional hours....' Instead of mother and father and sisters and brothers and friends and classmates, his world is peopled by guards, custodians, state employees, and 'delinquents' confined with him for anything from waywardness to rape and homicide.

In view of this, it would be extraordinary if our Constitution did not require the procedural regularity and the exercise of care implied in the phrase 'due process.'"

---

1. See Chapter 6, *infra* dealing with status offenders.

Rehabilitation, then, is the interest which the state has defined as being the purpose of confinement of juveniles. Due process in the adjudicative stages of the juvenile justice system has been defined differently from due process in the criminal justice system because the goal of the juvenile system, rehabilitation, differs from the goals of the criminal system, which include punishment, deterrence and retribution. Thus due process in the juvenile justice system requires that the post-adjudicative stage of institutionalization further this goal of rehabilitation. And whatever deviations, if any, from this goal of rehabilitation which might be tolerated as to those incarcerated juveniles convicted of violations of the criminal laws, such deviations are far less tolerable for the other classes of children incarcerated by the state.

. . . .

Annex B

Although defendants have voluntarily closed Annex B, the issue of confinement of juveniles at Annex B is not moot. In closing Annex B defendants did not concede any unconstitutionality or illegality in its operation. Because the situation may again be changed, the issue is not moot.

Conditions at Annex B were deplorable, as defendants themselves must have recognized in stopping its use. Lest defendants find themselves pressing Annex B into use again because of lack of adequate facilities elsewhere, this Court enjoins the use of Annex B and orders that it be closed.

. . . .

The fact that there is only some evidence of physical abuse of the boys does not immunize defendants from condemnation under the Eighth Amendment. The conditions in Annex B are insidiously destructive of the humanity of these boys. There were no or pitifully few "facilities or personnel for social services, exercise, recreation, reading, rehabilitation, or any other human resources to meet human needs." To confine a boy without exercise, always indoors, almost always in a small cell, with little in the way of education or reading materials, and virtually no visitors from the outside world is to rot away the health of his body, mind, and spirit. To then subject a boy to confinement in a dark and stripped confinement cell with inadequate warmth and no human contact can only lead to his destruction.

The prohibition on cruel and unusual punishment is not a static concept "* * * but may acquire meaning as public opinion becomes enlightened by a humane justice." The fact that juveniles are *in theory* not punished, but merely confined for rehabilitative purposes, does not preclude operation of the Eighth Amendment. The reality of confinement in Annex B is that it is punishment. It is punishment imposed on obdurate boys by defendant administrators of the Training School. The legislature could not constitutionally, and has not, directly authorized confinement of juveniles to the "bug-out" rooms of Annex B. Defendants cannot do, in their administrative discretion, that which the legislature could not constitutionally authorize.

. . . .

I hold that isolation of children under the circumstances as described in my findings of fact for the solitary confinement rooms of Annex B to be cruel and unusual punishment, and enjoin any use of these confinement cells.

Further this Court holds that because the conditions of confinement in Annex B are anti-rehabilitative, use of Annex B is enjoined as a violation of equal protection and due process of law. If a boy were confined indoors by his parents, given no education or exercise and allowed no visitors, and his medical needs were ignored, it is likely that the state would intervene and remove the child for his own protection. Certainly, then, the state acting in its *parens patriae* capacity cannot treat the boy in the same manner and justify having deprived him of his liberty. Children are not chattels.

Maximum Security-ACI

Plaintiffs attack confinement of juveniles at the ACI on two theories—that the administrative transfer procedures do not meet the requirements of due process and equal protection and that, regardless of the procedures used, confinement of juveniles with adults at a penal institution is constitutionally impermissible.

It appears that the original decision to transfer a boy to Maximum Security is made by defendant Devine and is subject to the approval of defendant Affleck. No rules have been promulgated defining the circumstances under which such a transfer would be deemed warranted, nor are there any other forms of institutionalized controls on defendants' discretion. The constitutionality of these transfer procedures was upheld by the Rhode Island Supreme Court in *Long v. Langlois*. *Long* appears to be decided on the theory that juveniles confined to the Training School have no claim to constitutional rights, and so has been overruled by *In re Gault*.

There is a substantial question whether a boy who has not been afforded the full protections of the criminal adjudicatory process may be confined to the ACI at all.

This Court is greatly disturbed by the testimony of two plaintiffs who have been confined to the ACI that they learned little there other than how to better commit crimes, that they were threatened with homosexual attacks, and that they had not participated in any rehabilitative programs. Such a situation surely cannot be in society's best interest. I note that a report by a committee appointed by the Governor of Rhode Island strongly recommended that the practice of incarcerating juveniles at the ACI be stopped.

The Court recognizes that some of these juveniles may be detrimental to the atmosphere of the Training School and are better confined elsewhere. Confinement with adult felons in a prison is not the only alternative open to defendants for dealing with these boys....

Annex C and Annex C Cellblock

It appears that Annex C is used primarily for two purposes; that is, to punish juveniles who have caused discipline problems and to detain juveniles who have run away in a somewhat more escape proof facility. According to defendants, the primary mission of Annex C is security from escape. Annex C cellblock serves the same purposes....

The class of inmates at the BTS consists of several subclasses according to the reasons for their confinement. There are boys there (1) who have been voluntarily committed by their parents; (2) who have been adjudicated dependent or neglected by their parents; (3) who have been convicted of delinquency[,] that is, who have committed an offense which, if committed by an adult, would be a felony, or otherwise more than once violated a law; (4) who have been adjudicated wayward, that is, deserted home without good cause, or habitually associated with dissolute, etc. persons, or leading an immoral or vicious life, or habitually disobedient, or truant, or violated a law; and (5) those awaiting trial. For all of these subclasses the legislature has decreed rehabilitative non-penal treatment.

The question is to what extent confinement in Annex C and in its cellblock can be justified as necessary to the ends of rehabilitation. The connection between this confinement and rehabilitation may be thought to exist through several links. First, as defendants have argued, they have to have the boys to treat them, that is, they cannot treat a boy who has run away. So they seek to justify this confinement as both actually necessary to stop yet another run away attempt and as a psychological deterrent to future attempts. They also argue their responsibility is to keep these boys out of the outside community until they have been reformed and are ready to return. Another link is the need to segregate boys, both to remove them as an obstacle to the rehabilitation of others, and to reform them. Presumably, segregated juveniles are themselves helped to reform by segregation by removing them from situations with which they cannot cope and by depriving them of "privileges" which they then presumably have incentive to earn back. There is also some evidence that on at least one occasion segregation has been necessary due to racial tensions. Defendants assert that Annex C and its cellblock are the only facilities they have in which they can segregate juveniles or keep them from running away.

Whatever the reasons, confinement in Annex C and its cellblock is punishment. The conditions of confinement are themselves detrimental to rehabilitation. It is conceivable perhaps, that this would not be so for security confinement in some other facility, but, as defendants assert, all they have is Annex C. Yet it is also clear that the conditions of confinement in Annex C and the cellblock are not the least restrictive means available to defendants for achieving their purposes of segregation and preventive detention, assuming arguendo these are permissible purposes.

Specifically, as to Annex C, I find no reason to deprive inmates of outdoors exercise. A well fenced exercise yard is available and is part of the institution. It should be used to provide a minimum of three hours of outdoors exercise daily, weather permitting. Defendants must provide daily outdoors exercise for all inmates of the BTS. I would note that this relief is in accord with testimony that the Assistant Director of the Department of Social and Rehabilitative Services wanted the inmates to have outdoors exercise.

As to education, there is a bitterly cruel irony in removing a boy from his parents because he is truant from school and then confining him to a small room, without exercise, where he gets no education because he already knows how to work the few math problems which constitute education at Annex C. Boys confined to Annex C are entitled to the same education received by inmates at the Training School proper....

This Court sees no reason for feeding boys on a schedule which will insure their hunger. So long as defendants adhere to the present feeding schedule, and/or serve dinner to inmates before 6 p. m., they are enjoined from confining inmates in Annex C without allowing them daily canteen rights and the right to keep food in their rooms.

Even with these changes in conditions at Annex C, confinement there will be worse than confinement in the cottages. Plaintiffs accordingly ask that all boys who were transferred to Annex C without a judicial hearing be sent back to the cottages and further seek to enjoin defendants from transferring any juvenile to Annex C and confining any juvenile to the Annex C cellblock. These motions are denied. The Court finds itself in need of considerably more expert testimony before it attempts to rule on these questions. The Court invites both sides to present expert evidence at the hearing on the merits. Considerable harm might result to the community were this Court to summarily deny defendants' use of Annex C.

Although these motions for preliminary injunction are denied, the Court would like to make some seminal observations. As to the transfer procedures, the loss of liberty entailed by a boy in a transfer to Annex C or the cellblock may well require that such transfers be done in accordance with due process of law.

It may also be that transfer to Annex C, if eventually found to be permissible at all, may well be limited to one or possibly two of the subclasses at the BTS, those adjudicated delinquent and those awaiting trial for delinquency. Assuming that no rehabilitative justification may be found for Annex C, then Annex C may only be justified in terms of society's need to be protected. It would be foolish to ignore the reality that society may have been harmed by a delinquent's offenses and should be protected against them. The same may be true for a juvenile awaiting trial for delinquency. But I take it that the presumption of innocence attaches to juveniles awaiting trial. It may be that the only permissible purpose for confining these awaiting trial juveniles is "to make certain that those detained are present when their cases are finally called for trial."

As to the other subclasses of inmates, society needs very little or no protection against them. "Wayward" children have not violated any criminal laws, except perhaps misdemeanor offenses. I doubt whether the legislature could pass laws to imprison a boy for truancy; yet for exactly this reason boys have been confined to the BTS and eventually to Annex C. As the Supreme Court has said, "[D]ue process requires that the nature and duration of commitment bear some reasonable relationship to the purpose for which the individual is committed." ...

Children who are committed to the BTS because they are dependent or have been neglected by their parents are confined on what must be a pure *parens patriae* theory. They are at the BTS because of their parents' actions, not their own. To cause them to suffer deprivations under law because of their status is constitutionally forbidden.

Solitary Confinement

Plaintiffs ask for an injunction restraining the isolation of a juvenile in a room for more than two hours unless a psychiatrist certifies in writing to the Court and counsel for the plaintiffs that the juvenile, if released, would be either a danger to himself or a danger to the others in the institution, but in no case may a juvenile be isolated in a room for more than 24 hours within a seven day period.

Plaintiffs have introduced some expert testimony by affidavit, arguing that isolation is contrary to rehabilitation. They argue that the effects of isolation on a juvenile are far worse than on an adult....

Plaintiffs have demonstrated probability of success in showing that plaintiff juveniles have a claim to rehabilitative treatment. This Court is convinced that solitary confinement may be psychologically damaging, anti-rehabilitative, and, at times inhumane.

However, the Court does not feel that there is sufficient expert testimony on the record of what constitutes solitary confinement as opposed to segregation and at what point it becomes destructive. In the absence of such evidence the Court finds it impossible to frame an equitable order and so denies the motion for preliminary injunction. From the record, however, it appears that solitary confinement is used as a solution to problems caused by juveniles at the BTS. The Court would urge defendants to find individualized methods of treatment for problem boys before final hearing on this matter.

Minimal Conditions of Confinement

Plaintiffs seek an injunction prohibiting confinement of juveniles in any facility without providing them the following:

a) A room equipped with lighting sufficient for an inmate to read by until 10:00 p. m.;

b) sufficient clothing to meet seasonal needs;

c) bedding, including blankets, sheets, pillows, pillow cases and mattresses; such bedding must be changed once a week;

d) personal hygiene supplies, including soap, toothpaste, towels, toilet paper, and a toothbrush;

e) a change of undergarments and socks every day;

f) minimum writing materials[:] pen, pencil, paper and envelopes;

g) prescription eyeglasses, if needed;

h) equal access to all books, periodicals and other reading materials located in the Training School;

i) daily showers;

j) daily access to medical facilities, including the provision of a 24-hour nursing service;

k) general correspondence privileges.

Although these minimal requirements may be provided in the cottages at the Training School, the record indicates that these have not been made available at all times in all facilities of the BTS. These are substantially the same as the regulations for minimal conditions of confinement of adult inmates at the ACI, which were promulgated by the State following this Court's order in *Morris v. Travisono*, final consent decree entered April 20, 1972.

The state has offered no reason to justify this discrimination against juveniles. The Court is hard pressed to think of any reason to justify this discrimination which would serve the purpose of rehabilitation. While defendants' carrot-and-stick program at the BTS which uses loss of privileges and gain of privileges to spur socially acceptable behavior from the juveniles might be thought to justify this, there are floors on the power of defendant administrators to deprive inmates of "privileges." It is clear that the state does not consider these minimal conditions of confinement to be "privileges" for adults, nor does this Court consider them to be "privileges" for juveniles. Society has bargained with these juveniles and it should be an honest bargain. They have been confined through a process offering them fewer protections than adults have; they may not now be treated worse than the adult inmates are. Defendants are ordered to provide these minimum conditions of confinement.

Morales v. Turman
364 F. Supp. 166 (E.D. Tex. 1973)

JUSTICE, District Judge:

Conclusions of Law
[The court's findings of fact are implicit in its conclusions of law.]

1. This court has jurisdiction of this civil action under the first, eighth, and fourteenth amendments to the United States Constitution, [and] 42 U.S.C.A. § 1983. Pendent jurisdiction also exists to decide questions arising from alleged violations of rights secured by state statutes in the context of this lawsuit.

2. The eighth amendment's prohibition against cruel and unusual punishment applies to state as well as federal government. The protection applies not only to convicted persons but also to non-convicted persons held in custody. Juveniles held in state institutions are protected by the eighth amendment.

3. The widespread practice of beating, slapping, kicking, and otherwise physically abusing juvenile inmates, in the absence of any exigent circumstances, in many of the Texas Youth Council facilities, particularly the Mountain View and Gatesville schools, violates state law, the avowed policies of the Texas Youth Council, and the eighth amendment to the United States Constitution. This kind of punishment, which is administered not merely in the absence of legislative authorization, whether express or implied, but rather in express derogation of state law, violates the eighth amendment because it is so severe as to degrade human dignity; is inflicted in a wholly arbitrary fashion; is so severe as to be unacceptable to contemporary society; and finally, is not justified as serving any necessary purpose.

4. The use of tear gas and other chemical crowd-control devices in situations not posing an imminent threat to human life or an imminent and substantial threat to property—but merely as a form of punishment—constitutes cruel and unusual punishment in violation of the eighth amendment.

5. Placing inmates in solitary confinement or secured facilities, in the absence of any legislative or administrative limitation on the duration and intensity of the confinement and subject only to the unfettered discretion of correctional officers, constitutes cruel and unusual punishment in violation of the eighth amendment.

6. Requiring inmates to maintain silence during periods of the day merely for purposes of punishment, and to perform repetitive, nonfunctional, degrading, and unnecessary tasks for many hours[—]the so-called make-work, such as pulling grass without bending the knees on a large tract of ground not intended for cultivation or any other purpose, or moving dirt with a shovel from one place on the ground to another and then back again many times, or buffing a small area of the floor for a period of time exceeding that in which any reasonable person would conclude that the floor was long since sufficiently buffed[—]constitutes cruel and unusual punishment in violation of the eighth amendment.

7. Racial segregation of any state-operated facility is unconstitutional.

8. The initial placement or subsequent transfer of inmates to Mountain View, the maximum security unit, absent any attempt through a hearing that comports with minimal due process requirements to determine which of the juvenile offenders pose a danger to society, constitutes a violation of the fourteenth amendment.

9. Although the limitation on permissible censorship of the mail of adult prisoners remains uncertain, it is clear that any restrictions upon the important first amendment freedom of communication must bear, at the very least, a rational relationship to the advancement of a legitimate state interest. The defendants have advanced no legitimate state interest, much less a compelling interest, that is served by the reading or censoring of incoming or outgoing mail or by limitation of the persons with whom inmates may correspond. A legitimate state interest in preventing the flow of contraband into Texas Youth Council institutions justifies only the least restrictive practices adequate to achieve that interest—in this case, the opening of incoming mail in the presence of the inmate to whom it is addressed for the sole purpose of examining it for contraband.

10. The practice of prohibiting or discouraging juveniles in TYC institutions from conversing in languages other than English, under circumstances that would not give rise to similar prohibitions on the speaking of English, is a violation of the first amendment to the Constitution.

11. The law of the state of Texas requires that the TYC adhere to its statutory duty to provide "a program of constructive training aimed at rehabilitation and reestablishment

in society of children adjudged delinquent." This law confers upon each juvenile committed to the custody of the Texas Youth Council a right to humane and rehabilitative treatment directed toward the ultimate purpose of reintegrating the child into society.

In addition to this state statutory right, the commitment of juveniles to institutions under conditions and procedures much less rigorous than those required for the conviction and imprisonment of an adult offender gives rise to certain limitations upon the conditions under which the state may confine the juveniles. This doctrine has been labeled the "right to treatment," and finds its basis in the due process clause of the fourteenth amendment. Thus juveniles committed to the custody of the Texas Youth Council enjoy both a state statutory and a federal constitutional "right to treatment."

12. The segregation by untrained correctional officers of some inmates from the general population on the basis of suspected homosexuality constitutes a violation of their state and federal right to treatment.

13. Failure to allow and encourage full participation of family and interested friends in the program of a youthful offender constitutes a violation of the juvenile's state and federal right to treatment.

14. The practice of withholding or neglecting to provide casework, nursing, and psychological or psychiatric services to juveniles confined in solitary confinement or security facilities constitutes a violation of their state and federal right to treatment.

15. Failure to provide inmates of a maximum security institution such as Mountain View, which has a history of brutality, neglect, and intimidation, with access to a person who can hear their complaints and seek administrative redress for their grievances without fear of reprisals, constitutes a violation of their state and federal right to treatment.

16. Confinement of juveniles in an institution in which a nurse is not available on the premises twenty-four hours a day constitutes a violation of their state and federal right to treatment.

17. The employment by the TYC of persons whose personalities, backgrounds, or lack of qualifications render them likely to harm the juveniles in their care either physically or psychologically, absent any attempt to administer the appropriate psychological testing or psychiatric interviews, constitutes a violation of the juveniles' state and federal right to treatment. In particular, failure to employ an individual who is qualified by education, experience, and personal attributes to superintend the rehabilitation of juveniles who have engaged in seriously delinquent behavior constitutes a violation of those juveniles' state and federal right to treatment.

18. The plaintiffs are without an adequate remedy at law that would protect them against the wrongs described in the foregoing findings of fact.

19. It is appropriate at this time for the court to enter a preliminary injunction to enjoin certain of the practices complained of by the plaintiffs, because their continuation would work irreparable injury, both physical and psychological, upon members of the plaintiff class.

Note

The *Morales* case has a convoluted history. The districts court's final 73-page order was appealed to the Fifth Circuit, which reversed on the ground that a three-judge district court was required. That conclusion went to the United States Supreme Court, which reversed, and remanded to the Fifth Circuit. The Fifth Circuit opinion follows. Ultimately, the parties entered into a consent decree.

Morales v. Turman

562 F.2d 993 (5th Cir. 1977)

AINSWORTH, Circuit Judge:

This matter is being considered by us on remand from the Supreme Court which held, contrary to our previous ruling, that determination of this case by a three-judge court was unnecessary....

On additional consideration we now conclude that this case must be remanded for a further evidentiary hearing concerning changes that have occurred in TYC. Extensive changes appear to have taken place. Thus an additional hearing is necessary to complete the record with TYC being afforded a full opportunity to present proof of such changes. Further, we have considerable doubts about the legal theory of a right to treatment that was relied on so heavily by the District Court.

The trial court's denial of the defendant's original motion to reopen the record was improper if TYC had sufficiently altered its operations at that time to warrant the receipt of additional evidence. Reopening the case for additional evidence is normally a discretionary matter for the trial court to decide. However, the circumstances of this case may render the denial of the motion an abuse of discretion.

Moreover, the changes in TYC's operation indicated in the defendants' brief are relevant to any injunctive relief that might be granted.... Many of the objectionable practices in the Texas juvenile system may already have been ended. Further, these changes may indicate a new attitude on the part of TYC that would eliminate the risk of further constitutional violations. Thus, new procedures adopted by the TYC would significantly alter or reduce the scope of any injunctive relief.

Consideration of additional evidence is especially important here as we are dealing with a significant federal intrusion into a state's affairs, and we should refrain from interference in state affairs unless necessary. State governments have wide discretion in dealing with their affairs. Hence, if Texas has already brought its detention facilities up to constitutional standards, we should be reluctant to impose additional restraints. Finally, limiting injunctive relief allows the state greater freedom to experiment with new programs for the treatment of juveniles.

These considerations which should have led to a reopening of the record in 1974 in the District Court have grown stronger with the additional passage of time. All of the arguments for permitting the state to show a change in circumstances continue to apply with greater force today.

While an evidentiary hearing will be necessary to determine the full magnitude of the changes in TYC, the supplemental brief for the TYC officials outlines some of the changes that allegedly have been made. A brief examination of a few of the major reforms alleged to have been made indicates, if true, a new attitude on the part of TYC and suggests that a fuller investigation of these claims would be useful.

Significant changes have allegedly taken place in the TYC's treatment of youths. Non-institutional settings for the care of juveniles has been emphasized to the extent that the declining institutional population has resulted in the state's closing three of the facilities at Gatesville and transferring the Mountain View facility, a major focus in the initial trial, to the Texas Department of Corrections. For those students who are still institutionalized new programs have been developed. For example, for those youths whose evaluation indicates the need for developing self-reliance TYC operates a therapeutic wilderness camp that includes both survival skills and academic instruction. For all juveniles in its care TYC is developing a treatment program that will develop living, learning and working skills. New staff members, often members of minority groups, have been hired to help implement these programs.

We are told that TYC has also made significant procedural changes to reduce the likelihood that a child will be abused while in custody. TYC has established a grievance system for the juveniles with time requirements to ensure the efficient processing of the complaints. In addition, a follow-up report determining the student's satisfaction or dissatisfaction with the action taken on his grievance must be obtained. Finally, the youth is provided with a full and fair opportunity to appeal an adverse decision on his grievance.

Admittedly, these statements in the defendant's brief, if proven, do not ensure that the serious abuses found by the District Court, such as beatings and prolonged solitary confinement, have been eliminated. However, they do indicate a new atmosphere within TYC which makes such conduct unlikely and suggest that further inquiry into the current conditions of these institutions should be made. Also the reforms noted here are highly relevant to many of the detailed minimum requirements set forth in the District Court opinion.

Although the District Court has only ordered the parties to negotiate a plan for final relief, negotiations between the parties could not adequately incorporate these changes in the operation of TYC. To guide the negotiations the District Court has set forth extremely detailed minimum standards for the operation of TYC's facilities. Under these standards, for example, TYC must: (1) administer to all youths newly committed to their case Leiter and Weschler IQ tests standardized for blacks and Mexican Americans; (2) have each student assessed by a language pathologist; (3) provide a coeducational living environment[;] and (4) provide a psychological staff with psychologists holding either masters or doctorates in psychology and experienced in work with adolescents. Many other similar requirements may be found in the District Court opinion. Because of this detail, TYC will lack the opportunity to show during negotiations that the changes they have initiated now satisfy constitutional standards even if all the specific requirements of the District Court opinion have not been met. Since the proper treatment of juveniles is a matter of dispute, the standards set forth by the District Court cannot be said to be the only constitutional method for rehabilitating juveniles. Therefore, the District Court must examine the new operations since only those aspects that continue to fail constitutional standards can be enjoined.

For the reasons stated above, we find it necessary to remand this case for further evidentiary hearings. Since additional hearings may influence the relief granted we do not now decide the legal issues presented. We do, however, have reservations concerning the right to treatment theory relied on by the District Judge. In order to expedite a final disposition of this action, our difficulties with this theory are set out below.

A right to treatment for juvenile offenders has not been firmly established. Only in recent years have courts discussed such a right. This right has been defended on two grounds. First, supporters of the doctrine argue that a permissible governmental goal must justify any nontrivial abridgement of a person's liberty. For instance, exercise of the state's *parens patriae* power to provide care or supervision is assumed as the permissible goal for committing juveniles or the mentally incompetent. Treatment must therefore be provided to prevent the exercise of the *parens patriae* power from merely being a pretext for arbitrary governmental action. Second, the right to treatment is viewed as a quid pro quo for reduced procedural protections. Whenever the state detains a person not in retribution for a specific offense, for an unlimited period of time or without the full procedural safeguards of a criminal trial, proponents of this right claim that due process requires that the person deprived of his liberty be in return entitled to treatment. To date most of the cases embracing this theory have involved the civil commitment of the mentally ill.

These rationales for a right to treatment for the mentally ill raise serious problems. The civil commitment of the mentally ill without treatment is not necessarily an impermissible exercise of governmental power. The Constitution does not specify in what manner a state may exercise its *parens patriae* power. Historically, the states merely provided custodial care for the incompetent or mentally ill. The second basis for the right to treatment doctrine, *i. e.*, compensation for reduced procedural protections, is also questionable. The interests of the individual and of society in the particular situation determine the standards for due process. A state should not be required to provide the procedural safeguards of a criminal trial when imposing a quarantine to protect the public against a highly communicable disease. Finally, treatment of the mentally ill is an extremely delicate task. Even experts in the field disagree as to the appropriate treatment and indeed if any treatment will be successful for a given patient. To attempt to specify the type of treatment that should be provided may well be beyond the competence of federal judges.

The case law has not universally accepted a right to treatment for the mentally ill. Further, in a recent case involving the right to treatment for the mentally ill, the Supreme Court held only that a nondangerous person could not be confined without treatment. *O'Connor v. Donaldson*. The Court did not, however, decide whether a nondangerous person could be confined with treatment or if a dangerous person could be confined without treatment.

The argument for a right to treatment is even less strong as related to juvenile offenders. Many of the detained juveniles will have committed acts that clearly pose a danger to society. *Donaldson* left open the appropriateness of confining such individuals without treatment. In addition, since many of the acts that result in a juvenile's detention would be crimes if committed by adults and since adult offenders do not have a right to treatment, a right to treatment for juveniles may be less appropriate than a similar right for the mentally ill. Of course, as a matter of social policy choosing a policy of rehabilitating juvenile offenders may be desirable.

While a right to treatment is doubtful, any constitutional abuses that may be found in the Texas juvenile program can be corrected without embracing such doctrine in this case. The eighth amendment prohibition of cruel and unusual punishment as the constitutional standard for the conditions of imprisonment can adequately remedy the conditions in TYC's institutions. For instance, the physical abuse of the students and degrading work assignments could be eliminated as cruel and unusual without adopting the questionable doctrine of a right to treatment. Admittedly the eighth amendment will not require the state to provide extensive vocational training, detailed personality assessments or coeducational facilities. The choice of providing these services properly remains with the State of Texas herein.

Finally, even if some form of right to treatment doctrine exists the minimum requirements established by the District Court are excessively detailed. A court is not in a position to monitor day-by-day changes that affect rehabilitation programs. New treatments and testing techniques will inevitably develop. A rigid set of requirements for the state will not enable the TYC to adequately adjust to these changes. The passage of time will render obsolete many of the requirements found in the District Court opinion.

Remanded for further proceedings.

Note

For additional cases that discuss conditions in juvenile long term correctional facilities, *see Nelson v Heynes*, 491 F.2d 352 (7th Cir. 1974) (prohibiting intramuscular injection of psychotropic drugs for disciplinary purposes and severe beatings with thick paddles); *Lollis v. N.Y. State Dep't. of Soc. Servs.*, 328 F. Supp. 1115 (S.D.N.Y. 1971) (prohibiting prolonged isolation in bare cells).

B. Do the More Things Change the More They Remain the Same?

1. Texan Calls for Takeover of State's Juvenile Schools

Ralph Blumenthal, N.Y. Times 2/28/07

A long-simmering scandal over sexual abuse of juveniles at schools for youthful offenders broke into the open on Tuesday with an outraged state senator calling for a takeover of the troubled Texas Youth Commission.

... [A] youth commission official acknowledged at a hearing of the State Senate Criminal Justice Committee [that the superintendent of a school in West Texas] ... was aware that two supervisors routinely awakened boys for late-night encounters behind closed doors in deserted offices.

The two supervisors — one of whom had been transferred from another state school after pornography was found on his work computer — were allowed to resign in 2005 without charges. One became the principal of a charter school in Midland, Texas, state officials said. The superintendent was promoted to director of juvenile corrections, a post he still holds, the youth commission confirmed.

"It's outrageous," said State Senator John Whitmire, chairman of the Criminal Justice Committee, who accused the commission of a cover-up.

Neil Nichols, the commission's general counsel and new acting executive director, named on Friday after the director, Dwight Harris, retired under pressure, voiced some contrition, saying at one point, "To say I'm disappointed about that is to say the least."

Mr. Whitmire, Democrat of Houston, was not mollified. "Why should this agency not be put in conservatorship and get a whole new management?" he asked.

He excoriated the commission board for not attending the hearing and canceled an appropriations session for the agency that had been scheduled for Wednesday.

Gov. Rick Perry, a Republican, called the revelations "absolutely reprehensible" and would not rule out a takeover, said a spokesman, Ted Royer. "The governor believes any time a very serious issue like this emerges, every option should be on the table," Mr. Royer said.

Accusations that staff members at the West Texas State School in Pyote (pronounced PIE-oht) were sexually preying on youths there were made to the youth commission as early as December 2003, according to a timeline presented at the hearing.

The complaints did not reach the Texas Rangers until February 2005 and remained largely secret until accounts began appearing in recent weeks on the Web site of the Texas Observer and the pages of The Dallas Morning News.

The problems were widespread at the agency, which annually places some 3,000 juveniles ages 10 to 17 at the time of their felonies in 13 secure schools, senators and witnesses said.

State Senator Juan Hinojosa, Democrat of McAllen, who investigated conditions at another school in his South Texas district in 2005, said, "We found out a lot of youths are kept seven or eight months longer than required, and we want to know why."

Mr. Hinojosa added: "If a young person refuses to have sex with a supervisor, they deduct a point and are required to stay longer."

At another state school in Brownwood in Central Texas, he said, "A supervisor was accused of having sex with a 15-year-old juvenile" — a girl, he said later. It was turned over to the Brownwood police, he said, "with no action — it was covered up."

Mr. Nichols, the acting director, said the commission investigated 1,300 cases of reported wrongdoing last year, including 98 cases of reported sexual abuse. In 78 of the cases, he said, staff members were fired or resigned.

"How about prosecuted?" Mr. Hinojosa asked.

Mr. Nichols did not say. But he said a "large number" of the 78 cases involved female staff members of the commission who had improper sexual contact with students, male and female.

Senators questioned Mr. Nichols about the transfer in 2003 of one supervisor, Ray Brookins, to the West Texas State School from another school for juvenile offenders at San Saba, after pornography had been found on his computer. Mr. Brookins later became assistant superintendent at Pyote and was cited by the Texas Rangers for sexual contact with juveniles there, senators said.

Another supervisor at Pyote, John Paul Hernandez, was also reported by the Texas Rangers to have engaged in sexual contact with students, senators said.

Both supervisors left the youth agency and are under investigation, said the Ward County district attorney, Randall Reynolds.

Mr. Brookins was said at the hearing to be working at a bar in Austin.

Mr. Hernandez became principal at a charter school in Midland, the Richard Milburn Academy, said Norman Hall, the school's superintendent. The school did not know of Mr. Hernandez's history when it hired him, Mr. Hall said, and put him on leave several weeks ago.

Mr. Hernandez did not return a call to his mobile phone.

The superintendent at Pyote, Chip Harrison, who knew of the accusations against Mr. Brookins and Mr. Hernandez and kept them on the staff, senators said, is now director of juvenile corrections for the commission, in charge of several schools.

"That's intolerable; that's unacceptable," Mr. Whitmire said.

Mr. Nichols called him "one of our most experienced superintendents," setting off a gasp from parents.

Mr. Harrison did not return a call.

Randall Chance, a former inspector general at the Pyote school and the author of a self-published book, "Raped by the State," said abuses were often covered up. "They're not a problem at the T.Y.C. unless you bring it up," Mr. Chance said, "and then you're the problem."

2. Abuse Claims Poured in Amid Debate

R.G. Ratcliffe, Houston Chronicle 4/29/07

After the Texas Youth Commission sex and physical abuse scandal broke, Gov. Rick Perry and legislative leaders debated for 16 days the best way to halt the violence in the juvenile corrections system before dispatching the Texas Rangers.

During those days, 82 complaints were lodged claiming that TYC youth[s] were victims of excessive force or sexual impropriety by staff and other youths in the system, according to records obtained by the Houston Chronicle under the Public Information Act.

House Democratic Caucus Chairman Jim Dunnam was among the legislators who called for immediately securing TYC facilities with Texas Rangers after the media reported the scandal. He said the state's leadership should have reacted faster to protect TYC's incarcerated youths.

"They (state leaders) should have first and foremost taken immediate action to protect the youth in the facilities from any additional wrongdoing," Dunnam said.

"Things to do with governing boards and restructuring, those are long-term solutions," Dunnam said. "You can't afford to have children neglected or abused while you are debating those long-term solutions."

Perry spokesman Ted Royer said the governor could not have acted more quickly than he did. Royer said Perry needed authorization from the Legislature to take over the agency, and several days were needed to coordinate a law enforcement response that included the Rangers, the Texas Department of Criminal Justice and the state's attorney general's office.

"It was swift by any standard," Royer said.

Lt. Gov. David Dewhurst said the problem was not how swiftly state leadership reacted, but how the agency heads tried to cover up abuse.

"This had nothing to do with Governor Perry. This had everything to do with an agency where the culture had gone bad among certain people," Dewhurst said. "The culture of the agency was to protect their own, was to protect their fellow employees (rather) than safeguard the young people incarcerated there."

The number of complaints that were filed during the initial legislative debate was not unusually high for a system that has logged more than 7,000 complaints of mistreatment of youths since 2000.

But the new TYC management officials, who took over in March, say the system became dramatically safer once the facilities were secured by law enforcement officers.

They said abusive employees are learning that complaints now will be investigated by law enforcement instead of agency administrators.

"This is not going to be a 'You're going to be suspended for a while. You may lose your job,'"said TYC Inspector General Bruce Tony, who has been on the job for two weeks. "It's, 'You're going to go to jail and possibly to prison if you do this kind of stuff.'"

Just how much safer the system is remains unclear because the abuse record-keeping has changed. The emphasis now is on the 2,793 complaints received on a TYC telephone hot line since March 6, when the auditors and Rangers arrived.

More than 800 calls involved complaints about food or uniforms and even homework. Of the remaining calls making criminal allegations, Tony said, some of those involve incidents that date as far back as 1965.

As of April 20, investigators had closed 1,320 cases, mostly by shifting administrative complaints back to the agency.

There have, however, been arrests for misconduct that occurred since Feb. 18.

An administrator of a San Antonio halfway house was arrested on a charge of destroying documents, and a superintendent in Marlin was arrested on a charge of lying to investigators about abuse in his facility.

A female corrections officer was arrested on a charge of having sex with a male inmate, and a male officer was arrested in Fort Worth last week on a charge of having sex with a female inmate.

"I do not believe that incident there (in Fort Worth) would have come to light three months ago," said TYC conservator Jay Kimbrough. "When people made allegations … it was such a vacuum, and nothing happened."

Rep. Jerry Madden, R-Richardson, chairman of the House Corrections Committee, said a real reduction in problems at TYC will not occur until the population is dramatically reduced, misdemeanor offenders are no longer sent there, and guards are better trained.

Madden said that will take time but that the current interventions already are improving the system.

Key events in the TYC investigation:

Feb. 18

The TYC scandal breaks in news accounts by the Texas Observer and Dallas Morning News.

At the Marlin facilities, a youth accused a female officer of fondling him, and a male officer was accused of obtaining oral sex from a female inmate in exchange for some chips.

Gainesville unit staffers reported to superiors that a worker was engaging in "predatory (sexual) behavior" toward youths.

A Gainesville youth said officers "body slammed" him. He had swelling to his right eyebrow and cheek.

Feb. 23

TYC Executive Director Dwight Harris resigns.

A father complained that his son was handcuffed at Victory Field and guards allowed other youths to punch him, knocking out his front tooth.

At the Al Price facility, a youth said other youths assaulted him while the corrections officers were asleep on their shift.

Feb. 26

Senate Criminal Justice Committee Chairman John Whitmire called for ousting TYC management.

Feb. 27

Legislative audit committee recommended a conservator for TYC and ordered state auditors to investigate TYC facilities.

At the John Shero facility, youths accused a female guard of asking male inmates to expose themselves and masturbate.

Feb. 28

Gov. Rick Perry ousted TYC board Chairman Pete Alfaro and defended remaining board members for their management of TYC. The Senate voted unanimously to put the agency into a conservatorship.

Security videos at Evins found a female officer was spending up to two hours at a time with a youth. Her name was tattooed on his upper arm, and her abbreviated first name was on his hand between his fingers.

A staff member at the West Texas State School said another staff member had sex with a student in a walk-in freezer.

March 2

Perry named Jay Kimbrough as special master for TYC but refused to put the agency into a conservatorship.

Youths at three facilities complained they were victims of excessive force. Male corrections officers at McLennan II claimed a female officer was talking to youths about pornography.

March 6

State auditors and Texas Rangers fanned out to TYC facilities.

The same day, youths at two facilities claimed they were victims of excessive force. A female youth at the Ron Jackson facility said male guards watched her shower. Male youths at the John Shero unit said a female guard asked them to masturbate in front of her.

March 29

Kimbrough was approved as conservator.

3. Inquiry Finds Abuse of Inmates in a Youth House

Alfonso A. Narvaez, N.Y. Times 10/15/83

The Hudson County New Jersey prosecutor charged today that inmates at the Hudson County Youth House had been physically and sexually abused.

Two guards have been indicted and, at the county's request, the state has temporarily taken over operation of the institution. It houses males and females from 10 to 17 years old who have been charged or convicted of crimes ranging from incorrigibility to murder.

The Prosecutor, Harold J. Ruvoldt Jr., said in an interview that an undercover investigator had recently been placed in the institution as a guard and had witnessed some of the abuses, such as guards overlooking attacks among inmates and some guards attacking inmates.

"As a result of the investigation, we feel that there is a pattern of physical and sexual abuse of children by inmates against inmates, by guards against inmates and the former occurring with the knowledge and non-intervention of the guards," Mr. Ruvoldt said. "We are concerned about the entire operation of the facility, every aspect of it—the financial, the custodial and the administrative," he said.

Officers of the State Department of Corrections are now running the house, pending a grand jury investigation. "We felt that to continue the situation while the grand jury investigation was going on might be inimical to the best interests of the children and might also present the opportunity for retaliation against the children who might become witnesses and against guards who might become witnesses," Mr. Ruvoldt said.

Earlier Problems Recalled

The guards who were indicted on charges of physically abusing youngsters on Sept. 12 are Robert McNulty, 33, and Ray Howard, 23, both of Jersey City. Mr. Howard was also charged with abusing an inmate on Sept. 21. They have been suspended without pay.

Mr. Ruvoldt said the grand jury was also investigating allegations that drugs and other contraband had been taken into the institution by guards and visitors.

He said it was the second time in three years that problems had been uncovered at the Youth House. In the past, he said, there had been little effort to check the backgrounds of people hired as guards. Three years ago, a number of officers were dismissed when they were found to have police records for crimes ranging from drug addiction to sexual abuse, he said.

James Stabile, a spokesman for the State Department of Corrections, said that investigators from the Internal Affairs Division had been checking conditions at the Youth House for the last month and that they would continue to do so. He said he expected three senior corrections officials sent by the state to continue to operate the institution for about three weeks.

He said officials from the Division of Youth and Family Services were also checking conditions there.

Investigators have been questioning guards and inmates. The facility now houses 44 male and 4 female inmates. The Youth House occupies two floors of the county mental institution, Meadowview Hospital, at 575 County Avenue in Secaucus. The Youth House has 59 employees—35 guards, 12 of whom are female; 5 supervisors, and 19 teachers.

4. Hard Time: A Special Report; Profits at a Juvenile Prison Come with a Chilling Cost

Fox Butterfield, N.Y. Times 7/15/98

Here in the middle of the impoverished Mississippi Delta is a juvenile prison so rife with brutality, cronyism and neglect that many legal experts say it is the worst in the nation.

The prison, the Tallulah Correctional Center for Youth, opened just four years ago where a sawmill and cotton fields once stood. Behind rows of razor wire, it houses 620 boys and young men, age 11 to 20, in stifling corrugated-iron barracks jammed with bunks.

From the run-down homes and bars on the road that runs by it, Tallulah [Louisiana] appears unexceptional, one new cookie-cutter prison among scores built in the United States this decade. But inside, inmates of the privately run prison regularly appear at the infirmary with black eyes, broken noses or jaws or perforated eardrums from beatings by the poorly paid, poorly trained guards or from fights with other boys.

Meals are so meager that many boys lose weight. Clothing is so scarce that boys fight over shirts and shoes. Almost all the teachers are uncertified, instruction amounts to as little as an hour a day, and until recently there were no books.

Up to a fourth of the inmates are mentally ill or retarded, but a psychiatrist visits only one day a week. There is no therapy. Emotionally disturbed boys who cannot follow guards' orders are locked in isolation cells for weeks at a time or have their sentences arbitrarily extended.

These conditions, which are described in public documents and were recounted by inmates and prison officials during a reporter's visit to Tallulah, are extreme, a testament to Louisiana's well-documented violent history and notoriously brutal prison system.

But what has happened at Tallulah is more than just the story of one bad prison. Corrections officials say the forces that converged to create Tallulah—the incarceration of more and more mentally ill adolescents, a rush by politicians to build new prisons while neglecting education and psychiatric services, and states' handing responsibility for juvenile offenders to private companies—have caused the deterioration of juvenile prisons across the country.

Earl Dunlap, president of the National Juvenile Detention Association, which represents the heads of the nation's juvenile jails, said, "The issues of violence against offenders, lack of adequate education and mental health services, of crowding and of poorly paid and poorly trained staff are the norm rather than the exception."

Recognizing the problem, the United States Justice Department has begun a series of investigations into state juvenile systems, including not only Louisiana's but also those of Kentucky, Puerto Rico and Georgia. At the same time, private juvenile prisons in Colorado, Texas and South Carolina have been successfully sued by individuals and groups or forced to give up their licenses.

On Thursday, the Juvenile Justice Project of Louisiana, an offshoot of the Southern Poverty Law Center, filed a Federal lawsuit against Tallulah to stop the brutality and neglect.

In the investigations by the Justice Department, some of the harshest criticism has been leveled at Georgia. The department threatened to take over the state's juvenile system, charging a "pattern of egregious conditions violating the Federal rights of youth," including the use of pepper spray to restrain mentally ill youths, a lack of textbooks, and guards who routinely stripped young inmates and locked them in their cells for days.

A surge in the inmate population forced Georgia's juvenile prison budget up to $220 million from $80 million in just four years, but the money went to building new prisons, with little left for education and psychiatric care. "As we went through a period of rapid increase in juvenile crime and record numbers of juvenile offenders," said Sherman Day, chairman of the Georgia Department of Juvenile Justice, it was "much easier to get new facilities from the Legislature than to get more programs."

After reacting defensively at first, Gov. Zell Miller moved quickly to avert a takeover by agreeing to spend $10 million more this year to hire teachers and medical workers and to increase guard salaries.

Louisiana, whose juvenile system is made up of Tallulah and three prisons operated by the state, is the Justice Department's latest target. In hundreds of pages of reports to a Federal judge who oversees the state's entire prison system under a 1971 consent decree, Justice Department experts have depicted guards who routinely resort to beatings or pepper spray as their only way to discipline inmates, and who pit inmates against one another for sport.

In June, two years after the Justice Department began its investigation and a year after it warned in its first public findings that Tallulah was "an institution out of control," consultants for the department filed new reports with the Federal judge, Frank J. Polozola of Federal District Court in Baton Rouge, warning that despite some improvements, conditions had deteriorated to "a particularly dangerous level."

Even a former warden at Louisiana's maximum-security prison, acting as a consultant to Judge Polozola, found conditions at Tallulah so serious that he urged the judge to reject its request to add inmates.

"I do not make these recommendations because of any sympathy for these offenders," wrote the former warden, John Whitley. "It shocks me to think" that "these offenders and their problems are simply getting worse, and these problems will be unleashed on the public when they are discharged from the system."

The Private Prison—When the Profits Are the Priority

Some of the worst conditions in juvenile prisons can be found among the growing number of privately operated prisons, whether those built specifically for one state, like Tallulah, or ones that take juveniles from across the country, like boot camps that have come under criticism in Colorado and Arizona.

Only 5 percent of the nation's juvenile prisons are operated by private, for-profit companies, Mr. Dunlap of the National Juvenile Detention Association estimates. But as their numbers grow along with privately operated prisons for adults, their regulation is becoming one of the most significant issues in corrections. State corrections departments find themselves having to police contractors who perform functions once the province of government, from psychiatric care to discipline.

In April, Colorado officials shut down a juvenile prison operated by the Rebound Corporation after a mentally ill 13-year-old's suicide led to an investigation that uncovered repeated instances of physical and sexual abuse. The for-profit prison housed offenders from six states.

Both Arizona and California authorities are investigating a privately operated boot camp in Arizona that California paid to take hundreds of offenders. A 16-year-old boy died there, and authorities suspect the cause was abuse by guards and poor medical care. California announced last Wednesday that it was removing its juveniles from the camp.

And recently Arkansas canceled the contract of Associated Marine Institutes, a company based in Florida, to run one juvenile institution, following questions of financial control and accusations of abuse.

A series of United States Supreme Court decisions and state laws have long mandated a higher standard for juvenile prisons than for adult prisons. There is supposed to be more schooling, medical care and security because the young inmates have been adjudged delinquent, rather than convicted of crimes as adults are, and so are held for rehabilitation instead of punishment.

But what has made problems worse here is that Tallulah, to earn a profit, has scrimped on money for education and mental health treatment in a state that already spends very little in those areas.

"It's incredibly perverse," said David Utter, director of the Juvenile Justice Project of Louisiana. "They have this place that creates all these injuries and they have all these kids with mental disorders, and then they save money by not treating them."

Bill Roberts, the lawyer for Tallulah's owner, Trans-American Development Associates, said that some of the Justice Department's demands, like hiring more psychiatrists, are "unrealistic." The state is to blame for the problems, he said, because "our place was not designed to take that kind of inmate."

Still, Mr. Roberts said, "There has been a drastic improvement" in reducing brutality by guards. As for fights between the inmates, he said, "Juveniles are a little bit different from adults. You are never going to stop all fights between boys."

In papers filed with Judge Polozola on July 7 responding to the Justice experts and Mr. Whitley, the State Attorney General's office disputed accusations of brutality and of high numbers of retarded and mentally ill inmates at Tallulah.

In a recent interview, Cheney Joseph, executive counsel to Gov. Mike Foster, warned there were limits to what Louisiana was willing to do. "There are certain situations the Department of Justice would like us to take care of," he said, "that may not be financially feasible and may not be required by Federal law."

The idea for a prison here was put forward in 1992 by James R. Brown, a Tallulah businessman whose father was an influential state senator.

One of the poorest areas in a poor state, Tallulah wanted jobs, and like other struggling cities across the country it saw the nation's prison-building spree as its best hope.

Louisiana needed a new juvenile prison because the number of youths being incarcerated was rising steeply; within a few years it more than doubled. Adding to that, mental health experts say, were hundreds of juveniles who had no place else to go because of cuts in psychiatric services outside of jail. Mental health authorities estimate that 20 percent of juveniles incarcerated nationally have serious mental illnesses.

To help win a no-bid contract to operate a prison, the company Mr. Brown formed included two close friends of Gov. Edwin W. Edwards—George Fischer and Verdi Adam—said a businessman involved in the venture's early stages, who spoke on the condition of anonymity.

None of the men had any particular qualification to run a prison. Mr. Verdi was a former chief engineer of the state highway department. Mr. Fischer had been the Governor's campaign manager, Cabinet officer and occasional business partner.

Tallulah opened in 1994, and the town of 10,000 got what it hoped for. The prison became its largest employer and taxpayer.

From the beginning, the company formed by Mr. Brown, Trans-American, pursued a strategy of maximizing its profit from the fixed amount it received from the state for each inmate (in 1997, $24,448). The plan was to keep wages and services at a minimum while taking in as many inmates as possible, said the businessman involved in the early stages.

For-profit prisons often try to economize. But the best-run companies have come to recognize that operating with too small or poorly trained a staff can spell trouble, and experts say state officials must pay close attention to the level of services being provided.

"Ultimately, the responsibility belongs to the state," said Charles Thomas, director of the Private Corrections Project at the University of Florida.

Louisiana officials say they monitored conditions at Tallulah and first reported many of the problems there. But in fiscal year 1996–97, according to the State Department of Public Safety and Corrections, Tallulah still listed no money for recreation, treatment or planning inmates' return to society. Twenty-nine percent of the budget went to construction loans.

By comparison, 45 percent of the $32,200 a year that California spends on each juvenile goes to programs and caseworkers, and none to construction. Nationally, construction costs average 7 percent of juvenile prison budgets, Mr. Dunlap said.

"That means either that Tallulah's construction costs are terribly inflated, or the services they are providing are extraordinarily low," he said.

The Inside—Hot, Crowded, Spartan, Neglectful

Part of Tallulah is a boot camp, with boys crammed so tightly in barracks that there is room only for double bunks, a television set and a few steel tables. Showers and urinals are open to the room, allowing boys who have been incarcerated for sexual assault to attack other inmates, according to a report in June by a Justice Department consultant, Dr. Bernard Hudson.

The only space for the few books that have recently been imported to try to improve education is a makeshift shelf on top of the urinals. Among the aging volumes that a reporter saw were "Inside the Third Reich," "The Short Stories of Henry James" and "Heidi."

From their wakeup call at 5:30 A.M., the inmates, in white T-shirts and loose green pants, spend almost all their time confined to the barracks. They leave the barracks only for marching drills, one to three hours a day of class and an occasional game of basketball. There is little ventilation, and temperatures in Louisiana's long summers hover permanently in the 90's.

The result, several boys told a visitor, is that some of them deliberately start trouble in order to be disciplined and sent to the other section of Tallulah, maximum-security cells that are air-conditioned.

Guards put inmates in solitary confinement so commonly that in one week in May more than a quarter of all the boys spent at least a day in "lockdown," said Nancy Ray, another Justice Department expert. The average stay in solitary is five to six weeks; some boys are kept indefinitely. While in the tiny cells, the boys are stripped of all possessions and lie on worn, thin mattresses resting on concrete blocks.

The crowding, heat and isolation are hardest on the 25 percent of the boys who are mentally ill or retarded, said Dr. Hudson, a psychiatrist, tending to increase their depression or psychosis.

Although Tallulah has made some improvements in its treatment of the emotionally disturbed over the last year, Dr. Hudson said, it remains "grossly inadequate."

The prison still does not properly screen new arrivals for mental illness or retardation, he reported. The part-time doctor and psychiatrist are there so infrequently that they have never met, Dr. Hudson said. Powerful anti-psychotic medications are not monitored. Medical charts often cannot be found.

And the infirmary is often closed because of a shortage of guards, whose pay is so low—$5.77 an hour—that there has been 100 percent turnover in the staff in the last year, the Justice Department experts said.

Other juvenile prisons that have come under investigation have also been criticized for poor psychiatric treatment. But at Tallulah this neglect has been compounded by everyday violence.

All these troubles are illustrated in the case of one former inmate, Travis M., a slight 16-year-old who is mentally retarded and has been treated with drugs for hallucinations.

Sometimes, Travis said in an interview after his release, guards hit him because his medication made him sleepy and he did not stand to attention when ordered. Sometimes they "snuck" him at night as he slept in his bunk, knocking him to the cement floor. Sometimes they kicked him while he was naked in the shower, telling him simply, "You owe me some licks."

Travis was originally sentenced by a judge to 90 days for shoplifting and stealing a bicycle. But every time he failed to stand for a guard or even called his grandmother to complain, officials at Tallulah put him in solitary and added to his sentence.

After 15 months, a judge finally ordered him released so he could get medical treatment. His eardrum had been perforated in a beating by a guard, he had large scars on his arms, legs and face, and his nose had been so badly broken that he speaks in a wheeze. A lawyer is scheduled to file suit against Tallulah on behalf of Travis this week.

One reason these abuses have continued, Mr. Utter said, is that juveniles in Louisiana, as in a number of states, often get poor legal representation. One mentally ill boy from Eunice was sentenced without a lawyer, or even a trial. Poorly paid public defenders seldom visit their clients after sentencing, Mr. Utter said, and so are unaware of conditions at places like Tallulah.

Another reason is that almost all Tallulah's inmates are from poor families and 82 percent are black, Mr. Utter noted, an imbalance that afflicts prisons nationwide to one degree or another. "They are disenfranchised and no one cares about them," he said.

The New Guard—A Retreat From Brutality

In September, Tallulah hired as its new warden David Bonnette, a 25-year veteran of Angola State Penitentiary who started there as a guard and rose to assistant superintendent. A muscular, tobacco-chewing man with his initials tattooed on a forearm, Mr. Bonnette brought several Angola colleagues with him to impose better discipline.

"When I got here, there were a lot of perforated eardrums," he said. "Actually, it seemed like everybody had a perforated eardrum, or a broken nose." When boys wrote complaints, he said, guards put the forms in a box and pulled out ones to investigate at random. Some were labeled, "Never to be investigated."

But allegations of abuse by guards dropped to 52 a month this spring, from more than 100 a month last summer, Mr. Bonnette said, as he has tried to carry out a new state policy of zero tolerance for brutality. Fights between boys have declined to 33 a month, from 129, he said.

In June, however, Ms. Ray, the Justice Department consultant, reported that there had been a recent increase in "youth defiance and disobedience," with the boys angry about Tallulah's "exceptionally high" use of isolation cells.

Many guards have also become restive, the Justice Department experts found, a result of poor pay and new restrictions on the use of force.

One guard who said he had quit for those reasons said in an interview: "The inmates are running the asylum now. You're not supposed to touch the kids, but how are we supposed to control them without force?" He has relatives working at Tallulah and so insisted on not being identified.

The frustration boiled over on July 1, during a tour by Senator Paul Wellstone, the Minnesota Democrat who is drafting legislation that would require psychiatric care for all incarcerated juveniles who need it. Despite intense security, a group of inmates climbed on a roof and shouted their complaints at Senator Wellstone, who was accompanied by Richard Stalder, the secretary of Louisiana's Department of Public Safety and Corrections.

Mr. Stalder said he planned to create a special unit for mentally ill juvenile offenders. One likely candidate to run it, he said, is Trans-American, the company that operates Tallulah.

5. United States and Georgia in Deal to Improve Juvenile Prisons

Fox Butterfield, N.Y. Times 3/22/98

Attorney General Janet Reno and Gov. Zell Miller of Georgia reached an unusual agreement on juvenile prisons last week under which the state pledged to spend millions of dollars and institute sweeping changes to improve what Justice Department investigators have called "egregious," "abusive" and "grossly substandard" conditions.

The agreement is part of a recent burst of activity by the civil rights division of the Justice Department in investigating constitutional violations in juvenile prisons in several states as well as abuse of mentally ill inmates in the Los Angeles County Jail. The department's actions have come at a time when anger at crime has led to a sharp increase in the number of convicted juvenile offenders, but often with little oversight of how prisons are run.

Other Justice Department inquiries into conditions at juvenile prisons in the past three years have led to a court order to ease overcrowding in Kentucky's juvenile prisons and revealed a pattern of brutality by guards in Louisiana's juvenile justice system who have inflicted sexual abuse, fractured jaws, noses, cheeks and eye sockets on young inmates.

The Federal investigators found that almost three-quarters of the young people confined in Georgia's Regional Youth Detention Centers, one of three main types of juvenile centers in the state, are charged with nonviolent offenses, contrary to the perception that most young criminals are violent predators.

Although Louisiana was already under a 1984 Federal court order to stop abuses in its all of prisons, Justice Department monitors in the past few months have reported that conditions in the state's four juvenile centers have actually "deteriorated" and the level of violence by guards in one privately owned institution has increased, according to court documents.

The agreement in Georgia was reached after whirlwind negotiations: Governor Miller rushed through a $10.8 million appropriations increase to hire teachers, guards and medical workers before the Legislature ended its session last week, a senior Justice Department official said. Georgia agreed to the spending increase as part of a package of changes, including the appointment of an independent monitor, to avert a threat by the Federal Government to take control of the state's 30 juvenile detention sites.

Governor Miller was infuriated last month by the Justice Department report, which found "a pattern of egregious conditions violating the Federal rights of youths in the Georgia juvenile facilities." And he wrote to the department that he was "appalled" at the way the investigation was conducted. Federal investigators said that the detention centers were "grossly overcrowded," that guards routinely stripped young inmates naked and then locked them in their cells for days, that education programs were virtually nonexistent and that many of the large number of mentally disturbed inmates "degenerated" because of a serious lack of appropriate care.

Often as many as five boys have been detained in cells intended for one inmate, the report said, with the guards frequently, especially on weekends, imposing lock-downs during which the corrections officers "take the youths' mattresses away during the day, leaving the youths with no choice but to lie on the cold, hard metal bed frames and concrete floors." During lock-downs, the "youths may not even have reading materials in their rooms" other than Bibles, the investigators found.

These punitive conditions are "particularly harmful," the investigators said, to an estimated one-third of the 25,000 inmates in Georgia's juvenile system each year who are locked up merely for being "status offenders," including runaways, truants and children whose parents say they are difficult to control.

The investigators, for example, found "a very small 11-year-old boy" detained for threatening his fifth-grade teacher, a 12-year-old boy with a seizure disorder incarcerated for making a harassing telephone call, a 14-year-old girl in solitary confinement for painting graffiti on a wall and a 16-year-old girl who had been locked up for "failing to abide by her father's rules," specifically, for throwing things in her room.

The detention of status offenders in state institutions is unusual and "an outrage," said Lois Whitman, director of the children's rights divisions of Human Rights Watch in New York. It was common practice to incarcerate runaways until the 1970's, but Federal law prohibits states from doing it if they want money from Congressional programs for juvenile justice.

"People forget that if you take kids who haven't committed a criminal offense and lock them up with kids who have, it means the chances are, you are going to create a criminal when they get out," she said.

One reason for the troubles in Georgia's juvenile system, said Gerry Weber, legal director of the Georgia branch of the American Civil Liberties Union, "is that Georgia has more of a philosophy of incarceration and punishment" for young people than other states. This leads to incarcerating runaways, he said, and contributes to the overcrowding, which in turns leads to some of the abuses by guards, who find themselves unable to cope with the sheer number of young offenders.

In some detention centers, two guards supervise as many as 90 youths in structures designed for 30, the report said. The result is that the guards are frequently unaware of sexual assaults or serious injuries incurred in fights for hours or days.

Up to 61 percent of the young inmates have psychiatric disorders, but "they are systematically denied access to adequate mental health care," the report said. Psychiatrists and psychologists seldom appear at the detention centers, anti-psychotic drugs are administered, without monitoring, by unqualified staff members and there are only five psychiatric hospital beds for the entire system.

Many mentally ill or retarded inmates are sent without screening to boot camps where they are forced to do 100 push-ups on asphalt that can burn their hands when it is 95 degrees and to finish their meals in five minutes. When mentally ill inmates cannot or do not conform to these orders, they are often placed in shackles, locked in solitary confinement or doused with pepper spray, the report said.

"The situation in Georgia reminds me of the descriptions of mental institutions in the early part of the century, with severe overcrowding, lack of trained staff and discipline by strapping people down," said Michael Faenza, the president of the National Mental Health Association. "I cannot imagine a more shameful situation in the country."

Mr. Faenza criticized the Justice Department's agreement with Georgia, which he said had been reached too quickly and lacked an enforcement mechanism, allowing the state to monitor its own abuses.

But Bill Lann Lee, the acting Assistant Attorney General for Civil Rights, defended the agreement, saying speed was important to secure the Legislature's approval of increased spending and that the Federal Government retained power because it filed a lawsuit last week, which could be activated if Georgia failed to carry out the accord.

6. Youth Prisons in California Stay Abusive, Suit Contends

Evelyn Nieves, N.Y. Times, 1/26/02

Two years ago, the California Youth Authority, which runs the state's juvenile prisons, acknowledged what critics had been saying for years: something was very wrong.

Instead of rehabilitation and education, the system of 11 prisons and four camps, with about 6,300 prisoners, had become known for brutality and other abuses. Reports that mentally ill youths were stripped to their underwear and isolated in cages 23 hours a day, that prisoners were subjected to biomedical experiments and sexually and physically abused by guards, and other problems led the state inspector general, Steven White, to conclude that "it would be impossible to overstate the problem." As a result, the California Board of Corrections ordered a review of the Youth Authority by more than 100 experts.

That review led to a four-inch-thick report in November 2000 that included scores of recommendations for reform, from when to place youths in isolation to what the cafeteria should serve. But on Thursday, a prison reform group and a disability rights group, with two San Francisco law firms, filed a class action lawsuit against the system contending that little had changed.

The suit, filed in federal court in Sacramento against the California Youth Authority on behalf of 11 prisoners, contends inhumane conditions are pervasive. It describes such practices as the use of cages as classrooms and the forcible injection of mind-altering drugs to control the behavior of inmates. It contends mental health care is virtually nonexistent and says prisoners with disabilities are sometimes isolated in dungeon-like holes splattered with feces and blood and that the inmates live in fear of physical and sexual violence. It asks the court to order state officials to make reasonable, prompt and sustained efforts to correct the conditions.

"I've been suing the adult prisons for 20 years for cruel and inhuman punishment, and the conditions in the youth facilities are as bad if not worse than any I've seen in the others," said Donald Spector, director of the Prison Law Office, a nonprofit legal services agency in San Quentin specializing in prisoner rights.

"Despite all the investigations and testimony before legislative committees over the last two years," Mr. Spector said, "there really haven't been substantial changes since the inspector general's report."

Mr. Spector said a lack of political will let the problems continue. Gov. Gray Davis, he said, ordered the agency to cut about $4 million for enhanced programs from its $437 million budget.

But a spokesman for the California Youth Authority said many of the charges were either being addressed or misrepresented conditions at the prisons.

"At first glance, it looks like they're rehashing a lot of old issues that we and others in the juvenile justice community are aware of and that have been a priority for the authority for some time," said the spokesman, George Kostyrko.

For example, Mr. Kostyrko said, when inmates older than 18 refuse psychotropic drugs, the Department of Corrections follows a legal process to administer the drugs. As for the use of cages as classrooms, he said, "in certain prisons, open-air small structures are used" to protect prisoners from violent classmates and to protect teachers, who stand outside the structures, from violent inmates.

Mr. Kostyrko denied assertions in the suit that students were not receiving required education or mental health accommodations.

The majority of the youths, 95 percent male, need mental health attention, he said. "Ninety percent of both our male and female wards have an identifiable mental health disorder," he said, "so mental health is one of our highest priorities."

7. Dismal California Prisons Hold Juvenile Offenders

John M. Broder, N.Y. Times 2/15/2004

The mission of the California Youth Authority, which runs the state's 10 juvenile prisons, housing 4,600 inmates, is to educate and rehabilitate offenders sentenced by juvenile courts. But state officials and outside experts brought in to study the system say it fails in its most basic tasks, because of antiquated facilities, undertrained employees and violence endemic within the walls.

Youths with psychological problems are ignored or overmedicated, classes are arbitrarily canceled, and inmates or whole institutions are locked down for days or weeks at a time because of recurring gang violence, according to the independent experts, retained by the state after it was sued two years ago in a class action brought on inmates' behalf.

Two wards committed suicide at one prison last month, and dozens more try to kill themselves every year, officials and parents of wards say. Conditions in many of the institutions were described by the experts as "deplorable," with blood, mucus and dried feces on the walls of many high-security cells.

Youths in solitary confinement are often fed what officials call "blender meals," in which a bologna sandwich, an apple and milk are pulverized and fed to the inmate by straw through a slit in the cell door.

The system's mental health programs are in "complete disarray," the experts found.

"The vast majority of youths who have mental health needs," one report said, "are made worse instead of improved by the correctional environment."

There are more than 4,000 serious assaults by wards on other wards each year throughout the California juvenile prison system, an average of more than 10 a day, according to Dr. Barry Krisberg, a nationally recognized criminologist who was among the experts reviewing the Youth Authority.

"These levels of ward-on-ward and ward-on-staff assaults are unprecedented in juvenile corrections across the nation," Dr. Krisberg wrote in a damning report released this month.

He said corrections leaders elsewhere were "astounded" to hear of the prevalence of violence in California juvenile prisons. Guards instigate fights among wards, he found, and fail to protect those who are singled out for rapes or beatings by other inmates.

"It is abundantly clear from a range of data that I collected as part of this review," Dr. Krisberg wrote, "that the Youth Authority is a very dangerous place and that neither staff nor wards feel safe in its facilities."

He also noted that California was the only state that used small cages, known as secure program areas, or SPA's, to isolate prisoners from one another and from members of the staff during instruction or counseling, a practice one prison pastor called "demonic."

State officials newly appointed to run the Youth Authority do not dispute most of the findings. They have promised quick action to remedy them, starting with the elimination of the security cages, which are in use in several of the juvenile prisons.

State Senator Gloria Romero, a Democrat who heads a special legislative committee overseeing the state's adult and juvenile prison networks, called conditions in the Youth Authority "barbaric" and "inhumane."

Senator Romero said that while the latest accounts were shocking, there was little new in them. She said that investigations and lawsuits over the last decade had uncovered similar abuses and that little had been done beyond hiring more guards and pouring vast sums of money into the system. The state now spends $80,000 a year on each imprisoned young offender, she said, and yet recidivism approaches 90 percent. "On all counts," she said of the system, "it's been a failure."

Karapet Darakchyan, an 18-year-old car thief, has been in the juvenile prison system for three years. For more than four months—he has not counted the days—he has been confined to the high-security lockup at the Fred C. Nelles Youth Correctional Facility here in Whittier, a result of an assault on a guard last fall.

Mr. Darakchyan, a former member of the notorious White Fence gang in East Los Angeles and a young man with an admitted "anger problem," spends 23 hours a day in a 4-by-8-foot cell. Other than for showers, he leaves the cell only to receive instruction or counseling, during which he is confined inside a steel mesh cage barely big enough to stand or turn around in.

Mr. Darakchyan, who was led from his cell in handcuffs for a brief interview, offered no specific complaints about his treatment at Nelles. "It's not a good place to be," he said matter-of-factly. "It's a jail. You've got to deal with it."

Asked whether he was receiving any useful treatment or training, he just shook his head.

The crisis in the Youth Authority, and similar problems in the vastly larger adult prison system, pose serious managerial and political challenges for Gov. Arnold Schwarzenegger. He has said he is "gravely concerned" about the California prison system, which costs $6 billion a year, and has already replaced the directors of youth and adult corrections. He has also proposed reductions in spending on prisons and wants to revamp the parole system to reduce the prison population, which now exceeds 160,000.

Mr. Schwarzenegger has vowed to renegotiate a contract that provides large raises over the next three years for prison guards. The guards' union, the California Correctional Peace Officers Association, which negotiated that contract with the governor's predecessor, Gray Davis, has been a heavy contributor to political campaigns and until now considered politically untouchable.

Walter Allen III, the new director of the Youth Authority, said that the reports so critical of the system were "substantially correct" and that he had ordered his staff to prepare remedies and a timetable for achieving them. He also said he had retained Dr. Krisberg to advise him and would work to settle the class-action lawsuit against his agency.

Laura Talkington of Fresno, whose 19-year-old son, David, has been held in Youth Authority prisons since he was convicted of arson four years ago, makes no excuses for his crime. But she is furious at the state for the treatment he has received, which has included beatings by the staff and fellow inmates. Attention deficit disorder has been diagnosed, she said, but he has received no treatment for it, or remedial education.

"There is no rehabilitation," Mrs. Talkington said. "There is only punishment and a lot of abuse."

Sara Norman, a staff lawyer with the Prison Law Office, one of the groups that brought the suit against the Youth Authority, said inmate advocates were seeking the appointment of a special master to ensure a top-to-bottom overhaul of juvenile corrections in California.

"The system is completely out of control," she said. "We don't want another blue-ribbon commission. The panel of experts' findings are right there. The system needs to be fixed now."

8. In New York, A Report Details Abuse and Neglect at 2 State-Run Centers for Girls

Lisa W. Foderaro, N.Y. Times at A25, 9/25/06

Lansing and Tryon. They are among the most secure facilities in New York State for girls who have crossed the law — remote state-run institutions located far from New York City, where most of their inmates are from. And to the girls who are sent there, the facilities are notorious.

"They restrain you for no reason," Antoinette, a 17-year-old, said in an interview last week. She was confined at Tryon Girls Center, near Albany, after she was found to have committed a robbery. "They throw you down and mush your face into the floor," she said. "It's just like having rug burns on your face. They make girls cry and are always doing strip searches."

Antoinette, whose last name was withheld to protect her privacy, was among 30 girls whose bleak accounts of life at Tryon and at Lansing Residential Center, near Ithaca, inform a harshly critical report about the centers released today by Human Rights Watch and the American Civil Liberties Union.

Human Rights Watch has investigated conditions at juvenile centers for boys elsewhere in the United States and other countries. But this was its first look at incarceration of girls, and the report's author, Mie Lewis, said she chose New York because of the size of its juvenile population and indications of problems at its institutions.

In New York State, girls represented 14 percent of the children taken into custody in 1994; 10 years later, the number had grown to more than 18 percent. A majority of the girls at Lansing and Tryon are 15 and 16, but some are as young as 12.

The 134-page report concludes that girls in the two centers, which together house about 150 girls, are being abused and neglected — violently restrained for minor infractions, subjected to sexual harassment and assault, cut off from families, and provided little rehabilitation.

Ms. Lewis, a lawyer and Aryeh Neier Fellow at Human Rights Watch and the A.C.L.U., said she was refused access to the facilities, which are operated by the State Office of Children and Family Services. But she combed through grievance reports and other documents obtained through the Freedom of Information Law and interviewed formerly and currently incarcerated girls.

"In other countries, we are always given access and we've been able to visit the facilities and talk to kids," she said. "With O.C.F.S., it's an incredibly closed and secretive agency. And then when kids are sent to these facilities, it's like they are dropped into a black hole."

The report calls on the state to curtail the use of a face-down restraint technique, in which girls are thrust to the floor and handcuffed. The report makes numerous other recommendations, from providing better education and assuring access to mental health services to limiting male staff members in girls' living quarters.

A spokesman for the Office of Children and Family Services, Brian Marchetti, criticized Human Rights Watch and the A.C.L.U. for not providing a copy of the report to the agency before its release, as the two groups did for the news media. "We have to question their motives," Mr. Marchetti said. "Is it to improve programs for children or is it to see their name in headlines and promote their agenda?"

Mr. Marchetti said the agency provided Ms. Lewis with 5,500 pages of material and granted her an interview in April with the agency's commissioner, John A. Johnson, and senior staff members. He said that access to the facilities themselves is granted to researchers only after receipt of a research proposal and that Ms. Lewis never presented one.

As for criticisms of Lansing and Tryon, Mr. Marchetti said the agency had "zero tolerance" for any kind of "sexual misconduct" between employees and residents.

The report quotes girls who had worked as prostitutes who felt they were singled out by male staff members. A number of those girls complained of harassment, unwanted touching and sexual contact.

One girl, identified as Ebony V., who was 16 at the time of her confinement, recalled in the report an episode in which she was having sex in the office of a male staff member at Lansing when another male employee walked in on them. "He said: 'Oh, oh, oh, oh I'm sorry' and closed the door. It's crazy, isn't it?" the report quotes her as saying.

Mr. Marchetti also defended the educational offerings at the centers. Across the agency's facilities in general, two-thirds of the young people score below grade level in reading and math upon entering. While at the institutions, he said, they improve on average by two grade levels.

One of the most stinging criticisms leveled by the report centers on the use of a face-down restraint. The report describes how girls are seized from behind and pushed to the floor, their arms held in place or put in handcuffs. The restraint is used for such infractions as not making a bed properly or not raising one's hand before speaking, the report said.

The agency's regulations say that such restraints are to be used to prevent children from harming themselves and others, but, Ms. Lewis said, the agency's internal policy is decidedly more lax.

Mr. Marchetti said restraints were used to prevent harm and also to "de-escalate situations." Asked whether they were used excessively, he said that "all staff in Office of Children and Family Services facilities are mandated reporters," meaning they must report abuse to the authorities.

Juanita Crawford, 19, who spent a year and a half at Lansing after she was found guilty of reckless endangerment and conspiracy and is now an intern at the A.C.L.U., said in an interview that she was restrained after not moving quickly enough to dispose of her food tray and talking back to a staff member.

"He takes you and hooks your arms backwards with a lot of force, and it hurts, and you're dropped face down," she said. "It's almost like getting tripped."

Notes

(a) Is it fair to say that the more things change the more they remain the same?

(b) Given the conditions prevailing in at least some juvenile facilities, is the court in *A.J. v. Kierst*, in Chapter 4, *supra*, correct in its conclusion that the Due Process clause of the Fourteenth Amendment provides greater protection for juveniles than the Eighth Amendment's cruel and unusual punishment clause?

(c) The extent to which juveniles committed to state correctional facilities have a due process "right to treatment" is unclear. In *Donaldson v. O'Connor*, 422 U.S. 563 (1975), the Court held that it was unconstitutional for the state to involuntarily commit a mentally ill man for treatment who was not a danger to himself or others, if the state then provided no treatment. This differs from the case of delinquents because the state may argue that children who have committed crimes are a danger to others. In *Youngberg v. Romeo*, 457 U.S. 307 (1982), the Court did find a substantive due process right to appropriate treatment in the case of mentally retarded persons involuntarily committed to state facilities. The protected liberty interest was, however, limited to safety and freedom of movement as well as "minimally adequate or reasonable treatment to insure safety and freedom from undue restraint."

> Furthermore, in *Kansas v. Hendricks*, 521 U.S. 346 (1997), the Court upheld a state law permitting involuntary civil commitment of a sex offender upon his release from prison. The constitutional liberty interest in avoiding physical restraint was trumped if the state "coupled proof of dangerousness with the proof of some additional factor, such as a 'mental illness' or 'mental abnormality.'"

> Finally, in *Ingraham v. Wright*, 430 U.S. 651 (1977), a majority concluded that even severe disciplinary corporal punishment of pubic school students did not violate the Eighth Amendment prohibition against cruel and unusual punishment because the Eighth Amendment was confined to criminal contexts. The Court dropped a footnote noting that it was not deciding whether the Eighth Amendment applied to juvenile correctional facilities. *See* 430 U.S. 651, 669 n. 37.

(d) Do the cases in this section support the abolitionists in Chapter 2, *supra*, who believe that juveniles would be better off tried in criminal courts in which they would receive full constitutional protections? Why?

Chapter 6

Status Offenders

Of PINS, MINS, JINS, CHINS, and YINS, a.k.a.
Incorrigibles, Ungovernables, Waywards,
Truants, Miscreants, and Persons, Minors,
Juveniles, Children and Youths in Need
of Supervision

A. Historical Roots

1. The Old Testament

Deuteronomy 21:18–21

If a man have a stubborn and rebellious son, that will not hearken to the voice of his father, or the voice of his mother, and though they chasten him, will not hearken unto them: then shall his father and his mother lay hold on him, and bring him out unto the elders of his city, and unto the gate of his place; and they shall say unto the elders of his city, "This our son is stubborn and rebellious, he doth not hearken to our voice; he is a glutton, and a drunkard." And all the men of his city shall stone him with stones, that he die: so shalt thou put away the evil from the midst of thee; and all Israel shall hear, and fear.

2. The Talmudic Gloss on the Stubborn and Rebellious Son — Deuteronomy Verse

a. Irene Merker Rosenberg & Yale L. Rosenberg, *The Legacy of the Stubborn and Rebellious Son*

74 MICH. L. REV. 1097, 1163–65 (1976)

According to the Talmud, the son was subject to prosecution only if he had defied both father and mother, and only if both parents concurred in the prosecution. Through the restrictive interpretation of the word "son," whose meaning was limited to one who was thirteen and thus sufficiently mature to bear criminal responsibility, but not yet old enough to be a "man," the period of indictment was limited to the three months following the thirteenth birthday.

The offense consisted of two elements: (1) repeated defiance and reviling of the parents, and (2) gluttony and drunkenness. The latter element could only be satisfied by consumption of specified minimum amounts of food and drink; because these quantities were so large that a child could not afford to purchase them, the law was further interpreted to require that the son have stolen money from his father for that purpose. Thus, while the Talmud recognized that the son's behavior would be predictive of future criminal conduct, that recognition was based on a finding of a criminal act by the son against the father and on a determination that his addictive gluttony could only be appeased by further criminal acts against his parents and others.

Moreover, prosecution was not allowed if the parents possessed certain characteristics. A son was not to be deemed stubborn and rebellious "if his mother [was] not fit for his father," as in the case of violation by the mother of the laws against incest. Thus, it can be inferred that if the parents had set a bad example for their son by themselves acting unlawfully, they were barred from leveling charges of illegality against him. In addition, a complaint of rebelliousness was precluded if the parents were not "alike in voice" when they admonished their son. This can be interpreted to mean that if the mother and father gave the son inconsistent directions, they were failing to provide him with a cohesive and disciplined home life, and that this parental shortcoming could be a defense to the charge that he was stubborn and rebellious.

Even if the son had committed all the elements of the "crime" and the parents were in no way deficient, he was brought first before a three-judge court where, upon conviction, he was flogged and warned of the consequences if he persisted in such conduct. It was only if he thereafter continued to violate the law that he could be brought before the elders of the city, which was a court of twenty-three persons, and be made subject to the death penalty.

There appears to be no recorded instance of the execution of a stubborn and rebellious son, [thus, suggesting that the law was hortatory and pedagogical].

b.   Irene Merker Rosenberg, Yale L. Rosenberg & Bentzion S. Turin, *Return of the Stubborn and Rebellious Son: An Independent Sequel on the Prediction of Future Criminality*

37 BRANDEIS L. J. 511, 514 (1998–99)

On the surface, the stubborn and rebellious son provision is either an ancient status offender statute or a pedagogical law that can be viewed as a "tough love" parental primer on raising children or, more whimsically, as a diet guide or a twelve-step program for youthful alcoholics. As the Jewish oral tradition makes clear, however, lurking beneath this provision is a utilitarian deterrence statute that seeks to eliminate those who will go on to commit very serious crimes in the future.

3.   1646 Mass. Bay Colony Stubborn and Rebellious Son Law

If a man have a stubborne or rebellious sonne, of sufficient yeares & undrstanding, viz, 16, wch will not obey ye voyce of his fathr or ye voyce of his mothr, & yt when they have chastened him will not harken unto ym, yn shall his fathr & mothr, being his naturall parents, lay hold on him, & bring him to ye matrates assembled in Corte, & testify unto ym, by sufficient evidence, yt ys their sonn is stubborne & rebellious, & will not obey their voyce & chasticemt, but lives in sundry notorious crimes, such a sonne shalbe put to death.

Commonwealth v. Brasher

270 N.E.2d 389 (Mass. 1971)

QUIRICO, Justice.

On May 3, 1969, a complaint issued from a District Court alleging that the defendant "being between seven and seventeen years of age, is a delinquent child in that during the one month last past before the making of this complaint, at Fall River * * * (she) was a stubborn child and did refuse to submit to the lawful and reasonable commands of * * * Michael T. Walsh whose commands said Dianne Brasher was bound to obey." The defendant was tried in the District Court and was adjudged a delinquent child. She appealed to the Superior Court where she was again tried and adjudged a delinquent child. On July 2, 1969, the court ordered the defendant committed to the custody of the Youth Service Board (now the Department of Youth Services), suspended execution of the order for three years, and placed her on probation on condition that she be placed in the home of a named individual at Lawell.

. . . .

The constitutional issue raised by the defendant is directed at the part of [General laws chap. 272, § 53], which provides punishment for stubborn children, and for this reason it will be helpful to review the history and development of this part of the statute. This provision appears to have originated in an act passed by the House of Deputies of the Colony of the Massachusetts Bay in New England on August 22, 1654, stating that 'it appeares by too much experience that divers children & servants doe behave themselves too disrespectively, disobediently, & disorderly towards their parents, masters, & gouvernors, to the disturbance of families, & discouragement of such parents & gouvernors," and providing "corporall punishment by whiping, or otherwise," for such offenders. Mass. Bay Records, Vol. III (1644–1657) 355. Mass. Col. Laws (1887 ed.) 27.

The next statutory reference to stubborn children is in Prov. St. 1699–1700, c. 8, §§ 2–6, permitting courts to commit various offenders, including stubborn children and other persons now included in G.L. c. 272, § 53, to houses of correction.

When the Constitution of Massachusetts was adopted in 1780, it then provided, and still provides, in Part II, c. 6, art. 6, that "All the laws which have heretofore been adopted, used and approved in the Province, Colony or State of Massachusetts Bay, and usually practised on in the courts of law, shall still remain and be in full force, until altered or repealed by the Legislature; such parts only excepted as are repugnant to the rights and liberties contained in this Constitution." By virtue of this provision, the part of the Province laws relating to the punishment of stubborn children and certain other offenders became a part of the law of this Commonwealth. Over the years the section of the statute which included the punishment of stubborn children was subjected to many amendments and it was included in a number of periodic consolidations and rearrangements of our statutes. Despite this, the provision relating to stubborn children as now contained in G.L. c. 272, § 53, has remained basically the same.

Notes

(a) Should the state have the power to punish children who are disobedient? Why and on what constitutional basis?

(b) To the extent the state's power to punish children for disobedience rests on its police power, should the state have the burden of proving that exercise of the status offender jurisdiction deters future criminality? Could such a burden be met? Why? See Yale Note, *Ungovernability,* in Section G of this Chapter, *infra.*

(c) If the status offender jurisdiction were repealed, would there be sufficient resources to treat children whose acting out did not rise to the level of criminal behavior? Do such children need help?

4. Note on Status Offenders

Every state has a separate juvenile court system that has jurisdiction over two forms of misconduct by children: criminal law violations and status offenses. The criminal law violators, delinquents, are ordinarily defined as minors who commit acts which if committed by adults would constitute crimes. Status offenders are those who commit acts that are criminal only for children, such as curfew violations, consumption of alcohol, truancy, and running away from home, and also encompass minors who are beyond parental control, incorrigible, ungovernable, or in need of supervision.

Prior to the 1960s, these two types of offenders were lumped together and designated delinquents and were treated almost exactly the same. See *In re Gault,* in Chapter 2, *supra.* Thus, runaways and truants were incarcerated in the same secure state facilities with rapists, murderers, and robbers. These practices drew extensive criticism and prompted legislative and judicial action. In particular, the Juvenile Justice and Delinquency Prevention Act of 1974 sought to give an impetus to deinstitutionalization of status offenders by conditioning receipt of federal funds on state plans to terminate status offenders' placement in detention and correctional facilities. In that same year, both the Department of Health, Education and Welfare and the National Council on Crime and Delinquency recommended elimination of the juvenile court jurisdiction over ungovernable children. Perhaps the most important set of proposals came in 1977 in a report issued by the American Bar Association, Institute of Judicial Administration, Juvenile Justice Standards Project. The ABA recommended that status offenders be removed from the jurisdiction of the juvenile courts. The Standards permitted limited custody of a juvenile for up to six hours if a substantial and immediate danger threatened the child's safety, and urged a broad range of services be made available to the child and his or her family. The status offender Standards, however, were never approved by the ABA House of Delegates because they were too controversial.

In addition to these proposals, intense scholarly criticism condemned the status offender jurisdiction and the way it operated in practice. Furthermore, several successful federal court class action suits attacked the inhumane and often barbaric treatment of both delinquents and status offenders in state training schools. See cases in Chapter 5, *supra.*

In response to widespread attacks on the juvenile court status offender jurisdiction, states have categorized status offenders separately and generally have treated them differently from delinquents. The main difference now between delinquents and status offenders is the latter are usually not incarcerated in secure state facilities, or, even if they are, they are not committed to secure facilities that also house delinquent criminal law violators. Furthermore, police officials and intake probation divert many status offender children from formal juvenile court action. The downside of this diversion is to force children into "treatment" options, including "voluntary" commitment to state mental hospitals, without a due process precommitment hearing. See *Parham v. J.R.,* 442 U.S. 584 (1979).

The other major change has been to define status offender misconduct with greater specificity. The older status offender statutes used very vague terminology to describe the underlying status offender misconduct, such as being "in danger of leading an idle, dissolute, lewd or immoral life." The conduct also was often expressed in terms of a condition or status (hence status offender), such as being "incorrigible" or "unruly" or "beyond parental control." Modern statutes instead tend to spell out the detrimental conduct, e.g., truancy, curfew violations, and running away from home.

The danger of the older, vaguer terms was that they failed to give fair notice of the proscribed acts. The purpose of the due process requirement that laws be framed with sufficient specificity so as to give notice of the underlying illegal conduct is not because we think criminals, adult or juvenile, will go to the law library to see if their intended behavior is unlawful. Rather, the notice requirement is a way of assuring compliance with certain institutional values. Amorphous language gives police and courts unlimited discretion to determine what behavior constitutes a violation of the law, the province of the legislature.

The modern trend of separately categorizing and punishing delinquents and status offenders is, however, often circumvented by manipulation of definitional terms. In almost all jurisdictions, criminal-law-violating delinquents can be placed in secure state training schools. The rub is that in some jurisdictions a delinquent is defined as either a criminal law violator or a child who has violated a lawful court order. This means that a status offender who has violated probation or a specific directive of the court not to engage in certain conduct (e.g., truancy), may be converted into a delinquent simply by engaging in further conduct that is in itself not criminal, and the status offender can then be committed to a state training school for delinquents who have committed true criminal acts. Analogous results occur in jurisdictions that define the crime of escape so as to include unauthorized departures by status offenders from facilities to which they have been judicially committed—conduct functionally equivalent to running away from home. By defining such conduct as "escape" under the penal law, the state makes possible the conversion of status offenders into criminal-law violators who can then be placed in secure state facilities with delinquents. The same result can be reached by labeling the violation of the court order criminal contempt. Not all states permit such circumvention, recognizing that it conflicts with the state's juvenile law policy.

To further complicate matters, the juvenile court also has jurisdiction over dependent, neglected and abused children. In those cases, the caregiver, usually the parent, is charged with harming the child physically, emotionally or sexually. In many states the behavior that can be the basis of a dependency or neglect action may also constitute status offender behavior. So, for example, if a young child is found wandering in the street at night, depending upon the circumstances, usually the age of the child, he or she can be treated as either a status offender or a neglected child. Many courts prefer the status offender route because it is easier than charging the parent with neglect, which often results in protracted proceedings. In contrast, most status offender cases are quickly resolved by the child admitting the allegations of the petition.

Some states combine status offenders and neglected children into one category, calling them "children in need of aid" or some variant thereof. In yet another twist, children in need of aid or care may also include children who commit a felony, but because of their "extreme youth" delinquency proceedings are deemed inappropriate. Thus, the separate categories are not airtight and give courts enormous discretion in determining the dispositions, which often depend on the available facilities rather than the appropriate treatment.

The status offender jurisdiction is subject to much abuse. As noted above, it enables courts to treat neglected children as status offenders and status offenders as delinquents.

Paradoxically, it also allows courts to circumvent the *Gault* and *Winship* cases. Some courts take the position that those rulings only apply to delinquent criminal law violators. Thus, if there is insufficient proof to permit adjudication for commission of a criminal act, some courts drop the delinquency charges and adjudicate the children as status offenders.

In one famous case, two girls, eleven and thirteen, were alleged to have engaged in sexual activities and drug use with adults. The adults were arrested and the children were identified as the victims. Nonetheless, the girls were charged as delinquents and status offenders. The evidence at the girls' adjudicatory hearings included statements that the girls had given to the police regarding the police investigation of the adults, and the testimony of one of the girls who had been called as a witness by the prosecutor at her hearing over counsel's objection. The trial judge found them to be status offenders. This was affirmed on appeal on the grounds that *Gault* did not apply to status offenders and therefore, there was no right against self-incrimination. The delinquency charges got lost in the shuffle. *In re Spalding*, 332 A. 2d 246 (Md. 1975). Similarly, in some states, the burden of proof in status offender cases is either a preponderance or clear and convincing evidence.

It is unclear if the status offender jurisdiction can be tamed so as to prevent its misuse. Many critics claim that it is the very nature of the jurisdiction itself that is the problem and that no amount of tinkering would help. On the other hand, for as long as the status offender jurisdiction is here to stay, zealous advocacy may ameliorate its most harmful effects.

B. Modern Statutes

1. Cal. Welf. & Inst. Code

§ 601. Minors habitually disobedient or truant; contact with minor in truancy program; notice to appear

(a) Any person under the age of 18 years who persistently or habitually refuses to obey the reasonable and proper orders or directions of his or her parents, guardian, or custodian, or who is beyond the control of that person, or who is under the age of 18 years when he or she violated any ordinance of any city or county of this state establishing a curfew based solely on age is within the jurisdiction of the juvenile court which may adjudge the minor to be a ward of the court.

(b) If a minor has four or more truancies within one school year as defined in Section 48260 of the Education Code or a school attendance review board or probation officer determines that the available public and private services are insufficient or inappropriate to correct the habitual truancy of the minor, or to correct the minor's persistent or habitual refusal to obey the reasonable and proper orders or directions of school authorities, or if the minor fails to respond to directives of a school attendance review board or probation officer or to services provided, the minor is then within the jurisdiction of the juvenile court which may adjudge the minor to be a ward of the court. However, it is the intent of the Legislature that no minor who is adjudged a ward of the court pursuant solely to this subdivision shall be removed from the custody of the parent or guardian except during school hours.

(c) To the extent practically feasible, a minor who is adjudged a ward of the court pursuant to this section shall not be permitted to come into or remain in contact with any minor ordered to participate in a truancy program, or the equivalent thereof, pursuant to Section 602 [which defines delinquency].

(d) Any peace officer or school administrator may issue a notice to appear to a minor who is within the jurisdiction of the juvenile court pursuant to this section.

§ 725. Judgment; placing minor on probation; adjudging minor ward of court

After receiving and considering the evidence on the proper disposition of the case, the court may enter judgment as follows:

(a) If the court has found that the minor is a person described by Section 601 or 602, by reason of the commission of an offense other than any of the offenses set forth in Section 654.3, it may, without adjudging the minor a ward of the court, place the minor on probation, under the supervision of the probation officer, for a period not to exceed six months. The minor's probation shall include the conditions required in Section 729.2 except in any case in which the court makes a finding and states on the record its reasons that any of those conditions would be inappropriate. If the offense involved the unlawful possession, use, or furnishing of a controlled substance, as defined in Chapter 2 (commencing with Section 11053) of Division 10 of the Health and Safety Code, a violation of subdivision (f) of Section 647 of the Penal Code, or a violation of Section 25662 of the Business and Professions Code, the minor's probation shall include the conditions required by Section 729.10. If the minor fails to comply with the conditions of probation imposed, the court may order and adjudge the minor to be a ward of the court.

(b) If the court has found that the minor is a person described by Section 601 or 602, it may order and adjudge the minor to be a ward of the court.

§ 727.5. Community service; habitually disobedient or truant minors

If a minor is found to be a person described in Section 601, the court may order the minor to perform community service, including, but not limited to, graffiti cleanup, for a total time not to exceed 20 hours over a period not to exceed 30 days, during a time other than his or her hours of school attendance or employment.

§ 207. Place of detention; contact with other detainees; records; reports; disclosure

(a) No minor shall be detained in any jail, lockup, juvenile hall, or other secure facility who is taken into custody solely upon the ground that he or she is a person described by Section 601 or adjudged to be such or made a ward of the juvenile court solely upon that ground, except as provided in subdivision (b). If any such minor, other than a minor described in subdivision (b), is detained, he or she shall be detained in a sheltered-care facility or crisis resolution home as provided for in Section 654, or in a nonsecure facility provided for in subdivision (a), (b), (c), or (d) of Section 727.

(b) A minor taken into custody upon the ground that he or she is a person described in Section 601, or adjudged to be a ward of the juvenile court solely upon that ground, may be held in a secure facility, other than a facility in which adults are held in secure custody, in any of the following circumstances:

(1) For up to 12 hours after having been taken into custody for the purpose of determining if there are any outstanding wants, warrants, or holds against the minor in cases where the arresting officer or probation officer has cause to believe that the wants, warrants, or holds exist.

(2) For up to 24 hours after having been taken into custody, in order to locate the minor's parent or guardian as soon as possible and to arrange the return of the minor to his or her parent or guardian.

(c) Any minor detained in juvenile hall pursuant to subdivision (b) may not be permitted to come or remain in contact with any person detained on the basis that he or she has been taken into custody upon the ground that he or she is a person described in Section 602 or adjudged to be such or made a ward of the juvenile court upon that ground.

(d) Minors detained in juvenile hall pursuant to Sections 601 and 602 may be held in the same facility provided they are not permitted to come or remain in contact within that facility.

(e) Every county shall keep a record of each minor detained under subdivision (b), the place and length of time of the detention, and the reasons why the detention was necessary. Every county shall report this information to the Board of Corrections on a monthly basis, on forms to be provided by that agency.

The board shall not disclose the name of the detainee, or any personally identifying information contained in reports.

2. Fla. Stat.

§ 984.03. Definitions

When used in this chapter, the term:

. . . .

(9) "Child in need of services" means a child for whom there is no pending investigation into an allegation or suspicion of abuse, neglect, or abandonment; no pending referral alleging the child is delinquent; or no current supervision by the Department of Juvenile Justice or the Department of Children and Family Services for an adjudication of dependency or delinquency. The child must also, pursuant to this chapter, be found by the court:

(a) To have persistently run away from the child's parents or legal custodians despite reasonable efforts of the child, the parents or legal custodians, and appropriate agencies to remedy the conditions contributing to the behavior. Reasonable efforts shall include voluntary participation by the child's parents or legal custodians and the child in family mediation, services, and treatment offered by the Department of Juvenile Justice or the Department of Children and Family Services;

(b) To be habitually truant from school, while subject to compulsory school attendance, despite reasonable efforts to remedy the situation pursuant to §§ 1003.26 and 1003.27 and through voluntary participation by the child's parents or legal custodians and the child in family mediation, services, and treatment offered by the Department of Juvenile Justice or the Department of Children and Family Services; or

(c) To have persistently disobeyed the reasonable and lawful demands of the child's parents or legal custodians, and to be beyond their control despite efforts by the child's parents or legal custodians and appropriate agencies to remedy the conditions contributing to the behavior. Reasonable efforts may include such things as good faith participation in family or individual counseling.

§ 984.22. Powers of disposition

(1) If the court finds that services and treatment have not been provided or utilized by a child or family, the court having jurisdiction of the child shall have the power to direct the least intrusive and least restrictive disposition, as follows:

(a) Order the parent, guardian, or custodian and the child to participate in treatment, services, and any other alternative identified as necessary.

(b) Order the parent, guardian, or custodian to pay a fine or fee based on the recommendations of the department.

(2) When any child is adjudicated by the court to be a child in need of services, the court having jurisdiction of the child and parent, guardian, or custodian shall have the power, by order, to:

(a) Place the child under the supervision of the department's contracted provider of programs and services for children in need of services and families in need of services. "Supervision," for the purposes of this section, means services as defined by the contract between the department and the provider.

(b) Place the child in the temporary legal custody of an adult willing to care for the child.

(c) Commit the child to a licensed child-caring agency willing to receive the child and to provide services without compensation from the department.

(d) Order the child, and, if the court finds it appropriate, the parent, guardian, or custodian of the child, to render community service in a public service program.

(3) When any child is adjudicated by the court to be a child in need of services and temporary legal custody of the child has been placed with an adult willing to care for the child, a licensed child-caring agency, the Department of Juvenile Justice, or the Department of Children and Family Services, the court shall order the natural or adoptive parents of such child, including the natural father of such child born out of wedlock who has acknowledged his paternity in writing before the court, or the guardian of such child's estate if possessed of assets which under law may be disbursed for the care, support, and maintenance of such child, to pay child support to the adult relative caring for the child, the licensed child-caring agency, the Department of Juvenile Justice, or the Department of Children and Family Services. When such order affects the guardianship estate, a certified copy of such order shall be delivered to the judge having jurisdiction of such guardianship estate. If the court determines that the parent is unable to pay support, placement of the child shall not be contingent upon issuance of a support order. The department may employ a collection agency for the purpose of receiving, collecting, and managing the payment of unpaid and delinquent fees. The collection agency must be registered and in good standing under chapter 559. The department may pay to the collection agency a fee from the amount collected under the claim or may authorize the agency to deduct the fee from the amount collected.

(4) All payments of fees made to the department pursuant to this chapter, or child support payments made to the department pursuant to subsection (3), shall be deposited in the General Revenue Fund.

(5) In carrying out the provisions of this chapter, the court shall order the child, family, parent, guardian, or custodian of a child who is found to be a child in need of services to participate in family counseling and other professional counseling activities or other alternatives deemed necessary for the rehabilitation of the child.

(6) The participation and cooperation of the family, parent, guardian, or custodian, and the child with court-ordered services, treatment, or community service are mandatory, not merely voluntary. The court may use its contempt powers to enforce its order.

3. Ga. Code

§ 15-11-2. Definitions

As used in this chapter, the term:

. . . .

(11) "Status offender" means a child who is charged with or adjudicated of an offense which would not be a crime if it were committed by an adult, in other words, an act

which is only an offense because of the perpetrator's status as a child. Such offenses shall include, but are not limited to, truancy, running away from home, incorrigibility, and unruly behavior.

(12) "Unruly child" means a child who:

(A) While subject to compulsory school attendance is habitually and without justification truant from school;

(B) Is habitually disobedient of the reasonable and lawful commands of his or her parent, guardian, or other custodian and is ungovernable;

(C) Has committed an offense applicable only to a child;

(D) Without just cause and without the consent of his or her parent or legal custodian deserts his or her home or place of abode;

(E) Wanders or loiters about the streets of any city, or in or about any highway or public place, between the hours of 12:00 Midnight and 5:00 A.M.;

(F) Disobeys the terms of supervision contained in a court order which has been directed to such child, who has been adjudicated unruly; or

(G) Patronizes any bar where alcoholic beverages are being sold, unaccompanied by such child's parents, guardian, or custodian, or possesses alcoholic beverages; and

(H) In any of the foregoing, is in need of supervision, treatment or rehabilitation; or

(I) Has committed a delinquent act and is in need of supervision, but not of treatment or rehabilitation."

C. Challenges to Incorrigibility Jurisdiction

1. Vagueness

Matter of Patricia A., A Person Alleged to Be in Need of Supervision
286 N.E.2d 432 (N.Y. 1972)

The appellant Patricia A. has been adjudicated a person in need of supervision (referred to at times as PINS) pursuant to the Family Court Act. Such a person is there defined as "a male less than sixteen years of age and a female less than eighteen years of age who does not attend school in accord with the provisions of the education law (relating to truancy or other nonattendance) or who is incorrigible, ungovernable or habitually disobedient and beyond the lawful control of parent or other lawful authority." The appellant, 16 years old at the time of her PINS adjudication, contends first that the statute offends against the requirements of due process in that it is unconstitutionally vague....

A statute is void for vagueness, the Supreme Court has stated, if it "fails to give a person of ordinary intelligence fair notice that his contemplated conduct is forbidden by the statute. The underlying principle is that no man shall be held criminally responsible for conduct which he could not reasonably understand to be proscribed." [W]e rejected the claim of vagueness in § 483 of the former Penal Law — which made it a misdemeanor to "cause" or "permit" the life of a child to be endangered or its health to be injured — and quoted the rule laid down in *Byron* that "[t]he test is whether a reasonable man subject to the statute would be informed of the nature of the offense prohibited and what is required of him. Such warning must be unequivocal but this requirement does not preclude the use of ordinary terms to express ideas which find adequate interpretation in common usage and understanding." ...

The appellant contends that the PINS statute does not meet essential tests or guidelines; more specifically, that it does not give potential offenders notice of what they may not do and that it does not provide adequate standards for the guidance of Family Court judges in applying the statute. In this connection, the appellant declares that what one parent or judge might consider grounds for a PINS adjudication—violation of midnight curfews, for example—another parent or another judge might be willing to overlook.

We find these arguments less than persuasive. The terms, "habitual truant," "incorrigible," "ungovernable," "'habitually disobedient and beyond * * * lawful control'", as well as the sort of conduct proscribed, are easily understood. The danger that Family Court judges may make an unduly restrictive application of the statute in marginal cases seems unrealistic.

2. Equal Protection

Matter of Patricia A., A Person Alleged to Be in Need of Supervision
286 N.E.2d 432 (N.Y. 1972)

Concluding, then, that the statute is sufficiently definite, we turn to the charge that it unconstitutionally discriminates against females.

Discrimination by the State between different classes of citizens must, at the very least, "have some relevance to the purpose for which the classification is made." Phrased somewhat differently, the classification "must be reasonable, not arbitrary, and must rest upon some ground of difference having a fair and substantial relation to the object of the legislation, so that all persons similarly circumstance[d] shall be treated alike."

The object of the PINS statute is to provide rehabilitation and treatment for young persons who engage in the sort of conduct there proscribed. This affords no reasonable ground, however, for differentiating between males and females over 16 and under 18. Girls in that age bracket are no more prone than boys to truancy, disobedience, incorrigible conduct and the like, nor are they more in need of rehabilitation and treatment by reason of such conduct.

The argument that discrimination against females on the basis of age is justified because of the obvious danger of pregnancy in an immature girl and because of out-of-wedlock births which add to the welfare relief burdens of the State and city is without merit. It is enough to say that the contention completely ignores the fact that the statute covers far more than acts of sexual misconduct. But, beyond that, even if we were to assume that the legislation had been prompted by such considerations, there would have been no rational basis for exempting, from the PINS definition, the 16 and 17-year-old boy responsible for the girl's pregnancy or the out-of-wedlock birth. As it is, the conclusion seems inescapable that lurking behind the discrimination is the imputation that females who engage in misconduct, sexual or otherwise, ought more to be censured, and their conduct subject to greater control and regulation, than males.

....

Consequently, since there is no justification for the age-sex distinction, [that much] of the Family Court Act as encompasses females between the ages of 16 and 18 must be stricken as unconstitutional.

SCILEPPI and JASEN, Judges, dissent and vote to affirm in the following memorandum:

> We dissent and vote to affirm on the ground that there is a rational basis for the distinction made between male and female offenders. The additional protection afforded females as provided for in the statute is realistic and reasonable and since the age differential applies to all females alike, there is no denial of equal protection.

Note

Is the *Patricia A.* holding relating to Equal Protection still valid in light of *Michael M. v. Superior Court*, 450 U.S. 464 (1981) (plurality opinion) (upholding the constitutionality of a statutory rape law punishing only the males; the Court found that the state had a "strong" interest in preventing illegitimate pregnancies)?

3. Substantive Due Process

Commonwealth v. Brasher

270 N.E.2d 389 (Mass. 1971)

....

The defendant argues ... it is beyond the limits of the police power of the Commonwealth to make laws for the punishment of stubborn children for the reasons (a) that they punish children for disobeying commands having only moral, but not legal sanctions, and (b) that they constitute an impermissible intrusion into the privacy of family life.

The fact that a child is under a moral obligation to obey his parents does not preclude the Legislature, in the exercise of its public power, from making that same obligation a legal one, with criminal penalties for its breach. It has never been contended, nor can it be properly contended, that because it is morally wrong to steal or to do harm to the person of another, or to kill him, the legislature is without power to make such conduct a crime and to prescribe penalties for the crime.

The argument that a law for the punishment of children who stubbornly disobey their parents is unconstitutional because it is an impermissible intrusion into the privacy of family life is without merit. While "[i]t is cardinal * * * that the custody, care and nurture of the child reside first in the parents, whose primary function and freedom include preparation for obligations * * * (in) the private realm of family life which the state cannot enter," such as religious teaching to children, "the family itself is not beyond regulation in the public interest." The rights and obligations of members of families in relation to each other have been regulated by laws for centuries. In that time the law has always imposed a duty upon parents to support, provide for and protect the children they bring forth. This is an obligation which they owe to their children, but its breach is also a crime against society. In more recent times the law in this regard has been expanded to include the obligation to provide educational guidance. To enable the parents to discharge that responsibility, the law gives them the custody of and right of control over their children. That carries with it the power to exercise whatever authority is reasonably necessary for the purpose, and to make all reasonable decisions for the control and proper functioning of the family as a harmonious social unit. It permits the parents to give reasonable commands to their children and to require the children to obey those commands. The children in turn owe the parents an obligation to acknowledge and submit to their authority and to obey their reasonable and lawful requests and commands. In short, the governing authority for the proper operation, control and discipline of the family unit is vested in the parents.

While the State defers to the parents with respect to most decisions on family matters, it has an interest in insuring the existence of harmonious relations between family members, and between the family unit and the rest of the public society. To protect this interest, the State may properly require that unemancipated children obey the reasonable and lawful commands of their parents, and it may impose criminal penalties on the children if they persistently disobey such commands. The State is not powerless to prevent or control situations which threaten the proper functioning of a family unit as an important segment of the total society. It may properly extend the protection of its laws in aid of the head of a family unit whose reasonable and lawful commands are being disobeyed by children who are bound to obey them. The making of such laws is within the power of the Legislature "to make, ordain, and establish, all manner of wholesome and reasonable Orders, laws, statutes, and ordinances, directions and instructions, either with penalties or without; * * * as * * * (it) shall judge to be for the good and welfare of this Commonwealth, and for the government and ordering thereof, and of the subjects of the same."

A substantial portion of the defendant's brief is devoted to the statement of facts and arguments of a sociological nature criticizing our present statutes governing proceedings against juvenile offenders, criticizing the physical facilities available for the detention of such offenders, and suggesting that many of the children confined in such facilities do not belong there. It also suggests that stubbornness in a child "may be symptomatic of a psychological defect in the child or inadequacy in the parent or both." Arguments of this type are not relevant to the legal issues presented for our decision. They would be more appropriate if addressed to the Legislature which has the power to change the statutes if it is persuaded that such changes are needed. We do not have that power.

4. Eighth Amendment

Blondheim v. Washington

529 P.2d 1096 (Wash. 1975)

STAFFORD, Associate Justice.

Petitioner was born August 21, 1956. On November 30, 1973, her mother filed a petition, in the King County Juvenile Court, alleging petitioner had run away from home or placements on[at least six occasions between April and August 1973], and that she had been AWOL from the Job Corps Center in Astoria, Oregon, on at least two occasions resulting in her termination from that program. Petitioner admitted the facts alleged in the petition. Her motion to dismiss the action was denied and she was declared an incorrigible dependent pursuant to [Revised Code chap.] 13.04.010(7). The Juvenile Court committed her to the Department of Social and Health Services, Division of Institutions. The commitment was suspended and she was placed on probation and released to herself, upon the condition she actively seek employment and cooperate with her probation officer.

Although admitting the facts, petitioner challenges RCW 13.04.010(7), defining incorrigibility, as unconstitutionally vague, overbroad, and, when coupled with RCW 13.04.095(6), punishing a mere status. Further, she asserts there is a violation of the eighth amendment to the United States Constitution prohibiting cruel or unusual punishment.

. . . .

[P]etitioner contends RCW 13.04.010(7) violates the Eighth Amendment in that it punishes the "status" of being incorrigible. In *Robinson v. California*, the United States Supreme Court found that a statute which made the "status" of being a narcotics addict a criminal offense inflicted a cruel and unusual punishment in violation of the eighth and fourteenth amendments to the United States Constitution. It was not the acts or behavior of the person thus afflicted that were being proscribed by the statute. Rather, it was the person's condition or state of being, over which he had little or no control, that was being punished. On the other hand, persons convicted of crimes for behavior in public which is proscribed by statute are not deemed convicted of a so-called "status" crime

Although incorrigibility is a condition or state of being, one acquires such a "status" only by reason of one's conduct or a pattern of behavior proscribed by the statute. An incorrigible is one "who is beyond the control and power," [of a parent or guardian]. The statute does not relate to a true "status". Rather, it relates to a cour[se] of conduct or the nature of the child which places it beyond the lawfully exercised control or lawfully exercised power of its parents, guardian, or custodian.

In the instant case, the petition filed by petitioner's mother alleged specific conduct on the part of her daughter. Petitioner admitted the allegations. The "status" of being incorrigible was established by proof of the facts alleged in the petition. But, it was not the "status" of being incorrigible for which petitioner was given a suspended commitment and placed on probation. Rather, it was her conduct which placed her beyond the lawfully exercised control or power of her mother, that led to her being found to be incorrigible, and, thus, resulted in the suspended commitment.

Petitioner also contends that RCW 13.04.010(7), when viewed in conjunction with RCW 13.04.095(6) (providing for the commitment of incorrigible dependents to the "Department of Institutions") is disproportionate to the conduct proscribed and thus violates the Eighth Amendment. Petitioner's position is based on the fact that a suspended commitment to the Division of Institutions gives rise to the possibility that she might be incarcerated in an institutional facility also housing juvenile delinquents. While this possibility apparently does exist, she has not been placed in such an institutional facility. Therefore, the issue is not before us. We cannot help but observe, however, that one who is a dependent, albeit an incorrigible dependent, should not be committed for treatment or confinement in the same immediate area of an institution where he or she may associate with children committed for delinquent behavior. This is not to say, however, that incorrigible dependents cannot be housed within the confines of the same institutional facility as delinquent children. Rather, an incorrigible dependent committed to an institutional facility also housing juvenile delinquents must be kept separate and apart from them.

D. Use and Misuse of the Status Offender Jurisdiction

1. Cases

In re Butterfield

253 Cal. App.2d 794 (Cal. App. Ct. 1967)

Petition for habeas corpus, challenging a juvenile court commitment to the California Youth Authority. The petitioner, a 15-year-old girl, is presently in custody at the Youth Authority Reception Center at Perkins, Sacramento County.

In May 1966 a petition was filed with the juvenile court alleging that she had run away from her parents' home. (The habeas corpus petition contains an undenied allegation that in February 1966 she had slashed her wrists in a suicide attempt. Other documents reveal an unstable family situation.) The juvenile court committed her to Napa State Hospital for the 90-day diagnostic period authorized by section 703, Welfare and Institutions Code. [T]wo additional 90-day periods followed. On April 12, 1967, after expiration of the third diagnostic commitment, the girl was declared a ward of the juvenile court under section 601. (Although no copy of the Napa Hospital report is included in the papers before us, the habeas corpus petition has an undenied allegation declaring that the diagnosis was "Schizophrenic Reaction, Schizoaffective Type.") The order took physical custody from her parents and placed the girl in the home of an aunt and uncle. Relatively minor behaviour problems occurred. In May 1967 she threatened another school pupil and was sent home from school. That evening she took an overdose of pills (referred to in the papers only as a "prescription drug") and was found in a coma. Later she said that although she did not want to die, it would be better to be dead than to be returned to the juvenile hall.

The probation officer then filed a second petition with the juvenile court, seeking a declaration of wardship under section 602.[4] It alleged: This person comes within the provisions of Section 602 of the Juvenile Court Law of California, in that: Said minor, Rachelle Teresa Butterfield, on or about the 19th day of May, 1967, at and in the County of Santa Clara, State of California, said minor is in danger of leading an immoral life, in that, said minor did ingest an unknown quantity of a prescription drug in an attempt to do bodily harm; thereby violating the Court Order of April 12, 1967."

A hearing was held at which the girl and her mother were present. At the hearing the court rendered the judgment under attack, finding that the minor came within section 602; finding that she had ingested an unknown quantity of a prescription drug in an attempt to do bodily harm, thereby violating the wardship order of April 12, 1967; directing her commitment to the Youth Authority and ordering her placement in Agnews State Hospital pending acceptance by the Youth Authority. After her acceptance by the Youth Authority, she was taken from the state hospital to the reception center at Perkins.

The judgment is appealable. Nevertheless, habeas corpus is an available means of inquiry into claims that constitutional guaranties have been violated. Such claims are made

---

4. Section 602 declares: "Any person under the age of 21 years who violates any law of this State or of the United States or any ordinance of any city or county of this State defining crime or who, after having been found by the juvenile court to be a person described by Section 601, fails to obey any lawful order of the juvenile court, is within the jurisdiction of the juvenile court, which may adjudge such person to be a ward of the court."

here. The girl is now in a Youth Authority reception center, a facility for temporary detention and processing of wards pending their assignment to institutions for long-term confinement and care. If petitioner's commitment is invalid, it should be interrupted before further migrations between institutions. Appeal is thus an inadequate remedy.

Due process of law is a requisite to the constitutional validity of juvenile court proceedings in which alleged misconduct may result in a determination of delinquency and commitment to a state institution. In that kind of proceeding due process demands such notice of hearing as would be constitutionally adequate in a civil or criminal proceeding; demands representation by counsel or waiver of that right; prohibits use against the juvenile of his self-incriminating statements unless he knows that he need not speak and will not be penalized for silence.

The papers before us demonstrate full compliance with the California statutes requiring advance service of a copy of the petition and notice of hearing (including information as to entitlement to counsel) upon the juvenile and her parents. At the inception of the hearing before the juvenile court, the probation officer again advised the juvenile and her mother of their right to counsel, including a court-appointed attorney. Both stated clearly and with apparent deliberation that they wished to proceed without an attorney. The clerk then read the basic allegation of the petition quoted earlier in this opinion. At that point, with no attempt to impart knowledge of the right to refrain from self-incrimination, the probation officer asked if the charges were true, the minor replied in the affirmative and the court immediately announced judgment.

No evidence other than the minor's admission was received. The adjudication was one of "delinquency" because it found her guilty of disobedience to a court order and committed her to confinement in a correctional institution. It was used "against" her in the sense that it formed the entire evidentiary basis for the judgment. The statement was self-incriminating. She had no prior warning and there is no evidence that she had any awareness of her right to refrain from self-incrimination. Evidentiary use of her self-incriminating statement without that awareness infected the hearing with a violation of due process.

The formal and literal waiver of counsel was ineffectual because not made with an intelligent understanding of its consequences. The girl's history was one of emotional disturbance and social maladjustment, not criminality. The facilities of the Youth Authority are inhabited primarily by "public offenders" who have violated the criminal laws. California designates a narrow class of youthful subjects who are innocent of law-breaking but committable to the Youth Authority along with the public offenders. After a juvenile has been made a ward under section 601 (for example, as one in danger of an immoral life) and has violated a lawful order of the court, he may be adjudged a ward under section 602. He may then be committed to the Youth Authority "as an additional alternative" under section 731. The statutory theory is that he has demonstrated a degree of incorrigibility which *may* warrant an indefinite commitment in an institution designed primarily for public offenders. Once in the institution, he may be confined until his 21st birthday; may be placed on parole as a "CYA parolee" or discharged. No matter how non-criminal in theory, an inevitable stigma accompanies such a commitment. Our present minor—with a history of emotional disturbance but not delinquency—uttered the words of waiver with no awareness that long-term confinement in a correctional institution was a possible consequence of the wardship order. Indeed, the girl entered upon the hearing in the hope that another foster home would be found for her. By proceeding without an intelligent waiver of counsel, the court deprived the minor of a second requisite of due process.

Although other aspects of the proceeding have been debated, the lack of effectual waiver of counsel and of the right to refrain from self-incrimination require that the commitment be set aside. Since further juvenile court proceedings will occur, one more aspect should be discussed. The court adjudged wardship under section 602 on the theory that the girl (being already a ward under section 601) had disobeyed a lawful order of the court. Wardship under section 602, in turn, would permit a commitment to the Youth Authority under section 731. The "disobedience" consisted of the girl's second suicide attempt. How this action violated the court's prior orders does not appear. In all realism, the suicide attempt was a repeated manifestation of emotional disturbance, not an act of disobedience. The proceeding appears to have been molded to the language of section 602 as a verbal technique leading to a pre-selected commitment, one offering a combination of physical security and psychiatric services. The array of facilities available for safeguarding and treating emotionally disturbed youngsters is woefully incomplete. In devising judicial commitments, crude compromises, diverging from the ideal, are a frequent necessity. A judge seeking an enlightened solution to the commitment problem deserves public and appellate sympathy. The demands of the Juvenile Court Law must be observed, however. The comparatively stringent wardship permissible under section 602 appears to be designed for delinquent youngsters. The present subject has violated no law and her second suicide attempt, like the first, is the apparent product of psychic imbalance rather than delinquency.

In the Matter of Lloyd

308 N.Y.S.2d 419 (N.Y. App. Div. 1970)

In this Family Court proceeding the appellant was adjudged a person in need of supervision and ordered to be placed in the Otisville Training School for a period of up to 18 months. There is little doubt that in so ordering the learned Family Court Judge was doing the best that he could for the appellant in a well-nigh impossible situation and one with which he never should have been faced. Frankly, we also are at a loss, and the disposition made is in the hope that conditions have so improved that a more suitable solution is possible.

The appellant, now just 15 years of age, together with his four sisters, first came to the attention of the Family Court on February 3, 1967, on a petition to have him declared a neglected child. It was incontrovertible that his situation necessitated such a disposition. He was then living with his sisters and parents in rooms reeking with the effluvia of neglect. The children were left alone and unsupervised. The mother, hostile to the educational process, encouraged them in truancy. It appears that both parents were inebriates. Following an adjudication, promises of reform led to their release in the mother's custody. Some weeks later aggravation of home conditions led to a second hearing, whereupon appellant was placed in the custody of the Department of Welfare and sent to the Children's Center. From that time on until May 13, 1969, he was in and out of the Children's Center, being released to his mother. (What became of his father is not revealed in the record.) On May 14, 1969, he was placed back in the Children's Center, where he has been officially consigned up to the date of this proceeding.

His stay at Children's Center has, however, been more a matter of official notation than actual residence. He has constantly eloped to his mother's home and remained there for extended periods. We have been informed that efforts to place him in private charitable institutions have been unsuccessful, as well as efforts to place him in a foster home. The situation presented to the Family Court upon the hearing under review was that release to his mother was unthinkable, placement in a suitable private institution unable of accomplishment, and retention at the Children's Center no longer possible. In this dilemma, and faced with the absolute necessity of providing some means of care for this boy, the finding was made that he was a person in need of supervision, and he was directed to be placed in Training School.

A careful review of this record indicates that this appellant is a "neglected child" rather than "a person in need of supervision" as defined in the Family Court Act. While there is ample support for the finding that appellant habitually absented himself from the Children's Center, this conduct does not warrant a finding that he was habitually disobedient or ungovernable. In each instance he went back to his mother's house because she had failed to visit him in the Center and feelings of neglect and rejection became unbearable. We appreciate the dilemma of the court but ... the provision of proper facilities is the responsibility of the Legislature and the legislative failure in that regard does not warrant circumvention of the statute. Incidentally, the Legislature has long recognized that the State training schools are hardly a beneficial haven for young people in need of supervision and such disposition was first interdicted and then allowed as a stopgap measure for three years until it was finally made permanent.

Is this child then to be relegated to the custody of his mother under conditions that the record shows have actually deteriorated since the original, and justified, finding of neglect? It is easy to say, as it is undoubtedly true, that it is not our problem. The court obviously cannot provide a facility where none exists. We do not give up, however, without a final gesture. Taking recourse in the Family Court Act, we direct a new adjudicatory and dispositional hearing in the hope that with the lapse of time a place in some authorized agency may be found or that the Children's Center may be able to make a viable adjustment.

In the Interest of Doe

26 P.3d 562 (Hawaii 2001)

....

Doe, born in Honolulu, Hawai'i on June 16, 1983, began attending the Wai'anae Intermediate School in 1995. Due to chronic truancy, Doe has repeated the seventh grade three years in a row.

On December 3, 1997, Doe's school counselor prepared a document, entitled "precourt interventions," listing the multiple unsuccessful "intervention efforts" by the school over the several previous years and recommending a plan of service including "[j]oint protective supervision to [family court and the Department of Education (DOE)]." On December 19, 1997, the State of Hawai'i (the State), through DOE, filed a petition against Doe alleging a violation of Hawai'i Revised Statutes based on 49 days of unexcused absences between September 3 and November 26, 1997.

A hearing was held on January 14, 1998....

After the hearing, the family court issued an order placing Doe under the protective supervision of the DOE and the court and requiring Doe to perform 20 hours of community service within 60 days of assignment. The order also provided: "Probation Officer shall make a referral to have minor undergo a psychological evaluation through [DOE];" and "DOE shall make a referral to the appropriate prosecuting attorney to file a contempt of court if minor fails to attend school."

In addition to its order, the court filed two documents stating the rules of protective supervision of the DOE and of the court. The DOE's rules provided in relevant part:

You have been placed under protective supervision to [DOE] until further order. This period may be extended by the Court.

While you are under this protective supervision, you must follow these rules:

1. You are to attend Wai'anae Int. School or any school or program as directed by the Department of Education.

* * *

2. You are to attend each day and every class.

* * *

. . . .

On January 29, 1998, Doe was arrested by the police and detained. On January 30, 1998, the prosecution filed a petition against Doe for violating rule 6 of the family court's rules, specifically, "le[aving] home without permission and remain[ing] away until apprehended." Later that day, the court issued an order authorizing Doe's early release to her mother after a psychological evaluation. The court also issued an order continuing Doe's protective supervision and providing that a "Contempt of Court hearing (petition) shall be set before [the court]. . . .

On February 9, 1998, Jean Anderson . . . , clinical psychology graduate student, and Patricia Harnish, Ph.D. . . . , clinical psychologist for the family court liaison branch, jointly submitted an extensive "psychological evaluation" of Doe based on interviews on January 27, 28, and 30, 1998. Based on a review of Doe's history and present status, Dr. Harnish and Anderson concluded that Doe "is aware of what she needs to do to improve her situation, but does not seem to have the self-discipline and self-motivation to follow through with what she needs to do* * *. Because of this, [she] may need a more structured environment to encourage school attendance on a daily basis." Dr. Harnish and Anderson recommended a detailed plan of treatment including mental health and support services, individual therapy, family therapy, school-based services, and, "if [Doe still] fails to attend school on a regular basis * * *, placement in a more structured setting, *i.e.*, group home, to monitor school attendance and behaviors in and out of school."

On April 3, 1998, the prosecution filed two petitions alleging that Doe violated Rule 4 of the family court's rules by failing to attend classes on February 3–17, 19–23, 25, 26, 1998 and March 2–31, 1998. On April 27, 1998, the prosecution filed another petition stating that "[Doe] appears to come within the purview of [the statute] in that [Doe] * * * did knowingly disobey and resist the process, injunction or other mandate of a court * * *, thereby committing the offense of Criminal Contempt of Court in violation of [the statute]."

Trial on the criminal contempt petition was held on July 1, 1998. The court took judicial notice of the records and files in this case, including the January 14, 1998 protective supervision order and rules. Doe's teacher and vice-principal at Wai'anae Intermediate testified regarding Doe's truancy.

. . . .

The court ruled that the protective supervision order was valid and that "[Doe] had actual proper notice of it." "[S]atisfied by proof beyond a reasonable doubt that the material allegations on the petition for criminal contempt of court have been proven," the court "adjudicated Doe as a law violator."

During the disposition phase of the trial, Gordean Akiona . . . , a court officer, recommended that Doe be placed on probation and confined to a detention home until July 5,

1998, that Doe and her family continue in counseling, and that the orders of protective supervision and community service be revoked. The representative of DOE joined the recommendation based on Doe's "willful and intentional disobedience of this Court." Doe disagreed, emphasizing her ongoing counseling program and recommending community service instead.

At the request of the DOE, the court received Doe's February 9, 1998 psychological report, her recent attendance records, and a progress report written by her school counselor, Linsey Ho * * *. Ho also addressed the court in person, raising her concern that Doe would be starting her fourth year as a seventh grader. Ho opined that "the only alternative we have, you know, because she is getting older * * *, we could be looking at [an alternative school]," but that, "again, the question is getting her to school."

The court adopted Akiona's recommended disposition, issuing an order revoking Doe's protective supervision and community service requirement, placing her on probation until further order of the court, mandating her confinement in a detention home until July 5, 1998, and directing her to continue counseling with the Department of Health. [Doe appealed to the Intermediate Court of Appeals].

. . . .

In its decision, the ICA ruled that the statutory distinction between "status offenders" and "law violators" precludes the family court from adjudicating a minor as a "law violator" for criminal contempt of court based on a violation of a court order of protective supervision. While this ruling focused on Doe's truancy, which would not be a crime if committed by an adult, in our view, it underemphasized Doe's willful violation of a lawful court order, which *would* be a criminal offense if committed by an adult. Balancing the policies of "deinstitutionalizing" status offenders, on the one hand, and ensuring effective administration of the family court's function, on the other, we hold that the family court may adjudicate status offenders under HRS § 571-11(1) for criminal contempt based on violations of court orders of protective supervision, subject to certain important limitations outlined below.

. . . .

The status offender who violates a court order of protective supervision does nothing other than violate the law, and contempt of court is nothing other than a crime if committed by an adult. *See In re D.L.D.* ("We believe that missing school as the occasion for [status offender] jurisdiction cannot be equated legally or factually with missing school in willful and contumacious defiance of a court order. Therefore, the remedies available pursuant to [a status offender] order are distinguishable from the remedies available to enforce that order."); *In re G.B.* ("The contempt proceedings * * * were filed because of a violation of [a court] order. * * * This, therefore, is not a case governed by the [family court statute]. Rather, the propriety of placing this minor on probation depends upon the court's power to impose punishment for contempt for the violation of its order."); *L.A.M. v. State* ("This behavior constitutes willful criminal contempt of the court's authority; were [appellant] an adult, her actions would be characterized as a 'crime' * * *."); ... [C]hapter 571 does not expressly bar the family court from dealing with violators of court orders of protective supervision under its inherent authority to punish contempts and its jurisdiction over "law violators." Absent such clear direction, "we should not presume that the Legislature intended to override such long-established power."

. . . .

Our interpretation, we observe, also stems from sensitivity to the overarching legislative intent to "promote the reconciliation of distressed juveniles with their families, foster the rehabilitation of juveniles in difficulty, render appropriate punishment to offenders, and reduce juvenile delinquency." "If a juvenile * * * can purposely or knowingly disregard Family Court orders without sanction and with impunity * * *, the legislation is a nullity, the court has no adequate remedy, [and] the juvenile remains at risk.* * * Such a result is clearly not in the best interest of the juvenile or the legislative intent."

In sum, "if family courts are to retain jurisdiction of [status offenders], they must have the authority to handle them. Their inherent contempt powers provide such tools." We therefore hold that the family court may adjudicate and punish status offenders in violation of a court order of protective supervision. At the same time, we do not ignore the general legislative policy of "deinstitutionalizing" status offenders. Accordingly, in line with other courts, we impose several limitations on the family court's contempt powers. First, the minor must receive sufficient notice to comply with the court's order and must understand its terms and operation, in particular, the possibility of secure detention for disobedience. Second, the court must consider less restrictive alternatives and determine them ineffective or inappropriate. "While the court need not necessarily have attempted lesser penalties before imposing secure confinement, the record should indicate that lesser alternatives were considered by the juvenile court before ordering incarceration." Third, contact between the minor and juvenile delinquents convicted of other crimes must "be kept to a minimum." These protective conditions strike the appropriate balance between the competing policies of limiting the secure detention of status offenders and preserving the dignity and authority of the family court.

In the Interest of S.S.

869 A.2d 875 (N.J. 2005)

PER CURIAM.

The question presented on these appeals is whether a juvenile, brought before the court under a juvenile family-in-crisis petition, may be adjudicated delinquent for criminal contempt. In each of the cases before us, the Appellate Division answered that question in the negative and reversed an adjudication of delinquency based upon a criminal contempt arising out of the juvenile's violation of a court order to "obey the rules of home and school."

We now affirm both Appellate Division judgments substantially for the reasons expressed in Judge Wecker's thorough and thoughtful opinion in *State of New Jersey in the Interest of S.S.* Like the Appellate Division, we have concluded that, on the backdrop of the legislative goals underlying the criminal contempt statute and our juvenile justice scheme, it was "error to subject a status offender * * * to an adjudication of delinquency based upon a repetition of the runaway conduct and truancy that brought her family to the court for help in the first place.

Our ruling does not leave the juvenile family-in-crisis judge impotent. [The statute] specifically provides: "In the case of failure of any person to comply with any orders entered pursuant to this section, the court may proceed against such person for the enforcement of litigants' rights." Pursuant to that authority, juvenile family-in-crisis judges have at their disposal civil proceedings that include the remedy of incarceration so long as the commitment order specifies "the terms of release." As that requirement underscores, incarceration in the civil context is a last resort intended to be primarily coercive.

Thus, the facts of each case require careful consideration to determine whether that remedy is appropriate in the first instance. Moreover, once incarceration is in play, the trial court must assure itself that juvenile status offenders are separated from those accused of being—or adjudicated as—delinquent. The inability to effectuate such segregation of the juvenile status offender would eliminate incarceration as an arrow in the judicial quiver.

We are fully aware, as was the Appellate Division, of the inherent "tension between the judiciary's power (and need) to enforce its own orders and its duty to provide appropriate protection for a juvenile—particularly one whose conduct has not violated any criminal law and has primarily endangered only herself." How to reconcile those competing interests is a difficult question that requires further review. We therefore refer the issue to the Conference of Family Presiding Judges for study and recommendations for the development of a schematic to harmonize those important concerns.

Note

For an analysis of the use and misuse of the status offender laws, see Irene Merker Rosenberg & Yale L. Rosenberg, *The Legacy of the Stubborn and Rebellious Son*, 74 Mich. L. Rev. 1097, 1110–21 (1976).

E. The Status Offender Laws and Parental Rights

In the Matter of the Welfare of Snyder
532 P.2d 278 (Wash. 1975)

Paul Snyder and Nell Snyder, petitioners, seek review of the King County Juvenile Court's finding that their daughter, Cynthia Nell Snyder, respondent, was an incorrigible child as defined under [Revised Code chap.] 13.04.010(7). The issue before this court is whether the Juvenile Court's determination is supported by substantial evidence.

Cynthia Nell Snyder is 16 years old, attends high school, and has consistently received above average grades. Prior to the occurrences which led to this action, she resided with her parents in their North Seattle home. The record shows that as Cynthia entered her teen years, a hostility began to develop between herself and her parents. This environment within the family home worsened due to a total breakdown in the lines of communication between Cynthia and her parents. Cynthia's parents, being strict disciplinarians, placed numerous limitations on their daughter's activities, such as restricting her choice of friends, and refusing to let her smoke, date, or participate in certain extracurricular activities within the school, all of which caused Cynthia to rebel against their authority. These hostilities culminated in a total collapse of the parent-child relationship. This atmosphere resulted in extreme mental abuse to all parties concerned.

On June 18, 1973, Mr. Snyder, having concluded that the juvenile court might be able to assist him in controlling his daughter, removed Cynthia from the family home and delivered her to the Youth Service Center. As a result, Cynthia was placed in a receiving home. On July 19, 1973, in an attempt to avoid returning home, Cynthia filed a petition in the Juvenile Department of the Superior Court for King County, alleging that she was a dependent child as defined by [chap.] 13.04.010(2) and (3), which provide:

This chapter shall be known as the "Juvenile Court Law" and shall apply to all minor children under the age of eighteen years who are delinquent or dependent; and to any person or persons who are responsible for or contribute to, the delinquency or dependency of such children.

For the purpose of this chapter the words "dependent child" shall mean any child under the age of eighteen years:

* * *

(2) Who has no parent, guardian or other responsible person; or who has no parent or guardian willing to exercise, or capable of exercising, proper parental control; or

(3) Whose home by reason of neglect, cruelty or depravity of his parents or either of them, or on the part of his guardian, or on the part of the person in whose custody or care he may be, or for any other reason, is an unfit place for such child; * * *.

On July 23, 1973, Cynthia was placed in the temporary custody of the Department of Social and Health Services and an attorney was appointed to be her guardian ad litem. On October 12, 1973, the Juvenile Court held that the allegations attacking the fitness of Cynthia's parents were incorrect, at least to the extent that they alleged dependency, and that Cynthia should be returned to the custody of her parents. Cynthia did return to the family residence, where she remained until November 16, 1973. At that time, following additional confrontations in her home, Cynthia went to Youth Advocates, a group which assists troubled juveniles, who in turn directed her to the Youth Service Center. On November 21, 1973, Margaret Rozmyn, who was in charge of the intake program at the center, filed a petition alleging that Cynthia was incorrigible as defined under [chap.] 13.04.010(7), which provides:

For the purpose of this chapter the words "dependent child" shall mean any child under the age of eighteen years:

* * *

(7) Who is incorrigible; that is, who is beyond the control and power of his parents, guardian, or custodian by reason of the conduct or nature of said child; * * *.

A hearing was held on December 3, 1973, to determine temporary custody. The court limited the proceedings to arguments of opposing counsel and ultimately decided that Cynthia should be placed in a foster home pending the outcome of the fact-finding hearing. This hearing was held on December 10 and 11, 1973. At that time, Commissioner Quinn found that Cynthia was incorrigible and continued the matter for one week in order for the entire family to meet with a counselor. Originally, the commissioner indicated that he was inclined to have Cynthia return home, while at the same time being placed under supervised probation. However, on December 18, 1973, Commissioner Quinn, upon hearing the comments and conclusions of the counseling psychiatrist chosen by the parents, decided that Cynthia was to be placed in a foster home, under the supervision of the probation department of the Juvenile Court, and that she and her parents were to continue counseling, subject to subsequent review by the court. The parents immediately filed a motion for revision of the commissioner's decision, which was denied by the Superior Court for King County in August of 1974.

. . . .

The sole issue presented by these facts is whether there is substantial evidence in the record, taken as a whole, to support the Juvenile Court's determination that Cynthia Nell Snyder is incorrigible. Her parents contend that Cynthia is not incorrigible, as a matter of law, since the only evidence to support such a finding is their daughter's own statements. We disagree.

A child is incorrigible when she is beyond the power and control of her parents by reason of her own conduct. In reviewing the record in search of substantial evidence, we must find "evidence in sufficient quantum to persuade a fair-minded, rational person of the truth of a declared premise." In applying this criteria for review, we are mindful that our paramount consideration, irrespective of the natural emotions in cases of this nature, must be the welfare of the child. When the questions of dependency and incorrigibility arise, "we have often noted what we think is a realistic and rational appellate policy of placing very strong reliance on trial court determinations of what course of action will be in the best interests of the child." In reviewing the record, we find no evidence which would indicate that Commissioner Quinn acted unfairly, irrationally, or in a prejudicial manner in reaching his conclusion. Therefore, we must give "very strong" credence to his determinations. We feel it is imperative to recognize that the issue of who is actually responsible for the breakdown in the parent-child relationship is irrelevant to our disposition of this case. The issue is whether there is substantial evidence to support a finding that the parent-child relationship has dissipated to the point where parental control is lost and, therefore, Cynthia is incorrigible. It is for this reason that Cynthia's conduct, her state of mind, and the opinion of Doctor Gallagher, the psychiatrist chosen by Mr. and Mrs. Snyder, are of such paramount importance. This child has established a pattern of refusing to obey her parents and, on two occasions, has, in effect, fled her home by filing petitions in the Juvenile Court in order that she might be made a ward of the court. Cynthia's adamant state of mind can be best understood by considering her clear and unambiguous testimony in response to her attorney's direct examination.

Q. Your petition alleges that you absolutely refuse to go home and obey your parents, is that correct? A. Yes. Q. You are under oath today, of course, and is that the statement you would make to the Court today? A. Yes. Q. Cindy, do you understand the consequences of filing a petition of this nature? A. Yes. Q. Did we discuss this matter? A. Yes. Q. Have we discussed this on several occasions? A. Yes. Q. What is your understanding of what might be the consequences of this type of petition? A. I could be put in the Youth Center or I could be put into another institution of some kind or I could go into the custody of the Department of Social and Health Services. Q. So you understand it is conceivable that you might not be able to go back home even if you want to go back home, is that correct? A. Yes. Q. In spite of all that, is it still your statement today that at the time of the petition anyway you refused to go back home? A. Yes. Q. Is that your position right now? A. Yes. Q. The position then, why don't you state that for the Court? A. I refuse to go back there. I just won't do it. Mr. Sanders [Attorney for parents]: I object to the whole line of testimony. I think it is irrelevant whether she refuses to go back home. That is not an issue in the case. The Court: Overruled. A. I just absolutely refuse to go back there. I can't live with them.

In addition, the parents and the older sister, by their testimony, admitted that a difficult situation existed in the home. The court also considered the testimony of the intake officer from the Youth Service Center as to the attitude of Cynthia. Finally, the court considered the opinion of Dr. Gallagher, who met with Cynthia and her parents, and reported that counseling would not be beneficial until all of the individuals concerned backed away from the hard and fast positions they now held in regard to this matter which, in his opinion, was the cause of the tension which resulted in overt hostility. In other words, the finding of incorrigibility is not supported solely by Cynthia's testimony and her refusal to return home. But in addition thereto, the commissioner's opinion finds support in the testimony of other individuals who were familiar with the situation, either from a personal or a professional standpoint. The fact that the commissioner gave serious consideration to the testimony of Cynthia, an interested party, is inconsequential since it only goes to the weight to be given to her statements as a witness. Furthermore, we have not deviated from the rule that when an interested party testifies, the rate at which that evidence is discounted, if at all, should be determined by the trial judge, who is far better qualified to make that judgment than we.

Having found the juvenile court's finding of incorrigibility to be supported by substantial evidence within the entire record, we are constitutionally bound to affirm the Juvenile Court's decision.

. . . .

It is implicit in the record that the petitioner parents believe the Juvenile Court has given sympathy and support to Cynthia's problems in disregard of their rights as parents, and that the Juvenile Court has failed to assume its responsibility to assist in the resolution of the parents' problems with their minor child. We find this presumption of the petitioners to be unsupported by the evidence. The record clearly shows that numerous attempts were made by the Juvenile Court commissioner to reconcile the family differences, as evidenced by its unsuccessful attempt at sending Cynthia home subsequent to the disposition of the first petition, the attempt to gain assistance through professional counseling, and the numerous and extensive exchanges between Commissioner Quinn and the Snyder family during the proceeding. The avenues for counseling were to remain open and counseling of both parties was to continue, which was interrupted by the interposition of the application by the parents for our review. In view of our disposition of this case, we are satisfied that the Juvenile Court, in exercising its continuing jurisdiction, will continue to review the progress of the parties to the end of a hoped-for reconciliation.

Notes

(a) For a contrary decision see *In re Polovchak*, 454 N.E.2d 258 (Ill. 1983) (reversing and finding that a 12-year-old boy's single act of leaving his parents' home and refusal to accompany them back to Russia did not constitute a basis for adjudging the child a minor in need of supervision; the child had filed the status offender petition to avoid returning to Russia).

(b) Given the underlying reasons for the constitutionality of in need of supervision laws, should the parents' objection to state intervention be a relevant factor in the court's decision to make a minor a ward of the court in an incorrigibility case?

(c) For an analysis of the rights of parents, children, and the state in status offender cases, see Irene Merker Rosenberg, *Juvenile Status Offender Statutes—New Perspectives on an Old Problem*, 16 U.C. DAVIS L. REV. 283, 322–23 (1983):

> The [status offender] laws have always been a source of danger to both parent and child. It seemed, however, that as long as the [status offender] laws were being invoked by parents and applied to children, they merely enhanced parental power. [Cases allowing juveniles to file status offender petitions] make clear that the power of the state is not so easily contained.

F. Beyond the Status Offender Jurisdiction

Colon v. Collazo

729 F.2d 32 (1st Cir. 1984)

PER CURIAM.

On appeal, the plaintiffs, "non-delinquent" youths committed on a temporary basis to juvenile institutions against their will, claim that their commitment without a hearing or a court order deprives them of a liberty interest without due process of law in violation of the United States Constitution and circumvents the laws of Puerto Rico. After a consideration of the evidence adduced at trial and the briefs of the parties, the United States District Court for the District of Puerto Rico denied the plaintiffs' request for injunctive and declaratory relief and entered judgment for the defendants. We affirm.

The plaintiffs filed a civil rights action for themselves and as representatives of a class consisting of all non-delinquent juveniles committed to juvenile institutions throughout the Commonwealth of Puerto Rico without a hearing or court order. The district court certified the class, dividing it, however, into two sub-classes, only the first of which is pertinent to this appeal: juveniles committed without a hearing or a court order to juvenile institutions pursuant to a classification of juveniles with behavioral problems.

On appeal, the plaintiffs raise two issues: (1) Does the commitment without a hearing or a court order of juveniles described in the certified sub-class violate the due process and equal protection clauses of the United States Constitution, and (2) Does such a commitment violate the statute of the Commonwealth of Puerto Rico governing judicial proceedings concerning minors. Both of these issues were raised in the district court and fully considered in an exhaustive opinion by the trial judge. We will therefore not engage in an extended discussion of the applicable principles of constitutional and statutory construction.

There appear to be two ways in which juveniles with problems are committed to institutions. The first is that if the Department of Social Services (the Department) deems a juvenile incorrigible or delinquent and in need of institutional care, it may use the adversarial process and obtain a court order after notice and hearing. The Department may then commit the juvenile to an institution without the parents' consent. The other method is utilized when the parents themselves request the commitment and the Department, after conducting a study of the child's problems, concurs.

The plaintiffs allege that the juvenile institutions where the sub-class is confined resemble detention-type institutions and that confinement there, even with parental consent, impinges on the juveniles' liberty interest. The commitment of the named representative, Ramon Negron Perez, to one of these institutions, Guaynabo State Home for Boys, pursuant to his classification as a juvenile with behavioral problems is typical of the Commonwealth's modus operandi. The district court found that the boy's behavioral problems were described as "defying parental and teacher authority, smoking marihuana, consuming alcoholic beverages, and truancy." The Department made a study of the boy's problems and obtained authorization for commitment from the juvenile's father.

When the commitment is with parental consent, the Department conducts its own investigation to determine "if the social condition of the minor's family justif[ies] his or her admission to any of said institutions." The district court found that the investigation includes, *inter alia*, a study performed by a social worker and, interviews "with the parents, the child, relatives, and other persons familiar with the child's situation, such as school teachers or neighbors." Once committed, a treatment plan is prepared by social workers and there is periodic review by an institutional panel consisting of social workers, psychologists, and supporting staff.

In analyzing the procedural due process required under the circumstances, the district court carefully and properly weighed the factors laid down in *Mathews v. Eldridge*:

First, the private interest that will be affected by the official action; second, the risk of an erroneous deprivation of such interest through the procedures used, and the probable value, if any, of additional or substitute procedural safeguards; and finally, the Government's interest, including the function involved and the fiscal and administrative burdens that the additional or substitute procedural requirement would entail.

The district court acknowledged that a juvenile has a substantial liberty interest in remaining free from confinement or commitment without due process of law, and that confinement "sometimes produces adverse social consequences" because of the stigma society attaches to it. On the other hand, the district court considered the interests of parents in their child's welfare. It rejected the plaintiffs' argument that the traditional interests and responsibilities of parents must be subordinated to the paramount concerns of the child to be determined after a hearing and a court order. The court found that the record demonstrates that the parents in this case acted in the best interests of their children by voluntarily committing them to the state institution. It concluded that the parents are best able to make a determination as to their children's needs and that the Department's authorization comes only after it conducts an exhaustive investigation. The court therefore held that an investigation by the Department of the juvenile's condition and family background supported by the parents' consent provides sufficient constitutional protection to safeguard the child's rights in the commitment. We agree.

Although *Parham* dealt with the process constitutionally due a minor child whose parents or guardian seek institutional mental health care for the child, we believe that the rationale of that case is directly applicable to a situation where the parents request administered care in an open institutional setting on a temporary basis for a "non-delinquent" child suffering from behavioral problems. In both situations, court proceedings prior to commitment "pose a significant intrusion into the parent-child relationship."

In *Parham*, the Court held that a state may commit a minor child to a mental institution on the recommendation of a "neutral factfinder" without a hearing or a court order if the state obtains the consent of the child's parents or legal guardian. The Court ruled that "the traditional presumption that the parents act in the best interests of their child should apply." To protect against the risks of error or hostility that may prompt the parents to act against the child's best interests, and to guard against wrongful parental assessment of their child's condition or needs, the Court required a "neutral factfinder" to determine whether the statutory and medical requirements for admission are satisfied. "Due process has never been thought to require that the neutral and detached trier of fact be law trained or a judicial or administrative officer."

We believe that *Parham* is instructive and that those persons who conduct the social study required by the Department prior to commitment constitute the "neutral factfinder" to determine whether the requirements for admission are met. We therefore hold that the procedures applied by the Department protect a juvenile from a faulty admission decision in a manner that neither unduly burdens the state nor inhibits parents from seeking state assistance. We reject plaintiffs' claim that their federal constitutional rights have been violated.

....

Notes

(a) Is the Court's reliance on *Parham* justified?

(b) Is or should *Gault* be relevant in this context?

G. Abolition of the Status Offender Jurisdiction

1. Note, *Ungovernability: The Unjustifiable Jurisdiction*

83 Yale L.J. 1383 (1974)

Case surveys and court observation [of juvenile courts in New York] demonstrate ... [that] the purpose of the ungovernability jurisdiction is being subverted in two ways. First, the court processes as ungovernable some youths who are in fact either "neglected" or "delinquent" in statutory terms and who should be processed under the provisions governing persons in those categories. Second, in ungovernability cases the family court allows itself to be used by angry parents to punish their children. Moreover, the ungovernability jurisdiction often fails to carry out its purpose: discerning and meeting the "needs" of a youth who is in conflict with an affectionate, non-neglecting parent.

These failures can be traced to judges' inability to exercise the jurisdiction's vast discretion over youths without extensive, if unwitting, abuse. Abolition of the jurisdiction would be a less detrimental alternative for the youths involved than any form of its continuation.

....

II. *The Failures*

A. *Jurisdictional Overreach: The Neglected and the Delinquent as Ungovernable*

....

In 37 percent of the cases, allegedly ungovernable youths are in fact neglected. When processed, these neglected youths are more likely to be referred to court and less likely to be adjusted [diverted from formal court intervention] than alleged ungovernables who are not neglected. Once in court, they are more likely to receive a finding. They also receive a higher percentage of such highly regulating dispositions as training school and placement. Thus, not only are many youths who are in fact neglected processed as ungovernable, but the presence of parental neglect seems to encourage the court to maintain control over a youth and to subject him to its full regulating power.

Court personnel readily admit that a high percentage of neglect cases are processed as ungovernable. Despite the option of treating such cases as neglects, they are handled as ungovernables because, observation suggests, judges in many cases do not want to face the delays and formalities that an accused parent and his or her lawyer will create in a neglect proceeding. There is also a reluctance in some cases to accuse an adult; it is simply easier to deal with a youth.

This practice of processing neglected youths as ungovernable may be criticized for two reasons. First, many of the private agencies which provide the best services available to the court are comparatively more likely to accept youths labeled neglected than those labeled PINS. Processing these youths as ungovernables limits their access to those services. Second, it is unfair to accuse a youth in connection with a matter in which fault, if it is to be placed, should be placed upon the adult. Penalizing the youth—even if only in such hidden ways as the greater stigma that attaches to being processed as ungovernable—can only be detrimental to the youth's interests.

Another group of allegedly ungovernable youths, perhaps fifteen to twenty percent, are accused of acts which would fall within the statutory definition of delinquency: acts (most often assault and drug possession) which would be criminal if committed by an adult. The decision to process these potential delinquents as ungovernable frequently represents a conscious determination by court personnel to obtain dispositional power over a youth with the comparative ease afforded by the ungovernability jurisdiction. [C]ircumvention of the goals and processes of handling criminal offenders is unfair to the youths concerned and is a distortion of the purposes of the ungovernability jurisdiction.

B. *Angry Parents—Pressured Decisions*

Misapplication of the ungovernability statute occurs not only when it is extended to encompass delinquent or neglected youths. It occurs as well when the court, though confronting a conflict between a non-neglecting parent and a noncriminal youth, allows itself to be used by the parent to punish the child and fails to make an independent determination of the youth's condition.

Animosity between parent and child is common in ungovernability cases. A case is usually triggered by emotionally charged struggles between a parent and a rapidly maturing adolescent. A higher percentage of all parental complaints are made against those over 15 years old than against any other age group. Parental complaints frequently mention such matters as refusal to obey, the youth's friends, sexual activity, verbal behavior. Such issues often become a test of wills in which the question of "saving face" plays no small part.

A parent who arrives at intake is often irate and hostile, a state that is aggravated by the admission of inadequacy which is implicit in a parent's seeking help from the court. Parents frequently recite a flood of allegations to the intake officer. While the officer may attempt to adjust matters and may even have a commendable success rate with the less insistent, often he simply acquiesces to a parental desire to see the youth in court.

Once in court, parents often insist on immediate punishment for their children. The statute interposes no definite barriers; as written it makes whatever the child has done unlawful as long as the parental order was lawful. Parental passions—"He is such a liar, his mind is bad and he needs to be put away," said a parent in one case—are on occasion powerful enough to divert judges and other court personnel from questioning whether the youth may have been acting justifiably or lawfully. The court typically responds according to the parent's wishes.

This response is, of course, difficult to measure statistically; it is often unwitting; court papers do not note "judge detained youth because parents so demanded." The degree to which the court functions in response to punitive parental desires can thus be statistically measured only obliquely, chiefly through examining detention decisions. This is the first major decision the court must make in any ungovernability case. Additionally, a comparison can be made of the judgments and dispositions of youths allegedly ungovernable and those brought to court by schools and other nonfamilial complainants.

The Family Court Act authorizes detention only when the youth is likely to abscond or to commit a criminal act. The drafting committee noted in its comments on detention that "[i]f the court is concerned that the respondent will not have a suitable place to stay until the return date, it should consider whether a neglect petition should be filed." The statute clearly does not authorize detention when a parent refuses to take a child home. However, detention is frequently ordered for this reason, in explicit contravention of the statute: Eleven percent of all detentions are so granted, according to the written records, and observation suggests that the actual rate may be close to 50 percent. Moreover, when such punitive detention occurs, in two out of three cases the youth is placed in a prison-like secure facility, a rate of secure detention as high as that for juveniles who the court fears will commit a criminal act.

Thus in many cases a vengeful parent can bypass the intake officer, have a child brought to court, and compel detention by refusing to take him home. This may be all that the parent wants from the court and most parental petitions are withdrawn or dismissed without any continuing sanction. Even here, however, statistical evidence implies that bitterness lingers: There is a very low parental withdrawal rate (in contrast to dismissal by the judge) for many of the allegations that involve questions of "saving face", particularly when a daughter is charged with sexual misbehavior, a highly sensitive and emotional matter for both parents and judges.

C. *Ungovernability Jurisdiction: Failure in General*

Finally, a general survey of ungovernability processing reveals that the court's assessments are frequently inaccurate, its dispositions usually provide little effective treatment, and the long-term effects on a youth and his family are often negative. The inaccuracies in assessment are evident in the illogical patterns of decisions concerning which cases to adjust, whom to detain, which cases are serious enough to merit formal adjudication, and what dispositions are appropriate.

At intake, the seriousness of the allegations bears little relation to whether a case is adjusted or referred to court. Rather, the decision to adjust an ungovernability case is principally a result of seemingly irrelevant secondary factors.

Detention decisions in the course of court processing also demonstrate a lack of logic and an apparent disregard of the nature of the youth's problems and needs. Detention is more likely to occur in cases involving relatively minor allegations of ungovernable behavior than in cases involving more serious runaway and assault charges. The overwhelming majority of detained youths are sent to secure facilities irrespective of the seriousness of the alleged actions. The reasons the court gives in support of its decision in selecting secure or non-secure facilities suggest that considerations other than the problems and needs of the particular youth govern the decision making at this stage of processing.

Formal adjudications also fail to reflect the seriousness of the allegations. Sexual misbehavior is treated with greater concern than criminal acts. Moreover, a case that has advanced this far in the process is almost automatically adjudicated. Chance and endurance are thus critical. Adjudications are more likely if parents do not weary of court hearings, the youth does not outgrow the court's jurisdiction, and the law guardian does not persuade parent and child to accept a "voluntary" referral.

When the court eventually decides upon an "appropriate" disposition, the degree of regulation and service it mandates for the youth often seems an incongruously small return on the court's investment of time and labor, especially in light of the imposition upon the youth and his family. After lengthy processing, two-thirds of the cases are withdrawn or dismissed. Moreover, the disposition ultimately reached often appears to be inappropriate, given the allegations made and previous court involvement.

Those who are subject to some type of regulating disposition are not thereby greatly benefitted. The primary disposition received by the majority of regulated youths is some form of generally ineffective probation supervision. Of the more highly regulating dispositions, private agency placement, the most desired, is available primarily on a discriminatory basis; and its value once attained is open to question. Nonsecure state facilities, frequently dispensed as next-best alternatives, are likewise of dubious value. Training schools are a last resort.

In the end most court processing is of limited utility. It effects little positive change for most youths, many of whom will soon reappear at intake with the same complainant and similar allegations. In other instances, the dispositions serve only to generate further business for the court. And whatever the dispositional outcome its value is eroded by various long-term aftereffects. For example, the research literature on stigma has proven the extent to which juvenile court adjudications tend to alter the juvenile's image not only in the eyes of others, but also in his own eyes; his changed perception of himself as "tarnished" and less valued than others is accompanied in the long run by a loss of respect for the institutions of law and authority in general.

Furthermore, observations suggest that ungovernability proceedings increase an embattled parent's already heavy burden by emphasizing the parent as the only source of rationality and competence within the family unit; by presuming the child helpless and incompetent, the court process cuts off the strength and support which the child might bring to the family were he treated as a responsible and contributing member of it. Thus, rather than strengthening the parent-child relationship in the child's interest, the ungovernability jurisdiction weakens the family and isolates the child-respondent from it.

III. *A Basic Flaw*

The frequent failures of the ungovernability jurisdiction stem from the inability of family court judges to exercise their wide discretion over youths without often serious mis-assessments. Unlike the problems of inadequate services and facilities which also plague the court, this problem is systemic and not susceptible to any simple solution.

In ungovernability cases a judge is given problems far more delicate and complex and far less subject to judicial solution than those in most areas of law. He must accurately assess a parent-child conflict and determine what kind of "help" the child involved may need. To permit the judge to understand and cope with problems of such intricacy, the statute gives him vast discretion with respect to what information he is to consider relevant and it sets no standards for decision making in order to avoid compromising this task.

However, in a court process which by its nature exists to decide cases, the absence of standards leaves a void as to how decisions should be made. In some cases, fortunately, the process works as intended. Because of the latitude which he is allowed, the judge is unable to assess accurately the youth and family before him. In many other cases, the judge in the absence of standards falls back, though often unwittingly and with the best intentions, upon personal feelings and predilections in making his decisions. He is, moreover, left vulnerable to inappropriate influences from court personnel and parents.

The ungovernability jurisdiction affords less protection against the intrusion of the judge's personal predilections than do other legal proceedings that consider narrower issues; and because the persons dealt with are youths, the personal predilections of judges as adult decisionmakers are more likely to be subject to inaccuracies and misconceptions. Youths are often seen as less than full persons, whose problems judges and adults generally assume are easily understood and readily remedied. Judges are also more likely to universalize unconsciously their own experiences and standards with juveniles than with adults; the consequence is a foreclosing of receptivity to the individual juvenile's particular social and personal circumstances. In addition, most judges, like other adults, possess an unconscious ambivalence toward youths.

The intrusion of personal feelings and predilections is exemplified in the presumption by some judges that the youth must be the erring party if a family conflict exists because a child owes obedience to parents under all circumstances. This presumption is discernible in the language of the statute, which proscribes as ungovernable *any* juvenile behavior that contravenes a lawful parental command. Only certain favorable middle class characteristics—a high I.Q., diligence in keeping appointments, deference to judicial authority—can lighten the burden of this presumption.

The absence of standards leaves the decisionmaking process in ungovernability cases vulnerable as well to the pressures of some adults who may not be fully devoted to the individual respondent's welfare. Such pressure may come in subtle form, as in the power exercised by groups of court personnel, or in more blatant form, as in the influence angry parents have upon decisions. In either case, such pressure has greater impact than it would if adults instead of youths were the respondents.

IV. *Abolition and Its Consequences*

Judicial processing of ungovernable youths has severe failings the causes of which are probably irremediable. It would be less detrimental for youths if they were dealt with, where appropriate, as delinquent or neglected, or indeed if they were not dealt with at all. The ungovernability jurisdiction should be abolished.

Were such a step taken, jurisdiction could of course be retained over those youths, now processed as ungovernable, who are in fact criminal or neglected. This step would afford delinquent youth the constitutional protections to which they are currently entitled. It would also probably yield an increase in services for neglected youths....

[N]oncriminal, nonneglected youths simply brought to court for "help" in the wake of disagreements with their parents would not, of course, receive the court's help. Rather, family members would have to fall back upon their own personal resources and upon the range of community resources that often go underutilized in the rush to bring children to court.

There are, of course, a few youths who need help and who might not receive it from other sources. But it must be remembered that many of the ungovernability cases which come to court involve issues of passing rather than ultimate significance in the lives of youths who are often competent enough to care for themselves. Furthermore, the failure to save a few unfortunate youths must be measured against the law's known and unavoidable negative consequences: the detention of youths in admittedly dangerous and deteriorated facilities for sorts of behavior that may be perfectly legal and sensible; the violation of the rights of youths who should be processed as delinquent and the isolation from available services of youths who should be processed as neglected; the illogical results of a court process vesting vast discretion in the hands of judges who are unable to exercise it without abuse; the increased intrafamily hostility that the process engenders in the short run; and the stigma suffered by youths as well as the negative attitude toward law and authority they develop in the long run. Juveniles should be "saved," of course, and "saving" them becomes an emotional issue whose lure no adult can easily ignore. But it is also important that the adolescents who in fact come before the court as allegedly ungovernable not be harmed as documented in this Note; the cost of such harm far exceeds any benefit that would be lost as a consequence of abolition of the jurisdiction.

2. John DeWitt Gregory, *Juvenile Court Jurisdiction Over Noncriminal Misbehavior: The Argument against Abolition*

39 Ohio St. L.J. 242 (1978)

[A]ttacks [against the status offender jurisdiction] and the demand for abolition are misguided. The juvenile courts should retain their jurisdiction over certain statutorily proscribed noncriminal misbehavior by children. The reasons supporting retention are clear and may be briefly summarized. First, the abolitionist proposals strike at the heart of the family autonomy tradition which is reflected in other statutes and judicial pronouncements relating to child-adult relationships. Second. although some critics charge that statutes proscribing noncriminal misbehavior by children discriminate unlawful[ly] against poor and minority groups, abolition may work to perpetuate such discrimination. Third, proponents of abolition have not devised or proposed truly realistic alternative approaches that will resolve the serious societal problems which are now addressed by the existing statutes; indeed, abolition is likely to give rise to a set of problems which could well make the cure worse than the disease. I do not suggest that the exercise of juvenile court jurisdiction over children's noncriminal misbehavior has been free of abuse, but continued efforts toward reform may go some distance toward alleviating the more egregious abuses.

3. Lois A. Weithorn, *Mental Hospitalization of Troublesome Youth: An Analysis of Skyrocketing Admission Rates*

40Stan. L. Rev.773, 785, 788–90 (1988)

Rates of admission of children and adolescents to inpatient mental health facilities have increased steadily during this century. Although deinstitutionalization policies of recent decades successfully reduced adolescent admission rates to state and county mental hospitals, adolescent admission rates to psychiatric units of private hospitals have jumped dramatically, increasing over four-fold between 1980 and 1984. In addition, data reveal that rates of psychiatric admission of children and adolescents to private hospitals are not only rising, but are doing so at a steadily accelerating pace.

....

There exist no criteria, commonly accepted or applied within the fields of child and adolescent psychiatry and psychology, to guide decisions about juvenile mental hospital admissions. Various professional and licensing/accreditation organizations have promulgated sets of standards, but neither the American Psychological Association nor the American Psychiatric Association has developed formal criteria.

In the absence of professional guidance in the form of standards, certain rather vague and overly broad criteria have been promulgated. These criteria may falsely convey a level of precision in admission decisions that does not exist....

....

[A]lthough many seriously emotionally disturbed adolescents benefit from the intensive and structured care of an inpatient treatment setting, a large proportion (perhaps as great as one-half to two-thirds) of recent juvenile admissions to psychiatric facilities are inappropriate. First, many adolescents admitted to psychiatric facilities in recent years did not have severe or acute mental illnesses, nor did their behavior require an inpatient environment in order to protect them or others from their potentially dangerous conduct. Second, in many cases psychiatric hospitalization provides less effective treatment than do outpatient alternatives. Early empirical findings suggest that certain family-oriented and community-based programs are quite successful at alleviating a range of serious or disturbing child, adolescent, and family problems. Third, psychiatric hospitalization inherently restricts liberty and invades privacy, rendering it less desirable than community-based treatment. It also entails other risks, such as the experience of physical or psychological trauma, to a degree not present in community-based treatment. Whereas these disadvantages of hospital-based psychiatric treatment may be justified when children require institutional restraint in order to protect them and others from their behavior, it clearly does not appear justified when other, less restrictive and equally effective options are available. Any one of these grounds alone may, in particular cases, render psychiatric hospitalization inappropriate. In combination, they provide powerful evidence that rising rates of juvenile psychiatric hospitalization reflect an overuse of a restrictive, sometimes dangerous, and often less effective service, and thus constitute a serious social problem.

. . . .

About two-thirds of juvenile inpatients receive initial diagnoses of conduct disorder, personality or childhood disorder, or transitional disorder. An examination of the various "symptoms" that characterize each type of disorder reveals that, in general, these categories describe troublemakers, children with relatively mild psychological problems, and children who do not appear to suffer from anything more serious than normal developmental changes.

For example, in order to assign a conduct disorder diagnosis, a clinician must note a persistent pattern of antisocial conduct for at least six months. Depending upon which of the enumerated behavioral problems a child exhibits, a clinician might diagnose the child as demonstrating a more "aggressive" versus "nonaggressive" conduct disorder, or a more socially oriented (such as gang-directed) or "solitary" conduct disorder. The more aggressive constellations of behavior may manifest as physical violence against persons or property, or thefts involving personal confrontation. As such, this "disorder" may mirror the type of behavior that could lead to an adjudication of delinquency in the juvenile justice system. The nonaggressive manifestations of this behavior problem include chronic violations of rules at home or at school, truancy, running away, persistent lying, or stealing not involving personal confrontation. Thus, the conduct required for this category is virtually parallel to conduct that could lead a judge to find that a minor is a status offender. These parallels have not escaped researchers, who have studied the similarities among juveniles in psychiatric and correctional facilities. Several have posited that rising rates of juvenile psychiatric admission result from the transinstitutionalization of children from the juvenile justice to the mental health system.

Notes

(a) See E. Schur, Radical Non-Intervention (1973), arguing that status offender laws are harmful because they label children as "problems" for non-criminal activity, thus stigmatizing them for behavior that they would likely outgrow.

(b) Is the status offender jurisdiction amenable to rehabilitation? How? In this connection, see Irene Merker Rosenberg & Yale L. Rosenberg, *The Legacy of the Stubborn and Rebellious Son*, 74 MICH. L. REV. 1097, 1144–1163 (1976) (urging lawyers representing minors in status offender cases to interpose defenses to the charges, e.g., the child's behavior was an isolated act, or that the parents have failed to utilize non-judicial remedies, or that the parents are not providing proper care).

Chapter 7

Waiver and Blended, Determinate, and Extended Jurisdiction Sentencing

A. The Three Types of Waiver Statutes: Judicial, Prosecutorial, and Legislative

Kent v. United States, the first of the Supreme Court cases "domesticating" the theretofore unregulated juvenile courts, involved a judicial waiver law in the District of Columbia. The Court held that the juvenile court judge must hold a hearing and receive evidence regarding the child's amenability to treatment as a juvenile offender. The importance of the waiver decision is reflected in the *Kent* opinion. The Court concluded that determining whether to transfer a juvenile to criminal court was a "critical stage of the proceedings," and therefore required that there be a hearing, a right to counsel who had access to the probation files, and a statement of reasons for the transfer so as to permit meaningful appellate review.

Many states were apprehensive about the injection of Due Process into what had been a perfunctory proceeding presided over by a judge whose discretion was insulated from any effective challenge. Although it was not initially clear whether *Kent* was of constitutional proportions, see *Harris v. Procunier*, in Section B of this Chapter, footnote 1 of Judge Hufstedler's opinion, the case prompted many states to reexamine their waiver statutes. Most jurisdictions revised their judicial transfer laws so as to incorporate *Kent's* Due Process protection in greater or lesser degrees.

In an appendix to its opinion, the *Kent* Court included a policy memorandum from the U.S. District Court for the District of Columbia listing eight factors that judges must consider in making such a decision. Over forty years later, many states use the same eight criteria in the *Kent* appendix; others have modified or added factors for consideration such as whether the alleged offense was related to gang activity, committed on school property, the child's mental condition, and catch all provisions that the judge consider any other relevant factors bearing on the transfer decision.

A few years after the *Kent* decision Congress revamped the Juvenile Code in the District of Columbia. The Code defined juvenile offenders as persons under the age of eighteen except for those sixteen and older who were charged by the United States Attorney with murder, rape, or other serious offenses. The D.C. Circuit in *United States v. Bland* upheld the statute against both Due Process and Equal Protection attacks, and noted that the new law was a response to the "substantial difficulties in transferring juvenile offenders charged with serious felonies to the jurisdiction of the adult court under present law."

The dissenters viewed the *Kent* decision as of constitutional dimension, and therefore, in their view, the government was prohibited from creating "a second parallel waiver procedure" by "definition." Indeed, argued the dissent, "the transfer of the waiver decision from the neutral judge to the partisan prosecutor increases rather than diminishes the need for Due Process protection for the child."

The *Bland* majority referred to the new code provisions both as a "legislative exclusion" and as an "exercise of prosecutorial discretion." The dissent also viewed the statute in those two ways, although it emphasized the prosecutorial discretion aspect of the law. This reflects the difficulty there often is in distinguishing between prosecutorial and legislative waivers.

After the Supreme Court denied certiorari in *Bland*, with three justices dissenting, many states followed suit and allowed prosecutors to file certain cases in either juvenile court or adult court. However, unlike judicial waiver, a juvenile cannot challenge a direct filing in criminal court, and there is no requirement of a hearing before such a decision is made by the prosecutor.

Judicial waiver requires a case by case analysis of each child. Indeed, most judicial waiver statutes mandate psychological and psychiatric examinations and a probation investigation of the child's home and background. To some extent that may be true with prosecutorial waiver, that is, presumably conscientious district attorneys weigh all factors regarding the child and the crime. Most states, however, do not demand such individualized determinations by the prosecutor and their decisions are not subject to appellate review unless the charging decision is based on race or other prohibited grounds.

The legislative waiver statutes simply exclude from juvenile court jurisdiction children of a certain age charged with certain crimes. As with prosecutorial waiver, such exclusion is typically based on the juvenile's age, the crime with which he or she is charged, and prior adjudications in juvenile court. Currently, at least twenty states allow for legislative waiver. Those statutes set the age at which transfer becomes automatic as early as thirteen and as late as seventeen. In Pennsylvania, there is no age minimum; any juvenile charged with murder or criminal homicide is automatically transferred. However, to the extent that such statutes consider the current offense it is not a true legislative waiver because ultimately the prosecutor decides the charges and thus can circumvent the legislative waiver determination. The only true legislative waiver is one based solely on age and prior adjudications.

Legislative waiver jurisdictions have effectively created an irrebuttable presumption that children of a certain age who are charged with certain crimes or who have previously been adjudicated delinquent are not really children. Analogously, although not usually considered a waiver, statutes that define adults for criminal purposes as persons over seventeen or sixteen, raise the same concerns that are presented in true legislative waiver statutes—an irrebuttable presumption that such children are to be treated as adults. Scientific and sociological studies, however, belie that assumption. At least as measured by brain development, a child is a child is a child until the age of twenty or twenty-five.

Notes

(a) Consider the following excerpt from Ellen Marrus & Irene Merker Rosenberg, *After Roper v. Simmons: Keeping Kids Out of Adult Criminal Court*, 42 San Diego L. Rev. 1151, 1153–55 (2005):

In *Roper v. Simmons*, the Supreme Court, again five-four, created an Eighth Amendment categorical bar against execution of persons who commit capital crimes when they are under the age of eighteen....

Although we recognize that capital cases are often sui generis and may not be of strong precedential value in other contexts, we think that the developmental and psychological distinctions between adults and adolescents, differences that the *Simmons* Court believed were constitutionally relevant regarding execution, should also be considered in determining the extent of punishment for juveniles who commit serious criminal acts. In particular, we argue that the Court's recognition of the growth capacity of juveniles, and their reduced moral culpability, should weigh heavily in favor of a categorical bar against waiver of children to criminal court. Furthermore, attempts to circumvent such a ruling by defining adults as sixteen or seventeen years of age for purposes of the criminal law should be prohibited.

If these proposals are not accepted, and a child is charged and convicted of a serious crime in criminal court, the kind and extent of punishment imposed should be heavily influenced by the type of evidence relied on by the *Simmons* Court in finding that youths are not death eligible. Either the Court should extend the *Simmons* rationale to prohibit life imprisonment without the possibility of parole or, at the least, create a presumption against such a sentence being imposed on an adolescent. As Justice Kennedy noted, "the punishment of life imprisonment without the possibility of parole is itself a severe sanction, in particular for a young person." Even life imprisonment is rapidly becoming life without possibility of parole. Defendants who use to be paroled in ten or twenty years are now dying in prison of old age.

When children kill, as they always have and probably always will, the state must juggle two distinct and often conflicting concerns: its police power and its parens patriae interest. These concerns are not, however, mutually exclusive. There is a delicate balance that must be maintained. Even during the more savage common-law era, children's diminished responsibility was reflected by the irrebuttable presumption of incapacity for children under seven, and the rebuttable presumption of incapacity for those between seven and fourteen. But we are not wedded to that more primitive assessment of culpability. Evolving standards of decency require that society takes a more refined approach in allocating responsibility and punishment for juveniles. Clearly, the state must incapacitate and punish children who commit serious criminal acts, but, as *Simmons* says, that does not mean that minors can be executed, nor, as we maintain, be consigned to a living death behind bars without any hope of respite. As the Court has said in another context, the legal system must somehow be adjusted "to account for children's vulnerability and their needs for 'concern, ... sympathy and ... paternal attention.'"

(b) What are the counter arguments to the authors' positions? Do such counter arguments reconcile the retribution basis for punishment with the purposes of the juvenile court system?

(c) As noted in this Chapter, *infra*, Article 37 of the Convention on the Rights of the Child prohibits life sentences without possibility of parole for persons who commit offenses when they are under eighteen years of age. See Evelynn Brown Remple & Mark E. Wojcik, *Capital Punishment and Life Sentences for Juvenile Offenders* in THE U.N. CONVENTION

ON THE RIGHTS OF THE CHILD: AN ANALYSIS OF TREATY PROVISIONS AND IMPLICATIONS OF U.S. RATIFICATION 277–91 (Todres, Wojcik, & Revaz, eds.) (2006):

> The United States is one of the countries that allow life imprisonment without possibility of parole for those who commit crimes when they are under the age of 18. The mantra of "adult time for adult crime" reflects a view that children should not be given any special treatment when the crimes they commit are especially horrible. Under federal law and the laws of 42 states, "the commission of a serious crime by children under eighteen — indeed in some states as young as ten — transforms them instantly into adults for criminal justice purpose."

> ....

> [T]he United States is ... one of the few countries to allow the imposition of life sentences without the possibility of release. In a survey of the practices of 154 countries, 132 countries were found to reject the sentence of life imprisonment without parole for juvenile offenders. In the countries that allowed the practice, it was reported to be relatively rare.

B. The Constitution and the Waiver Decision

Kent v. United States

Kent v. United States appears in Chapter 2, *supra*

Harris v. Procunier

498 F.2d 576 (9th Cir.) (en banc), *cert. denied*, 419 U.S. 970 (1974)

BARNES, Senior Circuit Judge:

The State of California (herein the State) appeals from the decision of the district court to grant a petition for writ of habeas corpus to appellee, Jackie Harris. In 1940, at the age of 14, Harris was charged with murder in a state court. The Juvenile Court had exclusive jurisdiction over him and conducted a hearing to examine Harris and determine whether he should be tried as an adult. Harris was not represented by counsel at that time, and there is no indication that he was informed of his right to same. The Juvenile Court found Harris to be unfit for juvenile proceedings and waived its jurisdiction. An information was subsequently filed against him in Superior Court; counsel was appointed for him and he entered a plea of guilty. He was placed in a state hospital as a sexual psychopath, and remained there for six years. After his release he was sentenced to life imprisonment.

In *Kent v. United States*, the Supreme Court held that a determination by a juvenile court on the issue of whether it should waive jurisdiction over a juvenile is a critical stage in a criminal proceeding. It therefore requires a hearing conforming to the basic requirements of due process, including assistance of counsel. Harris filed a petition for writ of habeas corpus in state court arguing that *Kent* should be given retroactive effect. The Supreme Court for the State of California denied the petition holding that retroactive application of *Kent* would seriously disrupt the administration of justice.

Subsequent to the filing of his petition in the United States district court, but before that court entered its order granting the petition, this Court filed its opinion in *Powell v. Hocker*, holding that *Kent* is to be given retroactive effect. *Powell* held that since *Harris* was not represented by counsel at the hearing before the Juvenile Court in 1940, *Kent* necessitates a ruling that that hearing was invalid. If the hearing is held invalid, the Superior Court did not have jurisdiction to entertain Harris's plea of guilty. Harris would be released from custody and the matter remanded back to the juvenile court, which would no longer have custody jurisdiction over him because he is over 18 years of age. (He should now be 47 years of age.)

The State argues that *Powell* should be overruled on the basis of *Adams v. Illinois....* In *Adams* the Supreme Court held that *Coleman v. Alabama* is not to be given retroactive effect. *Coleman* stands for the proposition that an accused is constitutionally entitled to the presence of counsel at a preliminary hearing. It is the State's position that a preliminary hearing for an adult (*Coleman*) is no less important a stage in the criminal proceedings than a certification hearing for a juvenile (*Kent*).

RETROACTIVITY:

The retroactivity of a rule concerning constitutional claims in criminal litigation turns, in a practical sense, on the exigencies of the situation.... In analyzing such a problem, three criteria are to be considered: "(a) the purpose to be served by the new standards, (b) the extent of the reliance by law enforcement authorities on the old standards, and (c) the effect on the administration of justice of a retroactive application of the new standards."

"Foremost among these factors is the purpose to be served by the new constitutional rule." The new constitutional rule enunciated in *Kent* was to insure that juveniles in certification proceedings were provided a full hearing and the right to counsel. Rules concerning the right to counsel have often been applied retroactively.... In distinguishing the right to counsel cases which require retroactive application from all other cases where retroactive application has been generally denied, the Supreme Court stated the following:

"Where the major purpose of new constitutional doctrine is to overcome an aspect of the criminal trial that substantially impairs its truth-finding function and so raises serious questions about the accuracy of guilty verdicts in past trials, the new rule has been given complete retroactive effect. Neither good-faith reliance by state or federal authorities on prior constitutional law or accepted practice, nor severe impact on the administration of justice has sufficed to require prospective application in these circumstances."

The question is therefore whether the purpose of *Kent* was to "overcome an aspect of the criminal trial that substantially impairs its truth-finding function?" We hold that it was not. First, a certification hearing is not a trial, but a hearing. Juvenile proceedings are not intended to be adversarial. Second, the function of a certification hearing is not to gather facts for the purpose of conducting criminal proceedings against the juvenile, but to determine whether it would be proper for the juvenile court to continue to assert jurisdiction over the juvenile. While we in no way discount the thrust of *Kent* to provide due process guarantees at the certification hearing, we do not see that it is the type of constitutional rule which is directed at, or in any way impairs, the truth-finding function.

With respect to the second criterion (the extent of reliance by law enforcement authorities on the old standards), we simply note that Harris's certification hearing occurred in 1940, while the rule in *Kent* was not made until 1966. We find this fact, in and of itself, sufficient factual proof that the law enforcement authorities have relied on the old rule for a period which meets the second criterion.

The third criterion, the effect on the administration of justice of a retroactive application of the new standards, would be devastating. The number of cases affected would be significant, and there would be numerous instances where the juvenile courts would no longer have jurisdiction over the person of the defendant by reason of age.

Perhaps even more importantly, the plaintiff-appellee is confined by reason of his own guilty plea in an adult court with all constitutional safeguards present. He thus has waived the failure of the state to provide counsel at the time of his juvenile court appearance.

For these reasons, we overrule *Powell v. Hocker* on the issue of retroactivity, and remand the action to the district court with instructions to dismiss the petition for writ of habeas corpus.

BROWNING, Circuit Judge (concurring):

....

The solution offered in dissent only highlights the problem. The dissent recognizes that a person of Harris's age (48) would not now be a fit and proper subject for juvenile court treatment. The alternative, it is suggested, is "a new trial in adult court." But Harris does not suggest that his adult court proceeding was in any way defective. The proposed remedy is wholly unrelated to the fault.

It is true that the same impossibility of affording a suitable remedy was present in *Kent* itself. However, retroactive application to *Kent* was necessitated by the Article III limitation of the power of federal courts to the decision of "Cases" and "Controversies."

CHOY, Circuit Judge (concurring):

While I concur in the majority opinion as to Jackie Harris' appeal, I feel it unnecessary that *Powell v. Hocker* be overruled in the process. The two cases are horses of different colors.

True, the juvenile offenders in both *Powell* and *Harris* were without counsel at their respective state certification proceedings, but the similarities between the cases end there.

Retroactivity of *Kent*

In *Harris* the California juvenile court did conduct a hearing in accordance with state statute before determining that Harris should be tried as an adult. But in *Powell*, certification for adult trial was admittedly made without any semblance of the "full investigation" mandated by the Nevada statute.

In *Harris*, the California Supreme Court expressly found that retroactive application of *Kent* would be devastating as to California. The record in *Powell* contains no similar finding as to Nevada and the briefs contain no such claim.

Harris' certification hearing occurred in 1940, twenty-six years before *Kent* was pronounced. Powell's non-hearing was in 1966, three weeks after *Kent*.

While the three criteria of *Stovall v. Denno*, negate retroactivity of *Kent* as applied by my Brother Barnes in *Harris*, those tests do not compel the same result in *Powell* because of the factual differences between the two cases above set forth.

Waiver by Guilty Plea

We held in *Powell*, that the failure of the Nevada juvenile court to comply with the Nevada statute in certifying the juvenile for trial as an adult, conferred no jurisdiction over Powell in the adult criminal court. We also quoted from a prior holding of this court, *Thomas v. United States*, that: "When a defendant voluntarily and knowingly pleads guilty at his trial this constitutes a waiver of all nonjurisdictional defenses...."

In *Harris* there having been compliance with the California hearing statute before the certification of Harris for adult trial, the superior court thereby acquired jurisdiction over the juvenile. Harris' subsequent guilty plea with advice and aid of counsel may thus be held to have waived failure of the state to provide him counsel in the juvenile court proceeding. But in Powell, the adult criminal court acquired no jurisdiction over the juvenile and so Powell's guilty plea waived nothing—the court could not even accept the plea.

. . . .

HUFSTEDLER, Circuit Judge, dissenting, with whom Judge ELY concurs:

At a hearing in which he was denied the assistance of counsel, Harris was found not to be a fit and proper subject for juvenile proceedings.[1] Nevertheless, the majority refuses to recognize Harris's right to counsel at the fitness hearing, holding that *Kent* is not to be given retroactive application. In so holding, the majority misconceives both the unique nature of the fitness hearing and the critical role that counsel can play at those hearings.

The fitness hearing has no direct counterpart in the usual adult criminal process. The purpose of the proceeding, unlike an indictment or preliminary hearing, is not to establish probable cause for the initiation of further action. The hearing is designed to determine, based on an evaluation of the youth, his background, and his criminal history, the nature of response the state should make upon a determination of guilt. Thus, to the extent that it can be analogized to a stage in the criminal prosecution, the fitness hearing most nearly resembles a sentencing proceeding by the trial judge. By finding that a youth is not a fit subject for exercise of juvenile court jurisdiction, the court determines that the accused, if found guilty, will be sentenced as an adult rather than receive non-punitive rehabilitation pursuant to the options available to the juvenile court under the Welfare and Institutions Code.

. . . .

In *Mempa v. Rhay*, the Court made it clear that the right to counsel applied to all disposition proceedings, even those that were not formally part of the "sentencing" hearing before the trial judge immediately after a finding of guilt. Although the Court acknowledged that there might be "fewer opportunities for the exercise of judicial discretion" in such non-traditional dispositional hearings, it nonetheless held that "the necessity for the aid of counsel in marshaling the facts, introducing evidence of mitigating circumstances and in general aiding and assisting the defendant to present his case as to sentence is apparent."

The Supreme Court has recognized that the need for counsel to marshal facts and introduce evidence of mitigating circumstances when dispositional determinations are being made is equally great in juvenile proceedings: "In all cases children need advocates to speak for them and guard their interests, particularly when disposition decisions are made. It is the disposition stage at which the opportunity arises to offer individualized treatment plans and in which the danger inheres that the court's coercive power will be applied without adequate knowledge of the circumstances." (*In re Gault*) ... The waiver hearing certainly calls as loudly for the "guiding hand" of counsel as does the sentencing hearing.

---

1. At the time of the *Kent* decision, there was some doubt that the requirement of counsel it announced was of constitutional dimension. The decision in *Kent* was based on a statute applicable to the District of Columbia, but the statute was "read in the context of constitutional principles relating to due process and the assistance of counsel." *In re Gault*, holding inter alia that due process requires that a minor be represented by counsel in proceedings to determine delinquency that may result in commitment to an institution, clarified the *Kent* decision: "Just as in *Kent* * * * we indicated * * * that the assistance of counsel is essential for purposes of waiver proceedings, so we hold now that it is equally essential for the determination of delinquency. * * *" The case at bench, accordingly, raises the question of the retroactivity of both *Kent* and portions of the decision in *Gault*.

The need for counsel at dispositional hearings has been found by the Supreme Court to be so compelling that it has held the right to counsel recognized in *Mempa* fully retroactive.... The majority fails to distinguish the role of counsel at sentencing proceedings, held to be so vital to the integrity of the criminal process, from the function that an attorney can perform at the proceedings to determine amenability to juvenile treatment at issue in *Kent* and the case at bench. Accordingly, I cannot agree with the majority's conclusion that because the juvenile fitness hearing is not a trial and its function is not to gather facts for the criminal guilt determination process—characterizations that are, of course, equally applicable to the dispositional proceedings in *Mempa*—the purpose of the constitutional rule announced in *Kent* and *Gault* does not require retroactive application.

Analyzing the fitness hearing as analogous to a sentencing proceeding in the usual criminal process, however, does not fully capture the unique nature of the decision as to the amenability of a minor to treatment by the juvenile court. In many ways, the youth of a juvenile offender is a defense to the offense charged, similar to a plea of diminished responsibility. The hearing which determines his fitness for treatment is the only stage at which a juvenile has an opportunity to assert this "defense," and is thus comparable to the arraignment proceeding considered in *Hamilton v. Alabama* which provided an accused the only opportunity he had to plead the defense of insanity. The right to counsel at a proceeding at which an accused must assert a defense or lose its benefit has also been found to relate to the "very integrity of the fact-finding process" and held fully retroactive.

The majority acknowledges, as it must, that the purpose served by a new constitutional ruling is the primary factor in determining the rule's retroactivity. Whether one focuses on the dispositional effect of the fitness hearing (and the close analogy to *Mempa v. Rhay*) or on its impact on a juvenile's "youth defense" (and the similarity to *Hamilton v. Alabama*), the purpose served by the right to counsel in this context argues strongly for the retroactive application of *Kent* and *Gault*. The majority opinion makes no attempt to distinguish the reasoning of the Supreme Court in *Mempa* and *Hamilton* and the decisions holding fully retroactive the right to counsel established in those cases. I do not believe that any such distinction can be made. Nor do the other two factors of the *Stovall* test preclude a finding of retroactivity; for, as the Supreme Court has repeatedly emphasized, when the purpose of a new constitutional right relates to the fundamental fairness of the criminal process—as it does at sentencing hearings, arraignment proceedings where unpleaded defenses are lost, and juvenile fitness hearings—"neither good-faith reliance by state or federal authorities on prior constitutional law or accepted practice, nor severe impact on the administration of justice has sufficed to require prospective application.***." (*Ivan V. v. City of New York*)

Even if the impact of retroactivity upon the administration of justice were relevant, however, the majority has failed to demonstrate that full retroactivity would have a significant adverse effect. Judicial opinion as to the number of cases that would be affected is in conflict. The statistics submitted by the state indicate that as of December 1971 there were slightly more than 300 defendants who had been committed to the custody of the Adult Authority at age 18 or younger between 1945 and the date of *Gault* who were still in prison or on parole. However, this figure is much larger than the actual number of cases that would be affected by holding *Kent* retroactive.

The state's figure includes youths committed at age 18, who may never have been within the jurisdiction of the juvenile court and thus not subject to a fitness hearing. The state's statistics also fail to exclude those prisoners and parolees who were represented by counsel at their fitness hearings. The 1961 revision of juvenile court law established a general right to counsel at juvenile hearings; hence, the number of offenders who were represented by counsel is potentially quite large. In addition, the number of cases that would be affected probably has been further reduced by termination of parole or unconditional release during the nearly 2½ years since these data were compiled. Thus, the actual number of cases that would be affected by a finding of retroactivity could be as small as ¼ or even 1/10 of the number suggested by the state. Even if nearly 300 cases in California could be affected by holding *Kent* and *Gault* retroactive, however, this is still a far cry from the potential for "devastating" impact on the administration of criminal justice that the Court has found in those instances in which it has relied on this factor in determining that a new standard should not be applied retroactively.

Neither is there any validity to the argument made by the majority that "there would be numerous instances where the juvenile courts would no longer have jurisdiction over the person of the defendant by reason of age." Juvenile court jurisdiction in California is restricted only by the age of the defendant at the time of the offense: "Any person who is under the age of 18 years when he violates any law of this state or of the United States or any ordinance of any city or county of this state defining crime * * * is within the jurisdiction of the juvenile court, which may adjudge such person to be a ward of the court." If the absence of counsel at the pre-*Gault* fitness hearing were held to invalidate the subsequent conviction, proceedings could again be initiated in the juvenile court—assuming that retrial was felt to be necessary for public safety. Presumably defendants like Harris who are substantially older than 18 could now properly be found not fit and proper subjects for juvenile court treatment and a new trial in adult court would then be appropriate. Thus, the passage of time has not made an appropriate remedy any more inconvenient or impracticable than in any other retroactivity case.

Even if California were not a jurisdiction in which retrial within juvenile court jurisdiction was possible, the argument premised on the lack of such jurisdiction would not be persuasive on the issue of retroactivity. The same jurisdictional difficulty inheres in applying retroactively any constitutional ruling that relates to juvenile court procedures. Yet in *Ivan V. v. City of New York*, the only juvenile procedure retroactivity case it has considered, the Supreme Court did not hesitate to make fully retroactive its decision in *In re Winship* concerning the standard of proof in juvenile proceedings. Moreover, in *Kent* itself the Supreme Court was faced with the identical problem. The Court recognized that "if on remand the decision were against waiver (of juvenile court jurisdiction), the indictment in the District Court would be dismissed. However, petitioner has now passed the age of 21 and the Juvenile Court can no longer exercise jurisdiction over him." Nevertheless, the Court accepted the fact that this might be the result of application of the new right to counsel to a fitness hearing held before *Kent* and remanded the case to the district court for a hearing de novo on waiver with directions to dismiss the indictment if waiver was found to be improper. In light of the Supreme Court's acceptance in *Kent* and *Ivan V.* of the possibility that juvenile defendants benefitting from a new constitutional standard might not be retriable, we cannot hold that the potential impact of the identical consequences would be so great as to outweigh the purpose served by the counsel requirement and thus preclude retroactive application of that requirement.

In sum, because of the similarity to the right to counsel at sentencing proceedings and certain types of arraignment hearings, the constitutional requirement of counsel at juvenile fitness hearings established by *Kent* and *Gault* relates to the "very integrity of the fact-finding process." When that is the purpose of a new constitutional rule, the rule is applied retroactively regardless of governmental reliance on the prior standard or impact of the new rule. Even if the effect of the new ruling were relevant, there has been no demonstration that retroactivity would have a significant effect on the administration of criminal justice.

In accordance with the standards announced by the Supreme Court in *Stovall v. Denno*, the counsel requirement of *Kent* and *Gault* should be held to be fully retroactive.

Apparently as an alternative basis for its decision, the majority also holds that even if *Kent* was retroactive, because of his guilty plea in Superior Court, Harris is not entitled to challenge the propriety of his juvenile fitness hearing. This holding is not supported by the Supreme Court's recent decisions on the effect of entry of a guilty plea on appellate review of antecedent constitutional violations.

In *Tollett v. Henderson* the Supreme Court said "When a criminal defendant has solemnly admitted in open court that he is in fact guilty of the offense with which he is charged, he may not thereafter raise independent claims relating to the deprivation of constitutional rights that occurred prior to the entry of the guilty plea." But it is clear that the Court in *Tollett* (and in *Brady v. United States*) was concerned with alleged constitutional defects in the process by which a defendant is apprehended and his guilt or innocence determined—that is, constitutional challenges to arrest, indictment, the admissibility of evidence, or the voluntariness of a confession. Once an effectively counseled defendant voluntarily and intelligently admits he violated the law, he can no longer object to anything done by the Government in bringing him through the guilt determination process. It is in this sense that "a guilty plea represents a break in the claim of events which has preceded it in the criminal process." The juvenile fitness hearing, as I have already indicated, is primarily a dispositional proceeding. Although in this case it occurred chronologically prior to the entry of the guilty plea, the fitness hearing logically involves a post-guilty-plea determination of the appropriateness of various forms of treatment. Thus, the determination of Harris's amenability to juvenile court process functionally succeeds the 'break in the chain of events' to which *Tollett* refers.

This distinction between an alleged defect in the fitness hearing and the constitutional errors at issue in *Tollett* and the *Brady* trilogy is consistent with the rationale of the Supreme Court's decisions. The danger of a trial based on an improper indictment, as alleged in *Tollett*, or on unconstitutionally obtained evidence, as in *McMann*, is that an innocent defendant will be convicted. Once the defendant waives his right to a trial and admits his guilt, that danger is obviated and there is no need to permit the defendant to attack antecedent constitutional violations. The error that Harris asserts, on the other hand, does not involve any element of the guilt determination process. The question is not whether Harris was guilty of an offense, but what disposition can be made. Whether or not the state was required to prove its case against Harris is completely irrelevant to his challenge to this dispositional determination. The danger that absence of counsel at the fitness hearing may have led the juvenile court to conclude erroneously that Harris should be treated as an adult offender is not cured by entry of a guilty plea. Indeed, entry of a plea highlights the importance of a correct determination of Harris's amenability to treatment by the juvenile process. Nothing in the reasoning of *Tollett* or the *Brady* trilogy suggests that this type of constitutional challenge is foreclosed by a guilty plea.

The impropriety of the majority's rigid reading of *Tollett* is suggested by the Supreme Court's decision to hear argument in *Blackledge v. Perry*. The Court must decide in *Perry* whether a guilty plea waives a defendant's right to contest double jeopardy—a defect which obviously arises prior to entry of the guilty plea. If the Majority's apparent assumption that *Tollett* precludes review of every alleged constitutional violation which occurred prior to entry of the guilty plea (except competency of counsel) were correct, plenary consideration of *Perry* would not be necessary. Instead, because the lower court decision to grant a writ of habeas corpus based on the double jeopardy argument was made before the Supreme Court's decision in *Tollett*, the decision of the Fourth Circuit would have been vacated and the Court would have remanded for reconsideration in light of *Tollett*.

Notes

(a) In *Blackledge v. Perry*, 417 U.S. 21 (1974), the Supreme Court concluded that a guilty plea does *not* waive a double jeopardy claim. How does that decision support Judge Hufstedler's waiver by guilty plea argument in *Harris*?

(b) What should be done with older defendants who in their teens were denied either a *Kent* hearing or the right to counsel at the waiver hearing? Although many such defendants are deceased or have been released from custody, the prior conviction obtained after a defective or nonexistent waiver hearing may be used to enhance punishment if the defendant is subsequently convicted of another crime. Asking and answering such questions helps to focus on the nature and purpose of the waiver hearing and the underlying objectives of the juvenile court system.

United States v. Bland
472 F.2d 1329 (1972)

WILEY, Circuit Judge.

The United States as statutory appellant seeks review of a memorandum opinion and order of the United States District Court for the District of Columbia, holding 16 D.C. Code § 2301(3)(A) unconstitutional as (1) an arbitrary legislative classification and (2) a negation of the presumption of innocence. Section 2301(3)(A) provides:

The term "child" means an individual who is under 18 years of age, except that the term "child" does not include an individual who is sixteen years of age or older and—

(A) charged by the United States Attorney with (I) murder, forcible rape, burglary in the first degree, robbery while armed, or assault with intent to commit any such offense, or (ii) an offense listed in clause (I) and any other offense properly joinable with such an offense. * * *

The appellee, born 30 July 1954, had been indicted pursuant to Section 2301(3)(A) as an adult (he was sixteen at the time of his arrest and indictment) on charges of armed robbery of a post office and related offenses on 8 February 1971. Appellee moved below to dismiss the indictment for lack of jurisdiction, asserting that the statutory basis for prosecuting him as an adult was constitutionally deficient in that it failed to provide him with procedural due process. The District Court dismissed the indictment.

I. *The Legislative Background*

Congress, pursuant to its constitutional authority to exercise exclusive jurisdiction over the District of Columbia, created the Family Division of the Superior Court of the District of Columbia. In defining the jurisdiction of the Family Division, Congress conferred on it exclusive jurisdiction of "proceedings in which a *child, as defined in section 16-2301*, is alleged to be delinquent, neglected, or in need of supervision." Thus, the Family Division's jurisdiction extends over a person—a child—alleged to have committed delinquent acts, a child being classified as a person not having yet reached the chronological age of 18 and not charged by the United States Attorney with certain specified crimes listed in 16 D.C. Code § 2301. As to any other individual, either one who has reached 18 or who has reached the age of 16 and has been charged by the United States Attorney with one or more of the enumerated felonies,[7] he is not a child and is to be prosecuted in the regular adult court system, whether it be the D.C. Superior Court or the United States District Court.

The legislative history accompanying 16 D.C. Code § 2301 reveals Congress' intent in enacting this legislation: To improve the operation of the juvenile justice system in the District of Columbia by removing from its jurisdiction certain individuals between the ages of 16 and 18 whom Congress concluded (1) were beyond rehabilitation in the juvenile justice system, and (2) whose presence in that system served as a negative influence on other juveniles. This represents a policy judgment of Congress, after gathering extensive appropriate evidence, as to how persons should be classified as "adult" and "child" for the purposes of rehabilitation following the commission of a criminal offense. We note that the policy judgment was both negative and positive: some previously classified as juveniles were beyond rehabilitation; others of the same chronological age were susceptible to special juvenile treatment, and for any chance of success these latter should be protected against the hard-core repeat offenders of the same chronological age.

While Congress easily could have established 16 as the age cutoff date (it is not clear what constitutional infirmities our dissenting colleague would have found in that less sympathetic approach), it concluded that some within the 16–18 age bracket were susceptible of rehabilitation, and determined that those age 16 and 17 whose offenses charged were minor were to be included within the juvenile system. As the Department of Justice made clear in its Memorandum to the Senate Committee:

The jurisdictional age for all juveniles was not lowered to 16 because there are still first offenders charged with minor offenses who may benefit from juvenile treatment up to the age of 18, and treating them as adults may be harsh and unnecessary. At the same time, experience has shown that in certain crime categories, juvenile treatment is unworkable. Accordingly, the jurisdictional age has been lowered with respect to these crimes.

Under the initial Senate version of Section 2301, the jurisdiction of the Family Division extends, in general, to persons under the age of 18. Excluded from the latter class, however, is any person 16 years of age or older in any case (1) where such person is [formally] charged with the commission of one or more of certain enumerated grave offenses, and (2) where such persons has [sic] previously had the benefit of special juvenile disposition after being charged with serious misconduct committed after attaining the age of 15.

The Senate Committee on the District of Columbia, in revealing its rationale for excluding such persons from the jurisdiction of the Family Division, stated:

The Committee has concluded that a juvenile can reliably be considered too well formed or sophisticated for, and beyond the reach of, mere juvenile therapy if the particular juvenile has already been exposed, in years of relative discretion, to the juvenile system and treated to the extent that his case required (as suggested by a prior finding of delinquency),

---

7. 16 D.C. Code § 2301(3) also provides: (3) The term "child" means an individual who is under 18 years of age, except that the term "child" does not include an individual who is sixteen years of age or older and—
   * * * * *
   (B) charged with an offense referred to in subparagraph (A)(I) and convicted by plea or verdict of a lesser included offense; or (C) charged with a traffic offense. For purposes of this subchapter the term "child" also includes a person under the age of twenty-one who is charged with an offense referred to in subparagraph (A)(I) or (C) committed before he attained the age of sixteen, or a delinquent act committed before he attained the age of eighteen.

and has nevertheless returned to serious misconduct (as suggested by a serious felony charge).[11]

The initial House version of Section 2301 provided that "a person, 16 years of age or older, who is charged by the United States attorney with an enumerated violent crime [a more extensive list than contained in the initial Senate version] is automatically subject to the jurisdiction of the adult court." The House Committee on the District of Columbia, referring to the same statistics on serious offenses committed by juveniles and to the growing recidivist rate among this group cited by the Senate Committee, gave the following as the basis for its exclusion of those 16 years of age or older charged with a certain serious crime from the Family Division's jurisdiction:

Because of the great increase in the number of serious felonies committed by juveniles and because of the substantial difficulties in transferring juvenile offenders charged with serious felonies to the jurisdiction of the adult court under present law, provisions are made in this subchapter for a better mechanism for separation of the violent youthful offender and recidivist from the rest of the juvenile community.

As finally enacted, Section 2301 reflects a compromise between the initial Senate and House versions. It provides that the Family Division shall have jurisdiction over "persons under 18 except those 16 and older charged by the United States attorney with murder, forcible rape, robbery while armed, burglary in the first degree, or assault with intent to commit one of these offenses, or any such offense and a properly joinable offense." As such, it eliminates the previous finding of delinquency required under the initial Senate version and shortens the list of serious crimes contained in the initial House version.

II. *The Due Process and Equal Protection of the Law Issue*

The District Court found Section 2301(3)(A) invalid as violative of due process of law:

The determination that a child should be tried as an adult cannot be made without the safeguard of basic due process. Without a provision in the new statute that would require some determination, reached after a fair hearing, that an individual is beyond the help of the Family Division, that statute must fall as violative of due process.

To the Government's objection below that the statute specifically classifies those individuals who are at least 16 years of age and charged with certain enumerated crimes by the United States Attorney as exempt from the Family Division's jurisdiction, the District Court found no standards in the statute to guide the United States Attorney in making this determination, hence it held that the statute denies due process to those individuals so charged.

A.

In relation to this holding of the District Court, we note in the first place that legislative classifications are entitled to a strong presumption of validity and may be "set aside only if no grounds can be conceived to justify them." As the Supreme Court has long held:

It is a salutary principle of judicial decision, long emphasized and followed by this Court, that the burden of establishing the unconstitutionality of a statute rests on him who

---

11. The Committee also noted, however: "Conversely, the committee did not take so dim a view of juveniles in the 16- to 18-year old age group generally as to presume sophistication in every case involving serious misconduct—and especially in cases involving first offenders or where any previous offense was committed before the onset of a relatively significant degree of discretion." As such, "[t]he committee was not inclined, therefore, to approve a lowering of the jurisdictional age limit (for the Family Division) in simple reaction to statistics indicating a greater incidence of crime committed by juveniles aged 16 to 18."

assails it, and that courts may not declare a legislative discrimination invalid unless, viewed in the light of facts made known or generally assumed, it is of such a character as to preclude the assumption that the classification rests upon some rational basis within the knowledge and experience of the legislators.

As the discussion on the legislative background of Section 2301(3)(A) indicates, Congress was well acquainted with the problems confronting the juvenile justice system in the District of Columbia; logically its definition of the Family Division's jurisdiction reflects its particular concern with the rise in the number of serious crimes committed by those 16 years of age and over coupled with the growing recidivist rate among this group.

Secondly, legislative exclusion of individuals charged with certain specified crimes from the jurisdiction of the juvenile justice system is not unusual. The Federal Juvenile Delinquency Act excludes offenses which are punishable by death or life imprisonment. Several states have similarly excluded certain crimes in defining the jurisdiction of their respective systems of juvenile justice, while others vest concurrent jurisdiction over enumerated crimes in both their adult and juvenile courts.

B.

The disagreement of our dissenting colleague arises almost solely from his fundamental unwillingness to accept Congress' power to define what is a "child." The words "child," "infant," and "minor" from early times in various legal systems have been susceptible to definition by statute; the critical "age" for specified purposes has varied, and differed between male and female. Before 1970 the District of Columbia Code (16 D.C. Code § 2301 (1967)), defined "child" as "a person under 18 years of age." Our dissenting colleague seems to consider this statute and its definition immutable, apparently because it was involved in *Kent v. United States*; we accept the fact that Congress has abolished this statutory definition and by statute substituted another, to which we simply give full effect.

We think the position of the appellee here would have more validity if it were possible to read (as apparently the dissenting opinion does) the word "child" as "child (as defined in the previous and now repealed statute)," but of course this is absurd. Yet it is necessary that the meaning of "child" be as defined in the repealed statute for the legal position of the appellee to be sustained. Believing that Congress has power to amend a statutory definition, we start with the definition of "child" currently on the statute books, and reach the legal conclusions set forth herein.

Similarly, the appellee's argument on an alleged "waiver" of the jurisdiction of the Family Court is based on the now outmoded definition. The District of Columbia Code states clearly that the jurisdiction of the Family Division of the Superior Court in delinquency cases is limited to those who come within the statutory definition of "child." 11 D.C. Code § 1101 provides:

> The Family Division of the Superior Court shall be assigned, in accordance with chapter 9, exclusive jurisdiction of—
>
> (13) proceedings in which a *child, as defined in* 16-2301, is alleged to be a delinquent * * * (emphasis supplied).

Until it is determined whether a person is a "child" within the statutory definition, there is no jurisdiction; therefore, *a fortiori* there can be no waiver of jurisdiction.

Nor is it true "a suspected juvenile remains a child until he is charged with an enumerated offense by the United States Attorney." There is just no classification of the person as a child or an adult until (1) his age is accurately ascertained, and (2) the decision on prosecution is made. Congress has incorporated more than one element in the definition of a "child." Until all the elements of the definition are ascertained, the status of the person is simply uncertain, just as under the 1967 definition the status of a person would be uncertain until his true age was established.

C.

The District Court's finding in the case at bar, and appellee's assertion to the same effect — that the exercise of the discretion vested by Section 2301(3)(A) in the United States Attorney to charge a person 16 years of age or older with certain enumerated offenses, thereby initiating that person's prosecution as an adult, violates due process — ignores the long and widely accepted concept of prosecutorial discretion, which derives from the constitutional principle of separation of powers. The Fifth Circuit, in holding that a court had no power to compel a United States Attorney to sign an indictment, stated:

Although as a member of the bar, the attorney for the United States is an officer of the court, he is nevertheless an executive official of the Government, and it is as an officer of the executive department that he exercises a discretion as to whether or not there shall be prosecution in a particular case. It follows, as an incident of the constitutional separation of powers, that the courts are not to interfere with the free exercise of the discretionary powers of the attorneys of the United States in their control over criminal prosecutions.

While there may be circumstances in which courts would be entitled to review the exercise of prosecutorial discretion, these circumstances would necessarily include the deliberate presence of such factors as "race, religion, or other arbitrary classification," not found in the case at bar. For example, in the absence of such factors, this court has held that the exercise of prosecutorial discretion, even when it results in different treatment of codefendants originally charged in the same case with the same offense, does not violate due process or equal protection of the law.

The District Court and appellee in the case at bar point to the acknowledged significant effect of the United States Attorney's decision whether to charge an individual 16 years of age or older with certain enumerated offenses, and conclude that, in the absence of a hearing, due process is violated when such a decision is made. This, however, overlooks the significance of a variety of other common prosecutorial decisions, *e. g.*, whether to charge one person but not another possible codefendant; whether to charge an individual with a misdemeanor or a felony; etc.[26] Furthermore, the decision whether to charge an individual with a misdemeanor or a felony has long determined the court in which that person will be tried. We cannot accept the hitherto unaccepted argument that due process requires an adversary hearing before the prosecutor can exercise his age-old function of deciding what charge to bring against whom. Grave consequences have always flowed from this, but never has a hearing been required.

---

26. Appellee's attempt to equate the United States Attorney's decision in the case at bar with the transfer of an individual from the jurisdiction of the juvenile court to that of adult court is unavailing. In contrast to such a situation, the case at bar involves *no* initial juvenile court jurisdiction; the United States Attorney's decision to charge an individual sixteen years of age or older with certain enumerated offenses operates automatically to exclude that individual from the jurisdiction of the Family Division. The cases cited by the appellee are equally inapposite: *In re Gault*, did not involve the question of adult court jurisdiction over persons sixteen years of age or over; *Kent v. United States* involved the "full investigation" requirement of 11 D.C. Code § 1553 (1967), the former local juvenile statute. Under former Section 1553, individual judgments were to be made by the Juvenile Court as to whether a particular youth should be "waived" for trial as an adult. The comparable transfer provision of the revised juvenile statute, is not at issue in the case at bar, which involves determination of which jurisdiction — adult or juvenile — attaches to appellee in the first instance. As such, it cannot involve a transfer from a nonexistent juvenile jurisdiction to adult court.

While the Supreme Court was presented with the precise question raised by this appeal on an earlier occasion, it declined to rule on the question because of "the barrenness of the record on this issue," including the failure of the Nebraska Supreme Court to pass on it, and the fact that "[s]o far as we have been made aware, this issue does not draw into question the validity of any Nebraska statute."[28] The Federal Juvenile Delinquency Act, however, presents an analogous situation on which courts have passed judgment. Section 5032 of the Act provides in relevant part:

A juvenile alleged to have committed one or more acts in violation of a law of the United States not punishable by death or life imprisonment, and not surrendered to the authorities of a state, shall be proceeded against as a juvenile delinquent if he consents to such procedure, unless the Attorney General, in his discretion, has expressly directed otherwise.

The discretion provided the Attorney General under this section can, of course, result in vastly different consequences for an individual subject to the Act since commitment of a juvenile adjudicated delinquent may continue under the Act, as under the comparable provision of the D.C. Code, only for the remainder of the youth's minority. Despite the significance of this decision, Judge Weinfeld of the District Court for the Southern District of New York stated:

*** [U]nder this section [§ 5032], which requires the juvenile's consent to such proceeding, the ultimate decision as to whether the Government will forego prosecution under the general criminal statutes rests in the sole discretion of the Attorney General. The Assistant Attorney General, who is authorized to exercise the Attorney General's discretion, has directed that this defendant be prosecuted under regular adult criminal procedures. The Court is without power to interfere with or overrule the exercise of this discretion.

As such, judicial consideration of the legitimate scope of prosecutorial discretion clearly encompasses the exercise of such discretion where it has the effect of determining whether a person will be charged as a juvenile or as an adult. In the absence of such "suspect" factors as "race, religion, or other arbitrary classification," the exercise of discretion by the United States Attorney in the case at bar involves no violation of due process or equal protection of the law.

III. *The Presumption of Innocence Issue*

The District Court and appellee assert that the exercise of discretion by the United States Attorney under Section 2301(3)(A) violates due process in that it denies the individual charged the presumption of innocence.

This, however, mistakes the nature of the United States Attorney's decision in the case at bar to charge appellee with an offense enumerated in Section 2301(3)(A). While the decision does have the effect of determining whether appellee is to be tried as an adult or a juvenile, it is not a judgment of guilt or an imposition of penalty. On the contrary, it is simply the result of a determination by the United States Attorney that there is sufficient evidence to warrant prosecution of the appellee for the offense charged and that adult prosecution is appropriate. It in no manner relieves the Government of its obligation to prove appellee's guilt beyond a reasonable doubt. Nor does it remove appellee's right to a jury trial. As the subsequent opinion of District Judge Gesell, ruling on this same issue under this statute, recognized:

---

28. *DeBacker v. Brainard*, 396 U.S. 28, 32(1969), in which the Supreme Court dismissed the grant of certiorari as "improvidently granted." In a subsequent case, the Nebraska Supreme Court considered the same question and found the exercise of such discretion did not violate due process.

It should be noted that all the traditional protections of grand jury presentment, preliminary hearing and jury trial are afforded this group of [alleged] offenders and that in the event of convictions the extraordinarily flexible provisions of the Federal Youth Correction Act designed to create programs for limited incarceration and effective rehabilitation are completely available.

The presumption of innocence, as the Supreme Court has long held, applies to the prosecution at trial and "* * * is a conclusion drawn by the law in favor of the citizen, by virtue whereof, *when brought to trial* upon a criminal charge, he must be acquitted, unless he is proven [beyond a reasonable doubt] to be guilty." As such, the District Court's opinion below and appellee's reliance on, *inter alia, Goldberg v. Kelly* and *Jones v. Robinson* is mistaken; in contrast to the summary adjudications found wanting in those cases, the United States Attorney's decision in the case at bar marks only the beginning of the process of adjudication of appellee's guilt, a process marked by the presence of all the traditional protections of procedural due process, followed by the extraordinarily liberal rehabilitation provisions of the Federal Youth Corrections Act.

IV. *Conclusion*

For these reasons, the order of the District Court dismissing appellee's indictment, on the basis of its opinion holding 16 D.C. Code § 2301(3)(A) unconstitutional as an arbitrary legislative classification and as a negation of the presumption of innocence, is accordingly reversed and the case remanded for trial.

Reversed and remanded.

J. SKELLY WRIGHT, Circuit Judge, dissenting:

As a matter of abstract legal analysis, the opinion of my brethren might appear to some degree persuasive. But we do not sit to decide questions in the abstract, and we are not writing on a clean slate. In 1966 the Supreme Court spoke clearly and specifically about this area. It held, in unmistakable terms, that before a child under 18 can be tried in adult court the Constitution requires a hearing "sufficient in the particular circumstances to satisfy the basic requirements of due process and fairness * * *."[1] I had not supposed that it was within our power as a lower federal court to change this mandate. Nor had I imagined that Congress could "overrule" this constitutional decision by a simple statutory enactment. Yet the majority holds that whereas before passage of the Court Reform Act of 1970 the Constitution required a hearing, after its passage the Constitution requires no such thing. While I must confess that this display of judicial legerdemain leaves me properly dazzled and mystified, I cannot quite persuade myself that the rabbit has really emerged from the hat. I would therefore hold that appellee is entitled to a hearing with counsel and a statement of reasons before he can be charged and tried as an adult.

I think it obvious that this second procedure was written into the Act in order to countermand the Supreme Court's decision in *Kent* as well as this court's rulings in *Watkins* and *Black*. Indeed, the House Committee primarily responsible for drafting the provision virtually admitted as much. The Committee Report explains 16 D.C. Code § 2301(3)(A) as follows:

"Because of the great increase in the number of serious felonies committed by juveniles *and because of the substantial difficulties in transferring juvenile offend-*

---

1. In my judgment, nothing better illustrates my brethren's fundamental misunderstanding of the issues presented in this case than their failure to consider *Kent* in the body of the opinion for the court.

ers charged with serious felonies to the jurisdiction of the adult court under present law, provisions are made in this subchapter for a better mechanism for separation of the violent youthful offender and recidivist from the rest of the juvenile community."

H.Rep. 91-907, 91st Cong., 2d Sess., at 50 (1970) (emphasis added.) While the surface veneer of legalese which encrusts this explanation need fool no one, a simultaneous translation into ordinary English might, perhaps, prove helpful. The "substantial difficulties * * * under present law" to which the Committee coyly refers are, of course, none other than the constitutional rights explicated in the *Kent* decision. And the "better mechanism" which the Committee proposes is a system for running roughshod over those rights in a manner which is unlikely to encourage those of us still committed to constitutionalism and the rule of law.

This blatant attempt to evade the force of the *Kent* decision should not be permitted to succeed. The result in *Kent* did not turn on the particular wording of the statute involved or on the particular waiver mechanism there employed. Rather, as the Court itself made clear, the rights expounded in *Kent* are fundamental and immutable. "The right to representation by counsel is not a formality. It is not a grudging gesture to a ritualistic requirement. It is of the essence of justice." I must confess, therefore, that I find myself unable to approach the majority's elaborate argumentation with an entirely open mind. As one who has long believed that our Constitution prohibits abrogations of due process "whether accomplished ingeniously or ingenuously," I react with a good deal of skepticism to an argument which supposes that "the essence of justice" can be defeated by a juggling of the definition of juvenile or a minor modification of Family Court jurisdiction. Nonetheless, I am willing to meet the majority on its own ground, since I am convinced that when its arguments are closely examined they must inevitably fall of their own weight.

II

I take it that my brethren and I begin our analysis of 16 D.C. Code § 2301(3)(A) with a common premise:[4] nothing in the Constitution prevents Congress from shifting the waiver decision from the Family Court judge to the United States Attorney or from establishing a supplemental waiver proceeding before the United States Attorney to complement the Family Court proceeding. There may be some decisions which are so peculiarly judicial in nature that they may not be transferred to an executive officer without running afoul of the Constitution. But, as the many cases cited by the majority demonstrate, this decision is simply not one of them.

It should be readily apparent, however, that this observation does little to advance the argument. The issue in this case is not *whether* the prosecutor should be permitted to make waiver decisions, but rather *how* he should go about making those decisions.[5] Put slightly

---

4. I am also ready to reject, for purposes of argument at least, appellee's contention that this statutory scheme undermines the presumption of innocence and violates equal protection. Since appellee's due process claim is, in my view, sufficient to dispose of this case, I find it unnecessary to reach the more difficult equal protection and presumption of innocence arguments.

5. Once this distinction is grasped, it becomes plain that virtually every decision cited by the majority is inapposite to the issues in this case. The majority relies exclusively on cases holding that the prosecutor may constitutionally make waiver decisions, *e. g., DeBacker v. Sigler,* or on cases holding that except in extreme situations prosecutorial discretion is not to be disturbed. My brethren fail to cite a single case where a prosecutorial waiver decision was challenged on the ground that the prosecutor failed to follow proper procedures before making the decision. So far as I have been able to determine, there is no such case. The only possible exception to this blanket statement is *Gentry v. Neil,* where a federal district judge rejected a *habeas corpus* petitioner's claim that he was entitled to a hearing before an adult court could assert jurisdiction over him. A careful reading of that case, however,

differently, the question is whether the shift in decision making responsibility from the court to the prosecutor eliminates the need for the procedural rights expounded in *Kent*. I would, of course, answer that question "no." The transfer of the waiver decision from the neutral judge to the partisan prosecutor increases rather than diminishes the need for due process protection for the child. In answering the question "yes" the Government and the majority here rely on essentially three lines of argument. Although these contentions are interrelated, for purposes of analysis they are best addressed *seriatim*.

A

The Government first argues that the *Kent* decision should be limited to situations in which the Government attempts to retract some pre-existing right, and that this is not such a situation. One gets a hint, I think, as to the merit of this argument from the fact that the majority barely mentions it in its otherwise eclectic defense of the statutory scheme. Nonetheless, since it is the contention chiefly relied upon by the Government and most forcefully pressed at oral argument, I think it deserves a few words of rebuttal.

As the Government reads *Kent*, its holding is restricted to cases where the Family Court has exclusive jurisdiction *ab initio* and the prosecutor attempts to wrest this jurisdiction from it. After passage of the Court Reform Act, it is argued, the Family Court is no longer vested with exclusive jurisdiction over persons between 16 and 18 who are suspected of committing serious felonies. Rather, the Government contends, this jurisdiction is now concurrent, and the United States Attorney is vested with the authority to determine the forum in which to proceed. Since there is no longer a pre-existing right to juvenile treatment, there is no longer a necessity to observe the procedural formalities which, under *Kent*, must accompany divestiture of such a right.

Despite the superficial plausibility of this argument, I think it plainly fallacious. In the first place, I can find nothing in *Kent* which speaks to Platonic distinctions between divestiture of an existing right and failure to grant a right not already in existence. *Kent* rested, not on some fine point of metaphysics, but on the crucially important distinction between the treatment afforded children in an adult court and that granted them in Family Court. Of course, that distinction is just as important whether the selection of the adult forum is spoken of as the divestiture of an existing, exclusive juvenile jurisdiction or as the initial choice of a concurrent adult jurisdiction. In either case, the consequences to the child are precisely the same and, hence, the procedural protections should be identical.

Moreover, even if one accepts the dubious vestiture-divestiture distinction as relevant, the Government's argument simply does not fit the contours of the statute. It is not true that the United States Attorney's decision to proceed in adult court negates no pre-existing right or that the Family Court lacks exclusive jurisdiction *ab initio*. In fact, the basic jurisdictional statute remains, for our purposes, unchanged since the Supreme Court's decision in *Kent*. Now, as then, the Juvenile Court is in terms granted *exclusive* jurisdiction over all children as defined in 16 D.C. Code § 2301. True, the definition of child contained in 16 D.C. Code § 2301 has now been modified. But under the new definition, a suspected juvenile remains a child until he is charged with an enumerated offense by the United States Attorney.[6] It follows that under 11 D.C. Code § 1101 the Family Court re-

---

makes clear that the petitioner was asserting a constitutional right to a preliminary hearing *by the juvenile court* before waiver could be effected. The petitioner did not challenge, and the court did not decide, the constitutional validity of the procedure used by the *prosecutor* in deciding to try the case in adult court.

6. Although the Government contests this point, a careful examination of the statute leaves no doubt as to its validity. The statute begins by defining a child as "an individual who is under 18 years

tains exclusive jurisdiction until the United States Attorney ends the defendant's status as a child by charging him with an enumerated crime. Thus the United States Attorney's charge acts to divest the Juvenile Court of its pre-existing exclusive jurisdiction in precisely the same manner as does the juvenile judge's waiver decision.[7] Since the divestiture is the same, the procedural rights accompanying it should be the same, and we need look no farther than *Kent* to determine what those rights are.

B

The majority wisely eschews substantial reliance on the Government's divestiture argument to distinguish *Kent*. But in its stead my brethren adopt two other arguments which, to me at least, seem equally unconvincing. First, the majority seems to contend that *Kent* is inapposite because it applied to a judicial decision, whereas 16 D.C. Code § 2301 contemplates a prosecutorial decision. Thus the majority apparently concedes, as it must, that *Kent* continues to guarantee procedural rights when the waiver is effected by a judge. But these rights do not attach when the same decision is made by a prosecutor, apparently because "the United States Attorney's decision * * * marks only the beginning of the process of adjudication of appellee's guilt, a process marked by the presence of all the traditional protections of procedural due process, followed by the extraordinarily liberal rehabilitation provisions of the Federal Youth Corrections Act." This argument will not stand analysis.[8] The decision by a juvenile judge or by the United States Attorney to treat the child as an adult for prosecution purposes marks the beginning of precisely the same process of adjudication. And it cannot be doubted that the United States Attorney is certainly a less disinterested decision maker than the Juvenile Court judge. It would seem then that, in order to compensate for lack of neutrality, procedural niceties should be *more* rather than less carefully observed when the prosecutor is the decision maker.

As long ago as 1935, the Supreme Court was presented with an argument that "the acts or omissions of the prosecuting attorney can [never] * * * amount either to due process of law or to a denial of due process of law." That contention was rejected in no uncertain terms. "Without attempting at this time to deal with the question at length, we deem it sufficient for the present purpose to say that we are unable to approve this nar-

---

of age." However, it then excepts from this definition individuals "charged by the United States attorney" with certain enumerated offenses. Obviously, a youth who has not yet been charged does not fall within this exception and, hence, remains a "child" until the charging decision is made. This legislative arrangement leads, in turn, to an interesting quirk in the statute which has apparently gone unnoticed by both the Government and appellee. 16 D.C. Code § 2302(a) (Supp. V 1972) provides: "If it appears to a[n adult] court, during the pendency of a criminal charge and before the time when jeopardy would attach in the case of an adult, that a minor defendant was a child *at the time of an alleged offense*, the court shall forthwith transfer the charge against the defendant, together with all papers and documents connected therewith, to the [Family] Division." (Emphasis added.) Obviously, the defendant fits within the 16 D.C. Code § 2301 definition of a child "at the time of the alleged offense" unless *at that time* he had been charged with one of the enumerated offenses in conjunction with some unrelated proceeding. It follows that even under the majority's decision appellee may be able to secure a 16 D.C. Code § 2302(a) transfer to the Family Division.

7. This interpretation of the statute is buttressed by the administrative practice of the D.C. police and corrections officials who, according to uncontested assertions in appellee's supplemental memoranda and affidavits, uniformly treat an arrested juvenile as a child until the U.S. Attorney divests him of that status by charging him with an enumerated offense.

8. To the extent that it is premised on the assumption that "all the traditional protections of procedural due process" compensate for the lack of an initial *Kent* hearing, the argument simply has no basis in fact. The traditional due process guarantees surrounding trial may assure a fair determination of guilt or innocence, but they do nothing to assure a fair choice between juvenile and adult procedures. That choice is made long before the trial begins in the privacy of the prosecutor's office.

row view of the requirement of due process. That requirement, in safeguarding the liberty of the citizen against deprivation though the action of the State, embodies the fundamental conceptions of justice which lie at the base of our civil and political institutions." In light of all that has occurred since *Mooney*—see, e. g., *Brady v. Maryland*—it is surprising to say the least to see resurrected the notion that conduct which has "no place in our system of law" when engaged in by a judge, *Kent v. United States*, is magically transformed into all the process which is due when engaged in by a prosecutor.

It should be clear, then, that the test for when the Constitution demands a hearing depends not on which government official makes the decision, but rather on the importance of that decision to the individual affected. "The extent to which procedural due process must be afforded * * * is influenced by the extent to which [an individual] may be 'condemned to suffer grievous loss.'" The test is not a precise one, and reasonable men may differ as to its application in close cases, but at least the underlying requirement is clear. "Certain principles have remained relatively immutable in our jurisprudence. One of these is that where governmental action seriously injures an individual, and the reasonableness of the action depends on fact findings, the evidence used to prove the Government's case must be disclosed to the individual so that he has an opportunity to show that it is untrue."

[There are many cases involving] decision[s] by executive, rather than judicial, officers. Yet in each case the Constitution was held to require a hearing, presumably because "the [individual's] interest in avoiding * * * loss outweigh[ed] the governmental interest in summary adjudication." In *Kent* the Supreme Court weighed the grievous consequences of a waiver decision against the Government's relatively meager interest in summary procedures. In the end the Court struck the balance in favor of fair procedures, and that balance is good enough for me.

The argument for why appellee should be entitled to representation by counsel at his waiver hearing is somewhat more elaborate but, in the end, no less persuasive. To the extent the contention is grounded on the Sixth Amendment right to counsel, it must be conceded that the majority's position seems to have some force. In a recent decision, a plurality of the Supreme Court has held that a right to counsel accrues only "at or after the initiation of adversary *judicial* criminal proceedings—whether by way of formal charge, preliminary hearing, indictment, information, or arraignment." *Kirby v. Illinois*. Hence, even though *Kent* held the waiver determination to be a "critically important" stage of the prosecution when made by a judge. Sixth Amendment rights may not attach if the decision is made by a nonjudicial officer at a precharge stage of the proceedings.

If that were the end of the matter, *Kirby* might pose a significant obstacle to an extension of the *Kent* counsel requirement to prosecutorial waivers. But it must be remembered that *Kent* was not solely, or even primarily, a Sixth Amendment decision. As argued above, *Kent's* requirement of a hearing and a statement of reasons was premised on the Fifth Amendment guarantee of procedural due process, a guarantee which has nothing to do with "critical stages," or with judicial as opposed to prosecutorial decision making.[11]

Once the right to a hearing is established, it follows, I think, that appellee also has a right to counsel—not because the Sixth Amendment requires it, but because it is neces-

---

11. Indeed, *Kirby* itself makes abundantly clear that, although the counsel requirement of *Wade* and *Gilbert* does not apply to precharge lineups, the *Wade-Gilbert* due process standards are fully effective at this stage.

sary to protect Fifth Amendment rights. Thus, in retrospect at least, it seems clear that there is no Sixth Amendment right to counsel during the precharge custodial interrogation discussed in *Miranda v. Arizona*. Yet a lawyer was required nonetheless "not to vindicate the constitutional right to counsel as such, but * * * 'to guarantee full effectuation of the privilege against self-incrimination. * * *'" Similarly, it could not conceivably be argued that Sixth Amendment rights attach to welfare termination proceedings, which are not even criminal in nature. Yet the Supreme Court held that there was a right to counsel nonetheless because counsel was necessary to "help delineate the issues, present the factual contentions in an orderly manner, conduct cross-examination, and generally safeguard the interests of the recipient."

I think all the arguments which influenced the Court to require counsel in *Goldberg* and *Miranda* are fully applicable here. "The right to be heard would be, in many cases, of little avail if it did not comprehend the right to be heard by counsel," and nowhere is this more true than when the individual presenting his case is a frightened juvenile confronted with the sometimes impersonal machinery of justice.

Congress itself seems to have realized that a waiver hearing would be a mockery without the presence of counsel. 16 D.C. Code § 2304 (Supp. V 1972) provides: "A child alleged to be delinquent or in need of supervision is entitled to be represented by counsel at all critical stages of [Family] Division proceedings * * *." The Senate Committee explained this provision as follows:

> "The proposed section guarantees representation at 'all critical stages' of the proceedings, the concept used in *Miranda v. Arizona*. * * * Further detail is left to the courts, and the statute is cast in terms which will absorb future court decisions without necessitating statutory change."

The citation to *Miranda* indicates that Congress did not use the term "critical stages" in its Sixth Amendment sense since, as argued above, *Miranda* was not a Sixth Amendment decision. Rather, Congress seems to have intended that counsel be provided the juvenile at all stages where critically important decisions affecting his case are made. *Kent* held that waiver proceedings are such a stage, and Congress was aware of the *Kent* decision when 16 D.C. Code § 2304 was drafted. I would therefore hold that counsel is required under statutory as well as constitutional compulsion.

C

Finally, the Government argues that extension of *Kent* to prosecutorial waivers would abrogate the ancient doctrine of prosecutorial discretion. It is, of course, still widely believed that prosecutors have a broad, unreviewable discretion to determine which offenders to charge and what crimes to charge them with, although even this notion is now widely challenged by the leading scholars. But it should be readily apparent that usual notions of prosecutorial discretion have nothing to do with this case. The defendant does not ask us to review the substance of the prosecutor's charging decision or to place limits on the scope of his discretion. Bland directs his complaint to the *procedures* the prosecutor uses rather than to the *merits* of the decision ultimately reached. Reference to the Supreme Court's decision in *Kent* is again instructive. The *Kent* majority recognized that "the Juvenile Court should have considerable latitude within which to determine whether it should retain jurisdiction over a child" and that the court had "a substantial degree of discretion as to the factual considerations to be evaluated, the weight to be given them and the conclusion to be reached." But, the Court continued, this admittedly broad discretion did not give the judge "a license for arbitrary procedure." Similarly, I think it plain here that the prosecutor's broad authority to choose between juvenile and criminal procedures provides no argument for the power to exercise that authority in a manner which does not comport with procedural due process.

The majority's opinion suggests reliance on a broad appeal to prosecutorial discretion, but ultimately comes to rest on the more specialized argument that the prosecutor has unreviewable discretion as to whether or not to grant a hearing. As should be readily apparent, this formulation merely assumes the answer to the very question before us for decision. The assumption is made, moreover, on the basis of flimsy evidence and a fallacious analogy.

My brothers point to "the significance of a variety of other common prosecutorial decisions, *e. g.*, whether to charge one person but not another possible codefendant; whether to charge an individual with a misdemeanor or a felony; etc. * * * Grave consequences have always flowed from this, but never has a hearing been required." With all respect, one could just as easily infer from the lack of authority provided to support this proposition that never has a hearing been *requested*. But even if one assumes, *arguendo*, that a hearing is not necessary in these situations, it hardly follows that a child may be summarily deprived of his right to juvenile treatment without being heard. As the majority itself indicates, there are dramatically real differences between run-of-the-mill charging decisions and prosecutorial waiver of Family Court jurisdiction. A normal charging decision is "only the beginning of the process of adjudication of [defendant's] guilt, a process marked by the presence of all the traditional protections of procedural due process * * *." A defendant has the opportunity to show that he was improperly charged—that is, that he is not guilty—at the preliminary hearing, at the trial itself, and, if necessary, on appeal.

In contrast, the waiver decision marks not only the beginning but also the end of adjudication as to the child's suitability for juvenile treatment. It is well established that, barring equal protection problems, a guilty person has no right not to be charged with a criminal offense. But a "guilty" child may, under certain circumstances, have a right to be charged as a juvenile. The question of juvenile treatment turns not on the issue of guilt, but on such factors as the maturity of the child and his susceptibility to rehabilitation. These factors, unlike the question of guilt, drop out of the case once the initial waiver decision is made. Hence it is especially vital that the procedures be fair at the one point in the criminal process where these matters are considered. The very fact that the prosecutor's decision is largely unreviewable and therefore final argues for, rather than against, making certain that he has all the facts before him when he exercises his great responsibility.

Nor is the majority on firm ground when it compares prosecutorial waiver to the decision "whether to charge an individual with a misdemeanor or a felony [which] has long determined the court in which that person will be tried." It trivializes the juvenile court system to suggest that it represents merely an alternative forum for the trial of criminal offenses. The Family Court is more than just another judicial body; it is another system of justice with different procedures, a different penalty structure, and a different philosophy of rehabilitation. We play a cruel joke on our children by arguing that the juvenile system is a nonadversary, noncriminal, beneficent instrument of rehabilitation when determining whether criminal procedures are to be required at trial, *see McKeiver v. Pennsylvania, supra,* while at the same time maintaining that it is just another criminal court when determining the procedures which must accompany waiver.

III

It will not do to minimize or ignore the consequences of the decision reached today. The majority suggests that youths tried in adult court will still receive a measure of protection, since conviction may be "followed by the extraordinarily liberal rehabilitation provisions of the Federal Youth Corrections Act." There is, however, more than a touch of irony in this suggestion. A similar point was made by District Judge Gesell in upholding 16 D.C. Code § 2301 in an unrelated case: "It should be noted that * * * in the event of convictions the extraordinarily flexible provisions of the Federal Youth Corrections Act designed to create programs for limited incarceration and effective re-habilitation are completely available." Yet Judge Gesell has also found that large num-bers of eligible youths are being denied Youth Corrections Act treatment precisely because there presently are no youth facilities available, and that "[t]he pressures from overcrowding [have resulted] in a complete frustration of the Youth Corrections Act program."

Thus I do not think we can escape the fact that after our decision today there will be many impressionable 16- and 17- year-olds who will be packed off to adult prisons where they will serve their time with hardened criminals. These children will be sentenced, moreover, without any meaningful inquiry into the possibility of rehabilitation through humane juvenile disposition. Sometimes I think our treatment of these hapless "crimi-nals" is dictated by the age-old principle "out of sight-out of mind." Yet there is no deny-ing the fact that we cannot write these children off forever. Some day they will grow up and at some point they will have to be freed from incarceration. We will inevitably hear from the Blands and Kents again, and the kind of society we have in the years to come will in no small measure depend upon our treatment of them now.

Perhaps I should add that I harbor no illusions as to the efficacy of our juvenile court system. I share Mr. Justice Fortas' view that "the highest motives and most enlightened impulses [have] led to a peculiar system for juveniles, unknown to our law in any com-parable context. The constitutional and theoretical bases for this peculiar system is — to say the least — debatable. And in practice * * * the results have not been entirely sat-isfactory." Nor do I believe that a fair and constitutional waiver system would rescue from the clutches of adult punishment every juvenile capable of rehabilitation in a more beneficent environment. As Chief Judge Bazelon has pointed out, "The job of saving the boy who has compiled a long juvenile record and then committed a serious offense after his sixteenth birthday may be so costly, or so difficult even if no cost were spared, that the [waiver procedures] required by statute cannot but be a pious charade in many cases."

I must admit, then, to considerable uncertainty as to the ultimately proper disposition of a case such as Bland's, given our scarce societal resources, our limited knowledge of ju-venile corrections, and the intractable nature of the root problems of poverty and social disintegration. I am certain of a few propositions, however. I am confident that a child is unlikely to succeed in the long, difficult process of rehabilitation when his teachers dur-ing his confinement are adult criminals. I am sure that playing fast and loose with funda-mental rights will never buy us "law and order": constitutional rights for children won in *Kent*, like other constitutional rights, are protected from "sophisticated as well as simple-minded" modes of revision or repeal. And I am convinced that the beginning of wisdom in this area, as in so many others, is a respect and concern for the individual—the kind of respect and concern which the due process clause guarantees. I would therefore hold that Congress may not abrogate a child's constitutional rights to a hearing, representation by counsel and a statement of reasons before he is charged and tried as an adult.

I must respectfully dissent.

Before BAZELON, Chief Judge, and WRIGHT, McGOWAN, TAMM, LEVENTHAL, ROBINSON, MacKINNON, ROBB and WILKEY, Circuit Judges.

ORDER

PER CURIAM.

On consideration of appellee's suggestion for rehearing *en banc*, it is

Ordered by the court, *en banc*, that appellee's aforesaid suggestion for rehearing *en banc* is denied.

Notes

(a) What type of waiver is involved in *Bland*? Although all the judges are clear that it is not a judicial waiver proceeding, it is ambiguous whether the statute is technically a legislative or prosecutorial waiver law. Given the prosecutor's almost untrammeled discretion to choose what charges to bring, does it make a difference whether a prosecutorial or legislative waiver is involved? Would the nomenclature affect the prosecutor's charging decisions? For example, if it is denominated a *legislative* waiver statute, would the prosecutor be more or less inclined to overcharge so as to meet the statutory definitions? If so, what result if the child is convicted of a lesser offense in criminal court, an offense that does not meet the legislative criteria?

(b) Presumably the state has no obligation to create a juvenile court system; that is, that it can decide that all children will be tried in criminal court. If the state has that greater power, why should it not have the lesser power to create a juvenile court system but restrict entry to it, as long as the restrictions are rational?

(c) Congress indicated that it was amending the statute in part because of the "substantial difficulties" in transferring juveniles to criminal court under the judicial waiver system. What is Congress saying about juvenile court judges?

Morgan Victor Manduley, et al. v. The Superior Court of San Diego County

27 Cal.4th 537 (Cal. 2002)

GEORGE, C. J.

Proposition 21, titled the Gang Violence and Juvenile Crime Prevention Act of 1998 made a number of changes to laws applicable to minors accused of committing criminal offenses. As relevant here, the initiative measure broadened the circumstances in which prosecutors are authorized to file charges against minors 14 years of age and older in the criminal division of the superior court, rather than in the juvenile division of that court, and upon prosecutors the discretion to bring specified charges against certain minors directly in criminal court, without a prior adjudication by the juvenile court that the minor is unfit for a disposition under the juvenile court law.

....

As we shall explain, we conclude that a prosecutor's decision to file charges against a minor in criminal court pursuant to § 707(d) is well within the established charging authority of the executive branch. Our prior decisions instruct that the prosecutor's exercise of such charging discretion, before any judicial proceeding is commenced, does not usurp an exclusively judicial power, even though the prosecutor's decision effectively can preclude the court from selecting a particular sentencing alternative. Accordingly, we disagree with the Court of Appeal's conclusion that § 707(d) is unconstitutional under the separation of powers doctrine.

....

II

....

The statute sets forth three situations in which the prosecutor may choose to file an accusatory pleading against a minor in either juvenile court or criminal court: (1) a minor 16 years of age or older is accused of committing one of the violent or serious offenses enumerated in § 707, subdivision (b) (§ 707(d)(1)); (2) a minor 14 years of age or older is accused of committing certain serious offenses under specified circumstances (§ 707(d)(2)); and (3) a minor 16 years of age or older is accused of committing specified offenses, and the minor previously has been adjudged a ward of the court because of the commission of any felony offense when he or she was 14 years of age or older (§ 707(d)(3)).

Where the prosecutor files an accusatory pleading directly in a court of criminal jurisdiction pursuant to § 707(d), at the preliminary hearing the magistrate must determine whether "reasonable cause exists to believe that the minor comes within the provisions of" the statute (§ 707(d)(4)) — e.g., reasonable cause to believe that a minor at least 16 years of age has committed an offense enumerated in § 707, subdivision (b), or that a minor at least 14 years of age has committed such an offense under the circumstances set forth in § 707(d)(2)(C). If such reasonable cause is not established, the case must be transferred to the juvenile court. (§ 707(d)(4).)

Section 602, subdivision (b), which specifies circumstances in which a minor must be prosecuted in a court of criminal jurisdiction, also was amended by Proposition 21. The revised statute decreases the juvenile's minimum age for such mandatory criminal prosecutions from 16 years to 14 years and alters in some respects the list of crimes for which a criminal prosecution is required.

....

Among the changes effected by Proposition 21, petitioners challenge only the aspect of § 707(d) that confers upon the prosecutor the discretion to file certain charges against specified minors directly in criminal court, without any judicial determination that the minor is unfit for a juvenile court disposition. We proceed to consider petitioners' various constitutional claims that § 707(d) is invalid.

III

Petitioners first contend that § 707(d) violates the separation of powers doctrine by vesting in the prosecutor the authority to make a decision — whether to initiate a proceeding in criminal court or juvenile court — that ultimately dictates whether minors charged with certain offenses, upon conviction, shall be sentenced under the criminal law or receive a disposition under the juvenile court law. The exercise of such authority by the executive branch, petitioners contend, invades the exclusive power of the judiciary to determine the appropriate sentence for individuals who commit criminal offenses. Petitioners' contention is based upon article III, section 3, of the California Constitution, which states: "The powers of state government are legislative, executive, and judicial. Persons charged with the exercise of one power may not exercise either of the others except as permitted by this Constitution."

The majority of the Court of Appeal agreed with petitioners that § 707(d) violates the separation of powers doctrine. The majority reasoned that resolution of this question depends upon whether the district attorney's choice between filing a petition in juvenile court or an accusatory pleading in criminal court is a charging decision properly allocated to the executive branch, or instead is a sentencing decision properly allocated to the judicial branch. According to the majority, "the fundamental nature of the decision given to district attorneys under § 707(d) is a decision that the adult sentencing scheme rather than the juvenile court dispositional scheme must be imposed if the juvenile is found guilty of the charged offenses." Section 707(d), the majority held, confers upon the prosecutor "the power to preemptively veto a court's sentencing discretion" and therefore violates separation of powers principles.

The dissent in the Court of Appeal, on the other hand, stated that prosecutors traditionally have possessed great discretion, largely unsupervised by the judiciary, to determine what charges to file against an individual, or whether to file charges at all. The dissent observed that a prosecutor's decision pursuant to § 707(d) whether to file charges in juvenile or criminal court is made before charges have been filed; therefore, the prosecutor exercises no veto over any judicial decision made after the proceeding is commenced. Because, in the dissent's view, the Legislature (or the voters through the initiative power) could abolish the juvenile justice system completely, or deny access to that system to juveniles of a certain age charged with certain crimes, the dissent concluded that § 707(d) properly could "take a more moderate approach" and delegate to the executive branch the discretion to determine where to file — in juvenile court or criminal court — charges against juveniles of a certain age accused of particular crimes. In this court, the People adopt a position similar to that reflected in the dissent in the Court of Appeal.

We believe that the majority of the Court of Appeal adopted an unduly restrictive view of the scope of the executive power traditionally vested in prosecutors to decide what charges shall be alleged, and against whom charges shall be brought. This broad power to charge crimes extends to selecting the forum, among those designated by statute, in which charges shall be filed. Contrary to the majority of the Court of Appeal, the circumstance that such a charging decision may affect the sentencing alternatives available to the court does not establish that the court's power improperly has been usurped by the prosecutor.

. . . .

IV

. . . .

Several amici curiae supporting petitioners contend that juvenile offenders possess a constitutionally protected liberty interest in remaining in the juvenile court system, and that this interest precludes the prosecutor from filing charges against minors in criminal court without first providing notice and a hearing. The authority upon which amici curiae rely, however, found liberty interests arising from statutes that created an expectation that adverse action by the state would occur only upon the occurrence of certain conditions. E.g., *Vitek v. Jones* (transfer of prisoner to mental hospital permitted only after a finding of mental illness). Section 707(d), in contrast, eliminates any expectation that a minor who commits an offense under the circumstances specified therein will be transferred to criminal court only upon an adverse fitness determination by the court. The predicate for filing charges in criminal court pursuant to § 707(d) is a determination by the prosecutor that the circumstances set forth in that statute are present. To the extent this provision creates a protected liberty interest that minors will be subject to the jurisdiction of the criminal court only upon the occurrence of the conditions set forth therein, the statute *does* require a judicial determination, at the preliminary hearing, "that reasonable cause exists to believe that the minor comes within the provisions" of the statute. (§ 707(d)(4).) Contrary to the contention of amici curiae, such a minor possesses no other protected interest in remaining in the juvenile court system. *Hicks v. Superior Court*(minors possess no constitutional or fundamental right to trial in juvenile court); *accord*, *State v. Angel C.*, 245 Conn. 93 (1998) (minors possess no liberty interest in juvenile status where applicable statutes authorize prosecutor to file charges directly in criminal court or to seek a transfer to juvenile court).

....

V

Petitioners next challenge § 707(d) on the ground that it violates their right to the equal protection of the laws (U.S. Const., 14th Amend.; Cal. Const., art. I, § 7; *id.*, art. IV, § 16, subd. (a)), because the statute permits identically situated minors to be subject to different laws and disparate treatment at the discretion of the prosecutor. Petitioners assert that minors of the same age and charged with the same crime under the circumstances enumerated in § 707(d) are subject either to the juvenile court law or to the criminal justice system, based solely upon a prosecutorial decision that is unguided by any statutory standards. According to petitioners, the creation of two classes of minors pursuant to § 707(d) implicates fundamental liberty interests, and the disparity in treatment of minors falling within the scope of the statute is neither justified by a compelling state interest nor rationally related to a legitimate interest. Therefore, they contend, § 707(d) is unconstitutional on its face. We conclude that petitioners' equal protection claim lacks merit.

To succeed on their claim under the equal protection clause, petitioners first must show that the state has adopted a classification that affects two or more similarly situated groups in an unequal manner. Petitioners do not challenge the classification expressly set forth in § 707(d)—that is, they do not contend that the disparate treatment of minors who meet the criteria set forth in § 707(d), and of minors who do not meet such criteria, is impermissible. Instead they assert that § 707(d) authorizes *prosecutors* to create two classes of minors, both of which satisfy the criteria set forth in the statute. One class consists of those minors against whom prosecutors choose to file criminal charges in criminal court; the other consists of minors accused of having committed the same offenses, but against whom prosecutors choose to file wardship petitions in juvenile court. These two classes of minors are affected in an unequal manner, petitioners observe, because application of the juvenile court law or the criminal law can give rise to significantly different rights and penalties for similarly situated minors.

As petitioners implicitly concede, all minors who meet the criteria enumerated in § 707(d) equally are subject to the prosecutor's discretion whether to file charges in criminal court. Any unequal treatment of such minors who commit the same crime under similar circumstances results solely from the decisions of individual prosecutors whether to file against particular minors a petition in juvenile court or instead an accusatory pleading in criminal court. Although, as petitioners assert, a prosecutor's decision in this regard can result in important consequences to the accused minor, so does a decision by a prosecutor to initiate criminal charges against *any* individual, including an adult. Claims of unequal treatment by prosecutors in selecting particular classes of individuals for prosecution are evaluated according to ordinary equal protection standards. These standards require the defendant to show that he or she has been singled out deliberately for prosecution on the basis of some invidious criterion, and that the prosecution would not have been pursued except for the discriminatory purpose of the prosecuting authorities. "[A]n invidious purpose for prosecution is one that is arbitrary and thus unjustified because it bears no rational relationship to legitimate law enforcement interests ***."

Section 707(d) contains no overtly discriminatory classification. In their challenge to §707(d), petitioners do not contend that the district attorney filed charges against them in criminal court on the basis of some invidious criterion or for a discriminatory purpose, or that §707(d) has had any discriminatory effect. Petitioners instead contend that §707(d) *might* result in invidious discrimination because it contains no standards guiding the prosecutor's discretion whether to file charges in criminal court. Similarly, several amici curiae assert that historical data regarding racial disparities in the juvenile justice system suggest that §707(d) *likely* will exacerbate such inequities. Such speculation is insufficient to establish a violation of the equal protection clause.

....

The decision to file charges in criminal court pursuant to §707(d) also is analogous to a prosecutor's decision to pursue capital charges against a defendant. It long has been held that "prosecutorial discretion to select those eligible cases in which the death penalty will actually be sought does not in and of itself ∗∗∗ offend principles of equal protection ∗∗∗. Many circumstances may affect the litigation of a case chargeable under the death penalty law. These include factual nuances, strength of evidence, and, in particular, the broad discretion to show leniency. Hence, one sentenced to death under a properly channeled death penalty scheme cannot prove a constitutional violation by showing that other persons whose crimes were superficially similar did not receive the death penalty. The same reasoning applies to the prosecutor's decisions to pursue or withhold capital charges at the outset."

Thus, petitioners cannot establish a violation of their right to the equal protection of the laws by showing that other minors in circumstances similar to those of petitioners can be prosecuted under the juvenile court law. Section 707(d) limits the prosecutor's discretion to file charges in criminal court to minors of a specified age who commit enumerated crimes under certain circumstances, and at the preliminary hearing the magistrate must find reasonable cause to believe that the minor has committed such a crime under those circumstances. In addition, the prosecutor's decision is subject to constitutional constraints against invidious discrimination. Therefore, contrary to petitioners' contention, the prosecutor's decision is not unfettered or entirely without standards. The prosecutor's discretion to select those statutorily eligible cases in which to seek a criminal disposition against a minor—based upon permissible factors such as the circumstances of the crime, the background of the minor, or a desire to show leniency, for example—does not violate the equal protection clause.

....

KENNARD, J., Dissenting

Historically, in California the decision whether to grant a district attorney's request that a minor be prosecuted in adult court instead of juvenile court has been a function of the judiciary, a neutral body. In 2000, however, the voters of this state enacted Proposition 21, an initiative measure that among other matters grants a prosecutor arbitrary and virtually unlimited discretion to decide whether a minor should be tried in juvenile or adult court. There is no hearing, and no right to counsel. No standards guide the exercise of discretion. There is no judicial review. This last omission is fatal, for by depriving the judiciary of any role in making or reviewing the decision, this portion of Proposition 21 eliminates an essential check to arbitrary executive power, and thus offends the principle of separation of powers embodied in the California Constitution.

....

IV

In my view, Proposition 21 unconstitutionally invaded a judicial function, for the following reasons:

First, almost from the inception of the juvenile court system in California, the decision whether a minor is unfit for juvenile court proceedings has been a judicial function. History alone may not be conclusive, but it is important, for the division of authority among the three coequal branches of government is largely a product of history.

Second, the decision whether to prosecute in juvenile or adult court is critical, and thus deserving of the due process protections of a judicial proceeding. In *Kent v. United States* the United States Supreme Court reviewed an arbitrary ruling of the District of Columbia juvenile court to waive jurisdiction and permit trial in adult court. Overturning that ruling, the high court repeatedly described the decision whether a minor should be tried as a juvenile or an adult as "critically important," one of "tremendous consequence," and thus deserving and requiring the protection of due process....

[C]ases do not suggest that the critically important decision whether to try the minor in adult or juvenile court should receive due process protections only if it is made after charges have been filed. Yet if the same decision, equally important and consequential, is made before charges are filed, then, according to the majority, the prosecutor has unreviewable discretion, subject only to the most minimal of constitutional constraints prohibiting invidious discrimination or vindictive or retaliatory prosecution. There is no judicial review to correct erroneous decisions, inconsistent decisions, or decisions that certain classes of minors, or all minors, will always be prosecuted in adult court.

Third, at the time of filing charges, the district attorney's office has limited information—the details of the particular crime, and the minor's prior criminal history, if any. It may not know the minor's family, school, or community history, all matters that are important in deciding whether the minor is suitable for juvenile court treatment. It may not know the minor's view of the matter, and probably has not heard from the minor's counsel, who has yet to be appointed. There has been no hearing, no testimony, and no receipt of evidence. As a result, the prosecutor, acting with limited information, may err in the decision, and although an error in submitting the minor to juvenile court jurisdiction is correctable, one in assigning the minor to adult court is not.

V

The separation of powers doctrine does not require that the prosecutor take no part in the decision whether a minor should be tried in adult or juvenile court. Because that doctrine envisions that each branch of government acts as a check upon the power of the other branches, the doctrine of separation of powers would be satisfied if the prosecutor's initial decision were subject to judicial review....

VI

In conclusion, the validity of Proposition 21's provision giving the prosecutor power to decide whether to prosecute a minor in adult court or juvenile court turns not on the timing of the prosecutor's decision, but "the substance of the power and the effect of its exercise." The power, as I have explained, is unrestrained by legislative standards and susceptible to arbitrary exercise; the effect is profound, determining whether the minor will be prosecuted in a system that stresses punishment or one that stresses rehabilitation. In this setting, the absence of judicial review brings that portion of Proposition 21 into conflict with article III, section 3 of the California Constitution.

C. A Typical Waiver Statute — Florida

Fla. Stat. §985.226

Criteria for waiver of juvenile court jurisdiction; hearing on
motion to transfer for prosecution as an adult

(1) Voluntary waiver. — The court shall transfer and certify a child's criminal case for trial as an adult if the child is alleged to have committed a violation of law and, prior to the commencement of an adjudicatory hearing, the child, joined by a parent or, in the absence of a parent, by the guardian or guardian ad litem, demands in writing to be tried as an adult. Once a child has been transferred for criminal prosecution pursuant to a voluntary waiver hearing and has been found to have committed the presenting offense or a lesser included offense, the child shall be handled thereafter in every respect as an adult for any subsequent violation of state law, unless the court imposes juvenile sanctions under §985.233(4)(b).

(2) Involuntary waiver. —

(a) *Discretionary waiver.* — Except as provided in paragraph (b), the state attorney may file a motion requesting the court to transfer the child for criminal prosecution if the child was 14 years of age or older at the time the alleged delinquent act or violation of law was committed.

(b) *Mandatory waiver.* —

1. If the child was 14 years of age or older, and if the child has been previously adjudicated delinquent for an act classified as a felony, which adjudication was for the commission of, attempt to commit, or conspiracy to commit murder, sexual battery, armed or strong-armed robbery, carjacking, home-invasion robbery, aggravated battery, aggravated assault, or burglary with an assault or battery, and the child is currently charged with a second or subsequent violent crime against a person; or

2. If the child was 14 years of age or older at the time of commission of a fourth or subsequent alleged felony offense and the child was previously adjudicated delinquent or had adjudication withheld for or was found to have committed, or to have attempted or conspired to commit, three offenses that are felony offenses if committed by an adult, and one or more of such felony offenses involved the use or possession of a firearm or violence against a person;

the state attorney *shall* request the court to transfer and certify the child for prosecution as an adult or shall provide written reasons to the court for not making such request, or proceed pursuant to §985.227(1). Upon the state attorney's request, the court shall either enter an order transferring the case and certifying the case for trial as if the child were an adult or provide written reasons for not issuing such an order.

(3) Waiver hearing. —

(a) Within 7 days, excluding Saturdays, Sundays, and legal holidays, after the date a petition alleging that a child has committed a delinquent act or violation of law has been filed, or later with the approval of the court, but before an adjudicatory hearing and after considering the recommendation of the juvenile probation officer, the state attorney may file a motion requesting the court to transfer the child for criminal prosecution.

(b) After the filing of the motion of the state attorney, summonses must be issued and served in conformity with § 985.219. A copy of the motion and a copy of the delinquency petition, if not already served, must be attached to each summons.

(c) The court shall conduct a hearing on all transfer request motions for the purpose of determining whether a child should be transferred. In making its determination, the court shall consider:

1. The seriousness of the alleged offense to the community and whether the protection of the community is best served by transferring the child for adult sanctions.

2. Whether the alleged offense was committed in an aggressive, violent, premeditated, or willful manner.

3. Whether the alleged offense was against persons or against property, greater weight being given to offenses against persons, especially if personal injury resulted.

4. The probable cause as found in the report, affidavit, or complaint.

5. The desirability of trial and disposition of the entire offense in one court when the child's associates in the alleged crime are adults or children who are to be tried as adults.

6. The sophistication and maturity of the child.

7. The record and previous history of the child, including:

　　a. Previous contacts with the department, the Department of Corrections, the former Department of Health and Rehabilitative Services, the Department of Children and Family Services, other law enforcement agencies, and courts;

　　b. Prior periods of probation;

　　c. Prior adjudications that the child committed a delinquent act or violation of law, greater weight being given if the child has previously been found by a court to have committed a delinquent act or violation of law involving an offense classified as a felony or has twice previously been found to have committed a delinquent act or violation of law involving an offense classified as a misdemeanor; and

　　d. Prior commitments to institutions.

8. The prospects for adequate protection of the public and the likelihood of reasonable rehabilitation of the child, if the child is found to have committed the alleged offense, by the use of procedures, services, and facilities currently available to the court.

(d) Prior to a hearing on the transfer request motion by the state attorney, a study and report to the court relevant to the factors in paragraph (c) must be made in writing by an authorized agent of the department. The child and the child's parents or legal guardians and counsel and the state attorney shall have the right to examine these reports and to question the parties responsible for them at the hearing.

(e) Any decision to transfer a child for criminal prosecution must be in writing and include consideration of, and findings of fact with respect to, all criteria in paragraph (c). The court shall render an order including a specific finding of fact and the reasons for a decision to impose adult sanctions. The order shall be reviewable on appeal under § 985.234 and the Florida Rules of Appellate Procedure.

(4) Effect of order waiving jurisdiction. —

(a) Once a child has been transferred for criminal prosecution pursuant to an involuntary waiver hearing and has been found to have committed the presenting offense or a lesser included offense, the child shall thereafter be handled in every respect as an adult for any subsequent violation of state law, unless the court imposes juvenile sanctions under § 985.233.

(b) When a child is transferred for criminal prosecution as an adult, the court shall immediately transfer and certify to the adult circuit court all felony cases pertaining to the child, for prosecution of the child as an adult, which have not yet resulted in a plea of guilty or nolo contendere or in which a finding of guilt has not been made. If the child is acquitted of all charged offenses or lesser included offenses contained in the original case transferred to adult court, all felony cases that were transferred to adult court pursuant to this paragraph shall be subject to the same penalties such cases were subject to before being transferred to adult court.

Fla. Stat. § 985.227

Prosecution of juveniles as adults by the direct filing of an information in the criminal division of the circuit court; discretionary criteria; mandatory criteria

(1) Discretionary direct file; criteria. —

(a) With respect to any child who was 14 or 15 years of age at the time the alleged offense was committed, the state attorney *may* file an information when in the state attorney's judgment and discretion the public interest requires that adult sanctions be considered or imposed and when the offense charged is for the commission of, attempt to commit, or conspiracy to commit:

1. Arson;

2. Sexual battery;

3. Robbery;

4. Kidnapping;

5. Aggravated child abuse;

6. Aggravated assault;

7. Aggravated stalking;

8. Murder;

9. Manslaughter;

10. Unlawful throwing, placing, or discharging of a destructive device or bomb;

11. Armed burglary in violation of § 810.02(2)(b) or specified burglary of a dwelling or structure in violation of § 810.02(2)(c), or burglary with an assault or battery in violation of § 810.02(2)(a).

12. Aggravated battery;

13. Any lewd or lascivious offense committed upon or in the presence of a person less than 16 years of age;

14. Carrying, displaying, using, threatening, or attempting to use a weapon or firearm during the commission of a felony;

15. Grand theft in violation of § 812.014(2)(a);

16. Possessing or discharging any weapon or firearm on school property in violation of § 790.115;

17. Home invasion robbery;

18. Carjacking; or

19. Grand theft of a motor vehicle in violation of § 812.014(2)(c)6 or grand theft of a motor vehicle valued at $20,000 or more in violation of § 812.014(2)(b) if the child has a previous adjudication for grand theft of a motor vehicle in violation of § 812.014(2)(c)6 or § 812.014(2)(b).

(b) With respect to any child who was 16 or 17 years of age at the time the alleged offense was committed, the state attorney *may* file an information when in the state attorney's judgment and discretion the public interest requires that adult sanctions be considered or imposed. However, the state attorney may not file an information on a child charged with a misdemeanor, unless the child has had at least two previous adjudications or adjudications withheld for delinquent acts, one of which involved an offense classified as a felony under state law.

(2) Mandatory direct file. —

(a) With respect to any child who was 16 or 17 years of age at the time the alleged offense was committed, the state attorney *shall* file an information if the child has been previously adjudicated delinquent for an act classified as a felony, which adjudication was for the commission of, attempt to commit, or conspiracy to commit murder, sexual battery, armed or strong-armed robbery, carjacking, home-invasion robbery, aggravated battery, or aggravated assault, and the child is currently charged with a second or subsequent violent crime against a person.

(b) With respect to any child 16 or 17 years of age at the time an offense classified as a forcible felony, as defined in § 776.08, was committed, the state attorney *shall* file an information if the child has previously been adjudicated delinquent or had adjudication withheld for three acts classified as felonies each of which occurred at least 45 days apart from each other. This paragraph does not apply when the state attorney has good cause to believe that exceptional circumstances exist which preclude the just prosecution of the juvenile in adult court.

(c) The state attorney *must* file an information if a child, regardless of the child's age at the time the alleged offense was committed, is alleged to have committed an act that would be a violation of law if the child were an adult, that involves stealing a motor vehicle, including, but not limited to, a violation of § 812.133, relating to carjacking, or § 812.014(2)(c) 6, relating to grand theft of a motor vehicle, and while the child was in possession of the stolen motor vehicle the child caused serious bodily injury to or the death of a person who was not involved in the underlying offense. For purposes of this section, the driver and all willing passengers in the stolen motor vehicle at the time such serious bodily injury or death is inflicted shall also be subject to mandatory transfer to adult court. "Stolen motor vehicle," for the purposes of this section, means a motor vehicle that has been the subject of any criminal wrongful taking. For purposes of this section, "willing passengers" means all willing passengers who have participated in the underlying offense.

(d)1. With respect to any child who was 16 or 17 years of age at the time the alleged offense was committed, the state attorney *shall* file an information if the child has been charged with committing or attempting to commit an offense listed in §775.087(2)(a)1.a.-q., [includes such serious felonies as murder, sexual battery, robbery, burglary, arson, escape, aggravated assault, kidnapping, carjacking and drug trafficking] and, during the commission of or attempt to commit the offense, the child:

>   a. Actually possessed a firearm or destructive device, as those terms are defined in §790.001.

>   b. Discharged a firearm or destructive device, as described in §775.087(2)(a)2.

>   c. Discharged a firearm or destructive device, as described in §775.087(2)(a)3., and, as a result of the discharge, death or great bodily harm was inflicted upon any person.

2. Upon transfer, any child who is:

>   a. Charged pursuant to sub-subparagraph 1.a. and who has been previously adjudicated or had adjudication withheld for a forcible felony offense or any offense involving a firearm, or who has been previously placed in a residential commitment program, shall be subject to sentencing under §775.087(2)(a) [minimum sentence of twenty years], notwithstanding §985.233.

>   b. Charged pursuant to sub-subparagraph 1.b. or sub-subparagraph 1.c., shall be subject to sentencing under §775.087(2)(a), notwithstanding §985.233.

3. Upon transfer, any child who is charged pursuant to this paragraph, but who does not meet the requirements specified in subparagraph 2., shall be sentenced pursuant to §985.233; however, if the court imposes a juvenile sanction, the court must commit the child to a high-risk or maximum-risk juvenile facility.

4. This paragraph shall not apply if the state attorney has good cause to believe that exceptional circumstances exist which preclude the just prosecution of the child in adult court.

5. The Department of Corrections shall make every reasonable effort to ensure that any child 16 or 17 years of age who is convicted and sentenced under this paragraph be completely separated such that there is no physical contact with adult offenders in the facility, to the extent that it is consistent with chapter 958 [dispositional guidelines for youthful offenders].

(3) Effect of direct file. —

(a) Once a child has been transferred for criminal prosecution pursuant to an information and has been found to have committed the presenting offense or a lesser included offense, the child shall be handled thereafter in every respect as if an adult for any subsequent violation of state law, unless the court imposes juvenile sanctions under §985.233.

(b) When a child is transferred for criminal prosecution as an adult, the court shall immediately transfer and certify to the adult circuit court all felony cases pertaining to the child, for prosecution of the child as an adult, which have not yet resulted in a plea of guilty or nolo contendere or in which a finding of guilt has not been made. If a child is acquitted of all charged offenses or lesser included offenses contained in the original case transferred to adult court, all felony cases that were transferred to adult court as a result of this paragraph shall be subject to the same penalties to which such cases would have been subject before being transferred to adult court.

(c) When a child has been transferred for criminal prosecution as an adult and has been found to have committed a violation of state law, the disposition of the case may be made under § 985.233 and may include the enforcement of any restitution ordered in any juvenile proceeding.

(4) Direct-file policies and guidelines.—Each state attorney shall develop written policies and guidelines to govern determinations for filing an information on a juvenile, to be submitted to the Executive Office of the Governor, the President of the Senate, and the Speaker of the House of Representatives not later than January 1 of each year.

(5) An information filed pursuant to this section may include all charges that are based on the same act, criminal episode, or transaction as the primary offenses.

D. Evidentiary Problems in Judicial Waiver Cases

In re Randolph T.
437 A.2d 230 (Md. 1981)

SMITH, Judge.

We shall here uphold against constitutional attack the requirement of the Maryland Code that "a preponderance of the evidence" is the standard to be used by a trial judge in determining whether to waive juvenile jurisdiction. Accordingly, we shall affirm the judgment of the Court of Special Appeals.

. . . .

A hearing was held on June 9, 1980, at which time the court's exclusive original jurisdiction was waived and it was ordered that Randolph T. be held for action under the appropriate criminal procedure. Among other things, in determining whether to waive jurisdiction, the trial judge took into consideration the fact that the juvenile was already incarcerated while awaiting trial in the Criminal Court of Baltimore on a murder charge. In response to a question from counsel, the judge indicated that he was using the preponderance of the evidence standard and that the nature of the events and the public safety were serious factors which he considered in determining whether to waive juvenile jurisdiction. He expressly rejected a contention that the [United States Supreme Court] decision in *Addington v. Texas* [holding that the Constitution required a clear and convincing standard of proof with commitments to state mental hospitals], required that he declare the Maryland act unconstitutional and that under the Due Process Clause the proper standard was proof beyond a reasonable doubt.

. . . .

Randolph first contends that § 3-817(c), when it states that "(t)he court may not waive its jurisdiction unless it determines, from a preponderance of the evidence presented at the hearing, that the child is an unfit subject for juvenile rehabilitative measures," does not require the preponderance standard. He emphasizes the use of the word "may" and suggests that a higher standard of proof therefore is not forbidden. We understand the statute to be saying that if the judge finds from a preponderance of the evidence that the child is an unfit subject for juvenile rehabilitative measures, then he is to bring his best judgment to bear in the weighing of the various factors.... A preponderance of the evidence is the standard specified by the statute.

Randolph next contends that by virtue of the Supreme Court's holding in *Addington*, the State is bound to prove beyond a reasonable doubt that he is an unfit subject for juvenile rehabilitative measures, and that waiver of juvenile jurisdiction without such proof constitutes a denial of due process of law. This contention is predicated upon the due process holdings in juvenile matters by the Supreme Court in *In re Winship*, *In re Gault*, and *Kent v. United States*.

Addington is not a juvenile case. Chief Justice Burger opened the opinion by saying for the Court:

"The question in this case is what standard of proof is required by the Fourteenth Amendment to the Constitution in a civil proceeding brought under state law to commit an individual involuntarily for an indefinite period to a state mental hospital."

After reviewing the background of that particular case, the Court began its discussion by saying:

"The function of a standard of proof, as that concept is embodied in the Due Process Clause and in the realm of factfinding, is to 'instruct the factfinder concerning the degree of confidence our society thinks he should have in the correctness of factual conclusions for a particular type of adjudication.' The standard serves to allocate the risk of error between the litigants and to indicate the relative importance attached to the ultimate decision."

The Court then discussed the three standards of proof:

"At one end of the spectrum is the typical civil case involving a monetary dispute between private parties. Since society has a minimal concern with the outcome of such private suits, plaintiff's burden of proof is a mere preponderance of the evidence. The litigants thus share the risk of error in roughly equal fashion.

"In a criminal case, on the other hand, the interests of the defendant are of such magnitude that historically and without any explicit constitutional requirement they have been protected by standards of proof designed to exclude as nearly as possible the likelihood of an erroneous judgment. In the administration of criminal justice, our society imposes almost the entire risk of error upon itself. This is accomplished by requiring under the Due Process Clause that the state prove the guilt of an accused beyond a reasonable doubt.

"The intermediate standard, which usually employs some combination of the words 'clear,' 'cogent,' 'unequivocal' and 'convincing,' is less commonly used, but nonetheless 'is no stranger to the civil law.' One typical use of the standard is in civil cases involving allegations of fraud or some other quasi-criminal wrongdoing by the defendant. The interests at stake in those cases are deemed to be more substantial than mere loss of money and some jurisdictions accordingly reduce the risk to the defendant of having his reputation tarnished erroneously by increasing the plaintiff's burden of proof. Similarly, this Court has used the 'clear, unequivocal and convincing' standard of proof to protect particularly important individual interests in various civil cases. See, e.g., *Woodby v. INS*, (deportation); and *Chaunt v. United States* (denaturalization).

In proceeding with its analysis and examination, the Court observed that it "must be mindful that the function of legal process is to minimize the risk of erroneous decisions"; that "civil commitment for any purpose constitutes a significant deprivation of liberty that requires due process protection"; that "involuntary commitment to a mental hospital after a finding of probable dangerousness to self or others can engender adverse social consequences to the individual" and "can have a very significant impact on the individual"; that the state "has a legitimate interest under its parens patriae powers in providing care to its citizens who are unable because of emotional disorders to care for themselves"; and that "the state ... has authority under its police power to protect the community from the dangerous tendencies of some who are mentally ill."

The Court rejected the preponderance standard because it "creates the risk of increasing the number of individuals erroneously committed...." It said "The individual should not be asked to share equally with society the risk of error when the possible injury to the individual is significantly greater than any possible harm to the state."

Addington argued to the Court "that the rationale of the *Winship* holding that the criminal law standard of proof was required in a delinquency proceeding applies with equal force to a civil commitment proceeding." The Court pointed out, "In a civil commitment state power is not exercised in a punitive sense."

In "conclud(ing) that it is unnecessary to require states to apply the strict, criminal standard," the Court reasoned:

"(T)he initial inquiry in a civil commitment proceeding is very different from the central issue in either a delinquency proceeding or a criminal prosecution. In the latter cases the basic issue is a straightforward factual question—did the accused commit the act alleged? There may be factual issues to resolve in a commitment proceeding, but the factual aspects represent only the beginning of the inquiry. Whether the individual is mentally ill and dangerous to either himself or others and is in need of confined therapy turns on the meaning of the facts which must be interpreted by expert psychiatrists and psychologists. Given the lack of certainty and the fallibility of psychiatric diagnosis, there is a serious question as to whether a state could ever prove beyond a reasonable doubt that an individual is both mentally ill and likely to be dangerous."

The Court then "turn(ed) to a middle level of burden of proof that strikes a fair balance between the rights of the individual and the legitimate concerns of the state," that of "clear and convincing" evidence, saying, "To meet due process demands, the standard has to inform the factfinder that the proof must be greater than the preponderance-of-the-evidence standard applicable to other categories of civil cases."

Randolph has correctly referred to *Winship, Gault*, and *Kent*. They do not dictate, however, the result he desires here.

Winship, as petitioner notes, requires proof beyond a reasonable doubt at the adjudicatory state of a juvenile proceeding where the juvenile is charged with an act which would be a crime if committed by an adult.

Gault, as summarized by Justice Brennan for the Court in *Winship*, "decided that, although the Fourteenth Amendment does not require that the hearing at (the adjudicatory) stage (of a juvenile proceeding) conform with all the requirements of a criminal trial or even of the usual administrative proceeding, the Due Process Clause does require application during the adjudicatory hearing of "the essentials of due process and fair treatment."

Kent involved a waiver under the District of Columbia juvenile statute. The holding of the Court was "that it is incumbent upon the Juvenile Court to accompany its waiver order with a statement of the reasons or considerations therefor" and "that an opportunity for a hearing which may be informal, must be given the child prior to entry of a waiver order," which "hearing must measure up to the essentials of due process and fair treatment."

Although a number of courts since *Addington* have referred to its standard of proof in various situations, we have been referred to no case nor have we encountered one in which the standard of proof in juvenile waiver proceedings has been changed because of *Addington*. The cases decided since *Addington*, when coupled with the examples given by the Supreme Court in *Addington*, do help to make a picture of the proper circumstances for the use of its standard, however.

Randolph focuses on what he calls the five reasons or factors used by the Supreme Court "(i)n rejecting the beyond a reasonable doubt standard for civil commitments to mental hospitals," which he says "distinguished the type of decision involved in *Addington* from the types of decisions involved where the reasonable doubt standard is required." Thus, Randolph submits that "application of these ... factors to juvenile waiver indicates that the reasonable doubt standard would best meet the requirements of Due Process." We shall discuss them seriatim.

He first points out the Court said that in "a civil commitment state power is not exercised in a punitive sense." He "recognizes that, under § 3-817(c), the juvenile's guilt or innocence and appropriate punishment are not at issue in a waiver proceeding." However, he contends that "(n)evertheless, a decision to waive jurisdiction leads to the punitive exercise of State power." What he seems to overlook is that there can be no such exercise until after a full trial in a court of law with a determination by the trier of fact that the accused is guilty beyond a reasonable doubt of any offense with which he is charged. Moreover, the accused has the full panoply of rights provided by the Constitution of the United States and that of the State of Maryland, including the right to assistance of counsel, which counsel will be provided at public expense should he be unable to afford the services of an attorney.

Secondly, Randolph says the Court recognized that "the 'beyond a reasonable doubt' standard historically has been reserved for criminal cases ... (in which it) is regarded as a critical part of the 'moral force of the criminal law'...." On this point he argues, "Since a juvenile waiver changes a delinquency proceeding into a criminal prosecution, the child should have the protection of the reasonable doubt standard." Applying the same argument one would be obliged to say that before a grand jury could indict it would be required to have proof beyond a reasonable doubt, since the indictment is the foundation for a criminal prosecution. Such is not the law and never has been.

Thirdly, he refers to the Court's statement that the "layers of professional review and observation of the patient's condition, and the concern of family and friends generally will provide continuous opportunities for an erroneous commitment to be corrected." On this point he states, "Although § 3-817(c) allows immediate appeal of the waiver decision, a waiver decision generally is final and the juvenile does not have continuous opportunities to correct an erroneous waiver." That is true, but as we have already pointed out, the juvenile will not be subject to a sanction until after due trial.

Fourthly, Randolph refers to the Court's statement that "it is not true that the release of a genuinely mentally ill person is no worse for the individual than the failure to convict the guilty (since) (o)ne who is suffering from a debilitating mental illness and in need of treatment is neither wholly at liberty nor free of stigma." To this Randolph observes, "The Supreme Court's point is correct. But in a juvenile waiver proceeding, it is the State which is trying to remove the juvenile from the care of a system, based on the State's role as parens patriae, designed to protect the juvenile." As Chief Judge Gilbert recognized for the Court of Special Appeals in this case:

"The stigma or labeling of a child as allegedly guilty of committing a criminal act does not attach automatically when a court determines that juvenile jurisdiction is waived, and the child is to be tried as an adult even though the waiver court presumes guilt for the purpose of the waiver hearing only. Rather, stigma results when the criminal court finds that the act was, in fact, committed by the one charged."

Finally, Randolph says the Supreme Court stated that "while a criminal prosecution involves the 'straightforward factual question—did the accused commit the act alleged?', a civil commitment involves the questions of whether a person is mentally ill and whether he is dangerous," questions which "usually turn on expert psychiatric testimony based on 'subjective analysis ... filtered through the experience of the diagnostician.'" On this point he "concedes that the waiver decision is not as straightforward as the decision on guilt or innocence since it involves a prediction as to how the child will respond to juvenile treatment." He goes on, however, to contend that "the waiver decision (is not) as speculative as the civil commitment decision" since the "Judge must assume the child did the criminal act alleged in the juvenile delinquency petition." The contention that waiver to the regular criminal process means enhanced punishment was also discussed by Chief Judge Gilbert for the Court of Special Appeals:

"That may or may not be so. The punishment, it is true, may be greater if meted out by a criminal court, but there is no iron-clad rule that it shall or must be more severe than that imposed by the juvenile court. Additionally, waiver does not mean that a conviction inevitably will follow. The juvenile is cloaked with the same presumption of innocence that attends every other person appearing in the criminal courts. Waiver followed by a verdict of guilty does subject the child to having a criminal record, with all the detriments thereto appertaining."

"The most acceptable meaning to be given to the expression, proof by a preponderance, seems to be proof which leads the jury to find that the existence of the contested fact is more probable than its nonexistence. Thus the preponderance of evidence becomes the trier's belief in the preponderance of probability."

Thus, our statute is requesting that a judge certify, after weighing all of the evidence adduced before him and considering the factors mandated by the statute, that it is probable that the child is an unfit subject for juvenile rehabilitative measures. In such a situation the juvenile is in a much different position than the individual about to be committed to a mental institution as in *Addington*, the parent to be permanently separated from his child, the young woman who is to be sterilized, or the persons subject to deportation or denaturalization which the Chief Justice mentioned in his discussion for the Court in *Addington*. The court proceeding in each of those cases is a final determination of the person's status. Randolph T. is being removed from the juvenile justice system, but that removal does not determine his ultimate status. That will come only after due trial.

We find nothing in *Addington* nor in any other case which requires the imposition of a reasonable doubt standard in this situation.

Note

Is it true that a child's status is not being finally determined in a waiver hearing? Review Judge Hufstedler's dissenting opinion in *Harris v. Procunier, supra.*

Collins v. State of Arkansas

908 S.W.2d 80 (Ark. 1995)

ROAF, Justice.

This is an interlocutory appeal from the granting of the State's motion to transfer appellant Ronald Collins' case from juvenile to circuit court. We affirm the trial court's decision to grant the motion to transfer.

On July 15, 1994, Ray Shoptaw, a criminal investigator with the Garland County Sheriff's Office, was conducting surveillance from an unmarked police car parked in front of the house next door to appellant's home in Hot Springs. Mr. Shoptaw testified that there had been numerous burglaries and thefts from homes in the area, and that appellant and his brother were considered by his office to be suspects in these burglaries. Shortly after noon, Mr. Shoptaw saw appellant, age 16, his brother and another adult male come out of appellant's home with nothing in their hands, and walk into some nearby woods; about an hour and a half later, he heard gunshots and muffled voices coming from the same area of the woods. A short while later, Mr. Shoptaw saw appellant and his two companions walk out of the wooded area carrying something in their hands. All three were arrested for residential burglary and searched incident to their arrest. One of appellant's companions had a .22 caliber revolver and numerous pieces of jewelry wrapped in an article of clothing, a pair of gloves and a large screwdriver. Appellant's brother had a .22 derringer and a pair of gloves with a diamond ring inside one glove. The arresting officers found a pair of gloves and a pistol holster on the appellant. The jewelry, guns and holster were later identified as items stolen in the burglary of a residence in the area. The companion of the Collins' brothers admitted to officers that the three had committed this burglary and another burglary on the previous day. Appellant was out on bond for a pending burglary charge at the time of his arrest.

On August 4, 1994, the transfer hearing was conducted; the arresting officer, appellant's probation officer and appellant's mother testified at this hearing. At the conclusion of the hearing the trial court made the following ruling:

THE COURT: Based upon the testimony that I've heard, I find that there is clear and convincing evidence that this matter should be transferred to the Circuit Court of Garland County, Arkansas.

I make the following findings: that first, this is indeed a serious offense. As I recall, there are just Y and A above a Class B felony, which is what the defendant's charged with. That there apparently were firearms involved, if not directly, at least collaterally; that this offense would appear to be part of a repetitive pattern of conduct on the part of the defendant. In fact as I see from the record here, this charge was alleged to have occurred while the defendant was charged with another Class B felony, the one to which he had pled last Thursday. And that repetitive pattern then would demonstrate that this individual may be beyond, or is in fact beyond the current rehabilitation available in this state.

That, coupled with the history of the defendant, his traits and maturity, all of which bear upon his prospects for rehabilitation, the Court finds that there is clear and convincing evidence to transfer this matter to Circuit Court. The bond will remain the same.

Appellant's sole argument on appeal is that the trial court's finding, by clear and convincing evidence, that appellant should be tried as an adult was clearly erroneous and against the preponderance of the evidence.

We have repeatedly stated that if a trial court determines a juvenile should be tried in circuit court as an adult, its decision must be supported by clear and convincing evidence.

Clear and convincing evidence is "that degree of proof which will produce in the trier of fact a firm conviction as to the allegation sought to be established." We will not reverse the trial court's decision on transfer unless we determine the decision was clearly erroneous.

Arkansas Code Annotated § 9-27-318 provides that in deciding whether to transfer the case or to retain jurisdiction, the court in which the criminal charges have been filed shall consider the following factors:

(1) The seriousness of the offense, and whether violence was employed by the juvenile in the commission of the offense;

(2) Whether the offense is part of a repetitive pattern of adjudicated offenses which would lead to the determination that the juvenile is beyond rehabilitation under existing rehabilitation programs, as evidenced by past efforts to treat and rehabilitate the juvenile and the response to such efforts; and

(3) The prior history, character traits, mental maturity, and any other factor which reflects upon the juvenile's prospects for rehabilitation.

(f) Upon a finding by clear and convincing evidence that a juvenile should be tried as an adult, the court shall enter an order to that effect.

In making its decision, the lower court is not required to give weight to each of the statutory factors, and proof need not be introduced by the prosecutor against the juvenile on each factor.

The evidence adduced at appellant's transfer hearing was as follows. Appellant's probation officer, Robert Evans, recounted that appellant had been in and out of court on numerous occasions. In April, 1992, appellant was charged with third degree battery; that case was dismissed with the appellant consenting to pay costs. Appellant's first conviction was in September, 1993, for failure to appear and for obstructing governmental operations; appellant agreed, once again, to pay costs and received probation and a suspended sentence. Appellant's record also contained a probation violation for failing to report and for leaving the county. At the time of his arrest, appellant had been charged with another burglary which had been transferred from circuit court to juvenile court, and was out on bond for that offense.

Mr. Evans testified that as a probationer, appellant was not at all cooperative and reported in only sporadically and his parents also failed to insure that he reported in as required. Further, counseling was available to appellant, but he had not availed himself of this service. Appellant had not been to the training school, but Mr. Evans opined that, considering appellant's degree of noncooperation, neither counseling nor the training school would do him any good.

Appellant argues that there is countervailing evidence to the appellant's alleged failure to cooperate while on probation. Appellant's mother testified that at times he did not have transportation to make the ten mile trip to the probation office, his younger sister had frequent surgery and dealing with her medical problems was a family priority, and there had been a death in the family which necessitated a trip out of state. Appellant also argues that the only attempt at rehabilitation was to place him on probation, he had only one felony adjudication, he had no weapon when arrested and there was no evidence that violence was involved in the offense with which he was charged. He further contends his family situation contributed to his lack of maturity; his mother testified that appellant had not completed the eighth grade and that he had failed either the seventh or eighth grade twice.

[We have held] that where there was evidence that the current felony charges were part of a repetitive pattern of offenses and where past efforts at rehabilitation in the juvenile court system have not been successful, these factors alone prevented us from holding the trial court's ruling on the transfer motion was clearly erroneous, even though no violence was used in the commission of the offense. Also, we determined that even though appellant was not accused of personally using a weapon in crimes that involved a pistol and gunfire, his association with the gunman in committing the alleged robberies and thefts was enough to satisfy the violence criterion.

Here, the trial court, in considering the factors outlined in § 9-27-318, found that appellant was charged with a serious offense, a class B felony, that there were firearms involved at least collaterally, that the offense appeared to be part of a repetitive pattern of conduct which would demonstrate that appellant was beyond the current rehabilitation available, and that appellant's history, traits and maturity also reflected adversely upon his prospects for rehabilitation. We cannot say the trial court was clearly erroneous in finding that there was clear and convincing evidence presented at the hearing to support transfer of this case to circuit court.

Affirmed.

McKaine v. Texas
170 S.W.3d 285 (Tex. Crim. App. 2005)

....

Background

The conviction from which McKaine appeals stems from the following events. On November 12, 2002, McKaine and three other people used force to unlawfully enter the residence of Charles and Amy in Cuero, Texas. McKaine entered the home carrying a twenty-gauge shotgun. His cohorts were armed with handguns. With their weapons drawn, the group forced Charles down onto the kitchen floor, threatening to kill him if he resisted. McKaine then pointed his shotgun at Charles's wife, Amy, and told her to take off her shirt. With her husband and three small children watching, Amy removed her shirt for McKaine, exposing her breasts. McKaine's companions then took Charles into the couple's bedroom, and McKaine took Amy and two of her children into a second bedroom. Once inside, he began to touch Amy, fondling her breasts and repeatedly telling her that he wanted to have sex and that he was going to have sex with her on her child's bed in front of her children. He threatened to kill her, her husband, and her children if she told anyone. McKaine then took Amy into the living room and in front of all three of her children, ordered her to pull down her pants. She refused. McKaine repeated his demand, and again, she refused, saying that she was "on her period." McKaine put his shotgun against the head of Amy's three year old son and said, "Pull down your pants and spread your legs, or I'm going to kill your son." She complied, but McKaine did not have sex with her. He and his companions left, taking a knife, cigarettes, and money belonging to the family. Before leaving, McKaine repeated his threat that he would kill all of them if they told anyone what happened.

At the time of the incident, McKaine was sixteen years old. He was originally charged as a juvenile, but the State petitioned the juvenile court to transfer the case to district court so that he could be prosecuted as an adult. After a hearing, the juvenile court certified McKaine as an adult and transferred the case. Before the district court, McKaine pleaded guilty to burglary of a habitation and committing aggravated assault therein, a first-degree felony. He requested that a jury determine his punishment. The jury sentenced him to seventy-five years' imprisonment.

McKaine raises two issues on appeal. First, he challenges the juvenile court's decision to transfer his case to district court for trial as an adult. Second, he argues that the trial court abused its discretion during the punishment phase of the trial by not allowing his attorney to question Amy and Charles regarding their involvement in drug activities.

I. Transfer to District Court

In his first issue, McKaine claims that the juvenile court erred in transferring his case to district court. He complains that the court erred by considering a psychological report because it amounted to inadmissible hearsay. McKaine also contends that the author of the report should have been present at the transfer hearing to explain her evaluation and the basis for her findings. Finally, he maintains that the juvenile court had insufficient evidence to transfer his case to district court for trial as an adult....

When the State requests a transfer, the juvenile court is required to conduct a hearing without a jury to consider transfer of the child for criminal proceedings. Tex. Fam.Code Ann. § 54.02(c). Before the transfer hearing, the court must order and obtain a complete diagnostic study, social evaluation, and full investigation of the child, his circumstances, and the circumstances of the alleged offense. Based on this information, the court must determine whether there is probable cause to believe that the child committed the offense alleged and whether the welfare of the community requires criminal proceedings because of the seriousness of the offense or the background of the child. The juvenile court's decision to transfer a case to district court is reviewed for abuse of discretion.

We first consider McKaine's argument that the trial court erred by considering a psychological report because it was inadmissible hearsay. Strict rules of evidence are not applied in transfer proceedings. Section 54.02(e) authorizes the juvenile court to "consider written reports from probation officers, professional court employees, or professional consultants in addition to the testimony of witnesses." In previous case involving the use of a psychiatric evaluation in a transfer hearing, this Court overruled an alleged hearsay error, noting that juvenile courts are authorized to consider such evidence. We reach the same conclusion in this case. The juvenile court did not err in admitting the psychological report into evidence.

McKaine also argues that Dr. Karan Redus, who conducted his psychological evaluation and authored the report, should have testified at the transfer hearing. He contends that the juvenile court's duty to conduct a "full investigation and hearing" is not complete without live testimony from the author of any reports relied upon under section 54.02(e). The State has not responded to this argument. Nevertheless, we cannot conclude that the juvenile court abused its discretion. The family code does not specifically require that the juvenile court hear live testimony from a professional consultant whose written report is considered under section 54.02(e). It allows the court to consider "written reports from * * * professional consultants in addition to the testimony of witnesses." Although McKaine makes compelling arguments regarding the court's duty to be fully informed of the juvenile's circumstances, he has cited no cases holding that the court must receive live testimony in addition to the written reports. Our research has unearthed no such authority. Thus, we cannot conclude that the trial court abused its discretion. In so holding, we note that although McKaine's trial counsel complained of Dr. Redus's absence at the hearing, the record does not show that he ever attempted to subpoena her or otherwise solicit her testimony. The record shows that McKaine's trial counsel received proper notice of Dr. Redus's report under section 54.02(e).

Finally, McKaine argues that the juvenile court erred in transferring his case to district court because the evidence was insufficient to support a transfer. McKaine argues that the evidence adduced at the transfer hearing was insufficient to support a transfer because it showed that (1) he had never been adjudicated of a felony as a juvenile, (2) he suffered from drug addiction and had not received treatment, and (3) the Texas Youth Commission offered services that could assist in rehabilitating him. The State has not responded to McKaine's sufficiency arguments. Assuming without deciding that McKaine has properly presented this issue for review, we hold that it does not warrant reversal because his arguments do not address all of the grounds for the juvenile court's decision. Specifically, McKaine has not addressed the court's finding that the seriousness of the offense necessitated criminal proceedings to protect the welfare of the community.

As noted above, the juvenile court has discretion to waive its jurisdiction and transfer a case to criminal court if it finds that there is probable cause to believe that the child committed the offense alleged and that the welfare of the community requires criminal proceedings because of the seriousness of the offense or the background of the child. In making this determination, the court is required to consider (1) whether the alleged offense was against a person or property, with greater weight in favor of transfer given to offenses against the person; (2) the sophistication and maturity of the child; (3) the record and previous history of the child; and (4) the prospects of adequate protection of the public and the likelihood of the rehabilitation of the child by use of procedures, services, and facilities available to the juvenile court. While the juvenile court must consider all of these factors before transferring the case to district court, it is not required to find that each factor is established by the evidence. The court is also not required to give each factor equal weight as long as each is considered.

In its order, the juvenile court discussed each of the foregoing factors and how they influenced its decision. The court also noted that "after conducting * * * [a] full investigation, including evidence and argument of counsel, the Court finds that the welfare of the community requires criminal proceedings, because of the seriousness of the offenses and the background of the child and * * * [because] there is probable cause to believe the child committed the offenses.* * *" On appeal, McKaine argues that his background did not require criminal proceedings for the protection of the community's welfare, but he does not challenge the court's finding that the seriousness of the offense warranted criminal proceedings. A court does not abuse its discretion by finding the community's welfare requires transfer due to the seriousness of the crime alone, regardless of the child's background. Thus, even if we were to sustain McKaine's challenge regarding his background, his failure to challenge the court's finding regarding the seriousness of the offense would preclude relief on his sufficiency arguments. Appellant's first issue is therefore overruled.

Notes

(a) Does the higher clear and convincing standard for waiver eliminate arbitrary decisions by trial judges? Note that the clear and convincing standard applies only to the trial court. The appellate court's standard of review is clearly erroneous, that is, was the trial court clearly erroneous in concluding that there was clear and convincing evidence to support the waiver. Is the problem, therefore, the standard of proof at trial or the standard of review by the appellate courts? Is there a way for appellate courts to exercise a more effective standard of review without unduly impinging on the trial court's discretion?

> Although statutes generally list several factors for the trial court to consider when making the waiver decision, trial courts are often swayed by the seriousness of the offense. If the appellate courts do not require that there be evidence as to each of the factors to support a waiver decision, in effect, trial courts are free to

waive children to criminal court based on only one factor, the seriousness of the offense.

(b) Does it make a difference who has the burden of proof at the waiver hearing—the state or the child? In some jurisdictions this shifts according to the age of the child and the nature of the offense, e.g., between the ages of twelve and fourteen in a homicide case the state has to prove by clear and convincing evidence that the child should be waived, whereas after the age of fourteen the burden shifts to the child to prove by clear and convincing evidence that he or she should not be waived.

(c) Draft a waiver statute that balances the public safety concerns and the role of the juvenile court as protector of the juvenile's interests.

E. What Happens after Waiver?

Ex Parte Powell
558 S.W.2d 480 (Tex. Crim. App. 1977)

This is an appeal from an order of the 181st District Court denying relief on petitioner's pretrial application for writ of habeas corpus.

On March 3, 1977, petitioner was respondent in a hearing under Family Code § 54.02 to determine whether the juvenile court should waive its exclusive original jurisdiction and transfer petitioner to the district for criminal proceedings. The juvenile court did order such a transfer in an order entered March 4 that appears regular on its face. On September 16, 1977, petitioner filed his application in the district court, alleging errors in the juvenile court hearing in the admission of evidence, the sufficiency of findings of fact and the sufficiency of evidence to support the findings....

At the outset we must determine whether habeas corpus jurisdiction should be exercised to review the matters asserted by petitioner as error in the juvenile court hearing.

Article 5, Section 8, of the Texas Constitution provides in part: "The District Court * * * and the judges thereof, shall have power to issue writes of habeas corpus, mandamus, injunction and certiorari, and all writs necessary to enforce their jurisdiction." From the district court's consideration of petitioner's habeas corpus application appeal was taken to this Court. The issue, then, is whether the district court properly entertained petitioner's claims relating to the juvenile court hearing.

Habeas corpus may be used to challenge any unlawful restraint. It is also true, however, that habeas corpus may not be used as a substitute for appeal.

Petitioner here does not challenge the validity of the indictment, nor does he contest probable cause. Neither is the facial validity of the order transferring jurisdiction challenged. He seeks instead a pre-trial review of the proceedings in the juvenile court. The Legislature has provided a statutory procedure for review of the issues petitioner seeks to raise by habeas corpus. Family Code § 56.01 provides in part: "(a) An appeal from an order of a juvenile court is to the Texas Court of Civil Appeals and the case may be carried to the Texas Supreme Court by writ of error or upon certificate, as in civil cases generally...."(c) An appeal may be taken by or on behalf of the child from: (1) an order entered upon § 54.02 of this code respecting transfer of the child to criminal court for prosecution as an adult, * * *."

We hold the proper procedure for petitioner to secure review of the matters challenged here lies not in habeas corpus, but by statutory appeal in the civil court system of this State under the above quoted provision of the Family Code. The record reveals that petitioner failed to perfect review under the State statutory procedure that was available to him.

While this Court's original habeas corpus jurisdiction is limited, and while regulatory legislative action is not required before this Court can exercise its habeas corpus powers, and is not capable of abolishing or restricting the substantive scope of those powers, the exercise of our original habeas corpus jurisdiction is discretionary.

In light of the available statutory appeals procedure through the civil courts, we hold that the district court should not have entertained the application for habeas corpus, and we decline to exercise our original habeas corpus jurisdiction. Accordingly, we order the application for habeas corpus be dismissed and petitioner be remanded to custody.

It is so ordered.

Notes

(a) Texas presents special problems regarding review of waiver decisions. Juvenile cases are civil and, therefore, go to the Texas Supreme Court. Criminal cases, on the other hand, go to the Texas Court of Criminal Appeals. The intermediate appellate courts are now unified. Note that notwithstanding this bifurcated jurisdiction, both the Texas Court of Criminal Appeals and the Texas Supreme Court hear issues regarding the Family Code.

(b) Can Powell appeal the waiver hearing decision after conviction in the adult criminal court? Why?

(c) What would have happened if Powell had promptly appealed the waiver decision, but because of a backlog he was tried and convicted in adult criminal court before the appellate court's decision? Is it likely that an appellate court would reverse the waiver order in such circumstances?

Griffin v. State

765 S.W.2d 422 (Tex. Crim. App. 1989) (en banc)

CLINTON, Judge.

Appellant, a sixteen year old juvenile at the time of the offense, was convicted as a party to murder. Her punishment was assessed by the jury at fifteen years in the Texas Department of Corrections. The Dallas Court of Appeals reversed her conviction, holding that her written confession had been involuntary, and hence its admission into evidence violated the Due Process Clause of the United States Constitution.

The court of appeals reasoned that because an oral statement appellant gave to police upon her arrest was not obtained in accordance with the dictates of V.T.C.A., Family Code § 51.09(b), a subsequent written statement, though taken in compliance with that same provision, was nevertheless rendered involuntary in that appellant was unaware her earlier oral statement could not be used as evidence against her. In short, the court of appeals reversed on the basis of the "cat-out-of-the-bag theory of involuntariness. . . .

....

We discern two purposes to which the court of appeals utilized provisions of the Family Code. First, it specifically grounded its holding that appellant's oral confession was inadmissable in § 51.09(b)(2). Secondly, it found support for its conclusion that appellant's written confession was involuntary at least in part upon a general legislative attitude embodied in the Family Code that rights of a juvenile should be accorded greater solicitude than the same rights for an adult. The State maintains the court of appeals erred in thus relying upon the provisions of the Family Code in its determination of the voluntariness of appellant's written confession. Although in a certain respect we agree with the State on this point, we reject the specific argument made here.

The State relies principally upon *Swink v. State*, 617 S.W.2d 203 (Tex. Cr. App. 1981), to contend that provisions of the Family Code do not apply once a juvenile is certified for trial as an adult offender. In *Swink* the juvenile defendant claimed he "could not validly waive his rights, and consent to a warrantless search" because the requisites of Family Code § 51.09(a) had not been met. Noting that the searches in issue had not been conducted by authority of the defendant's consent, and were therefore not predicated upon waiver of any of his rights, a panel for the Court continued: "Moreover, the section upon which [the defendant] relies speaks only in terms of proceedings under Title 3 of the Family Code. The complained of actions in this case did not occur under that title." The Court neither elaborated upon nor cited authority in support of this proposition.

In apparent conflict with this *ipse dixit* in *Swink,* is the Court's earlier decision in *Lovell v. State*, which the court of appeals herein found dispositive. There a juvenile's written confession was obtained in violation of § 51.09, as it read prior to amendment in 1975, in that no attorney had been present when he waived his *Miranda* rights. Because presence of an attorney is not a prerequisite to waiver of these rights under Article 38.22 [Code of Criminal Procedure], it became necessary for the Court to determine which provision would prevail in view of Family Code § 54.02(h), prescribing that upon transfer of a juvenile for criminal proceedings, he be dealt with as an adult in accordance with the Code of Criminal Procedure. Using principles of code construction now found in §§ 311.025 and 311.026 of the Government Code, the Court found § 51.09, to prevail, both because it was enacted at a later point in time than Article 38.22, and because it was found to be the more specific. Even though § 51.09 (now § 51.09(a)), the same provision construed in *Swink* is facially applicable only to "proceedings under this title," the Court in *Lovell* found it operable in the context of the eventual criminal trial, rendering the juvenile's confession inadmissible in that proceeding.

Relying on *Lovell* for authority, the Court recently expounded: "Until the moment transfer is ordered, the juvenile is cloaked with the trappings of a non-criminal proceeding with attendant safeguards such as greater protections in the areas of confession law and notice requirements. * * * After transfer to the criminal system, the juvenile retains any more protective safeguards afforded him as a juvenile * * * as well as other safeguards afforded him under the Code of Criminal Procedure." *Vasquez v. State.* Thus, since *Swink* the Court has spoken in even broader terms than in *Lovell* indicating that issues involving substantive rights of pretransfer juveniles, such as legality of detention or a confession, though raised in the criminal forum, shall be controlled by applicable provisions of the Family Code.

Because appellant was a juvenile when she made it, the court of appeals did not err in measuring legality of her oral confession against § 51.09(b)(2). Nor do we fault the court of appeals for invoking the greater protections afforded to juveniles by the Family Code in general, except inasmuch as it purported to rely upon the legislative attitude to define the parameters of federal due process analysis. To the extent it conflicts with our opinion today, *Swink v. State*, is overruled.

Vasquez v. Texas

739 S.W.2d 37 (Tex. Crim App. 1987) (en banc)

OPINION ON APPELLANT'S PETITION FOR DISCRETIONARY REVIEW

McCORMICK, Judge.

After appellant was certified as an adult, he was convicted of capital murder and assessed a mandatory life sentence. On direct appeal, he contended that his confession and a monogrammed cigarette lighter belonging to the deceased were improperly admitted into evidence as both were fruits of an illegal warrantless arrest. * * * We granted appellant's petition for discretionary review to determine whether § 52.01 impermissibly entitles a juvenile certified to be prosecuted as an adult fewer protections under the laws of arrest and search than other adults coming within the purview of Chapter 14 of the Texas Code of Criminal Procedure. We will affirm.

. . . .

The appeals court first determined that an apparent conflict exists between Article 14.04 [Code of criminal Procedure] and Family Code § 52.01. Construing the two provisions with regard to the Code Construction Act, the appeals court held § 52.01 to be the more specific statute pertaining to the arrest of minors. Applying the same construction principles to what it termed an apparent conflict between the provisions of § 52.01(a)(2) and (3) and (b), the appeals court was of the opinion that a child may be taken into custody if he meets any one of the four criteria of § 52.01(a). Finally, turning its attention to appellant's contention that his arrest violated the Fourth and Fourteenth Amendments to the United States Constitution and Article I, Section 9 of the Texas Constitution, that court concluded that no Fourth Amendment violation occurred since there was probable cause for the arrest, the less stringent detention requirements for children did not violate principles of equal protection or due process, and that appellant was entitled to no greater protection under Article I, Section 9 of the Constitution than under the Fourth Amendment.

In his sole ground for review, appellant contends that the appeals court erred in determining that a juvenile certified to be prosecuted as an adult "is entitled to fewer protections under the law of arrest and search than a similarly situated adult" by virtue of § 52.01. Appellant correctly points out that, had he been arrested as an adult, his warrantless seizure would have been in violation of Article 14.04 since the State was unable to demonstrate that some enumerated exception to the general warrant requirement applied.

At first blush appellant's argument appears meritorious, bringing into question fundamental issues of due process and equal protection. Upon further reflection, however, it becomes apparent that appellant's claim is based upon a faulty premise. Appellant would have this Court examine his "arrest" as a *juvenile* not at the time he was taken into custody but only after he was certified as an adult and the cause transferred to criminal district court. In arguing that he was denied the protection afforded *other* adults, appellant ignores the reality that his detention arose outside the adult criminal justice system.

Article 14.04, states:

"Where it is shown by satisfactory proof to a peace officer, upon the representation of a credible person, that a felony has been committed, and that the offender is about to escape, so that there is no time to procure a warrant, such peace officer may, without warrant, pursue and arrest the accused."

In comparison with Article 14.04, Family Code § 52.01, provides, in pertinent part:

"(a) A child may be taken into custody:

"(1) pursuant to an order of the juvenile court under the provisions of this subtitle;

"(2) pursuant to the laws of arrest;

"(3) by a law-enforcement officer if there are reasonable grounds to believe that the child has engaged in delinquent conduct or conduct indicating a need for supervision; or

"(4) by a probation officer if there are reasonable grounds to believe that the child has violated a condition of probation imposed by the juvenile court.

"(b) The taking of a child into custody is not an arrest except for the purpose of determining the validity of taking him into custody or the validity of a search under the laws and constitution of this state or of the United States."

Restated, the issue before us is whether Article 14.04 applies to the warrantless detention and taking into custody of a juvenile suspect and, if it does not apply to juveniles, whether a juvenile situated in the shoes of appellant is denied equal protection or due process of law.

The rule favoring arrest with warrant is not constitutionally mandated but is a product of legislative action. Article I, Section 9 of the Texas Constitution merely requires that an arrest conducted pursuant to a warrant shall be based upon probable cause.

Along with Article 14.04, the remainder of Chapter 14 of the Code of Criminal Procedure provides certain enumerated exceptions to the general warrant requirement mandated by Chapter 15 of the Code. Although these are not the only exceptions contained in our State statutes, Chapter 14 and especially Article 14.04 are the focus in this cause.

The cardinal rule of statutory construction is to ascertain the legislative intent in enacting a statute. Such intent and a determination of the meaning of a statute is to be based upon the language of the statute itself. As in the case of an adult arrested pursuant to Chapter 14 of the code, we believe that the Legislature, in adopting Article 52.01 of the Family Code, has expressed its intent to allow a juvenile suspect to be taken into custody without a warrant if certain predicate procedures are met. Subsection (b) of that article clearly states that the taking into custody of a juvenile suspect is not to be considered as an "arrest" except for purposes of determining the *validity* of that "arrest." The validity of the "arrest" is to be measured, in turn, according to the dictates of state law and the respective guarantees and protections found in the Fourth Amendment, Fourteenth Amendment and Article I, Section 9 of the Texas Constitution. By setting out four permissible methods of taking a juvenile into custody, the Legislature has demonstrated its intent to allow custodial detention of a minor suspect in a more liberal manner under the Family Code than other individuals arrested pursuant to the procedures outlined in the Code of Criminal Procedure.

At first glance, it would appear that the "arrest" provisions in the two Codes are in conflict since both generally provide for the custodial detention of an individual under various circumstances of state law. However, even though dealing with the same general subject of arrest, we find that the persons involved and the objects of the two provisions at issue are distinct. Article 14.04, along with the remainder of Chapter 14 of the Code of Criminal Procedure, provides for an action conducted pursuant to a criminal proceeding. Article 52.01 is by its very nature a civil statute and [lies] outside the criminal system. The purpose of the Legislature in enacting the sections of the Family Code pertaining to juvenile offenders is set out in §51.01 of that Code:

"This title shall be construed to effectuate the following public purposes:

"(1) to provide for the care, the protection, and the wholesome moral, mental, and physical development of children coming within its provisions;

"(2) to protect the welfare of the community and to control the commission of unlawful acts by children;

"(3) consistent with the protection of the public interest, to remove from children committing unlawful acts the taint of criminality and the consequences of criminal behavior and to substitute a program of treatment, training, and rehabilitation;

"(4) to achieve the foregoing purposes in a family environment whenever possible, separating the child from his parents only when necessary for his welfare or in the interest of public safety and when a child is removed from his family, to give him the care that should be provided by parents; and

"(5) to provide a simple judicial procedure through which the provisions of this title are executed and enforced and in which the parties are assured a fair hearing and their constitutional and other legal rights recognized and enforced."

In line with these general guidelines, the juvenile court has exclusive jurisdiction over a juvenile until it properly certifies its action and waives jurisdiction in accord with the provisions of Family Code §§51.04 and 54.02. Delinquency proceedings are civil in nature and the provisions of the Texas Code of Criminal Procedure do not apply unless the Legislature evinces a contrary intent.

The Legislature, in adopting the provisions relating to the custodial detention of a juvenile, has demonstrated its awareness of the rule favoring warrants by including subsection (a)(2) in Article 52.01, which allows a juvenile to be taken into custody "pursuant to the laws of arrest." This provision provides police necessary flexibility in making arrests where the age of the offender is not known. Subsection (a)(3), on the other hand, allows for a more liberal manner of taking a known juvenile into custody for further investigation without the formal stigmatizing procedures accompanying an adult arrest. At the same time, the procedure allows the State to exercise limited control over a juvenile whose conduct has demonstrated a need for supervision and some as yet unknown level of punishment or rehabilitation.

Given the dissimilar individuals covered by the two provisions, the different objectives sought and the fact that the Legislature has mandated that the child is not "arrested" for purposes of criminal action until a juvenile transfer order is entered, we do not find the two statutes to be in irreconcilable conflict so as to require the type of construction used by the Court of Appeals below. To the contrary, we find that the Legislature has evinced its intent to distinguish the "arrest" of juveniles from that of adult offenders as shown by the pertinent juvenile provision.

Even if the two provisions at issue were to be in conflict, the Code Construction Act applies generally to both the Family Code and the Code of Criminal Procedure. Pursuant to that act, we would agree that Article 52.01, because it more specifically addresses the custodial detention of *juvenile* offenders, is the more specific enactment and controls over Article 14.04 of the Criminal Code. We, therefore, hold that Article 14.04 does not apply to the warrantless "arrest" of a juvenile offender. Appellant, being detained pursuant to Article 51.02 of the Family Code, was not entitled by statute to the same protections his adult counterpart would expect as a detainee in a criminal prosecution. Indeed, after initial detainment for further investigation, appellant was entitled to and received greater protections than he would had he been arrested as an adult. Review of the record before us shows that appellant was treated in a manner entirely consistent with the procedures set out in the Family Code and was not denied his rights as a juvenile nor denied due process of the law.

We further find that appellant was not denied equal protection of the law by manner of his detention under § 52.01. Article I, Section 3 of the Texas Constitution and the Fourteenth Amendment to the Federal Constitution secure to all persons similarly situated equal protection under the laws of this State and the United States. In the absence of a suspect classification, a state law is not repugnant to either constitutional provision so long as unequal treatment of persons is based upon a reasonable and substantial classification of persons. Unequal treatment of persons under a state law which is founded upon unreasonable and unsubstantial classification constitutes discriminating state action and violates both the state and federal constitutions.

Juveniles and adult criminal defendants are not "similarly situated" until the former is certified as an adult and comes within the purview of the adult criminal system. But, even assuming a similar stance at point of trial, there is no difficulty in perceiving a rational basis for application of Article 52.01 to juveniles ultimately tried as adults. The provisions of the Family Code pertaining to delinquency are civil in nature and were enacted both to allow juveniles to avoid the stigmatizing effect of arrest and to ensure that any child who is without proper supervision may be placed back into a supervised environment for the protection of the child and of the rest of society. The detention itself must meet constitutional and statutory muster to be valid. Until the moment transfer is ordered, the juvenile is cloaked with the trappings of a non-criminal proceeding with attendant safeguards such as greater protections in the areas of confession law and notice requirements. After transfer to the criminal system, the juvenile still retains many more protective safeguards afforded him as a juvenile.

In enacting Article 52.01(a)(3), the Legislature has pursued a rational course in allowing further investigation of an incident involving a juvenile by requiring that the police may only take a juvenile into custody if the "arrest" meets statutory and constitutional muster. Article 52.01(a)(3), as a separate and distinct method of "arresting" a juvenile as compared to an adult suspect, provides a vehicle to be used in lieu of formal arrest procedures contemplated under the criminal code.

CLINTON, Judge, dissenting.

In the Houston (1st) Court of Appeals appellant presented two points of error arising out of what he contended is an illegal warrantless arrest in that it is not authorized by Article 14.04.

The Houston Court believed his contention "presumes that when a minor is taken into custody without a warrant that Article 14.04 is applicable to the detention rather than § 52.01 of the [Family Code]." For its part, the majority here flatly holds that Article 14.04 "does not apply to the warrantless 'arrest' of a juvenile offender." Neither is correct, in my judgment.

In the trial court, having been certified as an adult and transferred to a district court for trial, appellant objected as an adult to admission in evidence of fruits of an illegal arrest in a criminal action on an indictment for capital murder. Family Code § 54.02(h) provides that after being transferred the child "shall be dealt with as an adult and in accordance with the Code of Criminal Procedure, 1965," and that such "transfer of custody is an arrest." Neither the Houston Court nor the majority opinion here ever satisfactorily explains how it is that a certified child and an adult are not similarly situated upon being indicted for a penal offense. In Steele, *Delinquent Children and Children in Need of Supervision,* 13 Tex. Tech. L. Rev. 1145 (1982), also cited in the majority opinion, legislative intent is plainly stated, *viz:*

" 'Pursuant to the laws of arrest' in subsection (a)(2) means that a child may be taken into custody *under the same circumstances that a law enforcement officer is authorized to arrest an adult.* * * *

....

Subsection (b) is * * * designed to shelter the child from the stigmatizing effects of an arrest, *while providing him with the legal protections that surround the arrest of adults.* These include the right to exclude evidence seized pursuant to an unlawful arrest. * * *"

Although §54.02(a)(3) provides that a juvenile court may waive its exclusive original jurisdiction and transfer a child to district court for criminal proceedings if "after full investigation and hearing" it determines existence of a prescribed reason that "requires criminal proceedings," the courts have held that a transfer hearing is "like a grand jury proceeding and, therefore, is not the proper forum to litigate [such issues as] legal admissibility of a confession" or hearsay evidence "because it is not the function of a transfer proceeding to determine guilt."

Thus a child may not complain of an illegal arrest until he stands accused as an adult in district court. When he does then and there, the majority says his complaint will be decided under its own construction of his former status as a juvenile rather than his certified status as a adult.

Without its construction there would be no equal protection question raised. Since he has become similarly situated with any adult offender, it seems to me there is *great* "difficulty in perceiving a rational basis" for denying a certified adult equal rights of an adult under the law. The purported rationalization offered by the majority is woefully lacking in demonstrating there is one to justify stripping a certified adult of the protection afforded by Article 14.04 from a warrantless arrest that is vouchsafed to every adult citizen.

Notes

(a) Which opinion in *Vasquez* furthers the purposes of the juvenile court system?

(b) Note the goose-gander effect of holding that provisions of the juvenile code apply to juveniles waived over to criminal court. Does the *Griffin* decision mandate the result in *Vasquez?*

Ex Parte Green

688 S.W.2d 555 (Tex. Crim. App. 1985) (en banc)

OPINION

CLINTON, Judge.

This is a postconviction writ of habeas corpus brought before the Court pursuant to Article 11.07, [Code of Criminal Procedure]

To three separate indictments alleging aggravated robbery applicant plead guilty; thereupon he was convicted and sentenced to concurrent ten year sentences. Applicant here contends that he should be given credit on his sentences for time spent in a juvenile detention center between his having been taken into custody upon committing the robberies and his being sentenced in the causes.

At the time of the commission of these offenses applicant was sixteen years old. On the night of January 14, 1983 police officers observed applicant and an accomplice in the act of robbing and sexually molesting three young women in Dallas. Applicant was taken into custody and referred to the Dallas County Juvenile Department's detention center. On January 17, presumably as a result of a detention hearing pursuant to Family Code, §54.01, applicant was detained further on the order of the juvenile court. Applicant was released on March 21, 1983. Subsequently, on August 23, 1983 he was "re-arrested." The instant indictments were filed August 31. The judgment in each of the three robbery convictions grants applicant credit for time served in jail beginning August 23.

Applicant now contends that by operation of Article 42.03, §2(a)[2] he is entitled to credit for the 67 days, from January 14 until March 21, that he was confined in the juvenile detention center. He asserts that his detention under the court order "effectively held him in constructive custody," and that "[w]hen the applicant does not have a choice of custodian and is held on a particular cause, he is entitled to credit for time served."

The question is thus presented whether time spent by a juvenile in a detention center, where he was confined as a result of behavior which, if committed by an adult would constitute a penal offense, may be credited to a sentence he subsequently receives in a court of criminal jurisdiction to which the case has been transferred.

The district court recommended that relief be denied. In its conclusions of law the court reasoned that, because the policy considerations in detaining juveniles are not comparable to those which underly the incarceration of adult offenders, detention of a juvenile pursuant to Family Code, Chapters 52 and 53 should not be treated as "constructive custody" for purposes of implementing penal sanctions. The court concluded that "[b]ecause juvenile confinement is not considered punishment, see *Schall v. Martin,* the legislature [in enacting Article 42.03, §2(a)] could not have intended for that time to be applied towards a person's sentence."

We disagree.

To compare the respective policies behind juvenile confinement and adult incarceration in this context is to miss the point. More illuminating for purposes of construing Article 42.03, §2(a) is the comparison between pretrial detention of adults and the detention of a juvenile prior to his delinquency adjudication hearing.

That juvenile detention is not considered punishment is of no moment; adult confinement prior to trial is not for punishment either. As the Supreme Court pointed out in *Schall:* "It is axiomatic that '[d]ue process requires that a pretrial detainee not be punished. In *Bell* it was observed: "A person lawfully committed to pretrial detention has not been adjudged guilty of any crime. He has had only a 'judicial determination of probable cause as a prerequisite to [the] extended restraint of [his] liberty following arrest. Under such circumstances, the Government concedely may detain him to ensure his presence at trial and may subject him to the restrictions and conditions of the detention facility so long as those conditions and restrictions do not amount to punishment, or

---

2. Article 42.03, §2(a) reads:
   "In all criminal cases the judge of the court in which the defendant was convicted shall give the defendant credit on his sentence for the time that the defendant has spent in jail in said cause, from the time of his arrest and confinement until his sentence by the trial court."

otherwise violate the Constitution." *Schall* supports the proposition that neither adults *nor* juveniles may be constitutionally detained pretrial for purposes of *punishment*. Hence, the court's reliance on *Schall* proves inapposite, and its invocation of policy differences as a justification for denying relief, insubstantial.

Though it has been held that generally there is no Federal constitutional right to credit for time served prior to sentence, the Legislature has amended Article 42.03, § 2, to make it mandatory that the trial court award such credit. In so doing the Legislature recognized that pretrial confinement, though not instigated for purposes of punishment, nevertheless has an incidental punitive effect in that it deprives the detainee of his liberty. To compensate for this deprivation the Legislature provided that whenever that detainee is ultimately assessed a term of imprisonment the convicting court shall grant credit to his sentence for time spent in pretrial detention, even though the detention was not imposed *at the time* for purposes of punishment.

Once a juvenile is "certified" as an adult under V.T.C.A. Family code, § 54.02, it makes no difference that "said cause" began as a civil proceeding, since "[o]n transfer of the child for criminal proceedings, he shall be dealt with as an adult and in accordance with the Texas Code of Criminal Procedure, 1965." Section 54.02(h). We do not think that in enacting Article 42.03, § 2(a) the Legislature intended that an individual initially detained as a juvenile and later certified an adult, then prosecuted and sentenced accordingly, should be treated any differently than one who is initially detained as an adult.

We therefore hold applicant is entitled to the flat time credit he seeks from January 14, 1983 to March 21, 1983. A copy of this opinion will be forwarded to the Texas Department of Corrections.

It is so ordered.

Note

Is *Green* consistent with *Vasquez*?

Robinson v. State
707 S.W.2d 47 (Tex. Crim. App. 1986) (en banc)
OPINION

W.C. DAVIS, Judge.

After appellant was certified as an adult, a jury convicted him of aggravated robbery. The trial court assessed punishment at twenty years' confinement.

. . . .

On March 7, 1980 appellant was placed in a juvenile detention center after allegedly committing aggravated robbery, aggravated kidnapping and aggravated rape. He was sixteen years of age at the time. On June 17, 1980, the juvenile court waived jurisdiction of the case and transferred jurisdiction to the 248th Judicial District Court to deal with appellant as an adult. Appellant was arrested the same day and a felony complaint was filed. On August 27, 1980, he was indicted for aggravated robbery and aggravated kidnapping. The State announced ready on October 20, 1980, and a pre-trial hearing was held on October 21, on appellant's "Motion to Set Aside the Indictment for Failure to Grant a Speedy Trial." The court overruled the motion.

Appellant contends that his right to a speedy trial was violated if the time is calculated either from March 7, when he was first placed in a juvenile detention center, or from June 17, when he was certified to be tried as an adult.

The juvenile court has exclusive jurisdiction over a juvenile until it properly certifies its action and waives jurisdiction in accord with the provisions of the Family Code. Delinquency proceedings are civil in nature and the provisions of the Texas Code of Criminal Procedure do not apply. Thus, the provisions of the Code of Criminal Procedure, including Art. 32A.02, do not apply until a defendant is certified as an adult and is transferred to a criminal court.

In the instant case, appellant was certified as an adult, arrested, and a felony complaint filed against him, on June 17, 1980. Thus, June 17, 1980, is the date upon which the criminal action against appellant commenced for the purposes of the Texas Speedy Trial Act.

. . . .

The judgment is affirmed.

CLINTON, J., dissents.

TEAGUE, Judge, dissenting.

I am compelled to file this dissenting opinion because the majority opinion is in conflict with what a majority of this Court recently stated and held in *Ex parte Green* regarding the applicability of the Code of Criminal Procedure to juveniles. . . .

In *Ex parte Green,* a majority of this Court stated and held the following:

> Once a juvenile is "certified" as an adult under Family Code, Section 54.02, it makes no difference that "said cause" began as a civil proceeding ... since "[o]n transfer of the child for criminal proceedings, he shall be dealt with as an adult and in accordance with the Texas Code of Criminal Procedure, 1965." Section 54.02(h), supra. *We do not think that in enacting Article 42.03, Sec. 2(a) [Code of Criminal Procedure] the Legislature intended that an individual detained as a juvenile and later certified an adult, then prosecuted and sentenced accordingly, should be treated any differently than one who is initially detained as an adult.*

But, today, the majority opinion states the following:

> Delinquency proceedings are civil in nature and the provisions of the Texas Code of Criminal Procedure do not apply ... Thus, *the provisions of the Code of Criminal Procedure, including Art. 32A.02, do not apply until a defendant is certified as an adult and is transferred to a criminal court"* (my emphasis).

If the provisions of Art. 42.03, Sec. 2(a) of the Code of Criminal Procedure can be used to give a juvenile credit on his sentence for the time he was confined in a juvenile detention center, which was before he was certified to stand trial as an adult, then I must ask: Why isn't the time that a juvenile was confined in a juvenile detention center not to be considered when the provisions of Art. 32A.02, V.A.C.C.P., the Speedy Trial Act, are involved? Shouldn't the majority opinion at least explain to the members of the Bench and Bar of this State how in one instance the Code of Criminal Procedure can be invoked and applied to a criminal cause that involves a juvenile, before he is implicated in the adult criminal process, but in another instance, that also involves a juvenile who is implicated in the adult criminal process, the Code of Criminal Procedure does not become effective "until a defendant is certified as an adult and is transferred to a criminal court"? I think so.

Note

Note that the civil-criminal dichotomy we examined in Chapter 4 continues to plague both the juvenile and criminal courts after waiver of a child to adult criminal court.

F. Blended, Determinate and Extended Jurisdiction Sentencing

Patrick Griffin, *Trying and Sentencing Juveniles as Adults: An Analysis of State Transfer and Blended Sentencing Laws*

Published by the National Center for Juvenile Justice (2003)

Mechanisms for taking "hard cases" out of the juvenile justice system have been available for as long as there have been juvenile courts. But in recent years, and especially in the past decade, these mechanisms have become a much more prominent feature of states' approaches to serious juvenile offending. Transfer laws—which spell out conditions under which juveniles may be prosecuted in the same manner as adults—have tended to proliferate, to become more expansive in their scope and more automatic in their operation. And *blended sentencing* laws—which can expose even those who remain under juvenile court jurisdiction to the risk of adult criminal sanctions—have become commonplace as well.

The following discussion of state law in this area is intended to provide a broad overview of the current mechanisms by which juveniles may reach the criminal justice system as a result of offenses committed as juveniles. State transfer laws define categories of juveniles who, because of their ages, their past records, or the seriousness of the charges against them, may—or in some cases must—be tried in courts of criminal jurisdiction. Transfer laws are concerned exclusively with the forum in which cases against serious juvenile offenders will be heard.

Blended sentencing laws, on the other hand, focus not on the trial forum but on the correctional system (juvenile or adult) in which the serious juvenile offender will be sanctioned. Some blended sentencing provisions permit a juvenile who has been "moved up" to the criminal court system for trial to be "moved down" again for sanctioning. Others perform the reverse function, essentially giving juvenile court judges the power to send uncooperative juveniles to prison.

Transfer laws are classified primarily according to where they locate responsibility for determining the trial forum.... Although blended sentencing laws are sometimes considered as a single group, it is more useful to classify them according to whether they provide juvenile court judges with criminal sentencing options, or allow criminal court judges to impose juvenile dispositions:

15 states have *juvenile blended sentencing* schemes that empower juvenile courts to impose adult criminal sanctions on certain categories of serious juvenile offenders. Most of these laws authorize the court to combine a juvenile disposition with a suspended criminal sentence—which functions as a kind of guarantee of good behavior. If the juvenile cooperates, he or she will remain in the juvenile sanctioning system; if not, he or she may be sent to the adult one. Although the practical effect of a sentencing provision of this type

may depend on a number of factors—including how it interacts with the state's transfer laws—juvenile blended sentencing generally increases the overall hazard that a juvenile offender will receive an adult criminal sentence, either immediately or eventually. In that sense, although it may be more flexible, it functions somewhat like an expanded transfer law.

17 states have *criminal blended sentencing* laws, on the other hand, under which criminal courts, in sentencing transferred juveniles, may impose sanctions that would ordinarily be available only to juvenile courts. Criminal blended sentencing provides a mechanism whereby individual juveniles who have left the juvenile system for criminal prosecution may be returned to it for sanctioning purposes. Again, sometimes the return to the juvenile system is only conditional, with a suspended adult sentence serving as a guarantee of good behavior. But the overall tendency of criminal blended sentencing is to soften or mitigate the effects of existing transfer laws, at least in individual cases.

. . . .

A total of 15 states empower their juvenile courts to impose criminal sanctions on some category of serious juvenile offenders. Juvenile blended sentencing laws bear a broad resemblance to transfer laws—in that they define some group of juveniles who may be treated as though they were adults, at least for sanctioning purposes. Though the specific effects of juvenile blended sentencing laws may depend on many factors, their general tendency is to expand the sanctioning powers of the juvenile court, and thus to increase the hazards and penalties to which young offenders may be exposed.

The most common type of juvenile blended sentencing scheme—sometimes called "inclusive" blended sentencing—allows juvenile court judges to impose both juvenile and suspended adult sanctions on certain categories of offenders. In Kansas, for example, following a plea or finding of guilty in an "extended jurisdiction juvenile" (EJJ) prosecution, the court must impose a juvenile disposition and an adult criminal sentence, with the execution of the latter "stayed on the condition that the juvenile offender not violate the provisions of the juvenile sentence and not commit a new offense." Juvenile blended sentencing laws in 11 states follow this inclusive model. A juvenile offender subject to a combination sentence in one of these states is allowed to remain in the juvenile sanctioning system only conditionally, with a criminal sentence dangling overhead as a way of encouraging cooperation and discouraging future misconduct. Most of the states with inclusive blended sentencing statutes simply require courts to impose combination sentences in qualifying cases.

. . . .

Four states have juvenile blended sentencing schemes that do not feature combination sentences. New Mexico has an "exclusive" blended sentencing provision, which simply gives the juvenile court the option of imposing an immediately effective criminal sanction on a qualifying Youthful Offender, in lieu of a juvenile one. The three remaining states—Texas, Colorado, and Rhode Island—have variations on the "contiguous" form of blended sentencing, under which a juvenile court in certain types of cases is authorized to impose a sentence of commitment that would be in force beyond (sometimes far beyond) the age of its extended jurisdiction. At least initially, the commitment is to the juvenile correctional authority, but the offender may later be transferred to an adult facility. There is no combination sentence—and no assurance that the transfer to adult corrections will occur only in the event of misbehavior on the juvenile's part. In fact, the juvenile may well be required to serve out the whole sentence without any proof of subsequent misconduct. But at the time of any proposed transfer from juvenile to adult correctional authorities, the sentence must be formally reconsidered.

Statutes that define eligibility for juvenile blended sentencing focus on age, offense, and prior record characteristics, just as state transfer laws do. In fact, juvenile blended sentencing statutes in two states—Kansas and Minnesota—have the same eligibility criteria as existing transfer laws. Arguably, in these states, juvenile blended sentencing simply provides a more flexible, less severe, "last chance" alternative to transfer. In Minnesota, for example, a juvenile accused of a felony committed when he or she was at least fourteen may be certified for adult criminal prosecution at the juvenile court's discretion, or instead subjected to an extended juvenile jurisdiction (EJJ) prosecution in juvenile court. In Kansas, which authorizes waiver of juveniles as young as 10, the county or district attorney may instead move to have any waiver eligible case designated an EJJ prosecution. Not only the eligibility requirements, but the procedures, presumptions, and factors to be considered in determining whether to designate a case an EJJ prosecution are identical to those involved in a hearing to consider whether a juvenile should be prosecuted as an adult.

Juvenile blended sentencing eligibility criteria in two other states—Alaska and Illinois—are drawn more narrowly than transfer criteria, and thus cover only a subset of those who are technically eligible for transfer.

But juvenile blended sentencing provisions in ten states—Arkansas, Colorado, Connecticut, Massachusetts, Michigan, Montana, New Mexico, Ohio, Rhode Island, and Texas—*expand* the categories of juveniles for whom adult sanctions are a possibility, in some cases significantly. For example, Montana's EJJ statute simply leaves out the minimum age requirements that restrict the scope of the state's transfer laws. With limited exceptions, Montana's direct file law permits criminal prosecution only of 16-year-olds, and its statutory exclusions apply only to 17-year-olds. But EJJ provisions may be invoked at the prosecutor's option on juveniles of any age who are accused of offenses covered by the direct file and statutory exclusion laws.

Similarly, in Ohio, there are no transfer categories, discretionary or automatic, that apply to juveniles under 14. But under Ohio's blended sentencing law for "Serious Youthful Offenders" (SYOs), enacted in 2001, juveniles as young as 10 may receive suspended adult sentences following adjudication for certain serious offenses. It is true that the suspended adult portion of an SYO sentence may not be invoked until after the juvenile has reached the age of 14. But the offense/misconduct threshold that must be satisfied at that point is quite low: the adult sentence may be triggered, for example, by conduct that "creates a substantial risk to the safety or security" of the community, the victim, or (in the case of juveniles who are still in custody) the institution, as long as the misconduct "demonstrates that the person is unlikely to be rehabilitated during the remaining period of juvenile jurisdiction."

In states in which blended sentencing eligibility is broader than transfer eligibility, juvenile blended sentencing clearly expands the pool of offenders *potentially* at risk of adult sanctions. But whether it *actually* sends more juveniles to prison depends on many factors, including the way it is used by decision-makers—whether as a mitigating alternative to transfer, or as a new tool for an "in-between" category of cases that would not otherwise have merited transfer.

Conversely, even blended sentencing provisions that apply only to juveniles who are already technically at risk of adult sanctions (on account of transfer laws) may nevertheless increase their actual risk. In a state such as Kansas, for instance, in which virtually all cases are waiver eligible—at least on paper—it is possible that some set of juveniles will be found "EJJ-worthy" who would never be considered "waiver-worthy." For one thing, the EJJ designation is not nearly so final or irrevocable. Not only is the adult sanction stayed on condition of good behavior, but the juvenile is entitled at age 18 to a hearing reviewing the necessity of continuing the juvenile disposition. If necessary, another review must be held no more than three years later. However, if the court at any time finds by substantial evidence that the juvenile has violated the conditions of the juvenile disposition, it must revoke the stay and impose the adult sentence.

A total of 17 states authorize their criminal courts, in sentencing juveniles who have been tried and convicted as adults, to impose juvenile dispositions rather than criminal ones under some circumstances. Like blended sentences imposed by juvenile courts, criminal blended sentences may sometimes consist of a combination of juvenile and criminal sanctions — with the latter suspended as long as the offender cooperates in the dispositional program. But all criminal blended sentencing provisions permit individual juveniles who have already left the juvenile system for criminal prosecution to be returned to it, at least conditionally, for supervision, treatment, and rehabilitative programs available only to juveniles.

Criminal blended sentencing laws can be broadly divided into "exclusive" and "inclusive" types. Exclusive blended sentencing laws give courts an either/or choice between juvenile and adult sanctions. Inclusive laws allow them to impose both in combination.

The most common form of criminal blended sentencing scheme is exclusive. A provision of this kind can serve as a kind of "emergency exit" from the criminal justice system for those who, at the time of sentencing, appear to be still capable of benefitting from the juvenile one.

Ten states have exclusive criminal blended sentencing provisions of one kind or another. These laws vary considerably in scope, however. The broadest make juvenile sanctions available to the sentencing court whenever a juvenile has been prosecuted as an adult, regardless of the offense. In West Virginia, any juvenile who has been tried and convicted following transfer may receive a juvenile disposition in lieu of a criminal sentence. Similarly, Nebraska authorizes a criminal court to impose a juvenile disposition on any juvenile except one convicted of a crime for which a life term is required by law.

On the other hand, Kentucky and Massachusetts have the narrowest possible form of criminal blended sentencing, applicable only in one restricted set of circumstances — when a juvenile in criminal court pleads or is found guilty of a lesser offense that would not have been subject to criminal prosecution in the first place. In such cases, laws in both states give courts no option but to impose juvenile dispositions.

Some other states have exclusive criminal blended sentencing laws that apply only to juveniles being sentenced for offenses less serious than the ones for which they were prosecuted; however, they give courts somewhat more flexibility. For instance, in New Mexico, a juvenile who is prosecuted as an adult for first-degree murder but convicted of a lesser offense is subject to disposition as a "Youthful Offender" — and thus may receive either juvenile or criminal penalties. Wisconsin requires a criminal court to opt for a juvenile disposition when a juvenile is found to have committed an offense that would not have qualified for exclusion or waiver, but it also permits the court to consider the juvenile disposition option for offenses that *would* have qualified, if the juvenile demonstrates by clear and convincing evidence that "it would be in the best interests of the juvenile and of the public."

Several states, like Wisconsin, call for a kind of formal "fitness hearing" when a juvenile is to be sentenced for a lesser offense. An Illinois criminal court, when sentencing a juvenile who has been tried for an offense excluded from juvenile jurisdiction but found to have committed an offense that is not excluded, must impose a juvenile disposition, unless the state requests a hearing to determine if the juvenile should be sentenced as an adult. At the hearing, the court must consider factors similar to those the juvenile court takes into account in deciding whether to grant a motion to transfer a juvenile for criminal proceedings.

California has a provision that is similar in effect, but considerably more complicated in design. First, when a juvenile is convicted of an offense that, in combination with the juvenile's age, would not have qualified for transfer to criminal court in the first place, the sentencing court must choose a juvenile disposition—or else remand the matter to the juvenile court for a disposition hearing. If a juvenile who was criminally prosecuted without the benefit of a preliminary fitness hearing (that is, for an offense qualifying for direct file or statutory exclusion) is convicted of an offense that, in combination with the juvenile's age, would merely have permitted a transfer to criminal court upon a showing of unfitness, the juvenile is entitled to a juvenile disposition or a remand, unless the prosecutor requests a fitness hearing and shows by a preponderance of the evidence that the juvenile is not "a fit and proper subject to be dealt with under the juvenile court law." If the same juvenile is convicted of an offense that would have given rise to a rebuttable presumption of unfitness, the court may impose a criminal sanction unless the *juvenile* requests and prevails at a post-conviction fitness hearing. Finally, subject to certain limitations, the court may order a juvenile disposition in any case in which (1) the juvenile and prosecutor agree and (2) the court finds that the order "would serve the best interests of justice, protection of the community, and the person being sentenced."

The criminal blended sentencing schemes of seven states feature combination sentencing, in which a juvenile receives both a juvenile disposition and a suspended criminal sentence. In Missouri, for instance, a criminal court that does not wish to impose a straight criminal sentence on a juvenile must impose a combination sentence, with execution of the criminal portion of the sentence suspended pending successful completion of the juvenile disposition. If the juvenile thereafter commits a violation or a new offense, the court may continue the juvenile disposition or revoke it and impose the adult sentence, as it sees fit. When the juvenile reaches the age of 17, a hearing must be held, after which the court must (1) continue the juvenile disposition, (2) place the juvenile on probation, or (3) revoke the suspension and transfer the juvenile to the Department of Corrections.

There are a number of variations on this basic theme. In several, the sentence is not formally denominated a combination sentence, but it functions as one. So in Iowa, the criminal sentencing of a "Youthful Offender" following a plea or verdict of guilty is deferred, and the youth is transferred back to the juvenile court for disposition. Before turning 18, however, the juvenile is returned to the trial court for a reconsideration hearing. After considering the juvenile court's report on the juvenile, the services available, and the interests of the juvenile and the community, the trial court may either continue the juvenile on Youthful Offender status or enter a criminal sentence, which may be a suspended sentence.

Florida and Michigan are other states that authorize what are in effect, though not in form, conditional sentences. In Florida, a juvenile may receive a straight juvenile disposition following prosecution in the criminal division of the circuit court. But if the juvenile thereafter "proves not to be suitable" for the disposition, he or she is liable to be recalled and resentenced as an adult. Florida juveniles may be found unsuitable for juvenile sanctions if they break the law while under sanctions or violate conditions imposed as part of their sanctions. In such cases, following a hearing, the sentencing court "may revoke the previous adjudication [of delinquency], impose an adjudication of guilt, and impose any sentence which it may lawfully impose" under the criminal sentencing laws.

In Michigan, a juvenile tried in circuit court must be sentenced "in the same manner as an adult" if convicted of any of a number of specified crimes. Otherwise, the court must conduct a sentencing hearing to determine whether to impose an adult sentence or order the juvenile placed on probation and committed to a juvenile facility. The court must impose an adult sentence unless it finds by a preponderance of the evidence that "the best interests of the public would be served" by a juvenile commitment. However, even in such a case, the court retains jurisdiction over the juvenile throughout the disposition, and must "conduct an annual review of the services being provided to the juvenile, the juvenile's placement, and the juvenile's progress in that placement." The court may order changes in the juvenile's placement on the basis of these reviews, "including, but not limited to, committing the juvenile to the jurisdiction of the department of corrections."

Of the states that give criminal courts other options than combination sentences in dealing with juveniles tried as adults, only two permit them to impose a juvenile disposition and leave it at that. In Idaho, upon conviction of any juvenile tried as an adult, the sentencing court is authorized to impose either a juvenile disposition or a suspended criminal sentence combined with a commitment to the custody of the Department of Juvenile Corrections. Likewise, under Virginia law, if a juvenile who has been tried as an adult is convicted of a merely waivable nonviolent felony, the court may choose from among three sentencing options: (1) a juvenile disposition, (2) an adult sentence, or (3) an adult sentence suspended on condition of successful completion of a juvenile disposition. If the juvenile is convicted of a violent felony qualifying for mandatory waiver or direct file treatment, however, the court must choose from among (1) a juvenile disposition combined with a suspended criminal sentence, (2) a "serious juvenile offender" disposition (involving an extended juvenile commitment up to seven years or age 21, whichever comes first) followed by a criminal sentence, or (3) a straight criminal sentence.

The laws of most states either dictate criminal handling of certain defined categories of juvenile offenders, or else place decisions about that handling solely in the hands of prosecutors. However, many of these states also have what might be called judicial corrective or "failsafe" mechanisms, by means of which, at some point in the process, criminal court judges may review the circumstances and make individualized determinations of juveniles' suitability for criminal prosecution or criminal sanctions. The two basic forms of fail-safe mechanism are reverse waiver and criminal blended sentencing:

Reverse waiver. The laws of 25 states allow a juvenile subject to prosecution in criminal court to petition to have the case transferred — or transferred back — to juvenile court. Generally, a criminal court judge making such a reverse waiver decision is guided by the same kinds of broad standards and considerations as a juvenile court in a waiver proceeding. In most cases, a reverse waiver hearing is held prior to trial, and if the reverse waiver is granted, the case is adjudicated in juvenile court. But three states — California, Colorado, and Oregon — permit reverse waiver only after the offender's guilt has been established; reverse waiver in these states is for disposition only.

Criminal blended sentencing. Even juveniles whose cases are handled in the criminal court system may ultimately be *sanctioned* in the juvenile correctional system. As noted above, 17 states have criminal blended sentencing laws authorizing their criminal courts, at least under some circumstances, to impose juvenile dispositions rather than criminal ones. By enacting a reverse waiver or criminal blended sentencing law, a state may simultaneously define a broad category of cases that it believes merit criminal handling and also ensure that its courts will have an opportunity to consider whether such handling is actually appropriate in individual cases.

Note

What are the advantages and disadvantages of each sentencing method discussed in the above essay? Which would you choose? Why?

In the Matter of the Welfare of L.J.S. and J.T.K.

539 N.W.2d 408 (Minn. Ct. App. 1996)

LANSING, Judge.

These consolidated certified questions raise constitutional challenges to the new extended jurisdiction juvenile statute and to the new presumption of certification applied in certain juvenile delinquency proceedings. The trial court in each case denied defense challenges to the constitutionality of the statute, but certified the questions as important and doubtful. We conclude that the statutes are constitutional and answer the consolidated certified questions in the negative.

FACTS

In 1994 the legislature amended the laws pertaining to juveniles to provide extended jurisdiction that allows the juvenile court to retain jurisdiction until age twenty-one and to impose a juvenile disposition subject to a stayed adult penalty that can be imposed if the juvenile violates the conditions of his disposition or commits a new offense. A second amendment provides for presumptive certification for adult prosecution for certain offenses if the juvenile is sixteen or seventeen. Presumptive certification may be rebutted by clear and convincing evidence that retaining the proceeding in juvenile court serves the public interest.

J.T.K. appeals an order allowing the prosecutor to designate an extended jurisdiction juvenile offense, and L.J.S. appeals an order applying presumptive certification. The petition filed against sixteen-year-old J.T.K. alleged terroristic threats and second and third degree assault on January 19, 1995. The petitions filed against seventeen-year-old L.J.S. alleged first degree burglary, aggravated robbery, and possession of a shotgun on March 3, 1995; and robbery, property damage, and fleeing from police on March 12, 1995.

ISSUES

The following issues are certified as important and doubtful:

I. Is the provision in Minn.Stat. § 260.126, subd. 1(2) for prosecutor-designated extended jurisdiction juvenile proceedings unconstitutionally vague?

II. Does the prosecutor-designated extended jurisdiction juvenile provision violate the separation of powers?

III. Does the presumptive certification statute, Minn.Stat. § 260.125, subd. 2a, violate equal protection?

IV. Does the presumptive certification statute violate due process by creating a mandatory irrebuttable presumption of certification?

V. Does the presumptive certification statute violate due process by placing on the juvenile the burden of persuasion?

ANALYSIS

I

The section of Minn. Stat. § 260.126 at issue provides that a proceeding involving a child alleged to have committed a felony offense is an extended jurisdiction juvenile prosecution if:

* * *

(2) the child was 16 or 17 years old at the time of the alleged offense; the child is alleged to have committed an offense for which the sentencing guidelines and applicable statutes presume a commitment to prison or to have committed any felony in which the child allegedly used a firearm; *and the prosecutor designated in the delinquency petition that the proceeding is an extended jurisdiction juvenile prosecution.*

* * *

J.T.K. asserts that this language is unconstitutionally vague and violates due process by creating the potential for arbitrary and discriminatory enforcement.

A statute must define a criminal offense with sufficient definiteness to meet due process standards. A penal statute must define the offense so that ordinary people can understand what is prohibited and so that those charged with enforcing the statute have minimal guidelines that prevent arbitrary and discriminatory enforcement. Of these two requirements, the prevention of arbitrary and discriminatory enforcement is the more important.

A prosecutor can designate an extended jurisdiction juvenile proceeding only if the juvenile is sixteen or seventeen years old and only if the petition alleges an offense with a presumptively executed guidelines sentence or an offense involving use of a firearm. These criteria are very specific. They are neither vague nor conducive to arbitrary and discriminatory enforcement.

The Minnesota Supreme Court upheld the previous juvenile reference statute against a vagueness challenge when reference depended on suitability for juvenile treatment or whether public safety was served by proceeding in juvenile court. The criteria in the current statute for prosecutor-designated extended jurisdiction juvenile prosecutions are much more specific. The statute does not lack minimal guidelines for extended jurisdiction juvenile designation or give too much discretion to prosecutors in deciding what cases to designate. We reject J.T.K.'s suggestion that a higher standard of definiteness should apply because the designation is made by the prosecutor rather than the court. Criminal statutes generally are judged by the guidance they provide to law enforcement and to prosecutors....

II

J.T.K. argues that the prosecutor's exclusive role in designating the extended jurisdiction juvenile proceedings under Minn.Stat. § 260.126, subd. 1(2) violates the separation of powers. He maintains that only the court can constitutionally designate a juvenile case as an extended jurisdiction juvenile proceeding because the designation sharply restricts the court's sentencing powers.

J.T.K. characterizes the prosecutor's designation of an extended jurisdiction juvenile prosecution as essentially a sentencing determination because it prevents the court from imposing a purely juvenile disposition. The state counters that the decision is merely a charging decision.

The Minnesota Supreme Court, in analyzing a similar issue, discounted the significance of the charging/sentencing distinction in juvenile proceedings: "Our examination of the juvenile court statute leads us to conclude that the legislature had the clear intent to make laws dealing with juvenile delinquency *sui generis.*" The statute's provision for varying means of designation — by the court itself, by the court on the prosecutor's recommendation, or by the prosecutor based on the specific criteria — suggests that this decision is *sui generis,* with no analogue in criminal procedure.

Furthermore, the U.S. Supreme Court in recent years has emphasized a "flexible understanding of separation of powers" that does not require a "hermetic division among the Branches." Even if the prosecutor's extended jurisdiction juvenile designation restricts to some degree the court's ultimate sentencing options, some interplay between the responsibilities of the executive and judicial branches is permitted. For instance, the well-established executive parole power and pardon authority impinge on a court's sentencing powers.

In analyzing a challenge to a similar federal statute, the D.C. Circuit Court of Appeals concluded that the statute did not violate due process or equal protection. *United States v. Bland*. Although not directly addressing a separation-of-powers argument, *Bland* treated the prosecutor's discretion as merely a form of the charging discretion that had historically been accorded to the prosecutor. Courts in most other jurisdictions have followed the rationale of *Bland* and rejected separation-of-powers challenges to statutes giving a prosecutor absolute or conditional discretion to charge a juvenile as an adult.

. . . .

III

L.J.S. argues that the presumptive certification provision in Minn.Stat. § 260.125, subd. 2a violates equal protection because there is no rational basis for distinguishing those juveniles subject to the provision from those not within its definition.

The presumptive certification provision states:

It is presumed that a proceeding involving an offense committed by a child will be certified to district court if:

(1) the child was 16 or 17 years old at the time of the offense; and

(2) the delinquency petition alleges that the child committed an offense that would result in a presumptive commitment to prison under the sentencing guidelines and applicable statutes, or that the child committed any felony offense while using * * * a firearm.

If the presumption applies, then the juvenile bears the burden of rebutting it by clear and convincing evidence. L.J.S. concedes that the statute involves no suspect classification, and that the "rational basis" test is the appropriate standard for determining whether the statute violates equal protection.

L.J.S. is claiming only a violation of the Minnesota Constitution. Under Minnesota's "rational basis" test, there must be a genuine and substantial distinction between those included in the classification and those excluded, the classification must be relevant to the purpose of the law, and the statute must have a legitimate purpose. The court will not hypothesize a rational basis to justify a classification.

Both the offender-age and the offense criteria in the presumptive certification statute are relevant to the purpose of the statute. The purpose of the juvenile certification statute has been narrowed to protecting public safety.

The juvenile's age is highly relevant to whether juvenile jurisdiction serves public safety. If a juvenile's age curtails the length of time available for juvenile treatment, and if the offense indicates danger to the public, the public safety is not served.

The offense criteria are also directly related to the danger to public safety. Offenses carrying a presumptively executed sentence are generally crimes against the person, representing a greater threat to public safety.

L.J.S. argues that most adult offenders charged with offenses calling for presumptive prison sentences plead to lesser offenses or receive downward departures. But, even assuming that is true, the ways in which trial courts and attorneys view individual cases are not relevant to whether the guidelines' presumptive disposition adequately measures the seriousness of an offense. We conclude that the presumptive certification statute does not violate equal protection.

IV

L.J.S. argues that the presumptive certification statute violates due process because it creates a mandatory, irrebuttable presumption. *See Sandstrom v. Montana,* 442 U.S. 510 (1979) (due process prevents any presumption in a criminal case that shifts the burden of proof on an element of the offense or that establishes a conclusive, irrebuttable presumption). The presumptive certification statute does not affect the state's burden of proving an *element* of the offense, and so does not conflict with the presumption of innocence.

Neither does the presumptive certification statute create an irrebuttable presumption. The juvenile may rebut the presumption "by demonstrating by clear and convincing evidence that retaining the proceeding in the juvenile court serves public safety." The juvenile may present relevant evidence on several listed factors. L.J.S. cites no authority to support his claim that a presumption is irrebuttable if the basic facts giving rise to the presumption are beyond challenge. The statute still allows the juvenile to present evidence going beyond those basic facts to the broader issue of whether public safety is served.

V

Finally, L.J.S. argues that the presumptive certification statute violates due process by shifting the burden of persuasion to the juvenile. Shifts in the burden of persuasion on any element in a criminal offense violate due process. The certification presumption applies only to a pretrial procedure, although one that determines which court will try the juvenile. But criminal defendants routinely bear the burden of persuasion on some pretrial motions, such as constitutional challenges to statutes.

The state concedes that some presumptions, at least irrebuttable ones, may violate due process even though they occur in a civil context which does not implicate the presumption of innocence. But, the presumption of certification that applies to L.J.S. is not irrebuttable. Moreover, the presumption does not shift the burden of persuasion on any element of the offense. The presumption merely determines which court will try the case and evaluate the elements of the offense.

New Mexico v. Gonzales
24 P.3d 776 (N.M. Ct. App. 2001)

PICKARD, Chief Judge.

Defendant appeals his adult sentence as a consequence of the trial court's findings that he was not amenable to treatment as a juvenile or eligible for commitment to an institution for the mentally disordered or developmentally disabled pursuant to NMSA 1978, §2A-2-20 (1996). Defendant argues that the state and federal constitutions require the State to prove these findings to a jury beyond a reasonable doubt before a court may exercise its discretion to sentence a child as an adult. In support of his federal constitutional argument, Defendant relies on *Apprendi v. New Jersey*, in which the Supreme Court struck down a New Jersey law that allowed a court to increase a maximum criminal sentence based on facts not found by a jury beyond a reasonable doubt. In addition to his constitutional claims, Defendant argues that, whatever the applicable burden of proof, the evidence was insufficient to support the trial court's findings. We hold that (1) the *Apprendi* decision is inapplicable to the findings required by Section 32A-2-20(B), (2) the state constitution does not require the State to prove non-amenability or ineligibility for commitment by proof beyond a reasonable doubt, and (3) substantial evidence supported the trial court's findings that Defendant was not amenable to treatment as a child or eligible for commitment. We therefore affirm.

I. FACTS AND PROCEDURAL HISTORY

Defendant turned fourteen years old on December 14, 1996. On March 13, 1997, after breaking into and vandalizing several other houses, Defendant and an accomplice broke into and ransacked Victim's home while Victim and his wife were away. The two juveniles shot Victim's dog with a .22 caliber rifle, which they had stolen from another house. In addition, Defendant took a .30-30 rifle from a wall in Victim's home and fired several rounds into a wall.

When Victim and his wife returned home with their neighbors, they were alarmed to find that their dog had been shot while tied up in the yard. Victim went inside the house to call the police. The phone was next to a window outside of which Defendant and his accomplice were hiding. Defendant saw Victim, and assuming that Victim had likewise seen him, shot Victim in the chest with the .30-30 rifle. The accomplice then shot Victim in the head "to put him out of his misery."

Around the time that Victim was killed, Victim's wife went inside the house. She saw her husband's body and begged the boys not to kill her. One of the boys told her to give them money and the keys to a truck or they would kill her as well. Wife told them that she did not have any money or the keys. The boys then searched Victim's body, and Wife left the house in search of the neighbors. The boys came out of the house and fired 18 to 22 shots toward Wife and the neighbors. One of the neighbors was hit either by bullet fragments or fragments from a nearby car. The shot that hit the neighbor was fired from the .30-30 rifle that Defendant had stolen from Victim's home. At the time of his arrest, Defendant told the arresting officer that he had shot at the neighbor from about one-half mile away and that it was "a hell of a good shot" but "nothing to be proud of."

Defendant pleaded guilty to second degree murder, aggravated burglary, aggravated battery, and two counts of aggravated assault. Pursuant to Section 32A-2-20(A), the prosecutor had earlier filed a notice of intent to seek an adult sentence. At the amenability hearing, Defendant called eight witnesses, three of whom were experts. The expert witnesses agreed that, at the time of the murder, Defendant was suffering from a variety of mental disorders. These witnesses also testified that Defendant was amenable to psychiatric treatment. Nonetheless, the trial court found, by clear and convincing evidence, that Defendant was not amenable to treatment as a child and was ineligible for commitment to an institution, and exercised its discretion under Section 32A-2-20(A) to sentence Defendant to 22 years in an adult correctional facility. Defendant then moved for a reconsideration of the adult disposition based on recommendations made in a presentence report ordered by the court, arguing that the court's findings needed to be based on proof beyond a reasonable doubt. The court denied Defendant's motion for reconsideration, after stating that it was persuaded beyond a reasonable doubt.

II. DISCUSSION

....

B. Constitutional Arguments

Defendant argues that the federal constitution, as described in *Apprendi*, requires that the Section 32A-2-20(B) findings be made by a jury beyond a reasonable doubt. In addition, Defendant argues that the state constitution requires the application of the beyond a reasonable doubt standard, based on a comparison with other provisions of the Delinquency Act. In analyzing Defendant's claims, this Court applies the interstitial approach outlined in *State v. Gomez*. We first ask whether the right being asserted is protected under the federal constitution. If it is, the state constitutional claim is not reached. If the right is not protected under the federal constitution, we must then analyze whether the State constitution provides broader protection. We may diverge from federal precedent for three reasons: (1) the federal analysis of the issue is flawed, (2) distinctive state characteristics require a different result, or (3) the federal analogs are undeveloped.

1. Background

....

Prior to 1993, New Mexico maintained a system of transfer that was similar to systems developed within the federal and other state governments. However, the 1993 amendments to the Children's Code created a new system that is unique in this country. Whereas most jurisdictions have maintained provisions allowing a court to waive or transfer juvenile court jurisdiction, New Mexico has chosen to abolish the transfer system in favor of vesting the children's courts with the authority to sentence youthful offenders as adults.

In 1993, the Legislature created three "classes" of juvenile offenders: serious youthful offenders, youthful offenders, and delinquent offenders. *See* §§ 32A-2-3(C), (H), (I). These classifications reflect the rehabilitative purpose of the Delinquency Act, coupled with the realization that some juvenile offenders cannot be rehabilitated given the limited resources and jurisdiction of the juvenile justice system. Serious youthful offenders, namely children fifteen years or older charged with committing first degree murder, are excluded from the jurisdiction of the children's court unless found guilty of a lesser offense. Given the age of these offenders and the seriousness of the offense, including the requisite intent, the Legislature has determined that serious youthful offenders cannot be rehabilitated using existing resources in the time available. At the other end of the spectrum is the class of delinquent offenders, which includes all children under the age of fourteen, and children over the age of fourteen years who have been adjudicated guilty of less than four felonies in three years or have not been found guilty of an unenumerated offense. Given a delinquent child's young age or lack of a serious criminal history, the Legislature has determined that existing services and facilities most likely can rehabilitate these children within the time available. Under these circumstances, there is time to gauge progress, adjust treatment plans, and extend commitment if necessary.

The class of youthful offenders to which Defendant belongs includes children fourteen years or older who are adjudicated guilty of any one of twelve enumerated violent felonies or who have three prior felony adjudications in the previous three years in addition to their current felony offense, as well as children fourteen years of age who are adjudicated guilty of first degree murder. For these offenders, the determination of amenability to rehabilitation within the juvenile system is a more complicated question. Under the Delinquency Act, youthful offenders are entitled to be sentenced within the juvenile system unless the court makes the findings required. The provisions of Section 32A-2-20 apply if the prosecutor has filed an intent to seek an adult sentence and the child has been adjudicated guilty. Under Section 32A-2-20(B), a trial court has the discretion to sentence a youthful offender as an adult only if the court finds that "the child is not amenable to treatment or rehabilitation as a child in available facilities," and "the child is not eligible for commitment to an institution for the developmentally disabled or mentally disordered." In making these findings, a court is required by Section 32A-2-20(C) to consider the following factors:

(1) the seriousness of the alleged offense;

(2) whether the alleged offense was committed in an aggressive, violent, pre-meditated or willful manner;

(3) whether a firearm was used to commit the alleged offense;

(4) whether the alleged offense was against persons or against property, greater weight being given to offenses against persons, especially if personal injury resulted;

(5) the sophistication and maturity of the child as determined by consideration of the child's home, environmental situation, emotional attitude and pattern of living;

(6) the record and previous history of the child;

(7) the prospects for adequate protection of the public and the likelihood of reasonable rehabilitation of the child by the use of procedures, services and facilities currently available; and

(8) any other relevant factor, provided that factor is stated on the record.

If the court finds that a child is neither amenable to treatment as a child nor eligible for commitment, the court may impose either a juvenile disposition or an adult sentence. The findings trigger the court's discretion; they do not require the court to sentence a juvenile as an adult. By contrast, a finding of either amenability to rehabilitation or eligibility for commitment restricts the court's range of possible dispositions to those available within the juvenile system.

Although the consequences of the determination that a youthful offender is non-amenable to treatment and ineligible for commitment may be severe in that sentences under the Criminal Code are typically longer than commitments under the Delinquency Act, the purpose of the amenability hearing is not to punish a child or to increase the punishment, but rather to gauge the possibility for meaningful rehabilitation. The amenability hearing is a proceeding separate from both the adjudication of guilt and disposition or sentencing. A child may be found non-amenable to treatment or rehabilitation, yet the court may exercise its discretion by entering a disposition within the juvenile system. Similarly, a child may be found non-amenable and be sentenced as an adult, yet be given adult probation rather a sentence of incarceration.

With these considerations in mind, we now turn to Defendant's constitutional arguments. The issues presented by this case are whether the due process clause of the Fourteenth Amendment to the United States Constitution requires that the Section 32A-2-20(B) findings be made by a jury beyond a reasonable doubt or whether Article II, Section 4 of the New Mexico Constitution requires that the findings be made by the court pursuant to a reasonable doubt standard.

2. *Apprendi*

Defendant does not argue that federal law decided prior to *Apprendi* compels the application of the "beyond a reasonable doubt" standard to the Section 32A-2-20 findings. To the contrary, prior to *Apprendi,* most federal courts that have squarely addressed this issue hold that the proper standard for transfer is preponderance of the evidence.

In *Apprendi,* the Supreme Court held that, "[o]ther than the fact of a prior conviction, any fact that increases the penalty for a crime beyond the prescribed statutory maximum must be submitted to a jury, and proved beyond a reasonable doubt." After the defendant there pleaded guilty to second degree possession of a firearm, the prosecutor filed a motion seeking to enhance the sentence under the New Jersey "hate crimes" law.

The law provided for an extended term of imprisonment if the trial court found, by a preponderance of the evidence, that the defendant acted with the purpose to intimidate an individual or group because of an impermissible bias. The trial court found that the defendant had acted with racial bias and imposed a twelve-year sentence, which was two years longer than the maximum sentence allowed for a second degree felony. The Supreme Court reversed the sentence, holding that the hate crime statute defined an element of a criminal offense and, as such, due process required that a jury find beyond a reasonable doubt that the defendant acted with the purpose to intimidate.

Defendant argues that the *Apprendi* decision applies to the amenability determination, given the fact that the Section 32A-2-20(B) findings are necessary to expose a youthful offender to the possibility of an adult sentence. Defendant argues that the consequences of sentencing as an adult in terms of both the length of incarceration and removal of the protections of the juvenile system render the amenability determinations more like elements of a crime than sentencing factors. We disagree. We conclude that accepting Defendant's argument would require an overly broad interpretation of *Apprendi* that is unsupported by the Court's reasoning.

By way of introduction, we note that a determination that a child is not amenable to treatment within the juvenile system differs from findings related to the elements of crime in three significant ways. First, while findings of guilt are measures of the degree of an individual's criminal culpability, the finding that a child is or is not amenable to treatment is a measure of a child's prospects for rehabilitation. Second, while findings of guilt are based on historical facts susceptible of proof beyond a reasonable doubt, a finding that a child is not amenable to rehabilitation requires a prediction of future conduct based on complex considerations of the child, the child's crime, and the child's history and environment. Third, a determination of amenability or eligibility for commitment requires some foreknowledge of available facilities and the programs in them that trial judges who make sentencing decisions every day have, while juries do not.

Whether ultimately given a juvenile disposition or an adult sentence, every youthful offender has the constitutional right to the State's proof of every element of a criminal offense beyond a reasonable doubt. By contrast, whatever right a child may have to be treated as a child within the juvenile justice system is a statutory, not a constitutional, right. The United States Supreme Court has drawn a clear line between the process due during an adjudication of delinquency or guilt and the lesser process due during an amenability hearing. *Compare In re Winship,* ("The same considerations that demand extreme caution in factfinding to protect the innocent adult apply as well to the innocent child."), *with Kent,* (holding that amenability hearings "must measure up to the essentials of due process and fair treatment"), *and Breed v. Jones,* ("The [Supreme] Court has never attempted to prescribe criteria for, or the nature and quantum of evidence that must support, a decision to transfer a juvenile for trial in adult court."). The determination of a youthful offender's amenability to treatment within the juvenile system is a question of the prospects for rehabilitation of the child, not of the degree of a child's criminal culpability. The constitutional concerns expressed by the Supreme Court in *Winship* and *Apprendi* are satisfied by the jury's finding beyond a reasonable doubt that a child committed the offenses that form the foundation permitting the court to sentence the child as an adult.

The second difference between the Section 32A-2-20(B) findings and the elements of a crime is in the nature of the findings. The determination of a child's prospects for rehabilitation is a complicated and difficult question that requires consideration of a child's environment, age, maturity, past behavior, and predictions of future behavior as well as specifics of the offense as they relate to the prospects of rehabilitation. Unlike the finding that a child has committed a criminal offense, the finding that a child is not amenable to treatment as a child within the juvenile system requires a predictive, more than historical, analysis.

As such, a finding of non-amenability is different in nature from the type of findings discussed in *Apprendi*. Whether a defendant acts with the intention to intimidate another based on prejudice or bias is a fact susceptible to proof beyond a reasonable doubt. On the other hand, amenability or eligibility for commitment are not as susceptible to proof by this high standard. As the Supreme Court noted in *Addington v. Texas:*

> [T]he initial inquiry in a civil commitment proceeding is very different from the central issue in either a delinquency proceeding or a criminal prosecution. In the latter cases the basic issue is a straightforward factual question—did the accused commit the act alleged? There may be factual issues to resolve in a commitment proceeding, but the factual aspects represent only the beginning of the inquiry. Whether the individual is mentally ill and dangerous to either himself or others and is in need of confined therapy turns on the *meaning* of the facts which must be interpreted by expert psychiatrists and psychologists. Given the lack of certainty and the fallibility of psychiatric diagnosis, there is a serious question as to whether a state could ever prove beyond a reasonable doubt that an individual is both mentally ill and likely to be dangerous.

Additionally, a court, which has regular exposure to both the criminal and juvenile systems, is in a much better position to determine an individual child's amenability to treatment within existing programs. In their day-to-day interactions with sentencing decisions, presentence reports, probation violations, and the whole range of criminal and juvenile justice issues, trial courts become knowledgeable about the basic considerations governing appropriate dispositions for offenders.

With the foregoing as background, the important point is that the reasoning of the *Apprendi* decision itself supports our result. In reaching its holding, the Court distinguished and upheld trial courts' traditional discretion to consider factors relating both to the offense and the offender in imposing a sentence within the range set by statute. The Court also distinguished its holding from cases dealing with fact-finding in capital sentencing on the grounds that it is the jury's verdict of guilty of first degree murder that exposes a defendant to the possibility of a death sentence. The Court adopted the position that

"[o]nce a jury has found the defendant guilty of all the elements of an offense which carries as its maximum penalty the sentence of death, it may be left to the judge to decide whether that maximum penalty, rather than a lesser one, ought to be imposed. * * * The person who is charged with actions that expose him to the death penalty has an absolute entitlement to jury trial on all the elements of the charge."

The test for determining whether a particular fact is a sentencing factor or an element of the crime "is one not of form, but effect—does the required finding expose the defendant to a greater punishment than that authorized by the jury's guilty verdict?" This test is not merely whether a particular finding may result in a greater sentence than would have occurred without the finding, but whether the finding sets the maximum sentence to which a defendant may be subjected.

While a finding of non-amenability and ineligibility for commitment may expose a youthful offender to a longer period of deprivation of liberty than is possible under the Children's Code, only two factual findings are required to expose a child to the possibility of adult sentencing: (1) the child's age at the time of the offense and (2) the jury's verdict or a plea of guilty to a specifically enumerated felony or to any felony, provided it is in fact the child's fourth felony in three years. Under Section 32A-2-20(D), if the court invokes an adult sentence, the sentence may be "less than, but shall not exceed, the mandatory adult sentence." Therefore, at the time the child pleads or is adjudicated guilty of an offense, the range of possible sentences is fixed. In this case, the finding of non-amenability and ineligibility for commitment did not expose Defendant to a first degree sentence for a second degree crime as was the case in *Apprendi*. We note that the plea agreement signed by Defendant prior to the amenability hearing included the range of juvenile dispositions as well as the adult sentences applicable to the crimes committed. Under no circumstances do the Section 32A-2-20(B) findings result in the child being found guilty of or sentenced for a greater offense. Furthermore, no child will be subject to the possibility of sentencing as an adult if, at the time of the finding of guilt, the child does not meet the statutory definition of a youthful offender under Section 32A-2-3(I).

In conclusion, we hold that *Apprendi* is inapplicable to the Section 32A-2-20(B) findings.

3. State Constitution

New Mexico cases have never articulated the standard of proof pursuant to which the findings required by Section 32A-2-20 are to be made. Prior versions of the children's code statutorily established the very low standard of "reasonable grounds to believe" that the enumerated crime was committed and required simple consideration of whether the child was amenable to treatment as a juvenile. Under the current statute, the trial court must make a specific finding that the child is not amenable. Whatever the current standard of proof is for the trial court to make this specific finding, whether it is preponderance of the evidence as advocated by the State or something higher, we review the trial court's decision for substantial evidence or abuse of discretion.

Defendant argues that two provisions in the current Delinquency Act suggest the Legislature's intent to apply the beyond a reasonable doubt standard to the Section 32A-2-20 findings. These two provisions, Section 32A-2-24(B) (requiring proof beyond a reasonable doubt in probation revocation hearings), and Section 32A-2-16(E) (requiring proof beyond a reasonable doubt in a delinquency proceeding), are readily distinguishable from the amenability determination under Section 32A-2-20(B). First, the requirement of proof beyond a reasonable doubt in a delinquency proceeding is constitutionally mandated. *See In re Winship*. Second, a probation revocation hearing, like an adjudication, requires proof that a defendant is guilty of an act that occurred in the past. The Legislature's distinction between the proof required for a finding of guilt versus the proof required to find an adjudicated youthful offender non-amenable to treatment as a child is consistent with federal and state precedent.

We note that New Mexico courts have consistently held that the lack of a standard of proof for the amenability findings does not violate due process under the federal constitution.

Finally, when compared with the laws of other states, the lack of a discernible standard in Section 32A-2-20 appears in keeping with the majority rule. As of 1999, 47 states have statutes granting juvenile court judges the power to waive jurisdiction over cases involving juvenile offenders so that they may be transferred to an adult criminal court. The most prevalent transfer statute gives the juvenile courts complete discretion in deciding which cases are appropriate for transfer. In the 46 states with discretionary transfer statutes, the majority require proof by substantial or a preponderance of the evidence. In two states, the prosecution is required to prove non-amenability to treatment as a juvenile by clear and convincing evidence. In four states that combine discretionary and presumptive waiver provisions, the burden of proof by clear and convincing evidence rests upon the party seeking to rebut the presumption (for discretionary waivers, the prosecution; for presumptive waivers, the defendant). No states require proof beyond a reasonable doubt.

Based on the legislative history of the code, New Mexico case law, and statutes from other jurisdictions, we find no reason to hold that the New Mexico Constitution requires a "beyond a reasonable doubt" standard. We need not decide in this case whether to adopt the preponderance standard advocated by the State in view of the trial court's use of the "clear and convincing" standard and our upholding of its decision based on it in the next section of this opinion.

C. Sufficiency of the Evidence

Defendant argues that whatever standard of proof is applicable, the State failed to prove that Defendant was not amenable to treatment as a juvenile or eligible for commitment to an institution for the developmentally disabled or mentally disordered. We disagree.

1. Standard of Review

Defendant argues that this Court should review the entire record in a de novo type of manner to determine whether the evidence supported a finding that Defendant was not amenable to treatment as a juvenile or eligible for commitment. Defendant argues that *State v. Sheets,* and *Jackson v. Virginia*, require us to consider all the evidence presented to the trial court. We do not read either case as supportive of Defendant's claim. *Sheets* and *Jackson* stand for the unremarkable proposition, long accepted by New Mexico courts, that in reviewing the sufficiency of the evidence supporting a conviction, whatever evidence is reviewed by this Court must be viewed in the light most favorable to the prosecution. ("Once a defendant has been found guilty of the crime charged, the factfinder's role as weigher of the evidence is preserved through a legal conclusion that upon judicial review *all of the evidence* is to be considered in the light most favorable to the prosecution." (emphasis in original)).

In assessing a claim of evidentiary insufficiency, this Court asks whether substantial evidence supports the court's decision. Neither the basic formulation of the question nor the language we use in describing the trial courts' function changes depending on the standard of review. "Substantial evidence is relevant evidence that a reasonable mind would accept as adequate to support a conclusion." This Court views the evidence in the light most favorable to the trial court's decision, resolves all conflicts and indulges all permissible inferences to uphold the court's decision, and disregards all evidence and inferences to the contrary. We do not reweigh the evidence and will not substitute our judgment for that of the trial court. We recognize that the factfinder is entitled to disregard evidence presented by either party, and to disregard the testimony of experts. Our role is to review the evidence to determine whether any rational fact-finder could conclude that the proof requirement below was met. *See Jackson* ("the relevant question is whether, after viewing the evidence in the light most favorable to the prosecution, *any* rational trier of fact could have found the essential elements of the crime beyond a reasonable doubt"); *In re Termination of Parental Rights of Eventyr J.,* ("Our standard of review is therefore whether, viewing the evidence in the light most favorable to the prevailing party, the fact finder could properly determine that the clear and convincing standard was met."). In this case, because the trial court used the clear and convincing standard, we will evaluate whether, viewing the evidence in the light most favorable to the State, the trial court could have found that the clear and convincing standard was met.

2. Amenability to Treatment

Defendant challenges the trial court's finding of non-amenability on three grounds: (1) the court ignored the uncontradicted expert testimony that Defendant was amenable to treatment, (2) the court misunderstood or mischaracterized the expert testimony in its finding, and (3) the court misapplied the Section 32A-2-20(C) factors.

The evidence regarding Defendant's amenability to treatment or rehabilitation was not uncontradicted as Defendant suggests. Although the experts testified that Defendant had made some progress in therapy, the testimony indicated that he carried the risk of violence with him and that it was impossible to predict whether he would re-offend given that, at the time of the hearing, he was sheltered from his peers. At least one of the defense witnesses who had observed Defendant's progress while in treatment testified that Defendant's progress had been sporadic: some days Defendant seemed to work at getting better, other days he appeared to be just "playing the game." Furthermore, several expert witnesses expressed concern over Defendant's lack of remorse for the murder. Finally, most experts expressed an understanding that amenability to treatment or rehabilitation under Section 32A-2-20(B) is a bigger question than responsiveness to psychiatric care.

As stated above, "[i]t is well settled in New Mexico that a factfinder may disregard the opinions of experts." The trial court chose to disregard the testimony of most experts because their opinions of Defendant's prospects for rehabilitation were formed without knowledge of Defendant's history of destructive and aggressive behavior. In the case of Sonde Harley Grano, the expert witness whom the court did find credible and upon whose testimony the court relied in making its findings, the court was entitled to disregard her ultimate conclusions as to Defendant's amenability. As the court said, "[Ms.] Grano felt that he was amenable to treatment, but everything else she said indicated that she really had serious doubts."

Furthermore, although the trial court did appear to misunderstand or misremember some of Ms. Grano's testimony, other evidence supported the court's conclusions. For example, although the court seemed to misunderstand Ms. Grano's testimony regarding Defendant's appearance of passivity at the time of the hearing, Ms. Grano later testified that it was impossible to predict whether Defendant's passivity was a permanent change given that Defendant was sheltered from his peers at the time of the hearing.

Finally, Defendant argues that the court erred by using the seven factors set forth in Section 32A-2-20(C) to control, rather than guide, its finding that Defendant was not "amenable to treatment or rehabilitation as a child in available facilities." We note that the court was required to consider and balance these factors in making its finding. Furthermore, contrary to Defendant's assertion that factor (C)(7) is the only factor relevant to determining a child's amenability to treatment, we believe that every factor provides important information about the child and the child's prospects for rehabilitation.

Defendant pleaded guilty to second degree murder, aggravated battery, two counts of aggravated assault, and aggravated burglary. Any one of these offenses alone was sufficient to subject Defendant to the possibility of adult sentencing. *See* § 32A-2-3(I) (list of crimes subjecting child to youthful offender status). These offenses were clearly committed in a violent and aggressive manner. After killing Victim, Defendant and his accomplice fired 18–22 shots at Wife and the neighbors. In addition, Defendant purposefully damaged Victim's home. Furthermore, there was considerable evidence that Defendant had grown increasingly out-of-control and violent in the year preceding the murder. Several experts testified to an inability to predict whether Defendant would pose a threat of danger in the future, and Ms. Grano testified that rehabilitation was possible only with long term therapy at a high security facility. In his report to the court, Defendant's probation officer gave his opinion that Defendant was unwilling to accept responsibility for his behavior and that this unwillingness demonstrated Defendant's non-amenability to treatment or rehabilitation. Based on the above, we hold that there was substantial evidence to support the trial court's finding of non-amenability by clear and convincing evidence.

3. Eligibility for Commitment

Defendant appears to argue that if any expert deems a child eligible for commitment under NMSA 1978, § 32A-6-13(I) (1995), or if any treatment facility is willing and able to accept the child, then the court must find the child eligible for commitment to an institution. However, this is not the standard under Section 32A-2-20(B)(2). In deciding whether Defendant was eligible for commitment, the trial court was required by statute to consider the seven factors listed in Section 32A-2-20(C). The court's role in determining a child's eligibility is not as simple as tallying votes for and against commitment. The trial court must observe the child, measure the credibility of witnesses, consider the security and appropriateness of available facilities, and analyze all the evidence in light of the Section 32A-2-20(C) factors. It was not enough that Defendant made some progress in therapy; the question was whether he could be successfully rehabilitated or treated for his mental illnesses given available facilities and the time remaining before Defendant reached the age of twenty-one.

Furthermore, one expert witness testified that Defendant's mental status would need to decline significantly before Defendant could be committed under Section 32A-6-13(I). If, at age 21, Defendant was dangerous to himself or others, but was not mentally ill, the State would be severely limited in its efforts to protect the public. In addition, another defense witness testified that, while Defendant may be eligible for some degree of residential treatment, he was not eligible for high security residential treatment. Finally, several experts testified that Defendant was ineligible for commitment to an institution for the developmentally disabled. Based on these opinions and a review of the evidence considered under the seven factors of Section 32A-2-20(C), we hold that substantial evidence supported the trial court's finding that Defendant was not eligible for commitment by clear and convincing evidence.

III. CONCLUSION

We affirm.

....

BUSTAMANTE, Judge (specially concurring).

I agree with the majority that affirmance is appropriate. However, I would take the opportunity to finally determine the standard of proof required to establish that a youthful offender is not amenable to treatment or rehabilitation. I concur in the result the majority has reached as to the *Apprendi* issue, though I cannot agree with most of the analysis which produces it.

STANDARD OF PROOF

The majority declines to decide which standard of proof is appropriate for the amenability finding. I agree that the two provisions Defendant relies upon in the juvenile code do not support his argument, and I recognize that the majority accurately cites New Mexico case law on this issue, but I believe it is time to settle the issue.

In our last pronouncement on the issue — *In re Ernesto M., Jr.* — we rejected a constitutional challenge to Section 32A-2-20 by noting that the current provision gave more guidance than its predecessor, which had also passed constitutional muster. We held that the statute provided "elemental due process" (notice, hearing, assistance of counsel, and a statement of the judge's decision rationale) and did not address what standard of proof was required.

That discussion would have been particularly apropos in *In re Ernesto M., Jr.* in that the defendant there also challenged the manner in which the trial court weighed the statutory factors. In *In re Ernesto M., Jr.*, the trial judge indicated he felt the order of appearance of the seven factors in Section 32A-2-20 suggested they were to be read and weighed in "descending order of importance." Under this interpretation the most important and weighty factor would be the seriousness of the crime, and so forth. Weighing the factors in this manner has obvious implications for the nature of the inquiry; that is, whether the inquiry broadly speaking will emphasize rehabilitation or punishment. We did not address the issue substantively, finding instead no prejudice to the defendant in the context of that case regardless of how the trial court weighed the factors. I, of course, do not question the result in *In re Ernesto M., Jr.*, but the case does illustrate that there is a basic uncertainty as to the manner in which trial judges in New Mexico should consider and apply Section 32A-2-20. That uncertainty is exacerbated by failing to provide guidance as to one of the most basic issues in any factual assessment — the standard of proof guiding the fact finder's deliberations. As the Supreme Court in *In re Gault* noted: "Juvenile Court history has again demonstrated that unbridled discretion, however benevolently motivated, is frequently a poor substitute for principle and procedure."

A standard of proof has at least two functions: It serves to guide the fact finder as to the level of confidence it should have in its decision and it serves as a means of allocating the risk of error between the litigants.

By way of illustration, the [United States] Supreme Court in *Santosky* contrasted the bases for the preponderance of the evidence and beyond reasonable doubts standard as follows:

"Thus, while private parties may be interested intensely in a civil dispute over money damages, application of a "fair preponderance of the evidence" standard indicates both society's "minimal concern with the outcome," and a conclusion that the litigants should "share the risk of error in roughly equal fashion." When the State brings a criminal action to deny a defendant liberty or life, however, "the interests of the defendant are of such magnitude that historically and without any explicit constitutional requirement they have been protected by standards of proof designed to exclude as nearly as possible the likelihood of an erroneous judgment." The stringency of the "beyond a reasonable doubt" standard bespeaks the "weight and gravity" of the private interest affected, society's interest in avoiding erroneous convictions, and a judgment that those interests together require that "society impos[e] almost the entire risk of error upon itself."

I appreciate the concern the majority expresses concerning the propriety of imposing the criminal beyond a reasonable doubt standard to this particular finding. Amenability is more predictive than historical. It is an attempt to predict the future conduct of the juvenile defendant. Moreover, the statute makes it clear that it is not simply a medical or psychological question. It is a mixed bag of history, potential for treatment, and a straightforward need to protect the public. In addition, by the time the trial court is making the amenability assessment, the juvenile has already been convicted or has pled to criminal conduct making the sentencing necessary. The conviction must occur under the normal beyond a reasonable doubt standard. Thus, by the time of sentencing, the criminal policy objectives noted above have, for the most part, been fulfilled.

Employing the three-part test enunciated by the United States Supreme Court in *Mathews v. Eldridge*, I suggest that the amenability hearing should be determined on a clear and convincing evidence standard. I thus agree with the trial judge here who ruled that clear and convincing was the appropriate standard. The *Mathews* factors are: (1) the private interest affected by the proceeding, (2) the risk of error created by the State's chosen procedure, and (3) the countervailing governmental interest supporting use of the challenged procedure. The aim of the *Mathews* test is to assess what process is due in any given situation. Courts have employed the *Mathews* test in a variety of situations, including civil commitment proceedings, *Addington;* termination of parental rights, *Santosky;* worker compensation hearings, *United States v. Woods;* and tenured faculty termination hearings, *Patterson v. Bd. of Regents.*[1]

Applying *Mathews* points to the need for at least an intermediate standard of clear and convincing evidence. The weight or value of the private interest at stake is clear and significant. Personal liberty and freedom of movement have consistently been treated as surpassing values in the United States, and state initiated proceedings curtailing freedom have consistently called for heightened standards of proof. The criminal standard is the benchmark, but there are other types of actions involving curtailment of personal freedom which invoke an intermediate standard, i.e., civil commitments (*Addington,*), deportation (*Woodby v. INS*), denaturalization (*Schneiderman v. United States*).

Of course, by the time a juvenile defendant faces an amenability hearing, he or she has already forfeited the right to be free as such. The choice at this point is between the juvenile and adult systems. With the former, the juvenile likely faces a shorter time of incarceration and the potential for treatment and rehabilitation. With the latter sentence, the juvenile faces significantly longer incarceration in a harsher environment and the prospects of little or no treatment and rehabilitation. Thus, while the individual interest at the time of the amenability hearing is muted, it is still significant.

The risk of error is unquestionably heightened by the absence of a specific standard of proof which the trial courts know to apply. This is not to disparage the work, quality, or good faith of trial judges. It is simply a reflection of the difficulty of the task and a common sense observation that the lack of a specific standard makes the task that much harder. Faith in the quality of the children's court bench is simply not an entirely satisfactory substitute for appropriate due process standards.

The interests of the State are complex. Any adverse monetary impact created by meeting a higher standard of proof can be expected to be de minimis and should be discounted. The State's interest in the outcome of the amenability hearing are conflicting. On the one hand the State is dealing with a convicted juvenile. The societal policy preferring freeing the guilty to convicting the innocent which drives the criminal standard is no longer applicable in full force. The stronger societal interest is now self-protection and, frankly, punishment. On the other hand, the State has a continuing interest in attempting to salvage its youth from the sad consequences of their actions. Abandoning the goal of rehabilitation should not be made too easy through the mechanism of a too-low standard of proof. On balance, the *Mathews* factors call for a heightened standard of proof short of "beyond a reasonable doubt;" clear and convincing is the normal rubric for this level.

---

1. The United States Supreme Court also used *Mathews* in two criminal cases. *Ake v. Oklahoma,* and *United States v. Raddatz.* The Court recently retreated from use of *Mathews* in evaluating state procedural due process rules in the criminal area, recognizing a potential for undue federalization of the area beyond truly fundamental concerns. *Medina v. California.* The Court's concerns do not cast doubt on a state court's adaptation and use of the *Mathews* factors to determine "what procedures are due" in its own courts....

Breed is not to the contrary. In *Breed,* the United States Supreme Court held that double jeopardy applied to juvenile transfer proceedings if a determination that the juvenile had violated the law was made prior to or at the transfer hearing. Since jeopardy attached at that point, the Court held that the juvenile could not then be retried in adult court. In exploring the procedural consequences of its ruling, the Court observed that complying with its decision should not in and of itself change the nature of transfer hearings. The court noted that it had " … never attempted to prescribe criteria for, or the nature and quantum of evidence that must support, a decision to transfer a juvenile for trial in adult court." That statement in *Breed* is a little more than a descriptive statement of the then state of the law. The Court up to that time had not addressed the standard of proof required in what were then termed transfer hearings, and it still has not to this date. The Court's observation should not be read as a holding or acknowledgment by the court that no standard of proof is required. Rather, it is more appropriate to read it as assurance by the Court that no change of procedure—such as a showing of probable cause that the juvenile committed an offense—was required to comply with its double jeopardy ruling.

In sum, adopting a clear and convincing standard of proof would provide a welcome guide to the trial bench as they make these difficult decisions. It would also make the process more consistent and predictable for the state and defendants alike.

APPRENDI ISSUES

I am simply not as confident as the majority that the rule of *Apprendi* is inapplicable to our juvenile sentencing system.

The differences between the juvenile and adult justice systems are not in my view so dramatic or fundamental that *Apprendi* of necessity cannot be applied. To be sure the juvenile justice system places comparatively more emphasis on rehabilitation than the adult system does. But, the juvenile system has increasingly concerned itself with accountability and protection of the public, narrowing the gap between the two approaches. The gap almost disappears in cases such as this where the offenses are serious and the amenability determination can result in tripling the sentence imposed on the defendant. And, despite the theoretical possibility of imposing a juvenile sentence after a finding of non-amenability, I cannot imagine a situation where a trial judge would find any reason to do so. Whatever the ideal purposes of the amenability hearings may be, the end result is punishment, potentially if not probably, at adult levels.

Despite my reservations about the route taken by the majority, I must agree with the result. As the majority notes, juveniles have no constitutional right to be treated as a child within the juvenile system. Given that limitation, the legislature can set sentencing essentially as it pleases for juveniles. New Mexico's unique system has given the trial judge two sentencing options. The amenability determination helps guide which option a judge may employ, but it does not increase the maximum sentence allowed by the legislature. In this way, our system most closely resembles in operation the capital sentencing procedures approved by the Supreme Court in *Apprendi.*

Notes

(a) After the *Apprendi* ruling in 2000, the United States Supreme Court decided *Blakely v. Washington,* 542 US 296 (2004), extending *Apprendi* to a state law permitting the trial court to impose "an exceptional sentence," one above and beyond the statutory maximum, if he or she found that the defendant acted with "deliberate cruelty." The Court ruled that "the relevant 'statutory maximum' is not the maximum sentence a judge may impose after finding additional facts, but the maximum he may impose without any additional findings. When a judge inflicts punishment that the jury's verdict alone does not allow, the jury has not found all the facts 'which the law makes essential to the punishment.'"

In *United States v. Booker*, 543 U.S. 220 (2005), the Court extended *Blakely* to the Federal Sentencing Guidelines, holding that if the Guidelines were viewed as mandatory, it violated the Sixth Amendment right to a jury trial. Again the Court stressed that a sentence must be based solely on the jury's verdict, not upon some additional finding of fact.

(b) Do *Blakely* and *Booker* require further consideration of the constitutionality of extended jurisdiction sentencing?

In the Matter of the Welfare of D.M.D., Jr.
607 N.W.2d 432 (Minn. 2000)

This is an appeal from a court of appeals decision reversing the juvenile court's grant of the prosecutor's motion to designate the juvenile court proceedings as an Extended Jurisdiction Juvenile (EJJ) prosecution. We reverse the court of appeals and affirm the juvenile court's EJJ designation.

On March 18 or 19 and June 21 of 1997, respondent D.M.D., Jr., then fourteen, was alleged to have penetrated an eight-year-old girl digitally and with his penis while babysitting her and her two siblings. On January 23, 1998, respondent was charged with two counts of criminal sexual conduct in the first degree.

As required by [statute] the juvenile court ordered an EJJ study and a psychological study of respondent. The state presented testimony from two psychologists that the additional two years of juvenile jurisdiction associated with EJJ designation were necessary because respondent could not complete needed treatment before his 19th birthday, when the juvenile court's jurisdiction would otherwise cease. The state's psychologists' EJJ recommendations were based on the severity of respondent's offenses, his high risk to reoffend, and his refusal to admit to the offenses. In contrast, the psychologist called by respondent testified that respondent was capable of completing treatment before his 19th birthday. However, the juvenile court judge found that respondent's psychologist's conclusion was based on the questionable assumption that respondent would admit to the offenses.

After conducting an EJJ hearing, the juvenile court found that the statutory factors used to determine whether granting EJJ designation will serve public safety were split evenly. Nevertheless, the court found that EJJ designation was warranted, due primarily to the state's psychologists' testimony that EJJ was necessary for the full treatment of respondent. The court of appeals, however, reversed the juvenile court and held that in addition to the statutory factors, nonoffense related evidence of dangerousness is required for EJJ designation. Because the juvenile court did not specifically address nonoffense related evidence of dangerousness, the court of appeals reversed and remanded for findings of fact on such dangerousness.

I.

The question before us is whether the EJJ statute, requires evidence of nonoffense related dangerousness before an EJJ designation can be made on public safety grounds. The EJJ statute provides for extended jurisdiction in cases involving a juvenile alleged to have committed a felony. In an EJJ prosecution, upon a finding of guilt or entry of a guilty plea the juvenile is given both an adult criminal sentence and a juvenile disposition. The adult sentence is stayed on the condition that the juvenile does not violate the terms of the disposition or commit a new offense. EJJ designation extends the juvenile court's jurisdiction until the juvenile reaches 21 years of age, as opposed to the usual limit of 19 years. *See* Minn.Stat. § 260.181, subds. 4(a), (b) (1998).

The statute provides for three types of EJJ prosecution: automatic, presumptive, and designated. This case involves the third type, in which the prosecutor requests that a proceeding be designated an EJJ prosecution. On the prosecutor's motion, a pretrial hearing is held at which the prosecutor must show by clear and convincing evidence that EJJ designation will serve public safety. To guide courts in their determination of whether EJJ designation serves public safety, the statute references subdivision 2(b) of the adult certification statute, which sets forth six factors for courts to consider when certifying a juvenile for prosecution as an adult on public safety grounds. If the prosecutor proves that public safety will be served by EJJ designation, the court must grant the motion.

. . . .

Since the enactment of the EJJ statute, this court has not addressed whether our prior holding, that certification on public safety grounds requires nonoffense related evidence of dangerousness, is applicable to EJJ designation on public safety grounds.

Although this is a case of first impression for this court, the issue has been presented to the court of appeals in several cases. Starting with *S.W.N.*, the court of appeals has consistently held that nonoffense related evidence of dangerousness is required for EJJ designation on public safety grounds. ("We conclude that the same requirement of non-offense related evidence of dangerousness [in certification cases] applies to motions for EJJ designation."). Similarly, in the present case, the court of appeals followed *S.W.N.* in holding that nonoffense related evidence of dangerousness is required for EJJ designations on public safety grounds.

S.W.N.'s holding that nonoffense related evidence of dangerousness is required for EJJ designation on public safety grounds was based on the rationale that the legislature may have intended that the EJJ classification serve as a middle ground appropriate for some juveniles who could not be certified for adult prosecution. Such an intent would accommodate threshold requirements somewhat more relaxed than those required for certification. * * * A lower threshold does not necessarily mean, however, that EJJ designation should be permitted based solely on the charged offense * * *.

Therefore, the court of appeals concluded that the lower threshold for EJJ designation does not imply abandonment of the requirement of nonoffense related evidence of dangerousness.

In developing the "lower threshold" theme, the court noted that the lower EJJ threshold can be seen in a textual comparison of the EJJ and certification statutes: For nonpresumption certification cases, "the prosecutor must show that retaining the child in the juvenile system *does not serve public safety* * * *; for EJJ designation * * * the prosecutor need only show that such designation *serves public safety* * * *." While stated differently, the statutory language appears to be a distinction without a difference in that the thresholds for both statutes seem to be the same, i.e., the prosecutor must prove public safety will be served by either certifying a juvenile to adult court or by granting an EJJ designation.

Moreover, the court of appeals' concern in *S.W.N.* that the "lower threshold" of EJJ designation might allow designation based solely on the charged offense seems to be misplaced. While the 2(b) factors pertaining to public safety heavily weight the seriousness of the alleged offense, the factors also take into account the juvenile's prior history and the available programs and dispositions.

That being said, we emphasize that the *Dahl* requirement of nonoffense related evidence of dangerousness arose from our interpretation of the former certification statute. In short, *Dahl* simply recognized that in enacting the former statute, the legislature did not intend certification to be based solely on age or offense. Since *Dahl* was decided, however, the legislature has significantly amended the statutory framework and provided public safety factors for courts to consider. We therefore hold that nonoffense related evidence of dangerousness not required by the statutory factors is not necessary for EJJ designation on public safety grounds. To the extent *S.W.N.* and its progeny are inconsistent with this holding, those decisions are overruled.

In the Matter of D.S., A Minor
921 S.W.2d 383 (Tex. Crim. App. 1996)

This is an appeal from a Juvenile Court order transferring appellant to the custody of the Institutional Division of the Texas Department of Criminal Justice (TDCJ) for the completion of a 30 year sentence previously handed down in a jury trial adjudicating him a delinquent child and setting his punishment under the determinate sentencing provisions of the Texas Family Code.

. . . .

On December 21, 1990, at the age of 14 years, appellant was adjudicated in a jury proceeding in juvenile court of engaging in delinquent conduct, to wit: murder. He was sentenced to commitment to the Texas Youth Commission for 30 years. This commitment was appealed to this Court and the trial court's decision was affirmed.

. . . .

[A]ppellant complains that the hearing is unconstitutional in that: it allows a person to serve time in the penitentiary or be punished without ever being convicted of an offense; it denies appellant bail; it violates the separation of powers doctrine by delegating the executive branch function of commutation to the judiciary; it denies effective assistance of counsel; it violates double jeopardy by allowing two punishments for the same offense; and, it violates due process because it allows the State to punish appellant for his conduct while in TYC. These complaints will be addressed in turn. At the outset, we should note an act of the legislature is presumed to be constitutional, and the challenger bears the burden of demonstrating that it is unconstitutional.

D.S. complains he is being incarcerated without having been convicted of a crime. It is true that adjudication as a delinquent does not constitute conviction of a crime. This is intended to avoid branding a child a criminal for life and to allow him to retain certain rights that would be lost to an adult offender. In essence, a juvenile offender is afforded the important constitutional protections of the adult criminal justice system, but upon his release the juvenile will not have the same legal disabilities as an adult offender would. Under the juvenile system, a child is entitled to counsel, a twelve member jury, and proof of delinquency beyond a reasonable doubt. While a child is not labelled the same as an adult convicted of a crime, he is nevertheless afforded the basic constitutional protections of an adult. It is the process, and not the name given it, which is of the highest importance. We overrule appellant's contention that he is being incarcerated without a conviction.

Appellant claims he is denied the right to bail. Appellant asserts that he is entitled to bail pending the outcome of the release or transfer hearing. A child at the hearing is not being tried again; he is simply being given a second chance to persuade the court that he should not be imprisoned. Up to the point of the release or transfer hearing, appellant's transfer to TDCJ for completion of his sentence has remained only a conditional possibility, with numerous factors affecting the judge's decision. Appellant's contention that he is being wrongfully denied the right to bail is without merit.

....

Appellant also complains that the act violates double jeopardy by allowing two punishments for the same offense. As discussed earlier, a juvenile is not tried again at the release or transfer hearing. He has already been sentenced to a specific term at the adjudication proceeding. Now he has a second chance to persuade the court that he should not be imprisoned. The act does not allow two chances for the State to convict, but it does allow the juvenile two chances to stay out of prison. Appellant's contention that the act violates double jeopardy is without merit.

Appellant's last complaint ... is that the act violates due process by allowing the State to punish him for conduct, unrelated to the offense and while in TYC custody. The judge is allowed to consider a number of factors in making his decision at the release or transfer hearing, including, but not limited to, "the experiences and character of the person before and after commitment to the youth commission." The juvenile has already been sentenced to a specific term of 30 years. The release or transfer hearing, as stated earlier, represents a *second* chance for the juvenile, a chance for a release from such sentence. Clearly, the juvenile's behavior since commitment is a factor that should be considered in making this decision. The juvenile is being punished for his original conduct which was already adjudged delinquent. Appellant is not being denied due process....

In points of error nine through eleven, appellant raises various complaints about the admission of certain evidence at the release or transfer hearing. Specifically, appellant raises three complaints. First, that hearsay was admitted; second, that he was denied his right to confront witnesses against him; and third, that his prior record, including unadjudicated offenses, was improperly admitted. These arguments will be addressed individually. Once again, we should note that the release or transfer hearing is a "second chance hearing" after appellant had already been sentenced to a determinate number of years. It is not part of the guilt/innocence determination, consequently it need not meet the extensive due process requirements of an actual trial.

Appellant complains generally of evidence contained in State's Exhibits One and Two, which appellant characterizes as the "official records" from TYC, a description very similar to TYC "reports." Family Code section 54.11(d) authorizes the court, at the release or transfer hearing, to consider written reports from various persons, including TYC officials.

....

[A]ppellant complains that admission of the report containing the TYC official recommendation, which derives in part from a secret vote by an eight member panel of TYC officials, denies him his right of confrontation. As stated earlier, the Family Code authorizes use of TYC reports. The code also authorizes use, with identical language, of the same type of reports at a hearing for discretionary transfer to criminal court. Case law in this area is helpful. It has been held that in such proceedings, which are similar to release or transfer hearings in that no determination of guilt is made, admission of such reports does not offend confrontation rights, so long as defense counsel received copies of the reports before the hearing; if there was a doubt as to the genuineness of reports or a need to cross-examine the authors, the attorney should avail himself of the opportunity to raise the issue by calling the authors as witnesses or by otherwise submitting evidence. It has even been held that a juvenile has no right of confrontation whatsoever at a discretionary transfer hearing. Appellant's contention that his rights of confrontation have been abridged is overruled.

Lastly appellant complains, much in the same vein, that his prior record found in the TYC report, including unadjudicated offenses, should not have been admitted at the release or transfer hearing. D.S. complains specifically with regard to his prior record: the court made no relevancy finding; the court did no balancing; the information was unreliable; that D.S. had not received adequate warnings that his prior adjudications could be used against him; and, that equal protection is violated because a similar unadjudicated offense could not be used against an adult offender.

Once again, TYC reports are allowable. Appellant's prior record, including unadjudicated offenses, is a logical component of such a report. The statute deems the reports relevant and does not require any specific balancing or finding of reliability.

Appellant apparently complains that when he was previously adjudicated a delinquent because of conduct unrelated to the case at bar, he was not adequately warned of the possible use of such adjudications at a later release or transfer hearing for a subsequent offense. There is nothing in the record to suggest appellant was not adequately warned at the prior adjudications. Regardless, we have difficulty understanding how any such failure is relevant to the present case.

Finally, appellant's equal protection claim must also fail. *See* U.S. Const. amend. XIV; Tex. Const. art. I, § 3. Appellant's argument rests on his assertion that unadjudicated offenses would not be subsequently admissible against an adult offender. Without passing on the question of admissibility in the adult context, we would simply note that an adult offender, if anything, is in a less favorable position; there is no adult equivalent of the second chance hearing. Appellant is hardly in a position to complain of his advantage. Points of error nine through eleven are overruled.

The judgment is affirmed.

State v. IRA

43 P.3d 359 (N.M. Ct. App. 2002)

In this case, we are called upon to determine whether a 91½-year adult sentence imposed against the juvenile Defendant for brutally and repeatedly sexually abusing his younger stepsister over a two-year period is cruel and unusual punishment....

FACTUAL AND PROCEDURAL BACKGROUND

This appeal arises from a series of sexual assaults and other violent attacks committed by Defendant, when he was fourteen and fifteen years old, mostly upon his stepsister, who is nearly six years younger than he is. The State charged Defendant with ten counts of first-degree criminal sexual penetration, one count of aggravated battery against a household member, one count of aggravated battery, one count of battery against a household member, and one count of intimidation of a witness. The State also filed notice of its intent to invoke adult sanctions.

Under New Mexico's Children's Code, once the notice of intent to invoke adult sanctions is filed and the child is adjudged a youthful offender, the district court is given the discretion to impose either an adult sentence or juvenile disposition on the child.... To impose an adult sentence on an adjudicated youthful offender, the court must find that "(1) the child is not amenable to treatment or rehabilitation as a child in available facilities; and (2) the child is not eligible for commitment to an institution for the developmentally disabled or mentally disordered." In making such findings the court is required to consider several factors, focusing on the seriousness of the offense and the likelihood of a reasonable rehabilitation of the child that would provide adequate protection of the public.

Following a plea hearing at which Defendant was advised that he could be sentenced as an adult on all charges for a maximum sentencing exposure of 185 years, Defendant entered into a plea and disposition agreement in which he agreed to plead no contest to all charges except for one count of battery against a household member (his father), which the State agreed to dismiss. Under the plea agreement, the district court retained sentencing discretion, with the understanding that Defendant would argue for a juvenile disposition and the State would argue for adult sanctions.

The district court held an extensive sentencing hearing to determine whether to sentence Defendant as a child or an adult. The court began by hearing about the nature and seriousness of Defendant's offenses through the testimony of Defendant's stepsister (the Victim). The Victim testified that Defendant came to live with her family during 1995, when she was eight years old and Defendant was fourteen years old. The Victim testified that Defendant was nice to her at first, but he soon began to sexually abuse her.

The Victim recounted numerous instances of vaginal, oral, and anal sex that took place about every other day over the course of about two years. She also recalled times when Defendant forced her to swallow his urine and semen. The Victim described how Defendant's acts would sometimes cause her so much pain that she would stick her head into a pillow to scream, she would almost vomit at times, and she would bleed from her rectum. Defendant also had a method of signaling the Victim that another rape was about to occur; he would tap his fingers on the arm of his chair. In addition to the sexual abuse, Defendant physically abused the Victim on several occasions and frequently threatened to kill her if she ever told anyone about his actions. He once choked her to unconsciousness. The Victim also talked about Defendant's violent mistreatment of her dog and other creatures, and described how he liked to play with fire.

The Victim also testified about the mental and emotional toll that she suffered from the abuse....

In an effort to assess Defendant's amenability to treatment and the threat that he posed to society, the court also received testimony from a number of mental health and juvenile justice professionals. Defendant's juvenile probation officer recounted Defendant's extensive history of prior delinquency referrals for other offenses, and he described the extent to which Defendant did or did not comply with prior rehabilitation efforts. The juvenile probation officer further noted that Defendant lacked remorse, feeling that he did not do anything wrong in this case. In light of the seriousness of Defendant's current offenses, the juvenile probation officer did not believe that Defendant was amenable to treatment in the juvenile justice system and strongly urged the court to impose an adult sentence, remarking that Defendant's case was the first time he had ever recommended adult sanctions for a juvenile offender.

The court also heard testimony from the Director of Psychological Services at the New Mexico Boys' School. He opined that Defendant had a very low chance of rehabilitation and did not believe he would benefit from the treatment services offered at the Boys' School. Although the Boys' School does have a sex offender treatment program, Defendant is not the type of client the program treats because of his tendency toward combining sex with other violent, antisocial conduct. Because Defendant was abused to some degree as a young child, had a history of hurting animals, had a fascination with fire, and exhibited violent sexual behavior, the director suggested that Defendant fit the profile of a serial offender and was of the opinion that New Mexico has no facilities to treat Defendant.

The testimony received by the court from three other mental health experts who evaluated Defendant was remarkably consistent. One psychotherapist described Defendant as a pedophile who could not be successfully rehabilitated and would need a long-term institution. The other psychotherapist and clinical psychologist both diagnosed Defendant as having a severe conduct disorder, with tendencies towards violent sexual behavior and domination, that would require intensive, secured, long-term treatment. Perhaps most disturbing was their conclusion that Defendant is in effect a child without a conscience who lacks empathy or the ability to be concerned for others. All three experts noted that Defendant failed to show any remorse and refused to take responsibility for his actions. They also uniformly agreed that Defendant could not be treated successfully at the New Mexico Boys' School, and, that if sent there, he would surely re-offend upon release. To the extent that the experts believed Defendant might benefit from a long-term, intensive treatment program, the limited number of potentially available treatment programs were discussed and were generally deemed inadequate. However, even assuming that an adequate treatment program could be found, none of the experts could predict how long such treatment would take, nor could they give the court any degree of assurance that rehabilitation efforts would be successful.

After considering the evidence presented at the sentencing hearing, the court issued a thoughtful and detailed explanation of its sentencing decision....

....

DISCUSSION

Defendant does not argue that the district court abused its discretion, or lacked substantial evidence, to impose adult sanctions against him as a youthful offender. Rather, Defendant argues that his sentence of 91½ years constitutes cruel and unusual punishment. Defendant further argues that the district court abused its discretion in denying Defendant's motion to set aside his plea. We address each argument in turn.

Cruel and Unusual Punishment

Whether a particular sentence amounts to cruel and unusual punishment raises a constitutional question of law that we review de novo on appeal. However, because a cruel and unusual punishment challenge necessarily focuses on the factual circumstances of the particular case, we view the facts in the light most favorable to the district court's decision and defer to the district court on evidentiary matters of weight and credibility. Although Defendant argues that his sentence constitutes cruel and unusual punishment under both our state and federal constitutions, he does not suggest that the protections afforded under our state constitution are any greater than those provided under the federal constitution. We, therefore, will proceed without regard for whether Defendant's challenge is brought under the state or federal constitution.

To determine whether a sentence amounts to cruel and unusual punishment we must consider "'[w]hether in view of contemporary standards of elemental decency, the punishment is of such disproportionate character to the offense as to shock the general conscience and violate principles of fundamental fairness.'"

....

Without focusing on the gravity of his offenses, Defendant emphasizes that he was only fifteen years old at the time of the acts for which he was sentenced. To be sure, the decision to sentence a child as an adult is an extreme sanction that cannot be undertaken lightly. That said, however, the imposition of a lengthy, adult sentence on a juvenile does not, in itself, amount to cruel and unusual punishment.

. . . .

Although an overwhelming number of states have rejected cruel and unusual punishment challenges to adult sentences imposed on juvenile offenders, Defendant relies on *Workman v. Commonwealth*, 429 S.W.2d 374, 377–78 (Ky.1968), as support for his contention that the sentence in this case is unconstitutional. In *Workman,* the Kentucky Court of Appeals held that a mandatory sentence of life without possibility of parole imposed on a fourteen-year-old defendant convicted of first-degree sexual offenses amounted to cruel and unusual punishment under the Kentucky State Constitution. However, *Workman* is distinguishable for several reasons. First, *Workman* involved a life sentence without the possibility of parole. In contrast, Defendant was not given a life sentence in this case, and he does have the possibility of parole in this case, even though that possibility will not ripen for a very long time. Second, the defendant in *Workman* was fourteen years old at the time of the offense, while in this case adult sanctions were only imposed for offenses committed while Defendant was fifteen years old. Third, in *Workman,* the juvenile defendant committed a limited number of offenses during one attack on an elderly woman. Conversely, in this case Defendant committed multiple offenses against a very young child over the course of two years. Fourth, the opinion in *Workman* suggests that there was little, if any, evidence of record concerning the juvenile defendant's amenability to treatment. The opposite is true in this case in light of the substantial evidence in this case suggesting that Defendant is not amenable to treatment. And finally, the decision in *Workman* must be viewed within the context of circumstances as they existed over 30 years ago. In view of the qualitative differences in juvenile crime in today's society, we question the continued vitality of the *Workman* decision in light of contemporary standards and concerns. *See Green* (recognizing "the general consensus that serious youthful offenders must be dealt with more severely than has recently been the case in the juvenile system"). In short, we find no basis for relying on *Workman* to conclude that the sentence imposed against Defendant in this case constitutes cruel and unusual punishment.

[W]e must consider the gravity of Defendant's offenses and the severity of his punishment within the context of contemporary standards of elemental decency. Defendant implies that during the sentencing process the district court acted contrary to developing concepts of elemental decency. In particular, Defendant asserts that the district court ignored the possibility of juvenile treatment alternatives despite the existence of treatment programs and facilities throughout the country. However, Defendant's argument ignores the actual state of the record below. The expert testimony presented below was virtually unanimous in concluding that there were simply no programs or treatments available anywhere that could address the psychological and emotional problems that make Defendant a continuing danger to society. And while some of the experts may have held out a faint hope that rehabilitation might be possible if Defendant's treatment were intensive enough and prolonged enough, it is undisputed in the record below that no expert could give the court any reasonable degree of assurance that Defendant could be successfully rehabilitated by the time Defendant reached the age of twenty-one, which is the point at which the court would have lost jurisdiction over Defendant had he been sentenced as a juvenile.

Defendant also makes vague allegations that the district court's failure to provide Defendant with treatment alternatives was the result of a legislative unwillingness to fund adequate treatment alternatives for individuals like Defendant. Our review of the record reveals no indication that the district court's decision to forego treatment alternatives was the result of financial constraints. To the contrary, the district court's decision reflected a desire to pursue rehabilitation, but a grim realization that an attempt at rehabilitation would not be possible in this case without creating an unreasonable risk to the safety of Victim and the public at large because medicine and psychology have yet to develop reliable methods for rehabilitating individuals like Defendant.

Defendant also submits an alternate basis for finding that his sentence amounts to cruel and unusual punishment, arguing that his sentence is unconstitutional because it goes beyond what is necessary to achieve the aim of public intent expressed by the legislature in the New Mexico Children's Code. In this regard, Defendant seems to believe that the court's sentence was intended to exact retribution rather than encourage rehabilitation. Even if that were true, we question Defendant's assumption that a retributive sentence is somehow inconsistent with the sentencing of a juvenile as an adult. But in any event, the record simply does not support Defendant's assertion that the district court was interested in retribution to the exclusion of other considerations such as rehabilitation and protection of the public. Although Defendant's sentence is very long, the district court went to great lengths to explain that the sentence was intended as a means for protecting the public from Defendant in the face of a considerable amount of testimony demonstrating that Defendant was not amendable to current treatment methods and, as a result, would remain a threat to society. In short, we find no basis for agreeing with Defendant's contention that the district court's sentence was motivated by intentions inconsistent with contemporary standards of elemental decency or even with the legislative intent behind the Children's Code.

Although we find no basis for concluding that the district court imposed an unconstitutional sentence, we cannot ignore the apparent gap in our current statutory structure for sentencing children as adults that was brought into relief by the circumstances of this case. The district court was ultimately presented with the task of fashioning a sentence that would recognize the gravity of the Defendant's offenses, and the threat that he poses to society, without ignoring the possibility for rehabilitation. But as the district court noted in its thoughtful decision, the limited jurisdiction it has over offenders sentenced as juveniles is simply inadequate when the juvenile offender is extremely dangerous and in need of intensive treatment that, if there is any hope of rehabilitation, must extend well beyond the time that our current statutory scheme gives our courts to rehabilitate juvenile offenders.

After New Mexico's Children's Code was significantly revised in 1993, our state was recognized for its innovative response to the national movement to address what was perceived as an epidemic of violent juvenile criminals. Around the country, many states responded to violent juvenile crime with legislative initiatives that automatically transferred violent juvenile offenders to adult courts, or gave prosecutors unfettered discretion to transfer juvenile offenders into adult court, where they would be tried and sentenced as adults without regard to the individual circumstances of each child and his or her potential for rehabilitation. Other states responded with what are known as blended sentencing schemes that give a sentencing court the discretion to impose a juvenile disposition or an adult sentence, or both, depending on the individual circumstances of each case. New Mexico took the unique approach of providing for the trial of almost all juveniles in children's court, while still allowing the children's court to decide whether an adjudicated youthful offender should be sentenced as a juvenile or an adult.

Despite New Mexico's innovative approach to juvenile crime, the circumstances of this case reveal an inadequacy in our juvenile justice sentencing scheme. As noted above, when a youthful offender is sentenced as a child, the court's power over the child must end when the child reaches the age of twenty one. However, in some instances, successful rehabilitation would require a longer commitment to the rehabilitative resources of the juvenile justice system. And unfortunately, in some cases, despite providing the best treatment options available, rehabilitation will prove impossible. Because of these very real possibilities and the obligation that every sentencing court also has to protecting public safety, many courts, like the court in this case, will opt for a longer term of adult incarceration for a juvenile offender instead of risking a short-term, unsuccessful juvenile detention that would result in the premature release of a dangerous offender.

The district court's dilemma in this case is not an isolated phenomenon. Indeed, a number of commentators have written extensively on the shortcomings inherent in a juvenile justice system that focuses on harsher punishment as the primary means of protecting the public from violent juvenile offenders. For example, serious doubts exist concerning the extent to which a "get tough" approach is truly effective in protecting the public from future violent crime. To the extent that the movement toward the increased sentencing of juveniles as adults is an implicit recognition that violent juvenile offenders are just like adults, there is increasing evidence that many violent juvenile offenders currently sentenced as adults are in fact psychologically different from adults and, as such, are worthy of different treatment. Similarly, valid concerns exist regarding the extent to which the juvenile justice system may be relying too heavily on psychological experts to predict a child's amenability to treatment and future dangerousness.

Given the complexities involved in effectively dealing with violent juvenile offenders, it is easy to understand why the district court wanted an alternative that did not exist within New Mexico's current juvenile sentencing structure. While it would be unrealistic to expect a legislative solution that would completely eliminate all of the doubt and apprehension that accompanies the decision to sentence a child as an adult, a number of states around the country have enacted blended sentencing alternatives that do give the sentencing judge the option of pursuing a juvenile, rehabilitative approach in marginal cases without sacrificing the ability to impose a long-term, adult incarceration if rehabilitation attempts prove futile.

For example, in Texas the juvenile court is given the authority to impose lengthy, determinate sentences on juveniles for certain enumerated offenses. While the defendant is a juvenile, he remains confined in a youth facility focused on rehabilitative efforts. When the juvenile offender reaches the age of eighteen, the juvenile court is empowered to evaluate the juvenile's rehabilitative progress. At that point, the juvenile court can either continue to confine the offender in a juvenile facility for further rehabilitation efforts until the offender reaches the age of twenty one, or commit the offender to an adult prison to serve the remainder of his sentence if rehabilitation efforts are proving unsuccessful. Other states like Massachusetts, Rhode Island, and Colorado have similar sentencing procedures.

Another example of an innovative, flexible sentencing scheme exists in Minnesota. In that state, the juvenile court can simultaneously impose a juvenile disposition and an adult sentence for certain offenses. The adult sentence is stayed on the condition that the juvenile offender complies with the provisions of his juvenile disposition. If the juvenile does violate the conditions of his juvenile disposition or commits a new offense, the juvenile court can execute the adult sentence. But if the offender does successfully complete his juvenile disposition, he is released at the age of twenty one and the adult sentence is removed....

These are some of the options that could fill the gap that cases such as this one expose in our system and that could eliminate the dilemma faced by the court below. Additionally, we note that some states have extended the jurisdiction of the juvenile court to age twenty five. Despite the advisability of considering whether other states have adopted better ways of dealing with violent juvenile offenders, the decision to move toward such alternatives is fundamentally a policy-based decision for our Legislature. ("'We may not require the legislature to select the least severe penalty possible so long as the penalty selected is not cruelly inhumane or disproportionate to the crime involved.... In a democratic society legislatures, not courts, are constituted to respond to the will and consequently the moral values of the people.'") While we do not intend to suggest that the failure to provide such sentencing alternatives amounts to an unconstitutional sentencing scheme, we would be remiss if we did not urge our legislature to consider some of the flexible sentencing alternatives summarized above.

....

CONCLUSION

We affirm the judgment and sentence.

....

BOSSON, Chief Judge (specially concurring).

Although the law weighs in favor of affirming Joel's sentence, I have substantial concerns regarding a system that imposes long term, adult sentences on children without affording judges the tools necessary to make sound, informed decisions.

According to the record, the earliest Joel can expect to be considered for parole is after serving a sentence of forty-five years. For one so young, this is effectively a life sentence. One who goes into prison a teenager and comes out a man at the age of retirement has forfeited most of his life.

A sentence of ninety years, for acts committed while Joel was fourteen and fifteen years old, is likely one of the longest sentences ever imposed on one so young in the modern history of this state. And this was not even a murder case. If Joel had eventually killed his victim, perhaps to protect himself from prosecution for his other crimes, he could have received a life sentence as an adult, but would have become eligible for parole after a "mere" thirty years. Thus, although Joel commits crimes which, however gruesome, are less than first degree murder, he receives a sentence that is effectively fifty percent longer.

The problem with this sentence lies not just with the number of years, but more importantly with the process that seemingly made this sentence inevitable. As I read the record below, it was as much the lack of sentencing alternatives, as the particular merits of Joel's circumstances, that compelled this sentence. The Children's Court judge was put in a classic dilemma. If he wanted to afford Joel a reasonable chance to redeem himself, the judge had to put society at risk. If the judge sentenced Joel as a juvenile, Joel would go free at age twenty-one, regardless of whether or not he proved to be truly amenable to rehabilitation. If, on the other hand, the judge wanted to maximize the protection of society, the judge had to assume the worst—that Joel was not amenable to treatment and rehabilitation as a juvenile—and sentence him then, and forevermore, as an adult. Although, in a technical sense, the court could choose its sentence, the harsh reality of our flawed system made it a Hobson's choice. The court essentially had no choice but to protect society at the expense of the child.

The judge was not insensitive to this dilemma. At the final sentencing hearing, the court characterized its role as that of "a judge searching for options." Yet, he recognized the effective lack of any such options, thanks to the faulty amenability process. The judge emphasized the need for "a system that would allow us to experiment and protect the community at the same time," a decision that the court "dearly wish[ed he] could make ... in this case." Instead, the judge had "to make a prediction [now] ... as the only decision I'll get a chance to make." Forcing the judge to make that decision now meant that, in order to protect society, he had no choice but to sentence Joel as an adult and, in the court's own words (concurring in defense counsel's characterization), "throw away the child." The court was brutally frank in its reasoning. The sentence was ninety years so that, even with the possibility of meritorious time reductions and parole eligibility, Joel will not leave prison until he is at an age when, biologically speaking, he will be too old a man to pose a serious threat of re-offending. The court regretfully concluded, "I take no joy at all in finding that [this] is the only option I have."

I enthusiastically join that portion of the majority opinion that calls for improvements in the Children's Code. Children's Court judges need more flexible tools in order to adequately address the unique problems presented by youthful offenders. Judges need the power to sentence juveniles conditionally, first as juveniles and later as adults, depending upon whether subsequent review indicates that adult sentencing is warranted. With conditional sentencing, courts could take advantage of the therapeutic and rehabilitative services that are uniquely available for juveniles, and would have the opportunity to observe how a child actually performs until turning twenty-one. When the juvenile became of age, the judge would have a record of performance upon which to base a more informed, predictive decision about the probability for success versus the risk to society. Conditional sentencing affords the juvenile one last opportunity for redemption, while retaining institutional control over the juvenile for the protection of society; this seems to be a win-win proposition.

New Mexico, unfortunately, does not have such a system in place. Instead, we ask the impossible of our Children's Court. We expect judges to make life-long, predictive decisions, without the possibility of later review, about the kind of adults these juveniles will turn out to be, twenty, thirty, and forty years into the future. We do not, however, equip our judges with adequate and timely information to make such decisions as informed as they could be.

We demand that judges determine, now, whether a child is "amenable to treatment or rehabilitation as a child in available facilities." We do not, however, afford judges the opportunity to experiment, under controlled conditions, to see how a child actually responds to treatment. Thus, the amenability determination is fraught with risk and, as a practical matter, forces judges to err on the side of caution in making amenability decisions. A lot rides on the wisdom of these amenability decisions. In the interest of protecting society, judges have to assume the worst about a juvenile, which can translate into a lengthy adult sentence on the chance that a juvenile may re-offend. And let us not forget that, under the present system, sixteen-year-old boys, once they are deemed not "amenable" to rehabilitation in juvenile facilities, serve lengthy adult sentences in the company of full-grown and very dangerous men.

Thus, in my mind, the process that compelled this ninety-year sentence is what makes its severity in this case so suspect. It is not that the punishment does not fit the crime in the abstract. It is that the punishment exceeds the crime in the particular context of compelling a judge to act out of fear; to impose upon a child the worst possible sentence, instead of a sentence based upon what the court felt the child truly deserved. "The inquiry focuses on whether a person *deserves* such punishment, not simply on whether punishment would serve a utilitarian goal."

Defendant's status as a juvenile makes this flawed process all the more suspect in a constitutional sense. It is generally a tenet of constitutional law that children merit special consideration in assessing whether a punishment is cruel and usual under the Constitution....

The Children's Code, unlike adult sentencing codes, requires us first to consider whether the defendant is amenable to rehabilitation; this is because, constitutionally speaking, kids are different. "[O]ur courts are especially solicitous of the rights of juveniles...."

Before requiring judges to make a decision of such consequence, we owe it to the court, to the victim, to the juvenile, and to society as a whole, to inform these decisions as much as practicable. Conditional sentencing, subject to later review, would make those decisions infinitely more informed than our present system.

Regrettably, I must concur in affirming Joel's sentence, because existing constitutional authority gives me no choice. It ought to be different, and if it were in my power, I would elect to make it different. Suffice it to say that I concur with grave reservations about the lack of alternatives that make this sentence inevitable.

Note

In *Harmelin v. Michigan*, 501 U.S. 957 (1991) (plurality opinion), the United States Supreme Court rejected an Eighth Amendment proportionality claim and upheld a state law mandating life imprisonment without possibility of parole for those convicted of certain possessory drug offenses. There was no majority opinion in the case, but a reading of the dissent and the concurring and concurring in the judgment opinions indicates that prison sentences may be challenged on Eighth Amendment grounds only if they are *grossly* disproportionate.

Does *Harmelin* affect the *IRA* decision?

Index